Civil Procedure

ASPEN CASEBOOK SERIES

Civil Procedure

Howard M. Erichson
Professor of Law
Fordham University School of Law

J. Maria Glover
Professor of Law
Georgetown University Law Center

Wolters Kluwer

Printed in the United States of America.

1 2 3 4 5 6 7 8 9 0

ISBN 978-1-5438-2835-1

Library of Congress Cataloging-in-Publication Data application is in process.

About Wolters Kluwer Legal & Regulatory U.S.

Wolters Kluwer Legal & Regulatory U.S. delivers expert content and solutions in the areas of law, corporate compliance, health compliance, reimbursement, and legal education. Its practical solutions help customers successfully navigate the demands of a changing environment to drive their daily activities, enhance decision quality and inspire confident outcomes.

Serving customers worldwide, its legal and regulatory portfolio includes products under the Aspen Publishers, CCH Incorporated, Kluwer Law International, ftwilliam. com and MediRegs names. They are regarded as exceptional and trusted resources for general legal and practice-specific knowledge, compliance and risk management, dynamic workflow solutions, and expert commentary.

For Danny and Jake
HME

For Oliver and Teddy
JMG

Summary of Contents

Contents

Chapter 1: Introduction to Civil Procedure   1

Chapter 2: Pleadings   33

Chapter 3: Discovery   119

Chapter 4: Summary Judgment, Pretrial Adjudication, and Case Management   173

Chapter 5: Trial   225

Chapter 6: Appeals   261

Chapter 7: Joinder   295

Chapter 8: Enforcement and Preclusion   367

Chapter 9: Subject Matter Jurisdiction   443

Chapter 10: Personal Jurisdiction   507

Preface

As casebook authors, we see our job as priming students to engage with the material at a high level in the classroom. We ask hard questions, but we do not "hide the ball." Rather than keep students in the dark about legal doctrine, we have tried to offer clear explanations and to set up each case to help students get the most out of their reading. We want students to see, as clearly as possible, what is fascinating and important about civil procedure, including the many ways in which it is *unclear* and *unsatisfying*. By the time students arrive in the classroom having completed their assignment in this casebook, they should have a solid understanding not only of the basic mechanics of the topic, but also why the topic matters in the real world of litigation. Moreover, they should appreciate the questions of procedural design raised by each topic. Teachers who use this casebook, we hope, will find that they can spend less time in class explaining basic doctrine and clearing up misconceptions, and more time exploring the cases and helping students think about procedural policy and litigation strategy.

We have included many decisions by district judges and magistrate judges. Our goal is to help students see how civil procedure plays out in real disputes, and lower court decisions often show this more clearly than decisions that emerge from the rarefied air of the Supreme Court. But on certain topics, students must understand the law as it has evolved, and we have included the essential cases in the canon. In selecting cases of both sorts—those that demonstrate on-the-ground application and those that were instrumental in the development of the law—we have stuck to cases that actually deserve to be read by a smart-future-lawyer-learning-civil-procedure-for-the-first-time law student. Rather than choose cases that raise quirky legal issues at the periphery, we have chosen cases to help students understand the core purposes and difficulties of each aspect of civil procedure.

We have thoroughly edited cases to help students focus on each topic, but we have included enough facts and procedural history to provide context and a sense of how rules work in litigation. Deletions within cases are indicated by ellipses or brackets; additions and substitutions are indicated by brackets. To enhance readability, we have deleted or reduced footnotes and citations without indication, and we have altered citation format for consistency, including moving some citations into text from footnotes. Where we have retained footnotes within a case, we have kept their original numbering.

Civil procedure is hard. It is hard, in part, because it matters and because students need to learn that procedure is power. Procedural issues often are hard for judges and hard for lawyers, and they ought to be hard for students. Our goal in this casebook is to make the students' job no harder than necessary. We want students to experience civil procedure in all of its glory, without creating an unnecessary layer of struggle by obscuring the law or leading students down tangential paths. We hope students will find that our explanations, our cases, and our questions help them achieve as much clarity as the law permits.

In sum, we are two unabashedly enthusiastic proceduralists, and our goal is to make every law student love the subject and learn it well. We have seen plenty of students who entered the course dreading what they expected to be a dreary slog through technicalities, and who finished the course declaring procedure to be their favorite subject and realizing that these procedural "technicalities" are nothing less than our justice system at work. If the students who read our book come away with that sort of understanding, we will have done our job.

Howard M. Erichson & J. Maria Glover
December 2020

Acknowledgments

We could not have written this book this without the support of many individuals and institutions. We thank Fordham Law School and Georgetown Law School for their support of this project and for giving us the privilege of teaching. We thank our research assistants—Sami Helgason, Mitchell Mengden, Ryan Miller, Serhiy Moshak, Sean Airut Murphy, Alina Pastor-Chermak, Samara Perlman, Meg Tomlinson, and Catherine Tremble—not only for their meticulous work but also for never letting us forget that this book is for law students. We thank Richard Mixter and Shannon Davis at Aspen, and Kathy Langone and Sara Nies at The Froebe Group, for their faith in this project and their work in seeing it through to completion. We owe a debt of gratitude to Steven Benz, Edward Hartnett, David Shapiro, Suzanna Sherry, and Linda Silberman, who have been particularly instrumental in our understanding and appreciation of civil procedure, as well as countless other colleagues at our home institutions and in our fields of civil procedure and complex litigation. We thank Alex Reinert, Nancy Welsh, and outside reviewers who offered many valuable suggestions. Finally, we are indebted to our students, who have been a constant source of challenge and inspiration. Their questions, confusions, ideas, and insights are woven into every page.

Thanks are also in order for permission to reprint the following articles:

Andrew D Bradt, A Radical Proposal: The Multidistrict Litigation Act of 1968 (2017). 165 University of Pennsylvania Law Review 831.

Morton Denlow, Mediation 101: A Primer, Jams ADR Blog (August 3, 2017).

Kathleen Balthrop Havener, Discovering Lessons Your Mother Should Have Taught You (ABA GP / Solo Newsletter, July / August 2014). American Bar Association © 2014.

William W Schwarzer and Alan Hirsch, The Elements of Case Management, Third Edition (Federal Judicial Center 2017).

CHAPTER 1

Introduction to Civil Procedure

This is a book about justice. And truth. And peace.

. . . and lots of rules and statutes. For a book about justice, truth, and peace, you may find that some of it feels rather *technical*. But even as you learn the structures and the details, do not lose sight of what is at stake. In legal disputes, achieving justice requires a *process* for airing disagreements and bringing them to resolution. Reaching truth requires a *process* for uncovering facts and presenting them to decision makers. Achieving peace requires a *process* that not only facilitates negotiated resolutions, but also has the capacity to produce an enforceable and binding judgment. And since justice, truth, and peace are neither easy nor costless, the process for striving to reach them involves countless trade-offs and hard questions.

In the pursuit of justice, truth, and peace—and in the service of clients whose disputes are the workload of the justice system—one thing is always in demand: lawyers who understand how the process works, why it works that way, and how it might be made to work better. This is where you come in. Welcome to civil procedure.

A. LEARNING PROCEDURE

Let's begin at the beginning: What is civil procedure?

First, it is *civil*. This book does not address *criminal* procedure, the process by which the state seeks to impose punishments on those who are accused of committing crimes. Nor does it address *administrative* procedure, the process by which government agencies function. It concerns civil actions in the courts, or what many people simply call lawsuits. As you will see, civil actions vary tremendously in scope and subject matter. They may involve parties who are individuals, corporations, or government entities. They range from small-stakes disputes between neighbors to massive disputes over billions of dollars and demands for structural and legal reform. The subject matter may involve almost any area of law. But always, a civil action involves some person or entity that went to court seeking a remedy from some other person or entity.

Second, and more fundamentally, it is *procedure*. It is about how litigation proceeds rather than about what people sue over. Because it concerns procedure, your course on civil procedure will feel different from other typical first-year law school courses such as contracts, torts, property, and criminal law. Most of your other courses focus on "substantive law"—the rights and duties that the law establishes, whereas procedure is all about the process for resolving disputes that arise under those substantive rights and duties.

While procedure differs in kind from other topics in law, do not make the mistake of viewing procedure as secondary or insignificant. Any lawyer will tell you that the outcome of a matter often depends on its procedural path. As Representative John Dingell once said during a House of Representatives subcommittee hearing, "I'll let you write the substance . . . and you let me write the procedure, and I'll screw you every time." *Hearing on H.R. 2327*, 98th Cong. 312 (1983). Moreover, procedure interacts with substance in fascinating ways, and you will learn that you cannot really understand substantive rights and duties unless you understand the procedures that bring them to life. Finally, process matters for its own sake. We are talking, after all, about nothing less than our system of justice. Treating participants fairly and taking the resolution of disputes seriously rank among the most important things we do in a civilized society.

Civil procedure is the course that introduces you to the justice system and how it works. It is also the course—more than any other in the standard first-year curriculum—that introduces you to thinking strategically on behalf of clients. And it is the course that drives home the point that whatever the substantive law may say, it means nothing unless there are available procedures that can turn rights into reality.

Because procedure differs from other topics, you must learn it differently. When you read cases in torts or contracts, for example, you will focus primarily on the factual story of what happened among the parties and whether those facts give rise to certain duties or liabilities. By contrast, when you read cases in civil procedure, you will focus primarily on the story of the *litigation process*. In this book, you will read cases that involve torts, contracts, civil rights, and many other areas of substantive law. As you read each case, you will need to understand the factual story and the substantive claims and defenses so that you can comprehend the case (you should always be able to answer "Who is suing whom for what?"), but mostly your attention should be on what is going on in the litigation *process*. The judges in the cases in this book, rather than deciding substantive law questions such as whether a person breached a duty under tort law, will be deciding procedural questions such as whether the complaint suffices to survive a motion to dismiss, how much information the parties can obtain in discovery, and whether multiple plaintiffs can join together in a single lawsuit. Therefore, as you read each case, keep in mind that the procedural issue in the case could have arisen in a wide range of disputes in disparate areas of law, and that the case you are reading is just one example. While you are learning the procedural law from each case in the context of a particular dispute, you must be ready to apply the same procedural principles in disputes that involve completely different facts and substantive law.

This book focuses primarily on procedure in the U.S. federal courts. Each state has its own procedural rules that govern the litigation process in its state courts. We have chosen to focus on federal procedure for two reasons. First, U.S. law students may end up practicing in any state or multiple states, and as a practical matter it would be impossible to teach all state court variations in a single course. Federal civil procedure is largely uniform across the country, as all federal district courts apply the same Federal Rules of Civil Procedure (although each district also has its own "local rules," which you should *always* consult when practicing in a particular district court). Second, much civil procedure in the United States, even in state courts, follows the general model of the federal rules. A grounding in federal civil procedure gives law students an understanding of the architecture of civil procedure in the United States, which provides a framework for learning state variations.

Get in the lawyerly habit of reading rules and statutes directly. When this book refers to a particular rule of civil procedure, statute, or constitutional provision, *read it. Carefully.* If you do not have a supplemental book with the relevant rules and statutes, you can access these sources online.

As you learn about each topic, think about how you would *use* these procedures as a lawyer. Often, the procedural rules create multiple options and, over the course of litigation, lawyers make thousands of large and small choices about how to proceed. To serve your clients well in an adversary system of justice, you need to understand the strategies available under the rules of procedure. Lawyers often compare litigation to a chess game or some sort of ritualized battle. Chess and other games of strategy require players to see all available options, anticipate opponents' moves, and plan several moves ahead. Litigation requires a similar mindset, and a complex case with multiple claims and parties may feel like playing multiple interrelated chess games at once. Thinking about the ways in which you can use procedural tools for your clients will greatly enhance your understanding of each topic.

Finally, look for how each part fits into the whole. You cannot understand summary judgment, for example, without seeing how it relates to pleadings, discovery, and trial. Although this book necessarily teaches procedural topics one at a time, ultimately you have to understand civil procedure as a web in which each aspect of the litigation process relates to all of the others.

B. THE LITIGATION PROCESS: AN OVERVIEW

It always starts with a dispute. The dispute could be about nearly anything—an injury, a business disagreement, property ownership, government powers, employment, healthcare, the environment, civil rights, or anything else under the sun. The dispute could be between individuals, business entities, government entities, or others. If the disputants are unable to work things out on their own and if the stakes are high enough, one of them might seek the advice of a lawyer (or might consider filing a lawsuit *pro se*, without a lawyer). Consulting a lawyer does not necessarily lead to a lawsuit, as the lawyer may help the client negotiate a resolution or find an alternative solution, or the lawyer may advise that the prospective client has no viable claim worth pursuing. The lawyer could consider whether the client has a viable claim as a legal matter (not every dispute under the sun is a dispute under the law), as a factual matter, and as a matter of whether pursuing the claim is worth the cost. If the lawyer determines that the client has a viable claim, and if negotiations or other solutions are unavailing or unwarranted, then the lawyer might advise bringing a lawsuit. It is the client's decision whether to go forward with pursuing the legal action.

Suppose the client decides to go forward with a lawsuit. The following overview paints, in broad strokes, the steps involved in litigation. Not every action follows each of these steps, and the steps need not happen in the same order, though the order in which we present these steps might be fairly described as typical. We will explore in much greater detail each of the steps mentioned in this overview; for now, your goal is to understand the broad outline so that you can keep the big picture in mind as you fill in the details chapter by chapter.

> **Terminology Tip**
>
> The *plaintiff* is the one bringing a lawsuit. A *defendant* is a person from whom a plaintiff seeks a remedy. The most precise word for lawsuit is *action*, but lawyers and others often simply call it a suit, lawsuit, or case. The word *litigation* can refer to the entire process of a particular action, as in "the litigation between X and Y has been going on for a year," or it can refer to the process of lawsuits in general, as in "litigation is one way to resolve disputes." Do not use *trial* as a synonym for litigation; *trial* refers to a specific part of the litigation process when the parties appear in court to present evidence and when the jury or judge renders a decision.

(1) Claims, Parties, and Forum

When a plaintiff brings a lawsuit, certain decisions happen up front. The plaintiff must decide whether to sue, what claims to assert, and what remedies to seek. The plaintiff also must decide whom to sue, which may be one defendant or multiple defendants. If others have claims against the defendant arising out of the same situation, they may decide with the plaintiff to bring their claims together in a single lawsuit. In addition to deciding *whether* to sue, *what* claims to assert, and *against whom* and *with whom*, the plaintiff also must decide *where* to sue. Thus, certain procedural decisions about subject matter, structure, and forum occur even before the lawsuit gets started.

Later in the book, we will closely examine questions of claims and party structure (the topic of joinder, covered in Chapter 7) as well as questions of forum selection (the topics of subject matter jurisdiction, personal jurisdiction, and venue, covered in Chapters 9-11). For now, we will briefly note each of these topics before turning to our overview of how litigation proceeds.

(a) Claims

Two preliminary questions for a potential plaintiff are whether to sue and what claims to assert. As mentioned above, the decision to sue belongs to the client, but clients typically rely heavily on a lawyer's advice for this decision. Determining the viability of a claim requires legal research and factual investigation. The lawyer may advise the client on whether the client has a viable claim, its chance of success, and the costs and benefits of litigation as compared with other ways of addressing the client's problem. If the client chooses to file a lawsuit, a basic question is what *claims* to assert. Sometimes, the answer may be obvious, as in a simple breach-of-contract dispute. Often, however, a plaintiff has multiple potential claims to assert. A person injured by a defective product, for example, might assert claims for negligence, product liability, and breach of warranty, among other things. Each claim encompasses a set of elements that a plaintiff must establish, and may be accompanied by various defenses that a defendant can attempt to prove to avoid or reduce liability. Throughout law school, as you study various fields of substantive law, you will learn about a wide variety of legal claims, or *causes of action*, and the elements required for each one. A plaintiff need not choose only one claim to assert; a plaintiff may assert multiple claims against a defendant in a single lawsuit, as we will see in Chapter 2 on pleadings and in Chapter 7 on joinder.

Relatedly, the plaintiff decides what remedies to seek. Depending on the nature of the claim, a plaintiff might seek compensatory damages (monetary remedy to compensate for the harm), punitive damages (monetary remedy, on top of compensatory damages, to punish defendant for egregious conduct), an injunction (ordering a defendant to do something or to refrain from doing something), or other remedies. The plaintiff's demand for a remedy must be stated in the complaint, so it is a question that prospective plaintiffs must consider before embarking on litigation.

(b) Parties

Another preliminary question, alongside *whether* and *what*, is *who*. The plaintiff decides whom to sue and how many to sue, and this is more complicated than you might imagine. Many situations involve more than one potentially liable party, and it may require some work to determine exactly which persons ought to be named as defendants, especially if there are several related business entities. If the plaintiff wishes to sue multiple defendants in a single lawsuit, modern rules of civil procedure generally make it easy to do so as long as the claims arise out of the same transaction or occurrence. Indeed, *permissive joinder of parties* is common. But there are reasons why a plaintiff might choose not to sue a person against whom the plaintiff has a potential claim, including reasons of economic efficiency, litigation strategy, and the protection of relationships. Uncommonly, plaintiffs *must* include particular parties in their lawsuit, as a matter of *compulsory joinder of parties*. This joinder decision thus involves several questions: whether joinder of multiple defendants is *permitted*, and if so, whether the plaintiff chooses to join them; and whether joinder of certain parties is *required*, and, if so, whether it is achievable. We will explore both permissive joinder and compulsory joinder in Chapter 7.

The plaintiff also decides *with whom* to sue. If others have claims against the same defendants that arise out of the same transaction or occurrence, multiple plaintiffs may choose to join together in a single lawsuit. This type of joinder is governed by the same rules as decisions about whether to sue multiple defendants. The most extreme version of plaintiffs joining together is the *class action*, in which a plaintiff or group of plaintiffs sues as representatives on behalf of an entire defined class of persons.

Other types of claims may make the litigation structure more complex than a basic plaintiff-sues-defendant scenario. If a defendant has a claim against a plaintiff, the defendant may assert a *counterclaim*. If a party has a claim against its co-plaintiff or co-defendant that is transactionally related to the original suit, it may assert a *crossclaim*. If a defendant seeks to bring into the lawsuit a person who may be liable to pay the defendant if the defendant is liable to the plaintiff, the defendant may do so by asserting a *third-party claim*. We will explore all of these types of claims in Chapter 7.

(c) Forum

A final preliminary question is *where* to bring the dispute for resolution. That is, which court or other option will be the setting for resolving the dispute? Lawyers often refer to this as the *choice of forum*. Initially, the choice of forum belongs to the plaintiff, who is sometimes called "the master of the complaint." The plaintiff's lawyer considers what forum options are available and which of them would be most convenient or strategically advantageous.

The decision may involve a choice among different types of courts as well as a choice among geographical locations. Regarding which type of court, if a basis exists for federal court power over a case, the plaintiff often may choose whether to file in state court or federal court. As to geography, the plaintiff must decide whether to file the action, say, in Minneapolis or Miami or Milan. Some disputes are highly localized, leaving little doubt about the location for the lawsuit, while other disputes have interstate or international elements that open up multiple forum options. We will explore the constraints on plaintiffs' choice of forum in Chapters 9, 10, and 11.

After the plaintiff files the action in the plaintiff-selected court, the defendant has opportunities to object to the choice of forum. A defendant may move to dismiss for lack of subject matter jurisdiction, lack of personal jurisdiction, or improper venue. To have the power to decide a case, a federal court must have *subject matter jurisdiction* over the action. In general, federal subject matter jurisdiction requires either that the claim arise under federal law or that the suit be between citizens of different states and meet an amount-in-controversy requirement. Any court must have *personal jurisdiction* over the parties to have the power to enter a binding judgment. In general, personal jurisdiction depends on whether the connections between the defendant, the dispute, and the forum state suffice to support the exercise of the court's power over that defendant. Also, the court must be a proper *venue* for the action, which means it must comply with legislative restrictions on which districts are permissible based on the parties and events in the case. If the court dismisses the action on any of these grounds, then the plaintiff would have the opportunity to file the action in an appropriate court.

Aside from motions to dismiss, another way for a defendant to alter the forum is known as *removal*. Suppose the plaintiff filed the action in a state court but there is a basis for federal jurisdiction and the defendant would prefer to be in federal court. In this situation, the defendant may *remove* the action to federal court. Similarly, if the defendant believes there is a geographical location for the action that is more appropriate than the one the plaintiff chose, the defendant may *move to transfer* the action, or a court may transfer an action on its own initiative. To sum up, the plaintiff initially selects the forum, but that choice of forum is constrained by jurisdictional limits and venue rules. More than that, the plaintiff's original choice of forum may be disrupted by other parties or by the court.

While we are on the topic of choosing forums for resolving disputes, keep in mind that the forum need not be a court. Sometimes, parties submit their dispute to *arbitration*, which means that a private decision maker renders a binding decision. Typically, arbitration occurs because the parties have included an arbitration agreement as part of a contract between them. Sometimes, parties submit their dispute to *mediation*, which means that a private facilitator assists the parties in trying to reach a negotiated resolution of the dispute. And very often, parties are able to settle their dispute through *negotiation*. We will discuss forms of dispute resolution in Chapter 13.

(2) Pleadings

Now that a plaintiff has decided to file a lawsuit, has decided what claims to assert, has decided whom to name as parties, and has selected a forum, how does the actual litigation process begin? A plaintiff formally begins a lawsuit by filing a *complaint*. In addition to filing the complaint with the court, the plaintiff delivers, or *serves*, a copy of the complaint to the defendant, in accordance with detailed rules about service. Along with the complaint, the plaintiff serves on the defendant a *summons*, which is a document issued by the court that compels the defendant to respond to the complaint.

Now that an action is in court and the defendant has been notified of the proceeding, what is the next step? A defendant has several options. One option is to file an *answer*. In the answer, the defendant admits or denies the allegations in the complaint, and asserts any defenses to the plaintiff's claims. Together, the complaint and answer are known as *pleadings*. We will explore the pleading stage of litigation in Chapter 2.

(3) Motions to Dismiss

Instead of responding to the complaint with an answer, a defendant may file a *motion to dismiss*. By moving to dismiss, a defendant asks the judge to throw out the plaintiff's claims before the defendant has the burden of admitting or denying the plaintiff's factual allegations. If the defendant contends that the facts alleged by the plaintiff, even if true, do not give rise to liability on the part of the defendant, the defendant may file a *motion to dismiss for failure to state a claim upon which relief can be granted.* Or, if the defendant contends that the court lacks jurisdiction to hear the case, the defendant may move to dismiss for lack of subject matter jurisdiction or for lack of personal jurisdiction. We will explore these and other motions to dismiss in Chapter 2 in connection with pleadings.

(4) Discovery

Suppose the lawsuit survives the pleadings stage, either because the court denied a motion to dismiss or because the defendant decided simply to move forward with answering the complaint. The next step, typically, is for parties to pursue their investigation of the facts. Although the parties may know a lot about the facts already, at the outset of litigation neither side typically has the whole picture. An employee suing her employer may need access to a personnel file or to the employer's e-mails. Businesses in a dispute may need to see each other's relevant financial documents. Parties may need to ask questions of witnesses.

Parties and their lawyers gather information both informally, such as by seeking information from their clients and other willing witnesses, and formally, by using the tools of *discovery*. The Federal Rules of Civil Procedure provide a number of discovery mechanisms that parties can use to compel others to turn over relevant information, including *interrogatories* (written questions to elicit written answers), *depositions* (oral testimony by witnesses responding to lawyers' questions), and *document requests*. These and other discovery devices create a powerful opportunity for parties to gather the information they need.

The scope of discoverable information is broad but not infinite. It is limited by the concept of *relevance*: The requested information must matter to the claims or defenses in the action. It is limited as well by legal doctrines of *privilege*, such as the attorney-client privilege, which protects confidential communications between lawyers and clients. And it is limited by the principle of *proportionality*: Discovery requests must not be unreasonably burdensome in light of the costs and benefits of obtaining the information. We will explore discovery in Chapter 3.

(5) Summary Judgment

A party may move for *summary judgment*, arguing that the case is so clear, on the facts and the law, that it can only be decided in the party's favor. Summary judgment is a way for the court to enter judgment without conducting a trial. To win a motion for summary judgment, the moving party must show that there is "no genuine dispute as to any material fact" and that the moving party is entitled to judgment as a matter of law. For example, a plaintiff might argue that the undisputed facts establish the defendant's liability as a matter of law. Or a defendant might argue that the plaintiff has no evidence to support an essential element of the claim, and therefore the plaintiff must lose. Or a party may argue that there is a particular legal issue that, if decided in a particular way by the judge, disposes of the case. When arguing for summary judgment, a party is essentially saying that no reasonable judge or jury could find in the other party's favor, and therefore it is unnecessary for the judge to hold a trial. We will explore summary judgment, as well as other types of pretrial adjudication, in Chapter 4.

(6) Trial

Trials occur in only a small percent of civil actions, because most cases are settled, voluntarily dropped, or resolved by pretrial adjudications on motions to dismiss or summary judgment. But in the relatively small number of cases that reach this moment, trial is the main event. Trial is the part of the process when the parties appear in a courtroom to present their evidence, and when the jury or judge hears the evidence and renders a decision by making factual determinations and applying the law to the facts to decide the outcome.

Some trials in the United States have a jury and some do not, depending on whether the case is one in which a constitutional or statutory right to trial by jury exists, and also depending on whether either party demanded a jury. If the case has a *jury trial*, the court empanels a jury from a representative group of citizens. In a jury trial, the judge runs the trial, makes all legal rulings, decides what evidence is admissible, and instructs the jury on the law. The jury determines the facts, often in part by making credibility determinations about witnesses, and applies the law to those facts. If the case has a non-jury trial, or *bench trial*, the judge not only runs the process but also serves as fact-finder.

At a trial, typically each party's lawyer has the opportunity to give an opening statement. Each party then has the opportunity to present evidence by calling witnesses and introducing documents or other exhibits into evidence. Each witness, after taking an oath to testify truthfully, answers questions from the lawyer who called the witness (direct examination) and from lawyers for opposing parties (cross-examination). When lawyers object to whether certain evidence can be introduced, the judge decides whether to sustain or overrule the objection. In federal court, these decisions about admissibility are governed by the Federal Rules of Evidence. After all of the evidence has been taken, each party's lawyer may give a closing argument. If it is a jury trial, the judge then gives the *jury charge* or *jury instructions*, explaining the relevant legal principles to the jury so that the jury can make an informed decision. The next step is *jury deliberation*, when the members of the jury discuss the evidence and attempt to reach a conclusion together.

Finally, the jury renders a *verdict*, deciding who prevails and, if the plaintiff wins, how much. The judge enters judgment based on the verdict. We will explore trial procedure in Chapter 5.

(7) Post-Trial Motions

After evidence has been presented at trial, a party can move for *judgment as a matter of law*. This motion asks the judge to decide that the case need not be submitted to the jury because, based on the evidence at trial, there is only one way the case can reasonably be decided. In this regard, the motion resembles a motion for summary judgment, but the difference is that summary judgment is based on evidence gathered by the parties prior to trial, whereas the motion for judgment as a matter of law is based entirely on the evidence presented at trial. If the judge denies the motion for judgment as a matter of law and sends the case to the jury, and if the jury decides in favor of the other party, a party can make a *renewed motion for judgment as a matter of law*, also known as a motion for *judgment notwithstanding the verdict*. If the judge grants this motion, the judge takes the decision away from the jury and decides the case the opposite way, on the grounds that the relevant legal principles, applied to the facts based on the evidence at trial, reasonably permit only one result.

Alternatively, a party that is dissatisfied with the outcome may file a *motion for a new trial*. A motion for a new trial may be based on problems with the trial process, such as erroneous admission or exclusion of evidence, faulty jury instructions, or misconduct by lawyers or other trial participants. Or a motion for a new trial may be based on an argument that the verdict was against the great weight of the evidence. If the judge grants the motion for a new trial, then the trial starts again from the beginning. We will explore these motions in Chapter 5.

(8) Appeal

In federal court, a party that suffers an adverse judgment has a right to appeal the judgment. Appeals generally may only be taken from final judgments. Decisions made along the way—or *interlocutory rulings*—typically are not appealable. There are several exceptions to the final judgment rule, and in Chapter 6 we will explore the various situations in which interlocutory rulings may be appealed. Keep in mind that many cases reach final judgment without trial. Therefore, while some appeals are taken from judgments entered after trial, many other appeals are taken from judgments entered on motions to dismiss, summary judgment, or other forms of pretrial adjudication.

Appellate courts do not hold trials. In general, they do not take evidence. Rather, they hear arguments from the lawyers (or from the parties if they are proceeding *pro se*). Lawyers submit their written arguments in *briefs*, and often have the opportunity to present *oral arguments* as well. The federal courts of appeals generally decide cases in three-judge panels.

Courts of appeals apply different *standards of review* to different types of trial court decisions. They review trial judges' legal rulings *de novo*. That is, appellate courts give no deference to trial judges' decisions on matters of law, and instead simply apply the law as they think correct. However, they review trial judges' factual findings on a *clearly erroneous* standard. That is, appellate courts defer to trial judges' findings on matters of fact and do not overturn such decisions unless they are quite sure the trial judge erred. As to discretionary rulings by trial judges on many procedural matters, appellate courts apply an *abuse of discretion* standard. That is, they leave the trial judge plenty of room to make discretionary decisions about how the litigation should proceed.

The process within the courts of appeals is not governed by the Federal Rules of Civil Procedure, which address procedure in the district courts. Rather, procedures in the U.S. courts of appeals are governed by the Federal Rules of Appellate Procedure.

A losing party in the federal court of appeals, or on a federal issue in state court, may seek review in the United States Supreme Court by filing a *petition for certiorari*. The Supreme Court typically hears fewer than one hundred cases each year, choosing its cases primarily based on the importance of the legal issues presented and whether lower courts have reached divergent conclusions on the points of law. The vast majority of cases, therefore, end either in the district court or the court of appeals.

C. COURTS

Courts in the United States are not a unitary system, but rather multiple systems of multilayered courts. They include a federal court system and multiple state court systems, and each system comprises layers of trial courts and appellate courts.

(1) One Nation, Multiple Court Systems

Each of the 50 states has its own court system. So do U.S. districts and territories such as the District of Columbia, Puerto Rico, and the U.S. Virgin Islands. The state and territorial court systems employ their own judges, and are supported by the taxpayers of each state (except the courts of the District of Columbia, which are funded by the federal government). Some states hold judicial elections to select their judges, while others use an appointment process.

Each system of state or territorial courts includes courts of limited jurisdiction and courts of general jurisdiction. Courts of limited jurisdiction vary from state to state, but may include small claims courts, municipal courts, probate courts, traffic courts, and family courts. What makes them courts of limited jurisdiction is that they are empowered to hear only certain categories of cases. Municipal courts, for example, often handle traffic violations, small claims, and misdemeanors, but would not adjudicate felony criminal cases or civil lawsuits for substantial money damages. Courts of general jurisdiction, by contrast, can hear any type of case unless it is specifically excluded from the court's power. The name for the court of general jurisdiction varies from state to state.

In Texas, it is the District Court. In Tennessee, it is the Circuit Court. In New York, confusingly, it is called the Supreme Court. A number of states label their court of general jurisdiction the Superior Court, to draw a contrast between courts of general jurisdiction and courts of limited jurisdiction, or inferior courts. By whatever name, every state has at least one court of general jurisdiction.

In addition to the more than 50 state and territorial court systems in the United States, there is a separate court system that includes courts across the entire nation. These are the federal courts—the judicial branch of the U.S. government. In some cities, there is a federal courthouse literally across the street from a state courthouse. The state and federal courts function side by side, presenting different procedural opportunities depending on the nature of the lawsuit.

The federal courts are courts of limited jurisdiction. That is, they are only empowered to hear certain categories of cases. We will explore the topic of federal *subject matter jurisdiction* in Chapter 9. For now, it suffices to know that there are two main categories of cases over which the federal courts have subject matter jurisdiction. First, they have power to hear cases that arise under federal law, known as *federal question jurisdiction. See* 28 U.S.C. §1331. Second, they have power to hear cases between citizens of different states, known as *diversity jurisdiction.* For diversity jurisdiction, none of the plaintiffs may be citizens of the same state as any of the defendants, and the amount in controversy must exceed $75,000. *See* 28 U.S.C. §1332.

(2) Trial and Appellate Courts

Each of the state and territorial court systems, like the federal court system, comprises layers of trial courts and appellate courts. Cases begin in the trial court and make their way to an appellate court if a dissatisfied party appeals. In rare instances, courts other than trial courts have *original jurisdiction* (power to hear the case from the start) rather than merely *appellate jurisdiction* (power to review a lower court's decision).

The three-tiered federal court system includes the U.S. district courts, the U.S. courts of appeals, and the U.S. Supreme Court. With few exceptions, federal cases are filed originally in the district court, and the district judge oversees the pretrial and trial process. There are currently 94 federal districts, each of which has a number of judges. Some states and territories have only a single district, such as the District of Connecticut, the District of Minnesota, and the District of Puerto Rico. Others have multiple districts, such as the Northern, Central, Southern, and Eastern Districts of California.

If a party appeals the judgment of the district court, the appeal goes to the U.S. court of appeals. The courts of appeals are divided into 13 circuits; you will often hear lawyers refer to them as *circuit courts.* Twelve circuits cover geographically defined areas—the circuits numbered First through Eleventh, plus the District of Columbia Circuit. Appeals from the Southern District of Texas, for example, go to the U.S. Court of Appeals for the Fifth Circuit, which includes Texas and Louisiana. The Federal Circuit does not cover a specific geographical area, but instead hears appeals of patent cases and appeals from certain federal agencies and several specialized federal courts—the Court of International Trade, the Court of Federal Claims, and the Court of Appeals for Veterans Claims.

From these 13 U.S. courts of appeals, losing parties may attempt to take a further appeal to the U.S. Supreme Court, but as mentioned above, the Supreme Court hears very few cases each year.

Most of the state court systems contain three tiers just like the federal system, although the names vary significantly. We have already seen that some state trial courts use names that make it easy for a novice to confuse them with federal courts, such as the District Courts of Texas, the Circuit Courts of Tennessee, and the Supreme Court of New York. State intermediate courts of appeals, such as California's Courts of Appeal or New Jersey's Superior Court Appellate Division, hear appeals from the trial courts. Each state has a high court, often called the state supreme court, although again, New York manages to confuse things by naming its highest court the Court of Appeals. This responsibility may be divided; Texas has a nine-justice Supreme Court for civil cases and a separate nine-judge Court of Criminal Appeals. Some smaller states employ a two-tier system in which appeals go directly from the trial courts to the state's high court.

On questions of state law, there is no higher judicial authority than the state high court. But if a state court case involves a question of federal law—for example, if a party argues that a state statute violates the U.S. Constitution—then the U.S. Supreme Court has jurisdiction to hear an appeal from the state high court or whichever state court was the last to hear the case. Thus, most appeals to the Supreme Court come from the federal courts of appeals, but each year the Supreme Court hears a number of cases from the state courts that raise important federal issues.

FEDERAL AND STATE COURT SYSTEMS

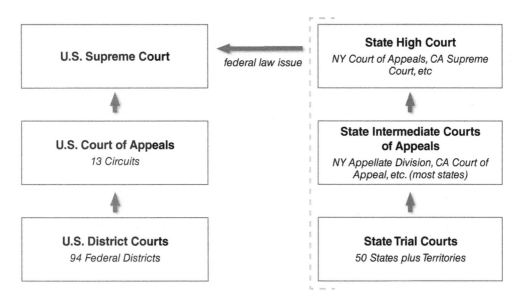

D. PROCEDURAL DUE PROCESS

The Fifth and Fourteenth Amendments to the U.S. Constitution provide that neither the federal government nor a state government may deprive any person of "life, liberty, or property, without due process of law." When a court renders a decision in a civil lawsuit, it may deprive a person of property, for example by imposing a judgment that requires a defendant to pay damages to a plaintiff. The court is an arm of the government. Therefore, the requirement of the Due Process Clause applies. But what process is due?

At a minimum, before being subjected to a civil judgment, a party is entitled to notice about the proceeding, an opportunity to be heard, and a neutral decision maker, but due process can require much more than this, depending on the circumstances. The Supreme Court has described procedural due process in terms of a balancing test:

> [O]ur prior decisions indicate that identification of the specific dictates of due process generally requires consideration of three distinct factors: First, the private interest that will be affected by the official action; second, the risk of an erroneous deprivation of such interest through the procedures used, and the probable value, if any, of additional or substitute procedural safeguards; and finally, the Government's interest, including the function involved and the fiscal and administrative burdens that the additional or substitute procedural requirement would entail.

Mathews v. Eldridge, 424 U.S. 319, 332-33 (1976) (citing *Goldberg v. Kelly*, 397 U.S. 254, 263-71 (1970)).

The axiom underlying the *Mathews v. Eldridge* balancing test is that process is not costless. Perhaps we could better find the truth in a $10,000 dispute by spending $1 million on a factual investigation, but it wouldn't be worth it. Costs may include not only monetary cost to the parties and to the taxpayers through support of the court system, but also the time of parties, witnesses, jurors, and others, as well as intangible costs such as intrusions on privacy and harm to relationships. As you encounter each aspect of civil procedure in this book, consider the costs as well as the benefits of each procedural opportunity. Even more, consider whether the current rules and doctrines of the law of civil procedure make good on the promise of the Due Process Clause.

THE BIG PICTURE

In the United States, the law of civil procedure comes from at least four different sources:

(1) **Constitution.** In addition to the Due Process Clause, the U.S. Constitution includes provisions on jury trial, jurisdiction, and other fundamental aspects of procedure. Similarly, each state has its own state constitution with provisions that relate

to state courts. Constitutional provisions can be changed only by the difficult process of amending the constitution, but courts, including the U.S. Supreme Court, engage in the ongoing process of constitutional interpretation.

(2) **Statutes.** An entire volume of the U.S. Code (Title 28) is devoted to statutes that govern federal courts, and state statutes similarly govern state courts. In nearly every chapter of this book, you will encounter statutes—laws passed by the U.S. Congress or by state legislatures—that regulate aspects of the litigation process.

(3) **Rules.** Most of this book will explore the Federal Rules of Civil Procedure. These rules govern most of the litigation process. The rules are technically adopted by the U.S. Supreme Court, but in reality are created and amended through a lengthy rule-making process that includes participation by judges, lawyers, and others, including an opportunity for Congress to reject proposed rules. Each state has its own rules of procedure for its state courts, many of which are modeled on the federal rules.

(4) **Common Law.** While other law school courses, such as torts, contracts, and property, are heavily based on common law, it plays a smaller role in civil procedure. However, a few aspects of procedure, such as the binding effect of court judgments, are based mostly on common law development through judicial decisions.

E. AN INTRODUCTORY CASE FILE

What follows is a set of litigation materials from an actual dispute between an injured guest and a hotel owner. The purpose of including these materials obviously is not for you to learn law about hotel owners' liability, nor is it even for you to learn any particular points about the law of civil procedure. Rather, the purpose is to offer you an overview of the litigation process in the form of a concrete, real world dispute. These documents are not models of perfect lawyering, nor are they models of bad lawyering; they are here simply to give you a litigation story line so that you can see how the pieces fit together. Each of these documents is heavily abridged and they were selected from among hundreds of items in the actual lawsuit—pleadings, motions, discovery requests and responses, judicial decisions, and so forth—but they should suffice to let you see the arc of the litigation. We hope that by seeing the forest before examining each tree, you will better comprehend details of civil procedure throughout the book.

COMPLAINT

IN THE UNITED STATES DISTRICT COURT
FOR THE DISTRICT OF UTAH

E. JAMES SPAHR and COLLEEN SPAHR Plaintiffs, vs. CHOICE HOTELS INTERNATIONAL, INC., a Corporation organized in Delaware; RODEWAY INN & SUITES; FERBER RESORTS, LLC, a Corporation organized in Utah; DOES 1 through 10; and ROE CORPORATIONS 1 through 10. Defendants.	**AMENDED COMPLAINT** Civil No.: 2:08cv00072 Judge: Ted Stewart

COME NOW the Plaintiffs, E. James Spahr and Colleen Spahr, by and through their attorney, A. Bryce Dixon of the Law firm of Dixon Truman, Fisher & Clifford, P.C. and allege and complains against Defendants as follows:

THE PARTIES

1. Plaintiffs E. James Spahr and his wife, Colleen Spahr, are both residents and citizens of the state of Michigan.

2. Upon information and belief, Defendant Choice Hotels International, Inc. (hereinafter "Choice Hotels") is a corporation organized in Delaware whose headquarters is in Maryland.

3. Defendant Rodeway Inn & Suites (hereinafter "Rodeway"), is a fictional entity doing business in Washington County Utah.

4. Defendant Ferber Resorts, LLC (hereinafter "Ferber") is a Utah corporation doing business in Washington County, Utah. . . .

6. The accident which is the subject matter of this law suit occurred in the County of Washington, State of Utah.

JURISDICTION AND VENUE

7. Plaintiffs file this action in the United States District Court for the District of Utah, on the basis of Diversity of Citizenship pursuant to 28 U.S.C. §1332.

8. Plaintiffs suffered personal injuries and medical and hospital expenses such that the case has an amount in controversy exceeding $75,000.00 exclusive of interest and costs and exceeding the sum specific by 28 U.S.C. section 1332(a).

FIRST CAUSE OF ACTION — NEGLIGENCE

9. Defendants Choice Hotels and/or Rodeway and/or Ferber owned and operated a motel on and before October 4, 2006 in Springdale, Utah.

10. The name of the motel at that time was Rodeway Inn & Suites.

11. Plaintiffs on October 4, 2006 were registered guests of the said lodging establishment.

12. In the early morning hours of October 4, 2006 while it was dark, E. James Spahr walked from his room toward the office of the motel.

13. He fell in an open culvert or ditch about six feet deep, landing directly on his knees on concrete at the bottom of the culvert.

14. Mr. Spahr did not see the open culvert because of the darkness.

15. There was no covering over the culvert opening nor any barriers to protect pedestrians from walking off into the culvert.

16. Mr. Spahr fell just a few feet away from the asphalt covering over the culvert that establishes the main path for patrons of the hotel to walk toward the office from the rooms on the other side of the culvert.

17. As a result of the fall Mr. Spahr suffered a patellar tendon rupture, an open laceration to his knee, back pain, chest pain and permanent disability.

18. Mr. Spahr suffered surgery to repair the patellar tendon but his recovery from that surgery was complicated by infection.

19. As a result of the fall Mr. Spahr incurred expenses for hospital and medical treatment and for physical therapy and rehabilitation amounting to $29,543.43.

20. He further incurred expenses for medical supplies of $419.74 and travel expenses of $200.

SECOND CAUSE OF ACTION — LOSS OF CONSORTIUM

21. Plaintiffs incorporate paragraphs 1 through 18 of the Complaint as though said paragraphs were fully set forth at this point herein.

22. As a result of the fall Mr. Spahr's wife, Colleen, lost income in the amount of $2,927.83 to care for her husband.

23. Ms. Spahr also lost the support, companionship, and consortium of her husband as well.

WHEREFORE, the plaintiffs demand judgment as follows:
1. General damages of $350,000
2. Special damages of $33,091.00
3. Such other and further relief as may be proper in the premises.

DATED this 12th day of March, 2008.

ANSWER

E. JAMES SPAHR and COLLEEN SPAHR,
 	
        Plaintiffs,
 	
vs.
 	
CHOICE HOTELS INTERNATIONAL,
INC., a Corporation organized in
Delaware; RODEWAY INN & SUITES;
FERBER RESORTS, L.L.C., a Corporation
organized in Utah; DOES 1 through 10;
and ROE CORPORATIONS 1 through 10,
 	
        Defendants.
	Case No. 2:08cv00072TS
	
	AMENDED ANSWER
	
	JURY DEMANDED

Defendant Rodeway Inn and Suites and Defendant Ferber Resorts, L.L.C. (*hereinafter* "Defendant"), by and through counsel of record Trent J. Waddoups, answers the Amended Complaint filed by Plaintiffs E. James Spahr and Colleen Spahr (*hereinafter* "Plaintiffs") on or about March 12, 2008 and admits, denies, and alleges as follows:

FIRST DEFENSE

Plaintiffs' Complaint fails to state a cause of action upon which relief can be granted.

SECOND DEFENSE

THE PARTIES

1. In response to the allegations contained in Paragraph 1, Defendant denies the allegations for lack of sufficient information upon which to form an opinion as to the truthfulness of the allegations.

2. In response to the allegations contained in Paragraph 2, Defendant denies the allegations for lack of sufficient information upon which to form an opinion as to the truthfulness of the allegations.

3. In response to the allegations contained in Paragraph 3, Defendant denies the allegations. Defendant affirmatively alleges that the business at which the alleged accident occurred was Rodeway Inn and Suites operated by Ferber Resorts International, L.L.C. and that, upon information and belief, Choice Hotels is a licensor (Defendant does not vouch for the precise legal description because it could properly be described as a franchisor

but Defendant denies the relevance of the precise legal description) of the trade name Rodeway Inn and Suites. Defendant Ferber Resorts admits it was doing business as Rodeway Inn & Suites at the time of the alleged incident in Washington County.

4. In response to the allegations contained in Paragraph 4, Defendant denies the allegations. Defendant affirmatively alleges that Ferber Resorts International, L.L.C. is a limited liability company organized under the laws of the State of Utah and that it conducted business in Washington County as set forth in Paragraph 3. . . .

6. In response to the allegations contained in Paragraph 6, Defendant admits that the place of business at which the alleged accident occurred is located in or near Springdale City, Washington County, State of Utah.

JURISDICTION AND VENUE

. . .

8. In response to the allegations contained in Paragraph 8, Defendant admits that the Plaintiffs claim damages in excess of the jurisdictional threshold and denies the remainder of the allegations for lack of personal knowledge.

FIRST CAUSE OF ACTION — NEGLIGENCE

9. In response to the allegations contained in Paragraph 9, Defendant admits the allegation that Ferber Resorts operated a Rodeway Inn in Springdale, Utah on October 4, 2006.

10. In response to the allegations contained in Paragraph 10, Defendant admits the allegations.

11. In response to the allegations contained in Paragraph 11, Defendant denies the allegations as stating a legal conclusion and admits that Plaintiffs stayed at the Rodeway Inn for a period of time including October 4, 2006.

12. In response to the allegations contained in Paragraphs 12 through 15, Defendant denies the allegations.

13. In response to the allegations contained in Paragraph 16, Defendant denies the allegations. Defendant affirmatively alleges that Plaintiff was familiar with the layout of the hotel and was fully aware of the culvert's existence prior to the accident. Defendant further alleges that, immediately before the accident in question, Plaintiff consciously elected not to use the clearly marked and illuminated pathway between the buildings which he had used on at least one prior occasion.

14. In response to the allegations contained in Paragraphs 17 through 20, Defendant denies the allegations for lack of sufficient information upon which to form an opinion as to their truthfulness.

SECOND CAUSE OF ACTION — LOSS OF CONSORTIUM

15. In response to the allegations contained in Paragraph 21, Defendant incorporates the admissions, denials, and allegations as set forth above.

16. In response to the allegations contained in Paragraph 22, Defendant denies the allegations for lack of sufficient information upon which to form an opinion as to their truthfulness.

17. In response to the allegations contained in Paragraph 23, Defendant denies the allegations.

18. In response to the allegations contained in Paragraphs 1 through 3 in Plaintiffs' prayer for relief, Defendant denies the allegations.

19. Defendant denies each and every allegation set forth in Plaintiffs' Amended Complaint that is not specifically admitted herein.

THIRD DEFENSE

As a separate and affirmative defense, Defendant alleges assumption of risk, estoppel, fraud, failure of consideration, release, laches, superseding cause, new and independent cause, lack of knowledge or notice, local regulation, trespass and waiver.

. . .

SIXTH DEFENSE

As a separate and affirmative defense, Defendant alleges that liability, if any, is limited to the proportionate share of fault attributable to a person, and the parties are entitled to an apportionment of fault of all parties and non-parties pursuant to UTAH CODE ANN. §78-27-37, *et seq.* This affirmative defense may be amended after discovery is provided. Potentially responsible parties include the county irrigation or drainage district. . . .

NINTH DEFENSE

As a separate and affirmative defense, Defendant alleges that any damage or injury sustained by Plaintiffs was caused or proximately contributed to by negligence or other culpable conduct of Plaintiffs, said negligence or culpable conduct being equal to or greater than the negligence or culpable conduct, if any, of the Defendant.

. . .

TWELFTH DEFENSE

As a separate and affirmative defense, Defendant alleges that the Plaintiffs had knowledge of the allegedly dangerous condition and made a calculated decision to assume the risk of crossing said condition. Defendant affirmatively denies that the condition was unreasonably dangerous. Defendant also affirmatively denies that it owed any duty of care relating to the condition alleged to have precipitated the injuries.

. . .

WHEREFORE, Defendant, having answered Plaintiffs' Complaint, prays that the same be dismissed, for no cause of action, that Plaintiffs take nothing therefor, for Defendant's costs of court incurred herein, and for such other and further relief as the Court deems just in the premises.

DEFENDANT REASSERTS ITS DEMAND FOR A TRIAL BY JURY.

DISCOVERY

Editors' Note: After the plaintiffs filed their Complaint and the defendants responded with Answers, the parties engaged in factual investigation and discovery. This included obtaining documents and medical records, posing questions to each other through written interrogatories, and taking depositions of several witnesses. The following is a brief excerpt from the transcript of one of the depositions:

> The deposition of **E. JAMES SPAHR,** a witness in the above-entitled cause, taken at the instance of the Defendants, at the Law Offices of Dixon, Truman, Fisher & Clifford, P.C., 20 North Main Street, Suite 205, St. George, Utah, on Monday, June 17, 2008, at the hour of 12:00 p.m., before Heidi Hunter, Certified Court Reporter, Registered Professional Reporter, in and for the State of Utah.

Q: **BY MR. WADDOUPS:** . . . You said the last thing you knew was you didn't have any ground under your foot. Can you remember any part of the fall?

A: Oh, yes.

Q: Take me through that.

A: Well, there's that split second when you wonder what's happened and what's going to happen, most definitely.

Q: And —

A: And then I hit and my legs were back, self-defense was hands down, because you know if you ever go through anything like that, I hope you never do, but you're going to hit something. So my hands went down, my legs were apparently back, I'm not sure if that's because I was walking or what, you know, my feet went straight down, but my legs were back and I landed on my knees.

. . .

Q: Did you hit your hands before — did your hands hit the ground before your knee did or is there any way to tell?

A: It all happened together. Yeah, I don't have any recollection of one and then the other, it was a total impact.

Q: And then you hit your head, we understand that from your wife's testimony, is that right?

A: What happened was when I hit the ground, I basically stopped and then I fell over.

. . .

Q: After you fell, what was the first thing you did?

A: Well, I guess I tried to take stock of what had happened, first of all, tried to get myself to my feet.

Q: And did you have any problem getting to your feet?

A: Yes, I did.

Q: How — how so?

A: Well, primarily the injury to my left knee.

Q: How did that affect your ability to stand up?

A: Well, I — I knew my left knee had more injury than anyplace else. I could tell that. I pulled myself up, I don't remember exactly how, but onto my right leg, and then tried to walk, tried to put pressure on my left leg, which I could not do.

. . .

Q: Going back a little bit, when you left the room, you decided to get ice for the cooler, correct?

A: I was going to check out and get ice.

. . .

Q: We talked to your wife and to you, and it seems like nearly every time you left the hotel room to go over toward the office you went around across the bridge. Isn't that a fair restatement of the testimony?

A: That's correct.

Q: Do you have any recollection of why you didn't go that direction this time?

A: The darkness.

Q: What do you mean?

A: I would not have walked over that stone path in the dark.

Q: Why not?

A: Irregular surface, grass, stone, grass, stone.

Q: Do you remember making that conscious decision or is that just what you do?

A: I do remember making that decision, yes.

Q: And do you remember thinking about the culvert running up to the ledge there to those rocks?

A: I had not seen the culvert.

Q: Well, you walked across the culvert several times according to your testimony across that bridge?

. . .

Q: You did know that there was the ditch there. Did you know that it ended at those rocks at the parking lot?

A: I had not paid attention to the ditch, no.

Q: But you had seen those rocks before?

A: I had not paid attention to the rocks.

. . .

Q: Besides the dark, what do you think was wrong with the condition of the ditch at the time that you fell into it?

MR. DIXON: I'm going to object inasmuch to the extent that it calls for a legal conclusion that this witness is not competent to give. He can certainly give a lay opinion. I think that's what you're asking him for. You can give your opinion.

A: No barrier.

. . .

Q: Did it occur to you at all to walk on the left-hand side of those as you're walking toward the office?

A: In the dark?

Q: Yeah, in the dark.

A: I don't know. When are you referring to?

Q: Did that ever occur to you as you're walking toward the office with the ice chest, to check out, that you should walk to the left of them?

A: No.

MOTION FOR SUMMARY JUDGMENT

E. JAMES SPAHR and COLLEEN SPAHR Plaintiffs, vs. CHOICE HOTELS INTERNATIONAL, INC., a corporation organized in Delaware; RODEWAY INN & SUITES; FERBER RESORTS, L.L.C., a corporation organized in Utah; DOES 1 through 10; and ROE CORPORATIONS 1 through 10, Defendants.	Case No. 2:08cv0072 **MEMORANDUM IN SUPPORT OF DEFENDANTS' MOTION FOR SUMMARY JUDGMENT**

Pursuant to FED R. CIV. P. 56, the Defendants (hereinafter "Defendant" and "Rodeway Inn") submit this brief in support of a Motion for Summary Judgment. . . .

The question on summary judgment is whether, if the record of the summary judgment proceeding were the record of a trial, a reasonable factfinder, whether judge or jury, could find in favor of the party opposing the motion for summary judgment. . . .

The undisputed facts demonstrate that the wash is not out of place in Springdale, Utah; it is large and deep, and the dangers of walking into it would have been perceived by any reasonable person. Moreover, Mr. Spahr had alternate routes he could have followed. He had previously taken other routes during his stay at the hotel.

The undisputed evidence does not support a reasonable inference that the Defendant should have expected Plaintiff to fail to discover, realize, or avoid danger, or should have anticipated harm despite Plaintiff's knowledge and awareness of the existence of the wash. . . .

Both the wash into which Mr. Spahr walked and the darkness into which Mr. Spahr walked were perspicuous warnings which discharged the Defendant's duty of care to its business invitee. The mere existence of the conditions were adequate warnings. Because the danger of an accident was itself a sufficient, and costless, warning, there was no need, and therefore no legal duty, to provide any additional warnings or protection. . . .

There is no duty, and therefore no cause of action for negligence, when the hazard in question is open and obvious. This is so regardless of how "negligent" the defendant's conduct ordinarily would appear to be. . . .

No reasonable person exercising due care for his own safety by observing what is there to be seen would walk into the wash. When courts apply the open and obvious danger rule, they must focus on the fact that the doctrine relates to the threshold issue of duty. By focusing on the duty prong of negligence, the rule properly considers the nature of the dangerous condition itself, as opposed to the nature of the plaintiff's conduct in encountering it.

The fact that a plaintiff was unreasonable in choosing to encounter the danger is not what relieves the property owner of liability. Rather, it is the fact that the condition itself is so obvious that it absolves the property owner from taking any further action to protect the plaintiff. . . .

Therefore, the Defendant owed no duty and a summary judgment is appropriate.

TRIAL

Editors' Note: The judge denied the summary judgment motion and eventually the case proceeded to trial, which lasted four days. At trial, the court empaneled a jury and each side's lawyer made an opening statement. Then the lawyers presented their evidence by calling witnesses, each of whom was subject to direct examination and cross-examination. Below is a short excerpt from the transcript of day two of the trial, including the testimony of plaintiffs' witness Sandra Trindel, a first responder:

Salt Lake City, Utah, Tuesday, October 20, 2009

. . .

THE COURT: Good morning. Thank you for being here on time. We're here in Spahr v. Ferber Resorts. Mr. Dixon you may proceed.

MR. DIXON: Thank you, Your Honor. We call Ms. Sandra Trindel as our next witness. Shall I go get her?

THE COURT: Yes, if you will please.

Q: I'm going to show you, ma'am, what we have marked as Exhibit 2. Take a look at that, if you would. Does that appear to be the report you filled out?

A: Yes, it does.

. . .

MR. DIXON: I move for the admission of Exhibit 2, Your Honor.

MR. WADDOUPS: No objection.

THE COURT: Exhibit 2 is received. (Whereupon, Plaintiff's Exhibit 2 was received into evidence.)

. . .

Q: (By Mr. Dixon) You've already said that upon arrival you saw the patient sitting on a ledge, or I guess a rock. It would be the same as a rock; is that right?

A: Correct.

. . .

Q: Then after that, there's a reference to the pain goes to 7 out of 10. What does that mean, what are you talking about there?

A: Well, in the emergency room they'll ask you if you're in pain on a scale of 1 to 10, with 1 being the lowest and 10 being the most excruciating pain, where you would put your pain level. And at that time Mr. Spahr put it at 7 over 10. So out of the possible 10 being the worst he's ever felt, he expressed being at number 7.

. . .

Q: All right. Now, the last note in your report before we go to that, it says that — you've written, Note: Light not working on site of injury. Do you remember what that diagram — can we pull up that diagram? All right. Did you mark the light on that diagram?

A: Yes, I did. It's in the upper left-hand corner.

Q: And that was close to the place where Mr. Spahr had fallen.

A: Correct.

Q: And you observed that light was not working when you were at the scene of the accident?

A: Correct.

Q: And then you also observed totally dark there.

A: Yes.

. . .

Q: Did you have occasion to go back to the scene of the accident in the daylight hours?

> **MR. WADDOUPS:** I'm going to object because he's calling for opinion testimony by a layman.
>
> **THE COURT:** Yes. Let's see what the question is, but so far we've just got her at the scene.

Q: (By Mr. Dixon) Did you go back to the scene of the accident?

A: Yes.

Q: All right. And did you go back in the daylight?

A: Yes, I did.

Q: Why did you go back to the scene of the accident?

A: To see for myself the exact — the culvert and the situation that had taken place because it was so dark.

. . .

Q: Now, after taking — after looking at all of those things, did you come to any feelings about whether this was foreseeable that this accident might happen?

> **MR. WADDOUPS:** Objection.
>
> **THE COURT:** Sustained.
>
> **MR. DIXON:** That's all the questions I have ma'am.
>
> **THE COURT:** Cross-examination?
>
> **MR. WADDOUPS:** Just a couple of items.

Q: (By Mr. Waddoups) . . . First of all, you were looking at your report and it listed 7:08 as the time that you initially gave the morphine; is that correct?

A: Correct.

Q: Where were you at the time, in the ambulance?

A: We were in route to the hospital, correct.

Q: Was it light outside at that time of the morning?

A: No.

Q: It was still dark?

A: Correct.

. . .

> **MR. WADDOUPS:** Okay. That's all I have.
>
> **THE COURT:** Any redirect?
>
> **MR. DIXON:** No, Your Honor.
>
> **THE COURT:** Thank you. You may step down.

JUDGMENT

IN THE UNITED STATES DISTRICT COURT
FOR THE DISTRICT OF UTAH

E. JAMES SPAHR and COLLEEN SPAHR,	
Plaintiffs,	JUDGMENT ON JURY VERDICT
vs.	Civil No.: 2:08cv00072
	Judge: Clark Waddoups
FERBER RESORTS, LLC, a Corporation organized in Utah	
Defendants.	

This action came on for trial on October 19, 2009 before the Court and a jury, Honorable Clark Waddoups, District Judge, presiding, the issues having been duly tried and the jury having duly rendered its verdict upon special interrogatories on October 23, 2009. The jury found that condition of the land where Plaintiff E. James Spahr fell was not known or obvious to him, that the negligence of Ferber Resorts, LLC (herein Ferber Resorts) caused harm to the Plaintiffs, that Mr. Spahr's own negligence caused harm to himself, that Ferber Resorts' percentage of fault was 99 percent of the total and Mr. Spahr's percentage of fault was one percent of the total, that Mr. Spahr suffered economic damages of $31,216.41 (from this figure the court deducts the sum of $10,000 in medical payments coverage from Ferber Resorts' insurance carrier for a total of $21,216.41 in economic damages) and noneconomic damages of $375,855.76, that Colleen Spahr suffered a loss of consortium caused by Ferber Resorts, that Colleen Spahr suffered economic damages of $2,927.83 and noneconomic damages of $40,000. The total of the damages found was $450,000 which sum must be reduced by the amount of Mr. Spahr's comparative negligence of 1%, yielding a discount for comparative negligence of $4,500.

It is ORDERED AND ADJUDGED that Plaintiff E. James Spahr recover of the Defendant Ferber Resorts, LLC the sum of $393,001.45 ($31,216.41 plus $375,855.76 less one percent less $10,000 med pay) and that Plaintiff Colleen Spahr recover of Defendant Ferber Resorts, LLC the sum of $42,498.55. Each sum shall accrue interest at the rate of .39% percent as provided by law. Plaintiff shall also recover of Defendant Ferber Resorts, LLC their costs of action.

Dated this 28th day of October 2009.

BY THE COURT:

CLARK WADDOUPS
U.S. District Judge

DECISION ON RENEWED MOTION FOR JUDGMENT AS A MATTER OF LAW

Editors' Note: Before the jury reached a verdict, the defendant had moved for "judgment as a matter of law," arguing that no reasonable jury could find for the Spahrs based on the evidence presented at trial. The judge denied the motion. After the jury reached a verdict in favor of the Spahrs, the defendant renewed its motion for judgment as a matter of law. On February 4, 2010, the district judge issued his decision, of which the following is an excerpt:

UNITED STATES DISTRICT COURT
FOR THE DISTRICT OF UTAH

E. JAMES SPAHR and COLLEEN SPAHR,	
Plaintiffs,	**ORDER and**
	MEMORANDUM DECISION
vs.	
FERBER RESORTS, LLC d/b/a RODEWAY INN,	Case No. 2:08-cv-72-CW
Defendant.	

Now before the court is Defendant Ferber Resort's motion for a judgment as a matter of law or, in the alternative, for a new trial or remittitur (Dkt. No. 26). For the reasons discussed below, this motion is DENIED in its entirety.

A. Judgment as a Matter of Law Under Rule 50
1. Ferber Resorts Owed a Legal Duty to Protect Mr. Spahr from a Dangerous Condition.

Ferber Resorts contends that Mr. Spahr knew that he was walking into the darkest part of the property and took the risk that he might be injured as a result. According to Ferber Resorts, Mr. Spahr's doing so relieved Ferber Resorts of any legal duty to Mr. Spahr.

The court concludes that the evidence does not compel a finding that, because Mr. Spahr knew it was dark, the dangerous condition at the Rodeway Inn should have been open and obvious to him. To the contrary, Mr. Spahr presented evidence that reasonably supported the jury's finding that Ferber Resorts had a legal duty to provide adequate lighting and otherwise protect against the risk that a person would not see the ditch while attempting to walk from the motel rooms to the motel office. For example, Mr. Spahr testified that while attempting to reach the office in the early morning hours he was not simply walking into a pitch dark area. Rather, he recalled that there was bright lighting near the guest buildings and ambient lighting as he walked away from the guest buildings. Moreover, there was a light on near the office which he testified he was walking directly toward. There was also evidence that the drive way light on the pole next to the ditch was not on, the automatic timer apparently having turned the light off long before day light. This testimony was corroborated by other evidence. Mr. Spahr further testified that the area of the ditch that he walked into appeared to him to be a continuation of the pavement, not simply an abyss. The photographs of the ditch and its surroundings, as well as other evidence, support this testimony. This testimony, along with other evidence, supports a finding that the darkness into which Mr. Spahr walked did not alone reasonably put him on notice of a danger.

2. The Evidence Supports the Verdict for Loss of Consortium.

Ferber Resorts asserts that Ms. Spahr did not prove a significant injury to Mr. Spahr sufficient to satisfy . . . the loss of consortium statute. Specifically, Ferber Resorts contends that Ms. Spahr did not present evidence that Mr. Spahr was "paralyzed," that he had a "significant disfigurement," or that he was "incapable" of performing the types of jobs he did before the injury.

Mr. Spahr did not claim to have been paralyzed and no evidence was offered to support such an assertion. Ms. Spahr did, however, present evidence of scars on Mr. Spahr's knee, a fact that Ferber Resorts concedes. . . . There was further testimony that Mr. Spahr was ashamed to be seen in shorts because people might see the scarring to his knee. While neither party has cited any Utah authority establishing what exactly is required to show a "significant disfigurement" . . . the court is convinced that the extreme scarring to Mr. Spahr's knee reasonably meets that definition.

Moreover, there was evidence that Mr. Spahr was unable to perform key aspects of the types of jobs he did before the injury. . . . In this case, the evidence reasonably supported a finding by the jury that Mr. Spahr was incapable of performing many of the jobs he had done before the injury. . . .

For the above reasons, the evidence supports a finding by a reasonable jury that Mr. Spahr was either significantly disfigured, incapable of performing jobs he did before the injury, or both. Either of these findings supports the conclusion that Mr. Spahr was significantly injured as defined by the Utah loss of consortium statute. Accordingly, Ms. Spahr was not precluded as a matter of law from proceeding on her loss of consortium claim.

APPEAL

Editors' Note: Ferber Resorts appealed the district court's denial of its motion for judgment as a matter of law. The following is an excerpt from the appellate court's decision:

UNITED STATES COURT OF APPEALS
FOR THE TENTH CIRCUIT

E. James SPAHR and Colleen Spahr,	
Plaintiffs,	ORDER and JUDGMENT
vs.	No. 10-4055
	(D.C. No. 2:08-cv-72-CW)
FERBER RESORTS, LLC,	(D. Utah)
Defendant.	

Before KELLY, TACHA, and LUCERO, Circuit Judges.

PAUL KELLY, JR., Circuit Judge.

Defendant-Appellant Ferber Resorts, LLC ("Ferber Resorts") appeals from a judgment on a jury verdict awarding $393,001.45 to Plaintiff-Appellee James Spahr on his negligence claim and $42,498.55 to Plaintiff-Appellee Colleen Spahr, his wife, for loss of consortium. After trial, Ferber Resorts unsuccessfully moved for judgment as a matter of law.... Utah law applies in this diversity case, and our jurisdiction arises under 28 U.S.C. §1291. We affirm.

Because this is an appeal from the denial of judgment as a matter of law, we view the facts in the light most favorable to the non-moving party—here, Mr. and Mrs. Spahr. [The court proceeded to describe the facts, the procedural history, and the arguments on appeal.]

Our review of the denial of a Rule 50 motion is *de novo*. Only when the evidence would not permit a reasonable jury to find in favor of the non-movant would judgment as a matter of law be required.

[The court stated the elements, under Utah law, for a claim against a possessor of land for liability for physical harm caused to an invitee by a condition on the land, citing *Hale v. Beckstead*, 116 P.3d 263 (Utah 2005) and Restatement (Second) of Torts §343 (1965).]

First, evidence supports the jury's finding that Ferber Resorts knew or should have known about the wash and should have realized that it involved an unreasonable risk of harm. Stewart Ferber—the principal of Ferber Resorts, LLC—testified that he bought the property and designed the layout of the hotel, that he knew the wash separated the office from the guest rooms, and that he "accept[ed] 100% responsibility" for safety at the hotel. . . . Evidence also showed that Ferber Resorts knew the lights were controlled by an automatic timer that required manual adjustment to keep up with changing daylight hours. Finally, evidence showed that Ferber Resorts considered the parking lot a safe means of ingress and egress—even at night, and even though the wash protruded into the parking lot and was surrounded by pavement on three sides.

Second, there was sufficient evidence for the jury to conclude that Ferber Resorts should have expected that the guests would not discover or realize the danger, or that they would fail to protect themselves against it. . . . Witnesses testified that the parking lot was part of the approved means of egress and ingress between the guest rooms and the office and that rocks had previously surrounded the entire culvert but had been removed where Mr. Spahr fell. Mr. Spahr also testified that there was minimal light at the time of the accident. The lights were set to turn off at 6:00 a.m.—even though it was still dark at that time—and in the low-light conditions, Mr. Spahr could not distinguish between the black of the asphalt and the darkness of the wash.

Finally, evidence supports the jury's conclusion that Ferber Resorts failed to exercise reasonable care to protect the Spahrs against the danger. . . . Ferber Resorts did not warn the guests or construct any sort of barrier to protect them from injury. Further, Ferber Resorts did not ensure that the wash was illuminated in low-light conditions—certainly a reasonable step that could have been taken. . . .

In sum, there is ample evidence from which the jury could conclude that Ferber Resorts was liable under the elements of [Utah law]. Therefore, the district court did not err in denying Ferber Resorts' motion for judgment as a matter of law.

[The court discussed the defendant's other arguments on appeal, rejecting each one.]

AFFIRMED.

Notes & Questions

The documents reprinted above from *Spahr v. Ferber*—complaint, answer, deposition transcript, summary judgment motion, trial transcript, judgment, decision on post-trial motion, and appellate opinion—reflect only a tiny selection from the many documents in that litigation. Even so, you should be able to follow the basic story of the litigation and understand the moves made by each party along the way. Take it step by step, using the following questions as a guide.

1. Who sued whom? What was the basis for the claim? What remedy did the plaintiffs seek?

2. What court did the plaintiffs choose? Was it a state court or a federal court? What was the basis for the court's jurisdiction?

3. Which of the plaintiffs' allegations did the defendants admit and which did they deny? In addition to denying some of the plaintiffs' allegations, what "affirmative defenses" did the defendants assert?

4. What sort of information did the parties seek during the discovery process, based on what you saw in the deposition excerpt? What other information do you suppose each side sought?

5. On what basis did the defendants (unsuccessfully) ask the court to grant summary judgment?

6. What sort of evidence did the parties introduce at trial, at least based on what you can tell from the short excerpt from the trial transcript? Who decided what questions to ask witnesses and what other evidence to put forward? Who ruled on disputes over whether evidence was admissible?

7. What did the jury decide?

8. On what basis did the defendant argue, after the jury verdict, that the court should grant judgment in the defendant's favor? Did the trial judge agree? What was the outcome of the case at the trial court level?

9. Which party appealed the trial court judgment, and on what basis? What court heard the appeal? How many judges heard the appeal? What was the nature of the information provided to the appellate court? Did witnesses testify? Was other evidence presented? If not, then on what basis did the appellate court make a decision? What did it decide?

10. Now step back. Having considered *Spahr v. Ferber* piece by piece, consider it more broadly, and use it as a starting point for establishing certain habits of learning. First, consider the case file from the perspective of procedural policy. Were you satisfied that each party had an adequate opportunity to assert claims and defenses, to gather information, to present factual evidence, and to assert

points of law? Did the process seem well suited to determine what happened and whether the facts establish a basis for liability? Did the process seem well suited for resolving this dispute efficiently? It is probably too early for you to have strong views on any of these questions, and you will have plenty of opportunity to consider whether various aspects of civil procedure are well designed for accuracy, efficiency, dispute resolution, and other objectives. But it is good to get in the habit of asking such questions about every case you read.

11. Next, consider the case file as a matter of strategy. Were there any steps in the process where you think the lawyers could have and should have handled the case differently? The case file gives you too little information for you to say with confidence whether either side made strategic errors. But again, it is good to get in the habit of asking such questions.

12. Finally, consider the case file as preparation for establishing certain habits for learning civil procedure. Why did we ask you to read this case file? Obviously the point is not for you to learn about lighted pathways and dangerous ditches. Nor is the point, in this book, for you to master substantive legal norms that govern liability of property owners for personal injuries. Rather, the point is to give you an overview of the litigation process, and the point of cases in the remainder of the book will be to teach you specific components of the litigation process. To understand the litigation process in *Spahr*, you needed to get comfortable with the facts (the ditch, the fall) and the substantive law (negligence liability of property possessors), but as a matter of your civil procedure education, those facts and law were merely a means to the end of understanding the procedural steps. As you embark on learning civil procedure through the cases in this book, get in the habit of looking for the procedural issues. Use the facts and substantive legal norms in each case as set-ups for thinking about procedure, keeping in mind that the same procedural issues arise in a wide variety of factual contexts.

CHAPTER 2

Pleadings

In every lawsuit, there are at least two sides to the story. That is what makes it a litigated dispute rather than a math problem. The pleadings are how each party tells its side of the story at the outset of the formal litigation process.

To initiate a lawsuit, the plaintiff files a *complaint* setting forth its allegations. The defendant then files an *answer* responding to the plaintiff's allegations. Alternatively, the defendant may file pre-answer motions. In some cases, after a defendant files an answer, the plaintiff files a *reply*.

These documents—the complaint, the answer, and (less commonly) the reply—are known as *pleadings*, and together they set out the framework for the litigation. The pleadings define the boundaries of the litigation by showing which issues are and are not in dispute. Moreover, the pleadings notify each party about the adversary's claims or defenses. Finally, the pleadings provide the information on which a court can decide whether a claim or defense should be dismissed at the outset.

Rules regarding pleading have huge implications for access to justice and the efficient functioning of our system of litigation. As you read this chapter, consider whether the pleading rules strike the appropriate balance between screening meritless lawsuits and providing access to the courts. Consider also whether the pleading rules provide the parties and the court with the right amount of information, and the right sorts of information, at the outset of litigation.

A. COMPLAINT

"A short and plain statement of the claim showing that the pleader is entitled to relief." According to Federal Rule of Civil Procedure 8, that is the heart of what is required to initiate a case in federal court. In broad historical context, this rule is a relatively easy standard to satisfy and to understand. Had you been studying law a century ago, more than half of this book might have been devoted to pleadings. The advent of newer rules and especially the adoption of the Federal Rules of Civil

Procedure greatly simplified the pleading process. However, law is rarely as simple as it appears, and as you will see, the law of pleadings is no exception.

(1) A Brief History of Pleadings

Despite the relative simplicity of modern pleading rules, those rules cannot be understood without some history. Modern pleading is not so much a system unto itself as it is a *reaction* to the common law system that preceded it. The famous legal historian F.W. Maitland wrote that "the forms of action we have buried, but they still rule us from their graves." The following short history reveals the truth behind Maitland's statement.

From about the thirteenth century through the late nineteenth century, the English legal system was divided into two kinds of courts: courts of common law and courts of equity. These two court systems had very different procedures. In the common law courts, pleadings and procedures were linked to a system of *writs*. A writ was what the court issued at the outset of the action, ordering the sheriff to compel the defendant either to appear in court or to satisfy the claim. Every type of claim had its own writ; what's more, every writ had its own procedural rules. In other words, the procedures differed depending on the type of claim.

The categories of liability and their procedures in common law courts were known as forms of action, some with names you might be familiar with, like debt and trespass. The plaintiff had to file a pleading setting forth a cognizable cause of action in whichever form of action she had used. If the plaintiff chose the incorrect form, the case would be thrown out. Over time, the statements required in these pleadings became formulaic.

In the common law pleading system, the defendant could choose one of four basic responses to plaintiff's complaint. One, the defendant could *demur*, meaning the defendant could contend that the plaintiff's pleading did not state a valid legal claim even if the allegations were true. To take a silly example, imagine that Z filed a complaint alleging that Y was liable to Z for wearing a blue shirt in Z's presence. Z hates the color blue, and Z would like to be compensated for having been subjected to the offensive color. Even if Z's allegations are true, *one*, that he detests the color blue; *two*, that Y wore a blue shirt in Z's presence; and *three*, that the blue shirt disgusted Z, you know that the following is also true: It is not unlawful to wear a blue shirt, no matter how much someone dislikes the sartorial choice. Z thus did not state a valid legal claim, even if Z's allegations are true.

Two, the defendant could also make a *dilatory plea*, a response that focuses on procedural issues such as objections to the court's jurisdiction. Here, the defendant did not directly attack either the validity or the veracity of the plaintiff's claims. Instead, the defendant contended that there was some reason, not stemming from the claims themselves, that the case could not be heard by this court, or perhaps by any court.

Three, the defendant could *traverse*. To traverse is to address plaintiff's claims directly by denying the factual allegations in the complaint. Assume that Z alleged that Y climbed his fence and entered his yard without permission—that Y trespassed. If Z's allegations are true, then Z has likely stated a valid legal claim for trespass. If Y chose to traverse, however, he would deny one or more of Z's factual allegations. Perhaps Y never climbed Z's fence; perhaps Y was out of town on the day of the alleged trespass. Both of these contentions are offered to deny the factual allegations in Z's complaint.

Finally, the defendant could make a *confession and avoidance*, wherein the defendant would admit the truth of the plaintiff's allegations but plead something additional as a defense. In the trespass example above, for instance, Y might plead that Z's claim for trespass is barred by the statute of limitations.

The idea behind this formal back-and-forth was to narrow the dispute to a single, precise issue. By forcing the plaintiff to choose a single legal theory and a set of facts, and by forcing the defendant to choose a single response, common law pleading essentially told the parties: Get your disagreement straight, and only then will the court resolve it. Common law pleading had the advantage of defining neatly the disputed issues. But it carried the cost of glossing over ambiguities that inevitably arise when there are at least two sides to a story. Increasingly, the common law pleading system was criticized as hyper-technical and unduly rigid.

During the same time period, courts of equity grew alongside (but entirely separate from) the courts of common law. These courts of equity grew out of the need for a more flexible system capable of filling the gaps left by the restrictive writ system. The courts of equity, as their name implies, were broadly empowered to create fairness in cases where the more mechanical writ system failed to offer parties a way to vindicate their rights. For instance, there were no writs for disputes related to trusts or divorce, so parties with these types of claims had no remedy in the courts of law, but they could pursue their claims before the courts of equity. Further, while the courts of law focused on relatively mechanical monetary damages as the sole remedy for claimants, the courts of equity had greater discretion to craft individualized, nonmonetary remedies such as injunctions and orders for specific performance. Courts of equity had no juries, so judges had heightened power and flexibility in their role as the sole triers of fact. Further, because equity judges were not restricted to a single writ or cause of action, they had freedom to engage in procedural innovations such as counterclaims and joinder.

The courts of law and equity have now largely merged. The procedural innovations of the courts of equity, as well as the spirit of judicial discretion, are dominant features of modern procedure. At the same time, the distinction between "remedies at law" such as money damages and "equitable remedies" such as injunctions remains significant, particularly for determining the right to a jury.

By the mid-nineteenth century, the flaws of common law pleading had grown significant enough to spur reform. Beginning with New York's Field Code in 1848, states abandoned the common law pleading system and adopted *code pleading* systems—so named because they were enacted by statutory codes as opposed to judicially developed common law. The codes abolished the forms of action and replaced them with a requirement that a complaint plead facts, a practice known as *fact pleading*. Under fact, or code, pleading, facts were required to be pleaded at the appropriate levels of specificity, called *ultimate facts*. If a pleading stated facts too generally, those allegations were *mere evidence*. If you find these terms less than illuminating, you are not alone. Judges and attorneys struggled to identify what constituted ultimate facts, and thus code pleading developed its own (ultimately unworkable) technicalities to address this struggle. While code pleading brought pleading closer to the actual facts of the case, continued technical difficulties in code pleading systems led to the need for additional reform. Indeed, only a few states retain code pleading systems today.

The Federal Rules of Civil Procedure ushered in a new era of pleading in federal courts (and in most state courts, which follow analogues of the federal rules). In 1934, Congress passed the Rules Enabling Act, authorizing the Supreme Court to create rules of procedure for the federal courts. This set in motion the process that would lead to the creation of the Federal Rules of Civil Procedure, which went into effect in 1938. The 1938 reformers sought to eliminate procedural technicalities and instead adopted a relatively simple model of adjudication: Cases were to be resolved on their merits at trial (by jury where appropriate), following plenary discovery and pretrial processes for weeding out claims and issues that lacked enough substance to go to trial.

With the new federal rules came not only a new approach to pleading, but also a system that flowed to a significant extent from that new approach to pleadings. Look at the first two rules. In Rule 1, the reformers spell out the overarching goals of the Federal Rules to achieve "the just, speedy, and inexpensive determination of every action." Rule 1 also states that "[t]hese rules govern the procedure in all civil actions and proceedings in United States district courts. . . ." That directive may seem obvious for something called the "Federal Rules of Civil Procedure," but the non-obvious part to the 1938 mindset was that the rules established the same pleadings and other procedures for *both* law and equity. This statement dovetails with Rule 2, which states that "[t]here is one form of action—the civil action." What does that mean? Again, return to the mindset of 1938. Rule 2 echoes, for the new Federal Rules of Civil Procedure, the abolition of the common law forms of action.

If the federal rules rejected the common law pleading system but also broke away from code pleading, what was put in their place? Quite simply, rules animated by new goals for pleading. In place of the former goal of pleadings—to reduce disputes to a single issue—came new aims of giving the parties *notice* of each other's claims and defenses, as well as providing a basis for motions to dismiss and other procedures to test whether the claims and defenses had enough substance to be allowed to proceed.

(2) Pleading Under the Federal Rules

Modern pleadings under the Federal Rules of Civil Procedure are governed by Rules 3 through 12. As you read these rules, pay especially close attention to Rule 8. Note first that Rule 8 applies to *any* "pleading that states a claim for relief." Usually, this means the plaintiff's complaint. However, a plaintiff is not the only one who may bring claims. *See* Fed. R. Civ. P. 7(a) (setting forth the various types of pleadings allowed). Defendants and others may bring counterclaims, crossclaims, and third-party claims, as we will explore in Chapter 7. For present purposes, know this: Rule 8(a) and its pleading standard apply equally to original claims by plaintiffs and to affirmative claims by parties other than the original plaintiff. Similarly, the dictates of Rule 8(b) and (c) regarding denials and defenses apply not only to responses by original defendants, but to *any* pleading that responds to a claim, regardless of who filed that response.

(a) Summons and Complaint

To initiate a lawsuit, a plaintiff must inform both the court and the defendant of the plaintiff's claim. To inform the court, the plaintiff files a complaint with the court. To inform the defendant, the plaintiff delivers a copy of the complaint to the defendant along with a court summons. The summons, governed by Rule 4(a), is an order obtained from the court, signed by the clerk of the court, and bearing the court's seal. The summons notifies the defendant of the exercise of the court's power, and it instructs the defendant to respond. The delivery of the summons and complaint to the defendant is known as *service of process*.

The complaint is the pleading in which the plaintiff sets forth her claims against the defendant as well as her demand for relief. Rule 8(a) requires three things for a complaint to be valid: (1) a statement of the basis for the court's jurisdiction over the claims; (2) a "short and plain statement of the claim showing that the pleader is entitled to relief"; and (3) a demand for relief. The second requirement in 8(a)(2)—a "short and plain statement of the claim(s)"—is the heart of Rule 8(a); it goes directly to the sufficiency of the complaint, and we will spend the bulk of Part A of this chapter on it. Before turning to 8(a)(2), though, let's make quick work of the other two requirements.

Rule 8(a)(1) requires every complaint to include a "short and plain statement of the grounds for the court's jurisdiction." As we will discuss in Chapter 9, federal courts are courts of *limited jurisdiction*. They

---

Terminology Tip

The word *pleading* is used by lawyers in at least three ways. First, as a noun, *pleading* refers to the document itself—the complaint or answer filed in court. Thus, one can say, "The complaint is the plaintiff's pleading." Rule 7 uses the word this way when it lists the pleadings that are allowed. Second, as a verb, *pleading* refers to the act of asserting claims, defenses, or facts. Thus, one can say "the plaintiff pleaded a claim for breach of contract" (or, in the criminal context, "the defendant pleaded not guilty"). Third, *pleading* refers to the stage of a lawsuit during which these documents are filed. Thus, lawyers might say that they have moved on to discovery, having completed the "pleading stage" or "pleadings stage" of the litigation.

Terminology Tip

Both *service* and *process* are common words in the English language, but in the legal phrase *service of process*, neither word is used in its everyday sense. *Service*, in this setting, refers to the formal delivery of a document to another person. *Process* refers to the summons and complaint. Thus, *service of process* is the procedure by which one party gives notice to another party (typically the plaintiff notifying the defendant) of the court proceedings. Rule 4 sets out the requirements for service of process in federal court actions. You will re-encounter Rule 4 in Chapter 10, when we explore the importance of service of process for a court's assertion of power over a party.

may only hear certain types of cases and certain types of claims. If the claims in the complaint do not fall within the federal court's subject matter jurisdiction, the court has no power to hear the case and must dismiss it. Given this dismissal require- ment, Rule 8(a) requires a statement of the court's jurisdiction up front—the court ought to find out about any jurisdictional defect immediately rather than after hav- ing wasted the court's and parties' time litigating the dispute in the wrong court. Note that, while a statement of jurisdiction is required by Rule 8(a), that require- ment applies only in *federal* court. State courts of general jurisdiction need not impose such a requirement because their jurisdiction is not limited like that of the federal courts.

Rule 8(a)(3) requires a complaint to include a "demand for the relief sought, which may include relief in the alternative or different types of relief." In other words, *every* complaint must state what remedy the plaintiff seeks. *Cf. Sholty v. Cavalry Portfolio Servs.*, 2019 WL 4394735 at *6 (C.D. Ill. Sept. 13, 2019) ("A com- plaint without a prayer for relief is nothing more than a[n] essay."). The complaint may demand whatever sort of remedy the plaintiff contends should be provided under applicable substantive law. Maybe the request is for an *injunction*, an order that the defendant do this or refrain from doing that. For instance, in an intellec- tual property case, maybe it is a request for an injunction prohibiting the defendant from infringing on the plaintiff's patent, trademark, or copyright. In a different case, maybe the request is for *specific performance* of a contract. Perhaps the request is for a *declaratory judgment*, which proclaims the legal rights of the parties. Usu- ally, however, the request is a demand for *monetary damages*. Note that Rule 8(a)(3) does not require that plaintiffs specify the precise amount of money requested, although the local rules of some district courts state whether a complaint should specify a dollar amount. In some cases, a complaint demands a specific sum, while other complaints simply demand fair compensation. As a strategic matter, if specifying an amount, plaintiffs' lawyers often demand a monetary judgment at the highest end of the range of damages that would be plausible in the case. As you will learn in Part D of this chapter, however, the demand must have a reason- able basis in law and fact.

(b) Sufficiency of the Complaint: Notice Pleading

Here we turn to the heart of the complaint—the statement of the claims. Rule 8(a)(2) requires that the complaint contain "a short and plain statement of the claim showing that the pleader is entitled to relief." This is a bit misleading. The statement does not necessarily have to be short. Or plain for that matter. Occasionally, a judge will rebuke a party for excessively lengthy or complex pleadings, and a few have actually dismissed complaints for extreme wordiness, but that is rare. In practice you will find that complaints are often not short and plain at all. A more realistic phrasing of Rule 8(a)(2) might go something like: "a statement of the claim showing that the pleader is entitled to relief (and feel free to keep it short and plain)."

When the rule was promulgated in 1938, this "short and plain" phrase was included not so much to provide a manual for drafting a complaint; rather, it was included to make clear that the requirements of common law pleading and code pleading did not apply. The modern approach, embodied in "short and plain," is often called *notice pleading*. This "notice pleading" label reinforced the concept that the purpose of the complaint is to give the defendant notice of the basis for the plaintiff's claim. The complaint did not have to include much detail or persuade anyone of the strength of the plaintiff's claim.

That said, good lawyers have long used the complaint to state a claim that is not merely sufficient as a matter of notice, but compelling as a matter of substance and advocacy. The intended audience is not only the judge, but also the defendant and her lawyers. If a plaintiff wishes to bring a defendant to the bargaining table, a complaint that tells a powerful story backed up with supporting factual detail and a clear command of the legal precepts is more likely to do the trick than one that merely notifies the defendant of the claims. Drafting a compelling complaint is an art, and thus is also trickier than it sounds. Among other things, lawyers must draw a delicate balance and not include too much detail in the complaint if doing so would either show their cards too early or box the plaintiff into a corner before all of the evidence has come to light.

Still, notice pleading acknowledges that, at the start of a lawsuit, the parties may not possess all of the information they need in order to set out their positions in detail. Thus, the complaint need only provide a "short and plain statement of the claim showing that the pleader is entitled to relief." But what does this mean? The answer lies in a series of Supreme Court cases that have fleshed out the pleading standard in Rule 8(a)(2). In each case, a defendant moved to dismiss the plaintiff's complaint for "failure to state a claim," and the Court had to determine whether the complaint's allegations sufficed under Rule 8.

In *Conley v. Gibson*, 355 U.S. 41 (1957), a group of African-American railroad workers sued their union for breaching its duty to represent them in good faith against their employer when the employer discriminated against them. The union moved to dismiss the suit, arguing that the plaintiffs had failed to set forth enough factual detail to make out their claim. The Supreme Court unanimously rejected the defendant's argument:

> The respondents also argue that the complaint failed to set forth specific facts to support its general allegations of discrimination and that its dismissal is therefore proper. The decisive answer to this is that the Federal Rules of Civil Procedure do not require a claimant to set out in detail the facts upon which he bases his claim. To the contrary, all the Rules require is "a short and plain statement of the claim" that will give the defendant fair notice of what the plaintiff's claim is and the grounds upon which it rests. . . . Such simplified "notice pleading" is made possible by the liberal opportunity for discovery and the other pretrial procedures established by the Rules to disclose more precisely the basis of both claim and defense and to define more narrowly the disputed facts and issues. . . . The Federal Rules reject the approach that pleading is a game of skill in which one misstep by counsel may be decisive to the outcome and accept the principle that the purpose of pleading is to facilitate a proper decision on the merits.

Id. at 47-48. The Supreme Court described the standard for motions to dismiss as follows:

> In appraising the sufficiency of the complaint we follow, of course, the accepted rule that a complaint should not be dismissed for failure to state a claim unless it appears beyond doubt that the plaintiff can prove no set of facts in support of his claim which would entitle him to relief.

Id. at 45-46. Thus, the *Conley* Court laid out a deferential standard for reviewing the sufficiency of complaints.

The following case, *Swierkiewicz v. Sorema N.A.*, similarly involved a defendant's motion to dismiss a plaintiff's claim of workplace discrimination. Be sure you understand why the Supreme Court unanimously ruled that the complaint sufficed and that the defendant's motion to dismiss therefore had to be denied.

SWIERKIEWICZ v. SOREMA N.A.
534 U.S. 506 (2002)

THOMAS, J., delivered the opinion of the Court.

This case presents the question whether a complaint in an employment discrimination lawsuit must contain specific facts establishing a prima facie case of discrimination under the framework set forth by this Court in *McDonnell Douglas Corp. v. Green*, 411 U.S. 792 (1973). We hold that an employment discrimination complaint need not include such facts and instead must contain only "a short and plain statement of the claim showing that the pleader is entitled to relief." Fed. Rule Civ. Proc. 8(a)(2).

I

Petitioner Akos Swierkiewicz is a native of Hungary, who at the time of his complaint was 53 years old.[1] In April 1989, petitioner began working for respondent Sorema N.A., a reinsurance company headquartered in New York and principally owned and controlled by a French parent corporation. Petitioner was initially employed in the position of senior vice president and chief underwriting officer (CUO). Nearly six years later, François M. Chavel, respondent's Chief Executive Officer, demoted petitioner to a marketing and services position and transferred the bulk of his underwriting responsibilities to Nicholas Papadopoulo, a 32-year-old who, like Mr. Chavel, is a French national. About a year later, Mr. Chavel stated that he wanted to "energize" the underwriting department and appointed Mr. Papadopoulo as CUO. Petitioner claims that Mr. Papadopoulo had only one year of underwriting experience at the time he was promoted, and therefore was less experienced and less qualified to be CUO than he, since at that point he had 26 years of experience in the insurance industry.

Following his demotion, petitioner contends that he "was isolated by Mr. Chavel . . . excluded from business

---

[1] Because we review here a decision granting respondent's motion to dismiss, we must accept as true all of the factual allegations contained in the complaint. *See, e.g., Leatherman v. Tarrant Cty.*, 507 U.S. 163, 164 (1993).

decisions and meetings and denied the opportunity to reach his true potential at SOREMA." Petitioner unsuccessfully attempted to meet with Mr. Chavel to discuss his discontent. Finally, in April 1997, petitioner sent a memo to Mr. Chavel outlining his grievances and requesting a severance package. Two weeks later, respondent's general counsel presented petitioner with two options: He could either resign without a severance package or be dismissed. Mr. Chavel fired petitioner after he refused to resign.

Petitioner filed a lawsuit alleging that he had been terminated on account of his national origin in violation of Title VII of the Civil Rights Act of 1964, and on account of his age in violation of the Age Discrimination in Employment Act of 1967 (ADEA).

[The complaint alleged, in relevant part:*

11. Mr. Swierkiewicz is a native of Hungary. He became a United States citizen in 1970.

12. Mr. Swierkiewicz is 53 years old.

13. SOREMA is a reinsurance company principally owned and controlled by a French parent corporation. At all times relevant hereto, SOREMA's Chief Executive Officer has been François M. Chavel, a French national.

16. On April 17, 1989 Mr. Swierkiewicz began his employment with SOREMA in the position of Senior Vice President and Chief Underwriting Officer ("CUO").

17. In all respects, Mr. Swierkiewicz performed his job in a satisfactory and exemplary manner.

18. Despite plaintiff's stellar performance, in February 1995 Mr. Chavel demoted him from his CUO position to a marketing and

---

*Editors' Note: Because the Supreme Court's opinion did not quote the complaint at length, these allegations are taken directly from the complaint.

services position and transferred the bulk of his underwriting responsibilities to another French national, Nicholas Papadopoulo, who was 32 years old at the time (and 16 years younger than plaintiff).

19. Mr. Chavel demoted Mr. Swierkiewicz on account of his national origin (Hungarian) and his age (he was 49 at the time).

20. A year later, in or about February 1996, Mr. Chavel formally appointed Mr. Papadopoulo as SOREMA's CUO.

21. Mr. Papadopoulo was far less experienced and less qualified to be SOREMA's CUO than was Mr. Swierkiewicz. Indeed, Mr. Papadopoulo had just one year of underwriting experience prior to being appointed CUO by Mr. Chavel. By contrast, plaintiff had more than 26 years of broad based experience in the insurance and reinsurance industry.

22. At the time Mr. Papadopoulo assumed plaintiff's duties as CUO, Mr. Chavel stated that he wanted to "energize" the underwriting department—clearly implying that plaintiff was too old for the job.

28. Mr. Swierkiewicz was isolated by Mr. Chavel following his demotion, excluded from business decisions and meetings and denied the opportunity to reach his true potential at SOREMA.

32. Mr. Chavel and Daniel E. Schmidt, IV, SOREMA's General Counsel, met with Mr. Swierkiewicz and gave him two options: either resign his job (with no severance package) or be fired.

33. Mr. Swierkiewicz refused to resign his employment with SOREMA.

34. As a result, he was fired by Mr. Chavel, effective that very day (April 29, 1997).

35. SOREMA had no valid basis to fire Mr. Swierkiewicz.

42. SOREMA terminated Mr. Swierkiewicz's employment on account of his national origin and thereby violated his

right to equal employment opportunity as protected by Title VII.

44. SOREMA terminated Mr. Swierkiewicz's employment on account of his age and thereby violated his right to equal employment opportunity as protected by the ADEA.]

The United States District Court for the Southern District of New York dismissed petitioner's complaint because it found that he "ha[d] not adequately alleged a prima facie case, in that he ha[d] not adequately alleged circumstances that support an inference of discrimination." The United States Court of Appeals for the Second Circuit affirmed the dismissal, relying on its settled precedent, which requires a plaintiff in an employment discrimination complaint to allege facts constituting a prima facie case of discrimination under the framework set forth by this Court in *McDonnell Douglas*, 411 U.S. at 802. The Court of Appeals held that petitioner had failed to meet his burden because his allegations were "insufficient as a matter of law to raise an inference of discrimination." 5 Fed. Appx. 63, 65 (2nd Cir. 2001). We granted certiorari to resolve a split among the Courts of Appeals concerning the proper pleading standard for employment discrimination cases, and now reverse.

II

Applying Circuit precedent, the Court of Appeals required petitioner to plead a prima facie case of discrimination in order to survive respondent's motion to dismiss. In the Court of Appeals' view, petitioner was thus required to allege in his complaint: (1) membership in a protected group, (2) qualification for the job in question, (3) an adverse employment action, and (4) circumstances supporting an inference of discrimination. *McDonnell Douglas*, 411 U.S. at 802. The prima facie case under *McDonnell Douglas*, however, is an evidentiary standard, not a pleading requirement. . . .

This Court has never indicated that the requirements for establishing a prima facie case under *McDonnell Douglas* also apply to the pleading standard that plaintiffs must satisfy in order to survive a motion to dismiss. . . . Consequently, the ordinary rules for assessing the sufficiency of a complaint apply. . . .

[I]mposing the Court of Appeals' heightened pleading standard in employment discrimination cases conflicts with Federal Rule of Civil Procedure 8(a)(2), which provides that a complaint must include only "a short and plain statement of the claim showing that the pleader is entitled to relief." Such a statement must simply "give the defendant fair notice of what the plaintiff's claim is and the grounds upon which it rests." *Conley v. Gibson*, 355 U.S. 41, 47 (1957). This simplified notice pleading standard relies on liberal discovery rules and summary judgment motions to define disputed facts and issues and to dispose of unmeritorious claims. "The provisions for discovery are so flexible and the provisions for pretrial procedure and summary judgment so effective, that attempted surprise in federal practice is aborted very easily, synthetic issues detected, and the gravamen of the dispute brought frankly into the open for the inspection of the court." 5 C. Wright & A. Miller, Federal Practice and Procedure §1202, p. 76 (2d ed. 1990).

Rule 8(a)'s simplified pleading standard applies to all civil actions, with limited exceptions. Rule 9(b), for example, provides for greater particularity in all averments of fraud or mistake. This Court, however, has declined to extend such exceptions to other contexts. In *Leatherman v. Tarrant Cty.*,

507 U.S. 163, 168 (1993), we stated: "[T]he Federal Rules do address in Rule 9(b) the question of the need for greater particularity in pleading certain actions, but do not include among the enumerated actions any reference to complaints alleging municipal liability under §1983. *Expressio unius est exclusio alterius*." Just as Rule 9(b) makes no mention of municipal liability, neither does it refer to employment discrimination. Thus, complaints in these cases, as in most others, must satisfy only the simple requirements of Rule 8(a).

Other provisions of the Federal Rules of Civil Procedure are inextricably linked to Rule 8(a)'s simplified notice pleading standard. Rule 8(e)(1) states that "[n]o technical forms of pleading or motions are required," and Rule 8(f) provides that "[a]ll pleadings shall be so construed as to do substantial justice." Given the Federal Rules' simplified standard for pleading, "[a] court may dismiss a complaint only if it is clear that no relief could be granted under any set of facts that could be proved consistent with the allegations." *Hishon v. King & Spalding*, 467 U.S. 69, 73 (1984). If a pleading fails to specify the allegations in a manner that provides sufficient notice, a defendant can move for a more definite statement under Rule 12(e) before responding. Moreover, claims lacking merit may be dealt with through summary judgment under Rule 56. The liberal notice pleading of Rule 8(a) is the starting point of a simplified pleading system, which was adopted to focus litigation on the merits of a claim. *See Conley, supra*, at 48 ("The Federal Rules reject the approach that pleading is a game of skill in which one misstep by counsel may be decisive to the outcome and accept the principle that the purpose of pleading is to facilitate a proper decision on the merits").

Applying the relevant standard, petitioner's complaint easily satisfies the requirements of Rule 8(a) because it gives respondent fair notice of the basis for petitioner's claims. Petitioner alleged that he had been terminated on account of his national origin in violation of Title VII and on account of his age in violation of the ADEA. His complaint detailed the events leading to his termination, provided relevant dates, and included the ages and nationalities of at least some of the relevant persons involved with his termination. These allegations give respondent fair notice of what petitioner's claims are and the grounds upon which they rest. *See Conley, supra*, at 47. In addition, they state claims upon which relief could be granted under Title VII and the ADEA.

Respondent argues that allowing lawsuits based on conclusory allegations of discrimination to go forward will burden the courts and encourage disgruntled employees to bring unsubstantiated suits. Whatever the practical merits of this argument, the Federal Rules do not contain a heightened pleading standard for employment discrimination suits. A requirement of greater specificity for particular claims is a result that "must be obtained by the process of amending the Federal Rules, and not by judicial interpretation." *Leatherman*, 507 U.S. at 168. Furthermore, Rule 8(a) establishes a pleading standard without regard to whether a claim will succeed on the merits. "Indeed it may appear on the face of the pleadings that a recovery is very remote and unlikely but that is not the test." *Scheuer v. Rhodes*, 416 U.S. 232, 236 (1974).

For the foregoing reasons, we hold that an employment discrimination plaintiff need not plead a prima facie case of discrimination and that petitioner's complaint is sufficient to survive respondent's motion to dismiss. Accordingly, the judgment of the Court of Appeals is reversed, and the case is remanded for further proceedings consistent with this opinion.

Notes & Questions

1. On a motion to dismiss for failure to state a claim upon which relief can be granted, the court must take the allegations of the complaint as true. Look at the allegations in Swierkiewicz's complaint. The ADEA protects employees 40 years of age and older from discrimination on the basis of age, and Title VII protects employees from discrimination on the basis of national origin (among other things). If Swierkiewicz's allegations are true, has he stated a claim that entitles him to relief? If so, why did the district judge and the Second Circuit think it appropriate to dismiss his complaint?

2. In *Swierkiewicz*, the Second Circuit held that the complaint must contain allegations to satisfy each element of the *McDonnell Douglas* standard. To understand why the Supreme Court rejected the Second Circuit's view, you must distinguish the *burden of pleading* from the *burden of proof*. The burden of pleading relates to what a plaintiff must *allege* in the complaint to avoid dismissal of a claim (or what a defendant must allege in an answer to avoid the striking of a defense). The burden of proof—which includes a burden of production and a burden of persuasion—is the requirement that a party present *evidence* to persuade the ultimate finder of fact. A plaintiff has the burden to plead allegations sufficient to make out a valid legal claim; otherwise, the plaintiff may lose on a motion to dismiss. If the complaint survives, however, then the plaintiff will have the burden of persuasion to convince the jury (or other fact-finder) of each element of the claim. Does the *McDonnell Douglas* standard speak to a burden of pleading or to burdens of production and persuasion? Which burden is the appropriate one to apply on a motion to dismiss a complaint for failure to state a claim?

3. In *Swierkiewicz*, how did the Supreme Court interpret the language of Rule 8(a)(2)? What functions must the complaint serve to be sufficient under Rule 8(a)(2)? How do those functions relate to other portions of the Federal Rules of Civil Procedure, according to the Court?

4. The Court in *Swierkiewicz* points out that there might be practical reasons for requiring heightened pleading of factual allegations. What might those practical reasons be? Why was the Court unwilling to engage in a discussion about those possible reasons?

5. In both *Conley* and *Swierkiewicz*, the issue of the complaint's sufficiency under Rule 8 arose on a motion to dismiss for failure to state a claim under Rule 12(b)(6). The 12(b)(6) motion is one of the most important procedural tools in the defendant's toolkit. Once a plaintiff files a complaint, a defendant may respond either with an answer or with a pre-answer motion. A motion to dismiss under Rule 12(b)(6) is the motion by which a defendant challenges the legal validity and factual sufficiency of a plaintiff's pleading.

   There are several ways that a complaint may fail. First, a complaint may be inadequate because, on the facts alleged, it simply does not state a valid legal claim. Recall our earlier example: Z alleges that Y wore a blue shirt, and that the blue shirt offended Z. Even if Z's allegations are true, that does not entitle Z to relief. He has not stated a valid legal claim. Surely Y would move to dismiss under Rule 12(b)(6), and surely the court would grant the motion.

Second, a complaint may fail because the allegations do not meet an essential element of a claim. Assume that Y, from New York, files a complaint alleging that on a particular date, at a particular intersection, Y and Z had an automobile collision in which Y suffered significant personal injury and property damage. While Y's complaint notifies Z of the incident that is the subject of the lawsuit, Y's complaint fails to meet an essential element of the claim. Can you see what is missing? Even if you have not yet studied tort law, you probably can appreciate that the complaint does not say whether the collision was Z's fault, Y's fault, or neither. In terms of tort law, Y's claim against Z sounds in negligence, which provides the only viable basis for liability in this scenario. Taking Y's claim of negligence element by element, which might be listed as breach of duty of reasonable care, actual and proximate causation, and damages, Y has not alleged breach. He has not satisfied his burden of pleading as to a required element of the claim.

Third, a complaint may fail because it states a mere legal conclusion, devoid of any factual basis for the claim. Take the following examples. First, and most ridiculously, suppose a plaintiff's complaint states: "The defendant (Z) is liable to the plaintiff (Y) in the amount of $100,000." The complaint would be dismissed for failing to state a claim upon which relief can be granted. Now, imagine that Y revises his complaint to read: "Z is liable to Y for driving negligently." Y's revision gets closer to suggesting a breach of duty of care by alleging that Z drove negligently. However, without more, this bare assertion of the legal claim of negligence would be dismissed for failure to state a claim. The complaint fails to give Z reasonable notice of the basis for the claim. When did the alleged accident occur? Where? What happened? The Supreme Court in *Swierkiewicz* emphasized that complaints need not include much detail, but even so, a complaint must contain sufficient allegations to notify the defendant of the factual basis for the claim. How much more would Y need to include for his complaint to survive under *Swierkiewicz*? After you read the next two cases, do your answers change?

STRATEGY SESSION

Rule 8 does not require that a complaint specify the *legal basis* for the claim. To satisfy the rule, a plaintiff merely needs to plead *factual allegations* that, if true, rise to a valid legal claim. As a practical matter, however, good lawyers nearly always assert the legal basis for their client's claims in the complaint. Why, if the rule does not require it? One, they do not want to risk dismissal by leaving the court to guess about their legal theory. Two, they want both the judge and the defendant to take the complaint seriously. Thus, a complaint generally states not only the facts that give rise to the plaintiff's claim, but also the legal theory that entitles the plaintiff to relief under the law. Often, each claim is listed as a separate "count" in the complaint, such as "Count One: Negligence," "Count Two: Product Liability." Thus, in our car accident example, although Rule 8 may not technically require the plaintiff to use the magic word "negligence," you can bet that the complaint will do so.

(c) Sufficiency of the Complaint: Plausibility Pleading

The notice pleading standard seemed simple enough until the Supreme Court shook things up in *Bell Atlantic v. Twombly*, 550 U.S. 544 (2007), and *Ashcroft v. Iqbal*, 556 U.S. 662 (2009). As you read these cases, think about what they add to the Rule 8(a)(2) analysis and how they would influence the way you draft a complaint or a motion to dismiss.

BELL ATLANTIC CORP. v. TWOMBLY
550 U.S. 544 (2007)

SOUTER, J., delivered the opinion of the Court.

Liability under §1 of the Sherman Act, 15 U.S.C. §1, requires a "contract, combination, . . . or conspiracy, in restraint of trade or commerce." The question in this putative class action is whether a §1 complaint can survive a motion to dismiss when it alleges that major telecommunications providers engaged in certain parallel conduct unfavorable to competition, absent some factual context suggesting agreement, as distinct from identical, independent action. We hold that such a complaint should be dismissed.

I

The upshot of the 1984 divestiture of the American Telephone & Telegraph Company's (AT&T) local telephone business was a system of regional service monopolies (variously called "Regional Bell Operating Companies," "Baby Bells," or "Incumbent Local Exchange Carriers" (ILECs)), and a separate, competitive market for long-distance service from which the ILECs were excluded. [Congress later withdrew approval of the ILECs' monopolies and required each ILEC to share its network with competitors, which came to be known as "competitive local exchange carriers" (CLECs).]

Respondents William Twombly and Lawrence Marcus (hereinafter plaintiffs) represent a putative class consisting of all "subscribers of local telephone and/or high speed internet services . . . from February 8, 1996 to present." In this action against petitioners, a group of ILECs, plaintiffs seek treble damages and declaratory and injunctive relief for claimed violations of §1 of the Sherman Act, which prohibits "[e]very contract, combination in the form of trust or otherwise, or conspiracy, in restraint of trade or commerce among the several States, or with foreign nations."

The complaint alleges that the ILECs conspired to restrain trade in two ways, each supposedly inflating charges for local telephone and high-speed Internet services. Plaintiffs say, first, that the ILECs "engaged in parallel conduct" in their respective service areas to inhibit the growth of upstart CLECs. Their actions allegedly included making unfair agreements with the CLECs for access to ILEC networks, providing inferior connections to the networks, overcharging, and billing in ways designed to sabotage the CLECs' relations with their own customers. According to the complaint, the ILECs' "compelling common motivatio[n]" to thwart the CLECs' competitive efforts naturally led them to form a conspiracy; "[h]ad any one [ILEC] not sought to prevent CLECs . . . from competing effectively, . . . the resulting greater competitive inroads into that [ILEC's] territory would have revealed the degree to which competitive entry by CLECs would have been successful in the other territories in the absence of such conduct."

Second, the complaint charges agreements by the ILECs to refrain from competing against one another. These are to be inferred from the ILECs' common failure "meaningfully [to] pursu[e]" "attractive business opportunit[ies]" in contiguous markets where they possessed "substantial competitive advantages," and from a statement of Richard Notebaert, chief executive officer (CEO) of the ILEC Qwest, that competing in the territory of another ILEC "might be a good way to turn a quick dollar but that doesn't make it right."

The complaint couches its ultimate allegations this way:

> In the absence of any meaningful competition between the [ILECs] in one another's markets, and in light of the parallel course of conduct that each engaged in to prevent competition from CLECs within their respective local telephone and/or high speed internet services markets and the other facts and market circumstances alleged above, Plaintiffs allege upon information and belief that [the ILECs] have entered into a contract, combination or conspiracy to prevent competitive entry in their respective local telephone and/or high speed internet services markets and have agreed not to compete with one another and otherwise allocated customers and markets to one another.

The United States District Court for the Southern District of New York dismissed the complaint for failure to state a claim upon which relief can be granted. The District Court acknowledged that "plaintiffs may allege a conspiracy by citing instances of parallel business behavior that suggest an agreement," but emphasized that "while [c]ircumstantial evidence of consciously parallel behavior may have made heavy inroads into the traditional judicial attitude toward conspiracy . . . conscious parallelism has not yet read conspiracy out of the Sherman Act entirely." 313 F. Supp. 2d 174, 179 (2003). Thus, the district court understood that allegations of parallel business conduct, taken alone, do not state a claim under §1; plaintiffs must allege additional facts that "ten[d] to exclude independent self-interested conduct as an explanation for defendants' parallel behavior." The District Court found plaintiffs' allegations of parallel ILEC actions to discourage competition inadequate because "the behavior of each ILEC in resisting the incursion of CLECs is fully explained by the ILEC's own interests in defending its individual territory." As to the ILECs' supposed agreement against competing with each other, the District Court found that the complaint does not "alleg[e] facts . . . suggesting that refraining from competing in other territories as CLECs was contrary to [the ILECs'] apparent economic interests, and consequently [does] not rais[e] an inference that [the ILECs'] actions were the result of a conspiracy."

The Court of Appeals for the Second Circuit reversed, holding that the District Court tested the complaint by the wrong standard. It held that "plus factors are not required to be pleaded to permit an antitrust claim based on parallel conduct to survive dismissal." 425 F.3d 99, 114 (2005). Although the Court of Appeals took the view that plaintiffs must plead facts that "include conspiracy among the realm of plausible possibilities in order to survive a motion to dismiss," it then said that "to rule that allegations of parallel anticompetitive conduct fail to support a plausible conspiracy claim, a court would have to conclude that there is no set of facts that would permit a plaintiff to demonstrate that the particular parallelism asserted was the product of collusion rather than coincidence." *Ibid.*

We granted certiorari to address the proper standard for pleading an antitrust conspiracy through allegations of parallel conduct, and now reverse.

II
A

[Section 1 of the Sherman Act prohibits "contract, combination, . . . or conspiracy" in restraint of trade. The crucial question is whether the anticompetitive conduct arose from independent decisions or from an agreement.] While a showing of parallel "business behavior is admissible circumstantial evidence from which the fact finder may infer agreement," it falls short of "conclusively establish[ing] agreement or . . . itself constitut[ing] a Sherman Act offense." *Id.* at 540-41. Even "conscious parallelism," a

common reaction of "firms in a concentrated market [that] recogniz[e] their shared economic interests and their interdependence with respect to price and output decisions" is "not in itself unlawful." *Brooke Group Ltd. v. Brown & Williamson Tobacco Corp.*, 509 U.S. 209, 227 (1993). . . .

B

This case presents the . . . question of what a plaintiff must plead in order to state a claim under §1 of the Sherman Act. Federal Rule of Civil Procedure 8(a)(2) requires only "a short and plain statement of the claim showing that the pleader is entitled to relief," in order to "give the defendant fair notice of what the . . . claim is and the grounds upon which it rests," *Conley v. Gibson*, 355 U.S. 41, 47 (1957). While a complaint attacked by a Rule 12(b)(6) motion to dismiss does not need detailed factual allegation . . . a plaintiff's obligation to provide the "grounds" of his "entitle[ment] to relief" requires more than labels and conclusions, and a formulaic recitation of the elements of a cause of action will not do. Factual allegations must be enough to raise a right to relief above the speculative level,[3] on the assumption that all the allegations in the complaint are true (even if doubtful in fact).

---

[3] The dissent greatly oversimplifies matters by suggesting that the Federal Rules somehow dispensed with the pleading of facts altogether. . . . While, for most types of cases, the Federal Rules eliminated the cumbersome requirement that a claimant "set out *in detail* the facts upon which he bases his claim," *Conley v. Gibson*, 355 U.S. 41, 47 (1957) (emphasis added), Rule 8(a)(2) still requires a "showing," rather than a blanket assertion, of entitlement to relief. Without some factual allegation in the complaint, it is hard to see how a claimant could satisfy the requirement of providing not only "fair notice" of the nature of the claim, but also "grounds" on which the claim rests. . . .

In applying these general standards to a §1 claim, we hold that stating such a claim requires a complaint with enough factual matter (taken as true) to suggest that an agreement was made. Asking for plausible grounds to infer an agreement does not impose a probability requirement at the pleading stage; it simply calls for enough fact to raise a reasonable expectation that discovery will reveal evidence of illegal agreement. And, of course, a well-pleaded complaint may proceed even if it strikes a savvy judge that actual proof of those facts is improbable, and "that a recovery is very remote and unlikely." *Scheuer*, 416 U.S. at 236. [However,] an allegation of parallel conduct and a bare assertion of conspiracy will not suffice. Without more, parallel conduct does not suggest conspiracy, and a conclusory allegation of agreement at some unidentified point does not supply facts adequate to show illegality. Hence, when allegations of parallel conduct are set out in order to make a §1 claim, they must be placed in a context that raises a suggestion of a preceding agreement, not merely parallel conduct that could just as well be independent action.

The need at the pleading stage for allegations plausibly suggesting (not merely consistent with) agreement reflects the threshold requirement of Rule 8(a)(2) that the "plain statement" possess enough heft to "sho[w] that the pleader is entitled to relief." . . . An allegation of parallel conduct gets the complaint close to stating a claim, but without some further factual enhancement it stops short of the line between possibility and plausibility of "entitle[ment] to relief."

. . . [W]hen the allegations in a complaint, however true, could not raise a claim of entitlement to relief, "this basic deficiency should . . . be exposed at the point of minimum expenditure of time and money by the parties and the court." *Id.* at 346.

Thus, it is one thing to be cautious before dismissing an antitrust complaint in advance of discovery, but quite another to forget that proceeding to antitrust discovery can be expensive. . . . That potential expense is obvious enough in the present case: plaintiffs represent a putative class of at least 90 percent of all subscribers to local telephone or high-speed Internet service in the continental United States, in an action against America's largest telecommunications firms (with many thousands of employees generating reams and gigabytes of business records) for unspecified (if any) instances of antitrust violations that allegedly occurred over a period of seven years.

It is no answer to say that a claim just shy of a plausible entitlement to relief can, if groundless, be weeded out early in the discovery process through "careful case management," given the common lament that the success of judicial supervision in checking discovery abuse has been on the modest side. *See, e.g.,* Judge Frank Easterbrook, *Discovery as Abuse*, 69 B.U. L. REV. 635, 638 (1989). And it is self-evident that the problem of discovery abuse cannot be solved by "careful scrutiny of evidence at the summary judgment stage," much less "lucid instructions to juries"; the threat of discovery expense will push cost-conscious defendants to settle even anemic cases before reaching those proceedings. Probably, then, it is only by taking care to require allegations that reach the level suggesting conspiracy that we can hope to avoid the potentially enormous expense of discovery in cases with no "reasonably founded hope that the [discovery] process will reveal relevant evidence" to support a §1 claim.[6] *Dura*, 544 U.S. at 347.

Plaintiffs do not, of course, dispute the requirement of plausibility and the need for something more than merely parallel behavior . . . and their main argument against the plausibility standard at the pleading stage is its ostensible conflict with an early statement of ours construing Rule 8. Justice Black's opinion for the Court in *Conley v. Gibson* spoke not only of the need for fair notice of the grounds for entitlement to relief but of "the accepted rule that a complaint should not be dismissed for failure to state a claim unless it appears beyond doubt that the plaintiff can prove no set of facts in support of his claim which would entitle him to relief." 355 U.S. at 45-46. This "no set of facts" language can be read in isolation as saying that any statement revealing the theory of the claim will suffice unless its factual impossibility may be shown from the face of the pleadings; and the Court of Appeals appears to have read *Conley* in some such way when formulating its understanding of the proper pleading standard.

On such a focused and literal reading of *Conley*'s "no set of facts," a wholly conclusory statement of claim would survive a motion to dismiss whenever the pleadings left open the possibility that a plaintiff might later establish some "set of [undisclosed] facts" to support recovery. . . .

Seeing this, a good many judges and commentators have balked at taking the literal terms of the *Conley* passage as a pleading standard. . . . To be fair to the *Conley* Court, the passage should be understood in light of the opinion's preceding summary of the complaint's concrete allegations, which the Court quite reasonably understood as amply stating a claim for relief. But the passage so often quoted fails to mention this understanding on the part of the Court, and after puzzling the profession for 50 years, this famous observation has earned its retirement. . . .

III

When we look for plausibility in this complaint, we agree with the District Court that plaintiffs' claim of conspiracy in restraint of trade comes up short. To begin with, the complaint leaves no doubt that plaintiffs rest their §1 claim on descriptions of parallel conduct and not on any independent allegation of actual agreement among the ILECs. Although in form a few stray statements speak directly of agreement, on fair reading these are merely legal conclusions resting on the prior allegations. Thus, the complaint first takes account of the alleged "absence of any meaningful competition between [the ILECs] in one another's markets," "the parallel course of conduct that each [ILEC] engaged in to prevent competition from CLECs," "and the other facts and market circumstances alleged [earlier]"; in light of these, the complaint concludes "that [the ILECs] have entered into a contract, combination or conspiracy to prevent competitive entry into their . . . markets and have agreed not to compete with one

---

[6] The dissent takes heart in the reassurances of plaintiffs' counsel that discovery would be "phased" and "limited to the existence of the alleged conspiracy and class certification." But determining whether some illegal agreement may have taken place between unspecified persons at different ILECs (each a multibillion dollar corporation with legions of management level employees) at some point over seven years is a sprawling, costly, and hugely time-consuming undertaking not easily susceptible to the kind of line drawing and case management that the dissent envisions.

another."[10] The nub of the complaint, then, is the ILECs' parallel behavior, consisting of steps to keep the CLECs out and manifest disinterest in becoming CLECs themselves.

We think that nothing contained in the complaint invests either the action or inaction alleged with a plausible suggestion of conspiracy. As to the ILECs' supposed agreement to disobey the 1996 Act and thwart the CLECs' attempts to compete, we agree with the District Court that nothing in the complaint intimates that the resistance to the upstarts was anything more than the natural, unilateral reaction of each ILEC intent on keeping its regional dominance. The 1996 Act did more than just subject the ILECs to competition; it obliged them to subsidize their competitors with their own equipment at wholesale rates. The economic incentive to resist was powerful, but resisting competition is routine market conduct, and even if the ILECs flouted the 1996 Act in all the ways the plaintiffs allege, there is no reason to infer that the companies had agreed among themselves to do what was only natural anyway; so natural, in fact, that if alleging parallel decisions to resist competition were enough to imply an antitrust conspiracy, pleading a §1 violation against almost any group of competing businesses would be a sure thing. . . .

Plaintiffs' second conspiracy theory rests on the competitive reticence among the ILECs themselves in the wake of the 1996 Act, which was supposedly passed in the "hop[e] that the large incumbent local monopoly companies . . . might attack their neighbors' service areas, as they are the best situated to do so." Contrary to hope, the ILECs declined "'to enter each other's service territories in any significant way,'" and the local telephone and high-speed Internet market remains highly compartmentalized geographically, with minimal competition. Based on this state of affairs, and perceiving the ILECs to be blessed with "especially attractive business opportunities" in surrounding markets dominated by other ILECs, the plaintiffs assert that the ILECs' parallel conduct was "strongly suggestive of conspiracy."

But it was not suggestive of conspiracy, not if history teaches anything. In a traditionally unregulated industry with low barriers to entry, sparse competition among large firms dominating separate geographical segments of the market could very well signify illegal agreement, but here we have an obvious alternative explanation. In the decade preceding the 1996 Act and well before that, monopoly was the norm in telecommunications, not the exception. The ILECs were born in that world, doubtless liked the world the way it was, and surely knew the adage about him who lives by the sword. . . . We [thus] agree with the District Court's assessment that antitrust conspiracy was not suggested by the facts adduced under either theory of the complaint, which thus fails to state a valid §1 claim.[14]

---

[10] If the complaint had not explained that the claim of agreement rested on the parallel conduct described, we doubt that the complaint's references to an agreement among the ILECs would have given the notice required by Rule 8. Apart from identifying a 7-year span in which the §1 violations were supposed to have occurred, the pleadings mentioned no specific time, place, or person involved in the alleged conspiracies. . . . [A] defendant seeking to respond to plaintiffs' conclusory allegations in the §1 context would have little idea where to begin.

---

[14] In reaching this conclusion, we do not apply any "heightened" pleading standard, nor do we seek to broaden the scope of Federal Rule of Civil Procedure 9, which can only be accomplished "by the process of amending the Federal Rules, and not by judicial interpretation." *Swierkiewicz v. Sorema N.A.*, 534 U.S. 506, 515 (2002). . . .

Plaintiffs say that our analysis runs counter to *Swierkiewicz*, 534 U.S. at 508, which held that "a complaint in an employment discrimination lawsuit [need] not contain specific facts establishing a prima facie case of discrimination. . . ." As the District Court correctly understood, however, "*Swierkiewicz* did not change the law of pleading, but simply reemphasized . . . that the Second Circuit's use of a heightened pleading standard for Title VII cases was contrary to the Federal Rules' structure of liberal pleading requirements." 313 F. Supp. 2d at 181. . . .

Here, in contrast, we do not require heightened fact pleading of specifics, but only enough facts to state a claim to relief that is plausible on its face. Because the plaintiffs here have not nudged their claims across the line from conceivable to plausible, their complaint must be dismissed.

* * *

The judgment of the Court of Appeals for the Second Circuit is reversed, and the case is remanded for further proceedings consistent with this opinion.

Justice STEVENS, with whom Justice GINSBURG joins except as to Part IV, dissenting.

[T]his is a case in which there is no dispute about the substantive law. If the defendants acted independently [even if in parallel], their conduct was perfectly lawful. If, however, that conduct is the product of a horizontal agreement among potential competitors, it was unlawful. The plaintiffs have alleged such an agreement and, because the complaint was dismissed in advance of answer, the allegation has not even been denied. Why, then, does the case not proceed? Does a judicial opinion that the charge is not "plausible" provide a legally acceptable reason for dismissing the complaint? I think not.

Respondents' amended complaint describes a variety of circumstantial evidence and makes the straightforward allegation that petitioners

> entered into a contract, combination or conspiracy to prevent competitive entry in their respective local telephone and/or high speed internet services markets and have agreed not to compete with one another and otherwise allocated customers and markets to one another.

The complaint explains that, contrary to Congress' expectation when it enacted the 1996 Telecommunications Act, and consistent with their own economic self-interests, ILECs have assiduously avoided infringing upon each other's markets and have refused to permit nonincumbent competitors to access their networks. . . . Moreover, respondents allege that petitioners "communicate amongst themselves" through numerous industry associations. In sum, respondents allege that petitioners entered into an agreement that has long been recognized as a classic *per se* violation of the Sherman Act.

Under rules of procedure that have been well settled, a judge ruling on a defendant's motion to dismiss a complaint "must accept as true all of the factual allegations contained in the complaint." *Swierkiewicz*, 534 U.S. at 508 n.1. But instead of requiring knowledgeable executives such as Notebaert to respond to these allegations by way of sworn depositions or other limited discovery—and indeed without so much as requiring petitioners to file an answer denying that they entered into any agreement—the majority permits immediate dismissal based on the assurances of company lawyers that nothing untoward was afoot. . . .

The Court and petitioners' legal team are no doubt correct that the parallel conduct alleged is consistent with the absence of any contract, combination, or conspiracy. But that conduct is also entirely consistent with the *presence* of the illegal agreement alleged in the complaint. And the charge that petitioners "agreed not to compete with one another" is not just one of "a few stray statements"; it is an allegation describing unlawful conduct. As such, the Federal Rules of Civil Procedure, our long-standing precedent, and sound practice mandate that the District Court at least require some sort of response from petitioners before dismissing the case.

Two practical concerns presumably explain the Court's dramatic departure from settled procedural law. Private antitrust litigation can be enormously expensive, and there is a risk that jurors may mistakenly conclude that evidence of parallel conduct has proved that the parties acted pursuant to an agreement when they in fact merely made similar independent decisions. Those concerns merit careful case management, including strict control of discovery, careful scrutiny of evidence at the summary judgment stage, and lucid instructions to juries; they do not, however, justify the dismissal of an adequately pleaded complaint without even requiring the defendants to file answers denying a charge that they in fact engaged in collective decision making. More importantly, they do not justify an interpretation of Federal Rule of Civil Procedure 12(b)(6) that seems to be driven by the majority's appraisal of the plausibility of the ultimate factual allegation rather than its legal sufficiency.

I

Rule 8(a)(2) of the Federal Rules requires that a complaint contain "a short and plain statement of the claim showing that the pleader is entitled to relief." ... Under the relaxed pleading standards of the Federal Rules, the idea was not to keep litigants out of court but rather to keep them in. The merits of a claim would be sorted out during a flexible pretrial process and, as appropriate, through the crucible of trial....

II

... [A]s the *Conley* Court well knew, the pleading standard the Federal Rules meant to codify does not require, or even invite, the pleading of facts.[6] The "pleading standard" label the majority gives to what it reads into the *Conley* opinion—a statement of the permissible factual support for an adequately pleaded complaint—would not, therefore, have impressed the *Conley* Court itself. Rather, that Court would have understood the majority's remodeling of its language to express an *evidentiary* standard, which the *Conley* Court had neither need nor want to explicate. Second, it is pellucidly clear that the *Conley* Court was interested in what a complaint *must* contain, not what it *may* contain. In fact, the Court said without qualification that it was "appraising

---

[6] The majority is correct to say that what the Federal Rules require is a "showing" of entitlement to relief. Whether and to what extent that "showing" requires allegations of fact will depend on the particulars of the claim. For example, had the amended complaint in this case alleged *only* parallel conduct, it would not have made the required "showing." Similarly, had the pleadings contained *only* an allegation of agreement, without specifying the nature or object of that agreement, they would have been susceptible to the charge that they did not provide sufficient notice that the defendants may answer intelligently. Omissions of that sort instance the type of "bareness" with which the Federal Rules are concerned. A plaintiff's inability to persuade a district court that the allegations actually included in her complaint are "plausible" is an altogether different kind of failing, and one that should not be fatal at the pleading stage.

the *sufficiency* of the complaint." 355 U.S. at 45 (emphasis added). . . . We can be triply sure as to *Conley*'s meaning by examining three Court of Appeals cases the *Conley* Court cited as support for the "accepted rule" that "a complaint should not be dismissed for failure to state a claim unless it appears beyond doubt that the plaintiff can prove no set of facts in support of his claim which would entitle him to relief." 355 U.S. at 45-46. . . .

We have consistently reaffirmed that basic understanding of the Federal Rules in the half century since *Conley*. . . . Most recently, in *Swierkiewicz* . . . [w]e reversed, in another unanimous opinion, holding that "under a notice pleading system, it is not appropriate to require a plaintiff to plead facts establishing a prima facie case because the *McDonnell Douglas* framework does not apply in every employment discrimination case." *Swierkiewicz*, 534 U.S. at 511. We also observed that Rule 8(a)(2) does not contemplate a court's passing on the merits of a litigant's claim at the pleading stage. Rather, the "simplified notice pleading standard" of the Federal Rules "relies on liberal discovery rules and summary judgment motions to define disputed facts and issues and to dispose of unmeritorious claims." *Id.* at 512.

As in the discrimination context, we have developed an evidentiary framework for evaluating claims under §1 of the Sherman Act when those claims rest on entirely circumstantial evidence of conspiracy. *See Matsushita Elec. Industrial Co. v. Zenith Radio Corp.*, 475 U.S. 574 (1986). Under *Matsushita*, a plaintiff's allegations of an illegal conspiracy may not, at the summary judgment stage, rest solely on the inferences that may be drawn from the parallel conduct of the defendants. In order to survive a Rule 56 motion, a §1 plaintiff "must present evidence 'that tends to exclude the

possibility' that the alleged conspirators acted independently." *Id.* at 588. . . .

Everything today's majority says would therefore make perfect sense if it were ruling on a Rule 56 motion for summary judgment and the evidence included nothing more than the Court has described. But it should go without saying in the wake of *Swierkiewicz* that a heightened production burden at the summary judgment stage does not translate into a heightened pleading burden at the complaint stage. The majority rejects the complaint in this case because—in light of the fact that the parallel conduct alleged is consistent with ordinary market behavior—the claimed conspiracy is "conceivable" but not "plausible." I have my doubts about the majority's assessment of the plausibility of this alleged conspiracy. But even if the majority's speculation is correct, its "plausibility" standard is irreconcilable with Rule 8 and with our governing precedents. . . .

[Further], this case is a poor vehicle for the Court's new pleading rule, for we have observed that "in antitrust cases, where the proof is largely in the hands of the alleged conspirators, dismissals prior to giving the plaintiff ample opportunity for discovery should be granted very sparingly." *Hospital Building Co. v. Trustees of Rex Hospital*, 425 U.S. 738, 746 (1976). . . .

III

. . . Even if I were inclined to . . . ignore the complaint's allegations [as the Majority does], I would dispute the Court's suggestion that any inference of agreement from petitioners' parallel conduct is "implausible." . . . To be clear, if I had been the trial judge in this case, I would not have permitted the plaintiffs to engage in massive discovery based solely on the allegations in this complaint. On the other hand, I surely would not have dismissed the complaint without requiring the defendants to answer the charge that they "have agreed not to compete with one another and otherwise allocated customers and markets to one another."...

Respondents... proposed a plan of phased discovery limited to the existence of the alleged conspiracy and class certification.... Whether or not respondent's [particular] plan was sensible, it was an appropriate subject for negotiation....[13]

---

[13] The potential for "sprawling, costly, and hugely time-consuming" discovery, *ante* n.6, is no reason to throw the baby out with the bathwater. The Court vastly underestimates a district court's case-management arsenal. Before discovery even begins, the court may grant a defendant's Rule 12(e) motion; Rule 7(a) permits a trial court to order a plaintiff to reply to a defendant's answer; and Rule 23 requires "rigorous analysis" to ensure that class certification is appropriate. Rule 16 invests a trial judge with the power, backed by sanctions, to regulate pretrial proceedings via conferences and scheduling orders, at which the parties may discuss, *inter alia*, "the elimination of frivolous claims or defenses," Rule 16(c)(1); "the necessity or desirability of amendments to the pleadings," Rule 16(c)(2); "the control and scheduling of discovery," Rule 16(c)(6); and "the need for adopting special procedures for managing potentially difficult or protracted actions that may involve complex issues, multiple parties, difficult legal questions, or unusual proof problems," Rule 16(c)(12). Subsequently, Rule 26 confers broad discretion to control the combination of interrogatories, requests for admissions, production requests, and depositions permitted in a given case; the sequence in which such discovery devices may be deployed; and the limitations imposed upon them. Indeed, Rule 26(c) specifically permits a court to take actions "to protect a party or person from annoyance, embarrassment, oppression, or undue burden or expense" by, for example, disallowing a particular discovery request, setting appropriate terms and conditions, or limiting its scope.

I fear that the unfortunate result of the majority's new pleading rule will be to invite lawyers' debates over economic theory to conclusively resolve antitrust suits in the absence of any evidence.... [The proper remedy for the antitrust defense bar] was to seek to amend the Federal Rules—not our interpretation of them.

IV

... Whether the Court's actions will benefit only defendants in antitrust treble-damages cases, or whether its test for sufficiency of a complaint will inure to the benefit of all civil defendants, is a question that the future will answer. But that the Court has announced a significant new rule that does not even purport to respond to any congressional command is glaringly obvious.

The transparent policy concern that drives the decision is the interest in protecting antitrust defendants—who in this case are some of the wealthiest corporations in our economy—from the burdens of pretrial discovery....

[And] if the allegation of conspiracy happens to be true, today's decision obstructs the congressional policy favoring competition that undergirds both the Telecommunications Act of 1996 and the Sherman Act itself. More importantly, even if there is abundant evidence that the allegation is untrue, directing that the case be dismissed without even looking at any of that evidence marks a fundamental—and unjustified—change in the character of pretrial practice.

Accordingly, I respectfully dissent.

Notes & Questions

1. As a matter of antitrust law, the defendants in *Twombly* could be held liable under the Sherman Act only if they *agreed* not to compete with each other, not if they merely engaged in the parallel conduct of each choosing not to compete with the others. Did Twombly's complaint allege that the defendants agreed not to compete with one another? If you consider Twombly's complaint in light of Rule 8(a) and *Swierkiewicz v. Sorema*, 534 U.S. 506 (2002), would you have thought that it stated a claim sufficiently to survive a motion to dismiss?

2. Why did the Supreme Court rule that the complaint must be dismissed? Did the majority reject, as a general principle, that courts must accept a complaint's allegations as true for purposes of deciding a motion to dismiss? Did the majority reject, as a general principle, that a complaint need only include a "short and plain" statement of the claim? How did the Supreme Court majority justify its ruling? Was the decision driven mostly by the text of Rule 8 or by policy concerns?

3. In *Twombly*, one of the majority's key concerns is that a lenient pleading standard opens the door to significant discovery costs, especially in a case like *Twombly*. Under the discovery rules, parties can compel others to turn over a great deal of information. Moreover, in the United States, each party generally pays its own litigation costs and attorneys' fees. This is widely known as the "American Rule," because it stands in contrast to the approach of a number of other countries' legal systems. The upshot is this: If a plaintiff gets to discovery, that plaintiff may begin requesting a large amount of information from the defendant, and the defendant must bear the cost of producing it. What sort of undue pressure do these costs place on defendants, according to the majority? (Consider that only about 2 percent of cases go to trial.)

    Could these discovery costs be contained by careful judicial management, as the dissent suggests in footnote 13, or is that an impossible task, as the majority asserts? You will be better equipped to answer this question after you have studied discovery in Chapter 3 and pretrial management in Chapter 4. As you learn about the litigation process, keep *Twombly* in mind and ask yourself *one*, whether the majority's concerns about discovery costs and settlement pressure are justified in general, in particular types of cases, or both; and *two*, whether such concerns are better addressed directly through discovery and pretrial rules, rather than indirectly through rules governing pleading.

4. To meet the "plausibility" requirement, what more did Twombly and Marcus need to allege? Does the majority believe that the plaintiffs could have crafted a "plausible" complaint with the information that they had in their possession?

THE BIG PICTURE

Twombly raises hard questions about information asymmetry and access to justice. On the one hand, the Court does not want meritless claims to go forward. On the other hand, if Twombly's claim of conspiracy is correct, then wouldn't the defendants possess information regarding the conspiracy that would be very difficult for Twombly to obtain before filing the lawsuit? Think of types of claims in which, at the outset, certain relevant information is possessed only by the defendant. Workplace discrimination and product liability are two examples. Can you think of others? Should courts consider such informational asymmetries when evaluating the sufficiency of complaints?

5. How far does the holding in *Twombly* go? The Court stated that it "granted certiorari to address the proper standard for pleading an antitrust conspiracy through allegations of parallel conduct." Moreover, the bulk of the discussion in both the majority opinion and the dissent centers on the features of antitrust law and litigation, including the high costs of discovery in antitrust class actions. Is the holding of *Twombly* limited to antitrust cases? Along similar lines, the Court's reasoning in *Twombly* is based in large part on concerns of high discovery costs in a massive and complex nationwide class action against the telecommunications industry. Is the holding of *Twombly* limited to class actions? Is it limited to complex cases with high anticipated discovery costs? Keep these questions in mind as you read the following case.

ASHCROFT v. IQBAL
556 U.S. 662 (2009)

KENNEDY, J., delivered the opinion of the Court.

Javaid Iqbal (hereinafter respondent) is a citizen of Pakistan and a Muslim. In the wake of the September 11, 2001, terrorist attacks he was arrested in the United States on criminal charges and detained by federal officials. Respondent claims he was deprived of various constitutional protections while in federal custody. To redress the alleged deprivations, respondent filed a complaint against numerous federal officials, including John Ashcroft, the former Attorney General of the United States, and Robert Mueller, the Director of the Federal Bureau of Investigation (FBI). Ashcroft and Mueller are the petitioners in the case now before us. As to these two petitioners, the complaint alleges that they adopted an unconstitutional policy that subjected respondent to harsh conditions of confinement on account of his race, religion, or national origin.

In the District Court petitioners raised the defense of qualified immunity and moved to dismiss the suit, contending the complaint was not sufficient to state a claim against them. The District Court denied the motion to dismiss, concluding the complaint was sufficient to state a claim despite petitioners' official status at the times in question. Petitioners brought an interlocutory appeal in the Court of Appeals for the Second Circuit. The court ... affirmed the District Court's decision.

[Iqbal's account of his ordeal could demonstrate unconstitutional conduct by some government officials, but this appeal does not involve Iqbal's claims against defendants other than Ashcroft and Mueller.] This case instead turns on a narrow question: Did respondent, as the plaintiff in the District Court, plead factual matter that, if taken as true, states a claim that petitioners [Ashcroft and Mueller] deprived him of his clearly established constitutional rights. We hold respondent's pleadings are insufficient.

I

Following the 2001 attacks, the FBI and other entities within the Department of Justice began an investigation of vast reach to identify the assailants and prevent them from attacking anew. . . .

In the ensuing months the FBI questioned more than 1,000 people with suspected links to the attacks in particular or to terrorism in general. Of those individuals, some 762 were held on immigration charges; and a 184-member subset of that group was deemed to be of high interest to the investigation. The high-interest detainees were held under restrictive conditions designed to prevent them from communicating with the general prison population or the outside world.

Respondent was one of the detainees. According to his complaint, in November 2001 agents of the FBI and Immigration and Naturalization Service arrested him on charges of fraud in relation to identification documents and conspiracy to defraud the United States. Pending trial for those crimes, respondent was housed at the Metropolitan Detention Center (MDC) in Brooklyn, New York. Respondent . . . was placed in a section of the MDC known as the Administrative Maximum Special Housing Unit (ADMAX SHU) [which] incorporates the maximum security conditions allowable under Federal Bureau of Prisons regulations. ADMAX SHU detainees were kept in lockdown 23 hours a day, spending the remaining hour outside their cells in handcuffs and leg irons accompanied by a four-officer escort.

Respondent pleaded guilty to the criminal charges, served a term of imprisonment, and was removed to his native Pakistan. He then filed a *Bivens* action in the United States District Court for the Eastern District of New York against 34 current and former federal officials and 19 "John Doe" federal corrections officers. . . .

The allegations against petitioners [Ashcroft and Mueller] are the only ones relevant here. The complaint contends that petitioners designated respondent a person of high interest on account of his race, religion, or national origin, in contravention of the First and Fifth Amendments to the Constitution. The complaint alleges that "the [FBI], under the direction of Defendant Mueller, arrested and detained thousands of Arab Muslim men . . . as part of its investigation of the events of September 11." It further alleges that "[t]he policy of holding post–September-11th detainees in highly restrictive conditions of confinement until they were 'cleared' by the FBI was approved by Defendants Ashcroft and Mueller in discussions in the weeks after September 11, 2001." Lastly, the complaint posits that petitioners "each knew of, condoned, and willfully and maliciously agreed to subject" respondent to harsh conditions of confinement "as a matter of policy, solely on account of [his] religion, race, and/or national origin and for no legitimate penological interest." The pleading names Ashcroft as the "principal architect" of the policy, and identifies Mueller as "instrumental in [its] adoption, promulgation, and implementation."

Petitioners moved to dismiss the complaint for failure to state sufficient allegations to show their own involvement in clearly established unconstitutional conduct. The District Court denied their motion. Accepting all of the allegations in respondent's complaint as true, the court held that "it cannot be said that there [is] no set of facts on which [respondent] would be entitled to relief as against" petitioners. Petitioners filed an interlocutory appeal in the United States Court of Appeals for the Second Circuit. While that appeal was pending, this Court decided *Bell Atlantic Corp. v. Twombly*, 550 U.S. 544 (2007), which discussed the standard for evaluating whether a complaint is sufficient to survive a motion to dismiss.

The Court of Appeals considered *Twombly*'s applicability to this case. Acknowledging that *Twombly* retired the *Conley* no-set-of-facts test relied upon by the District Court, the Court of Appeals concluded that *Twombly* called for a "flexible plausibility standard, which obliges a pleader to amplify a claim with some factual allegations in those contexts where such amplification is needed to render the claim *plausible.*" 490 F.3d at 157-58. The court found that petitioners' appeal did not present one of "those contexts" requiring amplification. As a consequence, it held respondent's pleading adequate to allege petitioners' personal involvement in discriminatory decisions which, if true,

violated clearly established constitutional law....

We granted certiorari, and now reverse.

II

[Part II addressed whether the Court of Appeals had jurisdiction over the appeal from the District Court's order denying the motion to dismiss.]

III

In *Twombly*, the Court found it necessary first to discuss the antitrust principles implicated by the complaint. Here too we begin by taking note of the elements a plaintiff must plead to state a claim of unconstitutional discrimination against officials entitled to assert the defense of qualified immunity.... Because vicarious liability is inapplicable [here], a plaintiff must plead that each Government-official defendant, through the official's own individual actions, has violated the Constitution....

Where the claim is invidious discrimination in contravention of the First and Fifth Amendments, our decisions make clear that the plaintiff must plead and prove that the defendant acted with discriminatory purpose.... [P]urposeful discrimination requires more than "intent as volition or intent as awareness of consequences." *Personnel Administrator of Mass. v. Feeney*, 442 U.S. 256, 279 (1979). It instead involves a decision maker's undertaking a course of action "because of, not merely in spite of, [the action's] adverse effects upon an identifiable group." *Ibid.* It follows that, to state a claim based on a violation of a clearly established right, respondent must plead sufficient factual matter to show that petitioners adopted and implemented the detention policies at issue not for a neutral, investigative reason but for the purpose of discriminating on account of race, religion, or national origin. . . .

IV

A

We turn to respondent's complaint. Under Federal Rule of Civil Procedure 8(a)(2), a pleading must contain a "short and plain statement of the claim showing that the pleader is entitled to relief." As the Court held in *Twombly*, the pleading standard Rule 8 announces does not require "detailed factual allegations," but it demands more than an unadorned, the-defendant-unlawfully-harmed-me accusation. *Id.* at 555. A pleading that offers "labels and conclusions" or "a formulaic recitation of the elements of a cause of action will not do." Nor does a complaint suffice if it tenders "naked assertion[s]" devoid of "further factual enhancement." *Id.* at 557.

To survive a motion to dismiss, a complaint must contain sufficient factual matter, accepted as true, to "state a claim to relief that is plausible on its face." *Id.* at 570. A claim has facial plausibility when the plaintiff pleads factual content that allows the court to draw the reasonable inference that the defendant is liable for the misconduct alleged. The plausibility standard is not akin to a "probability requirement," but it asks for more than a sheer possibility that a defendant has acted unlawfully. *Ibid.* Where a complaint pleads facts that are "merely consistent with" a defendant's liability, it "stops short of the line between possibility and plausibility of entitlement to relief." *Id.* at 557.

Two working principles underlie our decision in *Twombly*. First, the tenet that a court must accept as true all of the allegations contained in a complaint is

inapplicable to legal conclusions. Threadbare recitals of the elements of a cause of action, supported by mere conclusory statements, do not suffice. . . . Rule 8 . . . does not unlock the doors of discovery for a plaintiff armed with nothing more than conclusions. Second, only a complaint that states a plausible claim for relief survives a motion to dismiss. Determining whether a complaint states a plausible claim for relief will be a context-specific task that requires the reviewing court to draw on its judicial experience and common sense. But where the well-pleaded facts do not permit the court to infer more than the mere possibility of misconduct, the complaint has not "show[n]" that the pleader is entitled to relief." Fed. R. Civ. P. 8(a)(2).

In keeping with these principles a court considering a motion to dismiss can choose to begin by identifying pleadings that, because they are no more than conclusions, are not entitled to the assumption of truth. While legal conclusions can provide the framework of a complaint, they must be supported by factual allegations. When there are well-pleaded factual allegations, a court should assume their veracity and then determine whether they plausibly give rise to an entitlement to relief.

Our decision in *Twombly* illustrates the two-pronged approach. [There, the plaintiffs pleaded that the defendants "entered into a contract, combination or conspiracy to prevent competitive entry" and "agreed not to compete with one another."]

The Court held the plaintiffs' complaint deficient under Rule 8. In doing so it first noted that the plaintiffs' assertion of an unlawful agreement was a "legal conclusion" and, as such, was not entitled to the assumption of truth. *Id.* at 555. Had the Court simply credited the allegation of a conspiracy, the plaintiffs would have stated a claim for relief and been entitled to proceed perforce. The Court next addressed the "nub" of the plaintiffs' complaint—the well-pleaded, nonconclusory factual allegation of parallel behavior—to determine whether it gave rise to a "plausible suggestion of conspiracy." *Id.* at 565-66. Acknowledging that parallel conduct was consistent with an unlawful agreement, the Court nevertheless concluded that it did not plausibly suggest an illicit accord because it was not only compatible with, but indeed was more likely explained by, lawful, unchoreographed free-market behavior. Because the well-pleaded fact of parallel conduct, accepted as true, did not plausibly suggest an unlawful agreement, the Court held the plaintiffs' complaint must be dismissed.

B

Under *Twombly*'s construction of Rule 8, we conclude that respondent's complaint has not "nudged [his] claims" of invidious discrimination "across the line from conceivable to plausible." *Ibid.*

We begin our analysis by identifying the allegations in the complaint that are not entitled to the assumption of truth. Respondent pleads that petitioners "knew of, condoned, and willfully and maliciously agreed to subject [him]" to harsh conditions of confinement "as a matter of policy, solely on account of [his] religion, race, and/or national origin and for no legitimate penological interest." The complaint alleges that Ashcroft was the "principal architect" of this invidious policy, and that Mueller was "instrumental" in adopting and executing it. These bare assertions, much like the pleading of conspiracy in *Twombly*, amount to nothing more than a "formulaic recitation of the elements" of a constitutional discrimination claim, namely, that petitioners adopted a policy "because of, not merely in spite of, its adverse effects

upon an identifiable group." *Feeney*, 442 U.S. at 279. As such, the allegations are conclusory and not entitled to be assumed true. To be clear, we do not reject these bald allegations on the ground that they are unrealistic or nonsensical. . . . It is the conclusory nature of respondent's allegations, rather than their extravagantly fanciful nature, that disentitles them to the presumption of truth.

We next consider the factual allegations in respondent's complaint to determine if they plausibly suggest an entitlement to relief. The complaint alleges that "the [FBI], under the direction of Defendant Mueller, arrested and detained thousands of Arab Muslim men . . . as part of its investigation of the events of September 11." It further claims that "[t]he policy of holding post–September-11th detainees in highly restrictive conditions of confinement until they were 'cleared' by the FBI was approved by Defendants Ashcroft and Mueller in discussions in the weeks after September 11, 2001." Taken as true, these allegations are consistent with petitioners' purposefully designating detainees "of high interest" because of their race, religion, or national origin. But given more likely explanations, they do not plausibly establish this purpose.

The September 11 attacks were perpetrated by 19 Arab Muslim hijackers who counted themselves members in good standing of al Qaeda, an Islamic fundamentalist group. Al Qaeda was headed by another Arab Muslim—Osama bin Laden—and composed in large part of his Arab Muslim disciples. It should come as no surprise that a legitimate policy directing law enforcement to arrest and detain individuals because of their suspected link to the attacks would produce a disparate, incidental impact on Arab Muslims, even though the purpose of the policy was to target neither Arabs nor Muslims. On the facts respondent alleges the arrests Mueller oversaw were likely lawful and justified by his nondiscriminatory intent to detain aliens who were illegally present in the United States and who had potential connections to those who committed terrorist acts. As between that "obvious alternative explanation" for the arrests, *Twombly*, 550 U.S. at 567, and the purposeful, invidious discrimination respondent asks us to infer, discrimination is not a plausible conclusion.

But even if the complaint's well-pleaded facts give rise to a plausible inference that respondent's arrest was the result of unconstitutional discrimination, that inference alone would not entitle respondent to relief. . . . Respondent's   constitutional claims against petitioners rest solely on their ostensible "policy of holding post–September-11th detainees" in the ADMAX SHU once they were categorized as "of high interest." To prevail on that theory, the complaint must contain facts plausibly showing that petitioners purposefully adopted a policy of classifying post–September-11 detainees as "of high interest" because of their race, religion, or national origin.

This the complaint fails to do. Though respondent alleges that various other defendants [engaged in specific acts against him], his only factual allegation against petitioners accuses them of adopting a policy approving "restrictive conditions of confinement" for post–September-11 detainees until they were " 'cleared' by the FBI." Accepting the truth of that allegation, the complaint does not show, or even intimate, that petitioners purposefully housed detainees in the ADMAX SHU due to their race, religion, or national origin. All it plausibly suggests is that the Nation's top law enforcement officers, in the aftermath of a devastating terrorist attack, sought to keep suspected terrorists in the most secure conditions available until the suspects could be cleared of terrorist activity. Respondent does not argue, nor can he, that such a motive would violate petitioners' constitutional obligations. He would need to allege more by way of factual content to "nudg[e]" his claim of purposeful discrimination "across the line from conceivable to plausible." *Twombly*, 550 U.S. at 570.

To be sure, [unlike in *Twombly*,] here, the complaint alleges discrete wrongs—for instance, beatings—by lower level Government actors. [However,] petitioners cannot be held liable unless they themselves acted on account of a constitutionally protected characteristic. Yet respondent's complaint does not contain any factual allegation sufficient to plausibly suggest petitioners' discriminatory state of mind. His pleadings thus do not meet the standard necessary to satisfy Rule 8.

C

Respondent first says that our decision in *Twombly* should be limited to pleadings made in the context of an antitrust dispute. This argument is not supported by *Twombly* and is incompatible with the Federal Rules of Civil Procedure. Though *Twombly* determined the sufficiency of a complaint sounding in antitrust, the decision was based on our interpretation and application of Rule 8. That Rule in turn governs the pleading standard "in all civil actions and proceedings in the United States district courts." Fed. R. Civ. P. 1. . . .

V

We hold that respondent's complaint fails to plead sufficient facts to state a claim for purposeful and unlawful discrimination against petitioners. The Court of Appeals should decide in the first instance whether to remand to the District Court so that respondent can seek leave to amend his deficient complaint.

The judgment of the Court of Appeals is reversed, and the case is remanded for further proceedings consistent with this opinion.

Justice SOUTER, with whom Justice STEVENS, Justice GINSBURG, and Justice BREYER join, dissenting.

[The majority improperly weighs in on the issue of supervisory liability for federal officers.] The majority then misapplies the pleading standard under *Twombly* to conclude that the complaint fails to state a claim. I respectfully dissent.

... [T]he complaint satisfies Rule 8(a)(2). Ashcroft and Mueller admit they are liable for their subordinates' conduct if they "had actual knowledge of the assertedly discriminatory nature of the classification of suspects as being of high interest and they were deliberately indifferent to that discrimination." Iqbal alleges that after the September 11 attacks the FBI "arrested and detained thousands of Arab Muslim men," that many of these men were designated by high-ranking FBI officials as being "of high interest," and that in many cases, including Iqbal's this designation was made "because of the race, religion, and national origin of the detainees, and not because of any evidence of the detainees involvement in supporting terrorist activity[.]" The complaint further alleges that Ashcroft was the "principal architect of the policies and practices challenged," and that Mueller "was instrumental in the adoption, promulgation, and implementation of the policies and

practices challenged." According to the complaint, Ashcroft and Mueller "knew of, condoned, and willfully and maliciously agreed to subject [Iqbal] to these conditions of confinement as a matter of policy, solely on account of [his] religion, race and/or national origin and for no legitimate penological interest." ... If these factual allegations are true, Ashcroft and Mueller were, at the very least, aware of the discriminatory policy being implemented and deliberately indifferent to it.

Ashcroft and Mueller argue that these allegations fail to satisfy the "plausibility standard" of *Twombly*. They contend that Iqbal's claims are implausible because such high-ranking officials "tend not to be personally involved in the specific actions of lower-level officers down the bureaucratic chain of command." But this response bespeaks a fundamental misunderstanding of the enquiry that *Twombly* demands. *Twombly* does not require a court at the motion-to-dismiss stage to consider whether the factual allegations are probably true. We made clear, on the contrary, that a court must take the allegations as true, no matter how skeptical the court may be. The sole exception to this rule lies with allegations that are sufficiently fantastic to defy reality as we know it: claims about little green men, or the plaintiff's recent trip to Pluto, or experiences in time travel. That is not what we have here.

Under *Twombly*, the relevant question is whether, assuming the factual allegations are true, the plaintiff has stated a ground for relief that is plausible. That is, in *Twombly*'s words, a plaintiff must "allege facts" that, taken as true, are "suggestive of illegal conduct." 550 U.S. at 564 n.8. ... Here, by contrast [with *Twombly*], the allegations in the complaint are neither confined to naked legal conclusions nor consistent with legal conduct. The complaint alleges that FBI officials discriminated against Iqbal solely on account of his race, religion, and national origin, and it alleges the knowledge and deliberate indifference that, by Ashcroft and Mueller's own admission, are sufficient to make them liable for the illegal action. Iqbal's complaint therefore contains "enough facts to state a claim to relief that is plausible on its face." *Id.* at 570.

I do not understand the majority to disagree with this understanding of "plausibility" under *Twombly*. Rather, the majority discards the allegations discussed above with regard to Ashcroft and Mueller as conclusory, and is left considering only two statements in the complaint: that "the [FBI], under the direction of Defendant Mueller, arrested and detained thousands of Arab Muslim men . . . as part of its investigation of the events of September 11," and that "[t]he policy of holding post–September 11th detainees in highly restrictive conditions of confinement until they were cleared by the FBI was approved by Defendants Ashcroft and Mueller in discussions in the weeks after September 11, 2001." . . . I agree that the two allegations selected by the majority, standing alone, do not state a plausible entitlement to relief for unconstitutional discrimination.

But these allegations do not stand alone as the only significant nonconclusory statements in the complaint, for the complaint contains many allegations linking Ashcroft and Mueller to the discriminatory practices of their subordinates.

The majority says that these are "bare assertions" that, "much like the pleading of conspiracy in *Twombly*, amount to nothing more than a formulaic recitation of the elements of a constitutional discrimination claim" and therefore are "not entitled to be assumed true." The fallacy in the majority's position, however, lies in looking at the relevant assertions in isolation. The complaint contains specific allegations that, in the aftermath of the September 11 attacks, the Chief of the FBI's International Terrorism Operations Section and the Assistant Special Agent in Charge for the FBI's New York Field Office implemented a policy that discriminated against Arab Muslim men, including Iqbal, solely on account of their race, religion, or national origin. Viewed in light of these subsidiary allegations, the allegations singled out by the majority as "conclusory" are no such thing. Iqbal's claim . . . is that [Ashcroft and Mueller] "knew of, condoned, and willfully and maliciously agreed to subject" him to a particular, discrete, discriminatory policy detailed in the complaint. Iqbal does not say merely that Ashcroft was the architect of some amorphous discrimination, or that Mueller was instrumental in an ill-defined constitutional violation; he alleges that they helped to create the discriminatory policy he has described. Taking the complaint as a whole, it gives Ashcroft and Mueller "fair notice of what the . . . claim is and the grounds upon which it rests." *Twombly*, 550 U.S. at 555 (quoting *Conley v. Gibson*, 355 U.S. 41, 47 (1957)).

That aside, the majority's holding that the statements it selects are conclusory cannot be squared with its treatment of certain other allegations in the complaint as nonconclusory. . . . By my lights, there is no principled basis for the majority's disregard of the allegations linking Ashcroft and Mueller to their subordinates' discrimination.

I respectfully dissent.

Notes & Questions

1. Before *Twombly*, the decision whether to grant Ashcroft's and Mueller's motion to dismiss was straightforward. As the district court concluded in the *Iqbal* case on the motion to dismiss (before the Supreme Court decided *Twombly*), the complaint alleged that Ashcroft and Mueller acted with a discriminatory purpose and therefore the district court denied the defendants' motion. By the time the *Iqbal* appeal reached the Second Circuit and the Supreme Court, however, the Justices had decided *Twombly*. This presented two questions: (a) Did *Twombly* apply to cases like Iqbal's, an individual civil rights case, or was it limited to cases like *Twombly*, an antitrust class action with potentially massive discovery? (b) If the *Twombly* standard applied, did Iqbal's complaint suffice to meet the plausibility test and to survive a motion to dismiss?

2. *Iqbal* made it clear that the new "plausibility pleading" standard applied across the swath of cases and claims in federal court. Is the pleading standard set forth in *Iqbal* the same standard set forth in *Twombly*? Which Justice wrote the majority opinion in *Twombly*? Which way did that Justice go in *Iqbal*? What do you make of this? To whatever extent *Iqbal* clarifies the rule of *Twombly*, state the new rule as precisely as possible.

3. The Court in *Iqbal* says that *Twombly* was not limited to the antitrust context. Is that a fair read of *Twombly*? Recall one of the key concerns in *Twombly*—the *in terrorem* settlement pressure defendants face when the gates of discovery are thrown open. Are such concerns about settlement pressure likely to be present in a case like *Iqbal*?

   The Court in *Iqbal* also states that limiting *Twombly* to the antitrust context would be incompatible with the Federal Rules of Civil Procedure. Do you agree?

4. What renders an allegation in a complaint a mere conclusion "not entitled to the presumption of truth"? Can you distinguish those allegations in Iqbal's complaint that the majority held were bare "legal conclusions," not entitled to a presumption of truth, from those it deemed nonconclusory?

5. In *Twombly*, Justice Stevens in dissent said that the case was a poor vehicle for making a sweeping change to a Federal Rule of Civil Procedure. Are there arguments that *Iqbal* provides an even worse vehicle for such change?

6. After *Twombly* and *Iqbal*, many worried that a far greater number of complaints would be dismissed at the pleading stage. These fears were not just hypothetical. Indeed, studies have found that, after *Twombly*, courts granted motions to dismiss in a greater percentage of cases across various areas of the law. *See, e.g.,* Raymond H. Brescia, *The* Iqbal *Effect: The Impact of New Pleading Standards in Employment and Housing Discrimination Litigation*, 100 KY. L.J. 235, 261 (2011) (finding an increase in dismissal rates after *Twombly* from 61 percent to 72 percent in housing discrimination cases); Patricia W. Hatamyar, *The Tao of*

Pleading: Do Twombly *and* Iqbal *Matter Empirically?*, 59 AM. U. L. REV. 553, 607 (2010) (finding similar increases in dismissal rates after *Twombly* and *Iqbal* in torts cases, civil rights cases, and cases involving various statutory causes of action). Other studies, however, including a report submitted to the Judicial Conference Advisory Committee on Civil Rules, found that there was no significant change in dismissal rates for most kinds of cases after *Twombly*, making the impact of these cases less clear. *See* JOE S. CECIL ET AL., MOTIONS TO DISMISS FOR FAILURE TO STATE A CLAIM AFTER IQBAL: REPORT TO THE JUDICIAL CONFERENCE ADVISORY COMMITTEE ON CIVIL RULES 1, 21 (Fed. Judicial Ctr., 2011). Looking at dismissal rates alone may not tell the entire story. As Professor Gelbach has pointed out, tracking dismissal rates does not tell you whether *Twombly* and *Iqbal* have a chilling effect on the filing of complaints in the first place. Jonah B. Gelbach, *Material Facts in the Debate over* Twombly *and* Iqbal, 68 STAN. L. REV. 369, 374-75 (2016).

7. As you proceed through the course, ask yourself whether and to what extent changes to pleading rules adequately address the following possible concerns: (1) error costs of letting unmeritorious suits drive costs and settlement pressure; (2) error costs of over-screening meritorious suits; and (3) transaction cost barriers to claiming. Think about whether each of these concerns is more (or less) likely to come up with certain types of claims, certain types of plaintiffs, or certain levels of party resources.

STRATEGY SESSION

After *Twombly* and *Iqbal*, how much detail should you put in a complaint? As a matter of practice, more detail is not necessarily better. A complaint may be dismissed for lack of plausibility because the plaintiff unwittingly includes *too much* detail—adding factual allegations that *negate* the plausibility of the claim. This is sometimes referred to as "pleading yourself out of court." On the other hand, lawyers do not generally limit their complaints to the bare minimum needed to satisfy Rule 8 and the plausibility requirement. The allegations of the complaint shape the judge's and adversary's first impressions of the case. The complaint may dictate the course of discovery. And a compelling complaint may draw the defendant to the settlement table. Accordingly, litigators draft the complaint with an eye toward getting the judge on board with their factual and legal theories, as well as with an eye toward getting the defendant to see the strength of the plaintiff's claim. When crafting a complaint, you are telling a story to two important audiences—a judge and an adversary.

(3) Heightened Pleading

As a general rule, notice pleading does not require specificity. In both *Twombly* and *Iqbal*, the Supreme Court required enough factual content to nudge the complaints' conclusions "across the line from conceivable to plausible," but the Court insisted that it was not requiring "heightened fact pleading of specifics, but only enough fact to state a claim to relief that is plausible on its face." *Twombly*, 550 U.S. at 570. Whether this insistence is true in practice is a matter of some empirical and theoretical debate. When courts refer to "heightened pleading," however, what is typically being referenced are rules and statutes that require specificity for certain types of allegations.

Take a look at Fed. R. Civ. P. 9(b), which imposes a heightened pleading requirement for "fraud or mistake," whether in the complaint or in the answer to a complaint. Under Rule 9(b), it is not sufficient to allege, for instance, that a contract is unenforceable because it was induced fraudulently or was the product of the mistake. Instead, the rule requires that a party state "with particularity the circumstances constituting fraud or mistake." A fraud complaint, therefore, cannot merely allege that the defendant defrauded the plaintiff by making intentional misrepresentations on which the plaintiff relied. Rather, the complaint must give a more detailed account of the fraud, such as who said what to whom, when and where the representation was made, in what way the representation was false, and how the plaintiff relied on it.

UNITED STATES ex rel. HIRT v. WALGREEN COMPANY
846 F.3d 879 (6th Cir. 2017)

SUTTON, Circuit Judge.

[Andrew] Hirt owns two pharmacies, one of which is located in Cookeville, Tennessee. His Cookeville pharmacy competes with a Walgreens in the area. Between November 19, 2012, and August 25, 2014, Hirt alleges that Willow Walgreens offered $25 gift cards to lure his customers to Walgreens in violation of the Anti-Kickback Statute, 42 U.S.C. §1320a-7b(b), and that Walgreens submitted the resulting prescription-drug claims by Medicare and Medicaid recipients to the government in violation of the False Claims Act, 31 U.S.C. §3729.

Hirt filed this *qui tam* action under the whistleblower provision of the False Claims Act on behalf of himself and the United States. The government declined to intervene in the action, and Walgreens moved to dismiss it. The district court granted the motion, holding (among other things) that Hirt failed to state his claims with sufficient particularity under Civil Rule 9(b).

The False Claims Act imposes civil liability for "knowingly present[ing] . . . a false or fraudulent claim" to the government "for payment or approval." The statute provides for public enforcement and private (*qui tam*) lawsuits. *Id.* §3730(b). . . .

In addition to satisfying the False Claims Act's requirements, *qui tam* plaintiffs must meet the heightened pleading standards of Civil Rule 9(b). In all averments of "fraud or mistake," the plaintiff must state with "particularity the circumstances constituting fraud or mistake." Fed. R. Civ. P. 9(b). The identification of at least one false claim with specificity is "an indispensable element of a complaint that alleges a [False Claims Act] violation in compliance with Rule 9(b)." *U.S. ex rel. Bledsoe v. Cmty. Health Sys., Inc.*, 501 F.3d 493, 504 (6th Cir. 2007).

Hirt has not met this standard. His complaint does not identify a single false claim. He describes the unlawful distribution of gift cards in general but not the submission of any claims obtained with those gift cards. All that Hirt says is that "his [Medicaid and Medicare] customers accepted the $25.00 gift cards to move their business to (Willow) Walgreens in Cookeville during the period November 19, 2012 through August 25, 2014," and that Walgreens "induce[d] . . . false or fraudulent claims to the United States Government for the payment of pharmaceuticals." But he does not identify any false claim arising from any of those (allegedly) induced customers. He does not tell us the names of any such customers or their initials. He does not tell us the dates on which they filled prescriptions at Walgreens. He does not tell us the dates on which Walgreens filed the reimbursement claims with the government. He does not, indeed, even say that these unnamed customers filled any prescriptions at Walgreens at all, let alone that Walgreens processed them and filed reimbursement claims with the government. We are left to infer these essential elements from the fact that Hirt's customers moved their business from his pharmacies. But inferences and implications are not what Civil Rule 9(b) requires. It demands specifics—at least if the claimant wishes to raise allegations of fraud against someone. . . .

We have no more authority to "relax" the pleading standard established by Civil Rule 9(b) than we do to increase it. Only by following the highly reticulated procedures laid out in the Rules Enabling Act can anyone modify the Civil Rules, whether in the direction of relaxing them or tightening them. To the extent the words of Civil Rule 9(b) need elaboration, and it's not obvious that they do, the most that can be said is that "particular" allegations of fraud may demand different things in different contexts. . . .

[In the context of this case,] Hirt failed to provide the factual predicates necessary to convince us that "actual false claims" "in all likelihood exist." *Bledsoe*, 501 F.3d at 504 n.12. He does not allege personal knowledge of Walgreen's claim submission procedures [as required by the False Claims Act]. And he does not otherwise allege facts "from which it is highly likely that a claim was submitted to the government." *Chesbrough v. VPA, P.C.*, 655 F.3d 461, 472 (6th Cir. 2011). At the least, Hirt could have described a prescription filled by one of his previous customers at the Willow Walgreens. In the same way that Hirt discovered that his former customers had accepted the gift cards, he could have determined whether they used those gift cards when filling a prescription at Walgreens. And if that is somehow not the case, how could he know that Walgreens violated the False Claims Act—the first requirement for filing an action?

Hirt's general allegations that Walgreens offered gift cards and some Medicare and Medicaid recipients accepted them do not meet the particularity requirement. "To conclude that a claim was presented" in this setting "requires a series of assumptions," leaving only a "possibility" of fraudulent submissions rather than an establishment of them. *Id.* at 472. Hirt failed to describe even one unlawful prescription purchase— that customer X of his pharmacy filled prescription Y with Willow Walgreens on date Z after receiving a gift card from Walgreens. If Hirt lacked the information to do even this, he was not the right plaintiff to bring this *qui tam* claim—and almost certainly not the right one to do so in a way that would allow a court to decide whether the public-disclosure bar applies to the allegation. We have no basis for excluding a lack of personal knowledge when it comes to the essential—the primary—illegal conduct at issue. The point of Civil Rule 9(b) is to prevent, not facilitate, casual allegations of fraud....

For these reasons, we affirm.

Notes & Questions

1. As you think about justifications for requiring parties to plead fraud with particularity, consider whether those justifications distinguish fraud from other claims and defenses. If the justification is that fraud is a powerful and damaging accusation, yet easy to allege, is this not the case for many other allegations that arise in civil litigation? Indeed, are there reasons why one might wish to treat victims of fraud more *leniently*, rather than more strictly, in terms of the information they are expected to have in their possession prior to discovery?

2. The Supreme Court in *Twombly* and *Iqbal* emphasized that, in interpreting Rule 8(a), it was not imposing a heightened pleading requirement. Indeed, the Court specifically mentioned Rule 9(b) in both cases. But how clear is the distinction? While neither *Twombly* nor *Iqbal* set forth specific factual requirements for pleading the substantive claims in those cases, does the plausibility requirement nonetheless nudge the requirements for *any* type of claim closer to something resembling Rule 9(b)? (Compare the suggestion in *Hirt* that the plaintiff "[a]t the least ... could have described a prescription filled by one of his previous customers at Willow Walgreens" with the suggestion in footnote 10 of *Twombly*.)

3. In *Iqbal*, the Supreme Court held that, when analyzing a motion to dismiss, district courts should not treat "legal conclusions" as entitled to a presumption of truth. Can you distinguish this aspect of *Iqbal* from the application of Rule 9(b) in *Hirt*?

4. In *Hirt*, the Sixth Circuit asserts that "relaxing" Rule 9(b) would be incompatible with the Rules Enabling Act (REA). In what way would it be incompatible? Would it be equally incompatible to tighten the rule? If the court's point is that Federal Rules of Civil Procedure should be amended through the rule-making process spelled out in the REA rather than by judicial fiat, what does that say about *Twombly* and *Iqbal*?

5. Both before and after *Twombly* and *Iqbal*, some courts have attempted to impose a heightened pleading requirement on plaintiffs in civil rights cases. However, the Supreme Court has made it clear that unless Rule 9(b) is amended or Congress so legislates, no such heightened requirement exists. In *Leatherman v. Tarrant County*, 507 U.S. 163 (1993), plaintiffs sued a municipality and several of its police officers, alleging that the officers violated the plaintiffs' civil rights by killing their dogs and beating an elderly man in connection with a search. The defendants moved to dismiss under 12(b)(6), arguing that the complaint contained insufficient detail to state a claim. The district court granted the motion,

and the court of appeals affirmed, reasoning that heightened pleading should be required for civil rights claims because of the risk of frivolous suits and because defendants have qualified immunity. The Supreme Court reversed, citing the notice pleading standard of Rule 8(a). After *Leatherman*, though, the judicial impulse to require specificity for civil rights complaints remains, and some courts have found ways to impose such a requirement, such as by requiring plaintiffs to file a detailed reply if a defendant asserts qualified immunity as a defense. How might the decisions in *Twombly* and *Iqbal* affect the post-*Leatherman* reality for civil right claims?

B. DEFENDANT'S RESPONSE TO THE COMPLAINT

After a defendant has been served with a complaint, the defendant has a number of options. The defendant may make a responsive pleading, called an answer. The answer may include admissions, denials, and affirmative defenses. Fed. R. Civ. P. 8(b), (c). Alternatively, a defendant may file a pre-answer motion, such as a motion to dismiss for failure to state a claim, as you read about above, or a motion to dismiss for lack of jurisdiction, among others. *See* Fed. R. Civ. P. 12(b)(1)-(7). In addition, the defendant may assert claims of its own, whether as counterclaims, crossclaims, or third-party claims. You will learn more about these types of claims in Chapter 7 on joinder, but the important takeaway here is that, once a plaintiff files a complaint, that plaintiff is subject to having claims brought against it in that same lawsuit.

These response options are not mutually exclusive. Unlike common law pleading, which was more restrictive, modern pleading permits defendants to offer multiple responses to a complaint. For example, a defendant may object to the court's jurisdiction, argue that the complaint does not state a claim upon which relief can be granted, deny the truth of the plaintiff's allegations, offer affirmative defenses, and assert counterclaims.

(1) Admissions and Denials

Under Rule 8(b), a responsive pleading admits or denies each of the allegations in the complaint and asserts the defenses to each claim. The core component of this pleading—the defendant's answer—is a series of statements in which the defendant answers each paragraph of the complaint, one by one, by stating whether the defendant admits or denies the allegations in that paragraph. Under the rule, any allegation that is not denied is deemed admitted. In addition to admissions and denials, the answer can also contain affirmative defenses. To get a handle on the basic distinction between a denial and an affirmative defense, recall the common law practices of *traverse*, on the one hand (through which the defendant asserted that some or all of the plaintiff's allegations were untrue), and *confession and avoidance* on the other (through which the defendant accepted the plaintiff's allegations as true, but asserted that she was not liable for some other reason).

In almost any dispute, there is actually a lot that the parties agree about. Maybe the parties agree that they entered into a contract, but they disagree about whether the defendant breached it. Or the parties agree that a surgeon performed an appendectomy on the patient on a given day at a particular hospital, but they disagree about whether malpractice occurred. The admissions and denials clarify these points of agreement and disagreement, so that the litigation can focus on what is really in dispute. If an answer admits some of the complaint's allegations, those allegations are deemed true for purposes of the litigation. The upshot: Facts admitted in the pleadings need not be proved at trial; they are simply accepted as true.

What if a defendant does not have enough information to decide whether to admit or deny certain of the plaintiff's allegations? Rule 8(b)(5) contemplates this possibility. It provides that "[a] party that lacks knowledge or information sufficient to form a belief about the truth of an allegation must so state, and the statement has the effect of a denial."

Answering a complaint requires very careful work. Defendants must respond to each of the complaint's allegations. For instance, if you're drafting an answer, and the complaint contains a paragraph that you partly admit and partly deny, you cannot simply deny the whole thing because part of it is false. You must state which parts of the allegation you admit and which parts you deny. This is critical to remember given that any allegation *not* denied is deemed admitted. With this in mind, consider the following case.

SINCLAIR REFINING COMPANY v. HOWELL
222 F.2d 637 (5th Cir. 1955)

RIVES, Circuit Judge.

A father suing under the Alabama statute for the wrongful death of his nineteen year old son, secured a verdict and judgment for damages in the amount of $30,000 from which this appeal is prosecuted. Three questions are presented for decision. The first and most important is whether, within the issues tried, the deceased was subject to the Workmen's Compensation Act of Alabama [as the exclusive source of a remedy for his son's death], and whether, for that reason, the district court erred in denying the defendant's motions for a directed verdict and for *judgment non obstante veredicto....*

Hayward Howell, the brother of the deceased minor, John Arthur Howell, was in the process of opening a general store and gasoline filling station on U.S. Highway 231 in Montgomery County, Alabama, on the 17th day of November, 1951. John Arthur Howell was in the general employ of Hayward Howell on this date. One A.O. Hall, an employee of appellant as a maintenance mechanic, whose duties were to supervise and assist in the installation of equipment at various filling stations, was engaged in supervising and assisting in the installation of a pole at Hayward Howell's filling station.... Hall reported to the Howell filling station on the morning of November 17, 1951, with one helper Hargrove to assist in the erection of the pole.

There were some overhead electric power lines running parallel to the roadway and parallel to the pumps at the Howell station. Hall had a truck that had an "A" frame mounted on the rear of the truck bed with a pulley working through the "A" frame to be used in hoisting the pole into the air. The truck was between the pumps and the power lines. As Hall started hoisting the pole into the air Hargrove was unable to hold the larger end of the pole and requested that he have help. . . .

Sullivan Thomas came out to assist and the deceased also came out of the store to assist. Hall saw that the deceased was actually working and helping to lift or move the pole at the time the deceased was killed. Hall repeatedly gave instructions to the deceased, to Hargrove and others helping, about what they were to do. As Hall hoisted the pole in the air with the pulley, Hargrove, Thomas and the deceased had hold of the base of the pole and were holding the base down, attempting to lift it over some wooden frames, and place it in the hole where it was to rest. The deceased had nothing to do with the top of the pole hitting the high voltage line. Hall knew that the high voltage line was overhead, and, according to his own testimony, the duty rested on him to supervise the safe erection of the pole. He knew that if the pole touched the high voltage wire someone would probably [b]e killed. His worker, Hargrove, had on rubber boots, but no precaution or warning was observed as to the deceased and the other helpers. The top of the pole came in contact with the high voltage line and John Arthur Howell was electrocuted.

The general verdict for the plaintiff was based upon two counts, one charging the defendant with negligence, and the other charging it with wanton misconduct. Under the rulings of the court, the plaintiff was required to amend his complaint so as to aver "that the said John Arthur Howell was not subject to the Workmen's Compensation Laws of Alabama." There was no express denial of this averment in the defendant's answer, and the only way that it was even impliedly denied was by the concluding sentence of the answer: "Defendant denies that the plaintiff is entitled to recover any damages in this cause."

Rule 8(b) of the Federal Rules of Civil Procedure, provides: "A party shall state in short and plain terms his defenses to each claim asserted and shall admit or deny the averments upon which the adverse party relies."[*] Rule 8(d) provides: "Averments in a pleading to which a responsive pleading is required, other than those as to the amount of damage, are admitted when not denied in the responsive pleading."[**] The effect of the defendant's answer was to admit the averment that the deceased was not subject to the Workmen's Compensation Law of Alabama. If the issue of applicability of the Workmen's Compensation Act had been clearly drawn, as required by the rule, the appellee would have had the opportunity of developing that the deceased's working for his brother was at most a "casual" employment excluded from the terms of the Act, or that the Act did not apply because his brother regularly employed less than eight employees. Such possibilities illustrate the wisdom of the rule in requiring issues to be clearly drawn. . . .

Affirmed.

---

[*] *Editors' Note:* The current version of Rule 8(b) reads, in relevant part, "In responding to a pleading, a party must . . . admit or deny the allegations asserted against it by an opposing party."

[**] *Editors' Note:* The substance of this quoted portion of Rule 8 as it existed at the time of *Howell* is now embodied in Rule 8(b)(6), which provides, "An allegation—other than one relating to the amount of damages—is admitted if a responsive pleading is required and the allegation is not denied."

Notes & Questions

1. Some of the terminology in this opinion may be unfamiliar to you, especially at this stage in the course. For instance, a *judgment non obstante veredicto* is a judgment entered by the judge notwithstanding the jury's verdict. As we will cover in Chapter 5, to obtain such a judgment, a party must demonstrate that no reasonable jury could have found for the prevailing party. Here, the defendant had argued that it was entitled to such a judgment on the grounds that Howell could not recover on his tort claim because workers' compensation was his only available remedy. What answer does the court provide to the question of whether Howell was limited to recovery under that statute?

2. What value is served by the result in *Howell*? The key purpose of workers' compensation laws is to provide a form of insurance for workers in exchange for their right to sue employers under tort law. Is the court's interpretation of Rule 8 in *Howell* in tension with the purpose of workers' compensation laws or other statutes that provide alternative recourse to the tort system? Is the dictate of Rule 8—that allegations not denied are admitted—unduly harsh, or does it strike the appropriate balance between accuracy, fairness, and efficiency?

3. In theory, rather than making specific denials of particular allegations, a defendant has the option of making a general denial, by which the defendant denies all of the allegations in the complaint. Fed. R. Civ. P. 8(b)(3). Given the popular perception of litigation as a sort of sport in which the parties fight about everything, you might expect to see this sort of denial frequently. In reality, a general denial is very rare. It is almost never possible for a party to deny *all* of the adversary's allegations. For instance, Sinclair Refining could not deny that Howell worked for Sinclair. It could not deny that Howell was electrocuted. Rule 8(b)(3) makes this point by saying that "[a] party that intends in good faith to deny all the allegations of a party that does not intend to deny all the allegations must either specifically deny designated allegations or generally deny all except those specifically admitted." In other words, do not make a general denial unless you really mean to deny each and every allegation.

(2) Affirmative Defenses

In addition to admitting or denying the plaintiff's allegations in its answer, a defendant may also assert affirmative defenses. You might think of these defenses as "Yes, but..." responses. The "yes, but" characterization captures the critical distinction between a plain defense or denial and an affirmative defense: With a denial, a defendant asserts that the plaintiff's allegations are untrue. In contrast, with an affirmative defense, the plaintiff's allegations can be taken as true. Indeed, an affirmative defense is a response asserting that the defendant is not liable, *even if* the plaintiff's allegations are true and *even if* the plaintiff makes out a legally sufficient claim, for some reason independent of the plaintiff's allegations. When a defendant argues that the plaintiff's claim is barred by the statute of limitations, for example, the defendant argues that *even if* the plaintiff's allegations are true, the claim is untimely. That is an affirmative defense.

Another key distinction between plain and affirmative defenses is that, unlike plain defenses to the plaintiff's allegations—where the burden of proof for the allegations remains with the party making those allegations—the burden of proof for affirmative defenses falls squarely on the defendant. What, precisely, is the nature of the defendant's burden at the pleading stage? Courts are split on the question of whether the plausibility pleading standard of *Twombly* and *Iqbal* applies to affirmative defenses. Part of the disagreement stems from the text of Rule 8 itself: Rule 8(a), which sets for the standard by which the sufficiency of the complaint is judged, requires the pleader to "show" that it is entitled to relief. Rule 8(b), on the other hand, requires a defendant to "state" its defenses. Some courts have concluded that this difference in language, along with the longer time period a plaintiff has to craft a complaint (relative to the time a defendant has to respond to the complaint), means that the plausibility standard should *not* apply to affirmative defenses. Other courts have reached the opposite conclusion, in part on the grounds that the plausibility standard applies to anything for which the pleader bears the burden of proof—what's sauce for the goose is sauce for the gander.

Lawyers must proceed with care regarding affirmative defenses because they are waived if not pleaded. Rule 8(c) provides a *non-exhaustive* list of affirmative defenses, such as assumption of risk, contributory negligence, discharge, duress, failure of consideration, fraud, illegality, license, release, res judicata, statute of frauds, statute of limitations, and waiver. Emphasis on *non-exhaustive*. (You can see that this list is non-exhaustive because of the following language in Rule 8(c): "In responding to a pleading, a party must affirmatively state any avoidance or affirmative defense, *including...*"). Therefore, if you represent a defendant, and under the applicable law your client has an affirmative defense, be sure to plead it even if it is not listed in Rule 8(c). On the other hand, if you represent a plaintiff and wish to argue that the defendant waived a particular defense because it constitutes an affirmative defense and was not pleaded, do not be deterred by the fact that it is not listed in Rule 8(c).

Though non-exhaustive, the list of affirmative defenses in 8(c) is useful for two reasons. One, it contains many of the affirmative defenses you will likely encounter in practice. Two, the affirmative defenses listed in 8(c) will provide helpful analogues in your analysis of possible additional affirmative defenses. By seeing what a potential defense has in common with those on the list in Rule 8(c), you will better understand whether that potential defense is, in fact, an affirmative defense. For instance, at first glance, contributory negligence, failure of consideration, res judicata, and statute of limitations—all listed in Rule 8(c)—may seem about as different as any legal doctrines can be. To understand the nature of an affirmative defense, though, ask yourself what these doctrines have in common. Each of them involves (1) additional facts pleaded by the defendant that were not part of the plaintiff's pleading (the plaintiff was negligent; there was no quid pro quo for the contract; the claim was already litigated to a final judgment; and too much time has expired, respectively); and (2) the defendant's assertion that those additional facts undo the plaintiff's claim for reasons *independent* of that claim. Affirmative defenses therefore differ from denials or plain defenses, which attempt to undo the claim by negating the plaintiff's allegations; they also differ from the defense of failure to state a claim, which asserts that the plaintiff's allegations do not make out a valid legal basis for granting relief.

While defense attorneys must think carefully about all possible affirmative defenses before filing an answer, the pleading rules do not totally withhold second chances. If a party fails to plead an affirmative defense in its original answer, the party can often fix the problem by amending the answer pursuant to the requirements of Rule 15, which we will explore in Part C of this chapter.

(3) Motions to Dismiss and Other Motions on the Pleadings

An answer responds to the substance of a complaint. However, answering the complaint imposes a burden on the defendant. It requires time, money, and possible embarrassment. Defendants therefore often look for some basis to ask the court to dispose of the complaint without requiring an answer.

Any defense may be asserted in the answer, but certain defenses may also be raised by pre-answer motion if the party so chooses. For the most part, these are motions to dismiss, and they are listed in Rule 12(b). Other motions in response to the pleadings are the motion for a more definite statement (Rule 12(e)), motion to strike (Rule 12(f)), and motion for judgment on the pleadings (Rule 12(c)).

(a) Motions to Dismiss

Rule 12(b) lists seven defenses that can be raised by motion rather than in the answer. The first five address the choice of forum or the way the defendant was haled into the forum. The sixth is one you are already familiar with—a motion to dismiss for failure to state a claim upon which relief can be granted. The seventh addresses compulsory party joinder, which you will study in Chapter 7. There is a separate subdivision among these defenses you need to know as well: 12(b)(2), (3), (4), and (5) defenses are *waived* if not raised by the defendant in the *first response to the complaint. See* Fed. R. Civ. P. 12(g), (h).

> **Terminology Tip**
>
> What is a *motion?* A motion is simply a request that a court order something. There is no magic list of permissible motions. As an attorney, when you want the court to order something—whether it is dismissing the complaint, excluding certain evidence, rescheduling a hearing, or anything else—you make a motion. Be aware, though, *motion* is a noun. You do not "motion" something. The verb is *move.* Thus, it is correct to say that a party *moves* to dismiss the case or that a defendant makes a *motion* to dismiss. An embarrassing rookie error would be to say that the defendant *motions* to dismiss.

Dismissals Regarding Forum and Process (Rule 12(b)(1)-(5)). The first three of the Rule 12(b) defenses respond to the complaint by asserting that the action should be dismissed because it is filed in the wrong *place.* Rule 12(b)(1) permits a motion to dismiss for lack of subject matter jurisdiction. Recall from Chapter 1's overview that the wrong place, in the context of a motion to dismiss for lack of subject matter jurisdiction under 12(b)(1), is federal court versus state court. Although the court may raise subject matter jurisdiction on its own, in practice any party who objects to the court's jurisdiction and wants the case dismissed would move to dismiss rather than rely on the court to do so *sua sponte*. You will learn more about this jurisdictional problem in Chapter 9.

Rule 12(b)(2) and (3) permit motions to dismiss for lack of personal jurisdiction and for improper venue. In a Rule 12(b)(2) motion, the defendant argues that a court in the state where the plaintiff filed the action lacks power to adjudicate this claim against this defendant. On a Rule 12(b)(3) motion, the defendant argues that the federal district in which the plaintiff filed the action is an improper venue for the action. Unlike subject matter jurisdiction, these objections to the "wrong place" are waived if not asserted. Thus, if a defendant objects to the court's personal jurisdiction or venue, the defendant must raise the objection either by motion under Rule 12(b) or in the answer, whichever it chooses to file first. Personal jurisdiction and venue are explored in Chapters 10 and 11, respectively.

A defendant may also object to service of the summons and complaint upon the defendant. Specifically, under Rule 12(b)(4) and (5), a defendant may move to dismiss for "insufficient process" or "insufficient service of process." These may sound identical, but they are distinct. Insufficient process means that something was wrong with the summons itself, such as omitting the clerk's signature or misnaming the defendant. Insufficient service of process means that something was wrong with the way in which the summons and complaint were delivered to the defendant. If service of process was accomplished improperly—either because of a problem with the means of service or because the defendant was served beyond the territorial reach of the court's power—then the court lacks personal jurisdiction over the defendant. This is why motions to dismiss under Rule 12(b)(5) often accompany motions to dismiss for lack of personal jurisdiction under Rule 12(b)(2). We will explore service of process in more depth as part of our study of personal jurisdiction in Chapter 10. Like motions under 12(b)(2) and (3), if a defendant fails to object to insufficient process or insufficient service of process in its first response to the complaint, the defendant waives these objections. *See* Fed. R. Civ. P. 12(g), (h).

Dismissal for Failure to State a Claim (Rule 12(b)(6)). The defendant may move to dismiss for failure to state a claim upon which relief can be granted. This important motion, discussed in detail earlier in Part A of this chapter, tests the legal sufficiency of the complaint and is used frequently in litigation. At common law it was known as *demurrer*, and some states retain this name for the device. This motion, which is made under Rule 12(b)(6) under the federal rules, argues that even if the plaintiff's allegations are accepted as true, they do not give the plaintiff a right to relief. The defense of failure to state a claim upon which relief can be granted is typically raised in a 12(b)(6) motion, but it may also be raised in an answer, in a motion for judgment on the pleadings under Rule 12(c), or at trial. Fed. R. Civ. P. 12(h)(2).

Dismissal for Failure to Join a Party (Rule 12(b)(7)). If a party fails to include a party that the defendant believes is essential to the fair resolution of the litigation, then the defendant may move to dismiss for failure to join an indispensable party. In federal court, Rule 12(b)(7) authorizes the motion, and the court's analysis would follow the mandates of Rule 19, which addresses compulsory joinder. You will study compulsory party joinder in Chapter 7, but it is important to mention it here, as a Rule 12(b)(7) motion is the most common way by which parties raise that issue.

The Relationship Between Pre-Answer Dismissal Motions and Pleadings. To understand Rule 12(b) as it relates to pleadings, think about why these particular defenses might be pursued in a pre-answer motion (which is *not* a pleading), while denials and other defenses must go in the answer. Start with Rule 12(b)(1)-(5): If the court lacks power over the parties or the claims, or if the court is the wrong forum to adjudicate the case, then it makes no sense for the parties to continue with the litigation process in that forum. As a matter of efficiency and as a matter of legitimacy, the sooner the court dismisses the action, the better. Then, if a party wishes to proceed with that now-dismissed action, that party can file the action in a proper forum.

Now, consider Rule 12(b)(6): If the substance of the allegations in the complaint are insufficient to state a claim upon which relief can be granted, then going forward would be futile, and it would waste the resources of the court and the parties. If the complaint was insufficient because of a defect in *how* it was pleaded—as opposed to the substance of the claim—then the court should dismiss the complaint without prejudice. That way, the plaintiff has the opportunity to repair the pleading defect. Either way, it makes sense to address the problem before going forward with the litigation. That includes before going forward with the filing of an answer.

Finally, consider Rule 12(b)(7), using similar thinking: It makes sense to raise compulsory joinder issues at the outset of litigation. If a party is required and joinder is possible, then that party should join the litigation. If the party cannot be joined, and if the court decides that in that party's absence, dismissal is warranted, then requiring the defendant to submit a responsive pleading before the action is dismissed is—again—a waste of the time and resources of the defendant and the court.

Terminology Tip

When a court grants a motion to dismiss, the court often indicates whether that dismissal is *with prejudice* or *without prejudice*. A dismissal with prejudice precludes the plaintiff from bringing the same claim again. A dismissal without prejudice, on the other hand, has no claim preclusive effect. Thus, the plaintiff can try again by filing a new complaint. Sometimes a court refers to this type of dismissal without prejudice as *dismissal with leave to amend* or *with leave to replead*.

(b) Other Motions on the Pleadings

A party may move under other portions of Rule 12 for additional actions on the pleadings. If a complaint is particularly unclear, Rule 12(e) provides a mechanism for seeking clarification and refinement. If the complaint contains matters that the opposing party believes are included only to embarrass, harass, or for another improper purpose, that party may move under 12(f) to strike the inappropriate content. Finally, once the pleading stage is complete, either party may move for a judgment in its favor on the basis of the pleadings under Rule 12(c).

Motion for a More Definite Statement (12(e)). If a complaint is unintelligible or missing critical information, a defendant in federal court can seek refinement, clarification, or explanation by moving for a more definite statement under Rule 12(e). In some state courts, the objective is achieved with a procedural device known as a bill of particulars. The motion for more definite statement can be useful if a complaint omits basic information that would help the defendant formulate a response. For instance, in an action with multiple defendants and multiple claims, if the complaint fails to identify which defendants are charged with which claims, a Rule 12(e) motion could force the plaintiff to connect the dots.

On the whole, however, a Rule 12(e) motion is not terribly useful, functionally or strategically. As to the former, the motion is a narrow one: The point of the motion for a more definite statement is to remedy situations in which a pleading is, as Rule 12(e) puts it, "so vague or ambiguous that a party cannot reasonably be required to frame a responsive pleading." The way for a party to get more information about the claims and defenses, in general, is through the discovery process, not by asking for more information in the pleadings. As to the latter, imagine that you represent a client who has been served with a poorly drafted complaint. You know that because of the notice pleading standard, the court probably will not grant a Rule 12(e) motion as long as the complaint is comprehensible. Moreover, you know that if the court *does* grant the motion, the plaintiff almost assuredly gets a shot at re-drafting the complaint without any analysis of whether the complaint stated a legally sufficient claim. Thus, are you not better off moving to dismiss the complaint for failure to state a claim under Rule 12(b)(6), even if—perhaps especially if—the complaint is so lacking that you cannot understand it? If you win on the 12(b)(6), the court dismisses the complaint. Even if the dismissal is without prejudice, you have still gotten the complaint thrown out—a better result for your client than an order from the court that the plaintiff simply re-draft the complaint.

Motion to Strike (12(f)). A party can move to strike portions of the complaint or other pleading. In federal court, Rule 12(f) authorizes such motions before a required responsive pleading, or if a responsive pleading is not permitted, 21 days after being served with the pleading. Parties use this device to ask the court to strike "redundant, immaterial, impertinent, or scandalous matter" from their adversary's pleading. Fed. R. Civ. P. 12(f). In other cases, however, it is used by defendants a bit like a mini-Rule 12(b)(6) motion, wherein the defendant contends that certain aspects of the complaint—a demand for punitive damages, for instance—fail to state a legally sufficient claim and therefore ought to be thrown out. This strategy might be attractive when the complaint, as a whole, would likely survive a 12(b)(6) motion, but when the defendant believes it can home in on certain aspects of the complaint and get them thrown out. Note that this device is not just for defendants: Plaintiffs may use it to strike insufficient defenses.

Motion for Judgment on the Pleadings (12(c)). After the pleadings are completed, a party may move for judgment on the pleadings under Rule 12(c). This motion asks the court to decide the case as a matter of law, based solely on what is contained in the pleadings. If made by a defendant, a motion for judgment on the pleadings strongly resembles a Rule 12(b)(6) motion to dismiss for failure to state a claim, except that as a matter of timing, the Rule 12(c) motion comes later, and the court may consider both the complaint and the answer. If made by a plaintiff, a motion for judgment on the pleadings points to the admissions made in the answer and asserts that, as a matter of law, the plaintiff must prevail based on facts established by all of the pleadings.

STRATEGY SESSION

If a defendant has defenses to assert, should the defendant wait until the answer or proceed with a pre-answer motion to dismiss? It is important to take the time to decide if a motion to dismiss is really in your client's best interest. Filing a motion to dismiss for failure to state a claim has the potential benefit of ending the case early on. But if the grounds for dismissal are weak, filing may have adverse consequences. It could result in needless costs, not only for your client but for the plaintiff, which may impede the possibility of an early settlement. An adverse judicial opinion may also embolden the plaintiff or contain unfavorable pronouncements on the applicable law. Other grounds for dismissal may likewise result in Pyrrhic victories. For example, a successful challenge to venue may only result in the plaintiff's bringing the same suit in a less convenient or more plaintiff-friendly venue. The decision whether to file a motion to dismiss should be pursued deliberately, with a clear view of the client's objectives and the motion's likelihood of success.

(4) Waiver of Defenses

One of the most important issues attorneys must pay attention to in litigation is waiver. Certain defenses, such as lack of personal jurisdiction, must be asserted at the first opportunity or they are waived. If a defendant files an answer without filing a pre-answer motion, the defendant must include such defenses in the first responsive pleading—the answer—to avoid waiving them. If the defendant files a pre-answer motion such as a motion to dismiss, the motion must include these defenses to avoid waiver. While we have already noted which defenses under 12(b) are waivable, the mechanics of waiver warrant further attention, particularly given the detailed interaction between Rules 12(b), 12(g), and 12(h).

As a preliminary matter, how many pre-answer defenses may a defendant make? How many must a defendant make? Rule 12(g) not only provides the *permission* to include all Rule 12 defenses in the same motion; it also, along with Rule 12(h), *requires* that these defenses be combined, with certain exceptions. Rule 12(h)(1) makes clear that defenses of personal jurisdiction, venue, process, and service of process—the defenses contained in Rule 12(b)(2)-(5)—are waived if omitted from the answer or pre-answer motion, whichever comes first. Needless to say, you do not want to waive defenses that might be available to your client—at least not unintentionally!

Rule 12(h)(2) addresses the defenses of failure to state a claim upon which relief can be granted (Rule 12(b)(6)) and failure to join an indispensable party (Rule 12(b)(7)). These defenses, if not raised in the pleadings or pre-answer motion, may nonetheless be raised in a motion for judgment on the pleadings (12(c)) or may be raised at trial. Why are these two defenses given different treatment? Consider the Rule 12(b)(6) defense—failure to state a claim. If a defendant has a valid defense of failure to state a claim upon which relief can be granted, it would be a tad nonsensical to say that this particular defense can be waived. By definition, that defense means that the plaintiff does not have a cognizable legal claim. Waiver of the defense of failure to state a claim would require the court to ignore the substantive merits of a lawsuit. Next, consider the Rule 12(b)(7) defense—failure to join a required party. The idea of compulsory party joinder is that there are some parties whose absence from the lawsuit would make it unjust for the court to proceed. Sometimes this does not become clear until the litigation is underway. Rule 12(h)(2) therefore ensures that such party concerns can be raised later.

Finally, Rule 12(h)(3) addresses the defense of subject matter jurisdiction. It states simply: "If the court determines at any time that it lacks subject-matter jurisdiction, the court must dismiss the action." Rule 12(h)(3) simply gives procedural form to the fundamental principle that the *court's* power over an action cannot be waived by *parties*. For federal courts, the limits on subject matter jurisdiction protect the constitutional values of separation of powers—making sure that the courts do not encroach on the power of the legislative and executive branches of government—and values of federalism—making sure that the federal government does not encroach upon the powers of the states. In other words, subject matter jurisdiction is not up to the parties. Rule 12 gives parties the ability to raise the defense of subject matter jurisdiction by motion, but subject matter jurisdiction is bigger than the parties. The court *must* dismiss the case if it realizes that it lacks subject matter jurisdiction.

Working through the mechanics of Rule 12 can be tricky, and the only way to fully wrap your head around the functioning of the rule is to practice. Here are some problems to get you started:

1. Assume that after being served with a complaint, the defendant files a motion to dismiss under Rule 12(b)(4) for insufficient process. The court denies the motion. The defendant wishes to raise additional defenses by motion. Under Rule 12(g) and 12(h), may she? Does it depend upon which additional defenses she wishes to raise?
2. Y files a complaint for negligence against Z. Z files a timely motion to dismiss for lack of personal jurisdiction. The judge denies the motion four months

later. May Z now move for insufficient service of process? May Z answer the complaint and include the defense of insufficient service of process? File a motion to dismiss under Rule 12(b)(6)? File an answer that includes the defense of lack of subject matter jurisdiction?

(5) Claims by Defendants

In addition to the various responses defendants can make to a complaint—admissions and denials, affirmative defenses, motions to dismiss, motions to strike, or motions for a more definite statement—there are three types of *claims* defendants can assert when they have been sued: counterclaims, crossclaims, and third-party claims. You will explore these in more detail in Chapter 7, but they bear brief mention here to flesh out your understanding of the various options available to defendants at the pleading stage, and to distinguish these sorts of claims from defenses.

A *counterclaim* is a claim that a party asserts *against* a party that has brought a claim against it. In the simple plaintiff-defendant set-up, this is a claim a defendant asserts against the plaintiff. Federal Rules 13(a) and (b) provide for both compulsory (required) and permissive counterclaims. Be careful not to confuse counterclaims with defenses. A counterclaim is not an assertion that the defendant is not liable to the plaintiff; that would be a defense. Rather, a counterclaim is an assertion that the plaintiff is liable to the defendant; it is a separate claim for relief. Other than the fact that a counterclaim is being asserted by the defendant, a counterclaim is just like a claim asserted in the original complaint. That means that counterclaims must comply with the pleading requirements of Rule 8(a) and the interpretation of Rule 8(a) in *Swierkiewicz, Twombly*, and *Iqbal*. As a matter of strategy, though, counterclaims often relate to defenses in the following way: They emphasize and reinforce the defendant's denials and defenses. For example, in an automobile accident case in which each party accuses the other of running a red light at an intersection, the defendant could *deny* that she acted negligently (e.g., she did not run the red light), assert the *affirmative defense* of contributory or comparative negligence (e.g., the plaintiff ran the red light), and assert a *counterclaim* against the plaintiff for the defendant's own injuries and property damage. As a strategic matter, the denial, affirmative defense, and counterclaim—all of which would be included in the defendant's answer—reemphasize and reinforce the core message of defendant's responsive pleading: "The accident was plaintiff's fault, not mine."

A *crossclaim* is a claim asserted against a co-party. Imagine that the plaintiff sues multiple defendants. In that situation, one defendant may assert a crossclaim against a co-defendant that relates to the claims the plaintiff brought against the defendants. Specifically, Rule 13(g) states that crossclaims are only permitted if they arise out of the same "transaction or occurrence" as the original claim.

A *third-party claim*, also known as *impleader*, is a device by which a defendant can bring in an additional party (a third-party defendant, hence the name of the type of claim) and assert that if the defendant is liable to the plaintiff, then the third-party defendant should be liable to reimburse the defendant for some or all of what the defendant must pay the plaintiff. Rule 14 makes clear that third-party claims may be used only for claims such as contribution or indemnification, in which one party must pay another party who was held liable. In a product liability case, for instance, if the plaintiff originally sues only the retailer, the retailer may assert a third-party claim for indemnification against the manufacturer for the allegedly defective product.

You will learn about these mechanisms for joining additional claims and parties in litigation in Chapter 7. Here, you need to understand them as part of a defendant's overall set of reactions to a plaintiff's complaint, and you need to understand that they are subject to the same scrutiny vis-à-vis Rule 8 that the plaintiff's claims were subject to in *Swierkiewicz*, *Twombly*, and *Iqbal*.

C. AMENDMENT

Can a party change the contents of its pleading? Suppose the plaintiff's lawyer, through legal research and factual investigation, learns of an additional claim that she did not include in the original complaint. Or suppose the defendant's lawyer identifies a defense that was not included in the original answer. Or perhaps the discovery process has turned up factual information that alters or supplements the parties' allegations or denials. Amendment of pleadings—to add or delete a claim, to add or delete a defense, or to correct or supplement factual allegations or denials—is a routine part of the litigation process. It is not uncommon in lengthy cases to see pleadings with names like "Fifth Amended Complaint" or "Third Amended Answer and Counterclaim."

Rule 15 of the Federal Rules of Civil Procedure makes it easy to amend pleadings. The rule's liberal approach to amendment follows the same logic as the notice pleading standard of Rule 8. Parties are not expected to know everything at the outset of litigation. Notice pleading was a reaction against common law pleading's tendency to make outcomes depend on technicalities of pleading rather than the merits. The same reasoning leads to a liberal attitude toward amendment. The goal is to allow parties to get their claims and defenses right, even if the parties do not have complete information at the start. Even with the advent of plausibility pleading under *Twombly* and *Iqbal*, amendment remains a generally easy thing to do.

(1) Amending the Pleadings

Rule 15(a) offers three avenues by which amendment is permitted: amendment as a matter of course, amendment by consent, and amendment by leave of court. Look closely at the language of Rule 15(a), which spells out the circumstances when a party may amend as a matter of course and when a party needs leave of court or the adversary's consent.

Amendment as a Matter of Course. The easiest kind of amendment is when the rule allows a party to amend its pleading without asking the court's permission or the other party's consent. Rule 15(a) allows a party to amend its pleading once "as a matter of course" either 21 days after serving it or 21 days after the opposing party's response. This means, first, that a party is free to amend a complaint or answer within 21 days of serving it. The idea is to allow parties to correct their own mistakes and omissions promptly. It also means that, alternatively, a party can amend its complaint or counterclaim within 21 days of receiving the opposing party's answer or a responsive Rule 12 motion. This provides an opportunity to tweak the complaint when the party becomes aware of the adversary's response. Under these circumstances, a party simply files the amended pleading—no permission needed.

Amendment as a matter of course may be used not only for complaints and other pleadings with claims, but also for answers. Since ordinarily answers do not elicit further responsive pleadings, the time limit for amending an answer cannot be measured by whether a responsive pleading has been served. Therefore, as applied to answers, Rule 15(a) simply provides that a party may amend once as a matter of course within 21 days after serving the answer.

Amendment by Consent. Any pleading may be amended if the adverse party consents to the amendment in writing. It is an adversary system, after all, and if the opposing party states that it does not object to the amendment, there is no good reason for the court to reject the amended pleading.

STRATEGY SESSION

As a new law student, you might be skeptical about amendment by consent; perhaps you imagine that "zealous advocacy" means that it would be difficult to obtain an adversary's consent to anything. Actually, the norm is that lawyers often grant each other's requests for amendment and plenty of other courtesies in litigation. One reason is that lawyers understand that "what goes around comes around." Today your adversary is requesting your consent to amend a pleading; tomorrow you may be requesting your adversary's consent for an extension of time or some other courtesy. But the other reason lawyers consent to each other's reasonable requests is that lawyers know that if they withhold consent, the adversary will simply ask the judge, and the judge not only will grant the request but also will be annoyed at the lawyer who refused to accommodate the reasonable request. So a refusal may accomplish nothing other than to make the judge perceive one side as unreasonable, which is not a smart way to get a good result for one's client.

Amendment by Leave of Court. If it is too late to amend as a matter of course, and if the opposing party does not consent, a party must ask the court's permission to amend a pleading. In legal terms, the party must move for leave to amend the pleading. In the following case, be sure you understand why the plaintiff needed leave of court to amend its complaint, why the court permitted the amendment, and what sort of circumstances might lead a court to reject an amended pleading.

BLT RESTAURANT GROUP v. TOURONDEL
855 F. Supp. 2d 4 (S.D.N.Y. 2012)

DOLLINGER, Magistrate Judge.

Plaintiff BLT Restaurant Group ("BLT") commenced this lawsuit to assert a variety of claims—one federal and the others based on state law—in the wake of the departure of defendant Laurent Tourondel from his contractual relationship with plaintiff. Until Tourondel's withdrawal, he played a central role in designing the food and related practices of a number of restaurants opened under the name BLT. He now operates and is opening another series of restaurants in conjunction with other investors.

Currently before the court are three motions, two by defendants. [Defendants move to dismiss a portion of the complaint for lack of subject matter jurisdiction over the state law claims, and they move for summary judgment on some claims.] Plaintiff has moved for leave to serve a second amended complaint, which would add claims, reorganize some of the current claims, and insert some further factual allegations. For the reasons that follow, we deny defendants' motion to dismiss, grant plaintiff's motion to amend, and deny all but a sliver of defendants' motion for partial summary judgment.

PROCEDURAL BACKGROUND

Plaintiff filed suit in mid-2010. As embodied in its current pleading—the Amended Complaint—BLT asserted eight claims against Tourondel [and several related claims against LT Burger, Inc. and Michael Cinque]. In substance, plaintiff alleged that it had entered into a contractual arrangement with Tourondel, an accomplished French chef, under which Tourondel was to work with plaintiff in developing a series of restaurants using the trade name BLT (for Bistro Laurent Tourondel). According to BLT, after these restaurants had attained substantial critical and financial success, Tourondel left (as was his contractual right) to set up his own restaurants with other financiers under the trade name LT, and he has in fact opened one such establishment in Sag Harbor, and intends to open others. Plaintiff complained, however, that in doing so Tourondel had violated his contractual obligations in a variety of respects and has engaged in unfair competition by the use of "proprietary" or "confidential" information belonging to plaintiff. This alleged wrongful conduct is said to include the copying of recipes originally used in dishes featured in the BLT restaurants, the use of names for dishes that imitated the fanciful names utilized in the BLT menus, the choice of combinations of featured dishes that mimic those offered by plaintiff's eateries and a mimicking of plaintiff's pricing.

Based on these allegations, plaintiff asserted [eight claims: a claim for breach of contract, a claim for unfair competition under the federal Lanham Act, a claim for deceptive practices under New York's General Business Law, a claim seeking a declaratory judgment, a claim seeking reformation of the contract, a claim for unjust enrichment, a claim for breach of fiduciary duty, and a demand for attorneys' fees and costs].

Following the filing of plaintiff's amended complaint and a responsive pleading by defendants, defendants moved for judgment on the pleadings under Federal Rule of Civil Procedure 12(c). By memorandum and order filed July 19, 2011, the District Court granted the motion with respect to the General Business Law, contract-reformation and unjust-enrichment claims and otherwise denied defendants' application.

The parties have pursued written discovery, including principally the exchange of documents. While still engaged in that process, however, they filed the three motions now before us. We address these motions *seriatim.*

ANALYSIS
I. SUPPLEMENTAL JURISDICTION

[The court rejected defendant's argument that the court lacked subject matter jurisdiction over some of the plaintiff's state law claims.]

II. PLAINTIFF'S MOTION TO AMEND

Plaintiff has moved for leave to amend its most recent amended complaint in the form of a proposed Second Amended Complaint. The motion postdated Judge Daniels's dismissal of a portion of the current pleading, and the requested amendments would add factual averments and incorporate new claims under the rubric of the first, second, third and seventh causes of action. It would also substitute Think Burger, LLC as a defendant in place of LT Burger, Inc., which Think Burger owns. Defendants consent to the substitution, but oppose the balance of the motion. Before considering the merits of plaintiff's motion, we briefly reiterate the oft-cited standards for assessing Rule 15 applications.

A. RULE 15(A) STANDARDS

Where, as here, a plaintiff may no longer amend the complaint as a matter of right, Rule 15(a) of the Federal Rules of Civil Procedure specifies that courts should "freely give" leave to amend "when justice so requires." As explained by the Supreme Court, such leave is to be liberally granted:

> If the underlying facts or circumstances relied upon by a plaintiff may be a proper subject of relief, he ought to be afforded an opportunity to test his claim on the merits. In the absence of any apparent or declared reason—such as undue delay, bad faith or dilatory motive on the part of the movant, repeated failure to cure deficiencies by amendments previously allowed, undue prejudice to the opposing party by virtue of allowance of the amendment, futility of amendment, etc.—the leave sought should, as the rules require, "be freely given."

Foman v. Davis, 371 U.S. 178, 182 (1962).

As *Foman* suggests, one circumstance that justifies denial of a motion for leave to amend is a determination that the proposed amendment would be futile. Futility may be shown by demonstrating that the proposed new pleading fails to state a cognizable claim and thus would be subject to dismissal under Rule 12(b)(6).

As an alternative ground, a court may deny a requested amendment if it would unduly prejudice the other side or seriously interfere with the court's efforts to ensure the efficient and reasonably prompt conclusion of pretrial proceedings. Delay alone is generally not a sufficient basis for denying relief, but if that delay is particularly egregious or prejudicial, or the complications that it would impose on pretrial scheduling are sufficiently compelling, the court may decline the request for an amendment.

Citing two grounds, defendants oppose the proposed amended version of the four contract-breach claims as futile. First, they assert that the claims are barred for lack of subject-matter jurisdiction. Second, they argue that a number of the newly configured allegations fail to state any cognizable claim. Moreover, in a preliminary section of their memorandum of law they seem to suggest that discovery has turned up evidence that undercuts some, if not all, of the claims. Alternatively, defendants assert in fairly skeletal terms that granting the motion would cause them undue prejudice.

B. FUTILITY

Defendants first argue that the proposed amendments to add claims or portions of claims would be futile because of the previously discussed asserted lack of subject-matter jurisdiction. Since we have already rejected that argument in the context of defendants' motion to dismiss, and because they have not suggested that the proposed new claims differ from the challenged preexisting ones on any basis pertinent to the jurisdictional question, we reject defendants' argument for reasons already discussed.

Alternatively, defendants argue that some of the proposed new claims are futile because they fail to state a cognizable claim. This argument requires an examination of the proposed amendments through the prism that would apply to a Rule 12(b)(6) motion.

1. Rule 12(b)(6) Criteria

The traditional test on a Rule 12(b)(6) motion allowed the complaint to survive unless "it appears beyond doubt that the plaintiff can prove no set of facts in support of his claim which would entitle him to relief." *Conley v. Gibson*, 355 U.S. 41, 45-46 (1957). The Supreme Court has since rejected this formulation, however, and hence, "[t]o survive a motion to dismiss, a complaint must contain sufficient factual matter, accepted as true, to state a claim to relief that is plausible on its face." *Bell Atl. Corp. v. Twombly*, 550 U.S. 544, 570 (2007). Under this "plausibility standard," our analysis requires two steps. "First, although a court must accept as true all of the allegations contained in a complaint, that tenet is inapplicable to legal conclusions[,] and threadbare recitals of the elements of a cause of action, supported by mere conclusory statements, do not suffice." *Ashcroft v. Iqbal*, 556 U.S. 662, 677. "Second, only a complaint that states a plausible claim for relief survives a motion to dismiss." *Id.* at 1950. . . .

2. The Proposed Second Amended Complaint

In plaintiff's proposed Second Amended Complaint we find some alterations from its predecessor in the order of the narrative and in rhetoric used to describe defendants' alleged misdeeds. As for the factual allegations, apart from asserting in substance, as before, that Tourondel misappropriated proprietary and/or confidential information in the form of recipes, as well as combinations, names, and descriptions of dishes and pricing in the menus, and the use of a marketing magazine, plaintiff alludes to the copying of "preparation techniques" and "presentation style," and adds allegations to the effect that Tourondel improperly lured away from plaintiff "his personal assistant." Plaintiff also asserts that he refused to return, and then destroyed, "confidential and proprietary information" when he held on to a plaintiff-supplied laptop and then returned it only after erasing its hard drive.

As for the claims asserted in this newest version of the complaint, plaintiff pleads a somewhat updated version of its contract-breach theory, now encompassed in four separate claims, all asserted only against Tourondel. For the first claim, apart from the general mention of asserted breaches of the contractual bar on misappropriation of confidential and proprietary information, plaintiff refers to the opening of a steak restaurant by defendants in the Manrey Hotel in Panama, and it alleges that Tourondel copied dishes and forms of presentation as well as decor from the BLT steak restaurants.

Plaintiff's second contract claim focuses on a burger restaurant opened by defendants in Sag Harbor. It alleges that, at this location, Tourondel copied BLT's combination of offered dishes, the names of the dishes, and the ingredients of the dishes. As part of the same claim, plaintiff alleges similar misconduct in Tourondel's opening of a burger restaurant in the Manrey Hotel in Panama.

[The court described each of the remaining claims in the proposed Second Amended Complaint.]

3. Assessment of the Proposed Amendments

Defendants' Rule 12(b)(6) arguments do not justify dismissal. We address each set of targeted claims in turn.

Defendants first focus on the contract-breach claims that are premised on defendants' alleged use of plaintiff's proprietary and confidential information, an argument that implicates at least the first, second, and fourth claims. Defendants argue that the contractual provisions governing such information preclude plaintiff from succeeding on its claims that Tourondel breached their terms. . . .

At least with respect to the first and second claims—invoking the Panamanian and Sag Harbor restaurants—these arguments fail for several reasons. [First, contrary to the defendants' arguments, the contract does not clearly permit Tourondel to use proprietary materials. Second, defendants fail to explain why plaintiff may not assert Tourondel's misappropriation of proprietary material as a breach-of-contract claim.] Third, we cannot determine from the face of the complaint that Tourondel did not appropriate "confidential information," as defined in the contract, when he created his menus and otherwise designed his restaurants. If he did, then we cannot say as a matter of law that he did not breach the pertinent contractual provisions. This too precludes dismissal on the face of the pleading.

[The court proceeded to explain, as to plaintiff's other claims, its reasons for rejecting defendants' arguments that the claims would be subject to dismissal under Rule 12(b)(6), and thus its reasons for rejecting defendants' argument that it would be futile to permit amendment of the complaint.]

Finally, insofar as defendants may be arguing that pre-trial discovery has disproved some or all of plaintiff's claims, new or old, that is a matter that should be addressed in the context of a summary-judgment motion, not in opposition to a motion to amend. In any event, we note that defendants' factual arguments are not accompanied by the proffer of any concrete evidence, and plainly their opposition here does not demonstrate an absence of material and triable issues. . . .

C. UNDUE PREJUDICE AND DELAY

As for defendants' assertion of prejudice, we find it entirely unpersuasive. They first allude to the delay in completing discovery, but that delay is attributable in part to defendants' request—granted by the court—to pursue partial summary judgment in the midst of discovery and to stay deposition discovery during the pendency of their motion.[10] They then emphasize that one new set of allegations concerns the establishment of a restaurant in Panama, and they argue that allowing this claim to

proceed will engender burdensome and costly overseas discovery. There is nothing in the record, however, to indicate that the discovery triggered by this set of allegations will be prolonged or expensive, and the court retains adequate means of ensuring that proceedings not be unduly extended.

In sum, we grant plaintiff's motion to serve and file its second amended complaint.

III. DEFENDANTS' SUMMARY JUDGMENT MOTION

[The court largely rejected defendants' motion for summary judgment.]

CONCLUSION

For the reasons stated, we deny defendants' motion to dismiss, grant plaintiff's motion to amend, and deny defendants' motion for partial summary judgment except insofar as we have deemed a portion of the disputed contract to be unambiguous. Plaintiff's Second Amended Complaint is deemed served on defendants. They are to serve their responses to it within twenty-one days.

---

[10] We granted these requests on the representation that clarifying the meaning of the contract, insofar as it may limit what businesses Tourondel can now pursue, would be cost-efficient and conducive to possible resolution of the case. Those concerns were persuasive, but that does not mean that granting these requests should then preclude plaintiff from fine-tuning its pleading in the interim.

Notes & Questions

1. In *BLT*, the plaintiff sought leave of court to serve its Second Amended Complaint. Why did BLT need the court's permission? That is, why couldn't it make these amendments as a matter of course? Amendment as a matter of course is one of the least complicated things you will learn about civil procedure. Just be sure you get it right because it will prove useful in the common situation where you wish to make a prompt alteration to your client's pleadings.

   Test your understanding of amendments as a matter of course under Rule 15(a). In which of the following situations would you be able to amend as a matter of course (that is, without moving for leave to amend or obtaining the adversary's consent)?

a. You file a complaint. Twenty days later, the defendant files and serves a motion to dismiss for failure to state a claim. Twenty days after that, you seek to amend your complaint to add more factual allegations.

b. You file a complaint. Ten days later, you amend the complaint as a matter of course to assert an additional claim. Ten days after that, you seek to amend the complaint to correct an erroneous factual allegation.

c. You file an answer. Thirty days later, you seek to amend your answer to alter your admissions and denials and to add an affirmative defense.

2. Note that BLT did not need leave of court to amend its complaint to substitute Think Burger, LLC, as a defendant in place of LT Burger, Inc. Why not?

3. As to the remaining changes in its Second Amended Complaint, BLT needed to obtain leave of court. Note how the court framed the analysis in terms of Rule 15(a)'s instruction that the court "should freely give leave when justice so requires." It is interesting phrasing for a rule of civil procedure, isn't it? The rule does not simply state a standard—"when justice so requires"—for deciding whether to grant a motion for leave to amend. Rather, it actively encourages judges to grant such motions by adding the words "freely give." The rule tells the judge, in essence: Go ahead, let the parties amend their pleadings if amendment will help them get their pleadings right. The *BLT* court invoked the oft-quoted language of *Foman v. Davis*, 371 U.S. 178 (1962), emphasizing the liberality of the amendment rule. In *Foman*, the Supreme Court held that unless there is a good reason for the denial, it is reversible error for a district judge to deny leave to amend.

4. Despite the liberal standard under Rule 15(a), courts deny leave to amend if the amendment would be futile. The idea is that if the claims or defenses sought to be amended would be dismissed or struck anyway, then it is pointless to allow the amendment. In *BLT*, the defendants unsuccessfully argued futility as a basis for rejecting the plaintiff's proposed amendments. What standard did the court apply to analyze whether the proposed amendments were futile? Why was this a sensible standard to apply?

5. When a court considers arguments of futility on a motion for leave to amend a pleading, which party should have the burden of establishing its position? Did the *BLT* court treat it as the defendant's burden to demonstrate futility, or the plaintiff's burden to demonstrate non-futility by showing that the claims were viable?

6. Another basis for rejecting amendments is undue delay in seeking the amendment, or undue prejudice to the opposing party if the amendment were permitted. In *CMR D.N. Corp. v. City of Philadelphia*, 703 F.3d 612, 629-31 (3d Cir. 2013), for example, the court upheld a district court's denial of leave to amend where the plaintiff sought to add a new theory of liability to its complaint more than three years after the litigation began, and the plaintiff offered no good reason for the delay. Why did the defendants' argument of undue delay and undue prejudice fail in *BLT*?

(2) Statutes of Limitations and Relation Back

The most difficult issue concerning amended pleadings is not really about the pleadings at all, but rather about statutes of limitations.

Statutes of limitations set time limits for filing specific types of claims. For example, New York has a six-year statute of limitations for breach of contract claims, which means that if a plaintiff wishes to pursue a claim for breach of contract, the plaintiff must commence a lawsuit within six years of the date on which the claim accrued. If a plaintiff commences the suit too late, the court may dismiss the claim as untimely. Specifically, the defendant would assert the statute of limitations as an affirmative defense, and the court could grant the defendant's motion to dismiss on grounds of untimeliness.

Now, consider the connection between statutes of limitations and amendment of pleadings. Suppose a party wishes to amend its pleading to assert a new claim against a current party, or to add a claim by or against a new party, but the time for filing the claim has expired under the applicable statute of limitations. Maybe it was carelessness that led to the error or omission in the original pleading, or maybe the party learned of the error or omission only from information that came out during the discovery process. Either way, the pleader wishes to add the claim despite the apparent expiration of the limitations period. The pleader argues that it is simply a matter of amending an existing pleading. The opposing party argues that the limitations period has expired, and therefore the amendment should not be permitted.

This is where the doctrine of *relation back* comes into play. The party seeking to amend the pleading argues that the amended pleading "relates back" to the date of the original pleading, and therefore does not violate the statute of limitations. Usually, invocations of the relation back doctrine concern the amendment of a plaintiff's complaint, but the doctrine can apply to defenses as well as counterclaims and other claims for relief.

The timeline for relation back problems always looks like this:

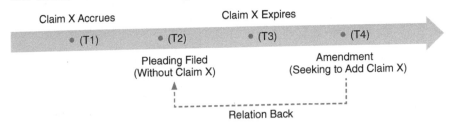

First, an occurrence gives rise to a claim ("Claim X"). That is the moment when Claim X accrues, which the timeline above calls T1. The time limit for filing Claim X runs from the date of accrual. If the applicable statute of limitations is two years, the party must file Claim X within two years from the accrual date. The timeline uses T2 for the date when the pleading is filed; the pleading does not include Claim X. After the lawsuit gets started, the limitations period for Claim X expires. This expiration date, T3, may occur quite soon after the lawsuit begins because plaintiffs sometimes file their cases shortly before time runs out, either as a matter of strategy and information-gathering or merely as a matter of procrastination and the power of deadlines. As the lawsuit proceeds, a party may realize that it should have asserted Claim X (or other, different claims, or named different parties, either in addition to or instead of those that were pleaded). The party, at time T4, seeks to amend its pleading to add a new claim or party. The question: If a claim would be time-barred under the statute of limitations, should a party nonetheless be allowed to amend its pleading to assert that claim, as long as the original pleading was filed within the limitations period?

Here is how the argument between the parties regarding a time-barred claim often goes. Suppose a plaintiff moves for leave to amend a complaint to add a new claim. The defendant argues that the court should reject the amendment on the grounds that the new claim is barred under the statute of limitations, which expired on T3. To be precise, the defendant argues futility: It would be futile for the plaintiff to amend the complaint because the new claim would simply be dismissed. (Recall that in *BLT*, the judge examined whether it would be futile to permit the amendments.) The plaintiff responds that the new claim is not untimely because even though the amended pleading is filed on T4, the amendment "relates back" to the complaint that the plaintiff filed on T2. For purposes of the statute of limitations, the plaintiff argues, the court should treat the amended pleading as if it were dated T2. The defendant, in turn, argues that the plaintiff's amendment should not be treated as if it were filed on T2 because the time-barred claim differs from those in the original pleading.

Rule 15(c) states the circumstances under which "[a]n amendment to a pleading relates back to the date of the original pleading." Relation back of a claim is permitted under Rule 15(c)(1)(B) if "the amendment asserts a claim or defense that arose out of the conduct, transaction, or occurrence set out—or attempted to be set out—in the original pleading." In the following case, a hospital moves to dismiss a claim on the grounds that the limitations period has expired, and the plaintiff argues that the claim relates back to the date of the original complaint. Keep track of the timeline (T1, T2, T3, and T4), and think about whether you agree with the judge's analysis of whether the medical injury claim against the hospital relates to the original complaint in a way that makes it reasonable to permit the claim despite the passage of time.

ORNELAS v. CITY OF MANCHESTER
2017 WL 2423512 (D.N.H. June 5, 2017)

McCafferty, District Judge.

Fernando Ornelas brings suit against the City of Manchester, the Manchester Police Department, Hillsborough County, Elliot Hospital, the Hillsborough County Department of Corrections, and several employees of those entities alleging claims arising out of serious injuries that he sustained while in their custody. Elliot Hospital moves to dismiss Ornelas's medical injury claim against it, arguing that the claim is barred by New Hampshire's three-year statute of limitations on personal actions. Ornelas objects. . . .

BACKGROUND
I. FACTUAL BACKGROUND

On October 15, 2013, Ornelas was admitted to Elliot Hospital's emergency room to be evaluated for possible head trauma following a car accident. Ornelas, who had a known mental health condition, was disoriented.... [Mental health professionals] diagnosed Ornelas with bipolar disorder, and, with his sister's consent, petitioned to have Ornelas involuntarily committed in a psychiatric hospital under state law. According to the petition completed by medical personnel, Ornelas was "displaying paranoia, hallucinations and mood swings, as a result of mental illness, sufficient to pose a likelihood of danger to himself or others."

While waiting for a bed to become available at the psychiatric hospital, Ornelas remained in the secured mental health section of Elliot Hospital's emergency room. While there, Ornelas had an altercation with ... a hospital security guard. During that altercation, Ornelas suffered severe head and facial injuries.... Officers from the [Manchester Police Department took] Ornelas to the police station and book[ed] him on charges for simple assault. Before being taken to the police station, however, the police officers requested that Elliot Hospital staff examine Ornelas to determine whether he was stable enough to be discharged....

Ornelas was discharged into the Manchester Police Department's custody at around 10:45 p.m. on October 16, 2013. After being booked, Ornelas was then placed in the custody of the Hillsborough County Department of Corrections and was taken to the Valley Street Jail. At the jail, Ornelas acted confused and could be heard by guards hitting the cell door with his forehead and running back and forth in his cell. After unsuccessfully attempting to get Ornelas to calm down, officers decided to forcibly extract Ornelas from his cell.

Three officers entered Ornelas's cell and eventually restrained him. During the extraction, Ornelas was slammed to the concrete floor and hit his head on the toilet. Other inmates heard Ornelas screaming and heard "sounds consistent with a person being struck." Following the extraction, Ornelas's cell contained visible pools of blood on the floor.

After being removed from his cell, Ornelas was placed in a restraint chair. A nurse later noticed that Ornelas was unresponsive and determined that he needed emergency medical care.... Emergency personnel arrived at the Valley Street Jail at 9:10 a.m. on October 17 and returned Ornelas to the Elliot Hospital emergency room. Once at the hospital, physicians determined that Ornelas had severely fractured his cervical vertebrae and was paralyzed.

II. PROCEDURAL BACKGROUND

Ornelas brought suit on September 11, 2014, alleging claims against several defendants, including claims for general negligence and negligent infliction of emotional distress against Elliot Hospital. Although Ornelas brought claims under RSA 507-E, New Hampshire's medical injury statute, against several defendants he did not bring such a claim against Elliot Hospital.

In support of his negligence claim, Ornelas alleged that Elliot Hospital had failed to, among other things, provide Ornelas proper psychological evaluations, "examine properly and diagnose" Ornelas, and "properly evaluate and recommend the appropriate discharge instructions and follow-up with the patient." Ornelas's original complaint did not contain any specific allegation of wrongdoing or negligence arising out of his second visit to Elliot Hospital. Rather, Ornelas alleged that he had already suffered the cervical fracture and was paralyzed when he returned to Elliot Hospital. Based on this theory, Ornelas alleged that he "suffered an injury sufficient to cause a fracture of his cervical spine" during either his first visit to Elliot Hospital, his booking at the Manchester Police Department, or his detention at Valley Street Jail.

On January 26, 2017, Ornelas moved for leave to amend his complaint. In that motion, Ornelas asserted that during discovery he had obtained additional information demonstrating that Ornelas was not paralyzed when he arrived at Elliot Hospital, the second time, but rather had become paralyzed there. Ornelas further asserted that based on that information, it was his position that he "suffered a cervical fracture which was unstable and which became progressively worse until the fracture caused complete paralysis." Because no defendants objected, the court granted Ornelas's motion for leave to amend.

Ornelas's amended complaint, which was filed on February 10, 2017, contained new factual allegations about his care at Elliot Hospital after he was returned to the emergency room. Specifically, the amended complaint provided that:

> Upon arrival at the Elliot Hospital, Mr. Ornelas did not have a neck brace on and none was placed until after he was paralyzed. . . . [H]e was not paralyzed upon his arrival at the hospital but did become paralyzed while at the hospital. Thereafter, it was confirmed that Mr. Ornelas had a severe cervical fracture that had gone undiagnosed and untreated by all persons responsible for his care.

In addition to that factual allegation, the amended complaint added a claim for medical injury under RSA 507-E against Elliot Hospital for providing negligent care during both of Ornelas's visits.

DISCUSSION

Elliot Hospital moves to dismiss Ornelas's medical injury claim, arguing that Ornelas brought that claim after New Hampshire's three-year statute of limitations expired. In response, Ornelas contends that his medical injury claim is based on recently-discovered evidence and thus is not barred by the statute of limitations. Ornelas further argues that the medical injury claim is permissible because it relates back to his original pleading.[4]

I. STATUTE OF LIMITATIONS

[The applicable New Hampshire statute of limitations] provides that "all personal actions, except actions for slander or libel, may be brought only within 3 years of the act or omission complained of." Here, there is no dispute that the acts causing Ornelas's injuries occurred at some point on or before October 17, 2013. Because Ornelas filed his amended complaint in February 2017, he did not bring his claim within the three years required under [the statute].

Ornelas contends, however, that his medical injury claim is not time-barred based on either the discovery rule exception to the statute of limitations or the relation-back doctrine. In response, Elliot Hospital contends that neither the discovery rule nor the relation back doctrine applies here.

II. DISCOVERY RULE

[Under the applicable statute of limitations,] the limitations period is tolled until the plaintiff discovers, or reasonably should have discovered, the injury and its causal connection to the negligent or wrongful act. . . .

In this case, Ornelas presumably knew that he had been treated in Elliot Hospital

---

[4] Ornelas also contends that Elliot Hospital waived any statute of limitations objections to his medical injury claim when it failed to object to his motion to amend his complaint. That theory, however, is incorrect.

after being found unresponsive at the Valley Street Jail. This fact likely alerted Ornelas to the possibility that Elliot Hospital's medical care was a cause of his injuries. Nevertheless, the court need not determine whether the discovery rule applies, an issue which could turn on factual inquiries, because it concludes that Ornelas's claim for medical injury against Elliot Hospital relates back to his original pleading.

III. RELATION BACK

Under the relation-back doctrine, a plaintiff may avoid the preclusive effect of a statute of limitations if his complaint relates back to a prior, timely-filed complaint. Under Federal Rule of Civil Procedure 15(c), an amended complaint adding an additional claim relates back to the original complaint if either "(A) the law that provides the applicable statute of limitations allows relation back" or "(B) the amendment asserts a claim or defense that arose out of the conduct, transaction, or occurrence set out—or attempted to be set out—in the original pleading." Fed. R. Civ. P. 15(c)(1)(A)-(B). The choice between these two provisions is "a one-way ratchet, meaning that a party is entitled to invoke the more permissive relation back rule." *Coons v. Indus. Knife Co.*, 620 F.3d 38, 42 (1st Cir. 2010).

Here, it is undisputed that Ornelas's original complaint was filed within the applicable statute of limitations. Ornelas contends that his medical injury claim relates back to that complaint under both New Hampshire and federal law.

A. FEDERAL RULE

Under the conduct, transaction, or occurrence test, "[s]o long as the original and amended petitions state claims that are tied to a common core of operative facts, relation back will be in order." *Frederick v. New Hampshire*, 2016 WL 4382692 (D.N.H. Aug. 16, 2016) (quoting *Mayle v. Felix*, 545 U.S. 644 (2005)). An amended complaint adding a new claim after the statute of limitations has expired will not relate back where the amendment "is so substantial that it cannot be said that [the] defendant was given adequate notice of the conduct, transaction, or occurrence that forms the basis of the claim or defense." *O'Loughlin v. Nat'l R. Passenger Corp.*, 928 F.2d 24, 26 (1st Cir. 1991).

Accordingly, courts deny amendments "to assert a claim which was not even suggested in the original complaint." *Id.* If, however, the original complaint "gives fair notice of the general fact situation out of which the claim or defense arises, an amendment which merely makes more specific what has already been alleged will relate back." *Id.* "This analysis is directed to conduct rather than causes of action and new legal theories may relate back to the original filing where . . . there is a shared basis in factual circumstances." *Iconics, Inc. v. Massaro*, 2016 WL 199407 (D. Mass. Jan. 15, 2016).

Ornelas asserts that the medical injury claim relates back because his original complaint provided notice that he was asserting such a claim against Elliot Hospital. In response, Elliot Hospital contends that Ornelas's medical injury claim does not arise from the same conduct, transaction, or occurrence because it is premised on different facts—Ornelas's return to its emergency room—than those asserted in the original complaint.

1. Medical Injury Claims Arising Out of First Visit

Although Ornelas's medical injury claim does rely on new allegations concerning his return to Elliot Hospital, it also expressly references the treatment he received during his first visit. In his original complaint, Ornelas plainly alleged that Elliot Hospital's treatment during his first visit constituted medical negligence. For example, Ornelas alleged that Elliot Hospital failed to properly examine and diagnose him, failed to provide appropriate psychological care, and failed to properly evaluate him before his discharge. Therefore, regardless of whether Ornelas asserted a formal claim under RSA 507-E, his original complaint in substance set out or attempted to set out a transaction or occurrence based on Elliot Hospital's alleged negligent care. . . .

Therefore, to the extent Ornelas's medical injury claim is based on Elliot Hospital's treatment during his first visit, it relates back to the original complaint.

2. Medical Injury Claims Arising Out of Second Visit

Ornelas's amended complaint also asserts a medical injury claim based on new allegations that Elliot Hospital failed to properly stabilize his neck upon his return to its emergency room. Ornelas contends that these new allegations relate back because they fall within the general fact pattern alleged in his original pleading. In response, Elliot Hospital argues that the allegations arise from a different occurrence because they rely on facts that differ in both time and type than those alleged in the original pleading.

In support, Elliot Hospital relies on *Mayle v. Felix*, 545 U.S. 644 (2005). In *Mayle*, the plaintiff filed a petition for a writ of habeas corpus, alleging a Sixth Amendment claim based on the government's introduction of out-of-court testimony during his criminal trial. After the relevant statute of limitations expired, the plaintiff amended his petition to allege a Fifth Amendment claim based on the government's introduction of statements that he made during a pretrial, police interrogation. On appeal, the Supreme Court held that the amended petition did not relate back to the original petition because the new Fifth Amendment claim arose from a different occurrence or transaction. In doing so, the court concluded that the plaintiff's new claim was not tied to a "common core of operative facts" because the essential predicate of that claim, the police interrogation, depended on facts that differed in type and time from those alleged in the original complaint. *Id.* at 659-61, 664.

Elliot Hospital contends that *Mayle* bars relation back here because Ornelas has alleged different conduct as the cause of his paralysis. The court disagrees. . . . *Mayle* itself does not hold that each distinct alleged act of wrongdoing underlying a claim is a separate transaction or occurrence for Rule 15 purposes.

That is evident from the *Mayle* court's conclusion that its decision does not conflict with *Tiller v. Atlantic Coast Line R. Co.*, 323 U.S. 574, 580-81 (1945). In *Tiller*, a railroad car struck and killed a railroad worker, whose wife sued on his behalf. She initially alleged several negligent acts and, after the statute of limitations had expired, amended her complaint to allege a different theory of negligence based on the railroad's failure to equip the locomotive with a rear light. The *Tiller* court held that the new claim related back to the original pleading, concluding that both claims "related to the same general conduct, transaction and occurrence which involved the death of the deceased." *Id.* at 581. The court further reasoned that "[t]here is no reason to apply a statute of limitations when, as here, the respondent has had notice from the beginning that petitioner was trying to enforce a claim against it because of the events leading up to the death of the deceased." *Id.*

The *Mayle* Court explained that although the amended pleading in *Tiller* "invoked a legal theory not suggested by the original complaint and relied on facts not originally asserted," it related back to the original pleading because there "was but one episode-in-suit, a worker's death attributed from the start to the railroad's failure to provide its employee with a reasonably safe place to work." *Mayle*, 545 U.S. at 660. The *Mayle* court further explained that unlike the plaintiff in its case, the plaintiff in *Tiller* "based her complaint on a single 'occurrence,' an accident resulting in her husband's death." *Id.*

Based on similar reasoning, courts have concluded that new factual allegations raised in an amended complaint will relate back when they are closely tied to the general factual situation alleged in the original complaint.

In this case, the occurrence at issue is the fracture of Ornelas's neck, the resulting paralysis, and the events that led to those conditions. In his original complaint, Ornelas alleged that Elliot Hospital's negligence, including its negligent provision of medical care, was in part responsible for his injuries. Just as in *Tiller*, Ornelas now alleges other conduct as an alternative cause of his injuries.

Those allegations relate back to the original complaint because they are tied to the common core of operative facts alleged therein. The new allegations concern the same injuries and involve the same type of conduct by Elliot Hospital—the negligent provision of medical care—that was alleged in the original complaint. Moreover, the new allegations share a close temporal proximity to the facts originally alleged. Ornelas's return to Elliot Hospital occurred within 24 hours of his initial discharge from that institution and nearly contemporaneously with the other allegations of misconduct alleged in the original complaint. Given these facts and that the original complaint gave notice that Ornelas was returned to and treated in its emergency room, Elliot Hospital cannot now claim that it was unaware of the general fact situation from which these new allegations arise.

Accordingly, the RSA 507-E claims alleged against Elliot Hospital relate back to the original pleading in this action.

B. NEW HAMPSHIRE RULE

Because the court concludes that the medical injury claim relates back under the federal test it need not assess whether it relates back under New Hampshire's standard.

CONCLUSION

For the foregoing reasons, Elliot Hospital's motion to dismiss is denied.

Notes & Questions

1. First, be clear on the timeline. When did Ornelas's medical injury claim against Elliot Hospital accrue? How long is the applicable statute of limitations, and on what date did this time period expire? On what date did Ornelas file the pleading in which he asserted his medical injury claim against the hospital? Based on your answers, you should see why the hospital argued that Ornelas's claim is

time-barred. What is Ornelas's argument that, notwithstanding these dates, his claim is not time-barred?

2. Next, consider Ornelas's relation back argument in light of the policies underlying the statute of limitations. Legislatures enact statutes of limitations to protect defendants from being forced to defend claims after memories have faded and evidence has become unavailable. Statutes of limitations allow courts to prioritize claims that plaintiffs care enough about to file promptly. And statutes of limitations also provide repose for defendants: After a period of time, the defendant need not worry about the potential claim hanging over its head. As the New York Court of Appeals has explained, "Statutes of limitation not only save litigants from defending stale claims, but also express[] a societal interest or public policy of giving repose to human affairs." *Ace Sec. Corp. v. DB Structured Prods., Inc.*, 25 N.Y.3d 581, 593 (2015). Consider how the relation back doctrine reflects these policies. If an amended pleading concerns the same dispute as the original pleading, and if the original pleading was filed within the limitations period, then the defendant cannot complain of inadequate warning to gather and preserve relevant evidence. Similarly, if the plaintiff filed a timely original complaint against the defendant, then the defendant can hardly feel repose about the situation, nor can the plaintiff be accused of carelessly sitting on the claim. Therefore, if a claim in an amended pleading arose out of the same underlying occurrence as the original pleading, the policies underlying the statute of limitations are not offended by permitting the claim to go forward. In light of the policies underlying the statute of limitations, what would you have argued on behalf of Elliot Hospital? Did the judge in *Ornelas* adequately consider these arguments?

3. In *Ornelas*, the plaintiff's amended complaint asserted a claim against a party who was already in the lawsuit. The plaintiff was not attempting to assert a claim against someone who had not previously been named as a party, which would present a more difficult situation. Recall that in *BLT*, where there was no statute of limitations problem, the defendants consented to an amendment that substituted Think Burger, LLC, as a defendant in place of a company that it owned. Would Think Burger have consented to the amendment if the time for the claim had expired under the statute of limitations?

Consider how the relation back doctrine might apply to a defendant who was not sued within the limitations period, and who argues that it is unfair to drag a new party into a lawsuit after the statute of limitations has expired. The newly named defendant argues that the claim is time-barred. The plaintiff argues that the claim relates back to the original complaint, which was filed within the statute of limitations. The new defendant replies that the original complaint was filed against someone else, and that the new defendant is entitled to rely on the protection of the statute of limitations. Unsurprisingly, courts are much more grudging about applying relation back to amendments that change the name of parties. If you want to amend a pleading to add a new party or change the name of a party, and you need relation back because the limitations period has passed, you will have to show that it was merely a case of mistaken identity and the new party already knew about the lawsuit and knew or should have known that it was the intended target.

Rule 15(c)(1)(C) lays out three requirements to get the benefit of relation back for an amendment that changes the party against whom a claim is asserted. First, the amendment must satisfy Rule 15(c)(1)(B); that is, it must arise out of the same conduct or occurrence as the original pleading. Second, within the 120-day period for service of process after the original pleading was filed, the new party must have known about the lawsuit so that it will not be at a disadvantage in defending the lawsuit. Third, it must be the case that within the same period, the new party "knew or should have known that the action would have been brought against it, but for a mistake concerning the proper party's identity." In practice, this means that if you failed to join a party within the statute of limitations, you are probably out of luck. You cannot use relation back to add a new party to the lawsuit if the party did not already know about the lawsuit. Rule 15(c)(1)(C) relation back works best for correcting simple misnomers, where the defendant actually was served with the complaint but the name was slightly incorrect, or for cases in which an amendment replaces a corporate defendant with its corporate parent or subsidiary.

4. In *Krupski v. Costa Crociere S.p.A.*, 560 U.S. 538 (2010), the Supreme Court addressed a fundamental question about how to interpret Rule 15(c)(1)(C). For purposes of relation back when naming a new party, does it matter whether the *plaintiff* knew or should have known the correct defendant's name, or does it only matter what the newly named *defendant* knew or should have known?

Wanda Krupski was injured on a cruise ship. Her lawyer notified Costa Cruise of Krupski's claim and attempted to negotiate a settlement. Unable to reach a settlement, and three weeks before the one-year limitations period expired, Krupski filed and served a negligence complaint against Costa Cruise in the Southern District of Florida (the venue required by the cruise ticket's forum-selection clause). Several months later, after the limitations period had expired, Costa Cruise informed Krupski that "Costa Cruise" was merely the North American sales and marketing agent for Costa Crociere, S.p.A., an Italian corporation, which was the actual vessel operator. Costa Cruise moved for summary judgment, stating that Costa Crociere was the proper defendant. Krupski moved to amend her complaint to add Costa Crociere as a defendant, which the district court granted. Costa Crociere—represented by the same lawyer who had represented Costa Cruise—moved to dismiss on the grounds that the claim was untimely. Krupski argued that the amended pleading related back to the original complaint. The district court rejected Krupski's relation back argument because the plaintiff knew or should have known about Costa Crociere from pleadings and corporate disclosure statements. Because of the plaintiff's knowledge, the court ruled, the failure to name Costa Crociere was not a "mistake" within the meaning of Rule 15(c)(1)(C), and therefore her claim against Costa

Crociere must be dismissed as untimely. The Eleventh Circuit affirmed, adding that Krupski's passenger ticket included information about Costa Crociere.

The Supreme Court reversed and ruled in favor of Krupski. Rejecting the Eleventh Circuit's focus on the plaintiff's knowledge, the Supreme Court explained its reasoning in terms of both the text and purpose of Rule 15(c)(1)(C):

> The question under Rule 15(c)(1)(C)(ii) is not whether Krupski knew or should have known the identity of Costa Crociere as the proper defendant, but whether Costa Crociere knew or should have known that it would have been named as a defendant but for an error. Rule 15(c)(1)(C)(ii) asks what the prospective defendant knew or should have known during the Rule 4(m) period, not what the plaintiff knew or should have known at the time of filing her original complaint. . . .
>
> This reading is consistent with the purpose of relation back: to balance the interests of the defendant protected by the statute of limitations with the preference expressed in the Federal Rules of Civil Procedure in general, and Rule 15 in particular, for resolving disputes on their merits. A prospective defendant who legitimately believed that the limitations period had passed without any attempt to sue him has a strong interest in repose. But repose would be a windfall for a prospective defendant who understood, or who should have understood, that he escaped suit during the limitations period only because the plaintiff misunderstood a crucial fact about his identity. Because a plaintiff's knowledge of the existence of a party does not foreclose the possibility that she has made a mistake of identity about which that party should have been aware, such knowledge does not support that party's interest in repose.

Costa Crociere had constructive notice of Krupski's complaint within the relevant time period, and Costa Crociere knew or should have known that it was not named as a defendant only because of Krupski's misunderstanding about which Costa entity was in charge of the ship. Therefore, under the Supreme Court's analysis, Krupski's amended complaint against Costa Crociere related back to the date of her original complaint against Costa Cruise.

D. ETHICAL CONSTRAINTS

Now that you have learned the pleading and amendment rules of the Federal Rules of Civil Procedure, as well as the difference between evidence and allegations, you might get the misimpression that in an adversary system parties can allege whatever they please. In fact, there are significant constraints on pleadings and advocacy. Both the rules of civil procedure and the rules governing lawyers' conduct impose limits on what can be asserted in the litigation process.

We turn now to these procedural and ethical constraints on pleadings and advocacy. In particular, we will examine the requirement that every factual assertion must have a basis in fact and every legal assertion must have a basis in law. These requirements, in turn, implicate not only the lawyer's duty of honesty and candor, but also the lawyer's duties of competence and diligence in making reasonable inquiries.

At the outset, we should draw a distinction between rules of professional conduct and rules of civil procedure. Each state has its own set of ethics rules for lawyers;

many of these are based on the American Bar Association's Model Rules of Professional Conduct. Violations of rules of professional conduct are punishable by disbarment, suspension, reprimand, or other penalties. The rules are enforced by disciplinary processes in each state, sometimes run by the state bar association. Most law students study the rules of professional conduct in a course on professional responsibility.

In this book, we will not focus primarily on the rules of professional conduct. Instead, we will focus on a procedural rule that embraces a similar set of norms—Rule 11 of the Federal Rules of Civil Procedure. Rule 11 is not enforced through lawyer disciplinary proceedings, but rather by judges as part of the litigation process. In essence, Rule 11 says that when you sign a pleading, motion, or other paper, or when you file it or present it to the court, you are certifying that it is not frivolous, false, or filed for some improper purpose. If you violate this rule, the court may punish you by imposing sanctions.

The heart of the rule is Rule 11(b), which explains what is entailed every time a lawyer or party signs or presents a pleading, motion, or other paper. Rule 11(b) states that the lawyer or party "certifies that to the best of the person's knowledge, information, and belief, formed after an inquiry reasonable under the circumstances. . . ." The first requirement of Rule 11(b) is embedded in that prefatory language—"an inquiry reasonable under the circumstances." Lawyers are forbidden to submit a pleading or other paper without first making a reasonable inquiry into the facts and law. Sometimes, this may require no more than asking appropriate questions to the client to elicit the facts and reviewing essential documents or other evidence. Other times, however, a reasonable inquiry may require more extensive factual investigation or legal research.

What exactly are you certifying, to the best of your knowledge? That is what subsections 11(b)(1) through (4) spell out.

Under Rule 11(b)(1), the presenting lawyer or party is certifying that the pleading, motion, or other paper "is not being presented for any improper purpose, such as to harass, cause unnecessary delay, or needlessly increase the cost of litigation." *Any* pleading or motion increases the cost of litigation, of course, and to a party being sued, it always feels like harassment. The point of Rule 11(b)(1) is not to undo the adversary system, but rather to emphasize that pleadings or motions may be presented only if the party actually seeks the relief requested in the pleading or motion, and not if the sole purpose is to harass, embarrass, intimidate, or to make the litigation needlessly burdensome.

Rule 11(b)(2) prohibits *legally* frivolous claims and defenses. The lawyer or party presenting the paper certifies that "the claims, defenses, and other legal contentions are warranted by existing law or by a nonfrivolous argument for extending, modifying, or reversing existing law or for establishing new law." If you do not have a legal basis to back up your claim, defense, motion, or other legal contention, then you are not allowed to present it. The "inquiry reasonable under the circumstances" requires reasonable legal research if you are unsure of whether the law supports your position. But if you have a good argument that the law *should* support your position, do not allow Rule 11 to deter you from asserting reasonable, creative legal arguments. The rule's language about "nonfrivolous argument for extending, modifying, or reversing existing law or for establishing new law" is important. Thurgood Marshall was not acting improperly when he argued, as the plaintiff's lawyer in *Brown v. Board of Education*, 347 U.S. 483 (1954), that racial segregation in education is unconstitutional despite precedent that permitted "separate but equal" schools. One of the dangers, if judges do not respect Rule 11(b)(2)'s protection of reasonable legal arguments, is that sanctions could be used to chill creative lawyering that seeks to move the law forward. The rule attempts to strike a balance by forbidding frivolous claims and defenses but permitting nonfrivolous arguments for changing the law.

Rule 11(b)(3) and 11(b)(4) prohibit *factually* baseless allegations and denials. Although the pleading standard of Rule 8 does not expect litigants to have gathered all of their evidence before the lawsuit begins, parties and their lawyers are expected not to allege things in their pleadings unless they have evidence to back up their statements or have at least made sufficient inquiry so that they have a basis to expect to find evidentiary support for the allegations. Rule 11(b)(3) concerns factual contentions: "[T]he factual contentions have evidentiary support or, if specifically so identified, will likely have evidentiary support after a reasonable opportunity for further investigation or discovery." Rule 11(b)(4) concerns denials: "[T]he denials of factual contentions are warranted on the evidence or, if specifically so identified, are reasonably based on belief or a lack of information." Remember that under Rule 8(b)(6), allegations of the complaint are ordinarily deemed admitted unless they are denied in the defendant's answer. This puts significant pressure on defendants to deny the plaintiffs' allegations. But Rule 11 imposes a check on careless denials. Denials must be based on the evidence; if the party lacks information to be able to admit or deny an allegation, the party may say so and treat it as a denial under Rule 8(b), but may not simply deny the opposing party's contentions without a factual basis for doing so.

Notice what Rule 11 does not say. It does not talk about "good faith" or "bad faith." With the exception of Rule 11(b)(1)'s treatment of improper purpose, the prohibitions of Rule 11(b) are not about subjective state of mind. The issue is whether the allegations, claims, and defenses have an objectively nonfrivolous basis in fact and law, not whether the person's intentions were good. As some courts have noted, Rule 11 does not contain a "good heart, empty head" defense.

Notice, too, that the requirements of Rule 11 are rather modest. Contentions must have *some* factual and legal basis, but that does not mean they all have to be winners. Every week, thousands of plaintiffs and defendants lose cases, but that does not mean that their positions were frivolous or that the lawyers behaved unethically by representing the clients to the best of their ability. It does not violate Rule 11(b)(2) to assert a claim or defense supported by some legal basis or reasonable argument, even if the position probably will lose because the weight of legal authority falls on the other side. Nor does it violate Rule 11(b)(3) to make allegations that have some factual basis, such as the client's plausible account of the facts, even if the contrary evidence appears stronger. Rule 11, in other words, obligates the lawyer to make a reasonable inquiry and to refrain from making baseless assertions, but it does not obligate the lawyer to serve as judge and jury rather than as the client's advocate.

If a lawyer or party violates Rule 11, the court may impose sanctions such as a monetary penalty to be paid to the court, nonmonetary directives, or an order directing the violator to pay the other side's legal fees or expenses. Rule 11(c) empowers the court to impose sanctions on the attorneys, law firms, or parties that bear responsibility for the violation. Although the rule permits sanctions against parties as well as lawyers, Rule 11(c)(5) specifies that "the court must not impose a monetary sanction . . . against a represented party for violating Rule 11(b)(2)." Think about the logic behind this limitation. For factually baseless allegations (Rule 11(b)(3)) or denials (Rule 11(b)(4)), the client may bear some or all of the responsibility because lawyers often rely in part on their clients' accounts of the facts. Likewise, the client may be wholly or partly responsible for papers submitted for an improper purpose such as harassment (Rule 11(b)(1)). But if a party retains a lawyer for legal representation in litigation, then the responsibility for avoiding frivolous *legal* contentions (Rule 11(b)(2)) should fall on the lawyer.

In the following two cases, courts imposed sanctions for violations of Rule 11. Be sure you understand which provision(s) of Rule 11 each court relied on, in what way each judge thought the lawyer or party violated those provisions, and why each judge thought sanctions were warranted. More generally, use these cases to think about the "rules of the game" in litigation and what constraints are needed for effective functioning of an adversary system of dispute resolution.

SHELTON v. ERNST & YOUNG, LLP
143 F. Supp. 2d 982 (N.D. Ill. 2001)

KEYS, Magistrate Judge

Before the Court is Defendants' Motion to Dismiss Plaintiff's First Amended Complaint, pursuant to Federal Rules of Civil Procedure 12(b)(1) and 12(b)(6), and Motion for Sanctions, pursuant to FRCP 11. For the following reasons, Defendants' Motion to Dismiss and Motion for Sanctions are granted.

BACKGROUND

In his First Amended Complaint, Plaintiff Carlton L. Shelton asserts various claims relating to the termination of his employment with Defendant Ernst &

Young, LLP ("Ernst & Young"): (1) sex and race[1] discrimination under Title VII

---

[1] It is not entirely clear from Plaintiff's Amended Complaint whether he is asserting both race and gender discrimination under Title VII and the Illinois Human Rights Act, or merely gender discrimination. While his charge to the Equal Employment Opportunity Commission ("EEOC") lists sex and race discrimination, and paragraph one of his Amended Complaint mentions both gender and racial discrimination, the remainder of the Amended Complaint, dealing with discrimination, only mentions allegations concerning gender discrimination. Furthermore, to add to the confusion, Plaintiff's Amended Complaint goes directly from the heading "Facts" to "Count III," and the Court (as well as Defendants) are left pondering what constitutes Counts I and II. Since Count III is for the state breach of contract claim, the Court assumes that

of the Civil Rights Act of 1964 ("Title VII") and/or the Illinois Human Rights Act, ("IHRA"), against Defendants Ernst & Young and Sylvia Pozarnsky; and (2) breach of an oral employment contract against Defendant Ernst & Young.

Plaintiff is an African-American male who was hired by Ernst & Young in its Personal Financial Counseling ("PFC") practice in July of 1998. Ms. Pozarnsky managed Ernst & Young's PFC practice, and terminated Plaintiff's employment on April 30, 1999. According to Plaintiff, however, he was not taken off Ernst & Young's payroll until June 15, 1999. On March 22, 2000, three hundred and twenty-seven (327) days after his discharge (on April 30, 1999), Plaintiff filed a charge with the EEOC, alleging race and gender discrimination. The EEOC issued a "Right to Sue" letter on June 5, 2000, and Plaintiff filed his original Complaint in federal court on September 5, 2000. (There is no evidence that Plaintiff filed a charge with the Illinois Human Rights Commission pursuant to IHRA.)

On October 16, 2000, Defendants' counsel sent Plaintiff's counsel a letter, explaining in depth (and citing the relevant cases and statutes) that many—if not all—of Plaintiff's claims were groundless, and likely in violation of Rule 11 of the FRCP.... Plaintiff's counsel responded by letter, stating that he would file a motion to voluntarily dismiss the appropriate claims (although he did not specify which ones) by November 13, 2000. Nonetheless,

by November 13, 2000, Plaintiff's counsel had not moved to dismiss any of the claims. However, on December 29, 2000, Plaintiff filed a Motion for Leave to Amend Plaintiff's Complaint and Jury Demand. In that Motion, Plaintiff's counsel stated that, based on discussions with Defendants' counsel, he agreed that some of the allegations were either time-barred, inapplicable, or that requiring Defendants to respond to them in their current form would be unfair to Defendants, and could detract from Plaintiff's meritorious allegations. By Order dated January 3, 2001, the Court granted Plaintiff's Motion to Amend the Complaint by January 16, 2001. On January 16, 2001, Plaintiff filed his Amended Complaint, which still contained many of the claims that were in the original Complaint—claims that had been specifically addressed by Defendants' counsel in his October 16th letter. On February 8, 2001, Defendants filed their present Motion to Dismiss and for Sanctions.

MOTION TO DISMISS STANDARD

The purpose of a motion to dismiss pursuant to Rule 12(b)(1) is to dismiss claims over which a federal court lacks subject matter jurisdiction. Jurisdiction is the "power to decide" and must be conferred upon a federal court. In reviewing a 12(b)(1) motion to dismiss, the court may look beyond the complaint and view any extraneous evidence submitted by the parties to determine subject matter jurisdiction. The plaintiff bears the burden of establishing that the jurisdictional requirements have been met. When a party moves for dismissal pursuant to Rule 12(b)(1), the nonmoving party must support its allegations with competent proof of jurisdictional facts.

Counts I and II are for the sex and gender discrimination claims. Nonetheless, as explained in depth infra, Plaintiff's discrimination claims—whether they are for both race and gender discrimination, or merely gender discrimination—are dismissed, with prejudice, because they are time-barred.

As for the Rule 12(b)(6) motion to dismiss for failure to state a claim upon which relief can be granted, the purpose of the rule is to test the sufficiency of the complaint and not to decide the merits of the case. In ruling on a motion to dismiss, the court must construe the complaint's allegations in the light most favorable to the plaintiff, and all well-pled facts and allegations in the plaintiff's complaint must be taken as true. . . .

DISCUSSION

I. PLAINTIFF'S TITLE VII CLAIMS ARE TIME-BARRED AND, THEREFORE, DISMISSED UNDER FRCP 12(B)(1)

Compliance with the limitations period under Title VII for filing a charge with the EEOC is jurisdictional. In order to pursue a Title VII claim, a plaintiff must file an EEOC charge within 300 days of the occurrence of the event that forms the basis of the complaint. 42 U.S.C. §2000e-5(e). Significantly, "[f]ailure to do so bars litigation over those claims." *Speer v. Rand McNally & Co.*, 123 F.3d 658, 662 (7th Cir. 1997).

Here, despite Plaintiff's assertion to the contrary, the event that forms the basis of his discrimination claims is his termination from Ernst & Young on April 30, 1999. Plaintiff filed his charge of discrimination with the EEOC on March 22, 2000—327 days after his termination. Nonetheless, Plaintiff asserts in his Response to Defendants' Motion to Dismiss ("Response") that he was not officially taken off Ernst & Young's payroll until June 15, 1999, and that, consequently, he timely filed his charge within the 300 day requirement. However, as the abundant case law undeniably shows, when Plaintiff was taken off Ernst & Young's payroll is totally irrelevant. The critical date—that starts the 300 day clock ticking—is when Plaintiff learned about the adverse decision, and not when the financial consequences (such as being taken off the payroll) are felt, or when the termination becomes effective. *See, e.g., Librizzi v. Children's Memorial Medical Center*, 134 F.3d 1302, 1306 (7th Cir. 1998) ("An adverse decision whose effect is deferred gives rise to a claim when the decision is made, not when the effect is felt. This is commonplace in the law of employment discrimination.").

Nonetheless, Plaintiff attempts to circumvent the prevailing case law by making several erroneous and frivolous arguments.[4] First, Plaintiff argues, in his Response, that he first had knowledge of Ernst & Young's adverse employment decision on June 15, 1999—when he was officially taken off the payroll—and that he felt the effects of this discrimination on June 30, 1999, the last pay date. He then cites *Delaware State College v. Ricks*, 449 U.S. 250 (1980), for this proposition. However, Plaintiff's counsel misunderstands and misapplies the relevant case law. *Ricks* and its progeny clearly hold that the statute of limitation begins to run when the plaintiff first learns of the adverse employment action. *See, e.g., Davidson v. Board of Governors of State Colleges and Univs.*, 920 F.2d 441, 443 (7th Cir. 1990) (citing *Ricks* for the proposition that "[t]he Supreme Court has held that the time for attacking a discriminatory practice begins to run when the practice is first applied to you, not when the application blossoms into a

---

[4] As explained *infra*, these arguments are particularly frivolous as Defendants' counsel specifically informed Plaintiff's counsel (and even cited the relevant cases) of the problems with his Title VII claims in an October 16, 2000 letter.

full-blown injury."). Significantly, in Plaintiff's Amended Complaint, he states, in paragraphs 11 and 16, that he was discharged on April 30, 1999. He also states, in his EEOC charge, that he was terminated on April 30, 1999. Therefore, April 30, 1999 is, undisputedly, when Plaintiff learned of the adverse employment action. Plaintiff has, essentially, pled himself out of Court. The fact that his termination may have become effective at a later date is irrelevant for statute of limitations purposes. His claims under Title VII are time-barred.

Plaintiff next argues that the continuing violation theory applies to his case, and that he should be allowed to obtain relief for time-barred acts (such as the April 30th termination date) by linking that act with an act that is within the limitations period (such as the June 15th date, when he was taken off the payroll). However, fatal to Plaintiff's use of the continuing violation theory is that he fails to allege that any discriminatory act took place within the limitations period.

Plaintiff argues in his Response that, between April 30, 1999 and June 15, 1999, he and Ernst & Young were engaged in ongoing conversations in an attempt to work out their differences without an interruption in pay. Although the Amended Complaint never states this theory, it is entirely irrelevant, because the case law clearly shows that failing to correct alleged previous discrimination is not a new act of discrimination. Therefore, assuming that Ernst & Young's decision to terminate Plaintiff on April 30th was, indeed, discriminatory, its failure to correct it is not a new act of discrimination. Consequently, as a preliminary matter, the continuing violation theory cannot even apply to the case *sub judice*, as there was no discriminatory act within the limitations period.

Furthermore, Plaintiff argues that equitable estoppel and/or equitable tolling should apply to the facts of this case. However, as with the continuing violation theory, these theories are not applicable to the case *sub judice.* For equitable estoppel to apply, Plaintiff would have to allege that Ernst & Young actively lulled him into inaction by promising not to plead the statute of limitations, or by hiding evidence. Here, however, there are no allegations that Ernst & Young impeded Plaintiff's ability to pursue his discrimination claims. Even if Plaintiff believed that, pursuant to their negotiations, Ernst & Young might change its April 30, 1999 termination decision, as explained in *Librizzi,* "neither denials of liability nor negotiations toll the period of limitations." 134 F.3d at 1307.

With respect to equitable tolling, Plaintiff would have to allege that he could not have obtained evidence of the discriminatory acts within the limitations period. Plaintiff cites *Davidson, supra,* to support his equitable tolling argument, but the facts of *Davidson* are distinguishable from the case at bar, and illustrate that equitable tolling is not applicable to the case *sub judice. Davidson* concerned a pay scheme that allegedly discriminated against older workers. In tolling the statute of limitations, the court held that the plaintiff did not have enough evidence to determine whether the compensation scheme was unlawful until new, younger employees were hired at higher salaries. Here, however, Plaintiff had all the evidence he needed when he was terminated on April 30, 1999. Indeed, no new evidence of discrimination emerged after April 30, 1999—being taken off the payroll on June 15th was merely the effect of the prior alleged discrimination and not new evidence of discrimination. Again, as with Plaintiff's other theories, this one is frivolous.

Plaintiff's termination on April 30, 1999 provided him with all the information he needed to pursue a discrimination claim.

II. ALL TITLE VII CLAIMS AGAINST MS. POZARNSKY ARE DISMISSED, BECAUSE INDIVIDUALS CANNOT BE HELD PERSONALLY LIABLE UNDER TITLE VII

Although Plaintiff's Title VII claims have been dismissed for the reasons discussed above—so this issue is moot—it is worth addressing, because Plaintiff's counsel refuses to accept the prevailing law that supervisors, such as Ms. Pozarnsky, cannot be held individually liable under Title VII. Liability for employment discrimination under Title VII can only be imposed against an individual who qualifies independently as an employer. *EEOC v. AIC Sec. Investigations, Ltd.*, 55 F.3d 1276, 1279-82 (7th Cir. 1995). Under Title VII, an employer is defined as "a person engaged in an industry affecting commerce who has fifteen or more employees . . . and any agent of such a person."[8] 42 U.S.C. §2000e(b). Because Ms. Pozarnsky does not qualify as an employer, the Title VII claims as to her must be dismissed.

---

[8] In his Response, Plaintiff argues that dismissing Ms. Pozarnsky from Title VII liability would be premature, as Ms. Pozarnsky's actions exceeded the scope of her employment, and constituted personal acts intentionally directed at Plaintiff. Plaintiff cites no legal authority for this proposition, and does not even address the abundant case law which says otherwise. As explained *infra*, refusing to dismiss Ms. Pozarnsky from this lawsuit, especially after Defendants' counsel, in his October 16th letter, apprized Plaintiff's counsel of the state of the law, is particularly troublesome, and serves as one of the bases for awarding sanctions against Plaintiff.

III. PLAINTIFF'S CLAIMS UNDER THE IHRA ARE DISMISSED, BECAUSE PLAINTIFF FAILED TO ALLEGE THAT HE EXHAUSTED ADMINISTRATIVE REMEDIES UNDER THE IHRA

[To the extent Plaintiff seeks relief under the Illinois Human Rights Act, his claims are dismissed for failure to state a claim, as he failed to allege that he filed a charge with the Illinois Department of Human Rights.]

IV. TO THE EXTENT PLAINTIFF SEEKS RELIEF FOR EMOTIONAL DISTRESS, THESE CLAIMS ARE PREEMPTED BY THE IHRA

[To the extent Plaintiff asserts claims for infliction of emotional distress, his claims are dismissed, as the Illinois Human Rights Act preempts state tort claims that are linked to civil rights violations listed in the IHRA.]

V. PLAINTIFF'S STATE BREACH OF CONTRACT CLAIM IS DISMISSED, BECAUSE HE FAILS TO ALLEGE DURATION OF THE EMPLOYMENT CONTRACT AND ADEQUATE CONSIDERATION

Under Illinois law, an oral or written contract that does not specify the duration of the employment is presumed to be terminable at will by either party, and an employment-at-will relationship may be terminated for good cause, bad cause, or no cause at all. This presumption of employment at-will, however, may be overcome by demonstrating that the parties intended to contract otherwise. Furthermore, "[o]ral employment contracts, at least under Illinois law, are viewed with more skepticism than their formal written counterparts." *Tolmie v. United Parcel Service, Inc.*, 930 F.2d 579, 581 (7th Cir. 1991).

Here, Plaintiff alleges the existence of an oral employment contract, where Ernst & Young promised to begin his employment at a management level higher than the level at which he began, and promised to give him a raise and a promotion within one year of his start date. Plaintiff also alleges that he turned down, and/or discontinued his pursuit of, other positions at the same or comparable level when he accepted the lower position at Ernst & Young.

There are two fundamental problems with Plaintiff's assertion that his employment with Ernst & Young was not at-will, and that he had an oral employment contract. First and foremost, Plaintiff has failed to allege that Ernst & Young specified a duration for his employment. Second, Plaintiff has not alleged sufficient consideration to support an employment contract.

Fatal to Plaintiff's breach of contract claim is its lack of a durational term. While Plaintiff alleges that he was promised a promotion within a year, he does not allege that he was promised employment for at least a year, or for any length of time. As explained in *Krieger v. Adler, Kaplan, & Begy*, 1996 WL 6540, at *6 (N.D. Ill. Jan. 5, 1996), . . . "the plaintiff must show that the employer made clear and definite oral promises concerning the terms and duration of his employment." However, in the case *sub judice*, Plaintiff fails to mention anywhere in his Amended Complaint the duration of the supposed employment contract.

Plaintiff also fails to allege sufficient consideration to support an employment contract. Under Illinois law, consideration for an employer's oral promise to employ a person for a period of time is provided when an employee makes in return some sacrifice that the employee probably would not have made absent the guarantee of continued permanent employment. Significantly, under Illinois law, an employee's mere waiving of a right to pursue or accept alternative employment opportunities does not constitute adequate consideration to support a promise to employ the employee for a certain period of time. Rather, the employee must forego a real and favorable job offer from another employer, or give up a secure position elsewhere. [The court cited recent cases from the Seventh Circuit and the Northern District of Illinois to emphasize this point.]

Here, Plaintiff's allegations are of the general nature—that he turned down and/or discontinued his pursuit of other job opportunities. He does not allege that he relinquished secure employment elsewhere, was solicited by Ernst & Young, relocated, or forewent a favorable job offer from another specific employer. Consequently, there is no consideration to support a contract for a specified duration (even if Plaintiff had alleged a specified duration, which he did not). Accordingly, Plaintiff's breach of contract claim is dismissed with prejudice.[14]

VI. SANCTIONS ARE APPROPRIATE AGAINST PLAINTIFF'S COUNSEL FOR BRINGING THE TITLE VII CLAIMS AFTER THEY WERE CLEARLY TIME-BARRED, AND FOR SUING MS. POZARNSKY, IN HER INDIVIDUAL CAPACITY, UNDER TITLE VII

FRCP 11 imposes an affirmative duty of reasonable investigation on an attorney

---

[14] Plaintiff's breach of contract claim is dismissed with prejudice (as opposed to without prejudice), because he has had ample time to plead allegations concerning duration and consideration. Therefore, the Court assumes that, if Plaintiff could have pled more specific allegations concerning duration and consideration, he would have done so in his Amended Complaint.

signing a court paper, such as a complaint. Specifically, Rule 11 provides two grounds for sanctions: the "frivolousness clause" and the "improper clause." In the case at bar, the "frivolousness" clause is implicated, as Plaintiff's counsel failed to conduct a reasonable inquiry into the relevant facts and law concerning the Title VII claims, even after Defendants' counsel specifically informed Plaintiff's counsel, in the October 16, 2000 letter, of the inherent problems with these claims. Although Plaintiff's counsel had an opportunity to withdraw these claims—and even indicated that he would do so in November 2000—he, nonetheless, filed an Amended Complaint, in January 2001, which still contained the Title VII claims.

Specifically, Plaintiff's counsel was warned that Plaintiff's Title VII claims were time-barred, and that individual supervisors could not be held liable under Title VII. Despite this admonishment, Plaintiff's counsel persisted with these frivolous claims. [The] Seventh Circuit [has] imposed sanctions under FRCP 11, where, as here, the plaintiff's claims were barred by the applicable statute of limitations, and where the plaintiffs, as here, had been previously warned. Accordingly, the Court orders that Plaintiff's counsel pay Defendants the reasonable expenses and attorneys' fees associated with defending Plaintiff's Title VII claims.

Furthermore, Plaintiff's counsel's insistence on suing Ms. Pozarnsky for individual liability, under Title VII, goes against well-established Seventh Circuit precedent, and at least one court within the Seventh Circuit has sanctioned counsel, under FRCP 11, for persisting with such a claim. Plaintiff's counsel's attempt to try to defend this claim, by asserting—with no legal authority—that Ms. Pozarnsky's actions exceeded the scope of her employment, only exacerbates the frivolousness of this claim. Accordingly, Plaintiff's counsel is also ordered to pay Defendants the reasonable expenses and attorneys' fees for not having dismissed Ms. Pozarnsky from individual liability, under Title VII, in the Amended Complaint.[17]

Finally, in response to Defendants' Motion for Sanctions, Plaintiff's counsel argues that Rule 11 provides for sanctions, not fee shifting, and that such sanctions should be used to deter and, if necessary, punish improper conduct, rather than to compensate the prevailing party. This Court is in complete agreement with counsel's argument in this regard, and it is extremely rare that it has granted motions for Rule 11 sanctions. However, where, as here, counsel has persisted in going forth with clearly legally baseless allegations and arguments—even after having been apprized of case law that clearly indicates their lack of merit—such sanctions are mandated. Contrary to counsel's argument, the effect of the sanction is not to penalize him for aggressively advocating Plaintiff's rights, but is meant as a partial recoupment by Defendants of their expenditures in defending these clearly legally baseless allegations. Those who merely engage in aggressive advocacy will have nothing to fear.

CONCLUSION

Accordingly, for the reasons set forth above, Defendants' Motion to Dismiss and Motion for Sanctions are granted. Plaintiff's claims in his Amended Complaint are dismissed with prejudice.

---

[17] Defendants, correctly, do not request that sanctions, under FRCP 11, be applied to Plaintiff's other claims (or potential claims), such as the breach of contract claim, claims under the IHRA, or claims for emotional distress. Accordingly, the Court only sanctions Plaintiff's counsel for his pursuit of the Title VII claims, and for refusing to dismiss Ms. Pozarnsky from individual liability under Title VII. The fees and costs are to be apportioned accordingly.

Notes & Questions

1. Be sure you understand the difference between Rule 11 violations that involve baseless factual assertions and Rule 11 violations that involve frivolous legal positions. Which type of violation did the court find in *Shelton*? Specifically, which parts of Rule 11(b) did the lawyer violate, and how?

2. What aspects of employment discrimination law did Shelton's lawyer get wrong? How should the lawyer have avoided these errors?

3. Judge Keys cites cases to show that Shelton's claims were contrary to controlling legal authority. How does the judge know that Shelton's lawyer lacks "a nonfrivolous argument for extending, modifying, or reversing existing law or for establishing new law," as permitted by Rule 11(b)(2)? Implicit in Rule 11 is the notion that not all arguments are equal. Just because a lawyer advances a position contrary to existing law, that does not mean the lawyer has a nonfrivolous argument for doing so. Given the judge's power to punish what the judge considers frivolous arguments, are you worried that Rule 11 might discourage lawyers from advancing important legal agendas that move the law forward in ways that make some judges uncomfortable? Isn't change always uncomfortable? Is *Shelton* such a case?

4. Does Judge Keys believe that Shelton's lawyer purposely ignored the law in pursuing these claims for his client? Or does the judge believe that Shelton's lawyer failed to understand the law? If the latter, does the judge believe that this was due to incompetence and ignorance, or that it was due to failure to conduct sufficiently diligent research? For purposes of determining whether Shelton's lawyer violated Rule 11, does it matter?

   The answer is yes, the lawyer's state of mind matters in certain respects, but be sure you understand the difference between where it matters and where it does not. For purposes of determining whether the lawyer violated Rule 11(b)(2) when he filed claims that were clearly time-barred, did the lawyer's state of mind matter? For purposes of determining whether the lawyer violated Rule 11(b)(2) when he filed claims against Pozarnsky that were barred by clear controlling legal authority, did the lawyer's state of mind matter? For purposes of determining whether the lawyer violated Rule 11(b)(1) by filing these claims, did the lawyer's state of mind matter? For purposes of determining whether there was an inquiry reasonable under the circumstances, did the diligence of the lawyer's research matter?

5. The sanctions provisions of Rule 11 have blown back and forth with the political winds. A few decades ago, Rule 11 was largely toothless and rarely invoked. The rule was toughened up in 1983, above all by amending Rule 11(c) to state that the court "shall" (rather than "may") impose sanctions for a violation. Over the following decade, courts and lawyers used Rule 11 more aggressively. They used it so much, in fact, that critics worried that Rule 11 motions had become a routine tactical maneuver and fee-shifting device, that lawyers were spending too

much time fighting over Rule 11 issues rather than litigating the merits of the case, and that the rule was having a chilling effect on civil rights cases. To address these problems, the rule was amended again in 1993. The word "shall" was changed back to "may," reinstating judicial discretion over whether to impose sanctions. The amendments specified that the sanction "shall be limited to what is sufficient to deter repetition of such conduct or comparable conduct," and made it clear that courts should not automatically impose attorneys' fees as the sanction. If the rule lacked teeth until 1983, perhaps we can say that in 1993, its teeth were filed down because they'd gotten too sharp. In recent years, there have been efforts in Congress—driven mostly by businesses that worry about frivolous litigation—to reform Rule 11, and the proposed reforms would return the rule in certain respects to its pre-1993 form.

LONE WOLF DISTRIBUTORS, INC. v. BRAVOWARE, INC.
2017 WL 874570 (D. Idaho Mar. 3, 2017)

WINMILL, Chief District Judge.

INTRODUCTION

The Court has before it plaintiff Lone Wolf's motion for sanctions. The motion is fully briefed and at issue. For the reasons explained below, the Court will grant the motion.

BACKGROUND

In its motion for sanctions, plaintiff Lone Wolf claims that defendants misrepresented that they had no connection with an entity named BravoTac. After Lone Wolf expended considerable time and effort to expose the falsity of these representations, defendants withdrew them. In this motion for sanctions, Lone Wolf seeks reimbursement for its efforts in uncovering the truth regarding defendants' connection to BravoTac.

Plaintiff Lone Wolf is an Idaho corporation. It makes aftermarket firearm accessories, including a thread cap protector that fits on the end of a gun barrel to protect the barrel's threads from damage during transport or storage.

Lone Wolf claims that the two defendants—Bravoware Inc. and Sopcom, Inc., both owned by Gino Shemesh—sold counterfeit Lone Wolf thread cap protectors over the internet through an alter ego named BravoTac. Lone Wolf accuses the defendants of trademark counterfeiting and unfair competition, among other claims.

In its original complaint, Lone Wolf did not name either BravoTac or Gino Shemesh as defendants. Instead, Lone Wolf claimed that BravoTac is conducting business as an alter-ego of the two named defendants, Bravoware Inc. and Sopcom Inc. [Lone Wolf's complaint alleged, among other things, that Shemesh conducted sales of counterfeit Lone Wolf products on eBay under the pseudonym BravoTac.]

Defendants responded on April 3, 2015, by filing a motion to dismiss alleging that this Court lacked personal jurisdiction over the two named defendants. Defendants argued that the two named defendants had no contacts with Idaho, and that any actions of BravoTac could not be attributed to them. Their brief alleged that "[n]either defendant operates a website. The website complained of by plaintiffs is not owned by either defendant." The brief was supported by a Declaration of Shemesh wherein he states that "[n]either Sopcom nor Bravoware owns the web site www.bravotac.com mentioned in the complaint." Shemesh also states that "[n]either Sopcom nor Bravoware was involved in any of the activities described in the Complaint."

Lone Wolf responded by filing a motion seeking to do discovery on the relationship between BravoTac and the defendants. On April 27, 2015, the defendants opposed that motion, and in their brief argued that discovery "would be futile because [Lone Wolf] could never prove that BravoTac is the 'alter ego' of either Defendant." Defendants filed another Declaration from Shemesh stating that Sopcom and Bravoware had "no subsidiaries or divisions." Defendants argued in their brief that Shemesh's statement "establishes that BravoTac cannot be an alter ego of either company because neither has any subsidiaries."

The attorney for the defendants, Paul Reidl, states that he prepared these Declarations after consulting with Shemesh. Reidl discussed the relationship between Bravoware, Sopcom, and BravoTac with Shemesh "in multiple telephone conversations and e-mails," and reviewed the Declarations "paragraph by paragraph with Shemesh over the telephone." Reidl states that Shemesh told him that Sopcom and Bravoware had nothing to do with BravoTac, and that BravoTac was Shemesh's personal eBay seller name.

Reidl conducted his own investigation into whether there was a connection between BravoTac and the two named defendants. He explains that he was aware of the BravoTac website but could find no connection between it and the two named defendants in his investigation. He discovered the BravoTac d/b/a/, but was told by Shemesh that "it was a d/b/a for his eBay business and that he had used it before Bravoware had been formed." When Reidl searched for the d/b/a, he saw that it was registered July 23, 2013, a date after Sopcom had been dissolved and before Bravoware had been formed. This chronology, Reidl explains, confirmed to him the truth of what Shemesh had told him. . . .

Turning back to Lone Wolf's motion for jurisdictional discovery, the Court granted that motion and allowed discovery into [the relationship between BravoTac and the defendants].

As a result of defendants' denials of any connection between them and BravoTac, Lone Wolf's counsel traveled to a hotel in California to take Shemesh's deposition.

In the hotel lobby, just thirty minutes before the deposition was set to begin, Reidl met with Shemesh and recalls that "[n]othing he told me was inconsistent with or contradicted anything" that he had said earlier concerning the relationship between BravoTac, Bravoware, and Sopcom.

[At the deposition, Shemesh stated that he filed BravoTac on behalf of Bravoware, that BravoTac conducted business for Sopcom, that Shemesh runs the BravoTac eBay store on behalf of Bravoware, and that Bravoware is doing business as BravoTac. According to Shemesh's deposition testimony, "the Bravoware company was the corporation, and the d/b/a was BravoTac."]

Reidl "was surprised" when Shemesh "testified [at his deposition] that Bravotac was a d/b/a of Bravoware because this contradicted the facts he had provided to me and the results of my investigation." Reidl "did not believe his [Shemesh's] recollection was accurate." But Reidl presents nothing to support this belief, and Shemesh has never retracted his deposition testimony.

About a month after this deposition, and despite Shemesh's admissions, defendants filed a second motion to dismiss arguing that neither defendant "operates a web site," and that the "web site complained of by plaintiffs [the BravoTac website] "is not owned by either defendant." Lone Wolf was forced to file a response brief and also filed a motion to amend its complaint to add Shemesh as a party defendant.

On June 13, 2016, Lone Wolf served but did not file a motion for Rule 11 sanctions. Lone Wolf sought reimbursement for all its expenses in revealing the false representations made by defendants that they had nothing to do with BravoTac.

On June 30, 2016, defendants filed a brief that withdrew their misrepresentations. Defendants also filed a notice that they were withdrawing their renewed motion to dismiss and not opposing Lone Wolf's motion to amend. Their withdrawal states as follows:

> Accordingly, even though there is considerable doubt about the accuracy of Mr. Shemesh's deposition testimony, Defendants hereby withdraw the following paragraphs from the previously filed declarations of Mr. Shemesh:
>
> - Docket No. 17-2, Paragraph 8: "Neither Sopcom nor Bravoware was involved in any of the activities described in the Complaint."
> - Docket No. 17-2, Paragraph 9: "Neither Sopcom nor Bravoware owns the website www.bravotac. com mentioned in the complaint."
> - Docket No. 18-1, Paragraphs 3 and 4: "[Bravoware, Inc. and Sopcom have] no subsidiaries or divisions."

> - Defendants also withdraw the contentions in the memoranda that were based on these paragraphs, inclusive of arguments to the effect that BravoTac was unrelated to Bravoware.

About a week after defendants withdrew their misrepresentations, Lone Wolf filed the motion for sanctions now before the Court. The motion seeks relief under Rule 11 because the defendants' misrepresentations required Lone Wolf to incur fees and costs to prove that they were false, and the withdrawal did nothing to cure that harm. Defendants respond that they timely withdrew the representations within Rule 11's safe harbor provision and thus cannot be liable for any sanctions. The Court will resolve this motion after reviewing the law governing Rule 11 motions.

LEGAL STANDARDS

Under Rule 11(b), an attorney, by signing any pleading or motion, certifies that "to the best of the [attorney's] knowledge, information, and belief, formed after an inquiry reasonable under the circumstances: . . .

(1) the factual contentions have evidentiary support or, if specifically so identified, will likely have evidentiary support after a reasonable opportunity for further investigation or discovery; and

(2) the denials of factual contentions are warranted on the evidence or, if specifically so identified, are reasonably based on belief or a lack of information."

Rule 11 is intended to deter baseless filings in district court and imposes a duty of "reasonable inquiry" so that anything filed with the court is "well grounded in fact, legally tenable, and not interposed for any improper purpose." *Islamic Shura Council v. F.B.I.*, 757 F.3d 870, 872 (9th Cir. 2014). A motion for sanctions may not be filed, however, unless there is strict compliance with Rule 11's safe harbor provision. That provision states that any motion for sanctions must be served on the offending party at least 21 days before the motion is filed with the court. Fed. R. Civ. P. 11(c)(2). The safe harbor provision further dictates that the motion may not be filed if the offending party timely "withdraw[s] or appropriately correct[s]" the challenged contention during the safe harbor period. *Id.*

If the Court finds a violation of Rule 11, it has the authority to make a monetary award that "should not exceed the expenses and attorney fees for the services directly and unavoidably caused by the violation of the certification requirement." *See 1993 Advisory Committee Notes.* That sanction can be imposed on "the persons—whether attorneys, law firms, or parties—who have violated the rule or who may be determined to be responsible for the violation." *Id.* The Ninth Circuit has affirmed an award of attorney fees against a party when that party was the "catalyst" behind the violations and was "well-positioned to investigate the facts supporting its claims." *Pan-Pacific & Low Ball Cable Television Co. v. Pacific Union*, 987 F.2d 594 (9th Cir. 1993).

ANALYSIS

In his Declarations, Shemesh denied that Sopcom and Bravoware were related to BravoTac. But in his deposition, he admitted that (1) BravoTac conducted business for Sopcom in 2013, (2) he is currently running BravoTac on behalf of Bravoware, and (3) Bravoware is doing business as BravoTac. Reidl claims that Shemesh might be mistaken, but Reidl has never presented any

evidence to support that claim, and Shemesh himself has never retracted his deposition testimony or even explained the blatant contradiction between his Declaration and his deposition. The only conclusion that can be drawn from this record is that Shemesh lied in his Declarations. His lies are attributed to Bravoware and Sopcom because he was speaking on their behalf as their owner. To uncover the truth, Lone Wolf was forced to expend substantial time and effort in discovery.

Reidl seeks to excuse himself because he was misled by his client, and because his own investigation appeared to confirm the truth of what Shemesh was telling him. The record supports Reidl's claim that he was misled by Shemesh up to a point. Reidl conducted his own investigation that seemed to confirm what Shemesh was telling him. But after the deposition on April 21, 2016, Reidl knew that the claims of no connection had no evidentiary support and yet he nevertheless filed the renewed motion to dismiss on May 19, 2016, advancing yet again Shemesh's lies that neither defendant "operates a web site" and that "the BravoTac website is not owned by either defendant." Rule 11 prohibits "reaffirming to the court and advocating positions contained in those pleadings and motions after learning that they cease to have any merit." *See 1993 Advisory Committee Notes.*

Reidl's filing of the renewed motion to dismiss violated Rule 11(b)(3) by making factual contentions without any evidentiary support. Prior to that, the Court finds that Reidl was misled by Shemesh. "[S]anctions should fall on the client rather than on counsel when the attorney has relied reasonably on the client's misrepresentations." Thus, Reidl is subject to sanctions only for the filing of the renewed motion to dismiss on May 19, 2016.

Rule 11(c)(1) also imposes sanctions on the party that is "responsible for the violation." Because Shemesh's lies are attributed to Sopcom and Bravoware, sanctions must also be imposed on these two defendants.

Reidl argues that because he withdrew the misrepresentations during Rule 11's safe harbor period, no sanctions can be awarded. But that argument misconstrues the purpose of the safe harbor. The immunity conferred during the safe harbor applies only if "the violation is corrected, as by withdrawing (whether formally or informally) some allegation or contention...." *See 1993 Advisory Committee Notes.* In other words, correction is the key—withdrawal is just one example of conduct that may, in some cases, completely correct the harm done. There is nothing magical about withdrawing allegations if the withdrawal does nothing to correct the harm. The conferral of immunity depends on correction.

Reidl's withdrawal did nothing to correct the harm here. Only an award of attorney fees can correct that harm.

As an independent ground for sanctions against Reidl, the Court relies on 28 U.S.C. §1927. This statute states that an attorney who "so multiplies the proceedings in any case unreasonably and vexatiously may be required by the court to satisfy personally the excess costs, expenses, and attorneys' fees reasonably incurred because of such conduct." To award fees under §1927, the court must find that an attorney acted "recklessly or in bad faith." *U.S. v. Blodgett*, 709 F.2d 608, 610 (9th Cir. 1983).... Reidl recklessly raised a frivolous argument when he filed his renewed motion to dismiss advancing Shemesh's lies. This multiplied the proceedings because Lone Wolf was forced to file a response. The sanctions for attorney fees against Reidl thus have an independent basis in §1927.

As an independent ground for sanctions against Bravoware and Sopcom, the Court relies on its inherent power to levy sanctions, including attorney fees, when a party has acted in "bad faith, vexatiously, wantonly, or for oppressive reasons." *Roadway Express, Inc. v. Piper*, 447 U.S. 752, 766 (1980). While the Court's inherent power extends to all litigation abuses, the litigant must have "engaged in bad faith or willful disobedience of a court's order." *Chambers v. NASCO, Inc.*, 501 U.S. 32, 46-47 (1991). Here, Shemesh lied in two Declarations forcing Lone Wolf to expend time and effort in discovery to uncover the truth. Shemesh therefore acted in bad faith, and that bad faith is attributed to Bravoware and Sopcom because he is their owner and lied on their behalf.

CONCLUSION

The Court will grant Lone Wolf's motion for sanctions. The Court will award sanctions against Reidl for violating Rule 11(b)(3) and 28 U.S.C. §1927, requiring payment to Lone Wolf of the attorney fees and costs it incurred in responding to the renewed motion to dismiss filed on May 19, 2016.

The Court will also award sanctions against defendants Bravoware and Sopcom pursuant to its inherent power, and under Rule 11(c)(1) because these defendants were responsible for violating Rule 11(b)(3), requiring payment to Lone Wolf of the attorney fees and costs it incurred for the following:

1. Responding to the first motion to dismiss;
2. Filing the motion to conduct discovery regarding BravoTac[;]
3. Responding to the renewed motion to dismiss[;]
4. Traveling and taking the deposition of Shemesh....

Notes & Questions

1. Consider again the difference between baseless factual assertions and frivolous legal positions. Which type of violation did the court find in *Lone Wolf*? Specifically, which part of Rule 11(b) did the court find was violated?

   Why did the court impose sanctions on Bravoware and Sopcom? Note the difference between *Lone Wolf*, in which Rule 11 sanctions were imposed on both the lawyer and his clients, and *Shelton*, in which only the lawyer faced Rule 11 sanctions.

   Why did the court impose sanctions on the lawyer, Reidl? If the misrepresentations were made by his client, Shemesh, why does the court find that the lawyer bears responsibility as well? What should Reidl have done differently?

2. Judge Winmill states that his imposition of sanctions does not violate the safe harbor provision of Rule 11(c)(2). Do you agree?

   The safe harbor provision of Rule 11(c)(2) was added in 1993 to address the concern that Rule 11 motions had become a tactical game in which parties engaged in finger pointing to gain leverage. Under the safe harbor provision, a party must *serve* a Rule 11 motion on the other party at least 21 days before the party may *file* the motion with the court. Because of the safe harbor provision, parties cannot go crying to the court every time they think the other side did something baseless. They can write their Rule 11 motion for sanctions, but they cannot present it to the court unless they have given the motion to the other party and given the party an opportunity to withdraw or amend the offending paper.

   In *Lone Wolf*, the defendants withdrew the statements that were said to have violated Rule 11. What is the judge's justification for imposing sanctions despite the withdrawal of the offending statements?

3. In addition to finding the conduct punishable under Rule 11, Judge Winmill cites two other bases for imposing sanctions in this case. First, he cites 28 U.S.C. §1927, the federal vexatious litigation statute, which provides:

   > Any attorney or other person admitted to conduct cases in any court of the United States or any Territory thereof who so multiplies the proceedings in any case unreasonably and vexatiously may be required by the court to satisfy personally the excess costs, expenses, and attorneys' fees reasonably incurred because of such conduct.

   Second, Judge Winmill cites his "inherent power" to impose sanctions under *Chambers v. NASCO*, 501 U.S. 32 (1991). In *Chambers*, the Supreme Court approved the power of a district judge to impose sanctions even if not authorized by a specific rule or statute, based on "the control necessarily vested in courts to manage their own affairs so as to achieve the orderly and expeditious disposition of cases." *Id.* at 43. The district judge in *Chambers* found that a litigant had engaged in fraudulent acts to deprive the court of jurisdiction, and had engaged in other abusive tactics outside of court to exhaust the other party into compliance. Rule 11 did not reach the conduct because it did not involve any papers filed with the court, and section 1927 did not reach the conduct because the perpetrator was not an attorney. Nevertheless, the Supreme Court upheld the imposition of sanctions based on the district judge's inherent power to control the litigation process.

Note that Judge Winmill relied on different sources of authority for different persons. Why did he rely on section 1927 as his back-up authority for sanctions against Reidl, but on inherent power as his back-up authority for sanctions against Bravoware and Sopcom?

More broadly, why did Judge Winmill feel the need to invoke any back-up authority at all? Didn't Rule 11 suffice for imposing sanctions on this lawyer and these litigants? Perhaps the judge simply took a belt-and-suspenders approach, as judges often do, citing each applicable basis even though one would have been enough. But another possibility is that the judge was concerned that his Rule 11 sanctions were subject to reversal on appeal for failure to comply with the letter of Rule 11's safe harbor provision, and he viewed section 1927 and inherent power as protection against reversal of the sanctions.

4. After the court imposed sanctions on the defendants and their lawyer, defense counsel withdrew and the defendants hired a new lawyer. The case proceeded to trial, where a jury found that defendants infringed Lone Wolf's trademark and awarded $37,500 in statutory damages. *See Lone Wolf Distributors, Inc. v. Bravoware, Inc.* (D. Idaho May 2, 2019).

5. As you read Rule 11, you may be surprised to see Rule 11(d), which declares that Rule 11 does not apply to the discovery process. Rest assured, this does *not* mean that lawyers and litigants are permitted to make factually baseless or legally frivolous discovery requests, responses, objections, and motions. Rather, this simply reflects the structure of the civil rules. The discovery rules contain their own provisions concerning certification and sanctions. If you look at Rule 26(g), you will see that it reads almost exactly like Rule 11, and additionally Rule 37 empowers courts to impose sanctions for discovery violations. We will explore discovery sanctions in Chapter 3.

6. At the outset of this section, we mentioned that each state has rules of professional conduct to govern lawyer conduct, and many of these rules are modeled on the American Bar Association's Model Rules of Professional Conduct (RPCs).

Of particular relevance to Rule 11, RPC 3.1 provides: "A lawyer shall not bring or defend a proceeding, or assert or controvert an issue therein, unless there is a basis in law and fact for doing so that is not frivolous, which includes a good faith argument for an extension, modification or reversal of existing law." Note how closely this ethics rule echoes Rule 11. In *Shelton* and in *Lone Wolf*, did the lawyers' conduct violate not only Rule 11, but also RPC 3.1? Whereas a judge enforces Rule 11 as part of the litigation process, rules of professional conduct such as RPC 3.1 are enforced through a separate lawyer disciplinary process. As a practical matter, which type of enforcement do you think is more likely to occur in situations like *Shelton* and *Lone Wolf*?

When thinking about Rule 11 and RPC 3.1, you may wonder about criminal defense lawyers. Is it prohibited for a lawyer to assist a criminal defendant in entering a not-guilty plea if the lawyer knows that the client committed the crime? No, it is not prohibited. The lawyer may defend the client and demand that the government meet its burden of proving each element of the crime beyond a reasonable doubt. Indeed, RPC 3.1 makes this point explicit: "A lawyer for the defendant in a criminal proceeding, or the respondent in a proceeding that could result in incarceration, may nevertheless so defend the proceeding as to require that every element of the case be established." In this regard, civil and criminal proceedings differ markedly. Unlike in criminal cases, Rule 11(b)(4) and RPC 3.1 make it clear that a lawyer cannot assert a denial on behalf of a civil defendant if the lawyer knows the denial is baseless. Remember that Rule 11, as a Federal Rule of Civil Procedure, applies only to civil proceedings.

7. In addition to RPC 3.1, as you learn about the litigation process you should be aware of several other ethics rules that bear on the lawyer's role as advocate. These rules impose duties that lawyers owe to clients as well as duties that lawyers owe to courts and to the legal system.

   Lawyers owe clients a duty of *competence, see* RPC 1.1 ("A lawyer shall provide competent representation to a client. Competent representation requires the legal knowledge, skill, thoroughness and preparation reasonably necessary for the representation."), a duty of *diligence, see* RPC 1.3 ("A lawyer shall act with reasonable diligence and promptness in representing a client."), a duty of *confidentiality, see* RPC 1.6 (imposing a duty of confidentiality with certain limited exceptions), and a duty of *loyalty, see, e.g.,* RPC 1.7 (prohibiting certain conflicts of interest regarding current clients), RPC 1.9 (prohibiting certain conflicts of interest regarding former clients).

   In addition to duties owed to clients, lawyers owe certain duties to the courts and the legal system, including a duty of *candor.* Specifically, under the Model Rules and the ethics rules of most states, lawyers are forbidden to lie to a judge, and lawyers are forbidden to knowingly offer false evidence. *See* RPC 3.3(a) ("A lawyer shall not knowingly: (1) make a false statement of fact or law to a tribunal . . . ; or (3) offer evidence that the lawyer knows to be false.").

   It is noteworthy that while some ethics rules are designed to protect clients from careless or predatory lawyers, other rules are designed to protect the integrity of the legal system itself. The duties created by Rule 11 fall into the latter category, and the threat of sanctions is intended to deter lawyers and litigants who might otherwise be tempted to make baseless allegations or to assert frivolous claims or defenses.

THE BIG PICTURE

Both Rule 11 and the Rules of Professional Conduct reflect an inherent tension in the lawyer's role. On the one hand, the client is entitled to a lawyer who serves as a loyal advocate—one who keeps the client's confidences and who uses professional skill to advance the client's objectives. The U.S. litigation process is an adversary system, and lawyers play a critical role as advocates on behalf of the disputants. On the other hand, the litigation process is not a game. The lawyer, as a professional with an important role in the legal system (or, as some describe it, as an "officer of the court"), not only owes duties to the client, but also owes duties as a protector of the integrity of the process. For most lawyers, these multiple duties come to feel natural over a career of representing clients; they likely will come to feel natural to you as you internalize the norms and regulations of the profession. Some beginning law students may crave the simplicity of a pure zealous-advocacy model of the lawyer's role, unconstrained by pesky details like facts and law and ethics, but that is not the reality of the lawyer's role in the litigation process, as both the ethics rules and Rule 11 emphasize.

CHAPTER 3

Discovery

As any litigator will tell you, it's all about the facts. Don't let a good legal education fool you into thinking that most case outcomes, particularly at the trial level, depend primarily on disputed questions of law. Mastery of the law is important, but when representing clients in the real world, mastery of the facts matters just as much and often much more.

To illustrate, suppose you represent Akos Swierkiewicz—the plaintiff in *Swierkiewicz v. Sorema N.A.*, 534 U.S. 506 (2002), from Chapter 2—on his claim of employment discrimination. The Supreme Court has ruled that your client's complaint suffices and his suit may move forward. Now what? How are you going to get the information you need to prove that your client was discriminated against on the basis of age and national origin? Some information, such as speaking with your client, is easily available to you. Other information, however, is in the possession of Sorema or others. You want to see the company's personnel file on Swierkiewicz. You want to see internal e-mails and other correspondence regarding the decision to demote and terminate your client, and regarding the selection of his replacement. You want data on the company's record with regard to hiring and firing employees of particular ages and national origins. You want to ask the CEO why he demoted and fired your client. If you cannot get your hands on this sort of information, it will be difficult indeed to prove your case.

Discovery refers to the process by which a party in a lawsuit requires other parties or witnesses to provide information relevant to the case. As compared with the legal systems of most other countries, United States discovery provides exceptionally broad access to information, and it places information-gathering power mostly in the hands of the litigants and their lawyers, rather than the judge. The Supreme Court has described the discovery process as "one of the most significant innovations of the Federal Rules of Civil Procedure" and has explained that its purpose is "for the parties to obtain the fullest possible knowledge of the issues and facts before trial." *Hickman v. Taylor*, 329 U.S. 495, 500-01 (1947). The Court also has described the American discovery process as expensive and potentially abusive. *See Bell Atlantic Corp. v. Twombly*, 550 U.S. 544, 558 (2007). As you learn about the discovery process, consider its power to help parties uncover facts and thus to help courts adjudicate cases on the merits. But consider, on the other hand, its potential for intrusion and expense, and the hard question of whether truth is always worth the price.

What is that price? The discovery process imposes costs on parties and witnesses in terms of money, time, and privacy. However, the amount and nature of discovery varies enormously from case to case. Some cases involve massive discovery involving millions of pages of documents, terabytes of electronically stored information, and many hours of witness depositions. Some cases, however, involve little formal discovery. According to a 2009 study by the Federal Judicial Center, the median cost of discovery in federal court civil actions, including attorneys' fees, was $15,000 to $20,000. At the tenth percentile, the cost of discovery was only $1,600 for plaintiffs and $5,000 for defendants, but at the ninety-fifth percentile the cost was $280,000 and $300,000. In other words, discovery can be a huge expense in document-heavy cases involving complex factual disputes, but there are plenty of other cases in which discovery costs are quite manageable. The study found that in most cases, alongside or in place of formal discovery, parties engaged in informal exchanges of documents and other information. Emery G. Lee III & Thomas E. Willging, *National, Case-Based Civil Rules Survey: Preliminary Report to the Judicial Conference Advisory Committee on Civil Rules* (Fed. Judicial Ctr. 2009).

There are several steps to understanding the discovery process. One, you need to learn how each discovery tool works. Two, you need to see how these tools can fit into an overall strategy of discovery and factual investigation. Three, you must grasp the scope of permissible discovery. This third step entails mastering the legal concepts of relevance, proportionality, privilege, and the work-product doctrine. Four, you need to understand the procedures by which discovery disputes get resolved, including motions to compel, motions for protective orders, and sanctions. Every lawyer—whether one who litigates disputes or one who advises clients about matters that may someday be topics of dispute—needs to understand how the discovery process works and the scope of information it can reach.

A. DISCOVERY DEVICES

Interrogatories. Oral depositions. Written depositions. Document production. E-discovery. Inspection of things and land. Mental and physical examinations. Requests for admission. Disclosures. The discovery rules hand lawyers a giant box full of powerful tools for extracting information. Learning to use the discovery devices is a lot like learning to wield a wrench, a screwdriver, and a hammer. Knowing what a wrench is and how it works is only the first step; you also must develop a sense of when a wrench is the right tool for the job. You can bang a nail into a wall with your wrench, but you will find it more effective to do it with a hammer. You get the point: If there is certain information you need in order to represent your client in litigation, there may be multiple discovery tools in your toolbox that could do the job, but the skilled lawyer knows whether a deposition, interrogatory, document request, informal investigation, or some other device is the most efficient and effective way to get the needed information.

As you learn about the mechanics of each of the discovery devices, take note of certain distinctions among them. For each discovery device, can you use it to get information only from the other parties in the lawsuit or from anyone who has the information? Can you use the device on an unlimited basis, constrained only by your client's budget and cost-benefit balancing, or does the rule impose a limit on the number of uses? Can you use it without seeking permission, or do you need leave of court? To the extent the device elicits answers to questions, are the answers provided directly by witnesses or are they filtered through the language of lawyers? For now, focus on these "how" questions—questions that go to the mechanics and uses of the various discovery devices. We will turn to the "what" questions—questions about what information you can demand—in Part B.

(1) Mandatory Disclosures

The mandatory disclosure provisions of Federal Rule of Civil Procedure 26(a) differ from all of the other discovery devices. The difference is so basic that a more precise title for this chapter would have been "Disclosures and Discovery." The discovery devices—interrogatories, depositions, document production, and others—start with a request from the party seeking the information, and the responding party is obligated to provide information in response to the request. The mandatory disclosure provisions require parties to disclose certain information to each other without even being asked. Pre-discovery discovery, if you will.

What must be provided in the mandatory initial disclosures? Rule 26(a) deserves a careful read. First, each party must disclose the name and contact information of every witness likely to have discoverable information that the disclosing party may use to support its position. Second, each party must provide a description, by category and location, of all documents and electronically stored information that the disclosing party has and may use to support its claims or defenses. Third, a party seeking damages must provide a computation of each category of damages, along with the material on which the computations are based. Fourth, the parties must disclose any applicable liability insurance policies.

The information in the mandatory initial disclosures is not as extensive as that which is available by using discovery tools, but the disclosures provide a starting point. The idea behind Rule 26(a) is that if basic information would be requested and provided as a matter of course in any lawsuit, it is faster and cheaper to make the disclosure automatic rather than to require parties to slog through the request-and-response process of discovery. Even so, the rule was controversial when it was first adopted on an experimental basis in 1993. Some lawyers objected that the whole idea of mandatory disclosures violated the spirit of the adversary system because it required parties to divulge information to the other side without even having been asked. Indeed, important language in Rule 26(a)—limiting witness disclosures and document disclosures to evidence that the disclosing party *may use* to support its own claims or defenses—was added by amendment in 2000 to mollify staunch adversarialists who objected to the prospect of disclosing information harmful to their client's position in the absence of a request from the other side. Under Rule 26(a) as amended, if a party plans to use at trial information from a particular witness, the party must disclose the name and contact information of that witness to the other side, but if the party does not plan to use any information from that witness in support of the party's position, then the rule does not require disclosure. The rule now largely avoids forcing a party to disclose at the outset information that harms the party's own position. Of course, each party will be required to reveal harmful information if asked about it in interrogatories, at depositions, or by document requests, but at least the party can withhold the damaging information until the adversary asks for it.

Rule 26, in combination with Rule 16, sets up rather elaborate provisions for the timing of initial disclosures. First, the parties (through their lawyers) develop a discovery plan. Note that this responsibility belongs to the parties, not the judge. The parties hold a discovery conference and then submit their proposed discovery plan to the judge. A judge typically issues a scheduling order at a scheduling conference, after the submission of a discovery plan. Mandatory initial disclosures occur either at the discovery conference or within 14 days afterwards. *See* Fed. R. Civ. P. 26(f); *see also* Fed. R. Civ. P. 16(b). Generally, parties cannot initiate discovery efforts until after they have met at the discovery conference.

In addition to the initial disclosures, Rule 26(a) requires *expert disclosures* and *pretrial disclosures*. These are also mandatory, but they occur later in the litigation process as the parties are getting ready for trial. If a party plans to use an expert witness at trial, Rule 26(a)(2) requires the party to disclose the identity of that expert to the other parties, along with a written report from the expert stating the expert's opinions, qualifications, and other information. The expert disclosures reduce surprise at trial and give opposing parties the opportunity to prepare for cross-examination or counter-testimony. Pretrial disclosures, addressed in Rule 26(a)(3), occur shortly before trial and require each party to provide the others with a list of witnesses the party expects to call at trial, depositions the party plans to present as evidence at trial, and the documents, exhibits, and summaries of any other evidence they plan to offer at trial.

(2) Interrogatories

Written questions, written answers. Rule 33 permits each party to serve each other party with a limited number of interrogatories (sometimes informally called *rogs*), and the responding party must answer in writing and under oath. If the responding party has the answer within its knowledge or control, then it must provide that answer unless it asserts an objection such as irrelevance, privilege, or undue burden—objections we will explore below in Part B.

Interrogatories offer a straightforward way to obtain objective information from other parties. Lawyers use them to get factual details, supporting data, names and contact information of witnesses, identity and location of documents, information about corporate structure, and other factual information that is susceptible to specific, well-defined questions.

Sometimes lawyers use interrogatories to ask about the other party's contentions in the case. For example, an interrogatory might say, "Please state all facts upon which you rely to support the allegation in paragraph 5 of the Complaint that defendant acted negligently." These are known as *contention interrogatories*, and they are what Rule 33 is referring to when it says that an "interrogatory is not objectionable merely because it asks for an opinion or contention that relates to fact or the application of law to fact." Contention interrogatories help flush out the who, what, when, where, why, and how of the other party's claims or defenses.

Rule 33 limits interrogatories to 25 questions, unless the parties stipulate otherwise or the court orders that the number be changed. *See* Rule 33(a)(1). In complex cases, it makes sense for parties to agree to a higher number, as interrogatories provide a relatively inexpensive way for both sides to obtain information. The rule makes it clear that you cannot circumvent the limit by breaking each interrogatory into multiple subparts; each discrete subpart counts as one of the 25 interrogatories, regardless of how they are numbered. Interrogatories, unlike some other discovery devices, are limited to the parties in the case. Each party may serve interrogatories on each other party, but to get information from nonparties, you must use other devices such as depositions and document requests.

STRATEGY SESSION

When thinking about how to use interrogatories, keep in mind who will probably write the answers. Interrogatory answers tend to be drafted by the responding party's attorney. The substance of the answers comes from the responding parties, who are under oath to provide truthful answers to the best of their knowledge, but the language is often filtered through lawyers. Fuzzy questions generate unhelpful responses. Don't use an interrogatory to ask: "Was your car in good condition at the time of the accident?" Do use an interrogatory to ask: "On what dates in the past five years has your car been serviced, who provided the service, and what services were performed?" Don't ask: "Does your company engage in employment discrimination?" Do ask: "State the number of employees in management positions, by race and gender, from January 1, 2019, to the present." For getting statistical data or other specific factual information, interrogatories are perfect. They are cheap and efficient, they provide written answers to your questions under oath, and the responding party can look things up to provide accurate information. They do not, however, give you an opportunity for follow-up questions as in oral depositions, so you'll get nowhere with interrogatories that allow evasive answers.

(3) Depositions

In a deposition, an attorney poses questions to a witness and the witness answers those questions under oath. Generally, a court reporter makes a verbatim transcript of the questions and answers; sometimes the deposition is videotaped. Of all the discovery devices, a deposition looks the most like a trial, except that it is not at the courthouse (depositions usually are held in conference rooms at lawyers' offices) and there is no judge present (except in rare situations like President Bill Clinton's deposition when he was sued by Paula Jones for sexual harassment).

> **Terminology Tip**
>
> The noun is *deposition*; the verb is *depose*. Do not say that a lawyer "depositioned" witness X. Rather, say that the lawyer *deposed* X. Alternatively, say that the lawyer *took X's deposition*. The person being deposed is called a *deponent*, but *witness* works too. And lawyers use *notice* not only as a noun as in the phrase *deposition notice*, but also as a verb to describe the act of formally announcing they will take someone's deposition. Thus, when a party has notified all of the other parties about the time and place of X's deposition, you would say that the party *noticed* the deposition of X.

To depose a witness, a party serves a deposition notice, informing the deponent and all of the other parties about the time and place of the deposition. May depositions be used to get information from anyone, or are they limited to parties? Look at Rule 30. The language in Rule 30(a)(1) that a party may depose "any person, including a party" makes it clear that depositions can be used not only to get information from other parties in the litigation, but also from anyone else. It is generally agreed that one may depose an individual who is a party simply by serving notice of the deposition (although the rules do not say so explicitly), but to depose a witness who is not a party to the lawsuit, you need a subpoena to compel the person's attendance at the deposition. *See* Rule 30(a)(1), Rule 45. The rules set parameters to avoid making the process too inconvenient for the deponent, but depositions nonetheless can be a burdensome process.

Rule 30 limits each party to ten depositions, and it limits each deposition to one seven-hour day, but like nearly all the details of the discovery rules, these limits can be altered by stipulation or by court order. *See* Rules 30(a)(2), Rule 30(d)(1).

In addition to the lawyer taking the deposition, often there is a lawyer "defending" the deposition. Typically, this is a lawyer who represents the opposing party to the side taking the deposition. For example, if the deponent is an employee of a corporation that is a party to the case, the lawyer defending the deposition may be a lawyer for the corporation. If the deponent is a plaintiff or defendant in the action, then the deponent's lawyer almost certainly would be present. In an action with multiple parties, there may be several lawyers who participate. Prior to the deposition, a defending lawyer typically would have prepared the witness by explaining how depositions work, helping the witness to anticipate questions, and emphasizing the duty to tell the truth but also encouraging the witness not to volunteer more information than each question calls for. During a deposition, defending or participating lawyers may object to questions. Except for objections on grounds of privilege, however, lawyers generally may not instruct the deponent not to answer the question. Instead, if the questioner persists with the question under objection, the deponent is expected to answer, and the lawyers may make motions to the court afterwards to sort out whether certain questions were permissible and whether the answers may be used as evidence. *See* Rule 30(c)(2).

Depositions have several advantages over interrogatories. First, depositions enable you to get answers straight from the horse's mouth, in contrast to interrogatories, which give the opposing lawyer time to phrase each answer in the least damaging way. At a deposition, you ask your question and the witness gives an answer in his or her own words. Notwithstanding the common practice of "deposition prep" described above, a deposition provides a less filtered response than an interrogatory. Deposition testimony is often used at trial to question the credibility of a witness who changes her testimony from the deposition to the trial. However, unlike interrogatories, depositions do not give deponents the chance to look things up or to double-check information, so interrogatories tend to work better for obtaining hard-to-remember detailed information. Look at any deposition transcript and you will see that one of the most common phrases is "I don't recall." Second, depositions give you the opportunity to size up the adversary's witnesses, to see how compelling they would be on the witness stand at trial. Third, at a deposition you can ask follow-up questions. If the deponent tries to be evasive, you can rephrase your question as necessary until you get the information you seek. When a deponent gives an incomplete response, you can follow up with further questions to nail down the information. You cannot do that with interrogatories. When an interrogatory response is evasive or incomplete, you can send another set of interrogatories (if you have not yet reached the limit), but that is a slow and unsatisfying way to get a complete answer. Fourth, at a deposition you can make on-the-spot decisions about where to go with your questions. A deponent's answers may lead you to fruitful lines of inquiry that you had not thought of.

Depositions may be the most powerful pretrial tool for extracting information, but they are also the most expensive. To take a deposition, you need the room, court reporter, and transcripts; each side pays lawyers for their time; and, depending on the location, there may be travel expenses as well. In big cases, there may be multiple lawyers for each of multiple parties. Picture a dozen lawyers sitting around a conference table with the deponent and court reporter, some lawyers asking questions, some defending, and some just there to observe and to ask follow-up questions if necessary. To think of the number of billable hours is painful (at least for the clients). Attorneys planning discovery need to think about the stakes of the case, as well as the importance of the witness, when deciding whether to take a particular deposition. Interrogatories, pretrial disclosures, and other sources of information help lawyers identify the most important witnesses to depose.

Frequently, parties need to obtain information from a corporation or other organization but do not know the name of the individual within the company who possesses the relevant knowledge. For a deposition, you need to pose your questions to an actual human being, but what if you don't know which human to ask? You need information about the company's chemical disposal policies, for example, but you do not know the name of the employee who bears that responsibility. This is where Rule 30(b)(6) comes in handy. Rule 30(b)(6) allows you to send a deposition notice to the company describing the topics to be addressed in the deposition, and the company must identify and produce a deponent with the knowledge to speak about those topics. As an alternative, you could use interrogatories to elicit the names of employees with specific responsibilities, and then you could notice the depositions of those individuals. The interrogatory-to-deposition approach is unavailable, however, if the company is not a party, and in any event Rule 30(b)(6) depositions accomplish the same objective more directly.

When lawyers think about depositions, they nearly always mean depositions by oral examination, the type of deposition governed by Rule 30. But there is another type of deposition, found in Rule 31: the deposition by written questions. Depositions by written questions look like a cross between a deposition and an interrogatory. A party delivers the questions to the court reporter, who in turn asks the deponent the questions and makes a verbatim transcript of the answers under oath. This process obviously loses one of the main advantages of depositions, the ability to ask follow-up questions. Seldom used, Rule 31 written questions are a way to get basic factual information, especially from nonparties because interrogatories can be used only on parties.

STRATEGY SESSION

Do lawyers depose every person who has relevant information? No, not even close, for at least three reasons. First, the rules impose a presumptive limit of ten depositions per party. Second, depositions are expensive, so unless the stakes are high, some depositions aren't worth the cost. Third—and this part is obvious to every lawyer but not so obvious to many law students—lawyers generally do not depose their own witnesses. A deposition is a tool for forcing a witness to answer your questions. If you need information from your own client or from a friendly witness, all you have to do is ask. An exception is if your witness may be unavailable for trial— perhaps the witness is ill or may be out of the country during the trial—in which case a deposition offers a way to preserve testimony for use at trial.

(4) Production of Documents, Electronically Stored Information, and Things; Inspection of Land

Unlike depositions and interrogatories, which involve asking questions and getting answers, Rule 34 requests are all about getting access to stuff. When you read Rule 34—indeed, even when you see its weirdly long title—you start to appreciate how many things lawyers need to get their hands on to investigate the facts of a dispute. Before turning to documents and data, the heart of Rule 34, start with tangible things and land. Some disputes involve physical evidence. In an auto accident case, a party may need access to the other party's crumpled vehicle and the opportunity to inspect it with a mechanic. In a pharmaceutical product liability case, it could be a bottle of pills. Rule 34 allows a party to "inspect, copy, test, or sample" items that are in another's "possession, custody, or control." Similarly, some disputes require inspection of property. A party may need to enter the opposing party's factory. Or in a toxic spill case, a party may need to test soil on another's land. Rule 34 provides the discovery tool for "entry onto designated land or other property possessed or controlled by the responding party, so that the requesting party may inspect, measure, survey, photograph, test, or sample the property or any designated object or operation on it."

Mostly, however, Rule 34 requests are about getting documents and their electronic equivalents. Nearly all litigation involves documentary evidence, although the amount varies widely. Depending on the type of dispute, document production may include business records, medical records, e-mails, memos, investigation reports, personnel records, contracts, deeds, or anything else in which information is stored on paper or electronically. The rule broadly describes "any designated documents or electronically stored information—including writings, drawings, graphs, charts, photographs, sound recordings, images, and other data or data compilations—stored in any medium from which information can be obtained."

Some document requests name particular documents that are needed, such as a specific contract. More often, requests identify categories of documents or subject matter, such as "all documents relating to the proposed joint venture between plaintiff and defendant." The risky thing about drafting document requests is this: Frame your request too narrowly, and you might miss the critical piece of evidence; frame your request too broadly, and you might spend weeks in a warehouse (physical or digital) full of useless documents. And if you frame your request carelessly, you might find yourself on the losing end of a battle over discoverability.

Discovery of electronically stored information—or *e-discovery*, as many lawyers call it—unsurprisingly has become a dominant aspect of Rule 34 discovery. Until not too long ago, lawyers simply treated electronic information as "documents" within the rule's meaning. The term "electronically stored information" was added to Rule 34 in 2006 to leave no doubt about the discoverability of electronic information and to establish a basis for several special e-discovery rules. For purposes of discoverability analysis, it usually should make no difference whether information happens to be stored on paper, hard drive, flash drive, network, cloud, CD, tape, laptop, handheld device, videotape, audiotape, or any other medium. If information is relevant, nonprivileged, and proportional (see Part B below), then in general it is discoverable regardless of its format. In fact, plenty of electronic discovery is easier to produce than hardcopy documents. Difficult-to-access forms of electronically stored information, however, are subject to a special proportionality analysis under Rule 26(b)(2), discussed later in this chapter. That rule specifically mentions that parties may refuse to provide e-discovery if the information is "not reasonably accessible because of undue burden or cost," and gives the court discretion to order discovery from such inaccessible electronic sources upon a showing of good cause.

The discovery rules allow parties to obtain evidence both from other parties and from nonparties, whoever has possession or control of the relevant documents, data, things, or property. For parties, you simply make a Rule 34 request. For nonparties, you must use a subpoena under Rule 45 to compel nonparties to produce documents, electronically stored information, or tangible things or to permit the inspection of premises.

(5) Physical and Mental Examinations

A party's physical or mental condition may be an issue in a case. In a personal injury lawsuit, to take the most obvious example, the defendant may wish to determine whether the plaintiff's injuries are as serious as the plaintiff alleges and whether the plaintiff's theory of causation is accurate. While information could also be obtained by requesting medical records and by deposing the plaintiff's physician, a defendant understandably may wish to have the plaintiff examined by a suitably licensed person of the defendant's choosing.

As a discovery tool, Rule 35 physical and mental examinations resemble Rule 34 requests for inspection. Instead of inspecting a crumpled car or a pile of documents, you need to inspect a person's body or mind. The rule limits such discovery to cases in which a party's physical or mental condition is "in controversy," which may include cases in which a party's blood type is relevant and disputed. Most people would find document requests less intrusive than being poked and prodded physically by a physician or mentally by a psychologist or some other qualified examiner. Therefore Rule 35 permits physical or mental exams only with a court order based on a showing of good cause. Unlike the other discovery tools, which can be used without making a motion to the court, a party must explain to the judge why a physical or mental examination is needed.

In *Sibbach v. Wilson & Co.*, 312 U.S. 1 (1941), when the discovery rules were very new, a party challenged the validity of Rule 35 under the Rules Enabling Act, 28 U.S.C. §2072, which provides that rules of civil procedure must actually regulate procedure and may not abridge substantive rights. The question was whether a rule that forced parties to submit to an intrusive physical examination violated substantive rights. The dissent contended, "I deem a requirement as to the invasion of the person to stand on a very different footing from questions pertaining to the discovery of documents, pre-trial procedure and other devices for the expeditious, economic and fair conduct of litigation." *Id.* at 18 (Frankfurter, J., dissenting). The majority, however, held that the rule on physical examinations was a legitimate rule of procedure, did not violate any substantive right, and was therefore valid under the Rules Enabling Act.

(6) Requests for Admission

The key to understanding requests for admission is to think of them functionally as a kind of pleading—like complaints, answers, and replies—rather than as a standard discovery device like interrogatories and depositions. Chronologically, the requests are used during the discovery process in litigation. And structurally, the federal rules place Rule 36 among the discovery rules (Rules 26-37). But their function resembles the admissions and denials of a defendant's answer during the pleading stage.

Requests for admission allow one party to ask another party to admit specific facts, and the responding party must admit, deny, or state exactly why the party cannot truthfully admit or deny. Anything admitted "is conclusively established unless the court, on motion, permits the admission to be withdrawn or amended." Fed. R. Civ. P. 36(b). Requests to admit, when used effectively, narrow the issues in dispute by establishing certain facts as uncontested. For instance, lawyers often use requests for admission to establish the authenticity of specific documents that may be used as evidence at trial.

Admissions apply only to the case in which they are requested; they may not be used against the party in any other proceeding. In this sense, their function is more limited than other discovery responses, which sometimes may be used as evidence in other cases. In the particular action, however, an admission completely resolves the admitted fact. In this sense, admissions are more conclusive than other discovery responses, which merely constitute evidence and may be refuted with contrary evidence. There is no numerical limit on the use of requests for admission, but they are limited to the actual parties to the action.

THE BIG PICTURE

You may wonder why some discovery devices can be deployed on nonparties while others can be used only on parties. The parties to a lawsuit are not the only ones with relevant information, so the discovery rules permit deploying document requests and depositions to get information from nonparties with the use of a subpoena. But some discovery devices are ill suited to use on nonparties. By limiting interrogatories to parties, the rule avoids burdening others with pressure to hire a lawyer to draft responses. Physical and mental exams are uniquely intrusive, and rarely do cases involve the disputed physical or mental condition of someone other than a party or someone in a party's custody or control. Finally, requests to admit, by definition, serve only to define the facts in contention between the actual parties; using them on nonparties would be nonsensical. Thus, while the discovery rules make it easy to obtain information from both parties and nonparties, only certain tools are available for the latter.

B. SCOPE OF DISCOVERY

How far can a party go in demanding information from others? That is, what is the scope of information that is available by using these discovery tools? Rule 26(b)(1) of the Federal Rules of Civil Procedure sets out the basic scope of discovery: "Parties may obtain discovery regarding any *nonprivileged* matter that is *relevant* to any party's claim or defense and *proportional* to the needs of the case, considering the importance of the issues at stake in the action, the amount in controversy, the parties' relative access to relevant information, the parties' resources, the importance of discovery in resolving the issues, and whether the burden or expense of the proposed discovery outweighs its likely benefit" (emphasis added). In other words, if some piece of information is *relevant*, if the burden of the discovery is not out of *proportion* to the needs of the case, and if the information does not fall within a legally recognized *privilege* or the work-product doctrine, then that information is discoverable.

(1) Relevance and Proportionality

(a) Relevance

The law of evidence, which provides a starting point for the relevance requirement in discovery, defines relevance broadly: "Evidence is relevant if (a) it has any tendency to make a fact more or less probable than it would be without the evidence; and (b) the fact is of consequence in determining the action." Fed. R. Evid. 401. If an item of information is just one piece of the puzzle, it is relevant. If it tends to make one story more plausible than another, it is relevant. If it makes a witness or a document a bit more credible, or a bit less credible, it is relevant. Note that evidence does not have to be direct to be relevant. Lots of relevant evidence is circumstantial.

If relevance potentially sweeps so broadly, you might ask what could make a piece of testimony or other evidence *ir*relevant? The law. Under the substantive law that applies to a dispute, each claim or defense requires certain elements or takes into account certain factors. To be relevant, the evidence must have some bearing, however slight, on facts that have some legal consequence in the matter. In an auto accident negligence lawsuit, for example, one party may wish to find out whether the adversary party is wealthy (both because that information could affect settlement negotiations and because it could affect a jury's perception of the other party), but an interrogatory inquiring into the party's net worth would be rejected as irrelevant because it has no bearing on the material issues in dispute.

Every word of Rule 26(b)(1) deserves attention. Take the last sentence, which drives home an important point about the breadth of relevance: "Information within this scope of discovery need not be admissible in evidence to be discoverable." For example, suppose a party seeks discovery from X about what X heard Y say about what happened. At trial, that would be considered hearsay. It would be inadmissible. In the discovery process, however, one cannot object to the request on grounds of hearsay (or any other basis of inadmissibility, other than relevance, privilege, and proportionality). One piece of info leads to another. By asking X what X heard, the discovering party may get information that will lead to other evidence. As long as the information is relevant, nonprivileged, and proportional, it is discoverable. Similarly, the rule allows discovery about where to find other evidence or witnesses.

Broad as the scope of discovery is, it used to be even broader. Before 2000, Rule 26(b)(1) permitted discovery "relevant to the *subject matter* involved in the pending action" (emphasis added). Out of concern that the "subject matter" language permitted excessively broad fishing expeditions, the rule was amended in 2000 to limit the general scope of discovery to information "relevant to any party's claim or defense." The amended rule still allowed a court to order discovery of "any matter relevant to the subject matter" if the requesting party showed good cause. In 2015, however, Rule 26(b)(1) was amended to eliminate the "relevant to the subject matter" language altogether. The current rule allows discovery regarding "any nonprivileged matter that is relevant to any party's claim or defense and proportional to the needs of the case." That is still a pretty broad standard, but when viewed in historical perspective, the shifts of the last two decades have made it easier for judges to deny discovery if a party cannot explain how the information relates to the claims or defenses in the case.

(b) Proportionality

The burden of discovery should not be disproportionate to its benefit. Remember the language of Rule 26(b)(1). It says that information is discoverable if it is relevant, nonprivileged, and "proportional to the needs of the case, considering the importance of the issues at stake in the action, the amount in controversy, the parties' relative access to relevant information, the parties' resources, the importance of the discovery in resolving the issues, and whether the burden or expense of the proposed discovery outweighs its likely benefit." Although the discovery rules had long included proportionality as a consideration, the basic rule on scope of discovery previously focused on relevance and privilege. In 2015, the proportionality language was moved into Rule 26(b)(1) to emphasize that proportionality is just as important as relevance and privilege in the analysis of whether information is discoverable.

The rule lists six factors. You can analyze them one by one if you like that sort of thing, but really it all comes down to a cost-benefit analysis. The final factor— "whether the burden or expense of the proposed discovery outweighs its likely benefit"—pulls them all together. Is the information more readily available from another source? Is the discovery request too burdensome or expensive given the stakes of the dispute and the importance of this piece of information? Sometimes the proportionality test means that information is discoverable only from certain sources rather than more difficult sources. Other times, it makes information completely non-discoverable because the burden outweighs the benefit. Note the closeness of the relevance and proportionality inquiries. A burdensome discovery request may be disproportionate if the information has only marginal relevance, but an equally burdensome request may be reasonable if the information bears on a key fact in the case. Thus, hard-to-reach information may not be worth the trouble if the case is small and the information tangential, but if the stakes are high and the hard-to-reach information is key, a court will allow discovery even if it is quite burdensome. The following case shows a district judge trying to strike the right balance, and offers a nice example of how to conduct an analysis of relevance and proportionality.

FASSETT v. SEARS HOLDING CORP.
319 F.R.D. 143 (M.D. Pa. 2017)

BRANN, District Judge.

Some personal injury cases spring from highly questionable circumstances, and others from undeniably life-altering events. Setting aside ultimate questions of liability and damages, this litigation is tragically one of the latter. When Plaintiff Daniel Fassett heard sputtering sounds emitting from his lawnmower, he attempted to relieve the pressure in its fuel tank by loosening the cap. As he did so, gasoline sprayed from the machine onto his body, igniting in flames. Mr. Fassett sustained serious injuries and shortly thereafter initiated this products liability action.

Although the litigation has progressed in a timely fashion since its inception in May 2015, the parties have recently reached a rather technical impasse. That quandary involves, among other questions, the extent to which material about alternative fuel cap designs and distinct lawnmower layouts may be discoverable. In other words, the parties have struggled to define the outer bounds of discovery in this case: what, if anything, can be discovered about parts or mowers not involved in the subject fire? By presenting such a question, this dispute necessarily calls upon the Court to apply the proportionality provision of recently amended Federal Rule of Civil Procedure 26 to the case's technologically nuanced facts.

As explained more fully below, I hold that in a products liability suit such as this one, faithful adherence to amended Rule 26(b)(1)'s renewed proportionality mandate is furthered considerably by implementation of a sliding scale analysis: material corresponding to alternative designs or components that exhibit significant similarities to the design or component at issue should be discoverable in the greatest quantities and for the most varied purposes; however, material corresponding to alternative designs or components that share less in common with the contested design or component should be incrementally less discoverable—and for more limited purposes—as those similarities diminish.

BACKGROUND

The alleged mechanism by which Mr. Fassett sustained his injuries, though difficult to recount, is central to an appropriate disposition. Mr. Fassett had been operating a Sears Craftsman "Zero Turn" riding lawnmower in May 2013 for about one hour when he heard what he described as "spitting" or "sputtering" in the gas tank. The noise reminded him of the sound of water having seeped into the gas. After moving the lawnmower into his garage and turning it off, Mr. Fassett lifted the seat so that he could reach the fuel tank. Upon visualizing the tank, he observed that the hissing was coming from underneath the gas cap, and he saw that the gas tank had visibly expanded.

In an effort to release what he believed was built-up pressure in the tank, he began to turn the gas cap. While the cap rotated, gasoline sprayed from the tank and "doused" his clothes and body. As he turned away from the machine to run, the gas cap burst off the tank, and more gasoline sprayed from within. Almost immediately, Mr. Fassett "heard the gas ignite and knew he was on fire." Flames covered his back and the left side of his body, traveling as high as the back of his head and portions of his face.

Two years later, on May 13, 2015, Plaintiffs filed the instant lawsuit [against Briggs & Stratton Corporation, the manufacturer of the lawn mower]. Averments central to their complaint identified "gas geysering from the mower" and "pressurized gas exploding from the gas tank" as alleged defects. In particular, Plaintiffs brought claims for ordinary and gross negligence, strict liability, breach of warranty, loss of consortium, and negligent infliction of emotional distress. On August 28, 2015, this Court granted Defendants' motion to dismiss as to the claims for breach of implied warranties and negligent infliction of emotional distress. Importantly, however, I concluded that a punitive damages claim could survive the motion to dismiss stage, as Plaintiffs alleged sufficient facts plausibly suggesting that the Defendants continued to design, manufacture, and sell the subject lawnmower "despite knowledge of the dangers." [Briggs & Stratton asserted a third-party claim for indemnification and contribution against Bemis Manufacturing Co., the manufacturer of the mower's gas cap.]

During the spring of 2016, counsel for Plaintiffs brought to the Court's attention what might initially have been described as a percolating discovery dispute. In essence, the parties disagreed about the extent to which material related to gas cap or lawnmower designs other than those specific ones involved in the accident should be discoverable. The Court held telephonic status conferences on May 5, July 26, and November 9 of that year. During each conference, I provided the parties with applicable legal citations upon which I would likely rely in reaching a determination and encouraged the parties to attempt to sort out the dispute without further judicial intervention.

After that guidance proved unsuccessful in resolving the pending disputes in their entirety, Plaintiffs filed the instant motions to compel. One motion seeks discovery primarily as to alternative cap designs from Bemis Manufacturing Company, the manufacturer of the gas cap at issue. The other seeks similar but more numerous discovery from Briggs & Stratton Corporation and Briggs & Stratton Power Products Group, LLC (referred to collectively as the Briggs & Stratton Defendants), the manufacturer of the lawnmower in question. Plaintiffs' motions to compel are granted in part and denied in part in accordance with the reasoning that follows. . . .

ANALYSIS

The starting point is amended Federal Rule of Civil Procedure 26(b)(1). From the outset, I note that the Court is mindful of Defendants' concerns about the mounting expense of unbridled discovery. Nevertheless, I cannot agree with the threshold assertion that what is discoverable is strictly limited to material that is ultimately relevant or otherwise admissible. As the parties well know, Rule 26(b)(1) envisions a broader universe of discoverable material than that. It makes clear, for instance, that "[i]nformation within this scope of discovery need not be admissible in evidence to be discoverable."

At the same time, however, "[t]his concept of relevance is tempered . . . by principles of proportionality." As amended Rule 26(b)(1)'s proportionality mandate provides:

> Parties may obtain discovery regarding any nonprivileged matter that is relevant to any party's claim or defense and proportional to the needs of the case, considering the importance of the issues at stake in the action, the amount in controversy, the parties' relative access to relevant information,

the parties' resources, the importance of the discovery in resolving the issues, and whether the burden or expense of the proposed discovery outweighs its likely benefit. . . .

Considering the factors set forth at Rule 26(b)(1), the parties' access to relevant information is undeniably lop-sided in this case: Defendants are repeat players in this genre of litigation, and they consequently enjoy the benefits of sweeping protective orders. On the other hand, the Plaintiffs lack nearly all avenues other than judicially-sanctioned ones to obtain the requisite records that rest in Defendants' possession.

Moreover, the importance of the issues at stake in the litigation militates slightly in Plaintiffs' favor. Although this is not a case involving, for instance, constitutional rights or matters of national significance, to these particular litigants, it is a matter of grave import. Further, its outcome may impact the marketability of a widely sold piece of home machinery or some of its components.

Just as important, I believe that the utility of the proposed discovery outweighs its attendant expenses. Certainly, the Defendants can readily produce electronically stored records relevant to the aforementioned models and can engage in a good faith effort to gather whatever data might not have been documented electronically. In the same vein, I am confident that production of the requested material will bear directly upon resolution of the core issues in this case. It may also clarify any lingering issues as to the most appropriate defendants.

Turning now to Rule 26(b)(1)'s application in product liability cases, the Plaintiffs here allege negligence and strict liability claims, two theories whose proof necessarily entails such questions as: what the Defendants knew or foresaw, what safety tests they conducted, and what designs they considered.

In product liability actions it is frequently difficult to judge which of a manufacturer's products are sufficiently similar to the allegedly defective product to be subject to discovery. Generally, different models of a product will be relevant if they share with the accident-causing model those characteristics pertinent to the legal issues raised in the litigation.

I will now proceed to consider the particular types of material requested, keeping in mind the factors set forth in Rule 26, including the importance of the discovery to the issues in dispute relative to the expenses that the Defendants would likely incur with production. . . .

Bemis contends that the only type of gas cap design about which the Plaintiffs may discover information is the open design, because that is the cap design used on Mr. Fassett's lawnmower. Although not outlandish, that suggestion is likely overly restrictive. . . .

Of great weight is the deposition testimony of Michael J. Holtz, a corporate designee and the gas cap's product design and engineering manager. In addition to the open style vent cap, Mr. Holtz identified three other variations: the screw vent cap, the duckbill cap, and the covered vent cap. Although the three variations are distinguishable from an open vent cap in that they possess different structural designs, all of these caps could function at a partly open setting. . . .

Plaintiffs' motion seeks the following information from Defendant Bemis:

> [A]ll previously demanded documents, including claims, litigation, warranty, testing data, or any other materials evidencing overpressurization and/or geysering, spewing, fountaining or other hazardous or catastrophic release of gasoline from a tank that has

become overpressurized due to inadequate venting. Plaintiffs therefore demand that Kelch/Bemis produce previously demanded documents for any of its free venting caps.

Because application of all of the aforementioned factors reveals that warranty information, testing data, and any other materials evidencing over-pressurization or geysering corresponding to each of the enumerated free venting caps designs (open, screw, covered, and duckbill) are relevant to a number of Plaintiffs' theories, those materials are discoverable so long as they are not work product.

My conclusion is different, however, insofar as Plaintiffs' requests for claims and other litigation material in all cases involving every variety of the free venting cap. "In products liability cases evidence of prior accidents involving the same product under similar circumstances is admissible to show notice to the defendant of the danger, to show existence of the danger, and to show the cause of the accident." *Gumbs v. Int'l Harvester, Inc.*, 718 F.2d 88, 97 (3d Cir. 1983). That being said, "[t]he almost universal requirement, however, is that the prior occurrence must involve facts and circumstances which are substantially similar to those involved in the case under consideration or they will be excluded." *Barker v. Deere & Co.*, 60 F.3d 158, 162 (3d Cir. 1995).

At a superficial level, it appears that all of the contested cap designs could be characterized generally as "free venting caps" because they contain a specified orifice that allows air to permeate them in some fashion or another. Nevertheless, the screw and covered vent caps appear most like the open vent cap in design and operation, with the duckbill being the most distinct as a consequence of its unique shaping. The notion that information relating to all

prior free venting claims is discoverable because all of those accidents involved failed venting is much too high a level of abstraction.

As for screw, covered, and duckbill caps, the differences in design and what tend to be the distinct factual circumstances render them beyond the scope of discovery. Specifically, each prior claim is capable of differing on a number of grounds: the age and prior history of the lawnmower; whether the lawnmower was a riding or push unit; the period of time for which lawnmower had been running on the date of the accident; the atmospheric conditions at the site of the accident; and the varied actions of the accident victims. In fact, Mr. Holtz recalled that at least one of the prior claims involved a missing gas cap altogether.

In my view, then, Plaintiffs have not met their burden of showing substantial similarity as to the accidents involving these other designs. Accordingly, although material unprotected by the work product doctrine in prior claims involving the open gas cap design is discoverable, the same is not true of prior claims or litigation involving screw, cover, or duckbill caps.

I consider this outcome to be an amenable compromise between the two overbroad and underinclusive proposals that have been presented. So often, discovery is not properly construed as an all-or-nothing game. Rather, it is a means for uncovering truth—the strengths and weaknesses of one's case—rationally bounded by efficiency and cost concerns. It is that dynamic that makes discovery a trade-off between knowledge and expenditure. The district court's role under Rule 26, then, is to discern that middle ground between two countervailing pressures, the optimal solution to the information-cost equations. It is my belief that the reasoning outlined above fulfills that dictate.

The parties have also raised a dispute regarding production of privilege logs. Consistent with the foregoing analysis, Defendants shall produce a privilege log detailing with sufficient specificity any items that would be discoverable but for the claiming of a valid privilege or protection. Obviously, Defendants need not log any items that fall beyond the scope of the discovery as detailed herein. Further, work product privilege should not be claimed for performance or testing results that were not truly prepared in preparation for litigation. However, Plaintiffs must also accept that materials shielded by good faith work product claims are likely beyond reach. It is this Court's belief and expectation that this Memorandum and the accompanying Order will sufficiently aid all parties in pinpointing the bounds of discovery and should thereby eliminate the need for subsequent motions to compel on these issues.

I now turn to the discovery requested from the Briggs & Stratton Defendants, those entities responsible for manufacturing the lawnmower at issue. Accordingly, the primary issue as to this subsequent motion is not the similarity of individual components but that of whole lawnmower units themselves. That being said, the applicable factors are largely similar, allowing, of course, for differences in scale. The motion also raises certain issues as to documents that came to light in connection with recent depositions.

Plaintiffs' first two requests deal with field and pressure testing documents relating to the fuel tank or gas cap used on the instant lawnmower model or on any of Defendants' other products. I tend to agree with the Defendants, however, that Plaintiffs fail to provide any information as to what constitutes a similar or comparable mower to the one at issue. According to the Briggs & Stratton Defendants, they have already provided or are in the process of providing documentation for four other lawnmowers that share similar characteristics with Mr. Fassett's mower[, a Craftsman ZT7000].

In persuasive fashion, those Defendants explain that the lawnmower models they selected "have the same gas cap, same tank, same frame, the same engine/gas tank layout, and the same heat shielding." In my view, those are particularly useful decision metrics for a district court sitting in precisely this discovery posture. . . .

In essence, the parties dispute whether having the same gas cap, tank, frame, and general layout are pertinent characteristics for "similar" products. I believe that in a case such as this, where the alleged injuries stemmed from the geysering and ignition of gasoline, similar products must share those attributes with the accident-causing product. This appears to be the case for several reasons: the layout and the frame dictate both the proximity of the tank to heat-emitting components and the space available for expansion of the gas tank. They control how easily the tank and cap may be accessed, or conversely, to what extent those parts are exposed. In my view, they also influence the likelihood of fire, given that they determine the closeness of the fuel cap and any attendant gasoline spills to the components of the lawnmower that are typically heated, such as a muffler or other exhaust component.

Plaintiffs' first two requests, as enumerated in their proposed order, seek discoverable material on "any other of Defendants products." An affidavit filed by a Briggs & Stratton representative indicates that this request could reasonably be read to include upwards of one hundred products. I therefore agree that Plaintiffs' first two discovery requests of the Briggs & Stratton Defendants are overbroad, unsupported by sufficient technical backing, and out of proportion with the needs of this case.

The Briggs & Stratton Defendants should produce or continue to produce only those non-privileged records associated with the Simplicity Axion, the Snapper 150Z, the Craftsman ZT7000, and the Craftsman ZT75000. They have also indicated that they are producing similar documents that correspond to the Coronet model, which documents they should also continue to produce. Accordingly, Defendants need not produce those documents requested in Categories 1 and 2, except and to the extent that they pertain to the five lawnmower models identified above.

Plaintiffs' Category 3 request seeks information relating to the Dortch/Reaves, Oliff, Milner, Reynolds, Steve Johnson, Timothy Johnson, James Thomas, O. Alexander, Ron Sheets, or Earl Vinson mowers and lawsuits, including all prior warranty claims. The Category 4 request seeks all "In Depth Investigation" (IDI) records from the Briggs & Stratton liability claims system. Consistent with my prior reasoning, those requests are denied, except and to the extent that any of the previously named actions or requests involved any of the five enumerated lawnmower models about which material has been deemed discoverable (the Simplicity Axion, the Snapper 150Z, the Craftsman ZT7000, the Craftsman ZT75000, and the Coronet). To the extent that the Defendants believe that any of these materials are protected by the work product doctrine or other rule or privilege, a log setting forth those protections in good faith and with sufficient specificity should be provided to counsel for Plaintiffs.

The next two requests (Categories 5 and 6) seek releases obtained by Thomas Wise, a Briggs & Stratton products safety and compliance manager, including drafts and any markups by Mr. Wise related to claims of venting clogging of fuel caps, fires, or near misses, as well as cover letter or cover email communications between Mr. Wise and claimants/owners from whom Mr. Wise obtained releases regarding such claims. These documents are beyond the scope of discovery, pursuant to Federal Rule of Evidence 408, which bars the introduction of evidence of offers or statements (accepted or otherwise) made in the settlement context when such evidence is offered to prove, among other things, "the validity . . . of a disputed claim."

Though the Plaintiffs contend that such material would be admissible for the alternative purpose of establishing the Defendants' knowledge, I cannot agree that the claimed admissible purpose is readily extricable from the inadmissible ones. I also remain wary of piercing the sanctity of settlement negotiations for fear that doing so would discourage extrajudicial resolution in future cases. This is particularly true where, as here, the Plaintiffs also have the opportunity to establish prior knowledge through a number of parallel avenues, such as internal testing and reports. Likewise, as Defendants point out, "numerous factors play a role in parties' decisions to settle claims, including risks and expenses of litigation, a party's policy towards settlement, and the confidentiality assured by settlement." . . .

Given the relatively low need for the material, their highly confidential nature, and their tendency to lack in probative value, the Category 5 and 6 requests are therefore denied. . . .

Category 10 requests the production of materials for all Briggs & Stratton gasoline engine products, whether they be lawnmowers, snowthrower, leafblowers, etc. For the reasons set forth above, I believe those requests are overly broad. Layout, frame, and other design specifications are critical to the propensities to heat and ignite in a case such as this, and even despite generalized similarities as to fueling, the entirely distinct patterns of usage among various power tools therefore render adequate comparison suspect as a matter of law. If similarity in fueling systems was the proper guideline for this Court to follow, it would seem exceptionally difficult to exclude just about any power tool from the scope of discovery. The line must be more acutely drawn than that. As such, the Category 10 request is denied, as Plaintiffs' discovery is appropriately limited to the five lawnmower models enumerated above.

Another issue central to this discussion is the proper temporal scope of discovery. In particular, Plaintiffs' proposed order seeking discovery from Bemis requests discovery from as early as 1970. Mr. Fassett purchased the subject lawnmower on or around March 2, 2007, and the Defendants approximate that this particular mower was manufactured between February 16, 2005 and June 29, 2005. As such, requiring the production of documents dating back to the 1970s would appear excessive in comparison with the needs of the case. As the Honorable Richard A. Posner of the United States Court of Appeals for the Seventh Circuit has described this dynamic generally:

> In most suits against corporations or other institutions, and in both *Twombly* and *Iqbal*—but also in the present case—the plaintiff wants or needs more discovery of the defendant than the defendant wants or needs of the plaintiff, because the plaintiff has to search the defendant's records (and, through depositions, the minds of the defendant's employees) to obtain evidence of wrongdoing. With the electronic archives of large corporations or other large organizations

holding millions of emails and other electronic communications, the cost of discovery to a defendant has become in many cases astronomical. And the cost is not only monetary; it can include, as well, the disruption of the defendant's operations. If no similar costs are borne by the plaintiff in complying with the defendant's discovery demands, the costs to the defendant may induce it to agree early in the litigation to a settlement favorable to the plaintiff.

Swanson v. Citibank, N.A., 614 F.3d 400, 411 (7th Cir. 2010) (Posner, J., dissenting). Thus, other courts have noticed that the lack of reasonable temporal bounds in a discovery request may render it "abusive" and "facially objectionable." *N.U. v. Wal-Mart Stores, Inc.*, 2016 WL 3654759, at *5 (D. Kan. July 8, 2016).

"[R]elevant information, which is otherwise discoverable, may be limited both geographically and temporally in order to avoid overly broad and unduly burdensome requests." *Briddell v. Saint Gobain Abrasives, Inc.*, 233 F.R.D. 57, 60 (D. Mass. 2005). "Thus, the task of the trial court is to balance the clear relevance of the information against the burden on the defendant." *Owens v. Sprint/United Mgmt. Co.*, 221 F.R.D. 649, 655 (D. Kan. 2004). Though the appropriate bounds will vary depending on the specific circumstances of each case, courts in this Circuit have often taken the default position of limiting discovery to no earlier than five years from the date on which the allegedly tortious conduct occurred. . . .

In regard to such lawsuits where a defendant is alleged to have knowingly designed, manufactured, or sold a defective product when safer, feasible alternatives existed, I hold that the temporal bounds of discoveries should be set not from the date of the accident but from the time period during which the product was manufactured and sold.

I believe that this determination rightly conforms to the nature of such actions. For instance, the tortious conduct is more properly construed as having occurred at the point of defective manufacture, design, or sale than at the point of injury. Further, a plaintiff should be able to gather information regarding a defendant's decision-making process, as the propriety of that risk-utility analysis occupies the core of such disputes. However, each case will present its own unique circumstances, and a defendant's showing that its production lines, components, or designs have materially changed during that same timeframe would perhaps justify a narrower tailoring of the discovery period.

Nevertheless, the timeline here is relatively clear: the lawnmower was manufactured sometime in the spring of 2005; it was purchased in 2007; the accident occurred in 2013; and this suit was filed in 2015. I will extend the discovery period to five years from the approximate time of its manufacture, thereby limiting the discovery of information and material relating to the manufacture, design, or sale of the subject lawnmower or its parts (or those comparable models and parts) to no earlier than January 1, 2000. . . .

Finally, I would caution that the purpose of this Memorandum is solely to resolve the instant discovery dispute and not to assess liability. Specifically, nothing herein should be read as concluding that the subset of similar components or designs for the purposes of discovery is coterminous with that subset of feasible alternative components or designs for the purposes of a merits determination. In fact, strong arguments can likely be made that merely as a consequence of the breadth of discovery, the former subset is typically more populous than the latter.

CONCLUSION

Consistent with the foregoing reasoning, Plaintiffs' motions to compel are granted in part and denied in part. An appropriate Order follows, which enumerates my rulings by motion and by individual requests. . . .

Notes & Questions

1. What discovery did the plaintiffs seek from Briggs & Stratton and from Bemis Manufacturing Co.? In what way did the defendants consider the requests too broad?

2. Consider the discovery requests from both perspectives. First, consider the plaintiffs' point of view. If you represent Daniel Fassett, why might you ask for information regarding all of the various lawn mower models and cap designs? What are you hoping to find? Think about the ways in which the requested information might help you prove the defendants' liability to your client.

Next, consider the defendants' point of view. If you represent Briggs & Stratton or Bemis, why not simply turn over all of the requested information? If it is irrelevant, then why worry about it? In other words, think about the ways in which providing the requested information may be costly to your client.

3. Note the process by which this discovery dispute reached the judge. In the Background portion of the opinion, the court describes the "percolating discovery dispute." While it was percolating—before the judge had heard about the discovery dispute—what do you suppose was going on? *See* Rule 34(b)(2)(C) (permitting a responding party to state objections to document requests); Rule 37(a)(1) (requiring a party that moves to compel discovery to certify that "the movant has in good faith conferred or attempted to confer with the person or party failing to make disclosure or discovery in an effort to obtain it without court action"). When the parties were unable to resolve the dispute on their own, note the way the judge offered some guidance but still encouraged the parties "to sort out the dispute without further judicial intervention." The judge wanted the parties to reach their own compromise about the scope of discovery regarding other models of lawn mowers and caps. When the parties in *Fassett* still could not reach agreement about the scope of this discovery, what sort of motion did the plaintiffs file? *See* Rule 37(a).

4. What was Judge Brann's ruling on the discoverability of the requested information? Essentially, he imposed his own compromise on the parties when they were unable to reach a compromise on their own. What compromise did the judge impose regarding discovery from Bemis involving various types of gas caps? Why was the answer different for documents regarding warranty and testing data, as opposed to documents regarding claims and litigation? What compromise did the judge endorse regarding discovery from Briggs & Stratton about pressure testing of gas caps? What compromise did the judge impose regarding the temporal scope of discoverable information? Note how one can break discovery requests down along lines of subject matter, types of materials, and time frame, and how each of these variables matters to the judge's analysis of relevance and proportionality.

5. In Categories 5 and 6, the plaintiffs sought releases and other communications involving settlements that Briggs & Stratton had reached with other claimants. Ruling that these documents were beyond the scope of discovery, Judge Brann cites Federal Rule of Evidence 408. What is the policy behind Rule 408? What is the argument that Rule 408 does not apply to Fassett's request? Recall that information may be discoverable even if it is inadmissible under the rules of evidence. Even so, one could view this decision in terms of proportionality analysis: Judge Brann saw little value and high cost in this request, noting his wariness about "piercing the sanctity of settlement negotiations."

STRATEGY SESSION

Skilled lawyers think ahead to discovery when drafting their pleadings. Because Rule 26(b) defines the scope of discovery in terms of relevance to the claims and defenses, parties exert some control over the scope of discoverable information by drafting pleadings broadly or narrowly. By asserting numerous and broad claims or defenses in a complaint or answer, a party expands the amount of available discovery. Conversely, by stating fewer claims or defenses or by framing them more specifically, a party contracts the scope of discovery. This can only carry a party so far. Daniel Fassett's claim involved a Craftsman ZT7000 with an open-cap design, and even if Fassett's complaint used different language to state the claim, the judge may have been unwilling to permit discovery that related to markedly different models. On the other hand, if you think of a case like *Swierkiewicz v. Sorema* from Chapter 2, the fact that Akos Swierkiewicz asserted claims for both age discrimination and national origin discrimination surely opened up more topics for discovery than if he had asserted just one of those claims.

(2) Privileges and the Work-Product Doctrine

(a) Privilege

Are some values more important than reaching the truth? That is the question underlying the law of privilege. If the only goal were to find the truth, then all relevant information would be open to discovery. The law, however, recognizes the importance of letting us keep some information private. In particular, the law recognizes that the value of certain relationships—such as lawyer-client, doctor-patient, and spouse-spouse—depends on the ability to speak candidly within those relationships, which in turn requires that certain communications be protected from compelled disclosure.

Note that privileges are not specific to civil litigation discovery. Privileges are part of the law of evidence, and in the case of the privilege against self-incrimination, a matter of constitutional law. They apply in both criminal and civil proceedings and in both discovery and trial. In this sense, privileges do not necessarily fall within the topic of "discovery" or even within "civil procedure." A detailed account of the law of privilege is beyond the scope of this book. Nonetheless, to understand the discovery process and its limitations, you need at least a basic understanding of evidentiary privileges.

(i) Attorney-Client Privilege and Other Relational Privileges

In civil litigation, the privilege that arises most often is the attorney-client privilege. The attorney-client privilege protects confidential communications between a lawyer and a client for purposes of giving or receiving legal advice or services. It protects communications from lawyer to client as well as from client to lawyer. It extends to oral, written, and electronic communications. If a communication is privileged, then neither the client nor the lawyer can be forced to reveal what was said.

The privilege protects *communications*, not the underlying *facts*. If a client in an auto accident case tells his lawyer that he was looking at his cell phone when he got into the crash, neither the client nor the lawyer can be compelled to disclose that conversation because the communication is privileged. But the privilege does not protect the fact itself. When opposing counsel at a deposition or trial asks the client whether he was looking at his phone when the accident occurred, the client must answer honestly. You should object on grounds of attorney-client privilege whenever someone asks your client, "What did you tell your lawyer about what happened?" But you have no objection on grounds of attorney-client privilege when someone asks your client, "What happened?"

Further, the privilege protects only *confidential* communications. If a client and lawyer have a conversation in a meeting with others present, the privilege does not apply. There is a limited exception for circumstances where the third person is necessary for the lawyer-client relationship, such as a paralegal, a translator, or a client's guardian.

Like most privileges, the attorney-client privilege can be waived. Disclosure outside the lawyer-client relationship waives the privilege. Not only must the communication have been made in confidence to get the benefit of the privilege, the lawyer and client must maintain its confidentiality. If they share the communication with others, then the privilege is lost. As a lawyer, be sure to instruct your clients to maintain the privacy of your communications to avoid inadvertently waiving the privilege.

If you find it surprising how easily the attorney-client privilege can be waived, keep in mind that privileges are obstacles to getting the truth. They run counter to the main thrust of discovery and trial, which is to bring out the evidence to enable the fact-finder to make accurate determinations. Blocking access to evidence is worth it, the thinking goes, only for communications in which privacy is essential. If the lawyer and client don't care enough about the confidentiality of a communication to keep it to themselves, then the legal system should not protect it from discovery.

The attorney-client privilege applies to lawyers' communications with corporations as well as individuals, but jurisdictions vary in exactly how they apply the privilege to corporations. Not every communication between a corporation's attorney and its employees is privileged. In *Upjohn v. United States*, 449 U.S. 383 (1981), the Supreme Court held, for purposes of federal law, that the privilege applies not merely to lawyers' communications with the corporation's "control group" (top officers), but to lawyers' communications with any employee concerning matters within the employee's corporate duties, where the communication is for the purpose of providing legal advice to the corporation.

Beyond the attorney-client relationship, several other relationships get the benefit of communications protected by privilege. The law on these relational privileges varies from one jurisdiction to another. Some of the common privileges are the doctor-patient privilege, the psychotherapist-patient privilege, the clergy-penitent privilege, and the spousal privilege. The doctor-patient privilege is well established, if not quite as firm as the attorney-client privilege. The spousal privilege, by contrast, is not universally accepted, and many states have eliminated the spousal privilege in civil cases.

(ii) Privilege Against Self-Incrimination

The Fifth Amendment to the U.S. Constitution says that no person "shall be compelled in any criminal case to be a witness against himself." The privilege against self-incrimination, for obvious reasons, arises in criminal cases more than in civil cases. Even in civil litigation, however, it plays a role. Suppose your client has been accused of killing someone, and faces both a criminal prosecution for homicide and a tort lawsuit for wrongful death. Or think of any other situation that may give rise to both criminal and civil liability, such as fraud, antitrust, physical assault, or driving under the influence. If your client faces possible criminal prosecution, and in the civil litigation is asked in discovery or at trial about what happened, the client could refuse to answer on grounds of the privilege against self-incrimination.

The privilege applies a bit differently in civil cases, however. In criminal cases, the prosecutor is not permitted to comment on the fact that the defendant refused to testify. As a matter of criminal procedure, the privilege would lose much of its value if prosecutors could encourage juries to draw adverse inferences from the fact of defendants' decision not to testify. In civil cases, however, such comments and inferences are allowed. *See Baxter v. Palmigiano*, 425 U.S. 308, 318 (1976) (explaining that "the Fifth Amendment does not forbid adverse inferences against parties to civil actions when they refuse to testify," in contrast to criminal cases, where Supreme Court precedent "prohibits the judge and prosecutor from suggesting to the jury that it may treat the defendant's silence as substantive evidence of guilt"). As a practical matter, this presents a serious downside to invoking the privilege against self-incrimination in civil litigation.

Note that the Fifth Amendment privilege deals only with in*crim*ination, that is, potential *criminal* liability. A client facing potential *civil* liability alone never gets Fifth Amendment protection. Suppose your client has been sued for breach of contract, and at her deposition the opposing attorney asks her whether she has complied with a particular requirement of the contract. She cannot refuse to answer on the ground that the information would make it more likely that she would be held liable for breach of contract. Her potential liability to the plaintiff is not a criminal matter; the state is not seeking to send her to prison or impose a fine or other criminal punishment. It is a civil matter, a question of whether she will be liable to the plaintiff for the alleged breach. She will be required to answer their questions in the deposition about whether she complied with the contract's terms. Litigants in civil cases routinely must produce evidence in discovery that harms their own interests. But if the alleged breach of contract involved a sale of narcotics that could expose your client to criminal punishment, then your client would have a basis to refuse to answer on grounds of the privilege against self-incrimination.

(iii) Other Privileges

In addition to attorney-client, doctor-patient, psychotherapist-patient, clergy-penitent, spousal, and self-incrimination privileges, courts have recognized several others. For example, courts have recognized an executive privilege, grounded in part on constitutional separation of powers, to protect certain communications within the executive branch of government. Likewise, courts have recognized a state secrets privilege to protect certain information relating to the military and national security. In each case, the holder of a recognized privilege may refuse to disclose information that otherwise would be discoverable.

Note that the recognized evidentiary privileges are few and each one is rather specific. Other than these recognized privileges, there is no general immunity that allows people to refuse to provide information on grounds that they consider the information private. The law does not recognize some general "mind your own business" doctrine. Discovery often requires parties and witnesses to answer questions about confidential business and personal matters. If information is relevant and not sought for improper purposes, then unless it fits within one of the legally recognized privileges, even highly sensitive information is discoverable. That said, the person or entity from whom such sensitive information is requested may seek a protective order to prohibit disclosure outside of the lawsuit or may object to the discovery if its sole purpose is to embarrass or harass. *See* Rule 26(c)(1), 26(g)(1)(B)(ii).

(b) The Work-Product Doctrine

Several years after the Federal Rules of Civil Procedure were adopted, an important question arose concerning the then-new discovery rules. Could lawyers use discovery tools to obtain work that the other side had done in preparation for the litigation? None of the traditional privileges addressed the issue. But surely discovery did not entitle a party to steal the other side's work. Or did it? This was the question the Supreme Court had to answer in the famous case of *Hickman v. Taylor*.

HICKMAN v. TAYLOR
329 U.S. 495 (1947)

Justice MURPHY delivered the opinion of the Court.

This case presents an important problem under the Federal Rules of Civil Procedure as to the extent to which a party may inquire into oral and written statements of witnesses, or other information, secured by an adverse party's counsel in the course of preparation for possible litigation after a claim has arisen. Examination into a person's files and records, including those resulting from the professional activities of an attorney, must be judged with care. It is not without reason that various

safeguards have been established to preclude unwarranted excursions into the privacy of a man's work. At the same time, public policy supports reasonable and necessary inquiries. Properly to balance these competing interests is a delicate and difficult task.

On February 7, 1943, the tug "J.M. Taylor" sank while engaged in helping to tow a car float of the Baltimore & Ohio Railroad across the Delaware River at Philadelphia. The accident was apparently unusual in nature, the cause of it still being unknown. Five of the nine crew members were drowned. Three days later the tug owners and the underwriters employed a law firm, of which respondent Fortenbaugh is a member, to defend them against potential suits by representatives of the deceased crew members and to sue the railroad for damages to the tug.

A public hearing was held on March 4, 1943, before the United States Steamboat Inspectors, at which the four survivors were examined. This testimony was recorded and made available to all interested parties. Shortly thereafter, Fortenbaugh privately interviewed the survivors and took statements from them with an eye toward the anticipated litigation; the survivors signed these statements on March 29. Fortenbaugh also interviewed other persons believed to have some information relating to the accident and in some cases he made memoranda of what they told him. At the time when Fortenbaugh secured the statements of the survivors, representatives of two of the deceased crew members had been in communication with him. Ultimately claims were presented by representatives of all five of the deceased; four of the claims, however, were settled without litigation. The fifth claimant, petitioner herein, brought suit in a federal court under the Jones Act on November 26, 1943, naming as defendants the two tug owners, individually and as partners, and the railroad.

One year later, petitioner filed 39 interrogatories directed to the tug owners. The 38th interrogatory read: "State whether any statements of the members of the crews of the Tugs 'J. M. Taylor' and 'Philadelphia' or of any other vessel were taken in connection with the towing of the car float and the sinking of the Tug 'John M. Taylor'. Attach hereto exact copies of all such statements if in writing, and if oral, set forth in detail the exact provisions of any such oral statements or reports."

Supplemental interrogatories asked whether any oral or written statements, records, reports or other memoranda had been made concerning any matter relative to the towing operation, the sinking of the tug, the salvaging and repair of the tug, and the death of the deceased. If the answer was in the affirmative, the tug owners were then requested to set forth the nature of all such records, reports, statements or other memoranda.

The tug owners, through Fortenbaugh, answered all of the interrogatories except No. 38 and the supplemental ones just described. While admitting that statements of the survivors had been taken, they declined to summarize or set forth the contents. They did so on the ground that such requests called "for privileged matter obtained in preparation for litigation" and constituted "an attempt to obtain indirectly counsel's private files." It was claimed that answering these requests "would involve practically turning over not only the complete files, but also the telephone records and, almost, the thoughts of counsel." . . .

The District Court for the Eastern District of Pennsylvania, sitting en banc, held that the requested matters were not privileged. 4 F.R.D. 479. The court then decreed that the tug owners and Fortenbaugh, as counsel and agent for the tug owners forthwith "answer Plaintiff's 38th interrogatory and supplemental interrogatories; produce all written statements of witnesses obtained by Mr. Fortenbaugh, as counsel and agent for Defendants; state in substance any fact concerning this case which Defendants learned through oral statements made by witnesses to Mr. Fortenbaugh whether or not included in his private memoranda and produce Mr. Fortenbaugh's memoranda containing statements of fact by witnesses or to submit these memoranda to the Court for determination of those portions which should be revealed to Plaintiff." Upon their refusal, the court adjudged them in contempt and ordered them imprisoned until they complied.

The Third Circuit Court of Appeals, also sitting en banc, reversed the judgment of the District Court. *Hickman v. Taylor*, 153 F.2d 212 (3d Cir. 1945). It held that the information here sought was part of the "work product of the lawyer" and hence privileged from discovery under the Federal Rules of Civil Procedure. The importance of the problem, which has engendered a great divergence of views among district courts, led us to grant certiorari.

The pre-trial deposition-discovery mechanism established by Rules 26 to 37 is one of the most significant innovations of the Federal Rules of Civil Procedure. Under the prior federal practice, the pre-trial functions of notice-giving issue-formulation and fact-revelation were performed primarily and inadequately by the pleadings. Inquiry into the issues and facts before trial was narrowly confined and was often cumbersome in method. The new rules, however, restrict the pleadings to the task of general notice-giving and invest the deposition-discovery process with a vital role in the preparation for trial. The various instruments of discovery now serve (1) as a device, along with the pre-trial hearing under Rule 16, to narrow and clarify the basic issues between the parties, and (2) as a device for ascertaining the facts, or information as to the existence or whereabouts of facts, relative to those issues. Thus civil trials in the federal courts no longer need be carried on in the dark. The way is now clear, consistent with recognized privileges, for the parties to obtain the fullest possible knowledge of the issues and facts before trial.

There is an initial question as to which of the deposition-discovery rules is involved in this case. Petitioner, in filing his interrogatories, thought that he was proceeding under Rule 33. That rule provides that a party may serve upon any adverse party written interrogatories to be answered by the party served. The District Court proceeded on the same assumption in its opinion, although its order to produce and its contempt order stated that both Rules 33 and 34 were involved. Rule 34 establishes a procedure whereby, upon motion of any party showing good cause therefor and upon notice to all other parties, the court may order any party to produce and permit the inspection and copying or photographing of any designated documents, etc., not privileged, which constitute or contain evidence material to any matter involved in the action and which are in his possession, custody or control. . . . [T]o the extent that petitioner was seeking the production of the memoranda and statements gathered by Fortenbaugh in the course of his activities as counsel, petitioner misconceived his remedy. Rule 33 did not permit him to obtain such memoranda and statements as adjuncts to the interrogatories addressed to the individual tug owners. . . .

But under the circumstances we deem it unnecessary and unwise to rest our decision upon this procedural irregularity, an irregularity which is not strongly urged upon us and which was disregarded in the two courts below. It matters little at this later stage whether [the appropriate device might have been an interrogatory, document request, or deposition]. The deposition-discovery rules create integrated procedural devices. And the basic question at stake is whether any of those devices may be used to inquire into materials collected by an adverse party's counsel in the course of preparation for possible litigation. . . .

In urging that he has a right to inquire into the materials secured and prepared by Fortenbaugh, petitioner emphasizes that the deposition-discovery portions of the Federal Rules of Civil Procedure are designed to enable the parties to discover the true facts and to compel their disclosure wherever they may be found. It is said that inquiry may be made under these rules, epitomized by Rule 26, as to any relevant matter which is not privileged; and since the discovery provisions are to be applied as broadly and liberally as possible, the privilege limitation must be restricted to its narrowest bounds. On the premise that the attorney-client privilege is the one involved in this case, petitioner argues that it must be strictly confined to confidential communications made by a client to his attorney. And since the materials here in issue were secured by Fortenbaugh from third persons rather than from his clients, the tug owners, the conclusion is reached that these materials are proper subjects for discovery under Rule 26.

As additional support for this result, petitioner claims that to prohibit discovery under these circumstances would give a corporate defendant a tremendous advantage in a suit by an individual plaintiff. Thus in a suit by an injured employee against a railroad or in a suit by an insured person against an insurance company the corporate defendant could pull a dark veil of secrecy over all the pertinent facts it can collect after the claim arises merely on the assertion that such facts were gathered by its large staff of attorneys and claim agents. At the same time, the individual plaintiff, who often has direct knowledge of the matter in issue and has no counsel until some time after his claim arises could be compelled to disclose all the intimate details of his case. By endowing with immunity from disclosure all that a lawyer discovers in the course of his duties, it is said, the rights of individual litigants in such cases are drained of vitality and the lawsuit becomes more of a battle of deception than a search for truth.

But framing the problem in terms of assisting individual plaintiffs in their suits against corporate defendants is unsatisfactory. Discovery concededly may work to the disadvantage as well as to the advantage of individual plaintiffs. Discovery, in other words, is not a one-way proposition. It is available in all types of cases at the behest of any party, individual or corporate, plaintiff or defendant. The problem thus far transcends the situation confronting this petitioner. And we must view that problem in light of the limitless situations where the particular kind of discovery sought by petitioner might be used.

We agree, of course, that the deposition-discovery rules are to be accorded a broad and liberal treatment. No longer can the time-honored cry of "fishing expedition" serve to preclude a party from inquiring into the facts underlying his opponent's case. Mutual knowledge of all the relevant facts gathered by both parties is essential to proper litigation. To that end, either party may compel the other to disgorge whatever facts he has in his possession. The deposition-discovery procedure simply advances the stage at which the disclosure can be compelled from the time of trial to the period preceding it, thus reducing the possibility of surprise. But discovery, like all matters of procedure, has ultimate and necessary boundaries. . . .

We also agree that the memoranda, statements and mental impressions in issue in this case fall outside the scope of the attorney-client privilege and hence are not protected from discovery on that basis. It is unnecessary here to delineate the content and scope of that privilege as recognized in the federal courts. For present purposes, it suffices to note that the protective cloak of this privilege does not extend to information which an attorney secures from a witness while acting for his client in anticipation of litigation. Nor does this privilege concern the memoranda, briefs, communications and other writings prepared by counsel for his own use in prosecuting his client's case; and it is equally unrelated to writings which reflect an attorney's mental impressions, conclusions, opinions or legal theories.

But the impropriety of invoking that privilege does not provide an answer to the problem before us. Petitioner has made more than an ordinary request for relevant, non-privileged facts in the possession of his adversaries or their counsel. He has sought discovery as of right of oral and written statements of witnesses whose identity is well known and whose availability to petitioner appears unimpaired. He has sought production of these matters after making the most searching inquiries of his opponents as to the circumstances surrounding the fatal accident, which inquiries were sworn to have been answered to the best of their information and belief. Interrogatories were directed toward all the events prior to, during and subsequent to the sinking of the tug. Full and honest answers to such broad inquiries would necessarily have included all pertinent information gleaned by Fortenbaugh through his interviews with the witnesses. Petitioner makes no suggestion, and we cannot assume, that the tug owners or Fortenbaugh were incomplete or dishonest in the framing of their answers. In addition, petitioner was free to examine the public testimony of the witnesses taken before the United States Steamboat Inspectors. We are thus dealing with an attempt to secure the production of written statements and mental impressions contained in the files and the mind of the attorney Fortenbaugh without any showing of necessity or any indication or claim that denial of such production would unduly prejudice the preparation of petitioner's case or cause him any hardship or injustice. For aught that appears, the essence of what petitioner seeks either has been revealed to him already through the interrogatories or is readily available to him direct from the witnesses for the asking. . . .

In our opinion, neither Rule 26 nor any other rule dealing with discovery contemplates production under such circumstances. That is not because the subject matter is privileged or irrelevant, as those concepts are used in these rules. Here is simply an attempt, without purported necessity or justification, to secure written statements, private memoranda and personal recollections prepared or formed by an adverse party's counsel in the course of his legal duties. As such, it falls outside the arena of discovery and contravenes the public policy underlying the orderly prosecution and defense of legal claims. Not even the most liberal of discovery theories can justify unwarranted inquiries into the files and the mental impressions of an attorney.

Historically, a lawyer is an officer of the court and is bound to work for the advancement of justice while faithfully protecting the rightful interests of his clients. In performing his various duties, however, it is essential that a lawyer work with a certain degree of privacy, free from unnecessary intrusion by opposing parties and their counsel. Proper preparation of a client's case demands that he assemble information, sift what he considers to be the relevant from the irrelevant facts, prepare his legal theories and plan his strategy without undue and needless interference. That is the historical and the necessary way in which lawyers act within the framework of our system of jurisprudence to promote justice and to protect their clients' interests. This work is reflected, of course, in interviews, statements, memoranda, correspondence, briefs, mental impressions, personal beliefs, and countless other tangible and intangible ways—aptly though roughly termed by the Circuit Court of Appeals in this case as the "work product of the lawyer." Were such materials open to opposing counsel on mere demand, much of what is now put down in writing would remain unwritten. An attorney's thoughts, heretofore inviolate, would not be his own. Inefficiency, unfairness and sharp practices would inevitably develop in the giving of legal advice and in the preparation of cases for trial. The effect on the legal profession would be demoralizing. And the interests of the clients and the cause of justice would be poorly served.

We do not mean to say that all written materials obtained or prepared by an adversary's counsel with an eye toward litigation are necessarily free from discovery in all cases. Where relevant and nonprivileged facts remain hidden in an attorney's file and where production of those facts is essential to the preparation of one's case, discovery may properly be had. Such written statements and documents might, under certain circumstances, be admissible in evidence or give clues as to the existence or location of relevant facts. Or they might be useful for purposes of impeachment or corroboration. And production might be justified where the witnesses are no longer available or can be reached only with difficulty. Were production of written statements and documents to be precluded under such circumstances, the liberal ideals of the deposition-discovery portions of the Federal Rules of Civil Procedure would be stripped of much of their meaning. But the general policy against invading the privacy of an attorney's course of preparation is so well recognized and so essential to an orderly working of our system of legal procedure that a burden rests on the one who would invade that privacy to establish adequate reasons to justify production through a subpoena or court order. That burden, we

believe, is necessarily implicit in the rules as now constituted. . . .

No attempt was made to establish any reason why Fortenbaugh should be forced to produce the written statements. There was only a naked, general demand for these materials as of right and a finding by the District Court that no recognizable privilege was involved. That was insufficient to justify discovery under these circumstances and the court should have sustained the refusal of the tug owners and Fortenbaugh to produce.

But as to oral statements made by witnesses to Fortenbaugh, whether presently in the form of his mental impressions or memoranda, we do not believe that any showing of necessity can be made under the circumstances of this case so as to justify production. . . .

Denial of production of this nature does not mean that any material, non-privileged facts can be hidden from the petitioner in this case. He need not be unduly hindered in the preparation of his case, in the discovery of facts or in his anticipation of his opponents' position. Searching interrogatories directed to Fortenbaugh and the tug owners, production of written documents and statements upon a proper showing and direct interviews with the witnesses themselves all serve to reveal the facts in Fortenbaugh's possession to the fullest possible extent consistent with public policy. Petitioner's counsel frankly admits that he wants the oral statements only to help prepare himself to examine witnesses and to make sure that he has overlooked nothing. That is insufficient under the circumstances to permit him an exception to the policy underlying the privacy of Fortenbaugh's professional activities. If there should be a rare situation justifying production of these matters, petitioner's case is not of that type. . . .

We therefore affirm the judgment of the Circuit Court of Appeals.

Justice JACKSON, concurring.

. . . The primary effect of the practice advocated here would be on the legal profession itself. But it too often is overlooked that the lawyer and the law office are indispensable parts of our administration of justice. Law-abiding people can go nowhere else to learn the ever changing and constantly multiplying rules by which they must behave and to obtain redress for their wrongs. The welfare and tone of the legal profession is therefore of prime consequence to society, which would feel the consequences of such a practice as petitioner urges secondarily but certainly. . . .

Counsel for the petitioner candidly said on argument that he wanted this information to help prepare himself to examine witnesses, to make sure he overlooked nothing. He bases his claim to it in his brief on the view that the Rules were to do away with the old situation where a law suit developed into "a battle of wits between counsel." But a common law trial is and always should be an adversary proceeding. Discovery was hardly intended to enable a learned profession to perform its functions either without wits or on wits borrowed from the adversary.

The real purpose and the probable effect of the practice ordered by the district court would be to put trials on a level even lower than a "battle of wits." I can conceive of no practice more demoralizing to the Bar than to require a lawyer to write out and deliver to his adversary an account of what witnesses have told him. Even if his recollection were perfect, the statement would be his language permeated with his inferences. . . .

Having been supplied the names of the witnesses, petitioner's lawyer gives no reason why he cannot interview them himself. If an employee-witness refuses to tell his story, he, too, may be examined under the Rules. He may be compelled on discovery as fully as on the trial to disclose his version of the facts. But that is his own disclosure—it can be used to impeach him if he contradicts it and such a deposition is not useful to promote an unseemly disagreement between the witness and the counsel in the case. . . .

It is true that the literal language of the Rules would admit of an interpretation that would sustain the district court's order. . . . But all such procedural measures have a background of custom and practice which was assumed by those who wrote and should be by those who apply them. . . . Certainly nothing in the tradition or practice of discovery up to the time of these Rules would have suggested that they would authorize such a practice as here proposed. . . .

Notes & Questions

1. What information did the plaintiff seek from Samuel Fortenbaugh, one of the lawyers for the tug owners? Was the information relevant? Was it covered by any of the then-existing privileges? Be sure you are clear on why the answer is that yes, the information was relevant, and no, it was not covered by any recognized privilege. In particular, be sure you are clear on why the information was not protected by the attorney-client privilege.

2. If the information was relevant and non-privileged, why did Fortenbaugh refuse to turn it over? And why did the Supreme Court agree with him? As a textual matter, did any then-existing Federal Rule of Civil Procedure support Fortenbaugh's position? As a policy matter, in what ways does the legal system function better if information like this is not discoverable?

3. *Hickman v. Taylor* is a landmark case in civil procedure not only because of its holding regarding work-product protection, but also because the case gave the Supreme Court an opportunity—when the Federal Rules of Civil Procedure were very young—to explain the purpose of discovery. Coming out of an era in which trial had been, at least in theory, the key moment for compelled revelations of fact, the discovery rules shifted the central occasion for factual revelation to the pretrial period. Looking at the majority opinion's broad dicta about the discovery rules, what was the Court's attitude about these rules and how they should be interpreted?

4. For 23 years, the doctrine of *Hickman v. Taylor* existed as a common law gloss on the federal discovery rules. In 1970, the doctrine was modified and added to the Federal Rules of Civil Procedure. Rule 26(b)(3) defines work product and gives it qualified protection. The rule defines the protected materials as "documents and other tangible things that are prepared in anticipation of litigation or for trial by or for another party or its representative (including the other party's attorney, consultant, surety, indemnitor, insurer, or agent)." Pay attention to three items embedded in Rule 26(b)(3)'s definition. First, the protection applies only to "documents and other tangible things," not to the underlying facts. Second, the materials must have been "prepared in anticipation of litigation or for trial." This may include materials prepared either before or after an actual lawsuit was filed. The doctrine concerns litigation-related work. It does not protect a client's or a lawyer's documents that were not prepared for litigation purposes (although some of those documents may be covered by the attorney-client privilege). Third, although you may hear lawyers refer to the doctrine as *attorney work product*, the rule explicitly covers litigation materials prepared not only by attorneys, but also by the client or other nonlawyers.

5. Rule 26(b)(3) grants only qualified protection for work product, not absolute protection. The rule carves out an exception for important information that is otherwise unavailable. Materials that fall within the definition of work product may nonetheless be discoverable if they are "otherwise discoverable under Rule 26(b)(1)" (that is, relevant, nonprivileged, and proportional) and if the requesting party "has substantial need for the materials to prepare its case and cannot, without undue hardship, obtain their substantial equivalent by other means." In *Hickman*, why did the plaintiff not need Fortenbaugh's work product?

6. There is one component of work product, however, that receives absolute protection under the rule—the lawyer's mental impressions. Even when the qualified protection of the work-product doctrine is overcome by a showing of substantial need, a lawyer's mental impressions remain non-discoverable. Rule

26(b)(3) requires the court to "protect against disclosure of the mental impressions, conclusions, opinions, or legal theories of a party's attorney or other representative concerning the litigation." As a policy matter, why should work product in general get only qualified protection? Why do mental impressions, by contrast, get absolute protection? Can you see possible difficulties with implementation of both the qualified-protection and the absolute-protection aspects of Rule 26(b)(3)?

7. Test your understanding of the work-product doctrine by applying Rule 26(b)(3) to the following problems, based on the *Hickman* story:

   a. Plaintiff seeks information by demanding document production of the signed witness statements obtained by Fortenbaugh from the four survivors of the tugboat sinking. Discoverable?

   b. Plaintiff seeks the same information by taking the survivors' depositions and asking them about the facts of the tugboat sinking. Discoverable?

   c. Plaintiff seeks the same information by serving interrogatories on the defendant, and much of the defendant's knowledge about the sinking came from the witness statements obtained by Fortenbaugh. Discoverable?

   d. Suppose Fortenbaugh interviewed the sole surviving crew member, who died shortly thereafter. Plaintiff seeks document production of the crew member's written statement obtained by Fortenbaugh. Discoverable?

   e. Same as the previous problem, except that Fortenbaugh made marginal notes with his thoughts about the crew member's statement. Plaintiff seeks production of the written statement including Fortenbaugh's notes. Discoverable?

8. In practice, the work-product doctrine often overlaps with the attorney-client privilege. A lawyer's memo to her client about trial strategy would be both privileged and work product. Despite their functional similarity, keep the doctrines distinct in your mind. The attorney-client privilege covers communications between lawyer and client. The work-product doctrine covers materials prepared in anticipation of litigation. Lawyer-client communications for nonlitigation legal services are privileged but not covered by the work-product doctrine. Trial preparation materials that are not lawyer-client communications (lawyers' notes, witness interviews, research memos, and so on) receive the qualified protection of the work-product doctrine but not the more absolute protection of the attorney-client privilege.

9. When withholding privileged documents from discovery, lawyers produce a *privilege log*. A privilege log identifies documents that would have been responsive to the document request but that have been withheld on the basis of privilege. Such a log may include the date, type, authors, and recipients of the document, as well as a description of the document explaining the basis for withholding the document. *See* Rule 26(b)(5) (requiring parties to state expressly

that materials were withheld based on privilege or work-product protection, and to describe the documents or other materials that were withheld). Recall that in *Fassett v. Sears*, above, the judge not only addressed the parties' dispute about relevance and proportionality, but also ruled, "Defendants shall produce a privilege log detailing with sufficient specificity any items that would be discoverable but for the claiming of a valid privilege or protection."

10. The rise of third-party litigation funding has led to novel questions concerning work-product protection. In litigation funding arrangements, a third party advances money to a party (usually a plaintiff) to enable her to proceed with her case, and in many arrangements the funder takes a cut of the winnings. Are materials created as part of such funding arrangements discoverable? These materials may include research by funders into the strengths and weaknesses of the plaintiff's case. Such materials may be highly relevant in the sense that they analyze the merits of the claims and defenses, and typically they are not attorney-client privileged because they are not communications between lawyer and client. Do litigation-finance materials fall within the work-product doctrine? Some courts have extended work-product protection to funding materials, but the issue remains hotly debated as defendants seek access to the information and as plaintiffs' lawyers and litigation funders seek to protect the information from discovery.

> **Terminology Tip**
>
> Rule 26(b)(3) never actually uses the term *work product*, but everybody else does. The phrase was introduced by the Third Circuit and repeated by the Supreme Court in *Hickman*. Some people call it the *work product privilege*, which is a reasonable way to describe its role as a constraint on discoverability of relevant information. However, because work product historically was not one of the law's recognized evidentiary privileges and because it offers only qualified protection, many lawyers and judges avoid the word *privilege* in this context and instead call it the *work-product doctrine*.

(3) Expert Witness Discovery

Expert witnesses—as contrasted with fact witnesses—are those who provide testimony to assist the judge or jury in understanding the evidence. Not every case involves experts, but they are a relatively common feature of U.S. litigation, especially in cases with high stakes or complex factual questions. Whereas fact witnesses generally cannot testify about their opinions, *see* Fed. R. Evid. 701, expert witnesses may do so if "the expert's scientific, technical, or other specialized knowledge will help the trier of fact to understand the evidence or to determine a fact in issue," and if the testimony is based on sufficient data, reliable methods, and reliable application. Fed. R. Evid. 702; *see also Daubert v. Merrell Dow Pharmaceuticals, Inc.*, 509 U.S. 579 (1993). Occasionally, judges use court-appointed experts, *see* Fed. R. Evid. 706, but much more often, experts are retained by the litigants.

Discovery from other parties' expert witnesses is closely related to the work-product doctrine because it raises similar concerns about the discoverability of litigation preparation. Lawyers, litigants, and experts may work together in discussions about the merits of claims and defenses. Earlier, we saw that the Rule 26(a) mandatory disclosures include information about expert witnesses, but what if a party wishes to take an opposing expert's deposition to get more information? Are communications with experts, as well as documents generated by or for experts in the context of litigation, available for discovery by other parties?

Rule 26(b)(4) draws a sharp distinction between *testifying* and *non-testifying* experts. One may depose any testifying expert ("any person who has been identified as an expert whose opinions may be presented at trial"). Rule 26(b)(4) was amended in 2010 to extend work-product protection to drafts and other communications between lawyers and expert witnesses, but one can still get discovery of any information that the expert relied on in forming opinions.

It is much tougher, however, to get discovery from a non-testifying expert ("an expert who has been retained or specially employed by another party in anticipation of litigation or to prepare for trial and who is not expected to be called as a witness at trial"). *See* Rule 26(b)(4)(D). Who are these non-testifying experts, and why would anyone hire them? They are people with expertise who serve as behind-the-scenes consultants to the parties and their lawyers. Often, they are experts whom a party considered but rejected as testifying expert witnesses because their opinions were not sufficiently helpful to the party to use at trial. Rule 26(b)(4)(D) permits taking the deposition of a non-testifying expert (or asking about the non-testifying expert's opinions by interrogatories) only in "exceptional circumstances." If it would be practically impossible for the requesting party to obtain facts or opinions on the same subject by other means—for example, if the expert is the only one with expertise on the subject—then the discovery is permissible. Otherwise, the non-testifying expert's opinions are not discoverable.

C. DISCOVERY PLANNING AND IMPLEMENTATION

(1) Discovery Planning

Now that you know each of the discovery tools, take a moment to think comprehensively about how you will wield them. When representing a client in litigation, how will you conduct your factual investigation? One way to approach discovery planning would be to look at each discovery tool and to decide how to use it in the particular case: What interrogatories should I ask? Whom should I depose? What sort of documents should I request? There is nothing embarrassing about that approach, but it is *not* the primary way great lawyers think about discovery planning. Great lawyers think about factual investigation more openly and proactively:

What information do I need?
Who has it?
How will I get it?

What information do I need? To answer the first question, look to the pleadings to understand each party's claims, defenses, and theory of the case, and look to your legal research to understand the elements or factors that bear on each of the claims and defenses. Until you know the claims, defenses, and the applicable law, you do not know what information you need. And until you know what information you need, you are not ready to use investigation and discovery wisely. Some litigators get into the right mindset by envisioning the jury instructions and closing arguments—long before trial—to ensure that they use the discovery process to obtain whatever information they will need at trial. When thinking about what information you need, remember that sometimes you need information to prove your theory of the case, sometimes you need information to decide what your theory of the case is, and, sadly for your client, sometimes you need information to realize that you have no viable theory of the case.

Who has the information? For each piece of information you need, you cannot get it until you figure out where it might be. Think broadly. Maybe the information is in the possession of another party, a nonparty, your own client, the government, or the public domain. Maybe there are multiple persons or places where you might find the information and you will use a multipronged approach.

Note that the third question is not "How will I try to get it?" but rather "How will I get it?" Given the broad scope of discovery and the powerful tools at your disposal, your expectation should be that if you need a piece of information, you will obtain it. The answer you find may not be one that helps your client's claims or defenses, but you will get an answer. At least, that is the mindset in a case with enough at stake to warrant a thorough factual investigation. You may have to adjust your attitude depending on the stakes of the dispute and your client's budget.

There is no required chronological order for the various discovery tools. With the exception of mandatory disclosures, whose timing is set forth in Rule 26(a), the other devices can be used in any combination and in any order. They are a set of available tools, not a series of steps. That said, many lawyers start with interrogatories to obtain basic information before turning to other devices, as interrogatory responses can provide names of potential deponents and can lead to better-defined document requests. Also, many lawyers obtain documents and e-discovery before taking depositions, because by reviewing the evidence the lawyer determines what questions to ask a deponent.

Do not forget that you have many ways to obtain information aside from the discovery devices. Useful sources include your own client, interviews with witnesses, the Internet, newspapers, government documents, private investigators, and any other type of research you can imagine. If a witness is willing to talk to you, there is no rule that says you must take a formal deposition, nor do you have to use a formal document request to get your hands on otherwise available information. (But be careful about talking to other represented parties without their lawyers, which raises ethics issues.) Your whole life, you have been figuring out facts for school, jobs, and life tasks. Effective lawyers use all of those skills of research and investigation, along with the tools in the discovery toolbox, to obtain whatever information is needed in representing a client.

(2) Discovery Implementation

The following article contains plenty of useful advice, from an experienced litigator's perspective, about how to engage in the discovery process.

Kathleen Balthrop Havener, *DISCOVERY LESSONS YOUR MOTHER SHOULD HAVE TAUGHT YOU*
American Bar Association GP/Solo Newsletter (July/Aug. 2014)

Take it from me. The most important things about discovery you learned in kindergarten, if you hadn't already learned them from your mother.

Know what you want. The first step of any discovery exercise is—considering as much as you know at the time about the claims and defenses—to put some quality time into figuring out what you want to know. I can't count the number of times I have received "form" discovery requests and read them with a mixture of puzzlement and astonishment. All too often, initial discovery requests ask a bucketful of questions that have absolutely nothing to do with the actual issues in the case. Especially in jurisdictions in which the number of interrogatories is limited, you can't afford to waste a single word on anything you don't really *need*. I always start with the elements of the claims and defenses and ask questions that relate only to facts needed to establish them.

Ask "why?" Pretrial discovery, properly accomplished, involves extreme care, minimal waste, constant weighing of the potential costs and benefits of anticipated discovery, and effective use of the fruits of discovery in dispositive motions and at trial.

Of course, the general purposes of discovery are to uncover evidence, avoid surprises, narrow the issues, lock in key testimony, and—on occasion—permit recovery of certain costs and fees where appropriate. It is important, however, to look beneath the surface of discovery and decide which activities you truly need to engage in to develop your case and which activities may be unnecessary, wasteful, or even damaging to your claims or defenses. If you pay attention to these few tips, your discovery should serve you in good stead for dispositive motions and trial. You should also find discovery to be a useful tool to understand fully the strengths and weaknesses of each party's case, which may move both sides toward the often more efficient and less expensive result of pretrial settlement.

Follow the rules. After contemplation, the most important thing to remember is to review carefully the local rules, along with any standing orders issued by the presiding judge. Do this in *every* case before you begin discovery. It will keep you on your toes when dealing with local opposing counsel if that is an issue, and you may even find more streamlined local discovery rules intended to make the process more straightforward and efficient.

Hide and seek. The primary purpose of discovery is to allow both sides to learn the evidence that best supports or most detracts from the claims and defenses. In some circumstances, your opponent or some other uncooperative party (or nonparty) certainly has the documents or other evidence that are essential for you to establish the elements of your claims or defenses. Carefully crafting each interrogatory or request for admission is the only way to avoid time-wasting objections and discovery motions. Moreover, it is critical to find out what evidence your opponent intends to use to establish its claims or defenses so that you can fully understand the entire case and make an objective assessment of it.

Pay attention. Often the pleadings are insufficient to allow you to know exactly what facts and issues are really in dispute. This is especially true when the language of a complaint is largely conclusory, in which case a *Twombly/Iqbal* motion may be appropriate, or where a defendant's general denial contains a laundry list of every imaginable affirmative defense without consideration of whether any particular defense may actually apply to your case. Properly formulated discovery will help you assess which contentions are merely foolishness and which contentions your opponent actually will rely on to address real issues in the case.

Take care of your stuff. Evidence vanishes. People disappear. People forget. Witnesses move from the jurisdiction. Documents may be misplaced or (even purposely) destroyed. Physical evidence may be lost or deteriorate to the point that it becomes useless. Loss of evidence presents difficult quandaries for attorneys and their clients.

To preserve evidence you need from your opponent, early requests to inspect documents or other materials are especially important. Once you make a formal request, the opposing party has an affirmative responsibility to preserve the documents and materials at issue. Your early request should limit your opponent's ability to claim that important documents or materials were inadvertently disposed of or lost in the regular course of business despite pending litigation. Early requests may even set up a spoliation claim if your opponent fails to preserve what appears to be benign information that later proves important.

Neutral nonparties, including banks, telephone companies, police departments, and brokerage firms, sometimes keep very useful records (e.g., tape recordings of telephone calls, security or surveillance videos) for a very short time. Failure to subpoena records promptly may result in your evidence being lost forever.

Early inspection of physical evidence allows you to memorialize its condition or perform tests before it is too late. For example, an accident investigator cannot inspect a car after it has been repaired or reduced to scrap metal. If you have the opportunity to inspect but fail to do so, you may lose key evidence and be left with no recourse.

If you are concerned that a witness may become unavailable before trial, you can perpetuate the witness's testimony by taking a deposition, either orally or through written questions. If the witness later becomes unavailable or just plain uncooperative, the record of the witness's responses to deposition questions (so long as any documents referenced are properly authenticated) should be admissible at trial under the rules of evidence and the civil rules. However, the testimony can be introduced only if all the parties have had a fair opportunity to question the witness. Mere declarations or other forms of recorded statements may not be admissible. Thus, you should consider noticing a troublesome witness's deposition as a trial deposition. Then approach the deposition as if you were questioning the witness in open court in front of the judge and jury. Be sure to attempt to keep your opponent's objections to a minimum by avoiding leading questions on direct examination. . . .

Know when to stop. "How much discovery is enough?" is a question that can't be answered. The opportunities and possible pitfalls in each case are different, as are your client's preferences, risk tolerance, and willingness or ability to pay for discovery. In certain cases your discovery strategy can be revised—some activities dispensed with it altogether. For example, if you are reasonably confident that a cooperative witness will testify on your client's behalf, consider obtaining an initial written statement or affidavit instead of noticing a deposition. If it's attached to a motion or opposition, rest assured, the opposing side will depose the witness and you will still have the opportunity to question, just on the other guy's nickel.

In a case that turns on conflicting testimony, you may even consider dispensing with the depositions of certain parties if you are confident that you have received satisfactory responses to interrogatories or if a party's discovery responses firmly establish a particular point or fail to preserve a defense.

On the other hand, some cases require huge investments of time and money in discovery. A detailed strategy and discovery plan—constructed with your client's goals and budget in mind—must be developed and continuously revised in every such matter you handle. If you and your client decide to forgo arguably useful discovery to save expense or for other reasons, be sure to document the risks involved and the client's decisions. Do so in letter form and retain a copy for your file. In other words, CYA.

Answer the question. Responding to discovery can be a dangerous enterprise. Take great care in preparing your answers to interrogatories, which in most jurisdictions must be verified under oath by your client. Failing to consider carefully the precise wording of interrogatory responses can lead to disaster.

Responses must be timely. If you fail to respond to written discovery requests by the applicable deadline, objections and claims of privilege may be waived. Even worse, if you fail to timely respond to requests for admissions, the requests may be deemed admitted. In that case you could be done for.

Failure to disclose some fact or to produce some evidence favorable to your case may preclude you from using it at trial. Therefore, be sure that your discovery responses reflect all the information that you and your client have or can reasonably obtain to support your claims or defenses.

Share your toys (but don't give them away). Stop and think when you receive a set of requests for production of documents. Analyze the requests. Ask yourself not only what your opponent is looking for but also what your opponent actually has requested. Ask your client to send you copies of everything remotely related to your claims or defenses and to your opponent's document requests. After you have closely reviewed these documents, select those that are responsive, note documents that are not clearly responsive but that may have some significance to your claims or defenses and therefore you want to produce, and remove and log any privileged documents. Then follow up with your client to confirm that nothing has been missed.

When you have reviewed and categorized the inevitable additional documents, all responsive documents, including the privileged documents, should be serially stamped for ease of reference later on. But be sure to remove the privileged documents and keep them separate from the produced documents in your file.

Only after you have collected and organized the documents for production should you begin to draft the written response to the document request. Reversing this order creates a risk that you will miss appropriate and applicable privileges or that you will fail to ascertain what objections you can safely omit because a complete response poses no danger. Finally, produce copies of the documents, together with your privilege log.

Plan ahead. It can be helpful to consider likely interrogatories during your initial evaluation of the case. Because your discovery responses should include all information your client has in its possession or can obtain with reasonable effort, it is neither wise nor safe to postpone investigation and information gathering until after discovery is underway. The often-seen response that information will be supplemented because "discovery is ongoing" ideally should not refer to your own internal investigation. To avoid ethical issues and Rule 11 concerns, the time to figure out that your case does not have a leg to stand on should not be while you and your client are responding to the opponent's discovery.

If you have a corporate client, be sure to talk to any individuals who contributed to your client's discovery responses to make sure that they are not overlooking any information that may be relevant to the responses, especially information that may be helpful in establishing a claim or defense.

Admit your mistakes. Responses to requests for admissions are binding and typically cannot be amended without leave of the court. But denying a fact without an adequate basis to do so can subject your client to liability for your opponent's costs and attorney fees and even risk sanctions on yourself. It is more critical to be careful about refusing to admit a fact than about admitting one.

Help the needy. The key to successfully defending a deposition is preparing your client to be deposed. A deposition is not your client's day in court. It is not for purposes of venting. It is not a therapy session. It is not the venue for telling her story. Make sure that your client understands that deposing counsel is not her friend. Instruct your client that her answers should be as short and careful as possible, responding only to the specific and limited question asked. Keep in mind that if your client relies on any documents, including privileged documents, to prepare for the deposition or while testifying, those documents may have to be turned over to opposing counsel in discovery.

The sample question I always use in preparing a client to be deposed is, "Do you remember what day the planes crashed into the Twin Towers in New York City?" When your client answers, as she inevitably will, "September 11, 2001," shake your head. "Too much information," you warn. "Listen to the question again." No matter how many tries it takes, allow her to come to the realization *by herself* that the question is not "What day?" but "Do you remember?" There are only two possible correct answers to the question posed, and they are "Yes" or "No." . . .

Follow the Golden Rule. No matter what, remember to play well with others. You can never go wrong by exercising cooperation and plain old common courtesy. But be sure to make your record and stick to your guns when appropriate and necessary for your client. If discovery disputes arise and become contentious, keep in mind that the more faithfully you conduct yourself in a collected and professional manner, the better.

(3) Supplemental Responses

As a case proceeds, parties may find new information that is responsive to earlier discovery requests. A party may realize that one of its interrogatory responses was incorrect, for example, or may realize that it failed to produce certain responsive documents or e-discovery. Under Rule 26(e), a "party who has made a disclosure under Rule 26(a)—or who has responded to an interrogatory, request for production, or request for admission—must supplement or correct its disclosure or response," unless the supplemental or corrective information has otherwise been made known to the other parties during discovery.

THE BIG PICTURE

Lawyers from other countries marvel at U.S. discovery. Both in the amount of information available and the extent to which the process is controlled by the parties rather than the court, U.S. procedure contrasts with nearly every other legal system in the world. In many countries, documents may be obtained from other parties only with the intervention of the judge. Pretrial depositions outside the United States are unusual. These differences create tension when foreign litigants face discovery in U.S. courts or when U.S. litigants need another country's assistance in obtaining information abroad. Many countries have signed the Hague Convention on the Taking of Evidence Abroad, which governs discovery in transnational litigation among the signatories.

D. ELECTRONIC DISCOVERY

As mentioned earlier in the chapter in connection with document requests, discovery of electronically stored information, or *e-discovery*, is an important aspect of Rule 34 practice. In general, the discoverability of information does not depend upon the medium. Relevant, nonprivileged information is generally discoverable whether stored on paper, in any electronic form, or otherwise. However, because of its sheer volume as well as accessibility issues, e-discovery raises special problems of proportionality. The discovery rules and judicial precedent have established a special set of considerations for dealing with electronically stored information that is "not reasonably accessible." Depending on the technology, inaccessible sources may include certain backup tapes, disaster-recovery systems, and electronic files created on older systems that are incompatible with current technology. With electronically stored information, access is rarely impossible, but it is a matter of cost. If translating data into usable form would be especially difficult or expensive, the rule gives the court the power to decide whether the discovery is worth it. The following case provides an example of a court weighing the need for electronically stored information against the cost of producing it, and deciding who should bear that cost.

HAWA v. COATESVILLE AREA SCHOOL DISTRICT
2017 WL 1021026 (E.D. Pa. 2017)

HEFFLEY, Magistrate Judge.

This matter has come before the Court on Defendant Coatesville Area School District's ("CASD") Motion for a Protective Order as to Electronically-Stored Information Sought in Discovery by Plaintiffs. For the reasons discussed below, the Motion will be denied.

I. BACKGROUND

This action involves claims of discrimination and retaliation arising out of Plaintiffs' employment by CASD. In the present Motion, CASD asks that it be relieved of all or, in the alternative, 80% of the costs of certain electronic discovery involving the hard drives of computers used by Plaintiffs, Defendant Romaniello, and a member of CASD's board of directors during the time in question, as well as a database called "GroupWise," which contains a backup of emails. CASD made the decision to store the documents in this fashion to preserve them in light of potential litigation and an ongoing grand jury investigation. The parties have engaged in extensive cooperative efforts to narrow and limit the scope of Plaintiffs' electronic discovery requests in order to reduce the costs of production. Those costs are exacerbated, however, by the fact that the materials in question are stored as pictorial images on unique proprietary software which is not searchable by word searches. CASD has submitted in support of its Motion an estimate provided by its third-party electronic discovery consultants, which reflects that the estimated charges for the production will range from $14,325 to $25,950 plus additional charges for hosting the processed files ranging from $900 to $3,500 per month.

II. DISCUSSION

Federal Rule of Civil Procedure 26(b)(2)(B) provides that:

A party need not provide discovery of electronically stored information from sources that the party identifies as not reasonably accessible because of undue burden or cost. On motion to compel discovery or for a protective order, the party from whom discovery is sought must show that the information is not reasonably accessible because of undue burden or cost. If that showing is made, the court may nonetheless order discovery from such sources if the requesting party shows good cause, considering the limitations of Rule 26(b)(2)(C). The court may specify conditions for the discovery.

As a general rule, parties must bear the costs of complying with discovery requests. Nevertheless, "[a] court may order a cost-shifting protective order only upon motion of the responding party to a discovery request and for good cause shown. The responding party bears the burden of proof on a motion for cost-shifting." *Zeller v. S. Cent. Emergency Med. Servs.*, 2014 WL 2094340, at *8 (M.D. Pa. May 20, 2014). Courts have interpreted Rule 26(b)(2)(B) as establishing . . . that "accessible data must be produced at the cost of the producing party; cost-shifting does not even become a possibility unless there is first a showing of inaccessibility." *Cochran v. Caldera Med., Inc.*, 2014 WL 1608664, at *2 (E.D. Pa. Apr. 22, 2014). "[I]t cannot be argued that a party should ever be relieved of its obligation to produce accessible data merely because it may take time and effort to find what is necessary." *Id.* CASD argues here that the data in question is inaccessible because it is stored on a separate server using proprietary software such that it will require extensive work to restore it to a searchable form. This Court agrees. Nevertheless, the inaccessibility of data merely raises the question of whether cost-sharing is appropriate, it does not mandate cost-sharing.

District courts in the Third Circuit have recognized a set of factors for determining whether cost-sharing is appropriate set out in *Zubulake v. UBS Warburg LLC*, 216 F.R.D. 280, 284 (S.D.N.Y. 2003). Those factors are as follows: (1) the extent to which the request is specifically tailored to discover relevant information; (2) the availability of such information from other sources; (3) the total cost of production, compared to the amount in controversy; (4) the total cost of production, compared to the resources available to each party; (5) the relative ability of each party to control costs and its incentive to do so; (6) the importance of the issues at stake in the litigation; and (7) the relative benefits to the parties of obtaining the information. *Id.*

Applying these factors in this case, the Court finds that CASD has not carried its burden to show that it should be relieved of the cost of producing its own records for discovery. As a result of the parties' efforts, Plaintiffs have pared down their requests so that they include only the hard drives of the individual parties to the litigation and of a school board member who was personally involved in the events at issue in the litigation as well as emails relating to the litigation. Those sources are likely to lead to the discovery of relevant information. CASD has not demonstrated that the same documents contained in the materials to be searched are available from other sources. The fact that CASD's outside counsel may have revealed the information contained in some of the documents sought in reporting the results of its school-district-wide investigation into a variety of alleged improprieties, which included a discussion of CASD's treatment of Plaintiffs, does not ensure that the documents most useful to Plaintiffs were fully disclosed in counsel's report. Similarly, the investigative grand jury report to which CASD refers addressed a variety of alleged improprieties in CASD's affairs and was not directed to Plaintiffs' claims in this litigation. Neither source provides an adequate substitute for Plaintiffs' right to conduct their own investigation of their claims.

The projected cost of the production is not excessive in comparison to the amount in controversy in this case. While neither side has provided the Court with any calculation of potential damages in this case, the Court notes that the Plaintiffs seek lost wages and benefits for the former director of CASD's information technology department and a school district administrator as well as loss of future earnings, emotional distress, potential punitive damages and statutory attorneys' fees and costs. An expenditure in the range of $14,325 to $25,950 plus additional hosting fees of $900 to $3,500 per month is not excessive in the context of the amount at stake in this litigation.[2] Moreover, it is clear that CASD has much greater resources to pay for the discovery sought than do the two individual Plaintiffs. The Court is satisfied that the parties have worked collaboratively to control the costs of the production motivated by the knowledge that the Court would be determining whether or the extent to which those costs would be imposed on either party. As to the sixth *Zubulake* factor—the importance of the issues at stake in the litigation—the Court notes that CASD is a public entity. This case involves alleged retaliation against CASD employees who undisputedly revealed important information regarding misconduct by CASD administrators. All of these factors weigh in favor of CASD bearing the costs of producing the electronically-stored information which is at issue here. Accordingly, the Motion is denied.

---

[2] CASD's argument that Plaintiffs' damages claims are "speculative," is unavailing. It is premature to make this assumption while discovery is ongoing in this case.

Notes & Questions

1. What e-discovery did the plaintiffs seek from the school district? The defendant's motion for a protective order, in this case, did not ask the court to rule that the information was non-discoverable. Rather, it asked the court to shift the costs of complying with the discovery request to the requesting party. Rule 26(b)(2)(B) addresses both discoverability and cost shifting for e-discovery. As to discoverability, it creates a special proportionality analysis for difficult-to-access electronically stored information, with a two-step analysis. First, the court decides if the information is "not reasonably accessible because of undue burden or cost." If the answer is yes, then the court must decide whether the requesting party has shown good cause to permit the discovery notwithstanding the accessibility difficulties. For the cost-shifting part of Rule 26(b)(2)(B), read the last sentence of the rule. Even if the court finds good cause to permit the discovery of information that is not reasonably accessible, the court may specify "conditions" for the discovery. There are a number of conditions for discovery that a court might specify—time, place, technology, and so on—but none is more important to the parties than who pays, particularly given how high the costs of e-discovery can run.

2. As the court notes, each party generally bears its own cost of complying with legitimate discovery requests. Each bears its own legal expenses in discovery, including the cost of having lawyers prepare discovery requests and responses.

For depositions, the party taking the deposition pays the costs of conducting the deposition, such as hiring the court reporter. For document requests and similar discovery, the producing party ordinarily bears the cost of locating the documents, electronic files, or other information responsive to the request and making it available to the requesting party. In exceptional cases, however, a court may order cost shifting, as the school district requested in *Hawa*. The opinion in *Hawa* cites the well-known *Zubulake* factors. In *Zubulake*, the court shifted 25 percent of the cost of certain difficult-to-access e-discovery to the plaintiff after reviewing a sample of the defendant's e-mail back-up records. *See Zubulake v. UBS Warburg LLC*, 217 F.R.D. 309 (S.D.N.Y. 2003) (explaining multifactor test for cost shifting and ordering sampling); *Zubulake v. UBS Warburg LLC*, 216 F.R.D. 280 (S.D.N.Y. 2003) (allocating cost of restoring back-up).

3. In *Hawa*, why did the court deny the school district's request to have the plaintiffs share the cost of e-discovery?

4. Note that, in *Hawa*, CASD submitted a cost estimate from its "third-party electronic discovery consultants." The use of outside vendors for e-discovery services has become a routine feature of litigation involving large amounts of information. As electronically stored information has grown as a component of discovery, the project of collecting potentially relevant documents from the client, identifying responsive documents, separating potentially privileged or work-product documents, and producing documents to the requesting party has become increasingly technology-driven. Unsurprisingly, lawyers routinely turn to nonlawyers for these technology services. As tech responds to tech, consider how the proportionality analysis might take into account both the cost of vendor services and potential efficiency gains in searching for relevant information.

E. DISCOVERY ENFORCEMENT

Mostly, lawyers handle discovery on their own. And mostly, the judge is happy to stay out of it. One side requests information; the other side either provides the requested information or objects, or a combination of the two. When there are objections to particular requests, the lawyers confer with each other to try to work out their differences. *See, e.g.*, Fed. R. Civ. P. 26(c)(1) (requiring conferral in good faith before asking court for protective order), Fed. R. Civ. P. 37(a)(1) (requiring conferral in good faith before asking court to compel discovery). If all goes well, initial disclosures are exchanged, interrogatories are asked and answered, documents are requested and produced, depositions are taken, and the judge remains blissfully unaware of all of it until the pretrial conference. But in the imperfect real world of the adversary system, sometimes the lawyers cannot work out their discovery disagreements and need the court's involvement. That is when motions to compel, motions for protective orders, and discovery sanctions come into play.

(1) Motions to Compel

When another party fails to comply with a discovery request, the requesting party may file a *motion to compel. See* Fed. R. Civ. P. 37(a). A motion to compel asks the court to order the other party to provide the discovery. Maybe the responding party objected to certain questions on grounds of relevance, maybe it gave evasive or incomplete responses, or maybe it failed to respond at all. One might move to compel a party to provide required disclosures, to compel a party to answer interrogatories, to compel a deponent to answer particular questions, or to compel a party to produce documents that were not turned over. Depending on why the responding party failed to comply with the initial discovery request, the legal issues raised by a motion to compel might include whether certain discovery is relevant, whether it is privileged or protected by the work-product doctrine, or whether it is unduly burdensome. In other words, the dispute might concern any aspect of discoverability or the proper use of the discovery tools. Rule 37 governs motions to compel disclosure or discovery. If the court grants the motion, then the responding party must comply with the court's order or face sanctions. If the court denies the motion, then the responding party need not provide the disputed disclosure or discovery.

(2) Motions for Protective Orders

Coming from the opposite direction, the other avenue for discovery disputes to get to court is the *motion for a protective order. See* Fed. R. Civ. P. 26(c). Whereas a motion to compel comes from the requesting party, a motion for a protective order comes from the responding party. A motion for a protective order asks the court to order that certain discovery not be had or to order some other constraint on discovery. Rule 26(c) permits a "party or any person from whom discovery is sought" to move for a protective order. A protective order may forbid certain discovery, such as by ordering that a particular deposition not go forward. It may order that certain topics are off limits or that certain categories of documents need not be produced. As with motions to compel, motions for a protective order might address any legal issues bearing on discoverability, including relevance, privilege, work product, and proportionality. More generally, Rule 26(c) empowers the court to issue protective orders "to protect a party or person from annoyance, embarrassment, oppression, or undue burden or expense."

Motions to compel and motions for protective orders require that the movant first attempt to confer in good faith with the other party to try to resolve the dispute without the court's involvement. Both types of motions are common in litigation, but they are intended as a last resort when the parties are unable to resolve their discovery dispute because of a genuine disagreement that they need the court to adjudicate.

In addition to limiting discovery at the behest of the responding party, protective orders can serve another important function—protecting the confidentiality of discovery materials. Even if information is discoverable, the responding party may consider the information highly confidential either for reasons of personal privacy or because it includes trade secrets or other confidential business information. Rule 26(c) includes confidentiality on its list of potential protective-order terms. Parties frequently ask courts to order that certain materials, even if subject to discovery, be kept confidential and not be revealed outside of the litigation.

(3) Sanctions and Ethical Duties

The discovery enforcement mechanisms—specifically Rule 37 and Rule 26(g)—provide for both minor and major punishments to give teeth to the disclosure and discovery requirements.

If a party fails to disclose required information such as the names of witnesses or descriptions of relevant documents, Rule 37(c) imposes a punishment: "the party is not allowed to use that information or witness to supply evidence on a motion, at a hearing, or at a trial, unless the failure was substantially justified or is harmless." Recall that the mandatory disclosures of Rule 26(a) require only that parties identify witnesses and documents that the party may use to support its own claims or defenses. Precluding the use of undisclosed witnesses and other information, therefore, creates a strong incentive for parties not to withhold names or information from the required disclosures.

More severe discovery sanctions—listed in Rule 37(b)—are normally reserved for parties who fail to comply with a court order. This rule gives added weight to the motion to compel. When a party responds to interrogatories incompletely or evasively, or makes unwarranted objections to document requests, or refuses to answer certain questions at a deposition, the requesting party may move to compel discovery. If the court grants the motion to compel, and the responding party persists in its noncompliance in violation of the court order, *then* a Rule 37 motion for sanctions would be proper. For parties who disobey a court's order compelling discovery, Rule 37(b) lists punishments for a court to consider imposing: directing that certain facts be taken as established for purposes of the action, prohibiting the disobedient party from making particular assertions or from using certain pieces of evidence, striking pleadings in whole or in part, staying the proceedings, dismissal, default judgment, and contempt of court. Generally, the most severe discovery sanction to impose on a disobedient plaintiff is dismissal (that is, judgment for the defendant), and the most severe discovery sanction to impose on a disobedient defendant is default (that is, judgment for the plaintiff). Courts reserve these extreme sanctions of dismissal and default for the most severe discovery violations. In addition or instead, courts order disobedient parties or their attorneys to pay the other side's attorneys' fees caused by the failure to provide discovery.

LEE v. MAX INTERNATIONAL, LLC
638 F.3d 1318 (10th Cir. 2011)

GORSUCH, Circuit Judge.

How many times can a litigant ignore his discovery obligations before his misconduct catches up with him? The plaintiffs in this case failed to produce documents in response to a discovery request. Then they proceeded to violate not one but two judicial orders compelling production of the requested materials. After patiently affording the plaintiffs chance after chance, the district court eventually found the intransigence intolerable and dismissed the case as sanction. We affirm. Our justice system has a strong preference for resolving cases on their merits whenever possible, but no one, we hold, should count on more than three chances to make good a discovery obligation.

The case started ordinarily enough. In February 2009, Markyl Lee and his wholly owned company, PTK, filed a complaint alleging that Max International had breached a contract with them. In the usual course discovery followed and Max propounded various document requests. Unsatisfied with the plaintiffs' production, Max filed a motion to compel.

So far, a little off track but nothing out of the ordinary. Soon, however, things got worse. In October 2009, a magistrate judge granted Max's motion and ordered production of a variety of documents. Despite the order, only a trickle of material followed. Plaintiffs still failed to turn over many items Max had requested and the court had ordered produced.

This led Max to file a motion for sanctions seeking dismissal of the case. As happens in these things, much motions practice followed. Eventually, the magistrate

judge in January 2010 confirmed that the plaintiffs had "blatant[ly]" and without apparent excuse flouted the October 2009 order. Even so, the magistrate stopped short of granting Max's request for dismissal. Instead, the court chose to give the plaintiffs one more chance to produce the requested documents. At the same time, the magistrate warned plaintiffs that "continued non-compliance will result in the harshest of sanctions." The magistrate gave plaintiffs until February 26, 2010 to produce the requested—and now twice compelled—discovery.

On January 25, 2010, the plaintiffs filed with the court a declaration certifying that they had now produced *all* the requested documents. But once again Max couldn't find all of the requested documents. So the very next day Max sent a letter claiming that various materials still remained missing. Receiving no reply to its letter, on February 3 Max renewed its motion for sanctions. Two days after Max filed its motion, plaintiffs produced some of the missing records. Later in the month, the plaintiffs sent along yet more discovery materials.

When the magistrate heard arguments on Max's renewed motion for sanctions, she was not well pleased. She issued a report and recommendation to the district court judge finding that the plaintiffs had violated not only her October 2009 but also her January 2010 order—and that the plaintiffs violated the latter order despite having been expressly warned that any further problems could result in dismissal. Pursuant to Rule 37 of the Federal Rules of Civil Procedure, the magistrate recommended to the district court that it grant

Max's motion and dismiss the case as sanction for plaintiffs' misconduct. In June 2010, the district court did just that, and it is from this order the plaintiffs now appeal.

We view challenges to a district court's discovery sanctions order with a gimlet eye. We have said that district courts enjoy "very broad discretion to use sanctions where necessary to insure . . . that lawyers and parties . . . fulfill their high duty to insure the expeditious and sound management of the preparation of cases for trial." *In re Baker*, 744 F.2d 1438, 1440 (10th Cir. 1984 (en banc). The Supreme Court has echoed this message, admonishing courts of appeals to beware the "natural tendency" of reviewing courts, far from the fray, to draw from fresh springs of patience and forgiveness, and instead to remember that it is the district court judge who must administer (and endure) the discovery process. *See Nat'l Hockey League v. Metropolitan Hockey Club*, 427 U.S. 639, 642 (1976). Commentators, too, have advised us to remember that "the district courts must have latitude to use severe sanctions for purposes of general deterrence." Charles Alan Wright, Arthur R. Miller, Mary Kay Kane & Richard L. Marcus, Federal Practice & Procedure §2284, at 444.

No doubt district judges enjoy such special discretion in this arena because of the comparative advantages they possess. In the criminal sentencing context, the district court receives special deference because it has a better vantage than we to assess the defendant, the crime, the credibility of all involved. And in some sense discovery disputes are analogous. The district court's active participation in the discovery motions practice affords it a superior position than we—with but a cold record to review—for deciding what sanction best fits the discovery "crime," both as a matter of justice in the individual case and "to

deter [others] who might be tempted to [similar] conduct." *Nat'l Hockey League*, 427 U.S. at 643. Discovery disputes are, for better or worse, the daily bread of magistrate and district judges in the age of the disappearing trial. Our district court colleagues live and breathe these problems; they have a strong situation sense about what is and isn't acceptable conduct; by contrast, we encounter these issues rarely and then only from a distance.

We hold that the district court's considerable discretion in this arena easily embraces the right to dismiss or enter default judgment in a case under Rule 37(b) when a litigant has disobeyed two orders compelling production of the same discovery materials in its possession, custody, or control. Plaintiffs in this case were given no fewer than three chances to make good their discovery obligation: first in response to Max's document requests, then in response to the October 2009 order, and finally in response to the January 2010 order. Plaintiffs failed at all three turns. And three strikes is more than enough to allow the district court to call a litigant out. Of course, our legal system strongly prefers to decide cases on their merits. Because of this, we have held that a dismissal or default sanctions order should be predicated on "willfulness, bad faith, or [some] fault" rather than just a simple "inability to comply." *Archibeque v. Atchison, Topeka & Santa Fe Ry.*, 70 F.3d 1172, 1174 (10th Cir. 1995) (*quoting Nat'l Hockey League*, 427 U.S. at 640). Likewise, the Federal Rules protect from sanctions those who lack control over the requested materials or who have discarded them as a result of good faith business procedures. Fed. R. Civ. P. 37(e) (providing a safe harbor for those who "fail[] to provide electronically stored information lost as a result of the routine, good-faith operation of an electronic information system"). But a party's thrice repeated failure to produce materials that have always been and remain within its control is strong evidence of willfulness and bad faith, and in any event is easily fault enough, we hold, to warrant dismissal or default judgment.

Back in 1937 the drafters of the Federal Rules promised that their project would help ensure "the just, speedy, and inexpensive determination of every action." Fed. R. Civ. P. 1. To date, that promise remains elusive, more aspirational than descriptive. But it is surely the case that if court orders can be repeatedly flouted we will only retreat further from the goal. When a party feels at liberty to disobey not just a discovery request but two court orders compelling production of the same material in its control, weeks or months (as in this case) pass without progress in the litigation. Hours, days, weeks of lawyers' time are consumed at great expense. Focus shifts from the merits to the collateral and needless. This is not speedy, inexpensive, or just. Just the opposite. And no doubt tolerating such behavior would encourage only more of it. But there is such thing as discovery karma. Discovery misconduct often may be seen as tactically advantageous at first. But just as our good and bad deeds eventually tend to catch up with us, so do discovery machinations. Or at least that's what Rule 37 seeks to ensure.

Of course, the plaintiffs urge us that theirs isn't a case warranting dismissal.

First, they note, the district court's dismissal order was expressly predicated on a finding that they violated two orders—and this, they say, they simply didn't do. To be more exact, the plaintiffs don't question that they failed to comply with the October 2009 order—and they admit that they don't "have a good explanation" for this misconduct. Instead, they argue only that they

did comply with the magistrate's January 2010 order, and that the district court's factual finding otherwise is clearly wrong. Because the district court rested its decision to dismiss their case on a factually faulty premise, they say, it should be reversed.

But it is the plaintiffs who are mistaken. For its part, Max claims the plaintiffs violated the January 2010 order in many ways. In reply, plaintiffs vigorously dispute Max's representations on each and every score. For our purposes, however, we don't need to wade too deeply into this heap of dispute upon dispute. To sustain the district court's factual finding that plaintiffs violated the January 2010 order against a challenge that it is clearly erroneous, it is enough for us to identify one violation. And one violation of the January 2010 order surely concerns Mr. Lee's tax returns. Max sought these documents in its May 2009 document requests, but plaintiffs failed to provide them. The court ordered the tax returns produced in October 2009, but still plaintiffs failed to yield. In January 2010, the court once again ordered the tax records produced. Responding to this latest order, on January 25 the plaintiffs filed with the court a declaration under the penalty of perjury certifying that they had produced all of the tax records. As it happened, they had not. Even the plaintiffs themselves now don't dispute this much. Neither does anyone dispute that the records were relevant to the case, the request for them reasonably tailored, and that the documents were always within the plaintiffs' control.

Instead, the plaintiffs shift ground. They try to convince us that their false declaration shouldn't matter. The magistrate gave them, they note, until February 26 to comply with the January 2010 order. And though their January 25 production was incomplete and their declaration of compliance false, they eventually produced the requested tax records by February 26. And all's well that ends well, they say.

We disagree. Once the plaintiffs chose to declare—under penalty of perjury, no less—that their production of tax records was now compliant with the January 2010 order, the game was up. The court and defendants were entitled to take that sworn declaration to the bank, to rely upon it, to consider the matter closed. Yet, the plaintiffs produced the tax records only *after* Max uncovered the falsity of the declaration and only *after* Max was forced to file yet *another* motion concerning their production. None of this should've been necessary. And none of this, in any reasonable sense, demonstrates "compliance" with the January 2010 order. Discovery is not supposed to be a shell game, where the hidden ball is moved round and round and only revealed after so many false guesses are made and so much money is squandered. Perhaps the district court could've exercised its discretion to allow the case to proceed despite the false declaration and the plaintiffs' repeated noncompliance. But it certainly did not err in finding that its January 2010 order was violated.

Second, the plaintiffs complain that the district court failed to explain in sufficient detail the reasons for its dismissal order. We have, the plaintiffs observe, previously suggested various factors a district court may wish to consider when deciding whether to exercise its discretion to issue a dismissal sanction: "(1) the degree of actual prejudice to the defendant; (2) the amount of interference with the judicial process; (3) the culpability of the litigant; (4) whether the court warned the party in advance that dismissal of the action would be a likely sanction for non-compliance; and (5) the efficacy of lesser sanctions." *Ehrenhaus v. Reynolds*, 965 F.2d 916, 921 (10th Cir. 1992).

Again the plaintiffs are in error. In *Ehrenhaus* we expressly stated the factors "do not represent a rigid test" that a district court must always apply. 965 F.2d at 921. The *Ehrenhaus* factors are simply a non-exclusive list of sometimes-helpful "criteria" or guide posts the district court may wish to "consider" in the exercise of what must always remain a discretionary function. *Id.* Accordingly, we have repeatedly explained that we will uphold a district court's sanctions order of dismissal or default—despite the "fact that . . . the court [has] not evaluate[d]" the *Ehrenhaus* factors, and despite the fact that not all the factors are satisfied in a particular case—so long as our independent review of the record confirms that the district court didn't abuse its discretion. *Archibeque*, 70 F.3d at 1174-75.

The dispositive question on appeal thus isn't whether the district court's order could or did touch every *Ehrenhaus* base. Instead, it is and always remains whether we can independently discern an abuse of discretion in the district court's sanctions order based on the record before us. The *Ehrenhaus* factors may sometimes help illuminate that question, just as they sometimes may assist a district court in exercising its discretion. But a district court's failure to mention or afford them extended discussion does not guarantee an automatic reversal. And where, as here, the record shows that a party failed to comply with a document request and two court orders compelling production of materials within the party's control, we are convinced a district court does not abuse its discretion by dismissing the case or entering default as sanction, regardless whether and to what extent the *Ehrenhaus* factors found their way into the court's order.

Notes & Questions

1. Note the steps in the story that had to occur before the moving party asked the court to impose sanctions. First, the defendant made document requests under Rule 34. Unsatisfied with the plaintiffs' responses, presumably the defendant's lawyer next made an effort to confer with the plaintiffs' lawyer to resolve the problem as required by Rule 37(a)(1). Still unsatisfied, the defendant moved to compel the plaintiffs to respond. All of this, so far, is neither uncommon nor problematic, as then-Judge Gorsuch explained. It is to be expected that sometimes parties will be unsatisfied with each other's discovery responses and will ask for more, and that sometimes the parties will be unable to resolve the dispute themselves even with a good faith effort to reach agreement on the scope of discovery. It is what happened next in *Lee* that made the case an appropriate scenario for sanctions. After the court granted the defendant's motion to compel, the plaintiffs should have complied with the discovery request. Instead, the plaintiffs produced "a trickle of material," failing to turn over many of the documents the court had ordered them to produce. And they did no better even after the magistrate judge gave them another chance. You can see where the story went from there.

2. Although in general the listed sanctions of Rule 37(b) apply only to parties who disobey court orders, certain failures are so basic that the rule allows sanctions even without a motion to compel and subsequent court order. If a party does not show up for a properly noticed deposition or utterly fails to respond to interrogatories or to a document request, Rule 37(d) permits the court to impose most of the listed sanctions.

3. Another discovery sanctions provision, Rule 26(g), punishes baseless discovery requests, responses, or objections. When you read Rule 26(g), it should look familiar because parts of it are nearly identical to Rule 11, which we addressed in Chapter 2. *Compare* Fed. R. Civ. P. 26(g)(1) *with* Fed. R. Civ. P. 11(a)-(b). Rule 26(g) requires attorneys or unrepresented parties to sign "every discovery request, response, or objection." The signature certifies that to the best of the person's knowledge after a reasonable inquiry, the request, response, or objection is legally warranted, not asserted for any improper purpose such as harassment or delay, and is "neither unreasonable nor unduly burdensome or expensive, considering the needs of the case, prior discovery in the case, the amount in controversy, and the importance of the issues at stake in the action." If a request, response, or objection is legally unjustified, asserted for an improper purpose, or unreasonable in violation of Rule 26(g), the rule instructs the court to impose an appropriate sanction.

4. Even if the parties have not sought sanctions, protective orders, or orders compelling discovery, judges have opportunities to manage the discovery process. In Chapter 4, we will cover pretrial case management, including pretrial conferences

under Rule 16. As you will see, judges treat discovery as an important area to address during pretrial conferences.

5. Recall from Chapter 2, in connection with our discussion of Rule 11 and ethical constraints on litigation, that each state has rules of professional conduct to govern lawyer conduct, and many of these rules are modeled on the American Bar Association's Model Rules of Professional Conduct (RPCs). Of particular relevance to discovery, RPC 3.4(a) states that a lawyer shall not "unlawfully obstruct another party's access to evidence or unlawfully alter, destroy or conceal a document or other material having potential evidentiary value. A lawyer shall not counsel or assist another person to do any such act," and RPC 3.4(d) states that a lawyer shall not "in pretrial procedure, make a frivolous discovery request or fail to make reasonably diligent effort to comply with a legally proper discovery request by an opposing party."

THE BIG PICTURE

Think about discovery in the context of the litigation process as a whole. Many commentators viewed the breadth of discovery under the Federal Rules of Civil Procedure as something that went hand in hand with liberal pleading and a vigorous summary judgment mechanism. As the Supreme Court explained in *Swierkiewicz*, the "simplified notice pleading standard relies on liberal discovery rules and summary judgment motions to define disputed facts and issues and to dispose of unmeritorious claims." *Swierkiewicz v. Sorema N.A.*, 534 U.S. 506, 512 (2002). In combination, these procedures made it easy for parties to assert claims and defenses, easy to gather information, and also reasonably easy to eliminate claims and defenses that could not stand up in light of the evidence discovered. Recent decades, however, have seen retrenchment on both pleadings and discovery. Among other things, the advent of plausibility pleading and the stepping-up of proportionality analysis for discovery were driven by concerns about the costs of discovery. Recall the Supreme Court's reasoning in *Twombly*: "[I]t is one thing to be cautious before dismissing an antitrust complaint in advance of discovery, but quite another to forget that proceeding to antitrust discovery can be expensive." *Bell Atlantic Corp. v. Twombly*, 550 U.S. 544, 546 (2007).

CHAPTER 4

Summary Judgment, Pretrial Adjudication, and Case Management

A. SUMMARY JUDGMENT

If a case reaches a trial, then each party presents its evidence in court and the jury or judge renders a decision. But what if it is clear even before trial, based on the applicable law and the available evidence, that there is only one way a reasonable decision maker could decide the case? Summary judgment gives the judge the power to decide such a lopsided case before it gets to trial.

Summary judgment plays a powerful part in the pretrial process. The motion is frequently made and granted often enough to make parties take it seriously. In certain cases where issues of law predominate or where jury sympathy or confusion may play a role, lawyers may think of summary judgment as the moment when a case is won or lost. For the party pursuing summary judgment, the opportunity to end the case favorably without the cost and uncertainty of trial is a happy prospect. For the party opposing the motion, summary judgment presents the unpleasant risk of losing before even getting the chance to present evidence and cross-examine witnesses at trial.

STRATEGY SESSION

Consider the impact of summary judgment motions on settlement dynamics. If a defendant has a strong chance of winning a summary judgment motion, is the defendant likely to settle? Or, to be more precise, is the defendant likely to settle unless the negotiated amount reflects downward pressure created by the possibility of a pretrial defense victory? If the court denies the defendant's summary judgment motion, then what happens to the plaintiff's leverage? Think about how the negotiating table might feel for each party when the next step is trial and when the judge, by denying summary judgment, has announced that the judge thinks the plaintiff could reasonably win.

The Summary Judgment Standard

Rule 56(a) of the Federal Rules of Civil Procedure states the standard for granting summary judgment:

> The court shall grant summary judgment if the movant shows that there is no genuine dispute as to any material fact and the movant is entitled to judgment as a matter of law.

The Rule 56 standard raises as many questions as it answers. What does it mean that a party is entitled to "judgment as a matter of law"? The movant must "show" such entitlement, but what exactly is required for such a showing? Above all, what does it mean for there to be "no genuine dispute as to any material fact"? This language—no genuine dispute as to any material fact—constitutes the heart of the summary judgment rule, and the cases in this chapter will help you grapple with its meaning.

Because summary judgment is all about the burden of proof, the analysis depends mightily on whether it is a motion by a plaintiff or by a defendant, since plaintiffs generally bear the burden of proof at trial.

Whenever you hear the phrase *burden of proof*, get in the habit of asking yourself whether the speaker is referring to a burden of persuasion, burden of production, or something else. We will take a deeper dive into these burdens in Note 4 after the *Celotex* case, because they will make more sense in the context of a real case, but for now, understand the basic distinction: *Burden of persuasion* refers to what a party must establish to prevail at trial. *Burden of production* refers to a requirement that a party show it has evidence so that a reasonable fact-finder *could* find in the party's favor at trial.

For a plaintiff to win summary judgment on a claim where the plaintiff would bear the burden of persuasion at trial, the plaintiff must establish every element of the claim and show that if the case were to go to trial, no reasonable jury could find for the defendant. For example, suppose a plaintiff sues a defendant for payment of a debt and moves for summary judgment. The plaintiff attaches to the motion a copy of a promissory note plus an excerpt from defendant's deposition transcript in which the defendant admitted that he has not paid. Unless the defendant offers some basis for finding the agreement unenforceable or presents some evidence that he in fact paid the amount owed, the court likely will grant summary judgment to the plaintiff. In the language of Rule 56, there is "no genuine dispute as to any material fact" because the material facts (whether the defendant owes the money and whether he paid it) are undisputed. Or, to be more precise, even if the defendant purports to dispute those facts, the dispute is not genuine unless the defendant presents some evidence to contradict the plaintiff's evidence of an unpaid debt.

For a defendant to win summary judgment, the defendant must show, for at least one element of the plaintiff's claim, that the plaintiff lacks sufficient evidence to raise a genuine dispute of material fact. In one sense, this is easy—the defendant need only show the plaintiff's failure as to a single element of the claim. Think about it this way: On a claim whose required elements are duty, breach, causation, and damages, the plaintiff cannot prevail unless the plaintiff proves *each* of these elements. Therefore, the plaintiff loses if the plaintiff cannot produce sufficient evidence regarding *either* the defendant's breach of a legal duty, *or* the causal link between breach and harm, *or* the fact that the plaintiff suffered harm.

But in another sense, showing the lack of a genuine dispute is quite hard—the defendant must show that the plaintiff's evidence is so utterly lacking that no reasonable jury could find for the plaintiff on that element of the claim. Courts deciding summary judgment cases often talk about viewing the evidence *in the light most favorable to the nonmoving party*. This means that if each side has enough evidence to support its version of the facts, the court's job on summary judgment is not to weigh the credibility of the conflicting stories. Even if a plaintiff's only supporting evidence is the plaintiff's own testimony (as shown by an affidavit or deposition transcript), summary judgment is improper unless no reasonable fact-finder could believe the plaintiff's version.

Alternatively, a defendant can win summary judgment by establishing an affirmative defense. For example, if a defendant points to undisputed facts showing the plaintiff's claim is untimely under the applicable statute of limitations, the court would grant summary judgment for the defendant rather than allow the plaintiff to proceed to trial. Recall from Chapter 2 that, for affirmative defenses, defendants generally bear the burden of proof—both the burden of production and the burden of persuasion. Thus, to take the route of moving for summary judgment based on an affirmative defense, a defendant must affirmatively establish each element of the defense, showing that no reasonable fact-finder could find otherwise. A defendant seeking summary judgment based on an affirmative defense therefore resembles a plaintiff seeking summary judgment on a claim, in the sense that it must establish each element beyond any reasonable dispute.

Summary Judgment Motion Practice

The party moving for summary judgment files the motion with the court and serves the motion on the other parties. *See* Rule 5(a)(1)(D); Rule 56. The motion ordinarily includes three parts: (1) The *notice of motion* takes only about a page and simply notifies the court and the other parties that the movant seeks summary judgment. (2) The *memorandum of law*, or the brief, contains the legal argument in favor of granting the motion. Along with the motion and brief, the moving party nearly always includes (3) *attachments*, pieces of evidence to show why the court should grant the motion. The nonmoving party responds with a memorandum of law in opposition to summary judgment, plus attachments to show why summary judgment should not be granted. The moving party may submit a reply brief, and the court may hear oral argument on the motion.

Attachments are key to understanding summary judgment. First of all, what exactly gets attached? Attachments may include affidavits (sworn written statements from witnesses), interrogatory responses, excerpts from deposition transcripts, copies of documents, or pretty much anything else to convince the judge to grant or deny summary judgment. The attachments reflect the difference between summary judgment and motions at the pleadings stage. Unlike on a Rule 12(b)(6) motion to dismiss for failure to state a claim or a Rule 12(c) motion for judgment on the pleadings, the judge at summary judgment looks at *evidence* or the lack thereof. The motion to dismiss or motion for judgment on the pleadings says to the judge, "The other party has not stated a legally valid claim (or defense). Just look at the pleadings and you'll see that we win." A summary judgment motion generally says to the judge, "The other party does not have the evidence to establish its claim (or defense). Just look at the evidence and you'll see that we win."

The attachments also reflect the difference between summary judgment and trial. On a summary judgment motion, unlike trial, witnesses do not testify in court. Witness testimony may figure prominently in the summary judgment decision, but it gets to the judge by way of affidavits or deposition transcripts attached to the motion or response. Similarly, documents are not "admitted into evidence" on a summary judgment motion. Rather, they are included as attachments to the motion or response.

If the party opposing the motion needs more time for discovery or to obtain affidavits, the party may ask the court to postpone ruling on the summary judgment motion. Rule 56(d) gives the court flexibility about how to handle such situations, but the basic idea is that a court may defer ruling on a summary judgment motion if the nonmoving party shows that it has been pursuing discovery diligently but needs more time to obtain evidence in opposition to the motion. Thus, while a party may move for summary judgment "at *any time* until 30 days after the close of all discovery," Fed. R. Civ. P. 56(b), as a practical matter, Rule 56(d) means that most summary judgment motions are not filed until at or near the close of all discovery.

A party responding to a summary judgment motion has one additional weapon to consider—the cross-motion for summary judgment. If a defendant moves for summary judgment, the plaintiff might cross-move. That is, the plaintiff might say to the judge, in essence, "Not only should you deny the defendant's motion, but you should grant summary judgment for me." (Note that cross-motions are not unique to summary judgment. Any time a party responds to another party's motion, it might make a motion of its own if it has sufficient legal and factual basis for doing so.) Cross-motions for summary judgment present the possibility that the judge may decide the case *either way* as a matter of law.

STRATEGY SESSION

When facing an adversary's summary judgment motion, keep in mind that as a litigator you have at least three different ways to respond, which you may use individually or in combination. First, you can address the legal argument directly. On this approach, you would use your brief to point out flaws in your adversary's legal argument and explain why, under a proper understanding of applicable law, your client's claim (or defense) is sound and why the court therefore should deny summary judgment. Second, you can focus on the sufficiency of the evidence. In your brief and with your attachments, you can point to evidence that meets your client's burden of production and thus defeats summary judgment. Third, if you have not had adequate opportunity for discovery and you need more time to gather evidence, you can say so and ask the court to deny summary judgment or defer ruling on the motion. Thus, as with so many aspects of litigation practice, the lawyer evaluates her strongest arguments and decides how much to emphasize the *law*, the *facts*, and the *process*.

In each of the following two cases, trial courts and appellate courts reached different conclusions on the appropriateness of summary judgment. The first case, *Celotex Corp. v. Catrett*, involved a summary judgment motion that focused on whether there was a genuine dispute regarding causation in a products-liability dispute. The second case, *Darden v. City of Fort Worth*, involved a summary judgment motion in a civil rights lawsuit alleging excessive force by police officers, but in which video evidence of the incident in question was offered for the purpose of conclusively demonstrating the absence of any dispute of material fact regarding excessive force.

CELOTEX CORP. v. CATRETT
477 U.S. 317 (1986)

REHNQUIST, J., delivered the opinion of the Court, in which WHITE, MARSHALL, POWELL, and O'CONNOR, JJ., joined. WHITE, J., filed a concurring opinion. BRENNAN, J., filed a dissenting opinion, in which BURGER, C.J., and BLACKMUN, J., joined. STEVENS, J., filed a dissenting opinion.

The United States District Court for the District of Columbia granted the motion of petitioner Celotex Corporation for summary judgment against respondent Catrett because the latter was unable to produce evidence in support of her allegation in her wrongful-death complaint that the decedent had been exposed to petitioner's asbestos products. A divided panel of the Court of Appeals for the District of Columbia Circuit reversed, however, holding that petitioner's failure to support its motion with evidence tending to *negate* such exposure precluded the entry of summary judgment in its favor. *Catrett v. Johns-Manville Sales Corp.*, 756 F.2d 181 (1985). This view conflicted with that of the Third Circuit. . . . We granted certiorari to resolve the conflict, and now reverse the decision of the District of Columbia Circuit.

Respondent commenced this lawsuit in September 1980, alleging that the death in 1979 of her husband, Louis H. Catrett, resulted from his exposure to products containing asbestos manufactured or distributed by 15 named corporations. Respondent's complaint sounded in negligence, breach of warranty, and strict liability. Two of the defendants filed motions challenging the District Court's *in personam* jurisdiction, and the remaining 13, including petitioner, filed motions for summary judgment. Petitioner's motion, which was first filed in September 1981, argued that summary judgment was proper because respondent had "failed to produce evidence that any [Celotex] product was the proximate cause of the injuries alleged within the jurisdictional limits of [the District] Court." In particular, petitioner noted that respondent had failed to identify, in answering interrogatories specifically requesting such information, any witnesses who could testify about the decedent's exposure to petitioner's asbestos products. In response to petitioner's summary judgment motion, respondent then produced three documents which she claimed "demonstrate that there is a genuine material factual dispute" as to whether the decedent had ever been exposed to petitioner's asbestos products. The three documents included a transcript of a deposition of the decedent, a letter from an official of one of the decedent's former employers whom petitioner planned to call as a trial witness, and a letter from an insurance company to respondent's attorney, all tending to establish that the decedent had been exposed to petitioner's asbestos products in Chicago during 1970-1971. Petitioner, in turn, argued that the three documents were inadmissible hearsay and thus

could not be considered in opposition to the summary judgment motion. . . .

[T]he District Court granted all of the motions filed by the various defendants. The court explained that it was granting petitioner's summary judgment motion because "there [was] no showing that the plaintiff was exposed to the defendant Celotex's product in the District of Columbia or elsewhere within the statutory period." Respondent appealed only the grant of summary judgment in favor of petitioner, and a divided panel of the District of Columbia Circuit reversed. The majority of the Court of Appeals held that petitioner's summary judgment motion was rendered "fatally defective" by the fact that petitioner "made no effort to adduce *any* evidence, in the form of affidavits or otherwise, to support its motion." According to the majority, Rule 56(e) of the Federal Rules of Civil Procedure and this Court's decision in *Adickes v. S.H. Kress & Co.,* 398 U.S. 144, 159 (1970), establish that "the party opposing the motion for summary judgment bears the burden of responding *only after* the moving party has met its burden of coming forward with proof of the absence of any genuine issues of material fact." The majority therefore declined to consider petitioner's argument that none of the evidence produced by respondent in opposition to the motion for summary judgment would have been admissible at trial. The dissenting judge argued that "[t]he majority errs in supposing that a party seeking summary judgment must always make an affirmative evidentiary showing, even in cases where there is not a triable, factual dispute." According to the dissenting judge, the majority's decision "undermines the traditional authority of trial judges to grant summary judgment in meritless cases."

We think that the position taken by the majority of the Court of Appeals is inconsistent with the standard for summary judgment set forth in Rule 56(c) of the Federal Rules of Civil Procedure. Under Rule 56(c), summary judgment is proper "if the pleadings, depositions, answers to interrogatories, and admissions on file, together with the affidavits, if any, show that there is no genuine issue as to any material fact and that the moving party is entitled to a judgment as a matter of law."* In our view, the plain language of Rule 56[] mandates the entry of summary judgment, after adequate time for discovery and upon motion, against a party who fails to make a showing sufficient to establish the existence of an element essential to that party's case, and on which that party will bear the burden of proof at trial. In such a situation, there can be "no genuine issue as to any material fact," since a complete failure of proof concerning an essential element of the nonmoving party's case necessarily renders all other facts immaterial. The moving party is "entitled to a judgment as a matter of law" because the nonmoving party has failed to make a sufficient showing on an essential element of her case with respect to which she has the burden of proof. "[T]h[e] standard [for granting summary judgment] mirrors the standard for a directed verdict under Federal Rule of Civil Procedure 50(a). . . ." *Anderson v. Liberty Lobby, Inc.*, 477 U.S. 242, 250 (1986).

Of course, a party seeking summary judgment always bears the initial

responsibility of informing the district court of the basis for its motion, and identifying those portions of "the pleadings, depositions, answers to interrogatories, and admissions on file, together with the affidavits, if any," which it believes demonstrate the absence of a genuine issue of material fact. But unlike the Court of Appeals, we find no express or implied requirement in Rule 56 that the moving party support its motion with affidavits or other similar materials *negating* the opponent's claim. On the contrary, [Rule 56 states that parties may move for summary judgment with or without supporting affidavits]. [T]he motion may, and should, be granted so long as whatever is before the district court demonstrates that the standard for the entry of summary judgment, as set forth in Rule 56[], is satisfied. One of the principal purposes of the summary judgment rule is to isolate and dispose of factually unsupported claims or defenses, and we think it should be interpreted in a way that allows it to accomplish this purpose.

Respondent argues, however, . . . that since petitioner did not "support" its motion with affidavits, summary judgment was improper in this case. But as we have already explained, a motion for summary judgment may be made pursuant to Rule 56 "with or without supporting affidavits." In cases like the instant one, where the nonmoving party will bear the burden of proof at trial on a dispositive issue, a summary judgment motion may properly be made in reliance solely on the "pleadings, depositions, answers to interrogatories, and admissions on file." Such a motion, whether or not accompanied by affidavits, will be "made and supported as provided in this rule," and Rule 56(e) therefore requires the nonmoving party to go beyond the pleadings and by her own affidavits, or

---

Editors' Note: The 2010 amendments to Rule 56 moved the summary judgment standard from Rule 56(c) to Rule 56(a) and changed the wording from "no genuine issue as to any material fact" to "no genuine dispute as to any material fact" (emphasis added). The amendment was not intended to alter the substantive standard for summary judgment, and courts continue to rely on the Celotex analysis to understand what this phrase means.

by the "depositions, answers to interrogatories, and admissions on file," designate "specific facts showing that there is a genuine issue for trial."

We do not mean that the nonmoving party must produce evidence in a form that would be admissible at trial in order to avoid summary judgment. Obviously, Rule 56 does not require the nonmoving party to depose her own witnesses. Rule 56(e) permits a proper summary judgment motion to be opposed by any of the kinds of evidentiary materials listed in Rule 56(c), except the mere pleadings themselves, and it is from this list that one would normally expect the nonmoving party to make the showing to which we have referred.

The Court of Appeals in this case felt itself constrained, however, by language in our decision in *Adickes*, 398 U.S. 144. [In *Adickes*, the Supreme Court held that summary judgment had been improperly entered in favor of the defendant, explaining that the rule puts "the burden of the moving party . . . to show initially the absence of a genuine issue concerning any material fact."] But we do not think the *Adickes* language quoted above should be construed to mean that the burden is on the party moving for summary judgment to produce evidence showing the absence of a genuine issue of material fact, even with respect to an issue on which the nonmoving party bears the burden of proof. Instead, as we have explained, the burden on the moving party may be discharged by "showing"—that is, pointing out to the district court—that there is an absence of evidence to support the nonmoving party's case. . . .

Our conclusion is bolstered by the fact that district courts are widely acknowledged to possess the power to enter summary judgments *sua sponte*, so long as the losing party was on notice that she had to come forward with all of her evidence. It would surely defy common sense to hold that the District Court could have entered summary judgment *sua sponte* in favor of petitioner in the instant case, but that petitioner's filing of a motion requesting such a disposition precluded the District Court from ordering it.

Respondent commenced this action in September 1980, and petitioner's motion was filed in September 1981. The parties had conducted discovery, and no serious claim can be made that respondent was in any sense "railroaded" by a premature motion for summary judgment. Any potential problem with such premature motions can be adequately dealt with under Rule 56(f),[**] which allows a summary judgment motion to be denied, or the hearing on the motion to be continued, if the nonmoving party has not had an opportunity to make full discovery.

In this Court, respondent's brief and oral argument have been devoted as much to the proposition that an adequate showing of exposure to petitioner's asbestos products was made as to the proposition that no such showing should have been required. But the Court of Appeals declined to address either the adequacy of the showing made by respondent in opposition to petitioner's motion for summary judgment, or the question whether such a showing, if reduced to admissible evidence, would be sufficient to carry respondent's burden of proof at trial. We think the Court of Appeals with its superior knowledge of local law is better suited than we are to make these determinations in the first instance.

[**] *Editors' Note*: The 2010 amendments moved this provision from Rule 56(f) to Rule 56(d).

The Federal Rules of Civil Procedure have for almost 50 years authorized motions for summary judgment upon proper showings of the lack of a genuine, triable issue of material fact. Summary judgment procedure is properly regarded not as a disfavored procedural shortcut, but rather as an integral part of the Federal Rules as a whole, which are designed "to secure the just, speedy and inexpensive determination of every action." Fed. R. Civ. P. 1. Before the shift to "notice pleading" accomplished by the Federal Rules, motions to dismiss a complaint or to strike a defense were the principal tools by which factually insufficient claims or defenses could be isolated and prevented from going to trial with the attendant unwarranted consumption of public and private resources. But with the advent of "notice pleading," the motion to dismiss seldom fulfills this function any more, and its place has been taken by the motion for summary judgment. Rule 56 must be construed with due regard not only for the rights of persons asserting claims and defenses that are adequately based in fact to have those claims and defenses tried to a jury, but also for the rights of persons opposing such claims and defenses to demonstrate in the manner provided by the Rule, prior to trial, that the claims and defenses have no factual basis.

The judgment of the Court of Appeals is accordingly reversed, and the case is remanded for further proceedings consistent with this opinion.

Justice WHITE, concurring.

I agree that the Court of Appeals was wrong in holding that the moving defendant must always support his motion with evidence or affidavits showing the absence of a genuine dispute about a material fact.

I also agree that the movant may rely on depositions, answers to interrogatories, and the like, to demonstrate that the plaintiff has no evidence to prove his case and hence that there can be no factual dispute. But the movant must discharge the burden the Rules place upon him: It is not enough to move for summary judgment without supporting the motion in any way or with a conclusory assertion that the plaintiff has no evidence to prove his case. . . .

Petitioner Celotex does not dispute that if respondent has named a witness to support her claim, summary judgment should not be granted without Celotex somehow showing that the named witness' possible testimony raises no genuine issue of material fact. It asserts, however, that respondent has failed on request to produce any basis for her case. Respondent, on the other hand, does not contend that she was not obligated to reveal her witnesses and evidence but insists that she has revealed enough to defeat the motion for summary judgment. Because the Court of Appeals found it unnecessary to address this aspect of the case, I agree that the case should be remanded for further proceedings.

Justice BRENNAN, with whom Chief Justice BURGER and Justice BLACKMUN join, dissenting.

This case requires the Court to determine whether Celotex satisfied its initial burden of production in moving for summary judgment on the ground that the plaintiff lacked evidence to establish an essential element of her case at trial. I do not disagree with the Court's legal analysis. The Court clearly rejects the ruling of the Court of Appeals that the defendant must provide affirmative evidence disproving the plaintiff's case. Beyond this, however, the Court has not clearly explained what is required of a moving party seeking summary judgment on the ground that the nonmoving party cannot prove its case. This lack of clarity is unfortunate: district courts must routinely decide summary judgment motions, and the Court's opinion will very likely create confusion. For this reason, even if I agreed with the Court's result, I would have written separately to explain more clearly the law in this area. However, because I believe that Celotex did not meet its burden of production under Federal Rule of Civil Procedure 56, I respectfully dissent from the Court's judgment.

I

Summary judgment is appropriate where the Court is satisfied "that there is no genuine issue as to any material fact and that the moving party is entitled to a judgment as a matter of law." Fed. R. Civ. P. 56(c). The burden of establishing the nonexistence of a "genuine issue" is on the party moving for summary judgment. This burden has two distinct components: an initial burden of production, which shifts to the nonmoving party if satisfied by the moving party; and an ultimate burden of persuasion, which always remains on the moving party. The court need not decide whether the moving party has satisfied its ultimate burden of persuasion unless and until the Court finds that the moving party has discharged its initial burden of production. *Adickes v. S.H. Kress & Co.*, 398 U.S. 144, 157-161 (1970).

The burden of production imposed by Rule 56 requires the moving party to make a prima facie showing that it is entitled to summary judgment. The manner in which this showing can be made depends upon which party will bear the burden of persuasion on the challenged claim at trial. If the *moving* party will bear the burden of persuasion at trial, that party must support its motion with credible evidence—using any of the materials specified in Rule 56[]—that would entitle it to a directed verdict if not controverted at trial. Such an affirmative showing shifts the burden of production to the party opposing the motion and requires that party either to produce evidentiary materials that demonstrate the existence of a "genuine issue" for trial or to submit an affidavit requesting additional time for discovery.

If the burden of persuasion at trial would be on the *non-moving* party, the party moving for summary judgment may satisfy Rule 56's burden of production in either of two ways. First, the moving party may submit affirmative evidence that negates an essential element of the nonmoving party's claim. Second, the moving party may demonstrate to the Court that the nonmoving party's evidence is insufficient to establish an essential element of the nonmoving party's claim. If the nonmoving party cannot muster sufficient evidence to make out its claim, a trial would be useless and the moving party is entitled to summary judgment as a matter of law. *Anderson v. Liberty Lobby, Inc.*, 477 U.S. 242, 249 (1986). . . .

If the moving party has not fully discharged this initial burden of production, its motion for summary judgment must be denied, and the Court need not consider whether the moving party has met its ultimate burden of persuasion. Accordingly, the nonmoving party may defeat a motion for summary judgment that asserts that the nonmoving party has no evidence by calling the Court's attention to supporting evidence already in the record that was overlooked or ignored by the moving party. In that event, the moving party must respond by making an attempt to demonstrate the inadequacy of this evidence, for it is only by attacking all the record evidence allegedly supporting the nonmoving party that a party seeking summary judgment satisfies Rule 56's burden of production. Thus, if the record disclosed that the moving party had overlooked a witness who would provide relevant testimony for the nonmoving party at trial, the Court could not find that the moving party had discharged its initial burden of production unless the moving party sought to demonstrate the inadequacy of this witness' testimony. Absent such a demonstration, summary judgment would have to be denied on the ground that the moving party had failed to meet its burden of production under Rule 56. . . .

II

I do not read the Court's opinion to say anything inconsistent with or different than the preceding discussion. My disagreement with the Court concerns the application of these principles to the facts of this case.

Defendant Celotex sought summary judgment on the ground that plaintiff had "failed to produce" any evidence that her decedent had ever been exposed to Celotex asbestos. Celotex supported this motion with a two-page "Statement of Material Facts as to Which There is No Genuine Issue" and a three-page "Memorandum of Points and Authorities" which asserted that the plaintiff had failed to identify any evidence in responding to two sets of interrogatories propounded by Celotex and that

therefore the record was "totally devoid" of evidence to support plaintiff's claim.

Approximately three months earlier, Celotex had filed an essentially identical motion. Plaintiff responded to this earlier motion by producing three pieces of evidence which she claimed "[a]t the very least . . . demonstrate that there is a genuine factual dispute for trial": (1) a letter from an insurance representative of another defendant describing asbestos products to which plaintiff's decedent had been exposed, (2) a letter from T.R. Hoff, a former supervisor of decedent, describing asbestos products to which decedent had been exposed, and (3) a copy of decedent's deposition from earlier workmen's compensation proceedings. Plaintiff also apparently indicated at that time that she intended to call Mr. Hoff as a witness at trial.

Celotex subsequently withdrew its first motion for summary judgment. However, as a result of this motion, when Celotex filed its second summary judgment motion, the record *did* contain evidence—including at least one witness—supporting plaintiff's claim. . . .

On these facts, there is simply no question that Celotex failed to discharge its initial burden of production. Having chosen to base its motion on the argument that there was no evidence in the record to support plaintiff's claim, Celotex was not free to ignore supporting evidence that the record clearly contained. Rather, Celotex was required, as an initial matter, to attack the adequacy of this evidence. Celotex' failure to fulfill this simple requirement constituted a failure to discharge its initial burden of production under Rule 56, and thereby rendered summary judgment improper. . . .

Notes & Questions

1. To see whether you understand the Supreme Court's analysis in *Celotex*, take it step by step, starting with the movant's argument. What was Celotex's argument that it was entitled to summary judgment? (Specifically, which element of Catrett's claim did Celotex argue she lacked evidence to establish?) How did Celotex attempt to show that Catrett lacked evidence to support this element of her claim? (Specifically, what did Celotex point to?) Keep in mind that rather than pointing to something, one might need to point to the *absence* of something. How does one show an absence?

   Now turn to the argument against summary judgment. The Supreme Court addresses two distinct arguments that summary judgment should be denied. First, there is the legal argument on which the D.C. Circuit relied—citing the Supreme Court's prior decision in *Adickes*—in holding that Celotex had failed to make the necessary showing to win summary judgment. What was this legal argument regarding Celotex's required showing under *Adickes*, and why did the Supreme Court reject it? Second, there is the argument that Catrett herself emphasized, and that Justice Brennan found convincing, regarding the sufficiency of her evidence. What were the pieces of evidence that Catrett pointed to in opposition to summary judgment?

2. Focus on the attachments—the documents that each party provides to the court in connection with the summary judgment motion—and consider the different role attachments play in the motion and the response. Celotex, in support of its motion, attached a copy of the interrogatory response in which Catrett failed to identify any evidence that her spouse was exposed to the company's asbestos products. Catrett, in her response to the motion, attached a letter from her spouse's former employer, a letter from an insurance company, and a transcript of her spouse's deposition from an earlier workers' compensation case. With these attachments, she sought to convince the court that she had enough evidence of her husband's exposure to the company's asbestos to meet her burden of production.

3. In *Celotex*, note that the Supreme Court did not ultimately answer whether summary judgment should be granted. The Supreme Court majority found that Celotex *might* be entitled to summary judgment, and therefore reversed the D.C. Circuit's ruling to the contrary. But the Court did not decide whether Catrett's evidence sufficed to meet her burden of production and thus to defeat summary judgment. The Supreme Court remanded the case for a determination of whether summary judgment should be granted.

   On remand, a majority of the Court of Appeals found that summary judgment should be denied. The majority opinion by Judge Kenneth Starr noted that Catrett had produced a letter indicating that her spouse supervised crews applying "Firebar Fireproofing" and that evidence in the record linked Firebar to Celotex in a way that could make Celotex liable. Judge Starr wrote:

> Considering the record before the District Court when it granted summary judgment—in particular, the four items discussed above—we believe that the issue of exposure was not so one-sided that Celotex was entitled to judgment as a matter of law. The record contains sufficient evidence to create a genuine issue of material fact with respect to Mr. Catrett's exposure to the asbestos product Firebar while working for Anning-Johnson. While the four items taken individually provide less than overpowering support for Mrs. Catrett's position, their cumulative effect is, we believe, sufficient to defeat the summary judgment motion.

Catrett v. Johns-Manville Sales Corp., 826 F.2d 33, 39-40 (D.C. Cir. 1987). In dissent, Judge Robert Bork maintained that the letter would be inadmissible as evidence at trial and therefore should not be considered on the question of summary judgment.

4. In *Celotex*, Justices Rehnquist, White, and Brennan each framed the analysis of summary judgment in terms of burdens. There are several burdens in play, and to understand how summary judgment works, you must understand how each burden plays a different role.

The common but unsatisfactorily vague phrase "burden of proof" encompasses at least two distinct concepts—(1) the burden of persuasion and (2) the burden of production. In general, the *burden of persuasion* refers to what must be established by a party to prevail at trial. In a civil case, the plaintiff typically bears the burden of persuasion to establish each element of the claim by a preponderance of the evidence. Note that this statement has two components. First, who bears the burden of production? (Answer: the plaintiff, as to each element of the claim.) Second, how high is this burden? (Answer: preponderance of the evidence, also described as "more likely than not.") In a criminal case, by contrast, the government bears the burden of persuasion to establish each element "beyond a reasonable doubt."

The *burden of production* generally refers to the requirement that a party produce sufficient evidence so that a reasonable fact-finder *could* find in the party's favor at trial. Burdens of production generally accompany burdens of persuasion. Thus, in a civil case, the plaintiff typically bears the burden of production. If a plaintiff fails to produce evidence from which a reasonable jury or judge could find in favor of the plaintiff, then the plaintiff has failed to meet the burden of production and may lose "as a matter of law." If the plaintiff fails to meet the burden of production *before trial*, the court may enter summary judgment under Rule 56. If the plaintiff fails to meet the burden of production *at trial*, the court may enter judgment as a matter of law under Rule 50, which we will cover in Chapter 5. In the less-common situations where the defendant bears the burden of production, such as affirmative defenses, it works the same way. If the defendant fails to meet its burden of production—that is, if the defendant has failed to produce sufficient evidence so that a reasonable jury or judge could find in favor of the defendant on that defense—then the court may enter partial summary judgment or judgment as a matter of law. Note the interplay between the burden of production and the burden of persuasion. When a court says that a plaintiff has failed to meet the *burden of production*, it means that the plaintiff has failed to produce enough evidence so that the fact-finder could reasonably find that the plaintiff has met its *burden of persuasion.*

In addition to the burden of persuasion and burden of production, courts sometimes refer to a *burden of pleading.* The burden of pleading is a useful frame for thinking about the Supreme Court's decisions in *Swierkiewicz, Twombly,* and *Iqbal,* and, indeed, for thinking about every motion to dismiss under Rule 12(b)(6). In a civil case, the plaintiff typically bears the burden of pleading each element of the claim—in Chapter 2 we explored the content of this burden—and the defendant typically bears the burden of pleading any affirmative defenses.

There is yet another burden that should be mentioned in the context of *Celotex.* This is the summary judgment *movant's* burden under Rule 56 to "show" that there is no genuine dispute as to any material fact. This is the burden to which Justice Rehnquist referred when he wrote for the *Celotex* majority that "the burden on the moving party may be discharged by 'showing'—that is, pointing out to the district court—that there is an absence of evidence to support the nonmoving party's case" and when he wrote that the movant "always bears the initial responsibility of informing the district court of the basis for its motion." Likewise, it is the burden Justice White referred to, in concurrence, when he wrote that "the movant must discharge the burden the Rules place upon him." And it is the burden Justice Brennan discussed at length in his dissent, calling it the "burden of production under Federal Rule of Civil Procedure 56." Justice Brennan's use of the phrase "burden of production" to refer to the Rule 56 movant's burden—a burden that stems from the party's status as the *movant*—differs from the more common usage, but when you examine the substance of his argument, note how Justice Brennan clearly distinguishes between plaintiff Catrett's burdens with regard to the underlying claims and defendant Celotex's burdens as the summary judgment movant.

5. In *Celotex,* both the majority opinion and the dissent offer helpful explanations of how to analyze a summary judgment motion, and Justice Brennan began his dissent by stating that he did "not disagree with the Court's legal analysis." But even though Justices Rehnquist and Brennan agreed on the law regarding summary judgment, note the difference in what they chose to emphasize. Which of them was more enthusiastic about the use of summary judgment? One of them emphasized the importance of summary judgment as an integral part of civil procedure, while the other emphasized the importance of the summary judgment movant's burden. Why the differences in emphasis?

6. Along with *Celotex*, the Supreme Court decided two other summary judgment cases in 1986. The others were *Matsushita Electric Industrial Co. v. Zenith Radio Co.*, 475 U.S. 574 (1986), and *Anderson v. Liberty Lobby, Inc.*, 477 U.S. 242 (1986). Lawyers sometimes refer to these three cases as the "summary judgment trilogy." The conventional wisdom is that before 1986, judges were reluctant to take cases away from the jury by granting summary judgment, and the trilogy raised the profile of summary judgment as a standard part of litigation practice. Some have questioned whether the trilogy actually had such a revolutionary impact. This much is clear: *Celotex*, *Matsushita*, and *Anderson* each moved the law of summary judgment in a way that made such motions easier to grant, and all three cases continue to be widely cited by lawyers and judges.

   Here is a nice piece of judicial trivia. On the all-time list of most-cited Supreme Court cases, the summary judgment trilogy cases rank one, two, and five: *Anderson* ranks first, *Celotex* second, and *Matsushita* fifth. *See* Adam Steinman, *The Rise and Fall of Plausibility Pleading*, 69 Vand. L. Rev. 333, 390 (2016) (ranking Supreme Court cases by number of federal court citations as of 2015). This should give you a sense of the centrality of the 1986 trilogy to summary judgment analysis as well as the sheer frequency of summary judgment motions in federal court. By the way, *Twombly* and *Iqbal* rank three and four respectively, *id.*, which similarly gives a sense of the significance of these cases, the frequency of motions to dismiss, and the ubiquity of procedural doctrine, no matter what the type of claims involved.

7. The Seventh Amendment to the U.S. Constitution guarantees a right to a jury trial in certain civil cases, as we will explore in Chapter 5. When a court grants summary judgment in a case that otherwise would have gone to a jury trial, the court shuts down preemptively the jury's power to decide the case. Courts have rejected the argument that the summary judgment procedure is unconstitutional under the Seventh Amendment, but when considering summary judgment motions, judges are sensitive to the implications of adjudicating a case as a matter of law rather than letting it go to the jury. A judge who grants summary judgment should not substitute her evaluation of the evidence for the jury's. At least in theory, on a summary judgment motion the judge does not decide which witnesses are credible and does not choose which inferences to draw from the evidence; these are jobs for the jury. Even if a judge personally believes that one party deserves to win the case because its evidence appears stronger, the judge should nonetheless deny summary judgment if evidence exists from which a reasonable jury *could* find the other way. This tension between the jury's role and the judge's role goes to the heart of the summary judgment procedure, even though summary judgment—a pretrial process—occurs before any jury has been assembled in a case.

8. Not all trials involve juries; some are "bench trials," in which the judge decides both the law and the facts. Rule 56 does not distinguish between jury trials

and bench trials. Thus, even if a case is heading toward a bench trial rather than a jury trial, summary judgment is available. In one obvious way, summary judgment looms larger in jury cases than in non-jury cases. When a judge grants summary judgment in a jury-trial case, the judge is taking power away from the (not-yet-assembled) jury. When a judge grants summary judgment in a bench-trial case, by contrast, the judge is not taking power away from a jury, but merely hastening the moment when the judge adjudicates the dispute.

A less obvious point, however, is that in one way it is easier to get summary judgment in non-jury cases than in jury cases. If a decision comes down to the judge drawing inferences or reaching conclusions based on undisputed evidence—that is, there are no issues of witness credibility or disputes of evidentiary fact, but only questions of what conclusion to reach based on the undisputed facts—then a judge may grant summary judgment in a non-jury case. By contrast, if the case were heading toward a jury trial and a jury could reasonably reach different conclusions, the judge must let the jury draw inferences and apply the law to the facts. For example, in a negligence case, suppose there is no dispute over what happened as a factual matter but the parties dispute whether those facts constitute negligence, and a reasonable jury could find either way. In a jury case, the judge would reject summary judgment because it is the jury's role to decide whether the defendant's conduct breached the duty of care. In a bench-trial case, however, the judge could grant summary judgment by reaching a conclusion based on the undisputed evidentiary record. *See, e.g., Stewart Title Guaranty Co. v. Residential Title*, 607 F. Supp. 2d 959 (E.D. Wis. 2009) (granting summary judgment for plaintiff in a bench-trial breach-of-contract action because "[i]n the present case, there are no disputed lay facts and no issues of witness credibility. The question for decision involves the evaluation of and drawing inferences from undisputed evidence."). In Chapter 5, we will explore other differences between jury trials and bench trials.

9. Summary judgment need not resolve an entire case. Often, it narrows the issues in dispute. If certain parts of claims or defenses are established or rejected clearly enough to meet the summary judgment standard, the court may grant *partial summary judgment* on those issues. There are two basic versions of partial summary judgment.

First, Rule 56(a) states that a party moving for summary judgment should identify "each claim or defense—or the part of each claim or defense—on which summary judgment is sought." In other words, the court need not grant summary judgment on every claim or defense. For instance, if an employee has sued her employer for race and gender discrimination, the court might grant summary judgment on one claim while allowing the other claim to proceed.

Second, partial summary judgment may be used to narrow the types of damages a jury may award, or, along similar lines, to reduce the jury's job simply to one of determining damages. Regarding the former, for example, if a plaintiff sues a defendant for both compensatory and punitive damages, the defendant might seek summary judgment as to punitive damages. If the defendant shows that the plaintiff lacks evidence on which a reasonable jury could award punitive damages, the court should grant partial summary judgment for the defendant. The case would move forward to trial on the compensatory damages claim. Regarding the latter, the evidence at the summary judgment stage may establish that the defendant is liable to the plaintiff, yet the extent of the plaintiff's damages may be disputed. In this situation, the judge should grant summary judgment on liability. At trial, the parties would present evidence only on the extent of the plaintiff's harm, and the jury would render a verdict on the amount of damages.

Third, summary judgment may reduce the number of factual issues for trial even if it does not fully resolve any claims. Rule 56(g) instructs judges that if the court does not fully grant summary judgment, the court may determine that certain facts have been established. In a case involving an auto accident, for example, a judge might determine that a genuine dispute exists concerning whether the defendant drove negligently but that no genuine dispute exists whether the plaintiff's broken ribs were caused by the crash. By determining some of the material facts at the summary judgment stage, the court streamlines the case for trial.

10. Summary judgment bears a resemblance to Rule 12(b)(6) dismissals for failure to state a claim and Rule 12(c) judgments on the pleadings. All three can be used to throw out claims that have no reasonable chance of prevailing on the merits. All three provide opportunities for the judge to rule on legal questions that go to the viability of plaintiffs' claims. Indeed, Rule 12(d) specifically instructs judges to convert a Rule 12(b)(6) motion or a Rule 12(c) motion into a Rule 56 summary judgment motion if the parties present matters outside the pleadings. The essential difference is that the 12(b)(6) motion looks only at the *allegations* in the complaint (or, for Rule 12(c), in the complaint and answer), whereas on a summary judgment motion the court may look at *evidence* presented in attachments to the motion and response.

11. How might the summary judgment analysis play out in a dispute involving *video* evidence? Does video evidence—increasingly common today—eliminate "genuine" disputes about the facts? Or does video evidence merely shift the way these disputes play out? Consider the following case involving allegations of police excessive force. As you read the case, ask what standards ought to apply to video evidence on a summary judgment motion, and what sorts of problems might arise—Authenticity? Reliability? Objectivity? Continuity? Other qualities? What if the video provides only part of the picture? And what if the non-movant submits affidavits from witnesses whose testimony contradicts the video or the inferences the movant would draw from it?

DARDEN v. CITY OF FORT WORTH
880 F.3d 722 (5th Cir. 2018)

PRADO, Circuit Judge.

Fort Worth Police Officers W.F. Snow and Javier Romero arrested Jermaine Darden, a black man who was obese, while executing a no-knock warrant at a private residence. In arresting Darden, the officers allegedly threw him to the ground, tased him twice, choked him, punched and kicked him in the face, pushed him into a face-down position, pressed his face into the ground, and pulled his hands behind his back to handcuff him. Darden suffered a heart attack and died during the arrest. The administrator of Darden's estate subsequently brought this 42 U.S.C. §1983 case against Officers Snow and Romero and the City of Fort Worth (the "City"). The district court granted summary judgment in favor of the officers and the City and dismissed all claims. We REVERSE in part, VACATE in part, and REMAND.

I. BACKGROUND

In 2013, the Fort Worth Police Department investigated claims that cocaine was being sold from a private residence. A magistrate judge issued a warrant that allowed the officers to enter the residence without first knocking and announcing themselves. On May 16, 2013, a large team of heavily armed police officers executed the warrant. Officer Snow was assigned to the entry team, which was tasked with breaking down the front door, entering the residence, and securing the premises. Officer Romero drove the van that transported the team to the residence. He was also assigned to stand guard near the front door while other officers entered the residence and arrested the people inside. Two other members of the team wore cameras on their helmets, which captured on video some but not all of the events that transpired as the warrant was executed.

When the police first arrived at the house, the entry team broke down the front door with a battering ram, yelled that they were police, and ordered everyone to get down. A large man, later identified as Darden, was kneeling on the seat of a couch near the door when the officers first entered, and he immediately raised his hands in the air. Darden weighed approximately 340 pounds. Several other people were sitting and standing in a nearby dining room. As Officer Snow entered the residence, he reached out and ripped the shirt off Darden's back, apparently in an attempt to get Darden from the couch to the ground. The videos do not show what happened during the twenty-five seconds that followed, and there is conflicting testimony about what transpired. According to witnesses for the plaintiff, Darden "had no time to react" before "[h]e was thrown on the ground" by the officers. Witnesses also testified that Darden never made any threatening gestures and did not resist arrest. . . .

After approximately twenty-five seconds, it became apparent that some sort of incident was occurring in the front room. One of the videos shows Darden lying on the ground face up. An officer in the front room yelled, "Roll over on your face," at which point, Darden appeared to follow directions and rolled over onto his stomach. The video then pans away from the scene and does not turn back for approximately fifteen seconds. The second video shows that Officer Romero then ran into the house to assist. However, in that video, much of the interaction between Darden and the officers is totally obscured by the couch. Although not captured by the video, eyewitnesses testified that Officer Romero proceeded to choke Darden and to repeatedly punch and kick Darden in the face.

At one point, Darden's body appeared to come up off the ground for a moment, but it is not clear from the video footage whether he came up of his own volition or was pulled up by police. The officers then backed away, and Officer Snow used a Taser on Darden. Shortly thereafter, Darden rolled over onto his stomach and appeared to push himself up on his hands. He was immediately pushed back down into the ground by police. Throughout these events, other people in the house repeatedly yelled, "He's got asthma," and "He can't breathe." Eyewitnesses also testified that Darden himself told the officers he could not breathe.

A few seconds later, the videos briefly show Darden on his knees, with his hands in the air, before Officer Snow tased him a second time. Darden fell to the ground and rolled onto his back, where he lay face up for a few seconds. Officer Romero then pushed Darden over onto his stomach and pressed his face into the ground. As Officer Romero tried to pull Darden's left arm behind his back, Darden seemed to pull his arm away. The officers then pushed Darden back into the ground, and one officer appeared to put him in a choke hold.

At that point, other people in the residence were still yelling that Darden could not breathe. Nevertheless, several officers continued to push Darden's body into the ground face down, pressed his face and neck into the floor, and pulled his arms behind his back so that Officer Romero

could handcuff him. As Officer Romero finished securing the handcuffs, Darden's body went limp. The officers then pulled Darden's debilitated body up into a sitting position and left him there. Darden appeared to be unconscious, and his head hung down on his chest. It was subsequently determined that Darden had suffered a heart attack and died.

The administrator of Darden's estate brought suit under 42 U.S.C. §1983, claiming that Officers Snow and Romero used excessive force in arresting Darden and that the City was liable for failing to adequately train the officers. All of the defendants filed motions for summary judgment, and the district court granted their motions and dismissed the case. The district court determined that the officers had not violated clearly established law and were thus entitled to qualified immunity. In addition, the district court stated that the plaintiff had failed to show that Darden's death resulted only from the officers' use of force. Because it held that the officers had not violated Darden's constitutional rights, the district court likewise dismissed the municipal liability claims. This appeal followed.

II. DISCUSSION

"We review a summary judgment *de novo*, using the same standard as that employed by the district court under Rule 56." *Newman v. Guedry*, 703 F.3d 757, 761 (5th Cir. 2012). Summary judgment is appropriate "if the movant shows that there is no genuine dispute as to any material fact and the movant is entitled to judgment as a matter of law." Fed. R. Civ. P. 56(a).

A. OFFICERS SNOW AND ROMERO

The Supreme Court has "mandated a two-step sequence for resolving government officials' qualified immunity claims." *Pearson v. Callahan*, 555 U.S. 223, 232 (2009). We must determine (1) "whether the facts that a plaintiff has alleged . . . make out a violation of a constitutional right" and (2) "whether the right at issue was clearly established at the time of defendant's alleged misconduct." *Id. . . .* In the excessive force context, a constitutional violation is clearly established if no reasonable officer could believe the act was lawful. . . .

Once an official pleads qualified immunity, "the burden then shifts to the plaintiff, who must rebut the defense by establishing a genuine fact issue as to whether the official's allegedly wrongful conduct violated clearly established law." *Brown v. Callahan*, 623 F.3d 249, 253 (5th Cir. 2010). Still, at the summary judgment stage, we must "view the facts in the light most favorable to . . . the nonmoving party." *City & Cty. of San Francisco v. Sheehan*, 135 S. Ct. 1765, 1769 (2015). "The evidence of the non-movant is to be believed, and all justifiable inferences are to be drawn in his favor." *Anderson v. Liberty Lobby, Inc.*, 477 U.S. 242, 255 (1986). . . .

1. INJURY AND CAUSATION

The district court held that the "plaintiff could not establish an excessive force claim because he cannot show that Darden's death resulted directly and only from the use of force that was clearly excessive to the need." According to the plaintiff's medical expert, "Darden died as a result of the application of restraint (physical struggle, 4 taser dart strikes, prone position with the weight of police officers on top of Mr. Darden) and consequential hypoxia and increased cardiac demand." But the medical expert went on to explain that "[t]he application of restraint [was] a contributing causal factor along with

natural disease." The other contributing factors were focal coronary artery disease, "which can increase the likelihood of developing an arrhythmia during a struggle," and chronic lung disease, which "can impede air exchange causing hypoxia (low oxygen) and increase the risk of cardiac arrhythmia during exertion such as a struggle." Thus, the district court's conclusion that the injury did not result directly and only from the use of force was essentially based on the fact that Darden had preexisting medical conditions that increased his risk of death during the incident.

The district court erred in reaching this conclusion. According to the "eggshell skull" rule, "a tortfeasor takes his victim as he finds him." *Dunn v. Denk*, 54 F.3d 248, 251 (5th Cir. 1995), *rev'd on other grounds*, 79 F.3d 401 (5th Cir. 1996) (en banc). The eggshell skull rule is applicable in §1983 excessive force cases. Darden's preexisting medical conditions increased his risk of death during a struggle, and in that way, they contributed to his death. However, the evidence suggests that Darden would not have suffered a heart attack and died if the officers had not tased him, forced him onto his stomach, and applied pressure to his back. Indeed, the medical expert ultimately concluded that "Darden's manner of death should not have been ruled as Natural." Accordingly, the plaintiff can show that the use of force was the direct and only cause of Darden's death.

2. CLEARLY EXCESSIVE AND CLEARLY UNREASONABLE USE OF FORCE

"Excessive force claims are necessarily fact-intensive; whether the force used is 'excessive' or 'unreasonable' depends on 'the facts and circumstances of each particular case.'" *Deville v. Marcantel*, 567 F.3d

156, 167 (5th Cir. 2009) (quoting *Graham v. Connor*, 490 U.S. 386, 396 (1989)). In making this determination, a court should consider the totality of the circumstances, "including the severity of the crime at issue, whether the suspect poses an immediate threat to the safety of the officers or others, and whether he is actively resisting arrest or attempting to evade arrest by flight." *Graham*, 490 U.S. at 396. . . .

a. Severity of the Crime

The magistrate judge who issued the warrant determined that there was probable cause to believe that suspects at the residence were dealing drugs. These types of drug crimes are certainly serious offenses. Thus, the severity of the crime at issue weighs in favor of the officers.

b. Immediate Safety Threat

There is a genuine factual dispute over whether Darden posed an immediate safety threat to the officers. There were certainly inherent dangers associated with executing a narcotics warrant, and the officers were aware that lookouts were positioned in the house across the street. Still, Darden "was not suspected of committing a violent offense," *Cooper v. Brown*, 844 F.3d 517, 522 (5th Cir. 2016), and testimony suggests that Darden did not threaten the officers in any way when they entered the residence. Eyewitnesses testified that Darden put his hands in the air, and indeed, the video shows Darden raising his hands when the officers enter the home. Witnesses also testified that Darden made no threatening gestures and did not resist arrest. Therefore, a jury could conclude that no reasonable officer would have perceived Darden as posing an immediate threat to the officers' safety.

c. Resisting Arrest

The district court's analysis largely turned on an assessment that Darden was actively resisting arrest when Officers Snow and Romero used force on him. . . . According to the district court, "[t]he video makes clear that Darden did not get on the ground as ordered by the officers and that the taser was employed to assist them in getting Darden to the ground."

"When opposing parties tell two different stories, one of which is blatantly contradicted by the record, so that no reasonable jury could believe it, a court should not adopt that version of the facts for purposes of ruling on a motion for summary judgment." *Scott v. Harris*, 550 U.S. 372, 380 (2007) [(evaluating video evidence and concluding that there was no genuine dispute of fact regarding a lack of excessive police force in a high-speed car chase)]. Thus, in *Scott*, the Supreme Court held that because the nonmovant's version of events was "so utterly discredited" by a videotape "that no reasonable jury could have believed him," the court of appeals "should have viewed the facts in the light depicted by the videotape." *Id.* at 380-81. Yet the standard imposed by the Supreme Court is a demanding one: a court should not discount the nonmoving party's story unless the video evidence provides so much clarity that a reasonable jury could not believe his account.

In the instant case, the videos do not meet that difficult standard because they do not show whether Darden got onto the ground when he was commanded to do so. After the officers entered the house and ripped off Darden's shirt, the next shot of Darden shows him lying on the ground approximately twenty-five seconds later. Neither video shows what transpired between those two events. Nor do the videos make clear how Darden transitioned from kneeling on the couch to lying on the floor. The parties offer conflicting accounts of Darden's actions during those twenty-five seconds: witnesses for the plaintiff claim that Darden was compliant with the officers' commands and was thrown to the ground by police, whereas Officer Snow claims that Darden was attempting to stand up and was resisting the officers' attempts to get him on the ground. In contrast to *Scott*, however, the videos do not favor one account over the other and do not provide the clarity necessary to resolve the factual dispute presented by the parties' conflicting accounts.

Based on the evidence in the record, a jury could conclude that no reasonable officer on the scene would have thought that Darden was resisting arrest. The videos show that Darden raised his hands when the officers entered the residence, and it appears that he rolled over onto his face at one point after the officers instructed him to do so. Moreover, eyewitnesses testified that Darden was thrown to the ground before he could react, that he complied with the officers' commands, and that he did not resist arrest. From the video recordings, it appears that Darden later pushed himself up on his hands, and eventually onto his knees, and he seemed to pull his arm away from the officers when they were trying to handcuff him. But those events occurred while other people in the house were loudly and repeatedly yelling that Darden had asthma and was trying to breathe. In addition, Darden allegedly told the officers he could not breathe.

Snow argues that the officers "had no way of knowing in that tense, uncertain, and rapidly evolving situation" if it was "true or false" that Darden was struggling to breathe. He contends that "a police

officer need not credit everything a suspect tells him." However, the issue of whether reasonable officers in this situation would have credited the warnings from Darden and the other suspects is a factual question that must be decided by a jury. As the Supreme Court has made clear, "at the summary judgment stage the judge's function is not himself to weigh the evidence and determine the truth of the matter." *Liberty Lobby*, 477 U.S. at 249. Rather, "[t]he evidence of the non-movant is to be believed, and all justifiable inferences are to be drawn in his favor." *Id.* at 255. A jury could conclude that all reasonable officers on the scene would have believed that Darden was merely trying to get into a position where he could breathe and was not resisting arrest.

d. Officer Snow's Use of Force

At this juncture, we must analyze the officers' actions separately. In cases where the defendants have not acted in unison, "qualified immunity claims should be addressed separately for each individual defendant." *Kitchen v. Dallas Cty.*, 759 F.3d 468, 480 (5th Cir. 2014).

First, we consider whether a jury could conclude that Officer Snow used excessive force when he allegedly threw Darden to the ground and tased him. We have previously suggested that a constitutional violation occurs when an officer tases, strikes, or violently slams an arrestee who is not actively resisting arrest. Thus, if a jury finds that Darden was not actively resisting arrest, then a jury could likewise conclude that Officer Snow used excessive force by throwing Darden to the ground and tasing him twice. The facts the plaintiff has alleged therefore make out a violation of a constitutional right. . . .

In the present case, eyewitnesses claim that Darden put his hands in the air when the officers entered the residence, complied with the officers' commands, and did not resist arrest. Yet Officer Snow allegedly threw Darden to the ground and twice shocked him with a Taser while he was being beaten by Officer Romero. In light of our prior case law, Officer Snow should have known that he could not use that amount of force on an individual who was not resisting arrest.

It is worth pointing out that a jury may ultimately conclude that Darden did not comply with the officers' commands and was actively resisting arrest. Under those facts, Officer Snow's decisions to force Darden to the ground and tase him might have been reasonable. However, on the record before us, there are genuine disputes of material fact as to whether Darden was actively resisting arrest and whether the force Officer Snow used was clearly excessive and clearly unreasonable. Thus, we hold that Officer Snow was not entitled to qualified immunity, and the district court erred in granting his motion for summary judgment.

e. Officer Romero's Use of Force

Next, we must determine whether a jury could find that Officer Romero used excessive force when he allegedly choked, kicked, and punched Darden and forced Darden into a prone position to handcuff him behind his back. . . .

As stated, we have found that a police officer uses excessive force when the officer strikes, punches, or violently slams a suspect who is not resisting arrest. Thus, if a jury finds that no reasonable officer on the scene would have perceived Darden to be actively resisting arrest, then a jury could also conclude that Officer Romero used excessive force by choking Darden and repeatedly punching and kicking him in the face.[8] . . .

In the case at bar, eyewitnesses testified that Officer Romero choked, punched, and kicked Darden, even though Darden was purportedly complying with the officers' orders and not resisting arrest. Officer Romero also forced Darden—an obese man—onto his stomach, pushed his face into the floor, and pulled Darden's hands behind his back. All the while, other people in the residence were repeatedly yelling that Darden could not breathe. If the plaintiff's version of events is true, Officer Romero's actions were plainly in conflict with our case law at the time of the alleged misconduct. . . .

[A] jury could conclude that no reasonable officer would have perceived Darden as posing an immediate threat to the officers' safety or thought that he was resisting arrest. Therefore, viewing the facts in the light most favorable to Darden, Officer Romero's actions—choking, punching, and kicking Darden—were objectively unreasonable in light of clearly established law at the time of the incident. Accordingly, we hold that a reasonable jury could conclude that Officer Romero used excessive force. Officer Romero was not entitled to qualified immunity, and the district court erred in granting his motion for summary judgment.

---

[8] We also find relevant, but not dispositive, the fact that Officer Romero's alleged conduct appears to have violated Fort Worth Police Department policies requiring officers to exercise "[e]xtreme caution" when arresting "a prisoner that is obese . . . since cuffing behind the back and laying the prisoner in a prone position could lead to positional asphyxia" (otherwise known as hypoxia).

B. THE CITY OF FORT WORTH

In the proceedings below, the plaintiff also brought claims against the City, including a claim that the City had failed to properly train its officers. The district court did not reach the merits of the plaintiff's municipal liability claims. Because it held that the officers did not violate Darden's constitutional rights, the district court likewise held that the City could not be liable and granted the City's motion for summary judgment. As discussed above, we hold that the plaintiff has adequately alleged facts that make out violations of a clearly established constitutional right. Therefore, we vacate the district court's dismissal of the claims against the City and remand the case for further consideration of municipal liability. We express no opinion on the merits of that claim.

III. CONCLUSION

For the foregoing reasons, we REVERSE the district court's dismissal of the claims against Snow and Romero, VACATE the dismissal of the claims against the City, and REMAND the case for further proceedings consistent with this opinion.

Notes & Questions

1. The Darden case went to trial in 2020, and the jury found in favor of the defendants.

2. Government officials often invoke "qualified immunity" as a basis for summary judgment. As the *Darden* court explains, police officers and other government officials are immune from liability for civil rights violations unless they violated a clearly established right. According to the court in *Darden*, who has the burden of pleading qualified immunity? Once the defense has been pleaded, who has the burden of production on the issue of whether the defendant's conduct violated a clearly established right? In light of this burden of production, what must a defendant show in order to win a summary judgment motion based on qualified immunity? The judicially created doctrine of qualified immunity has come under criticism for making it difficult for plaintiffs to succeed in claims against officers, and bills have been introduced in Congress to alter or eliminate the doctrine.

3. In *Darden*, two of the police officers wore helmet cameras that captured the events on video. These videos were used as evidence in the case. With the growing ubiquity of cell phone cameras, security video cameras, body cams, dashboard cams, and the like, such evidence is available in an ever-growing range of cases. Think about the significance of such evidence for summary judgment motions. If the relevant events are captured on video, shouldn't it be easier for one party to show that there is no genuine dispute as to the facts? Even leaving aside questions of the authenticity of video evidence, *Darden* shows that it is not so simple.

    There are cases in which a video or other powerful piece of evidence so fully discredits one side's story that the difference between the parties' accounts cannot be considered a "genuine" dispute for purposes of the summary judgment analysis. The Supreme Court decided that *Scott v. Harris*, 550 U.S. 372 (2007), cited in *Darden*, was such a case, and held that summary judgment should be granted for a police officer who was accused of using excessive force in an automobile chase. We see in *Darden*, however, that even when video evidence is available, the "facts" are not necessarily clear, much less conclusions on mixed questions of law and fact such as the reasonableness of police conduct.

4. In *Tolan v. Cotton*, 572 U.S. 650 (2014), the Supreme Court emphasized the importance of the principle that, on a summary judgment motion, the evidence must be viewed in the light most favorable to the non-moving party. Like *Darden*, the case involved a civil rights claim under 42 U.S.C. §1983 alleging that a police officer used excessive force. The district court granted summary judgment in favor of the police officer, and the Fifth Circuit affirmed. In affirming, the Fifth Circuit noted a number of facts, including that the location was dimly lit and that the plaintiff was moving in a way that could have caused the officer to fear for his own safety. The Supreme Court summarily vacated and remanded because "the Fifth Circuit failed to view the evidence at summary judgment in the light most favorable to Tolan with respect to the central facts of this case. By failing to credit evidence that contradicted some of its key factual conclusions, the court improperly 'weigh[ed] the evidence' and resolved disputed issues in favor of the moving party." *Id.* at 657 (citing *Anderson v. Liberty Lobby*, 477 U.S. 242 (1986)). As the Supreme Court saw it, the Fifth Circuit believed Officer Cotton's testimony about what happened and disbelieved Tolan. Disputes over credibility, the Supreme Court said, should be resolved at trial, not on summary judgment:

> The witnesses on both sides come to this case with their own perceptions, recollections, and even potential biases. It is in part for that reason that genuine disputes are generally resolved by juries in our adversarial system. By weighing the evidence and reaching factual inferences contrary to Tolan's competent evidence, the court below neglected to adhere to the fundamental principle that at the summary judgment stage, reasonable inferences should be drawn in favor of the nonmoving party.

Id. at 660. Ultimately, the case settled as jury selection was about to begin.

5. Now that you have seen courts analyze summary judgment in *Celotex* and *Darden*, try the following problems to test your application of Rule 56:

a. An automobile driven by X collides with a FedEx truck at an intersection, damaging X's automobile and leaving X with serious personal injuries. X sues FedEx for negligence. The complaint alleges that the FedEx driver drove through a red light, causing the collision. After discovery, FedEx moves for summary judgment, contending that its driver did not run the red light. In its motion, FedEx attaches an excerpt from the truck driver's deposition in which he testifies that the light was green when he drove into the intersection, as well as affidavits from three witnesses, each of whom states that they saw that X, rather than the truck driver, ran the red light. In her response to the motion, X attaches an excerpt of her own deposition in which she testifies that she had a green light when she drove into the intersection, and that the truck driver ran the red light. Should the court grant the motion for summary judgment?

b. Same as problem (a), but instead of attaching an excerpt from her deposition, X attaches only a copy of her complaint in which she alleged that the FedEx driver ran the red light and thereby caused the collision.

c. Same as problem (a), but FedEx makes an additional argument that even if its truck driver ran the red light, the company cannot be held liable because the driver was making an emergency delivery of supplies to a hospital and a newly enacted state statute protects the company from liability under these circumstances. X does not dispute that the truck was making an emergency delivery of supplies to a hospital, but as a matter of statutory interpretation, the parties dispute whether the statute applies to bar liability under these circumstances. The judge considers this question a close call, but believes FedEx has the better argument on this question.

B. OTHER FORMS OF PRETRIAL ADJUDICATION

In addition to summary judgment, several other procedural devices end cases before trial. These include voluntary dismissal, involuntary dismissal, and default.

(1) Voluntary Dismissal

Voluntary dismissal means exactly what it says. The plaintiff voluntarily dismisses the lawsuit. Why would a plaintiff want to drop the suit? Often, it is because the parties have negotiated a settlement. When parties settle, the defendant agrees to pay money or provide some other benefit in exchange for the plaintiff's agreement to dismiss the action and release the claims. Sometimes, even in the absence of any settlement, voluntary dismissal occurs because the plaintiff—or the plaintiff's lawyer—realizes that the claim lacks merit. This realization may come from legal research or factual discovery, or may be prompted by a Rule 11 motion from the defendant. As we saw in Chapter 2, when a party is served with a Rule 11 motion for sanctions, the party has 21 days (the "safe harbor" period) to correct the problem before the motion is filed with the court. For a plaintiff who has brought a factually baseless or legally frivolous claim, the way to correct the problem is a voluntary dismissal. Finally, some plaintiffs may attempt to deploy voluntary dismissal tactically if they hope a different court will be more favorable than the one they originally chose, but judges frown on what they derisively call "judge shopping."

Rule 41(a), which governs voluntary dismissals, strikes a delicate balance. It makes it easy for plaintiffs to drop their claims for any reason, but it tries to limit plaintiffs' ability to use dismissal for strategic gamesmanship. Courts do not want plaintiffs to engage in "judge shopping" by dropping and refiling an action repeatedly in the hope of getting a more favorable judge assigned to the case. And courts do not want plaintiffs to drop and refile an action in the hope of getting a fresh start whenever it appears the plaintiff is about to lose. But courts *do* want plaintiffs to drop an action when the plaintiff reaches a settlement with the defendant, when the plaintiff realizes the claim has no merit, or when the plaintiff for any other reason prefers not to pursue the claim.

Without even asking the court's permission, a party may voluntarily dismiss an action if all of the parties agree and sign a "stipulation of dismissal," or if the opposing party has not yet served an answer or a summary judgment motion. Rule 41(a). If the parties have not all stipulated to the dismissal, and the opposing party has already either answered or moved for summary judgment, then a party may ask the court for permission to dismiss. This makes it easy for plaintiffs to drop their claims early on, but more difficult for a plaintiff to avoid an adverse adjudication by dropping a lawsuit when it appears that the plaintiff is about to lose.

When a party voluntarily dismisses a lawsuit, may the party later file the same claim? To put this in the language of preclusion, addressed in Chapter 8, do courts treat voluntary dismissals as judgments on the merits for purposes of claim preclusion? Rule 41 declares that the first voluntary dismissal is without prejudice. That is, a plaintiff may voluntarily dismiss a claim once and file the same claim a second time without a problem. However, if the plaintiff decides to voluntarily dismiss the action a second time, the second dismissal is with prejudice, precluding the party from bringing the claim a third time. The message of Rule 41(a) is clear: If you have decided to drop your case, fine, but don't play games.

Notes & Questions

1. If a plaintiff seeks to drop one of multiple claims in a lawsuit, may the plaintiff voluntarily dismiss the unwanted claim under Rule 41(a) without dropping the entire action? What other procedural mechanism can you think of for accomplishing the same objective?

   In *Perry v. Schumacher Group of Louisiana*, 891 F.3d 954 (11th Cir. 2018), the Eleventh Circuit held that Rule 41(a) cannot be used for anything short of dismissing the entire action. The plaintiff asserted eight employment discrimination claims and the district court granted dismissal, summary judgment, or judgment as a matter of law in favor of the defendants on every claim except one. Rather than proceed to trial on that claim alone, the plaintiff wanted to appeal the adverse rulings. However, because one claim remained pending, there was not yet an appealable final judgment. So the plaintiff—to make the judgment final and therefore appealable—attempted to voluntarily dismiss her remaining claim by entering into a Rule 41(a) stipulation of dismissal. The Eleventh Circuit ruled that the stipulation of dismissal was invalid: "Rule 41(a)(1), according to its plain text, permits voluntary dismissals only of entire actions, not claims." The court's analysis contained some good advice for the plaintiff on remand:

> There are multiple ways to dismiss a single claim without dismissing an entire action. The easiest and most obvious is to seek and obtain leave to amend the complaint to eliminate the remaining claim, pursuant to Rule 15. Rule 15 states that an amendment to the pleadings is permitted upon permission from the other party or leave of the district court, and that "[t]he court should freely give leave when justice so requires." Fed. R. Civ. P. 15(a)(2). In this case, we cannot foresee how leave to amend could be denied given the circumstances.

Id. at 958.

2. *Microsoft Corp. v. Baker*, 137 S. Ct. 1702 (2017), similarly involved an attempt by plaintiffs to obtain appellate review by voluntarily dismissing a claim. The plaintiffs had filed a class action against Microsoft asserting products-liability claims concerning the Xbox 360 videogame console. The district court struck the plaintiffs' class allegations from the complaint. That is, the district court ruled against allowing a class action and decided the plaintiffs could go forward only with their individual claims. The plaintiffs first attempted to appeal the district court's decision under Rule 23(f), which allows class certification appeals at the discretion of the court of appeals, but the court of appeals declined to hear the appeal. Instead of pursuing their individual claims, the plaintiffs voluntarily dismissed their claims and then sought to appeal the district court's order striking their class allegations. The Ninth Circuit accepted the appeal, but the Supreme Court reversed on the grounds that appellate jurisdiction was lacking. The Court noted that Rule 23(f) creates a procedure for appealing some district court rulings on class certification, and held that plaintiffs should not be able to use Rule 41(a) to circumvent the final judgment rule and the Rule 23(f) appeal process: "Plaintiffs in putative class actions cannot transform a tentative interlocutory order into a final judgment . . . simply by dismissing their claims with prejudice." *Id.* at 1715. Where did this leave plaintiffs?

(2) Involuntary Dismissal

You have already encountered several types of involuntary dismissals. These include the Rule 12(b)(6) motion to dismiss for failure to state a claim, as well as all the other pre-answer motions to dismiss listed in Rule 12(b), including lack of subject matter jurisdiction, lack of personal jurisdiction, improper venue, insufficient process, improper service of process, and failure to join an indispensable party. You also have encountered the possibility of dismissal as a sanction for egregious conduct under Rule 11 or for discovery abuse under Rule 37. All of these are "involuntary" dismissals in the sense that the dismissed party does not voluntarily relinquish the claim, but instead gets thrown out unwillingly. In this section, we complete our look at pretrial dismissals by turning to Rule 41(b), which addresses involuntary dismissals for failure to prosecute or for noncompliance with rules or orders.

Involuntary dismissal for failure to prosecute is the court's tool for forcing plaintiffs to proceed with their case. It would be unfair to the defendant and to the court for a plaintiff to file a complaint and then to sit on it, leaving the defendant with a lawsuit hanging over her head and leaving the court with an extra case on its docket. After the plaintiff files a complaint and the defendant answers, the plaintiff should move forward with discovery and preparation for trial. If the plaintiff fails to move forward, the court may dismiss for failure to prosecute.

> **Terminology Tip**
>
> Do not be confused by the word *prosecute* as used in Rule 41(b). Although the word most often is used to refer to the government's role in criminal cases, it also denotes what plaintiffs do in moving forward with civil cases.

Rule 41(b) also permits a defendant to move for dismissal if the plaintiff fails to comply with a court order or with the rules of civil procedure. The following case involves a dismissal both for failure to prosecute and for failure to comply with rules and orders. As you read it, think about how frustrating the experience must have been for the district judge. But also think about the harshness of dismissal as a sanction, the difficulty of punishing a client for the attorney's failures, and the hard question of when a court should give up on resolving an action on its merits.

KOVACIC v. TYCO VALVES & CONTROLS
433 Fed. Appx. 376, 2011 WL 3289737 (6th Cir. 2011)

SILER, Circuit Judge.

The plaintiffs appeal the district court's dismissal with prejudice of their product liability case under Federal Rule of Civil Procedure 41(b), for failure to prosecute and failure to comply with the court's rules and orders. For the following reasons, we affirm.

I

In 2001, a steam engine owned and operated by Clifford Kovacic and his son, William Kovacic, exploded at the Medina County, Ohio fairgrounds, killing five people and injuring forty-seven. Clifford and William were among the deceased. In 2006, family members Delores Kovacic and Elizabeth Kovacic sued Tyco, the manufacturer of a safety valve within the steam engine. The Kovacics alleged that the safety valve was "defective and unreasonably dangerous in its design, manufacture, representations, instructions or warnings," and caused the fatal explosion.

For several years, there were delays in the discovery process primarily based on issues surrounding the destructive testing of the steam engine's safety valve. After both parties requested and received multiple extensions of time for discovery, the court set trial for June 2009. The parties jointly moved for a further extension of discovery deadlines and to postpone trial until August 2009 or later. After conferencing with the parties to find a mutually agreeable trial date, the court set the trial for December 8, 2009. The court "would have preferred to conduct the trial in the summer months," but postponed trial "in part to accommodate plaintiffs' counsel's work and travel schedule." The court then issued a trial order establishing deadlines for the parties' pretrial obligations.

On October 13, 2009, Tyco timely filed a *Daubert* motion to exclude the Kovacics' liability expert, Michael Clemens. Pursuant to the deadlines in the trial order, the Kovacics' response was due on October 20, 2009. Three weeks after the deadline, however, the plaintiffs had not filed a response. On November 6, 2009, Tyco filed a motion for leave to file a motion for summary judgment. . . . The Kovacics never filed a response to the motion for leave. They also failed to file a witness and exhibit list as requested by the trial order. As of November 10, the docket reflected that there had been no activity by the plaintiffs since July 31, 2009. . . .

[T]he court *sua sponte* scheduled a telephone status conference on November 10. Counsel for both parties discussed by telephone the circumstances of the Kovacics' failure to file a timely witness list, exhibit list, and *Daubert* response. Plaintiffs' counsel explained that he had been out of the country during the latter weeks of October, and when he returned on October 27 to find the *Daubert* motion pending, he contacted defense counsel the same day to schedule Clemens's deposition. He stated that the parties spoke during the first week of November and agreed upon alternative dates to depose Clemens. He also stated that, in light of the impending deposition, he did not think a response to the *Daubert* motion was necessary. He argued that his failure to file a response should be excused, because he understood his discussions with defense counsel to constitute an implicit waiver by the defendant of its obligation to adhere to the court-imposed deadlines. He also stated that he merely overlooked the deadline for filing witness and exhibit lists.

Based on this discussion, the district court ordered the Kovacics to file a *Daubert* response, witness list, and exhibit list by the end of the following day, and ordered Tyco to provide a written explanation of the parties' communications regarding expert depositions. [The parties complied with this order.] . . .

Meanwhile, November 10 was the deadline for filing a proposed voir dire, trial brief, and other motions in limine. Tyco timely filed these documents and motions. The Kovacics did not file anything on November 10, and never filed a proposed voir dire or trial brief.

On November 17, the court dismissed the Kovacics' case with prejudice pursuant to Fed. R. Civ. P. 41(b). First, it granted Tyco's *Daubert* motion and excluded Clemens's expert testimony from trial. The court treated Tyco's motion as unopposed because of the Kovacics' failure to file a timely response. [The court precluded Clemens from offering expert testimony at trial because Clemens's expert report of July 10, 2007 failed to comply with Rule 26(a)(2)(B) and made it impossible to assess the reliability of his opinions.]

In reaching this conclusion, the court noted that even if it excused plaintiffs' untimeliness, their response in opposition failed to supplement the expert report or bring it into conformity with Fed. R. Civ. P. 26. Although plaintiffs' counsel asserted that taking the expert's deposition would cure any deficiencies in his report, Tyco had attempted to schedule his deposition for months, and the court determined that conducting such an important deposition one week before trial would be "unfair."

Second, the court granted Tyco's motion in limine to preclude the Kovacics from calling any witnesses or presenting any exhibits. The court cited its express instructions in the trial order that "[n]o witness will be permitted to testify at trial if his or her name is not provided to opposing counsel" by November 3, 2009. Plaintiffs' counsel did not file these lists until a week after the deadline, and only upon prompting by the court.

Finally, "[i]n light of the above rulings," the court held that the Kovacics had failed to prosecute their case. First, it found that counsel consciously chose not to oppose the *Daubert* motion and could not articulate any reason for his failure to file witness and exhibit lists. Moreover, he never sought an extension of time to file these documents. Second, the court determined that Tyco was prejudiced by the untimeliness and would be forced to prepare for trial without a complete understanding of the nature of the key expert's opinions. Third, the court pointed out that it initiated the telephone conference to discuss the missed deadlines *sua sponte*, and that, even after the conference, plaintiffs' counsel continued to miss filing deadlines for their proposed voir dire and trial brief. Fourth, the court found less drastic sanctions inappropriate because further delay would "undermine the effect of the Court's Orders and the Civil Rules." Because the "judicial system depends on these procedural rules to allow the Court to facilitate fair and just resolution of disputes submitted to the Court," it dismissed the case with prejudice pursuant to Rule 41(b).

II
A

We review a district court's decision to dismiss a case under Rule 41(b) for abuse of discretion.... Nevertheless, the "dismissal of a claim for failure to prosecute is a harsh sanction which the court should order only in extreme situations showing a clear record of contumacious conduct by the plaintiff." *Wu v. T.W. Wang, Inc.*, 420 F.3d 641, 643 (6th Cir. 2005).

B

We review four non-dispositive factors in evaluating the district court's dismissal for failure to prosecute:

> (1) whether the party's failure is due to willfulness, bad faith, or fault; (2) whether the adversary was prejudiced by the dismissed party's conduct; (3) whether the dismissed party was warned that failure to cooperate could lead to dismissal; and (4) whether less drastic sanctions were imposed or considered before dismissal was ordered.

United States v. Reyes, 307 F.3d 451, 458 (6th Cir. 2002).

In *Link* [*v. Wabash R.R. Co.*, 370 U.S. 626 (1962)], the Supreme Court concluded that the district court had not abused its discretion when it dismissed the plaintiff's complaint for failure to prosecute. The Court stated that there is "certainly no merit to the contention that dismissal of petitioner's claim because of his counsel's unexcused conduct imposes an unjust penalty on the client." [*Id.* at 633.] "Any other notion would be wholly inconsistent with our system of representative litigation, in which each party is deemed bound by the acts of his lawyer-agent." *Id.* at 634.

The *Link* principle remains valid, but "we have increasingly emphasized directly sanctioning the delinquent lawyer rather than an innocent client." *Coleman v. Am. Red Cross*, 23 F.3d 1091, 1095 (6th Cir. 1994). Accordingly, we apply the factors "more stringently in cases where the plaintiff's attorney's conduct is responsible for the dismissal." *Harmon v. CSX Transp., Inc.*, 110 F.3d 364, 367 (6th Cir. 1997).

1. WILLFULNESS, BAD FAITH, OR FAULT

The first factor is whether the party's conduct is due to willfulness, bad faith, or fault. . . .

Here, counsel . . . "could not articulate any reason for his failure to file witness and exhibit lists," even though these deadlines were set well in advance of his travel abroad. *See Link*, 370 U.S. at 633. He also continued to miss pretrial filing deadlines, even after the court initiated a remedial conference. These actions indicate both fault and willfulness on the part of Kovacics' counsel. . . .

Accordingly, this factor weighs in favor of affirming the district court.

2. PREJUDICE

The second factor is whether the adversary was prejudiced by the dismissed party's conduct. . . .

The district court found that Tyco was prejudiced by the Kovacics' untimeliness, because it "forced [the defendants] to prepare to defend their case at trial without a complete understanding of the nature of the plaintiffs' key liability expert witness' opinions and the basis thereof." Clemens's report failed to provide Tyco with "the basis and reasons" for his opinions, which are required by Fed. R. Civ. P. 26(a). Moreover, "conducting the key deposition one week before trial is unfair, especially given the deadlines established by the Trial Order in June and [Tyco's] repeated efforts to schedule the deposition prior to October, efforts to which plaintiffs' counsel largely did not even respond." . . .

Here, as the district court explained, Tyco spent time and effort preparing its *Daubert* motion and pretrial documents, attempting to schedule Clemens's deposition, and continuously complying with court-imposed deadlines. Accordingly, this factor weighs in favor of affirming the district court's dismissal.

3. PRIOR NOTICE

Although the district court has the power to dismiss a claim as the first and only sanction, *Link*, 370 U.S. at 631-33, [a court generally should not impose "the extreme sanction of dismissal" unless it has given the party sufficient notice that noncompliance would result in dismissal].

The district court provided plaintiffs' counsel with some notice that it was contemplating dismissal. It included a warning in its trial order that the failure to timely file witness and exhibit lists would result in exclusion of witnesses from trial. . . .

Because counsel was on notice that the court was contemplating sanctions and nevertheless continued to miss pretrial filing deadlines, this factor weighs in favor of affirming.

4. LESS DRASTIC SANCTIONS

The fourth factor is whether the district court "imposed or considered" less drastic sanctions before ordering dismissal. [District courts have the power to dismiss a complaint as the first sanction on the basis of plaintiff's counsel's neglect.]

However, the district court abuses its discretion if it dismisses a case under Rule 41(b) "mechanically." *Freeland v. Amigo*, 103 F.3d 1271, 1279 (6th Cir. 1997). . . . Thus, we have found an abuse of discretion where the district court did not first impose alternative sanctions on plaintiff's counsel, such as "levying a fine, barring him from participating in oral argument, or any other disciplinary action." *Mulbah v. Detroit Bd. of Educ.*, 261 F.3d 586, 593 (6th Cir. 2001).

The district court appears to have considered less drastic sanctions in this case. First, the court called a status conference *sua sponte*, providing counsel with an opportunity to explain the missed deadlines. The court then allowed the Kovacics to file an untimely *Daubert* response. After reviewing the parties' submissions, the court held that "less drastic sanctions are not appropriate under the particular circumstances of this case." Specifically, the Kovacics failed to "satisfy the requirements for introducing expert testimony on the key issue of liability and then failed to oppose the Defendants' *Daubert* motion to that effect." The court noted that trial had already been pending for three years, and further delaying it to allow the parties to depose Clemens "would undermine the effect of the Court's Orders and the Civil Rules." . . .

The dismissal of the Kovacics' case was a harsh sanction, and the court could have imposed alternative sanctions on the attorney rather than dismissing the case. Indeed, "it is difficult to define the quantity or quality of the misconduct which may justify dismissal with prejudice as the first and only sanction." *Harmon*, 110 F.3d at 368. However, "[t]his difficulty is no doubt part of the reason that we review a district court's judgment in such cases only for an abuse of discretion." *Id.* The court's order, as well as its actions, indicate that it did not dismiss the case "mechanically," but only after considering alternatives.

Notes & Questions

1. Are you troubled by the fact that the clients, the Kovacics, were penalized for the misconduct of their lawyer? The court cites *Link v. Wabash R.R. Co.*, 370 U.S. 626 (1962), for the proposition that clients may be penalized for their lawyer's misconduct. The nature of agency relationships—that is, relationships between agents and principals such as the lawyer-client relationship—means that principals (the clients) are bound by the acts of their agents (the lawyers). If clients could disavow their lawyers' acts, it would be impossible for lawyers to do much of their work. As the Supreme Court explained in *Link*, it is built into our system of representative litigation that "each party is deemed bound by the acts of his lawyer-agent." *Link*, 370 U.S. at 634. Nonetheless, even as it reaffirms the *Link* principle, the *Kovacic* court backs away from it by stating a preference for "directly sanctioning the delinquent lawyer rather than an innocent client." In the *Kovacic* case, would a direct sanction

> **Terminology Tip**
>
> In *Kovacic*, the court mentioned "motions in limine" and a "*Daubert* motion." *In limine* means "at the threshold" in Latin. A *motion in limine* is a motion made before the start of a trial concerning what will happen at trial. Mostly, these motions are requests to exclude evidence. A "*Daubert* motion" is a type of motion in limine. Referring to *Daubert v. Merrell Dow Pharmaceuticals*, 509 U.S. 579 (1993), it is a motion to exclude expert testimony on the grounds that the witness lacks the required expertise or used unreliable methods.

against the lawyer have been an adequate solution? When the Sixth Circuit said that "[t]he district court appears to have considered less drastic sanctions in this case," were you persuaded?

2. In the final paragraph of the opinion, did you get the sense that Judge Siler would have decided the matter differently from the district judge? If so, then why did he vote to affirm? We will explore standards of appellate review in Chapter 6, but for now, consider why it is important that appellate courts apply the "abuse of discretion" standard when reviewing Rule 41(b) dismissals. Recall that in *Darden*, the appellate court applied a de novo standard—the court gave zero deference to the district judge—when reviewing a summary judgment ruling. Why should appellate judges defer to the district judge in *Kovacic* but not in *Darden*?

3. Suppose the Kovacics were to file a new lawsuit against Tyco, asserting the same products-liability claim. Would a court allow them to go forward with their new lawsuit? The answer, of course, is no. The district court dismissed the Kovacics' suit "with prejudice," which means that the Kovacics are barred from pursuing the claim. As we will see in Chapter 8, a new action by the Kovacics would be dismissed on grounds of claim preclusion.

   Compare this to voluntary dismissals. Recall that Rule 41(a) instructs that a voluntary dismissal is treated as a dismissal without prejudice, at least for the first one. Think about the difference between the purpose of voluntary dismissals and the purpose of involuntary dismissals, and why this should translate into different rules governing the preclusive effect of such dismissals.

   In *Kovacic*, the district court stated explicitly that it dismissed the case "with prejudice." What if the court had not specified whether the dismissal was with or without prejudice? Rule 41(b) speaks to the question of how dismissals should be treated if the court does not specify: "Unless the dismissal order states otherwise, a dismissal under this subdivision (b) and any dismissal not under this rule— except one for lack of jurisdiction, improper venue, or failure to join a party under Rule 19—operates as an adjudication on the merits." Note that the rule addresses *every* type of involuntary dismissal: dismissals "under this subdivision" (failure to prosecute and noncompliance) plus dismissals "not under this rule" (all other involuntary dismissals, such as those under Rule 12(b) or Rule 37). With a few exceptions, the rule states that every involuntary dismissal "operates as an adjudication on the merits." This language links the rule to the principle that judgments "on the merits" have claim preclusive effect. Thus, if a claim is involuntarily dismissed, Rule 41(b) generally means that the claim cannot be brought again.

   However, Rule 41(b) offers several exceptions. If the case is dismissed for "lack of jurisdiction, improper venue, or failure to join a party," the dismissal does not constitute adjudication on the merits. Think about the logic behind each of these exceptions. After dismissal for lack of federal subject matter jurisdiction, the plaintiff may refile the case in state court. After dismissal for lack of personal jurisdiction or improper venue, the plaintiff may refile the case in a court with jurisdiction over the parties and where venue is proper. And after dismissal for failure to join a required party, the plaintiff may refile the case and include the missing party.

(3) Default

As you saw in *Kovacic*, dismissal for failure to prosecute is what can happen when a plaintiff fails to move forward with a lawsuit. The penalty, under Rule 41(b), is precisely what plaintiffs fear most—dismissal with prejudice. But what if the opposite happens? What if a *defendant* fails to move forward? Suppose the deadline passes and the defendant has neither filed an answer nor made any pre-answer motion. Dismissal obviously will not suffice as a solution. Dismissal of the lawsuit is what defendants *want*. Rather, the legal system's response to the defendant's failure is to enter a default in favor of the plaintiff.

Default occurs when the defendant fails to answer or otherwise respond to the complaint. As you know from Chapter 2, a defendant has several options when responding to the complaint. The defendant may file an answer, admitting or denying each allegation in the complaint. Alternatively, the defendant may file a pre-answer motion such as a Rule 12(b) motion to dismiss or a Rule 12(e) motion for a more definite statement. What the defendant may not do, however, is ignore the complaint and do nothing, tempting as that may be. If a defendant fails to respond to the complaint within the time limits established by Rule 12(a), then the defendant risks losing by default.

Under Rule 55, default in federal court involves a two-step process. First, the court clerk "enters" the default, which is an administrative notation that the defendant failed to plead or otherwise defend. After the entry of default, the plaintiff requests a default judgment by applying either to the court clerk or to the judge. The clerk enters the default judgment, at the plaintiff's request, only if the amount of damages is "a sum certain or a sum that can be made certain by computation." For example, if the defendant defaults in a lawsuit on a $100,000 debt, the clerk may enter default judgment in the amount of $100,000 (or, more realistically, a specific higher amount after computing the interest). Many claims, however, are not for a "sum certain," and the plaintiff must apply to the judge for a default judgment. The court may hold a hearing to determine the amount of damages. At such a hearing, the defendant may not contest whether liability will be imposed, but does have the opportunity to argue that the plaintiff's damages are less than what the plaintiff requested.

When a case ends in default, there is a risk that the result does not correspond with the merits of the dispute on the law and the facts. Perhaps the defendant failed to respond because the defendant never actually knew about the lawsuit, or perhaps for some other reason justice would be better served by permitting the defendant to continue defending the lawsuit. Rule 55 addresses this concern by permitting a court to "set aside" a default when justice requires. Rule 55(c) permits the court to "set aside an entry of default for good cause," and if default judgment has already been entered, the court may "set aside a default judgment under Rule 60(b)." Often in the law there is a tension between accuracy and finality, and it can be difficult to ascertain whether justice, fairness, and efficiency are maximized by emphasizing finality or by providing second chances. In Chapter 8, you will learn that in general courts are quite stingy about setting aside judgments under Rule 60(b) because of the importance of finality. But you will also learn that a major exception is cases involving default judgments against defendants who did not receive actual notice of the lawsuit or who had some other sound explanation for why they failed to respond to the complaint.

The following case shows a judge struggling with the tension inherent in default. On the one hand, the judge knows that a default procedure is necessary to keep litigation moving and to ensure that defendants cannot delay justice simply by dragging their feet. On the other hand, the judge is loath to resolve the case on any basis other than the merits.

AZ DNR, LLC v. LUXURY TRAVEL BROKERS, INC.
2014 WL 1356050 (D. Kan. Apr. 7, 2014)

LUNGSTRUM, District Judge.

This matter comes before the Court on plaintiff's Request for Entry of Default and defendants' Motion for Extension of Time to File Responsive Pleading. For the reasons set forth below, defendants' motion is granted, and plaintiff's request is denied as moot, on the condition that defendants pay attorney fees and costs incurred by plaintiff, as set forth herein.

Plaintiff filed this action in November 2013 and effected service upon defendants in January 2014. Defendants responded to the amended complaint by filing a motion to dismiss or for more definite statement pursuant to Fed. R. Civ. P. 12, and the Court denied that motion by Memorandum and Order of February 19, 2014. On March 10, 2014, plaintiff filed a request that the Clerk enter defendants' default in this case, on the basis that defendants had failed to file a response to the amended complaint

after the Court's order. The following day, defendants filed an opposing brief and a motion for an extension to March 18, 2014, of the time in which to file an answer. In the motion, defendants explained their failure to file a timely answer as follows: "Weather, distance, and competing schedules of individual defendants, corporate counsel and trial counsel have conspired to delay the creation of an answer to the Amended Complaint." Plaintiff filed a brief in opposition to defendants' motion and a reply brief in support of its request for entry of default, but defendants did not file a reply brief in support of their motion for an extension. On March 18, 2014, defendants filed their answer to the amended complaint.

After the Court denied defendants' Rule 12 motion, defendants' responsive pleading was due on March 5, 2014. *See* Fed. R. Civ. P. 12(a)(4) (if the court denies a motion under Rule 12, the responsive pleading is due 14 days after notice of the denial). Rule 55(a) provides that when a defendant fails to plead, the Clerk is obligated to enter the party's default. *See* Fed. R. Civ. P. 55(a). Thus, plaintiff is entitled to entry of defendants' default in this case. Rule 55 further provides as follows: "The court may set aside an entry of default for good cause, and it may set aside a default judgment under Rule 60(b)." *See* Fed. R. Civ. P. 55(c). Thus, in determining whether defendants should be permitted to file their untimely answer and to proceed in the case, the Court must consider whether it would, for good cause, set aside the entry of default to which plaintiff is entitled. Because plaintiff has not requested a default judgment, *see* Fed. R. Civ. P. 55(b) (in the event of a defendant's default, a plaintiff may request a default judgment from the clerk or the court), Rule 60(b)'s standards for setting aside a judgment do not apply here.

The "good cause" standard under Rule 55(c) is not particularly onerous. The Tenth Circuit has noted that "it is well established that the good cause required by Fed. R. Civ. P. 55(c) for setting aside entry of default poses a lesser standard for the defaulting party than the excusable neglect which must be shown for relief from judgment under Fed. R. Civ. P. 60(b)." *Dennis Garberg & Assocs. v. Pack-Tech Int'l Corp.*, 115 F.3d 767, 775 n.6 (10th Cir. 1997). In determining whether good cause exists under Rule 55(c), judges in this district (including the undersigned) have considered factors relating to the defendant's willfulness or degree of culpability, the prejudice to the plaintiff, and whether the defendant has a meritorious defense. . . . Setting aside an entry of default is addressed to the discretion of the district court, which has "a great deal of latitude" in exercising that discretion. *See Nikwei v. Ross School of Aviation*, 822 F.2d 939, 941 (10th Cir. 1987).

In this case, the Court concludes that, if default were entered against defendants, good cause would exist to set aside that entry of default. "The preferred disposition of any case is upon its merits and not by default judgment." *See Gomes v. Williams*, 420 F.2d 1364, 1366 (10th Cir. 1970). Most significantly, plaintiff has suffered little prejudice from the 13-day delay in receiving defendants' answer. In this case, the delay occurred very early in the case, and there has been no suggestion that discovery or any other deadlines have been affected. The only prejudice identified by plaintiff in its briefs is the fact that plaintiff expended resources to seek the entry of default, and that prejudice will be cured by defendants' satisfaction of the condition imposed below. The Court agrees with plaintiff that defendants' reason for their failure to file a timely answer is vague and is not especially compelling, but it does not appear that defendants acted willfully. The Court can make no judgment concerning whether defendants have a meritorious defense, as defendants have failed to address that factor (except to call this case "vigorously-contested"). Nevertheless, the Court concludes in its discretion that, in light of the lack of prejudice to plaintiff, the early stage of the case, and the preference for deciding cases on their merits, good cause would exist here to justify setting aside any entry of default in the interests of justice. Accordingly, the Court grants defendants' motion for an extension, and it denies plaintiff's request for entry of default as moot.

The Court further concludes, however, that such rulings are most appropriately conditioned on defendants' payment of fees and costs incurred by plaintiff as a result of defendants' failure to file a timely answer. Requiring defendants to redress plaintiff's prejudice in incurring costs and fees is warranted in light of defendants' failures here. As noted above, defendants' stated reason for their delay was vague and was not supported by affidavit. Defendants did not address the meritorious-defense factor usually applied in this district, and defendants did not see fit to file a reply brief in support of their motion to address these shortcomings, even after plaintiff raised the issues in its response. Defendants offered no explanation for their failure to seek an extension before their answer deadline expired.

The Court also notes that this behavior by defendants and their counsel appears to continue a pattern begun with their filing of the motion under Rule 12. As the Court noted in its previous order, defendants' Rule 12 motion was utterly without merit; defendants did not cite a single case in support of that motion, but instead filed a brief containing the word "CITE" as a placeholder in several places; and defendants did not bother to file a reply brief in support of the motion. Defendants and their counsel are admonished that such a lack of diligence in the future litigation of this case will likely be treated harshly by this Court.

Accordingly, plaintiff is awarded its costs and reasonable attorney fees incurred in seeking the entry of default. If defendants do not comply with that condition, the Court shall enter default in favor of plaintiff on its claims. The parties shall consult on the amount of such fees and expenses, and if they reach agreement on the amount, defendant shall pay such amount and shall file a notice of compliance with this Court on or before April 14, 2014. If they cannot agree on the amount, the parties shall file, by that same date, short briefs with the Court addressing the issue.

Notes & Questions

1. Needless to say, the conduct of defendants' attorney described in this case is hardly a model of good lawyering, and we trust that no reader of this casebook will think that it is okay for a lawyer to miss deadlines or to submit a brief containing the word "CITE" as a placeholder. Indeed, two years after this case, the defendants' lawyer was disbarred. In an ironic but perhaps unsurprising twist, the disbarment order notes that the lawyer failed to respond to the disciplinary complaint and therefore defaulted in the professional misconduct proceeding. *See In re Phillip R. Gibson*, No. SC95852 (Mo. Sept. 1, 2016).

2. But how about the case as a model of good judging? Would you have handled the situation the same way Judge Lungstrum did? Was Judge Lungstrum too lenient in giving the defendant a second chance rather than entering default? Or, conversely, was he too harsh in requiring that the defendant pay the plaintiff's costs and fees despite the lack of prejudice to the plaintiff?

3. Despite giving them a second chance, Judge Lungstrum ultimately entered a default judgment against the defendants. Following the April 7, 2014, order reprinted above, the defendants filed an answer stating they lacked sufficient

knowledge to admit or deny certain allegations that were, in fact, within their knowledge. A magistrate judge found that the answer likely violated Rule 11 and ordered defendants "to file a revised answer by July 7, 2014, or to show cause by that same date why the current answer does not violate Rule 11(b)." The defendants failed to meet the deadline. On July 8, 2014, the defendants attempted to file an amended answer, but not only was it late, it also failed to address the deficiencies found by the magistrate judge. Eventually, after a string of delays by defendants, the court decided to strike the original answer and the amended answer and to enter a default judgment. *See AZ DNR, LLC v. Luxury Travel Brokers, Inc.*, 2014 WL 5430224 (D. Kan. Oct. 24, 2014).

4. After entering a default judgment, the court conducted a Rule 55(b)(2) hearing to determine the amount of the plaintiff's damages. The lawsuit was a dispute between two businesses over the sale of credit card points and frequent flier miles. At the hearing on damages, the judge heard testimony from an expert witness in accounting presented by the plaintiff. The defendants, represented by new counsel, argued that the expert's calculations were too high. The judge rejected several of the defendants' arguments on the grounds that the defendants were not permitted to contradict any of the facts that comprised the basis for their liability under the default judgment:

> As noted in the Court's prior order by which it ordered the default judgment on liability, defendants are precluded at this stage from arguing the merits of their liability on plaintiff's claims. By the default, defendants are deemed to have admitted plaintiff's well-pleaded allegations of fact.

AZ DNR, LLC v. Luxury Travel Brokers, Inc., 2015 WL 2412757 (D. Kan. May 21, 2015). Although the plaintiff bears the burden of proving damages, the court reasoned that, by defaulting, the defendant had admitted all of the complaint's factual allegations concerning the scope of liability. Ultimately, the court awarded the plaintiff damages of $502,543.46.

5. In Chapters 9 and 10, you will learn about jurisdictional constraints on courts' power. Suppose a court lacks personal jurisdiction over the defendant but nonetheless enters a default judgment. Can the defendant challenge the validity of the judgment? That is, may the defendant *collaterally attack* the default judgment for lack of personal jurisdiction (as opposed to *directly attacking* the judgment by appealing to the appropriate appellate court)? This question matters because a defendant might choose not to appear in an action if the defendant is confident that the court lacks power to enter a binding judgment. In Chapter 10, you will read the famous case of *Pennoyer v. Neff*, 95 U.S. 714 (1878), in which a party successfully challenged the validity of a judgment on the grounds that the rendering court lacked personal jurisdiction over him. However, if the defendant litigates the jurisdictional issue in the first action, loses on that issue, and then defaults, the default judgment is binding and may not be collaterally attacked. *See Baldwin v. Iowa State Traveling Men's Association*, 283 U.S. 522 (1931). As the Supreme Court restated the point in

a later case, "A defendant is always free to ignore the judicial proceedings, risk a default judgment, and then challenge that judgment on jurisdictional grounds in a collateral proceeding." *Insurance Corp. of Ireland v. Compagnie des Bauxites do Guinée*, 456 U.S. 694 (1982) (citing *Baldwin*).

If the court lacked subject matter jurisdiction (as opposed to personal jurisdiction), the result is less clear. Generally, a default judgment is not subject to collateral attack based on an argument that the rendering court lacked subject matter jurisdiction over the action. *See Chicot County Drainage District v. Baxter State Bank*, 308 U.S. 371 (1940). This result follows from the reasoning that courts are obligated to determine their own subject matter jurisdiction, so it should be presumed that every court has determined its own power over the action even if no party has raised the issue and even if the defendant has not appeared in the action. Whether or not this is a realistic assumption, it has provided a basis for courts to treat problems of personal jurisdiction and subject matter jurisdiction differently when considering the binding effect of default judgments.

6. So far, we have discussed default as something that occurs when a defendant fails to respond to a plaintiff's complaint. But there is another important use of default. Default is sometimes imposed as a punishment. Just as dismissal is an extreme sanction that can be imposed on plaintiffs for serious misconduct, default is an extreme sanction that can be imposed on defendants for serious misconduct. In particular, Rule 37 includes "rendering a default judgment against the disobedient party" in its list of potential sanctions for discovery abuse.

7. In terms of damages, default judgments are treated differently from all other judgments. Rule 54(c) provides: "A default judgment must not differ in kind from, or exceed in amount, what is demanded in the pleadings. Every other final judgment should grant the relief to which the party is entitled, even if the party has not demanded that relief in its pleadings." For example, if a jury finds that a plaintiff's claim is worth $100,000, it should award that amount even if the complaint only demanded $50,000, but if the defendant defaults, the default judgment may not exceed the $50,000 demanded in the complaint. As a matter of policy, why does Rule 54(c) treat defaults differently from litigated judgments in terms of capping the remedy? What is it about default judgments that warrants this different treatment?

STRATEGY SESSION

Rule 54(c) creates an intriguing option for defendants. Default may be an appealing route in the rare case in which the complaint demands too little relief. This strategy depends on the strength of plaintiff's case and how clear it is that a trial verdict would exceed the amount sought in the pleading. If the defendant is worse off going to trial than simply providing the relief demanded in the complaint, the defendant may decide to default. Of course, a smart plaintiff should never put the defendant in the strategic position of being able to elect smaller damages by defaulting. Therefore, when plaintiffs specify the relief sought in their complaint, they ordinarily demand an amount at the high end, keeping in mind Rule 11's requirement that the amount have a reasonable factual and legal basis.

C. PRETRIAL CASE MANAGEMENT

In addition to summary judgment and other forms of pretrial adjudication, judges have at their disposal a variety of tools for "managing" cases. Judges did not always think of themselves as managers, as opposed to adjudicators, but many of them do now. When the Federal Rules of Civil Procedure were adopted in 1938, the basic concept was a system for moving cases efficiently to trial so that disputes could be decided on the merits. Over the years, as discovery and pretrial practice grew in complexity and importance, judges began to play a more active role asserting control over the pretrial process.

The 1983 amendments to Rule 16 shined a spotlight on pretrial management and gave judges several important tools for managing cases. Rule 16 gives district judges wide discretion in managing the pretrial process by using preliminary pretrial conferences, scheduling orders, and final pretrial conferences. In addition to the management tools provided by Rule 16, judges also run the pretrial process by ruling on motions to dismiss, discovery motions, summary judgment, sanctions, and other matters.

The following reading is an excerpt from a handbook for judges published by the Federal Judicial Center (FJC) as part of its "pocket guide" series. The FJC is the research arm of the federal judiciary. In addition to conducting research about federal courts, the FJC publishes guides for judges. Wise lawyers understand the importance of knowing how judges think about their job. Thus, while judges are its intended audience, this handbook—like many other FJC publications—provides a nice introduction to the topic for lawyers and law students.

William W Schwarzer & Alan Hirsch, *THE ELEMENTS OF CASE MANAGEMENT, THIRD EDITION*
Federal Judicial Center (2017)

Introduction

Rule 1 of the Federal Rules of Civil Procedure describes the goal of the judicial system: "to secure the just, speedy, and inexpensive determination of every action." If judges are to achieve this goal despite limited judicial resources and the rising cost of litigation, particularly discovery, they must manage the litigation process.

Case management means different things to different people, and there is no single way to do it. In fact, there are substantial differences of opinion about many of the subjects we discuss here. But there is general agreement that case management, in essence, involves trial judges using the tools at their disposal with fairness and common sense (and in a way that fits their personalities and styles) in order to achieve the goal described in Rule 1. These tools include the Federal Rules of Civil and Criminal Procedure, the Federal Rules of Evidence, local rules, some provisions in Title 28, and the inherent authority of the court. Although judges operate in an environment largely shaped by local practice and custom, innovation and adaptation to circumstances also contribute to effective case management.

Faced with busy dockets, some federal judges say that they simply don't have time to meet with lawyers to discuss case management. In fact, however, a relatively modest amount of a judge's time devoted to case management early in a case can save very significant amounts of time later on. Saving time also means saving costs, both for the court and for the litigants. Judges who think they are too busy to manage cases probably are too busy not to. Indeed, the busiest judges with the heaviest dockets are often the ones most in need of sound case-management practices.

This manual briefly describes techniques that judges have found effective in managing their cases at various stages of the litigation process. It begins with a discussion of the Rule 16 conference, outlining how proper use of this conference enables judges to establish control of cases at the outset. It then provides separate discussions of several items on the Rule 16 agenda—settlement, discovery, and motions—that continue to play an important role in case management after the conference and are, in any event, important enough to warrant discrete consideration. The manual next turns to case management during the final pretrial conference. . . .

This manual is not intended to suggest that there is one preferred approach to case management. Its suggestions are offered as food for thought—a foundation for thinking about techniques and methods that will best suit the individual judge. Finally, a word of caution: local rules and the law of the circuit may affect some of what is said here.

The Rule 16 Conference

A judge's initial contact with the lawyers normally comes at the Rule 16 conference, known in some districts as a preliminary pretrial conference, scheduling conference, or status conference. The purpose of the conference is to launch the case-management process. The specific rules or practices in each district will influence the precise nature and scope of the conference. Regardless of variations, however, the culture of each court should further the central principle underlying Rule 16: that a judicial officer take charge of the case early on and, together with the lawyers, establish a program appropriate for its just, speedy, and inexpensive resolution. . . .

Timing and procedural matters

Rule 16 requires the court to issue a scheduling order within 60 days after the appearance of a defendant or within 90 days after the complaint has been served on a defendant. It is advantageous to schedule the first conference as early as possible, before the lawyers become bogged down in discovery or motions. Though some cases obviously require less attention than others, it makes good sense to schedule conferences in all cases with potential discovery and motion activity. Some types of cases, such as government collection cases or Social Security appeals, usually are so routine that no conference is needed.

Rule 16 conferences should not be perfunctory scheduling exercises. Judges who use conferences in that way miss out on its substantial benefits. The conference should be a moment of truth for the pleader and an opportunity for thoughtful discussion among the parties. The lawyers responsible for the case—not junior associates—should be there and should be prepared to explain their claims and defenses and to discuss future proceedings.

Although Rule 16(c) provides an agenda for the conference, judges may think of additional items appropriate for a particular case. Many judges issue a standard status conference order in advance, notifying the lawyers of what is expected of them. Many judges ask the lawyers to submit a joint case-management statement prior to the conference, summarizing the essentials of the case in simple terms, stating their position on the various agenda items, and proposing a joint scheduling plan. In addition to laying the groundwork for a complete and specific conference agenda, this procedure requires lawyers to prepare for the conference, to think about the case, and to reach agreements. This kind of analysis often eliminates meritless claims or defenses. A judge's reputation for insisting that lawyers be on top of a case from the beginning works wonders in reducing dockets and moving them along. Of course, the judge too should be prepared for the conference, having read the pertinent pleadings and the lawyers' statements.

In some cases, it also can be advantageous to have the parties present. This gives them an opportunity to hear opposing counsel and to learn firsthand what may be involved in the litigation, including the likely cost. Such knowledge can engender a more receptive attitude toward settlement. On the other hand, there is a risk that clients' presence will discourage candor on the part of the attorneys, or that some clients will attach too much significance to casual remarks. In some cases, it may be advantageous to have the parties available at the courthouse though not necessarily present during all of the conference.

While some judges hold Rule 16 conferences in open court with a court reporter present, others hold them in chambers and off the record, encouraging greater informality and a more searching and productive discussion.

Some conferences (and even motion hearings) can be conducted by telephone, saving time and money. But there is much to be said for having the case's first conference in person, bringing the lawyers and the judge face to face. Quite often, lawyers will not have talked to each other about the case beforehand. Bringing them together to engage with the litigation early on is one of the most useful aspects of case management.

Establishing jurisdiction and identifying pivotal issues

The primary objective of the Rule 16 conference is for the judge and the lawyers to discern what the case is really about. Pleadings often do more to obscure the real issues than to identify them. Before getting to the issues, however, the judge should always explore subject-matter jurisdiction, the absence of which is, of course, a non-waivable defect. It sometimes happens that the absence of jurisdiction is not recognized until well into a case—occasionally not until the appeal. The pretrial conference can prevent proceedings that will later prove fruitless.

Once federal jurisdiction has been established, the most important function of the conference is the identification of pivotal issues. This process reduces many seemingly complex cases to simple, clearly defined disputes that can be resolved more easily than appeared at first. For example, the Rule 16 conference may reveal that the plaintiff's right to recover ultimately turns on whether a legal defense bars the claim. Resolving that defense by motion, or perhaps by a separate trial, can save time and expense.

Detecting the underlying issues in dispute sometimes requires vigorous questioning of the attorneys by the judge to get beyond the pleadings. Parties may raise assorted claims or defenses that create the impression of a complex lawsuit when, upon probing, it turns out that the entire case hinges on a straightforward factual or legal question—or no triable issue at all. . . .

An important function of the conference is to disclose just what relief the plaintiff seeks—what damages it expects to prove and on what basis, and what other relief is sought. This helps to define what is at stake in the litigation. Undertaking this process at the outset can substantially reduce discovery. A commercial dispute, for example, may turn on an ordinary business record that has never been shown to the opponent. No discovery is needed. The judge can direct that the record be made available promptly and that the lawyers report back by telephone on a specified date. Similarly, if a defendant pleads all of the boilerplate defenses, the plaintiff may be in the position of having to conduct costly and unnecessary discovery; by using the conference to clarify which issues are genuinely in dispute, the judge can prevent such waste.

The Rule 16 conference should also be used to screen out cases or claims that lack any factual basis. While notice pleading means that parties need not allege all the evidentiary detail, it does not entitle them to litigate issues for which they have no evidence. Parties may not look wholly to discovery to make a case or defense. There must be some showing of a factual basis, or at least a strong likelihood of one, as a condition for permitting a party to go forward.

Careful definition of issues early in a case may also disclose issues susceptible to resolution by summary or partial summary judgment. Discussion can reveal some threshold legal issue that may not have appeared clearly to the lawyers or perhaps was swept under the rug by one of them. Judges who familiarize themselves with a case can usually determine whether there are disputed evidentiary facts requiring trial or whether the issue can be resolved on motion.

The conference not only lays the groundwork for motions but also provides an invaluable opportunity to identify and assess the proportionality of the discovery needed before motions can be made, thereby avoiding premature motions and building the foundation for proper ones. The conference can streamline or head off the filing of summary judgment motions that involve disputed factual issues and would only waste the parties' money and the court's time. . . .

Setting dates for future proceedings

Rule 16 directs the judge to set dates for completion of discovery, filing motions, joining other parties, and amending the pleadings. The judge may also modify the times for disclosure under Rule 26 and the extent of discovery, and set dates for a final pretrial conference and trial. It is important that these dates be set at the outset of the case if feasible. Sometimes not enough is known about a case to set meaningful dates, and another conference may be necessary. Some judges set firm discovery cutoff and trial dates at the first conference and never depart from those dates. Such rigidity can be effective for disposing of civil cases rapidly, but it is not always practical for courts whose heavy criminal dockets may affect trial dates for civil cases. However, most judges agree that a firm trial date is the most effective tool in case management. Therefore, every effort should be made to keep the scheduled trial date.

Judges should always set a firm date for the next event in the case, be it another conference, the filing of a motion, or any date requiring action by the lawyers. Every case in a judge's inventory should have a specific date calendared that will bring it to the court's attention.

Setting a firm schedule at the conference is no substitute for defining and narrowing issues. Focusing lawyers' attention on the issues from the outset avoids unnecessary discovery, promotes early settlement, prevents pointless trials, and, where a trial is needed, furthers efficiency and economy.

Settlement

The Rule 16 conference also should explore the possibility of settlement, and in most cases it should include a specific discussion of an appropriate time for and process of alternative dispute resolution. Most cases will eventually settle anyway, but often only after unnecessary cost, delay, and judicial effort. The traditional settlement on the courthouse steps, after much discovery and motion activity, not only is wasteful but also leaves the parties feeling dissatisfied with their experience as litigants. Judges should try to facilitate early settlement where practical.

Lawyers are generally not in a good position to evaluate settlement possibilities at the first conference, knowing too little of the case. Once the issues have been identified and narrowed, however, relatively little discovery may enable them to make a reasonable evaluation. The deposition of the plaintiff and perhaps the defendant or a key witness, and the exchange of a few documents, may be all that is necessary. This can be readily arranged, and the lawyers can be directed to return at a specified date if they have not settled. Such "phased discovery" frequently leads to an early settlement.

At the outset of a case, lawyers have rarely thought much about damages. Judges should focus attention on this subject early because it is crucial to a realistic evaluation. Many lawyers give insufficient consideration to the economics of their case, plunging into litigation without making a cost-benefit calculation. A client may have a meritorious claim, but the time and money necessary to establish it may be out of proportion to the potential reward. The Rule 16 conference should provide lawyers with a "reality check," and discussion about settlement should focus their attention on what would be an acceptable outcome for the client.

The judge's role

It is useful for a judge to inquire about settlement whenever meeting with the lawyers. Lawyers are often interested in settling (particularly in view of the rising cost of litigation), but may consider raising the subject an admission of weakness. A judge's questions offer a graceful opening.

Different judges take different approaches to settlement. Some judges become actively involved in settlement negotiations in their own cases, thinking that another judge would lack the necessary familiarity. Others choose not to, believing it may compromise them if the case goes to trial. This is a legitimate concern, because participation in the negotiations sooner or later may require the judge to evaluate and express a view on the strength of a claim or defense. Doing so will jeopardize the appearance of impartiality in future proceedings, and may cause both the judge and the parties to feel uncomfortable. This is less of a problem in a jury trial than in a bench trial. Nevertheless, in all cases, unless both parties urge the judge to act as settlement judge and waive disqualification, there is much to be said for recruiting a colleague on the court—another district judge or a magistrate judge—as a settlement judge. Many courts also have established alternative dispute resolution (ADR) programs, to which cases may be referred.

Of course, settlement is not desirable in every case. The dispute may involve a principle of importance to the parties or an issue whose resolution on the merits will help guide the conduct of other parties. Moreover, a party with a meritless claim should not be assisted in extracting a nuisance settlement by threatening protracted and costly litigation. Judges who are actively involved in settlement negotiations should be sensitive to such considerations and should avoid using their position of authority to apply undue pressure on parties to settle. Judges should facilitate, not coerce, settlement.

Discovery

Discovery, while often a critically important means of getting at the truth, also is probably the single greatest source of cost and delay in civil litigation. Judges can do much to mitigate this problem. Rule 26(b) gives judges great power and discretion to control discovery. This power can be used to prevent duplication, to require lawyers to use the least expensive way to get necessary information, including discovery of information stored electronically, and, particularly in light of the 2015 amendments to Rule 26(b), to keep discovery costs from becoming disproportionate to what is at stake in the lawsuit.

At the initial conference, the judge should review the lawyers' discovery plans with these considerations in mind and keep the discovery program in line with the objectives of Rule 26(b). Judges generally should not use valuable conference time to develop a detailed discovery plan with the lawyers. Instead, the lawyers should be asked to propose an agreed-upon plan, which the judge should review with care. Although the civil rules limit the number of depositions and interrogatories and the length of depositions, the court may alter those limits. The judge should therefore require justification as to the need for particular discovery and explore alternatives for getting information less expensively. Abuse of the discovery process is a ground for sanctions, but sanctions will rarely be needed when sound case management is applied.

Special care is required to manage expert discovery. The parties will usually exchange experts' reports before their depositions are taken—the reports can focus the deposition, and may even obviate the need for it. An expert should not be permitted to testify at trial unless he or she has been made available for deposition before the trial. Therefore, in some cases it makes sense to defer expert discovery until other discovery is completed, giving the parties a clearer sense of what expert testimony may be needed.

Some district judges assign supervision of discovery matters to magistrate judges. Whoever handles discovery disputes should have a program for keeping them under control. The most effective method may be having the judicial officer available to resolve any discovery dispute by telephone. This is particularly effective when a dispute develops during the taking of a deposition. Knowing that the judge is only a phone call away has a wonderful tendency to make lawyers more reasonable. It is surprising how quickly disagreements are resolved when they must be presented to the judge in a succinct statement. Telephone conferences eliminate the opportunity to use discovery disputes to obstruct the litigation. Establishing this procedure at the outset of a case greatly reduces the number of discovery disputes.

Many districts have local rules that preclude the filing of discovery motions unless the parties certify that they have met and conferred in a good-faith attempt to resolve the dispute. Even without such a rule, the judge can require that such a conference take place, and such practices are expressly encouraged in the 2015 Committee Notes to amended Rule 26(b).

Motions

Motions play an important role in litigation. They can prevent unnecessary trials or at least narrow issues so as to expedite trials. Pointless motions, however, waste time and money; whenever possible, the judge should discourage them. The classic example is the Rule 12(b)(6) motion for failure to state a claim. More often than not, the asserted defect is readily cured by an amendment. At the Rule 16 conference, the judge can ask the parties to specify any grounds they might have for such a motion and can determine in advance whether a defect is curable. Curable defects should generally be brought to the opponent's attention before a motion is filed. Similarly, lawyers should be discouraged from filing Rule 11 motions. There is a tendency to misuse this rule, which generally should be directed only at abusive conduct.

A hearing is unnecessary if a motion is routine and the outcome obvious. If the motion presents a difficult or close issue, the lawyers should come to court to answer questions and address the judge's concerns. Local rules or the Rule 16 scheduling order will provide a schedule for filing motions and oppositions. The time limits should be observed so that the judge has sufficient time to prepare for a hearing, if there is to be one.

If at all possible, the judge should be prepared to decide the motion from the bench. Most disputes do not become easier to resolve once taken back to chambers. In fact, as time passes the matter becomes cold, and the judge will need more time to refresh his or her recollection. While the litigants are entitled to the court's best effort, they will generally prefer a prompt decision to a perfect but belated one.

Trial courts should write no more than necessary, but often the legal issue involved in a summary judgment motion may be of great importance to the case before the court and to other cases. In those cases a written opinion is necessary. Otherwise, ruling from the bench orally after argument will be adequate and expeditious.

The Final Pretrial Conference

The final pretrial conference can be valuable in two respects. First, it is the last good shot at settlement. Second, it is a dress rehearsal for the trial. Delay and expense in civil litigation result not only from unnecessary trials but also from trials lasting too long and involving too many witnesses and exhibits. At the final pretrial conference, the judge and the lawyers can ascertain in advance what issues have to be tried and what evidence is necessary. This will also help ensure that the lawyers are prepared for trial.

Despite its potential, some judges treat the final pretrial conference as little more than a scheduling conference to set the final trial date. Others go to the opposite extreme and require preparation of elaborate statements, summaries, and stipulations. There is much to be said for a middle course: doing whatever is necessary, given the circumstances of the case, to lay the groundwork for a fair and efficient trial. Here are some of the agenda items the judge should consider.

Defining and narrowing the issues

The judge should have attempted to define and narrow the issues at the initial conference, but by the time of the final pretrial conference everyone will have a clearer understanding of the case. This conference presents the last and best opportunity to prevent waste of valuable trial time on pointless or undisputed matters. A good way to focus the issues is to require the parties to submit proposed jury instructions (or proposed findings of fact and conclusions of law in bench trials) that set forth clearly the governing rules of law and the factors controlling their application.

Previewing the evidence

By hearing and ruling on motions in limine, the judge can head off admissibility disputes during trial. The final pretrial conference provides an opportunity to hold a hearing under Rule 104 of the Federal Rules of Evidence to determine the admissibility of expert testimony under *Daubert* [*v. Merrell Dow Pharmaceuticals, Inc.*, 509 U.S. 579 (1993)], and to exercise the authority conferred by Rules 403 and 611. The judge can bar duplicative testimony (by limiting each side's expert or character witnesses, for example). So, too, the judge can eliminate testimony about matters not in dispute. For example, there is no point in having a handwriting expert if there is no dispute over who was the writer. Many foreseeable objections to testimony— such as hearsay objections—can be resolved before trial, as can issues concerning the permissible scope of opening statements.

Proposed exhibits should be previewed with a view to holding down their number and volume. There is little point in inundating jurors with a mass of exhibits beyond their capacity to read and absorb. (In post-trial interviews, jurors often complain that the lawyers presented too much evidence.) The judge may suggest that voluminous exhibits be redacted to eliminate unnecessary portions and cumulative exhibits be eliminated. Sometimes information from numerous exhibits can be presented in a summary exhibit (as authorized by Federal Rule of Evidence 1006). Previewing proposed exhibits can also save valuable trial time, since the judge can rule on evidentiary objections and receive into evidence unobjectionable exhibits.

Considering limits on the length of the trial

Trials that last too long are costly, exhaust jurors, and hinder comprehension. When a trial threatens to be protracted, some judges find it useful to limit the number of witnesses or exhibits each side may offer. Other judges sometimes limit the amount of time allowed each side for direct and cross-examination, using a chess clock or similar means to keep a running account of the time used by each party. Such limits can be helpful to the court and the parties but should be imposed with care and only after consultation with counsel.

Establishing the ground rules for the trial

The final conference can fix the procedures for trial, including the conduct of voir dire and method of jury selection, the order of witnesses, and daily trial schedules.

Considering the use of special procedures

The judge can discuss with counsel and determine the propriety of bifurcation, the return of sequential verdicts by the jury, use of special verdicts or interrogatories, and any other phasing arrangements or special procedures that may be appropriate.

Exploring once more the opportunities for settlement

Now that the parties are completely familiar with the case, they may be ready to settle if the judge provides the opening.

The results of the final pretrial conference should be memorialized in a pretrial order. To save time, the judge can dictate the order to the court reporter at the end of the conference with counsel present. . . .

Notes & Questions

1. Were you surprised to see so many references to *settlement* in this handbook for judges about how to manage cases? At nearly every turn, the guide encourages judges to prod lawyers about settlement. Think about the phrase "out-of-court settlement," often used to describe the resolution of litigation by agreement. The

"out-of-court" modifier is only partly correct. A settlement, by definition, is out of court in the sense that it resolves a dispute by negotiation rather than adjudication. But this does not mean that judges play no role in settlement. Many judges encourage parties and lawyers to explore settlement, and judges manage the pretrial process to generate information and opportunities to facilitate such negotiated resolutions.

We will return to the topic of settlements in Chapter 13, including the judge's role in encouraging settlement. For now, simply note the importance that judges place on settlement when they think about the functions of the pretrial process and in particular when they think about the functions of pretrial conferences.

2. *The Elements of Case Management* offers an unapologetically positive view of pretrial management by judges. Its original lead author, Judge Schwarzer, was an outspoken advocate of active judicial management. Not everyone views judicial management so positively. Some critics argue that management may not improve efficiency; it may merely create more hoops for lawyers to jump through in the litigation process. On this view, judges should spend their time ruling on motions and conducting trials rather than running meetings with lawyers, and lawyers should spend their time actually litigating cases rather than complying with judges' pretrial management demands.

Other critics raise a deeper set of concerns. What is the proper role of judges? What is the basis for the legitimate exercise of judicial power? When judges exercise power, what checks does our legal system provide to ensure that judicial power is not abused? The term "managerial judges" was coined by Professor Judith Resnik, and she did not mean it mostly as a compliment. In a famous law review article, Professor Resnik noted various ways in which judges had moved away from traditional adjudication. Unlike traditional adjudicatory acts that require reasoned explanation and are subject to appellate review, she argued, judicial acts of pretrial management are more subject to the whims of particular judges:

> [D]uring pretrial supervision, judges make many decisions informally and often meet with parties ex parte, and appellate review is virtually unavailable. The judge has vast influence over the course and eventual outcome of the litigation. As a result, litigants have good reason to capitulate to judicial pressure rather than risk the hostility of a judge who, under the individual calendar system, has ongoing responsibility for the case. During pretrial management, judges are restrained only by personal beliefs about the proper role of judge-managers.

Managerial Judges, 96 HARV. L. REV. 374, 413 (1982). She concluded with a reference to depictions of the goddess Justice wearing a blindfold and carrying scales:

> I want to take away trial judges' roving commission and to bring back the blindfold. I want judges to balance the scales, not abandon them altogether in the press to dispose of cases quickly. No one has convincingly discredited the virtues of disinterest and disengagement, virtues that form the bases of the judiciary's

authority. . . . I fear that, as it moves closer to administration, adjudication may be in danger of ceasing to be.

Id. at 445. Look again at the advice to judges in *The Elements of Case Management*, but this time do it with Professor Resnik's concerns in mind. Consider the danger of judges pressuring parties to abandon claims or defenses that have not yet been adjudicated on the merits, or pressuring parties to settle even if the parties prefer to have the court adjudicate the matter. It puts a rather different spin on the reading, doesn't it?

3. The language of Rule 16 gives judges plenty of discretion about whether, why, and how to conduct pretrial conferences. But the rule offers guidance on the functions and topics of such conferences. Rule 16(a) mentions, without limitation, five purposes of pretrial conferences:

(1) expediting disposition of the action;
(2) establishing early and continuing control so that the case will not be protracted because of lack of management;
(3) discouraging wasteful pretrial activities;
(4) improving the quality of the trial through more thorough preparation; and
(5) facilitating settlement.

Rule 16(c) offers a long list of topics that may be raised at a pretrial conference. These include formulating the issues, eliminating frivolous claims or defenses, obtaining stipulations of facts, controlling and scheduling discovery, identifying witnesses and documents, disposing of pending motions, adopting special procedures for complex issues, and, of course, settlement.

4. At the end of the section on final pretrial conferences, *The Elements of Case Management* mentions that the results from a final pretrial conference should be memorialized in a pretrial order. This is the *final pretrial order*. Although Rule 16 does not require a final pretrial order or even a final pretrial conference ("The court may hold a final pretrial conference to formulate a trial plan . . ."), the rule leaves no doubt about the standard for modifying a final pretrial order. Rule 16(e) states, "The court may modify the order issued after a final pretrial conference only to prevent manifest injustice." Courts have made it clear that "manifest injustice" is a high standard. After the plan for trial has been formulated and memorialized in a court order—including such matters as witnesses, exhibits, claims, and defenses—it is difficult to persuade a judge to alter it. Thus, when preparing for a final pretrial conference and when proposing language for a final pretrial order, a lawyer should have done all of the necessary work to know what evidence and arguments the lawyer intends to present at trial.

To a large extent, the final pretrial order supplants the pleadings at the end stage of litigation that makes it this far. Think about the relationship between the pleadings and the final pretrial order. In what ways does the final pretrial order resemble the complaint and answer? In what ways does it differ?

THE BIG PICTURE

If one were to list the most important developments in civil litigation of the last half-century, the shift toward judicial case management would be high on the list. Think of this phenomenon as it relates to both *adjudication* and *settlement*. Regarding adjudication, judges in the early days of the Federal Rules of Civil Procedure were more inclined to sit back, allow the lawyers to conduct discovery and prepare for trial, and then adjudicate claims at trial. Now, judges are more inclined to lean in, conduct pretrial conferences, and assert control over aspects of the pretrial process. Regarding settlement, many judges now do not view settlement merely as something that might occur along the road to trial if the parties choose to negotiate, but rather as an outcome judges should actively encourage.

CHAPTER 5

Trial

Trial is what nonlawyers imagine lawyers spend a lot of their time doing. While trial occurs a lot in movies and on television legal dramas, in the real world, trial represents only one segment of the litigation process. It is an important part of the process, but it is uncommon. Of all the civil cases filed in federal court, only about 2 percent reach trial. Most cases are settled, dropped by the plaintiff, or resolved before trial by summary judgment or other procedures. Nonetheless, the United States legal system is designed around trial. Indeed, the procedures you have learned about thus far are aimed in large part at developing a case for trial or weeding out cases before trial. Every lawyer must understand how trials work, and every successful litigator must be prepared to take cases to trial with skill.

This chapter does not teach you how to be a trial lawyer. Many law schools offer a separate course on trial practice where you can learn the skills of direct and cross-examination, opening and closing statements, evidentiary foundations, and objections. Even then, any good trial lawyer will tell you that the only way to hone and perfect those skills is through years of observation and experience.

This chapter, instead, focuses on the aspects of civil procedure that relate to how trials proceed. In particular, it first covers the jury: the constitutional right to a trial by jury, certain rules governing jury selection, and the role of the jury in our litigation system. Second, it covers the basic contours of the trial process. Third, it focuses on the power struggle between the judge and jury that plays out on motions for judgment as a matter of law or motions for a new trial.

As you read this chapter—and especially as you consider the role of the jury—ask yourself some big questions. First, what are the benefits of juries in civil cases? What are the costs? Second, consider the alternatives. Would other modes of resolving the facts be preferable to civil jury trials? Would you give the same answer regarding criminal cases? Third, if civil jury trials are such a rarity, does it seem odd that the civil litigation system is designed around trial as the endpoint? Or, to the contrary, are there benefits to designing a procedural system around a moment in which a fact-finder hears evidence, resolves factual disputes, and applies law to facts? Along these lines, is there a certain logic of history and political culture that explains why in the United States—unlike virtually every other country—that fact-finder is sometimes a jury of ordinary citizens? Does that logic still hold today?

A. JURY TRIAL

(1) Civil Jury Right

In the United States, we are so accustomed to the civil jury system that it is easy to forget what a unique and peculiarly American institution it is. Instead of charging a government bureaucrat with the responsibility for determining the facts, we obtain a representative sample of ordinary citizens and given them the power—and the civic duty—to decide the case. In most other countries, civil jury trials are virtually nonexistent. Some countries use juries or other forms of lay participation in *criminal* cases, where concerns about government overreaching run strong. However, *civil* cases around the world are nearly always decided by the judge. Even in England—the historic source of the jury trial—civil juries have largely been abandoned except in a few categories of cases.

In a jury trial, the jury and the judge play different roles. The judge runs the trial process, makes all the legal rulings, decides what evidence is admissible, and instructs the jury on the law. The jury determines the facts and applies the law to those facts. The jury hears the witnesses' testimony and sees the documentary or physical evidence presented by both sides. In some courts, jurors are allowed to submit questions for the judge to ask witnesses, but mostly, the jury sits and listens to the testimony as elicited by the lawyers' questions on direct and cross-examination. Indeed, because much must be discussed outside the jury's presence, it is not uncommon for jurors to be shuttled in and out of the courtroom. Traditionally, juries had 12 members, but these days juries range in size from 6 to 12 depending on the court. In a federal case, the jury's decision must be unanimous unless the parties agree otherwise. Some states, on the other hand, do not require unanimity.

Even in the United States, though, not all civil trials involve juries. In what is known as a *bench trial*, the judge plays the role of both fact-finder and legal decision maker. In Part B of this chapter, we will look at the procedural aspects of bench trials. We begin, however, by studying when the right to jury trial is in play.

(a) The Constitutional Right to a Jury

Not all civil cases come with a right to trial by jury. In some civil cases, however, parties have a right to a jury, and this right may arise under a statute or the Constitution. Regarding the former, occasionally Congress provides that a jury trial right accompanies a particular statute.[1] Many statutes, however, do not explicitly provide for a right to a trial by jury. If a statute is silent on the issue, or if a claim is non-statutory, such as a common law claim for a tort or breach of contract, then the right to a jury depends on application of the Seventh Amendment.

The Constitution enshrines the jury right in two separate provisions of the Bill of Rights. The Sixth Amendment establishes the right to a jury trial in criminal cases, along with other protections for criminal defendants. The Seventh Amendment preserves the right to a jury trial in certain civil cases. The text of the Seventh Amendment reads as follows: "In Suits at common law, where the value in controversy shall exceed twenty dollars, the right of trial by jury shall be preserved. . . ." Note the word *preserved*. Unlike most of the Bill of Rights, the Seventh Amendment explicitly preserves a right as it already existed in the common law courts of England and the fledgling United States.

Because of that backward-looking feature of the Seventh Amendment, the constitutional right to a jury trial in civil cases depends on history. In 1791, when the Seventh Amendment was ratified, and for a long time after, courts were divided into courts of *equity* (also known as chancery) and courts of *law* (also known as common law courts), as we saw in the short history of pleadings in Chapter 2. Recall also from Chapter 2 that the common law courts only had the power to hear certain categories of cases. Common law courts had jurisdiction to hear most cases for money damages. Other categories of cases, most notably those seeking injunctive relief, were sent to the courts of equity. Further, and critical here, common law courts had juries; courts of equity did not. This is where a careful reading of the Seventh Amendment text is key: Note that it begins with the words "[i]n suits at common law." Those words refer to the distinction between courts of common law and equity that existed in 1791 and that we mentioned in our brief history of pleadings Chapter 2. Thus, under the Seventh Amendment, if a case would have fallen within the jurisdiction of the courts of common law in the eighteenth century, then the parties have a constitutional right to a jury.

The historical nature of the text of the amendment often makes it easy to determine whether a party has a right to a jury trial. A tort claim or breach of contract claim for money damages, for example, carries a right to a jury trial because those cases would have been heard in the common law courts in 1791. By contrast, a claim for an injunction prohibiting certain conduct by the defendant or a claim seeking specific performance of a contract does not carry a right to a jury trial, as those claims would have been heard by the courts of equity in 1791. Other cases, though, are a little trickier. For instance, although replevin (demanding recovery of goods taken unlawfully from the plaintiff's possession) looks a lot like a form of injunctive relief, historically, it was a common law action and therefore carries a right to a jury trial.

---

[1] *See, e.g.,* 42 U.S.C. §1981a(c) (permitting jury trial of claims for compensatory or punitive damages for intentional discrimination in employment); 28 U.S.C. §1873 (permitting jury trial for tort claims concerning any vessel weighing 20 or more tons that trades between the coasts of the several states); 28 U.S.C. §2402 (permitting jury trial for claims against the United States that federal taxes or penalties were erroneously assessed or collected).

However, the trickiest cases arise when there is no clear historical answer. Much has happened in the centuries since the Seventh Amendment was ratified, and many claims available today had not even been imagined in 1791. How does the Seventh Amendment apply to a cause of action that was created *after* the Seventh Amendment's adoption? Consider the following case.

CHAUFFEURS, TEAMSTERS AND HELPERS, LOCAL NO. 391 v. TERRY
494 U.S. 558 (1990)

MARSHALL, J., delivered the opinion of the Court, except as to Part III-A.

This case presents the question whether an employee who seeks relief in the form of backpay for a union's alleged breach of duty of fair representation has a right to trial by jury. We hold that the Seventh Amendment entitles such a plaintiff to a jury trial.

I

McLean Trucking Company and the Chauffeurs, Teamsters, and Helpers Local No. 391 (Union) were parties to a collective-bargaining agreement that governed the terms and conditions of employment at McLean's terminals. The 27 respondents were employed by McLean as truckdrivers in bargaining units covered by the agreement, and all were members of the Union. In 1982 McLean implemented a change in operations that resulted in the elimination of some of its terminals and the reorganization of others. As part of that change, McLean transferred respondents to the terminal located in Winston-Salem and agreed to give them special seniority rights in relation to "inactive" employees in Winston-Salem who had been laid off temporarily.

After working in Winston-Salem for approximately six weeks, respondents were alternately laid off and recalled several times. Respondents filed a grievance with the Union, contesting the order of the lay-offs and recalls, [challenging] McLean's policy of stripping any driver who was laid off of his special seniority rights, [and claiming] that McLean breached the collective bargaining agreement by giving inactive drivers preference over respondents. After these proceedings, the grievance committee ordered McLean to recall any respondent who was then laid off and to lay off any inactive driver who had been recalled; in addition, the committee ordered McLean to recognize the respondents' special seniority rights until the inactive employees were properly recalled.

[McLean flouted the grievance committee's orders, but the committee did not respond to respondents' further requests to order McLean to reinstate the workers' statuses. The Union declined to refer any further charges to the grievance committee.]

In July 1983, respondents filed an action in District Court, alleging that McLean had breached the collective-bargaining agreement in violation of §301 of the Labor Management Relations Act, 1947, 29 U.S.C. §185 (1982 ed.), and that the Union had violated its duty of fair representation. Respondents requested a permanent injunction requiring the defendant[] [employers] to cease their illegal acts and to reinstate them to their proper seniority status; in addition, they sought compensatory damages for lost wages and health benefits. In 1986 McLean filed for bankruptcy; subsequently, the action against it was voluntarily dismissed, along with all claims for injunctive relief [leaving only the claims against the Union].

Respondents had requested a jury trial in their pleadings. The Union moved to strike the jury demand on the ground that no right to a jury trial exists in a duty of fair representation suit. The District Court denied the motion to strike. After an interlocutory appeal, the Fourth Circuit affirmed the trial court, holding that the Seventh Amendment entitled respondents to a jury trial of their claim for monetary relief. We granted the petition for certiorari to resolve a Circuit conflict on this issue, and now affirm the judgment of the Fourth Circuit.

II

The duty of fair representation is inferred from unions' exclusive authority under the National Labor Relations Act (NLRA), 29 U.S.C. §159(a) (1982 ed.), to represent all employees in a bargaining unit. *Vaca v. Sipes*, 386 U.S. 171, 177 (1967). The duty requires a union "to serve the interests of all members without hostility or discrimination toward any, to exercise its discretion with complete god faith and honesty, and to avoid arbitrary conduct." *Ibid.* A union must discharge its duty both in bargaining with the employer and in its enforcement of the resulting collective-bargaining agreement. Thus, the Union here was required to pursue respondents' grievances in a manner consistent with the principles of fair representation. . . .

[T]o recover money damages, [the employee must prove two facts]: that the employer's action violated the terms of the collective-bargaining agreement and that the union breached its duty of fair representation. *Id.* at 164-65.

III

We turn now to the constitutional issue presented in this case—whether respondents are entitled to a jury trial.[3] The Seventh Amendment provides that "[i]n Suits at common law, where the value in controversy shall exceed twenty dollars, the right of trial by jury shall be preserved." The right to a jury trial includes more than the common-law forms of action recognized in 1791; the phrase "Suits at common law" refers to "suits in which *legal* rights [are] to be ascertained and determined, in contradistinction to those where equitable rights alone [are] recognized, and equitable remedies [are] administered." *Parsons v. Bedford*, 28 U.S. 433 (1830). The right extends to cause of action created by Congress. *Tull v. United States*, 481 U.S. 412, 417 (1987). Since the merger of the systems of law and equity, *see* Fed. Rule Civil Proc. 2, this Court has carefully preserved the right to trial by jury where legal rights are at stake. As the Court noted in *Beacon Theatres v. Westover*, 359 U.S. 500, 501 (1959), "Maintenance of the jury as a fact-finding body is of such importance and occupies so firm a place in our history and jurisprudence that any seeming curtailment of the right to a jury trial should be scrutinized with the utmost care."

To determine whether a particular action will resolve legal rights, we examine both the nature of the issues involved and the remedy sought. "First, we compare the

---

[3] Because the NLRA, 29 U.S.C. §159(a) (1982 ed.), does not expressly create the duty of fair representation, resort to the statute to determine whether Congress provided for a jury trial in an action for breach of that duty is unavailing.

statutory action to 18th-century actions brought in the courts of England prior to the merger of the courts of law and equity. Second, we examine the remedy sought and determine whether it is legal or equitable in nature." *Tull*, 481 U.S. at 417-418. The second inquiry is the most important in our analysis. *Granfinanciera, S.A. v. Nordberg*, 492 U.S. 33, 42 (1989).[4]

A

An action for breach of a union's duty of fair representation was unknown in 18th-century England; in fact, collective bargaining was unlawful. We must therefore look for an analogous cause of action that existed in the 18th century to determine whether the nature of this duty of fair representation suit is legal or equitable.

The Union contends that this duty of fair representation action resembles a suit brought to vacate an arbitration award because respondents seek to set aside the result of the grievance process. In the 18th century, an action to set aside an arbitration award was considered equitable....

The arbitration analogy is inapposite, however, to the Seventh Amendment question posed in this case. No grievance committee has considered respondents' claim that the Union violated its duty of fair representation; the grievance process was concerned only with the employer's alleged breach of the collective-bargaining agreement. Thus, respondents' claim against the Union cannot be characterized as an action to vacate an arbitration award because

"[t]he arbitration proceeding did not, and indeed, could not, resolve the employee's claim against the union.... Because no arbitrator has decided the primary issue presented by this claim, no arbitration award need by undone, even if the employee ultimately prevails." *DelCostello v. Teamsters*, 462 U.S. 151, 167 (1983).

The Union next argues that respondents' duty of fair representation action is comparable to an action by a trust beneficiary against a trustee for breach of fiduciary duty. Such actions were in the exclusive jurisdiction of the courts of equity. This analogy is far more persuasive than the arbitration analogy. Just as a trustee must act in the best interests of the beneficiaries, a union, as the exclusive representative of the workers, must exercise its power to act on behalf of the employees in good faith, *Vaca*, 386 U.S. at 177. Moreover, just as a beneficiary does not directly control the actions of a trustee, an individual employee lacks direct control over a union's actions taken on his behalf. The trust analogy extends to a union's handling of grievances [as well]....

Respondents contend that their duty of fair representation suit is less like a trust action than an attorney malpractice action, which was historically an action at law, *see e.g., Russell v. Palmer*, 95 Eng. Rep. 837 (1767).... [T]his Court in *DelCostello* noted in dictum that an attorney malpractice action is "the closest state-law analogy for the claim against the union." 462 U.S. at 167. The Court in *DelCostello* did not consider the trust analogy, however. Presented with a more complete range of alternatives, we find that, in the context of the Seventh Amendment inquiry, the attorney malpractice analogy does not capture the relationship between the union and the represented employees as fully as the trust analogy does....

---

[4] Justice Stevens' analysis emphasizes a third consideration, namely whether "the issues [presented by the claim] are typical grist for the jury's judgment." This Court, however, has never relied on this consideration [as a basis for determining whether there is a jury trial right].

Nevertheless, the trust analogy does not persuade us to characterize respondents' claim as wholly equitable. The Union's argument mischaracterizes the nature of our comparison of the action before us to 18th-century forms of action. As we observed in *Ross v. Bernhard*, 396 U.S. 531 (1970), "The Seventh Amendment question depends on the nature of the *issue* to be tried rather than the character of the over-all action." *Id.* at 538 (emphasis added). As discussed above, to recover from the Union here, respondents must prove both that McLean violated §301 by breaching the collective-bargaining agreement and that the Union breached its duty of fair representation. When viewed in isolation, the duty of fair representation is analogous to a claim against a trustee for breach of fiduciary duty. The §301 issue, however, is comparable to a breach of contract claim—a legal issue.

Respondents' action against the Union thus encompasses both legal and equitable issues. The first part of our Seventh Amendment inquiry, then, leaves us in equipoise as to whether respondents are entitled to a jury trial.

B

Our determination under the first part of the Seventh Amendment analysis is only preliminary. In this case, the only remedy sought is a request for compensatory damages representing backpay and benefits. Generally, an action for money damages was "the traditional form of relief offered in the courts of law." *Curtis v. Loether*, 415 U.S. 189, 196 (1974). This Court has not, however, held that "any award of monetary relief must *necessarily* be legal relief." *Ibid.* (emphasis added). Nonetheless, because we conclude that the remedy respondents seek has none of the attributes that must be

present before we will find an exception to the general rule and characterize damages as equitable, we find that the remedy sought by respondents is legal.

First, we have characterized damages as equitable where they are restitutionary, such as in "action[s] for disgorgement of improper profits," *Tull*, 481 U.S. at 424. The backpay sought by respondents is not money wrongfully held by the Union, but wages and benefits they would have received from McLean had the Union processed the employees' grievances properly. Such relief is not restitutionary.

Second, a monetary award "incidental to or intertwined with injunctive relief" may be equitable. *Tull, supra*, 481 U.S. at 424. Because respondents seek only money damages, this characteristic is clearly absent from the case.

The Union argues that the backpay relief sought here must nonetheless be considered equitable because this Court has labeled backpay awarded under Title VII, of the Civil Rights Act of 1964, as equitable. . . . [T]he Union's argument does not persuade us that respondents are not entitled to a jury trial here. Congress specifically characterized backpay under Title VII as a form of "equitable relief." 42 U.S.C. §2000e-5(g) (1982 ed.). Congress made no similar pronouncement regarding the duty of fair representation. Furthermore, the Court has noted that backpay sought from an employer under Title VII would generally be restitutionary in nature, in contrast to the damages sought here from the Union. Thus, the remedy sought in this duty of fair representation case is clearly different from backpay sought for violations of Title VII. . . .

We hold, then, that the remedy of backpay sought in this duty of fair representation action is legal in nature. Considering both parts of the Seventh Amendment inquiry, we find that respondents are entitled to a jury trial on all issues presented in their suit.

IV

On balance, our analysis of the nature of respondents' duty of fair representation action and the remedy they seek convinces us that this action is a legal one. Although the search for an adequate 18th-century analog revealed that the claim includes both legal and equitable issues, the money damages respondents seek are the type of relief traditionally awarded by courts of law. Thus, the Seventh Amendment entitles respondents to a jury trial, and we therefore affirm the judgment of the Court of Appeals.

Justice BRENNAN, concurring in part and concurring in the judgment.

I agree with the Court that respondents seek a remedy that is legal in nature and that the Seventh Amendment entitles respondents to a jury trial on their duty of fair representation claims. I therefore join Parts I, II, III-B, and IV of the Court's opinion. I do not join that part of the opinion which reprises the particular historical analysis this Court has employed to determine whether a claim is a "Sui[t] at common law" under the Seventh Amendment, because I believe the historical test can and should be simplified.

The current test ... requires a court to compare the right at issue to 18th-century English forms of action to determine whether the historically analogous right was vindicated in an action at law or in equity, and to examine whether the remedy sought is legal or equitable in nature. However, this Court, in expounding the test, has repeatedly discounted the significance of the analogous form of action for deciding where the Seventh Amendment applies. I

think it is time we dispense with it altogether. I would decide Seventh Amendment questions on the basis of the relief sought. If the relief is legal in nature, *i.e.*, if it is the kind of relief that historically was available from courts of law, I would hold that the parties have a constitutional right to a trial by jury unless Congress has permissibly delegated the particular dispute to a non-Article III decisionmaker and jury trials would frustrate Congress' purposes in enacting a particular statutory scheme.

I believe that our insistence that the jury trial right hinges in part on a comparison of the substantive right at issue to forms of action used in English courts 200 years ago needlessly convolutes our Seventh Amendment jurisprudence. For the past decade and a half, this Court has explained that the two parts of the historical test are not equal in weight, that the nature of the remedy is more important than the nature of the right. Since the existence of a right to jury trial therefore turns on the nature of the remedy ... there remains little purpose to our rattling through dusty attics of ancient writs. . . .

[The concurrence of Justice Stevens, in which he agreed with the majority's conclusion that the plaintiff was entitled to a jury trial, but in which he also expressed his views that *one*, the majority overstated the importance of finding a precise historical analogue, and *two*, the court needed to consider the functional capabilities of the jury in determining whether a claim carried the right to a jury trial (*see* footnote 4, *supra*), is omitted.]

Justice KENNEDY, with whom Justice O'CONNOR and Justice SCALIA join, dissenting.

This case asks whether the Seventh Amendment guarantees the respondent union members a jury trial in a duty of fair representation action against their labor union. The Court is quite correct, in my view, in its formulation of the initial premises that must govern the case. Under *Curtis v. Loether*, 415 U.S. 189 (1974), the right to a jury trial in a statutory action depends on the presence of "legal right and remedies." To determine whether rights and remedies in a duty of fair representation action are legal in character, we must compare the action to the 18th-century cases permitted in the law courts of England, and we must examine the nature of the relief sought. I agree also with those Members of the Court who find that the duty of fair representation action resembles an equitable trust action more than a suit for malpractice.

I disagree with the analytic innovation of the Court that identification of the trust action as a model for modern duty of fair representation actions is insufficient to decide the case. The Seventh Amendment requires us to determine whether the duty of fair representation action "is more similar to cases that were tried in courts of law than to suits tried in courts of equity." *Tull*, 481 U.S. at 417. Having made this decision in favor of an equitable action, our inquiry should end. Because the Court disagrees with this proposition, I dissent. . . .

The Court must adhere to the historical test in determining the right to a jury because the language of the Constitution requires it. The Seventh Amendment "preserves" the right to jury trial in civil cases. We cannot preserve a right existing in 1791 unless we look to history to identify it. Our precedents are in full agreement with this reasoning and insist on adherence to the historical test. No alternatives short of rewriting the Constitution exist. If we abandon the plain language of the Constitution to expand the jury right, we may expect Courts with opposing views to curtail it in the future.

It is true that a historical inquiry into the distinction between law and equity may require us to enter into a domain becoming less familiar with time. . . . [However,] [t]he historical test, in fact, resolves most cases without difficulty. . . . I would hesitate to abandon or curtail the historical test out of concern for the competence of the Court to understand legal history. We do look to history for the answers to constitutional questions. . . .

If Congress has not provided for a jury trial, we are confined to the Seventh Amendment to determine whether one is required. . . . Our whole constitutional experience teaches that history must inform the judicial inquiry. Our obligation to the Constitution and its Bill of Rights, no less than the compact we have with the generation that wrote them for us, do not permit us to disregard provisions that some may think to be mere matters of historical form.

Notes & Questions

1. Make sure you understand whether the majority classified the employees' claim against the union as equitable, legal, or something else in nature, as a matter of the historical-analogue prong of the Seventh Amendment test. Why did that classification not settle the jury-trial issue?

2. Why did the Court even have to reach the Seventh Amendment historical analysis in the first place? What is the relationship to and role of Congress in this respect?

3. Although Justice Brennan agrees with the majority's result, he sets out a different Seventh Amendment test than the one used by the majority. What, precisely, is Justice Brennan's test? Why does he think his test ought to govern Seventh Amendment analysis? In what ways does the dissent disagree with Justice Brennan's test? Disagree with the majority's approach?

4. In his omitted concurrence (but quoted in footnote 4 of the majority opinion), Justice Stevens suggested an additional consideration be included in the Seventh Amendment test:

> [T]he commonsense understanding of the jury, selected to represent the community, is appropriately invoked when disputes in the factory, the warehouse, and the garage must be resolved. In most duty of fair representation cases, the issues, which require understanding of the realities of employment relationships, are typical grist for the jury's judgment. Indeed, the law defining the union's duty of fair representation has developed in cases tried to juries.

How does the majority react to Justice Stevens' suggestion of this sort of functional analysis? Keep this disagreement in mind when you read *Markman v. Westview Instruments*, 517 U.S. 370 (1996), later in this chapter.

5. What if a case involves multiple issues: some legal, some equitable? Suppose the plaintiff alleges wrongdoing by the defendant and demands both an injunction against the wrongful conduct and monetary compensation for the damages it has caused. Or suppose the plaintiff asserts a common law claim and the defendant responds with an equitable counterclaim. How can the court protect the Seventh Amendment right to a jury for the common law issues when neither party has a right to a jury on the equitable ones? The Court took up this thorny problem in *Beacon Theatres, Inc. v. Westover*, 359 U.S. 500 (1959), and held that a jury must decide all the legal claims first before the remaining equitable claims are decided. The jury's findings are then binding in the non-jury proceedings on the equitable issues. *Id.*

6. The Seventh Amendment applies only to federal courts, not state courts. As a matter of constitutional law, many provisions of the Bill of Rights have been applied to the states by "incorporating" those rights into the Due Process Clause of the Fourteenth Amendment, but the Supreme Court has treated the Seventh Amendment differently, applying it to federal courts alone. Nearly every state, however, has an analogous state constitutional provision for a civil jury right, and many state courts apply historical tests along the lines of the Seventh Amendment to effectuate those provisions.

(b) The Demand for a Jury

As you just learned, certain statutes provide a right to a jury trial, and if no right is provided by statute, the Seventh Amendment may provide a right to jury trial. However, neither substantive statutes nor the Seventh Amendment spells out how a party should assert that right—and a party *must* assert that right or it will be waived. This is where Federal Rule of Civil Procedure 38 comes into play.

The most important things to draw from Rule 38 are the related concepts of *demand* and *waiver*. If a party wishes to have a jury trial, the party must *demand* it within the time limit set by the rule. A party demands a jury trial by "serving the other parties with a written demand—which may be included in a pleading," and filing the demand with the court. Parties often make jury demands by including a prominent statement on the first page of their complaint or answer. The statement is usually very straightforward, for example: "The Plaintiff Demands a Trial by Jury." Look again at the defendants' answer in the *Spahr* case file in Chapter 1, and note how the defendants demanded a jury at the top and bottom of that document.

The jury right belongs to any party. Although as a strategic matter plaintiffs often prefer juries, this is by no means universally true, and both plaintiffs and defendants have the right to demand a jury trial. If the plaintiff demands a jury, and if it is a case in which the jury right applies, it will be a jury trial. If the defendant demands a jury, again assuming the jury right applies, it will be a jury trial. The parties do not have to agree. As long as any party properly demands a jury trial, that party's right will be respected, even if every other party would prefer a bench trial.

The corollary to the *demand* requirement is the doctrine of *waiver*. Like many other constitutional and statutory rights, the right to trial by jury is waivable. As Rule 38 puts the point: "A party waives a jury trial unless its demand is properly served and filed." Therefore, if neither party requests a jury, the trial will be a bench trial, even if the right to a jury trial would have been available under a statute or the Seventh Amendment. As a matter of litigation strategy, then, in any action where the Constitution or a statute provides the right to a jury trial, the lawyers must consider the tactical question of whether they would prefer a jury trial or bench trial.

THE BIG PICTURE

The civil jury right is controversial. Opponents (and even some supporters, like Justice Stevens) of civil juries worry about whether jurors can grasp complex factual disputes that depend on scientific, technical, or financial evidence. They worry about whether jurors adequately comprehend and apply nuanced legal instructions. They worry about whether jurors are swayed by sympathy or bias. Such criticisms, particularly from lobbyists representing business interests, have led to calls for reform (often tort reform in general, and then statutory caps on certain types of damages in particular) as well as calls for repeal of the Seventh Amendment. Proponents of civil juries, meanwhile, praise juries as a check on government overreach and as a key component of our democratic form of government. They argue that 12 (or 6) heads are better than one, and that ordinary citizens are well positioned to evaluate witness credibility and to understand the wide range of everyday situations that give rise to lawsuits. Proponents also argue that juries help litigants accept outcomes because juries bring legitimacy to resolutions in a way that judges, as governmental actors, cannot. Empirical evidence does not provide a great deal of support for the perception of the "runaway" jury opponents lament, but neither does it provide much support for the idea that jurors skillfully identify untruthful witnesses or that jurors comprehend complex jury instructions. When thinking about controversies over the civil jury, always ask yourself, compared to what? Do judges bring their own limitations and biases? Moreover, keep in mind that judges have various tools to control juries and to mitigate unfair outcomes, as you will learn later in this chapter. As you gain experience in your own studies and career, perhaps you will reach your own conclusions about the merits of the jury institution. As you do, we encourage you to bring a healthy skepticism to claims—from either side—that this ancient and complex institution is either all good or all bad.

(2) Jury Selection

The jury selection process serves multiple, sometimes competing, goals. First, the process aims to provide the court with a representative jury, or at least a jury that is drawn from a representative sample of the population in the court's district. Second, the process aims to give litigants some assurance of protection from biased jurors. Third, the process aims to provide the jurors themselves with an opportunity to exercise civil responsibility by participating in the process.

As a first step, the court summons citizens to appear for jury duty. The group of people from whom the jury will be selected, known as the *jury venire*, is then narrowed until the jury is finally seated for a particular trial. During this narrowing process, the judge or lawyers ask the potential jurors questions to elicit bias or other reasons why a person might be unable to decide the case fairly. (And some potential jurors try to get out of jury service by explaining to the judge why their personal or work obligations make it impossible for them to serve.) This questioning process is known as *voir dire*—French for "to see to say," as in "let us see what the potential jurors are going to say." Courts vary in how they conduct this process. In some, the judge does most of the questioning, while in others, lawyers have more leeway to ask their own questions.

During the *voir dire* process, the court excuses potential jurors who might be unable to listen fairly to the evidence and decide the case based on their independent, unbiased judgment. For example, jurors who have personal relationships with the litigants or who have had personal experiences that might prejudice them about the case are generally excused.

Litigants have the right to challenge particular jurors, either for good reason or no reason at all. First, they may make *challenges for cause*, in which a party argues that a particular juror should be excused because the juror would be unable to decide the case fairly. In addition, each side may make several *peremptory challenges*, in which the party gets rid of a particular juror without offering any reason. A federal statute limits each party to three peremptory challenges, 29 U.S.C. §1870, in contrast to challenges for cause, which are unlimited. The idea is to give each litigant greater confidence in the fairness of the jury by excluding the specific jurors about whom each side feels most uncomfortable. The Supreme Court has addressed constitutional questions about peremptory challenges, declaring that peremptory challenges on the basis of race or gender are unconstitutional as violations of the Equal Protection Clause. *J.E.B. v. Alabama*, 511 U.S. 127 (1994) (gender); *Edmonson v. Leesville Concrete Co.*, 500 U.S. 614 (1981) (race). If a party believes the other party has used a peremptory challenge to exclude a juror based on race or gender, the party may object and the court may require the party using the challenges to show that their challenge is not based on race or gender.

STRATEGY SESSION

For many trial lawyers, the favorability of a forum depends on the jurors. Although stereotypes cannot predict any individual juror's mindset, many trial lawyers would agree that a jury pool as a whole may have demographic characteristics that make it more favorable for a particular litigant. Federal district courts draw jury pools from a broader area; differences in jury pools tend to be most pronounced in state courts where jurors are selected from a specific county in which the court is located. Some courts develop reputations among lawyers as being relatively plaintiff-friendly or defendant-friendly based in part on jury demographics. How might jury demographics play a role, then, in forum-selection strategy? How might the ultimate forum for the case—along with the relevant jury demographics—impact settlement negotiations? And how might forum-selection strategy and settlement dynamics differ in a case where there is no right to a jury trial?

(3) Jury Role

Thus far, you have explored the contours of the constitutional right to a jury trial as well as the procedural and constitutional parameters for jury selection. Inquiries regarding the existence of a right to a jury or who is empaneled on the jury, however, do not speak directly to the practical abilities and limitations of juries. Indeed, there is debate about whether particular issues within an otherwise jury-triable case are, as a practical matter, best left to determination by the judge instead of the jury. The historical test gives no clear answer to this pragmatic question of the comparative skills of judges and juries; moreover, the Court in *Chauffeurs* declined Justice Stevens' invitation to include such considerations in the jury-right analysis. Consider then the following case, in which the Supreme Court *did* consider the practical abilities of juries in determining whether a particular issue in patent litigation must be decided by a jury.

MARKMAN v. WESTVIEW INSTRUMENTS, INC.
517 U.S. 370 (1996)

SOUTER, J., delivered the unanimous opinion of the Court.

The question here is whether the interpretation of a so-called patent claim, the portion of the patent document that defines the scope of the patentee's rights, is a matter of law reserved entirely for the court, or subject to a Seventh Amendment guarantee that a jury will determine the meaning of any disputed term of art about which expert testimony is offered. We hold that the construction of a patent, including terms of art within its claim, is exclusively within the province of the court.

I

The Constitution empowers Congress "[t]o promote the Progress of Science and useful Arts, by securing for limited Times to Authors and Inventors the exclusive Right to their respective Writings and Discoveries." Art. 1, §8, cl. 8.... It has long been understood that a patent must describe the exact scope of an invention and its manufacture to "secure to [the patentee] all to which he is entitled, [and] to apprise the public of what is still open to them." *McClain v. Ortmayer*, 141 U.S. 419, 424 (1891).... A patent [must] include[] one or more "claims," which "particularly poin[t] out and distinctly clai[m] the subject matter which the applicant regards as his invention." 35 U.S.C. §112.... The claim "define[s] the scope of a patent grant"... and functions to forbid not only exact copies of an invention, but products that go to "the heart of the invention".... In this opinion, the word "claim" is only used in this sense peculiar to patent law.

Characteristically, patent lawsuits charge what is known as infringement.... Victory in an infringement suit requires a finding that the patent claim "covers the alleged infringer's product or process," which in turn necessitates a determination of "what the words in the claim mean." H. Schwartz, Patent Law & Practice 80 (2d ed. 1995).

Petitioner in this infringement suit, Markman, owns United States Reissue Patent No. 33,054 for his "Inventory Control and Reporting System for Drycleaning Stores." The patent describes a system that can monitor and report the status, location, and movement of clothing in a dry cleaning establishment....

Markman brought an infringement suit against Westview and Althon Enterprises, an operator of dry cleaning establishments using Westview's products (collectively, Westview). Westview responded that Markman's patent is not infringed by its system because [it] functions merely to record an inventory of receivables by tracking invoices and transaction totals, rather than to record and track an inventory of articles of clothing. Part of the dispute hinged upon the meaning of the word "inventory."... The case was tried before a jury, which heard, among others, a witness produced by Markman who testified about the meaning of the claim language.

After the jury compared the patent to Westview's device, it found an infringement of Markman's [patent claim]. The District Court nevertheless granted Westview's deferred motion for judgment as a matter of law [and vacated the jury's determination].... Under the trial court's construction of the patent, the production, sale, or use of a tracking system for dry cleaners would not infringe Markman's patent unless the product was capable of tracking articles of clothing throughout the cleaning process and generating reports about their status and location. Since Westview's system cannot do these things, the District Court directed a verdict [for Westview]. . . .

Markman appealed, arguing it was error for the District Court to substitute its construction of the disputed claim term "inventory" for the construction the jury had presumably given it. The United States Court of Appeals for the Federal Circuit affirmed, holding the interpretation of claim terms to be the exclusive province of the court and the Seventh Amendment to be consistent with that conclusion. Markman sought our review on each point, and we granted certiorari. We now affirm.

II

The Seventh Amendment provides that "[i]n Suits at common law, where the value in controversy shall exceed twenty dollars, the right of trial by jury shall be preserved. . . ." U.S. Const., Amdt. 7. . . . In keeping with our longstanding adherence to th[e] "historical test" [of the Seventh Amendment], we ask, first, whether we are dealing with a cause of action that either was tried at law at the time of the founding or is at least analogous to one that was, *see, e.g., Tull v. United States*, 481 U.S. 412, 417 (1987). If the action in question belongs in the law category, we then ask whether the particular trial decision must fall to the jury in order to preserve the substance of the common-law right as it existed in 1791. . . .

A

As to the first issue, going to the character of the cause of action, "[t]he form of our analysis is familiar. First, we compare the statutory action to 18th-century actions brought in the courts of England prior to the merger of the courts of law and equity." *Granfinanciera, S.A. v. Nordberg*, 492 U.S. 33, 42 (1989). Equally familiar is the descent of today's patent infringement action from the infringement actions tried at law in the 18th century, and there is no dispute that infringement cases today must be tried to a jury, as their predecessors were more than two centuries ago. *See, e.g., Bramah v. Hardcastle*, 1 Carp. P.C. 168 (K.B. 1789).

B

This conclusion raises the second question, whether a *particular issue* occurring within a jury trial (here the construction of a patent claim) is itself necessarily a jury issue, the guarantee being essential to preserve the right to a jury's resolution of the ultimate dispute [emphasis added]. In some instances the answer to this second questions may be easy because of clear historical evidence that the very subsidiary question was so regarded under the English practice of leaving the issue for the jury. But when, as here, the old practice provides no clear answer . . . we are forced to make a judgment about the scope of the Seventh Amendment guarantee without the foolproof test. . . .

III

Since evidence of common-law practice at the time of the framing does not entail application of the Seventh Amendment's jury guarantee to the construction of the claim document, we must look elsewhere to characterize this determination of meaning in order to allocate it as between court or jury. We accordingly [A.] consult precedent and [B.] consider both the relative interpretive skills of judges and juries and the statutory policies that ought to be furthered by the allocation.

A

[In Part III-A, the Court concludes that neither history nor precedent answers the question regarding whether a judge or jury should determine the meaning of a patent claim.]

B

Where history and precedent provide no clear answers, functional considerations also play their part in the choice between judge and jury to define terms of art. We said in *Miller v. Fenton*, 474 U.S. 104, 114 (1985), that when an issue "falls somewhere between a pristine legal standard and a simple historical fact, the fact/law distinction at times has turned on a determination that, as a matter of the sound administration of justice, one judicial actor is better positioned than another to decide the issue in question." So it turns out here, for judges, not juries, are the better suited to find the acquired meaning of patent terms.

The construction of written instruments is one of those things that judges often do and are likely to do better than jurors unburdened by training in exegesis. Patent construction in particular "is a special occupation, requiring, like all others, special training and practice. The judge, from his training and discipline, is more likely to give a proper interpretation to such instruments than a jury; and he is, therefore, more likely to be right, in performing such a duty, than a jury can be expected to be." *Parker v. Hulme*, 18 F. Cas. 1138, 1140 (E.D. Pa. 1849). Such was the understanding nearly a century and a half ago, and there is no reason to weigh the respective strengths of

judge and jury differently in relation to the modern claim; quite the contrary, for the "claims of patents have become highly technical in many respects as the result of special doctrines relating to the proper form and scope of claims that have been developed by the courts and the Patent Office." Woodward, Definiteness and Particularly in Patent Claims, 46 Mich. L. Rev. 755, 756 (1948).

Markman would trump these considerations with his argument that a jury should decide a question of meaning peculiar to a trade or profession simply because the question is a subject of testimony requiring credibility determinations, which are the jury's forte. It is, of course, true that credibility judgments have to be made about the experts who testify in patent cases, and in theory there could be a case in which a simple credibility judgment would suffice to choose between experts whose testimony was equally consistent with a patent's internal logic. But our own experience with document construction leaves us doubtful that trial courts will run into many cases like that. In the main, we expect, any credibility determinations will be subsumed within the necessarily sophisticated analysis of the whole document. . . . Thus, in these cases a jury's capabilities to evaluate demeanor . . . to sense the "mainsprings of human conduct," *Commissioner v. Duberstein*, 363 U.S. 278, 298 (1960), or to reflect community standards, *United States v. McConney*, 728 F.2d 1195, 1204 (9th Cir. 1984) (en banc), are much less significant than a trained ability to evaluate the testimony in relation to the overall structure of the patent. . . . We accordingly think there is sufficient reason to treat construction of terms of art like many other responsibilities that we cede to a judge in the normal course of trial, notwithstanding its evidentiary underpinnings.

C

Finally, we see the importance of uniformity in the treatment of a given patent as an independent reason to allocate all issues of construction to the court. As we noted in *General Elec. Co. v. Wabash Appliance Corp.*, 304 U.S. 364, 369 (1938), "[t]he limits of a patent must be known for the protection of the patentee, the encouragement of the inventive genius of others and the assurance that the subject of the patent will be dedicated ultimately to the public." Otherwise a "zone of uncertainty which enterprise and experimentation may enter only at the risk of infringement claims would discourage invention only a little less than unequivocal foreclosure of the field." *United Carbon Co. v. Binney Smith Co.*, 317 U.S. 228, 236

(1942), and "[t]he public [would] be deprived of rights supposed to belong to it, without being clearly told what it is that limits these rights." *Merrill v. Yeomans*, 94 U.S. 568, 573 (1877). It was just for the sake of such desirable uniformity that Congress created the Court of Appeals for the Federal Circuit as an exclusive appellate court for patent cases, H.R. Rep. No. 97-312, pp. 20-23 (1981), observing that increased uniformity would "strengthen the United States patent system in such a way as to foster technological growth and innovation." *Id.* at 20....

Accordingly, we hold that the interpretation of the word "inventory" in this case is an issue for the judge, not the jury, and affirm the decision of the Court of Appeals for the Federal Circuit.

Notes & Questions

1. Given the Court's unwillingness to embrace functional analysis in *Chauffeurs* for purposes of determining whether the Seventh Amendment right applies to a particular cause of action, were you surprised to see the Court engaging in such analysis in *Markman*? What explains the difference in approach? Is this functional analysis grounded in the Seventh Amendment? Some other constitutional directive? The patent claim statute itself (35 U.S.C. §112)?

2. The decision in *Markman* greatly increased the focus on the construction of the patent claim in patent litigation. So much so, in fact, that a hearing now referred to specifically as a "*Markman* hearing" takes place after preliminary discovery in almost every patent case. John R. Allison & Lisa Larrimore Ouellette, *How Courts Adjudicate Patent Definiteness and Disclosure*, 65 Duke L.J. 609, 658 (2016).

   These *Markman* hearings, in turn, created a difficult question of how patent claims, construed by judges, should be decided on appeal. Should the trial judge's construction be reviewed *de novo*, as a question of law? Or should it be reviewed for *clear error*, as a judge's finding of fact? In *Teva Pharmaceuticals USA, Inc. v. Sandoz*, 810 F. Supp. 2d 578 (S.D.N.Y. 2011), the district judge construed Teva's patent as valid. On appeal, the United States Court of Appeals for the Federal Circuit applied a de novo standard of review, ignored the district judge's factual findings and conclusions regarding expert testimony, and held to the contrary. 723 F.3d 1363 (Fed. Cir. 2013). The Supreme Court reversed the opinion of the Federal Circuit, holding that a court of appeals " 'must not ... set aside' a district court's 'findings of fact'... unless they are 'clearly erroneous.'" *Teva Pharmaceuticals USA, Inc. v. Sandoz*, 574 U.S. 318 (2015) (quoting Fed. R. Civ. P. 52(a)(6)). The Court emphasized that a court of appeals may not depart from its role to review under a clear error standard findings of fact made by a judge (including subsidiary facts)—even a judge "sitting without a jury." *Id.* We will explore appellate standards of review in Chapter 6.

3. Three years after *Markman*, the Supreme Court again engaged in functional analysis to determine whether certain issues should go to the judge or jury, but not in the same way it had done in *Markman*. In *City of Monterey v. Del Monte Dunes, Ltd.*, 526 U.S. 687, 693-694 (1999), the Court found that the classic Seventh Amendment historical test did not provide a clear answer to whether a jury or judge should decide whether a city's rejection of a development plan constituted a regulatory taking. The Court did not discuss the relative capabilities of judge and jury; instead, it analyzed whether the city's justifications for rejecting the development plan were "essentially fact-bound in nature" (and thus appropriate for jury consideration). Though the Court in *Del Monte Dunes* described its analysis as "functional," its decision hinged on a formalistic law-fact distinction about the evidence and the claims, rather than upon the relative abilities of the judge and jury. Although occasionally the comparative skills of judges and juries may come into play in a court's jury-right or jury-role analysis, generally that inquiry hews to the two-part historical test.

4. Some scholars have advocated for considering issue complexity and the functional capabilities of the jury in the right-to-jury-trial analysis more generally. *See, e.g.*, Daniel Crane, *Antitrust Antifederalism*, 96 Cal. L. Rev. 1, 33-38 (2008) (arguing that ordinary juries are not competent to decide complex antitrust issues); Thomas M. Jorde, *The Seventh Amendment Right to Jury Trial of Antitrust Issues*, 69 Cal. L. Rev. 1 (1981) (arguing that factual complexity should be considered in determining whether there is a right to a jury trial in any particular antitrust case). Think about the sorts of factual issues that arise in civil litigation. Some are almost perfectly suited to the institution of the jury—issues like the "reasonable person" standard of negligence law or a "consumer expectations" test in products liability. Other issues, however, seem less perfectly suited to the jury—questions of scientific causation, complex technical questions, and corporate finance questions, to name a few. But does that necessarily mean a judge is well suited? Or is it simply the nature of an all-purpose public dispute-resolution system that some issues will be beyond the decision maker's comprehension and capabilities? To decide whether a judge is better suited than a jury to resolve complex factual issues, what would you need to know about a particular judge's background and experience (or about the background and experience of judges and jurors in general)? More generally, what values might be served by handing more complex issues to judges, rather than juries? What values would be sacrificed? If you were to design a better system for fact-finding regarding complex issues that arise in litigation, who would be the decision makers, and how would it work?

B. TRIAL PROCESS

(1) The Course of a Trial

The details of the course of a trial vary from court to court and case to case. Thus, this section provides only a general and brief description of trial proceedings.

After jury selection is completed (if it is a jury trial), the parties present their case to the judge and jury. First, the lawyer for each side makes an *opening statement* describing the case and setting the stage for the evidence that will follow. Following these opening statements, the plaintiff presents witnesses and other evidence. Each witness, after taking an oath to testify truthfully, answers questions on *direct examination* from the lawyer who called the witness. Opposing counsel then has the opportunity to ask the witness questions on *cross-examination*. After completion of the plaintiff's case, the defendant presents the case in opposition. During the questioning of witnesses and the presentation of documentary and other evidence, the lawyers may *object* to certain questions or to the admissibility of certain evidence. Common objections include hearsay, relevance, and privilege. The judge rules on each objection to decide whether the evidence will be admitted. (You can learn a great deal more about these and other evidentiary issues in an upper-level evidence course.) After both sides have presented their evidence, the lawyers give *closing arguments* summing up the case and explaining why their client should prevail.

At that point, the judge instructs the jury on the law to be applied in the case. These *jury instructions*, also known as the *jury charge*, explain the substantive law that the jurors must apply in reaching their decision. Many jurisdictions have *pattern jury instructions* available to judges either as the exact instructions to use or as a starting point for writing instructions in a particular case. The language of jury instructions becomes a point of contention in some cases, with lawyers for each side presenting the judge with the version they hope the court will adopt. Jury instructions provide fertile ground for appeals, too, as a losing party may blame the loss on a jury charge that the party argued was erroneous. Finally, the jurors return to the jury room to deliberate in private, discussing the evidence until they reach a verdict.

STRATEGY SESSION

Skilled lawyers think about jury instructions early in a case, even though trial is a long way off and unlikely actually to occur. There are several reasons to consider the possible jury instructions at the outset of litigation. Jury instructions generally track the elements that need to be proven for each claim or defense. Therefore, at the pleading stage, imagining future jury instructions is helpful for drafting the complaint *and* for challenging its sufficiency as a matter of law under Rule 12(b)(6). Similarly, during discovery, imagining jury instructions is one way to get a handle on exactly what must be proved for each claim or defense, and thus to see what information you need to gather.

(2) Verdict

Finally, the moment everyone has been waiting for: the verdict. First, though, how is a verdict reached? In a jury trial, after applying the law to the facts, and considering the parties' arguments, the jury must determine whether the party who bears the ultimate burden of persuasion on any given issue has met that burden. Answering that question depends critically upon how strong that burden of persuasion is, as defined by the associated burden of proof. In other words, a party may well have presented a strong case, but that alone is not sufficient. The party with the burden of persuasion on an issue or claim must convince the jury or judge *enough*—as defined by the relevant burdens of proof—in order to prevail. Second, which (of three) forms does a jury verdict take? Third, how is a verdict reached in a bench trial, where there is no jury?

(a) The Burden of Persuasion

When the judge instructs the jury, the judge must be clear about the *burden of persuasion*: Who has it, and how strong is it? Without knowing the burden of persuasion, the jury would lack a critical piece of analytical guidance. And without knowing how strong that burden is (the burden of proof), the jury will not know how strong a case the party must present to prevail.

Who bears the burden of persuasion? The plaintiff, mostly. However, recall from Chapter 2 that defendants have the burden to prove affirmative defenses. Further, certain types of claims, including many claims of discrimination, involve burden shifting in which the plaintiff bears the initial burden of establishing a prima facie case, but then the burden shifts to the defendant. But as a general matter, the plaintiff bears the burden of persuasion in civil cases. The real question for the jury, in other words, is not "What happened?" but rather "Did the plaintiff prove the case?" Or, to be even more precise, "Did the plaintiff prove each element of its claim?"

How strong is the burden? In civil cases, in general, the plaintiff must establish each element of the claim by a *preponderance of the evidence*. In other words, the jury decides whether the fact is more likely than not. Some lawyers describe it as a 51 percent standard (although mathematically speaking, it would be more accurate to call it something like 50.0000001 percent). In a breach of contract case, for instance, if the jury decides that probably the defendant breached the contract, then the plaintiff prevails. If the jury decides that probably the defendant did not breach the contract, then the defendant prevails. If the jury cannot decide—if the evidence for each side is so equal that the jurors are in perfect equipoise on the matter—then the defendant prevails because the plaintiff failed to meet the burden of persuasion.

The preponderance standard in civil cases contrasts starkly with the burden of proof in a criminal case. In criminal cases, the prosecution has the burden of proving its case beyond a reasonable doubt, a high burden intended to make it difficult to convict the innocent. Civil lawsuits are different. The plaintiff in a civil case need not remove all reasonable doubt, but need only convince the jury that the plaintiff's version of the facts is more likely than the defendant's version. Whereas criminal justice policy strongly favors protecting defendants from wrongful convictions, civil justice policy does not reflect any consensus that the civil litigation process should systematically favor either plaintiffs or defendants. More fundamentally, in a criminal case, the defendant's freedom is frequently at risk, hence an insistence on a higher burden of proof than in civil cases.

In certain types of civil proceedings, you will encounter an in-between burden of persuasion and proof requiring parties to establish the elements of their claims by *clear and convincing evidence*. Falling somewhere between the high burden of "beyond a reasonable doubt" and the lower burden of "preponderance of the evidence," the clear and convincing evidence standard often applies in quasi-criminal proceedings such as attorney disciplinary matters. In many states, punitive damages must be established by clear and convincing evidence.

(b) Forms of Jury Verdicts

The most basic form of verdict, the *general verdict*, simply asks the jury to decide who wins and how much. The jury either returns a verdict for the defendant or a verdict for the plaintiff in the amount of X dollars. In addition to the general verdict, Rule 49 gives courts two alternative forms of verdicts: the special verdict and the general verdict with questions.

The *special verdict* does not ask the jury to state which party should prevail, but instead asks the jury to answer specific factual questions. The judge then enters judgment for the appropriate party based on the answers given by the jury. For example, a special verdict form in a negligence case might begin with "Do you find by a preponderance of the evidence that the defendant failed to exercise reasonable care?" If a jury answers yes to the first question, then the form would instruct the jury to answer similar questions about proximate causation, damages, and any other essential issues. The more complex the case, the more useful courts find the special verdict. Special verdicts are not only useful to guide the jury through the elements of a single claim, they are also helpful to provide juries with structure in cases involving numerous claims and parties. By asking the jury to render its verdict in the form of answers to specific questions, the court is able to sort out liability on varied legal claims, damages of multiple plaintiffs, responsibility of multiple defendants, and other individualized issues that could easily get lost in a jury's deliberations over a general verdict.

The third type of verdict, known as a *general verdict with answers to written questions* or a *general verdict with interrogatories*, is basically a combination of the first two. In this type of verdict, the jury renders a verdict stating which party prevails, just like a general verdict, but in addition, the jury answers specific questions presented by the court. This type of verdict gives the court a tool for making sure the jury understood what it was doing and followed the court's instructions. You might think that this type of verdict is the best of both worlds. In some ways, it might be; in other ways, it might actually be the worst of both worlds. To wit: Sometimes the jury's answers reveal that the jury did not understand what it was doing or did not follow (or understand) the court's instructions. Thus, when a court uses a general verdict with interrogatories, there is always the risk that the jury's verdict will be inconsistent with the jury's answers to the specific questions. In that event, the court has several options, some more onerous than others, depending on the extent of the jury's confusion. If the jury's answers are consistent with one another but not with the verdict, the court may enter judgment according to the answers notwithstanding the verdict, it may send the case back to the jury for further consideration, or it may even order a new trial. If the answers are inconsistent with one another and one or more is inconsistent with the verdict, then the court will either return the jury for further consideration or order a new trial. Some courts view it as a downside of general verdicts with answers that these forms of verdicts have the potential to highlight jury confusion. One could also imagine similar confusion being revealed in a special verdict; jurors could well provide answers to questions in a special verdict that are internally inconsistent, therefore not leading to an obvious verdict. Such problems do not *appear* in general verdicts, but let's not kid ourselves: Jurors could be equally confused in a case with a simple general verdict; the difference is that the judge would never know about it. Which values are served by using the simpler general verdict? The special verdict? The general verdict with answers to written questions?

(3) Bench Trials

Bench trials—trials without juries—occur under two circumstances. First, when there is no right to a jury trial, the judge conducts the trial alone. Second, even if the lawsuit is one that entails a right to jury, if no party makes a timely jury demand, the judge does it alone.

Some cases involve aspects of both a jury trial and a bench trial. As you learned earlier in the chapter, if a case involves some issues that entail a right to jury trial and some that do not, the jury issues *must be* decided first to preserve the Seventh Amendment right. The jury's findings on those overlapping issues are then binding on the judge when she decides the non–jury triable issues. *Beacon Theatres Inc. v. Westover*, 359 U.S. 500 (1959).

To a large extent, bench trials proceed just like jury trials. Each side presents its case in open court, with opening statements, witnesses, and closing arguments. The witnesses testify under oath through direct and cross-examination. Lawyers assert objections and the court rules on the admissibility of evidence. In the end, the fact-finder assesses the evidence and decides the case by applying the law to the facts in light of the burden of persuasion. The salient difference between bench and jury trials—that the fact-finder is a judge rather than a jury—does not alter the basic function of the trial.

Two fundamental and obvious differences between bench and jury trials are that *one*, bench trials naturally skip the entire jury selection process, including issues of peremptory challenges and excusals for cause. *Two*, a trial judge is assigned for every trial—both jury trials and bench trials—but the assignment of the judge takes on additional significance because the judge in a bench trial is also the fact-finder. The judicial assignment process varies among courts. An assigned judge must recuse herself from any proceeding in which her impartiality may reasonably be questioned, 28 U.S.C. §455(a), or if the judge has expressed an opinion on the case or has a financial interest, 28 U.S.C. §455(b). Parties may move to disqualify a judge under such circumstances. California's code of civil procedure permits each party one "peremptory" challenge to the judge, but only if the party alleges that the judge is biased. Cal. Civ. Proc. Code §170.6.

Another important difference between jury and bench trials comes at the end of the trial. A jury announces its decision by rendering a verdict. As discussed above, there are several forms of verdicts, but the most basic—the general verdict—is completely opaque. With a general verdict, the jury declares who prevails but does not explain its reasoning. A special verdict or general verdict with answers to written questions obligates the jury to answer specific questions about the case, but even there, the jury does not have to explain its logic or which evidence it considered credible. By contrast, a judge in a bench trial must state his or her *findings of fact* and *conclusions of law*. As Fed. R. Civ. P. 52 puts it, "the court must find the facts specially and state its conclusions of law separately." The judge may state these findings and conclusions on the record in court after the close of the evidence or may put them in writing in the decision.

Finally, conducting a trial entirely in front of a judge does affect the feel of the trial—both in terms of how lawyers conduct themselves and the efficiency of the process. Jury trials bring out a certain theatricality by some trial lawyers; bench trials tend to be more subdued and businesslike. Bench trials tend to treat the rules of evidence with somewhat less formality than jury trials (particularly given that many rules of evidence are designed largely to protect against jury error and to safeguard the integrity of the jury). Bench trials also avoid the need to spend time ushering the jury in and out of the courtroom out of concern about what the jury may and may not hear.

The transparency of the bench trial decision makes it both less powerful and more powerful than a jury verdict. A judge's decision is less powerful than that of a jury in that it is more vulnerable to reversal on appeal. An appeals court may reverse a trial judge's factual findings if they are "clearly erroneous," which is a high standard, but reversal is not impossible. Jury verdicts, by contrast, are largely immune from appellate review. But a bench trial decision carries the potential to be more powerful than a jury's general verdict because of issue preclusion. Issue preclusion, discussed in Chapter 8, permits courts in later proceedings to bind parties to certain factual determinations reached in an earlier case. General verdicts make it difficult in some cases to figure out precisely what issues the jury determined, but judicial findings of fact are explicit (like special verdicts), making it easier to afford those findings issue preclusive effect in other cases.

One final note: Unlike a jury trial, there is *no* constitutional right to a bench trial. If a case falls outside the parameters of the Seventh Amendment, no party has a constitutional right to insist that there *not* be a jury. Thus, statutes can provide jury rights beyond the scope of the right granted by the Seventh Amendment.

C. JUDGMENT AS A MATTER OF LAW AND NEW TRIAL

Even if a case is tried to a jury, the jury might not get the final word. If a party believes that the evidence is so one-sided that a jury could reasonably decide only one way, that party may move for a *judgment as a matter of law*. Fed. R. Civ. P. 50. Alternatively, or in addition, if a party believes that there were serious defects with the trial itself, that party may move for a new trial. Fed. R. Civ. P. 59. As you study the following material, pay careful attention to both the timing requirements for these motions and the standards for granting these motions. Moreover, think critically about whether these motions take too much (or too little) authority away from the jury and give too much (or too little) power to the judge.

(1) Judgment as a Matter of Law

If the evidence at a trial is so lopsided that only one party can reasonably prevail, Federal Rule of Civil Procedure 50 can come into play. Specifically, a party may move for a *judgment as a matter of law* "[i]f a party has been fully heard on an issue during a jury trial and the court finds that a reasonable jury would not have a legally sufficient evidentiary basis to find for the party on that issue." Fed. R. Civ. P. 50(a)(1). Notice that the effect of this language, if the motion is granted, is to shift the jury's authority to the judge. In a jury trial, the judge and jury have different jobs. The job of ruling on questions of law belongs to the judge. The job of resolving disputed facts and applying the law to those facts to reach a verdict belongs to the jury. Whenever a judge grants judgment as a matter of law, the judge is taking the decision-making authority away from the jury. The justification is that the jury may decide the case within the bounds of reason, but juries are not empowered to decide civil cases without regard to the evidence and the applicable law.

The "no reasonable jury" standard for granting judgment as a matter of law is the same as the summary judgment standard. When a plaintiff or defendant moves for judgment as a matter of law, the court must look at the evidence in the light most favorable to the nonmoving party, drawing all reasonable inferences and resolving credibility disputes in favor of the nonmoving party. If, by believing certain witnesses and disbelieving others, a jury could reasonably find in favor of the nonmoving party, then the court must deny the motion for judgment

---

Terminology Tip

Older cases use the terms *directed verdict* and *judgment notwithstanding the verdict* (or *j.n.o.v.*, an abbreviation for *judgment non obstante veredicto*, Latin for "notwithstanding the verdict") to describe what is now called "judgment as a matter of law" in Rule 50. More specifically, *directed verdict* is the older term for a judgment as a matter of law before the verdict is rendered; *j.n.o.v.* is the older term for a judgment as a matter of law issued after the verdict is rendered, which is obtained through a renewed motion for judgment as a matter of law. Get comfortable with all these terms because earlier cases and some state court use the older terminology, as do many lawyers and judges.

as a matter of law. Given that the standard in Rule 50 and Rule 56 is the same, you might think the two rules are strangely redundant. As you read on, think about why and when a judge might deny summary judgment but grant a motion for judgment as a matter of law.

Judgment as a matter of law can occur before *or* after the jury has rendered a verdict. Look closely first at the language in Rule 50(a)(2): "A motion for judgment as a matter of law may be made at any time before the case is submitted to the jury." Then read the language in Rule 50(b): "If the court does not grant a motion for judgment as a matter of law made under Rule 50(a), the court is considered to have submitted the action to the jury. . . ."

Before the verdict, a party may move under Rule 50(a) for judgment as a matter of law, but only after the nonmoving party "has been fully heard on an issue." Fed. R. Civ. P. 50(a)(1). Therefore, the timing to move for judgment as a matter of law under Rule 50(a) depends on whether the moving party is a plaintiff or a defendant. For a plaintiff, judgment as a matter of law ordinarily must wait until the close of all the evidence because the court does not know whether the defendant should lose until the defendant has had an opportunity to present its evidence. For a defendant, however, judgment as a matter of law can occur either at the close of all the evidence or at the close of plaintiff's case. Once the plaintiff has had a full opportunity to present her case, the defendant can argue that the plaintiff has failed to meet her burden.

If the court grants judgment as a matter of law before the verdict, then the judge sends the jurors home. The jury never has the chance to render a verdict, which must be rather frustrating for jurors who have just spent many hours or days listening to the evidence. That is one major difference between Rule 50 (judgment as a matter of law) and Rule 56 (summary judgment). Although both take the decision away from the jury, at the Rule 56 stage, the jury is just an idea. By granting summary judgment, the court ensures that no actual jury will be empaneled for the case. At the Rule 50 stage, however, the case is at trial. There is an actual group of jurors sitting in the jury box in the courtroom, and they have listened to evidence. Although as a matter of procedural theory, Rule 56 and Rule 50 motions function almost identically, the fact that Rule 50 motions occur during trial is a more concrete and significant exercise of judicial power.

After the jury has rendered a verdict, the losing party may ask the judge to take the decision away from the jury and decide it the opposite way, arguing that based on the evidence and the applicable law, no reasonable jury could have decided the way this jury did. This is what traditionally has been called *judgment notwithstanding the verdict (j.n.o.v.)*. Rule 50(b) calls it the *renewed motion for judgment as a matter of law*.

The "renewed motion" terminology points to a critical procedural detail about Rule 50(b). Recall that a motion for judgment as a matter of law may be filed before *or* after the jury enters a verdict. However, it is also true that such a motion must be made before *and* after the verdict, if the original motion is denied. The first sentence of Rule 50(b) states that "*[i]f the court does not grant a motion for judgment as a matter of law made under Rule 50(a), the court is considered to have submitted the action to the jury subject to the court's later deciding the legal questions raised by the motion*" (emphasis added). This language is significant; it means that a party cannot *renew* its motion for judgment as a matter of law under Rule 50(b) after the verdict was rendered if no motion for judgment as a matter of law was made under Rule 50(a) before the verdict was rendered. Again, as you read on, think about when and why a judge would deny a Rule 50(a) motion for judgment as a matter of law and later grant that same party's Rule 50(b) renewed motion for judgment as a matter of law.

(2) New Trial

A trial may have problems serious enough that the court cannot allow the result to stand, but the circumstances do not warrant granting judgment as a matter of law for one party or the other. In such cases, the court may order a new trial. Federal Rule of Civil Procedure 59 spells out the procedure for new trial motions in federal court: "The court may, on motion, grant a new trial on some or all of the issues—and to any party . . . after a jury trial, for any reason for which a new trial has heretofore been granted in an action at law in federal court." Fed. R. Civ. P. 59(1) and (1)(A).

Note that Rule 59 is pretty cryptic about what are adequate grounds for granting the motion. The case law, however, fleshes out the grounds upon which a new trial may be granted. These grounds fall into two basic categories: process problems and outcome problems.

Process problems, to justify a new trial, must be serious enough to raise significant questions about the fairness of the proceedings. For instance, the judge's instructions to the jury may have reflected an erroneous interpretation of the law, or important evidence may have been erroneously admitted or excluded. Or a lawyer might have engaged in misconduct such as an improper closing argument. Perhaps the jurors themselves engaged in misconduct that raises questions about their objectivity and independence. If a judge believes that allowing the trial result to stand would be unjust in light of the error in the conduct—the process—of the trial, then the judge has the discretion under Rule 59 to order a new trial.

Outcome problems, as a basis for new trial motions, tend to go hand in hand with motions for judgment as a matter of law. Courts say that a new trial may be granted if the jury verdict is "against the weight of the evidence." Some courts emphasize the high standard by using the phrase "against the *great* weight of the evidence." Judges have wide discretion when deciding whether to grant a new trial. However, the judge may not substitute her own judgment for that of the jury. The question is not what the judge would have decided, but rather whether the jury's decision was so clearly contrary to the evidence that the verdict cannot stand.

Judges also use the power to grant new trials as a way to lower the amount of damages awarded by the jury. When a judge finds the amount of damages awarded by the jury irrationally high, the judge may order a conditional new trial, telling the plaintiff that there will be a new trial unless the plaintiff accepts a reduced amount of damages. For example, if the jury awarded $300,000 and the judge thinks that a reasonable amount, based on the evidence, must fall in the range of $50,000 to $100,000, then the judge might inform the plaintiff that the judge will grant a new trial unless the plaintiff accepts $100,000 in damages. Judges should not simply substitute their measure of damages for the jury's. Courts sometimes state that the judge should alter the damages only if the amount "shocks the conscience" of the court. *See, e.g., Lore v. City of Syracuse*, 670 F.3d 127, 177 (2d Cir. 2012). Known as *remittitur*, this type of conditional new trial order is permitted in both federal and state courts. (In *Gasperini v. Center for Humanities, Inc.*, 517 U.S. 1102 (1996), which we will study in Chapter 12, the Supreme Court grappled with differences between the federal-court remittitur process and the procedures in New York courts for handling excessively high jury verdicts.)

Turn remittitur upside-down and you get *additur*, which allows a judge to address damages that are irrationally low. Some state courts permit additur, but for the federal courts, the Supreme Court has declared additur unconstitutional as a violation of the Seventh Amendment. *See Dimick v. Schiedt*, 293 U.S. 474, 482 (1935). You might wonder about the logic of permitting remittitur but not additur, a difference that tilts the field in favor of defendants on the question of damages. The explanation for this difference lies in part in the historical test for applying the Seventh Amendment right to a jury trial. According to the Supreme Court in *Dimick*, something akin to remittitur but not additur was permitted in 1791. *Id.*

Rule 50 and Rule 59 motions often go hand in hand. When a losing party believes the jury's verdict was unsupported by the evidence, the party may make a Rule 50(b) renewed motion for judgment as a matter of law, and in the alternative, a Rule 59 motion for a new trial. The trial judge must decide the renewed motion for judgment as a matter of law before the new trial motion. If the court denies the Rule 50 motion, then the court must decide the new trial motion. Even if the court grants the Rule 50 motion, Rule 50(c) asks the judge to provide a conditional ruling on the new trial motion. That way, in case the judgment on the Rule 50 motion is reversed on appeal, the court of appeals knows whether to reinstate the original jury verdict or to remand for a new trial. Consider the following case, which involves motions for judgment as a matter of law and for a new trial, as well as a motion for remittitur.

GARDNER v. SIMPSON FINANCING LIMITED PARTNERSHIP

963 F. Supp. 2d 72 (D. Mass. 2013)

SAYLOR, District Judge

In May 2008, the apartment building in which plaintiffs lived was destroyed by fire. Plaintiffs Gayle Gardner, Tanya Pulisciano, Crystal Caissie, and Louise Felteau brought an action for negligence against defendant Simpson Financing Limited Partnership, the entity that owned and operated the apartment complex. The case was tried to a jury in April 2013; the jury found that Simpson was negligent in maintaining the premises and awarded each plaintiff compensatory damages for loss of property and emotional distress.

Pending before the Court is Simpson's motion for judgment as a matter of law, or, in the alternative, a remittitur or new trial. For the reasons set forth below, the motion will be granted in part and denied in part.

I. PROCEDURAL BACKGROUND

Plaintiffs brought separate actions in the Massachusetts Housing Court, Northeast Division, against Simpson, [as well as liability insurance companies] alleging negligence, negligent infliction of emotional distress, intentional and negligent misrepresentation, breach of contract, breach of the covenant of quiet enjoyment, nuisance, and violation of Mass. Gen. Laws ch. 93A. On October 26, 2009, defendants removed the actions to this Court on the basis of diversity of citizenship. The actions were then consolidated.

On March 30, 2012, this Court granted summary judgment in favor of the insurance company defendants. The Court also granted partial summary judgment in favor of Simpson with only the claims for negligence, negligent infliction of emotional distress, and breach of the covenant of quiet enjoyment surviving.

A jury trial was held from April 1 through April 5, 2013. The evidence at trial consisted of testimony indicat[ing] that there had been multiple fires in the landscaping mulch at the apartment complex prior to the one that burned down plaintiffs' building. During the testimony of Peabody Fire Inspector Joseph DiFranco, Peabody Fire Department reports were offered into evidence that described the department's response to mulch fires at the Highlands at Dearborn on May 19, 21, and 25, 2008. Inspector DiFranco also testified that he suggested to Simpson employees that they could address the fire risk by pulling the mulch away from the buildings, as well as better controlling the disposal of cigarette butts. Andrew Filippone, who was employed by Simpson as the maintenance supervisor for the Highlands at Dearborn, testified that while he was at the scene of one of the smaller mulch fires on the property, someone from the Peabody Fire Department "recommended bringing the mulch back away from the building a little bit." He further testified that he passed this recommendation on to Simpson property manager Victoria Jackman and that the mulch was never in fact pulled away from the buildings before the fire that destroyed Building 8 on May 29, 2008.

Also in evidence were two notices, one from the Peabody Fire Department and one issued by the property manager. The notice from the fire department, which was dated May 27, 2008, acknowledged the repeated mulch fires and instructed the property manager to address improper disposal of cigarette butts and matches; it did not, however, mention moving the mulch away from the buildings. The notice issued by the property manager was dated March 29, 2008, months before the mulch fires occurred, and asked residents not to throw cigarette butts on the ground. There was no evidence of any other notices having been issued to residents prior to the May 29 fire. . . .

Plaintiffs also testified . . . [and] each provided a list of items lost in the fire and attributed values to those items; those lists were admitted into evidence without objection. They also testified extensively about the mental and physical effects of the fire on their persons. They each testified that they saw Building 8, which was the building wherein their apartments were located, burning from Route 1, the entrance to the apartment complex, and/or a nearby parking lot. Plaintiffs Caissie, Gardner, and Felteau all testified about the loss of their pets in the fire.

Defendant moved for a directed verdict, which the Court denied. The jury then found in favor of plaintiffs on all counts and awarded compensatory damages for loss of property to plaintiff Gardner in the amount $74,128.00; to plaintiff Pulisciano in the amount of $41,355.57; to plaintiff Caissie in the amount of $47,331.43; and to plaintiff Felteau in the amount of $188,992.02. The jury also awarded emotional distress damages to each plaintiff in the amount of $450,000. Defendant has moved for an order of judgment as a matter of law, or in the alternative, for an order of remittitur or new trial.

II. STANDARD OF REVIEW

Judgment as a matter of law may be granted when the evidence, considered in the light most hospitable to the verdict, "is so one-sided that [the moving party] is plainly entitled to judgment, for reasonable minds could not differ as to the outcome." *Reeves v. Sanderson Plumbing Prods., Inc.*, 530 U.S. 133, 149-51 (2000).

Similarly, a court may grant a new trial when "the outcome is against the clear weight of the evidence such that upholding the verdict will result in a miscarriage of justice." *Goulet v. New Penn Motor Express, Inc.*, 512 F.3d 34, 44 (1st Cir. 2008). "[However,] a trial judge may order a new trial "even where the verdict is supported by substantial evidence." *Jennings v. Jones*, 587 F.3d 430, 439 (1st Cir. 2009).

As an alternative to ordering a new trial, a court may order a remittitur of damages in certain rare circumstances. The First Circuit has held that a district court is "obligated . . . to grant a remittitur or a new trial on damages only when the award exceeds any rational appraisal or estimate of the damages that could be based upon the evidence before it." *Eastern Mountain Platform Tennis, Inc. v. Sherwin-Williams Company, Inc.*, 40 F.3d 492, 502 (1st Cir. 1994). Courts have interpreted this standard to hold that a damages award must stand unless it is "grossly excessive,

inordinate, shocking to the conscience of the court, or so high that it would be a denial of justice to permit it to stand." *Correa v. Hosp. San Francisco*, 69 F.3d 1184, 1197 (1st Cir. 1995). When a remittitur is warranted, the plaintiff is given the option of either accepting the remitted damages figure, which is determined by the court to be the maximum amount that could have been awarded based upon the evidence presented at trial, or moving forward with a new trial.

III. ANALYSIS
A. JUDGMENT AS A MATTER OF LAW
1. NEGLIGENCE AND BREACH OF IMPLIED COVENANT OF QUIET ENJOYMENT

As to the claims for negligence, the Court instructed the jury that the plaintiffs had to prove four separate elements: (1) that defendant owed a duty of care to them; (2) that Simpson breached that duty; (3) that the plaintiffs each suffered injuries; and (4) that Simpson's breach of duty was a cause of the injuries. The jury was also told that it had to decide "whether Simpson exercised the degree of care that a reasonable landlord (that is, a landlord of ordinary caution and prudence) would have exercised under similar circumstances."

As to the claims for breach of the implied covenant of quiet enjoyment, the Court instructed the jury that the plaintiffs had to prove three separate elements: (1) that defendant leased the premises to them; (2) that acts or omissions of Simpson caused the premises to be substantially unsuitable for use; and (3) that defendant knew, or reasonably should have known, that its acts or omissions were likely to cause the premises to be substantially unsuitable for use. The first element was undisputed at trial. As to the second element, the Court instructed the jury that "[t]he meaning of causation for the breach of implied covenant claim is the same as for the negligence claim." Defendant thus contends, as explained more fully below, that if plaintiffs failed to prove the existence of a duty or that breach of that duty caused the fire, the jury's verdict on both claims must be reversed.

In the present motion, defendant challenges the jury's verdict as to the existence of a specific duty to pull back the mulch, and as to defendant's alleged breach of that duty being a cause of the plaintiffs' injuries.

a. Specific Duty of Care

Defendant first contends that the plaintiffs had to prove the existence of a specific duty of care with respect to the placement of the mulch and that expert testimony was required to establish that duty of care. Defendant contends that without expert testimony establishing the industry standard for the distance flammable mulch should be placed from a building, the members of the jury had no basis for determining whether the landscaping at issue complied reasonably with proper standards of care. . . .

Defendant here contends that the placement of the mulch here is . . . a "technical matter" that the jury would have no basis for evaluating without the aid of expert testimony. Because no expert testimony was offered, defendant argues, the jury was improperly left to "conjecture and surmise" in reaching their verdict.

Plaintiffs respond that they were not required to prove that defendant had a specific duty to pull back the mulch. They contend that they only had to prove that defendant had knowledge of a known risk and that a reasonable landlord would have taken steps to address that risk, which

defendant did not. Furthermore, they point to the testimony of inspector DiFranco as evidence that defendant was, in fact, specifically warned about the proximity of the mulch to the buildings.

First, the Court notes that the jury instructions included the statement, "[i]t is undisputed that defendant owed a duty to the plaintiffs as their landlord." The instruction also explained that "a landlord has a duty to take action when it becomes aware, or reasonably should become aware, of an unreasonably dangerous condition on the premises . . . and the nature of the action required to be taken . . . depends upon the circumstances of each case." Defendant did not object to those instructions. . . . Accordingly, at a minimum it appears that defendant has waived its right to move for a judgment as a matter of law on the basis that plaintiffs failed to prove that defendant had a specific duty to pull back the mulch. However, because defendant's contentions can be construed as challenging plaintiffs' ability to prove "the nature of the action to be taken" in response to a dangerous condition, the Court will address the merits of the motion on this issue.

In a negligence action, the plaintiff must prove the contours of a duty of care with expert testimony when "lay persons could not easily appraise the . . . alleged negligence as a matter of common knowledge." 3 Personal Injury §11.09 (MB, 2013). Defendant's position misconstrues the theory of the case and inappropriately narrows the duty of care at issue, which was a landlord's duty to address a known risk. Plaintiffs did not have to prove that[, as defendants contend], in the absence of notice of a risk, a landlord has a duty to place mulch a particular distance from a building [with expert testimony]. . . .

Here, the question of whether defendant's duty of care as landlord included [simply] moving the mulch away from the buildings, after having experienced multiple fires in the mulch over a short period of time, is similarly ascertainable by drawing on common knowledge and experience. In addition, inspector DiFranco testified that he specifically suggested pulling the mulch away from the building. Under the circumstances, the Court finds that the jury could have had a reasonable basis in the evidence for its decision.

b. Causation

Defendant contends that expert testimony was also necessary to prove that the proximity of the mulch to the building caused the fire to spread to the building. . . .

[We disagree,] where there [is] evidence [of the sort] here[:] that defendant was aware both of this specific fire before it spread to the building and of the increased risk of mulch fires on the premises generally. Defendant thus had the obligation to exercise reasonable care to ensure that the fire, or any potential fire created by the dangerous condition, did not spread to the building. There was evidence here that the mulch was up against the building's siding and next to the gas meter. Inspector DiFranco testified that the proximity to the gas line caused the fire to spread more quickly. A reasonable jury could have found, based on this evidence and their common knowledge, that it was more likely than not that the proximity of the mulch to the building, which included the gas line, was a cause of the fire spreading and ultimately engulfing the entire building.

Furthermore, the initial cause of the fire was not at issue. In many of Massachusetts cases specifically requiring expert testimony on the issue of a fire's cause, the claims were based on an allegation that a defective product or condition caused the fire. In those cases, the courts generally required expert testimony to establish that the alleged defect was the most likely source of the fire, as opposed to other potential sources. . . .

Here, plaintiffs conceded that the initial cause of the fire in the mulch was not a defect or even defendant's negligence, but rather the careless disposal of smoking materials. Inspector DiFranco also testified to that fact. Plaintiffs proceeded on a theory that the known risk of a mulch fire caused by the careless disposal of smoking materials imposed a duty on the landlord to address it, and that defendant's failure to address that risk caused the fire to spread to the building. As noted, there was sufficient evidence from which the jury could reasonably conclude that defendant's failure to act caused the fire to spread quickly to the building. The jurors were also entitled to rely on their "common knowledge of the nature of fire" in determining what facilitated the spread of the fire in terms of the mulch's proximity to other flammable materials on the building. *Commonwealth v. Levesque*, 436 Mass. 443, 454 (2002).

Here, the Court instructed the jury that plaintiffs had to prove that . . . "the harm would not have occurred absent the defendant's breach of duty." Again, defendant did not object to this instruction or offer a proposed alternative that required plaintiffs to prove specific causation as to the spreading of the fire. In any event, plaintiffs did offer evidence of the specific reasons that fire spread and spread quickly, and the jury could reasonably credit that evidence.

Accordingly, the defendant's motion for judgment as a matter of law will be denied as to the claims for negligence and breach of the implied covenant of quiet enjoyment.

2. Emotional Distress

The Court instructed the jury that in order to award compensatory damages for emotional distress, each plaintiff had to prove that (1) she suffered emotional distress and (2) she experienced an objective manifestation of that emotional distress. The Court explained that objective manifestations of emotional distress are physical symptoms such as severe headaches, insomnia, muscle tension, fatigue, nausea, vomiting, depression, shortness of breath, uncontrollable crying spells, or loss of appetite. The Court did not instruct the jury that objective manifestations had to be proved by corroborating evidence. Defendant did not propose that such an instruction be given.

Defendant now contends that the jury's verdict must be set aside as to the awards of emotional distress damages, because plaintiffs failed to corroborate their physical symptoms with objective evidence, instead relying only their own testimony. . . .

[A]s defendant concedes . . . evidence that the plaintiffs watched their home burn to the ground might be sufficient, in and of itself, to corroborate the physical manifestations of emotional distress. . . . Although it is certainly true that . . . testimony as to these symptoms may have been self-serving and therefore less credible, the jury was entitled to credit it. Accordingly, defendant's motion for judgment as a matter of law on the emotional distress claims will be denied.

B. NEW TRIAL AS TO LIABILITY
1. WEIGHT OF THE EVIDENCE

The first ground on which defendant bases its request for a new trial is the contention that the verdict was against the weight of the evidence as to liability. For the reasons set forth above, the Court finds that a reasonable jury could have found for plaintiffs as to liability and thus "the outcome was not against the clear weight of the evidence such that upholding the verdict will result in a miscarriage of justice." *Goulet*, 512 F.3d at 44. Accordingly, defendant's motion for a new trial as to liability will be denied.

2. EVIDENCE OF SUBSEQUENT REMEDIAL MEASURES

The second ground on which defendant bases its request for a new trial is the admission of evidence concerning the subsequent remedial measure of pulling back the mulch. Defendant argues that such evidence was admitted to prove negligence in contravention of Fed. R. Evid. 407, which prejudiced the defendant such that a new trial is warranted.

The first such evidence came in the form of testimony of Victoria Jackman, a defense witness, while she was being cross-examined by plaintiffs' counsel. Ms. Jackman was asked when the decision to pull back the mulch was made, and the Court permitted the question, not immediately understanding that plaintiff was seeking to elicit evidence of subsequent remedial measures. Jackman then testified that the decision was made shortly after the fire. The Court then immediately (indeed, without being requested to) gave the following curative instruction to the jury:

> Let me caution the jury. Obviously everyone is encouraged to make things safer after something has happened, and *you cannot use evidence that something was done after the fact to make something safer as proof it wasn't safe before the incident happened*. We expect and want everyone

to learn from incidents and to improve things as time goes on.

No objection was made to that instruction, and there was no request for further instruction as to that issue. No further testimony concerning subsequent remedial measures was elicited from Jackman.

The next witness was Dave Homan. On direct testimony, defense counsel asked more specifically about why and when he actually ordered the mulch pulled back. When plaintiffs' counsel attempted to impeach that testimony on cross-examination, defense counsel objected. The Court then ruled in a sidebar conference that defendant had opened the door during direct examination of Homan at least to a limited extent, and permitted the testimony. . . .

Defendant overstates the effect of this small portion of [Homan's] testimony, and understates its own counsel's role in bringing it before the jury. Defense counsel admitted that his purpose in eliciting the testimony from Homan was to show that it was defendant's idea, and not the fire department's, to pull back the mulch. Counsel was certainly permitted to waive the protection of [Evidence] Rule 407 and adopt such a strategy. Implicit in counsel's decision to pursue that strategy is a determination that the information about the subsequent remedial measure was not particularly prejudicial to his client. It would be illogical and unfair, with the benefit of hindsight, to permit defendant to use the admission of that evidence to vacate the jury verdict.

It is true that Jackman's testimony about the timing of the decision to pull back the mulch—which preceded Homan's testimony—should not have been elicited. However, that testimony was limited, and the Court immediately gave a curative instruction. . . . [Further,] if defense counsel had not elicited additional information,

the matter would have ended there. Instead, defense counsel chose to reintroduce the subject.

Under the circumstances, the Court finds that the admission of evidence of subsequent remedial measures does not warrant a new trial. . . .

C. REMITTITUR

Defendant also seeks an order of remittitur of the emotional distress damages, giving plaintiffs the option of accepting lower damages awards or going forward with a new trial as to damages alone. Defendant contends that the emotional distress damages should be remitted because they were (1) impermissibly punitive in nature, (2) excessive and against weight of evidence, and (3) impermissibly based on the loss of pets.

All of the plaintiffs were awarded exactly the same large amount of emotional distress damages despite their differing testimony as to the effects of the fire on them. There was no psychiatric, psychological, or other expert testimony as to the extent of any of the emotional distress experienced by plaintiffs; all of the evidence came in the form of plaintiff's own, often emotionally charged, testimony. No plaintiff claimed permanent physical injury. No plaintiff was hospitalized. That is at least some indication that the damages were not grounded in the evidence, but rather excessive and perhaps punitive.

There was also a significant amount of testimony about the loss of pets. The Court did give a limiting instruction informing the jury that pets are considered property under the law of Massachusetts and therefore emotional distress damages could not be awarded for their loss; however, considering the content and emotional nature of the testimony, there is at least some doubt that the jury heeded the instruction. . . .

As stated at the outset, a district court is "obligated . . . to grant a remittitur or a new trial on damages only when the award exceeds any rational appraisal or estimate of the damages that could be based upon the evidence before it." *Eastern Mountain*, 40 F.3d at 502. "Although determining whether damages for emotional distress are excessive is difficult, such damages are not immune from review." *Koster v. TWA*, 181 F.3d 24, 34 (1st Cir. 1999). The First Circuit [and other courts] ha[ve] held that it is appropriate for a district court to take the absence of medical or psychiatric evidence into account in fashioning a remittitur. . . .

Here, the jury awarded emotional distress damages of $450,000 per plaintiff, notwithstanding the absence of evidence of medical or psychiatric diagnoses or expenses. After a careful review of the record and a compendium of analogous cases, the Court concludes that the awards for emotional distress damages in this case were excessive and not supported by the

weight of the evidence. In most of the cases reviewed in the course of making this determination similarly excessive damages awards were remitted by $150,000 to $800,000.

Accordingly, the Court will order a new trial on the sole issue of emotional distress damages unless plaintiffs agree to accept remitted emotional distress damages of $100,000 each.

IV. CONCLUSION

For the foregoing reasons, defendant's motion for judgment as a matter of law, or, in the alternative, for a new trial as to liability will be DENIED. Defendant's motion for a new trial or remittitur as to emotional distress damages will be GRANTED; plaintiffs shall inform the court by August 29, 2013, whether they seek a new trial. If not, judgment shall enter in the amount of $100,000 in emotional distress damages as to each plaintiff, plus their already determined damages as to loss of property and prejudgment interest.

Notes & Questions

1. In *Gardner*, one of the arguments the defendant made in support of its motion for a new trial was that the trial judge erred in admitting evidence regarding the defendant's remedial measure of pulling back the mulch. As you will learn in an upper-level evidence course, a judge may not allow certain types of evidence to go before the jury. In *Gardner*, the defendant cited Federal Rule of Evidence 407, which states that "evidence of [subsequent] measures" that "would have made an earlier injury or harm less likely to occur" are not admissible to prove negligence (among other things). The trial judge in *Gardner* did not exclude this very sort of evidence, yet the district court did not grant the defendant's motion for a new trial on this ground. Why not?

2. The defendant pointed to numerous errors in the trial in support of its motion for a new trial. Which errors would be considered "process-based" and which ones would be considered "outcome-based"?

3. The defendant in *Gardner* moved for judgment as a matter of law *and* for a new trial. Make sure you know the difference between the two standards. Which standard is harder for the movant to satisfy? Which motion do you think the movant would prefer be granted? Which motion do you think the judge would be more likely to grant, of the two? Does your answer stem from the difference in the two standards, or does it stand in tension with that difference?

4. Why would a judge ever grant a *renewed* motion for judgment as a matter of law? After all, if the case was so clear-cut based on the evidence at trial, the judge would have granted the original motion for judgment as a matter of law, no? Judges sometimes deny (or defer decisions on) motions for judgment as a matter of law at the close of evidence and then grant the renewed motion after the jury verdict. Why might this be? As a matter of judicial power, think back to the way in which a judge's verdict in a bench trial is *less* powerful than a jury verdict. How might this help you answer this question? Also, think back to "The Big Picture" regarding the vices and virtues of juries. What virtues of the jury might a judge be thinking of when denying the initial Rule 50 motion? Finally, as a matter of efficiency and finality, consider the consequences of two separate actions the judge could take in this situation. Say the judge lets the jury render a verdict and then the judge grants a Rule 50(b) motion because the judge believed that the jury's verdict was unreasonable. If the judge's grant of the Rule 50(b) motion is reversed on appeal, what result? By contrast, if the judge grants a Rule 50(a) motion and thus does not let the jury render a verdict, and the judge's Rule 50(a) decision is then reversed on appeal, what result?

5. Another puzzle about the standard governing Rule 50 is that it mirrors that of Rule 56 for summary judgment. Given that, why would a Rule 50 motion *ever* be granted if a Rule 56 motion was denied? (Hint: Even if Rule 50 and Rule 56 demand exactly the same legal standard, do they rely on exactly the same evidence?)

CHAPTER 6

Appeals

Judges are human, and humans make mistakes. And even if judges were perfect, litigants are human and humans dislike losing. By allowing disappointed litigants to seek review from a higher authority, the appeals process not only creates an opportunity for the judicial system to correct its own errors, but also provides a path for dissatisfied parties. In addition to error correction and litigant satisfaction, appeals serve another important function—they enhance uniformity in the law by bringing legal issues to courts with power to create binding precedent over numerous trial courts.

This chapter will examine how appeals fit into the litigation process as a whole. First, we will review the structure of appellate courts. Then we will cover appealability—the question of when an appeal may be taken and what may be appealed—and the related topic of reviewability, which addresses which issues may be presented to the appellate court. Finally, we will turn to standards of review, concerning the level of deference that appellate judges give to trial judges' decisions.

A. THE STRUCTURE OF APPELLATE COURTS

(1) Overview

In the federal court system, each court of appeals hears appeals from the district courts within its circuit. The U.S. Court of Appeals for the Second Circuit, for example, hears appeals from district courts in New York, Connecticut, and Vermont. These geographically defined circuits are numbered one through eleven, plus a circuit for the District of Columbia. One additional circuit—the Federal Circuit—does not cover a particular geographic area but instead hears appeals involving patents, international trade, veterans' claims, and certain other categories of cases.

GEOGRAPHIC BOUNDARIES OF UNITED STATES COURTS OF APPEALS

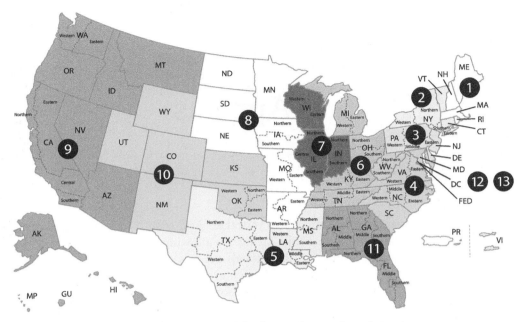

Source: https://www.uscourts.gov/about-federal-courts/court-role-and-structure.

The jurisdiction of the U.S. courts of appeals is governed largely by statute but constrained by Article III of the Constitution, which establishes the outer limits of federal court jurisdiction. In Part B of this chapter, we will explore the statutes, rules, and doctrines that govern appealability to the federal appellate courts.

The final authority in the federal system is, of course, the U.S. Supreme Court. Its jurisdiction comes from both the Constitution and federal statutes. For the most part, the Supreme Court gets to decide which cases to hear. Therefore, in the vast majority of cases that are appealed, the final word comes from the court of appeals.

In the state courts, each state has its own rules, statutes, and constitutional provisions concerning the structure and powers of its appellate courts. Recall that most state court systems contain three tiers like the federal courts. However, some smaller states have only a trial court and a high court, and still other systems are structured with more than three tiers and divisions. In some states, the intermediate appellate courts are divided into geographic regions, similar to the federal courts of appeals.

Taking an appeal to a state's high court generally is not a matter of right. Rather, the highest court of the state ordinarily has the power to select which appeals to hear, similar to the U.S. Supreme Court. Some states allow exceptions for particularly important types of appeals (in the criminal area, for example, many states allow automatic appeals to the state high court in death penalty cases) or for appeals in which a judge dissented at the intermediate appellate level.

Appellate courts normally hear appeals in multi-judge panels, unlike trial courts where, with rare exceptions, a single judge handles the case. The U.S. courts of appeals use three-judge panels, as do some state appellate courts. The total authorized number of court of appeals judges within each circuit ranges from 6 in the First Circuit to 29 in the enormous Ninth Circuit, which encompasses California and much of the western United States. In extraordinary cases, the court of appeals judges within a circuit may vote to hold a rehearing *en banc*, which means that the entire group of judges reconsiders the appeal after the original decision by the three-judge appellate panel.

State supreme courts often have five, seven, or nine justices (or judges, depending on the state's terminology) who decide each case *en banc*. For instance, the New York Court of Appeals has seven judges, the California Supreme Court has seven justices, and the Texas Supreme Court has nine justices. The U.S. Supreme Court, of course, currently has nine Justices. The Judiciary Act of 1789 set the original number of Supreme Court Justices at six, and over the next 80 years that number fluctuated multiple times by statute, but since 1869 the number has stood at nine. In the Supreme Court, if one or more Justices recuse themselves from a case because of conflicts of interest, the Court hears the case with fewer than nine Justices and may reach a tie. When a tie occurs, the judgment below is affirmed but the Court issues no opinion and the affirmance has no precedential value.

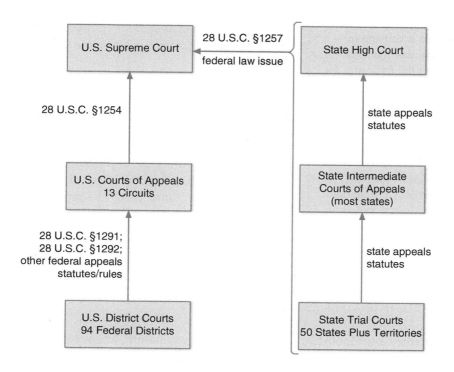

En banc (French for "in bench") refers to a decision by all the judges of a court rather than by a subset of them. The Supreme Court and state high courts usually decide matters as full courts, so the phrase *en banc* does not tell you anything surprising when used to describe them. But when you see *en banc* describing a decision of a U.S. court of appeals, it means the decision carries special weight because the judges rehear the case as a full group rather than rely on the original decision by a three-judge panel.

The word *bench*, by the way, is used both to refer to the place in the courtroom where the judge sits, and to refer collectively to members of the judiciary. Modern judges don't really sit on benches, so when a lawyer asks to "approach the bench," what they approach is the raised desk where the judge works.

While we are on the topic of courtroom interiors, the word *bar*, as used to refer collectively to lawyers, has a similar derivation. The bar in a courtroom is a low railing that separates the area for public spectators from the front area for judge, jury, court personnel, witnesses, and lawyers. In modern usage, *bar* can refer to lawyers in general (as in "relations between bench and bar"), lawyers who are licensed to practice in a particular state or court ("members of the Texas bar"), professional associations for lawyers ("the American Bar Association"), the bar exam ("Yay, I passed the bar!"), and sometimes a place where lawyers grab a beer after a hard day of work.

Consider how the pyramidal hierarchy of the judiciary furthers the goal of enhancing uniformity and predictability in law. In the federal system, there is one Supreme Court with nine Justices who work *en banc*; 13 courts of appeals with a current total of 179 authorized judgeships and judges who work mostly in three-judge panels; and 94 district courts with a current total of 673 authorized judgeships and judges who work mostly solo. Each state court system roughly mirrors this sort of pyramidal structure. On a close question of law—whether a matter of common law decision making, statutory construction, constitutional interpretation, or any other legal question—any two trial judges might reach different conclusions. Thus, parties in different actions may get different answers to the same legal question simply because their cases were assigned to different judges. When the same question of law makes its way up to the court of appeals, the appellate court renders a decision that is binding precedent for all of the judges within the circuit. This imposes greater uniformity within the circuit on that particular legal question. If another court of appeals reaches a different conclusion on the same legal question, creating a "circuit split," then at some point the Supreme Court might grant certiorari to resolve the question for all circuits.

Appellate courts have their own rules of procedure. In the federal court system, you need look no further than Rule 1 of the Federal Rules of Civil Procedure to be reminded that those rules govern procedure in the *district* courts. The Federal Rules of Civil Procedure say nothing about procedure in the courts of appeals. A separate set of rules—the *Federal Rules of Appellate Procedure* (FRAP)—regulate proceedings in the U.S. courts of appeals. The FRAP are where you will find rules on how to file appeals, what to include in briefs, when oral arguments are allowed, and so forth.

(2) The United States Supreme Court

The Supreme Court looms large in the popular imagination, in law school casebooks, and in the U.S. political system. It is a body with enormous influence over virtually every facet of American life because of its (self-declared but now thoroughly established) power "to say what the law is." *Marbury v. Madison*, 5 U.S. (1 Cranch) 137 (1803). The Supreme Court has been instrumental in shaping civil procedure just as it has been instrumental in shaping every other area of federal law. Indeed, in every chapter of this book, you can see examples of the Supreme Court's sway over the law of civil procedure.

But in terms of which courts actually participate in lawsuits, the Supreme Court is nearly always absent. Thus, while the Supreme Court looms large as a law-giver, it does not loom large as an actual participant in litigation because so few actions get there. The Supreme Court chooses which appeals to hear, granting only a small percentage of the thousands of *petitions for certiorari* filed each year by litigants vying for the Court's attention. The Justices decide whether to grant the petition—that is, whether to permit the appeal—based primarily on whether the petition presents an important legal issue that needs to be resolved.

The U.S. Supreme Court hears appeals from federal courts and from state courts. Note, however, that on questions of *state* law, the highest authority is the top court of the relevant *state*. The U.S. Supreme Court has no authority to tell the state courts how they should interpret their own state law. Appeals from state courts to the U.S. Supreme Court, therefore, are limited to questions of federal law. Under 28 U.S.C. §1257, if a state court case raises a federal law issue, a party may seek Supreme Court review. For example, in a New Jersey state court medical malpractice case, the losing party may appeal from the trial court to the Appellate Division of the New Jersey Superior Court, raising whatever issues of state or federal law the party considers significant. After the appellate court decides the case, the losing party might attempt to appeal to the New Jersey Supreme Court, and if that court grants certification to hear the case, the parties may raise state and federal issues. But if a party then wishes to appeal to the U.S. Supreme Court, the appellant may not ask the U.S. Supreme Court to reexamine the New Jersey Supreme Court's interpretation of New Jersey common law tort doctrines, New Jersey statutes, or New Jersey's constitution. The appellant could, however, ask the U.S. Supreme Court to determine whether New Jersey law, as applied by the state courts, violates the U.S. Constitution or some other aspect of federal law.

Terminology Tip

The party who filed the appeal is the *appellant*; the party against whom an appeal is filed is the *appellee*. An appellant or appellee might be plaintiff or defendant depending on who prevailed below, so you will see the terms plaintiff-appellant, defendant-appellant, and so forth. In the Supreme Court, where a party seeks review by petitioning for certiorari, the parties are more accurately referred to as *petitioner* and *respondent*, but sometimes these words are used interchangeably with appellant and appellee.

Terminology Tip

For case names, at the trial court level the plaintiff's name goes first: Plaintiff v. Defendant. Federal courts of appeals now retain the case name from the district court (in older cases, the appellant's name went first), but for Supreme Court cases, the name of the petitioner goes first. Thus, for example, in the Supreme Court case of *Bell Atlantic Corp. v. Twombly*, Twombly was the original plaintiff but Bell Atlantic and the other defendants appealed the Second Circuit's decision to the Supreme Court.

Appeals under section 1257 need not come from the state high court. Rather, the statute permits appeal of a final judgment from the highest state court in which a decision could be had. In the example above, if the case went all the way to the New Jersey Supreme Court, then any appeal to the U.S. Supreme Court would wait until after the state supreme court had decided the case. But if the New Jersey Supreme Court declined to hear the case, then the Appellate Division would have been the highest state court in which a decision could be had. If state law does not provide an appeal for a particular proceeding, then the trial court may be the highest state court in which a decision could be had. In such circumstances, when a party seeks review on a federal law issue, section 1257 permits a party to seek certiorari in the U.S. Supreme Court directly from the intermediate state appellate court or even from a state trial court.

Most Supreme Court appeals, however, come up through the federal courts. In recent years, about 10 to 20 percent of the Supreme Court's docket has come from state courts, and nearly all the rest comes from the U.S. courts of appeals. Under 28 U.S.C. §1254, cases from the courts of appeals may be reviewed by the Supreme Court either by "writ of certiorari granted upon the petition of any party to any civil or criminal case, before or after rendition of judgment or decree" or "certification at any time by a court of appeals of any question of law in any civil or criminal case as to which instructions are desired, and upon such certification the Supreme Court may give binding instructions or require the entire record to be sent up for decision of the entire matter in controversy."

In addition to this appellate jurisdiction, the Supreme Court has a small slice of original jurisdiction. Everyone thinks of the Supreme Court as the ultimate appellate court, and thinks of trial courts as the ones that possess original jurisdiction—that is, where the case gets filed originally. But actually things are a bit more complicated. Article III of the Constitution grants the Supreme Court original jurisdiction over "all Cases affecting Ambassadors, other public Ministers and Consuls, and those in which a State shall be Party." In practice, the Court's original docket has been dedicated mostly to controversies between state governments. By statute, the Court possesses *exclusive* original jurisdiction over controversies between two or more states, so these cases cannot be brought originally in a lower court. 28 U.S.C. §1251. When New York and New Jersey both claimed territorial ownership of the filled parts of Ellis Island in the 1990s, for example, they took their dispute directly to the Supreme Court. *New Jersey v. New York*, 523 U.S. 767 (1998).

B. APPEALABILITY AND REVIEWABILITY

There is no constitutional right to appeal in civil cases. *See Pennzoil v. Texaco, Inc.*, 481 U.S. 1, 31 & n.4 (1987) (Stevens, J., concurring) (noting that the Court's "precedents do tend to support" the proposition that "States are under no constitutional duty to provide for civil appeals"); *see also Cobbledick v. United States*, 309 U.S. 323, 324-25 (1940) ("the right to a judgment from more than one court is a matter of grace and not a necessary ingredient of justice").

As a statutory matter, however, both the federal and state court systems tend to give a losing party at least one chance to seek review of legal errors. *See, e.g.,* 28 U.S.C. §1291 (granting jurisdiction over appeals from all final decisions of district courts). To understand the right to appeal, you must get comfortable with a set of procedural doctrines that constrain the *who, when,* and *what* of appeals. We turn now to these three important aspects of the law governing appeals, focusing on appeals from the federal district courts to the courts of appeals:

1. *Who* may appeal—the topics of adversity and standing
2. *When* may decisions be appealed—the final judgment rule and its exceptions
3. *What* may be appealed—the topics of waiver and harmless error

(1) *Who* May Appeal: Adversity and Standing

To appeal, a party must have lost. This is the requirement of *adversity* or *aggrievedness.* It sounds like an obvious point. After all, why would a winning party even want to appeal? But it turns out that winning and losing are not always so simple.

Suppose a plaintiff wins a judgment but the relief granted by the court differs from what the plaintiff requested in the complaint. Perhaps the damages are lower than the plaintiff sought, or the plaintiff was denied injunctive relief in addition to damages, or the court awarded compensatory but not punitive damages. Even though the plaintiff "won" the lawsuit, the plaintiff may appeal the denial of the requested remedy. As a strategic matter, the plaintiff may decide that an appeal is not worth the risk and expense if the relief awarded was satisfactory, but as a legal matter, the plaintiff would have the right to appeal. Similarly, in a case involving multiple claims, the plaintiff may succeed on some claims but lose on others, and both the plaintiff and defendant could consider appealing the aspects of the case on which the other side prevailed.

Frequently, both sides emerge dissatisfied with the outcome of a case because no one entirely got what they wanted. You should not be surprised, therefore, to encounter *cross-appeals,* in which opposing parties appeal the judgment on different grounds.

What does *not* count as adversity? Mere dissatisfaction with the court's reasoning. If a defendant prevails and the plaintiff is awarded nothing, but the defendant dislikes the court's opinion because the defendant believes it creates a bad precedent for the defendant in future cases, the defendant has no right to appeal. Similarly, if a plaintiff prevails and gets the full remedy demanded in the complaint, but the plaintiff dislikes the court's opinion because it does not lambaste the defendant's conduct, the plaintiff has no right to appeal. A party appeals from the *judgment,* not from the *opinion.* Thus, if a plaintiff sues under multiple legal theories and obtains the full relief requested, the plaintiff cannot appeal simply because the court awarded the relief pursuant to one theory rather than the other. For example, suppose a plaintiff sues for damages of $100,000, asserting both a common law claim and a statutory claim. If the plaintiff wins a judgment of $100,000 on one claim but not the other, the plaintiff cannot appeal on the grounds that the plaintiff would have preferred to win on the other theory or both theories. If the plaintiff got exactly what the complaint demanded (a judgment for $100,000), then the plaintiff has not suffered an *adverse judgment*. If, however, some additional remedy (such as attorneys' fees) were available on the statutory claim but not on the common law claim, then the plaintiff would be able to appeal a rejection of the statutory claim. In *Aetna Cas. & Surety Co. v. Cunningham*, 224 F.2d 478 (5th Cir. 1955), an insurance company sued for fraud and breach of contract, and won full damages under the breach-of-contract theory while its fraud claim was rejected. The insurer appealed the rejection of the fraud claim, successfully arguing that it was entitled to appeal because the defendant was going bankrupt and, as a matter of bankruptcy law, the insurer was actually more likely to recover for fraud than for breach of contract. In sum, to establish adversity for purposes of bringing an appeal, a party must show that, in some way, it did not obtain the *result* it sought.

Nonparties ordinarily lack *standing* to appeal. Standing, in general, refers to the principle that only those who have suffered injury to their own interests may seek redress from a court. In the context of appeals, it means that a person may appeal a judgment only if the judgment is legally binding on them. Outsiders may be unhappy about the outcome of a case and their personal interests may somehow be affected, but they have no right to appeal the judgment if they were not actually parties to the lawsuit. A nonparty may ask the court's permission to participate as *amicus curiae*—"friend of the court"—which allows the nonparty to submit a brief and possibly to participate in oral argument, but it does not give a party standing to file the appeal. If a nonparty wishes to become a party for purposes of bringing an appeal, it may apply to intervene under Rule 24. In a class action, however, even though class members are not parties in the usual sense unless they choose to intervene in the action, a class member who objects to a settlement may appeal from the court's approval of that settlement. *Devlin v. Scardelletti*, 536 U.S. 1, 14 (2002).

(2) *When* May Decisions Be Appealed: The Final Judgment Rule and Exceptions

(a) *The Final Judgment Rule*

Only final judgments may be appealed—that is the general rule. Master that general rule, then get ready for a slew of exceptions and alternatives.

Start with the statutory grant of jurisdiction to the U.S. courts of appeals in 28 U.S.C. §1291: "The courts of appeals . . . shall have jurisdiction of appeals from all final decisions of the district courts of the United States. . . ." Note the key word—*final*. What counts as a final decision? According to the Supreme Court, it ordinarily means "one that ends the litigation on the merits and leaves nothing for the court to do but execute the judgment." *Ray Haluch Gravel Co. v. Central Pension Fund*, 571 U.S. 177, 183 (2014) (quoting *Caitlin v. United States*, 324 U.S. 229, 233 (1945)). During the trial court process, judges make plenty of interlocutory rulings—decisions along the way—but these do not constitute final judgments. For a litigator faced with adverse rulings, this calls for fortitude. Think of it as a Jedi rule: Patience, young Padawan.

To test your understanding of what constitutes a final judgment within the meaning of section 1291, try the following examples. The question for each is whether the court's decision is *final* or merely *interlocutory*:

(a) Case goes to trial and court enters judgment based on the jury verdict, with no post-trial motions pending.
(b) Court grants motion to compel discovery.
(c) Court denies motion to compel discovery.
(d) Court grants defendant's motion for summary judgment on all claims.
(e) Court denies motion for summary judgment.
(f) Court grants motion to dismiss for failure to state a claim.
(g) Court denies motion to dismiss for failure to state a claim.

Now check your answers. Items a, d, and f are final, and items b, c, e, and g are interlocutory. Be sure you understand why. As you can see from these examples, certain types of rulings, such as discovery motions, are interlocutory regardless of which way the court rules. Other types of rulings, such as motions to dismiss or for summary judgment, may be final judgments if granted but interlocutory if denied.

Note that in every one of these examples, one of the parties is unhappy about the court's decision and possibly anxious to get it reversed. In the last example, the defendant may be utterly convinced that the judge erred in denying the Rule 12(b)(6) motion and deeply annoyed at having to go forward with litigating what the defendant believes is a meritless case. But at that point, there is no final judgment. Denial of the motion to dismiss means that the defendant must file an answer and the litigation continues. After the case has been decided, if the defendant loses, *then* the defendant may raise the issue on appeal and argue that the trial court erred as a matter of law in failing to grant the motion to dismiss.

That last point is important. The final judgment rule does not prevent parties from raising on appeal all sorts of issues that may have come up during the litigation. On appeal, a losing party may argue that the trial court made erroneous rulings about pleadings, discovery, pretrial motions, admissibility of evidence, or other interlocutory decisions. The fact that those trial court decisions are *interlocutory* does not insulate them from review; it simply means that they cannot be reviewed immediately. Instead, their review must wait until after the case has reached a final judgment. Note one interesting exception: A denial of summary judgment is not appealable after a full trial, because the trial record supersedes the record that existed at the time of the summary judgment motion. *Ortiz v. Jordan*, 562 U.S. 180, 184 (2011).

Why does the federal court system (as well as many state courts) impose the final judgment rule? Why not permit parties to appeal each decision along the way if a party has reason to believe a decision was erroneous? Mostly, it is about efficiency. If parties routinely could seek review of interlocutory decisions, it would extend litigation and raise costs as parties go repeatedly up to the appellate court in a series of piecemeal appeals. Moreover, if routine interlocutory appeals were allowed, the appellate courts would decide numerous issues unnecessarily, as parties lose countless battles along the way to winning the war. Suppose a trial court denies a plaintiff access to certain discovery. If interlocutory appeal were permitted, the plaintiff might seek appellate review of the discovery decision, imposing delay and cost on both parties and the courts. But the plaintiff might win the case even without the discovery, in which case the appeal would be unneeded. By forcing parties to wait until the case concludes and then allowing the losing party to raise whatever points of error the party considers most important, the court system avoids the cost and delay associated with piecemeal and unnecessary appeals.

There is another perspective, however. When a trial judge makes a serious error, there is something to say for reversing the error as expeditiously as possible. If a trial court erroneously denies a motion to dismiss, justice and efficiency arguably are better served by a prompt reversal, rather than forcing the parties to slog through the entire litigation only to find on appeal that the action should have been dismissed at the outset. Also, most cases settle before reaching a final judgment. Given the frequency of settlement, many trial court decisions thus are unappealable as a practical matter: The trial judge makes a decision that may be erroneous, that decision factors into the anticipated outcome and thus into the settlement dynamic, and then the case settles. Without interlocutory appeal, a trial judge's erroneous decisions become unappealably embedded in a negotiated outcome. Because of these concerns, some state courts strike a different balance from the federal courts, permitting interlocutory appeals more liberally. In New York, for example, parties may appeal not only from a final judgment, but also from an order that "involves some part of the merits" or "affects a substantial right." N.Y. Civ. Prac. L. & R. §5701.

(b) Exceptions to the Final Judgment Rule

If it were absolute, the final judgment rule would be too harsh. Sometimes parties need appellate review of interlocutory decisions and forcing them to wait would be untenable. Congress, federal rule makers, and the courts therefore have carved out exceptions to the final judgment rule of appealability. Litigators know that in these circumstances, they can seek review of adverse decisions without awaiting a final judgment.

We will look at six scenarios in which trial court decisions may reach an appellate court's review prior to the conclusion of trial court proceedings: (i) interlocutory orders of injunctive relief; (ii) certified interlocutory appeals; (iii) interlocutory appeal from class certification decisions; (iv) the writ of mandamus; (v) appeal from partial final judgment; and (vi) the collateral order doctrine. Three of these are true exceptions to the final judgment rule: injunctive relief, certified interlocutory appeals, and class certification. Two are best understood as expansions of what counts as a "final decision": partial final judgment and the collateral order doctrine. And one of them—mandamus—really is neither an exception to nor an expansion of the final judgment rule, but rather a workaround by means of a separate proceeding.

(i) Interlocutory Orders Regarding Injunctive Relief

The statutory grant of authority to the courts of appeals, section 1292(a) of Title 28, gives the courts of appeals jurisdiction over interlocutory orders by district courts "granting, continuing, modifying, refusing or dissolving injunctions, or refusing to dissolve or modify injunctions." Injunctions—orders that tell parties what they must or must not do—have an immediacy that differs from money damages. Imagine a lawsuit to stop the defendant from running his ice cream shop based on a noncompete agreement that the parties dispute. If the court grants injunctive relief, the defendant must stop operating his business. If the court denies injunctive relief, the plaintiff must face business competition possibly in violation of the agreement. Even if the grant or denial of injunctive relief is interlocutory—a preliminary injunction rather than a permanent one, or perhaps the lawsuit seeks money damages as well and that issue has not been resolved—the impact of the injunction decision is so immediate and tangible that interlocutory appeal is permitted.

(ii) Certified Interlocutory Appeals

Section 1292(b) builds flexibility into the final judgment rule by allowing a district judge to certify that an important issue needs to be resolved by the appellate court right away. When the district judge makes an interlocutory order, the judge may state in writing that the order "involves a controlling question of law as to which there is substantial ground for difference of opinion and that an immediate appeal from the order may materially advance the ultimate termination of the litigation." 28 U.S.C. §1292(b). Note the three requirements embedded in that sentence. First, the interlocutory order must involve a controlling question of law. Second, there must be substantial basis for disagreement about that question of law. Third, the district judge must believe that immediate appellate review would help bring the lawsuit to a close.

Even if the district judge certifies an issue for interlocutory appeal under section 1292(b), the court of appeals gets to decide whether to accept it. As the statute puts it, the court of appeals "may thereupon, in its discretion, permit an appeal to be taken from such order." The process for certified interlocutory appeal thus involves two gatekeepers. First, a district judge must acknowledge that her decision on a crucial issue may be wrong, and then the court of appeals judges must choose to accept the appeal.

Section 1292(b) works particularly well in lawsuits with claims or defenses based on novel legal theories. If a plaintiff brings a claim based on a legal theory that no one has ever tried before, the district judge might think the claim questionable but deny the defendant's motion to dismiss for failure to state a claim. The district judge expects that ultimately the appellate court will decide the legal viability of the plaintiff's claim. Rather than go through discovery and trial without the benefit of the appellate court's input, the district judge might prefer to allow the parties to take an immediate appeal of the Rule 12(b)(6) decision before going forward.

Certified interlocutory appeals turn the final judgment rule's efficiency explanation on its head. The standard justification for the final judgment rule holds that interlocutory appeals decrease efficiency by multiplying proceedings. This justification makes sense with regard to most interlocutory decisions because usually the district judge's ruling will be affirmed, and even if reversed it may not matter to the outcome. However, when the appeal involves a controlling question of law on which there is a solid chance the district judge's ruling may be overturned—the set-up for a section 1292(b) certification—an interlocutory appeal may reduce rather than multiply proceedings. By obtaining a definitive answer to a key legal question, the court reduces the chance that proceedings will have to be redone, increases the chance of reaching a judgment on a Rule 12(b)(6) motion or summary judgment motion that will withstand appeal, and positions the parties to be able to negotiate a settlement with confidence about the legal framework that applies to their dispute.

Interlocutory appeals under section 1292(b) occur infrequently. The district courts certify only a few hundred interlocutory appeals each year, and the courts of appeals accept about half of those. Think again about each of the two gatekeepers. It is understandable that both the district and circuit judges reserve these appeals for special cases. Despite their rarity, certified interlocutory appeals carry a dispro-portionate impact because they tend to occur in important cases on the most interest-ing and controversial issues. As a law student, if you pay attention to the procedural histories of cases in your various casebooks, you may begin to notice cases that reached appellate courts as certified interlocutory appeals under section 1292(b).

(iii) Interlocutory Appeals of Class Certification Decisions

In class actions, many lawyers consider the single most important moment to be the court's decision on class certification. A grant of class certification propels an enor-mous litigation forward and places massive settlement pressure on the defendant. A denial of class certification often sounds a death knell for the litigation. Either way, the court's decision on the motion for class certification matters profoundly to both sides. But it is interlocutory. If the court grants class certification, the case does not end; it proceeds as a class action. If the court denies class certification, the case does not end; at least in theory, it proceeds as an individual action. Until 1998, class certi-fication decisions remained unappealable until after a final judgment. To avoid the harshness of the final judgment rule as applied to class certification, litigants and judges often used either section 1292(b) interlocutory appeals or the writ of manda-mus to obtain review of class certification decisions.

In 1998, the Supreme Court adopted an amendment to the class action rule to permit interlocutory appeals of class certification decisions at the discretion of the court of appeals. Rule 23(f) says that a court of appeals may permit, in its discretion, an appeal of a class action certification decision if a party files a petition for permis-sion to appeal within 14 days of the ruling.

(iv) Writs of Mandamus

The writ of mandamus dates back about 700 years in English legal history. In Latin, *mandamus* means "we command," and that is exactly what the writ does—it allows an appellate court to command a government official to perform a mandatory duty. What does this have to do with appeals? Remember that government officials include lower court judges. When a trial judge fails to perform a judicial duty correctly, a superior court can use the writ of mandamus to force the judge to apply the law. *See, e.g., Citibank, N.A. v. Fullam*, 580 F.2d 82 (3d Cir. 1978) (granting a writ of mandamus to compel a district judge to comply with the Third Circuit's earlier order prohibiting the use of particular funds to pay for reorganizing a debtor's estate); *see also Cheney v. U.S. Dist. Ct. for D.C.*, 542 U.S. 367 (2004) (holding that the D.C. Circuit had the authority, if it so decided, to issue a writ of mandamus to compel a district judge to protect the Vice President of the United States from vexatious litigation).

Mandamus is not an *appeal* from the trial court to the appellate court. Rather, the applicant for the writ brings a separate proceeding directly in the appellate court asking the court to grant a writ of mandamus. Courts insist that parties may use the writ of mandamus only in exceptional circumstances, when standard procedures do not suffice. In appropriate cases, however, parties find mandamus useful as way around the final judgment rule. When a party wishes to appeal an interlocutory decision but cannot find a basis for an interlocutory appeal, sometimes the only way to get the appellate court's attention is to bring a separate proceeding asking the appellate court to order the trial court to do its duty.

STRATEGY SESSION

Do not think of mandamus as a free pass to bypass the final judgment rule. Courts emphasize that mandamus "is a drastic and extraordinary remedy reserved for really extraordinary causes," justified only in "circumstances amounting to a judicial usurpation of power." *Cheney v. U.S. District Court for D.C.*, 542 U.S. 367, 380 (2004). Appellate courts are not afraid to sanction lawyers who frivolously apply for the writ. And running to another court to accuse the district judge of usurpation is no way to win friends at the district court. Absent significant justification, you can imagine how well such a request might go over with the district judge. So tread carefully. Reserve this tool for the rare situation where the judge's ruling violates a clear legal duty and your client's interest depends upon your getting the ruling changed promptly rather than waiting for appeal.

(v) Appeals of Partial Final Judgments

Litigation often includes multiple claims, multiple parties, or both, as we will explore in Chapter 7. Suppose a case is completely finished with regard to one of those claims or one of those parties, even if other parts of the case remain to be decided. May a party seek appeal of that decision, even though the entire action has not concluded? On the one hand, the decision is interlocutory because the case is still going on. On the other hand, it feels much like a final judgment because, at least with regard to that particular claim or party, nothing else remains to be done.

Federal Rule of Civil Procedure 54(b) resolves this conundrum by permitting a district court to enter a final judgment as to a particular claim or party. Rule 54(b) says that when there are multiple claims or parties, "the court may direct entry of a final judgment as to one or more, but fewer than all, claims or parties only if the court expressly determines that there is no just reason for delay." Unless the judge does this explicitly, however, a decision as to each claim or party is interlocutory until the whole case is resolved. To be clear about it, judges ordinarily use the exact language of the rule. Thus, if the judge grants a motion to dismiss or summary judgment as to a particular claim or party, and if the judge thinks that it makes sense to permit the appeal right away, the judge's order would say something like, "Finding no just reason for delay, the court directs that final judgment be entered as to [particular claim or particular party]."

Consider several scenarios in which Rule 54(b) might come into play. First example: A plaintiff sues Defendants X and Y, and the plaintiff wins summary judgment against X while the case against Y is still pending and heading to trial. If the claim against X has been fully resolved, the court could choose to enter a final judgment against Defendant X, which would permit X to appeal without waiting for Y's trial to conclude. Second example: Plaintiffs A and B sue a defendant and the defendant prevails against A on a motion to dismiss. Because the claim by A has been fully resolved, the court could choose to enter a final judgment against Plaintiff A, which would permit A to appeal the dismissal without waiting for B's claim to conclude. Third example: A plaintiff asserts two claims against a defendant, and the court has adjudicated one claim in favor of the defendant. If the claims are related, then most likely the court would not enter final judgment until both claims were fully resolved. If the claims are quite distinct, however, the court might choose to enter final judgment as to the one completed claim, which would permit the plaintiff to appeal that decision without waiting for the rest of the case to finish.

Note that Rule 54(b) does not exactly create an exception to the final judgment rule, at least not in the same way that sections 1292(a) and 1292(b) do. Rather than carving out an exception to the final judgment rule, Rule 54(b) empowers the district court to enter a *final judgment* that is appealable under the ordinary operation of section 1291. Conceptually, Rule 54(b) operates as a way to define finality rather than as an exception to the final judgment rule. But functionally, it is another tool that lawyers can use, with a district judge's support, to bring adverse decisions promptly to the court of appeals.

(vi) Collateral Order Doctrine

What if a trial judge's erroneous decision affects an important right aside from—*collateral* to—the outcome of the lawsuit itself? In that situation, the final judgment rule may perpetuate an injustice because the erroneous decision cannot be repaired by altering the final outcome of the case. Courts have developed a workaround for this problem by treating certain decisions as "final" for purposes of appeal even though they are not final in the sense of resulting in a judgment. This judge-made workaround is known as the collateral order doctrine. In the following case, the Supreme Court explains the collateral order doctrine and considers how far it should extend.

MOHAWK INDUSTRIES v. CARPENTER

558 U.S. 100 (2009)

SOTOMAYOR, J., delivered the opinion of the Court, in which ROBERTS, C.J., and STEVENS, SCALIA, KENNEDY, GINSBURG, BREYER, and ALITO, JJ., joined, and in which THOMAS, J., joined, as to Part II-C. THOMAS, J., filed an opinion concurring in part and concurring in the judgment.

Section 1291 of the Judicial Code confers on federal courts of appeals jurisdiction to review "final decisions of the district courts." 28 U.S.C. §1291. Although "final decisions" typically are ones that trigger the entry of judgment, they also include a small set of prejudgment orders that are "collateral to" the merits of an action and "too important" to be denied immediate review. *Cohen v. Beneficial Indus. Loan Corp.*, 337 U.S. 541, 546 (1949). In this case, petitioner Mohawk Industries, Inc., attempted to bring a collateral order appeal after the District Court ordered it to disclose certain confidential materials on the ground that Mohawk had waived the attorney-client privilege. The Court of Appeals dismissed the appeal for want of jurisdiction.

The question before us is whether disclosure orders adverse to the attorney-client privilege qualify for immediate appeal under the collateral order doctrine. Agreeing with the Court of Appeals, we hold that they do not. Postjudgment appeals, together with other review mechanisms, suffice to protect the rights of litigants and preserve the vitality of the attorney-client privilege.

I

In 2007, respondent Norman Carpenter, a former shift supervisor at a Mohawk manufacturing facility, filed suit in the United States District Court for the Northern District of Georgia, alleging that Mohawk had terminated him in violation of 42 U.S.C. §1985(2) and various Georgia laws. According to Carpenter's complaint, his termination came after he informed a member of Mohawk's human resources department in an e-mail that the company was employing undocumented immigrants. At the time, unbeknownst to Carpenter, Mohawk stood accused in a pending class-action lawsuit of conspiring to drive down the wages of its legal employees by knowingly hiring undocumented workers in violation of federal and state racketeering laws. *See Williams v. Mohawk Indus., Inc.*, No. 4:04-cv-00003-HLM (N.D. Ga. Jan. 6, 2004). Company officials directed Carpenter to meet with the company's retained counsel in the *Williams* case, and counsel allegedly pressured Carpenter to recant his statements. When he refused, Carpenter alleges, Mohawk fired him under false pretenses.

After learning of Carpenter's complaint, the plaintiffs in the *Williams* case sought an evidentiary hearing to explore Carpenter's allegations. In its response to their motion, Mohawk described Carpenter's accusations as "pure fantasy" and recounted the "true facts" of Carpenter's dismissal. According to Mohawk, Carpenter himself had "engaged in blatant and illegal misconduct" by attempting to have Mohawk hire an undocumented worker. The company "commenced an immediate investigation," during which retained counsel interviewed Carpenter. Because Carpenter's "efforts to cause Mohawk to circumvent federal immigration law" "blatantly violated Mohawk policy," the company terminated him.

As these events were unfolding in the *Williams* case, discovery was underway in Carpenter's case. Carpenter filed a motion to compel Mohawk to produce information concerning his meeting with retained counsel and the company's termination decision. Mohawk maintained that the requested information was protected by the attorney-client privilege.

The District Court agreed that the privilege applied to the requested information, but it granted Carpenter's motion to compel disclosure after concluding that Mohawk had implicitly waived the privilege through its representations in the *Williams* case. The court declined to certify its order for interlocutory appeal under 28 U.S.C. §1292(b). But, recognizing "the seriousness of its [waiver] finding," it stayed its ruling to allow Mohawk to explore other potential "avenues to appeal, . . . such as a petition for mandamus or appealing this Order under the collateral order doctrine."

Mohawk filed a notice of appeal and a petition for a writ of mandamus to the Eleventh Circuit. The Court of Appeals dismissed the appeal for lack of jurisdiction under 28 U.S.C. §1291, holding that the District Court's ruling did not qualify as an immediately appealable collateral order within the meaning of *Cohen,* 337 U.S. 541. "Under *Cohen,*" the Court of Appeals explained, "an order is appealable if it (1) conclusively determines the disputed question; (2) resolves an important issue completely separate from the merits of the action; and (3) is effectively unreviewable on appeal from a final judgment." 541 F.3d 1048, 1052 (2008). According to the court, the District Court's waiver ruling satisfied the first two of these requirements but not the third, because "a discovery order that implicates the attorney-client privilege" can be adequately reviewed "on appeal from a final judgment." *Id.*

The Court of Appeals also rejected Mohawk's mandamus petition, finding no "clear usurpation of power or abuse of discretion" by the District Court. *Id.* at 1055. We granted certiorari to resolve a conflict among the Circuits concerning the availability of collateral appeals in the attorney-client privilege context.

II

A

By statute, Courts of Appeals "have jurisdiction of appeals from all final decisions of the district courts of the United States, . . . except where a direct review may be had in the Supreme Court." 28 U.S.C. §1291. A "final decisio[n]" is typically one "by which a district court disassociates itself from a case." *Swint v. Chambers Cty. Comm'n,* 514 U.S. 35, 42 (1995). This Court, however, "has long given" §1291 a "practical rather than a technical construction." *Cohen,* 337 U.S. at 546. As we held in *Cohen,* the statute encompasses not only judgments that "terminate an action," but also a "small class" of collateral rulings that, although they do not end the litigation, are appropriately deemed "final." *Id.* at 545-46. "That small category includes only decisions that are conclusive, that resolve important questions separate from the merits, and that are effectively unreviewable on appeal from the final judgment in the underlying action." *Swint,* 514 U.S. at 42.

In applying *Cohen's* collateral order doctrine, we have stressed that it must "never be allowed to swallow the general rule that a party is entitled to a single appeal, to be deferred until final judgment has been entered." *Digital Equip. Corp. v. Desktop Direct, Inc.,* 511 U.S. 863, 868 (1994). Our admonition reflects a healthy respect for the virtues of the final-judgment rule. Permitting piecemeal, prejudgment appeals, we have recognized, undermines "efficient judicial administration" and encroaches upon the prerogatives of district court judges, who play a "special role" in managing ongoing litigation. *Firestone Tire & Rubber Co. v. Risjord*, 449 U.S. 368, 374 (1981).

The justification for immediate appeal must therefore be sufficiently strong to overcome the usual benefits of deferring appeal until litigation concludes. This requirement finds expression in two of the three traditional *Cohen* conditions. The second condition insists upon "*important questions separate from the merits.*" *Swint*, 514 U.S. at 42 (emphasis added). More significantly, "the third *Cohen* question, whether a right is 'adequately vindicable' or 'effectively reviewable,' simply cannot be answered without a judgment about the value of the interests that would be lost through rigorous application of a final judgment requirement." *Digital Equip.*, 511 U.S. at 878-79. . . .

B

In the present case, the Court of Appeals concluded that the District Court's privilege-waiver order satisfied the first two conditions of the collateral order doctrine—conclusiveness and separateness—but not the third—effective unreviewability. Because we agree with the Court of Appeals that collateral order appeals are not necessary to ensure effective review of orders adverse to the attorney-client privilege, we do not decide whether the other *Cohen* requirements are met.

Mohawk does not dispute that "we have generally denied review of pretrial discovery orders." *Firestone*, 449 U.S. at 377. Mohawk contends, however, that rulings implicating the attorney-client privilege differ in kind from run-of-the-mill discovery

orders because of the important institutional interests at stake. According to Mohawk, the right to maintain attorney-client confidences—the *sine qua non* of a meaningful attorney-client relationship—is "irreparably destroyed absent immediate appeal" of adverse privilege rulings.

We readily acknowledge the importance of the attorney-client privilege [to encourage full and frank communication]. The crucial question, however, is not whether an interest is important in the abstract; it is whether deferring review until final judgment so imperils the interest as to justify the cost of allowing immediate appeal of the entire class of relevant orders. We routinely require litigants to wait until after final judgment to vindicate valuable rights, including rights central to our adversarial system. *See, e.g., Richardson-Merrell Inc. v. Koller*, 472 U.S. 424, 436 (1985) (holding an order disqualifying counsel in a civil case did not qualify for immediate appeal under the collateral order doctrine).

We reach a similar conclusion here. In our estimation, postjudgment appeals generally suffice to protect the rights of litigants and assure the vitality of the attorney-client privilege. Appellate courts can remedy the improper disclosure of privileged material in the same way they remedy a host of other erroneous evidentiary rulings: by vacating an adverse judgment and remanding for a new trial in which the protected material and its fruits are excluded from evidence.

Dismissing such relief as inadequate, Mohawk emphasizes that the attorney-client privilege does not merely "prohibi[t] use of protected information at trial"; it provides a "right not to disclose the privileged information in the first place." Mohawk is undoubtedly correct that an order to disclose privileged information intrudes on the confidentiality of attorney-client communications. But deferring review until final judgment does not meaningfully reduce the *ex ante* incentives for full and frank consultations between clients and counsel.

One reason for the lack of a discernible chill is that, in deciding how freely to speak, clients and counsel are unlikely to focus on the remote prospect of an erroneous disclosure order, let alone on the timing of a possible appeal. Whether or not immediate collateral order appeals are available, clients and counsel must account for the possibility that they will later be required by law to disclose their communications for a variety of reasons—for example, because they misjudged the scope of the privilege, because they waived the privilege, or because their communications fell within the privilege's crime-fraud exception. Most district court rulings on these matters involve the routine application of settled legal principles. They are unlikely to be reversed on appeal, particularly when they rest on factual determinations for which appellate deference is the norm. *See, e.g., Richardson-Merrell*, 472 U.S. at 434 ("Most pretrial orders of district judges are ultimately affirmed by appellate courts."); *Reise v. Board of Regents*, 957 F.2d 293, 295 (7th Cir. 1992) (noting that "almost all interlocutory appeals from discovery orders would end in affirmance" because "the district court possesses discretion, and review is deferential"). The breadth of the privilege and the narrowness of its exceptions will thus tend to exert a much greater influence on the conduct of clients and counsel than the small risk that the law will be misapplied.

Moreover, were attorneys and clients to reflect upon their appellate options, they would find that litigants confronted with a particularly injurious or novel privilege ruling have several potential avenues of review apart from collateral order appeal. First, a party may ask the district court to certify, and the court of appeals to accept, an interlocutory appeal pursuant to 28 U.S.C. §1292(b). The preconditions for §1292(b) review—"a controlling question of law," the prompt resolution of which "may materially advance the ultimate termination of the litigation"—are most likely to be satisfied when a privilege ruling involves a new legal question or is of special consequence, and district courts should not hesitate to certify an interlocutory appeal in such cases. Second, in extraordinary circumstances—*i.e.*, when a disclosure order "amount[s] to a judicial usurpation of power or a clear abuse of discretion," or otherwise works a manifest injustice—a party may petition the court of appeals for a writ of mandamus. *Cheney v. United States Dist. Court for D.C.*, 542 U.S. 367, 390 (2004). While these discretionary review mechanisms do not provide relief in every case, they serve as useful "safety valve[s]" for promptly correcting serious errors.

Another long-recognized option is for a party to defy a disclosure order and incur court-imposed sanctions. District courts have a range of sanctions from which to choose, including "directing that the matters embraced in the order or other designated facts be taken as established for purposes of the action," "prohibiting the disobedient party from supporting or opposing designated claims or defenses," or "striking pleadings in whole or in part." Fed. R. Civ. P. 37(b)(2)(i)-(iii). Such sanctions allow a party to obtain postjudgment review without having to reveal its privileged information. Alternatively, when the circumstances warrant it, a district court may hold a noncomplying party in contempt. The party can then appeal directly from that ruling, at least when the contempt citation can be characterized as a criminal punishment. *See, e.g., Church of*

Scientology of Cal. v. United States, 506 U.S. 9, 18, n.11 (1992).

These established mechanisms for appellate review not only provide assurances to clients and counsel about the security of their confidential communications; they also go a long way toward addressing Mohawk's concern that, absent collateral order appeals of adverse attorney-client privilege rulings, some litigants may experience severe hardship. Mohawk is no doubt right that an order to disclose privileged material may, in some situations, have implications beyond the case at hand. But the same can be said about many categories of pretrial discovery orders for which collateral order appeals are unavailable. . . . Section 1292(b) appeals, mandamus, and appeals from contempt citations facilitate immediate review of some of the more consequential attorney-client privilege rulings. . . .

In short, the limited benefits of applying "the blunt, categorical instrument of §1291 collateral order appeal" to privilege-related disclosure orders simply cannot justify the likely institutional costs. *Id.* at 883. Permitting parties to undertake successive, piecemeal appeals of all adverse attorney-client rulings would unduly delay the resolution of district court litigation and needlessly burden the Courts of Appeals. . . . Were this Court to approve collateral order appeals in the attorney-client privilege context, many more litigants would likely choose that route. They would also likely seek to extend such a ruling to disclosure orders implicating many other categories of sensitive information, raising an array of line-drawing difficulties.

C

In concluding that sufficiently effective review of adverse attorney-client privilege rulings can be had without resort to the *Cohen* doctrine, we reiterate that the class of collaterally appealable orders must remain "narrow and selective in its membership." *Will v. Hallock*, 546 U.S. 345, 350 (2006). This admonition has acquired special force in recent years with the enactment of legislation designating rulemaking, "not expansion by court decision," as the preferred means for determining whether and when prejudgment orders should be immediately appealable. *Swint*, 514 U.S. at 48. Specifically, Congress in 1990 amended the Rules Enabling Act, 28 U.S.C. §2071 *et seq.*, to authorize this Court to adopt rules [defining when a decision is final for purposes of appeal, and creating exceptions that permit interlocutory appeals]. These provisions, we have recognized, "warran[t] the Judiciary's full respect." *Swint*, 514 U.S. at 48. . . .

* * *

In sum, we conclude that the collateral order doctrine does not extend to disclosure orders adverse to the attorney-client privilege. Effective appellate review can be had by other means. Accordingly, we affirm the judgment of the Court of Appeals for the Eleventh Circuit.

THOMAS, J., concurring in part and concurring in the judgment.

I concur in the judgment and in Part II-C of the Court's opinion because I wholeheartedly agree that "Congress's designation of the rulemaking process as the way to define or refine when a district court ruling is 'final' and when an interlocutory order is appealable warrants the Judiciary's full respect." *Swint v. Chambers Cty. Comm'n*, 514 U.S. 35, 48 (1995). It is for that reason that I do not join the remainder of the Court's analysis.

The scope of federal appellate jurisdiction is a matter the Constitution expressly commits to Congress, *see* Art. I, §8, cl. 9, and that Congress has addressed not only in 28 U.S.C. §§1291 and 1292, but also in the Rules Enabling Act amendments to which the Court refers. The Court recognizes that these amendments "designat[e] rulemaking, not expansion by court decision, as the preferred means of determining whether and when prejudgment orders should be immediately appealable." Because that designation is entitled to our full respect, and because the privilege order here is not on all fours with orders we previously have held to be appealable under the collateral order doctrine, *see Cohen v. Beneficial Indus. Loan Corp.*, 337 U.S. 541 (1949), I would affirm the Eleventh Circuit's judgment on the ground that any "avenue for immediate appeal" beyond the three avenues addressed in the Court's opinion must be left to the "rulemaking process." . . .

Notes & Questions

1. Mohawk wished to appeal a decision from the Northern District of Georgia, and thus sought review in the U.S. Court of Appeals for the Eleventh Circuit. What, exactly, was the decision that Mohawk sought to appeal? Why wasn't this decision appealable under a standard application of 28 U.S.C. §1291?

2. Mohawk's lawyers attempted to obtain Eleventh Circuit review of this district court decision in three different ways. What were the three ways in which Mohawk attempted to obtain review notwithstanding the final judgment rule? Of the six exceptions, extensions, and workarounds discussed in this chapter, you should see that three of them were clearly inapplicable but three were at least worth a shot for Mohawk.

3. Why is the collateral order doctrine better understood not as an exception to the requirement of a final decision, but rather as an alternative definition of finality?

4. The Supreme Court in *Mohawk* recites the required elements of the collateral order doctrine. For the doctrine to apply, the decision must (1) conclusively determine the disputed question, (2) resolve an important issue completely separate from the merits of the action, and (3) be effectively unreviewable on appeal from a final judgment. What is the strongest argument for Mohawk that the district court's order granting the motion to compel is an appealable decision under the collateral order doctrine? Why did the Supreme Court ultimately reject this argument?

5. The district court in *Mohawk* declined to certify the issue for appeal under section 1292(b). Why was this case a poor fit for a section 1292(b) certified interlocutory appeal?

6. The court of appeals in *Mohawk* rejected the petition for a writ of mandamus. Why?

7. Perhaps a hypothetical example will help to bring the collateral order doctrine into even clearer focus. Suppose a judge orders a party to submit to a blood test in discovery. The party objects that the court erroneously treated it as a Rule 34 request for inspection and thus failed to make any finding of good cause as required in Rule 35 for physical exams, and that the court failed to take into account the party's frail condition which makes it dangerous for her to give a blood sample. May the party appeal the court's decision? The order is interlocutory. But imagine telling this litigant that she can appeal the order after the case has reached a final judgment. She might say: "How sweet that you'll let me appeal *later*, but right *now* I don't want my health endangered, I don't want to get poked with that needle. What's the appellate court going to do later—*unpoke* me?" Note how her argument would invoke the three elements of the collateral order doctrine. First, the court's order conclusively determined whether the party must provide the blood sample. Second, the party's right not to be involuntarily subjected to a blood test without a showing of good cause (a legal question for the court to resolve) is separate from the merits of the lawsuit. Third, the decision is effectively unreviewable on appeal because by then the party already will have submitted to the blood test. Whether a court ultimately would accept the application of the collateral order doctrine to allow interlocutory appeal in this case might depend on whether the court considered the blood test a significant enough intrusion to justify special treatment for purposes of appealability.

8. One important application of the collateral order doctrine is to the issue of sovereign immunity. As we explained in Chapter 4 in connection with *Darden v. City of Fort Worth*, police officers and other government officials have qualified immunity that shields them unless they violated a clearly established right. Courts have held that such immunity not only protects officials from being held *liable*, it also protects officials from the burdens of *trial*. Suppose a civil rights defendant moves for summary judgment based on qualified immunity and the court denies the motion. The defendant would like to appeal the court's rejection of the immunity defense, but the denial of summary judgment constitutes an interlocutory order, not a final judgment. Using the collateral order doctrine, the defendant would argue that his immunity from trial exists apart from his immunity from liability, and that this right is effectively unreviewable after final judgment because he would already have been forced to endure the trial process. *See Mitchell v. Forsyth*, 472 U.S. 511, 524-530 (1985).

   Recall from Chapter 2 that in *Ashcroft v. Iqbal*, 556 U.S. 662 (2009), the district court had *denied* Ashcroft's and Mueller's motion to dismiss under Rule 12(b)(6). That decision was interlocutory. So how did it get appealed? The collateral order doctrine. *Iqbal*, 556 U.S. at 669 ("Invoking the collateral-order doctrine petitioners [Ashcroft and Mueller, who asserted the defense of qualified immunity,] filed an interlocutory appeal in the United States Court of Appeals for the Second Circuit.").

9. In *Mohawk*, both Justice Sotomayor and Justice Thomas mention the difference between the rule-making process and judge-made law through court decisions. To understand this point, consider the sources of law that govern appealability. In general, federal court jurisdiction—including appellate jurisdiction—is governed by statutes. The final judgment rule of section 1291 and its two most fundamental exceptions—injunctions under 28 U.S.C. §1292(a) and certified interlocutory appeals under 28 U.S.C. §1292(b)—are statutory. Jurisdiction traditionally was off limits as a topic for Federal Rules of Civil Procedure. *See* Fed. R. Civ. P. 82 ("These rules do not extend or limit the jurisdiction of the district courts or the venue of actions in those courts."). However, in 1990, Congress amended the Rules Enabling Act to say that when the Supreme Court makes rules of procedure pursuant to the rule-making process, "[s]uch rules may define when a ruling of a district court is final for purposes of appeal under section 1291 of this title." 28 U.S.C. §2072(c). Two years later, Congress amended the interlocutory appeals statute to specify that "[t]he Supreme Court may prescribe rules, in accordance with section 2072 of this title, to provide for an appeal of an interlocutory decision in the courts of appeals that is not otherwise provided for. . . ." 28 U.S.C. §1292(e). In combination, these statutes give the Supreme Court the power, through the rule-making process, to alter the scope of the final judgment rule and to create rules for interlocutory appeals. Thus, appealability has become a subject for rule making pursuant to the Rules Enabling Act process. A prime example is the Rule 23(f) provision for appealing class certification decisions. The collateral order doctrine, by contrast, is neither statutory nor rule-based. It was developed by courts as a judicial gloss on the final judgment rule. In *Mohawk*, both the majority and the concurrence saw the judge-made aspect of the collateral order doctrine—and the availability of the rule-making process to address questions of appealability—as an important reason not to expand the collateral order doctrine by judicial fiat.

(3) *What* May Be Appealed: Reviewability

Not every trial court error may be raised on appeal, and not every raised error leads to reversal. Even if an appellant has standing to appeal, even if the appeal is from a final judgment (or fits into an exception to the final judgment rule), even if the appellant is correct that the trial judge made an error, that does not necessarily mean the appeals court will reverse the trial court decision. To warrant appellate attention the error must be *reviewable*, and to warrant reversal the error must not have been *harmless*.

(a) Waiver

In Chapter 2, we highlighted waiver as an issue that deserves lawyers' attention. In the context of the pleadings chapter, we were talking mostly about waiver of defenses under Rules 12(g) and 12(h), as well as waiver of affirmative defenses under Rule 8(c). For example, under Rule 12(h)(1), a defendant waives the defenses of personal jurisdiction and venue unless the defendant raises them at the outset of the case. Naturally, this sort of waiver persists into the appeals process. If a defendant fails to raise its objection to personal jurisdiction or venue on a timely basis, then the defendant cannot raise those issues on appeal or otherwise. *But waiver on appeal goes much further.* Think of nearly any decision a trial judge might make during the pretrial or trial process—setting a discovery cutoff date, bifurcating the trial, admitting or excluding certain evidence, instructing the jury. If a party believes the judge got it wrong, but fails to raise that objection in the trial court, then the appeals court will refuse to hear about it.

Indeed, as a general matter, a party may not raise an issue on appeal unless the party raised that issue at the trial court level. If a trial lawyer has objections to the trial judge's decisions, the lawyer should point out those concerns promptly. For example, if a lawyer objects to the admission of a certain piece of evidence, the lawyer must state the objection. If the lawyer waits until after the trial judge has completed her work, and then on appeal accuses the trial judge of having made various errors, the trial judge is deprived of the opportunity to correct the problems. Also, if a lawyer believes his client will probably lose at trial, and the trial judge makes an erroneous decision along the way, the lawyer should not be allowed to keep that error in his pocket to obtain reversal on appeal rather than objecting to the error at the trial court level. Therefore, if an appellant seeks to raise issues on appeal that were not raised in the trial court, the appellate court ordinarily will refuse to hear those arguments on the ground that the issues were waived.

Courts allow certain exceptions to the general rule that issues are waived if not raised below. Some courts permit parties to raise arguments on appeal if the arguments stem from a change in the law that occurred after the judgment. Also, if the trial court mistake was *plain error*, appellate courts may permit a party to raise the point on appeal even if it was not raised explicitly in the trial court. The Federal Rules of Civil Procedure mention "plain error" only once—in the rule on jury instructions. Under Rule 51(d), if parties wish to raise arguments on appeal concerning errors in the jury instructions, they ordinarily must have made timely objections, but even if the party did not properly preserve the issue by objecting, a court "may consider a plain error in the instructions . . . if the error affects substantial rights."

STRATEGY SESSION

Remember that effective litigators think several moves ahead. Because of the doctrine of waiver, skilled trial lawyers never lose sight of the possibility that they will need to raise issues on appeal, and they are careful to preserve errors for appeal by making the proper objections during the pretrial and trial process. When a trial court makes a decision adverse to your client and you believe the court erred, you should object for two different reasons: first, to persuade the trial judge to change course, and second, to preserve the issue for appeal in case your effort to persuade the trial judge fails. This explains why trial lawyers sometimes make what appear to be futile motions or objections during pretrial or trial. Even if the trial judge has made it clear that she will reject the lawyer's argument, the lawyer hopes for a better result on appeal and must raise the objection to avoid waiving it.

(b) Harmless Error

Causation matters. In torts, if a driver behaves negligently but does not hurt anyone, no private plaintiff has a claim against the driver. The same holds true in procedural law. If a trial judge makes an error but the error causes no harm, then an appellate court will not reverse the judgment. It is *harmless error*.

Suppose in a case for money damages the trial court, over the plaintiff's objection, instructed the jury incorrectly on how to calculate the amount of damages. The jury then reached a verdict for the defendant finding no liability, and the court entered judgment accordingly. If the plaintiff were to appeal, the plaintiff would meet the requirement of adversity (the trial court entered judgment for the defendant), appealability (it was a final judgment), and reviewability at least in the sense of non-waiver (plaintiff objected to the court's instruction). But as a basis for reversal, the plaintiff's argument about the trial court's erroneous instruction would fall flat. On the question of whether the defendant was liable at all to the plaintiff, the court's error about how to calculate damages is beside the point.

The harmless error doctrine is not absolute. Despite the general principle that errors should lead to reversal only if they may have altered the outcome, some errors impinge on rights that are too fundamental to yield to the harmless error doctrine. One appeals court, for example, held that a trial court's erroneous failure to strike a juror for cause must lead to reversal, even if exclusion would have made no difference. As that court put it, "[d]enial of the right to an unbiased tribunal is one of those trial errors that is not excused by being shown to have been harmless." *Thompson v. Altheimer & Gray*, 248 F.3d 621 (7th Cir. 2003).

C. STANDARDS OF REVIEW

To get reversed, how wrong must the trial court be? Some errors are more egregious than others. Suppose a decision was a close call, but the appellate court happens to disagree with the trial court—should the appellate court reverse the trial court's decision? That depends on how much deference the appellate court gives to the trial judge's decisions. In other words, it depends on what *standard of review* the appeals court applies. In the following case, note the court's decisions about whether each issue on appeal is a question of law or a question of fact, and how this affects the standard of review.

HUSAIN v. OLYMPIC AIRWAYS

316 F.3d 829 (9th Cir. 2002), *aff'd*, 540 U.S. 644 (2004)

MOLLOY, District Judge.*

I. INTRODUCTION

After a non-jury trial, the district court determined that Dr. Abid M. Hanson's death on Olympic Airways ("Olympic") Flight 417 was caused by an accident as defined by Article 17 of the Warsaw Convention. The trial judge also found the accident resulted from willful misconduct by Olympic's employees. The district court awarded $1,400,000 in damages. Olympic appeals the determinations of the district court and the award of damages. We hold that the district court's findings are not clearly erroneous and we AFFIRM.

II. FACTUAL AND PROCEDURAL BACKGROUND
A. OVERVIEW

On January 4, 1998, 52 year-old Dr. Abid M. Hanson died while a passenger on Olympic Flight 417 between Athens, Greece and New York City. His death occurred after he suffered complications when he was exposed to ambient second-hand smoke while seated in the airplane's non-smoking section three rows in front of the smoking section. The plane had clearly demarcated sections for seating, one for smokers and one for non-smokers, though no partition separated the two. Dr. Hanson's wife, Rubina Husain, had asked Olympic's employees on multiple occasions with increasing urgency to move Dr. Hanson to

another seat away from the smoking section. She explained the critical reasons Dr. Hanson had to move and made her concerns known about the consequences of leaving him exposed to the offensive smoke. Ms. Husain's requests were ignored, primarily by flight attendant Maria Leptourgou. Dr. Hanson died from a severe asthma attack caused by the smoke exposure.

Plaintiffs filed suit in California Superior Court for Alameda County on December 24, 1998. Olympic removed the action to the United States District Court for the Northern District of California on March 23, 1999. On February 25, 2000, Olympic moved for summary judgment claiming Dr. Hanson's death was not caused by an accident as defined by Article 17 of the Warsaw Convention. The district court denied the motion for summary judgment without a written opinion on March 24, 2000. A three-day bench trial was held May 30 through June 1, 2000. After the parties presented evidence, the district court asked for post-trial briefs and agreed to hear closing arguments on July 20, 2000. Findings of fact and conclusions of law were entered on August 8, 2000 finding Ms. Leptourgou's failure to move Dr. Hanson to a new seat was an accident under Article 17 of the Warsaw Convention and proximately caused his death. The trial judge found Ms. Leptourgou's refusal to help Dr. Hanson constituted willful misconduct under Article 25 of the Warsaw Convention.

The district court awarded Plaintiffs $1,400,000, but reduced the award by 50% due to Dr. Hanson's comparative negligence. On October 2, 2000, the district court issued amended findings of fact and conclusions of law. Supplemental findings of fact and conclusions of law were issued on

---

*The Honorable Donald W. Molloy, United States District Judge for the District of Montana, sitting by designation.

November 28, 2000 awarding Plaintiffs an additional $700,000 in non-pecuniary damages. Final judgment was entered on November 28, 2000. Olympic timely appealed.

B. FACTS AS DETERMINED BY THE DISTRICT COURT

[Dr. Hanson had asthma and was sensitive to secondhand smoke. He also had food allergies. Before his death, Dr. Hanson had suffered two medical emergencies, both involving breathing difficulties, that may have been caused by either asthma or food allergies. After the first emergency, Dr. Hanson began carrying epinephrine. Dr. Hanson, Ms. Husain and their family flew to Athens and Cairo for a vacation. During a stop in New York, Dr. Hanson learned for the first time that Olympic allowed smoking on international flights. Dr. Hanson and his family asked to be seated in the non-smoking section and their request was honored.]

On January 4, 1998, Dr. Hanson and his family began the return trip from Cairo to the United States via Athens.... Upon boarding Olympic Airways Flight 417 from Athens to New York, Dr. Hanson and his family discovered that they were seated in non-smoking seats, but only three rows ahead of the smoking section which was not partitioned off. Immediately after finding their seats, Ms. Husain approached flight attendant Maria Leptourgou, informed her that Dr. Hanson could not be near the smoking section, and asked Ms. Leptourgou to move him. Ms. Leptourgou responded by telling Ms. Husain to "have a seat."

After all of the passengers were seated, but before take-off, Ms. Husain once again approached Ms. Leptourgou and adamantly asked that she move Dr. Hanson to another seat, explaining that he was allergic to smoke. Ms. Leptourgou refused, stating that she was "too busy" and the flight was "totally full." [The court notes in a footnote that, despite Leptourgou's statements, Flight 417 was not full.]

Immediately after take-off, passengers in the smoking area were allowed to begin smoking.... After Dr. Hanson indicated that the smoke was bothering him, Ms. Husain approached Ms. Leptourgou and, for the third time on the airplane, told her that she needed to move Dr. Hanson for health reasons. Ms. Leptourgou again refused stating that the plane was full. She did tell Ms. Husain that she and Dr. Hanson could ask other passengers to switch seats, but they would not be assisted by the flight crew. Despite one last plea for help by Ms. Husain, Ms. Leptourgou refused to help Dr. Hanson find another seat.

The amount of smoke floating around row 48 only increased as the flight progressed, especially after a meal was served. While Dr. Hanson ordered a meal, he did not eat much, and shared his meal with his daughter and another passenger. After the meal, Dr. Hanson's breathing problems worsened. He had emptied one inhaler and asked Ms. Husain to get another one. After telling his daughter that the smoke was bothering him, he walked to the front of the cabin to get some fresh air. [Dr. Hanson became weaker and collapsed, received shots of epinephrine, and was given CPR and oxygen, but despite the best efforts of family friend Dr. Umesh Sabharwal and other passengers, Dr. Hanson died.]

Because of religious reasons, there was no autopsy to determine the direct cause of death. In the district court and here, Plaintiffs argued that Dr. Hanson died from a severe asthma attack caused by inhaling secondhand smoke. Defendants believe that Dr. Hanson's death was the result of an allergic reaction to food or some other medical problem unrelated to the smoke.

The district court determined that the smoke exposure during Flight 417 was the primary cause of Dr. Hanson's death. We abide by and defer to those findings.

Of major significance to the district court was the timing of the events. First, Dr. Hanson was complaining about the secondhand smoke before the meal was served. Second, while Dr. Hanson had some food allergies and he did eat some food on the flight, there was no evidence that he ate any foods to which he was allergic. Third, experts for both parties and Dr. Sabharwal testified that smoke was a contributing factor, though the degree to which it contributed was disputed. Nonetheless, it is for the district court to resolve the factual disputes and to draw inferences from the proof.

III. ANALYSIS
A. STANDARD OF REVIEW

A district court's findings of fact are reviewed for clear error. Clear error review is deferential to the district court, requiring a "definite and firm conviction that a mistake has been made." *See Easley v. Cromartie*, 532 U.S. 234, 242 (2001). Thus, if the district court's findings are plausible in light of the record viewed in its entirety, the appellate court cannot reverse even if it is convinced it would have found differently.

A district court's conclusions of law are reviewed de novo. However, if the application of the law to the facts requires an inquiry that is "essentially factual," review is for clear error. *Koirala v. Thai Airways Int'l, Ltd.*, 126 F.3d 1205, 1210 (9th Cir. 1997). A district court's determination of proximate cause is reviewed for clear error. *Tahoe-Sierra Pres. Council, Inc. v. Tahoe Reg. Planning Agency*, 216 F.3d 764, 783 (9th Cir. 2000), *aff'd*, 535 U.S. 302 (2002). Likewise, a district court's finding of "willful misconduct" under Article 25 of the Warsaw Convention is reviewed for clear error.

B. DR. HANSON'S DEATH WAS PROXIMATELY CAUSED BY AN "ACCIDENT" UNDER ARTICLE 17 OF THE WARSAW CONVENTION
(1) ARTICLE 17 "ACCIDENT"

Liability for harm to international air travelers is established by Article 17 of the Warsaw Convention. Article 17 provides [in relevant part] that "[t]he carrier shall be liable for damage sustained in the event of death . . . [of] a passenger . . . if the accident which caused the damage so sustained on board the aircraft. . . ." Warsaw Conv. art. 17.

For a carrier to be liable to an injured passenger, the passenger must prove an accident caused the injury. *Air France v. Saks*, 470 U.S. 392, 396 (1985). As defined by the Supreme Court, an accident is "an unexpected or unusual event or happening that is external to the passenger." *Id.* at 405.

When determining whether an accident has occurred, the definition of accident "should be flexibly applied after assessment of all the circumstances surrounding a passenger's injuries." *Id.* Where there is contradictory evidence, "it is for the trier of fact to decide whether an 'accident' . . . caused the passenger's injury." *Id.* If the passenger's injury "indisputably results from the passenger's own internal reaction to the usual, normal, and expected operation of the aircraft," it is not the result of an accident as envisioned under Article 17. *Id.* at 406.

The district court found Ms. Leptourgou's refusal to move Dr. Hanson to another seat, despite three increasingly desperate requests by Ms. Husain, was an accident under Article 17. It did so because

Ms. Leptourgou (1) violated the recognized standard of care for flight attendants on international flights by refusing to assist; (2) violated Olympic's policy; and (3) failed to alert the chief cabin attendant or another flight attendant to help Dr. Hanson find another seat. The district court found that Ms. Husain specifically told Olympic workers, including Ms. Leptourgou, that Dr. Hanson was "susceptible to smoke," "allergic to smoke," and "could not be in any smoke." Despite these warnings, Ms. Leptourgou refused to assist Dr. Hanson. Considering the warnings and knowledge of the doctor's medical problems, Ms. Leptourgou's actions constituted an unusual or unexpected event. Ultimately, the district court concluded that Ms. Leptourgou's actions created a foreseeable risk of injury and therefore constituted an accident under Article 17.

Olympic argues Dr. Hanson's death resulted from "internal reactions to the usual, normal, and expected operation of the aircraft" and therefore cannot have resulted from an accident. A predicate of the argument is that the presence of ambient smoke in the cabin is "an expected and normal aspect of international air travel." Consequently, Olympic argues it had no duty to move Dr. Hanson. Olympic further contends that Dr. Hanson's pre-existing allergies, not his exposure to ambient secondhand smoke, led to his death.

Plaintiffs in essence contend that a flight attendant who does nothing to deal with a known risk to a passenger's health-related travel problems is negligent. Because Ms. Leptourgou's conduct was negligent, it fits the definition of accident under Article 17. Plaintiffs argue that crew negligence is external to the passenger and is not a reasonably expected part of international travel. . . .

The district court found, after examining evidence establishing industry standards and Olympic's policies regarding passengers with medical needs, that this failure to act was a "blatant disregard of industry standards and airline policies." *Husain*, 116 F. Supp. 2d 1121, 1134 (N.D. Cal. 2000). Ms. Leptourgou's failure to act was more egregious in light of the simple nature of Ms. Husain's request, which could easily have been satisfied without interference with the airplane's normal operation. Combined, these factors bring Ms. Leptourgou's failure to assist Dr. Hanson within the meaning of an "accident" for Article 17 purposes. Her conduct was clearly external to Dr. Hanson, and it was unexpected and unusual in light of industry standards, Olympic policy, and the simple nature of Dr. Hanson's requested accommodation. The failure to act in the face of a known, serious risk satisfies the meaning of "accident" within Article 17 so long as reasonable alternatives exist that would substantially minimize the risk and implementing these alternatives would not unreasonably interfere with the normal, expected operation of the airplane.

Because the district court's conclusion that Ms. Leptourgou's failure to help Dr. Hanson constituted an unexpected or unusual event is inextricably intertwined with the facts in this case, it is reviewed for clear error. Based on the record before the district court, we cannot conclude that it clearly erred.

(2) ACCIDENT AS PROXIMATE CAUSE OF DR. HANSON'S DEATH

For a carrier to be liable to a passenger for an injury, the passenger must prove the accident caused the injury. "Any injury is the product of a chain of causes" and the passenger need only prove "some link in the chain was an unusual or unexpected event external to the passenger." *Saks*, 470 U.S. at 406. . . .

In its findings of fact, the district court rejected the assertion that Dr. Hanson died as a result of food-related anaphylaxis. Rather, the district court found Dr. Hanson died as a result of exposure to secondhand smoke. . . .

Further, the district court considered Dr. Hanson's previous reactions to food and the food served on the plane, yet found Dr. Hanson was suffering breathing difficulties before the meal on the airplane was served and that there was not any testimony that Dr. Hanson ate any of the foods he was allergic to while on Flight 417.

As discussed above, it is apparent that the failure to move Dr. Hanson caused exposure to the smoke that led to his death. There was testimony at trial that the smoke around Dr. Hanson was particularly thick. Olympic personnel were aware of Dr. Hanson's condition, yet they did nothing to assist him. Under *Saks*, the accident need not be the sole cause of the injury, but it must be a "link in the chain." 470 U.S. at 406. In this case, the exposure to smoke and failure to move Dr. Hanson is such a link. The facts as determined by the district court, and confirmed by the record, establish that seats were available and that Ms. Leptourgou's failure to help Dr. Hanson resulted in continued exposure to second hand smoke. The district court concluded that had Ms. Leptourgou heeded Ms. Husain's requests for help, Dr. Hanson would not have been exposed to second hand smoke and would not have died. In other words, the minimization of the risk of smoke exposure would have prevented the physiological response that caused his death.

Whether Dr. Hanson's death was caused by a reaction to second hand smoke resulting from Ms. Leptourgou's failure to assist or by a reaction to food allergies may appear to be a close call. However, the district court, as the trier of fact, was in the best position to determine which of two plausible explanations was correct. The district court's determination here is plausible in light of the record before the district court, thus is not clearly erroneous, and will not be disturbed on appeal.

C. DR. HANSON'S DEATH WAS PROXIMATELY CAUSED BY OLYMPIC'S "WILLFUL MISCONDUCT" UNDER ARTICLE 25 OF THE WARSAW CONVENTION

[Carrier liability for injuries is usually limited to $75,000 per passenger, but Article 25 sets aside the limit for injuries that result from willful misconduct.] Willful misconduct has been defined as "the intentional performance of an act with knowledge that the . . . act will probably result in injury or damage or the intentional performance of an act in such a manner as to imply reckless disregard of the probable consequences." *Koirala*, 126 F.3d at 1209. . . .

Ms. Leptourgou's failure to take action, either by moving Dr. Hanson or by notifying the chief cabin attendant of Ms. Husain's request to have her husband moved, was willful misconduct. The district court concluded "Ms. Leptourgou *must have known* that the cabin was not full, that Dr. Hanson had a medical problem and a special susceptibility to smoke, and that her failure to move him would aggravate his condition and cause him probable injury." *Husain*, 116 F. Supp. 2d at 1139. This conclusion is supported by the record in this case, including the highly credible testimony of Ms. Husain. Additionally, because Ms. Leptourgou did not testify in person or by deposition, Ms. Husain's version of events was uncontradicted.

Of equal import was testimony by Plaintiffs' expert that Ms. Leptourgou was aware of the industry standard of care and Olympic policy regarding passengers requesting seat transfers for medical reasons. This established that Ms. Leptourgou should have assisted Dr. Hanson in finding a new seat, especially since there were available seats further away from the smoking section. Ms. Leptourgou's duty to act was compounded by the urgency of Ms. Husain's requests . . . .

[Further,] as the district court determined, Ms. Husain "was not merely a typical passenger complaining about an inconvenient seat assignment," because her repeated requests became increasingly "emphatic and desperate." *Id.* Based on Ms. Husain's testimony, the district court found Ms. Leptourgou could not have "failed to recognize that Dr. Hanson's problem was a medical one and that sitting near the smoking section was likely to cause him injury." *Id.* Despite this, Ms. Leptourgou "deliberately closed her eyes to the probable consequences of her acts." *Id.*

The district court, as the trier of fact in this matter, was in a superior position to appraise and weigh the evidence, and its determination regarding the credibility of witnesses is entitled to special deference. *See Anderson v. City of Bessemer*, 470 U.S. 564, 573-75 (1985). The district court's decision was based on the testimony of Ms. Husain, Plaintiffs' expert, and Olympic's own employees, and is well-grounded in the record. While establishment of willful misconduct requires a party to satisfy a high burden, the evidence before the district court in this case is sufficient to meet that burden. The facts in the record establish that Ms. Leptourgou was aware that Dr. Hanson was in a desperate situation that required immediate assistance, yet despite this knowledge and increasingly emphatic pleas from Ms. Husain, Ms. Leptourgou ignored Olympic's policy and industry standards and refused to assist Dr. Hanson. This amounts to a dereliction of duty that is not only unusual and unexpected on an international flight, but willful.

The district court's conclusion that Ms. Leptourgou's actions were willful misconduct cannot be disturbed on review unless we are left with a "definite and firm conviction that a mistake has been made." *Security Farms v. Int'l Bhd. of Teamsters*, 124 F.3d 999, 1014 (9th Cir. 1997). Based on facts in the record and the exhaustive findings by the district court, we cannot conclude that a mistake has been made.

IV. CONCLUSION

We decide that the district court's findings and conclusions are well-grounded in the record. Olympic's argument asks this Court to substitute its judgment and second guess the district court. This we cannot do. Olympic failed to meet its burden of showing that the district court's findings are clearly erroneous and that the district court erred in its application of the law. Therefore, we affirm the judgment of the district court.

Notes & Questions

1. ***De novo review.*** In *Husain*, the Ninth Circuit states, "A district court's conclusions of law are reviewed de novo." Consider the reasons for this. The primary function of appellate courts is to review the legal decisions of the trial court to ensure that the law was properly interpreted and applied. Appellate courts are charged with greater authority to decide and develop the law; they have more expertise in legal decision making; they have more time to consider the briefs and to write careful opinions; and, because they have authority over multiple trial courts, they can ensure greater uniformity in legal application. Therefore, on questions of law, appellate courts give zero deference to the trial judge's decisions. Rather, appellate courts review a trial court's legal rulings de novo, which means that the appellate judges take a fresh look at each legal issue that has been raised and decide it for themselves. Suppose the appellate judges think that a legal issue in the case was very close, but they decide—just barely—that the trial judge decided it the wrong way. Under the de novo standard of review, the appellate court applies its own interpretation of the law rather than defer to the trial judge's interpretation.

2. ***Clear error review.*** Facts are a different story. With regard to factual findings in a specific case, we do not worry about uniformity across different courts. Nor do we assume that appellate judges have greater expertise than trial judges at figuring out the facts. To the contrary, trial judges gain experience at hearing factual evidence, while appellate judges spend more time reading briefs and analyzing legal nuances. And in any specific case, the trial judge—not the appellate judges—actually heard the witnesses. Thus, as the Ninth Circuit states in *Husain*, when trial judges make findings of fact, appellate courts defer to those findings unless they are clearly erroneous. In bench trials, Rule 52 requires the district court to state the court's findings of fact and conclusions of law, and it goes on to declare the standard of review: "Findings of fact, whether based on oral or other evidence, must not be set aside unless clearly erroneous, and the reviewing court must give due regard to the trial court's opportunity to judge the witnesses' credibility." The Supreme Court has explained that "clearly erroneous" means that even if some evidence supports the lower court's finding, the reviewing court based on the entirety of the record is left with the definite and firm conviction that a mistake has been committed. *United States v. United States Gypsum Co.*, 333 U.S. 364, 395 (1948). The idea is not for the appellate court to substitute its judgment for that of the trial court (in sharp contrast to the de novo review applied to legal rulings), but rather for the appellate court to step in to correct errors only when the trial court clearly got it wrong.

3. In *Husain*, on the issue of whether the airline's refusal to move Dr. Hanson's seat was an "accident" within the meaning of Article 17 of the Warsaw Convention, what is the argument that this is a question of law, and therefore that the court of appeals should have reviewed the district court's decision de novo? What is

the argument that this is a question of fact, and therefore that the court of appeals should have reviewed the district court's decision on a clear error standard? Which argument is more compelling? That is, if the court of appeals believed that the employee's refusal to move Dr. Hanson's seat probably should not be considered an accident within the meaning of Article 17, but did not think the district judge's finding to the contrary was clearly erroneous, which way should the appellate court have decided? As you consider this question, be careful not merely to apply your own notion of the definition of "law" and "fact" (which will not get you very far on a mixed question like this one), but rather to think about the reasons why legal decisions are reviewed de novo and factual decisions are reviewed on a clearly erroneous standard.

The Supreme Court has described "mixed questions of law and fact" as those that ask whether "the historical facts . . . satisfy the statutory standard, or to put it another way, whether the rule of law as applied to the established facts is or is not violated." *Pullman-Standard v. Swint*, 456 U.S. 273, 289 n.19 (1982). To help unpack that, consider the following example: In *U.S. Bank Nat'l Ass'n v. Village at Lakeridge, LLC*, 138 S. Ct. 960 (2018), the Supreme Court considered whether a bankruptcy court's finding that a particular person was an "insider" of a debtor should be treated as a question of law or a question of fact for purposes of Rule 52's clearly erroneous standard. The Court identified it as a mixed question and asked, "What is the nature of the mixed question here and which kind of court (bankruptcy or appellate) is better suited to resolve it?" *Id.* at 966. Noting that some mixed questions "require courts to expound on the law," while others "immerse courts in case-specific factual issue," *id.* at 967, the Court held that the standard of review for a mixed question depends "on whether answering it entails primarily legal or factual work." *Id.* Ultimately, the Court decided that the issue of insider status in the case was more factual than legal, so it was subject to review for clear error. *Id.* at 968-69.

4. On the issue of whether the airline's refusal to move Dr. Hanson was a proximate cause of his death, ask yourself the same questions we posed in Note 3. That is, if the court of appeals believed that probably Dr. Hanson died from a food allergy rather than from secondhand smoke, but did not think the district judge's finding to the contrary was clearly erroneous, which way should the appellate court have decided? Again, think about it in terms of the reasons for the different standards of review.

5. Finally, on the issue of whether the airline's refusal to move Dr. Hanson was "willful misconduct" within the meaning of Article 25 of the Warsaw Convention, same questions as in Note 3.

6. After the Ninth Circuit's decision, Olympic Airways sought review in the Supreme Court. The Court granted certiorari on the question of whether the airline's conduct constituted an "accident" under the Warsaw Convention. *Olympic Airways v. Husain*, 540 U.S. 644, 646 (2004). The Supreme Court stated, "The issue we must decide is whether the 'accident' condition precedent to air carrier

liability under Article 17 is satisfied when the carrier's unusual and unexpected refusal to assist a passenger is a link in a chain of causation resulting in a passenger's pre-existing medical condition being aggravated by exposure to a normal condition in the aircraft cabin. We conclude that it is." The Supreme Court recited the facts based on "the District Court's findings, which, being unchallenged by either party, we accept as true." After reciting the facts and procedural history, the Court began its analysis with the language of the Warsaw Convention. It next examined in detail the precedent of *Air France v. Saks*, 470 U.S. 392 (1985), and finally considered the logic of action versus inaction and whether inaction can ever be considered an accident under the Warsaw Convention. "For the foregoing reasons," the Court said, "we conclude that the conduct here constitutes an 'accident' under Article 17 of the Warsaw Convention." *Olympic Airways*, 540 U.S. at 657. The opinion does not mention the standard of review. But based on how the Supreme Court addressed the issue of whether the airline's conduct constituted an accident, does it seem that the Supreme Court treated it as an issue of fact or as an issue of law?

7. ***Abuse of discretion review.*** In addition to the de novo standard for reviewing legal conclusions and the clear error standard for reviewing factual findings, there is a third standard of review that appellate courts regularly use. This is the abuse of discretion standard. As we have seen and will see throughout this book, trial judges make numerous discretionary decisions—decisions that the law permits but does not compel—and these include some of the most important decisions during the litigation process. These include Rule 11 sanctions, leave to amend pleadings, consolidation or separation of trials, venue transfer, proportionality decisions in discovery, decisions on motions for a new trial, and a host of other procedural rulings. You can spot the discretionary decisions by the language in the rules and statutes—words like "may" or "when justice so requires" or "for good cause." When an appellant seeks review of a trial court's discretionary decision, the appellate court will reverse only for abuse of discretion. In other words, the appellate court defers to the trial judge's decision unless the decision falls outside the scope of what a reasonable judge would have done under the circumstances.

8. ***Review of jury decisions.*** What about fact-finding by a jury? As you would expect, jury verdicts get even greater protection than judicial findings of fact. Indeed, the second clause of the Seventh Amendment commands that "no fact tried by a jury, shall be otherwise re-examined in any Court of the United States, than according to the rules of the common law." An appellate court does not review a jury's determinations. A losing party cannot appeal on the ground that the jury got it wrong. Instead, the appeal must focus on what the *judge* did or did not do. Even so, jury verdicts may get reviewed on appeal, indirectly, in the following manner: A party moves for judgment as a matter of law at trial, which the court denies. The jury finds against that party. The party then renews the motion for judgment as a matter of law, or in the alternative for a new trial, which the court denies. On appeal, the party does not simply argue that the *jury*

got it wrong. Rather, the party argues that the *judge* got it wrong by denying the Rule 50 motion for judgment as a matter of law or the Rule 59 motion for a new trial. The argument that the court erred by denying judgment as a matter of law requires the appellant to argue that no reasonable jury could have found as the jury did. The argument that the court erred by denying a new trial requires the appellant to argue that the jury's verdict was against the great weight of the evidence.

It is tough to win such an appeal. As to the Rule 50 denial, the appellate court reviews the denial de novo because whether to grant judgment as a matter of law is a legal decision, but the underlying question is whether *any* reasonable jury could have reached the same conclusion. Thus, in reviewing the denial of judgment as a matter of law, the court of appeals does not ask whether the jury was correct but only whether any reasonable jury could have found that way—an extremely deferential standard, even more so than the clearly erroneous standard applied to judicial fact-finding. As to the Rule 59 denial, the underlying question is whether the verdict was against the great weight of the evidence, but the appellate court reviews the decision for abuse of discretion. Thus, the jury's verdict is doubly protected—first by the high standard for a trial judge to grant a new trial, and second by the deferential review of the trial court's discretionary decision to deny a new trial.

CHAPTER 7

Joinder

Having learned the steps in the litigation process from pleading through appeals, you are ready to add a layer of complexity. In this chapter, rather than focus on a particular step in the process, we explore the rules that govern inclusion of multiple claims or multiple parties in a single action. In some cases, these multiple claims and parties are included at the outset of the action. In others, claims and parties are added later. Either way, you need to understand the circumstances under which it is permissible—or mandatory—to include multiple claims and parties.

In theory, a litigated dispute might involve only a single plaintiff suing a single defendant over a single claim. In reality, while some lawsuits fit this description, most lawsuits involve multiple claims, multiple parties, or both. An action may be as simple as a plaintiff suing a defendant for both breach of contract and breach of warranty (*joinder of claims*), or two passengers suing a driver for negligence in an auto accident (*joinder of parties*). Or it may be as complex as thousands of plaintiffs asserting claims against numerous defendants in a class action or other mass lawsuit, with defendants who in turn assert third-party claims against additional parties and crossclaims against each other. The rules of joinder attempt to balance the benefits of comprehensive proceedings against competing values such as litigant autonomy and the danger that procedural complexity may interfere with accomplishing justice.

As you learn about various forms of joinder, think about how each device affects the strategic dynamic of a lawsuit. Consider, for example, how a counterclaim may strengthen a defendant's position, but also how it may play into a plaintiff's hands. Consider how joinder of parties may strengthen plaintiffs' leverage by permitting plaintiffs to pursue claims jointly against a defendant, but also how each plaintiff gives up some control over her claim. As you read the cases in this chapter, ask yourself why the lawyers chose to join claims and parties the way they did, and why their adversaries decided to challenge their use of joinder.

A. JOINDER OF CLAIMS

(1) Permissive Joinder of Claims

A plaintiff may have more than one claim against a defendant. A wrongfully termi-nated employee, for example, may simultaneously have claims against her employer for race discrimination, gender discrimination, breach of contract, and other legal violations. These claims, moreover, may have a basis in federal statutes, state statutes, and common law. Similarly, a consumer injured by a defective product may have claims against the manufacturer for negligence, strict liability, breach of warranty, and consumer fraud. A plaintiff may bring these claims against the defendant in a single complaint.

Under modern rules of pleading and joinder, a party may assert claims under each legal doctrine that applies to the party's circumstances. Imagine telling a wrong-fully terminated employee that he can sue for discrimination or breach of contract, but not both. Or imagine telling an injured consumer that she can sue for negligence or breach of warranty, but not both. Maybe it *was* both. Or maybe it was one and not the other, but to determine which, the parties need discovery and trial. Given that a plaintiff may have multiple legal theories, it would be inefficient and unjust to require a separate lawsuit for each one.

What if the claims do not arise out of the same factual situation? Businesses in ongo-ing relationships may have multiple disputes. A retailer, for example, may have many contracts with a supplier for shipments of merchandise. Suppose one shipment never arrived, and an entirely different shipment, under a different contract, arrived with the wrong merchandise. Although these two claims do not arise out of the same transaction, the retailer may wish to assert both claims as part of a single lawsuit. The federal rules per-mit joinder of claims even if the claims are utterly unrelated. Rule 18(a) says that "[a] party asserting a claim, counterclaim, crossclaim, or third-party claim may join, as inde-pendent or alternate claims, as many claims as it has against an opposing party." One thing it does *not* say—unlike so many other joinder rules—is "arising out of the same transaction or occurrence." Permissive joinder of claims, in other words, is *unlimited*. As long as the plaintiff and defendant are in litigation, they may assert whatever claims they have against each other at the same time. So if you represent a plaintiff with property damage from a neighbor's septic tank overflow, and the neighbor also happens to owe your client money on an unrelated debt, the permissive joinder rule allows your client to file a single complaint asserting both the property damage claim and the debt claim.

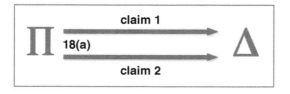

Bringing the claims together is not mandatory. If your client decides to sue the neighbor on both claims, then you and your client will analyze as a matter of strategy and practicality whether to assert the claims together or separately.

(2) Counterclaims

Defendants may have claims against plaintiffs, too. In an automobile collision case in which one driver sues another, for example, the defending driver also may have suffered vehicle damage, personal injury, or both. If each driver blames the other for the accident, a *counterclaim* is all but inevitable. Similarly, in a commercial dispute after a business relationship has gone sour, each party may have legal claims to assert against the other. The federal rules provide for permissive counterclaims in Rule 13(b) and compulsory counterclaims in Rule 13(a).

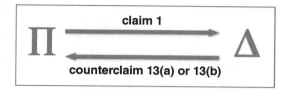

(a) Permissive Counterclaims

A defendant may assert, as a counterclaim, any claim that the defendant has against the plaintiff, even if it is completely unrelated to the plaintiff's claim. Rule 13(b) expressly permits a pleading to "state as a counterclaim against an opposing party any claim that is not compulsory." The logic of permissive counterclaims mirrors Rule 18(a)'s unlimited permissive joinder of claims—the plaintiff and defendant are in litigation anyway, so there's some efficiency in letting both of them assert whatever claims they have against each other. But the efficiency is relatively slight since the allegations and evidence may barely overlap, so the rule permits a defendant to choose either to assert the claim as a counterclaim or to file it as a separate lawsuit.

(b) Compulsory Counterclaims

Rule 13(a) states that "[a] pleading must state as a counterclaim any claim that—at the time of its service—the pleader has against an opposing party if the claim: (A) arises out of the transaction or occurrence that is the subject matter of the opposing party's claim; and (B) does not require adding another party over whom the court cannot acquire jurisdiction." The word *must* is what makes this a rule of compulsory counterclaims. If the claim arises out of the same transaction or occurrence, then the defending party must assert it as a counterclaim. What, exactly, is *compulsory* about it? If the defending party fails to assert the counterclaim, will the court order the party to do so because it's compulsory? No. What makes the counterclaim "compulsory" is the fact that a later court in a separate lawsuit will throw out the claim on the grounds that the party passed up the opportunity to assert it as a counterclaim. When we explore claim preclusion in Chapter 8, we will look again at compulsory counterclaims in that context.

By forcing parties to assert in a single action whatever claims they have against each other arising out of the same transaction, the legal system enhances efficiency, consistency, and finality. The compulsory counterclaim rule protects against the inefficiency of presenting the same evidence and relitigating the same disputes in two separate lawsuits. It protects against the potential inconsistency of having related claims adjudicated by different decision makers. And it serves the goal of finality by letting parties know that the adjudication of their action precludes relitigation of claims between the same parties arising out of the same factual situation.

For example, suppose Company A complains that Company B delivered goods of lower quality than specified in their contract, so Company A rejects the goods and refuses to pay. Unable to work out their differences amicably, A sues B for breach of contract. B counterclaims for breach of contract based on A's failure to pay. In this example, B's claim—that A breached the contract by failing to pay for the goods—is a compulsory counterclaim. It arises from the same transaction as A's original claim that B delivered unsatisfactory goods. Therefore, if B fails to bring its claim as a counterclaim and later files a separate lawsuit against A for nonpayment, B's claim will be dismissed for failure to bring the counterclaim in the first action.

Rule 13(a)(2)(A) creates a sensible exception to compulsory counterclaims: "[T]he pleader need not state the claim if: when the action was commenced, the claim was the subject of another pending action." So if, in our example, B had *already* sued A for nonpayment, and *then* A filed its suit for unsatisfactory goods, B would not be required to assert the counterclaim in A's lawsuit. By the way, notice that if B had filed the first suit, then A's claim would have been a compulsory counterclaim in B's lawsuit. Therefore, this exception to the compulsory counterclaim rule is unlikely to come up except when the first case was filed in a state court system that does not have compulsory counterclaims.

STRATEGY SESSION

Think about the considerations that come into play when deciding whether to assert a potential counterclaim. If your client has a *compulsory* counterclaim, you must explain to your client the use-it-or-lose-it situation, and your client will decide either to assert it or forgo the claim. If your client has a *permissive* counterclaim, the situation is more complicated. Precisely because they are not compulsory, permissive counterclaims present a strategic choice: assert the counterclaim now, file a separate action, or hold the claim in reserve? Litigators may find counterclaims advantageous on the theory that the best defense is a good offense (what military strategists call the strategic offensive principle). Whether at trial or at a bargaining table to discuss settlement, it helps to have something of your own to assert. On the other hand, whenever you assert a counterclaim, you have allowed the opposing party to choose your forum and timing. If your client has a claim that is unrelated to the plaintiff's claim and that would be better asserted in a different court or at a different time, you may forgo the counterclaim and file a new action at the time and place you choose. Forgoing a counterclaim is risky, however, because it may be difficult to predict whether a later court will deem it to have been compulsory. Therefore, you may choose to err on the side of caution and assert the counterclaim rather than risk losing it. The bottom line: Whether to sit on a claim or assert it as a counterclaim depends on the weight you and your client place on the strategic offensive, the extent to which your client wishes to pursue the claim immediately, the value you place on choosing your own forum, and your confidence level that the counterclaim is not compulsory.

(3) Crossclaims

Many cases involve multiple plaintiffs, multiple defendants, or both. May co-parties assert claims against each other? Rule 13(g) permits such crossclaims as long as they are transactionally related to the claims already asserted in the action: "A pleading may state as a crossclaim any claim by one party against a coparty if the claim arises out of the transaction or occurrence that is the subject matter of the original action or of a counterclaim, or if the claim relates to any property that is the subject matter of the original action."

In the case of co-defendants, crossclaims often involve claims for contribution or indemnification in which one defendant asserts that if it is held liable to the plaintiff, the other defendant should have to pay all or some of the damages. In a product-liability case, for example, if the plaintiff sues both the retailer and the manufacturer of a defectively manufactured product, the retailer may assert a crossclaim against the manufacturer. Indeed, Rule 13(g) anticipates such crossclaims by stating that they "may include a claim that the coparty is or may be liable to the crossclaimant for all or part of a claim asserted in the action against the crossclaimant." This type of crossclaim among co-defendants substantively resembles a third-party claim under Rule 14, but procedurally the third-party claim differs in that it is used to bring in someone who has not already been made a party to the lawsuit.

Similarly, co-plaintiffs may assert crossclaims against each other. For example, consider an automobile accident case in which an injured driver and passenger sue the driver of the other car. As discovery proceeds, the passenger decides that the driver of her own car was at fault as well. If the passenger asserts a negligence claim against her own driver, she may do so either by bringing a separate lawsuit or by filing a crossclaim against her co-plaintiff in the initial action.

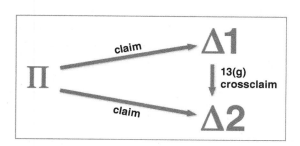

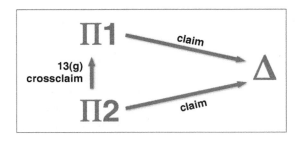

Although a few states have made related crossclaims compulsory in their state court rules, just like compulsory counterclaims, the federal rules and most states treat crossclaims as purely permissive. This means that if your client has a potential crossclaim, you and your client decide whether to assert it as a crossclaim, independently, or not at all. As with permissive joinder of claims and permissive counterclaims, the decision depends on strategy as well as practical considerations such as cost and timing. But with crossclaims, lawyers face an additional strategic layer, the risk that crossclaims may undermine an otherwise united front by co-parties.

It is easy to understand why courts permit related crossclaims. If the claims arise out of the same transaction or occurrence or relate to the same property, resolving those claims in the same action improves efficiency and consistency. But you should also understand the answer to the opposite question, which is why the rules impose greater constraints on crossclaims than on claims or counterclaims. Permissive joinder of claims is unlimited under Rule 18. So are permissive counterclaims under Rule 13(b). A plaintiff and defendant may assert whatever claims they have against each other, even *unrelated* claims. Why may co-parties assert crossclaims only if they arise out of the same transaction? Not only that, but claim preclusion and the compulsory counterclaim rule *require* a plaintiff and defendant to assert claims against each other if they arise out of the same transaction, whereas the federal crossclaim rule is merely permissive. Why?

The answer takes you beyond the efficiency and consistency rationales for joinder of related claims and into the complexity of the adversary system. Claims and counterclaims between the original plaintiff and defendant may add factual and legal disputes to an action, but they involve the original adversary relationship between the parties. Crossclaims, on the other hand, create an additional axis of adversariness. Parties who previously were merely co-plaintiffs or co-defendants become, with the assertion of a crossclaim, adversaries as well as allies. The efficiency gain may outweigh the cost of additional complexity for related crossclaims but not for unrelated crossclaims.

Terminology Tip

The federal rules use the word *crossclaim* to refer to a claim against a co-party (by a plaintiff against a co-plaintiff or by a defendant against a co-defendant), and *counterclaim* to refer to a claim by a defendant against a plaintiff (or, more precisely, a claim by a party against whom a claim was asserted, against the party asserting the claim). In some state courts, however, *crossclaim* or *cross-complaint* refers not only to claims between co-parties, but also to what the federal rules call a counterclaim and, less commonly, to what the federal rules call a third-party claim.

Notes & Questions

1. When looking at litigation with multiple claims or multiple parties, keep in mind the difference between *joinder* and *jurisdiction*. The joinder rules establish *procedural mechanisms* for including multiple claims and parties in a lawsuit. They do not, however, automatically give the court power over those claims and parties. Recall from Chapter 1's overview that a court needs subject matter jurisdiction over the case and personal jurisdiction over the parties—concepts we will explore in much greater detail in Chapters 9 and 10. Even if a claim complies with the procedural requirements of the joinder rules, the claim may be dismissed if the court lacks jurisdiction. Suppose a plaintiff sues a defendant in federal court under federal law and the defendant asserts a counterclaim. The counterclaim is *procedurally* proper under Rule 13, but the court still needs jurisdiction. If the counterclaim arises under federal law, then the court has federal question jurisdiction (28 U.S.C. §1331) over the counterclaim. If the parties are citizens of different states and the counterclaim meets the amount-in-controversy requirement, then the court has diversity jurisdiction (28 U.S.C. §1332) over the counterclaim. If the counterclaim arises out of the same transaction as the federal claim—that is, if it is a compulsory counterclaim—then the court may have supplemental jurisdiction (28 U.S.C. §1367) over the counterclaim. You will learn about federal question jurisdiction, diversity jurisdiction, and supplemental jurisdiction in Chapter 9. For now, as you learn the joinder mechanisms, keep in mind that you also will need to consider jurisdiction to know whether a court would have the power to adjudicate the additional claims.

2. Even more basic, keep in mind the difference between joinder and the *merits* of the dispute. The joinder rules establish procedural mechanisms for including multiple claims and parties in a lawsuit, but they do not tell the court anything about whether the claims and defenses should prevail on the law and the facts. If a claim is properly joined but the defendant believes that the claim lacks merit, the defendant should not argue that joinder is improper but rather should move to dismiss for failure to state a claim or for summary judgment. By the same token, if a claim is improperly joined in an action, the defendant may seek severance or dismissal, depending on the circumstances, even if the claim has merit as a matter of substantive law and fact.

3. Learn to deploy joinder rules in combination. For example, think about this question: When a litigant asserts a crossclaim against a co-party, may the litigant assert additional unrelated claims against the co-party? Having learned that crossclaims are permitted only if they arise out of the same transaction or occurrence as an original claim or counterclaim, you might think that the answer is no. But the answer is yes. Remember that Rule 18 (permissive joinder of claims) allows a plaintiff to assert multiple claims against a defendant even if the claims are unrelated. Look at the language of Rule 18(a) and note that it applies not only to original plaintiffs, but also to counterclaimants, crossclaimants, and third-party

plaintiffs: "A party asserting a claim, counterclaim, crossclaim, or third-party claim may join, as independent or alternative claims, as many claims as it has against an opposing party." If Defendant 1 asserts a permitted crossclaim against Defendant 2 (that is, a claim that arises out

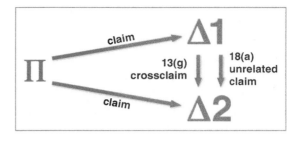

of the same facts as the original claim), then Defendant 1 also may assert unrelated claims against Defendant 2. The plaintiff joins the two defendants as a matter of permissive party joinder under Rule 20, which we will cover in the next section. The related claim is a crossclaim under Rule 13(g), and the unrelated claims are permitted as additional claims under Rule 18(a).

4. You will not find any Federal Rule of Civil Procedure labeled "compulsory joinder of claims." As a practical matter, however, compulsory joinder of claims exists in the common law doctrine of *claim preclusion* or *res judicata*, which we will examine in Chapter 8. If a plaintiff brings a lawsuit and chooses not to assert her entire claim, then a final judgment on the merits will preclude her from asserting the missing piece of claim in a subsequent lawsuit. Thus, just as defendants must assert transactionally related counterclaims or else lose them, so must plaintiffs assert transactionally related claims or else lose them.

B. PERMISSIVE PARTY JOINDER

So far, we have looked at joinder of *claims* among those who are already parties. We turn now to joinder of *parties*. Under what circumstances may a complaint include multiple plaintiffs or multiple defendants? That is the question of permissive party joinder.

Rule 20(a) permits joinder of parties if the claims by or against them arise out of the same circumstances. Rule 20(a)(1) states when multiple plaintiffs may sue together: "Persons may join in one action as plaintiffs if: (A) they assert any right to relief jointly, severally, or in the alternative with respect to or arising out of the same transaction, occurrence, or series of transactions or occurrences; and (B) any question of law or fact common to all plaintiffs will arise

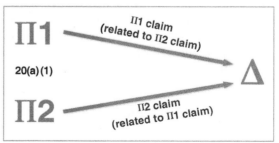

in the action." Think of the enormous range of disputes in which more than one plaintiff may share claims against a defendant arising out of the same transaction or occurrence: employees challenging an employer's policy, property owners harmed by environmental wrongdoing, corporations suing over a business deal gone sour, inmates challenging prison conditions, and so on. It could be two plaintiffs or it could be thousands; either way, the permissibility of joinder is governed by the two-part test of Rule 20(a)(1).

Permissive joinder not only allows multiple *plaintiffs* to sue together, but also allows plaintiffs to sue multiple *defendants*. For example, torts committed in the course of employment often generate claims against both the individual and the company for which that individual works. Securities cases

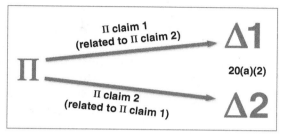

often involve claims against a company as well as individual officers and directors. Product-liability cases may involve claims against each company in a chain of distribution, such as a manufacturer, distributor, and retailer. Rule 20(a)(2) applies the same test—(A) same transaction, occurrence, or series; and (B) common question of law or fact—to joinder of defendants.

Determining whether claims arise out of the same circumstances can be trickier than it seems. What constitutes "the same transaction, occurrence, or series of transactions or occurrences"? Courts often describe it as a "logical relationship" test: Are the claims logically related to such an extent that it makes sense to package them together for trial? As you read the following case, ask yourself why these plaintiffs decided to join together in their lawsuit, why Yamaha fought to prevent them from joining together, and whether you agree with the court's application of Rule 20 to these facts.

KEHR ex rel. KEHR v. YAMAHA MOTOR CORP.
596 F. Supp. 2d 821 (S.D.N.Y. 2008)

McMahon, District Judge

Bruce Kehr, on behalf of his son Charles Kehr, a minor, and husband and wife, Grover and Shirley Taber ("Plaintiffs") filed this lawsuit on August 20, 2008 against Yamaha Motor Corporation, U.S.A., Yamaha Motor Manufacturing Corporation of America, Yamaha Motor Co., LTD. ("Yamaha") seeking damages for strict product liability, negligence, breach of implied warranty, fraudulent concealment, violation of the Consumer Product Safety

Act, violation of N.Y. Gen. Bus. L. §349, and loss of consortium. Plaintiffs also make a claim for punitive damages.

Before this Court is Yamaha's motion to dismiss, transfer, or sever the claims of the Taber plaintiffs. . . .

Yamaha's motion to dismiss, transfer or sever the claims of the Taber plaintiffs is DENIED.

BACKGROUND

This case involves the Yamaha Rhino, a side-by-side, all terrain utility vehicle (the

"Rhino"). In two separate incidents, plaintiffs allege that design defects in the Rhino caused it to tip over while being operated, injuring plaintiffs.

On June 21, 2007, 16 year-old Charles Kehr was riding in the passenger seat of a 2007 Rhino in Dutchess County, New York. The vehicle rolled over while making a turn, causing the Rhino's rollbar to crush and sever Charles Kehr's right fingers. Charles Kehr's leg was also injured in the accident. Since the accident, Charles Kehr has undergone five surgeries to repair and reattach his fingers. At all times referenced herein, Charles Kehr, and his father and legal guardian, Bruce Kehr, were residents of the State of New York and the County of Dutchess.

On August 20, 2005, 59 year-old Grover Taber was driving a 2005 Rhino in Oswego County, New York, when the vehicle tipped over, and caused injuries to Grover Taber's left foot, leg and shoulder. Since the accident Grover Taber has undergone several surgeries and other medical treatment for these injuries. Shirley Taber, Grover Taber's wife, also alleges that her husband's injuries have had a serious and detrimental impact on their relationship. At all times referenced herein, Grover and Shirley Taber were residents of the State of New York and the County of Oswego.

Yamaha began selling the Rhino within the United States in or around 2003. Plaintiffs allege that, due to inherent defects in the Rhino's design, including having a narrow track width, high platform, high center of gravity and wheels too small to maintain vehicle stability, the Rhino is excessively prone to tip over while being operated, even at low speeds. According to plaintiffs, when the Rhino does tip over, its unpadded, heavy steel roll cage, outlining both occupant compartments, can itself become very dangerous to vehicle occupants, causing severe crushing injuries and even death. Plaintiffs maintain that the Rhino's design and construction is in spite of the availability of safer design alternatives and vehicle testing methods that can reduce operator and occupant morbidity and mortality. [Plaintiffs further allege that Yamaha knew or should have known of the defects and that Yamaha concealed information about the Rhino's dangers.]

Finally, plaintiffs claim that "Since 2003, Yamaha has misled the government, the public, and consumers about the safety of the Yamaha Rhino" and that "Had the users of the Yamaha Rhino, including plaintiffs, known the full extent of the risks and dangers associated with the use of the Yamaha Rhino, including that they were not safe to operate even at low speeds and in flat areas, said users would never have used the Yamaha Rhino and received the injuries that they did."

DISCUSSION
I. YAMAHA'S MOTION TO DISMISS THE CLAIMS OF THE TABER PLAINTIFFS FOR IMPROPER VENUE IS DENIED

[Yamaha moved to dismiss for improper venue. The court found that venue was proper under the federal venue statute and denied the motion.]

II. YAMAHA'S MOTION TO TRANSFER THE CLAIMS OF THE TABER PLAINTIFFS TO THE UNITED STATES DISTRICT COURT, NORTHERN DISTRICT OF NEW YORK IS DENIED

[Yamaha argued, under the federal venue transfer statute, that the Taber claims should be severed and transferred to the Northern District of New York, which includes the county where the Taber accident occurred. The court found that although some evidence may be located there, much of the proof for the Kehr and Taber claims would overlap. Moreover, there were other Yamaha Rhino cases pending in 34 district courts around the country, and plaintiffs had moved to centralize all of the cases in a single court as Multidistrict Litigation (MDL). The court decided, "There is simply no sense in entangling yet another district court in litigation that may soon be transferred to a yet-to-be-determined MDL venue." The court therefore denied the motion to transfer.]

III. YAMAHA'S MOTION TO SEVER THE CLAIMS OF THE TABER PLAINTIFFS PURSUANT TO FED. R. CIV. P. RULE 20 AND RULE 21 IS DENIED

Yamaha argues that the claims of Grover and Shirley Taber were improperly joined in this action under Fed. R. Civ. P. 20 and moves for their severance under Fed. R. Civ. P. 21.

Rule 20(a) permits the joinder of multiple plaintiffs if: (1) "they assert any right to relief jointly, severally, or in the alternative in respect of or arising out of the same transaction, occurrence or series of transactions or occurrences" and (2) "if any questions of law or fact common to all these persons will arise in the action." Fed. R. Civ. P. 20(a). "The purpose of Rule 20 is to promote trial convenience and to expedite the resolution of disputes, thereby preventing multiple lawsuits." *Blesedell v. Mobil Oil Co.*, 708 F. Supp. 1408, 1421 (S.D.N.Y. 1989).

Pursuant to Rule 21, "Any claim against a party may be severed and proceeded with separately." Fed. R. Civ. P. 21. The decision of whether to sever a claim is left to the discretion of the trial court. However, "Federal courts view severance as a procedural device to be employed only in exceptional circumstances." *Laureano v. Goord*, No. 06-cv-7845, 2007 WL 2826649, at *8 (S.D.N.Y. Aug. 31, 2007). In considering a severance motion, a trial court will consider the two requirements of Rule 20 and additional factors, including: (1) whether severance would serve judicial economy; (2) whether prejudice to the parties would be caused by severance; and (3) whether the claims involve different witnesses and evidence.

A. PLAINTIFFS' CLAIMS ARISE OUT OF THE SAME "TRANSACTION OR OCCURRENCE" UNDER RULE 20

What will constitute the same transaction or occurrence under the first prong of Rule 20(a) is approached on a case by case basis. The interpretation of the terms "transactions or occurrences" as applied to the context of Rule 13(a) counterclaims offers guidance to the application of those terms under Rule 20. Under Rule 13(a), "Transaction is a word of flexible meaning. It may comprehend a series of many occurrences, depending not so much on the immediateness of their connection as upon their logical relationship." *Moore v. New York Cotton Exch.*, 270 U.S. 593, 610 (1926). Applying this reasoning to the terms used in Rule 20 ". . . would permit all 'logically related claims' by or against different parties to be tried in a single proceeding." *Blesedell*, 708 F. Supp. at 1421.

Yamaha urges this Court to sever the claims of the Taber plaintiffs, arguing that the Taber accident is an independent and unrelated event from the Kehr accident. Yamaha argues that because the two incidents alleged in the complaint involve distinct factual scenarios, including, *inter alia*, differing issues of the manner of operation, differing environments and differing resulting injuries, they are not the same "transaction or occurrence" for purposes of Rule 20. Plaintiffs counter that their claims arise from common design defects in the Rhino and that although the two Rhinos involved in the accidents are different, plaintiffs allege that all Rhinos sold in the United States suffer from the same defects, regardless of model or year.

Plaintiffs have met their burden of demonstrating that their claims arise out of the same transaction or occurrence for purposes of Rule 20(a). The Second Circuit has specifically held that an allegation of a common design defect in automobiles satisfies the requirement of logically related transactions for the purposes of permissive joinder under Rule 20. *Abraham v. Volkswagen of America, Inc.*, 795 F.2d 241, 247 (2d Cir. 1986). In *Abraham*, the Second Circuit considered a motion to sever 119 plaintiffs whose various cases arose from their use of Volkswagen "Rabbit" cars of model years 1975 to 1979. All the cars were equipped with a faulty valve stem seal that had resulted from a design defect in the vehicle, but not all the cars exhibited the same defect and some models were more likely than others to break down sooner. The Second Circuit reversed the district court's conclusion that the plaintiffs could not be joined under Rule 20(a). *Id.* at 251.

The Court found that the plaintiffs' allegation of "the faulty valve stem seal as a single defect that caused various damages, satisfied the same transaction or occurrence (or series thereof) requirement." *Id.*

Similarly, the plaintiffs in this case claim damages stemming from alleged design defects common to all Yamaha Rhinos on the market in the relevant time period. Both the Kehrs and the Tabers allege as a basis for their complaint an accident in a Rhino, which due to such design defects, was unreasonably dangerous and prone to tip over. These allegations readily satisfy the requirement of a series of logically related transactions under Rule 20(a).

B. PLAINTIFFS' CLAIMS PRESENT SEVERAL COMMON QUESTIONS OF LAW AND FACT

At the core of both the Kehr and Taber claims is the question of whether the Yamaha Rhino's design was defective. Related to and correlated to that central question are numerous other questions common to both sets of plaintiffs, including: (1) whether Yamaha failed to adequately warn the plaintiffs or the public of the dangers of the design defect, if one is found to exist; (2) Whether Yamaha failed to exercise ordinary care and breach[ed] their duty to purchasers of the Rhino; (3) Whether Yamaha intentionally concealed or failed to disclose the true nature of the problems with the Rhino for the purpose of inducing plaintiffs to purchase the product; and (4) Whether Yamaha is liable for its failure to comply with the reporting requirements of the Consumer Product Safety Act.

Yamaha argues that because the case involves two separate, unrelated accidents, with distinct factual patterns, that they cannot be joined under Rule 20(a). There is no requirement, however, that all questions of law and fact be *identical* in order for there to be permissive joinder under Rule 20(a). Indeed, the Rule provides for joinder as long as there is *any* question or fact common to all. The interpretation of Rule 20(a) urged by Yamaha is unworkably narrow and completely subverts the goals of judicial economy and efficiency underlying the Rule. *See, e.g., United Mine Workers of America v. Gibbs*, 383 U.S. 715, 724 (1966) ("Under the Rules, the impulse is toward entertaining the broadest possible scope of action consistent with fairness to the parties; joinder of claims, parties and remedies is strongly encouraged.").

C. JOINDER IN THIS CASE FACILITATES JUDICIAL ECONOMY AND EFFICIENCY

Proceeding with the Kehr and Taber claims as a single case would no doubt promote judicial economy and efficiency as it is anticipated that much of the discovery and depositions will be identical for both plaintiffs. It is also uncontested that there will be overlap between the witnesses and documentary proof used at trial. Further, as discussed *supra*, a motion has been made by plaintiffs in this case for consolidation and transfer of this case under 28 U.S.C. §1407. It would surely be a waste of judicial resources to now sever the claims of these two plaintiffs into two separate cases, begin separate discovery and trial preparation and discovery, only to have both cases then transferred to an MDL judge.

D. NO PREJUDICE WILL RESULT IF SEVERANCE IS DENIED

Yamaha's claim of prejudice amounts to an argument that if the claims of the Taber and Kehr plaintiffs are tried together that there is a likelihood of juror confusion. I do not find this to be argument to be credible. The core issue of whether the Rhino has a design defect, which causes it to tip over while being operated, will be the same for both plaintiffs. Further, I am unconvinced that jurors will be unable to separate the different fact patterns presented by the Kehr and Taber claims during trial or that trying the claims together will result in prejudice to either party.

E. THERE IS AN OVERLAP OF WITNESSES AND DOCUMENTARY PROOF IN THE TWO PLAINTIFFS' CASES

As discussed *supra*, it is anticipated that there will be significant overlap between both plaintiffs' discovery from Yamaha and their pretrial preparation. Plaintiffs submit that both the Kehr and Taber plaintiffs will require discovery from and possibly call as witnesses identical Yamaha employees. Severing the claims of the Kehr and Taber plaintiffs will force the duplication of efforts by the parties, counsel and this Court. . . .

CONCLUSION

Yamaha's motion to dismiss, transfer or sever the claims of the Taber plaintiffs is denied.

Notes & Questions

1. Why did these plaintiffs decide to file their claims together in a single action? What advantages do you think they saw in joining together?

2. Take the Rule 20 analysis step by step. Under Rule 20(a)(1)(A), do the Kehr and Taber claims arise out of the same transaction, occurrence, or series of transactions or occurrences? What is the strongest counterargument? Under Rule 20(a)(1)(B), what common questions are presented by each plaintiff's claim?

3. To make a persuasive argument for or against joinder under Rule 20, a lawyer must think carefully about how to frame the "transaction or occurrence." If you represented the *Kehr* plaintiffs, how would you describe the occurrence out of which the claims arose? If you represented Yamaha, how would you describe it?

4. In *Corley v. Google, Inc.*, 316 F.R.D. 277 (N.D. Cal. 2016), 879 university students, faculty, and staff sued Google, claiming that the company violated their privacy rights by intercepting and scanning e-mails when they used Gmail through Google Apps for Education. Google moved to sever the claims, arguing that joinder was improper under Rule 20. Plaintiffs argued that all of the claims arose out of Google's policy of processing the content of e-mails. The court, however, agreed with Google's argument that the claims arose out of different scanning policies across different educational institutions, and that a key issue for each plaintiff would be whether the plaintiff consented to Google's conduct. The court therefore granted the motion to sever and ordered that each plaintiff would have to file a separate complaint.

In a case like *Corley*, consider the economies of scale and the settlement leverage generated by joinder. A lawyer who represents 879 plaintiffs can invest a lot more time and money in the litigation than a lawyer who represents a single plaintiff. Moreover, the threat of liability to numerous plaintiffs may drive a defendant to the negotiating table. In *Corley*, the amount of damages for each plaintiff would be quite small. Unless the plaintiffs can bring a large number of claims collectively, it is hard to see how the lawsuit could be economically viable for any lawyer. In *Corley*, as a practical matter, was the court

> **Terminology Tip**
>
> Some students get the wrong idea that "joinder" refers only to the *addition* of claims or parties *after* a lawsuit has commenced. Do not assume the word joinder is defined chronologically. It is true that some forms of joinder (counterclaims, crossclaims, third-party claims, and intervention) are reactive in the sense that, by definition, they occur *after* an original plaintiff has commenced an action. But other forms of joinder (joinder of claims, joinder of parties, interpleader, and class actions) occur either in the original complaint or in an amended pleading. In *Kehr*, the plaintiffs filed their lawsuit jointly against Yamaha in the original complaint. The word *joinder* applies to this, and Rule 20 establishes the test for whether they are permitted to do so. Had Kehr filed a solo complaint initially and had the Tabers later joined in an amended complaint, this too would be called joinder, and again, the test is Rule 20.

really deciding whether the litigation should be 879 separate lawsuits versus one lawsuit, or whether these claims would be pursued at all?

5. Litigation party structure gets complex because of how rules work in combination. Think about how joinder of parties grows with joinder of claims. Plaintiffs may assert multiple claims with multiple co-plaintiffs and against multiple defendants, but the possibilities are much bigger than that. Each time a party asserts a counterclaim or a crossclaim, the party may add additional parties. Rule 13(h) provides that the rules on party joinder apply to counterclaims and crossclaims just as they apply to plaintiffs' original claims.

C. COMPULSORY PARTY JOINDER

The compulsory joinder rule dictates who *must* be joined in an action and empowers the court to order joinder of such a required party. The rule also offers guidelines for determining whether a case should be dismissed if such a required party *cannot* be joined. Think about compulsory party joinder from both sides. If you represent a plaintiff, you need to know whether you are required to join particular parties. If you represent a defendant, and the plaintiff has not joined someone, you need to know whether you can ask the court to order that the person be joined, or better yet, whether the nonjoinder provides a basis for dismissal.

Rule 19 establishes a two-step process for analyzing compulsory party joinder. The first question is whether a person must be joined. Rule 19(a) lays out the analysis for whether the absent person is a required party. If so, the court must order that the person be joined. Suppose, however, that the person seems to be a required party under Rule 19(a) but cannot be joined because of immunity, the court's jurisdictional limits, or some other constraint. Then, the question is whether the person is so critical to the lawsuit that, in the person's absence, the lawsuit should be dismissed. Rule 19(b) offers factors for courts to consider when making the determination whether to dismiss the action or to proceed without the absent party.

(1) The Rule 19(a) Analysis: Who Is a Required Party

Rule 19(a) defines "persons required to be joined if feasible" and instructs the court to order their joinder: "If a person has not been joined as required, the court must order that the person be made a party." A required party, depending on the circumstances, may be aligned as a plaintiff or as a defendant. Required parties are those who are so inextricably linked to the case that their absence could create real problems. The rule spells out three circumstances under which a person will be deemed a required party. First, Rule 19(a)(1)(A) requires joinder if "in that person's absence, the court cannot accord complete relief among existing parties." Second, Rule 19(a)(1)(B)(i) requires joinder if "that person claims an interest relating to the subject of the action and is so situated that disposing of the action in the person's absence

Terminology Tip

Lawyers and judges often use the term *necessary party* to describe a party whose joinder is required under Rule 19(a). And they often use the term *indispensable party* to describe a required party who cannot be joined and whose absence warrants dismissal under Rule 19(b). Neither *necessary* nor *indispensable* appears in the current federal rule, but some people still use the older terminology as shorthand for the two steps in the compulsory party joinder analysis.

may: as a practical matter impair or impede the person's ability to protect the interest." Third, Rule 19(a)(1)(B)(ii) requires joinder if "that person claims an interest relating to the subject of the action and is so situated that disposing of the action in the person's absence may . . . leave an existing party subject to a substantial risk of incurring double, multiple, or otherwise inconsistent obligations because of the interest." These three provisions often overlap, but they are analytically distinct and you must apply each one on its own. That is, they are not mere *factors* to be considered as part of an analysis to decide whether a party is required. Nor are they *elements*, each of which must be established in order to show that a party is required. Rather, each of these three pieces of Rule 19(a) spells out a circumstance that, in itself, suffices to show that a party is required. But do not be fooled into thinking that this makes compulsory joinder a broad rule. Quite the opposite. Rule 19(a) is surprisingly narrow, as shown by the following case in which the Supreme Court reversed a court of appeals that interpreted Rule 19(a) too broadly.

TEMPLE v. SYNTHES CORPORATION, LTD.

498 U.S. 5 (1990)

PER CURIAM.

Petitioner Temple, a Mississippi resident, underwent surgery in October, 1986, in which a "plate and screw device" was implanted in his lower spine. The device was manufactured by respondent Synthes Corp., Ltd. (U.S.A.) (Synthes), a Pennsylvania corporation. Dr. S. Henry LaRocca performed the surgery at St. Charles General Hospital in New Orleans, Louisiana. Following surgery, the device's screws broke off inside Temple's back.

Temple filed suit against Synthes in the United States District Court for the Eastern District of Louisiana. The suit, which rested on diversity jurisdiction, alleged defective design and manufacture of the device. At the same time, Temple filed a state administrative proceeding against Dr. LaRocca and the hospital for malpractice and negligence. At the conclusion of the administrative proceeding, Temple filed suit against the doctor and the hospital in Louisiana state court.

Synthes did not attempt to bring the doctor and the hospital into the federal action by means of a third-party complaint, as provided in Federal Rule of Civil Procedure 14(a). Instead, Synthes filed a motion to dismiss Temple's federal suit for failure to join necessary parties pursuant to Federal Rule of Civil Procedure 19. Following a hearing, the District Court ordered Temple to join the doctor and the hospital as defendants within 20 days or risk dismissal of the lawsuit. According to the court, the most significant reason for requiring joinder was the interest of judicial economy. The court relied on this Court's decision in *Provident Tradesmens Bank & Trust Co. v. Patterson*, 390 U.S. 102 (1968), wherein we recognized that one focus of Rule 19 is "the interest of the courts and the public in complete, consistent, and efficient settlement of controversies." *Id.* at 111. When Temple failed to join the doctor and the hospital, the court dismissed the suit with prejudice.

Temple appealed, and the United States Court of Appeals for the Fifth Circuit affirmed. 898 F.2d 152. The court deemed it "obviously prejudicial to the defendants to have the separate litigations being carried on," because Synthes' defense might be that the plate was not defective, but that the doctor and the hospital were negligent, while the doctor and hospital, on the other hand, might claim that they were not negligent, but that the plate was defective. The Court of Appeals found that the claims overlapped and that the District Court therefore had not abused its discretion in ordering joinder under Rule 19. A petition for rehearing was denied.

In his petition for certiorari to this Court, Temple contends that it was error to label joint tortfeasors as indispensable parties under Rule 19(b) and to dismiss the lawsuit with prejudice for failure to join those parties. We agree. Synthes does not deny that it, the doctor, and the hospital are potential joint tortfeasors. It has long been the rule that it is not necessary for all joint tortfeasors to be named as defendants in a single lawsuit. *See Lawlor v. National Screen Service Corp.*, 349 U.S. 322, 329-30 (1955); *Bigelow v. Old Dominion Copper Mining & Smelting Co.*, 225 U.S. 111, 132 (1912). Nothing in the 1966 revision of Rule 19 changed that principle. The Advisory Committee Notes to Rule 19(a) explicitly state that "a tortfeasor with the usual 'joint-and-several' liability is merely a permissive party to an action against another with like liability." 28 U.S.C. App., p.595. There is nothing in Louisiana tort law to the contrary.

The opinion in *Provident Bank* does speak of the public interest in limiting multiple litigation, but that case is not controlling here. There, the estate of a tort victim brought a declaratory judgment action against an insurance company. We assumed that the policyholder was a person "who, under §(a), should be joined if *feasible*," 390 U.S. at 108, and went on to discuss the appropriate analysis under Rule 19(b), because the policyholder could not be joined without destroying diversity. After examining the factors set forth in Rule 19(b), we determined that the action could proceed without the policyholder; he therefore was not an indispensable party whose absence required dismissal of the suit. *Id.* at 116, 119.

Here, no inquiry under Rule 19(b) is necessary, because the threshold requirements of Rule 19(a) have not been satisfied. As potential joint tortfeasors with Synthes, Dr. LaRocca and the hospital were merely permissive parties. The Court of Appeals erred by failing to hold that the District Court abused its discretion in ordering them joined as defendants and in dismissing the action when Temple failed to comply with the court's order. For these reasons, we grant the petition for certiorari, reverse the judgment of the Court of Appeals for the Fifth Circuit, and remand for further proceedings consistent with this opinion.

Notes & Questions

1. First, note how Rule 19 is used in litigation. It is not a rule used by plaintiffs who desire to join with other plaintiffs or who desire to sue multiple defendants; that would be permissive joinder under Rule 20. Rather, it is a rule used by *defendants* seeking to get a case dismissed because the plaintiff failed to include someone, or asking a court to order that a party be joined against the plaintiff's wishes. In *Temple*, which party raised the Rule 19 issue?

2. Next, note how emphatically the Supreme Court made its point regarding the narrowness of Rule 19. Both the district court and court of appeals held that the surgeon and hospital were required parties under Rule 19(a), and even went a step further and dismissed the action, finding the surgeon and hospital indispensable under Rule 19(b). The Supreme Court disagreed and held that the surgeon and hospital were not required parties. As if to put an exclamation point on it, the Court issued a summary reversal in a unanimous *per curiam* opinion. Look again at the last sentence of the opinion: "For these reasons, we grant the petition for certiorari, reverse the judgment. . . ." In other words, rather than go through the usual process of granting certiorari, receiving briefs on the merits, hearing oral argument, and then deciding the case, the Justices found this one so easy that they did not even need to hear arguments; they granted certiorari and simultaneously reversed the Fifth Circuit.

3. Be sure you understand why the surgeon and hospital were *not* required parties in Temple's products-liability case against Synthes. As always when considering whether someone is a required party, take it through the three pieces of Rule 19(a).

    Rule 19(a)(1)(A): Is the surgeon needed in order to accord complete relief among those already parties? No. The manufacturer may argue that the injury was the surgeon's fault, so the plaintiff cannot get "complete relief" unless the surgeon is joined as a defendant. But that is not the point. The rule talks about complete relief *among those already parties*. As between the plaintiff and manufacturer, the product-liability dispute can be completely resolved whether or not the surgeon is a party. Either the manufacturer is liable or not. The manufacturer may argue that the surgeon is needed because he knows what happened in the operating room. But a person can be subpoenaed to testify as a *witness* even if not a party to the case. The surgeon may be a critical witness in the product-liability case, but that does not mean he is a required *party*.

    Rule 19(a)(1)(B)(i): Will the lawsuit impair the surgeon's interests? No. Whatever happens in the product-liability lawsuit, the surgeon remains free to assert any defenses against a potential malpractice claim. The manufacturer may argue that the surgeon's interests will be impaired if the jury in this action decides that the implant was not defective and the injury was the surgeon's fault. But remember that as long as the surgeon is not a party, he is not legally bound by the judgment.

    Rule 19(a)(1)(B)(ii): Is the surgeon needed to prevent a risk of inconsistent obligations? No. The manufacturer may argue that if the plaintiff brings two separate lawsuits, one jury may blame the injury entirely on the surgeon and another jury may blame it entirely on the manufacturer, and that would be "inconsistent."

But what the rule means by *inconsistent obligations* is truly incompatible orders, not merely results that differ from each other.

4. The rule of *Temple v. Synthes* is clear: Joint tortfeasors are not required parties. But isn't it efficient for claims against joint tortfeasors to be adjudicated together? To understand the logic of *Temple*, you must remember the difference between permissive joinder (Rule 20) and compulsory joinder (Rule 19). *May* the plaintiff bring the product-liability claim against the manufacturer and the malpractice claim against the surgeon in a single action? Yes, most likely this would be allowed as permissive party joinder under Rule 20. The claims arise out of the same transaction or occurrence (the surgical implantation), and the claims involve common questions. *Must* the plaintiff sue both defendants together? No, it is up to the plaintiff.

5. How can we reconcile the breadth of permissive party joinder under Rule 20—and the breadth of permissive joinder of claims and counterclaims under Rules 18 and 13(b)—with the narrowness of compulsory party joinder under Rule 19? The answer lies in modern American procedure's emphasis on *party autonomy*. The rules *permit* parties to create the party structure they desire by joining additional claims and parties, but for the most part, the rules do not *require* the parties to do so. Party structure therefore does not depend on a top-down judicial mandate or preconceived notion about what the structure of the case ought to look like, but rather depends on what the parties choose to do.

(2) The Rule 19(b) Analysis: Whether to Dismiss If a Required Party Cannot Be Joined

If a court finds that an absentee is a required party, then under Rule 19(a) the court should order that the person be joined. But what happens when a required party cannot be joined?

There are at least four reasons why it might be impossible to join a required party. Recall from Chapter 1's overview that a court must have *subject matter jurisdiction* over the case, must have *personal jurisdiction* over the parties, and must be a proper *venue*; we will explore these topics further in Chapters 9, 10, and 11. If a federal court's subject matter jurisdiction is based on diversity of citizenship, and joinder of the party would destroy complete diversity, then the court cannot order that the party be joined. If the absent person is beyond the court's territorial reach as a matter of personal jurisdiction, then the court is powerless to order that the party be joined. The addition of a party may make the court an improper venue. Also, if a party has sovereign immunity or some other immunity from suit, then the party may be beyond the court's power.

Suppose a case fits this description. The absent party is needed under the Rule 19(a) analysis, but cannot be joined because of a jurisdictional or other barrier. In this sad situation of "we must, but we cannot," the court's choices are to go forward without the required party or to dismiss the action. Rule 19(b) instructs the court to "determine whether, in equity and good conscience, the action should proceed among the existing parties or should be dismissed." It forces the judge to make a hard decision: Under the circumstances, would it be better to go forward with the case to do at least *some* justice,

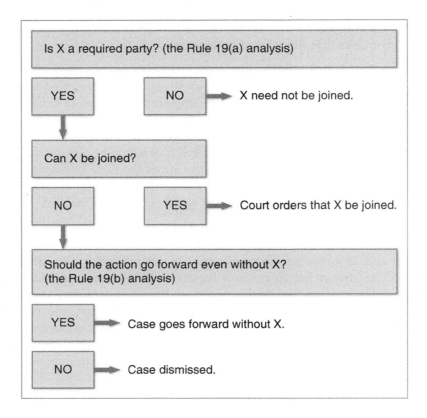

or would it be so unjust to proceed in the party's absence that it is better not to adjudicate at all? Rule 19(b) offers factors for courts to consider when deciding whether to dismiss a case on the grounds that a required party cannot be joined.

In the following case, be sure you understand why the Red Devils baseball team and the Mexican League were required parties under Rule 19(a), why the Red Devils and the Mexican League could not be joined in David Gonzalez Camacho's lawsuit, and why the judge decided dismissal was warranted under Rule 19(b).

CAMACHO v. MAJOR LEAGUE BASEBALL

297 F.R.D. 457 (S.D. Cal. 2013)

LORENZ, District Judge.

On November 30, 2012, Plaintiffs David Gonzalez Camacho and Daniel Arrellano Pesqueira commenced this tort action against multiple defendants.[1] This action

arises from allegations that Major League Baseball conspired with the Mexican Major Leagues to prevent baseball prospect Daniel

---

[1] The defendants in this action are Major League Baseball, Major League Baseball Enterprises, Inc., Major League Baseball Properties, Inc., Office of the Commissioner of Baseball, National Association of Professional Baseball Leagues, National Association of Professional Baseball Leagues, Inc., and Minor League Baseball.

Pesqueira from playing baseball in the United States. Pending before the Court is the Office of the Commissioner of Baseball (d/b/a Major League Baseball), Major League Baseball Enterprises, Inc., and Major League Baseball Properties, Inc.'s motion to dismiss pursuant to Federal Rule of Civil Procedure 12(b)(7). Plaintiffs oppose the motion. . . . For the following reasons, the Court GRANTS Defendants' motion to dismiss.

I. BACKGROUND

[David Gonzalez Camacho ("Gonzalez") is a citizen of Mexico who is domiciled and does business in Tijuana, Mexico and who resides and does business in San Diego County, California. He trains, supports, promotes, and represents Mexican baseball players for placement in international major and minor leagues, including Major and Minor League baseball in the United States. Daniel Pesqueira is a citizen of Mexico who resides in Tijuana. In 2010, Gonzalez began representing Pesqueira in his efforts to be drafted by a major or minor baseball team in any country. On February 17, 2012, the Boston Red Sox invited Pesqueira to train with the team for spring training in Florida. On March 6, 2012, a scout for the Boston Red Sox notified Gonzalez that Major League Baseball had directed that Pesqueira be returned to Mexico because Pesqueira "belonged to a Mexican league team and could not play in the major leagues without the consent of the Mexican league team." Major League Baseball also advised Gonzalez that Pesqueira "was and is on the reserve list of the Association of Professional Baseball Teams of the Mexican Leagues, therefore, he was ineligible to play for the Boston Red Sox."]

At Mr. Gonzalez's request, Major League Baseball forwarded a copy of the "contractual documentation" between Mr. Pesqueira and the Mexican League team called the Diablos Rojos ("Red Devils"). . . . One page—titled Contract for Professional Services"—includes Mr. Pesqueira's signature dated January 1, 2010 with a start date of March 22, 2009, and a second page with the same title includes Mr. Pesqueira's signature from and with a start date of March 21, 2011. . . . Plaintiffs allege that at both times Mr. Pesqueira was under 18 years old, having been born on April 6, 1994. [According to Plaintiffs, neither Pesqueira nor his father signed the documents, and the signatures were fraudulently lifted from another document. Plaintiffs allege that Major League Baseball "confirmed that Pesqueira in fact was not committed to in any way, nor under contract with, the Association of Professional Baseball Teams of the Mexican Leagues and the Red Devils of Mexico."]

Plaintiffs commenced this action on November 30, 2012. They subsequently amended their complaint after it was dismissed without prejudice for lack of subject matter jurisdiction. In the [first amended complaint], they assert the following claims against all of the defendants for: (1) intentional interference with economic relations; (2) intentional interference with prospective economic advantage; (3) negligent interference with economic relations; (4) negligent interference with prospective economic relations; (5) declaratory relief; (6) negligence; and (7) unfair business practices. Defendants now move to dismiss under Rule 12(b)(7). Plaintiffs oppose.

II. LEGAL STANDARD

A party may move to dismiss a case for "failure to join a party under Rule 19." Fed. R. Civ. P. 12(b)(7). Rule 19 imposes a three-step inquiry: (1) Is the absent party necessary (i.e., required to be joined if feasible) under Rule 19(a)?; (2) If so, is it feasible to order that absent party to be joined?; and (3) If joinder is not feasible, can the case proceed without the absent party, or is the absent party indispensable such that the action must be dismissed? The terms "necessary" and "feasible" are "terms of art in Rule 19 jurisprudence": "Necessary" refers to a party who should be joined if feasible; and "indispensable" refers to "a party whose participation is so important to the resolution of the case that, if the joinder of the party is not feasible, the suit must be dismissed." *Disabled Rights Action Comm. v. Las Vegas Events, Inc.*, 375 F.3d 861, 867 n.5 (9th Cir. 2004). The failure to join a party under Rule 19 can only lead to dismissal of a suit where the court cannot obtain jurisdiction over the necessary party and that party is determined to be indispensable to the action. . . .

III. DISCUSSION

Defendants argue that both the Red Devils and the Mexican League are necessary parties that cannot be feasibly joined to this action because (1) a determination of the validity of Mr. Pesqueira's alleged contracts with the Red Devils is necessary, and (2) joining the parties would vitiate this Court's subject-matter jurisdiction and Plaintiffs cannot establish personal jurisdiction over these absent parties in this Court. Plaintiffs present their claims very differently in their opposition brief compared to the allegations in the complaint. In a disingenuous early-inning strategic shift, they direct the focus of this action on Mr. Gonzalez's agency contract with Mr. Pesqueira, arguing that the Red Devils and Mexican League are "joint tortfeasors" that are not necessary parties to litigate the claims asserted in this action. Plaintiffs

swing for the fences, but ultimately come up short.

Upon reviewing the allegations in the complaint, it is clear that the threshold issue in this action is the validity of the alleged contracts entered into between Mr. Pesqueira and the Red Devils. Plaintiffs proceed with their action under the presumption that those contracts are invalid—because Mr. Pesqueira was a minor at the time the contracts were executed, or because the signatures were "fraudulently lifted from another document and transferred onto these documents." These allegations in the complaint overwhelmingly demonstrate that this entire action hinges on one game-winning issue—the validity of the Red Devils contracts. The Court emphasizes that determining the validity of the alleged contracts between Mr. Pesqueira and the Red Devils is outside the scope of this series. Therefore, the Court rejects the disingenuous shifted premise that Plaintiffs present in their opposition brief, and shall proceed analyzing Defendants' motion while recognizing that the validity of the alleged contracts entered into between Mr. Pesqueira and the Red Devils is the go-ahead run.

A. THE RED DEVILS AND THE MEXICAN LEAGUE ARE NECESSARY PARTIES

A party is necessary if: (1) complete relief cannot be granted in the party's absence; or (2) the district court determines that "the absent party's participation is necessary to protect its legally cognizable interests or to protect other parties from a substantial risk of incurring multiple or inconsistent obligations because of those interests." Such a legally cognizable interest must be more than a financial stake in the outcome of the litigation. Defendants demonstrate that the Red Devils and the Mexican League are necessary parties under the latter of the two aforementioned definitions.

Under Rule 19(a)(1)(B)(i), an absent party is necessary if it "has a *legally protected interest* in the suit" and "that interest will be *impaired or impeded* by the suit." *Makah Indian Tribe v. Verity*, 910 F.2d 555, 558 (9th Cir. 1990). "Impairment may be minimized if the absent party is adequately represented in the suit." *Id.* It is also a "fundamental principle" that "a party to a contract is necessary, and if not susceptible to joinder, indispensable to litigation seeking to decimate that contract." *Dawavendewa v. Salt River Project Agric. Improvement & Power Dist.*, 276 F.3d 1150, 1157 (9th Cir. 2002).

Plaintiffs unequivocally seek a judicial determination of their rights and duties under the alleged contracts between Mr. Pesqueira and the Red Devils. In the complaint, Plaintiffs explicitly state that they desire "a declaration as to whether or not Pesqueira is bound to the Red Devils of Mexico." They even go as far as to state that a "judicial declaration is *necessary* and appropriate at this time under the circumstances" because without the declaration, they are "financially burdened by the wrongful position taken by defendants Major League Baseball, and unable to work in their chosen professions." In other words, determining the validity of the Red Devils contracts is necessary to resolve essentially all of the wrongful conduct alleged in this action. The same applies to the Mexican League because of its bylaws and regulations that require disputes between players and member teams to be resolved by binding arbitration before the Executive President of the Mexican League.

Neither the Red Devils nor the Mexican League are represented in this action, and a determination by this Court regarding the validity of the Red Devils contracts may impair and impede the Red Devils' and the Mexican League's legally protected interest in this suit. *See Makah Indian Tribe*, 910 F.2d at 558. . . .

Alternatively, under Rule 19(a)(1)(B)(ii), an absent party is also necessary if there is a potential risk that adjudicating an action without the absent party could leave an existing party open to "incurring double, multiple, or otherwise inconsistent obligations." Fed. R. Civ. P. 19(a)(1)(B)(ii). The Ninth Circuit has stated that

"[i]nconsistent obligations" are not . . . the same as inconsistent adjudications or results. Inconsistent obligations occur when a party is unable to comply with one court's order without breaching another court's order concerning the same incident. Inconsistent adjudications or results, by contrast, occur when a defendant successfully defends a claim in one forum, yet loses on another claim arising from the same incident in another forum.

Cachil Dehe Band of Wintun Indians of the Colusa Indian Cmty. v. California, 547 F.3d 962, 976 (9th Cir. 2008) (*quoting Delgado v. Plaza Las Americas, Inc.*, 139 F.3d 1, 3 (1st Cir. 1998)).

Defendants argue that "the Red Devils could still sue others in the Mexican courts and elsewhere for wrongfully interfering with its contract with Mr. Pesqueira[,]" and "[t]his action will not have any binding effect on the Red Devils unless the team is made a party to this case." The concern that Defendants suggest is important, but for the purposes of Rule 19, the paramount concern is a Mexican court or another in the United States determining that the Red Devils contracts are valid if this Court finds that they are not, or vice versa. That would produce inconsistent obligations for all of the parties in this action in addition to the Red Devils because operating under one court's determination would then necessarily cause the parties to breach another court's determination regarding the same issue, i.e., the validity of the Red Devils contracts. Therefore, because of the risk of inconsistent obligations, the Red Devils are a necessary party to this action.

Swing and a miss—strike one.

B. JOINING THE RED DEVILS AND THE MEXICAN LEAGUE IS NOT FEASIBLE

"If an absentee is a necessary party under Rule 19(a), the second stage is for the court to determine whether it is feasible to order that the absentee be joined." *Equal Emp't Opportunity Comm'n v. Peabody W. Coal Co.*, 400 F.3d 774, 779 (9th Cir. 2005). . . . Defendants argue that "[t]he Red Devils and the Mexican League cannot be joined both because their joinder would destroy this Court's subject-matter jurisdiction, and because Plaintiffs cannot establish personal jurisdiction over them in this Court." Plaintiffs do not address feasibility in their opposition brief. In fact, the words "feasible" and "feasibility" do not appear anywhere in their brief. Consequently, Plaintiffs concede that joining the Red Devils and the Mexican League is not feasible under the second and third circumstances that Rule 19 enumerates. *See* [C.D. Cal. Civ. R. 7.1(f.3.c)]. They took this pitch and it went right down the middle—strike two.

C. THE RED DEVILS AND MEXICAN LEAGUE ARE INDISPENSABLE PARTIES

If the necessary party cannot be joined, the court must then determine whether

the party is indispensable. Under Rule 19(b), indispensable parties are "persons who not only have an interest in the controversy, but an interest of such a nature that a final decree cannot be made without either affecting that interest, or leaving the controversy in such a condition that its final termination may be wholly inconsistent with equity and good conscience." *Shields v. Barrow*, 58 U.S. 130, 139 (1854). Rule 19(b) provides the factors that courts should consider in determining if an action should be dismissed because an absent party is indispensable: (1) prejudice to any party or to the absent party; (2) whether relief can be shaped to lessen prejudice; (3) whether an adequate remedy, even if not complete, can be awarded without the absent party; and (4) whether there exists an alternative forum. Fed. R. Civ. P. 19(b). . . .

Plaintiffs' primary arguments addressing indispensability are: (1) Defendants fail to meet their burden, in part, because all of the cases cited are distinguishable, and (2) in equity and good conscience, this case should be allowed to proceed regardless of whether the Red Devils and the Mexican League are indispensable. The Court rejects these arguments. Plaintiffs either misread or misunderstand the cited case law, and they also fail to provide any law themselves that provides an avenue for this Court to bypass Rules 12(b)(7) and 19 and all of the related case law as they implore the Court do.

Rather, in seeking a determination that the Red Devils contracts are invalid, Plaintiffs are, for all practical purposes, attempting to set aside a contract. And it is evident from the allegations in the complaint that the Red Devils, as a party to the alleged contracts, and by extension the Mexican League, are parties that will be affected by any determination regarding the validity of the contracts.... [Thus,] the Red Devils and the Mexican League are indispensable parties to this action. Consequently, all four of the Rule 19(b) factors weigh in favor of dismissal. *See* Fed. R. Civ. P. 19(b). And finally, strike three—out.

IV. CONCLUSION & ORDER

In light of the foregoing, the Court GRANTS Defendants' motion to dismiss under Rule 12(b)(7) and DISMISSES this action in its entirety.

Notes & Questions

1. Do you see why Gonzalez and Pesqueira argued that the Red Devils and the Mexican League were "joint tortfeasors" with Major League Baseball and the other defendants? The plaintiffs hoped to get the benefit of the rule of *Temple v. Synthes* that joint tortfeasors are not required parties under Rule 19. The problem was that, unlike in *Temple*, the plaintiffs in *Camacho* did not merely assert liability against multiple alleged wrongdoers; they sought to invalidate a contract. In terms of the policies underlying Rule 19, why does that difference matter?

2. The *Camacho* court usefully breaks down its Rule 12(b)(7) analysis into three steps: (1) Is the absentee a required party under Rule 19(a)? (2) If so, can the absentee be joined as a party? (3) If the absentee is required but joinder is impossible, then should the court proceed without the absentee or dismiss the action? Be sure you understand each step and how it played out in *Camacho*.

   Start with the first step: Are the Red Devils and Mexican League required parties in Gonzalez's and Pesqueira's lawsuit? Having read both *Camacho* and *Temple*, you should be able to explain why the Red Devils and Mexican League in *Camacho* were required parties under Rule 19(a)(1)(B)(i) and why the surgeon and hospital in *Temple* were not. You should be able to do the same under Rule 19(a)(1)(B)(ii). And, although the court did not choose to go there, you should be able to make a plausible argument that the Red Devils and Mexican League also were required parties under Rule 19(a)(1)(A), in contrast to the surgeon and hospital in *Temple*.

3. Next, turn to the transition step: Given that the Red Devils and Mexican League were required parties, why didn't the court order that they be joined? The defendants offered two reasons why the Red Devils and the Mexican League could not be joined, and the court found that the plaintiffs conceded this point by failing to address it.

   First, if the Red Devils and Mexican League were joined, the federal court would lack *subject matter jurisdiction*. As you will see in Chapter 9, one basis for jurisdiction is diversity of citizenship, *see* 28 U.S.C. §1332, but the diversity requirement is not met in "actions between a United States citizen and an alien on one side and all aliens on the other side." *Guan v. Bi*, 2014 WL 953757, at *5 (N.D. Cal. Mar. 6, 2014). Since Gonzalez and Pesqueira were Mexican citizens, adding the Mexican defendants to the other side would ruin the court's diversity jurisdiction over the action.

Second, the court accepted the defendants' argument that, as a court in California, it lacked *personal jurisdiction* over the Red Devils and the Mexican League. As you will see in Chapter 10, courts lack power to adjudicate claims against parties unless those parties have adequate contacts with the forum state or some other basis for the court to assert power over them, which was missing here.

4. Now turn to the final step in analyzing a Rule 12(b)(7) motion to dismiss: Given that the Red Devils and Mexican League were required parties, and given that they could not be joined, should the court dismiss the action? In *Camacho*, the judge weighed the Rule 19(b) factors and decided to dismiss. If you represented the plaintiffs, what would you have argued to try to persuade the court not to dismiss?

This final step—the Rule 19(b) multi-factor analysis—should feel different from the first part. Rule 19(a) captures the idea that there is a *possibility* of unfairness to an existing party or absentee. Rule 19(b) takes it to the next step. Now that the court knows there is the possibility of prejudice but also knows the absentee cannot be joined, the question is whether the risk is so high that it justifies dismissal.

Also, note the difference between the highly technical Rule 19(a) analysis and the relatively unguided Rule 19(b) analysis. In the language of jurisprudence, Rule 19(a) offers a *rule* while Rule 19(b) offers a *standard*. Rule 19(b) provides factors for courts to consider when deciding whether to dismiss, but ultimately the question is "whether, in equity and good conscience, the action should proceed among the existing parties or should be dismissed." This, inevitably, is fact-sensitive and contextual.

5. In some cases, the dismissal question comes down to the fourth Rule 19(b) factor: Would the plaintiff have an adequate remedy if the action were dismissed? If the plaintiff can bring the action in a different forum, dismissal may be appropriate. For example, if the obstacle to joinder was diversity jurisdiction, can all of the parties be joined in state court? If the obstacle was personal jurisdiction, can all of the parties be joined in a different state? As the Supreme Court explained in *Provident Tradesmens Bank & Trust Co. v. Patterson*, 390 U.S. 102, 111 (1968), one goal of Rule 19 is "the interest of the courts and the public in complete, consistent, and efficient settlement of controversies." In *Camacho*, did the judge dismiss the action because he thought the plaintiffs could bring their case in Mexico? Or was he saying, regardless of whether the plaintiffs could bring their case in Mexico, that it would be unjust for him to proceed in the absence of the required parties?

6. Consider the mechanisms by which required joinder is enforced. Lawyers often refer to compulsory counterclaims and compulsory party joinder, but rarely pause to think about the difference in what actually makes them *compulsory*. There are at least three ways to compel joinder. First and most simply, a court can *order* joinder. That is the approach of Rule 19(a) for joinder of required

parties. Violation of a court order is grounds for dismissal and potentially punishable as contempt, so there is an implicit threat behind such an order. Second, a court can *dismiss* an action for failure to join. That's the approach of Rule 19(b) and the Rule 12(b)(7) motion to dismiss for failure to join an indispensable party. Third, failure to join can result in *preclusion*. That's the approach of compulsory counterclaims under Rule 13(a), as well as claim preclusion.

7. David Gonzalez Camacho did not give up on the claim after this dismissal. He refiled the lawsuit in 2014 in California state court, asserting claims against Major League Baseball, affiliates, and the commissioner, and this time he added Mexican Major League Baseball as a defendant. However, the court dismissed the Mexican League for lack of personal jurisdiction, and the claims against the other defendants were ultimately dismissed without prejudice.

STRATEGY SESSION

Defendants can wield Rule 19 to ask the court to bring another party into the action, but that is not the usual reason they invoke the rule. Typically, defendants invoke Rule 19 in a motion to dismiss under Rule 12(b)(7), as we saw in both *Temple* and *Camacho*. Yes, there are times when a defendant actually wants another person to be joined as a party; Rule 19(a) can accomplish this. But more likely, the defendant wants the case dismissed, and Rule 19(b) provides grounds for dismissal. If you represent a defendant, keep your eyes open for required parties that the plaintiff failed to join in the complaint. And if you represent a plaintiff, consider whether any parties are required, and if so, take this into account in your decisions about choice of forum and whom to name in the lawsuit.

D. THIRD-PARTY CLAIMS

When a defendant is sued, the most predictable response is some version of "I'm not liable." That is the stuff of denials, affirmative defenses, motions to dismiss, motions for summary judgment, and trial. But there is another common response that may not be quite as obvious: "If I am liable, then this other person should have to pay for all or part of my liability." This is what third-party claims accomplish.

With a third-party claim, a defendant joins a new party—the third-party defendant—and asserts a claim against that party for indemnification or contribution in case the defendant is held liable to the original plaintiff. As Rule 14 puts it, a "defending party may, as third-party plaintiff, serve a summons and complaint on a nonparty who is or may be liable to it for all or part of the claim against it." Many lawyers and judges still use the older terminology of *impleader*: The defendant *impleads* the third party.

Asserting a third-party claim does not mean that a defendant admits liability on the underlying claim. Rather, the third-party claim is conditional: *If* I am liable, then the third-party defendant must reimburse me for all or part of my liability. For example, if a

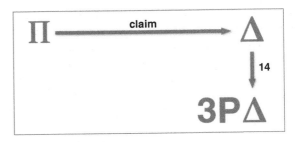

consumer sues a retailer for selling a defective product, the retailer might assert a third-party claim against the manufacturer, contending that the manufacturer should indemnify the retailer for any damages the retailer has to pay. The retailer prefers not to be held liable at all, but if the retailer is liable to the plaintiff, then the retailer wants to be reimbursed by the manufacturer. By using the third-party claim procedure of Rule 14, the retailer brings the manufacturer into the action so the manufacturer's duty to indemnify the retailer can be determined in the same proceeding as the plaintiff's product-liability claim.

Rule 14 does not itself create substantive liability. Like every other joinder rule, it offers a procedural mechanism by which to assert claims permitted by applicable substantive law.

SMERDON v. GEICO CASUALTY CO.
2017 WL 2506421 (M.D. Pa. June 9, 2017)

Brann, District Judge.

I. BACKGROUND

While shopping at her local Wal-Mart in Mansfield, Tioga County, Pennsylvania, Plaintiff Brenda G. Smerdon allegedly observed an unidentified individual rob the store. Upon witnessing the robbery, Ms. Smerdon, along with several other patrons, chased the robber outside to the store's parking lot. The robber then ran into a nearby vehicle, attempting to flee the scene. When she reached the purported getaway car, Ms. Smerdon stretched her arm through the passenger side window and attempted to grab the keys.

Unfortunately for Ms. Smerdon, the car sped off, ejected her from the vehicle, and ran her over. The alleged robber was never apprehended, and the subject vehicle turned out to be stolen. Ms. Smerdon contends that, as a result of this incident, she sustained skull fractures, traumatic brain injury, right knee injuries, and lower extremity injuries.

Further, according to Ms. Smerdon she maintained an automobile insurance policy with Defendant GEICO Casualty Company at the time of the accident, which included uninsured motorist coverage. Nevertheless, GEICO refused to provide coverage to Ms. Smerdon for her uninsured motorist claim by virtue of her alleged "assumption of the risk" under the policy.

On October 13, 2016, Ms. Smerdon initiated breach of contract and bad faith claims against GEICO in the Court of Common Pleas of Tioga County. Just over one week later, GEICO removed the case to this Court. Thereafter, on November 15, 2016, GEICO filed a Third Party Complaint against Wal-Mart. On February 28, 2017, Wal-Mart filed a motion to dismiss the Third Party Complaint. Because the Third Party Complaint fails to plead sufficient factual matter to state a plausible claim for relief, Wal-Mart's motion to dismiss is granted.

II. LAW

[Before turning to the Rule 14 analysis, the court set forth the standard for deciding a Rule 12(b)(6) motion.]

III. ANALYSIS

"Where . . . substantive law recognizes a right of contribution and/or indemnity, impleader under Rule 14 is the proper procedure by which to assert such claims." *In re One Meridian Plaza Fire Litig.*, 820 F. Supp. 1491, 1496 (E.D. Pa. 1993). Federal Rule of Civil Procedure 14 (entitled "Third-Party Practice") provides at subpart (a)(1) that "[a] defending party may, as third-party plaintiff, serve a summons and complaint on a nonparty who is or may be liable to it for all or part of the claim against it." "Third-party practice, also known as impleader, is generally permitted when the third party's liability is dependent upon the outcome of the main claim or when the third party is potentially secondarily liable to the defendant." *Blais Const. Co. v. Hanover Square Assocs.*, 733 F. Supp. 149, 152 (N.D.N.Y. 1990). Neither of those prerequisites is satisfied here, as GEICO's liability in contract is wholly independent of Wal-Mart's alleged premises liability in tort.

This link between the third-party and underlying claims is crucial, given that

"Rule 14 creates no substantive rights. Unless there is some substantive basis for the third-party plaintiff's claim he cannot utilize the procedure of Rule 14." *Robbins v. Yamaha Motor Corp.*, 98 F.R.D. 36, 37 (M.D. Pa. 1983). Impleader, therefore, "is not proper when the third-party plaintiff alleges only that the third-party defendant is solely liable to the plaintiff." *Pitcavage v. Mastercraft Boat Co.*, 632 F. Supp. 842, 845 (M.D. Pa. 1985).

"A defendant may not use Rule 14 to implead a third-party defendant who may have liability to the plaintiff *instead* of the defendant or in *addition* to the defendant. Rather, a defendant may use Rule 14 to implead a third-party defendant only if that third party will be liable to the *defendant* if the defendant is found liable to the plaintiff." *United States v. Bailey*, 516 F. Supp. 2d 998, 1020 (D. Minn. 2007), *aff'd*, 571 F.3d 791 (8th Cir. 2009). "In other words, a third party claim is not appropriate where the defendant and putative third party plaintiff says, in effect, 'It was him, not me.'" *Watergate Landmark Condo Unit Owners' Ass'n v. Wiss, Janey, Elstner Assocs.*, 117 F.R.D. 576, 578 (E.D. Va. 1987). . . .

GEICO's Third Party Complaint contains two substantive claims against Wal-Mart. The first is that Wal-Mart is solely liable for Ms. Smerdon's damages based on negligence in failing to provide adequate security, to properly train its security staff, and to warn its patrons accordingly. In its responsive briefing, GEICO concedes that impleader of this first claim is procedurally invalid.

Second, GEICO claims that, if Plaintiffs are entitled to recover on their underlying Complaint, Wal-Mart must also be liable to GEICO for contribution and/or indemnification. GEICO concedes that this conclusion applies only to Plaintiffs' breach of contract claim and not their bad faith allegations.

Accordingly, the narrow question that this motion presents is whether GEICO may properly implead Wal-Mart on the theory that Wal-Mart could be liable to GEICO for contribution and/or indemnification on Plaintiffs' underlying breach of contract claim. The law compels the conclusion that Wal-Mart is not properly impleaded under that theory.

A federal court sitting in diversity must apply state substantive law. *See Chamberlain v. Giampapa*, 210 F.3d 154, 158 (3d Cir. 2000) (citing *Erie R.R. v. Tompkins*, 304 U.S. 64 (1938)). "In Pennsylvania, indemnification is limited to those situations in which defendants' liability is secondary or when an indemnification contract exists." *Pitcavage*, 632 F. Supp. at 846 & n.2. Consequently, where "no such contract exists" and in cases that do not involve secondary liability, "the court proceeds with the analysis as if [the third-party plaintiff] seeks contribution from the third-party defendants." *Id.* at 846 n.1. Because GEICO had not contracted with Wal-Mart for indemnification and because no facts suggesting secondary liability for the underlying breach of contract have been alleged, impleader on that ground is inappropriate.

That leaves impleader by way of a claim for contribution. Although this is perhaps GEICO's strongest avenue in theory, it nevertheless is also unavailing. . . . Contribution in Pennsylvania is governed by the Pennsylvania Uniform Contribution Among Tortfeasors Act. Under that Act, contribution is only available between (or among) "joint tortfeasors." 42 Pa. C.S. §8324(a). The Act defines "joint tortfeasors" as "two or more persons jointly or severally liable *in tort* for the same injury to persons or property." 42 Pa. C.S. §8322 (emphasis added). Thus, courts have recognized that "contribution is not available for breach of contract claims," like that upon which GEICO relies here. *EQT Prod. Co. v. Terra Servs., LLC*, 179 F. Supp. 3d 486, 493 (W.D. Pa. 2016). . . . [T]he "wrongdoing" alleged against GEICO is the subsequent contractual breach of its policy with Ms. Smerdon, whereas the "wrongdoing" alleged against Wal-Mart sounds in tort and is limited to the circumstances of the original accident itself.

Neither do concerns for judicial economy militate in favor of impleader. To the contrary, any suggestion that overlapping issues transcend the two complaints appears more illusory than GEICO lets on. For instance, although Ms. Smerdon's claims against GEICO may require this Court to address *contract* principles like "assumption of the risk" under the policy's terms, any negligence action against Wal-Mart might address "assumption of the risk" and contributory or comparative negligence—as those terms have been interpreted in the applicable *tort* law. . . .

IV. CONCLUSION

For the foregoing reasons, Wal-Mart's motion to dismiss GEICO's Third Party Complaint is granted with prejudice.

Notes & Questions

1. As a matter of litigation strategy, why did GEICO want to bring in Walmart as a party to the action? What did it hope to achieve?

2. Why did the court reject GEICO's attempt to bring Walmart into the action by Rule 14? Focus on the crucial difference between two questions: whether the

plaintiff Brenda Smerdon herself had a tort claim that she could pursue against Walmart, and whether the defendant GEICO had a claim against Walmart that provided a sufficient basis to join Walmart as a third-party defendant.

3. Note that the assertion of a third-party claim does not establish a claim by the original plaintiff against the third-party defendant. The plaintiff may decide to add a related claim directly against the third-party defendant, *see* Rule 14(a)(3), but unless the plaintiff does so, the third-party claim runs strictly between the defendant/third-party plaintiff and the third-party defendant. Examine the language of Rule 14(a). Suppose the third-party defendant wishes to assert a related claim against the original plaintiff; under Rule 14, may she? What if a plaintiff wishes to assert an *unrelated* claim against the third-party defendant, or the third-party defendant wishes to assert an unrelated claim against the plaintiff?

4. To test your understanding of these joinder rules—as well as what you learned about pleadings in Chapter 2—decide which procedural mechanism you would use in each of the following situations. For each situation, consider these options (remember that you can use them in combination):

- denial (Rule 8(b))
- affirmative defense (Rule 8(c))
- motion to dismiss for failure to state a claim (Rule 12(b)(6))
- counterclaim (Rule 13(a))
- crossclaim (Rule 13(g))
- third-party claim (Rule 14)

You represent a client who has been sued in federal court for negligence. The claim arises out of a collision between your client, who was driving an automobile, and a bicyclist. The bicyclist's complaint alleges that your client caused the collision by running a red light, and that the bicyclist suffered significant injuries.

a. Your client has informed you that she did not run the red light, and in fact it was the bicyclist who caused the collision by carelessly riding into the side of the car. Your client also has informed you that the collision caused expensive damage to her car.

b. The accident took place four years ago. The applicable statute of limitations is three years.

c. At the time of the accident, your client was driving to deliver a package as part of her job. Her employment contract provides that the company will indemnify her for any liability she incurs in the scope of her employment.

d. Your client has informed you that she did not run the red light, and in fact it was the bicyclist who caused the collision by carelessly riding into the side of the car. Your client also has informed you that she did not herself suffer any personal injury or property damage from the collision.

e. The bicyclist sued not only your client, but also Other Driver (OD), because it was a three-way collision among OD, your client, and the bicyclist. In the collision, your client's car was badly damaged. Your client has informed you that the collision was caused by OD carelessly swerving into your client's lane.

f. The bicyclist's complaint actually does not allege that your client ran a red light. Indeed, although the complaint states that there was a collision and that the plaintiff suffered significant injuries, it does not state that your client did anything wrong.

5. Now, let's try a challenging question that requires creative use of joinder rules. Suppose you represent D, who has been sued by P. D wishes to assert a related claim against X. How many different ways can you think of by which D may be able to assert the claim against X, and what would be required for each option to succeed? First, try spinning out your own ideas, brainstorming as D's lawyer. If you're stuck, use these questions as hints to point you toward a number of possibilities.

a. Can D pursue the claim against X as a separate lawsuit?

Now, assume D prefers to assert the claim against X as part of the same action as P's claim against D.

b. If D's claim against X is a claim for contribution or indemnity, what rule should D employ?

c. If D has a direct claim against X as well as a claim for contribution or indemnity, what rules should D employ to bring both claims against X?

d. If D has a counterclaim to assert against P, how might D use the counterclaim as a foundation for joinder of D's claim against X?

e. If X is a required party, how would that help D to assert D's claim against X?

f. If P has a potential claim against X, how might that help D to assert D's claim against X?

Of course, each of these options is available only if your client's claim has a basis in fact and law; when thinking about joinder options, never forget Rule 11's prohibition on legally frivolous or factually baseless claims. There is no single right way to go about asserting D's claim against X. It depends on your client's situation. The joinder rules open up many possibilities, and it is the litigator's job to think creatively, realistically, strategically, and ethically about how to use them.

E. INTERVENTION

Intervention is the procedural mechanism by which someone seeks to become a party to an action that has already commenced. Although the plaintiff did not join the person as a plaintiff or as a defendant, the person chooses to be part of the lawsuit and therefore intervenes in the action.

One way to think about intervention is as a counterpoint to compulsory party joinder. In each situation, there is someone who could have been a party to the litigation but who was not joined. The difference is that with required parties, it is the defendant who drags the outsider into the litigation (or who moves to dismiss based on the infeasibility of joining the required party), whereas with intervention, it is the outsider who wants to jump in. Who would *want* to jump into ongoing litigation? Isn't litigation something people (with the possible exception of the plaintiff) try to avoid? As Judge Learned Hand once commented, "I must say that, as a litigant, I should dread a lawsuit beyond almost anything else short of sickness and death." 3 Lectures on Legal Topics, Association of the Bar of the City of New York 106 (1926). Mostly, outsiders to a lawsuit want to jump in only if they have some substantial interest that may be affected by the outcome of the litigation and they cannot depend upon any of the current parties to protect their interest.

Rule 24 divides intervention into two types: *intervention of right* and *permissive intervention*. If a would-be intervenor satisfies the requirements for intervention of right under Rule 24(a), then a court must allow the party to intervene. Rule 24(a), in other words, gives the would-be intervenor a *right* to intervene in the action. Permissive intervention, by contrast, is discretionary. If the would-be intervenor satisfies Rule 24(b), then it is up to the court whether to permit the party to intervene.

The following opinion on intervention comes from a lawsuit concerning Harvard University's admissions policy. The Harvard litigation attracted a lot of attention. Indeed, perhaps you heard about it as the litigation was proceeding, and perhaps you had a point of view about the merits of the underlying claim. Perhaps it even occurred to you that the outcome of the case could affect your own educational prospects in one direction or another, given the widespread impact the case could have, whichever way it was decided. If you had sought to become a party to the litigation, would you have been allowed to do so? As you read the opinion below, think about the difficult task a judge faces when deciding where to draw the line between those persons who should be allowed to intervene and those whose desired intervention, though understandable, might unnecessarily complicate the matter.

STUDENTS FOR FAIR ADMISSIONS v. PRESIDENT & FELLOWS OF HARVARD COLLEGE

308 F.R.D. 39 (D. Mass.), *aff'd*, 807 F.3d 472 (1st Cir. 2015)

BURROUGHS, District Judge.

I. INTRODUCTION

In this action, Plaintiff Students for Fair Admissions, Inc. ("SFFA") alleges that Defendant Harvard College ("Harvard) employs racially and ethnically discriminatory policies and procedures in administering its undergraduate admissions program, in violation of Title VI of the Civil Rights Act of 1964 and the Equal Protection Clause of the Fourteenth Amendment to the United States Constitution. SFFA's Complaint sets forth two types of allegations. First, SFFA asserts that the general manner in which Harvard considers race in its undergraduate admissions program violates the Equal Protection Clause. As opposed to using race as a mere "plus" factor in admissions decisions, SFFA alleges that Harvard engages in prohibited "racial balancing." Second, SFFA alleges that Harvard's policies invidiously discriminate against Asian-American applicants in particular....[1] Harvard denies these allegations, insists that its admissions policies fully comply with federal law, and maintains its intention to mount a vigorous defense to SFFA's claims.

Presently before the Court is a Motion to Intervene in Defense of Harvard's Admission Policy, which was filed on April 29, 2015.

The movants and proposed intervenors are nine minority high-school students who intend to apply for admission to Harvard College at some time in the future (the "Future Applicants"), and five minority college students who are currently enrolled in Harvard's full-time undergraduate program (the "Harvard Students") (collectively, the "Students"). In contrast to SFFA, these Students support Harvard's consideration of race in its admissions process, and they seek to intervene "in order to ensure that Harvard retains the right to consider race in its admissions decisions to the full extent allowed by law." For the reasons set forth herein, the Court finds that the Students do not meet the criteria for intervention as of right pursuant to Fed. R. Civ. P. 24(a), and it declines to allow permissive intervention pursuant to Fed. R. Civ. P. 24(b). Consequently, the Court will deny the Students' Motion to Intervene, but allow them to participate in this litigation as *amici curiae.*

II. RELEVANT FACTS

SFFA filed its Complaint with this Court on November 17, 2014, and Harvard filed its Answer on February 18, 2015. On May 4, 2015, the Court issued a Scheduling Order governing the timing of discovery, dispositive motions, and other matters. At this point, the case has not advanced beyond the early stages of discovery. On April 29, 2015, the Students filed their Motion to Intervene with the Court, along with a supporting Memorandum of Law. In addition, each of the Students filed a declaration explaining their purported interest in this case.

---

[1] SFFA purports to be a coalition of applicants and prospective applicants to institutions of higher education, along with their parents and other individuals. It further alleges to have at least one Asian-American student member who applied for and was denied admission to Harvard's 2014 entering class.

[One group of intervenors was comprised of nine minority high school students who stated that they intend to apply for admission to Harvard's undergraduate program (the "Future Applicants"). The Future Applicants detailed their academic accomplishments and connection with their heritage. The second group of intervenors was comprised of five current minority Harvard students (the "Harvard Students"). The Harvard Students described the academic and personal benefits they experienced as a result of Harvard's racially diverse student body, and expressed the belief that their education would be harmed if Harvard stopped considering race.]

III. SUMMARY OF THE STUDENTS' POSITION

The Students argue that Harvard must remain free to address the underrepresentation of certain racial and ethnic minority groups in its student body, so as to secure for these students access to opportunities associated with attending Harvard. Further, the Students believe they are in the best position to advance these interests, because their educational goals, career aspirations, and life experiences would be adversely affected if Harvard were prohibited from considering race in its admissions process. They seek to intervene because they believe that Harvard may not adequately represent their interests in this litigation, for a number of reasons. First, the Students wish to emphasize certain arguments that they fear Harvard may not present to the Court [including the need to consider race and ethnicity to offset the disparate impact of other criteria in Harvard's admissions policy.]

Second, the Students suggest that Harvard's defense of its admissions procedures "may be affected by concern over its public perception or by the need to serve myriad constituencies such as alumni, faculty, and the academic community. . . ." Essentially, the Students argue that Harvard would not be as zealous an advocate as they, and "[t]o the extent Harvard would seek to settle or would otherwise avoid politically sensitive topics," their intervention would ensure that those arguments are presented as fully and forcefully as possible.

Third, the Students claim that Harvard lacks the ability to defend its race-conscious admissions policy adequately because "Harvard, as an institution, does not have the personal experiences that Movants do with respect to race and ethnicity."

The Students argue that these considerations entitle them to intervene in this matter as of right, pursuant to Fed. R. Civ. P. 24(a). Alternatively, they argue that the Court should allow permissive intervention pursuant to Fed. R. Civ. P. 24(b).

IV. SUMMARY OF SFFA AND HARVARD'S POSITIONS

Both SFFA and Harvard oppose the Students' full-fledged intervention in this action, and both argue that the Students are not entitled to intervene as of right under Fed. R. Civ. P. 24(a). Harvard submits that intervention is not warranted because Harvard will adequately represent the Students' interests. SFFA agrees, and it further argues that the Students lack a "demonstrated interest" in this litigation, and that the Students' motion to intervene was not timely filed. In addition, both parties are concerned that full-scale intervention could interfere with the expeditious and orderly resolution of this case, by adding additional parties, broadening the scope of discovery, and engendering delays. Harvard has also cited concerns for the privacy of its students and applicants, which would be exacerbated by the intervention of additional parties.

However, neither SFFA nor Harvard opposes a more limited form of participation by the Students. SFFA suggests that the Students be permitted to participate as *amici curiae*. Harvard submits that if the Court permits intervention, it should limit the Students' participation to the submission of briefs, the presentation of their own declarations, and participation in any oral argument that the Court may choose to hear. Alternatively, Harvard is not opposed to the Students' participation as *amici curiae*, as suggested by SFFA.

V. ANALYSIS
A. *LEGAL STANDARD*

The Federal Rules of Civil Procedure contemplate two types of motions to intervene: intervention as of right, as set forth in Fed. R. Civ. P. 24(a), and permissive intervention, pursuant to Fed. R. Civ. P. 24(b). *R&G Mortg. Corp. v. Fed. Home Loan Mortg. Corp.*, 584 F.3d 1, 8 (1st Cir. 2009). "The differences are significant." *Id.* Faced with a motion to intervene as of right, the court must apply a four-factor test, and its discretion is "somewhat more constrained than in the case of a motion for permissive intervention." In contrast, when deciding whether permissive intervention is warranted under Fed. R. Civ. P. 24(b), the district court "can consider almost any factor rationally relevant," and "enjoys very broad discretion" in allowing or denying the motion. *Daggett v. Comm'n on Governmental Ethics & Election Practices*, 172 F.3d 104, 113 (1st Cir. 1999).

1. FED. R. CIV. P. 24(a) — INTERVENTION AS OF RIGHT

Federal Rule of Civil Procedure 24(a) provides an "authoritative recipe" that lists the "essential ingredients" for intervention as of right. *Ungar v. Arafat*, 634 F.3d 46, 50 (1st Cir. 2011). In the absence of a federal statute providing for a right to intervene, and on a timely motion, the court must permit anyone to intervene who:

> claims an interest relating to the property or transaction that is the subject of the action, and is so situated that disposing of the action may as a practical matter impair or impede the movant's ability to protect its interest, unless existing parties adequately represent that interest.

Fed. R. Civ. P. 24(a). "It follows that a would-be intervenor must demonstrate that: (i) its motion is timely; (ii) it has an interest relating to the property or transaction that forms the foundation of the ongoing action; (iii) the disposition of the action threatens to impair or impede its ability to protect this interest; and (iv) no existing party adequately represents its interest." *Ungar*, 634 F.3d at 50. . . .

2. FED. R. CIV. P. 24(b) — PERMISSIVE INTERVENTION

In contrast to the four-factor test for intervention as of right, permissive intervention has only two criteria. Upon a timely motion, the court has discretion to allow permissive intervention "when an applicant's claim or defense and the main action have a question of law or fact in common." *Daggett*, 172 F.3d at 112-13; *see* Fed. R. Civ. P. 24(b)(1)(B).[2] Permissive intervention, however, is "wholly discretionary," and when exercising its discretion, the court may consider "almost any factor

---

[2] In addition, the claim or defense asserted by the proposed intervenor must be supported by independent jurisdictional grounds.

rationally relevant. . . ." *Daggett*, 172 F.3d at 113. In addition, Rule 24(b)(3) expressly provides that the court must consider "whether intervention will prejudice the existing parties or delay the action." Fed. R. Civ. P. 24(b)(3).

B. THE STUDENTS' MOTION TO INTERVENE IS TIMELY

[The court found that the Students' Motion to Intervene was timely under Fed. R. Civ. P. 24(a) and (b) because it was not unreasonably delayed and would not prejudice the parties. The students moved to intervene when the case was in early stages of discovery and before an initial scheduling conference had taken place.]

C. THE STUDENTS LACK A SUFFICIENTLY PROTECTABLE INTEREST TO WARRANT INTERVENTION AS OF RIGHT

To satisfy intervention as of right, however, [the proposed intervenor must have a "significantly protectable interest" that is direct rather than contingent].

1. FUTURE APPLICANTS

The Court agrees with SFFA that the Future Applicants do not have a direct, protectable interest in this litigation that warrants intervention as of right under Rule 24(a). As a practical matter, although each of the Future Applicants has stated his or her intent to apply to Harvard at some point in the future, none of them has even a pending application. Therefore, there is little that distinguishes the proposed intervenors currently before the Court from any other minority student in America, or indeed, the world, who may potentially be affected by Harvard's consideration or non-consideration of race and ethnicity in its admissions decisions, if he or she should decide to apply. This is not a case where the proposed intervenors "belong to a small group, quite distinct from the ordinary run of citizens," who would be affected directly by the outcome of the case. *Daggett*, 172 F.3d at 110. These students' purported interests in Harvard's admissions policies are simply too removed, too speculative, and too contingent, to justify intervention as of right under Rule 24(a). . . .

The Court also finds that the Future Applicants' purported interest is not sufficiently "protectable" to warrant intervention as of right. The Students concede that they have "no constitutional right to have their race considered by Harvard," assuming that they eventually apply. . . .

In addition, though the Students argue that courts "routinely" grant intervention as of right to parties "seeking to protect their interests in race-conscious programs from which they benefit," the cases they cite are largely distinguishable. *See, e.g., Johnson v. San Francisco Unified Sch. Dist.*, 500 F.2d 349, 352 (9th Cir. 1974) (parents of children of Chinese ancestry had a right to intervene in action challenging compulsory desegregation program in their public school district); *Black Fire Fighters Ass'n of Dallas v. City of Dallas*, 19 F.3d 992, 994 (5th Cir. 1994) (group of city firefighters had right to intervene in action, where consent decree would affect their promotional opportunities). In *Johnson*, the intervenors were not simply "potential" applicants to a private university and possible beneficiaries of its resources—they were established residents of a public school district, whose children would be compelled to follow the district's reassignment policies. In *City of Dallas*, the intervenors were firefighters, presently employed by the city, whose opportunities for promotional advancement would be immediately and directly impacted by the outcome of a racial discrimination suit. Thus, these intervenors' interests were not speculative, indirect, or contingent.

[The court acknowledged that in *Grutter v. Bollinger*, 188 F.3d 394 (6th Cir. 1999), the Sixth Circuit held, under similar circumstances to the Harvard case, that prospective minority applicants had a right to intervene in an action challenging the University of Michigan's admissions policy. The First Circuit, however, does not follow the expansive approach used by the Sixth Circuit. Applying the First Circuit approach,] the Court finds that the Future Applicants do not, on these facts, have a sufficient interest in this litigation to warrant intervention as of right under Rule 24(a).

2. HARVARD STUDENTS

The current Harvard Students are in a different posture. In contrast to the Future Applicants, these students were admitted to Harvard, chose to matriculate, and are currently enrolled in the full-time undergraduate program at the College. Therefore, they have no remaining interest in Harvard's continued consideration of race and ethnicity with respect to their own applications. Rather, their purported interest is in continuing to enjoy the academic and personal benefits that they believe arise out of Harvard's racially diverse student body, and their desire to see an increase in the number and diversity of underrepresented minority groups admitted to Harvard. Although this interest is less speculative and less contingent than the interest articulated by the Future Applicants, it is still not a significantly protectable interest. For the same reasons that the Future Applicants lack a protectable interest in Harvard's continued consideration of race in its admissions policies, so too do the current

Harvard Students. Further, to the extent that the current Harvard Students have any interest in the continued consideration of race in Harvard's admissions process, they have not established that Harvard may not adequately represent those interests, as more fully set forth below.

D. THE STUDENTS HAVE NOT ESTABLISHED INADEQUATE REPRESENTATION

Both Harvard and SFFA argue that the Students are not entitled to intervene as of right, because the Students have not demonstrated that Harvard may not adequately represent their interests. The Court agrees. The Students claim that their ultimate goal in this litigation is to "ensure that Harvard retains the right to consider race in its admissions decisions to the full extent allowed by law." Harvard shares this same objective and intends to mount a "vigorous defense" of its admissions policies. . . .

First, the Students suggest that their interests would not be adequately represented should Harvard decide to settle this suit, or decline to appeal an unfavorable outcome. However, merely speculating about this possibility does not establish inadequacy. Harvard has argued that it would be "inconceivable" for Harvard to accede to SFFA's demands, and the Court agrees that this possibility currently appears to be "extremely remote." *Patch*, 136 F.3d at 208. Moreover, in the unlikely event that Harvard settled this action or failed to appeal, the Students could renew their motion to intervene at that point in time.

In addition, the Students allege that even if Harvard is not inclined to settle, it may want to "avoid politically sensitive topics" surrounding racial and ethnic diversity when defending its admissions policies. In other words, the zealousness and thoroughness of Harvard's defense may be compromised by "concern over its public perception or by the need to serve myriad constituencies such as alumni, faculty, and the academic community, who may all have differing opinions about the propriety of the goal of achieving racial and ethnic diversity." The Students, however, do not cite any evidence to substantiate this fear. . . .

The Students further argue that Harvard lacks the ability to defend its race-conscious admissions policy adequately because "Harvard, as an institution, does not have the personal experiences that Movants do with respect to race and ethnicity." This argument is also unavailing. Harvard is perfectly capable of gathering and presenting evidence of its students' interests and experiences, and it is not necessary for these Students to intervene as full-fledged litigants for this to occur. However, to the extent that the Students' individual experiences and viewpoints may be enlightening, the Court is more than willing to permit the Students to participate as *amici curiae*, and to submit these views through declarations, substantive briefs and, in appropriate cases, oral argument.

Next, the Students identify specific arguments that they claim Harvard is unlikely to make in this litigation, and that the Students wish to present to the Court. For example, although the Students support Harvard's continued consideration of race and ethnicity, they oppose other aspects of Harvard's admissions policies and programs, including (1) Harvard's reliance on SAT scores; (2) the school's "early admission" program; and (3) the so-called "legacy" factor, pursuant to which Harvard sometimes considers whether an applicant's parent(s) are alumni of the school. The Students wish to argue that all of these policies have a negative impact on minority applicants' chances for admission, and that Harvard should be able to consider race and ethnicity in its admissions decisions in order to offset or "remedy" the disparate impact of these criteria. As a preliminary matter, the Students do not clearly explain why this "remedy" theory would be a constitutionally sufficient reason to uphold Harvard's admissions practices. Furthermore, the Students' interest in exposing the allegedly disparate impact of other admissions criteria is already represented in this case, if not by Harvard, then by SFFA. For example, SFFA alleges in its Complaint that Harvard's alleged use of "legacy" preferences, as well as other policies, has a disparate impact on minorities, and it suggests that Harvard can achieve diversity in its student body without using race as a factor in admissions decisions, by simply eliminating policies such as legacy preferences. Thus, such issues are likely to surface over the course of discovery, even absent the Students' intervention. . . .

Overall, the Students have identified only relatively minor, and very speculative divergences in interests, which do not establish that Harvard's representation may be inadequate. . . . Given the relative weakness of the Students' purported interests, the potential inadequacies they cite are not sufficiently compelling to warrant intervention as of right. The Students' Motion to Intervene as of right pursuant to Fed. R. Civ. P. 24(a) is therefore DENIED.

E. THE COURT DECLINES TO ALLOW PERMISSIVE INTERVENTION

In the alternative, the Students have moved for permissive intervention under Fed. R. Civ. P. 24(b), which provides that a court may allow intervention upon a timely motion, "when an applicant's claim or defense and the main action have a question of law or fact in common." *Daggett*, 172 F.3d at 112-13. Permissive intervention, however, is "wholly discretionary," and the court should consider "whether intervention will prejudice the existing parties or delay the action." *Glass Dimensions, Inc. Profit Sharing Plan & Trust v. State St. Bank & Trust Co.*, 290 F.R.D. 11, 14 (D. Mass. 2013).

The Court declines to allow permissive intervention here, for a number of reasons. First, as discussed earlier in this Memorandum, Harvard should adequately represent the interests of both the Future Applicants and the Harvard Students in this litigation. Second, both SFFA and Harvard have objected to the Students' full-fledged intervention, citing concerns for expediency, and, in Harvard's case, privacy. Harvard is also concerned that the Future Applicants could become privy to the inner workings of Harvard's admissions process, which could pose an unfair advantage. The Court shares the parties' concerns. In their moving papers, the Students suggest that if permitted to intervene, they will be "present and involved" in fact discovery, and that they may gather evidence and present expert testimony beyond that sought by the parties. In all likelihood, allowing fourteen Students to intervene as parties would further complicate proceedings, lengthen the discovery process, add expense, and significantly delay the ultimate resolution of this case.

In sum, the Court finds that the Students' intervention would add undue delay, cost, and complexity to these proceedings, and that such intervention is unwarranted where Harvard adequately represents the Students' interests.

Consequently, the Students' Motion to Intervene pursuant to Fed. R. Civ. P. 24(b) is also DENIED.

F. AMICUS CURIAE STATUS

Although the Students may not intervene in this case as parties, the Court will permit the Students to participate as *amici curiae*. The role of an *amicus curiae*, meaning "friend of the court," is to "assist the court 'in cases of general public interest by making suggestions to the court, by providing supplementary assistance to existing counsel, and by insuring a complete and plenary presentation of difficult issues so that the court may reach a proper decision.' " *Sierra Club v. Wagner*, 581 F. Supp. 2d 246, 250 n.1 (D.N.H. 2008). The Court finds that *amicus* status will be sufficient for the Students to present their views and arguments in this case. As *amici curiae*, the Students will be permitted to submit their own declarations, file substantive briefs on dispositive motions, and participate in oral arguments on those motions. . . .

VI. CONCLUSION

For the foregoing reasons, the Proposed Intervenors' Motion to Intervene is DENIED. . . .

Notes & Questions

1. Do you agree with the court's finding that neither the future applicants nor the current students had a sufficient interest in the case for intervention of right under Rule 24(a)? As the court notes, the intervenor's interest must be a "significantly protectable interest." Often this means an economic interest as opposed to

a moral or political concern about the issues in the lawsuit. In the Harvard case, were the proposed intervenors expressing political views or were they seeking to protect their own interests in educational opportunities? If the latter, why did the court find this interest insufficient? The would-be intervenors argued that their interest in supporting Harvard's policy was just as real as the interest of the plaintiffs in opposing Harvard's policy. Do you see why the court rejected this argument? Would the result have been different if the would-be intervenors offered an argument that the university was legally obligated to use a race-conscious policy?

2. The students sought to intervene to *support* Harvard's policy. It is easy to see why SFFA opposed their intervention. But why did Harvard oppose intervention? Locked in battle, the one thing Harvard and SFFA agreed upon was that they did not want these students to intervene. If you represented Harvard in this litigation, would you want the students to intervene? Even if they were strongly "on your side," think of ways in which their participation as parties could make your job more complicated, more expensive, more time-consuming, and more public.

3. The court was satisfied that Harvard would adequately represent the interests of the proposed intervenors. This may seem straightforward since the students sought to intervene to support Harvard's policy. But if you were the future applicants or the current students, would you be satisfied that Harvard's interests are identical to your own?

   Determining whether current parties adequately represent the interests of would-be intervenors requires a realistic assessment of the interests of the parties. Often, it is helpful to think about what sort of settlement might satisfy each party and whether such a settlement would adequately protect the interests of the party applying to intervene. In an environmental lawsuit by the Sierra Club against the secretary of agriculture, for example, two timber trade associations intervened under Rule 24(a) to protect the interests of the trade association members, because the lawsuit could affect their economic interests, and neither the environmental group nor the government adequately protected the interests of the timber industry. *Sierra Club v. Espy*, 18 F.3d 1202 (5th Cir. 1994).

4. The court found the students' motion timely. Applications to intervene may be denied for being untimely. Interestingly, Rule 24 does not specify the time limit for applying to intervene, which is noteworthy in a set of procedural rules that contains dozens of specific time limits, as well as rules on precisely how to compute the number of days. Instead, Rules 24(a) and 24(b) each begin with "On timely motion. . . ." Rather than stating a certain number of days, the rule requires a context-specific inquiry to determine timeliness. This is because the situations for intervention vary so widely. When did the intervenor learn about the lawsuit? When should the intervenor have realized that its interests were at stake? When did it become clear that the existing parties would not adequately protect the intervenor's interests? The upshot is that it can be difficult to analyze whether

an application is timely, but if you represent a potential intervenor, be sure you file the application promptly once you realize that intervention is warranted, just as the students did in the Harvard case.

5. In addition to rejecting intervention as of right, the court also rejected the students' motion for permissive intervention under Rule 24(b). Take a moment to think about the various uses of the word *permissive*. *Permissive intervention* uses the word in a different sense from permissive counterclaims, permissive joinder of claims, and permissive party joinder. In each of those instances, *permissive* refers to a party's discretionary decision. A permissive counterclaim is one that the defending party *may*, but need not, assert. Permissive joinder refers to claims or parties that the pleader *may*, but need not, join. In this sense of the word, *all* intervention should be considered "permissive." There is no such thing as *compulsory* intervention under the federal rules, a point emphasized by the Supreme Court in *Martin v. Wilks*, 490 U.S. 755 (1989). Unless a statute dictates otherwise, *see, e.g.*, Civil Rights Act of 1991, 42 U.S.C. §2000e-2(n)(1), the decision whether to intervene is up to the potential intervenor. The distinction between Rules 24(b) and 24(a) is not between permissive and *compulsory*, but rather between permissive and *of right*. Whereas Rule 24(a) describes when a person *has a right* to intervene, Rule 24(b) describes when a *court may permit* intervention at the court's discretion.

6. The court denied the students' motion to intervene, but stated that they could participate as amici curiae. Why did the students prefer to intervene rather than participate as amici? Amicus curiae ("friend of the court") is a status that allows a nonparty, with the court's permission, to offer input on the issues by submitting briefs and sometimes by oral argument. When a nonparty wishes to provide input on a legal issue, filing an amicus brief often suffices. Participation as amicus, however, does not make someone a party to the action. Parties enjoy procedural opportunities unavailable to nonparties, such as taking discovery, making motions, presenting evidence at trial, and filing an appeal. To participate fully in the action, one must become a party, and for someone who has not been joined by the parties, intervention is the ticket.

7. After the district court denied their motion to intervene, the students appealed to the U.S. Court of Appeals for the First Circuit. They did not appeal the denial of permissive intervention under Rule 24(b); given the discretionary nature of permissive intervention, they surely knew there was little chance of persuading the appellate court to overturn this aspect of the district court's decision. Rather, the students appealed the denial of intervention under Rule 24(a). Among other things, the students argued that the district judge erred in finding the students' interests were adequately represented by Harvard. The First Circuit rejected this argument, noting "that Harvard has the resources necessary to litigate the case, that it has retained counsel of whom Students offer no criticism, and that it has publicly characterized the lawsuit through its highest officials as a threat to its

'most fundamental values.'" *Students for Fair Admissions v. President & Fellows of Harvard College*, 807 F.3d 472, 475 (1st Cir. 2015). Therefore, the First Circuit affirmed the denial of intervention.

8. The case went to trial in October 2018. During the three-week bench trial, the court heard testimony not only from Harvard employees and various expert witnesses, but also from eight current or former Harvard students who testified as amici curiae. *See Students for Fair Admissions v. President & Fellows of Harvard College*, 397 F. Supp. 3d 126, 132 (D. Mass. 2019). In 2019, Judge Burroughs issued her findings of fact and conclusions of law, ruling that Harvard's race-conscious admissions program did not violate the law. *Id.* at 203-04. A year later, the First Circuit affirmed the decision on the merits. *Students for Fair Admissions v. President & Fellows of Harvard College*, 2020 WL 6604313 (Nov. 12, 2020).

F. INTERPLEADER

Interpleader is an action brought by a stakeholder against multiple claimants. Although it is a relatively obscure joinder mechanism, it can prove useful in the right situation. Here is the situation: Someone (the stakeholder, often called the *plaintiff in interpleader*) is holding something (the stake) that others (the claimants, often called the *claimants in interpleader*) claim. Maybe it is an insurance company holding the proceeds of an insurance policy and facing multiple persons claiming to be the beneficiary. Maybe it is a parking garage holding an automobile that multiple persons claim to own. The stakeholder needs to know whether it must give the stake to one of the claimants, and if so, to whom. Interpleader provides the procedural mechanism by which the stakeholder can bring an action against the claimants and thereby obtain a judgment that will be binding on all of them.

Without interpleader, a stakeholder might find itself subject to multiple liability or inconsistent obligations. Fundamentally, the problem flows from the principle that nonparties are not bound by a judgment. If claimant 1 sues the stakeholder and prevails, it remains possible that claimants 2 and 3 will sue the stakeholder for the same thing. Compulsory party joinder under Rule 19 offers one solution to this problem, but for some stakeholders that option is too reactive and uncertain. Interpleader allows the stakeholder to take the situation into its own hands to obtain a judicial resolution.

An example may help. Suppose Acme Life Insurance Co. wrote a $500,000 life insurance policy on the life of person X. The policy named "my spouse" as the beneficiary. X died, and now two people have submitted claims. One is X's ex-spouse, S1, who was married to X when X bought the insurance policy. The other is X's new spouse, S2, whom X married a year ago. Acme knows

Stakeholder (π in interpleader) — Claimant 1 — Claimant 2

that it owes $500,000, but it does not know to whom. This is the perfect occasion to use interpleader. Interpleader would be permissible even if Acme itself had a claim to keep the money, such as an argument that the insurance policy was void for nonpayment of premiums. Whether or not the stakeholder claims an interest, interpleader allows a court to resolve the claims of competing claimants.

To see why no option other than interpleader fully resolves Acme's conundrum, consider the other procedural possibilities. Suppose S1 sues Acme and wins a judgment. Can the insurance company simply pay the money to S1, relying on the judgment? Not comfortably. S2 could sue Acme demanding payment of the life insurance proceeds. Because S2 was not a party to S1's lawsuit, S2 would not be bound by the judgment, as we will see in Chapter 8. Thus, Acme would remain vulnerable to being ordered in to pay $500,000 to S2, even though Acme was already ordered in to pay $500,000 to S1.

How about impleader as a solution? If S1 sues Acme, can Acme file a third-party claim to bring in S2? Be sure you understand why that approach will not work: To assert a third-party claim under Rule 14, Acme would have to contend that if it is liable to S1, then S2 must reimburse Acme for all or part of that liability, which would be nonsensical under these circumstances.

A better option might be compulsory party joinder under Rule 19. If S1 sues Acme, Acme could move to have S2 joined as a required party or could make a Rule 12(b)(7) motion to dismiss for failure to join S2. The Rule 19 motion *might* solve the problem. Thinking about the compulsory party joinder analysis, S2 undoubtedly would qualify as a required party, especially under Rule 19(a)(1)(B)(ii). As long as S2's joinder would not present jurisdictional problems, the court would order that S2 be joined, and this would resolve Acme's problem. But what if the court lacked jurisdiction to join S2? Then, under Rule 19(b), the court would decide whether to proceed or to dismiss. To Acme, both of those options are unsatisfactory. Acme doesn't want a dismissal; it wants a *binding resolution* in an action that includes both S1 and S2.

Interpleader allows Acme to take control of the situation. Acme can commence an interpleader action against S1 and S2, seeking a binding judgment from the court on who is the rightful beneficiary under the insurance policy. Even if the action began with S1's filing a lawsuit against Acme for the insurance proceeds, Acme could commence the interpleader action by bringing an interpleader counterclaim against S1 and joining S2 as an additional claimant.

Interpleader does not work as an all-purpose tool for potential defendants who want to preempt multi-plaintiff litigation. Imagine a company that faces a large number of potential lawsuits. It may seem like a clever idea for the company to commence a huge interpleader action against all of the potential plaintiffs. The strategic advantage would be to eliminate plaintiffs' power to choose the forum or to bring multiple individual lawsuits. When a party tried this tactic in a bus accident case, however, the Supreme Court stated that interpleader cannot be used as a general aggregation mechanism to bring together claims in mass litigation. *State Farm Fire & Casualty Co. v. Tashire*, 386 U.S. 523 (1967).

Federal law establishes two types of interpleader: *rule interpleader* and *statutory interpleader*. Both offer the same procedural mechanism—an action by a stakeholder against multiple claimants—but statutory interpleader alters the provisions on jurisdiction and venue to facilitate gathering all the claimants in a single forum.

Rule interpleader refers to interpleader pursuant to Rule 22 of the Federal Rules of Civil Procedure. Akin to other joinder rules, Rule 22 simply establishes a procedural mechanism for interpleader in federal court. It does not alter the requirements of subject matter jurisdiction, personal jurisdiction, and venue. When you represent a stakeholder facing multiple inconsistent claims, you could use rule interpleader in federal court if there is a basis for federal subject matter jurisdiction, if the chosen court has personal jurisdiction over each of the claimants, and if venue is proper. We will explore these topics in Chapters 9, 10, and 11. Unless the underlying claims arise under federal law, subject matter jurisdiction for rule interpleader ordinarily depends on diversity jurisdiction under 28 U.S.C. §1332, which requires that the stakeholder's citizenship be diverse from the claimants and that the amount in controversy exceed $75,000.

> **Terminology Tip**
>
> Despite the similar-sounding names, do not confuse *interpleader* with *impleader*. Impleader refers to third-party claims under Rule 14, in which a defendant brings in a party who may be liable to pay the defendant contribution or indemnification if the defendant is liable to the plaintiff. Interpleader refers to something completely different—a claim by a stakeholder to determine which of multiple potential claimants is entitled to the asset.

Statutory interpleader, by contrast, operates according to a federal statute that expands subject matter jurisdiction, personal jurisdiction, and venue for interpleader proceedings. Remember that interpleader's goal is to enable stakeholders to obtain a resolution of the competing claims of inconsistent claimants to an asset. For such a resolution to carry finality, the stakeholder needs to join all of the claimants in the action. Statutory interpleader does three things to help stakeholders achieve finality. First, the federal interpleader statute, 28 U.S.C. §1335, alters the requirements for federal subject matter jurisdiction based on diversity of citizenship. It lowers the amount-in-controversy requirement from over $75,000 to $500, and instead of requiring complete diversity between plaintiffs and defendants, it requires only minimal diversity of citizenship among the claimants themselves. The requirement is met as long as any claimant is a citizen of a different state from any other claimant. Second, another provision of the interpleader statute, 28 U.S.C. §2361, grants nationwide personal jurisdiction for statutory interpleader. Rather than facing the usual constraints on personal jurisdiction, a court has much wider reach for statutory interpleader. Third, the statute's venue provision, 28 U.S.C. §1397, permits a statutory interpleader action to be brought in any district where at least one claimant resides. By reducing the jurisdictional and venue obstacles, statutory interpleader tries to make good on the promise of the interpleader device—to allow a stakeholder to obtain a resolution that will bind all of the known claimants in one fell swoop.

Notes & Questions

1. If statutory interpleader lowers the obstacles, why would a stakeholder ever use rule interpleader? It is true that statutory interpleader generally offers greater benefits to a stakeholder by making it easier to bring all claimants into a single forum. Sometimes, however, the special provisions of statutory interpleader are unnecessary because jurisdiction and venue are satisfied under the usual rules. Moreover, one particular set of circumstances renders *statutory* interpleader unavailable but leaves *rule* interpleader working fine. This occurs when the amount in controversy exceeds $75,000 and all of the claimants are citizens of the same state but diverse from the stakeholder. In that situation, no minimal diversity of citizenship exists among the claimants, but there is complete diversity in the usual sense required for diversity jurisdiction under 28 U.S.C. §1332.

2. For an example of interpleader and how it relates to other forms of joinder, consider the saga of *John v. Sotheby's, Inc.*, 141 F.R.D. 29 (S.D.N.Y. 1992). A married couple—Erica John and Harry John—had purchased a painting in 1960 that was attributed to Rembrandt. The couple divorced in 1985. In 1989, Erica John entered a contract with Sotheby's auction house to sell the painting. Prior to the scheduled auction, however, another person—Julian Nava—came forward and claimed ownership of the painting, asserting that he had purchased the painting from Harry John in 1985 before the divorce. Nava filed an action in California state court against Sotheby's, Erica John, and Harry John, demanding possession of the painting. The California court dismissed the claim against Erica John for lack of personal jurisdiction. Erica John then filed an action against Sotheby's in the U.S. District Court for the Southern District of New York, seeking compensatory and punitive damages for breach of the contract to sell the painting. Sotheby's filed an answer responding, as the district judge summarized it, "that Sotheby's has retained the painting because it is unsure who is the rightful owner, and it fears becoming liable to the rightful owner if it relinquished the painting to the wrong individual." 141 F.R.D. at 32. The defendant Sotheby's then "moved to interplead Dr. Nava pursuant to Rule 22, or, in the alternative, to dismiss the action for failure to join an indispensable party pursuant to Rules 19 and 12(b)." *Id.* At the same time, Nava moved to intervene as of right under Rule 24(a)(2). The court granted Sotheby's motion to institute an interpleader action by way of a counterclaim, and it also granted Nava's motion to intervene. Thus, in two ways, Nava became a party to the action, and the court was able to resolve the competing claims to the painting. By the time the case reached trial in 1994, both John and Nava had individually settled their claims against Sotheby's, so the only claims remaining to be resolved at trial were the competing claims of John and Nava to ownership of the painting. After a bench trial, the judge found that Erica John and Julian Nava were each entitled to a one-half interest in the net proceeds from a sale of the painting. *See John v. Sotheby's, Inc.*, 858 F. Supp. 1283 (S.D.N.Y. 1994).

G. CLASS ACTIONS

This chapter has looked at a number of joinder devices that bring multiple parties together in a single lawsuit—permissive party joinder, compulsory party joinder, impleader, intervention, and interpleader. Each involves a different structure and arises in a different situation, but so far, they all have this in common: Every party is included by name.

Class actions work differently. A class action is *representative litigation.* In a class action, a party sues on behalf of herself and on behalf of all others who are similarly situated. The class members may have no desire to pursue their claims—indeed they may be totally unaware that they even have claims—but if they are part of the defined class in a certified class action, then their claims are represented by the class representative and class counsel. When a class action reaches judgment, the judgment is binding on all the class members as long as they were adequately represented.

Class actions, in other words, run contrary to civil procedure's usual notions of autonomy, consent, and participation. Why would the law allow such a strange procedure? Three answers: efficiency, consistency, and empowerment. When large numbers of claimants share essentially the same claim, a class action can resolve the dispute much more efficiently than individual litigation or even non-class mass joinder. Class actions also yield more consistent results than individual litigation because all class members are bound by the outcome of a single lawsuit. Consistency matters in cases involving money damages, but it is especially crucial in cases involving common injunctive relief. Finally, class actions empower plaintiffs to pursue claims that are not worth pursuing individually but are worth pursuing in the aggregate. Suppose a company with a million customers imposes $5 of illegal extra charges on each customer's monthly bill. Over the course of a year, that is a $60 million violation. But probably not a single customer would sue because it would cost much more to litigate than the $60 that each plaintiff has at stake. The class action device enables a lawyer and a class representative to pursue the claims on behalf of all of the customers. Even if none of the class members really cares about her individual monetary recovery, the class action creates a mechanism for enforcing the law and furthering the policies of disgorgement and deterrence.

Because class actions bind persons who may not have participated in the litigation, the law imposes a number of special procedures to protect the interests of class members. First, a case does not proceed as a class action unless the court certifies the class. *See* Rule 23(a)-(b). Second, the court has the power to appoint the lawyer for the class, *see* Rule 23(g), and the court has power over the class counsel's fees, *see* Rule 23(h). Third, settlement of a class action requires court approval. *See* Rule 23(e). Fourth, in most money damages cases, class members have the right to opt out of the class action. *See* Rule 23(c)(2)(B). Fifth, a class action is binding on the class members only if they were adequately represented. *See Hansberry v. Lee*, 311 U.S. 32 (1940).

Many law schools offer an upper-level course on class actions or complex litigation. Here, we offer a brief introduction to the topic, focusing on class certification and class action settlements.

(1) Class Certification

Filing a class action complaint does not create a class action; it merely creates a "putative class action" that the plaintiff hopes will be certified. The only thing that creates a class action is class certification. When a party moves to certify the class, the judge must decide whether the case meets the class certification requirements of Rules 23(a) and 23(b).

For class certification, a class action must meet all four of the prerequisites stated in Rule 23(a): numerosity, commonality, typicality, and adequate representation. In addition, class certification requires that the class action meet the requirements of at least one of the class action categories identified in Rule 23(b).

(a) Rule 23(a) Prerequisites

Numerosity. If the number of class members is not too large, then the parties can simply join together in a single lawsuit under the permissive joinder rule. Rule 23(a)(1) therefore requires that the number of class members be so large that joinder is impracticable. Courts emphasize that no magic number exists; numerosity requires case-by-case determination. In general, classes in the hundreds usually meet the numerosity requirement, and classes below 40 rarely meet the requirement. Big class actions involve thousands or even millions of class members; in the big cases, nobody disputes numerosity.

Commonality. Rule 23(a)(2) requires common questions of law or fact. Lawyers used to consider Rule 23's commonality requirement easy to meet, but in 2011, the Supreme Court in *Wal-Mart Stores v. Dukes*, 564 U.S. 338 (2011), made it clear that the commonality requirement is a non-trivial constraint on class certification. Rejecting a gender discrimination class action against Walmart, the Court emphasized that the claims were not unified enough: "Their claims must depend upon a common contention—for example, the assertion of discriminatory bias on the part of the same supervisor. That common contention, moreover, must be of such a nature that it is capable of classwide resolution—which means that determination of its truth or falsity will resolve an issue that is central to the validity of each one of the claims in one stroke." A party seeking class certification must show that there is "some glue" holding the claims together.

Typicality. For the class representative to sue on behalf of the entire group of similarly situated plaintiffs, the representative's situation must be like that of the rest of the class. Rule 23(a)(3) therefore requires that the named party's claim be typical of the class. Although some variation may exist within the class, the class representative should not be an outlier.

Adequacy of Representation. This is the most fundamental requirement of them all. It has a basis not only in the language of the class action rule, but also in the Due Process Clause of the Constitution. Rule 23(a)(4) requires, for class certification, that the class representative will adequately represent the interests of the entire class. Courts rarely worry about the class representative's skills or knowledge or ability to handle the litigation because, as a practical matter, class representatives often function as figureheads while the lawyers for the class actually handle the litigation. Courts do worry, however, about whether the class representatives have any conflicts of interest that prevent them from being adequate representatives. In this way, the adequacy requirement becomes another means of ensuring that the class is cohesive enough to justify a class action. The adequacy requirement transcends Rule 23. Without adequate representation, a class action would violate the constitutional guarantee of due process. In the landmark case of *Hansberry v. Lee*, 311 U.S. 32 (1940), the Supreme Court held that a class action judgment can bind the members of the class, but only if they were adequately represented.

(b) Rule 23(b) Categories

For class certification, the court must find not only that the class meets all four of the Rule 23(a) prerequisites, but also that it fits into at least one of the Rule 23(b) categories. The categories are significant not only for class certification, but also because different procedural requirements attach to them. In particular, Rule 23(b)(3) class actions have a notice requirement and give class members the right to opt out, while (b)(1) and (b)(2) class actions do not permit opt-outs and carry a more flexible notice provision. Because they do not allow opt-outs, class actions under Rule 23(b)(1) and 23(b)(2) are sometimes called *mandatory class actions*, in contrast to Rule 23(b)(3)'s *opt-out class actions*.

(i) Rule 23(b)(1) Class Actions

Rule 23(b)(1) actually includes two subcategories of class actions, (b)(1)(A) and (b)(1)(B). The main thing they have in common is that their language and logic strongly resemble the compulsory party joinder analysis of Rule 19(a).

Rule 23(b)(1)(A) permits class certification if individual adjudications would create a risk of "incompatible standards of conduct" for the defendant. For example, suppose a company has issued a bond that is owned by thousands of investors, and an investor sues the company for a declaratory judgment that the bond may be converted to common stock. It would make no sense to address that issue individually, because if the bond is convertible to common stock, then it must be so for all of the investors. Without a class action, the company might face inconsistent rulings and would not know how it should treat the security. The 23(b)(1)(A) class action permits a single adjudication or settlement that applies to all of the investors who own that security.

Rule 23(b)(1)(B) permits class certification if individual adjudications might impair the ability of other class members to protect their own interests. The typical (b)(1)(B) class action involves a limited fund. For example, suppose a large number of individuals have claims to money that is held in a trust. The maximum amount available for all of the claims is the amount in the trust. As a practical matter, individual adjudications for some of the claimants would limit the amount of money for the remaining claimants and might even exhaust all of the available funds.

The 23(b)(1)(B) class action permits a single adjudication or settlement that attempts to deal fairly and consistently with all of the claimants.

"Limited fund class actions" under Rule 23(b)(1)(B) were once considered a useful device for sorting out claims of money damages when the parties doubted the defendant's ability to pay the entirety of the claims. In 1999, however, the Supreme Court in *Ortiz v. Fibreboard Corp.*, 527 U.S. 815 (1999), imposed strict requirements for limited fund class actions, emphasizing that they may be certified only if the fund is clearly inadequate and if the entire fund is applied to paying the claims.

(ii) Rule 23(b)(2) Class Actions

Some class actions seek injunctive or declaratory relief rather than money damages. Most notably, civil rights class actions often have sought prison reform, school desegregation, voting rights enforcement, changes in hiring practices, and other types of institutional reform. If a court orders such injunctive relief, the remedy applies to all members of the class. Rule 23(b)(2) permits certification of a class action when the defendant has acted with respect to the entire class so that injunctive or declaratory relief "is appropriate respecting the class as a whole." The Supreme Court has held that money damages cannot be recovered in a Rule 23(b)(2) class action unless the monetary relief is incidental to the claims for injunctive relief. *Wal-Mart Stores v. Dukes*, 564 U.S. 338, 339 (2011).

(iii) Rule 23(b)(3) Class Actions

Rule 23(b)(3) permits a class action if common questions predominate and if the court finds that a class action is the superior way to adjudicate the controversy. For the most part, class actions for money damages—whether they involve antitrust, securities, product liability, consumer fraud, or other claims—are handled under Rule 23(b)(3).

Because class actions for divisible remedies such as money damages seem less necessary than class actions under (b)(1) and (b)(2), Rule 23(b)(3) adds the two requirements that define this category: *predominance* and *superiority*. First, the court must find that "questions of law or fact common to class members predominate over any questions affecting only individual members." Common questions often involve the defendant's conduct and classwide defenses, while individual questions often relate to individual causation and damages as well as individual defenses such as consent or comparative fault.

Second, the court must find that "a class action is superior to other available methods for fairly and efficiently adjudicating the controversy." The rule spells out factors for courts to consider when deciding whether a class action is superior. One important factor is "the class members' interests in individually controlling" their cases. If each claim involves high enough stakes that individual class members might pursue the claims themselves, a court is less likely to find superiority, in contrast to cases where each claim is too small to make an economically viable individual lawsuit. The rule also instructs courts to consider "the likely difficulties in managing a class action." If the court cannot see how it will be able to manage the case if it gets to trial, then the court may reject class certification.

The predominance and superiority inquiries often overlap. If the class action would require the court to apply the laws of different states to different class members, for example, the court may find that the various laws are individual issues and thus reject predominance, and the court may also find that applying the various laws would be unmanageable and thus a class action is not superior. Similarly, if the class action would require individualized determinations of causation, the court may find that common issues do not predominate, and also find that the individual causation analysis makes the class action an inferior way to handle the dispute.

In the following two cases, plaintiffs moved for certification of Rule 23(b)(3) classes, and the judges reached opposite conclusions on whether to grant class certification.

JOHNSON v. GENERAL MILLS, INC.
275 F.R.D. 282 (C.D. Cal. 2011)

CARNEY, District Judge.

I. INTRODUCTION

Mr. [Jeremiah] Johnson has brought claims on behalf of himself and putative class members asserting General Mills, Inc. and Yoplait USA, Inc. (collectively "General Mills") violated California's Unfair Competition Law ("UCL") and Consumers Legal Remedies Act ("CLRA") by falsely representing that YoPlus yogurt products promote digestive health. Mr. Johnson alleges that General Mills communicated these misrepresentations through product packaging and other forms of marketing including television, newspaper, magazine, internet, and direct mail advertisements. Before the Court is Mr. Johnson's motion for class certification of these claims. For the reasons explained below, Mr. Johnson's motion for class certification is GRANTED.

II. ANALYSIS
A. LEGAL STANDARD FOR CLASS CERTIFICATION

. . . Federal Rule of Civil Procedure 23(a) sets forth four requirements for maintenance of a class action. Under that rule, a class may only be certified if: (1) the class is so numerous that joinder of all members is impracticable, (2) there are questions of law or fact common to the class, (3) the claims or defenses of the representative parties are typical of the claims or defenses of the class, and (4) the representative parties will fairly and adequately protect the interests of the class. Fed. R. Civ. P. 23(a). In addition, the party seeking certification must show that the action falls within one of the three subsections of Rule 23(b). In this case, Mr. Johnson seeks certification pursuant to 23(b)(3). Rule 23(b)(3) permits certification of cases in which "the court finds that the questions of law or fact common to class members predominate over any questions affecting only individual members, and that a class action is superior to other available methods for fairly and efficiently adjudicating the controversy." Fed. R. Civ. P. 23(b)(3). Mr. Johnson bears the burden of demonstrating that he has met the four requirements of Rule 23(a) as well as the predominance and superiority requirements of Rule 23(b)(3).

B. STANDING

As an initial matter, Mr. Johnson has standing under the UCL and CLRA.... Mr. Johnson has UCL and CLRA standing because he alleges that he bought YoPlus in reliance on General Mills' allegedly deceptive representations concerning the digestive health benefit of YoPlus as communicated by the second generation YoPlus packaging and a television commercial for YoPlus. He further asserts that he suffered economic injury because he purchased YoPlus but did not receive the promised digestive health benefit.

C. RULE 23(A) REQUIREMENTS
1. NUMEROSITY

Numerosity is satisfied where "the class is so numerous that joinder of all members is impracticable." Fed. R. Civ. P. 23(a)(1). Mr. Johnson seeks to certify a class consisting of thousands of persons that purchased YoPlus in California over a period of several years. Although General Mills contests other Rule 23 requirements, it does not genuinely dispute that Mr. Johnson's proposed class satisfies the numerosity requirement. The numerosity requirement is met here.

2. COMMONALITY

To prevail under Rule 23(a)(2)'s commonality inquiry, the plaintiff must establish common questions of law and fact among class members....

Mr. Johnson's UCL and CLRA claims raise common issues regarding General Mills' allegedly deceptive representation that YoPlus promotes digestive health. *See* Cal. Bus. & Prof. Code §17200 (UCL prohibiting unfair competition in the form of "unlawful, unfair or fraudulent business act[s] or practice[s] and unfair, deceptive, untrue or misleading advertising"); Cal. Civ. Code §1770(a) (providing that misrepresenting the characteristics or benefits of products constitutes an unfair method of competition or unfair or deceptive act or practice under the CLRA).

Mr. Johnson may bring these UCL and CLRA claims on behalf of a class. Although [California law] requires that Mr. Johnson actually relied on General Mills' alleged misrepresentations to bring his UCL claim, that requirement does not apply to absent class members. *See In re Tobacco II Cases*, 46 Cal. 4th 298, 321, 326 (2009). Indeed, "relief under the UCL is available without individualized proof of deception, reliance and injury." *Id.* at 320.

As the Supreme Court of California has explained in the UCL context, " 'a presumption, or at least an inference, of reliance arises whenever there is a showing that a misrepresentation was material.' " *Id.* at 327. Similarly, a CLRA claim can be litigated on a classwide basis when the "record permits an 'inference of common reliance' to the class." *McAdams v. Monier, Inc.*, 182 Cal. App. 4th 174, 183 (2010)....

Accordingly, Mr. Johnson's UCL and CLRA claims present core issues of law and fact that are common and suitable for adjudication on a classwide basis. These issues include: (1) whether General Mills communicated a representation—through YoPlus packaging and other marketing, including television and print advertisements—that YoPlus promoted digestive health; (2) if so, whether that representation was material to individuals purchasing YoPlus; (3) if the representation was material, whether it was truthful; in other words, whether YoPlus does confer a digestive health benefit that ordinary yogurt does not; and (4) if reasonable California consumers who purchased YoPlus were deceived by a material misrepresentation as to YoPlus' digestive health benefit, what is the proper method for calculating their damages. The commonality requirement is also met here.

3. TYPICALITY

Mr. Johnson's claims are sufficiently typical to satisfy Rule 23(a)(3).... Mr. Johnson claims that he, like other reasonable consumers, purchased YoPlus in reliance on General Mills' representation that YoPlus promotes digestive health. He asserts that this representation was communicated by the packaging of YoPlus and by General Mills' marketing and advertising efforts including a television commercial that he saw. He further contends that YoPlus did not live up to this representation and that he suffered damages as a result. These assertions combined with Mr. Johnson's supporting evidence recently withstood General Mills' motion for summary judgment. General Mills conceded at the March 7, 2011 hearing on the motion for class certification that it does not genuinely dispute that Mr. Johnson's claims are typical. The typicality requirement is also met here.

4. ADEQUACY

Under Rule 23(a)(4)'s adequacy requirement, Mr. Johnson must establish that he "will fairly and adequately protect the interests of the class." Fed. R. Civ. P. 23(a)(4). In determining whether a proposed class representative will fairly and adequately protect the interests of the class, the Court asks two questions. First, do the proposed class representative and his counsel "have any conflicts of interest with other class members"? *Staton v. Boeing Co.*, 327 F.3d 938, 957 (9th Cir. 2003). Second, will the proposed class representative and his counsel "prosecute the action vigorously on behalf of the class"? *Id.* There is no evidence that Mr. Johnson or his counsel have any conflicts of interest with proposed class members. In fact, Mr. Johnson's claims, as explained with respect to the typicality requirement, are aligned with the claims of proposed class members. Moreover, Mr. Johnson is represented by attorneys that have significant class action experience—including class action experience with respect to this particular product—that are capable of fairly and adequately representing Mr. Johnson and the proposed class. Indeed, General Mills further conceded at the March 7, 2011 hearing that it does not genuinely dispute that Mr. Johnson and his counsel satisfy the adequacy requirement. Accordingly, the adequacy requirement is also met here.

D. RULE 23(b)(3) REQUIREMENTS

Mr. Johnson must also satisfy the predominance and superiority requirements of Rule 23(b)(3). For the reasons explained below, he meets those requirements.

1. PREDOMINANCE

"The Rule 23(b)(3) predominance inquiry tests whether proposed classes are sufficiently cohesive to warrant adjudication by representation." *Amchem Prods., Inc. v. Windsor*, 521 U.S. 591, 623 (1997). It is similar to the commonality requirement of Rule 23(a)(3). *Id.* at 623 n.18. But predominance is a more rigorous requirement than the Rule 23(a)(3) commonality prerequisite....

In this case, common issues underlying Mr. Johnson's UCL and CLRA claims predominate. As explained, the central issues raised by this suit concern an allegedly overriding, material misrepresentation that YoPlus promotes digestive health in a way that ordinary yogurt does not. According to Mr. Johnson, this misrepresentation was communicated by the packaging of YoPlus and further amplified by General Mills' marketing including television, newspaper, magazine, and internet advertisements. At this stage of the suit, Mr. Johnson has made a sufficient showing that the issues of (1) whether General Mills made such a common and pervasive representation and (2) if so, whether that representation was material and would have deceived reasonable consumers, can be litigated on a classwide basis. General Mills' argument is unpersuasive that individual issues predominate because purchasers of YoPlus have been exposed to different mixes of packages and advertisements since General Mills has, over time, modified the packaging of YoPlus and the content and emphasis of its marketing materials. Contrary to General Mills' suggestion, individualized proof of deception and reliance are not necessary for Mr. Johnson to prevail on the class claims. Again, the common issue that predominates is whether General Mills' packaging and marketing communicated a persistent and material message that YoPlus promotes digestive health.[4]

Other common issues of great importance to this litigation are also subject to classwide litigation and common proof, further evidencing that common issues predominate. Most importantly, General Mills could defeat the claims of the entire class by proving that YoPlus promotes digestive health in the manner that General Mills

---

[4] Ultimately, whether Mr. Johnson or General Mills is right on these issues need not be determined at this stage. What matters is that these significant common issues can be litigated on a classwide basis. General Mills may file the appropriate motion to decertify or for partial summary judgment if after conducting discovery it believes the class is overinclusive.

allegedly represented. The digestive health benefit of YoPlus, or the lack thereof, is a common issue that is particularly appropriate for classwide resolution because it will turn on complex and expensive scientific evidence and expert testimony. Litigation of this issue in individual cases would not only be extraordinarily duplicative and wasteful, it would exponentially increase the likelihood that courts and juries would reach inconsistent decisions. The predominance requirement is satisfied here.

2. SUPERIORITY

Finally, it is apparent that a class action would be a superior method for resolving these common issues. A class action may be superior "[w]here classwide litigation of common issues will reduce litigation costs and promote greater efficiency." *Valentino v. Carter-Wallace, Inc.*, 97 F.3d 1227, 1234 (9th Cir. 1996). It is also superior when "no realistic alternative" to a class action exists. *Id.* at 1234-35. In deciding whether a class action would be a superior method for resolving the controversy, the Court considers factors including: (1) the class members' interest in individually controlling the prosecution or defense of separate actions, (2) the extent and nature of any litigation concerning the controversy already begun by or against class members, (3) the desirability or undesirability of concentrating the litigation of the claims in the particular forum, and (4) the likely difficulties in managing a class action. Fed. R. Civ. P. 23(b)(3)(A)-(D).

These factors clearly favor classwide resolution of Mr. Johnson's UCL and CLRA claims. In a consumer class action of this type involving the purchase of a relatively inexpensive food product, injured consumers are extremely unlikely to pursue their claims on an individual basis. That is especially true here given the great expense that would fall on individual class members if each class member had to provide scientific evidence and expert testimony in separate cases. Although there are similar YoPlus actions pending against General Mills in other jurisdictions, it does not appear that those suits raise California state law claims on behalf of a class of California purchasers. This forum is appropriate for the resolution of such claims. Additionally, the likely difficulties of managing this suit on a classwide basis are manageable and should be undertaken in light of the significant common issues that exist and predominate over individual issues.

III. CONCLUSION

For the foregoing reasons, Mr. Johnson's motion for class certification is GRANTED. The Court GRANTS Mr. Johnson's motion to certify his UCL and CLRA claims for all persons who purchased YoPlus in the State of California from the date YoPlus was first sold in California to the date notice is first provided to the Class. The Court also GRANTS Mr. Johnson's request that he be appointed as the class representative as well as his request that Blood Hurst & O'Reardon, LLP and Robbins Gellar Rudman & Dowd, LLP be appointed as class counsel.

COLE v. GENE BY GENE, LTD.
322 F.R.D. 500 (D. Alaska 2017), *aff'd*, 735 Fed. Appx. 368 (9th Cir. 2018)

GLEASON, District Judge.

Before the Court is Plaintiff Michael Cole's Motion for Class Certification and Appointment of Class Counsel. Defendant Gene by Gene opposed the motion. . . .

BACKGROUND

Gene by Gene sells at-home DNA testing kits, which allow for comparisons between individuals to determine whether the individuals are related. There are three varieties of tests: Y-DNA, mtDNA, and autosomal DNA. Along with one of the three tests, Gene by Gene sends its customers an at-home testing kit containing two vials, two cheek swabs, an optional release form, a welcome letter, instructions, and a return envelope. The release form grants Gene by Gene permission to provide the customer's name and email address to "genetic matches," along with sufficient information about the customer's DNA test results to explain the nature of the genetic matches. After the customer has returned the kit and the sample has been tested, the customer can view his results on the Family Tree DNA website. The customer then has the option of joining "projects," which are websites run by volunteer administrators that allow customers to connect to individuals with similar surnames, genetic characteristics, or regional histories. Terry Barton, a project administrator for Gene by Gene, runs the website WorldFamilies.net, which hosts more than 1600 projects sites, and offers varying degrees of support to the volunteer administrators. When a customer joins a project, such as those hosted by WorldFamilies.net, Mr. Cole alleges that the customer's name, email address, oldest known ancestor, DNA testing kit number, and DNA test results are automatically shared with the group administrators. Mr. Cole alleges that this information is shared without the customer's consent. Moreover, Mr. Cole asserts that by default, customers' kit numbers and DNA test results are posted on publicly available project websites. Mr. Cole specifically alleges that if a customer joins a project administered by Terry Barton, the customer's test results and contact information are transmitted to WorldFamilies.net servers and databases, where the results may be displayed on World Families' public website. Mr. Cole maintains that he is one of hundreds of individuals in Alaska who "purchased a test from Gene by Gene and joined a project, only to find that doing so had resulted in the disclosure of his Genetic Information."

Mr. Cole now moves the Court to certify the following class:

> Project Membership Class: all individuals who purchased a DNA test from Gene by Gene, Ltd. and who executed a release form and joined a Family Tree DNA "project" between May 13, 2012 and August 1, 2016, while residing in the State of Alaska.

Mr. Cole further moves to certify the following subclass:

> Worldfamilies Subclass: all Project Membership Class members who joined a Family Tree DNA "project" administrated or co-administered by Terry Barton and/or WorldFamilies.net.

Gene by Gene opposes Mr. Cole's motion and argues that class certification must be denied because: (1) Mr. Cole's claim is unique: therefore, there are issues with commonality and typicality; (2) other class members might be entitled to actual damages that Mr. Cole is "expressly uninterested in representing"; (3) individual interests predominate over potential class interests and a class action is not superior to other methods to adjudicate this controversy; and (4) "the application of solely punitive damages, in the absence of alternate harm, is overly burdensome and disproportionate."

DISCUSSION
I. JURISDICTION

This Court has diversity jurisdiction pursuant to 28 U.S.C. §1332.

II. LEGAL STANDARD

"The class action is 'an exception to the usual rule that litigation is conducted by and on behalf of the individual named parties only.'" *Wal-Mart Stores, Inc. v. Dukes*, 564 U.S. 338, 348 (2011) (quoting *Califano v. Yamasaki*, 442 U.S. 682, 700-01 (1979)). Pursuant to Federal Rule of Civil Procedure 23(a), a district court may certify a class only if (1) it is so numerous that joinder of all members is impracticable, (2) there are questions of law or fact common to the class, (3) the claims of the representative party are typical of the claims of the class, and (4) the representative party will fairly and adequately protect the interests of the class.

Before certifying a class, a court must also find that one of the requirements of Rule 23(b) has been meet. Here, Mr. Cole relies on Rule 23(b)(3), which requires finding (1) that questions of law or fact common to the class predominate over any questions affecting individual class members: and (2) that a class action is superior to other available methods for resolving the controversy.

The party seeking class certification [bears the burden of demonstrating that the requirements of Rule 23(a) and (b) are met]. Here, as explained below, the Court finds that Mr. Cole has not satisfied the requirements of Rule 23(b)(3)—predominance and superiority—and will deny the motion on that basis.[19]

---

[19] Accordingly, the Court does not reach the Rule 23(a) requirements.

A. PREDOMINANCE

The predominance requirement is met where the proposed class's interests are "sufficiently cohesive to warrant adjudication by representation." *Amchem Prods., Inc. v. Windsor*, 521 U.S. 591, 623 (1997). The presence of commonality alone, as required under Rule 23(a), is not sufficient to fulfill Rule 23(b)(3)'s predominance requirement. "Rule 23(b)(3) imposes a 'far more demanding' standard than [Rule] 23(a)(2)." *Stockwell v. City & Cty. of San Francisco*, 749 F.3d 1107, 1113 (9th Cir. 2014). Rule 23(b)(3) requires that common questions predominate over individual questions. . . .

Mr. Cole brings this action against Gene by Gene for violating Alaska's Genetic Privacy Act. To prevail in a class action, each plaintiff must demonstrate that Gene by Gene disclosed the results of that customer's DNA analysis and that it did so without that customer's informed and written consent.

Mr. Cole has demonstrated that this case involves certain questions common to the proposed class and subclass. [Common questions include whether Gene by Gene's testing constitutes a DNA analysis under the Act, whether Gene by Gene's alleged disclosures were for profit, and whether Gene by Gene's sharing of genetic information constitutes a disclosure.]

To show that the alleged disclosures were uniform and automatic, Mr. Cole cites Elliott Greenspan's deposition testimony. He testified, "[W]hen the customer's results come back, they will get notified, the customer themselves, as well as a group administrator that is managing that sample, if there is one." Mr. Greenspan did not testify that group administrators automatically receive each customer's full test results. Rather, it appears the notification simply informs the administrator whenever "a new result has come in that matches [their group]." Whether additional information is provided depends on several factors, including whether the customer "signed the release form," whether the customer joined any projects, and whether the customer kept his privacy settings on private, public, or group. These issues are significant aspects of the case and require individualized proof, weighing against a finding that common questions predominate.

Whether each proposed class member gave informed and written consent to disclosure could depend on several individualized determinations: whether the customer signed a release form, the precise language of that particular customer's form, and the information provided to that customer about potential disclosures of genetic information. . . . In short, individualized determinations may be required as to the consent form each customer signed, which could be different for each project the customer joined.

The individualized proof that would be required to establish each customer's consent, together with the individualized proof needed to demonstrate Gene by Gene's disclosure of each customer's test results, supports a finding that individual questions predominate over common questions, as both consent and disclosure are key elements of the Genetic Privacy Act.

[Gene by Gene also argues that the calculation of damages is an individual issue. Individual differences in class members' damages do not generally defeat a finding of predominance, but in particular cases, courts may find that individual damage concerns are unusually pertinent, particularly if the damages cannot be measured on a classwide basis.] A proposed method for measuring individual damages should translate "the *legal theory of the harmful event* into an analysis of the economic impact *of that event.*" *Comcast Corp. v. Behrend*, 133 S. Ct. 1426, 1435 (2013) (quoting Federal Judicial Center, Reference Manual on Scientific Evidence 432 (3d ed. 2011)) (emphasis in original).

To the extent that any of the approximately 900 proposed class members sustained actual damages such as employment, health, or insurance discrimination, Mr. Cole has not proposed any method for measuring such damages. A trial within a trial would likely ensue for each class member seeking actual damages so as to establish the proximate cause of the alleged actual damages and the extent of that customer's injury as it relates to Gene by Gene's liability. While Mr. Cole does not need to show that each members' damages are identical, he must establish a means for measuring damages on a classwide basis that is traceable to Gene by Gene's conduct. With respect to actual damages, he has failed to present any such method.

The present case is distinguishable from the case Mr. Cole cites in his motion, *Harris v. comScore, Inc.*, 292 F.R.D. 579 (N.D. Ill. 2013). In *Harris*, each class and subclass member agreed to the same form contract and engaged in a substantively identical process when they downloaded the defendant's software. The software then collected the same information from all computers on which it was downloaded. Based on these similarities, the district court determined that common questions predominated and class certification was appropriate.

But here, the record indicates that proposed class members received different release forms, joined different projects run by different administrators, and could adjust the privacy settings to different degrees of disclosure. And to the extent that any of the approximately 900 proposed class members claims actual damages, such plaintiff would need to individually establish actual harm and connect that harm to Gene by Gene's alleged violation of the Genetic Privacy Act. The potential variance among the proposed class is substantially at odds with the uniformity of the proposed class in *Harris*. For the foregoing reasons, the Court finds that Mr. Cole has not demonstrated that questions common to the class predominate over questions that require individualized proof.

B. SUPERIORITY

"The policy at the very core of the class action mechanism is to overcome the problem that small recoveries do not provide the incentive for any individual to bring a solo action prosecuting his or her rights." *Amchem*, 521 U.S. at 617. In the superiority analysis, a court determines whether a class action is the best vehicle for the litigation of the plaintiffs' claims. A class action is superior when the claimed damages for each individual claimant are too small to be pursued individually. A class action may also be superior to other forms of litigation when it "achieve[s] econom[y] of time, effort, and expense" by consolidating duplicative individual lawsuits. *See* W. Rubenstein, *Newberg on Class Actions* §4:67 (5th ed.) (citing Advisory Committee Note to 1966 Amendments, 39 F.R.D. 69, 102 (1966)). In making a determination as to whether a class action is the superior method of adjudication, Rule 23(b) directs a court to evaluate the following four factors: (1) the class members' interests in individually controlling the prosecution; (2) the extent and nature of any already-pending litigation concerning the controversy; (3) the desirability of concentrating claims in one judicial forum; and (4) the likely difficulties in managing a class action.

The first factor asks whether the cost of pursuing individual litigation is prohibitive, thereby rendering a class action the presumptively superior method of adjudication. . . . Here, unlike securities law or patent litigation, this case involves a direct application of a relatively straightforward and concise law. There is no indication in the record that Gene by Gene has been unduly litigious. And Alaska Rule of Civil Procedure 82 provides that "the prevailing party in a civil case shall be awarded attorney's fees," which may incentivize a plaintiff's attorney to pursue this type of case.

Moreover, the available remedy under the Alaska Genetic Privacy Act for a for-profit violation would appear to be sufficient to make an individual suit economical. Mr. Cole has alleged that Gene by Gene's violations resulted in profit, which could render him entitled to a minimum of $100,000 for his claim alone. His claim satisfies the $75,000 threshold for diversity jurisdiction so that it may be individually pursued in federal court. Accordingly, the Court finds that given the amount of Mr. Cole's individual claim, this factor weighs strongly against class certification.

The second factor, the extent and nature of any already-pending litigation, [serves judicial economy by reducing multiple lawsuits]. Here, neither party has apprised the Court of any other pending litigation against Gene by Gene for alleged violations of Alaska's Genetic Privacy Act. Accordingly, there is no indication that a class action would achieve greater economy of time, effort, or expense. Therefore, this factor weighs against finding that a class action is the superior method of adjudication.

The third factor evaluates the advantages of concentrating litigation in this forum. Here, the Genetic Privacy Act is an Alaska statute and each proposed class member is an Alaska resident. And yet there is no other case of this nature pending in the District of Alaska. The Court finds that, if there were to be other claims, concentrating litigation in one class action in the District of Alaska could be desirable, unless, as discussed above, there were variations in the releases, privacy settings, actual damages sought, or other individualized determinations that made a class action unwieldy.

The fourth factor examines the difficulties in managing the class action. . . . Here, as discussed above, there may be many individual issues that predominate in the case regarding disclosure, informed consent, and actual damages. Given this likelihood, together with the magnitude of each individual plaintiff's potential damages award, the Court does not find that Mr. Cole has demonstrated that a class action is superior.

In light of the foregoing, the Court finds that a class action is not the superior method for adjudicating this dispute.

3. DUE PROCESS CONCERNS

Gene by Gene also argues that "even if Plaintiff can meet his burden to establish the elements of Rule 23," the Court should deny class certification because the potential "damages are overly excessive." The Ninth Circuit instructs it is "not appropriate to evaluate the excessiveness of the award [when deciding whether to certify a proposed class]." *Bateman v. American Multi-Cinema, Inc.*, 623 F.3d 708 (9th Cir. 2010); *see also Stockwell v. City & Cty. of San Francisco*, 749 F.3d 1107, 1111-12 (9th Cir. 2014) (quoting *Amgen Inc. v. Conn. Ret. Plans & Trust Funds*, 568 U.S. 455 (2013)) ("Merits questions may be considered to the extent—but only to the extent—that they are relevant to determining whether the Rule 23 prerequisites for class certification are satisfied."). This

Court has carefully considered available remedies under Alaska's Genetic Privacy Act to determine whether individual litigation or a class action is the preferable method for adjudication in this case. But the Court has not considered the distinct issue of whether the overall potential damages award at stake if the proposed class were certified would violate Gene by Gene's right to due process.[61] In light of

---

[61] In *Bateman*, the Ninth Circuit reviewed a district court's decision to deny class certification. There, despite the small amount of statutory damages available—$100 to $1,000 if willful—the district court was troubled by the magnitude of the defendant's potential liability, which if the class were certified may have amounted to $29 million to $290 million due to the number of alleged violations. The district court denied class certification on that basis, holding that "class treatment could result in enormous liability completely out of proportion to any harm suffered by the plaintiff." 623 F.3d at 711. The Ninth Circuit reversed the district court's decision, holding that

the Court's determination under Rule 23(b)(3), the Court does not reach this issue.

CONCLUSION

Because Mr. Cole has not established that common questions predominate and that a class action is the superior method of adjudication, the Court finds that class certification is inappropriate for the proposed Class and Subclass at this time. Therefore, Mr. Cole's Motion for Class Certification at Docket 138 is hereby DENIED. The class action claims in Mr. Cole's Complaint are DISMISSED. This action shall proceed with respect to Mr. Cole's individual claims only.

---

consideration of the total potential liability is not appropriate at the class certification stage of the litigation. *Id.* at 723.

Notes & Questions

1. On the surface, *Johnson* and *Cole* seem similar. In each case, individual consumers sued companies for alleged wrongdoing that affected large numbers in a parallel way. In each case, plaintiffs moved for class certification under Rule 23(b)(3) to represent the entire group of affected consumers. Why was class certification granted in *Johnson* but denied in *Cole*? Are the cases distinguishable in ways that warrant different answers on class certification?

2. Why did the plaintiffs in *Johnson* and *Cole* seek class certification? Would plaintiffs have pursued these claims individually? Is your answer the same for both cases? Even if plaintiffs might have pursued claims individually, what are some potential advantages of proceeding by way of a class action?

3. In thinking about why these plaintiffs sought class certification, to what extent do you think the decision was driven by the plaintiffs themselves as opposed to their lawyers? Supposing the decision was largely in the hands of the lawyers, do you find this off-putting or inspiring? Class actions tend to be lawyer-driven rather than client-driven. In a class action, aggregate stakes are high but individual stakes are often low. Thus the lawyers nearly always have a larger stake than

any individual class member. Each class member may stand to gain a small amount while the lawyers may spend years working on the litigation and hope to earn a substantial fee out of the judgment or settlement. Some critics view such lawyers as agitators stirring up litigation that few clients have any interest in pursuing. Others view such lawyers as reformers serving an essential function in rooting out wrongdoing. That class actions are lawyer-driven—and that many class actions are driven in significant part by the prospect of large fees for class counsel—is a fact. Whether such entrepreneurial lawyering is a bug or a feature of modern litigation depends on one's attitudes about litigation in general and about class actions in particular.

4. Both *Johnson* and *Cole* were federal court cases even though they involved state law claims. Before 2005, many state law class actions were brought in state courts. In 2005, Congress passed a statute that dramatically expanded federal court jurisdiction over class actions. The Class Action Fairness Act (CAFA), which we will encounter in Chapter 9 when we explore subject matter jurisdiction, permits federal jurisdiction over class actions based on minimal diversity (rather than the usual complete diversity requirement) and over a $5 million aggregate amount in controversy (rather than over $75,000 for each individual). Because of CAFA, most large-scale class actions may now be brought in federal court by the plaintiff or removed to federal court by the defendant, even if the action involves only state law claims.

5. The district court's decision on class certification often looms as the single most important ruling in a case. If the court grants class certification, it creates massive litigation and places pressure on the defendant to settle. If the court denies class certification, in theory the lawsuit proceeds as a non-class action, but in reality the denial often amounts to a death knell for the litigation. Either way, the party on the losing side of the class certification motion usually would like to appeal the decision before proceeding with the case. In general, only final judgments are appealable, as discussed in Chapter 6. Grants or denials of class certification are interlocutory rulings rather than final judgments, and thus would not be appealable under the final judgment rule. But because class certification is a critical moment in the case, Rule 23(f) permits interlocutory appeals of class certification rulings at the discretion of the court of appeals. Thus, the defendant in *Johnson* could attempt to appeal the district court's grant of class certification, subject to the discretion of the court of appeals, and in parallel fashion, the plaintiff in *Cole* could attempt to appeal the district court's denial of class certification, again subject to the appellate court's discretion as to whether to permit the appeal.

6. Indeed, Michael Cole took an appeal under Rule 23(f), but the Ninth Circuit affirmed the denial of class certification. It held that the district court did not abuse its discretion in finding that individualized determinations predominated with respect to disclosure, consent, and damages. Similarly, it held that the district court did not abuse its discretion by denying class certification on

superiority grounds, noting not only the difficulties inherent in managing a class action with significant individual issues, but also the substantial damages available to aggrieved Gene by Gene customers under the Alaska Genetic Privacy Act. *Cole v. Gene by Gene, Ltd.*, 735 Fed. Appx. 368 (9th Cir. 2018).

7. Some of the most famous examples of mass litigation—but not necessarily class actions—involve mass torts. Mass tort litigation may arise out of disasters such as air crashes, environmental spills, building collapses, and terrorist attacks. Even more prominently, much mass tort litigation involves product-liability claims, such as disputes over asbestos, tobacco, defective automobiles, guns, medical devices, and pharmaceutical products.

   Courts generally refuse to certify class actions in mass tort litigation involving personal injuries or death, mostly because individual questions concerning injuries and causation tend to overwhelm common questions concerning liability. During the 1980s and 1990s, some courts experimented with class actions as a way to resolve mass torts, but several important appellate decisions squelched the movement. In *Castano v. American Tobacco Co.*, 84 F.3d 734 (5th Cir. 1996), the Fifth Circuit decertified a nationwide class action that plaintiffs had brought against the six leading cigarette manufacturers. Among other reasons, the court found that the class action failed the predominance requirement of Rule 23(b)(3) because of differences in smokers' factual situations and variations in state tort law. In *Amchem Products, Inc. v. Windsor*, 521 U.S. 591 (1997), the Supreme Court similarly rejected class certification in a nationwide asbestos settlement class action. Based on these and other cases, district judges now generally decline to grant class certification in cases involving personal injuries or death, even when the cases share significant common questions concerning the basis for liability against a defendant.

8. One of the biggest areas of class action practice is securities litigation. When investors sue a corporation over a misrepresentation or omission in the company's financial disclosures that affected the company's stock price, the financial harm may impact large numbers of investors similarly. Courts often find such cases suitable for class certification under Rule 23(b)(3). Defendants have fought class certification by arguing that each investor's reliance on a misrepresentation or omission is an individual question. Courts, however, have held that reliance in securities fraud cases can be a common question based on the fraud-on-the-market doctrine, which allows investor plaintiffs to prevail by showing that a company's misrepresentation or omission affected the market price of a security and investors were harmed by relying on the market price. By making reliance a common question, the fraud-on-the-market doctrine permits securities fraud plaintiffs to meet the predominance requirement of Rule 23(b)(3), which would be very difficult to satisfy if reliance were an individual question. *See, e.g., Amgen, Inc. v. Connecticut Retirement Plans & Trust Funds*, 568 U.S. 455 (2013).

   Securities class actions operate a bit differently from other class actions. Under the Private Securities Litigation Reform Act (PSLRA), a federal statute passed in 1995, plaintiffs face a higher pleading standard in securities cases, even beyond Rule 9(b)'s general heightened pleading standard for fraud. *See* 15 U.S.C. §78u-4(b)(1)(B). The PSLRA also establishes a different process for appointing the class representative and class counsel. Under the PSLRA, the class member with the largest financial interest—which usually means an institutional investor such as a pension fund or investment company—presumptively serves as class representative and selects class counsel. *See* 15 U.S.C. §77z-1(a)(3)(B).

9. Class actions have long been an important mechanism for pursuing civil rights litigation. Civil rights class actions typically are brought under Rule 23(b)(2), which permits class certification where plaintiffs seek classwide injunctive or declaratory relief. *Brown v. Board of Education*, 347 U.S. 483 (1954), which held racially segregated schools unconstitutional, was a class action. Over the years, many other cases involving voting rights, prison reform, employment discrimination, and other civil rights have similarly been litigated as class actions. The Supreme Court made discrimination cases somewhat harder to certify with its decision in *Wal-Mart Stores, Inc. v. Dukes*, 564 U.S. 338 (2011), in which the Court found that the plaintiffs' gender-discrimination claims failed the commonality test because the claims were not sufficiently capable of a single classwide resolution.

   Note one difference between Rule 23(b)(3) class actions for monetary damages and Rule 23(b)(2) class actions for declaratory or injunctive relief. For claims of money damages, only named parties or class members get the direct benefit of the remedy. For civil rights claims seeking declaratory or injunctive relief, by contrast, potentially all affected individuals reap the benefit even if the case is litigated on an individual basis. If a court grants an injunction that prohibits a particular employment practice at a company, bans a prison policy, or alters voting rights in a district, all affected persons likely get the benefit even if no class action was filed or certified. Even more broadly, a legal pronouncement can bestow a benefit that transcends the parties in the action. For example, consider *Obergefell v. Hodges*, 135 S. Ct. 2584 (2015), in which the Supreme Court held that same-sex couples have a constitutional right to marry. It was not a class action. Rather, it was a consolidated appeal of several cases that had been filed by 14 couples and by 2 men whose partners were deceased. These plaintiffs filed their lawsuits against various state officials. As a matter of procedural form, the outcome in each lawsuit was a judgment for the benefit of the specific parties in that case. But the actual impact was to establish a constitutional right to marry for every same-sex couple in the United States. Despite the fact that individual civil rights cases may have broad impact, can you think of some reasons why civil rights plaintiffs sometimes choose to file class actions rather than individual actions?

10. *Johnson* and *Cole* each involved an attempt to certify a *plaintiff* class. Look again at the language of Rule 23(a): "One or more members of a class may sue *or be sued* as representative parties on behalf of all members only if..." (emphasis

added). Those words "or be sued" mean that, at least in theory, a court can certify a defendant class if all of the requirements of Rule 23(a) and 23(b) are satisfied. In practice, defendant class actions are exceedingly rare. For an example, see *Thillens, Inc. v. Community Currency Exchange Ass'n of Ill.*, 97 F.R.D. 668 (N.D. Ill. 1983) (certifying a class of hundreds of members of the Illinois Currency Exchange Association, and naming the association as the class representative, in an action brought by a check-cashing company alleging that the association and its members conspired to prevent the plaintiff from obtaining licenses).

STRATEGY SESSION

In class actions that are litigated (as opposed to class actions that are certified solely for settlement), it is nearly always the plaintiffs who seek class certification and defendants who oppose it. Plaintiffs find strength in numbers, and class actions empower plaintiffs to pursue claims with greater efficiency and leverage. To maximize the chance of winning class certification, class action lawyers seek to frame their clients' claims in a way that lends itself to classwide resolution. A court is more likely to grant class certification if claims focus on a defendant's uniform policy or systemic practice as opposed to mistreatment of particular individuals. And a court is more likely to grant class certification if the claims are governed by federal law or a single state's substantive law, rather than by the law of multiple states. When drafting a complaint and in every step thereafter, the class action lawyer must think about the implications for class certification.

(2) Class Action Settlements

Class action settlements, unlike most settlements, require court approval. Outside of class actions, settlements usually require only the parties' agreement. As we will explore in Chapter 13, a settlement is a contract in which the plaintiff agrees to drop the lawsuit and release claims in exchange for the defendant's agreement to provide a remedy. Settlements need a judge's approval only in special situations such as when one of the parties is a minor or mentally incompetent to consent to the settlement. The requirement of judicial approval of class settlements makes sense by analogy to settlements involving minors or incompetent persons. In a class action, some of the persons bound by the settlement are incapable of consent—not because they are minors or lack the mental competence to consent, but because they are not there. The absent class members will be bound by a settlement even though they did not agree to it.

Rule 23(e) requires that the court hold a hearing to determine whether the proposed settlement is "fair, reasonable, and adequate." Class members must get reasonable notice of the proposed settlement, and they may voice any objections. When the court approves a proposed class action settlement, that outcome becomes a judgment of the court. An approved class action settlement is binding on all of the parties, including absent class members.

In some cases, the parties negotiate a classwide settlement even before seeking class certification. These cases are known as "settlement class actions" or "settlement-only class actions." The parties ask the court to certify a class action solely for purposes of the settlement that they already negotiated. Simultaneously, they ask the court to approve the class settlement they negotiated but only on the condition that the class is certified. Settlement class actions arise when a defendant faces widespread potential liability and seeks to dispose of the entire dispute with a single massive settlement. The defendant may be willing to pay a large amount of money to settle the dispute, but only if the settlement resolves the whole thing. Settling cases one by one cannot bring that sort of finality, but a class action settlement can. Two settlement class actions reached the Supreme Court in the late 1990s, both arising out of asbestos litigation. *Amchem Products v. Windsor*, 521 U.S. 591 (1997), presented a Rule 23(b)(3) opt-out settlement class action, and *Ortiz v. Fibreboard Corp.*, 527 U.S. 815 (1999), presented a Rule 23(b)(1)(B) limited fund settlement class action. In each case, the Court found that the proposed class actions failed to meet the requirements of Rule 23, but the Court did not reject the idea of settlement class actions. The Supreme Court expressed concerns about the fact that plaintiffs' lawyers lack leverage when negotiating a settlement class action (since the class action has not yet been certified, the plaintiffs' lawyer cannot make a realistic threat of taking the class action to trial). Nonetheless, a court may approve a settlement class action as long as it finds the settlement fair under Rule 23(e) *and* finds that the class meets the requirements of Rule 23(a) and 23(b) for class certification.

To decide whether a class settlement is "fair, reasonable, and adequate," judges consider several factors. Rule 23 was amended in 2018 to state these factors explicitly: (A) whether the class was adequately represented by the representatives and by class counsel; (B) whether the proposal was negotiated at arm's length; (C) whether the relief provided for the class is adequate, taking into account the risks and benefits of taking the claims to trial; and (D) whether the proposal treats class members equitably relative to each other. *See* Rule 23(e)(2)(A)-(D).

STRATEGY SESSION

Most people think of class actions as a weapon for plaintiffs, but class actions also can serve defendants. It depends on whether the class action is used for litigation or for settlement. In litigation, class actions mostly benefit plaintiffs. But in settlement, class actions help defendants resolve mass disputes. Indeed, *settlement class actions* (class actions certified solely for settlement) often are driven by defendants' desire for peace in the face of potential liability. By binding an entire group of claimants with a single negotiated resolution, the settlement class action allows defendants to obtain more protection from future litigation than they could obtain by settling with claimants individually.

H. CONSOLIDATION AND MULTI-DISTRICT LITIGATION

(1) Consolidation

Although not technically a joinder mechanism, consolidation has a similar practical effect. Rule 42(a) empowers a court to pull multiple cases together for a joint trial or other joint proceedings: "If actions before the court involve a common question of law or fact, the court may: (1) join for hearing or trial any or all matters at issue in the actions; (2) consolidate the actions." The minimal requirement ("a common question of law or fact") leaves the consolidation decision almost entirely to the court's discretion. A major obstacle to consolidation, however, is that under Rule 42(a), consolidation works only if the actions are pending in the same court.

The flipside of consolidation is separation. Under Rule 42(b), a court may order separate trials of any claims, crossclaims, counterclaims, third-party claims, or even of separate issues, "[f]or convenience, to avoid prejudice, or to expedite and economize." Rule 20(b) reminds the court, in the context of permissive party joinder, that even if a party is properly joined under the rule, the court retains the power to order separate trials.

The upshot of Rule 42(a) consolidation and Rule 42(b) separation is that joinder of claims and joinder of parties does not always dictate whether the claims will be tried together. Judges have significant discretion to consolidate actions that were brought separately or to separate claims that were brought in a single action.

(2) Multi-District Litigation

Multi-district litigation (MDL) allows the federal judicial system to handle related actions together even if the actions were filed in different districts. MDL plays a much bigger role than you might think just by reading the statute.

The MDL statute, 28 U.S.C. §1407, provides:

> (a) When civil actions involving one or more common questions of fact are pending in different districts, such actions may be transferred to any district for coordinated or consolidated pretrial proceedings. Such transfers shall be made by the judicial panel on multidistrict litigation authorized by this section upon its determination that transfers for such proceedings will be for the convenience of parties and witnesses and will promote the just and efficient conduct of such actions. Each action so transferred shall be remanded by the panel at or before the conclusion of such pretrial proceedings to the district from which it was transferred unless it shall have been previously terminated. . . .
>
> (b) Such coordinated or consolidated pretrial proceedings shall be conducted by a judge or judges to whom such actions are assigned by the judicial panel on multidistrict litigation. . . .

In the illustration to the right, civil actions were pending in the Central District of California, the Northern District of Illinois, the Southern District of New York, and the Southern District of Florida. The Judicial Panel on Multidistrict Litigation—a group of seven judges appointed by the Chief Justice of the United States—decided to transfer all four cases for pretrial

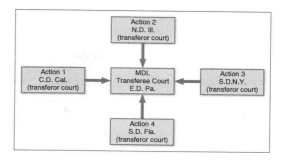

purposes to a judge in the Eastern District of Pennsylvania. Perhaps the four cases involve the same plaintiff or the same defendant, or perhaps not, but the Panel must have found that the actions share at least one common question of fact, and must have decided that pretrial centralization would serve the interests of efficiency and justice. Now that the actions have been transferred pursuant to 28 U.S.C. §1407, the MDL judge in the Eastern District of Pennsylvania (the transferee court) will manage the litigation and decide any pretrial matters such as motions to dismiss, discovery disputes, summary judgment, and class certification. If discovery and other pretrial matters are completed, then the MDL statute provides that each case will be remanded to its original district (the transferor court) for trial.

Technically, the MDL statute establishes a venue transfer mechanism. It allows the Panel to transfer related actions to a single federal district judge for pretrial proceedings. But in reality, MDL is much more than venue transfer, and its most important functions mirror consolidation and joinder. In obvious ways, MDL resembles Rule 42(a) consolidation. Not only does the statute use the word "consolidated," it also relies on a "common question" test, but note that while Rule 42(a) allows consolidation where there is any common question of law or fact, MDL requires a common question of fact. As a functional matter, however, many lawyers experience MDL above all as an alternative or accompaniment to class actions. Particularly in mass tort litigation, but also in other areas of large-scale litigation such as securities, antitrust, employment, and civil rights, MDL has become a prominent form of aggregate litigation.

The following excerpt from a law review article about the history of the MDL statute offers an introduction not only to how MDL works, but also to its recent growth and to controversies about how it functions in practice.

Andrew D. Bradt, *"A RADICAL PROPOSAL": THE MULTIDISTRICT LITIGATION ACT OF 1968*
165 U. Pa. L. Rev. 831 (2017)

As recently as a decade ago, it would have been reasonable to say that multidistrict litigation, the statutory authorization for consolidating cases filed around the country in a single federal district court for pretrial proceedings, was a second banana to the class action, which had long demanded the lion's share of public and scholarly attention. Despite several high-profile examples, scholars have characterized the device, commonly referred to as "MDL," as an obscure device or "disfavored judicial backwater."

To the extent MDL was ever appropriately considered a bit player, things have changed. With the Supreme Court and lower courts cutting back the viability of the class action under Rule 23 for decades and with Congress providing for expanded jurisdiction over class actions in the federal courts, MDL has become the leading mechanism for resolving mass torts. As of June 2014, 36% of all filed federal civil cases were part of a pending MDL, up from 16% in 2002. That now amounts to over 120,000 cases, the vast majority of which are mass-tort matters, including products liability or defective drugs—cases that had been considered by some courts, at least for a brief period, as appropriate subjects for class actions. . . .

A natural way to begin to understand MDL's effectiveness in tort cases is by comparing it to its more famous and now-much-diminished cousin, the class action. In a class suit, a representative files and pursues litigation on behalf of a group of absent plaintiffs. By contrast, in MDL, a panel of federal judges transfers already pending and to-be-filed cases sharing a common question of fact to a single district judge for "pretrial proceedings." After pretrial proceedings are concluded, the statute mandates that cases be remanded to the courts from which they were transferred for trial. Remand, however, happens less than 3% of the time—like most cases, in or out of an MDL, the vast majority of transferred cases are terminated or settled before pretrial proceedings conclude, that is, while they are within the control of the MDL judge. In a world where trials are exceedingly rare, pretrial proceedings are the main event.

In sum, this structure makes MDL, according to one prominent federal district judge, "a 'once-in-a-lifetime' opportunity for the resolution of mass disputes by bringing similarly situated litigants from around the country, and their lawyers, before one judge in one place at one time." Indeed, as another prominent district judge has described it, "[I]t is almost a point of honor among transferee judges . . . that cases so transferred shall be settled rather than sent back to their home courts for trial." While the concept of the "settlement class" under Rule 23(b)(3) has withered under Supreme Court scrutiny and after the passage of the Class Action Fairness Act of 2005, MDL has begun to accomplish essentially the same end.

Courts and lawyers on both sides of the "v." appear to be adjusting to this new era of MDL ascendancy. Plaintiff-side firms have come to appreciate the ability to join forces to achieve parity with well-resourced defendants. Defendants recognize the opportunity to litigate all claims in a single forum where they can both efficiently perform discovery and motion practice and eventually achieve peace, whether through victory on a dispositive motion or through settlement. And, for judges, the power of MDL to vacuum thousands of cases filed nationwide into one courtroom carries significant docket-clearing benefits.

Scholars' reactions are more mixed. Some laud MDL for its success in achieving settlement of massive cases and for the flexibility it provides transferee judges. But others contend that MDL is a raw deal for individual plaintiffs, who, compared to those in a class action, have fewer formal protections from unfairness but equally little control over the day-to-day conduct of the litigation. For instance, although an MDL is not a representative suit, unlike a class action, there is no right to opt out of an MDL proceeding—once you're in, you're in, often for years until "pretrial proceedings" have concluded. Moreover, while the litigation is within the jurisdiction of the MDL court, the cases are prosecuted primarily by "steering committees" of lawyers appointed by the court. These lawyers, who receive additional fees, take charge of discovery and motion practice and eventually play the most prominent role in negotiating global settlements. In addition, unlike a class action, there is no requirement that a judge review a settlement for fairness. But judges nevertheless play an active role in brokering global settlement deals, and some of those agreements (most notably in the massive set of cases arising from the use of the drug Vioxx) have been criticized as unduly coercive to the individual plaintiffs. MDL, to these critics, presents the worst of both worlds—a statute that provides inadequate power to protect plaintiffs but also no real limitations on judges acting imperially to manage cases and essentially mandate settlement. . . .

I. What Is MDL, and Why Is It Important and Controversial?

To set the stage, consolidation and coordination of multidistrict litigation in the federal courts is authorized by 28 U.S.C. §1407. The statute provides, "When civil actions involving one or more common questions of fact are pending in different districts, such actions may be transferred to any district for coordinated or consolidated pretrial proceedings." To accomplish these transfers, the statute mandates creation of a panel of seven federal judges, appointed by the Chief Justice of the Supreme Court, called the Judicial Panel on Multidistrict Litigation. Upon its own motion, or the motion of any party in any action to potentially be transferred, the Panel may initiate proceedings to create an MDL. After notice to any affected party and a hearing, if the Panel decides that it "will be for the convenience of parties and witnesses and will promote the just and efficient conduct of [the] actions," it may transfer all of the pending cases to a single district judge of its choosing, commonly referred to as the "MDL judge," for pretrial proceedings. All later-filed cases involving the same subject matter are transferred rather seamlessly as "tagalong cases" to the MDL judge. The Panel's transfer orders are reviewable only by extraordinary writ; the Panel's orders denying transfer are not reviewable at all. The statute mandates that the cases be remanded to the districts from which they came at the conclusion of pretrial proceedings.

During pretrial proceedings, all actions in the transferor courts are stayed, and the MDL judge possesses all of the powers of any district judge, including the power to manage discovery, dismiss cases, exclude evidence, and grant summary judgment or other dispositive motions. The result is that the MDL judge has complete authority over the mass of cases, whose numbers can run into the thousands, until pretrial proceedings have concluded and the cases have to be returned to their original courts. In practice, however, the MDL judge actively attempts to guide the litigation to a conclusion, typically through a "global settlement" that resolves most, if not all, of the component cases in the litigation. As a result of the MDL judge's power to terminate and assist in settling the cases, very few cases are ultimately remanded to their home districts. Historically, the remand rate is around 3%. Moreover, when cases involving the same subject matter are pending in both federal MDL proceedings and state court MDL analogs, the state court judges often coordinate with and defer to the federal MDL judges to reach a resolution.

Although the MDL statute was little noticed when it was passed in 1968 and remained that way for the first decades of its existence, today it is central. The numbers are staggering—and become more so every year. According to a recent report by the Duke Law School Center for Judicial Studies,

> More than one-third of the civil cases pending in the nation's federal courts are consolidated in multidistrict litigations. In 2014, these MDL cases make up 36% of the civil case load. In 2002, that number was 16%. Removing 70,328 prisoner and social security cases from the total, cases that typically (though not always) require relatively little time of Article III judges, the 120,449 pending actions in MDLs represented 45.6% of the pending civil cases as of June 2014.

Strikingly, 96% of these cases are what are commonly considered "mass tort" cases—that is, tort claims involving similar claims by a large group of plaintiffs—and the vast majority of those are state-law products liability cases. Some MDLs are enormous. For instance, the pelvic-mesh product liability cases, consolidated in the Southern District of West Virginia, contain nearly 50,000 cases. Those are at the high end of the spectrum, but there are currently twenty pending MDLs containing more than one thousand component cases, amounting to over 115,000 cases.

Without belaboring the point, it is fair to say that MDL has exploded, particularly in the area of mass-tort products cases. Why the recent surge? It is apparently because such cases, at least for a brief period, were class actions (typically settlement class actions) brought under Rule 23(b)(3) in federal court or, when those class actions became more difficult to maintain in federal court, were class actions brought in state court. Rule 23(b)(3) class actions have become harder to maintain in federal court due to restrictive lower appellate court decisions and the Supreme Court's decisions in *Amchem Products, Inc. v. Windsor* [521 U.S. 591 (1997)] and *Ortiz v. Fibreboard Corp.* [527 U.S. 815 (1999)]. When lawyers turned to comparatively friendly state courts, Congress responded by extending federal jurisdiction over class actions in the Class Action Fairness Act of 2005. The catch-22 created by that combination (there is federal jurisdiction over these class actions, but under Rule 23 they cannot be certified as class actions) created a vacuum for aggregate mass-tort litigation. Hiding in plain sight was the MDL statute, which has emerged as the primary alternative for mass-tort litigation. Although it is not as blunt an aggregation tool as the class action because the plaintiffs file and formally pursue their own cases rather than being represented by a class representative, MDL achieves many of the same efficiencies—namely, coordinated discovery and motion practice controlled by small committees of lawyers appointed by the court and gathering most parties together into a single proceeding for a potential global resolution. From an efficiency standpoint, there is much to be said for the flexibility offered by the MDL process. The MDL judge has the ability to coordinate and manage the litigation to its ultimate conclusion, relieving the federal courts of the burden of resolving the cases individually. The parties and courts get a lot of bang for their aggregation buck without having to surmount the many hurdles to class certification.

Although many courts and lawyers have come to embrace MDL, it has come under attack in the academy. Why? It is precisely *because* MDL achieves many of the efficiencies of class actions without all of the procedural protections for absent plaintiffs. By way of comparison, in order to sustain a mass-tort class action under Rule 23(b)(3), a class representative must fulfill all of the prerequisites of Rule 23(a), plus show that the common questions predominate over individual questions, demonstrate that the class action is a superior way of proceeding, and provide notice and the opportunity to opt out to class members. MDL requires none of that. All that is necessary for consolidation is one common question of fact, and there is no opportunity to opt out. Once a plaintiff's case has been transferred into an MDL, it remains there until pretrial proceedings have been concluded, which, in practice, typically means until the MDL is terminated or settled.

In a class action, all of these procedural hurdles are thought to be necessary because most of the plaintiffs are not actively participating in the litigation. Instead, they are represented by the class representative and must be protected from incompetent or unscrupulous representation. In MDL, it is said that none of these additional protections need to exist because the plaintiff prosecutes her own case with her own attorney. This, however, is not an accurate portrayal of how MDL actually works. In practice, the MDL process looks, in many ways, very much like the class action process, with judge-appointed steering committees of attorneys representing the plaintiffs as a whole, many of whose cases have been transferred to a far-flung location selected by the Panel.

The three most prominent strands of criticism of MDL are that (1) MDL insufficiently protects individual plaintiffs' due process rights, including the right to a meaningful day in court, (2) there are no established rules governing MDL judges' procedures, resulting in inconsistency, and (3) MDL cases take a very long time to litigate. These critiques are detailed and complex, but for brevity's sake, I will boil them down: critics think that the MDL statute gives MDL judges unlimited discretion and deprives plaintiffs of control over their cases with little procedural protection. The result for many plaintiffs is a coercive global settlement negotiated in a distant court by someone else's lawyer that the plaintiffs have little practical choice but to accept. In sum, what makes MDL such an effective means of resolving mass litigation is also what provokes intense criticism: the almost unlimited discretion of the district judge that the Panel puts in charge of the litigation. Yet, unlike the class action, the MDL structure has been unmolested by due process-based attacks to its legitimacy. In one sense, the crackdown on alleged lawlessness of class actions has facilitated a shift to MDL and potential lawlessness in the *other* direction.

Notes & Questions

1. At first glance, one might look at the MDL statute and suppose that the transferee judge is relatively insignificant. The statute limits MDL to pretrial matters and states that actions will be remanded for trial to their transferor courts. But think about all of the things that happen *pretrial*. Motions to dismiss, discovery, and summary judgment fall within the power of the MDL judge. The vast majority of settlements occur pretrial. The MDL judge decides joinder issues including class certification, and also has the power to approve class action settlements, thus potentially resolving an entire mass dispute. This combination of powers—the power of pretrial adjudication such as dismissal or summary judgment, the power to facilitate settlement negotiations, and the power to certify class actions and approve class settlements—make the MDL judge a powerful player in large-scale litigation. Transferee judges in large MDLs do not mostly see themselves as mere pretrial processers

whose job is to get cases ready for trial by their original judges, but rather, as Professor Bradt makes clear, as judges whose job is to bring disputes to resolution.

2. Not only do MDL judges bring cases to resolution by virtue of their pretrial powers, sometimes they conduct trials. The statute does not authorize MDL judges to try the cases transferred to them by the Panel. And the Supreme Court made it clear that MDL judges may not circumvent this constraint by self-transferring cases under another venue transfer statute. *See Lexecon v. Milberg Weiss Bershad Hynes & Lerach*, 523 U.S. 26 (1998). However, an MDL judge may try actions that were filed in the judge's own district—even if they are related cases that are being handled as part of the MDL—because such actions fall within the judge's trial power, unlike actions that are transferred pursuant to the MDL statute.

When an MDL judge oversees a large number of actions, the judge may aim to help the parties reach a settlement that resolves many or all of the claims at the same time. For lawyers to negotiate such a settlement with confidence, often they need information about the likely outcome of individual cases if the cases were to be tried. One way a judge can provide this information is by scheduling "bellwether trials." A bellwether trial is a trial of an individual action with the goal not merely of adjudicating the particular action but also of providing a bit of information—the data point of this particular outcome—to help parties reach a global settlement of a widespread dispute. MDL judges may do this by trying cases over which they have direct power, by readying and remanding cases for trial in their transferor courts, or both.

3. Even if many actions are being handled on a coordinated basis through MDL, each action remains a civil action in federal court, and its procedures are governed by the Federal Rules of Civil Procedure. Thus, an MDL judge decides summary judgment under Rule 56, class certification under Rule 23, and so on. Some procedural questions, however, are unique to MDL and not addressed by the general civil procedure rules. Some observers have suggested that there ought to be special rules to govern procedures within MDL, while others have said that such matters are better left to the discretion and creativity of transferee judges.

CHAPTER 8

Enforcement and Preclusion

We have followed the litigation process from start (pleadings) to finish (trial and appeal), and then added complexity by considering joinder. What, exactly, is the end result of this process? It is a *judgment*. The court's judgment is the decision that concludes the matter, and typically it is issued as a separate document. In a case that settles or where the plaintiff chooses to drop the claim, the plaintiff may voluntarily dismiss the action, *see* Fed. R. Civ. P. 41(a), but in cases that reach adjudication, the court "enters judgment" reflecting the outcome.

A judgment, ultimately, is just a piece of paper or an electronic document in the court's records. Its power comes from the fact that authorities are willing to *enforce* it, ultimately backed up by the physical power of the state if necessary. For a litigant, the first step is getting a favorable judgment, but ultimately what matters is the judgment's binding effect. One might ask a number of different questions about the binding effect of a judgment. First, if a judgment states that the plaintiff is entitled to a particular remedy from a defendant, what if the defendant does not voluntarily comply? If the judgment is for monetary relief, what if the defendant simply does not pay? And if the judgment is for injunctive relief, how does one compel the party to obey the injunction? This is the topic of *enforcement of judgments*, which we explore in Part A of this chapter. Second, what if a plaintiff is at risk of immediate and irreparable harm such that it requires a remedy *prior* to final judgment? The possibility of obtaining preliminary remedies to prevent such harm, or to preserve the court's ability to render a meaningful final judgment, is the subject of Part B. Third, regardless of whether the plaintiff or defendant prevails, what if a party attempts to relitigate the claims or issues underlying the judgment? These are the topics of *claim preclusion* and *issue preclusion*, which we explore in Parts C, D, and E. Fourth, can a judgment be undone? This is the topic of *relief from judgment*, which we discuss in Part F. Note that there is an additional aspect of the binding effect of judgments that this chapter does not address—the precedential effect of a judgment as a matter of *stare decisis*. Rather than look at outcomes of litigation as they affect the development of the law, this chapter focuses on outcomes of litigation as they relate directly to the participants in the action.

A. ENFORCEMENT OF JUDGMENTS

Entry of judgment by the district court is a formalized procedure governed by Federal Rule of Civil Procedure 58. "Every judgment and amended judgment must be set out in a separate document [except for orders disposing of certain motions]." Rule 58(b) governs entry of judgment—with or without the court's direction, Fed. R. Civ. P. 58(b)(2) (with); 58(b)(1) (without), as well as the time of entry (Rule 58(c)), and the procedure for requesting entry of judgment (Rule 58(d)).

After a judgment is entered, the expectation is that party against whom that judgment is entered will comply with it. However, that is not always the case. What is the prevailing party to do? For judgments to amount to anything more than words on paper, courts must have both the *power* and the *mechanisms* to actually enforce judgments. As to the former, every court with the power to enter a judgment has the power to enforce it. *Peacock v. Thomas*, 516 U.S. 349, 356 (1996) ("Without jurisdiction to enforce a judgment . . . the judicial power would be incomplete and entirely inadequate to the purposes for which it was conferred by the constitution.") (quoting *Riggs v. Johnson City*, 6 Wall. 166, 187 (1868)). As to the mechanisms for enforcing a judgment, this section provides a brief overview of *how* courts enforce a judgment when faced with a defendant who is unwilling or unable to pay a monetary judgment, or who fails to abide by an injunctive or other equitable judgment. The Federal Rules of Civil Procedure paint with a broad brush in this regard, and they provide procedures for enforcing monetary remedies (Fed. R. Civ. P. 69) and remedies for specific acts, such as compliance with an injunction (Fed. R. Civ. P. 70).

(1) Enforcing Monetary Judgments

Often, a party with a monetary judgment against her (a debtor) will simply pay without any further action by the court. If the debtor does not pay of her own accord, however, the court must get involved again to enforce its judgment and ensure that the creditor gets paid. Federal Rule of Civil Procedure 69 governs the enforcement of monetary judgments in federal court. Under Rule 69, the means of enforcing a monetary judgment is through an instrument called a "writ of execution." Fed. R. Civ. P. 69(a)(1). The creditor must secure this writ of execution in order to collect a judgment from a recalcitrant debtor. A writ of execution is simply an order from the court that rendered or registered the judgment directing a U.S. marshal, state sheriff, or other similar official to seize the debtor's property and sell it or give it to the creditor. In order to get a writ of execution, the creditor must file an application with the clerk of the district court in which the creditor is trying to enforce the judgment.

State law sets forth what must be included in these requests, so the specifics will vary. Typically, however, these requests must include the amount of the judgment, the date of the judgment, the property to be seized, and the identity of both the creditor and the debtor. The creditor may also be required to submit supporting affidavits or declarations to show that the writ is necessary or that the creditor is actually entitled to the money that the debtor has refused to pay. The request also generally must contain a draft of the writ of execution itself, and state law also specifies what this must contain.

But what happens once a creditor obtains a writ of execution? Take another look at Rule 69. Despite playing such an important role in ensuring that victorious parties actually get the money they are entitled to, the rule is quite short. Notably, while it specifies that the writ of execution is the means of enforcing a monetary judgment, it does not describe what procedure parties must go through once they obtain the writ. Instead, the rule says only that enforcement should follow state procedures, unless there is some federal statute on point. As a result, just *how* a writ of execution is used to enforce a judgment can vary from state to state.

> **Terminology Tip**
>
> We usually think of "debtors" as people who have taken out loans. (Given your status as a law student, you likely have a ready example of this type of debtor.) However, in the context of enforcing judgments, the party who has not paid the judgment against it is also referred to as a "debtor." The debt consists of the money that it has been ordered to pay but is either unwilling or unable to offer to the winning side. Similarly, the party trying to enforce the judgment is called the "creditor," as it is awaiting the payment of the debt that is owed to it in the form of the outstanding judgment.

In general, though, most states enforce a writ of execution by executing a lien on the debtor's property as a way to secure the debt that is owed to the creditor. A lien is a legal device that gives a creditor a property interest in some piece of property that is held by the debtor. A home mortgage is perhaps the most familiar type of lien; it gives the creditor, in this case the bank, the right to take the mortgaged piece of property if the debtor, in this case the homebuyer, cannot make payments on the house. The same basic idea is used for enforcing monetary judgments. The court may grant the creditor a lien on some piece of the debtor's property that is valuable enough to satisfy the judgment. If the debtor still does not pay the judgment, the creditor may then "execute on the lien," which means that the property is seized by a federal marshal and sold at a foreclosure sale. The proceeds from the sale are then given to the creditor to satisfy the judgment. While executing on a lien is a fairly common method of enforcement among the states, it is not the only one. Various states have other mechanisms for enforcing writs of execution, and Rule 69 permits enforcement of writs using any method that has been approved by the state in which the court sits.

Notably, some states do not provide *any* methods for enforcing a writ of execution, at least in certain cases. These states still have enforcement mechanisms of course, but they may have decided that a device such as contempt of court is more appropriate in some cases than the more "standard" writ of execution. Rule 69 takes these scenarios into account by specifying that a money judgment is to be enforced by a writ of execution, *unless the court directs otherwise.* Fed. R. Civ. P. 69(a)(1). While the language here suggests that courts are free to choose other methods of enforcement whenever it suits them, this exception is actually quite narrow: It allows for deviation from the use of writs of enforcement *only* when the state's rules, not the court's preferences, so require.

Further, some states have special procedures that simply are not used in federal courts. For example, New York's standard procedure for enforcing a writ of execution involves use of a "special proceeding," a type of procedure unique to New York law that would have required the creditors to start a whole new proceeding even though the issue of enforcement was already before the federal court. *Mitchell v. Lyons Professional Services, Inc.*, 727 F. Supp. 2d 120 (E.D.N.Y. 2010). Instead of forcing the creditors to start all over, the federal district court took a "common sense approach" and allowed the enforcement action to proceed without conforming to New York's laws requiring a "special proceeding." *Id.* This "common sense approach" has become the standard among most federal courts; they will rely on state procedures as mandated by the rule up to the point where conforming to these procedures would be unwieldy and unnecessary to enforce the judgment.

Rule 69(a)(1) also notes that, in some cases, federal enforcement statutes may control instead of state enforcement procedures. The notes to Rule 69 include some examples of these statutes, which set forth their own procedures in certain specific cases that then override existing state procedures. These federal statutes apply only in narrowly defined situations, meaning that state laws will generally control enforcement procedures. However, it is important to check any potentially relevant federal statutes to see whether they contain enforcement provisions that modify the usual state procedures.

As with most procedural tools you have read about, there are time limits in place for when creditors may enforce a judgment. And as with most procedures regarding the enforcement of judgments, the specifics of these time limits are set by state law. Timing considerations will thus vary depending on the state in which the creditor is trying to enforce the debt. That said, there are some timing commonalities that most states observe. Many states will not issue a writ of execution for judgments that have become "dormant," a state of affairs that occurs once a specified amount of time passes from the date of the judgment. For example, in Texas, a judgment becomes dormant if no enforcement action is taken within ten years of the date of the judgment. Tex. Civ. Prac. & Rem. Code §34.001 (1995). However, dormant status does not necessarily prevent the creditor from ever enforcing the judgment. In some jurisdictions, a judgment can be "revived" if an action is brought within some specified amount of time after the judgment became dormant. *See id.* §31.006 (two

---

Terminology Tip

Although you will hear some of these words used interchangeably, especially by nonlawyers, learn to be precise with *judgment, order, verdict,* and *opinion.* A *judgment* is a court's final determination of the parties' rights and obligations. *See* Fed. R. Civ. P. 54(a). Note the standard spelling of *judgment* (not *judgement*) when used in law. *Order* is a broader word referring to any ruling by a judge about what is required to happen. In the course of litigation there may be hundreds of orders (discovery orders, pretrial management orders, etc.) along the way to a single judgment at the action's conclusion. A *verdict* is a jury's determination. While all sorts of cases end in judgments, only jury-trial cases have verdicts. After a jury trial, a judge typically enters judgment based on the jury's verdict. An *opinion* is a court's explanation of its reasoning. And at the risk of stating the obvious, although nonlawyers sometimes use the word *settlement* as if it were synonymous with judgment, a settlement is a negotiated resolution rather than adjudication by the court.

years). Other jurisdictions have set statutory limitations on the execution of judgment and only allow extension with a showing of good cause. *See, e.g.,* Va. Code Ann. §8.01-251. If the creditor fails to enforce the judgment before the date set by the limitations period, not only can the creditor no longer seek a writ of execution, but the debt itself is sometimes extinguished. Thus, it is critical for attorneys to learn what the various time limits are for the various jurisdictions in which they are trying to enforce a judgment. The last thing your client wants is to win a case and be granted damages only to lose the opportunity to actually collect the money she won because of an error with entry or registration of that winning judgment.

Finally, Rule 69(a)(2) provides for discovery procedures to facilitate the enforcement of judgments. Specifically, the creditor is permitted to obtain discovery in order to help it enforce the judgment. Fed. R. Civ. P. 69(a)(2). Discovery might seem unnecessary at this stage; after all, the parties likely already requested vast amounts of information from each other as part of the litigation that led to the judgment in the first place. However, depending on the content of the litigation, the parties may know very little about what assets the other party has (much less where those assets are located) that could be used to satisfy the judgment. This kind of information could be not only useful, but also vital to enforcing monetary judgments. Note that rather than set out its own, new practices for discovery, Rule 69(a)(2) simply allows the use of any of the discovery methods set out in other parts of the Federal Rules of Civil Procedure, meaning that the rules you learned in Chapter 3 still apply here.

(2) Enforcing Judgments for Specific Acts

While Rule 69 outlines the process for enforcing monetary judgments, Rule 70 sets out the procedure for enforcing judgments that require the performance of some action. Similar to the requirement in Rule 69 that a creditor must request a writ of execution to enforce a judgment against a recalcitrant debtor, Rule 70 directs the party seeking enforcement against an unwilling party to file a motion for enforcement. Unlike in Rule 69, however, Rule 70, not various state laws, controls the enforcement of a judgment for specific acts.

Once a court grants a party's motion for enforcement under Rule 70, the court has a few options to enforce its judgment. Rule 70(a) empowers the court to appoint another party to perform whatever act the disobedient party was supposed to perform. If the court decides to do this, the disobedient party is not off the hook; it must pay whatever expenses are incurred by the "substitute" party that the court chose. Fed. R. Civ. P. 70(a). If the disobedient party was ordered to convey title in a piece of property but refused to do so, the court may enter another judgment under 70(b) that divests the disobedient party's title and vests it with the other party.

Alternatively, upon motion, the court may issue a writ of attachment or writ of sequestration in order to compel obedience. Fed. R. Civ. P. 70(c). If the judgment mandated that the disobedient party give possession of some piece of property to the other party, Rule 70(d) empowers the court to issue a writ of execution or a writ of assistance that allows law enforcement to take the property and give it to the other party. Finally, if all else fails, Rule 70(e) allows the court, under certain conditions, to hold the disobedient party in contempt.

While Rule 70 thus provides courts with multiple ways of enforcing judgments for specific acts, note that, in general, only one of these options will be suited to the specific case at hand. For example, imagine that a judgment ordered the losing party to give a unique and valuable painting to the prevailing party. In this case, it would not make sense for the court to try and order some "substitute" party to take this action under Rule 70(a), since no other party would have the painting to give. Instead the court would use Rule 70(d) to order law enforcement to seize the painting from the disobedient party and give it to the prevailing one. On the other hand, if the judgment to be enforced ordered the losing party to paint a portrait of the prevailing party, a U.S. marshal likely could not convince the disobedient party to do so regardless of whether or not she had a writ of assistance. In this case, a court would be more likely to use Rule 70(a) and appoint another painter to do the portrait at the losing party's expense.

B. PRELIMINARY REMEDIES

In some instances, a party may suffer irreparable harm if a remedy is not granted before trial or other final judgment. In such instances, that party may move for a preliminary remedy prior to any final decision on the merits. Typically, preliminary remedies are injunctive in nature and are usually issued to restore the status quo ante (the state of affairs before the suit), when not doing so would cause irreparable injury to the plaintiff. However, sometimes a party will seek preliminary injunctive relief ordering a change in a current situation in order to prevent future injury. Preliminary relief may be afforded to protect a wide variety of interests. Three common examples are *one*, interests involving tangible or intangible property; *two*, interests related to economic or contract rights *not* based on property interests; and *three*, interests involving constitutional, personal, and public rights.

There are two types of pretrial injunctive orders: preliminary injunctions and temporary restraining orders (TROs). In the federal system, Federal Rule of Civil Procedure 65 governs the *procedures* on an application for a preliminary injunction or TRO; the states have their own procedural analogues. However, the *standards* for granting a plaintiff's request for such remedies are governed by historical equitable practice. Section 1 below discusses the procedures and standards for obtaining preliminary injunctions; Section 2 discusses those for obtaining TROs. Operating in the background of the procedures and standards for obtaining preliminary orders are constitutional due process concerns, which are addressed directly in Section 3.

(1) Preliminary Injunctions

Preliminary injunctions, by definition, are issued *before* a trial on the merits or a full hearing, and *before* a plaintiff's right to permanent relief is certain. Preliminary injunctions are therefore distinct from permanent injunctions as a matter of process and timing. However, the two are closely linked as a matter of content: A court may not issue a preliminary injunction unless it is of the same character and within the same subject matter as the plaintiff's underlying suit. Further, preliminary injunctions have all the force of a permanent injunction during their duration. A preliminary injunction stays in effect until a final judgment is rendered or the complaint dismissed; until it expires by its own terms; or until it is modified, stayed, or reversed by the court.

In the federal system, both 28 U.S.C. §1651 (All Writs Act) and Federal Rule of Civil Procedure 65 govern the procedures for requesting and issuing a preliminary injunction. The All Writs Act authorizes the United States federal courts to "issue all writs necessary or appropriate in aid of their respective jurisdictions and agreeable to the usages and principles of law." Federal Rule of Civil Procedure 65 (which has counterparts in many states) provides that "[t]he court may issue a preliminary injunction *only on notice* to the adverse party." Fed. R. Civ. P. 65(a)(1) (emphasis added). The motion for a preliminary injunction may serve as part of the written notice of a hearing on the preliminary injunction. *See* Fed. R. Civ. P. 65(a)(2). In terms of timing, note how Rule 65 interacts with Federal Rule of Civil Procedure 6(c), which provides that the motion must be served, along with a notice of the preliminary injunction hearing, at least 14 days prior to the hearing date, unless the court modifies the period for giving advance notice. Fed. R. Civ. P. 6(c)(1)(C).

A hearing for a preliminary injunction is typically quite abbreviated. For instance, evidence is often taken by affidavits and treated differently from summary judgment under Rule 56, which requires that affidavits set out facts that would be admissible at trial. In a typical preliminary injunction hearing, the court determines whether to grant the motion after all parties have presented testimony. *See, e.g., Flynt Distributing Co., Inc. v. Harvey*, 734 F.2d 1389, 1394 (9th Cir. 1984). However, Rule 65 does *not* require an oral hearing. Indeed, many courts (but not all) allow parties to rely upon written evidence alone, which is presumed true if not contradicted. *See, e.g., Williams v. San Francisco Unified School Dist.*, 340 F. Supp. 438 (N.D. Cal. 1972); Fed. R. Civ. P. 78(b) ("the court may provide for submitting and determining motions on briefs, without oral hearings"); *but see Murray v. Kunzig*, 426 F.2d 871 (D.C. Cir. 1972); *Industrial Electronics Corp. v. Cline*, 330 F.2d 480, 483 (3d Cir. 1964) (excluding written affidavits if affiant is unavailable to testify in person). In addition to affidavits, the court may consider additional written evidence, such as verified pleadings and depositions. If there *are* facts in dispute, however, oral testimony is preferable, and in such a case, a motion for preliminary injunction supported only by written evidence will typically be denied.

Given the significant impact of a preliminary injunction and the concomitant absence of procedural safeguards in obtaining one, courts *may* "advance the trial on the merits and consolidate it with the hearing [for preliminary injunction]." Fed. R. Civ. P. 65(a)(2)). This consolidation helps conserve judicial resources, reduce delay, and minimize the potential harm to the defendant of the issuance of a preliminary injunction before a fuller opportunity to be heard on the merits. The decision to consolidate (or not) is within the discretion of the trial court, upon reasonable and fair notice to the litigants. Fed. R. Civ. P. 65(a)(2). Pay close attention to the last sentence of Rule 65(a)(2), though: "[T]he court must preserve any party's right to a jury trial." Thus, any issue on which a party demands and is entitled to a jury trial (see Chapter 5) that pertains to both the request for preliminary injunction and the merits of the claim itself may not be determined by the judge alone in the consolidated hearing under Rule 65. *See Beacon Theatres, Inc. v. Westover*, 359 U.S. 500, 511 (1959). Importantly, though, Rule 65(a)(2) does *not* limit the trial court's power to issue a preliminary injunction prior to a full hearing on the merits. In other words, a court may issue a preliminary injunction based on its initial determination regarding issues that ultimately must be decided by a jury.

The preliminary injunction is often described by courts as an "extraordinary" remedy; thus, the standards for obtaining one are stringent. The plaintiff seeking a preliminary injunction carries the burden of persuasion, which requires the plaintiff to demonstrate by a "clear showing" that (1) there is a significant threat of irreparable harm to the plaintiff if the injunction is not granted; (2) the balance between this harm and the injury to the defendant in granting the requested injunction cuts in the plaintiff's favor; (3) the plaintiff is likely to succeed on the merits; and (4) the public interest warrants such an injunction. *See Winter v. Natural Resources Defense Council, Inc.*, 555 U.S. 7 (2008). No single factor of the "balance-of-the-harms" test described in *Winter* is talismanic. The decision to issue a preliminary injunction is performed on a case-by-case basis and granted at the trial court's discretion. Depending on the facts of the case, a court may require that all factors be satisfied; conversely, a court may find the risk of harm to, say, the public interest, so compelling that it alone justifies an injunction. Unsurprisingly, in many cases, the analysis of the factors intersects. For example, the more likely the plaintiff is to succeed on the merits, the higher the probability of irreparable harm (and vice versa). The trial court's discretion to issue a preliminary injunction includes the discretion to grant all or part of the total relief plaintiff seeks. Indeed, the trial court can (and should) tailor a preliminary injunction to the needs of any particular case or set conditions upon the preliminary injunction. Fed. R. Civ. P. 65(a).

THE BIG PICTURE

Obtaining a preliminary injunction is a huge win for the plaintiff. The grant of a preliminary injunction creates a strong presumption that a permanent injunction will issue. Indeed, if a preliminary injunction is granted, defendants often read the writing on the wall and discontinue the litigation. Given the abbreviated procedures involved in granting preliminary relief, is this practical effect troubling as a matter of fairness to defendants? Keep in mind that preliminary injunctive relief is decided by the judge, even in cases where issues pertaining to liability would ultimately have to be decided by a jury. Does this raise concerns about the Seventh Amendment right to jury trial, which may be extinguished as a practical (if not a formal) matter?

(2) Temporary Restraining Orders

Plaintiffs seeking injunctive relief are sometimes faced with the possibility that irreparable harm will occur before a preliminary injunction hearing can take place. In such situations, a plaintiff may seek a temporary restraining order (TRO). The primary difference between a TRO and a preliminary injunction is that a TRO is issued *ex parte*, meaning "without written or oral notice to the adverse party." Fed. R. Civ. P. 65(b). Because procedural protections for the defendant are even further diminished in the context of obtaining a TRO, the plaintiff moving for a TRO must demonstrate that "*immediate and irreparable injury*, loss or damage will result . . . before the adverse party can be heard in opposition," Fed. R. Civ. P. 65(b)(1)(A) (emphasis added), and the movant's attorney must certify in writing "any efforts made to give notice and the reasons why it should not be required." Fed. R. Civ. P. 65(b)(1)(B). In addition to the analyzing "irreparable injury" requirement, courts often perform the "balance-of-the-harms" test used to decide motions for preliminary injunctions, though necessarily in a more cursory fashion than with a preliminary injunction, given that a TRO is an emergency remedy.

Another key difference between TROs and preliminary injunctions is their duration. TROs are designed as stop-gap measures to enjoin the defendant until there is an opportunity to hold a hearing on the motion for preliminary injunction, and as such, TROs are much more limited in duration. To protect the adverse party and to expedite the preliminary injunction hearing, the restrained party must be informed of the order as soon as possible, and the TRO itself remains in effect for a maximum of 14 days. Fed. R. Civ. P. 65(b)(2). In contrast, a preliminary injunction may stay in effect until the court decides whether to issue a permanent injunction.

Once the adverse party receives notice of the TRO, the procedures for a hearing are functionally the same as those for a preliminary injunction. Under Rule 65(b)(3), that hearing must be held at the earliest possible time. Once a hearing takes place, a TRO may be treated as a preliminary injunction, if the circumstances warrant. Consider the following TRO and related preliminary injunction to see this connection in play. As you read, keep in mind the standards and procedures for granting TROs and preliminary injunctions.

SWIFT v. MATTHEWS

U.S. District Court, Middle District of Tennessee
Civil Action No. 3:09-0442 (May 19, 2006)

TEMPORARY RESTRAINING ORDER AND ORDER OF SEIZURE OF COUNTERFEIT GOODS

This matter comes before the Court upon Plaintiff Taylor Swift's Verified Complaint, *Ex Parte* Motion for Temporary Restraining Order, Motion for Preliminary Injunction and Application for Order of Seizure of Counterfeit Goods.... After due consideration thereof, the Court makes the following findings of fact and conclusions of law and grants Plaintiff's Motion for Temporary Restraining Order and Application for Order of Seizure of Counterfeit Goods:

1. Plaintiff owns and controls the trademark TAYLOR SWIFT....
2. Plaintiff also owns and controls the trademark FEARLESS.... Plaintiff's trademarks TAYLOR SWIFT and FEARLESS are collectively referred to in this Order as "Plaintiff's Trademarks."...
3. Defendants are not licensed or otherwise authorized by Plaintiff to use Plaintiff's Trademarks.
4. It appears to this Court that Defendants have been, are and will be present on the premises or within a five-mile radius of the venues where Plaintiff will perform during her concert tour in 2009 ... for the purpose of manufacturing, distributing, offering for sale, and selling merchandise and products that bear marks, words and/or names identical or confusingly similar to, or are counterfeits of, Plaintiff's Trademarks, without authorization from Plaintiff ("Counterfeit Goods")....

5. Defendant's distribution, offering for sale, and sale of Counterfeit Goods would ... cause confusion or mistake or be likely to deceive and would constitute trademark infringement....
6. This Court has the power under Rule 65 of the Federal Rules of Civil Procedure, and under the All Writs Act, 28 U.S.C. §1651, to grant an *ex parte* seizure order for goods that are infringing but not counterfeits within the meaning of 15 U.S.C. §1116(d).
7. No order other than an *ex parte* seizure order would adequately achieve the objectives of the Trademark (Lanham) Act, 15 U.S.C. §§1115, 1116, and 1125(a).
8. Plaintiff is likely to succeed in showing that Defendants have used and, unless enjoined, will continue to use counterfeit or infringing marks in connection with the sale, offering for sale and/or distribution of Counterfeit Goods.
9. Notice of this Motion need not be given to Defendants prior to *ex parte* hearing because: (a) the identities and whereabouts of certain Defendants are currently unknown; (b) many Defendants have no business identity or stable place of business before or after Plaintiff's concert performances and cannot be identified; and (c) Defendants who can be located and identified, if notified, likely will

cause immediate concealment or destruction of Counterfeit Goods or removal of Counterfeit Goods outside the access of the Court.

10. Plaintiff will suffer immediate and irreparable injury and will have no adequate remedy at law if this Court declines to grant an *ex parte* restraining and seizure order. . . .

11. Should this Court not grant the requested relief, the harm to Plaintiff clearly outweighs any harm that Defendant may suffer if the relief is granted. . . .

It is accordingly ORDERED and ADJUDGED that:

1. Defendants . . . are temporarily ENJOINED and RESTRAINED from:

   a. manufacturing, distributing, offering to distribute, offering for sale, or selling any Counterfeit Goods. . . .

   b. representing by any method that Counterfeit Goods are sponsored, manufactured, sold or licensed by Plaintiff; and

   c. otherwise taking any action likely to cause confusion, mistake or deception as to the origin of Counterfeit Goods.

2. Any federal, state, or local law enforcement officer ("Enforcement Official") may seize and maintain in their custody and control any and all Counterfeit Goods and counterfeit marks, and the means of making them, and records documenting the manufacture, sale or receipt of things relating thereto, in the possession, dominion or control of Defendants. . . .

3. Enforcement Officials are authorized to carry out the foregoing on the premises or within a five-mile radius of any venue where Plaintiff will perform live concert events that will be occurring at any time during the duration of this Order, from twenty-four hours before each concert begins and until twenty-four hours following the completion of each concert. . . .

4. Simultaneously with seizure hereunder, or as soon thereafter as practical under the circumstances, each named Defendant shall be served with a copy of (i) this Order and (ii) a Summons and the Verified Complaint in this action. . . .

5. Plaintiff shall post security . . . in the amount of $10,000.00 for the payment of such costs and damages as may be incurred or suffered by any party who is found to have been wrongfully restrained, pending the hearing and determination of the continuation of this Order.

6. Unless extended by the Court, the temporary restraining order shall become valid upon the posting of bond and shall expire ten (10) business days after the issuance of this Order.

7. IT IS FURTHER ORDERED that a hearing on Plaintiff's Motion for Preliminary Injunction shall be set by the District Judge to whom this case is assigned. . . .

Entered this 19th day of May, 2009, at 4:00 p.m.

Notes & Questions

1. On June 17, 2009, the district court held a hearing and granted Taylor Swift's motion for preliminary injunction. The injunction itself contained language identical to the TRO provided here. While in this case both the TRO and preliminary injunction were granted, when might a court grant a TRO but *not* a preliminary injunction? In answering this question, think about how rapidly a court needs to issue a TRO. Consider also the interplay between Rule 65(b) and Rule 52. While Rule 65(b)(2) permits the court to extend a TRO for "good cause" or upon the consent of the adverse party, under Rule 52(b), a party may move for the court to amend its findings of fact or law no later than 28 days after the issuance of an order. The interplay of these two provisions suggests not only that a TRO extended in excess of 28 days must become an appealable preliminary injunction, but also that it must then meet the standards governing a court's findings of fact and law contained in Rule 52(a).

2. Note that the court in *Swift* mentioned an *ex parte* hearing in the TRO (as well as in the ultimate order granting a preliminary injunction). Why, in the court's view, was no such hearing required? At what point, if ever, would defendants in *Swift* receive notice of the TRO or preliminary injunction, according to the district court?

3. In both the TRO and the ultimate preliminary injunction, the court ordered Taylor Swift to "post security, in the form of a cash bond or corporate surety bond" in order to pay any damages that might be suffered by the defendants if it turns out that they were ultimately "wrongfully restrained or enjoined." *See* Fed. R. Civ. P. 65(c). Rule 65(c) uses mandatory language on this score: "The court may issue a preliminary injunction or a temporary restraining order *only if* the movant gives security. . . ." However, while many courts have held that Rule 65(c) requires that plaintiff post a bond or other form of security once the court decides to grant relief under Rule 65, *see, e.g., Hoechst Diafoil Co. v. Nan Ya Plastics Corp.*, 174 F.3d 411 (4th Cir. 1999) (district court's failure to require a bond from plaintiff as security for a preliminary injunction was reversible error), other courts have held that the district court is only required to consider the question of requiring a bond and may exercise its discretion as to whether one is required. *See, e.g., Rathmann Group v. Tatenbaum*, 889 F.2d 787 (8th Cir. 1989).

4. What if, unlike a wealthy entertainer like Taylor Swift who could easily shake off the bond requirement of Rule 65(c), the plaintiff requesting preliminary relief lacks the resources to do so? Rule 65(c) states that a district court may require a security "in an amount that the court considers proper to pay the costs and damages sustained by any party wrongfully enjoined or restrained." Many courts have taken the position that this language gives district courts the discretion to set the amount of the security at a level below the actual costs and damages that the enjoined or restrained party may suffer, particularly if the plaintiffs are financially unable to post a bond. *See, e.g., Bass v. Richardson*, 338 F. Supp. 478 (S.D.N.Y. 1971).

5. Both the TRO and the ultimate preliminary injunction granted Taylor Swift's request for the *ex parte* seizure of counterfeit goods. Assuming the court complied with the procedural requirements of Rule 65 in *Swift*, are the processes in Rule 65 itself sufficient to satisfy constitutional due process requirements of notice and opportunity to be heard before "any person is deprived of life, liberty, or property"? U.S. Const. amend. V, XIV. Keep these questions in mind as you read Section 3 below.

(3) Preliminary Remedies and Due Process

As you have learned, in the federal system, Rule 65 provides the procedures for obtaining preliminary remedies; the states provide their own procedures (sometimes mirroring Rule 65) that likewise provide procedures for the issuance of preliminary remedies by state courts. And while these rules and statutes provide the procedures, historical equitable practice provides the standards for obtaining preliminary remedies. Both these procedures and standards, to be constitutional, must satisfy the requirements of the Due Process Clause.

Recall from Chapter 1 that the Fifth and Fourteenth Amendments of the United States Constitution each contains a Due Process Clause. The Fifth Amendment applies to the federal government. It provides that "[n]o person shall . . . be deprived of life, liberty, or property, without due process of law." The Fourteenth Amendment imposes the same due process limitations upon state actors. Procedural due process has long been understood to require, at a minimum, notice and opportunity to be heard. *See, e.g., Mullane v. Central Hanover Bank & Trust Co.*, 339 U.S. 306 (1950). Nonetheless, the Supreme Court has held that *actual* notice is not required by due process as long as the party attempting to provide notice used a means that was reasonably calculated to notify adverse parties of the pending action. *Id.*

When Rule 65 was amended in 1966, the Rules Advisory Committee anticipated that the Supreme Court might have procedural due process objections to the rule (particularly sub-section (b), which permits the issuance of *ex parte* TROs). The Advisory Committee therefore included the following language in the 1966 Advisory Committee Note to Rule 65(b):

> In view of the possibly drastic consequences of a temporary restraining order, the opposition should be heard, if feasible, before the order is granted. Many judges have properly insisted that, when time does not permit of formal notice of the application to the adverse party, some expedient, such as telephonic notice to the attorney for the adverse party, be resorted to if this can reasonably done. On occasion, however, temporary restraining orders have been issued without any notice when it was feasible for some fair, although informal, notice to be given.

The Supreme Court has implicitly approved of Rule 65(b), initially by adopting the 1966 Amendment, and then by stating three years later that "there is a place in our jurisprudence for the *ex parte* issuance, without notice, of temporary restraining orders of short duration." *Carroll v. President & Commissioners of Princess Anne,*

393 U.S. 175 (1968). While the Supreme Court has never explicitly stated that Rule 65 has a constitutional dimension, it has, in a line of famous cases, emphasized that *any* court considering issuing a preliminary remedy without notice and hearing (whether under Rule 65 in federal court, or a state statute in state court) must find that the plaintiff has produced very compelling evidence of "irreparable injury" and that, in the context of an *ex parte* preliminary injunction, has exhausted all reasonable efforts to provide notice to the adverse party. *Sniadach v. Family Finance Corp. of Bay View*, 395 U.S. 337 (1969); *Boddie v. Connecticut*, 401 U.S. 371 (1971); *Fuentes v. Shevin*, 407 U.S. 67 (1972); and *Connecticut v. Doehr*, 501 U.S. 1 (1991). That said, and especially given that preliminary remedies are determined on a case-by-case basis, what *precisely* does due process require? Consider the following case, one of the latest in the Supreme Court's line of procedural due process decisions regarding preliminary remedies:

CONNECTICUT v. DOEHR

501 U.S. 1 (1991)

WHITE, J., delivered the opinion, Parts I, II, and III of which are the opinion of the Court.

This case requires us to determine whether a state statute that authorizes prejudgment attachment of real estate without prior notice or hearing, without a showing of extraordinary circumstances, and without a requirement that the attachment post a bond, satisfies the Due Process Clause of the Fourteenth Amendment. We hold that, as applied to this case, it does not.

I

On March 15, 1988, petitioner John F. DiGiovanni submitted an application to the Connecticut Superior Court for an attachment in the amount of $75,000 on respondent Brian K. Doehr's home in Meriden, Connecticut. DiGiovanni took this step in conjunction with a civil action for assault and battery that he was seeking to institute against Doehr in the same court. The suit did not involve Doehr's real estate,

nor did DiGiovanni have any pre-existing interest either in Doehr's home or any of his other property.

Connecticut law authorizes prejudgment attachment of real estate without affording prior notice or the opportunity for a prior hearing to the individual whose property is subject to the attachment. The State's prejudgment remedy statute provides, in relevant part:

> The court or a judge of the court may allow the prejudgment remedy to be issued by an attorney without hearing as provided in sections 52-278c and 52-278d upon verification by oath of the plaintiff or of some competent affiant, that there is probable cause to sustain the validity of the plaintiff's claims and . . . that the prejudgment remedy requested is for an attachment of real property. . . . Conn. Gen. Stat. §52-278e (1991).

The statute does not require the plaintiff to post a bond to insure the payment of damages that the defendant may suffer should the attachment prove wrongfully issued or the claim prove unsuccessful.

As required, DiGiovanni submitted an affidavit in support of his application. In five one-sentence paragraphs, DiGiovanni stated that the facts set forth in his previously submitted complaint were true; that "I was willfully, wantonly and maliciously assaulted by the defendant, Brian K. Doehr" that "[s]aid assault and battery broke my left wrist and further caused an ecchymosis to my right eye, as well as other injuries"; and that "I have further expended sums of money for medial care and treatment." The affidavit concluded with the statement, "In my opinion, the foregoing facts are sufficient to show that there is probable cause that judgment will be rendered for the plaintiff."

On the strength of these submissions the Superior Court Judge, by an order dated March 17, found "probable cause to sustain the validity of the plaintiff's claim" and ordered the attachment on Doehr's home "to the value of $75,000." The sheriff attached the property four days later, on March 2. Only after this did Doehr receive notice of the attachment. He also had yet to be served with the complaint, which is ordinarily necessary for an action to commence in Connecticut. *Young v. Margiotta*, 136 Conn. 429, 433 (1950). As the statute further required, the attachment notice informed Doehr that he had the right to a hearing: (1) to claim that no probable cause existed to sustain the claim; (2) to request that the attachment be vacated, modified, or dismissed or that a bond be substituted; or (3) to claim that some portion of the property was exempt from execution. Conn. Gen. Stat. §52-278e(b) (1991).

Rather than pursue these options, Doehr filed suit against DiGiovanni in Federal District Court, claiming that §52-278(a)(1) was unconstitutional under the Due Process Clause of the Fourteenth Amendment.

The district court upheld the statute and granted summary judgment in favor of DiGiovanni. On appeal, a divided panel of the United States Court of Appeals for the Second Circuit reversed.

II

With this case we return to the question of what process must be afforded by a state statute enabling an individual to enlist the aid of the State to deprive another of his or her property by means of the prejudgment attachment or similar procedure. . . .

"[D]ue process, unlike some legal rules, is not a technical conception with a fixed content unrelated to time, place, and circumstances." *Mathews v. Eldridge*, 424 U.S. 319, 334 (1976). In *Mathews*, we drew upon our prejudgment remedy decisions to determine what process is due when the government itself seeks to effect a deprivation on its own initiative. 424 U.S. at 334. That analysis resulted in the now familiar threefold inquiry requiring consideration of "the private interest that will be affected by the official action"; "the risk of an erroneous deprivation of such interest through the procedures used, and the probable value, if any, of additional or substitute safeguards"; and lastly "the Government's interest, including the function involved and the fiscal and administrative burdens that the additional or substitute procedural requirement would entail." *Id.* at 335.

Here the inquiry is similar, but the focus is different. Prejudgment remedy statutes ordinarily apply to disputes between private parties rather than between an individual and the government. Such enactments are designed to enable one of the parties to "make use of state procedures with the overt, significant assistance of state officials," and they undoubtedly involve state action "substantial enough to implicate the

Due Process Clause." *Tulsa Professional Collection Services, Inc. v. Pope*, 485 U.S. 478, 486 (1988). Nonetheless, any burden that increasing procedural safeguards entails primarily affects not the government, but the party seeking control of the other's property. For this type of case, therefore, the relevant inquiry requires, as in *Mathews*, first, consideration of the private interest that will be affected by the prejudgment measure; second, an examination of the risk of erroneous deprivation through the procedures under attack and the probable value of additional or alternative safeguards; and third, in contrast to *Mathews*, principal attention to the interest of the party seeking the prejudgment remedy, with, nonetheless, due regard for any ancillary interest the government may have in providing the procedure or forgoing the added burden of providing greater protections.

We now consider the *Mathews* factors in determining the adequacy of procedures before us. . . .

III

We agree with the Court of Appeals that the property interests that attachments affect are significant. For a property owner like Doehr, attachment ordinarily clouds title; impairs the ability to sell or otherwise alienate the property; taints any credit rating; reduces the chance of obtaining a home equity loan or additional mortgage; and can even place an existing mortgage in technical default where there is an insecurity clause. Nor does Connecticut deny that any of these consequences occurs.

Instead, the State correctly points out that these effects do not amount to a complete, physical, or permanent deprivation of real property; their impact is less than the perhaps temporary total deprivation of household goods or wages. But the Court has never held that only such extreme deprivations trigger due process concern. To the contrary, our cases show that even the temporary or partial impairments to property rights that attachments, liens, and similar encumbrances entail are sufficient to merit due process protection. . . .

We also agree with the Court of Appeals that the risk of erroneous deprivation that the State permits here is substantial. By definition, attachment statutes premise a deprivation of property on one ultimate factual contingency—the award of damages to the plaintiff which the defendant may not be able to satisfy. For attachments before judgment, Connecticut mandates that this determination be made by means of procedural inquiry that asks whether "there is probable cause to sustain the validity of the plaintiff's claim." Conn. Gen. Stat. §52-278e(a) (1991). The statute elsewhere defines the validity of the claim in terms of the likelihood "that the judgment will be rendered in the matter in favor of the plaintiff." Conn. Gen. Stat. §52-278c(a)(2) (1991). What probable cause means in this context, however, remains obscure. The State initially took the position . . . that the statute requires a plaintiff to show the objective likelihood of the suit's success. Doehr, requiring no more than that a plaintiff demonstrate a subjective good-faith belief that the suit will succeed. At oral argument, the State shifted its position to argue that the statute requires something akin to the plaintiff stating a claim with sufficient facts to survive a motion to dismiss.

We need not resolve this confusion since the statute presents too great a risk of erroneous deprivation under any of these interpretations. . . .

Even if the provision requires the plaintiff to demonstrate, and the judge to find, probable cause to believe that judgment will be rendered in favor of the plaintiff, the risk of error was substantial in this case. As the record shows, and as the state concedes, only a skeletal affidavit need be, and was, filed. The State urges that the reviewing judge normally reviews the complaint as well, but concedes that the complaint may also be conclusory. It is self-evident that the judge could make no realistic assessment concerning the likelihood of an action's success based upon these one-sided, self-serving, and conclusory submissions. And as the Court of Appeals said, in a case like this involving an alleged assault, even a detailed affidavit would give only the plaintiff's version of the confrontation. Unlike determining the existence of a debt or delinquent payments, the issue does not concern "ordinarily uncomplicated matters that lend themselves to documentary proof." *Mitchell v. W.T. Grant Co.*, 416 U.S. 600, 609 (1974). The likelihood of error that results illustrates that "fairness can rarely be obtained by secret, one-sided determination of facts decisive of rights. . . . [And n]o better instrument has been devised for arriving at truth than to give a person in jeopardy of serious loss notice of the case against him and opportunity to meet it." *Joint Anti-Fascist Refugee Comm. v. McGrath*, 341 U.S. 123, 170-72 (1951) (Frankfurter, J., concurring).

What safeguards the State does afford do not adequately reduce this risk. Connecticut points out that the statute also provides an "expeditiou[s]" postattachment adversary hearing, §52-278e(c); notice for such a hearing, §52-278e(b); judicial review of an adverse decision, §52-278l(a); and a double damages action if the original suit is commenced without probable cause, §52-568(a)(1). Similar considerations were present in *Mitchell*, where we upheld Louisiana's sequestration statute despite the lack of predeprivation notice and hearing. But in *Mitchell*, the plaintiff had a vendor's lien to protect, the risk of error was minimal because the likelihood of recovery involved uncomplicated matters that lent themselves to documentary proof, 416 U.S. at 609-10, and the plaintiff was required to put up a bond. None of these factors diminishing the need for predeprivation hearing is present in this case. It is true that a later hearing might negate the presence of probable cause, but this would not cure the temporary deprivation that an earlier hearing might have prevented. "The Fourteenth Amendment draws no bright lines around three-day, 10-day or 50-day deprivations of property. Any significant taking of property by the State is within the purview of the Due Process Clause." *Fuentes v. Shevin*, 407 U.S. 67, 86 (1972).

Finally, we conclude that the interests in favor of an *ex parte* attachment, particularly the interest of the plaintiff, are too minimal to supply such a consideration here. The plaintiff had no existing interest in Doehr's real estate when he sought the attachment. His only interest in attaching the property was to ensure the availability of assets to satisfy his judgment if he prevailed on the merits of his action. Yet there was no allegation that Doehr was about to transfer or encumber his real estate or take any other action during the pendency of the action that would render his real estate unavailable to satisfy a judgment. Our cases have recognized such a properly supported claim would be an exigent circumstance permitting postponing any notice or hearing until after the attachment is effected. Absent such allegations, however, the plaintiff's interest in attaching the property does not justify the burdening of Doehr's ownership rights without a hearing to determine the likelihood of recovery.

No interest the government may have affects the analysis. The State's substantive interest in protecting any rights of the plaintiff cannot be any more weighty than those rights themselves. Here the plaintiff's interest is *de minimis*. Moreover, the State cannot seriously plead additional financial or administrative burdens involving predeprivation hearings when it already claims to provide an immediate post-deprivation hearing. Conn. Gen. Stat. §§52-278e(b) and (c) (1991).

Historical and contemporary practices support our analysis. . . . Connecticut's statute appears even more suspect in light of current practice. A survey of state attachment provisions reveals that nearly every State requires either a preattachment hearing, a showing of some exigent circumstance, or both, before permitting an attachment to take place. . . .

IV

[Section IV, in which a plurality of the Court—Justice White, joined by Justices Marshall, Stevens, and O'Connor—discuss the possibility that due process requires a party requesting attachment to post a bond, has been omitted.]

V

Because Connecticut's prejudgment remedy provision, Conn. Gen. Stat. §52-278e(a)(1), violates the requirements of due process by authorizing prejudgment attachment without prior notice or a hearing, the judgment of the Court of Appeals is affirmed, and the case is remanded to that court for further proceedings consistent with this opinion.

Notes & Questions

1. In *Doehr*, the Supreme Court applied the due process test from *Mathews v. Eldridge*, 424 U.S 319 (1976), a chestnut of administrative law jurisprudence, to Connecticut's prejudgment attachment statute. The Court made an important change to the *Mathews* test in *Doehr* to adapt it to the context of private civil litigation; namely, the Court substituted the adversary's interest for the government's interest in part three of the test. Nonetheless, the crux of the *Mathews* analysis (in either context) is a comparison between the existing procedures (in *Doehr*, those contained in Connecticut's prejudgment attachment statute) and alternative procedures. What alternative procedures did the Court suggest were required in *Doehr* for the *Mathews* due process test to be satisfied? Pay attention to the Court's comparison of the statute in *Doehr* to the Louisiana statute involved in *Mitchell v. W.T. Grant Co.*, 416 U.S. 600 (1974).

2. In constitutional law, there are two types of challenges to a statute. One is a facial challenge, which challenges the statute itself and contends that the statute is unconstitutional in *all cases*. The other is an as-applied challenge, which argues that the *particular application* of a statute in a particular case is unconstitutional. Which type of challenge was raised in *Doehr*? What does your answer tell you about the breadth of the Court's holding for due process protections in the

context of preliminary remedies? Pay close attention to the Court's discussion of the nature of Doehr's claim, which sounds in tort, versus other types of claims, like those involved in *Mitchell. See also, e.g., Shaumyan v. O'Neill*, 987 F.2d 122 (1993) (upholding the same prejudgment attachment statute considered in *Doehr* as applied in the creditor-debtor dispute before it).

3. Two years after the decision in *Doehr*, the Connecticut legislature amended its statutory requirements for the issuance of preliminary remedies. Among other things, the revisions eliminated the possibility of the attachment of defendant's property without some showing of exigency by the plaintiff. 1993 Conn. Acts 93-413 §3 (Reg. Sess.) (codified at 52 Conn. Gen. Stat. §52-278e) (exigent circumstances under the revised statute include a showing by the plaintiff that the defendant will hide to avoid service of process, will leave the state, or will soon fraudulently dispose of property or other assets that could otherwise be used to satisfy a judgment in favor of the creditor). What were the alleged "exigent circumstances" for the plaintiff in *Doehr*? Why did the Court find those insufficient, as a matter of due process?

4. Notice that the Court in *Doehr* does not describe the showing required to demonstrate a likelihood of success on the merits. Most courts evaluate the likelihood-of-success factor alongside the injury-to-the-plaintiff factor. One informs the other: The higher the likelihood of success on the merits, the more likely there will be irreparable harm to the plaintiff if the preliminary remedy is withheld. This interconnected balance is often referred to as a "sliding scale," whereby the plaintiff's burden to show likely success on the merits "slides" either lower or higher depending on the strength of its showing of probable harm, and vice versa.

5. Along these lines, the Court in *Doehr* suggests that the plaintiff's complaint is an insufficient basis upon which to make a finding that the plaintiff is likely to succeed on the merits (at least in a tort case like *Doehr*), in large part because allegations in complaints are permitted to be conclusory. *Doehr* was decided in 1991, long before the Court's decisions in *Twombly* and *Iqbal*. Should the Court's decisions in those pleading cases change the Court's analysis on this point?

6. In Parts IV and V of *Doehr*, Justice White wrote for a plurality of the Court and asserted that due process also required that a plaintiff obtaining an attachment of property must post a bond or other form of security for any damages the defendant might suffer if the attachment turns out to have been wrongfully obtained. In his concurrence, Justice Rehnquist, joined by Justice Blackmun, objected to the plurality's "hypothetical" discussion of what due process would require in cases not before the Court in *Doehr*. Recall that Rule 65 requires the movant to post a bond, but it is an open question whether and to what extent that requirement is constitutionally mandated.

C. CLAIM PRECLUSION

When a court enters judgment, parties may enforce the judgment in the ways described above. One might assume that this concludes the matter. But what if someone attempts to litigate the claim *again* with the hope of obtaining a different result? Or to litigate an arguably different claim that arises out of the same circumstances addressed in the first action? Or to relitigate a question of fact or law that was answered in the first action? These are questions of claim preclusion and issue preclusion. *Claim preclusion* addresses whether parties are prohibited from asserting a claim on the ground that they already received a judgment on the same claim. *Issue preclusion*, which we will cover in Part D, addresses whether parties are prohibited from relitigating a particular issue that was decided in a prior lawsuit.

The doctrine of claim preclusion can be pretty well summed up in one sentence: A valid, final judgment "on the merits" precludes relitigation of the same claim between the same parties. Applying this sentence in practice, however, requires some exploration. The sentence contains at least four components that take effort to understand: (a) How do courts decide whether lawsuits present the *same claim*, and in particular, to what extent are related but nonidentical claims treated as the same? (b) What makes a judgment *valid* and *final*? (c) What types of adjudication count as "*on the merits*"? (d) How do courts decide whether lawsuits involve the *same parties*, and in particular, to what extent are related but nonidentical parties treated as the same? We will address these four questions one by one, and then we will look briefly at the preclusive aspect of compulsory counterclaims, a cousin of claim preclusion.

(1) Requirements for Claim Preclusion

(a) Same Claim

First, and most importantly, consider what counts as the "same claim." Just because A sued B in the past, that obviously does not mean A can never sue B again on any claim. For example, if employee A sued employer B for unpaid wages, that would not prevent A from suing B later on an unrelated claim for sexual harassment, or, for that matter, on a claim for new unpaid wages that occur later. If it is a different claim, then there is no problem. Claim preclusion only prevents relitigation of the *same claim*. But how exactly do we know what is the same claim? What if the second lawsuit is related to the first but asserts a different legal theory, or adds new factual allegations, or seeks a different remedy?

The following case should, first, help you see how the doctrine of claim preclusion differs from the doctrine of issue preclusion. And then you will see the court grapple with a basic question about how broadly to define "same claim" for purposes of claim preclusion.

RUSH v. CITY OF MAPLE HEIGHTS
147 N.E.2d 599 (Ohio 1958)

HERBERT, J.

[Lenore Rush was a passenger on a motorcycle, which she owned, when her husband (who was driving the motorcycle) hit a pothole in the road, damaging the motorcycle and injuring Rush. Rush sued the City of Maple Heights for damages to the motorcycle, alleging negligent street maintenance by the city. The Municipal Court found the city negligent and awarded $100 in property damages. The judgment was affirmed by the Court of Appeals and the Supreme Court of Ohio.

Rush then sued the City of Maple Heights to recover damages for personal injuries suffered in the same accident, arguing that the issue of negligence was determined in the previous litigation. The trial court agreed, holding that the issue of negligence was binding against the defendant, and sent the case to a jury on the issue of damages alone. The jury awarded $12,000 in personal injury damages. The Court of Appeals affirmed.]

The eighth error assigned by the defendant is that "the trial and appellate courts committed error in permitting plaintiff to split her cause of action and to file a separate action in the Cleveland Municipal Court for her property damage and reduce same to judgment, and, thereafter, to proceed, in the Cuyahoga County Common Pleas Court, with a separate action for personal injuries, both claims arising out of a single accident."

Other facets of this question have been before the court before.

In the case of *Vasu v. Kohlers, Inc.*, 145 Ohio St. 321 (1945), plaintiff operating an automobile came into collision with defendant's truck, in which collision he suffered personal injuries and also damage to his automobile. . . . The insurance company paid the plaintiff a sum covering the damage to his automobile, whereupon, in accordance with a provision of the policy, the plaintiff assigned to the insurer his claim for such damage. [The insurance company sued Kohlers to recoup the money it paid for damage to Vasu's automobile, but the insurance company lost at trial. In the meantime, Vasu sued Kohlers for his personal injuries from the collision. Kohlers argued that Vasu's personal injury action was barred because of the judgment in the insurance company's case. The court rejected this argument and, at trial, Vasu won. The Court of Appeals reversed, but the Ohio Supreme Court reversed again, reinstating the judgment for Vasu. The Ohio Supreme Court's syllabus in *Vasu* explained the reasoning, in part, as follows:]

1. If the owner of a single cause of action arising out of a single tortious act brings an action against his tortfeasor, he may have but one recovery; and, in case he fails to recover, he may not maintain a subsequent action on the same cause of action, even though he has failed to include his entire cause of action or elements of damage in his original action.

2. If an owner of a single cause of action has a recovery thereon, the cause of action is merged in the judgment; but if he fails to recover on his claimed cause of action and judgment goes against him, such judgment is *res judicata* and a bar to a second action on the same cause of action. . . .

overruled

4. Injuries to both person and property suffered by the same person as a result of the same wrongful act are infringements of different rights and give rise to distinct causes of action, with the result that the recovery or denial of recovery of compensation for damages to the property is no bar to an action subsequently prosecuted for the personal injury, unless by an adverse judgment in the first action issues are determined against the plaintiff which operate as an estoppel against him in the second action. . . .

[Subsequent Ohio cases,] distinguishing and explaining the *Vasu* case, have not changed the rule established in paragraph four of the syllabus of [*Vasu*], holding that injuries to both person and property suffered by the same person as a result of the same wrongful act are infringements of different rights and give rise to distinct causes of action.

However, it is contended here that that rule is in conflict with the great weight of authority in this country and has caused vexatious litigation. The following quotation from 1 American Jurisprudence, 494, Section 114, states this question well:

It sometimes happens that a single wrongful or negligent act causes damage in respect of both the person and the property of the same individual, as, for instance, where the owner of a vehicle is injured in a collision which also damages the vehicle. In such a case, the question arises as to whether there are two causes of action or only one, and the authorities are in conflict concerning it. The majority rule is that only one cause of action arises, the reason of the rule being that as the defendant's wrongful act is single, the cause of action must be single, and that the different injuries occasioned by it are merely items of damage proceeding from the same wrong. . . .

In other jurisdictions, the rule is that two causes of action result from a negligent act which inflicts injury on a person and his property at the same time. This conclusion has been reached in different jurisdictions by different lines of reasoning.

Upon examination of decisions of courts of last resort, we find that the majority rule is followed in [cases from 21 states]. The minority rule, that separate actions may be maintained to recover for personal injuries and for damages to property resulting from the same wrongful act, is set forth in [cases from five states]. . . .

The reasoning behind the majority rule seems to be well stated in the case of *Mobile & O.R. Co. v. Matthews*, 115 Tenn. 172 (1906), as follows:

The negligent action of the plaintiff in error constituted but one tort. The injuries to the person and property of the defendant in error were the several results and effects of one wrongful act. A single tort can be the basis of but one action. It is not improper to declare in different counts for damages to the person and property when both result from the same tort, and it is the better practice to do so where there is any difference in the measure of damages, and all the damages sustained must be sued for in one suit. This is necessary to prevent multiplicity of suits, burdensome expense, and delays to plaintiffs, and vexatious litigation against defendants. . . .

Indeed, if the plaintiff fail to sue for the entire damage done him by the tort, a second action for the damages omitted will be precluded by the judgment in the first suit brought and tried.

The minority rule would seem to stem from the English case of *Brunsden v. Humphrey*, 14 Q.B. 141 (1884). The facts in that case are set forth in the opinion in the *Vasu* case, concluding with the statement:

> The Master of the Rolls, in his opinion, stated that the test is "whether the same sort of evidence would prove the plaintiff's case in the two actions," and that, in the action relating to the cab, "it would be necessary to give evidence of the damage done to the plaintiff's vehicle. In the present action it would be necessary to give evidence of the bodily injury occasioned to the plaintiff, and of the sufferings which he has undergone, and for this purpose to call medical witnesses. This one test shows that the causes of action as to the damage done to the plaintiff's cab, and as to the injury occasioned to the plaintiff's person, are distinct."

The fallacy of the reasoning in the English court is best portrayed in the dissenting opinion of Lord Coleridge, as follows:

> It appears to me that whether the negligence of the servant, or the impact of the vehicle which the servant drove, be the technical cause of action, equally the cause is one and the same: that the injury done to the plaintiff is injury done to him at one and the same moment by one and the same act in respect of different *rights*, i.e. his person and his goods, I do not in the least deny; but it seems to me a subtlety not warranted by law to hold that a man cannot bring two actions, if he is injured in his arm and in his leg, but can bring two, if besides his arm and leg being injured, his trousers which contain his leg, and his coatsleeve which contains his arm, have been torn.

There appears to be no valid reason in these days of code pleading to adhere to the old English rule as to distinctions between injuries to the person and damages to the person's property resulting from a single tort. It would seem that the minority rule is bottomed on the proposition that the right of bodily security is fundamentally different from the right of security of property and, also, that, in actions predicated upon a negligent act, damages are a necessary element of each independent cause of action and no recovery may be had unless and until actual consequential damages are shown. . . .

Apparently, much of the vexatious litigation, with its attendant confusion, which has resulted in recent years from the filing of separate petitions by the same plaintiff, one for personal injuries and one for property damage although sustained simultaneously, has grown from that one decision [in *Vasu*], this case presenting a good example.

In the light of the foregoing, it is the view of this court that the so-called majority rule conforms much more properly to modern practice, and that the rule declared in the fourth paragraph of the syllabus in the *Vasu* case, on a point not actually at issue therein, should not be followed.

We, therefore, conclude and hold that, where a person suffers both personal injuries and property damage as a result of the same wrongful act, only a single cause of action arises, the different injuries occasioned thereby being separate items of damage from such act. It follows that paragraph four of the syllabus in the *Vasu* case must be overruled.

Accordingly, the judgment of the Court of Appeals is reversed, and final judgment is entered for defendant.

ZIMMERMAN, J., dissenting.

I am not unalterably opposed to upsetting prior decisions of this court where changing conditions and the lessons of experience clearly indicate the desirability of such course, but, where those considerations do not obtain, established law should remain undisturbed in order to insure a stability on which the lower courts and the legal profession generally may rely with some degree of confidence.

Much may be said in support of the position taken in the majority opinion herein. However, there is a sharp division in the cases as to whether injuries to both person and property suffered by the same person as a result of the same wrongful act give rise to distinct causes of action or to a single cause of action. Less than 13 years ago that question was discussed at some length in the opinion in the case of *Vasu v. Kohlers, Inc.*, 145 Ohio St. 321 (1945), and the rule in favor of distinct causes of action was carried into the fourth paragraph of the syllabus and approved by a unanimous court. . . .

There is abundant and respectable authority for both viewpoints. Ohio has deliberately adopted one of them, and I can find no impelling reason for changing the rule at the present time. . . .

Notes & Questions

1. Preclusion issues always involve at least two actions: a prior case in which a judgment was rendered and a subsequent case in which the preclusion issue arises. Before tackling any preclusion issue, be sure you get the two cases straight so that you can see the preclusion question clearly. In *Rush*, who sued whom for what in case 1? What was the outcome of the first case? In case 2, who sued whom for what?

    In case 2, each of the parties attempted to use the case 1 judgment to their advantage. How did Rush try to make use of the former suit? Do you see how she argued, based on the outcome of case 1, that she should prevail in case 2? You should see that Rush's argument in case 2—which was a winning argument for her at the trial court level—was based on *issue preclusion* (also known as *collateral estoppel*). What, precisely, was the issue that Rush said had already been determined and should not be relitigated?

    By contrast, how did the City of Maple Heights try to use the former suit? Do you see how the city argued, based on the outcome of case 1, that it should prevail in case 2? The city's contention—that Rush had already sued the city over the motorcycle accident and had gotten a final judgment, and that she should not be able to sue again over the same incident—was an argument based on *claim preclusion*. The idea of claim preclusion is that a plaintiff gets one bite at the apple. If a party asserted a claim and a court entered judgment, the party may not bring the same claim again. It is a "thing decided"—or to say it in Latin, it's *res judicata*.

2. On the question of claim preclusion, what was Rush's argument that her claim in case 2 should *not* be precluded by the judgment in case 1? What authority did she cite in support of this argument? Why did the Ohio Supreme Court reject her argument?

3. For purposes of claim preclusion, did it matter whether Rush won or lost case 1? In *Rush*, the plaintiff prevailed in case 1 (the $100 judgment for property damage), and ultimately the state supreme court determined that she was precluded from bringing case 2. Suppose instead that Rush had lost case 1. In applying claim preclusion, the result in case 2 would be the same. But the terminology differs, at least in older cases like *Rush* that use the terms *merger* and *bar*. If a plaintiff wins the first suit but comes back for more, claim preclusion tells the plaintiff: "You brought your claim, you won, now that's enough." That is what courts used to call *merger*. The idea is that the entire claim merges into the judgment. If, instead, the plaintiff loses the first suit and then tries again, claim preclusion tells the plaintiff: "You brought your claim, you lost, now go away." That is what courts called *bar*. The judgment against the plaintiff bars the plaintiff from reasserting the losing claim. The distinction between merger and bar makes no difference; claim preclusion applies equally whether the plaintiff won or lost.

4. Why did Rush bring two separate suits? Consider the possibility that, as a matter of strategy, Rush hoped the city would defend weakly in case 1 since the amount of property damage was small, and that Rush hoped to use the judgment in case 1 for its issue preclusive effect in case 2, where the stakes were higher. Indeed, why did the city appeal the judgment in case 1 all the way to the state supreme court even though the damages were only $100? Is it possible that the city understood the risk posed by the $100 judgment if a later court were to give it issue preclusive effect? Note how a broad approach to claim preclusion, such as the one adopted by the Ohio Supreme Court in *Rush*, prevents such strategic claim-splitting by forcing the plaintiff to bring the entire claim in one lawsuit.

> **Terminology Tip**
>
> The terminology of preclusion law is a mess. In addition to *merger* and *bar*, you will encounter a host of other names. Claim preclusion used to be called (and is still often called) *res judicata*. Issue preclusion encompasses what used to be called *collateral estoppel* and *direct estoppel* (see Terminology Tip later this chapter for more on the language of estoppel). You will see *res judicata* and *collateral estoppel* not only in older cases and authorities; many lawyers and judges continue to use these terms. One more complication: Although the phrase *res judicata* usually is synonymous with claim preclusion, sometimes it is used to encompass the entire set of prior adjudication doctrines, including both claim and issue preclusion, capturing the most general sense of *res judicata* as "thing decided."

5. States have adopted various tests for determining whether the claim in the second lawsuit is the same as the claim in the first lawsuit. The *primary rights test* asks whether the same rights are involved in the two actions. The *same evidence test* focuses on whether the same evidence could be used to prove each of the claims. The majority approach and the modern trend is to apply a broad *transactional test*.

This was the approach that the Ohio Supreme Court adopted in *Rush*. Federal courts and most modern state courts apply the transactional test for claim preclusion, often citing this passage from the American Law Institute's influential Restatement (Second) of Judgments:

> (1) When a valid and final judgment rendered in an action extinguishes the plaintiff's claim pursuant to the rules of merger or bar, the claim extinguished includes all rights of the plaintiff to remedies against the defendant with respect to all or any part of the transaction, or series of connected transactions, out of which the action arose.
>
> (2) What factual grouping constitutes a "transaction," and what groupings constitute a "series," are to be determined pragmatically, giving weight to such considerations as whether the facts are related in time, space, origin, or motivation, whether they form a convenient trial unit, and whether their treatment as a unit conforms to the parties' expectations or business understanding or usage.

Restatement (Second) of Judgments §24 (1982). The "convenient trial unit" aspect of the transactional test makes it function similarly to the same evidence test.

The transactional test casts a wide net. It makes claim preclusion a strong tool for defendants to get claims dismissed in the second case. Moreover, it creates a powerful incentive for a plaintiff to join all related claims in a single lawsuit. If you represent a plaintiff and you are deciding what claims to include in the complaint, claim preclusion tells you that you cannot "split the claim" and pursue it in multiple actions. You could not, for example, split theories by bringing a breach-of-contract claim first and a promissory estoppel claim later based on the same promise. Nor could you split remedies by bringing separate actions for money damages and for specific performance.

To apply the transactional test, resist the temptation to think about lawsuits in purely legal terms. Do not focus too much on what *legal theories* the complaint invokes (strict liability, breach of contract, negligence, antitrust, and so on). Do not focus, either, on what *remedies* the complaint demands (damages, injunctive relief, and so on). Such focus on legal categories or remedial components will lead you toward the sort of claim-splitting that was rejected in *Rush*. Instead, ask what the dispute was actually about as a *factual* matter. What was alleged to have *happened* that gave rise to the claim? Maybe it was a business deal, or an employment termination. In *Rush*, it was a motorcycle accident. The transactional test asks whether the claim asserted in the second lawsuit arises out of the same factual situation as the first.

> **Terminology Tip**
>
> The word *claim* figures prominently in claim preclusion, and courts have devised various tests for defining what constitutes a claim. But note that this use of *claim* differs from how we have used the word for other aspects of civil procedure, such as pleadings and joinder. When Rule 18 says that a party may join multiple claims, keep in mind that some of those *claims* (plural) may constitute the *same claim* (singular) for purposes of claim preclusion, especially under the transactional test of *Rush* and the Second Restatement.

6. Claim preclusion covers not only those claims that were actually asserted, but also those that could have been asserted and that arose out of the same

transaction. By encouraging joinder of related claims, claim preclusion advances goals of efficiency, consistency, and finality. Indeed, although the Federal Rules of Civil Procedure lack any rule labeled "compulsory joinder of claims," claim preclusion has the effect of turning the permissive joinder of Rule 18 into compulsory joinder for claims that arise out of the same transaction or occurrence. Unlike issue preclusion's message of "been there, done that," claim preclusion says to litigants, "woulda, shoulda, coulda."

7. You may have noticed that, unlike every previous primary case in this book, *Rush* was decided by a state court rather than a federal court. You may have noticed, as well, that it was decided without reference to rules or statutes. The law of claim preclusion and issue preclusion is mostly common law. Each state has developed its own body of judicially created preclusion law, as have the federal courts. The American Law Institute's Restatement (Second) of Judgments (1982) was influential in explaining, modernizing, and harmonizing the law of preclusion across jurisdictions, but significant variations remain.

(b) Valid and Final Judgment

The point of claim preclusion, one might say, is that parties should not get to try again after they have gotten a valid, final judgment that adjudicates the claim. But what makes a judgment valid and final? Or to put it differently, what entitles a judgment to *recognition* as something worthy of preclusive effect?

(i) Validity

For a judgment to have preclusive effect, it must be valid. What makes a judgment valid? Your first instinct might be to say that a judgment is valid if it decides the case correctly. On that view, we would call a judgment "valid" only if it gets the facts straight and applies the law appropriately to those facts. But obviously this definition will not work as a rule for guiding the application of claim preclusion. The very nature of litigation is that there are conflicting views on the facts and the law, and the objective of adjudication is to resolve the dispute as soundly as possible. If claim preclusion depended on whether the first court got it right, then every collateral attack would lead right back into the underlying dispute and would require a new trial or other proceedings to examine the facts and the law.

Validity of a judgment as a condition of claim preclusion cannot be based on the substantive merits or the outcome of a dispute. Rather, think of "validity" as a structural and procedural notion. What entitles a judgment to recognition ultimately is the legitimacy of the court to render a decision that is binding in this particular dispute on these particular parties. This brings us to the requirements of personal jurisdiction, notice, and subject matter jurisdiction, and to this question: Can a party in case 2 avoid the effect of a judgment in case 1 by arguing that the court in case 1 lacked jurisdiction? With several exceptions, the general answer is *no*.

As you know from Chapter 1 and will study in Chapter 10, if a court lacks personal jurisdiction over a party or if adequate notice has not been provided, then the judgment does not bind the party. However, as you know from Chapter 2, personal jurisdiction and notice are waivable defenses, *see* Fed. R. Civ. P. 12(g)-(h), so if a party litigates an action without objecting to jurisdiction or notice, then the party will be unable to challenge the validity of the judgment in a later action on personal jurisdiction or notice grounds. If the court in the first action rejects the party's personal jurisdiction challenge, then the court's jurisdictional determination will be binding—preclusive—in a subsequent action. *See Baldwin v. Iowa State Traveling Men's Ass'n*, 283 U.S. 522 (1931). This means that, in general, a subsequent challenge to the validity of a judgment based on personal jurisdiction or notice can come only from a party who defaulted in the first action, that is, a party who never appeared in the action at all.

Recall also that for a court to have power to render a decision, it must have subject matter jurisdiction to adjudicate the case. You might think this would mean that if the court lacks subject matter jurisdiction, then the judgment would not be entitled to preclusive effect, but it turns out to be more complicated. If a party objected to jurisdiction in the first action and the court rejected the challenge, then the court's jurisdictional determination is binding. *See Durfee v. Duke*, 375 U.S. 106 (1963). What if the jurisdictional question was not litigated in the first action? In *Chicot Cty. Drainage Dist. v. Baxter State Bank*, 308 U.S. 371 (1940), the Supreme Court held defendants bound by a decree even though the particular defendants had not appeared in the action and the statute establishing federal subject matter jurisdiction over the action was later found unconstitutional. According to the Restatement (Second) of Judgments, a judgment may not be collaterally attacked on grounds of subject matter jurisdiction—that is, attacked in a subsequent action rather than in the action itself at the trial court or on direct appeal—with a few exceptions. *See* Restatement (Second) of Judgments §12. An exception applies for cases in which the first court abuses its authority or substantially infringes on the authority of another court. *See id.* §12(2). One author suggests the example of a traffic court that enters a judgment granting a divorce and awarding child custody. David L. Shapiro, Civil Procedure: Preclusion in Civil Actions 28 (Foundation Press 2001). If a party later sought to enforce the traffic court's judgment, the judgment's validity could be challenged for lack of subject matter jurisdiction. The logic of the general rule of giving binding effect to the judgment in a litigated action, rather than allowing collateral attack in a later action on the subject-matter-jurisdiction validity of the prior judgment, is that courts are expected to police their own subject matter jurisdiction. A court that renders judgment in a litigated action, therefore, is generally presumed to have determined that it possessed subject matter jurisdiction.

When thinking about the validity requirement for preclusion, recognize the clash of fundamental values. On one side is the value of legitimacy—a court that lacks jurisdiction should not resolve a dispute. On the other side is the value of finality—once a judgment has been entered and appeals are concluded, the decision should not be reopened. Court decisions on validity of judgments reflect a balance of these competing values.

One key takeaway here is that the "validity" of a judgment does not depend on the correctness of the court's judgment, but rather on structural factors relating to the court's power (which, with a few exceptions, is presumed to have existed once a judgment is rendered on the merits). The point of claim preclusion is finality, not perfection. If parties could relitigate claims whenever they dislike the result, there would be nothing left of claim preclusion (and, with the onslaught of filings, courts would grind to a halt). If a party thinks the court got it wrong, the proper course is to challenge the judgment on direct appeal. In rare extenuating circumstances, as discussed later in the chapter, parties can move to reopen a judgment. But in general, parties cannot avoid the preclusive effect of a final judgment merely by showing that it was erroneous. As the Supreme Court has explained, "an 'erroneous conclusion' reached by the court in the first suit does not deprive the defendants in the second action 'of their right to rely upon the plea of res judicata.'" *Federated Dep't Stores v. Moitie*, 452 U.S. 394 (1981) (quoting *Baltimore S.S. Co. v. Phillips*, 274 U.S. 316, 325 (1927)).

(ii) Finality

At first glance, the finality requirement may look like circular logic: For a judgment to be entitled to finality, it must be "final." *See, e.g.*, Restatement (Second) of Judgments §17 ("A valid and final personal judgment is conclusive between the parties...."). But the finality requirement is not as meaningless as it may seem.

Litigation often proceeds for quite a while before adjudication ultimately resolves the dispute. During that time, the court may make many decisions in the litigation. The court may deny a motion to dismiss, resolve discovery disputes, grant partial summary judgment, rule on the admissibility of evidence, and so forth. Such interlocutory orders—decisions by the court during the course of litigation—do not finally resolve the action. Because they remain subject to modification, interlocutory orders are not considered final enough to be given preclusive effect.

Suppose a trial court enters judgment in a case after trial, summary judgment, or some other adjudication that resolves the case. It sure seems like a final judgment. But now the losing party files an appeal. Is there a "final judgment" for purposes of preclusion? Or suppose the trial court enters judgment, and no party has yet filed an appeal but the time for filing an appeal has not expired. The question is whether finality means completion at the trial court level or whether it means the unavailability of further review. In other words, is a judgment considered "final" pending appeal? In the federal courts and the majority of state courts, a judgment is considered final even if an appeal is pending. *See, e.g.*, *Tripati v. Henman*, 857 F.2d 1366, 1367 (9th Cir. 1988) ("The established rule in the federal courts is that a final judgment retains all of its res judicata consequences pending decision of the appeal.") (quoting 18 WRIGHT, MILLER & COOPER, FEDERAL PRACTICE AND PROCEDURE §4433 (1981)); *Joseph v. Linehaul Logistics, Inc.*, 2013 WL 2019513 (D. Mont. 2013); *Wyatt v. Wyatt*, 65 P.3d 825 (Alaska 2003). The reasoning is that most cases are affirmed on appeal, and a trial court's judgment is entitled to respect unless it is actually reversed or vacated. As the Ninth Circuit explained, "[t]o deny preclusion in these circumstances would lead to an absurd result: Litigants would be able to refile identical cases while appeals are pending, enmeshing their opponents and the court system in tangles of duplicative litigation." *Tripati*, 857 F.2d at 1367. Treating a judgment as final pending appeal also meshes nicely with the final judgment rule of appealability, discussed in Chapter 6, which states that in general a decision can be appealed only if it is a final judgment. In California and several other jurisdictions, however, a judgment is not considered final for purposes of preclusion until after appeal or the time for appeal has passed. *See, e.g., Kay v. City of Rancho Palos Verdes*, 504 F.3d 803 (9th Cir. 2007) ("Unlike the federal rule and that of several states, in California the rule is that the finality required to invoke the preclusive bar of res judicata is not achieved until an appeal from the trial court judgment has been exhausted or the time to appeal has expired.") (quoting *Franklin & Franklin v. 7-Eleven Owners for Fair Franchising*, 85 Cal. App. 4th 1168, 1174 (2000)). As a practical matter, a court faced with such a situation could stay the proceedings in case 2 until the appeal in case 1 is completed, at which point case 2 could be dismissed on grounds of claim preclusion.

THE BIG PICTURE

How does claim preclusion fit into the picture if a case settles? Settlement provides a final resolution of a dispute, but its finality comes mostly from contract law, not preclusion. A settlement is not a judgment—at least, not typically. It is a contract in which, generally, a defendant agrees to pay a sum of money or provide some other remedy in exchange for the plaintiff's agreement to release the claims against the defendant. Claim preclusion may enter the picture as additional protection because the settling plaintiff normally agrees to dismiss the complaint with prejudice, and such a dismissal is a final judgment with claim preclusive effect. Certain settlements, such as consent decrees and class-action settlements, require judicial approval. In such cases, a court-approved settlement is entered as a judgment that has claim preclusive effect on the parties, including all the class members in a certified class action. Despite these ways in which claim preclusion supports certain settlements, in general lawyers correctly think of settlement and adjudication as two different paths for achieving finality in a dispute—settlement with binding effect supplied by contract law, and adjudication with binding effect supplied by claim preclusion.

(c) "On the Merits"

Many cases and authorities on preclusion state that claim preclusion applies only to judgments "on the merits." If parties have received an adjudication on the merits of their dispute, a dissatisfied party should not be permitted to try again for a better result. If, on the other hand, a lawsuit is dismissed on a threshold procedural issue, and if the procedural flaw in the first action can be repaired, then there is no good reason to prevent a litigant from refiling the same claim. What, though, does "on the merits" mean? Again, your first instinct might be to say that a judgment "on the merits" is one that reached the right result on the facts and law. As with the validity requirement, the definition of "on the merits" does not (and cannot) turn on whether the judgment reflects a "correct" result. Consider the following examples—some trickier than others—that illustrate the contours of the "on the merits" requirement.

Suppose A and B have a business dispute, giving rise to state law breach-of-contract claims as well as a federal antitrust claim. A sues B in federal court, asserting the state law contract claims. In general, federal courts have power to decide a dispute only if it arises under federal law or if the parties are of diverse citizenship. In A's lawsuit against B, there is no diversity of citizenship and no federal question, so when B moves to dismiss for lack of subject matter jurisdiction, the court grants the motion and dismisses A's case. Subsequently, A sues B again in federal court, this time asserting the claim under federal antitrust law. Will the court in case 2 throw out A's claim on the ground that it is claim precluded because of the judgment in case 1? Of course not. Even assuming that the antitrust claim arose from the same transaction as the contract claim and thus would be considered the same claim, the first judgment simply was not on the merits. The court dismissed for lack of subject matter jurisdiction. That dismissal means that in the absence of diversity of citizenship or some other basis for federal jurisdiction, A's breach-of-contract claim did not belong in federal court. It means that A should go to federal court only if the court's limited jurisdiction permits it to adjudicate A's claim. Therefore, it makes sense that A would be allowed to come back to the federal court in order to assert the federal antitrust claim. Note that if A had returned to federal court to file the same state law contract claim rather than the federal antitrust claim, then the court would dismiss A's complaint again for lack of subject matter jurisdiction.

Here is a similar example, looking at personal jurisdiction rather than subject matter jurisdiction: A sues B in Oklahoma. In general, a court's personal jurisdiction over the defendant depends upon the defendant's contacts with the state. B is a New York company that lacks contacts with Oklahoma, so the court grants B's motion to dismiss for lack of personal jurisdiction. Subsequently, A sues B on the same claim, but this time files the suit in New York rather than Oklahoma. The court in case 2 will not dismiss on grounds of claim preclusion, even though A had previously filed the exact same claim against the same party and had received a final judgment. The judgment of dismissal for lack of personal jurisdiction was not on the merits. Consider the meaning of the Oklahoma court's dismissal for lack of personal jurisdiction. It is saying, in essence, "You cannot sue B here. We have no power over this defendant. If you want to sue B, go do it in New York."

If a case has been tried to a jury verdict and the court enters judgment based on the verdict, or if a court enters judgment after reaching findings of fact and conclusions of law in a bench trial, then naturally the judgment is "on the merits" for purposes of preclusive effect. Similarly, if a case is resolved on summary judgment or judgment as a matter of law, the judgment is "on the merits."

A more difficult question is whether a judgment is "on the merits" when a court grants a motion to dismiss for failure to state a claim upon which relief can be granted. Rule 12(b)(6), you will recall, allows a defendant to move to dismiss a complaint if the allegations in the complaint fail to state a valid claim. If a court dismisses an action for failure to state a claim, should the plaintiff be permitted to try again? Well, that depends.

Consider this example. A sues B. B moves to dismiss for failure to state a claim under Rule 12(b)(6). The court grants the motion and dismisses the action. Subsequently, A sues B again based on the same dispute, but with more extensive factual allegations in support of the claim. The question is whether A's second action is claim precluded. It is the *same claim*, brought between the *same parties*, and it resulted in a *valid, final judgment*. But was the judgment *on the merits*? That depends on why the court granted the motion to dismiss in the first case.

First, suppose the court granted the motion because A's claim simply has no basis in law (recall the example from Chapter 2 in which a plaintiff sued because the defendant wore a blue shirt). In that case, the dismissal reflects the court's determination that A has no meritorious claim, and there is no reason to allow A to bring the same claim again. Therefore, claim preclusion should apply. To make this clear, the court might state in the original order of dismissal that the dismissal is "with prejudice."

Now suppose the court granted the dismissal because of A's failure to plead adequately. Perhaps the allegations in the complaint fail to meet all of the elements of the claim, but leave open the possibility that A has a valid claim but simply forgot to include all of the necessary allegations. Or perhaps the complaint was dismissed due to a technical pleading error, such as failing to include a demand for judgment as required by Rule 8(a). In that case, the dismissal does not reflect a determination that A has no meritorious claim, but rather the court's determination that this complaint has not been drafted properly. Recall from Chapter 2 that the goal of modern pleading, as embodied in the federal rules, is to attempt to resolve disputes on the merits rather than on the technicalities of pleading. Under modern pleading theory, it would not make sense to apply claim preclusion to a dismissal that was intended to tell the plaintiff to get the pleading right, rather than to tell the plaintiff that she had no case. To make this clear, the court might state that the dismissal is "without prejudice" or "with leave to amend."

What if the court dismisses the claim but the order does not state whether the dismissal is "with prejudice" or "without prejudice"? If the order simply says "dismissed," what preclusive effect then? In the federal courts, the answer may be found in Rule 41(b), which states: "Unless the dismissal order states otherwise, a dismissal . . . —except one for lack of jurisdiction, improper venue, or failure to join a party under Rule 19—operates as an adjudication on the merits." In other words, if a dismissal order does not specify that it is *not* on the merits, then the dismissal is considered an adjudication on the merits and is entitled to claim preclusive effect. Two caveats: First, although the federal courts and most state courts follow this interpretation of Rule 41(b), a few state court systems take the opposite approach; in those state courts, a dismissal is considered to be without prejudice unless the court specifies otherwise. Second, in *Semtek Int'l v. Lockheed Martin*, 531 U.S. 497 (2001), the Supreme Court offered a more modest interpretation of the "adjudication upon the merits" language of Rule 41(b): that the same claim cannot be refiled in the same court, at least where the claim in the first case was based on state law. *See id.* at 506.

STRATEGY SESSION

To your client, there is a big difference between a dismissal that is claim preclusive and one that is not. If you represent a defendant, you would nearly always prefer a dismissal on the merits, and vice versa if you represent a plaintiff. Therefore, if you represent a plaintiff whose claim is dismissed on the pleadings, and if the problem was a pleading error rather than that plaintiff had no valid case, then it is essential to ask that the court's order of dismissal state "without prejudice" or "with leave to amend." Otherwise, claim preclusion may well prevent your client from bringing the claim (and you may find yourself looking down the wrong end of a malpractice suit).

So far, our examples have presented situations in which you can figure out claim preclusion by asking yourself whether the judgment was "on the merits" in the everyday sense of those words. Claim preclusion naturally applies to a judgment based on a trial verdict or a dismissal based on a determination that the plaintiff's case is legally without merit. Such judgments go to the merits of the lawsuit. And claim preclusion does not apply to dismissals for lack of jurisdiction, improper venue, or technical pleading problems. But our next example proves that "on the merits" is a term of art, and you have to be careful about applying it.

Suppose A sues B, and B seeks discovery from A. A refuses to comply with B's discovery requests. B moves to compel discovery, and the court grants the motion. A refuses to comply with the court order. Finally, the court grants discovery sanctions under Rule 37, and because of the extent of A's misconduct, the court imposes a severe sanction—dismissal of A's action—just as the district court did in *Lee v. Max International*, which we saw in Chapter 3. Subsequently, A files a new complaint asserting the same claim. In the second action, B argues claim preclusion, pointing out that it is the same claim between the same parties and that there is a valid, final judgment. But A argues that claim preclusion applies only to judgments on the merits, and the dismissal in case 1 had nothing to do with the merits of A's lawsuit. Although A's argument sounds logical, you can see that if A's argument were to prevail, it would render the Rule 37 dismissal meaningless. For a sanction of dismissal to have any teeth—whether in the context of discovery or otherwise—it must be given claim preclusive effect even though the judgment is not based on the actual merits of the lawsuit.

(d) Same Parties

Claim preclusion applies to claims between the same parties. If A sues B and a court enters judgment on A's claim, then A is precluded from reasserting the same claim against B. In general, claim preclusion does not prevent A from asserting a similar claim against a *different defendant*. Nor does it generally prevent a *different plaintiff* from asserting a claim against B, even if it arises out of the same event. The "same parties" requirement, however, is not absolute. How far does the principle extend and what are its exceptions? This was the question the Supreme Court faced in the following case.

TAYLOR v. STURGELL

553 U.S. 880 (2008)

GINSBURG, J., delivered the opinion for a unanimous Court.

"It is a principle of general application in Anglo-American jurisprudence that one is not bound by a judgment *in personam* in a litigation in which he is not designated as a party or to which he has not been made a party by service of process." *Hansberry v. Lee*, 311 U.S. 32, 40 (1940). Several exceptions, recognized in this Court's decisions, temper this basic rule. In a class action, for example, a person not named as a party may be bound by a judgment on the merits of the action, if she was adequately represented by a party who actively participated in the litigation. In this case, we consider for the first time whether there is a "virtual representation" exception to the general rule against precluding nonparties. Adopted by a number of courts, including the courts below in the case now before us, the exception so styled is broader than any we have so far approved.

The virtual representation question we examine in this opinion arises in the following context. Petitioner Brent Taylor filed a lawsuit under the Freedom of Information Act seeking certain documents from the Federal Aviation Administration. Greg Herrick, Taylor's friend, had previously brought an unsuccessful suit seeking the same records. The two men have no legal relationship, and there is no evidence that Taylor controlled, financed, participated in, or even had notice of Herrick's earlier suit. Nevertheless, the D.C. Circuit held Taylor's suit precluded by the judgment against Herrick because, in that court's assessment, Herrick qualified as Taylor's "virtual representative."

We disapprove the doctrine of preclusion by "virtual representation," and hold, based on the record as it now stands, that the judgment against Herrick does not bar Taylor from maintaining this suit.

I

The Freedom of Information Act (FOIA or Act) accords "any person" a right to request any records held by a federal agency. 5 U.S.C. §552(a)(3)(A). No reason need be given for a FOIA request, and unless the requested materials fall within one of the Act's enumerated exceptions, the agency must "make the records promptly available" to the requester. If an agency refuses to furnish the requested records, the requester may file suit in federal court and obtain an injunction "order[ing] the production of any agency records improperly withheld." §552(a)(4)(B).

The courts below held the instant FOIA suit barred by the judgment in earlier litigation seeking the same records. Because the lower courts' decisions turned on the connection between the two lawsuits, we begin with a full account of each action.

A

The first suit was filed by Greg Herrick, an antique aircraft enthusiast and the owner of an F-45 airplane, a vintage model manufactured by the Fairchild Engine and Airplane Corporation (FEAC) in the 1930's. In 1997, seeking information that would help him restore his plane to its original condition, Herrick filed a FOIA request asking the Federal Aviation Administration (FAA) for copies of any technical documents about the F-45 contained in the agency's records.

. . . The FAA denied Herrick's request, however, upon finding that the documents he sought are subject to FOIA's exemption for "trade secrets and commercial or financial information obtained from a person and privileged or confidential." In an administrative appeal, Herrick urged that FEAC and its successors had waived any trade-secret protection. The FAA thereupon contacted FEAC's corporate successor, respondent Fairchild Corporation (Fairchild). Because Fairchild objected to release of the documents, the agency adhered to its original decision.

Herrick then filed suit in the U.S. District Court for the District of Wyoming. Challenging the FAA's invocation of the trade-secret exemption, Herrick placed heavy weight on a 1955 letter from FEAC to the Civil Aeronautics Authority [(the FAA's predecessor)]. The letter authorized the agency to lend any documents in its files to the public "for use in making repairs or replacement parts for aircraft produced by Fairchild." This broad authorization, Herrick maintained, showed that the F-45 certification records held by the FAA could not be regarded as "secre[t]" or "confidential" within the meaning of [the Act].

Rejecting Herrick's argument, the District Court granted summary judgment to the FAA. The 1955 letter, the court reasoned, did not deprive the F-45 certification documents of trade-secret status. . . .

[On appeal, the Tenth Circuit] affirmed the entry of summary judgment for the FAA.

B

The Tenth Circuit's decision issued on July 24, 2002. Less than a month later, on August 22, petitioner Brent Taylor—a friend of Herrick's and an antique aircraft enthusiast in his own right—submitted a FOIA request seeking the same documents Herrick had unsuccessfully sued to obtain. When the FAA failed to respond, Taylor filed a complaint in the U.S. District Court for the District of Columbia. Like Herrick, Taylor argued that FEAC's 1955 letter had stripped the records of their trade-secret status. . . .

After Fairchild intervened as a defendant, the District Court in D.C. concluded that Taylor's suit was barred by claim preclusion; accordingly, it granted summary judgment to Fairchild and the FAA. The court acknowledged that Taylor was not a party to Herrick's suit. Relying on the Eighth Circuit's decision in *Tyus v. Schoemehl*, 93 F.3d 449 (8th Cir. 1996), however, it held that a nonparty may be bound by a judgment if she was "virtually represented" by a party. . . .

The record before the District Court in Taylor's suit revealed the following facts about the relationship between Taylor and Herrick: Taylor is the president of the Antique Aircraft Association, an organization to which Herrick belongs; the two men are "close associate[s]"; Herrick asked Taylor to help restore Herrick's F-45, though they had no contract or agreement for Taylor's participation in the restoration; Taylor was represented by the lawyer who represented Herrick in the earlier litigation; and Herrick apparently gave Taylor documents that Herrick had obtained from the FAA during discovery in his suit.

Fairchild and the FAA conceded that Taylor had not participated in Herrick's suit. The D.C. District Court determined, however, that Herrick ranked as Taylor's virtual representative. . . . Accordingly, the District

Court held Taylor's suit, seeking the same documents Herrick had requested, barred by the judgment against Herrick.

The D.C. Circuit affirmed. *Taylor v. Blakey*, 490 F.3d 965 (D.C. Cir. 2007). . . .

We granted certiorari to resolve the disagreement among the Circuits over the permissibility and scope of preclusion based on "virtual representation."

II

The preclusive effect of a federal-court judgment is determined by federal common law. *See Semtek Int'l Inc. v. Lockheed Martin Corp.*, 531 U.S. 497, 507-508 (2001). For judgments in federal-question cases—for example, Herrick's FOIA suit— federal courts participate in developing "uniform federal rule[s]" of res judicata, which this Court has ultimate authority to determine and declare.[4] The federal common law of preclusion is, of course, subject to due process limitations. *See Richards v. Jefferson County*, 517 U.S. 793, 797 (1996). . . .

A

The preclusive effect of a judgment is defined by claim preclusion and issue preclusion, which are collectively referred to as "res judicata."[5] Under the doctrine of claim preclusion, a final judgment forecloses "successive litigation of the very same claim, whether or not relitigation of the claim raises the same issues as the earlier suit." *New Hampshire v. Maine*, 532 U.S. 742, 748 (2001). Issue preclusion, in contrast, bars "successive litigation of an issue of fact or law actually litigated and resolved in a valid court determination essential to the prior judgment," even if the issue recurs in the context of a different claim. By "preclud[ing] parties from contesting matters that they have had a full and fair opportunity to litigate," these two doctrines protect against "the expense and vexation attending multiple lawsuits, conserv[e] judicial resources, and foste[r] reliance on judicial action by minimizing the possibility of inconsistent decisions." *Montana v. United States*, 440 U.S. 147, 153-54 (1979).

A person who was not a party to a suit generally has not had a "full and fair opportunity to litigate" the claims and issues settled in that suit. The application of claim and issue preclusion to nonparties thus runs up against the "deep-rooted historic tradition that everyone should have his own day in court." *Richards*, 517 U.S. at 798. Indicating the strength of that tradition, we have often repeated the general rule that "one is not bound by a judgment *in personam* in a litigation in which he is not designated as a party or to which he has not been made a party by service of process." *Hansberry*, 311 U.S. at 40.

B

Though hardly in doubt, the rule against nonparty preclusion is subject to exceptions. For present purposes, the recognized exceptions can be grouped into six categories.

---

[4] For judgments in diversity cases, federal law incorporates the rules of preclusion applied by the State in which the rendering court sits. *See Semtek Int'l Inc. v. Lockheed Martin Corp.*, 531 U.S. 497, 508 (2001).

[5] These terms have replaced a more confusing lexicon. Claim preclusion describes the rules formerly known as "merger" and "bar," while issue preclusion encompasses the doctrines once known as "collateral estoppel" and "direct estoppel." *See Migra v. Warren City School Dist. Bd. of Ed.*, 465 U.S. 75, 77 n.1 (1984).

First, "[a] person who agrees to be bound by the determination of issues in an action between others is bound in accordance with the terms of his agreement." 1 Restatement (Second) of Judgments §40 (1980). For example, "if separate actions involving the same transaction are brought by different plaintiffs against the same defendant, all the parties to all the actions may agree that the question of the defendant's liability will be definitely determined, one way or the other, in a 'test case.'" D. Shapiro, *Civil Procedure: Preclusion in Civil Actions* 77-78 (2001).

Second, nonparty preclusion may be justified based on a variety of pre-existing "substantive legal relationship[s]" between the person to be bound and a party to the judgment. Shapiro at 78. *See also Richards*, 517 U.S. at 798. Qualifying relationships include, but are not limited to, preceding and succeeding owners of property, bailee and bailor, and assignee and assignor. These exceptions originated "as much from the needs of property law as from the values of preclusion by judgment." 18A C. Wright, A. Miller, & E. Cooper, Federal Practice and Procedure §4448, p. 329 (2d ed. 2002).[8]

Third, we have confirmed that, "in certain limited circumstances," a nonparty may be bound by a judgment because she was "adequately represented by someone with the same interests who [wa]s a party" to the suit. *Richards,* 517 U.S. at 798. Representative suits with preclusive effect on nonparties include properly conducted class actions, *see Martin v. Wilks*, 490 U.S. 755, 762 n.2 (1989) (citing Fed. R. Civ. P. 23), and suits brought by trustees, guardians, and other fiduciaries, *see Sea-Land Services, Inc. v. Gaudet*, 414 U.S. 573, 593 (1974).

Fourth, a nonparty is bound by a judgment if she "assume[d] control" over the litigation in which that judgment was rendered. *Montana*, 440 U.S. at 154. Because such a person has had "the opportunity to present proofs and argument," he has already "had his day in court" even though he was not a formal party to the litigation.

Fifth, a party bound by a judgment may not avoid its preclusive force by relitigating through a proxy. Preclusion is thus in order when a person who did not participate in a litigation later brings suit as the designated representative of a person who was a party to the prior adjudication. *See Chicago, R.I. & P.R. Co. v. Schendel*, 270 U.S. 611, 620 (1926). And although our decisions have not addressed the issue directly, it also seems clear that preclusion is appropriate when a nonparty later brings suit as an agent for a party who is bound by a judgment.

Sixth, in certain circumstances a special statutory scheme may "expressly foreclos[e] successive litigation by nonlitigants . . . if the scheme is otherwise consistent with due process." *Martin*, 490 U.S. at 762 n.2. Examples of such schemes include bankruptcy and probate proceedings, and *quo warranto* actions or other suits that, "under [the governing] law, [may] be brought only on behalf of the public at large," *Richards*, 517 U.S. at 804.

---

[8] The substantive legal relationships justifying preclusion are sometimes collectively referred to as "privity." *See, e.g., Richards v. Jefferson County*, 517 U.S. 793, 798 (1996). The term "privity," however, has also come to be used more broadly, as a way to express the conclusion that nonparty preclusion is appropriate on any ground. To ward off confusion, we avoid using the term "privity" in this opinion.

III

Reaching beyond these six established categories, some lower courts have recognized a "virtual representation" exception to the rule against nonparty preclusion. . . . The D.C. Circuit, the FAA, and Fairchild have presented three arguments in support of an expansive doctrine of virtual representation. We find none of them persuasive.

A

The D.C. Circuit purported to ground its virtual representation doctrine in this Court's decisions stating that, in some circumstances, a person may be bound by a judgment if she was adequately represented by a party to the proceeding yielding that judgment. But the D.C. Circuit's definition of "adequate representation" strayed from the meaning our decisions have attributed to that term.

In *Richards*, we reviewed a decision by the Alabama Supreme Court holding that a challenge to a tax was barred by a judgment upholding the same tax in a suit filed by different taxpayers. 517 U.S. at 795-97. The plaintiffs in the first suit "did not sue on behalf of a class," their complaint "did not purport to assert any claim against or on behalf of any nonparties," and the judgment "did not purport to bind" nonparties. *Id.* at 801. There was no indication, we emphasized, that the court in the first suit "took care to protect the interests" of absent parties, or that the parties to that litigation "understood their suit to be on behalf of absent [parties]." *Id.* at 802. In these circumstances, we held, the application of claim preclusion was inconsistent with "the due process of law guaranteed by the Fourteenth Amendment." *Id.* at 797.

The D.C. Circuit stated, without elaboration, that it did not "read *Richards* to hold a nonparty . . . adequately represented only if special procedures were followed [to protect the nonparty] or the party to the prior suit understood it was representing the nonparty." 490 F.3d at 971. As the D.C. Circuit saw this case, Herrick adequately represented Taylor for two principal reasons: Herrick had a strong incentive to litigate; and Taylor later hired Herrick's lawyer, suggesting Taylor's "satisfaction with the attorney's performance in the prior case." *Id.* at 975.

The D.C. Circuit misapprehended *Richards*. As just recounted, our holding that the Alabama Supreme Court's application of res judicata to nonparties violated due process turned on the lack of either special procedures to protect the nonparties' interests or an understanding by the concerned parties that the first suit was brought in a representative capacity. *Richards* thus established that representation is "adequate" for purposes of nonparty preclusion only if (at a minimum) one of these two circumstances is present. . . .

Our decisions recognizing that a nonparty may be bound by a judgment if she was adequately represented by a party to the earlier suit thus provide no support for the D.C. Circuit's broad theory of virtual representation.

B

Fairchild and the FAA do not argue that the D.C. Circuit's virtual representation doctrine fits within any of the recognized grounds for nonparty preclusion. Rather, they ask us to abandon the attempt to delineate discrete grounds and clear rules altogether. Preclusion is in order, they contend, whenever "the relationship between a party and a non-party is 'close enough' to bring the second litigant within the judgment." Courts should make this "close enough" determination, they argue, through a "heavily fact-driven" and "equitable" inquiry. . . .

We reject this argument for three reasons. First, our decisions emphasize the fundamental nature of the general rule that a litigant is not bound by a judgment to which she was not a party. *See, e.g., Richards*, 517 U.S. at 798-799. Accordingly, we have endeavored to delineate discrete exceptions that apply in "limited circumstances." *Id.* at 762 n.2. Respondents' amorphous balancing test is at odds with the constrained approach to nonparty preclusion our decisions advance. . . .

Our second reason for rejecting a broad doctrine of virtual representation rests on the limitations attending nonparty preclusion based on adequate representation. A party's representation of a nonparty is "adequate" for preclusion purposes only if, at a minimum: (1) The interests of the nonparty and her representative are aligned, *see Hansberry*, 311 U.S. at 43, 61; and (2) either the party understood herself to be acting in a representative capacity or the original court took care to protect the interests of the nonparty, *see Richards*, 517 U.S. at 801-802. In addition, adequate representation sometimes requires (3) notice of the original suit to the persons alleged to have been represented, *see Richards*, 517 U.S. at 801. In the class-action context, these limitations are implemented by the procedural safeguards contained in Federal Rule of Civil Procedure 23. . . .

Third, a diffuse balancing approach to nonparty preclusion would likely create more headaches than it relieves. Most obviously, it could significantly complicate the task of district courts faced in the first instance with preclusion questions. An all-things-considered balancing approach might spark wide-ranging, time-consuming, and expensive discovery tracking factors potentially relevant under seven- or five-prong tests. And after the relevant facts are established, district judges would be called upon to evaluate them under a standard that provides no firm guidance. Preclusion doctrine, it should be recalled, is intended to reduce the burden of litigation on courts and parties. *Montana*, 440 U.S. at 153-154. "In this area of the law," we agree, " 'crisp rules with sharp corners' are preferable to a round-about doctrine of opaque standards." *Bittinger v. Tecumseh Prods. Co.*, 123 F.3d 877, 881 (6th Cir. 1997).

C

Finally, relying on the Eighth Circuit's decision in *Tyus*, 93 F.3d at 456, the FAA maintains that nonparty preclusion should apply more broadly in "public-law" litigation than in "private-law" controversies. . . .

The FAA . . . argues that "the threat of vexatious litigation is heightened" in public-law cases because "the number of plaintiffs with standing is potentially limitless." FOIA does allow "any person" whose request is denied to resort to federal court for review of the agency's determination. 5 U.S.C. §552(a)(3)(A), (4)(B). Thus it is theoretically possible that several persons could coordinate to mount a series of repetitive lawsuits.

But we are not convinced that this risk justifies departure from the usual rules governing nonparty preclusion. First, *stare decisis* will allow courts swiftly to dispose of repetitive suits brought in the same circuit. Second, even when *stare decisis* is not dispositive, "the human tendency not to waste money will deter the bringing of suits based on claims or issues that have already been adversely determined against others." Shapiro at 97. This intuition seems to be borne out by experience: The FAA has not called our attention to any instances of abusive FOIA suits in the Circuits that reject the virtual representation theory respondents advocate here.

IV

For the foregoing reasons, we disapprove the theory of virtual representation on which the decision below rested. The preclusive effects of a judgment in a federal-question case decided by a federal court should instead be determined according to the established grounds for nonparty preclusion described in this opinion. . . .

In some cases, however, lower courts have relied on virtual representation to extend nonparty preclusion beyond the latter doctrine's proper bounds. We now turn back to Taylor's action to determine whether his suit is such a case, or whether the result reached by the courts below can be justified on one of the recognized grounds for nonparty preclusion.

A

It is uncontested that four of the six grounds for nonparty preclusion have no application here: There is no indication that Taylor agreed to be bound by Herrick's litigation, that Taylor and Herrick have any legal relationship, that Taylor exercised any control over Herrick's suit, or that this suit implicates any special statutory scheme limiting relitigation. Neither the FAA nor Fairchild contends otherwise.

It is equally clear that preclusion cannot be justified on the theory that Taylor was adequately represented in Herrick's suit. Nothing in the record indicates that Herrick understood himself to be suing on Taylor's behalf, that Taylor even knew of Herrick's suit, or that the Wyoming District Court took special care to protect Taylor's interests. Under our pathmarking precedent, therefore, Herrick's representation was not "adequate." *See Richards*, 517 U.S. at 801-02.

That leaves only the fifth category: preclusion because a nonparty to an earlier litigation has brought suit as a representative or agent of a party who is bound by the prior adjudication. Taylor is not Herrick's legal representative and he has not purported to sue in a representative capacity. He concedes, however, that preclusion would be appropriate if respondents could demonstrate that he is acting as Herrick's "undisclosed agen[t]."

Respondents argue here, as they did below, that Taylor's suit is a collusive attempt to relitigate Herrick's action. The D.C. Circuit considered a similar question in addressing the "tactical maneuvering" prong of its virtual representation test. The Court of Appeals did not, however, treat the issue as one of agency, and it expressly declined to reach any definitive conclusions due to "the ambiguity of the facts." We therefore remand to give the courts below an opportunity to determine whether Taylor, in pursuing the instant FOIA suit, is acting as Herrick's agent. Taylor concedes that such a remand is appropriate. . . .

* * *

For the reasons stated, the judgment of the United States Court of Appeals for the District of Columbia Circuit is vacated, and the case is remanded for further proceedings consistent with this opinion.

Notes & Questions

1. As always before tackling a preclusion issue, be sure you are clear on the two actions. In *Taylor*, who sued whom for what in case 1? What was the outcome? Who sued whom for what in case 2? Which party sought to use the prior judgment for its preclusive effect?

2. *Taylor* is an example of a case in which arguments of claim preclusion and issue preclusion go hand in hand. In case 2, Fairchild and the FAA could frame their argument in terms of claim preclusion—that there was a valid, final judgment on the merits regarding this claim in case 1 and therefore the plaintiff should be barred from pursuing the same claim in case 2. Or they could frame their argument in terms of issue preclusion—that the question of whether the requested documents are protected from disclosure under FOIA was already answered in case 1 and the answer should be binding in case 2. Thus, while this casebook offers the case in the section on claim preclusion, one can as easily think of *Taylor* as an issue preclusion case. Either way, the Supreme Court in *Taylor* had to address the fundamental question of whether Brent Taylor could be bound by the judgment in Greg Herrick's case.

3. What aspects of the Herrick-Taylor story made this a strong case for applying preclusion based on a theory of "virtual representation"? Why did the Supreme Court nonetheless reject this argument?

4. The Supreme Court emphatically rejected the "virtual representation" theory on which the lower courts had relied in *Taylor*, driving home the principle that a nonparty is not bound by a judgment. Even so, the Court was careful to spell out a number of exceptions to this general principle. All are worth knowing, and several are especially worth highlighting.

   The opinion mentions a set of exceptions based on preexisting substantive legal relationships. For example, a successor in interest, such as someone who purchases an ongoing business, is bound by the outcomes of its predecessor's litigation. In footnote 8, Justice Ginsburg explains why her opinion avoids the word *privity*, which is often used as a conclusory, broad catch-all to describe the sorts of relationships that permit a nonparty to be treated as an extension of a party and thereby bound.

   The opinion also mentions a set of exceptions involving representative litigation. For example, a person is bound by a judgment in a case brought on her behalf by a guardian or other legal representative. The grand version of this exception is the class action. One way to conceptualize class actions is as a giant exception to the rule that nonparties are not bound by judgments. By setting out the circumstances when "[o]ne or more members of a class may sue or be sued as representative parties on behalf of all members," Rule 23 explicitly sets up a form of litigation that is intended to bind all class members, not only the named parties.

Last, the opinion mentions a set of exceptions based on "special statutory scheme[s]." Two prominent examples are bankruptcy and probate. The end result of bankruptcy is a discharge of the debtor's debts; for the scheme to be effective, it must bind all would-be creditors. Similarly, when a will is probated, the finality of the process depends upon the power of a probate decree to bind all potential claimants to the assets of the estate.

5. The Supreme Court remanded for a determination of whether the fifth exception (relitigating through a proxy) applied to Greg Herrick and Brent Taylor. That is, in case 2, was Taylor litigating as a proxy for Herrick? Note that this is sort of the opposite of the theory on which the lower courts had relied—that Taylor was bound because Herrick had represented Taylor when Herrick litigated case 1.

6. Focus on the core principle of *Taylor v. Sturgell*—that a new party generally is not precluded by a judgment in a different party's case—and consider why this is so. There are at least two levels at which to think about it.

   Suppose A sues B, and the case reaches a valid, final judgment on the merits. Then C sues B on a claim arising out of the same facts. If B were to assert a claim preclusion argument ("We already had a lawsuit about this, and the court entered judgment, so go away."), C's response would be irrefutable: "*I* haven't had a lawsuit about this. *You* and A did." One way to think about this is that B's claim preclusion argument fails to meet two of the claim preclusion requirements. It fails to meet the same-parties requirement, because C was not a party to the first action. And it fails to meet the same-claim requirement, because even though their claims arise out of the same event, different plaintiffs necessarily possess separate claims.

   The other way to think about this is more fundamental and ultimately more important to your understanding. C cannot be bound by judgment 1 because C was not a party to the case. As a functional matter, even if A failed, C might have a better lawyer, a different strategy, more resources, or other reasons for which C wants her own shot. More fundamentally, as a due process matter, if C was not made a party to case 1, then the court never had the power to enter a binding judgment against C. In Chapter 10, you will see the Supreme Court articulate this principle in *Pennoyer v. Neff* as the foundational idea behind constraints on personal jurisdiction under the Due Process Clause.

7. The Supreme Court in *Taylor* cites *Martin v. Wilks*, 490 U.S. 755 (1989). In *Martin*, a group of African-American firefighters had sued the City of Birmingham, Alabama, for employment discrimination. Eventually, the parties reached a consent judgment, pursuant to which the city was required to implement a remedial scheme to improve the racial balance in hiring and promotions. A group of white firefighters then sued the city, claiming that the remedial scheme discriminated against them on the basis of race. The district court held that the new plaintiffs were bound by the terms of the consent judgment, but the Supreme Court held otherwise, quoting the same language from *Hansberry v. Lee* that you see in the opening line of *Taylor*, and permitting the firefighters to go forward with their claims of unlawful discrimination. In a dispute like the discrimination litigation

in *Martin*, what argument could you make for the new litigants that it is especially important to allow them to assert their own claims? And, looking at it from the other side, what argument could you make for the city that it is especially important *not* to allow the claims?

Congress responded to *Martin* by enacting the Civil Rights Act of 1991, 42 U.S.C. §2000e-2(n)(1). That statute, among other things, provides that a litigated or consent judgment in an employment discrimination dispute is binding on nonparties (like the white firefighters who brought case 2 in *Martin*) as long as they had actual notice and an opportunity to be heard, or as long as their interests were adequately represented by someone who challenged the judgment on the same grounds. Is this provision of the Civil Rights Act constitutional? If so, does this mean that the principle in *Taylor*—that nonparties are not bound by a judgment—operates at a sub-constitutional level rather than as a requirement imposed by the Due Process Clause? Or does it mean that, although a constitutional due process principle, it admits of several exceptions as enunciated in *Taylor*? Which exception does the Civil Rights Act of 1991 fit?

(2) Compulsory Counterclaims

The "woulda, shoulda, coulda" message of claim preclusion extends not only to parties who assert claims, but also to those defending against claims. Recall what you learned about compulsory counterclaims in Chapter 7: If a defendant fails to assert a claim against the plaintiff that arises out of the same transaction or occurrence as the plaintiff's claim against the defendant, then in general the defendant is barred from asserting that claim in a separate lawsuit. In this regard, the compulsory counterclaim rule functions somewhat like claim preclusion.

Note a couple of important differences, however, between claim preclusion and the compulsory counterclaim rule. First, the obvious difference: Claim preclusion precludes those who were plaintiffs (or, more precisely, those who asserted claims) in the first action, whereas compulsory counterclaim preclusion precludes those who were defendants (or those against whom claims were asserted). Second, and less obviously, claim preclusion operates based on a final judgment on the merits, whereas compulsory counterclaim preclusion operates based on the defendant's responsive pleading. Thus, after a defendant has filed an answer in the first action, it may be barred from asserting a related claim in a separate action even if no final judgment has yet been reached in the first action.

Despite these differences, one can think of the compulsory counterclaim rule and claim preclusion as complementary rules that preclude litigation of certain claims that could have been brought in a prior action. What claim preclusion does for plaintiffs, the compulsory counterclaim rule does for defendants. The policies underlying the claim preclusion rule—efficiency, consistency, finality—all weigh in favor of not allowing a defendant to assert a claim in a separate action that arises out of the same facts as the plaintiff's claim. Both claim preclusion and the compulsory counterclaim rule encourage parties to resolve a dispute in a single action rather than piecemeal.

estoppel may seem harsh. But there are considerations on the other side of the balance as well. A plaintiff should not need to prove the same facts over and over again in order to obtain meaningful relief. As a result, the requirements of collateral estoppel call for the moving party to demonstrate that the issue is substantially identical, that the issue was actually litigated and determined, that the party to be estopped had a full and fair opportunity to litigate the issue, and that the determination of the issue was necessary to the first court's final judgment. These are challenging requirements, and each must be satisfied for a defendant to be barred from re-litigating an issue. But where—as here—these requirements are met, then the plaintiff should not be required to litigate the issue again. . . .

BACKGROUND
THE BANKRUPTCY CASE

On December 12, 2011, David Birnbaum filed a petition for relief under Chapter 7 of the Bankruptcy Code. Birnbaum's bankruptcy petition notes several aliases, including David Guggenheim, David B. Guggenheim, and David Birnbaum Guggenheim. In his Statement of Financial Affairs, Birnbaum indicated that in the year preceding his bankruptcy filing, he was a defendant in an action captioned *Guggenheim Capital, LLC v. Catarina Pietra Toumei,* pending in the U.S. District Court for the Southern District of New York (the "District Court Action").

THE DISTRICT COURT ACTION

On November 22, 2010, Guggenheim commenced the District Court Action against Birnbaum and others by filing a complaint alleging [among other things] trademark infringement and trademark counterfeiting. . . . [O]n December 17, 2010, the District Court converted [a] temporary restraining order into a preliminary injunction, enjoining Birnbaum from using Guggenheim's marks.

After those orders were entered, the District Court found that Birnbaum continued to counterfeit and infringe the Guggenheim marks as part of a scheme to defraud investors. Four months later, the District Court issued an order to show cause why contempt sanctions should not be imposed for Birnbaum's alleged failure to comply with that court's preliminary injunction order.

Birnbaum participated in the District Court Action in several ways. He appeared at the December 17, 2010 preliminary injunction hearing and the December 30, 2010 contempt hearing. Birnbaum also sought and received extensions of time to respond to Guggenheim's discovery requests, sought and was denied a stay of discovery pending the resolution of the related criminal investigation, and sought and was denied a modification of the District Court's preliminary injunction.

THE DISTRICT COURT JUDGMENT

On July 14, 2011, based on Birnbaum's continuing conduct within and outside the District Court Action, including his violations of the preliminary injunction and discovery orders, and his continuing counterfeiting and infringement of Guggenheim's trademarks, the District Court sanctioned Birnbaum and entered a default judgment against him [and an entity he controlled] (the "District Court Judgment" or "Judgment"). The District Court determined that Birnbaum intentionally injured Guggenheim by his counterfeiting and infringement of Guggenheim's trademarks, and that his conduct was willful. . . .

[T]he District Court made several findings concerning Birnbaum's intent and state of mind. The District Court found, among other things, that Birnbaum's conduct was "a bad faith attempt" to exploit the "goodwill and reputation" of the Guggenheim trademarks, that Birnbaum's actions amounted to "intentional trafficking in counterfeit marks," and that his actions were "willful, intentional, and in bad faith." The District Court also found that Birnbaum's use of the Guggenheim marks created a "likelihood of confusion" and that there were "no 'extenuating circumstances'" that warranted his conduct.

The District Court's award of damages, fees, and costs also reflects its findings concerning Birnbaum's intent and state of mind. The District Court awarded Guggenheim "statutory damages for trademark counterfeiting in the amount of $1.25 million in lieu of an award of actual damages and profits, pursuant to 15 U.S.C. §1117(c)." Concluding that Birnbaum's "unlawful conduct [was] knowing and intentional and there are no 'extenuating circumstances' for such conduct," the District Court also awarded Guggenheim attorneys' fees and costs "under the Lanham Act and New York law," and directed Guggenheim to file a declaration documenting their costs and attorneys' fees. On January 31, 2012, the District Court entered an order (the "Fees Order") awarding Guggenheim attorneys' fees of $405,901.75 and costs of $42,967.92. . . .

[The Second Circuit affirmed.]

THIS ADVERSARY PROCEEDING AND THE RELIEF SOUGHT

Birnbaum commenced this Chapter 7 bankruptcy case on December 12, 2011, some five months after the District Court entered the Judgment, and some two months before the District Court entered the Fees Order. On January 12, 2012, Guggenheim commenced this adversary proceeding by filing a complaint, and on February 9, 2012, Guggenheim filed an amended complaint (the "Complaint"), seeking a determination that the debt arising from the District Court Judgment and Fees Order is nondischargeable [in Birnbaum's bankruptcy] under Bankruptcy Code Section 523(a)(6) . . . on grounds that it arises from willful and malicious injury to Guggenheim's property.

The Complaint describes the history of the District Court Action, and alleges that Birnbaum infringed Guggenheim's trademarks and falsely used the name "Guggenheim" in furtherance of his nationwide scheme to defraud investors by offering "bogus" financial consultation and investment services. The Complaint alleges that Birnbaum's actions included conducting business meetings and discussions with potential investors and "distributing advertising materials, emails, letters of intent, investment proposals, and purchase agreements replete with unauthorized uses of Plaintiffs' marks." The Complaint also alleges that the District Court issued the temporary restraining order and the preliminary injunction enjoining Birnbaum from using the Guggenheim names and trademarks, and that Birnbaum continued to use those names and trademarks despite the entry of these and other orders.

In addition, the Complaint describes Birnbaum's participation in the District Court Action. This participation includes appearing with counsel on December 17, 2010 at a preliminary injunction hearing; appearing on December 30, 2010 at a contempt hearing concerning his continued use of Guggenheim's marks in violation of the temporary restraining order and the preliminary injunction; making a motion on January 26, 2011 to modify the preliminary injunction for permission to use the "David Guggenheim" and "David B. Guggenheim" names in connection with importing and distributing distilled spirits; and appearing on April 4, 2011 at a hearing to show cause why a default judgment should not be entered against him based on his continuing use of the "Guggenheim" name in violation of the temporary restraining order and preliminary injunction. . . .

[In the present proceeding,] Birnbaum asserts several "affirmative defenses" to Guggenheim's Section 523 claims. These include that Guggenheim is Birnbaum's mother's name, that he has used the name Guggenheim throughout his life, and that his actions in using his family name "at all times lacked malice or willfulness to cause injury." Birnbaum also states, in substance, that the District Court Judgment and Fees Order are not entitled to preclusive effect here because he "did not substantially participate in the underlying litigation," due to "procedural irregularities and other issues," and that he was not represented by counsel in certain of the District Court Action proceedings.

In response to Guggenheim's Section 523(a)(6) claim, Birnbaum states that Guggenheim does not allege and cannot prove actual injury, and that Guggenheim does not allege and cannot prove malice, "as is required to allege a claim of willful or malicious injury" under Bankruptcy Code Section 523(a)(6).

THE MOTION FOR SUMMARY JUDGMENT

By this motion, Guggenheim seeks summary judgment solely on its Section 523(a)(6) claim, and only that claim is addressed here. This claim states that "[t]he claims and findings embodied in the District Court Judgment and the Fees Order constitute claims against Defendant for willful and malicious injury by Defendant to Plaintiffs or to their property," and should be excepted from Birnbaum's discharge pursuant to Bankruptcy Code Section 523(a)(6). Guggenheim argues that the District Court Judgment and Fees Order are entitled to preclusive effect under the doctrine of collateral estoppel, and that the District Court's findings establish each element of this claim.

Guggenheim also argues, among other things, that Birnbaum "substantially participated" in the District Court Action and had the opportunity to defend on the merits, although he did not always choose to do so. Guggenheim asserts that this satisfies the "actually litigated" requirement for collateral estoppel to apply. And Guggenheim argues that the same standard of proof by a preponderance of the evidence applies in the District Court Action and here. That is, Guggenheim argues that this Court should give preclusive effect to the District Court's determination that there is no genuine dispute of material fact as to each element of its Section 523(a)(6) claim, and that it is entitled to a determination that the District Court Judgment and Fees Order debts are nondischargeable as a matter of law.

Birnbaum filed a response (the "Response") and argues, in substance, that this Court should not give preclusive effect to the District Court's determinations because he did not have an opportunity to litigate the underlying claims in that forum. As a consequence, he argues that the matters were not "actually litigated" and collateral estoppel cannot apply. Birnbaum denies "the claims of trademark counterfeiting which formed the basis of the judgment against him," and asserts that this is the "first time" he has had the opportunity to deny these claims.

Specifically, Birnbaum asserts, among other things, that the District Court Judgment and Fees Order were "entered based on a number of purported defaults by [Birnbaum] . . . which were the direct result of the Debtor's assertion of . . . his privilege against self-incrimination under the Fifth Amendment." And Birnbaum states that the District Court mischaracterized his assertion of that privilege as a failure to oppose Guggenheim's motion for a default judgment.

On these grounds, among others, Birnbaum argues that there are "unresolved factual disputes that relate to . . . issue[s] which [are] material to the outcome of the litigation." Birnbaum also argues that the burden of proof in this nondischargeability action is the more stringent clear and convincing standard, as opposed to the lower preponderance of evidence standard that applies in a civil trademark infringement proceeding. For these and other reasons, Birnbaum argues that collateral estoppel does not apply, and that Guggenheim is not entitled to summary judgment on its Section 523(a)(6) claim. . . .

DISCUSSION
THE SUMMARY JUDGMENT STANDARD

Federal Rule of Civil Procedure 56[], made applicable to this Adversary Proceeding by Bankruptcy Rule 7056, provides that summary judgment is appropriate "if the movant shows that there is no genuine dispute as to any material fact and the movant is entitled to judgment as a matter of law." Fed. R. Civ. P. 56(a). . . . [T]he moving party must first demonstrate that there is no genuine dispute of material fact as to each element of its claim. . . . If the moving party meets this initial burden, [the burden shifts to the non-moving party to produce sufficient evidence to create a genuine dispute as to a material fact].

THE COLLATERAL ESTOPPEL DOCTRINE

. . . A "judgment in the prior suit precludes relitigation of issues actually litigated and necessary to the outcome of the first action." *Parklane Hosiery Co. v. Shore,* 439 U.S. 322, 327 n.5 (1979). . . .

The Supreme Court has confirmed that . . . "collateral estoppel principles do indeed apply in discharge exception proceedings pursuant to §523(a)." *Grogan v. Garner,* 498 U.S. 279, 284 n.11 (1991). The Supreme Court also determined that "the ordinary preponderance standard . . . govern[s] the applicability of all the discharge exceptions." *Id.* at 288. As a consequence, the Supreme Court observed, "a bankruptcy court could properly give collateral estoppel effect to those elements of the claim that are identical to the elements required for discharge and which were actually litigated and determined in the prior action. *See* Restatement (Second) of Judgments §27 (1982)." *Grogan,* 498 U.S. at 284. . . .

Courts recognize that the application of the collateral estoppel doctrine differs based on the forum in which first judgment was entered. As several courts have found, "[when] the issues sought to be precluded were decided by a *federal* court, as in the case at bar, the Bankruptcy Court must apply the theoretically uniform federal common law of collateral estoppel." *FTC v. Wright,* 187 B.R. 826, 832 (Bankr. D. Conn. 1995). . . .

Several requirements must be met in order for a prior federal judgment to have preclusive effect. As the Second Circuit has observed:

Federal principles of collateral estoppel, which we apply to establish the preclusive effect of a prior federal judgment, require that "(1) the identical issue was raised in a previous proceeding; (2) the issue was actually litigated and decided in the previous proceeding; (3) the party had a full and fair opportunity to litigate the issue; and (4) the resolution of the issue was necessary to support a valid and final judgment on the merits."

Ball v. A.O. Smith Corp., 451 F.3d 66, 69 (2d Cir. 2006). . . .

Substantial Identity of Issues. The first requirement, that the issues are substantially identical in the pending and prior proceedings, calls for the court to ascertain:

> whether the issues presented by this litigation are in substance the same as those resolved [in the prior litigation]; whether controlling facts or legal principles have [not] changed significantly since the [prior litigation]; and finally, whether special circumstances warrant exception to the normal rules of preclusion.

Montana v. U.S., 440 U.S. 147, 155 (1979). . . .

Actual Litigation and Determination of the Issue. The second requirement, that the issue was actually litigated and decided in the prior proceeding, is satisfied where the issue was "raised by the pleadings or otherwise placed in issue. . . ." *Evans v. Ottimo,* 469 F.3d 278, 282 (2d Cir. 2006). Courts recognize that where the defendant does not appear or participate in the proceedings in any way, and a default judgment is entered, that judgment may not merit preclusive effect. At the same time, a full trial on the merits is not a prerequisite for collateral estoppel to apply. Rather, preclusion is appropriate where [the issue was raised by the pleadings, or otherwise placed in issue, and actually determined]. . . .

Full and Fair Opportunity to Litigate the Issue. The third requirement, that the party against whom collateral estoppel is invoked had a full and fair opportunity to litigate the issue, calls for the court to determine whether that party "was fully able to raise the same factual or legal issues" in the prior litigation. *LaFleur v. Whitman,* 300 F.3d 256, 274 (2d Cir. 2002).

As distinct from the "actually litigated" element, the requirement that the party opposing collateral estoppel had a full and fair opportunity to litigate the issue requires the court to examine whether the party "was fully able to raise the same factual or legal issues . . . assert[ed in the prior proceeding]." *Id.* So, for example, the Second Circuit declined to apply principles of collateral estoppel where the defendant was deprived of a fair opportunity to litigate based on, among other considerations, the trial judge's statements that "clearly abrogated his 'responsibility to function as a neutral, impartial arbiter'" and demonstrated "fundamental misunderstanding of the basis" of the defendant's claim. *Ali v. Mukasey,* 529 F.3d 478, 491 (2d Cir. 2008). . . .

Necessity of the Issue to Support the Final Judgment. The fourth and final requirement for collateral estoppel to apply, that the issue previously determined was necessary to support the final judgment, requires the court to consider the elements of the prior claim and whether a final judgment was entered. This assures that matters that were ancillary to the first determination, and matters that were not finally determined, will not be invoked to bar the consideration of a disputed issue by the second court. As one Court of Appeals noted, "'for purposes of issue preclusion . . . "final judgment" includes any prior adjudication of an issue in another action that is determined to be sufficiently firm to be accorded conclusive effect.'" *Wolstein v. Docteroff (In re*

Docteroff), 133 F.3d 210, 216 (3d Cir. 1997) (quoting *Restatement (Second) of Judgments*).

THE ELEMENTS OF A SECTION 523(a)(6) CLAIM

In order to establish that a debt should not be discharged under Bankruptcy Code Section 523(a)(6), . . . a plaintiff must establish three elements to succeed on a Section 523(a)(6) claim—first, that the debtor acted willfully, second, that the debtor acted maliciously, and third, that the debtor's willful and malicious actions caused injury to the plaintiff or the plaintiff's property. . . . [T]he standard of proof necessary in a Section 523 nondischargeability action is by a preponderance of the evidence. . . .

WHETHER GUGGENHEIM HAS SHOWN THAT THERE IS NO GENUINE DISPUTE OF MATERIAL FACT THAT BIRNBAUM ACTED WILLFULLY

The first element of a Section 523(a)(6) claim is whether the defendant acted willfully. To succeed on this claim, Guggenheim must establish that Birnbaum's conduct was willful. And to succeed on this motion for summary judgment, Guggenheim must establish that there is no genuine dispute of material fact as to Birnbaum's willful conduct. . . .

As to the first requirement of collateral estoppel, whether the issues are substantially identical in this action and the prior proceeding, the record shows that the District Court Judgment contains a number of findings and conclusions that [explicitly reference the court's determination that the infringement was intentional]. And the Judgment memorializes the District Court's determinations as to Birnbaum's willfulness in the prior proceeding. As a consequence,

these issues are substantially identical in this case and in the District Court Action, and this requirement is met.

As to the second requirement of collateral estoppel, whether the issue was actually litigated and determined in the prior proceeding, the record shows that the issue of Birnbaum's willfulness was "raised by the pleadings or otherwise placed in issue" in the District Court Action. *Dolan*, 325 F. Supp. 2d at 133. The record also shows that it was the subject of extensive proceedings, including the December 17, 2010 preliminary injunction hearing and the December 30, 2010 contempt hearing, and was addressed in detail in the District Court Judgment. For these reasons, this issue was actually litigated and determined in the District Court Action, and this requirement is met.

As to the third requirement of collateral estoppel, whether there was a full and fair opportunity to litigate the issue, the record shows that, as noted above, Birnbaum's willfulness was the subject of extensive proceedings in the District Court, and Birnbaum had the opportunity to participate in these proceedings. For example, Birnbaum appeared at preliminary injunction and contempt hearings, sought and received extensions of time to respond to discovery requests, and sought and was denied a modification of the District Court's preliminary injunction. Birnbaum argues that because he asserted his Fifth Amendment privilege against self-incrimination in the District Court Action, he did not have a full and fair opportunity to litigate there. But case law in this Circuit holds that the choice to assert one's Fifth Amendment privilege in a prior litigation may bind that party in subsequent litigation, and does not serve as a bar to the application of collateral estoppel. Accordingly, Birnbaum had a full and fair opportunity to litigate the issue of willfulness, and this requirement is also met.

And as to the fourth requirement of collateral estoppel, whether determination of the issue was necessary to the final judgment, the record shows that the District Court's findings as to Birnbaum's willfulness formed the basis for its conclusions in several significant respects. These include with respect to the District Court's determinations that Birnbaum's conduct was in bad faith and that his conduct amounted to the intentional trafficking in counterfeit marks. The District Court's findings with respect to Birnbaum's willfulness also form the basis for that court's award of statutory damages and attorneys' fees and costs. As a result, determination of this issue was necessary to the District Court Judgment, and this requirement of collateral estoppel is met.

Based on the entire record, the Court finds that Guggenheim has established that each of the requirements of collateral estoppel has been met as to the District Court's determination that Birnbaum acted willfully. For these same reasons, the Court finds that Guggenheim has established that there is no genuine dispute of material fact as to the first element of its Section 523(a)(6) claim, whether Birnbaum acted willfully.

WHETHER GUGGENHEIM HAS SHOWN THAT THERE IS NO GENUINE DISPUTE OF MATERIAL FACT THAT BIRNBAUM ACTED MALICIOUSLY

The second element of a Section 523(a)(6) claim is whether the defendant's conduct was malicious. To succeed . . . on this motion for summary judgment, Guggenheim must establish that there is no genuine dispute of material fact as to Birnbaum's malicious conduct. . . .

As to the first requirement of collateral estoppel, whether the issues are substantially identical in this action and the prior proceeding, courts have noted that for collateral estoppel to apply in this context, "the non-bankruptcy court need not have made a finding of malice *per se*. Rather, the bankruptcy court can infer from the prior factual findings whether a debtor's pre-bankruptcy conduct was 'malicious' sufficient to satisfy Section 523(a)(6)." *Indo-Med Commodities v. Wisell*, 494 B.R. 23, 42 (Bankr. E.D.N.Y. 2011). And as the court found in *Yash Raj Films v. Ahmed*, 359 B.R. 34 (Bankr. E.D.N.Y. 2005), "[t]he facts supporting a finding that the debtor's conduct was malicious, specifically his 'deliberate disregard' of warnings [not to engage in certain specific conduct] were found in the context of determining the willfulness of his [trademark] infringement." 359 B.R. at 43. Here, the record shows that the District Court found that Birnbaum disregarded its orders and deliberately continued to use counterfeit Guggenheim marks, and concluded that Birnbaum intentionally and willfully used the Guggenheim marks. This equates with acting maliciously for purposes of Bankruptcy Code Section 523(a)(6). For these reasons, these issues are substantially identical in this case and in the District Court Action, and this requirement is met.

As to the second requirement of collateral estoppel, whether the issue was actually litigated and determined in the prior proceeding, the record shows that the issues of Birnbaum's intent and state of mind were presented in the pleadings before the District Court and among the matters decided by that court, including in the context of the District Court's findings that Birnbaum continued to use the Guggenheim marks in knowing violation of court orders. In particular, the District Court described Birnbaum's conduct as the "unauthorized use" of marks "identical and similar" to Guggenheim marks, and as willful "acts undertaken with intent." For these reasons, the issue of maliciousness was actually litigated and determined in the District Court Action, and this requirement is met.

As to the third requirement of collateral estoppel, whether there was a full and fair opportunity to litigate the issue, the record shows that, as with Birnbaum's willfulness, the issue of maliciousness was the subject of extensive proceedings in the District Court, in which Birnbaum either participated or had the opportunity to participate. . . . [A]s noted above, Birnbaum's assertion of his Fifth Amendment privilege against self-incrimination in the District Court Action does not mean that he did not have a full and fair *opportunity* to litigate this issue, or that he may not be barred from re-litigating the issue by the collateral estoppel doctrine. As a result, Birnbaum had a full and fair opportunity to litigate the issue of whether he acted maliciously in the District Court Action, and this requirement is also met.

As to the fourth requirement of collateral estoppel, whether determination of the issue was necessary to the final judgment, the record shows that as with the element of willfulness, the District Court's findings as to Birnbaum's malicious acts were necessary to several aspects of its rulings [including the award of statutory damages and attorneys' fees]. Accordingly, determination of this issue was necessary to the District Court's final judgment, and this requirement of collateral estoppel is met.

[The court found that Guggenheim met the requirements for collateral estoppel, so Birnbaum was estopped from relitigating the District Court's determination that Birnbaum acted maliciously.]

WHETHER GUGGENHEIM HAS SHOWN THAT THERE IS NO GENUINE DISPUTE OF MATERIAL FACT THAT BIRNBAUM'S WILLFUL AND MALICIOUS ACTS INJURED GUGGENHEIM OR ITS PROPERTY

The third element of a Section 523(a)(6) claim is whether the debtor's willful and malicious conduct caused an injury to the plaintiff or the plaintiff's property. . . . Here too, Guggenheim relies on the District Court Judgment and the collateral estoppel doctrine to demonstrate that there is no genuine dispute of material fact as to this element of its claim. . . .

As to the first requirement of collateral estoppel, whether the issues are substantially identical in this action and the prior proceeding, the record shows that the District Court made several findings to the effect that Guggenheim was injured by Birnbaum's willful and malicious use of its marks. These include the determinations that Birnbaum attempted in bad faith to trade off of the goodwill and reputation of Guggenheim's marks, that Guggenheim suffered irreparable injury as a result of Birnbaum's use of these marks, and that unless Birnbaum was permanently enjoined from these acts, Guggenheim would continue to suffer such injury. [The court explained that the issue of injury was actually litigated and determined, that Birnbaum had a full and fair opportunity to litigate the issue, and that the determination of injury was necessary to the judgment because, among other things, it formed the basis for the court's imposition of a permanent injunction.]

[The court found that Guggenheim met the requirements for collateral estoppel, so Birnbaum was estopped from relitigating the District Court's determination of injury and causation.]

CONCLUSION

Based on the entire record, and for all the reasons reflected in the record and as set forth in this Memorandum Decision, Guggenheim Capital, LLC and Guggenheim Partners, LLC have established that they are entitled to summary judgment on their claim under Bankruptcy Code Section 523(a)(6) that the District Court Judgment and Fees Order debts are not dischargeable in this Chapter 7 bankruptcy case because they arise from a willful and malicious injury to Guggenheim or its property. An order in accordance with this Memorandum Opinion will be entered simultaneously herewith.

Notes & Questions

1. Just as you did with claim preclusion, before tackling the issue preclusion question, be clear on the two actions. In *Guggenheim*, who had sued whom for what in case 1? What was the outcome, and what specific findings did the court reach? What type of proceeding was case 2, and who asserted what claim against whom?

> ### Terminology Tip
>
> Issue preclusion is the newer term and *collateral estoppel* is older, but the old terminology is still used frequently by judges, lawyers, and professors. *Estoppel* is an equitable doctrine; the word comes from Middle English. *Estoppel* is the noun; the verb is *estop*. Broadly speaking, estoppel means that if someone is entitled to rely on something based on another person's acts, the person who acted is prevented—"estopped"—from claiming otherwise. The notion behind *collateral estoppel* is that if a party has litigated an issue, others are entitled to rely on the fact that the party already had its shot at the question, so the party is *estopped* from relitigating the issue. The "collateral" part of collateral estoppel distinguishes it from *direct estoppel*, which prevents relitigation of an issue on the *same* claim. Collateral estoppel prevents relitigation of an issue in a subsequent action on a *different* claim.

2. What are the required elements for a party to prevail on a claim that a debt is non-dischargeable under Bankruptcy Code §523(a)(6)? Guggenheim sought summary judgment on this claim of non-dischargeability. As you know from Chapter 4, summary judgment should be granted only if there is no genuine dispute as to any material fact. Are the facts disputed regarding the elements of the section 523(a)(6) claim? In particular, did Birnbaum dispute that he acted willfully or maliciously? For Guggenheim to obtain summary judgment, it had to show that these issues were no longer legitimately in dispute. This, of course, is where issue preclusion enters the picture. Do you see how, by using issue preclusion, Guggenheim turned disputed issues into ones on which there was no "genuine dispute" for purposes of summary judgment?

3. Recall that in *Rush v. City of Maple Heights*, the lower court applied issue preclusion in favor of the plaintiff motorcyclist. That court had rejected claim preclusion based on the *Vasu* precedent and therefore allowed Rush to proceed with her claim for personal injury. On Rush's personal

injury claim, the court held that Rush was not required to prove the city's neg-ligence, since that question had already been answered in Rush's prior case for property damage. Consider each of the elements of issue preclusion as applied to *Rush*. The question of the city's negligence in leaving the pothole, as well as the issue of whether the city's negligence was a proximate cause of the motor-cycle accident, is the same issue in both cases. That issue was actually litigated in case 1, and it was actually determined, because unless the city was found negligent, Rush would not have been awarded damages for the harm to the motorcycle. By the same reasoning, the determination of the city's negligence was essential to the judgment in case 1. Thus far, it seems that Rush could sat-isfy the requirements for issue preclusion in case 2. As you know, however, the Ohio Supreme Court ruled that *claim* preclusion applied in favor of the city, so ultimately Rush did not get the benefit of issue preclusion. Had the court not overturned *Vasu*, the issue preclusion question would have been front and center. Was there a full and fair opportunity to litigate in case 1 in *Rush*?

(2) Requirements for Issue Preclusion

In the following sections, drawing upon both *Rush* and *Guggenheim*, we explore in greater depth three of the required elements of issue preclusion. We will not revisit the requirements of *validity* and *finality* as prerequisites for issue preclusion, as we explored them regarding claim preclusion, and they operate in much the same way in both contexts. The other elements, however, raise issues uniquely applicable to issue preclusion: (a) How do courts decide whether a subsequent lawsuit raises the *same issue* that was decided in a prior case? (b) What does it mean for an issue to be *actually litigated*, and how can courts tell what issues were *actually determined*, especially if there was a general jury verdict rather than answers to specific questions? (c) What makes an issue *essential to the judgment*?

(a) Identical Issue

For a determination to be given preclusive effect in a subsequent lawsuit, the very same question must be at issue in both actions. If the issue that was decided in the first case differs from the issue that is disputed in the second case, then issue preclu-sion does not apply.

When you think about issue preclusion, your first step should be to define as crisply as possible the issue or issues that might be precluded. In *Guggenheim*, those issues might be articulated as "Did Birnbaum act willfully in using Guggenheim's trademarks?" "Did Birnbaum act maliciously in using Guggenheim's trademarks?" and "Did Birnbaum's use of Guggenheim's trademarks cause injury to Guggenheim's property?" In *Rush*, they might be stated as "Did the city fail to exercise reasonable care by failing to repair the pothole?" and "Was the city's negligence in leaving the pothole a proximate cause of Rush's motorcycle accident?" The issue may be major or minor, it may be simple or complex, but for issue preclusion to apply, the issue must be identical—not merely similar or related—in both proceedings.

(b) Actually Litigated and Determined

Issue preclusion applies only to issues that were actually litigated and determined in the first action. The point of issue preclusion is to avoid relitigating questions that already have been answered after adequate consideration. If the question was not answered, or if it was not actively considered, then issue preclusion does not apply.

Notice the difference here between issue preclusion and claim preclusion. Claim preclusion prevents parties not only from pursuing claims that were *actually* litigated, but also those that *could have been* litigated as part of the prior action, as long as they constitute part of the "same claim." Again, claim preclusion tells the plaintiff: "Woulda, shoulda, coulda. You already had a lawsuit about this dispute. If you had other legal theories or other remedies to seek, you should have asserted them at that time."

It is different with issue preclusion. Issue preclusion never tells litigants: "You *could have* presented evidence about this issue in the earlier lawsuit, so now you are precluded from raising it." Rather, issue preclusion says: "This exact issue was already raised in a prior lawsuit. It has been litigated and answered. So we are going to take that answer and use it. You are precluded from relitigating the issue." Been there, done that.

How does the court in case 2 know what issues were (a) actually litigated and (b) determined in case 1? Note that those are two separate questions. Figuring out what was *litigated* involves seeing what was pleaded, what evidence was presented, and what arguments were advanced. Pleadings, motion papers, hearing transcripts, trial transcripts, or other clues from the prior action reflect what the parties actually litigated.

Figuring out what was *determined* is easy in some cases. In a bench trial, the judge is required to make specific findings of fact and conclusions of law. Therefore, it is usually easy to know what issues were actually determined when the fact-finder in case 1 is a judge. The prior judge in *Guggenheim*, for example, had made explicit findings that Birnbaum's conduct was "willful, intentional, and in bad faith." Similarly, if case 1 was a jury trial in which the jury rendered a special verdict or a general verdict with interrogatories, as we discussed in Chapter 5, then the jury's determinations are stated explicitly in the answers to the special verdict questions or interrogatories.

In other cases, however, it is harder to know exactly what issues were determined, particularly if case 1 was a jury trial in which the jury rendered a general verdict. Recall from Chapter 5 that a general verdict reveals only whether the plaintiff or defendant prevails on each claim, and if the plaintiff prevails, then the amount of damages. General verdicts do a perfectly good job of resolving the case at hand, but they can be frustrating later on if you are a lawyer trying to figure out whether a prior judgment has any value as a matter of issue preclusion.

To illustrate, suppose plaintiff X sues defendant Y for negligence, and Y asserts an affirmative defense such as contributory negligence in a traditional contributory negligence jurisdiction. (The traditional common law rule of contributory negligence, as a matter of tort law, was that a plaintiff cannot get *any* damages for a defendant's negligence if the plaintiff was partly at fault for the plaintiff's own injury. A few states still apply this rule as a complete bar to recovery even if the plaintiff's negligence was slight in comparison to the defendant's.) The jury renders a verdict for Y. If a later case raises the same questions about who was negligent in this incident, can issue preclusion be used? The problem is that we simply do not know what the jury actually determined because the verdict form does not say *why* the jury found in favor of Y. Maybe the jury decided for Y because it determined that Y did not act negligently. Maybe the jury decided for Y because it determined that the plaintiff was contributorily negligent. Or maybe the jury decided for Y because, although Y acted negligently, the jury determined that Y's negligence did not cause X's alleged injury. In the end, we know nothing about what the jury found, other than the outcome that the Y is not liable to X.

Jury verdicts may seem like inscrutable black boxes, but do not assume that the "actually determined" requirement can never be satisfied with a general verdict. With a bit of deductive logic, sometimes it is possible to see what the jury determined, even when the first case was decided by general verdict. A helpful case for illustrating this point is *Illinois Central Gulf Railroad v. Parks*, 390 N.E.2d 1078 (Ind. App. 1979). Jessie Parks was driving with his spouse Bertha. At a railroad crossing, their car collided with a train. Bertha sued the railroad for her injuries, and Jessie joined Bertha's case as a plaintiff seeking damages for loss of consortium. The plaintiffs claimed that the railroad was negligent. The railroad denied that it was negligent and asserted Jessie's contributory negligence as an affirmative defense. Under Indiana law at the time, a plaintiff's contributory negligence constituted a complete bar to a claim. The case went to a jury trial. On Bertha's claim, the jury found the railroad liable for $30,000. On Jessie's claim, the jury found for the defendant. Subsequently, Jessie brought a lawsuit against the railroad for his own injuries.

Think about what preclusion arguments the parties should make in case 2. Start with claim preclusion. Which party would you expect to assert claim preclusion in case 2? Indeed, just as you would expect, the railroad argued that Jessie should be barred from bringing the second case. Run through the elements of claim preclusion. Does the claim arise out of the same factual occurrence? Were both Jessie and the railroad parties to the first case? Did the first case result in a valid, final judgment on the merits? In most jurisdictions, the railroad would have a winning argument to get Jessie's second case dismissed on grounds of claim preclusion. Under Indiana law of claim preclusion, however, "same claim" was not defined by the transactional test, but rather by a narrower test that treated Jessie's personal injury claim as separate from his claim for loss of consortium. So the court rejected the railroad's claim preclusion argument.

Now, what about issue preclusion? Both Jessie and the railroad sought to use issue preclusion in case 2. Start with Jessie. What issues would you expect Jessie to say were already determined in case 1? As you might have guessed, Jessie argued that it was already determined that the railroad was negligent and that the railroad's negligence was a proximate cause of the accident. He wanted the railroad to be precluded from relitigating those issues. Were those issues actually determined in case 1? Logically, the answer has to be yes. Do you see why? Therefore, the court agreed with Jessie that the railroad was precluded from relitigating the issues of negligence and proximate cause.

But that is not the end of the story. The railroad, too, sought to use issue preclusion in case 2. The railroad argued that it was already determined that Jessie was contributorily negligent. If the jury found in favor of Bertha but against Jessie, the railroad argued, the reason must be that the jury agreed with the railroad's contributory negligence defense against Jessie. Do you see the flaw in the railroad's argument? It is not clear that the jury in case 1 found Jessie negligent, because maybe instead the jury found that he had not suffered any loss-of-consortium damages. Logically, either finding—contributory negligence or zero damages—could have resulted in the jury's verdict for the defendant on Jessie's loss of consortium claim. The court agreed that it was impossible to determine why the jury found against Jessie in case 1 and therefore rejected the railroad's use of issue preclusion on the question of contributory negligence.

The upshot was that case 2 was allowed to go forward (because claim preclusion was denied). The next step would be a trial solely on the issues of contributory negligence (because the railroad's issue preclusion argument failed) and damages. At trial, no evidence would be required on the issues of the railroad's negligence and proximate cause, both of which were taken as conclusively established (because Jessie's issue preclusion argument succeeded).

Remember that the *actually litigated and determined* requirements are no mere technicalities. Issue preclusion means that certain determinations from one case may be taken as conclusively established in another case, and the parties will not be allowed to relitigate those questions. The point of the requirement is to prevent the unfairness that would occur if parties were precluded from presenting evidence on issues that had not truly been litigated in the prior action, or that the fact-finder in the prior action did not actually decide.

(c) *Essential to the Judgment*

Even if an issue was actually litigated and determined in case 1, it would not make sense to apply issue preclusion in case 2 if there is a significant risk that the fact-finder in the first case treated the issue cavalierly rather than carefully. That is the reason for the requirement that the determination be essential to the judgment. If a determination was not necessary to the disposition of the case, then the judge or jury may not have considered the issue thoroughly. Also, to whatever extent the parties foresee that an issue will not be essential, they may not advocate their positions as vigorously as they would with regard to issues that are more likely to determine the outcome. Finally, if the determination was not essential to the judgment, then it could not have formed a basis for appeal, and the possibility of appellate review is one guarantor that an issue has been treated with care.

Consider the following example. A and B are involved in an accident in which both are injured and each blames the other. A sues B for negligence, and B asserts the defense of contributory negligence; as in *Parks*, the jurisdiction follows the doctrine of pure contributory negligence. In a special verdict, the jury finds that both parties were at fault in the accident. The verdict states that defendant B was negligent and also that plaintiff A was contributorily negligent. The court therefore enters judgment for the defendant because, under the pure contributory negligence doctrine, the plaintiff's negligence acts as an absolute bar to recovery. Subsequently, B sues A for negligence based on the same accident. (Surely you are thinking, "How can B bring a separate action against A based on the same accident? Wouldn't that be a compulsory counterclaim?" You are correct. In federal court and most state courts, it would be a compulsory counterclaim and therefore the second action would be precluded. But to use this hypothetical case for understanding the essential-to-the-judgment requirement, assume that this takes place in the state courts of one of the few jurisdictions that does not have compulsory counterclaims.)

In the second action, A argues that a jury already determined that B was negligent, and issue preclusion should apply. Therefore, A contends, B should lose the second action based on B's contributory negligence. Would issue preclusion apply to the determination of B's negligence? No. Although it is the identical issue and it was actually litigated and determined, the determination of B's negligence was not essential to the judgment in case 1. Do you see why? The outcome in the first case would have been the same regardless of whether the jury found B negligent because the jury's finding of A's contributory negligence ensured a defense verdict. In the presence of a finding of contributory negligence (in a contributory negligence jurisdiction), the finding of contributory negligence renders the defendant's conduct—negligent or otherwise—of no real consequence to the outcome. Since the finding of B's negligence was not essential to the judgment in the first case, issue preclusion would not apply.

Meanwhile, B is also thinking about how to use issue preclusion. B argues that a jury already determined that A was negligent, and issue preclusion should apply to that finding. The issue of A's negligence was essential to the judgment in case 1—contributory negligence is why A lost the first case. Therefore, issue preclusion would apply to the finding that A was negligent. The upshot: In case 2, it will be taken as conclusively established that A was negligent. Note that this does not necessarily mean B will win the lawsuit. B still has to prove damages. Also, now the tables have turned: A can pursue the defense of contributory negligence by presenting evidence that B was negligent. But as far as issue preclusion goes in case 2, it will establish A's negligence but not B's negligence, because B's negligence was not essential to the judgment in case 1.

Alternative holdings present a difficult twist on the *essential to the judgment* requirement. Sometimes, a jury or judge makes multiple findings, any one of which would be sufficient to support the outcome. For example, in *Halpern v. Schwartz*, 426 F.2d 102 (2d Cir. 1970), a bankruptcy judge granted a petition for an involuntary bankruptcy against Evelyn Halpern. The judge made three separate findings relating to Halpern's transfer of a bond and mortgage to her son, any *one* of which would have sufficed to grant the petition. The court found, first, that Halpern had transferred property with the intent to hinder creditors; second, that she had transferred property without fair consideration; and third, that she had made a preferential payment. Subsequently, the bankruptcy trustee brought an action to deny Halpern a discharge of her debts, on the grounds that she had transferred property with the intent to hinder her creditors. For the denial of a bankruptcy discharge, intent would be a key issue. The trustee moved for summary judgment, arguing that issue preclusion should apply to the earlier proceeding's finding that Halpern had transferred property with the intent to hinder creditors. At first, it looks like issue preclusion should apply. The question of whether Halpern transferred property with the intent to hinder creditors is the identical issue in the first and second proceedings. We know that the issue was actually litigated and determined. Unlike the jury verdict in *Parks*, the court in *Halpern* spelled out its findings in the first action. Nonetheless, the court in *Halpern* decided that issue preclusion did not apply because the finding of intentional hindrance was not essential to the judgment in the first action. Because it was one of several alternative grounds, the court reasoned, the issue may not have received sufficiently careful attention, vigorous advocacy, or appellate review.

That said, courts are not in agreement regarding whether issue preclusion applies to alternative holdings. The *Halpern* court's view, adopted in the Second Restatement of Judgments, gives no issue preclusive effect to alternative holdings because they are not essential to the judgment. *See* Restatement (Second) of Judgments §27 cmt. i. But some courts continue to follow the view of the First Restatement of Judgments, which states that alternative holdings should be given issue preclusive effect. *See* Restatement (First) of Judgments §68 cmt. n; *see also, e.g., Jean Alexander Cosmetics, Inc. v. L'Oreal USA, Inc.*, 458 F.3d 244 (3d Cir. 2006). The justification behind the First Restatement position, in short, is that if an issue has been fully litigated and determined, and if the determination was part of the logic that supported the outcome (as opposed to a superfluous issue), then giving preclusive effect to the determination serves the interests of efficiency, consistency, and finality. The federal courts of appeals have split on this question. *See id.* at 251-52 (collecting cases). A lawyer faced with a question of whether issue preclusion applies to alternative holdings therefore must pay careful attention to how the question has been treated in that particular jurisdiction or circuit.

STRATEGY SESSION

The split regarding issue preclusion for alternative holdings has interesting implications for litigation strategy *in the first case*. Plenty of lawsuits include multiple issues that could determine the outcome, whether various bases for a claim or various defenses that could defeat the claim. If courts follow the First Restatement approach of giving issue preclusive effect to each alternative holding, then litigants who are concerned about future implications of a particular issue will want their lawyers to litigate each issue to the hilt. In the *Halpern* case, for example, had the First Restatement applied, even if it were clear that the involuntary bankruptcy would be granted based on a transfer without fair consideration, the debtor would be well advised to litigate vigorously the issue of intent to hinder creditors. Even if, as a practical matter, the intent issue made no difference to the involuntary bankruptcy petition in the first action, she might choose to fight hard on that issue for fear that an adverse determination would come back to haunt her through issue preclusion in a later proceeding.

Be careful not to confuse the problem of alternative holdings with the more straightforward problem of nonessential determinations. Although the two look similar at first glance, our earlier example—in which the jury found both the plaintiff and defendant negligent—does not involve alternative holdings. Alternative holdings are multiple determinations, any one of which could support the outcome. Contrast these with determinations that play no role in supporting the outcome. In our example, the finding of B's negligence did not support the case 1 judgment at all. It was, as the case played out, simply an extraneous finding that did not matter to the outcome. The problem of alternative holdings would arise if the jury in case 1 answered that A was negligent and B was not negligent, and the court therefore entered judgment for the defendant B. The two determinations—the defendant's non-negligence and the plaintiff's contributory negligence—would be alternative bases for the judgment. In that situation, whether the determinations would be given issue preclusive effect would depend on whether the court followed the First Restatement or Second Restatement approach to alternative holdings.

THE BIG PICTURE

Do not assume that issue preclusion is based on some naïve notion that the first court necessarily got it right. The premise of issue preclusion is that if a question has been answered after being fully and fairly litigated, there is no justification for allowing a party to relitigate the same question. The "actually litigated and determined" and "essential to the judgment" requirements are meant to ensure that only carefully considered issues are given finality. But don't confuse this with certainty about the truth. The fact that a court actually determined an issue does *not* mean the first court got it right. After all, how much certainty was required of the judge or jury in the first case? In most civil cases, the burden of persuasion is by a preponderance of the evidence. So behind that verdict, the fact-finder's level of certainty might have been a mere 51 percent. Moreover, the determination in case 1 may have been a result of jury compromise or some other factor other than truth. The bottom line is that issue preclusion is not about certainty. It's not about perfection. It's about finality.

(3) Issue Preclusion with Different Parties

As a practical matter, issue preclusion does not usually arise in subsequent actions between the same parties. This is because a subsequent action between the same parties based on the same events would likely be barred either by claim preclusion or by the compulsory counterclaim rule. Rather, issue preclusion tends to arise when a different party litigates against one of the parties to the original action in which an issue was decided.

With limited exceptions, only parties can be *bound* by a judgment. But on the question of who can *assert* preclusion, we will see that most modern courts treat issue preclusion differently from claim preclusion, and issue preclusion often is deployed by persons who were not parties to the prior action.

(a) Who Is Bound by Issue Preclusion

Before we turn to the question of who can *assert* issue preclusion, let's consider whom issue preclusion can be *used against*. On this question of who is "bound" by a judgment—that is, against whom the judgment can be invoked for its issue preclusive effect—apply the reasoning of *Taylor v. Sturgell*, above. In general, only parties are bound by a judgment, with the limited exceptions that the Supreme Court enumerated in *Taylor*.

To see this in the context of issue preclusion, consider this example: A three-car collision occurs among drivers A, B, and C. A sues B for negligence. The jury does not find that B was negligent, and therefore returns a verdict for the defendant. The court enters judgment accordingly. Subsequently, C sues B for negligence in the same collision.

Could B assert issue preclusion in case 2? Absolutely not. If B were to say, "It was already decided that I was not negligent in causing the collision," B would encounter several problems. First, C might respond that it is not the identical issue: As a matter of tort law, whether B acted negligently toward A may be a different question from whether B acted negligently toward C. But let's assume that the collision occurred in such a way that the negligence issue was indeed identical with regard to both A and C. And assume it is clear that in case 1 the issue of B's negligence was actually litigated and determined, and was essential to the judgment. Even so, B could not use issue preclusion against C in case 2, because C was not a party to case 1. If the court in the first case never acquired power over C because C was not made a party, then C is not legally bound by the judgment—either as a matter of claim preclusion or as a matter of issue preclusion. This is the key takeaway from *Taylor v. Sturgell*, rooted in due process concerns.

Just as with claim preclusion, and as described by the Supreme Court in *Taylor*, there are exceptions when a nonparty may be deemed to be represented by a party for purposes of issue preclusion. As a matter of both claim preclusion and issue preclusion, for example, a successor in interest may be bound by its predecessor's litigation, or a person may be bound by a judgment in a case brought on his behalf by a legal representative. But these are exceptions. The general rule is that only parties are bound by a judgment.

(b) Who Can Assert Issue Preclusion: The Mutuality Doctrine

Now we turn to what many students find the toughest part of learning preclusion—the mutuality doctrine and the rise of nonmutual issue preclusion. Nonmutual issue preclusion occurs when someone who was *not* a party to the first case seeks to use the judgment for issue preclusion against someone who *was* a party to the first case. Most modern courts permit at least some nonmutual issue preclusion, but under more limited circumstances than mutual issue preclusion.

To illustrate, let's return to the example of the three-car collision, but this time we shall let the plaintiff win the first case: A three-car collision occurs among drivers A, B, and C. A sues B for negligence. The jury returns a verdict for the plaintiff A, and the court enters judgment accordingly. Subsequently, C sues B for negligence in the same collision. This time, it is C who tries to use issue preclusion. In case 2, C argues that it was already established in case 1 that B was negligent in causing the collision. Unlike C in our earlier version of the story, B cannot use the "you can't bind a non-party" argument, because, well, B *was* a party in case 1. That is precisely what makes this *nonmutual* issue preclusion. C is seeking to bind B with the judgment from case 1, but B would not be able to bind C if the case had gone the other way. So the possibility of issue preclusion does not go both directions; only one of the parties has the possibility of binding the other. It is not mutual.

The question is: Can C use issue preclusion against B? Until the mid-twentieth century, the answer would have been no. That is because courts would have applied what was known as the mutuality doctrine. Under the mutuality doctrine, a person could not assert issue preclusion unless that person could also be bound by the same doctrine. It had to be mutual. This meant that the only ones who could use issue preclusion were those who were parties to the first case. Effectively, the mutuality doctrine imposed a "same parties" requirement on issue preclusion.

Starting with the California Supreme Court's 1942 decision in *Bernhard v. Bank of America*, 122 P.2d 892 (Cal. 1942), however, the mutuality doctrine began to erode. In that opinion, Justice Roger Traynor reasoned that if a party had a full and fair opportunity to litigate an issue in the first case, there was no justification for allowing the same party to relitigate the issue against a different adversary in a later case. It took some time for other courts to follow suit. Almost 30 years after *Bernhard*, the U.S. Supreme Court abandoned the mutuality doctrine in *Blonder-Tongue Laboratories v. University of Illinois Foundation*, 402 U.S. 313 (1971). The federal courts and a substantial majority of the states now allow at least some nonmutual issue preclusion, although several states still cling to the traditional mutuality doctrine.

You need to know a bit more about the *Blonder-Tongue* case to understand the next piece of the nonmutuality puzzle. That piece is the difference between defensive and offensive nonmutual issue preclusion. In *Blonder-Tongue*, a patent holder sued another company, alleging that the company had infringed its patent. The defendant prevailed in its argument that the patent was invalid, so the court entered judgment for the defendant. The same patent holder subsequently sued a different alleged infringer—call it Infringer 2. In case 2, Infringer 2 asserted issue preclusion: "Patent Holder, your patent is not valid. You already litigated that very issue, and you lost." Patent Holder's response to Infringer 2's issue preclusion argument? In a word, mutuality. "Infringer 2, you weren't a party to case 1, so you have no right to use that judgment for your own advantage. After all, if the first court had decided our patent was valid, you would not have been bound by that decision. It's just not fair to preclude us from relitigating the issue of patent validity, when you would have been free to relitigate the issue if it had come out the other way in the first case." Although there is some force to the fairness argument in favor of the traditional mutuality rule, the Supreme Court decided that the policies in favor of issue preclusion—efficiency, consistency, finality—apply even when the party asserting issue preclusion in the second action was not a party to the first action. Therefore, the Court allowed Infringer 2 to use issue preclusion to establish that Patent Holder's patent was not valid.

Blonder-Tongue involved *defensive* nonmutual issue preclusion. Infringer 2 used issue preclusion as a shield to defend itself against Patent Holder's infringement claim, not as a sword to pursue a claim of its own. Similarly, the *Bernhard* case in California involved defensive use of nonmutual issue preclusion. Our three-car-collision example, by contrast, illustrates an attempt to use *offensive* nonmutual issue preclusion. A sued B in case 1, and B was found to have negligently caused the three-car collision. In case 2, C sues B, and C seeks to use issue preclusion to establish B's negligence in causing the collision. C is trying to use issue preclusion as a sword to establish a negligence claim against B. Courts are far more receptive to the use of defensive nonmutual issue preclusion. Offensive use raises rather different concerns, which the Supreme Court addressed in the following case.

PARKLANE HOSIERY CO. v. SHORE
439 U.S. 322 (1979)

STEWART, J., delivered the opinion of the Court.

This case presents the question whether a party who has had issues of fact adjudicated adversely to it in an equitable action may be collaterally estopped from relitigating the same issues before a jury in a subsequent legal action brought against it by a new party.

The respondent brought this stockholder's class action against the petitioners in a Federal District Court. The complaint alleged that the petitioners, Parklane Hosiery Co., Inc. (Parklane), and 13 of its officers, directors, and stockholders, had issued a materially false and misleading proxy statement in connection with a merger. The proxy statement, according to the complaint, had violated §§14(a), 10(b), and 20(a) of the Securities Exchange Act of 1934, as well as various rules and regulations promulgated by the Securities and Exchange Commission (SEC). The complaint sought damages, rescission of the merger, and recovery of costs.

Before this action came to trial, the SEC filed suit against the same defendants in the Federal District Court, alleging that the proxy statement that had been issued by Parklane was materially false and misleading in essentially the same respects as those that had been alleged in the respondent's complaint. Injunctive relief was requested. After a 4-day trial, the District Court found that the proxy statement was materially false and misleading in the respects alleged, and entered a declaratory judgment to that effect. *SEC v. Parklane Hosiery Co.*, 422 F. Supp. 477. The Court of Appeals for the Second Circuit affirmed this judgment. 558 F.2d 1083.

The respondent in the present case then moved for partial summary judgment against the petitioners, asserting that the petitioners were collaterally estopped from relitigating the issues that had been resolved against them in the action brought by the SEC. The District Court denied the motion on the ground that such an application of collateral estoppel would deny the petitioners their Seventh Amendment right to a jury trial. The Court of Appeals for the Second Circuit reversed, holding that a party who has had issues of fact determined against him after a full and fair opportunity to litigate in a nonjury trial is collaterally estopped from obtaining a subsequent jury trial of these same issues of fact. 565 F.2d 815. The appellate court concluded that "the Seventh Amendment preserves the right to jury trial only with respect to issues of fact, [and] once those issues have been fully and fairly adjudicated in a prior proceeding, nothing remains for trial, either

with or without a jury." *Id.* at 819. Because of an intercircuit conflict, we granted certiorari.

I

The threshold question to be considered is whether, quite apart from the right to a jury trial under the Seventh Amendment, the petitioners can be precluded from relitigating facts resolved adversely to them in a prior equitable proceeding with another party under the general law of collateral estoppel. Specifically, we must determine whether a litigant who was not a party to a prior judgment may nevertheless use that judgment "offensively" to prevent a defendant from relitigating issues resolved in the earlier proceeding.[4]

A

Collateral estoppel, like the related doctrine of res judicata,[5] has the dual purpose of protecting litigants from the burden of relitigating an identical issue with the same party or his privy and of promoting judicial economy by preventing needless litigation.

---

[4] In this context, offensive use of collateral estoppel occurs when the plaintiff seeks to foreclose the defendant from litigating an issue the defendant has previously litigated unsuccessfully in an action with another party. Defensive use occurs when a defendant seeks to prevent a plaintiff from asserting a claim the plaintiff has previously litigated and lost against another defendant.

[5] Under the doctrine of res judicata, a judgment on the merits in a prior suit bars a second suit involving the same parties or their privies based on the same cause of action. Under the doctrine of collateral estoppel, on the other hand, the second action is upon a different cause of action and the judgment in the prior suit precludes relitigation of issues actually litigated and necessary to the outcome of the first action.

Blonder-Tongue Laboratories, Inc. v. U. of Ill. Found., 402 U.S. 313, 328-29 (1971). Until relatively recently, however, the scope of collateral estoppel was limited by the doctrine of mutuality of parties. Under this mutuality doctrine, neither party could use a prior judgment as an estoppel against the other unless both parties were bound by the judgment. Based on the premise that it is somehow unfair to allow a party to use a prior judgment when he himself would not be so bound,[7] the mutuality requirement provided a party who had litigated and lost in a previous action an opportunity to relitigate identical issues with new parties.

By failing to recognize the obvious difference in position between a party who has never litigated an issue and one who has fully litigated and lost, the mutuality requirement was criticized almost from its inception.[8] Recognizing the validity of this criticism, the Court in *Blonder-Tongue* abandoned the mutuality requirement, at least in cases where a patentee seeks to relitigate the validity of a patent after a federal court in a previous lawsuit has already declared it invalid. . . .

---

[7] It is a violation of due process for a judgment to be binding on a litigant who was not a party or a privy and therefore has never had an opportunity to be heard. *Blonder-Tongue*, 402 U.S. at 329.

[8] This criticism was summarized in the Court's opinion in *Blonder-Tongue Laboratories, Inc. v. University of Illinois Foundation*, 402 U.S. 313, 322-27 (1971). The opinion of Justice Traynor for a unanimous California Supreme Court in *Bernhard v. Bank of America Nat. Trust & Savings Ass'n*, 19 Cal. 2d 807, 812 (1942), made the point succinctly:

> No satisfactory rationalization has been advanced for the requirement of mutuality. Just why a party who was not bound by a previous action should be precluded from asserting it as res judicata against a party who was bound by it is difficult to comprehend.

B

The *Blonder-Tongue* case involved defensive use of collateral estoppel—a plaintiff was estopped from asserting a claim that the plaintiff had previously litigated and lost against another defendant. The present case, by contrast, involves offensive use of collateral estoppel—a plaintiff is seeking to estop a defendant from relitigating the issues which the defendant previously litigated and lost against another plaintiff. In both the offensive and defensive use situations, the party against whom estoppel is asserted has litigated and lost in an earlier action. Nevertheless, several reasons have been advanced why the two situations should be treated differently.

First, offensive use of collateral estoppel does not promote judicial economy in the same manner as defensive use does. Defensive use of collateral estoppel precludes a plaintiff from relitigating identical issues by merely "switching adversaries." *Bernhard v. Bank of America Nat. Trust & Savings Ass'n*, 19 Cal. 2d 807, 813 (1942).[12] Thus defensive collateral estoppel gives a plaintiff a strong incentive to join all potential defendants in the first action if possible. Offensive use of collateral estoppel, on the other hand, creates precisely the opposite incentive. Since a plaintiff will be able to rely on a previous judgment against a defendant but will not be bound by that judgment if the defendant wins, the plaintiff has every incentive to adopt a "wait and see" attitude, in the hope that the first action by another plaintiff will result in a favorable judgment.

---

[12] Under the mutuality requirement, a plaintiff could accomplish this result since he would not have been bound by the judgment had the original defendant won.

Thus offensive use of collateral estoppel will likely increase rather than decrease the total amount of litigation, since potential plaintiffs will have everything to gain and nothing to lose by not intervening in the first action.[13]

A second argument against offensive use of collateral estoppel is that it may be unfair to a defendant. If a defendant in the first action is sued for small or nominal damages, he may have little incentive to defend vigorously, particularly if future suits are not foreseeable. Allowing offensive collateral estoppel may also be unfair to a defendant if the judgment relied upon as a basis for the estoppel is itself inconsistent with one or more previous judgments in favor of the defendant.[14] Still another situation where it might be unfair to apply offensive estoppel is where the second action affords the defendant procedural opportunities unavailable in the first action that could readily cause a different result.[15]

C

We have concluded that the preferable approach for dealing with these problems in the federal courts is not to preclude the use of offensive collateral estoppel, but to grant trial courts broad discretion to determine when it should be applied. The general rule should be that in cases where a plaintiff could easily have joined in the earlier action or where, either for the reasons discussed above or for other reasons, the application of offensive estoppel would be unfair to a defendant, a trial judge should not allow the use of offensive collateral estoppel.

In the present case, however, none of the circumstances that might justify reluctance to allow the offensive use of collateral estoppel is present. The application of offensive collateral estoppel will not here reward a private plaintiff who could have joined in the previous action, since the respondent probably could not have joined in the injunctive action brought by the SEC even had he so desired.[17] Similarly, there is no unfairness to the petitioners in applying offensive collateral estoppel in this case. First, in light of the serious allegations made in the SEC's complaint against the petitioners, as well as the foreseeability of subsequent private suits that typically follow a

---

[13] The Restatement (Second) of Judgments §88(3) (Tent. Draft No. 2, Apr. 15, 1975) provides that application of collateral estoppel may be denied if the party asserting it "could have effected joinder in the first action between himself and his present adversary."

[14] In Professor Currie's familiar example, a railroad collision injures 50 passengers all of whom bring separate actions against the railroad. After the railroad wins the first 25 suits, a plaintiff wins in suit 26. Professor Currie argues that offensive use of collateral estoppel should not be applied so as to allow plaintiffs 27 through 50 automatically to recover. Currie, *Mutuality of Estoppel: Limits of the Bernhard Doctrine*, 9 STAN. L. REV. 281, 304 (1957). *See* Restatement (Second) of Judgments §88(4).

[15] If, for example, the defendant in the first action was forced to defend in an inconvenient forum and therefore was unable to engage in full scale discovery or call witnesses, application of offensive collateral estoppel may be unwarranted. Indeed, differences in available procedures may sometimes justify not allowing a prior judgment to have estoppel effect in a subsequent action even between the same parties, or where

---

defensive estoppel is asserted against a plaintiff who has litigated and lost. The problem of unfairness is particularly acute in cases of offensive estoppel, however, because the defendant against whom estoppel is asserted typically will not have chosen the forum in the first action. *See id.*, §88(2) and Comment d.

[17] *SEC v. Everest Management Corp.*, 475 F.2d 1236, 1240 (2d Cir. 1972) ("[T]he complicating effect of the additional issues and the additional parties outweighs any advantage of a single disposition of the common issues"). Moreover, consolidation of a private action with one brought by the SEC without its consent is prohibited by statute. 15 U.S.C. §78u(g).

successful Government judgment, the petitioners had every incentive to litigate the SEC lawsuit fully and vigorously.[18] Second, the judgment in the SEC action was not inconsistent with any previous decision. Finally, there will in the respondent's action be no procedural opportunities available to the petitioners that were unavailable in the first action of a kind that might be likely to cause a different result.[19]

We conclude, therefore, that none of the considerations that would justify a refusal to allow the use of offensive collateral estoppel is present in this case. Since the petitioners received a "full and fair" opportunity to litigate their claims in the SEC action, the contemporary law of collateral estoppel leads inescapably to the conclusion that the petitioners are collaterally estopped from relitigating the question of whether the proxy statement was materially false and misleading.

[Part II of the opinion addressed whether the use of collateral estoppel in this case would violate Parklane Hosiery's right to a jury trial. The majority concluded that the Seventh Amendment does not prevent the use of offensive nonmutual collateral estoppel, even if it prevents presentation of an issue to a jury.]

The judgment of the Court of Appeals is Affirmed.

REHNQUIST, J., dissenting.

It is admittedly difficult to be outraged about the treatment accorded by the federal judiciary to petitioners' demand for a jury trial in this lawsuit. . . . It may be that if this Nation were to adopt a new Constitution today, the Seventh Amendment guaranteeing the right of jury trial in civil cases in federal courts would not be included among its provisions. But any present sentiment to that effect cannot obscure or dilute our obligation to enforce the Seventh Amendment, which was included in the Bill of Rights in 1791 and which has not since been repealed in the only manner provided by the Constitution for repeal of its provisions.

The right of trial by jury in civil cases at common law is fundamental to our history and jurisprudence. . . . Over 35 years ago, Mr. Justice Black lamented the "gradual process of judicial erosion which in one hundred fifty years has slowly worn away a major portion of the essential guarantee of the Seventh Amendment." *Galloway v. United States*, 319 U.S. 372, 397 (1943) (dissenting opinion). Regrettably, the erosive process continues apace with today's decision.[1] . . .

I think it is clear that petitioners were denied their Seventh Amendment right to a jury trial in this case. Neither respondent nor the Court doubts that at common

---

[18] After a 4-day trial in which the petitioners had every opportunity to present evidence and call witnesses, the District Court held for the SEC. The petitioners then appealed to the Court of Appeals for the Second Circuit, which affirmed the judgment against them. Moreover, the petitioners were already aware of the action brought by the respondent, since it had commenced before the filing of the SEC action.

[19] It is true, of course, that the petitioners in the present action would be entitled to a jury trial of the issues bearing on whether the proxy statement was materially false and misleading had the SEC action never been brought—a matter to be discussed in Part II of this opinion. But the presence or absence of a jury as factfinder is basically neutral, quite unlike, for example, the necessity of defending the first lawsuit in an inconvenient forum.

---

[1] Because I believe that the use of offensive collateral estoppel in this particular case was improper, it is not necessary for me to decide whether I would approve its use in circumstances where the defendant's right to a jury trial was not impaired.

law as it existed in 1791, petitioners would have been entitled in the private action to have a jury determine whether the proxy statement was false and misleading in the respects alleged. The reason is that at common law in 1791, collateral estoppel was permitted only where the parties in the first action were identical to, or in privity with, the parties to the subsequent action. It was not until 1971 that the doctrine of mutuality was abrogated by this Court in certain limited circumstances. *Blonder-Tongue Laboratories, Inc. v. University of Illinois Foundation*, 402 U.S. 313 (1971).[14] But developments in the judge-made doctrine of collateral estoppel, however salutary, cannot, consistent with the Seventh Amendment, contract in any material fashion the right to a jury trial that a defendant would have enjoyed in 1791. In the instant case, resort to the doctrine of collateral estoppel does more than merely contract the right to a jury trial: It eliminates the right entirely and therefore contravenes the Seventh Amendment. . . .

Even accepting, *arguendo*, the majority's position that there is no violation of the Seventh Amendment here, I nonetheless would not sanction the use of collateral estoppel in this case. The Court today holds:

> The general rule should be that in cases where a plaintiff could easily have joined in the earlier action or where, either for the reasons discussed above or for other reasons, the application of offensive estoppel would be

unfair to a defendant, a trial judge should not allow the use of offensive collateral estoppel.

In my view, it is "unfair" to apply offensive collateral estoppel where the party who is sought to be estopped has not had an opportunity to have the facts of his case determined by a jury. Since in this case petitioners were not entitled to a jury trial in the Securities and Exchange Commission (SEC) lawsuit, I would not estop them from relitigating the issues determined in the SEC suit before a jury in the private action. . . .

The ultimate irony of today's decision is that its potential for significantly conserving the resources of either the litigants or the judiciary is doubtful at best. That being the case, I see absolutely no reason to frustrate so cavalierly the important federal policy favoring jury decisions of disputed fact questions. The instant case is an apt example of the minimal savings that will be accomplished by the Court's decision. As the Court admits, even if petitioners are collaterally estopped from relitigating whether the proxy was materially false and misleading, they are still entitled to have a jury determine whether respondent was injured by the alleged misstatements and the amount of damages, if any, sustained by respondent. Thus, a jury must be impaneled in this case in any event. The time saved by not trying the issue of whether the proxy was materially false and misleading before the jury is likely to be insubstantial. It is just as probable that today's decision will have the result of coercing defendants to agree to consent orders or settlements in agency enforcement actions in order to preserve their right to jury trial in the private actions. In that event, the Court, for no compelling reason, will have simply added a powerful club to the administrative agencies' arsenals that even Congress was unwilling to provide them.

---

[14] The Court's decision in *Blonder-Tongue Laboratories, Inc. v. University of Illinois Foundation*, is, on its facts, limited to the defensive use of collateral estoppel in patent cases. Abandonment of mutuality is a recent development. The case of *Bernhard v. Bank of America Nat. Trust & Sav. Assn.*, 19 Cal. 2d 807, generally considered the seminal case adopting the new approach, was not decided until 1942.

Notes & Questions

1. As always, begin by charting the two actions. In *Parklane Hosiery*, notice that "case 1" (the action that resulted in the judgment to which preclusive effect may attach) was actually the second-filed case. What matters for purposes of preclusion is not which action was *filed* first, but which reached *judgment* first.

   In case 2 (the class action), who sought to use issue preclusion, and on precisely what issue? By now, you should be able to walk through the general test for issue preclusion step by step: (a) Is it the same issue? (b) Was it actually litigated and determined? (c) Was there a valid and final judgment? (d) Was the determination essential to the judgment? Regarding *Parklane Hosiery*, you likely answered yes to each of these questions, making this an attractive scenario for applying issue preclusion, aside from the mutuality question. The problem is that, in this case, issue preclusion would be nonmutual. The class representatives and class members were not parties to the SEC's action, so they would not have been bound had the prior case gone in favor of the defendants. In *Blonder-Tongue Laboratories*, the Supreme Court had already taken the step of rejecting the traditional mutuality doctrine as a matter of federal law. *Parklane Hosiery*, however, presented a harder version of the question because, whereas *Blonder-Tongue Laboratories* involved *defensive* use of issue preclusion, *Parklane Hosiery* involved *offensive* use.

2. The Supreme Court in *Parklane Hosiery* conveyed a strong message that, while offensive nonmutual issue preclusion is not forbidden, courts should be more reluctant to allow offensive use than defensive use. Why? Consider some of the reasons why courts might find offensive nonmutual issue preclusion more troubling than the defensive version.

   a. First, consider the joinder incentives created by issue preclusion. Defensive nonmutual issue preclusion promotes judicial economy by encouraging plaintiffs to join all potential defendants in one action. Do you see how it does this? Offensive nonmutual issue preclusion creates the opposite incentive. If courts were to freely allow offensive nonmutual issue preclusion, potential plaintiffs might choose to wait rather than join. Do you see why?

   b. Second, consider several situations in which offensive nonmutual issue preclusion would be especially unfair to the defendant. Suppose the stakes in the second case dwarf those in the first. The danger is that a party may not have defended case 1 vigorously if the stakes were low. Offensive nonmutual issue preclusion would have the unfortunate effect of forcing a party to litigate case 1 as if it were for much bigger stakes, which would increase the cost to both of the litigants as well as to the public. Similarly, it could be unfair to bind a defendant to an issue determination if the procedural opportunities in the first court—for example, the right to gather information through discovery or the opportunities to present evidence at trial—were more constrained than in the second court.

c. Another situation involving potential unfairness is when there have been multiple cases with inconsistent determinations concerning the particular issue. The *Parklane Hosiery* Court, in footnote 14, cites Professor Brainerd Currie's famous railroad example in which a train wreck results in 50 lawsuits against the railroad brought by 50 different plaintiffs, each of whom was injured in the wreck. The railroad wins cases 1 through 25. In each case, the jury finds that the railroad was not negligent. But in case 26, the jury finds that the railroad was negligent, so Plaintiff 26 wins. Can Plaintiff 27 use issue preclusion to establish that the railroad was negligent? Obviously, it would be ridiculous to permit issue preclusion to establish negligence under these circumstances. On the question of whether the railroad was negligent, the score is 25-1 in favor of the railroad. Case 26 was the aberration. Even if only one jury had found the railroad not negligent before the conflicting finding of negligence, most courts would not allow a plaintiff to use offensive nonmutual issue preclusion in the face of inconsistent determinations.

d. Finally, consider which party is bound by each type of issue preclusion. Defensive nonmutual issue preclusion binds the party who chose the time and place of the first lawsuit. It was the patent holder in *Blonder-Tongue*, not the alleged infringer, who selected the venue for case 1 and who controlled the timing of the lawsuit. It hardly seems unfair to hold a litigant to the decisions of a tribunal that was selected by that litigant. Offensive nonmutual issue preclusion, by contrast, would bind a party who, by virtue of being a defendant, presumably was dragged into case 1 unwillingly.

3. In *Parklane Hosiery*, how did the Supreme Court handle each of the concerns set forth above in Note 2? On the facts of the case, why did the Court permit the use of offensive nonmutual issue preclusion?

4. Recall from *Rush v. City of Maple Heights*, above, that Lenore Rush's husband was with her on the motorcycle when the accident happened. His name was Wilson Rush. In case 1, Lenore Rush sued the city and won a judgment for compensatory damages based on a finding that the city was negligent in leaving the pothole. Then, in case 2, suppose Wilson Rush sued the city for his own injuries. He would not be claim precluded, as he is a different person and has his own claim. *See Taylor v. Sturgell*, above. But what about issue preclusion? In case 2, Wilson would attempt to use issue preclusion to get the benefit of the determination of the city's negligence in case 1. Would he succeed?

To answer this question, walk through the entire analysis, step by step: (a) Is it the same issue? (b) Was it actually litigated and determined? (c) Was there a valid and final judgment? (d) Was the determination essential to the judgment? (e) Would this be mutual or nonmutual issue preclusion? (f) If nonmutual, is it

action to federal court based on diversity jurisdiction. The federal court dismissed "on the merits and with prejudice" based on California's two-year statute of limitations. Semtek proceeded to file the same claim in Maryland state court, because in Maryland the applicable statute of limitations was three years, which had not yet expired. In case 2, Lockheed moved to dismiss on grounds of claim preclusion.

Was Semtek precluded from pursuing the action in Maryland state court after the first action had been dismissed by the federal court? It is the same claim, between the same parties, and there was a valid and final judgment. But the point of contention was whether the judgment in case 1 was "on the merits." The dismissal was based on the statute of limitations, which arguably does not go to the merits of the lawsuit. Indeed, under California law such a dismissal would not be entitled to claim preclusive effect for that very reason. In other words, California's statute of limitations would bar plaintiff's suit; Maryland's statute of limitations would not; but California's claim-preclusion law would not give the California statute-of-limitations judgment preclusive effect. As between the preclusion law of Maryland and of California, whose preclusion law would you expect the court would apply, if the analysis in *Semtek* had stopped here?

Alas, the analysis could not stop there, because case 1 was ultimately decided by a *federal* court in California, not by a California state court. And not only did the federal court in case 1 state explicitly that the dismissal on statute-of-limitations grounds was "on the merits," but also, even if the court had not said so, Federal Rule of Civil Procedure 41(b) would seem to treat the dismissal as a judgment on the merits ("Unless the dismissal order states otherwise, a dismissal under this subdivision (b) . . . operates as an adjudication on the merits."). Thus, a third possible source of preclusion law is involved—federal preclusion law. And if *federal* preclusion law applied (because a federal court issued the judgment in case 1), the dismissal would be considered "on the merits" and claim preclusion would apply. But if *California* preclusion law applied (because case 1 was decided under California substantive law), claim preclusion would not apply.

The Supreme Court first explained that the preclusive effect of the judgment must be determined by looking to the first case. Preclusion concerns the binding effect of a judgment, so the relevant forum is the one that rendered the judgment. In other words, as you likely concluded above, *Maryland* preclusion law was entirely beside the point, because Maryland is merely the forum of case 2, not the forum that rendered the judgment in case 1. But that did not resolve the question of whether California preclusion law or federal preclusion law applied. Because case 1 was a state law case in federal court, the question of whose law governed the preclusive effect of the judgment was a question that implicated the *Erie* doctrine on whether federal or state law applies in federal court, a doctrine we will explore in Chapter 12. The Court concluded that "federal common law governs the claim-preclusive effect of a dismissal by a federal court sitting in diversity." 531 U.S. at 508.

Nonetheless, that conclusion *still* did not end the inquiry. The Court went on to hold that, for purposes of determining the effect of a federal court decision grounded in state substantive law, the federal common law of preclusion should incorporate state standards unless an overriding federal interest demands otherwise. Finding no clear overriding federal interest, the Court held that the Maryland state court in case 2 should apply the California rule that the statute-of-limitations dismissal was not claim preclusive.

F. RELIEF FROM JUDGMENT

After an order or judgment has been entered, a party may ask the court for relief from the judgment. If the court grants the motion, then the judgment has no claim preclusive or issue preclusive effect on the party. You would expect courts to be extremely reluctant to grant such motions, and you would be right. In the federal rules, Rule 60(b) defines narrowly the situations in which a party can obtain relief from a judgment. For example, if the judgment was obtained by an adverse party's fraud, the court may grant relief. Newly discovered evidence does not provide a basis for relief unless it could not have been discovered in time to include in a motion for a new trial.

For instance, *Spurgin-Dienst v. United States*, 359 F.3d 451 (7th Cir. 2004), involved a fatal air crash, and the plaintiffs contended that the judgment should not stand because there had been a delay in providing the plaintiffs certain data used for the pilot's weather briefing. However, the district court rejected the plaintiffs' Rule 60(b) motion and the Seventh Circuit affirmed, finding that the defendant did not use this data in its case-in-chief at trial and the plaintiffs' lawyer had sufficient time to review the data to use it at trial. By contrast, in *Ebersole v. Kline-Perry*, 292 F.R.D. 316 (E.D. Va. 2013), a court granted the defendant's Rule 60(b) motion. *Ebersole* was a defamation case against a defendant who had accused the plaintiff, a pet care facility owner, of mistreating animals. After trial, the court entered judgment for the plaintiff. Several months later, the defendant's lawyer received videos that showed the plaintiff abusing dogs, which could have demonstrated that the plaintiff's trial testimony was false. The plaintiff had failed to produce these videos in discovery. The defendant filed a motion to vacate the judgment. The court granted the motion under Rule 60(b)(3) and ordered a new trial, finding that the plaintiff had engaged in misconduct that prevented the defendant from fully presenting her case. The court explained that "given the highly relevant content of the videos at issue here, the Court finds that the consideration of finality of judgments is outweighed by the Court's interest in justice being done in view of all the facts." *Id.* at 323.

"Excusable neglect" can also provide a basis for relief from judgment in rare cases; parties cannot expect relief from a judgment simply because they or their attorneys were careless or confused. One situation in which courts are somewhat more willing to grant relief is to give defendants relief from default judgments in cases where the defendant can show good cause for defaulting, prompt correction of the default, and a meritorious defense. With the possible exception of default judgments, lawyers should not think of motions for relief from judgment as an easy way for their clients to avoid the preclusive effect of a judgment. Finality is the overriding goal of preclusion doctrines, and Rule 60(b) creates a relatively small exception to finality to avoid serious injustice.

Subject Matter Jurisdiction

Now that we have explored the litigation process from beginning to end, added joinder, and examined enforcement and preclusion, we turn to a different aspect of civil procedure: Which court will decide the dispute?

A court's authority to adjudicate a particular dispute depends upon three sets of forum-selection doctrines. Here in Chapter 9, we examine *subject matter jurisdiction—* in particular, the question of whether the dispute fits into a category that federal courts (as distinguished from state courts) have the power to hear. Chapter 10 explores *personal jurisdiction*, the question of whether a court has power to render a decision that binds the parties, which depends in part on whether the defendant falls within the territorial reach of the court's authority. Chapter 11 considers *venue*, a set of statutory rules for determining which district or districts are appropriate forums for a particular dispute, as well as related doctrines that allow courts to transfer or decline to hear a dispute if a more appropriate forum exists. After exploring subject matter jurisdiction, personal jurisdiction, and venue, we turn in Chapter 12 to the question of what law applies to the dispute. Finally, in Chapter 13, we compare courts with other forums in which disputes may be resolved, such as private arbitration.

STRATEGY SESSION

One of the first strategic decisions in any case is choosing the forum. By analyzing subject matter jurisdiction, personal jurisdiction, and venue, a lawyer figures out which courts are available. Sometimes, these constraints leave only one court to choose. Often, however, multiple courts could properly hear the case, and the lawyer faces a choice. As a matter of strategy for a particular case, the lawyer may prefer state court or federal court, and may prefer a specific state, county, or district. Forum-selection strategy may depend on the convenience of the location, differences in courts' procedures or resources, differences in the individual judges who comprise the court, the demographic makeup of the potential jury pool, speed of the docket, choice of law, or other factors. Initially, the plaintiff chooses the forum, and at that stage forum-selection strategy is mostly a question for the plaintiff's lawyer. But defense lawyers, too, engage in forum strategy. Defendants decide whether to seek transfer to another court, whether to "remove" an action from state court to federal court, and whether to move to dismiss based on an improper forum choice. As you learn about forum-selection doctrines, think about them on two levels: first, as a set of legal rules that allocate judicial authority, and second, as a set of strategic constraints and opportunities when choosing where to litigate.

A. INTRODUCTION TO SUBJECT MATTER JURISDICTION

Different courts have different powers. To start with an easy example, suppose a judge in traffic court entered a judgment purporting to grant divorce and award child custody. No one would consider the judgment legitimate because the judge's power does not extend to that category of cases. In other words, a traffic court lacks *subject matter jurisdiction* over a family law case. For traffic court, family court, probate court, or other subject-specific tribunals within state or municipal court systems, these case-category distinctions are somewhat self-explanatory. But there is another aspect of subject matter jurisdiction that is neither obvious nor self-explanatory, yet it carries enormous significance within the United States litigation system—the subject matter jurisdiction of *federal courts*. Federal courts have limited subject matter jurisdiction. Knowing the limits on the jurisdictional power of federal courts is essential to understanding United States civil procedure.

Terminology Tip

Jurisdiction refers to an institution's authority to make legal decisions. Etymologically, it comes from *jur-* (law) + *dictio* (saying): the power to say law. In civil procedure, the word mostly refers either to *subject matter jurisdiction* (a court's power over certain categories of cases) or *personal jurisdiction* (a court's power over the parties). But lawyers and judges often use the word *jurisdiction* to refer to the state or other territory over which legal authority extends, as in the sentence, "The law varies from one jurisdiction to another."

Recall a few points from our introduction to court systems in Chapter 1. Each state and territory within the United States has its own court system, including both courts of limited jurisdiction and courts of general jurisdiction. Courts of *limited jurisdiction* may include small claims courts, municipal courts, probate courts, and family courts, among others. What makes them courts of limited jurisdiction is that they are authorized to hear only particular categories of cases. Courts of *general jurisdiction*, by contrast, can hear any type of case unless specifically excluded. Alongside all of these state court systems, the United States government has its own system—the federal courts.

The starting point for your study of federal subject matter jurisdiction is this: *Federal courts are courts of limited jurisdiction.* The U.S. Constitution establishes the judicial branch of the federal government and defines the outer limits of the powers of the federal judiciary. According to Article III, Section 2, the judicial power of the United States extends only to certain categories of cases. These categories include "all Cases, in Law and Equity, arising under this Constitution, the Laws of the United States, and Treaties," as well as "Controversies between two or more States;—between a State and Citizens of another State;—between Citizens of different States; . . . and between a State, or the Citizens thereof, and foreign States, Citizens or Subjects." It also includes cases in which the United States is a party, cases involving ambassadors or consuls, and maritime cases.

Inclusion in Article III, however, does not automatically confer that power on the federal district courts. The Constitution declares which categories of cases *may* fall within federal judicial power, but the framers of the Constitution left it up to Congress to decide whether to create any lower federal courts and, if so, which powers to grant to those courts. Congress promptly created the lower federal courts in the Judiciary Act of 1789 and gave the federal courts original jurisdiction over certain types of cases within the constitutional limits of Article III, including cases between citizens of different states (diversity jurisdiction, now codified at 28 U.S.C. §1332). Congress later enacted statutes authorizing the federal courts to hear additional types of cases within the constitutional limits, most significantly the power to hear cases arising under federal law (federal question jurisdiction, now codified at 28 U.S.C. §1331).

You might wonder why such jurisdictional statutes are necessary at all. If Article III of the Constitution says that the "judicial Power shall extend to" cases between citizens of different states and to cases arising under federal law, why isn't that enough to give the federal district courts power to adjudicate such cases? The answer is that the Constitution established only one federal court—the Supreme Court of the United States. As far as the Constitution goes, it would have been possible for no federal district courts or courts of appeals to exist at all. Article III, Section 1, states, "The judicial Power of the United States, shall be vested in one supreme Court, and in such inferior Courts as the Congress may from time to time ordain and establish." Since the very existence of federal district courts and courts of appeals was left to Congress, the implication is that Congress decides what powers to grant to these "inferior Courts." But Congress cannot give powers to the federal courts that go beyond what the Constitution permits, just as it cannot enact other unconstitutional laws. The bottom line is that for a federal court to exercise jurisdiction over a case, it must have not only constitutional authority but also statutory authority to do so.

To understand the relationship between Article III and the jurisdictional statutes, consider the Venn diagram to the right. We could clutter up the picture by including dozens of jurisdictional

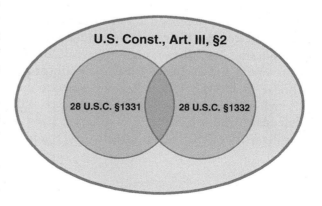

statutes, but this should suffice to convey the concept. The circles represent statutory grants of jurisdiction (such as section 1331's grant of federal question jurisdiction and section 1332's grant of diversity jurisdiction), which cannot exceed the bounds permitted by Article III of the Constitution. The jurisdictional circles overlap because a dispute that arises under federal law may also be a dispute between citizens of different states. In addition to sections 1331 (federal question jurisdiction) and 1332 (diversity jurisdiction), there are federal statutes that grant the federal courts power to hear cases in which the United States government is a party, admiralty cases, bankruptcy cases, and others. If you find the diagram helpful, you can visualize these other statutory grants as additional circles that fall within the permissible reach of Article III jurisdiction.

THE BIG PICTURE

Understanding the limits on the power of federal courts is fundamental not only as a building block in civil procedure, but also as a matter of constitutional law. Federal courts have two attributes, constitutionally speaking, that imply constraints on power—they are *federal*, and they are *courts*. Because they are federal, their powers are limited to avoid encroaching on the sovereignty of the states as a matter of *federalism*. Because they are courts, their powers are limited to avoid encroaching on the legislative and executive branches as a matter of *separation of powers*. Federal subject matter jurisdiction, at a constitutional level, flows from both of these principles as embodied in Article III, which delimits the power of the Supreme Court and the federal judiciary just as Article I spells out the power of Congress and Article II spells out the power of the executive branch. Some find it useful to picture these limits as being both *vertical* (federal versus state) and *horizontal* (judicial versus legislative and executive).

Most federal jurisdictional statutes grant the federal courts subject matter jurisdiction concurrently with the jurisdiction of the state courts. With *concurrent jurisdiction*, a party may choose to file the action either in state court or in federal court. For example, if a plaintiff seeks to assert an employment discrimination claim under Title VII (a federal antidiscrimination statute), the plaintiff may choose federal court because the case arises under federal law and therefore the court has federal question jurisdiction under section 1331. But jurisdiction under section 1331 is *concurrent*, not exclusive, so if the plaintiff prefers state court, the plaintiff may choose to file the Title VII claim in state court rather than federal court even though the claim arises under federal law. Likewise, if a plaintiff seeks to sue a defendant who is a citizen of a different state and the case meets the requirements for diversity of citizenship jurisdiction, the plaintiff may choose federal court; the court would have diversity jurisdiction under section 1332. But jurisdiction under 1332 is concurrent, not exclusive, so if the plaintiff prefers state court, the plaintiff may choose to file the action in state court even though it is between citizens of different states.

A few jurisdictional statutes, however, grant the federal courts *exclusive jurisdiction* over certain types of claims, which means that such cases may be brought only in federal court. *See, e.g.,* 15 U.S.C. §78aa(a) (securities); 28 U.S.C. §1334 (bankruptcy); 28 U.S.C. §1337 (antitrust); 28 U.S.C. §1338(a) (patent and copyright). Thus, for example, a plaintiff may bring a patent infringement suit only in federal court, not in state court.

B. FEDERAL QUESTION JURISDICTION

(1) Introduction to Federal Question Jurisdiction

Unsurprisingly, federal courts have jurisdiction to hear cases that arise under federal law. The general federal-question-jurisdiction statute, 28 U.S.C. §1331, gives the U.S. district courts original jurisdiction over "all civil actions arising under the Constitution, laws, or treaties of the United States." Thus, when plaintiffs sue under federal statutes governing civil rights, securities, antitrust, or other federal laws, they may file their cases in federal court.

What seems surprising from the perspective of the twenty-first century is that the general federal-question-jurisdiction statute was not enacted until 1875. For the first century of our nation's existence, most federal law claims could be brought only in the state courts, and the federal courts were reserved largely for cases between citizens of different states. By expanding federal question jurisdiction in the wake of the Civil War and Reconstruction, Congress ensured the availability of a forum not hostile toward federally created rights.

The growth of federal statutory claims fueled an expansion in the types and number of cases adjudicated in federal court. Federal statutes have established private rights of action in a wide range of legal disputes, including antitrust, banking, civil rights (including voting, employment, housing, disability accommodation, and education), environment, prisons, labor, intellectual property, and securities. The federal district courts hear large numbers of cases in all of these areas. *See* U.S. District Courts: Civil Federal Judicial Caseload Statistics (Mar. 31, 2019), https://www.uscourts.gov/statistics/table/c-2/federal-judicial-caseload-statistics/2019/03/31.

Originally, the statute granted federal question jurisdiction only in disputes that involved more than a certain dollar amount. By 1980, however, the amount-in-controversy requirement was removed. Currently, federal courts have jurisdiction over cases arising under federal law regardless of the amount at stake.

(2) "Arising Under" Federal Law

The concept of federal question jurisdiction is deceptively simple—federal courts have power to adjudicate claims that arise under federal law. Determining which cases fall within its ambit, however, requires some analysis. What exactly does it mean for a case to "arise under" federal law?

(a) State Law Claim with Federal Defense

The Supreme Court addressed a fundamental aspect of this question in the case that follows. If the determination of a dispute depends entirely on resolution of a question of federal law, does that mean that the case *arises under* federal law? Or does "arising under," as used in the federal-question-jurisdiction statute, require something different?

LOUISVILLE & NASHVILLE RAILROAD CO. v. MOTTLEY
211 U.S. 149 (1908)

MOODY, J.

[Erasmus and Annie Mottley were injured when two trains collided in 1871 at Randolph's Station, Jefferson County, Kentucky. The Mottleys agreed to settle all claims against the Louisville & Nashville Railroad Company in exchange for lifetime passes for free transportation. The Railroad renewed the lifetime passes every year until January 1, 1907, when the Railroad refused to renew the passes. The Railroad argued that it could not renew the passes because Congress passed an act on June 29, 1906 forbidding free passes. The Mottleys sued seeking specific performance of their settlement. They argued, first, that the act of Congress does not prohibit the giving of passes under the circumstances of this case; and, second, that, if the law is to be construed as prohibiting such passes, it conflicts with the Fifth Amendment of the Constitution, because it deprives the plaintiffs of their property without due process of law. The Railroad demurred to the Mottleys' complaint. The trial court overruled the demurrer and entered judgment in favor of the Mottleys. The Railroad appealed to the Supreme Court.]

Two questions of law were raised by the demurrer to the bill, were brought here by appeal, and have been argued before us. They are, first, whether that part of the act of Congress of June 29, 1906, which forbids the giving of free passes or the collection of any different compensation for transportation of passengers than that specified in the tariff filed, makes it unlawful to perform a contract for transportation of persons who, in good faith, before the passage of the act, had accepted such contract in satisfaction of a valid cause of action against the railroad; and, second, whether the statute, if it should be construed to render such a contract unlawful, is in violation of the Fifth Amendment of the Constitution of the United States. We do not deem it necessary, however, to consider either of these questions, because, in our opinion, the court below was without jurisdiction of the cause. Neither party has questioned that jurisdiction, but it is the duty of this court to see to it that the jurisdiction of the circuit court, which is defined and limited by statute, is not exceeded. This duty we have frequently performed of our own motion.

There was no diversity of citizenship, and it is not and cannot be suggested that there was any ground of jurisdiction, except that the case was a "suit . . . arising under the Constitution or laws of the United States." 25 Stat. 434, c.866. It is the settled interpretation of these words, as used in this statute, conferring jurisdiction, that a suit arises under the Constitution and laws of the United States only when the plaintiff's statement of his own cause of action shows that it is based upon those laws or that Constitution. It is not enough that the plaintiff alleges some anticipated defense to his cause of action, and asserts that the defense is invalidated by some provision of the Constitution of the United States. Although such allegations show that very likely, in the course of the litigation, a question under the Constitution would arise, they do not show that the suit, that is, the plaintiff's original cause of action, arises under the Constitution. In *Tennessee v. Union & Planters' Bank*, 152 U.S. 454 (1894), the plaintiff, the state of Tennessee, brought suit in the circuit court of the United States to recover from the defendant certain taxes alleged to be due under the laws of the state. The plaintiff alleged that the defendant claimed an immunity from the taxation by virtue of its charter, and that therefore the tax was void, because in

violation of the provision of the Constitution of the United States, which forbids any state from passing a law impairing the obligation of contracts. The cause was held to be beyond the jurisdiction of the circuit court, the court saying, by Mr. Justice Gray: "A suggestion of one party, that the other will or may set up a claim under the Constitution or laws of the United States, does not make the suit one arising under that Constitution or those laws." Again, in *Boston & M. Consol. Copper & S. Min. Co. v. Montana Ore Purchasing Co.*, 188 U.S. 632 (1903), the plaintiff brought suit in the circuit court of the United States for the conversion of copper ore and for an injunction against its continuance. The plaintiff then alleged, for the purpose of showing jurisdiction, in substance, that the defendant would set up in defense certain laws of the United States. The cause was held to be beyond the jurisdiction of the circuit court, the court saying, by Mr. Justice Peckham:

> It would be wholly unnecessary and improper, in order to prove complainant's cause of action, to go into any matters of defense which the defendants might possibly set up, and then attempt to reply to such defense, and thus, if possible, to show that a Federal question might or probably would arise in the course of the trial of the case. To allege such defense and then make an answer to it before the defendant has the opportunity to itself plead or prove its own defense is inconsistent with any known rule of pleading, so far as we are aware, and is improper.

The rule is a reasonable and just one that the complainant in the first instance shall be confined to a statement of its cause of action, leaving to the defendant to set up in his answer what his defense is, and, if anything more than a denial of complainant's cause of action, imposing upon the defendant the burden of proving such defense.

Conforming itself to that rule, the complainant would not, in the assertion or proof of its cause of action, bring up a single Federal question. The presentation of its cause of action would not show that it was one arising under the Constitution or laws of the United States.

The only way in which it might be claimed that a Federal question was presented would be in the complainant's statement of what the defense of defendants would be, and complainant's answer to such defense. Under these circumstances the case is brought within the rule laid down in *Tennessee v. Union & Planters' Bank*, 152 U.S. 454 (1894). That case has been cited and approved many times since.

Id. at 638, 639. . . . The application of this rule to the case at bar is decisive against the jurisdiction of the circuit court.

It is ordered that the judgment be reversed and the case remitted to the circuit court with instructions to dismiss the suit for want of jurisdiction.

Notes & Questions

1. The Mottleys claimed they had the right to continue receiving passes for free travel on the Railroad based on their earlier settlement. The Railroad argued that, as a matter of law, it could no longer issue the Mottleys' free passes. To resolve the dispute, a court would have to decide two legal issues—one statutory and one constitutional. What was the *statutory interpretation* question a court would have to decide in order to resolve whether the Railroad must continue to provide passes to the Mottleys? What was the *constitutional* question a court would have to decide to resolve this dispute? Is each of these questions a matter of state law or of federal law?

   If the only thing for a court to decide was a pair of questions about federal law—an interpretation of the congressional prohibition on railroad passes and an application of the Due Process Clause—why did the Supreme Court decide that the case did not "arise under" federal law for purposes of federal question jurisdiction?

2. Did the Supreme Court's decision depend on whether the Mottleys mentioned federal law in their complaint? Not exactly. The Mottleys' complaint alleged (a) that the Railroad refused to reissue their passes on the grounds that the passes were prohibited by the new federal statute, (b) that the federal statute does not actually apply to the Mottleys' passes, (c) that if the statute did apply to them it would violate their due process rights, and (d) therefore, the Mottleys are legally entitled to continue getting passes. Despite the fact that the Mottleys' complaint

explicitly mentioned federal law in this way, the Supreme Court's decision makes it clear that the federal court lacked jurisdiction over the Mottleys' claim. Why?

3. Is the *Mottley* rule a matter of statutory or constitutional law? In other words, did the Supreme Court decide the case based on its interpretation of the federal-question-jurisdiction statute or its interpretation of Article III of the Constitution?

   Remember that for a federal court to have jurisdiction, not only must the case fall within the range of permissible jurisdiction under Article III, it also must fall within a statutory grant of jurisdiction. In *Osborn v. Bank of the United States*, 22 U.S. 738 (1824), decided half a century before the adoption of the general federal-question-jurisdiction statute, the Supreme Court gave a broad interpretation of the words "arising under" in Article III. The Court held that the *constitutional* "arising under" clause extends to any case in which there is a federal "ingredient." Neither *Mottley* nor any other case has overruled *Osborn*'s broad definition of "arising under" in

> ## Terminology Tip
>
> Federal question jurisdiction, under *Mottley*, cannot depend on an anticipated defense; rather, the claim itself must arise under federal law. Many authorities refer to this as the *well-pleaded complaint rule*. But the phrase is misleading if you take it too literally. Jurisdiction does not depend on whether a complaint is "well pleaded" in the sense of verbal clarity or eloquence. Rather, the idea is to suppose that the complaint states nothing more than the bare minimum needed to state the basis for the plaintiff's claim, and to ask whether such a complaint—the essentials of the claim—raises the federal issue.

Article III. But in *Mottley*, the Court decided that the words "arising under" in the *statute* had a narrower meaning that excluded cases in which the federal question comes up only as a defense. Thus, under *Osborn*, it would be constitutional for Congress to pass a statute that gives federal courts the power to adjudicate a claim like the Mottleys' on the grounds that the action "arises under" federal law because there is a federal ingredient. But, under *Mottley*, the federal-question-jurisdiction statute does not give federal courts power over such a claim because the claim does not "arise under" federal law within the meaning of the statute.

4. Under the Declaratory Judgment Act, 28 U.S.C. §2201, a party may file an action to ask a court to declare the legal relationship of the parties with regard to an actual controversy. Suppose the Railroad had filed a lawsuit against the Mottleys in federal court, seeking a declaratory judgment that under federal law the Railroad was not permitted to renew the Mottleys' free passes. Would the court have had jurisdiction? After reading *Mottley*, you might think that the answer would be yes, because the federal issue would appear on the face of the Railroad's declaratory judgment complaint. But the Supreme Court has decided otherwise. In *Skelly Oil Co. v. Phillips Petroleum Co.*, 339 U.S. 667 (1950), the Court held that the Declaratory Judgment Act expanded the range of *remedies* available in federal courts but did not expand federal subject matter jurisdiction. Thus, to determine whether a court has federal question jurisdiction in a declaratory judgment action, courts look to the underlying dispute. That is, the court envisions what a standard coercive lawsuit would look like in the dispute between the

parties. If the court would have subject matter jurisdiction when the dispute is framed as a coercive action, then the court has subject matter jurisdiction over the declaratory judgment action. In our *Mottley* variation, even if the Railroad had preemptively filed an action seeking a declaratory judgment, the underlying dispute was the Mottleys' claim against the Railroad for breach of contract. Therefore, the court lacked federal question jurisdiction regardless of whether the action was filed by the Mottleys as a breach-of-contract action or by the Railroad as a declaratory judgment action.

5. Just as federal question jurisdiction cannot depend upon an anticipated federal defense, it cannot depend on a counterclaim asserted by the defendant. *See Vaden v. Discover Bank*, 556 U.S. 49 (2009); *Holmes Group, Inc. v. Vornado Air Circulation Systems, Inc.*, 535 U.S. 826 (2002). Thus, if a plaintiff asserts a state law claim and a defendant responds by filing a federal law counterclaim, the action does not arise under federal law.

6. In *Mottley*, which party objected to the court's subject matter jurisdiction, and how did that party assert its objection? (Hint: It's a trick question.)

   If the defendant did not move to dismiss for lack of jurisdiction, and if the plaintiff chose to be in federal court, why did the Supreme Court order that the case be dismissed? Why not go ahead and resolve the parties' dispute if both parties want the court to resolve it? The answer is that subject matter jurisdiction can never be waived. The parties, in other words, cannot simply agree to give a court power over their case if the court's jurisdiction does not extend to that type of case. A federal court's power over a case comes from the Constitution and from Congress, not from parties. Whenever a court realizes that it lacks subject matter jurisdiction, the court *must* dismiss the case even if no party has objected. Recall from Chapter 2, Part B(4) that Rule 12(h) addresses waiver of defenses, and unlike the treatment of other defenses, Rule 12(h)(3) emphatically rejects the possibility that subject matter jurisdiction can be waived: "If the court determines at any time that it lacks subject-matter jurisdiction, the court must dismiss the action."

   Think about the "time bomb" aspect of this. In *Mottley*, the parties litigated the case on the merits, all the way to the Supreme Court on appeal. When the Supreme Court recognized that the federal courts had no jurisdiction, it threw out the case despite all the time and effort the parties already had expended in litigating it.

7. After the Supreme Court ordered that the Mottleys' action be dismissed from federal court, the Mottleys filed their case in Kentucky state court. They litigated the case in the state courts and won, but the Railroad successfully appealed to the U.S. Supreme Court based on its federal law defense. *Louisville & Nashville R. Co. v. Mottley*, 219 U.S. 467 (1911).

8. Mostly, the *Mottley* rule means that federal question jurisdiction is reserved for claims that are created by federal law. Federal statutes have created numerous

causes of action in such areas as antitrust, civil rights, employment, environment, intellectual property, labor, and securities. Under the federal-question-jurisdiction statute, 28 U.S.C. §1331, federal courts have jurisdiction over these federal law claims. By contrast, claims created by state law, such as common law claims involving contracts, torts, or property, or claims under a myriad of state statutes, ordinarily do not fall within federal question jurisdiction. The following section, however, describes an exception to this general rule.

(b) State Law Claim with Embedded Federal Issue

The *Mottley* rule and its implications get you most of the way there in terms of understanding federal question jurisdiction. If a claim is created by federal law, then federal question jurisdiction follows, and if a claim is created by state law, then in general federal question jurisdiction does not follow. And, therefore, if a federal issue arises because of a defense or counterclaim rather than as part of the claim itself, the claim does not "arise under" federal law. But it would be an oversimplification to say that federal question jurisdiction *never* gives jurisdiction over state law claims. Occasionally, state law claims involve federal law so centrally that the federal courts will exercise federal question jurisdiction. Some call it "type two" federal question jurisdiction ("type one" would be claims that are created by federal law, which constitute the overwhelming majority of federal question cases).

Here is how it comes up. A plaintiff sues on a state law claim such as negligence, breach of contract, or a state statutory claim. But an essential piece of the plaintiff's claim, as pleaded in the complaint, is that the defendant violated some federal law. In one sense, such a case satisfies the *Mottley* requirement that federal law appear in the basic statement of the claim and not merely as an anticipated defense. But can one really say that a claim "arises under" federal law if it is a claim created by state law?

In *Merrell Dow Pharmaceuticals v. Thompson*, 478 U.S. 804 (1986), plaintiffs sued Merrell Dow, a drug manufacturer, for injuries that the plaintiffs claimed were caused by the defendant's product. It was a state law tort claim, but the plaintiffs' assertion of negligence was that Merrell Dow breached its duty under the Food, Drug and Cosmetic Act, a federal statute. That statute regulated the drug industry but it did not create a federal cause of action for private plaintiffs. The Supreme Court decided 5-4 that even though the plaintiffs' case relied on federal law for an element of the claim, it did not "arise under" federal law for purposes of federal question jurisdiction.

The Supreme Court's decision in *Merrell Dow* did not rule out the possibility of federal question jurisdiction over state law claims with embedded federal issues, a possibility the Supreme Court had earlier recognized in *Smith v. Kansas City Title & Trust Co.*, 255 U.S. 180 (1921). The Court returned to this elusive type of jurisdiction in the following case.

GRABLE & SONS METAL PRODS., INC. v. DARUE ENGINEERING & MANUFACTURING

545 U.S. 308 (2005)

SOUTER, J.

The question is whether want of a federal cause of action to try claims of title to land obtained at a federal tax sale precludes removal to federal court of a state action with nondiverse parties raising a disputed issue of federal title law. We answer no, and hold that the national interest in providing a federal forum for federal tax litigation is sufficiently substantial to support the exercise of federal-question jurisdiction over the disputed issue on removal, which would not distort any division of labor between the state and federal courts, provided or assumed by Congress.

I

In 1994, the Internal Revenue Service seized Michigan real property belonging to petitioner Grable & Sons Metal Products, Inc., to satisfy Grable's federal tax delinquency. [After notifying Grable by certified mail, the IRS sold the property to Darue Engineering & Manufacturing.]

Five years later, Grable brought a quiet title action in state court, claiming that Darue's record title was invalid because the IRS had failed to notify Grable of its seizure of the property in the exact manner required by [26 U.S.C. §6335], which provides that written notice must be "given by the Secretary to the owner of the property [or] left at his usual place of abode or business." Grable said that the statute required personal service, not service by certified mail.

Darue removed the case to Federal District Court as presenting a federal question, because the claim of title depended on the interpretation of the notice statute in the federal tax law. The District Court declined to remand the case after finding that the "claim does pose a 'significant question of federal law,'" and ruling that Grable's lack of a federal right of action to enforce its claim against Darue did not bar the exercise of federal jurisdiction. On the merits, the court granted summary judgment to Darue, holding that although §6335 by its terms required personal service, substantial compliance with the statute was enough. 207 F. Supp. 2d 694 (W.D. Mich. 2002).

The Court of Appeals for the Sixth Circuit affirmed. [T]he panel thought it sufficed that the title claim raised an issue of federal law that had to be resolved, and implicated a substantial federal interest (in construing federal tax law). The court went on to affirm the District Court's judgment on the merits. We granted certiorari on the jurisdictional question alone to resolve a split within the Courts of Appeals on whether *Merrell Dow Pharmaceuticals, Inc. v. Thompson*, 478 U.S. 804 (1986), always requires a federal cause of action as a condition for exercising federal-question jurisdiction. We now affirm.

II

Darue was entitled to remove the quiet title action if Grable could have brought it in federal district court originally, 28 U.S.C. §1441(a), as a civil action "arising under the Constitution, laws, or treaties of the United States," 28 U.S.C. §1331. This provision for federal-question jurisdiction is invoked by and large by plaintiffs pleading a cause of action created by federal law. There is, however, another long-standing, if less frequently encountered, variety of federal "arising under" jurisdiction, this Court having recognized for nearly 100 years that in certain cases federal-question jurisdiction will lie over state-law claims that implicate significant federal issues. *Hopkins v. Walker*, 244 U.S. 486, 490-491 (1917). The doctrine captures the commonsense notion that a federal court ought to be able to hear claims recognized under state law that nonetheless turn on substantial questions of federal law, and thus justify resort to the experience, solicitude, and hope of uniformity that a federal forum offers on federal issues.

The classic example is *Smith v. Kansas City Title & Trust Co.*, 255 U.S. 180 (1921), a suit by a shareholder claiming that the defendant corporation could not lawfully buy certain bonds of the National Government because their issuance was unconstitutional. Although Missouri law provided the cause of action, the Court recognized federal-question jurisdiction because the principal issue in the case was the federal constitutionality of the bond issue. *Smith* thus held, in a somewhat generous statement of the scope of the doctrine, that a state-law claim could give rise to federal-question jurisdiction so long as it "appears from the [complaint] that the right to relief depends upon the construction or application of [federal law]." *Id.* at 199.

The *Smith* statement has been subject to some trimming to fit earlier and later cases recognizing the vitality of the basic doctrine, but shying away from the expansive view that mere need to apply federal law in a state-law claim will suffice to open the "arising under" door. . . . It has in fact become a constant refrain in such cases that federal jurisdiction demands not only

a contested federal issue, but a substantial one, indicating a serious federal interest in claiming the advantages thought to be inherent in a federal forum.

But even when the state action discloses a contested and substantial federal question, the exercise of federal jurisdiction is subject to a possible veto. For the federal issue will ultimately qualify for a federal forum only if federal jurisdiction is consistent with congressional judgment about the sound division of labor between state and federal courts governing the application of §1331. . . .

These considerations have kept us from stating a "single, precise, all-embracing" test for jurisdiction over federal issues embedded in state-law claims between non-diverse parties. We have not kept them out simply because they appeared in state raiment, . . . but neither have we treated "federal issue" as a password opening federal courts to any state action embracing a point of federal law. Instead, the question is, does a state-law claim necessarily raise a stated federal issue, actually disputed and substantial, which a federal forum may entertain without disturbing any congressionally approved balance of federal and state judicial responsibilities.

III

A

This case warrants federal jurisdiction. Grable's state complaint must specify "the facts establishing the superiority of [its] claim," and Grable has premised its superior title claim on a failure by the IRS to give it adequate notice, as defined by federal law. Whether Grable was given notice within the meaning of the federal statute is thus an essential element of its quiet title claim, and the meaning of the federal statute is actually in dispute; it appears to be

2. What type of claim did Grable assert? Is this claim created by state law or by federal law? If the plaintiff's claim—an action to quiet title to real property—is one created by state law, then why didn't the Court find that the *Mottley* rule answered the question of whether federal question jurisdiction exists in this case? Note the critical difference between *Grable* and *Mottley*. In *Grable*, did the federal issue arise as part of an anticipated federal defense?

3. In both *Merrell Dow* and *Grable*, unlike in *Mottley*, the plaintiff asserted a state law claim with an embedded federal issue. In each case, the federal issue arose as part of the plaintiff's original claim, rather than as part of an anticipated defense or counterclaim. Yet the cases yielded opposite results on the question of jurisdiction. Why did the Supreme Court find that federal question jurisdiction existed in *Grable* but not in *Merrell Dow*?

4. The Supreme Court helpfully summed up the *Grable* test a few years later in *Gunn v. Minton*, 568 U.S. 251, 258 (2013):

> [F]ederal jurisdiction over a state law claim will lie if a federal issue is: (1) necessarily raised, (2) actually disputed, (3) substantial, and (4) capable of resolution in federal court without disrupting the federal-state balance approved by Congress.

The *Gunn* case presented a twist on the usual set-up. In *Gunn*, the question was whether exclusive jurisdiction for patent claims applied to a legal malpractice action that raised an issue of federal patent law. The plaintiff, Minton, first brought a patent infringement suit in federal court and lost on summary judgment, which was affirmed on appeal. Minton blamed the loss on his attorney's failure to raise a particular argument of patent law. Minton sued his lawyers for malpractice. Legal malpractice is a state law claim, and Minton brought the legal malpractice action in Texas state court. After his malpractice claim lost on summary judgment, Minton argued on appeal that the Texas court lacked jurisdiction because the claim arose under federal patent law and therefore was subject to exclusive federal jurisdiction under 28 U.S.C. §1338(a). The Texas Supreme Court agreed with Minton that the action "arose under" federal patent law and therefore was subject to exclusive federal jurisdiction.

Applying the *Grable* test, the United States Supreme Court reversed. First, the Court acknowledged that resolution of a federal patent law issue was *necessary* to determine the legal malpractice claim, and that the patent issue was *actually disputed* in the legal malpractice suit. However, the Supreme Court found the federal issue not *substantial* because, whatever the resolution of the malpractice suit, it would not change the result of Minton's original patent infringement suit, and the resolution of the case-within-a-case patent question in the malpractice suit would not bind other courts considering patent issues in the future. Thus, the Court concluded that Minton's malpractice suit did not "arise under" federal patent law: "There is no doubt that resolution of a patent issue in the context of a state legal malpractice action can be vitally important to the particular parties in that case. But something more, demonstrating that the question is significant to the federal system as a whole, is needed. That is missing here." *Gunn*, 568 U.S. at 264.

In light of *Merrell Dow* and *Gunn*, you can appreciate the narrowness of *Grable*-type jurisdiction. In the real world of federal court litigation, nearly all federal question cases involve claims *created by* federal law rather than claims created by state law that include an embedded federal issue; *Grable* represents an interesting but uncommon exception.

5. "Jurisdictional rules should be clear," says Justice Thomas in his concurrence. Having read *Grable* and having learned about *Merrell Dow* and *Gunn*, you may find yourself agreeing with him that this little corner of federal-question-jurisdiction doctrine is *anything but* clear. He issued an invitation to future litigants to argue that the Court should embrace the rule set forth by Justice Oliver Wendell Holmes in *American Well Works Co. v. Layne & Bowler Co.*, 241 U.S. 257 (1916). In *American Well Works*, the plaintiff sued defendant Layne & Bowler Co. on the state law claims of libel and slander. Specifically, the plaintiff alleged that the defendant had falsely disparaged the plaintiff's title to a particular type of pump by stating that the pump infringed the defendant's patents. The plaintiff sued in Arkansas state court, and the defendant removed the action to federal court on the grounds that federal courts have jurisdiction over patent cases. The Supreme Court held that the federal court lacked jurisdiction over the action. Writing for the majority, Justice Holmes explained, "A suit arises under the law that creates the cause of action." *Id.* at 260. Is the "creation test" of *American Well Works* consistent with the outcome in *Mottley*? Is it consistent with the outcome in *Grable*? In the law's never-ending battle between clarity and nuance, Justices Holmes and Thomas made a plea for clarity. The *Grable* majority, however, went with nuance.

C. DIVERSITY JURISDICTION

The framers of the Constitution worried that state courts might favor their own citizens over out-of-staters. This concern led the framers to authorize federal courts to hear cases between citizens of different states. In modern times, some have questioned whether local bias remains as significant a problem as it was when Congress enacted the Judiciary Act of 1789, and in recent decades some federal judges and others have advocated abolishing diversity jurisdiction. With the passage of time and as Americans have become more mobile, perhaps the 50 states are not as different from each other as the original 13 states were when they formed a union, and perhaps the individual identity of most Americans is less wrapped up in state citizenship than it would have been two centuries ago. On the other hand, state identity has not disappeared. There are plenty of cases—particularly disputes between a local individual and an out-of-state corporation—in which the out-of-stater feels more comfortable in federal court than in a state court with locally elected judges. In any event, despite calls for its abolition, diversity jurisdiction—federal jurisdiction based on diversity of citizenship—has remained a staple of the federal courts ever since

Terminology Tip

The name *subject matter jurisdiction* is a bit misleading. Diversity jurisdiction is part of subject matter jurisdiction even though the citizenship of the parties has nothing to do with the "subject matter" of the action. A more accurate descriptor would be *jurisdiction over particular categories of actions.* But nobody calls it that; everybody calls it *subject matter jurisdiction*, so get used to it. *See, e.g.*, Rule 12(b)(1) (motion to dismiss for lack of subject matter jurisdiction).

their founding, and parties regularly avail themselves of the opportunity this creates to litigate disputes in federal court.

For federal diversity jurisdiction, a case must meet two requirements. First, the parties must have diverse citizenship as defined in the statute. Second, the amount in controversy must be more than $75,000. We will explore each of these requirements in turn.

(1) Diversity of Citizenship

To determine whether a federal court has subject matter jurisdiction based on diversity of citizenship, one must understand what is meant by *diversity* and what is meant by *citizenship*.

(a) Types of Diversity

Diversity jurisdiction applies not only to cases between citizens of different states, but also to several other scenarios involving diverse citizenship. The diversity jurisdiction statute, 28 U.S.C. §1332(a), lists four types of diversity. First and most basically, it grants jurisdiction over cases between citizens of different states (New York plaintiff suing a South Carolina defendant). Second, it covers cases between citizens of a state and citizens of a foreign state (New York plaintiff suing a Brazilian defendant), unless the foreigner is a permanent resident alien who is domiciled in the same state. Third, it includes cases between citizens of different states in which foreign citizens are additional parties (New York plaintiff suing a South Carolina defendant and a Brazilian defendant). Finally, it grants jurisdiction over cases between a foreign state as plaintiff and citizens of a state or of different states (the country Brazil suing a South Carolina defendant).

Notice what this leaves out. There is no diversity jurisdiction over cases between citizens of foreign states. If a Nigerian plaintiff tries to sue a French defendant in a U.S. federal court, the court would not have subject matter jurisdiction based on diversity of citizenship, although the court might have federal question jurisdiction if the case arises under federal law. Do not make the mistake of assuming that any form of diverse citizenship gives rise to federal jurisdiction. "Diversity of citizenship"—like much of civil procedure—is more technical than that, so read the statute carefully before jumping to conclusions.

For diversity jurisdiction, no plaintiff can have the same citizenship as any defendant. We will look at this "complete diversity" requirement in more detail after seeing how citizenship is defined for different types of litigants, but keep the requirement in mind as you think about these various configurations.

Type of Diversity	Statute	Example
Citizens of different states	§1332(a)(1)	NY π v. SC Δ
Citizen of state and foreigner	§1332(a)(2)	NY π v. Brazil Δ
Citizens of different states, plus foreigner	§1332(a)(3)	NY π v. SC Δ, Brazil Δ
Foreign state versus citizen of state	§1332(a)(4)	Brazil v. SC Δ

(b) Complete Diversity

For jurisdiction based on diversity of citizenship, *complete diversity* is required. No plaintiff may have the same citizenship as any defendant. As a practical matter, this is a very significant limitation on diversity jurisdiction. Many cases involve multiple parties, and corporations may have dual citizenship. Therefore, even in cases between citizens of different states, the federal courts often lack diversity jurisdiction because some party on one side of the *v* is a citizen of the same state as some party on the other side of the *v*.

You won't find the complete diversity requirement in the plain language of section 1332(a). But for over two centuries, since the Supreme Court's decision in *Strawbridge v. Curtiss*, 7 U.S. 267 (1806), this is how courts have interpreted the diversity jurisdiction statute. The Supreme Court has held that the complete diversity requirement applies only to the statute, not to Article III, Section 2 of the Constitution, even though the language is essentially identical. *See State Farm Fire & Casualty Co. v. Tashire*, 386 U.S. 523, 530-31 (1967) (upholding federal jurisdiction in a statutory interpleader action based on minimal diversity). This means that Congress has the constitutional power to enact statutes that allow diversity jurisdiction based on minimal diversity (any plaintiff's citizenship differs from any defendant's citizenship), even though, absent such a specific statute, the standard analysis under section 1332(a) requires complete diversity.

Applying the complete diversity requirement is mostly straightforward. Look at the state citizenship of each of the plaintiffs and see whether any state of citizenship is the same as that of any of the defendants. If any plaintiff is a citizen of the same state as any defendant, then complete diversity is lacking. Corporations, as we will explain in the next section, are citizens of both their state of incorporation and the state of their principal place of business. Consider how the complete diversity requirement intersects with the types of diversity described above ("citizens of different states," etc.). For diversity jurisdiction in general, the parties must be diverse in one of the ways identified by the statute, plus the diversity must be complete. One interesting twist applies to cases involving foreign parties. Diversity jurisdiction applies to a case between citizens of different states even if an alien is on one or both sides, but does not apply to a case with a state citizen plus an alien on one side and only aliens on the other side.

To test your understanding of what constitutes complete diversity, try the following examples. The question for each is whether a federal court has diversity jurisdiction under 28 U.S.C. §1332, assuming the amount-in-controversy requirement is met:

(a) Florida π v. Florida
(b) Florida π v. Texas Δ
(c) Florida π v. Texas Δ, Louisiana Δ
(d) Florida π v. Texas Δ, Florida Δ
(e) Florida π, Texas π v. Texas Δ
(f) Florida π v. Texas Δ, Texas Δ
(g) Florida π v. Delaware/Michigan Δ (corporation incorporated in Delaware, with principal place of business in Michigan)
(h) Delaware π v. Delaware/Michigan Δ
(i) Florida π, Florida π, Michigan π v. Texas Δ, Texas/Louisiana Δ, Delaware/Florida Δ
(j) Mexico π v. France Δ
(k) Florida π, Mexico π v. Texas Δ, Mexico Δ
(l) Florida π, Mexico π v. France Δ

Now check your answers. Cases b, c, f, g, and k meet the requirements for diversity jurisdiction. Cases a, d, e, h, i, j, and l do not.

STRATEGY SESSION

Consider the strategic choices created by the complete diversity requirement. Suppose you represent plaintiff A, a citizen of Florida. Your client has a state law claim greater than $75,000 that she could assert against defendant X (a citizen of Texas), against defendant Y (a citizen of Florida), or both. If you believe your client has a better chance of success in federal court, you might advise A to assert the claim solely against X. This would maintain complete diversity and make the action amenable to federal court jurisdiction. If, on the other hand, you believe your client has a better chance of success in state court, you might advise A to assert the claim against both X and Y (or solely against Y). This would destroy complete diversity and make the action unamenable to federal jurisdiction. Don't forget Rule 11: These options exist only if you have a factual and legal basis to assert claims against X and Y. And don't lose sight of other considerations. You would not advise a plaintiff to forgo either X or Y if there are significant remedial or evidentiary reasons to include both. But in a situation with multiple potential defendants who could plausibly be included or not, forum considerations may drive the decision. Note that a similar analysis applies to joinder of plaintiffs. Suppose A and B both have potential claims against X arising out of the same transaction or occurrence, and B is a citizen of

Texas. If A wants to file the case against X in federal court, then A might choose not to join with B, in order to maintain complete diversity. And if A wants to keep the case against X in state court, then A might choose to join with B, destroying complete diversity. In sum, when lawyers think about party structure, one of their considerations is how joinder of particular plaintiffs or defendants affects federal jurisdiction based on the parties' citizenship.

(c) Determining Citizenship

To determine whether a court has diversity-of-citizenship jurisdiction you obviously have to know the citizenship of the parties. Not so obviously, determining a party's citizenship can get complicated.

(i) Corporations

When the litigant is a corporation, the diversity jurisdiction statute defines citizenship two ways. *See* 28 U.S.C. §1332(c). First, a corporation is considered a citizen of its state of incorporation, which means the state under whose laws the corporation was formed. In addition, a corporation is considered a citizen of the state of its principal place of business. This means that a corporation can have more than one state of citizenship for purposes of diversity jurisdiction. General Motors Corporation is incorporated in Delaware, and has its principal place of business in Detroit, Michigan. For diversity jurisdiction, General Motors is considered a citizen of both Delaware and Michigan. Starbucks Corporation is a Washington corporation with its principal place of business in Seattle, Washington. For diversity jurisdiction, Starbucks is simply a citizen of Washington. If a corporation has been incorporated under the laws of multiple states or countries, it is considered a citizen of each one, but a corporation has only one principal place of business for purposes of diversity jurisdiction.

Whereas the state of incorporation is very straightforward, the principal place of business has the potential to be more ambiguous. How do courts determine a company's principal place of business? In the past, some courts used a "nerve center" test, focusing on the location of corporate headquarters, while others used a "muscle" test, focusing on where the bulk of the company's day-to-day operations were located. In *Hertz Corp. v. Friend*, 559 U.S. 77 (2010), the Supreme Court adopted the nerve center test.

In *Hertz*, two California citizens sued Hertz Corporation in California state court, and Hertz removed the case to federal court. Hertz argued that the federal court had diversity jurisdiction because the plaintiffs were citizens of California and Hertz was incorporated in Delaware and headquartered in New Jersey. The plaintiffs argued that complete diversity was lacking because, despite Hertz's corporate headquarters in New Jersey, the company had more car rental locations in California.

The district court decided that Hertz was a citizen of California because of its significant business operations there, and the court of appeals affirmed, but the Supreme Court unanimously vacated the judgment. The Supreme Court ruled that the principal place of business, for purposes of diversity jurisdiction, is the nerve center of the corporation, not necessarily the place where most of its business is conducted:

> We conclude that "principal place of business" is best read as referring to the place where a corporation's officers direct, control, and coordinate the corporation's activities. It is the place that Courts of Appeals have called the corporation's "nerve center." And in practice it should normally be the place where the corporation maintains its headquarters—provided that the headquarters is the actual center of direction, control, and coordination, *i.e.,* the "nerve center," and not simply an office where the corporation holds its board meetings (for example, attended by directors and officers who have traveled there for the occasion).

The Court justified its decision, in part, on its preference for simple jurisdictional rules:

> [A]dministrative simplicity is a major virtue in a jurisdictional statute. Complex jurisdictional tests complicate a case, eating up time and money as the parties litigate, not the merits of their claims, but which court is the right court to decide those claims. Complex tests produce appeals and reversals, encourage gamesmanship, and, again, diminish the likelihood that results and settlements will reflect a claim's legal and factual merits. . . . Simple jurisdictional rules also promote greater predictability. Predictability is valuable to corporations making business and investment decisions. Predictability also benefits plaintiffs deciding whether to file suit in a state or federal court.

The bottom line is that to determine a corporation's principal place of business for purposes of defining its state of citizenship under the diversity jurisdiction statute, look for the company's main corporate headquarters. Thus, even though Starbucks has over 3,000 coffee shops in California and fewer than 1,000 in Washington (as of 2019), the principal place of business of Starbucks Corporation for purposes of determining its citizenship for diversity jurisdiction is Washington, where its headquarters are located.

(ii) Unincorporated Associations

Partnerships, labor unions, and other unincorporated associations are treated differently from corporations. For purposes of diversity jurisdiction, such entities are considered citizens of every state in which any member is a citizen. In other words, if partners are citizens of Minnesota, Wisconsin, and Illinois, then the partnership is a citizen of all three states. The Supreme Court recently applied this concept to a real estate investment trust, holding that for purposes of diversity jurisdiction, the trust (which is not a corporation) possessed the citizenship of all of its shareholders, and therefore the federal court lacked diversity jurisdiction. *Americold Realty Trust v.*

ConAgra Foods, Inc., 136 S. Ct. 1012 (2016). As a practical matter, this definition of citizenship, combined with the complete diversity requirement, makes it relatively unlikely that diversity jurisdiction will exist in disputes involving nationwide unions, large multistate partnerships, or other unincorporated entities with widespread membership.

(iii) Individuals

For purposes of diversity jurisdiction, courts determine the citizenship of individual United States citizens based on their *domicile*. Domicile means a person's home. More precisely, it means physical presence plus intent to remain indefinitely. At any given moment, every individual has a single domicile. No one is without domicile, and no one has multiple domiciles. You can see why this is a useful way to define citizenship for purposes of jurisdiction.

Suppose X owns a vacation house in Maine and often travels to New York, but X's primary home is in New Jersey. On these facts, X's domicile is New Jersey. If X leaves New Jersey to wander the country for a year, X remains a New Jersey domiciliary unless and until X takes up residence in another state with an intent to remain there indefinitely. If X leaves New Jersey to take a two-year position in California, but does not intend to remain in California after the job ends, then X is still a New Jersey domiciliary even while living in California. Even if X never intends to return to New Jersey—"I don't know where I'll end up when I leave California after this job, but I'm never going back to Jersey!"—X is still a New Jersey domiciliary until the moment when X takes up residence somewhere with an intent to stay there.

As you read the following case, consider the difficulties that arise when courts apply the concept of domicile to individuals whose lives touch multiple states.

APONTE-DÁVILA v. MUNICIPALITY OF CAGUAS
828 F.3d 40 (1st Cir. 2016)

Lynch, Circuit Judge.

José Aponte-Dávila appeals from the district court's dismissal of his negligence suit for lack of subject-matter jurisdiction. Aponte-Dávila invokes the federal courts' diversity jurisdiction, arguing that because he was domiciled in Texas and the defendants were domiciled in Puerto Rico at the time the suit was filed, there was complete diversity. The district court found, instead, that both Aponte-Dávila and the defendants were domiciled in Puerto Rico and dismissed the case.

We conclude otherwise, that Aponte-Dávila had not abandoned his Texas domicile while receiving medical care in Puerto Rico, and, that in any event, he had reinstated his Texas domicile before suit was filed. We reverse and remand.

I

On May 9, 2013, Aponte-Dávila filed a complaint in the Puerto Rico federal district court against the Municipality of Caguas ("Municipality"), Consolidated Waste Service

Corporation ("ConWaste"), and MAPFRE/ PRAICO, ConWaste's insurance provider. The issue in this case is where Aponte-Dávila was domiciled as of May 9, 2013.

[The complaint alleged that Aponte-Dávila suffered injuries when he slipped and fell while trying to pass a dumpster obstructing a sidewalk. Aponte-Dávila alleged that the Municipality and ConWaste, the owner of the dumpster, were negligent. The district court granted the defendants' motion to dismiss for lack of subject matter jurisdiction under Federal Rule of Civil Procedure 12(b)(1).]

The dispute between the parties boils down to whether on May 9, 2013, the date the complaint was filed, Aponte-Dávila was domiciled in Texas, creating complete diversity and affording the federal district court jurisdiction, or Puerto Rico, defeating complete diversity and depriving the federal district court of jurisdiction.

II

The facts relevant to Aponte-Dávila's domicile, which are largely undisputed, are as follows. Aponte-Dávila was born in Río Piedras, Puerto Rico, in 1963. In the late 1980s, after service with the U.S. Army Reserve in Puerto Rico and the Puerto Rico National Guard, he moved to Florida to work as a professional truck driver. After a few years as a commercial dump truck driver in Florida, he moved back to Puerto Rico.

In 1998, he moved to Arkansas and obtained an Arkansas commercial driver's license. From 1999 to 2004, he worked as an interstate truck driver based in Arkansas. In 2004, Aponte-Dávila left his job in Arkansas, moved to Laredo, Texas, and began working for a trucking company called Landstar. Later that year, Aponte-Dávila left Landstar and relocated to Puerto Rico to help his father, who had fallen ill,

with his asphalt business. In 2007, after his father's health improved, he returned to Texas to continue his truck driving career and purchased, with the help of a loan from First National Bank in Laredo, a third semi-trailer truck, a 2001 Freightliner Condo. From 2007 to 2010, Aponte-Dávila, based out of Laredo, worked for a trucking company called Land Carrier. He stated that because he was a truck driver, he would frequently stay in Laredo at a hotel, at the trucking company's terminal, or in a small utility apartment, and while on the road he often lived out of his truck. In 2008, he obtained a Texas Class "A" commercial driver's license.

On July 13, 2009, while in Puerto Rico to marry his second wife, María Teresa Báez, Aponte-Dávila suffered the injury giving rise to the instant lawsuit. He remained bedridden in Puerto Rico until he was able to return to Texas. After the accident, he obtained medical coverage through Puerto Rico's government health plan, then known as "Reforma." When applying for benefits, Aponte-Dávila provided Báez's address in Caguas, Puerto Rico. He explained that he gave Báez's address because that was where he was staying while recovering. He and Báez divorced two years later in September of 2011.

Aponte-Dávila returned to Texas in late 2009 after recuperating from his accident. The back pain caused by his accident prevented him from completing his truck routes with Land Carrier on schedule, so he eventually left Land Carrier and began working for another trucking company called Hotfoot Logistics, which had a terminal in Laredo. His time at Hotfoot Logistics was short lived; after three months, he found that his persistent back pain prevented him from continuing driving.

In September 2010, about a month after he left Hotfoot Logistics, and still based out of Laredo, he started working for Warren Transport. On a personnel form that Aponte-Dávila filled out for Warren Transport titled "Warren Transport wants to get to know you!!!" he wrote "Caguas, Puerto Rico" in the blank space following "I make my home in." He later explained that he had been directed by Warren Transport to do so. The form also asked him to provide the names of his family members as well as a list of interests and hobbies. During his deposition, Aponte-Dávila stated that a dispatcher had told him that the purpose of the form was to list the names of individuals who would be authorized to ride along with him in his truck and so he listed Caguas because that is where Báez, to whom he was still married at that point, lived. According to Aponte-Dávila, Warren Transport management already knew that he lived in Laredo. On other Warren Transport forms, he listed his address as a P.O. Box in Laredo.

For the tax years 2007 to 2012, Aponte-Dávila filed all of his federal tax returns using his Texas address. From 2000 to 2014, he never filed state personal income tax returns in Puerto Rico.

Starting in 2010, Aponte-Dávila began traveling back to Puerto Rico for longer visits to receive physical therapy, staying at Báez's residence in Caguas. In September 2011, he applied for and received a disability parking permit in Puerto Rico. In the application for the permit, he stated that his address was in Puerto Rico. In January 2012, he obtained a Puerto Rico driver's license, which also listed his address as being in Caguas. He explained that the address he provided was Báez's, even though by that point they had been divorced for several months.

On May 27, 2012, Aponte-Dávila suffered a bout of paralyzing back pain that left him immobile on the ground of a parking lot in Laredo. A week later, he resigned from Warren Transport, sold his truck, threw away everything he had in the truck including clothes and documents, and returned to Puerto Rico to recover at his parents' house in Canóvanas. In early 2013, he filed a Merchant's Registry Certificate with the Puerto Rico Department of Treasury, listing his address as being in Caguas. He also submitted an application to the Medicaid Program of the Puerto Rico Department of Health. In February 2013, his Texas commercial driver's license expired.

Aponte-Dávila returned to Laredo at the end of April 2013. He stayed with a friend and began looking for work as an interstate trucker. . . .

On May 9, 2013, the day the instant lawsuit was filed in federal district court in Puerto Rico, Aponte-Dávila says that he "was physically present in Laredo, Texas organizing his personal and professional affairs to continue residing and working there as he had done the previous nine (9) years since approximately 2004."

In July 2013, Aponte-Dávila leased an apartment in Laredo. Around the same time, he set up electric and cable services with local Texas providers. According to Aponte-Dávila, once he moved into his apartment, he notified the Texas Department of Public Safety of his new address, and on September 30, 2013, a new Texas commercial driver's license was issued to him listing the new address. He says that the Texas Department of Public Safety took and kept the license that had been issued to him on May 6, 2013.

Aponte-Dávila found a job as a contract driver for a company operating out of Laredo in July 2013, but because of his back pain he was only able to complete a handful of trips by early 2014. In September 2013, he filled out a Texas voter registration application, and in November 2013 he voted in Texas. . . .

In July 2014, unable to work and declared disabled by the Social Security Administration, he returned to Puerto Rico. He rented an apartment in Puerto Rico in December 2014 and as of January 2015 had not returned to Texas.

III

On June 23, 2015, the district court granted the defendants' motion to dismiss for lack of diversity jurisdiction, finding that Aponte-Dávila was domiciled in Puerto Rico on the date that his case was filed. The court found that while Aponte-Dávila "was not a resident of Puerto Rico from the early 1980s until around 2007," after his 2009 injury he reestablished domicile in Puerto Rico because "he refocused his life to obtain medical treatment in Puerto Rico." The district court noted that by 2012 Aponte-Dávila had "sold his Freightliner Condo truck, thr[own] away everything he owned, . . . traveled to Puerto Rico," "let his Texas Commercial Driver's License expire," and "severed relevant links to Texas, making Puerto Rico his home." The court also placed particular emphasis on forms that Aponte-Dávila submitted to several entities between 2009 and 2013 in which he listed his residence as Puerto Rico. According to the district court, though he "may have sought to reestablish links with Texas in July 2013 (lease agreement); September 2013 (car purchase, and Consumer Account Application with Wells Fargo Bank); and October 2013 (voting registration certificate)," these events all occurred after May 2013 and therefore could not support a finding that he had abandoned his domicile in Puerto Rico and established a new domicile in Texas before the filing of the instant lawsuit.

This appeal followed.

IV

Though the issue of domicile is a mixed question of law and fact, we nevertheless review the district court's determination of the plaintiff's domicile for clear error. This standard applies where, as here, the district court did not hold an evidentiary hearing but instead relied on a paper record. . . .

V

Federal courts have subject-matter jurisdiction over cases in which the amount in controversy exceeds $75,000 and where the parties are "citizens of different States."[2] 28 U.S.C. §1332(a)(1). Diversity must be complete—"the presence of but one nondiverse party divests the district court of original jurisdiction over the entire action." *Strawbridge v. Curtiss*, 7 U.S. 267, 267 (1806). "For purposes of diversity, a person is a citizen of the state in which he is domiciled." *Padilla-Mangual* [*v. Pavía Hosp.*, 516 F.3d 29, 31 (1st Cir. 2008)]. "A person's domicile 'is the place where he has his true, fixed home and principal establishment, and to which, whenever he is absent, he has the intention of returning'." *Rodriguez-Diaz v. Sierra-Martinez*, 853 F.2d 1027, 1029 (1st Cir. 1988). Proving domicile requires two showings: (1) "physical presence in a place," and (2) "the intent to make that place one's home." *Valentin* [*v. Hosp. Bella Vista*, 254 F.3d 358, 366 (1st Cir. 2001)]. Necessarily then, domicile and residence are not the same thing. After it is established, a domicile "persists until a new one is acquired." *Id.*

---

[2] For the purpose of §1332, Puerto Rico is a "State[ ]." 28 U.S.C. §1332(e).

"Once challenged, the party invoking diversity jurisdiction must prove domicile by a preponderance of the evidence." *García Pérez v. Santaella*, 364 F.3d 348, 350 (1st Cir. 2004). There are a variety of factors that are relevant to determining a party's domicile: "current residence; voting registration and voting practices; location of personal and real property; location of brokerage and bank accounts; membership in unions, fraternal organizations, churches, clubs and other associations; place of employment or business; driver's license and other automobile registration; [and] payment of taxes." *Id.* at 351. . . .

VI

We believe that the district court committed clear error. In a nutshell, the evidence establishes that Aponte-Dávila was domiciled in Texas before his 2009 accident, that his stays in Puerto Rico while obtaining medical care needed in the aftermath of the accident were insufficient to effect a change of domicile from Texas to Puerto Rico, and that accordingly he was domiciled in Texas on the date his case was filed.

No one seriously disputes that Aponte-Dávila was domiciled in Texas before his accident. He first moved to Laredo, Texas, in 2004 and began working for Landstar. Though he left Texas in late 2004 to go to Puerto Rico, it is undisputed that the purpose of this relocation was to help his sick father with his business. There is nothing to suggest that this move was intended to be permanent. In fact, once his father's health improved in 2007, Aponte-Dávila returned to Laredo. He then obtained a loan from the First National Bank in Laredo to purchase a 2001 Freightliner Condo truck, and he spent the next two and a half years working out of Laredo for a trucking

company called Land Carrier. In 2008, he obtained a Texas Class "A" commercial driver's license. Laredo was his base of operations during his tenure at Land Carrier. Moreover, for tax years 2007 to 2012, he filed all of his federal tax returns using his Texas address. As of the date of his accident, July 13, 2009, Aponte-Dávila was clearly domiciled in Texas.

Where the district court erred was in concluding that Aponte-Dávila had changed his domicile from Texas to Puerto Rico after his accident, as of the time he filed suit in Puerto Rico.

The bulk of the district court's justification for finding that Aponte-Dávila was domiciled in Puerto Rico is based on representations that Aponte-Dávila made about his residence in various forms including an application to participate in Puerto Rico's "Reforma" health plan,[3] an application for Medicaid benefits, an application for a disability parking permit, a form submitted to the Puerto Rico Department of Treasury, and a form submitted to Warren Transport. He also obtained a Puerto Rico driver's license that listed an address in Caguas. The district court reasoned that "[s]trong evidence of domicile is found in representations a party has made on reports and documents submitted to third parties," and, citing a treatise, that "[a]lthough residence alone is not the equivalent of

---

[3] The district court and the defendants add that the "Reforma" health plan is limited to residents of Puerto Rico. Aponte-Dávila disagrees. We need not resolve this dispute. For the purposes of our inquiry, it does not matter whether [Puerto Rico's "Reforma" health plan] is actually limited to residents or not—residence is not the same as domicile. Rather, his participation in the plan is relevant to the extent that it demonstrates his intent, by claiming Puerto Rican residence, to make Puerto Rico his domicile.

domicile, the place of residence is prima facie evidence of a party's domicile."[4]

While the district court was certainly correct that residence is relevant to the question of domicile and that representations of one's residence in certain instances "are entitled to significant weight," the court erred by placing altogether too much emphasis on this factor in light of the circumstances. When considered in the context of Aponte-Dávila's reason for being in Puerto Rico in the first place—medical treatment—these representations about his residence, many tied to getting such treatment, do not themselves result in a change in domicile.

Aponte-Dávila shuttled back and forth between Texas and Puerto Rico between 2009 and 2013 so that he could obtain medical care and assistance from his family as he attempted to recover from the injuries from his fall. The district court concluded that Aponte-Dávila "severed relevant links to Texas." But the record shows that he never stopped returning to Texas to work and that he continued to file his federal taxes from Texas. He never filed tax returns in Puerto Rico. When he was in Puerto Rico, he stayed with his parents or with his ex-wife, Báez. After his last stay in Puerto Rico from May 2012 to April 2013, he returned to Texas where he renewed his Texas commercial driver's license, leased an apartment in Laredo, reactivated his bank accounts at Wells Fargo, and registered to vote in Texas. While several of these actions occurred after the filing of the lawsuit, "subsequent events may bear on the sincerity of a professed intention to remain." In this case, the actions that Aponte-Dávila took in Texas after filing his lawsuit are strong evidence that he never harbored an intention to change his domicile to Puerto Rico. . . .

"Jurisdictionally speaking, residency and citizenship are not interchangeable." *Valentin*, 254 F.3d at 361 n.1. . . . Indeed, "[w]hile a person may have more than one residence, he can only have one domicile." *Bank One v. Montle*, 964 F.2d 48, 53 (1st Cir. 1992). This is why residence is not dispositive of the domicile inquiry but rather one of many factors that the federal courts consider when determining a party's domicile. Given the circumstances of Aponte-Dávila's ongoing medical treatment in Puerto Rico, the unremarkable fact that he claimed a residence in Puerto Rico and listed it on a variety of forms, several of which pertain directly to his medical condition and treatment, is weak evidence of an intent to remain in Puerto Rico indefinitely and give up his Texas domicile, particularly in light of his continued ties to Texas while he was recovering in Puerto Rico. . . .

In the end, that Aponte-Dávila, within days of returning to Texas, renewed his commercial driver's license in order to return to his truck-driving career in Texas is evidence that he never intended to forego his Texas domicile in favor of Puerto Rico.[6]

---

[4] The Supreme Court long ago stated that "[t]he place where a person lives is taken to be his domicil until facts adduced establish the contrary." *Anderson v. Watt*, 138 U.S. 694, 706 (1891). This principle, however, does not provide an end run around the longstanding test for domicile. Looking at residency alone is an insufficient analysis if there are other facts, and this court has consistently required analysis of a variety of factors to determine a party's domicile.

[6] We also believe the district court erroneously disregarded the significance of Aponte-Dávila's license renewal. The district court appeared to equate Aponte-Dávila's commercial license with a noncommercial one. Aponte-Dávila's renewal of his commercial license, a more onerous task than renewing a noncommercial driver's license, is indicative of his intent to return to his longstanding career in Texas despite obtaining medical care in Puerto Rico.

We find that on the evidence presented, Aponte-Dávila has shown that he did not abandon his Texas domicile in favor of a Puerto Rico domicile after his accident in 2009, and that Texas necessarily remained his domicile until at least the date that his lawsuit was filed. We add, however, that even if we were to agree that Aponte-Dávila had shifted his domicile to Puerto Rico for the period during which he was seeking medical treatment, we believe that the district court erred in concluding that Aponte-Dávila had not reestablished Texas as his domicile before filing his complaint. Aponte-Dávila returned to Texas, his prior domicile, and immediately took the significant step of renewing his commercial driver's license in order to resume his truck-driving career. Shortly thereafter, he rented an apartment, reactivated his bank accounts, registered to vote, and voted in Texas. Though events that happen after the filing of the complaint are "not part of the primary calculus," they still "bear on the sincerity of a professed intention to remain."

VII

The judgment of the district court is reversed and the case is remanded for further proceedings consistent with this opinion.

Notes & Questions

1. Whenever you consider diversity jurisdiction under section 1332, chart the citizenship of the parties to see whether the complete diversity requirement is met. Each of the defendants in *Aponte-Dávila* is a citizen of what state, commonwealth, or territory? What does José Aponte-Dávila assert is his own citizenship? What do the defendants assert is Aponte-Dávila's citizenship?

2. Note how domicile works when a person moves from one place to another. Until a new domicile is established, the person remains a domiciliary of the prior state of domicile, even if the person resides in a new place. What evidence did the court find most useful on the question of whether Aponte-Dávila had established a new domicile?

3. The court states that "the issue in this case is where Aponte-Dávila was domiciled as of May 9, 2013." Why is that the relevant date?
    Citizenship can change over time. An individual may change domicile by moving from one state to another, or a corporation's principal place of business may shift. Suppose a litigant was a citizen of state A during the time period when the events occurred that gave rise to the claim, but the litigant was a citizen of state B on the date the complaint was filed. For purposes of diversity jurisdiction, should the court consider the litigant a citizen of state A or state B? Why? Now, suppose a litigant's citizenship changes during the course of the litigation. Suppose that on the date the complaint is filed, the litigant was a citizen of state A, but by the time a party moves to dismiss for lack of jurisdiction, the litigant had become a citizen of state B. For purposes of diversity jurisdiction, should the court consider the litigant a citizen of state A or state B? A long-standing rule

holds that the moment for determining citizenship is when the case was filed—not some earlier moment when the underlying facts occurred, and not some later moment when the court is asked to decide the jurisdictional issue. *See, e.g., LeBlanc v. Cleveland,* 248 F.3d 95, 99-100 (2d Cir. 2001). If complete diversity exists at the time of filing, the federal court retains jurisdiction even if one of the parties later changes citizenship. What justifications can you see for this rule?

4. Domicile issues often arise with regard to persons who are in transitional periods in their lives. Consider your own living situation and those of your law school classmates. You probably know people who moved to a new state to attend law school, and who may or may not remain in that state after completing law school. What facts would you need to know to determine their domicile?

In litigation over whether Mark Zuckerberg stole the idea for Facebook, a district court ruled in 2007 that Zuckerberg was still domiciled at his parents' house in New York even though he had moved to California. At the time the case was filed, Zuckerberg's intent "was to stay in California for a semester or maybe two to work on Facebook and see how it would go, but then he planned to return to school at Harvard." *ConnectU LLC v. Zuckerberg,* 482 F. Supp. 2d 3, 31 (D. Mass. 2007), *rev'd on other grounds,* 522 F.3d 82 (1st Cir. 2008).

5. The *Aponte-Dávila* court noted that once jurisdiction has been challenged, the party invoking diversity jurisdiction must prove domicile by a preponderance of the evidence. Ultimately, domicile comes down to the specific facts. What if the party that needs to establish the opposing party's domicile lacks relevant information? A court may order limited discovery into the jurisdictional facts. Thus, even if the jurisdictional issue arises on a motion to dismiss and discovery on the merits has not yet begun, a court can allow parties to access information relevant to the jurisdictional issue.

6. If complete diversity is lacking, can a party create diversity jurisdiction by making someone else the owner of the claim? Suppose a Texas plaintiff wishes to sue a Texas defendant in federal court. She assigns her claim to a friend who is domiciled in California and lets the Californian file the case on her behalf. While there are plenty of legal ways for plaintiffs and defendants to alter the presence or absence of diversity jurisdiction, this blatant attempt to manufacture jurisdiction would fail. Under 28 U.S.C. §1359, a "district court shall not have jurisdiction of a civil action in which any party, by assignment or otherwise, has been improperly or collusively made or joined to invoke the jurisdiction of such court."

7. Courts have recognized two longstanding exceptions to diversity jurisdiction: the "domestic relations exception" and the "probate exception." Although neither exception is compelled by the test of the statute or the Constitution, federal courts have declined to take diversity jurisdiction over divorce, child custody, and probate matters. The Supreme Court, while recognizing these exceptions, has rejected expansive applications of them. *See Marshall v. Marshall,* 547 U.S. 293 (2006) (probate); *Ankenbrandt v. Richards,* 504 U.S. 689 (1992) (domestic relations).

(2) Amount in Controversy

In addition to the requirement of complete diversity, section 1332 imposes an amount-in-controversy requirement. The point is to reserve federal judges for high-stakes work. Remember that federal district courts are a limited resource—each federal judge under Article III is appointed by the President and confirmed by the Senate, and these federal judges are vastly outnumbered by state judges. If a case arises under federal law, the current thinking goes, it makes sense to give litigants the right to have the case decided by a federal judge. But if a case does not arise under federal law, and the basis for jurisdiction is diversity of citizenship, then federal judges should not be burdened with the case unless the stakes are high enough. Currently, for diversity jurisdiction, the amount in controversy must be greater than $75,000. *See* 28 U.S.C. §1332(a) ("civil actions where the matter in controversy *exceeds* the sum or value of $75,000, exclusive of interest and costs") (emphasis added). Over the years, Congress has amended the statute occasionally to increase the amount. The amount was raised in 1988 from in excess of $10,000 to in excess of $50,000, and again in 1996 to in excess of $75,000.

[handwritten margin note: $75,000.01]

How do courts determine the amount in controversy? Often, it is simply a matter of looking at the amount demanded by the plaintiff in the complaint. Complications arise in four situations: (a) when a complaint demands an impossible amount, (b) when a party seeks nonmonetary relief such as an injunction, (c) when a lawsuit includes multiple claims or parties, or (d) when the lawsuit is a class action.

(a) Plaintiff's Demand

As a starting point, courts generally consider the amount in controversy to be whatever amount the complaint demands. If the complaint demands a specific dollar amount that is at least $75,000.01, then it satisfies the requirement. In some courts, a plaintiff may simply state that "plaintiff demands an amount in excess of $75,000." The question is not whether or how much the plaintiff actually wins, but rather how much the complaint demands. If an Oregon plaintiff sues a Texas defendant for negligence, demanding $100,000 in damages, then a federal court has subject matter jurisdiction, even if the plaintiff ultimately recovers only $50,000, or even if the plaintiff loses the case.

The plaintiff's demand does not control, however, if it appears *to a legal certainty* that the claim is really for less. If the plaintiff *cannot* recover an amount that meets the amount-in-controversy requirement, then the court lacks jurisdiction. Here is how the Supreme Court stated the rule in *St. Paul Mercury Indemnity Co. v. Red Cab Co.*, 303 U.S. 283, 288-89 (1938):

> [T]he sum claimed by the plaintiff controls if the claim is apparently made in good faith. It must appear to a legal certainty that the claim is really for less than the jurisdictional amount to justify dismissal. The inability of plaintiff to recover an amount adequate to give the court jurisdiction does not show his bad faith or oust the jurisdiction. Nor does the fact that the complaint discloses the existence of a valid defense to the claim. But if, from the face of the pleadings, it is apparent to a legal certainty that the plaintiff cannot

recover the amount claimed or if, from the proofs, the court is satisfied to a like certainty that the plaintiff never was entitled to recover that amount, and that his claim was therefore colorable for the purpose of conferring jurisdiction, the suit will be dismissed.

For example, if an applicable statute caps the damages at $10,000 or if the lawsuit is to recover on an exact $10,000 debt, but the complaint implausibly demands more than $75,000, the court will ignore the impossible amount demanded in the complaint and hold the amount-in-controversy requirement unmet.

STRATEGY SESSION

Just as plaintiffs may exercise some control over diversity jurisdiction by choosing which parties to join among those available, they also may exercise some control by deciding what relief to demand in the complaint. Suppose complete diversity exists and the plaintiff could reasonably claim an amount slightly over $75,000. The plaintiff has the power to avoid diversity jurisdiction by demanding an amount no greater than $75,000. Such a move would be unlikely, though, if the plaintiff has a basis to demand a substantially larger amount.

(b) Nonmonetary Relief

What if the plaintiff seeks injunctive or declaratory relief rather than money damages? That is more challenging because the court must place a dollar value on ordering the defendant to do (or not to do) something. If a plaintiff seeks an order requiring specific performance of a contract, or an injunction that the defendant be required to stop disposing of chemicals in a particular way, or a declaration that the defendant's employment practices are illegal under state law, what is the amount in controversy? When the complaint does not seek a monetary remedy, how should a court determine whether "the matter in controversy exceeds the sum or value of $75,000"?

Some courts have measured the value of the remedy by its monetary value to the plaintiff. Other courts have held that either the value to the plaintiff *or* the cost to the defendant may satisfy the requirement. *See Olden v. Lafarge Corp.*, 383 F.3d 495, 503 n.1 (6th Cir. 2004) (describing the circuit split and citing cases). In *McCarty v. Amoco Pipeline Co.*, 595 F.2d 389 (7th Cir. 1979), for example, a homeowner sued to enjoin an energy company from putting an oil pipeline across the plaintiff's property. The court adopted the either-view approach and decided that even if the value of the injunction to the plaintiff was under the jurisdictional amount, the cost of the injunction to the defendant was greater than the jurisdictional amount, and therefore the jurisdictional requirement was met.

(c) Aggregation of Claims

Often, a complaint includes multiple claims or multiple parties. Can stakes be added up to meet the amount-in-controversy requirement? Courts refer to this as the question of whether the amounts may be *aggregated*. The answer depends on whether one seeks to aggregate the claims of a particular plaintiff against a particular defendant or whether one seeks to aggregate claims involving multiple parties.

A plaintiff may aggregate as many claims as he or she has against a single defendant in order to satisfy the amount. Suppose a plaintiff has a $40,000 negligence claim and a separate $40,000 breach-of-contract claim against a particular defendant. If the plaintiff joins these two claims in a single lawsuit, then the amount in controversy is $80,000, which exceeds $75,000 and therefore meets the requirement for diversity jurisdiction, even though each claim by itself would be jurisdictionally insufficient.

However, claims by or against multiple parties may not be aggregated for purposes of the amount-in-controversy requirement (the "no-aggregation rule"). *See Walter v. Northeastern Railroad Co.*, 147 U.S. 370 (1893). If Plaintiff 1 and Plaintiff 2 each have $40,000 claims against a defendant, their claims do not satisfy the amount-in-controversy requirement, even if they are joined in a single lawsuit. Similarly, if a plaintiff has claims against multiple defendants, those amounts may not be aggregated to meet the jurisdictional amount requirement. For the amount in controversy, look at each plaintiff's claims against each defendant.

AMOUNT-IN-CONTROVERSY REQUIREMENT MET

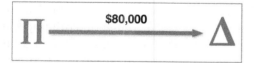 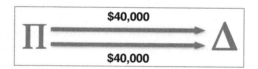

AMOUNT-IN-CONTROVERSY REQUIREMENT NOT MET

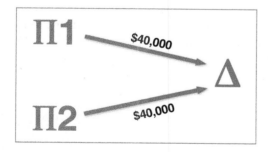 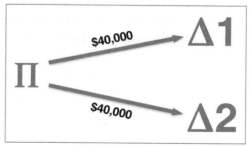

Often a plaintiff asserts a claim against multiple defendants to recover for an indivisible injury. For example, a medical malpractice plaintiff might sue both a doctor and a hospital, as well as others whose negligent conduct may have caused the plaintiff's injury. As a matter of substantive law, in some cases the defendants may be subject to joint and several liability, which means that the plaintiff can collect the full amount of damages from any of the defendants, and then the defendants may seek contribution from each other. The question arises how courts should treat claims against multiple defendants for an indivisible injury for purposes of the jurisdictional amount. When a plaintiff asserts a claim against several defendants for the same damages, the court does not divide the amount in controversy among the defendants, but rather considers the entire amount of the plaintiff's claim against each defendant. For example, suppose a plaintiff asserts a product-liability claim against both the manufacturer and the retailer of a defective automobile, and the plaintiff seeks compensatory damages of $100,000. The plaintiff is not entitled to recover twice for the same harm; rather, the plaintiff seeks to recover her damages from either defendant. This case meets the amount-in-controversy requirement because it is a $100,000 claim against each of the defendants. It is *not* a $50,000 claim against each of them. The no-aggregation rule addresses something different—the situation where damages are separable and therefore must be counted separately.

An exception to the no-aggregation rule applies to claims involving a common undivided interest, where multiple parties assert joint rather than individual rights. *See Troy Bank of Troy, Ind. v. G.A. Whitehead & Co.*, 222 U.S. 39 (1911). For example, if co-owners sue to recover property worth $100,000, alleging they own it jointly, their claim would be treated as a single $100,000 claim for purposes of the amount in controversy, rather than as two $50,000 claims. Courts have struggled with whether to extend this "common undivided interest" approach to claims by partnerships and other scenarios. Be aware that some courts may interpret it more broadly than others, but in general, think of this as a relatively infrequent exception to the general rule against aggregating claims by or against multiple parties when determining the amount in controversy. Note that the "common undivided interest" situation involves the relatively uncommon situation of joint rights asserted by plaintiffs, whereas the indivisible injury situation discussed in the prior paragraph involves the more common scenario of a plaintiff's assertion of claims against multiple defendants alleged to be liable for the plaintiff's injury.

There is one other important exception to the no-aggregation rule. In class actions, federal courts possess jurisdiction over certain class actions in which the *total* stakes are over $5 million, as the next section explains.

(3) Diversity Jurisdiction over Class Actions

Congress expanded federal subject matter jurisdiction over class actions by enacting the Class Action Fairness Act of 2005 (CAFA). In a class action, as we saw in Chapter 7, a party sues as a representative on behalf of all others who are similarly situated. For diversity jurisdiction over class actions, CAFA eliminates the complete diversity requirement and alters the amount-in-controversy requirement. This portion of the diversity jurisdiction statute is codified at 28 U.S.C. §1332(d). CAFA does not affect federal question jurisdiction; under section 1331, federal courts have the power to hear class actions that arise under federal law.

Under CAFA, any class action with at least one hundred class members is subject to federal jurisdiction if it meets minimal diversity and the aggregate amount in controversy exceeds $5 million, unless it fits into certain narrow exceptions. Minimal diversity means that at least one member of the class is a citizen of a different state from any defendant. 28 U.S.C. §1332(d)(2)(A). In class actions, it is nearly impossible *not* to satisfy minimal diversity, and intentionally so, as the point of the statute was to extend federal jurisdiction to all large class actions. As long as any two class members are citizens of different states, minimal diversity will be met because at least one of the class members must be diverse from a defendant. Similarly, as long as any two defendants are citizens of different states, minimal diversity will be satisfied because at least one of them must be diverse from a plaintiff.

Rather than the usual in-excess-of-$75,000-per-plaintiff requirement, CAFA requires over a $5 million *aggregate* amount in controversy. This means that in a class of hundreds, thousands, or millions of plaintiffs, the amounts of their claims are combined to determine the total amount. For example, if a class action includes 50,000 class members with claims averaging over $100, it meets the requirement. You can appreciate the significance of this provision when you think about how often class actions involve very large numbers of low-value claims. Not many class actions are comprised of individual claims in excess of $75,000, but lots of class actions involve over $5 million in the aggregate.

CAFA spells out a few narrow exceptions, denying diversity jurisdiction in cases where the defendants and many of the plaintiffs are from the same state. *See* 28 U.S.C. §1332(d)(3)-(4).

CAFA is the most important basis for federal jurisdiction over state law class actions, but it is not the only one. In addition to jurisdiction under CAFA, 28 U.S.C. §1332(d) (minimal diversity and $5 million aggregate amount in controversy), federal courts also may have jurisdiction over class actions based on standard diversity jurisdiction, 28 U.S.C. §1332(a) (complete diversity and $75,000 amount in controversy). For purposes of determining whether complete diversity exists for jurisdiction under section 1332(a), unlike CAFA, only the citizenship of the class representatives is considered. *See Supreme Tribe of Ben Hur v. Cauble*, 255 U.S. 356 (1921). For purposes of the amount-in-controversy requirement, the claim of each class member is considered and, unlike CAFA, the amounts cannot be added up. *See Zahn v. International Paper Co.*, 414 U.S. 291 (1973). However, supplemental jurisdiction (addressed in Part E below) may provide a basis for jurisdiction as long as at least one class member asserts a claim over $75,000. *See Exxon Mobil Corp. v. Allapattah Services, Inc.*, 545 U.S. 546 (2005). Thus, if the class representatives are completely diverse from the defendants, then the amount-in-controversy requirement can be satisfied either by showing that each class member has a claim over $75,000 (thus meeting diversity jurisdiction under *Zahn*) or by showing that at least one class member has a claim over $75,000 and the others meet the test for supplemental jurisdiction (thus satisfying diversity jurisdiction plus supplemental jurisdiction under *Allapattah*). Although technically CAFA does not override these rules for determining whether a court has standard diversity jurisdiction over a class action, as a practical matter CAFA offers a path to federal jurisdiction that is generally much easier to satisfy.

THE BIG PICTURE

In theory, neither federal courts nor state courts are superior to the other, but in practice, many lawyers perceive differences. This is one reason lawyers care about federal subject matter jurisdiction. On the whole, federal courts have greater resources than state courts. The federal judiciary is relatively small, the selection process is intense, and Article III judges have life tenure. State judges are more numerous and, in many states, elected rather than appointed. Years ago, in a famous law review article, a prominent civil liberties lawyer argued the parity of federal and state courts was a myth, at least for plaintiffs asserting constitutional rights. *See* Burt Neuborne, *The Myth of Parity*, 90 HARV. L. REV. 1105 (1977). He argued not only that federal judges were more respectful of federal constitutional rights, but also that federal judges had greater technical competence and more independence from political pressures. Not everyone agreed with Neuborne's assessment, and some said that such comparisons are unprovable. *See, e.g.,* Erwin Chemerinsky, *Parity Reconsidered: Defining a Role for the Federal Judiciary*, 36 UCLA L. REV. 233 (1988). Nonetheless, it remains common for lawyers to perceive differences and it remains true that many state courts lack the resources of federal courts. Interestingly, whereas in the 1960s and 1970s it was civil rights and civil liberties plaintiffs in particular who favored federal courts, these days large corporate defendants often favor federal courts and many plaintiffs' lawyers choose state courts. But whatever particular litigants may prefer as a strategic matter, the broader debates over whether federal courts provide a superior system of justice, rather than merely an alternative forum, are not likely to disappear anytime soon.

D. OTHER BASES FOR FEDERAL JURISDICTION

In addition to the two dominant bases for federal jurisdiction—federal question and diversity of citizenship—federal courts have several other bases for subject matter jurisdiction. Significantly, federal jurisdiction extends to cases in which the United States government is a party. *See* 28 U.S.C. §§1345 (United States as plaintiff), 1346 (United States as defendant). It extends as well to cases involving ambassadors and other public ministers. *See* 28 U.S.C. §§1251(b)(1), 1351.

Congress has enacted dozens of jurisdiction-granting statutes that establish federal subject matter jurisdiction in various areas of law. *See, e.g.,* 28 U.S.C. §§1333 (admiralty and maritime), 1334 (bankruptcy), 1337 (commerce and antitrust), 1338 (patent, trademark, and copyright), and 1343 (civil rights). Some of these statutes constitute specific applications of the general federal question jurisdiction of section 1331 and can be explained mostly as historical remnants that predate the enactment of the general federal-question-jurisdiction statute. Others, such as the statute on patent and copyright jurisdiction, retain significance because they grant *exclusive* federal jurisdiction, allowing the federal courts to be the sole arbiters of these areas of federal law.

For controversies between states, Congress not only granted exclusive federal jurisdiction but made it *original* jurisdiction in the Supreme Court. *See* 28 U.S.C. §1251(a). Thus, unlike other federal court cases that originate in district court, controversies between states go straight to the Supreme Court. For example, as we mentioned in Chapter 6, in *New Jersey v. New York*, 526 U.S. 589 (1998), the two states asserted competing claims to a portion of Ellis Island in New York Harbor. The Supreme Court appointed a prominent attorney to serve as "special master" in the case. The special master conducted a trial and made recommendations to the Court, but ultimately the decision belonged to the Supreme Court pursuant to its original jurisdiction.

E. SUPPLEMENTAL JURISDICTION

If a federal court has subject matter jurisdiction over a claim, may the federal court also adjudicate related claims that do not have an independent basis for federal jurisdiction? This is the question of supplemental jurisdiction.

(1) Fundamentals of Supplemental Jurisdiction

Supplemental jurisdiction began as a set of judicially created doctrines. The Supreme Court set forth the basic principles in *United Mine Workers v. Gibbs*, 383 U.S. 715 (1966), and *Owen Equipment & Erection Co. v. Kroger*, 437 U.S. 365 (1978). When Congress passed the supplemental jurisdiction statute in 1990, it followed the outline laid out by the Supreme Court in *Gibbs* and *Kroger* but added some twists. We will start with *Gibbs* and *Kroger* and then turn to the statute and its application.

UNITED MINE WORKERS v. GIBBS
383 U.S. 715 (1966)

BRENNAN, J.

Respondent Paul Gibbs was awarded compensatory and punitive damages in this action against petitioner United Mine Workers of America (UMW) for alleged violations of §303 of the [federal] Labor Management Relations Act and of the common law of Tennessee. The case grew out of the rivalry between the United Mine Workers and the Southern Labor Union over representation of workers in the southern Appalachian coal fields. [Tennessee Consolidated Coal Company had laid off one hundred miners. Its subsidiary, Grundy Co., then hired Paul Gibbs as a mine superintendent to attempt to open a new mine and, as part of the arrangement, gave Gibbs a contract to haul the mine's coal to a railroad loading point. Armed union members, believing Consolidated had promised them the jobs at the new mine, forcibly prevented the opening of the mine.]

Respondent lost his job as superintendent, and never entered into performance of his haulage contract. He testified that he soon began to lose other trucking contracts and mine leases he held in nearby areas. Claiming these effects to be the result of a concerted union plan against him, he sought recovery [against UMW]. The suit was brought in the United States District Court for the Eastern District of Tennessee, and jurisdiction was premised on allegations of secondary boycotts under §303. The state law claim, for which jurisdiction was based upon the doctrine of pendent jurisdiction, asserted "an unlawful conspiracy and an unlawful boycott aimed at him and (Grundy) to maliciously, wantonly and willfully interfere with his contract of employment and with his contract of haulage." [The jury concluded that the UMW had violated both section 303 and state law, and awarded Gibbs compensatory and punitive damages.]

A threshold question is whether the District Court properly entertained jurisdiction of the claim based on Tennessee law. . . .

The Court held in *Hurn v. Oursler*, 289 U.S. 238 (1933), that state law claims are appropriate for federal court determination if they form a separate but parallel ground for relief also sought in a substantial claim based on federal law. The Court distinguished permissible from non-permissible exercises of federal judicial power over state law claims by contrasting "a case where two distinct grounds in support of a single

cause of action are alleged, one only of which presents a federal question, and a case where two separate and distinct causes of action are alleged, one only of which is federal in character. In the former, where the federal question averred is not plainly wanting in substance, the federal court, even though the federal ground be not established, may nevertheless retain and dispose of the case upon the nonfederal ground; in the latter it may not do so upon the nonfederal cause of action." *Id.* at 246. . . .

Under the Rules, the impulse is toward entertaining the broadest possible scope of action consistent with fairness to the parties; joinder of claims, parties and remedies is strongly encouraged. Yet because the *Hurn* question involves issues of jurisdiction as well as convenience, there has been some tendency to limit its application to cases in which the state and federal claims are, as in *Hurn*, "little more than the equivalent of different epithets to characterize the same group of circumstances." *Id.*

This limited approach is unnecessarily grudging. Pendent jurisdiction, in the sense of judicial power, exists whenever there is a claim "arising under (the) Constitution, the Laws of the United States, and Treaties made, or which shall be made, under their Authority. . . ." U.S. Const. art. III, §2, and the relationship between that claim and the state claim permits the conclusion that the entire action before the court comprises but one constitutional "case." The federal claim must have substance sufficient to confer subject matter jurisdiction on the court. *Levering & Garrigues Co. v. Morrin*, 289 U.S. 103 (1933). The state and federal claims must derive from a common nucleus of operative fact. But if, considered without regard to their federal or state character, a plaintiff's claims are such that he would ordinarily be expected to try them all in one judicial proceeding, then, assuming substantiality of the federal issues, there is power in federal courts to hear the whole.[13]

That power need not be exercised in every case in which it is found to exist. It has consistently been recognized that pendent jurisdiction is a doctrine of discretion, not of plaintiff's right. Its justification lies in considerations of judicial economy, convenience and fairness to litigants; if these are not present a federal court should hesitate to exercise jurisdiction over state claims, even though bound to apply state law to them. *Erie R. Co. v. Tompkins*, 304 U.S. 64 (1938). Needless decisions of state law should be avoided both as a matter of comity and to promote justice between the parties, by procuring for them a surer-footed reading of applicable law. Certainly, if the federal claims are dismissed before trial, even though not insubstantial in a jurisdictional sense, the state claims should be dismissed as well. Similarly, if it appears that the state issues substantially predominate, whether in terms of proof, of the scope of the issues raised, or of the comprehensiveness of the remedy sought, the state claims may be dismissed without prejudice and left for resolution to state tribunals. There may, on the other hand, be situations

in which the state claim is so closely tied to questions of federal policy that the argument for exercise of pendent jurisdiction is particularly strong. In the present case, for example, the allowable scope of the state claim implicates the federal doctrine of preemption; while this interrelationship does not create statutory federal question jurisdiction, *Louisville & N.R. Co. v. Mottley*, 211 U.S. 149 (1908), its existence is relevant to the exercise of discretion. Finally, there may be reasons independent of jurisdictional considerations, such as the likelihood of jury confusion in treating divergent legal theories of relief, that would justify separating state and federal claims for trial, Fed. R. Civ. P. 42(b). If so, jurisdiction should ordinarily be refused....

We are not prepared to say that in the present case the District Court exceeded its discretion in proceeding to judgment on the state claim.... [T]he state and federal claims arose from the same nucleus of operative fact and reflected alternative remedies. Indeed, the verdict sheet sent in to the jury authorized only one award of damages, so that recovery could not be given separately on the federal and state claims.

It is true that the §303 claims ultimately failed and that the only recovery allowed respondent was on the state claim. We cannot confidently say, however, that the federal issues were so remote or played such a minor role at the trial that in effect the state claim only was tried. Although the District Court dismissed as unproved the §303 claims that petitioner's secondary activities included attempts to induce coal operators other than Grundy to cease doing business with respondent, the court submitted the §303 claims relating to Grundy to the jury. The jury returned verdicts against petitioner

---

[13] While it is commonplace that the Federal Rules of Civil Procedure do not expand the jurisdiction of federal courts, they do embody "the whole tendency of our decisions... to require a plaintiff to try his... whole case at one time," and to that extent emphasize the basis of pendent jurisdiction.

on those §303 claims, and it was only on petitioner's motion for a directed verdict and a judgment n.o.v. that the verdicts on those claims were set aside. The District Judge considered the claim as to the haulage contract proved as to liability, and held it failed only for lack of proof of damages. Although there was some risk of confusing the jury in joining the state and federal claims—especially since, as will be developed, differing standards of proof of UMW involvement applied—the possibility of confusion could be lessened by employing a special verdict form, as the District Court did. Moreover, the question whether the permissible scope of the state claim was limited by the doctrine of pre-emption afforded a special reason for the exercise of pendent jurisdiction; the federal courts are particularly appropriate bodies for the application of pre-emption principles. We thus conclude that although it may be that the District Court might, in its sound discretion, have dismissed the state claim, the circumstances show no error in refusing to do so. . . .

Notes & Questions

1. Be sure you understand why the Supreme Court had to consider an alternative basis for the federal court to have jurisdiction over both of Paul Gibbs' claims. Gibbs asserted two claims against the United Mine Workers union—a statutory claim under the federal Labor Management Relations Act, and a state common law claim for tortious interference with contract. The federal court had subject matter jurisdiction over the labor law claim because it arose under federal law. But what about the tort claim? There was no federal question jurisdiction over the tort claim because the claim did not arise under federal law. Nor was there diversity jurisdiction. Do you see why? (Hint: How is citizenship defined for unions and other unincorporated associations?)

2. The *Gibbs* "common nucleus of operative fact" test for supplemental jurisdiction bears a striking resemblance to the transactional test for claim preclusion (discussed in Chapter 8), as well as the "same transaction or occurrence" tests for compulsory counterclaims, crossclaims, and permissive party joinder (discussed in Chapter 7). Indeed, look at how the Supreme Court explained the policy underlying its decision: "Under the Rules, the impulse is toward entertaining the broadest possible scope of action consistent with fairness to the parties; joinder of claims, parties and remedies is strongly encouraged." These doctrines work together and reflect similar policies to facilitate bringing related claims into a single lawsuit. Joinder rules and supplemental jurisdiction make it possible for litigants to assert transactionally related claims in the same action, and claim preclusion gives litigants a strong reason to avail themselves of that opportunity.

OWEN EQUIPMENT & ERECTION CO. v. KROGER
437 U.S. 365 (1978)

STEWART, J.

In an action in which federal jurisdiction is based on diversity of citizenship, may the plaintiff assert a claim against a third-party defendant when there is no independent basis for federal jurisdiction over that claim? The Court of Appeals for the Eighth Circuit held in this case that such a claim is within the ancillary jurisdiction of the federal courts. We granted certiorari because this decision conflicts with several recent decisions of other Courts of Appeals.

I

[James Kroger was electrocuted when the boom of a steel crane next to which he was walking came too close to an electric power line. Kroger's widow filed a wrongful-death action, alleging negligence, in the United States District Court for the District of Nebraska against the Omaha Public Power District (OPPD). Federal jurisdiction was based on diversity of citizenship because Kroger was a citizen of Iowa and OPPD was a Nebraska corporation.]

OPPD then filed a third-party complaint pursuant to Fed. Rule Civ. Proc. 14(a) against the petitioner, Owen Equipment and Erection Co. (Owen), alleging that the crane was owned and operated by Owen, and that Owen's negligence had been the proximate cause of Kroger's death. [Before the District Court granted OPPD's motion for summary judgment, Kroger was granted leave to file an amended complaint naming Owen as an additional defendant. Thus, the case proceeded between Kroger and Owen alone. Owen moved to dismiss for lack of jurisdiction because its principal place of business was in Iowa, not Nebraska, and thus Owen and Kroger were both citizens of Iowa. The District Court denied the motion, and the jury thereafter returned a verdict in favor of Kroger.]

[The Court of Appeals affirmed, holding] that under this Court's decision in *Mine Workers v. Gibbs*, 383 U.S. 715 (1966), the District Court had jurisdictional power, in its discretion, to adjudicate the respondent's claim against the petitioner because that claim arose from the "core of 'operative facts' giving rise to both [respondent's] claim against OPPD and OPPD's claim against Owen." It further held that the District Court had properly exercised its discretion in proceeding to decide the case even after summary judgment had been granted to OPPD. . . .

II

It is undisputed that there was no independent basis of federal jurisdiction over the respondent's state-law tort action against the petitioner, since both are citizens of Iowa. And although Fed. R. Civ. P. 14(a) permits a plaintiff to assert a claim against a third-party defendant, it does not purport to say whether or not such a claim requires an independent basis of federal jurisdiction.

In affirming the District Court's judgment, the Court of Appeals relied upon the doctrine of ancillary jurisdiction, whose contours it believed were defined by this Court's holding in *Mine Workers v. Gibbs*, 383 U.S. 715 (1966). The *Gibbs* case differed from this one in that it involved pendent jurisdiction, which concerns the resolution of a plaintiff's federal- and state-law claims against a single defendant in one action. By contrast, in this case there was no claim based upon substantive federal law, but rather state-law tort claims against two different defendants. Nonetheless, the Court of Appeals was correct in perceiving that *Gibbs* and this case are two species of the same generic problem: Under what circumstances may a federal court hear and decide a state-law claim arising between citizens of the same State? But we believe that the Court of Appeals failed to understand the scope of the doctrine of the *Gibbs* case. . . .

[Precedent makes] clear that a finding that federal and nonfederal claims arise from a "common nucleus of operative fact," the test of *Gibbs*, does not end the inquiry into whether a federal court has power to hear the nonfederal claims along with the federal ones. Beyond this constitutional minimum, there must be an examination of the posture in which the nonfederal claim is asserted and of the specific statute that confers jurisdiction over the federal claim, in order to determine whether "Congress in [that statute] has . . . expressly or by implication negated" the exercise of jurisdiction over the particular nonfederal claim. *Aldinger v. Howard*, 427 U.S. 1 (1976).

III

The relevant statute in this case, 28 U.S.C. §1332(a)(1), confers upon federal courts jurisdiction over "civil actions where the matter in controversy exceeds the sum or value of [requisite amount in controversy] . . . and is between . . . citizens of different States." This statute and its predecessors have consistently been held to require complete diversity of citizenship. That is, diversity jurisdiction does not exist unless *each* defendant is a citizen of a different State from *each* plaintiff. Over the years Congress has repeatedly re-enacted or amended the statute conferring diversity jurisdiction, leaving intact this rule of complete

diversity. Whatever may have been the original purposes of diversity-of-citizenship jurisdiction, this subsequent clearly demonstrates a congressional mandate that diversity jurisdiction is not to be available when any plaintiff is a citizen of the same State as any defendant.

Thus it is clear that the respondent could not originally have brought suit in federal court naming Owen and OPPD as codefendants, since citizens of Iowa would have been on both sides of the litigation. Yet the identical lawsuit resulted when she amended her complaint. Complete diversity was destroyed just as surely as if she had sued Owen initially. In either situation, in the plain language of the statute, the "matter in controversy" could not be "between . . . citizens of different States."

It is a fundamental precept that federal courts are courts of limited jurisdiction. The limits upon federal jurisdiction, whether imposed by the Constitution or by Congress, must be neither disregarded nor evaded. Yet under the reasoning of the Court of Appeals in this case, a plaintiff could defeat the statutory requirement of complete diversity by the simple expedient of suing only those defendants who were of diverse citizenship and waiting for them to implead nondiverse defendants.[17]

---

[17] This is not an unlikely hypothesis, since a defendant in a tort suit such as this one would surely try to limit his liability by impleading any joint tortfeasors for indemnity or contribution. Some commentators have suggested that the possible abuse of third-party practice could be dealt with under 28 U.S.C. §1359, which forbids collusive attempts to create federal jurisdiction. The dissenting opinion today also expresses this view. But there is nothing necessarily collusive about a plaintiff's selectively suing only those tortfeasors of diverse citizenship, or about the named defendants' desire to implead joint tortfeasors. Nonetheless, the requirement of complete diversity would be eviscerated by such a course of events.

If, as the Court of Appeals thought, a "common nucleus of operative fact" were the only requirement for ancillary jurisdiction in a diversity case, there would be no principled reason why the respondent in this case could not have joined her cause of action against Owen in her original complaint as ancillary to her claim against OPPD. Congress' requirement of complete diversity would thus have been evaded completely.

It is true, as the Court of Appeals noted, that the exercise of ancillary jurisdiction over nonfederal claims has often been upheld in situations involving impleader, cross-claims or counterclaims. But in determining whether jurisdiction over a nonfederal claim exists, the context in which the nonfederal claim is asserted is crucial. And the claim here arises in a setting quite different from the kinds of nonfederal claims that have been viewed in other cases as falling within the ancillary jurisdiction of the federal courts.

[T]he nonfederal claim here was asserted by the plaintiff, who voluntarily chose to bring suit upon a state-law claim in a federal court. By contrast, ancillary jurisdiction typically involves claims by a defending party haled into court against his will, or by another person whose rights might be irretrievably lost unless he could assert them in an ongoing action in a federal court. A plaintiff cannot complain if ancillary jurisdiction does not encompass all of his possible claims in a case such as this one, since it is he who has chosen the federal rather than the state forum and must thus accept its limitations.

It is not unreasonable to assume that, in generally requiring complete diversity, Congress did not intend to confine the jurisdiction of federal courts so inflexibly that they are unable to protect legal rights or effectively to resolve an entire, logically entwined lawsuit. Those practical needs are the basis of the doctrine of ancillary jurisdiction. But neither the convenience of litigants nor considerations of judicial economy can suffice to justify extension of the doctrine of ancillary jurisdiction to a plaintiff's cause of action against a citizen of the same State in a diversity case. Congress has established the basic rule that diversity jurisdiction exists under 28 U.S.C. §1332 only when there is complete diversity of citizenship. To allow the requirement of complete diversity to be circumvented as it was in this case would simply flout the congressional command.

Accordingly, the judgment of the Court of Appeals is reversed.

Notes & Questions

1. Take the claims in *Kroger* one by one, and consider whether the federal court has subject matter jurisdiction over each claim.

   First, Kroger sued the power company, OPPD. It was a state law claim so there was no federal question jurisdiction. But the court had diversity jurisdiction over this claim. Kroger was a citizen of Iowa, and the power company was

Terminology Tip —————

In *Gibbs* and *Kroger*, the Supreme Court used the terms *pendent jurisdiction* and *ancillary jurisdiction*. To understand the cases, it helps to know the terms. *Pendent jurisdiction* referred to federal court jurisdiction over state law claims that arose out of the same facts as federal law claims over which the court had power. *Ancillary jurisdiction* referred to a wide variety of other situations in which a federal court had jurisdiction over claims that arose out of the same facts as claims over which the court had power, including counterclaims, crossclaims, and third-party claims. *Gibbs* was an example of pendent jurisdiction. The third-party claim in *Kroger* was an example of ancillary jurisdiction, and Kroger's claim against Owen was an unsuccessful attempt at ancillary jurisdiction. When Congress in 1990 enacted the supplemental jurisdiction statute, 28 U.S.C. §1367, it abandoned the language of pendent and ancillary jurisdiction. Instead, Congress adopted the all-encompassing term *supplemental jurisdiction.*

incorporated in Nebraska with its principal place of business in Nebraska, and the amount in controversy sufficed. Thus, the court had diversity jurisdiction over Kroger's claim against the power company.

Next, OPPD impleaded the equipment company, Owen. It was a state law indemnity claim, so there was no federal question jurisdiction. Owen was incorporated in Nebraska with its principal place of business in Iowa. Therefore the court lacked diversity jurisdiction over OPPD's third-party claim against Owen—both were Nebraska citizens, so complete diversity was lacking. But the court had ancillary jurisdiction over the third-party claim since it arose out of the same occurrence as Kroger's original claim against OPPD.

Finally, Kroger asserted a claim directly against Owen. Again, it was a state law claim and therefore did not give rise to federal question jurisdiction. And this claim, too, did not meet complete diversity—both Kroger and Owen were Iowa citizens. Thus, the Supreme Court had to address whether ancillary jurisdiction could apply to a claim by a plaintiff against a third-party defendant.

2. The Supreme Court's decision that the federal court lacked jurisdiction over Kroger's claim against Owen may at first seem surprising in light of *Gibbs*, since Kroger's claim against Owen arose out of the same "common nucleus of operative fact" as her claim against OPPD. But it makes sense if you look at it in terms of the requirements of diversity jurisdiction. Suppose Kroger originally sued both OPPD and Owen. Would a federal court have had jurisdiction? Do you see why the Supreme Court worried that parties might attempt to use supplemental jurisdiction as an end run around constraints on diversity jurisdiction?

(2) The Supplemental Jurisdiction Statute

In *Finley v. United States*, 490 U.S. 545 (1989), the Supreme Court acknowledged the *Gibbs* line of cases extending federal court jurisdiction to claims that arise out of the same facts as claims over which the court has original jurisdiction, but the Court raised questions about whether such jurisdiction was permissible in the absence of legislation explicitly granting such power to the federal courts:

> [T]wo things are necessary to create [federal court] jurisdiction, whether original or appellate. The Constitution must have given to the court the capacity to take it, *and an act of Congress must have supplied it.* ... To the extent that such action is not taken, the power lies dormant.

Id. at 548 (quoting *The Mayor v. Cooper*, 6 Wall. 247, 252 (1868)). In the absence of a statute, the Supreme Court in *Finley* rejected an extension of *Gibbs*, but noted that "[w]hatever we say regarding the scope of jurisdiction conferred by a particular statute can of course be changed by Congress." *Id.* at 556.

One year later, Congress accepted the implicit invitation and enacted a statute establishing supplemental jurisdiction. The federal supplemental jurisdiction statute, 28 U.S.C. §1367, grants power to the federal district courts to hear additional claims that arise out of the same facts as a claim over which the court has jurisdiction and spells out the boundaries of such jurisdiction, applying the principles the Supreme Court laid out in *Gibbs* and *Kroger*.

(a) Section 1367(a): The Grant of Jurisdictional Power

The grant of supplemental jurisdiction in section 1367(a) uses language that seems cryptic unless you understand that the statute codifies the principle of *United Mine Workers v. Gibbs*:

> Except as provided in subsections (b) and (c) or as expressly provided otherwise by Federal statute, in any civil action of which the district courts have original jurisdiction, the district courts shall have supplemental jurisdiction over all other claims that are so related to claims in the action within such original jurisdiction that they form part of the same case or controversy under Article III of the United States Constitution. Such supplemental jurisdiction shall include claims that involve the joinder or intervention of additional parties.

The reference to "the same case or controversy under Article III" links to the analysis in *Gibbs* and ratifies the holding by granting federal courts power to decide related claims even if they lack an independent jurisdictional basis. Section 1367(a)'s grant of supplemental jurisdiction over "claims that are so related ... that they form part of the same case or controversy" depends on whether the claims arise out of a "common nucleus of operative fact," as the Court expressed it in *Gibbs*.

The basic grant of supplemental jurisdiction in section 1367(a) does not distinguish between different bases of original jurisdiction or between different types of related claims, so it can work in a wide variety of situations. One useful application of supplemental jurisdiction is the *Gibbs*-type scenario in which a court has federal question jurisdiction over one claim and supplemental jurisdiction over a related state law claim. Another is a federal claim and a related state law counterclaim, crossclaim, or third-party claim. Yet another is when the court has diversity jurisdiction over an original claim and a party asserts a related counterclaim, crossclaim, or third-party claim that does not satisfy complete diversity or the amount-in-controversy requirement. As long as the additional claim arises out of the same facts as the claim over which the court has original jurisdiction, the statute's grant of supplemental jurisdiction applies.

(b) Section 1367(b): Carve-Out in Diversity Cases

The most difficult aspect of supplemental jurisdiction to master is section 1367(b)'s rejection of jurisdiction over certain claims in diversity cases. Just as one cannot really understand the section 1367(a) grant without knowing *United Mine Workers v. Gibbs*, it is hard to understand the section 1367(b) carve-out unless you know *Owen Equipment & Erection Co. v. Kroger*. Section 1367(b) codifies and extends *Kroger* by disallowing supplemental jurisdiction in particular situations where permitting jurisdiction would circumvent the complete diversity and amount-in-controversy requirement for diversity jurisdiction. Section 1367(b) therefore denies supplemental jurisdiction over certain claims for failure to meet the usual diversity jurisdiction requirements, even if the claim otherwise would have fallen within the jurisdictional grant of section 1367(a). The cases have applied this section quite literally, so pay attention to section 1367(b)'s language:

> In any civil action of which the district courts have original jurisdiction founded solely on section 1332 of this title, the district courts shall not have supplemental jurisdiction under subsection (a) over claims by plaintiffs against persons made parties under Rule 14, 19, 20, or 24 of the Federal Rules of Civil Procedure, or over claims by persons proposed to be joined as plaintiffs under Rule 19 of such rules, or seeking to intervene as plaintiffs under Rule 24 of such rules, when exercising supplemental jurisdiction over such claims would be inconsistent with the jurisdictional requirements of section 1332.

Thus, for example, under section 1367(b), if the case is in federal court solely because of diversity jurisdiction, plaintiffs may not use supplemental jurisdiction for claims against additional defendants (joined under Rule 19 or 20) or third-party defendants (joined under Rule 14). Rather, such claims must independently meet the requirements for diversity jurisdiction—complete diversity and amount in controversy—or have some other independent basis for federal jurisdiction, such as federal question jurisdiction.

The policy underlying section 1367(b), following the logic of the Supreme Court in *Kroger*, is that without this carve-out, parties might use supplemental jurisdiction to circumvent the limits on diversity jurisdiction. For example, under section 1332, a Florida plaintiff cannot sue a Texas defendant and a Florida defendant on state law claims in federal court, because complete diversity is lacking. But suppose the plaintiff argues that the court has diversity jurisdiction over the claim against the Texas defendant and supplemental jurisdiction over the claim against the Florida defendant. Section 1367(b) prevents the plaintiff from doing this end run around the complete diversity requirement. (Applying section 1367(b), this would be a claim by a plaintiff against a person made party under Rule 20.) Or suppose the Florida plaintiff sued only the Texas defendant, expecting the defendant to implead the Florida third-party defendant, and then the plaintiff asserted a claim directly against the Florida third-party defendant. Again, section 1367(b) prevents the plaintiff from achieving this end run around complete diversity. (Applying section 1367(b), this would be a claim by a plaintiff against a person made party under Rule 14.)

EXAMPLES OF PROHIBITED USES OF SUPPLEMENTAL JURISDICTION UNDER SECTION 1367(b)

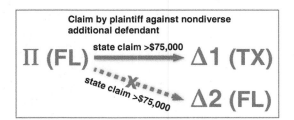

Three warnings about section 1367(b): First, remember that it does not grant jurisdiction; it merely takes it away. When analyzing supplemental jurisdiction, your starting point is always the jurisdictional grant of section 1367(a). Section 1367(b) carves out situations in which supplemental jurisdiction would otherwise have been allowed. Second, it applies *only* in diversity cases. If a case is in federal court on federal question jurisdiction, section 1367(b) is irrelevant. Third, as mentioned above, it is a sparsely worded but highly technical statute, so pay attention to its exact terms.

On a careful reading, you will see that the first part of section 1367(b) applies only to claims "by plaintiffs" (not, for example, claims by defendants against third-party defendants). You will also see that it applies only to claims "against persons made parties under Rule 14, 19, 20, or 24." The Supreme Court has interpreted this language literally. Consider the following example to try your hand at applying this portion of section 1367(b):

> Plaintiffs X and Y (both citizens of State A) sue Defendant Z (citizen of State B) in federal court on state law claims that arise out of the same set of facts. X's claim exceeds $75,000, but Y's claim does not. Does the federal court have subject matter jurisdiction over both claims?

The starting point is easy: The federal court has diversity jurisdiction over X's claim against Z (it meets the complete diversity requirement and it meets the amount-in-controversy requirement). And, as a matter of procedural *mechanism*, joinder of X and Y is permitted under Rule 20 (their claims arise out of the same transaction or occurrence and raise common questions). But now it gets hard: Does the federal court have jurisdiction over Y's claim against Z? It does not have diversity jurisdiction over Y's claim because the claim fails to meet the amount-in-controversy requirement of section 1332, and because different parties cannot aggregate amounts. How about supplemental jurisdiction? Walk through sections 1367(a) and 1367(b) carefully to address this question. Does the *logic* of section 1367(b) and *Kroger* lead you to a different conclusion from where the *language* of section 1367(b) leads you?

In *Exxon Mobil Corp. v. Allapattah Services, Inc.*, 545 U.S. 546 (2005), the Supreme Court addressed this very situation. An injured child asserted a claim of more than $75,000 against the maker of a product that had caused her injury, and her parents joined as plaintiffs to assert a claim for loss of consortium; the parents' claim was under $75,000. The Supreme Court held that the federal court not only had diversity jurisdiction over the child's claim, but also supplemental jurisdiction over the parents' claims. Although the girl and her parents were joined under Rule 20, the section 1367(b) carve-out did not apply because the parents' claims were not claims by plaintiffs *against* persons joined under Rule 20. Do you see why the Court's ruling seems contrary to the logic of *Kroger*? Do you also see the plain-language argument that supports the Court's reading of the statute?

Suppose, instead, that the issue was not that a plaintiff's claim failed to meet the *amount-in-controversy* requirement, but rather that one of the plaintiffs was not of *diverse citizenship* from the defendant:

> Plaintiff X (citizen of State A) and Plaintiff Y (citizen of State B) sue Defendant Z (citizen of State B) in federal court on state law claims that arise out of the same set of facts. Both

X's claim and Y's claim exceed $75,000. Does the federal court have subject matter jurisdiction over both claims?

One might have thought, in light of the Court's holding in *Allapattah* regarding the parents' under-amount claims, that the Court would apply similar reasoning to this question. This reasoning might lead you to imagine that a federal court would have diversity jurisdiction over X's claim against Z, and would have supplemental jurisdiction over Y's claim against Z. The Supreme Court in *Allapattah*, however, stated in dicta that the lack-of-complete-diversity situation should be treated differently from the amount-in-controversy situation. According to the Court, where complete diversity is lacking, the federal court has no original basis for jurisdiction under section 1332. The supplemental jurisdiction statute requires some initial "hook" for being in federal court—this is the point of section 1367(a)'s language about a "civil action over which the district courts have original jurisdiction"—and in the absence of complete diversity, this hook is missing. Do you agree that, for purposes of applying the supplemental jurisdiction statute, one can draw a distinction between a failure to meet the amount-in-controversy requirement and a failure to meet the complete diversity requirement?

In *Allapattah*, the Supreme Court also addressed whether a class action could be brought in federal court based on diversity jurisdiction if the class representative met the amount-in-controversy requirement, even if other class members' claims were below the amount. The Court held that when at least one class member meets the amount-in-controversy requirement, the plain language of section 1367 permits supplemental jurisdiction over the claims of the other class members. Thus, as mentioned above in our discussion of diversity jurisdiction in class actions, as long as one class member meets the amount-in-controversy requirement for diversity jurisdiction, the rest of the class need not satisfy the amount requirement because their claims are susceptible to supplemental jurisdiction. The *Allapattah* opinion explained, however, that jurisdiction still required complete diversity between the class representatives and the defendants. The significance of *Allapattah*'s holding on class action jurisdiction would have been greater had it not been for the enactment of the Class Action Fairness Act (CAFA), which, as we saw earlier in the chapter, provides an easier path to federal jurisdiction for many class actions.

(c) Section 1367(c): Discretion to Decline Jurisdiction

Just because a federal court *can* use supplemental jurisdiction doesn't mean the court *must* use it. When the Supreme Court embraced the idea of supplemental jurisdiction in *United Mine Workers v. Gibbs*, 383 U.S. 715, 726 (1966), it stated that "pendent jurisdiction is a doctrine of discretion, not of plaintiff's right." Congress included this discretion component in section 1367(c), allowing federal courts to decline to exercise supplemental jurisdiction.

Section 1367(c) describes three main circumstances under which a federal court "may decline to exercise supplemental jurisdiction over a claim." It also allows a court to decline supplemental jurisdiction for other "compelling reasons." First, a court may decline jurisdiction if "the claim raises a novel or complex issue of State law." If Paul Gibbs' tort claim had raised a cutting edge issue of state tort law, the federal court might have decided not to exercise jurisdiction over that claim because it would make more sense to allow a state court to decide the issue. The federal court would proceed to hear the federal labor law claim and would dismiss the tort claim so that it could be brought in state court if Gibbs wanted to pursue it.

Second, a court may decline jurisdiction if "the claim substantially predominates over the claim or claims over which the district court has original jurisdiction." Suppose Gibbs' federal labor law claim was limited to statutory damages of a hundred dollars but his tort claim was potentially worth tens of thousands of dollars. Under those circumstances, a court might decide that the main event was really the state law claim and might prefer not to treat it as a tag-along with the smaller federal claim.

Third, a court may decline jurisdiction if "the district court has dismissed all claims over which it has original jurisdiction." Suppose that early in the litigation, the court dismissed Gibbs' federal claim on a motion to dismiss for failure to state a claim. At that point, all that would remain is the tort claim over which the court has neither federal question nor diversity jurisdiction. Rather than proceed through discovery and trial purely on the state law claim, the court might decline jurisdiction over the pendent state claim. The plaintiff would then decide whether to pursue the claim in state court.

(d) Applying the Supplemental Jurisdiction Statute

In some ways, the supplemental jurisdiction statute clarified this corner of jurisdictional law. Instead of a bundle of evolving judge-made principles under *Gibbs*, *Kroger*, and other cases, the adoption of section 1367 put this type of jurisdiction squarely into the realm of statutory application. But that does not mean the enactment of section 1367 made the topic of supplemental jurisdiction easy. Particularly in cases involving section 1367(b), the statute presents difficult questions of statutory interpretation, and the very nature of supplemental jurisdiction means that it can arise in procedurally complex scenarios. Consider the following case, in which application of section 1367 arose as part of a Rule 19 analysis to determine whether a required party could be joined.

VIACOM INTERNATIONAL, INC. v. KEARNEY
212 F.3d 721 (2d Cir. 2000)

SOTOMAYOR, Circuit Judge.

Plaintiff-appellant Viacom International, Inc. ("Viacom") brought this diversity action in federal court against defendant-appellee Michael W. Kearney ("Kearney") seeking indemnification for costs arising from the environmental cleanup of the facilities at Taylor Forge Stainless, Inc. ("Taylor Forge"). Kearney filed counterclaims against Viacom and third-party complaints against two additional parties, one of whom filed a fourth-party complaint against Taylor Forge.

On June 21, 1999, the district court granted Kearney's motion to dismiss the action pursuant to Fed. R. Civ. P. 19, holding that Taylor Forge was a necessary and indispensable party who could not join in Kearney's counterclaims against Viacom without also destroying the court's diversity jurisdiction. We find that the district court erred in granting defendant's motion to dismiss because Taylor Forge was already present in the case as a fourth-party defendant and could file any claims necessary to protect its interests under the court's supplemental jurisdiction without destroying diversity jurisdiction.

BACKGROUND

Prior to October 1984, Gulf & Western Manufacturing Company ("G&W") owned Taylor Forge, a steel manufacturing business located in Somerville, New Jersey and incorporated under the laws of Delaware. On October 26, 1984, G&W concluded an agreement ("October Agreement") with Michael Kearney—Taylor Forge's manager—whereby G&W sold all of its shares in Taylor Forge to Kearney. In order to obtain regulatory approval for the sale, G&W and Kearney entered into a consent order with the New Jersey Department of Environmental Protection ("NJDEP") which provided that G&W would undertake a NJDEP-approved cleanup plan for the Taylor Forge facilities. Under the October Agreement, G&W assumed the responsibility for implementing the cleanup plan and Kearney agreed to indemnify G&W for third-party costs and expenses in excess of $1.75 million.

In August 1993, Kearney and Taylor Forge sued G&W's successor, Paramount Communication Realty Corporation ("Paramount"), in New Jersey state court. The complaint sought declaratory and other relief, claiming that: (1) G&W procured Kearney's

contractual indemnity commitment by fraud and misrepresentation regarding the extent of the environmental contamination and cleanup costs; and (2) the cleanup plan had not yet been implemented, thus damaging the value of Taylor Forge's business. In May 1994, the parties agreed to dismiss the New Jersey action, without prejudice, in order to explore the possibility of settlement.

On September 3, 1998, Viacom—the corporate successor of G&W and Paramount—filed this diversity action against Kearney in the United States District Court for the Southern District of New York. Viacom's complaint stated claims against Kearney for: (1) breach of his contractual indemnity obligations under Section 7.7(iii) of the October Agreement; (2) breach of Section 7.7(i) of the October Agreement, which required Kearney to prevent Taylor Forge from further contaminating the site; and (3) declaratory relief requiring Kearney to indemnify Viacom for all existing and future costs of implementing the cleanup plan in excess of $1.75 million. Significantly, Viacom's complaint stated no claim against Taylor Forge.

On November 30, 1998, Kearney answered and filed 22 counterclaims against Viacom. The thrust of Kearney's contentions was that: (1) G&W misrepresented the extent of the contamination and the projected cost and time required to clean up the Taylor Forge site; (2) G&W and its successors failed to carry out the NJDEP-approved cleanup plan in a diligent and timely manner; and (3) the cleanup costs covered by Kearney's indemnification duty refer only to the actual physical remediation of the facility and exclude tests, studies, evaluations, plans, and other similar expenses that Viacom and its predecessors incurred.

On November 20, 1998, Kearney filed a third-party complaint against Conolog Corporation ("Conolog"), Taylor Forge's neighbor, alleging that Conolog had contaminated the Taylor Forge site and was therefore liable for contribution. On March 19, 1999, Kearney filed a second third-party complaint against Camp, Dresser & McKee ("CDM"), Viacom's environmental consultant who had managed Viacom's cleanup operations at the Taylor Forge site. Kearney alleged that CDM's misfeasance exacerbated the site's environmental problems and frustrated the normal business operations of Taylor Forge. Finally, Conolog filed a fourth-party complaint against Taylor Forge on March 15, 1999, seeking contribution and indemnification.[1] Taylor Forge answered Conolog's complaint on April 15, 1999, thus becoming a fourth-party defendant in the instant litigation. Significantly, Taylor Forge has not filed any claims against any of the parties in this federal action.

Following the filing of this federal action, on November 20, 1998, Kearney and Taylor Forge reinstated their (amended) complaint in New Jersey state court against Viacom, asserting 22 claims that exactly mirrored the 22 counterclaims which Kearney filed in this action against Viacom. In April 1999, Kearney filed a motion to dismiss this action pursuant to Fed. R. Civ. P. 19, arguing that Taylor Forge was a necessary and indispensable party to the litigation.

In an opinion and order dated June 21, 1999, the district court granted Kearney's motion to dismiss, finding that Taylor Forge was a necessary and indispensable party under Rule 19 who could not join in Kearney's counterclaims against Viacom because doing so would destroy the court's diversity jurisdiction. Viacom appeals from that order.

---

[1] Conolog also filed a counterclaim against Kearney and a third-party claim against Viacom.

DISCUSSION

Fed. R. Civ. P. 19 sets forth a two-step test for determining whether the court must dismiss an action for failure to join an indispensable party. First, the court must determine whether an absent party belongs in the suit, *i.e.*, whether the party qualifies as a "necessary" party under Rule 19(a). *Provident Tradesmens Bank & Trust Co. v. Patterson*, 390 U.S. 102, 124 (1968). Rule 19(a) provides that the absent party should be joined, if feasible, where:

> (1) in the person's absence complete relief cannot be accorded among those already parties, or (2) the person claims an interest relating to the subject of the action and is so situated that the disposition of the action in the person's absence may (i) as a practical matter impair or impede the person's ability to protect that interest or (ii) leave any of the persons already parties subject to a substantial risk of incurring double, multiple, or otherwise inconsistent obligations by reason of the claimed interest.

Fed. R. Civ. P. 19(a). If a party does not qualify as necessary under Rule 19(a), then the court need not decide whether its absence warrants dismissal under Rule 19(b).

But where the court makes a threshold determination that a party is necessary under Rule 19(a), and joinder of the absent party is not feasible for jurisdictional or other reasons, Fed. R. Civ. P. 19(b), the court must finally determine whether the party is "indispensable." If the court determines that a party is indispensable, then the court must dismiss the action pursuant to Rule 19(b). . . .

Applying this analytical framework, the district court first concluded that Taylor

Forge was a "necessary" party under Rules 19(a)(2)(i) and (a)(2)(ii):

> While it is true that the only parties to the [October] Agreement are Kearney and Viacom, Taylor Forge is directly implicated as an active, if not the primary, participant in the transaction. . . . Therefore, Taylor Forge's non-party status under the Agreement should not bar its joinder as a necessary party. . . . Taylor Forge has a substantial legal interest in the environmental management of its own facility and the disposition of the action in its absence may as a practical matter impede or impair its ability to protect that interest. . . . In addition, Taylor Forge is seeking injunctive relief on nearly identical grounds from these same parties in the parallel state action, thus causing a substantial risk that multiple parties may incur inconsistent obligations should this action continue.

Viacom Int'l, Inc. v. Kearney, 190 F.R.D. 97, 101 (S.D.N.Y. 1999).

Upon finding that Taylor Forge qualified as a necessary party, the district court next determined that, for jurisdictional reasons, it would not be feasible for Taylor Forge to join with Kearney in his counterclaims against Viacom. Specifically, the district court concluded that "the joinder of Taylor Forge, which like Viacom is a Delaware-chartered corporation, would deprive this Court of its jurisdiction" under 28 U.S.C. §1332. Finally, the district court dismissed the action under Rule 19(b) because it found that "Taylor Forge is an indispensable party to this action and it must be joined."

This Court reviews a district court's Rule 19 dismissal under the abuse of discretion standard. Moreover, "[w]hen reviewing a district court's determination of its subject matter jurisdiction, we review factual findings for clear error and legal conclusions *de novo*." *Conntech Dev. Co. v. U. of Conn. Educ. Props., Inc.*, 102 F.3d 677, 681 (2d Cir. 1996).

Reviewing this matter on appeal, we find a serious question as to whether Taylor Forge qualifies as a "necessary" party under Rule 19(a) and, whether Taylor Forge is an "indispensable" party within the meaning of Rule 19(b). We need not decide these issues here, however, because we conclude that Taylor Forge was already present in the litigation and could have joined with Kearney in asserting its 22 claims against Viacom without destroying the court's subject matter jurisdiction. In other words, we hold that, as a jurisdictional matter, it is feasible for Taylor Forge to file any claims necessary to protect its interests in this case.

Viacom brought its original complaint against Kearney under 28 U.S.C. §1332, which provides that "[t]he district courts shall have original jurisdiction of all civil actions where the matter in controversy exceeds the sum or value of $75,000, exclusive of interests and costs, and is between . . . citizens of different States." 28 U.S.C. §1332(a)(1). The statute further provides that "a corporation shall be deemed to be a citizen of any State by which it has been incorporated and of the State where it has its principal place of business." 28 U.S.C. §1332(c)(1). Because Viacom and Kearney are citizens of different states[3] and the amount in controversy exceeds $75,000, Viacom's original

---

[3] The parties do not dispute the citizenship of the various entities in this case. Plaintiff Viacom is a Delaware corporation with its principal place of business in New York and defendant Kearney is a citizen of Florida. Third-party defendant CDM is a citizen of Massachusetts and third-party defendant Conolog is a Delaware corporation with its principal place of business in New Jersey. Finally, fourth-party defendant Taylor Forge is a Delaware corporation with its principal place of business in New Jersey.

complaint—and Kearney's counterclaims—clearly fell within the district court's diversity jurisdiction. *Wisconsin Dep't of Corrections v. Schacht*, 524 U.S. 381, 388 (1998) ("A case falls within the federal district court's original diversity jurisdiction only if diversity of citizenship among the parties is complete, *i.e.*, only if there is no plaintiff and no defendant who are citizens of the same State.").

In its June 19, 1999 opinion, the district court concluded that, if Taylor Forge were to join with Kearney in asserting claims against Viacom, such participation in the lawsuit would divest the court of subject matter jurisdiction. We disagree. Reviewing this legal question *de novo*, we find that the district court could have exercised supplemental jurisdiction over Taylor Forge's claims against Viacom without destroying the court's original diversity jurisdiction.

In cases where a district court has original jurisdiction, it may also exercise "supplemental jurisdiction over all other claims that are so related to claims in the action within such original jurisdiction that they form part of the same case or controversy." 28 U.S.C. §1367(a). Section 1367(b) limits the scope of that jurisdictional grant in diversity cases, providing that:

> In any civil action of which the district courts have original jurisdiction founded solely on section 1332 of this title, the district courts shall not have supplemental jurisdiction under subsection (a) over claims *by plaintiffs* against persons made parties under Rule 14, 19, 20, or 24 of the Federal Rules of Civil Procedure, or over claims by persons proposed to be joined *as plaintiffs* under Rule 19 of such rules, or seeking to intervene *as plaintiffs* under Rule 24 of such rules, when exercising supplemental jurisdiction over such claims would be

inconsistent with the jurisdictional requirements of section 1332.

28 U.S.C. §1367(b).

Significantly, §1367(b) reflects Congress' intent to prevent original plaintiffs—but not defendants or third parties—from circumventing the requirements of diversity.

By contrast, "[b]ecause defendants are involuntarily brought into court, their [claims a]re not deemed as suspect as those of the plaintiff, who is master of his complaint." *United Capitol Ins. Co. v. Kapiloff*, 155 F.3d 488, 493 (4th Cir. 1998).

Under this analysis, a non-diverse fourth-party defendant such as Taylor Forge may bring claims against plaintiff Viacom ("downsloping claims"), but Viacom may not bring claims—or counterclaims—against Taylor Forge ("upsloping claims").

Accordingly, we find that §1367(b) poses no bar to the exercise of supplemental jurisdiction over Taylor Forge's downsloping Rule 14(a) claims against Viacom, and the only issues for adjudication are (1) whether such claims are "part of the same case or controversy" under §1367(a), and (2) whether §1367(c) counsels against the exercise of such jurisdiction.[4] 28 U.S.C. §1367(a), (c).

The §1367(a) analysis gives us little pause because, just as in the New Jersey action, the substance of Taylor Forge's claims are identical to Kearney's 22 compulsory counterclaims. Therefore, Taylor Forge's claims are, by definition, "part of the same case or controversy."

Furthermore, although §1367(c) provides that the exercise of supplemental jurisdiction is discretionary, we see no reason for declining to exercise supplemental

---

[4] [T]his same supplemental jurisdiction analysis would apply to Conolog's downsloping Rule 14(a) claims against Viacom and any other claims between third-party litigants.

jurisdiction over Taylor Forge's claims in the instant case. Specifically, we note that Viacom's complaint states no claim against Taylor Forge in federal court, just as it asserted no (counter)claims against Taylor Forge in the New Jersey action. Indeed, Viacom stated at oral argument that it waives any potential claims (or counterclaims) against Taylor Forge in federal court. The exercise of supplemental jurisdiction over Taylor Forge's claims against Viacom therefore threatens no prejudice to Viacom. Moreover, the exercise of supplemental jurisdiction over Taylor Forge's claims promotes judicial economy because, if this litigation is allowed to proceed, the district court will be required to adjudicate Kearney's 22 (sister) counterclaims against Viacom.[6]

---

[6] It would appear that, through the exercise of supplemental jurisdiction over the various third-party claims in this case, this federal action could potentially duplicate the universe of parties and claims before the New Jersey state court and eliminate the need for litigation in dual fora. We express no opinion here regarding the appropriateness of a stay pending resolution of the parties' claims in the New Jersey action.

In light of the foregoing, we find that Taylor Forge could have filed any claims against Viacom necessary to protect its interests without destroying the district court's subject matter jurisdiction. This Court has emphasized in the Rule 19 context that " 'the parties actually before the court are obliged to pursue any avenues for eliminating the threat of prejudice.' " In the instant case, we view as dispositive Taylor Forge's presence in the action coupled with its failure to avoid any potential prejudice to itself by attempting to file claims against Viacom under the court's supplemental jurisdiction. We therefore hold that the district court's dismissal of this action under Rule 19 for failure to join Taylor Forge as an indispensable party constituted an abuse of discretion.

CONCLUSION

For the foregoing reasons, we vacate the district court's June 22, 1999 order granting defendant Kearney's motion to dismiss this action and remand for further proceedings consistent with this opinion.

Notes & Questions

1. To follow the analysis in *Viacom*, you must understand the party structure as well as the jurisdictional question. Start with the party structure, and use the case to check your understanding of several of the joinder rules from Chapter 7. You may find it helpful to draw a diagram of the litigation, as suggested in Chapter 7, to keep track of the various parties and claims. The case began with Viacom's complaint against Kearney. Kearney then asserted counterclaims against Viacom. Under Rule 13, were they compulsory counterclaims or permissive counterclaims? Kearney also asserted third-party claims against Conolog and CDM. What claims did Kearney assert against these third-party defendants, and why were these claims a proper use of third-party practice under Rule 14? Conolog then asserted a "fourth-party claim" against Taylor Forge. What provision of Rule 14 permitted this?

2. Next, understand Kearney's Rule 19 argument. Kearney did not merely argue that Taylor Forge was a required party (after all, Taylor Forge *was* a party), but rather that Taylor Forge was a required party to assert claims against Viacom. The Second Circuit expressed skepticism about whether Taylor Forge was a required party but ultimately found it unnecessary to decide the issue. Under Rule 19(a), what was Kearney's argument that Taylor Forge was a required party to join in Kearney's counterclaims against Viacom?

3. Do you see why Kearney wanted to argue that Taylor Forge was a required party to join Kearney in asserting claims against Viacom? The reason is *diversity jurisdiction.* What is Taylor Forge's citizenship for purposes of section 1332? What is Viacom's citizenship for purposes of section 1332? If Kearney and Taylor Forge are asserting claims against Viacom, do they meet the complete diversity requirement? Kearney's argument—which the district court found convincing—was that Taylor Forge was required in the claims against Viacom under Rule 19(a), that Taylor Forge could not join in the claims against Viacom because of the lack of subject matter jurisdiction under 28 U.S.C. §1332, and that therefore the entire action ought to be dismissed under Rule 19(b).

4. The Second Circuit reversed the district court's dismissal on the grounds that Taylor Forge could assert its claims against Viacom so dismissal was unwarranted. This is where supplemental jurisdiction enters the picture. Let's take the subject matter jurisdiction analysis step by step.

   First, what was the basis for original jurisdiction over Viacom's claim against Kearney? Did Viacom's claim arise under federal law? If not, was there diversity jurisdiction (what were Viacom's and Kearney's states of citizenship)?

   Second (but incidental to the court's analysis of the issue here), note that the federal court had both diversity jurisdiction and supplemental jurisdiction over the third-party claims against Conolog and CDM.

   Third (also incidental to the court's analysis of the issue here), note that the federal court did not have diversity jurisdiction over Conolog's fourth-party claim against Taylor Forge. Do you see why not? Even so, the federal court did have supplemental jurisdiction over this claim. Do you see why?

   Finally, turn to the question of subject matter jurisdiction that was the key to this case: Would the federal court have jurisdiction over Taylor Forge's claims against Viacom? They were state law claims, so no federal question jurisdiction. Nor was there diversity jurisdiction for Taylor Forge's claims against Viacom, as discussed in Note 3 above. How about supplemental jurisdiction? Under 1367(a), did the federal court have a basis for original jurisdiction, and did Taylor Forge's claims against Viacom form part of the same case or controversy? Under 1367(b), was this one of the situations in which supplemental jurisdiction is prohibited? And under 1367(c), was there a basis for declining supplemental jurisdiction?

5. Focus on the 1367(b) issue. Can you make an argument, in the spirit of *Kroger,* that supplemental jurisdiction ought not to be permitted for Taylor Forge's

claims against Viacom? If the original lawsuit had been filed by Kearney and Taylor Forge against Viacom, would a federal court have had jurisdiction? The Second Circuit, however, did not see it this way. Looking at the language of section 1367(b), why did the Second Circuit conclude that supplemental jurisdiction existed for Taylor Forge's claims against Viacom?

6. Suppose, after Conolog joined Taylor Forge as a fourth-party defendant, Viacom asserted a state law claim against Taylor Forge in this action. Consider whether the court would have had subject matter jurisdiction over Viacom's claim: Federal question jurisdiction? Diversity jurisdiction? Supplemental jurisdiction? If your answer is that the federal court would lack subject matter jurisdiction over Viacom's claim against Taylor Forge, why did the Second Circuit reach the opposite conclusion with regard to Taylor Forge's claim against Viacom? Does your answer change if Viacom asserted its claim against Taylor Forge *after* Taylor Forge asserted a claim against Viacom?

F. REMOVAL TO FEDERAL COURT

(1) Introduction to Removal

For a defendant, the misery of being sued is compounded by the realization that the plaintiff chose the time and place for the battle. This is where *removal* comes into play. Removal is one of defendants' most powerful counter-weapons to plaintiffs' forum selection. If the case could have been brought in federal court but the plaintiff chose to file it in state court, the removal statute, 28 U.S.C. §1441, gives a defendant the right to switch the case from state court to federal court.

When a case is removed from state court, it goes to the federal district court "for the district and division embracing the place where such action is pending." 28 U.S.C. §1441(a). A case removed from Pennsylvania state court in Philadelphia, for example, would go to the U.S. District Court for the Eastern District of Pennsylvania.

Figuring out whether a defendant may remove a case from state court to federal court largely involves going through the subject matter jurisdiction analysis explained throughout this chapter. If the claim arose under federal law, the defendant may remove the case based on federal question jurisdiction. If the parties satisfy complete diversity of citizenship and the amount in controversy exceeds $75,000, the defendant may remove the case based on diversity jurisdiction. If the case is a class action that meets minimal diversity and involves more than $5 million, the defendant may remove the case under CAFA, which includes its own removal provisions at 28 U.S.C. §1453.

When a case includes multiple defendants, removal ordinarily requires agreement among all the defendants who have been served. 28 U.S.C. §1446(b)(2). This prevents the confusion that would erupt if removal could split defendants between state and federal court. As a practical matter, this unanimity requirement usually does not create problems because co-defendants often see eye to eye on the question of whether it makes strategic sense to remove a case.

(2) Forum Defendant Exception

There is one important exception to diversity removal. In-state defendants who are sued in their home state cannot remove a case based on diversity jurisdiction. This is what section 1441(b) means when it says that a diversity action "may not be removed if any of the parties in interest properly joined and served as defendants is a citizen of the State in which such action is brought." For example, suppose a Florida plaintiff sues a Texas defendant and a Louisiana defendant in Texas state court, and the claims against each defendant exceed $75,000. Although the case meets the standard requirements of diversity jurisdiction, the defendants would not be allowed to remove the case from Texas state court to federal court because a defendant is a Texas citizen. For the same reason, they would not be allowed to remove it if it had been brought in Louisiana state court. But if the case were filed in Florida state court, or indeed any state court besides Texas and Louisiana, then the defendants could remove the case to federal court, invoking diversity of citizenship jurisdiction.

The logic behind the forum defendant rule of section 1441(b) is that a defendant should not be worried about unfavorable local bias in the defendant's "home court." Therefore, the defendant should have no need to remove based on diversity jurisdiction, which is intended to provide a federal forum to protect out-of-staters against local bias. That logic sounds reasonable as far as it goes, but note that it creates a double standard. If diversity jurisdiction should be reserved for the protection of out-of-staters, why are plaintiffs allowed to file diversity cases in federal court within their home states? In our example, if the Florida plaintiff files the case in federal court in Florida, the court would have diversity jurisdiction under section 1332. But if the defendants try to remove the case to federal court from either a Texas or Louisiana state court, they are barred by the in-state defendant rule of section 1441(b). This is one way in which the law favors a plaintiff's autonomy in choosing the forum over a defendant's desire to alter the forum. The forum defendant rule does not apply to removal of class actions under CAFA. See 28 U.S.C. §1453(b). Some defendants have found a clever way to avoid the forum defendant rule if they act quickly enough. Suppose a defendant is sued by an out-of-state plaintiff in state court in the defendant's home state, and the defendant would prefer to litigate in federal court. Assume it is a state law claim for over $75,000. Even though the action meets the complete diversity and amount-in-controversy requirements for diversity jurisdiction, one might think the defendant would be unable to remove the action to federal court because of the forum defendant rule of section 1441(b). But recall the statutory language. It says that an action may not be removed based on diversity jurisdiction if "any of the parties in interest properly joined and served as defendants" is a citizen of the forum state. Often, there is a time lag between the moment a complaint is filed and the moment the defendant is served. Under Rule 4(m) in federal court, defendants generally must be served within 90 days after the complaint is filed, and analogous state court rules similarly permit a gap between filing and service. Some in-state defendants have removed cases after the complaint was filed but before they were served, arguing that they are not barred from removal because they are not "properly joined and served as defendants." Some have labeled this technique "snap removal." You may wonder how a defendant would even know about the case if it has not yet been served with the summons and complaint. The answer is that some corporations monitor state court dockets (which are public information) electronically so they know when a complaint has been filed. The Third Circuit upheld snap removal in *Encompass Insurance Co. v. Stone Mansion Restaurant, Inc.*, 902 F.3d 147 (3d Cir. 2018). The court acknowledged that the "result may be peculiar in that it allows [the defendant] to use pre-service machinations to remove a case that it otherwise could not," but nonetheless applied the plain language of the statute to permit removal. *Id.* at 153-54. *See also Gibbons v. Bristol-Myers Squibb Co.*, 919 F.3d 699 (2d Cir. 2019) (similarly upholding such removal).

STRATEGY SESSION

Litigants sometimes go to great lengths to secure their forum selection. Plaintiffs who file in state court never like removal; if they wanted to be in federal court, they would have sued there in the first place. To make a case non-removable, a plaintiff with potential state and federal claims sometimes forgoes the federal claim to avoid removal based on federal question and supplemental jurisdiction. A plaintiff suing a defendant of diverse citizenship sometimes joins another plaintiff or another defendant to ruin complete diversity, or adds an in-state defendant to render the case non-removable under the forum defendant rule. Defendants occasionally remove these cases anyway, arguing that the non-diverse parties or in-state defendants were improperly or fraudulently joined. What ensues is a battle over removability, typically fought out in federal court on the plaintiff's motion to remand the case to state court.

(3) Removal Procedure

The most fundamental thing to know about removal procedure is this: It is not up to the state court to give permission. The defendant's lawyer does not ask the state court judge for permission to remove; rather, the lawyer simply removes the action to federal court. To put it differently, no one makes a *motion* to remove, because a motion means a request that a court order something.

Here is how it works. The defendant files a *notice of removal* in federal court. The details are spelled out in the removal procedure statute, 28 U.S.C. §1446, but the basic point is to notify the federal court of the new case on its docket. Then, the defendant notifies the other parties and the state court to let them know that the case has been removed. The defendant gives the state court a copy of the notice of removal—sometimes awkwardly called a *notice of notice of removal.* Understand what the defendant is saying with that notice of notice of removal: "Dear state court: This case is no longer yours. It's now in federal court. I'm not asking you; I'm telling you. Good-bye. Yours truly, Defendant." Don't use those exact words.

What if the plaintiff disputes the removal of the case, arguing either that the federal court lacks jurisdiction or that the defendant failed to abide by the proper procedure for removal? The plaintiff may *move to remand* the case back to state court. *See* 28 U.S.C. §1447(c). If the parties basically fight the same fight over removability on a plaintiff's motion to remand, you might wonder what difference it makes that the defendant did not have to *move* to remove. The difference is *where* the motion is made. The plaintiff moves to remand in federal court after the case has been removed. This gives the federal court, not the state court, the power to decide the question of federal subject matter jurisdiction. Remand decisions generally are not appealable. *See* 28 U.S.C. §1447(d).

Good litigators stay keenly aware of time limits that govern each aspect of civil procedure, and removal is no exception. When reading the removal procedure statute, pay attention to section 1446(b), which imposes a 30-day time limit for defendants to remove.

There is an interesting twist concerning the timeliness of removal, accounting for the possibility that a case might become removable after the initial pleading. If the original complaint does not meet the requirements for federal subject matter jurisdiction, at that point the defendant cannot remove the case. But suppose the plaintiff amends the complaint to add a federal law claim. Or suppose the plaintiff adds a claim that increases the amount in controversy to over $75,000. Or suppose the plaintiff drops one of the defendants or a co-plaintiff, and the remaining parties are completely diverse. Suddenly the case becomes removable. It would be unfair to the defendant to prohibit removal simply because more than 30 days had passed since the initial pleading, since the case was not removable at the outset. The statute therefore allows a defendant to remove within 30 days of when "it may first be ascertained that the case is one which is or has become removable." 28 U.S.C. §1446(b)(3). To avoid forum changes far into the litigation, however, the statute imposes a one-year time limit on removal based on diversity of citizenship. A recent amendment provides that the one-year time limit does not apply if a plaintiff acted in bad faith to prevent removal. 28 U.S.C. §1446(c)(1).

Problem: Test your understanding of removal and subject matter jurisdiction with the following examples. In each case, the plaintiff filed the action in Texas state court, the defendant then removed the action to U.S. District Court, and the plaintiff moved to remand the case to state court. The question in each case is whether the court should rule that removal was improper and thus grant the plaintiff's motion to remand.

a. P (an individual domiciled in Texas) sued D (a company incorporated in Delaware and headquartered in Illinois) on a state law breach-of-contract claim for $100,000.

b. P (an individual domiciled in Texas) sued D (a company incorporated in Delaware and headquartered in Texas) on a federal law civil rights claim for $50,000.

c. P (an individual domiciled in Texas) sued D1 (a company incorporated in Delaware and headquartered in Texas) and D2 (an individual domiciled in Ohio) on a state law breach-of-contract claim for $100,000, jointly and severally, in which D1 and D2 contend that their contract with P is unenforceable because it violates federal law.

d. P (an individual domiciled in California) sued D (a company incorporated in Delaware and headquartered in Texas) on a state law breach-of-contract claim for $100,000.

e. P (an individual domiciled in Texas) sued D1 (a company incorporated in Delaware and headquartered in Illinois) and D2 (an individual domiciled in Ohio) on a state law claim for $100,000. D2 prefers state court. Over D2's objection, D1 removed the case.

f. P (an individual domiciled in Texas) sued D1 (a company incorporated in Delaware and headquartered in Illinois) and D2 (an individual domiciled in Texas) on a state law claim for $100,000, jointly and severally. After two years of litigation, P amended the complaint to drop all claims against D2, and then D1 removed the case.

g. P (an individual domiciled in Texas) sued D (a company incorporated in Delaware and headquartered in Texas) asserting two claims—a federal law claim and a state law claim that arises out of the same transaction—seeking $100,000 in damages.

h. P (an individual domiciled in Texas) filed a class action against D (a company incorporated in Delaware and headquartered in Texas), asserting state law claims on behalf of a nationwide class of consumers, seeking $10,000,000 in damages for the class.

G. ANALYZING SUBJECT MATTER JURISDICTION

Let's try to pull this chapter together to see how you might analyze whether a federal court has subject matter jurisdiction. Perhaps you represent a prospective plaintiff and you are deciding whether to file suit in state or federal court. Or perhaps you represent a defendant who has been sued in state court and you are deciding whether to remove the case to federal court. Or you represent a defendant who has been sued in federal court and you are deciding whether to file a motion to dismiss for lack of subject matter jurisdiction. Or maybe you are a judge or law clerk (or even a law student) who has been presented with a question of whether federal jurisdiction exists. The following flowchart necessarily oversimplifies pieces of the analysis, but you may nonetheless find it useful as you try to incorporate the statutes and cases into a step-by-step analysis of subject matter jurisdiction.

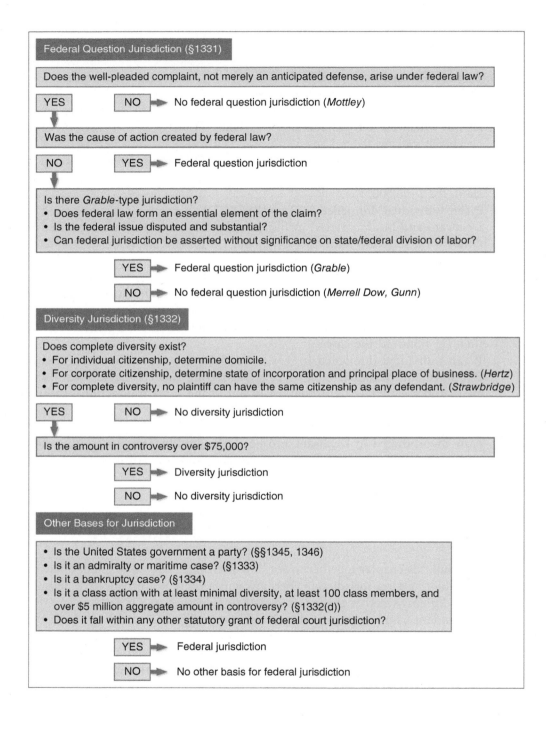

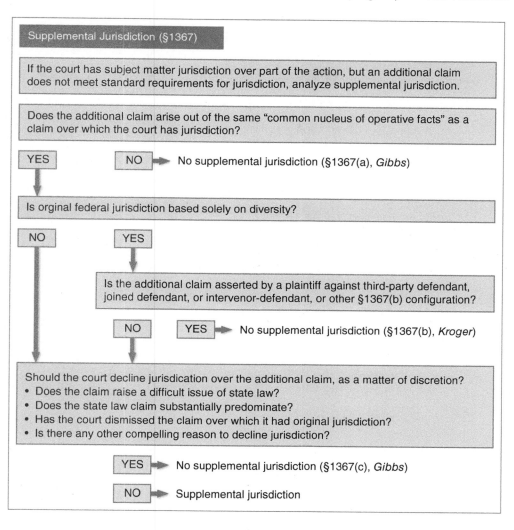

Supplemental Jurisdiction (§1367)

If the court has subject matter jurisdiction over part of the action, but an additional claim does not meet standard requirements for jurisdiction, analyze supplemental jurisdiction.

Does the additional claim arise out of the same "common nucleus of operative facts" as a claim over which the court has jurisdiction?

YES   NO ➡ No supplemental jurisdiction (§1367(a), *Gibbs*)

Is orginal federal jurisdiction based solely on diversity?

NO   YES

Is the additional claim asserted by a plaintiff against third-party defendant, joined defendant, or intervenor-defendant, or other §1367(b) configuration?

NO   YES ➡ No supplemental jurisdiction (§1367(b), *Kroger*)

Should the court decline jurisdication over the additional claim, as a matter of discretion?
- Does the claim raise a difficult issue of state law?
- Does the state law claim substantially predominate?
- Has the court dismissed the claim over which it had original jurisdiction?
- Is there any other compelling reason to decline jurisdiction?

YES ➡ No supplemental jurisdiction (§1367(c), *Gibbs*)

NO ➡ Supplemental jurisdiction

CHAPTER 10

Personal Jurisdiction

Does this particular court have *power* over these particular parties in this particular lawsuit? That, in short, is what the law of personal jurisdiction addresses. Without jurisdiction over the parties, a court cannot enter a judgment that binds those parties.

The power of a court over parties depends, in part, upon whether the parties were properly *notified* about the proceeding; we will consider this aspect of personal jurisdiction at the end of the chapter. Above all, however, personal jurisdiction addresses the *territorial reach* of the courts of particular states over a party. Suppose, for instance, that X is domiciled in Virginia and gets into an auto accident in Maryland. If a plaintiff (say, the other driver) sues X in *Virginia*, you might not be surprised that X would be bound by a Virginia court's decision since X is a Virginia citizen. Similarly, if the plaintiff sues X in *Maryland*, you might not be surprised that a Maryland court has power to adjudicate this claim against X because the accident occurred in Maryland. Suppose, however, that Y sues X in New York, or for that matter in France. If the New York or French court purported to exercise power over X despite X's lack of connection with those places, X would be understandably annoyed. Even before reading the cases on personal jurisdiction, you probably can understand, at an intuitive level, why a Virginia court or Maryland court probably could assert power to adjudicate the claim against X regarding this auto accident, and why a New York court or a French court probably could not.

A plaintiff, by the very fact of filing a lawsuit in a particular state, consents to the power of that state's courts. Thus, nearly every case about personal jurisdiction focuses on a question of power over a *defendant*. Defendants typically raise the issue of personal jurisdiction by filing a motion to dismiss. In federal court, this is the Rule 12(b)(2) *motion to dismiss for lack of personal jurisdiction*, one of the Rule 12 pre-answer motions we discussed in Chapter 2. In state courts, it may likewise be labeled a motion to dismiss for lack of personal jurisdiction, or sometimes a *special appearance* or a *motion to quash service of process*. Plaintiffs' lawyers, however, should anticipate any possible objections to personal jurisdiction. Thus, plaintiffs' lawyers analyze personal jurisdiction to figure out where to file their clients' lawsuits, and defendants' lawyers analyze personal jurisdiction to figure out whether to object to the court's power.

To have personal jurisdiction over a defendant, a court needs both *statutory authority* and *constitutional authority*. Questions of statutory authority focus largely on state statutes known as long-arm statutes (because they extend the "long arm of the law" to reach parties beyond the state's borders). *Out-of-state* defendants are the ones who assert personal jurisdiction objections, because in-state defendants are virtually always subject to the power of the courts of the state in which they are domiciled. Some state long-arm statutes list specific bases for personal jurisdiction over out-of-state defendants, such as a contract entered into within the state, a tortious act committed within the state, or an intentional tortious act committed elsewhere that caused injury within the state.[1] When analyzing personal jurisdiction in a state with one of these enumerated-act long-arm statutes, the first step is to determine whether the defendant fits within the meaning of the statute. If not, then the court lacks jurisdiction; the analysis is over. If yes, then the long-arm statute provides a basis for jurisdiction, and the next question is whether the assertion of jurisdiction would be constitutional. Other state long-arm statutes, rather than enumerating specific bases for jurisdiction, simply provide that the courts may assert personal jurisdiction to the full extent permitted by the Constitution.[2] When analyzing personal jurisdiction in a state with a long-arm statute that reaches to the full extent of the Constitution, the statutory step in the analysis merges with the constitutional analysis.

How does a court determine whether a state's assertion of personal jurisdiction is *constitutional*? The very short answer is that it comes down to an interpretation of the Due Process Clause, which states that no person may be deprived of "life, liberty, or property, without due process of law." U.S. Const. amend. XIV; *see also* U.S. Const. amend. V. The long answer, frankly, is that this question is the main topic we will explore in this chapter, and you just have to learn it case by case.

---

[1] *See, e.g.,* Colo. Rev. Stat. §13-1-124:

13-1-124. Jurisdiction of Courts

(1) Engaging in any act enumerated in this section by any person, whether or not a resident of the state of Colorado, either in person or by an agent, submits such person ... to the jurisdiction of the courts of this state concerning any cause of action arising from:
(a) The transaction of any business within this state;
(b) The commission of a tortious act within this state;
(c) The ownership, use, or possession of any real property situated within this state;
(d) Contracting to insure any person, property, or risk residing or located within this state at the time of contracting;
(e) The maintenance of a matrimonial domicile within this state [related to issues of child support, divorce, etc.] ...;
(f) The engaging of sexual intercourse in this state as to an action brought under article 4 or article 6 of title 19, C.R.C., with respect to a child who may have been conceived by that act. ...

[2] *See, e.g.,* Cal. Code Civ. Proc. §410.10: "A court of this state may exercise jurisdiction on any basis not inconsistent with the Constitution of this state or of the United States."

One thing you will learn is that, fundamentally, the constitutional due process analysis for purposes of personal jurisdiction asks whether it is fair to hale a defendant into a court in a particular state. What does "fair" mean in the context of personal jurisdiction? In your short time in law school, you have no doubt already learned that words like "fair" are hardly self-executing and almost always context-specific. In the context of personal jurisdiction, not only is the answer elusive, it has changed over time. The Supreme Court's interpretation of the Due Process Clause, as applied to personal jurisdiction, continues to evolve. This has two important implications for your study of personal jurisdiction. First, the law of personal jurisdiction will make sense to you only if you first understand its historical underpinnings, and then follow the unraveling, evolution, and partial resurgence of those underpinnings over time. Second, the law of personal jurisdiction, as it exists today, will not necessarily be the law of personal jurisdiction tomorrow. Of course, this is true of every area of law, but personal jurisdiction is particularly in flux, surprisingly so for a doctrine with deep historical roots and a constitutional foundation. As you study personal jurisdiction, look to the values, concerns, and purposes the Supreme Court has articulated in its personal jurisdiction jurisprudence, and watch for shifting ground.

The origins of the law of personal jurisdiction—at least as a matter of constitutional due process—start with a case called *Pennoyer v. Neff*, which is one of the most famous cases you will read in law school. The case is famous for a number of reasons, chief among them this: *Pennoyer* stands for the principle that *a person is not bound by a judgment unless the court properly acquired power over that person*. We will introduce the underpinnings of personal jurisdiction, as articulated in *Pennoyer* and as then reworked by the Supreme Court, in Part A. This chapter will then explore, in Part B, the modern development of the law of personal jurisdiction and the various ways that courts may have jurisdiction over a party or over property. Finally, in Part C, we will explore the requirement that a party must be properly notified about a lawsuit, as both a statutory and a constitutional matter.

THE BIG PICTURE

Unlike subject matter jurisdiction, personal jurisdiction is a waivable defense. What does that tell us about due process (the constitutional foundation for personal jurisdiction) as a limit on courts' power? The fact that the defense is waivable suggests that due process in this context is about fairness to a defendant. If a defendant does not object to being haled into the plaintiff's choice of forum, then it can hardly be said that it would offend the "fundamental fairness that is the touchstone of due process" for that court to render a judgment that would bind the defendant. *Burger King v. Rudzewicz*, 471 U.S. 462 (1985). Subject matter jurisdiction, by contrast, is not about the defendant's rights as a matter of due process, but rather about limits on the court's power as a matter of federalism and separation of powers. As you read about judicial *power* in the personal jurisdiction cases to follow, try to understand the difference between, on the one hand, constraints on the power of a judicial institution within a governmental framework (subject matter jurisdiction limits for federal courts), and, on the other hand, constraints on the power of a court because a party has a liberty interest in being free from that court's power (personal jurisdiction limits based on notions of territorial power and notice).

A. PERSONAL JURISDICTION ORIGINS

As you learn about the evolution of personal jurisdiction jurisprudence in Parts A and B, ask yourself what values the Court cares about when it determines whether it would be "fair" for a court to exercise personal jurisdiction over a defendant. Should "fairness" be about where a defendant could reasonably expect to be sued? Where a defendant could reasonably afford to litigate? Convenience to the defendant? The benefits a defendant derived from a forum state? Further, ask yourself what else, if anything, matters (or should matter) to the due process "fairness" inquiry. Does it take into account the interests of the plaintiff? The interests of the forum state itself? The interests of the judicial system? Finally, ask yourself whether and to what extent concepts of fairness have changed—or should change—with modern developments in travel, technology, and commerce.

The Beginning: *Pennoyer v. Neff* and Territorial Power   Before diving into *Pennoyer v. Neff*, a bit of background explanation will help. The lawsuit that gave rise to this opinion is the second of two lawsuits. The first lawsuit, *Mitchell v. Neff*, began with a simple dispute over legal fees. Attorney John Mitchell sued his former client Marcus Neff for an unpaid fee. Mitchell brought his lawsuit in Oregon state court. Neff did not appear—as it turns out, he was seeking his fortune in California—and the court entered a default judgment against Neff. To enforce the judgment, or, in other words, to get his money, Mitchell had the sheriff seize land that Neff owned in Oregon and put it up for sale. At the sheriff's sale, Mitchell bought the land and then sold it to Sylvester Pennoyer. Eight years later, Neff returned and sued Pennoyer, claiming that Neff still owned the property. The ultimate question in Neff's case against Pennoyer was whether Neff was bound by the judgment in *Mitchell v. Neff*. That question turned on whether the court in *Mitchell v. Neff* had power—jurisdiction—over Neff and his land in the first place. If there was no such power, the judgment in *Mitchell v. Neff* was a nullity—not binding on Neff, thus rendering the sale of Neff's land invalid. To Pennoyer himself, this was a dispute about a tract of land that he thought was legally his (a dispute that made Pennoyer so upset, in fact, that when he was later governor of Oregon, Pennoyer criticized this case in his inaugural address!). To Neff and to the rest of us, this is a foundational case about the power of courts over people and property.

PENNOYER v. NEFF
95 U.S. 714 (1878)

Justice FIELD delivered the opinion of the court.

This is an action to recover the possession of a tract of land, of the alleged value of $15,000, situated in the State of Oregon. The plaintiff asserts title to the premises by a patent of the United States issued to him in 1866, under the act of Congress of Sept. 27, 1850, usually known as the Donation Law of Oregon. The defendant claims to have acquired the premises under a sheriff's deed, made upon a sale of the property on execution issued upon a judgment recovered against the plaintiff in one of the circuit courts of the State. The case turns upon the validity of this judgment.

[The] judgment [at issue] was rendered in February, 1866, in favor of J. H. Mitchell, for less than $300, including costs, in an action brought by him upon a demand for services as an attorney; that, at the time the action was commenced and the judgment rendered, the defendant therein, the plaintiff here, was a non-resident of the State that he was not personally served with process, and did not appear therein; and that the judgment was entered upon his default in not answering the complaint, upon a constructive service of summons by publication.

The Code of Oregon provides for such service when an action is brought against a non-resident and absent defendant, who has property within the State. It also provides, where the action is for the recovery of money or damages, for the attachment of the property of the non-resident. And it also declares that no natural person is subject to the jurisdiction of a court of the State, "unless he appear in the court, or be found within the State, or be a resident thereof, or have property therein; and, in the last case, only to the extent of such property at the time the jurisdiction attached." Construing this latter provision to mean, that, in an action for money or damages where a defendant does not appear in the court, and is not found within the State, and is not a resident thereof, but has property therein, the jurisdiction of the court extends only over such property, the declaration expresses a principle of general, if not universal, law. The authority of every tribunal is necessarily restricted by the territorial limits of the State in which it is established. Any attempt to exercise authority beyond those limits would be deemed in every other forum, as has been said by this court, an illegitimate assumption of power, and be resisted as mere abuse. In the case against the plaintiff, the property here in controversy sold under the judgment rendered was not attached, nor in any way brought under the jurisdiction of the court. Its first connection with the case was caused by a levy of the execution. It was not, therefore, disposed of pursuant to any adjudication, but only in enforcement of a personal judgment, having no relation to the property, rendered against a non-resident without service of process upon him in the action, or his appearance therein. . . .

The several States of the Union are not, it is true, in every respect independent, many of the right and powers which originally belonged to them being now vested in the government created by the Constitution. But, except as restrained and limited by that instrument, they possess and exercise the authority of independent States, and the principles of public law to which we have referred are applicable to them. One of these principles is, that every State possesses exclusive jurisdiction and sovereignty over persons and property within its territory. . . .

The other principle . . . is that no State can exercise direct jurisdiction and authority over persons or property without its territory. The several States are of equal dignity and authority, and the independence of one implies the exclusion of power from all others. And so it is laid down by jurists, as an elementary principle, that the laws of one State have no operation outside of its territory, except so far as is allowed by comity; and that no tribunal established by it can extend its process beyond that territory so as to subject either persons or property to its decisions. . . .

So the State, through its tribunals, may subject property situated within its limits owned by non-residents to the payment of the demand of its own citizens against them; and the exercise of this jurisdiction in no respect infringes upon the sovereignty of the State where the owners are domiciled. Every State owes protection to its own citizens; and, when non-residents deal with them, it is a legitimate and just exercise of authority to hold and appropriate any property owned by such non-residents to satisfy the claims of its citizens. It is in virtue of the State's jurisdiction over the property of the non-resident situated within its limits that its tribunals can inquire into that non-resident's obligations to its own citizens, and the inquiry can then be carried only to the extent necessary to control the disposition of the property. If the non-resident have no property in the State, there is nothing upon which the tribunals can adjudicate.

These views are not new. They have been frequently expressed, with more or less distinctness, in opinions of eminent judges, and have been carried into adjudications in numerous cases. Thus, in *Picquet v. Swan*, 5 Mas. 35, Mr. Justice Story said:

> Where a party is within a territory, he may justly be subjected to its process, and bound personally by the judgment pronounced on such process against him. Where he is not within such territory, and is not personally subject to its laws, if, on account of his supposed or actual property being within the territory, process by the local laws may, by attachment, go to compel his appearance, and for his default to appear judgment may be pronounced against him, such a judgment must, upon general principles, be deemed only to bind him to the extent of such property, and cannot have the effect of a conclusive judgment *in personam*, for the plain reason, that, except so far as the property is concerned, it is a judgment *coram non judice*.

[I]n *Boswell's Lessee v. Otis*, 9 U.S. (How.) 336 (1850), where the title of the plaintiff in ejectment was acquired on a sheriff's sale, under a money decree rendered upon publication of notice against non-residents, in a suit brought to enforce a contract relating to land, Mr. Justice McLean said:

> Jurisdiction is acquired in one of two modes: first, as against the person of the defendant by the service of process; or, secondly, by a procedure against the property of the defendant within the jurisdiction of the court. In the latter case, the defendant is not personally bound by the judgment beyond the property in question. And it is immaterial whether the proceeding against the property be by an attachment or bill in chancery. It must be substantially a proceeding *in rem*.

... [And] in *Cooper v. Reynolds*, reported in the 10th of Wallace... Justice Miller said: "[In some instances,] the plaintiff is met at the commencement of his proceedings by the fact that the defendant is not within the territorial jurisdiction, and cannot be served with any process by which he can brought personally within the court. For this difficulty the statute has provided a remedy. It says that, upon affidavit being made of that fact, a writ of attachment may be issued and levied on any of the defendant's property, and a publication may be made warning him to appear; and that thereafter the court may proceed in the case, whether he appears or not. If the defendant appears, the cause becomes mainly a suit *in personam*, with the added incident, that the property attached remains liable, under the control of the court, to answer to any demand which may be established against the defendant by the final judgment of the court. But if there is no appearance of the defendant, and no service of process on him, the case becomes in its essential nature a proceeding *in rem*, the only effect of which is to subject the property attached to the payment of the demand which the court may find to be due to the plaintiff. [In this type of situation,] first[,] the judgment of the court, though in form a personal judgment against the defendant, has no effect beyond the property attached in that suit. No general execution can be issued for any balance unpaid after the attached property is exhausted. No suit can be maintained on such a judgment in the same court, or in any other; nor can it be used as evidence in any other proceeding not affecting the attached property; nor could the costs in that proceeding be collected of defendant out of any other property than that attached in the suit. Second, the court, in such a suit, cannot proceed, unless the officer finds some property of defendant on which to levy the writ of attachment. A return that none can be found is the end of the case, and deprives the court of further jurisdiction, though the publication may have been duly made and proven in court."...

Substituted service by publication, or in any other authorized form, may be sufficient to inform parties of the object of proceedings taken where property is once brought under the control of the court by seizure or some equivalent act. The law assumes that property is always in the possession of its owner, in person or by agent; and it proceeds upon the theory that its seizure will inform him, not only that it is taken into the custody of the court, but that he must look to any proceedings authorized by law upon such seizure for its condemnation and sale. Such service may also be sufficient in cases where the object of the action is to reach and dispose of property in the State, or of some interest therein, by enforcing a contract or a lien respecting the same, or to partition it among different owners, or, when the public is a party, to condemn and appropriate it for a public purpose. In other words, such service may answer in all actions which are substantially proceedings *in rem*. But where the entire object of the action is to determine the personal rights and obligations of the defendants, that is, where the suit is merely *in personam*, constructive service in this form upon a non-resident is ineffectual for any purpose. Process from the tribunals of one State cannot run into another State, and summon parties there domiciled to leave its territory and respond to proceedings against them. Publication of process or notice within the State where the tribunal sits cannot create any greater obligation upon the non-resident to appear. Process sent to him out of the State, and process published within it, are equally unavailing in proceedings to establish his personal liability.

The want of authority of the tribunals of a State to adjudicate upon the obligations of non-residents, where they have no property within its limits, is not denied . . . but where they have property within the State, it is immaterial whether the property is in the first instance brought under the control of the court by attachment or some other equivalent act. . . . But the jurisdiction of the court to inquire into and determine [the defendant's] obligations at all is only incidental to its jurisdiction over the property. Its jurisdiction in that respect cannot be made to depend upon facts to be ascertained after it has tried the cause and rendered the judgment. If the judgment be previously void, it will not become valid by the subsequent discovery of property of the defendant, or by his subsequent acquisition of it. The judgment, if void when rendered, will always remain void; it cannot occupy the doubtful position of being valid if property be found, and void if there be none. . . .

[T]he validity of every judgment depends upon the jurisdiction of the court before it is rendered, not upon what may occur subsequently. In *Webster v. Reid*, 52 U.S. 437 (1851), . . . the court said: ". . . No person is required to answer in a suit on whom process has not been served, or whose property has not been attached. In this case, there was no personal notice, nor an attachment or other proceeding against the land, until after the judgments. The judgments, therefore, are nullities and did not authorize the executions on which the land was sold." . . .

Since the adoption of the Fourteenth Amendment to the Federal Constitution, the validity of judgments may be directly questioned, and their enforcement in the State resisted, on the ground that proceedings in a court of justice to determine the personal rights and obligations of parties over whom that court has no jurisdiction do not constitute due process of law. . . . To give such proceedings any validity, there must be a tribunal competent by its constitution—that is, by the law of its creation—to pass upon the subject-matter of the suit; and, if that involves merely a determination of the personal liability of the defendant, he must be brought within its jurisdiction by service of process within the State, or his voluntary appearance. . . .

It follows from the views expressed that the personal judgment recovered in the State court of Oregon against the plaintiff herein, then a non-resident of the State, was without any validity, and did not authorize a sale of the property in controversy. . . .

Notes & Questions

1. Before you can understand the ways in which the law has evolved from *Pennoyer*, you must first understand how personal jurisdiction worked in the *Pennoyer* world. Start with four easy questions: Under *Pennoyer*, did a state court have power over persons within the state's boundaries? Did it have power over persons outside the state's boundaries? Did it have power over property within the state's boundaries? Did it have power over property outside the state's boundaries? That is the starting point.

2. Now turn to the question of what mechanisms a plaintiff would use, in the *Pennoyer* world, to subject a person or property to the court's authority. If a defendant were found within the state, what step did a plaintiff take to give the court power over the *person*? If the defendant owned property within the state, what step did a plaintiff take to give the court power over the *property*?

The *Pennoyer* opinion repeatedly mentions "service of process." Service of process, as we briefly discussed in Chapter 2, refers to the delivery of the summons and complaint. In the time of *Pennoyer* (and still today, to some extent), this was accomplished by personally handing the documents to the defendant. We will look more closely at service of process later in this chapter.

The opinion also speaks a lot about "attachment" of property. In short, attachment means that the property is frozen by court order—that is, the property cannot be sold or otherwise transferred—so that it will be available to the plaintiff to satisfy a judgment against the defendant.

While the technicalities of service and attachment may seem quaint, the fundamental notion of the timing of the court's acquisition of power over a person or property is not. A court cannot adjudicate the liabilities of a person or the ownership of property until it has power over that person or property.

> **Terminology Tip**
>
> The Court in *Pennoyer* discusses three types of personal jurisdiction. The first, *in rem* jurisdiction, refers to the court's power over property located in the forum state. The second, *in personam* jurisdiction, refers to the court's power over the defendant herself (or, in the case of a corporation, the defendant itself), that is, the power to render a judgment that is personally binding on the defendant. The third—and the type primarily at issue in *Pennoyer*—is usually called *quasi-in-rem* jurisdiction (a term the *Pennoyer* Court does not use). *Quasi-in-rem* jurisdiction refers to a court's power to adjudicate personal obligations of the defendant through attachment of the defendant's in-state property.

3. In *Mitchell v. Neff*, the Oregon court did not have true *in rem* jurisdiction because Mitchell's lawsuit was about an unpaid debt, not about ownership of Oregon property. Nor did the Oregon court have *in personam* jurisdiction, because Neff was not served with process in Oregon, nor had Neff voluntarily appeared to litigate or consented to the court's power. But what about the third type of jurisdiction? Mitchell attached Neff's Oregon property to enforce the default judgment and get his money. Why didn't the attachment of Neff's property suffice to give the court *quasi-in-rem* jurisdiction to adjudicate Mitchell's claim up to the value of Neff's property?

4. Neff owed Mitchell approximately $300, but the property attached was worth approximately $15,000 at the time of Pennoyer's suit. In theory, when the attached property is worth more than the plaintiff's claim, the excess value still belongs to the defendant. But what if those numbers had been reversed? What if Neff had owed Mitchell $15,000, but the property attached had only been worth $300? Assuming Mitchell had attached the property *before* the lawsuit began, could Mitchell have recovered more than the value of the land?

5. In the *Pennoyer* world, there is more than one way a court might have *in personam* jurisdiction over a defendant. One of those ways is if the defendant is served with process within the state boundaries. What are other ways the Court states or implies would suffice for *in personam* jurisdiction?

6. From a modern vantage point, it might seem that the biggest problem with the Oregon court's assertion of power over Neff was that, as far as we can tell, Neff had no clue that there was a lawsuit against him. Notice was published in fine print in a newspaper, and Neff in California never learned of the proceeding. But is Neff's lack of actual notice what the Supreme Court was really worried about in *Pennoyer*? Consider these two questions: First, in the *Pennoyer* world, is actual notice *necessary* for a court to have personal jurisdiction over a defendant? (Consider whether notice of suit by publication was permissible under the Oregon statute for purposes of establishing personal jurisdiction. If Neff's property had been attached at the outset of the lawsuit, and if notice were published in accordance with the statute, would the court have had jurisdiction?) Second, in the *Pennoyer* world, is actual notice *sufficient* for a court to have personal jurisdiction over a defendant? (Suppose Mitchell had sent a messenger to California to find Neff and tell him that Mitchell was suing him in Oregon for unpaid legal fees, and to give Neff a copy of the complaint. Would that have sufficed to give the Oregon court personal jurisdiction over Neff?) If actual notice of the lawsuit is neither necessary nor sufficient for personal jurisdiction under *Pennoyer*, that tells you something about whether the case was more about notice or power. The Supreme Court later returned to the question of notice in *Mullane v. Central Hanover Bank & Trust Co.*, 339 U.S. 306 (1950), and spelled out a due process requirement of notice reasonably calculated to reach the defendant, as we will discuss later in the chapter.

7. In the most enduring passage of the *Pennoyer* opinion, Justice Field invokes the Due Process Clause of the Fourteenth Amendment as a basis on which a judgment may be attacked for lack of jurisdiction. Why does it matter that the Court made personal jurisdiction a constitutional imperative, as opposed to merely a set of statutory or common law constraints? In thinking about Justice Field's invocation of due process, consider the newness of that clause (the Fourteenth Amendment was ratified in 1868), and the significance of the Court's use of the Fourteenth Amendment in *Pennoyer* to impose a federal constitutional constraint on the states. Think also of the time period in American history (the Civil War concluded in 1865). Even if it is hard, from a modern vantage point, for us to think of each state as a separate sovereign entity, do you suppose that state sovereignty had a different resonance in that period?

From Territoriality to Contacts: The Decline of *Pennoyer*.   In its approach to the territorial power of state courts, *Pennoyer* assumed that each state was essentially separate and that interstate activity was the exception (to be fair, it was 1878). The modern doctrine of personal jurisdiction emerges from the unraveling of the assumptions and realities that underlie the rigid *Pennoyer* scheme. A framework whereby states are all-powerful vis-à-vis what rests within their boundaries (be it people or property) but virtually impotent otherwise perhaps made sense at the time of *Pennoyer*, but what happened after 1878? The automobile was introduced. And the airplane. The telephone. Interstate highways. The global economy and global financial markets. The Internet. Amazon. Google. Cyber currency. State boundaries are not what they once were.

Changes in personal jurisdiction doctrine, however, did not come quickly. *Pennoyer*'s theory of territorial limits of judicial power endured for nearly 70 years; courts simply found ways to bend—but not break—the *Pennoyer* scheme. As an example, consider the issue of nonresident motorists—a problem that did not exist when *Pennoyer* was decided. Under the rigid scheme of *Pennoyer*, an out-of-state motorist who entered another state and caused an accident could not be sued in that state unless (1) the out-of-state driver was served with process inside the state borders (*in personam*); or (2) the out-of-state driver owned property in the state in which the accident occurred, and the plaintiff attached the property at the outset of the suit (*quasi-in-rem*). You can imagine that these two options would leave many plaintiffs completely out of luck. Instead of jettisoning the territorial framework of *Pennoyer*, both state legislatures and the Supreme Court "adapted" *Pennoyer* to the problem of nonresident motorists. Specifically, in 1916, the Court upheld a New Jersey state statute that required out-of-state motorists to appoint a New Jersey agent for service of process before using New Jersey's highways (thus enabling nonresident motorists to be served in New Jersey). *Kane v. New Jersey*, 242 U.S. 160 (1916).

Of course, the New Jersey statute imposed a rather onerous requirement upon anyone who simply wanted to drive in New Jersey. In 1927, Massachusetts responded with its own, less onerous, nonresident motorist statute, which said that by using a Massachusetts highway, a nonresident motorist is *deemed* to have appointed a state officer as an agent to accept service of process. The Supreme Court approved, *Hess v. Pawloski*, 274 U.S. 352 (1927), while steadfastly holding to the *Pennoyer* framework. The Massachusetts statute, by "deeming" the driver to have appointed an in-state agent for service, satisfied *Pennoyer*'s requirements as a technical matter. The statute shoehorned the situation into the consent basis for jurisdiction that the Court acknowledged in *Pennoyer*, as well as satisfied the need for in-state service. What was Massachusetts' true interest in appointing an agent for service for nonresident motorists? Some commitment to the theory undergirding *Pennoyer*? No. The statute was drafted not to endorse *Pennoyer*, but to deal with its practical annoyances. Massachusetts' interest was in protecting its citizens and regulating its roads. There is no room under *Pennoyer*, however, for such reasoning. Thus, the legal fiction of implied consent.

Another scenario that arose in the years after *Pennoyer* was the problem of suing an *in-state* defendant who happened to be out of state when a lawsuit was brought. In 1940, the Supreme Court bent *Pennoyer* once more when it decided *Milliken v. Meyer*, 311 U.S. 457, a case in which a plaintiff sued a defendant—a Wyoming citizen—in Wyoming state court. The defendant was in Colorado at the time the suit was brought. The defendant argued that the Wyoming court lacked personal jurisdiction over him because *Pennoyer* required in-state service. The Supreme Court upheld personal jurisdiction despite the lack of in-state service, reasoning that *Pennoyer* addressed personal jurisdiction over nonresidents; it was implicit in *Pennoyer* that a state can exercise power over its own citizens.

Milliken was the last opinion in which the Court bent over backwards to preserve *Pennoyer*. In 1945, the rigid framework of *Pennoyer*, ill-suited for the twentieth century, finally broke. The next case, *International Shoe v. Washington*, a case at least as famous as *Pennoyer*, at long last decoupled the due process analysis from the strict territorial thinking of the *Pennoyer* era of a given state in favor of an inquiry into the defendant's connections with the forum state. That contact-based inquiry remains the foundation of due process analysis in personal jurisdiction cases today.

INTERNATIONAL SHOE CO. v. WASHINGTON
326 U.S. 310 (1945)

STONE, C.J., delivered the opinion of the Court.

The questions for decision are (1) whether, within the limitations of the due process clause of the Fourteenth Amendment, appellant, a Delaware corporation, has by its activities in the State of Washington rendered itself amenable to proceedings in the courts of that state to recover unpaid contributions to the state unemployment compensation fund exacted by state statutes, and (2) whether the state can exact those contributions consistently with the due process clause of the Fourteenth Amendment.

The statutes in question set up a comprehensive scheme of unemployment compensation, the costs of which are defrayed by contributions required to be made by employers to a state unemployment compensation fund.

The contributions are a specified percentage of the wages payable annually by each employer for his employees' services in the state. The assessment and collection of the contributions and the fund are administered by appellees. [The statute] authorizes appellee Commissioner to issue an order and notice of assessment of delinquent contributions upon prescribed personal service of the notice upon the employer if found within the state, or, if not so found, by mailing the notice to the employer by registered mail at his last known address. [The statute establishes a process for collecting unpaid contributions, subject to review by the state courts.]

In this case notice of assessment for the years in question was personally served upon a sales solicitor employed by appellant in the State of Washington, and a copy of the notice was mailed by registered mail to appellant at its address in St. Louis, Missouri. Appellant appeared specially before the office of unemployment and moved to set aside the order and notice of assessment on the ground that the service upon appellant's salesman was not proper service upon appellant; that appellant was not a corporation of the State of Washington and was not doing business within the state; that it had no agent within the state upon whom service could be made; and that appellant is not an employer and does not furnish employment within the meaning of the statute. . . .

The facts, as found by the appeal tribunal and accepted by the state Superior

Court and Supreme Court, are not in dispute. Appellant is a Delaware corporation, having its principal place of business in St. Louis, Missouri, and is engaged in the manufacture and sale of shoes and other footwear. It maintains places of business in several states, other than Washington, at which its manufacturing is carried on and from which its merchandise is distributed interstate through several sales units or branches located outside the State of Washington.

Appellant has no office in Washington and makes no contracts either for sale or purchase of merchandise there. It maintains no stock of merchandise in that state and makes there no deliveries of goods in intrastate commerce. During the years from 1937 to 1940, now in question, appellant employed eleven to thirteen salesmen under direct supervision and control of sales managers located in St. Louis. These salesmen resided in Washington; their principal activities were confined to that state; and they were compensated by commissions based upon the amount of their sales. The commissions for each year totaled more than $31,000. Appellant supplies its salesmen with a line of samples, each consisting of one shoe of a pair, which they display to prospective purchasers. On occasion they rent permanent sample rooms, for exhibiting samples, in business buildings, or rent rooms in hotels or business buildings temporarily for that purpose. The cost of such rentals is reimbursed by appellant.

The authority of the salesmen is limited to exhibiting their samples and soliciting orders from prospective buyers, at prices and on terms fixed by appellant. The salesmen transmit the orders to appellant's office in St. Louis for acceptance or rejection, and when accepted the merchandise for filling the orders is shipped f.o.b. from points outside Washington to the purchasers within the state. All the merchandise shipped into Washington is invoiced at the place of shipment from which collections are made. No salesman has authority to enter into contracts or to make collections. . . .

Appellant . . . insists that its activities within the state were not sufficient to manifest its "presence" there and that in its absence the state courts were without jurisdiction, that consequently it was a denial of due process for the state to subject appellant to suit. . . .

Historically the jurisdiction of courts to render judgment *in personam* is grounded on their de facto power over the defendant's person. Hence his presence within the territorial jurisdiction of court was prerequisite to its rendition of a judgment personally binding him. *Pennoyer v. Neff*, 95 U.S. 714, 733 (1878). But now that the capias ad respondendum has given way to personal service of summons or other form of notice, due process requires only that in order to subject a defendant to a judgment *in personam*, if he be not present within the territory of the forum, he have certain minimum contacts with it such that the maintenance of the suit does not offend "traditional notions of fair play and substantial justice." *Milliken v. Meyer*, 311 U.S. 457, 463 (1940).

Since the corporate personality is a fiction, although a fiction intended to be acted upon as though it were a fact, it is clear that unlike an individual its "presence" without, as well as within, the state of its origin can be manifested only by activities carried on in its behalf by those who are authorized to act for it. To say that the corporation is so far "present" there as to satisfy due process requirements, for purposes of taxation or the maintenance of suits against it in the courts of the state, is to beg the question to be decided. For the terms "present" or "presence" are used merely to symbolize those activities of the corporation's agent within the state which courts will deem to be sufficient to satisfy the demands of due process. *Hutchinson v. Chase & Gilbert*, 45 F.2d 139, 141 (2d Cir. 1930). Those demands may be met by such contacts of the corporation with the state of the forum as make it reasonable, in the context of our federal system of government, to require the corporation to defend the particular suit which is brought there. An "estimate of the inconveniences" which would result to the corporation from a trial away from its "home" or principal place of business is relevant in this connection. *Id.* at 141.

"Presence" in the state in this sense has never been doubted when the activities of the corporation there have not only been continuous and systematic, but also give rise to the liabilities sued on, even though no consent to be sued or authorization to an agent to accept service of process has been given. Conversely it has been generally recognized that the casual presence of the corporate agent or even his conduct of single or isolated items of activities in a state in the corporation's behalf are not enough to subject it to suit on causes of action unconnected with the activities there. To require the corporation in such circumstances to defend the suit away from its home or other jurisdiction where it carries on more substantial activities has been thought to lay too great and unreasonable a burden on the corporation to comport with due process.

While it has been held, in cases on which appellant relies, that continuous activity of some sorts within a state is not enough to support the demand that the corporation be amenable to suits unrelated to that activity, there have been instances in which the continuous corporate operations within a state were thought so substantial and of such a nature as to justify suit against it on causes of action arising from dealings entirely distinct from those activities.

Finally, although the commission of some single or occasional acts of the corporate agent in a state sufficient to impose an obligation or liability on the corporation has not been thought to confer upon the state authority to enforce it, other such acts, because of their nature and quality and the circumstances of their commission, may be deemed sufficient to render the corporation liable to suit. *Cf. Kane v. New Jersey*, 242 U.S. 160 (1916); *Hess v. Pawloski*, 274 U.S. 352 (1927). True, some of the decisions holding the corporation amenable to suit have been supported by resort to the legal fiction that it has given its consent to service and suit, consent being implied from its presence in the state through the acts of its authorized agents. But more realistically it may be said that those authorized acts were of such a nature as to justify the fiction.

It is evident that the criteria by which we mark the boundary line between those activities which justify the subjection of a corporation to suit, and those which do not, cannot be simply mechanical or quantitative. The test is not merely, as has sometimes been suggested, whether the activity, which the corporation has seen fit to procure through its agents in another state, is a little more or a little less. Whether due process is satisfied must depend rather upon the quality and nature of the activity in relation to the fair and orderly administration of the laws which it was the purpose of the due process clause to insure. That clause does not contemplate that a state may make binding a judgment *in personam* against an individual or corporate defendant with which the state has no contacts, ties, or relations.

But to the extent that a corporation exercises the privilege of conducting activities within a state, it enjoys the benefits and protection of the laws of that state. The exercise of that privilege may give rise to obligations; and, so far as those obligations arise out of or are connected with the activities within the state, a procedure which requires the corporation to respond to a suit brought to enforce them can, in most instances, hardly be said to be undue.

Applying these standards, the activities carried on in behalf of appellant in the State of Washington were neither irregular nor casual. They were systematic and continuous throughout the years in question. They resulted in a large volume of interstate business, in the course of which appellant received the benefits and protection of the laws of the state, including the right to resort to the courts for the enforcement of its rights. The obligation which is here sued upon arose out of those very activities. It is evident that these operations establish sufficient contacts or ties with the state of the forum to make it reasonable and just according to our traditional conception of fair play and substantial justice to permit the state to enforce the obligations which appellant has incurred there. Hence we cannot say that the maintenance of the present suit in the State of Washington involves an unreasonable or undue procedure. . . .

Appellant having rendered itself amenable to suit upon obligations arising out of the activities of its salesmen in Washington, the state may maintain the present suit *in personam* to collect the tax laid upon the exercise of the privilege of employing appellant's salesmen within the state. . . .

BLACK, J., delivered the following opinion.

. . . [I]t is unthinkable that the vague due process clause was ever intended to prohibit a State from regulating or taxing a business carried on within its boundaries simply because this is done by agents of a corporation organized and having its headquarters elsewhere. To read this into the due process clause would in fact result in depriving a State's citizens of due process by taking from the State the power to protect them in their business dealings within its boundaries with representatives of a foreign corporation. Nothing could be more irrational or more designed to defeat the function of our federative system of government. Certainly a State, at the very least, has power to tax and sue those dealing with its citizens within its boundaries, as we have held before. Were the Court to follow this principle, it would provide a workable standard for cases where, as here, no other questions are involved. The Court has not chosen to do so, but instead has engaged in an unnecessary discussion in the course of which it has announced vague Constitutional criteria applied for the first time to the issue before us. It has thus introduced uncertain elements confusing the simple pattern and tending to curtail the exercise of State powers to an extent not justified by the Constitution. . . .

I believe that the Federal Constitution leaves to each State, without any "ifs" or "buts," a power to tax and to open the doors of its courts for its citizens to sue corporations whose agents do business in those States. Believing that the Constitution gave the States that power, I think it a judicial deprivation to condition its exercise upon this Court's notion of "fair play," however appealing that term may be. Nor can I stretch the meaning of due process so far as to authorize this Court to deprive a State of the right to afford judicial protection to its citizens on the ground that it would be more "convenient" for the corporation to be sued somewhere else.

There is a strong emotional appeal in the words "fair play," "justice," and "reasonableness." But they were not chosen by those who wrote the original Constitution or the Fourteenth Amendment as a measuring rod for this Court to use in invalidating State or Federal laws passed by elected legislative representatives. No one, not even those who most feared a democratic government, ever formally proposed that courts should be given power to invalidate legislation under any such elastic standards. There is no reason for reading the due process clause so as to restrict a State's power to tax and sue those whose activities affect persons and businesses within the State, provided proper service can be had.

[T]he rule announced means that tomorrow's judgment may strike down a State or Federal enactment on the ground that it does not conform to this Court's idea of natural justice. I therefore find myself moved by the same fears that caused Mr. Justice Holmes to say in 1930:

> I have not yet adequately expressed the more than anxiety that I feel at the ever increasing scope given to the Fourteenth Amendment in cutting down what I believe to be the constitutional rights of the States. As the decisions now stand, I see hardly any limit but the sky to the invalidating of those rights if they happen to strike a majority of this Court as for any reason undesirable.

Baldwin v. Missouri, 281 U.S. 586, 595 (1930).

Notes & Questions

1. Before turning to the constitutional analysis, consider the statutory step. What is the statutory authority for the Washington state court to assert power over International Shoe Co. regarding the state's claim to collect unpaid contributions to the unemployment fund? How did the State of Washington notify International Shoe Co. about the proceeding?

2. Now, turning to the question of due process, start by applying the *Pennoyer* analysis to this case. In the *Pennoyer* world, could a Washington court constitutionally assert jurisdiction over the International Shoe Co.? *In rem* jurisdiction obviously does not fit. This is not a case about ownership of property located in Washington; it is a case about the company's liability for unpaid contributions to the unemployment fund. Next, consider *quasi-in-rem* jurisdiction. Does International Shoe have property in Washington that could be attached for purposes of adjudicating the company's liability? (Attach a pile of left shoes, perhaps?) All that remains is *in personam* jurisdiction. Consider the traditional bases for *in personam* jurisdiction from *Pennoyer*. Was the defendant served within the state borders? Is the defendant present within the state? Did the

defendant consent to the jurisdiction of the state? These are easier questions to answer regarding an individual like Marcus Neff than regarding a corporation like International Shoe. What argument could you make that the company was "present" in the state? What argument could you make that the company "consented" to the state's power? And what would be the strongest counter-arguments? In trying to apply the traditional analysis, consider the difficulties presented by the fact that, as Chief Justice Stone aptly noted, "corporate personality is a fiction."

3. Rather than apply *Pennoyer* and evaluate jurisdiction over International Shoe accordingly, the Court announced a new test. Consider the Court's formulation of the new test and its impact on the law of personal jurisdiction. Did the Court in *International Shoe* expand or contract a state's power under the Constitution to exercise personal jurisdiction over an out-of-state defendant? Or did it do both?

> **Terminology Tip**
>
> In *International Shoe*, appellant "appeared specially." What does that mean? The term *special appearance*, as used in older cases and in some current state court cases, distinguished the participation from a *general appearance*. General appearance means that the party showed up to litigate, for example by filing an answer or a motion. Special appearance, by contrast, means that the party showed up not to litigate the merits, but only to argue that the court lacks personal jurisdiction. In essence, the party making a special appearance is saying: I'm here (to contest jurisdiction) but I'm not *really* here, so don't treat me as having consented to jurisdiction by virtue of the fact that I'm here. The modern equivalent of a special appearance in federal court is the Rule 12(b)(2) motion to dismiss for lack of personal jurisdiction.

4. The *Pennoyer* Court grounded its due process analysis in principles of sovereignty and territorial boundaries. Upon what principles did the *International Shoe* Court base its due process analysis?

5. Justice Black's concurrence reads like a dissent. He agreed that Washington has the power to tax the company and to enforce its taxes through a judicial process, but he emphatically disagreed with the new test announced by the Court. What was it about the new personal jurisdiction test that Justice Black found so objectionable?

6. Part of the logic animating *International Shoe* is the notion of reciprocity. If a person or company receives the benefits of a state—such as the protection of its laws—it should expect to be subject to the power of that state's courts. Embedded in that notion of reciprocity are two separate ideas: (1) the notion that, when a person (individual or corporation) benefits from its activities in a state, *it is fair* to impose on that person certain burdens that correspond to the benefits; and (2) a person who benefits from a state *can reasonably expect* to be haled into that state's courts. Note that the second notion is more about the expectations of the defendant than it is about pure reciprocity. Which of these concerns seemed to most influence the majority? Which seemed to most influence Justice Black?

7. The opinion in *International Shoe* describes two types of contact-based *in personam* jurisdiction. Recall this paragraph:

> While it has been held in cases on which appellant relies that continuous activity of some sorts within a state is not enough to support the demand that the corporation be amenable to suits *unrelated to that activity*, there have been instances in which the continuous corporate operations within a state were thought so substantial and of such a nature as to justify suit against it on causes of action arising from dealings entirely distinct from those activities.

Id. at 308 (emphasis added). The following section (Part B(1)) will focus on the first type of *in personam* jurisdiction introduced in *International Shoe*—jurisdiction over a defendant for a claim that arises out of or relates to the defendant's contacts with the forum state. This is known as specific jurisdiction or case-linked jurisdiction. Later (Part B(2)), we will explore the second type of *in personam* jurisdiction alluded to in *International Shoe*, known as general, or all-purpose, jurisdiction. For general jurisdiction, a defendant's contacts with the state must be "so substantial" and of "such a nature" that it would not violate due process for the court to exercise jurisdiction over that defendant in *any* suit. In other words, even in suits *unrelated* to the defendant's contacts with the state. Which type of jurisdiction was present in *International Shoe*?

B. TYPES OF PERSONAL JURISDICTION

(1) Specific Jurisdiction

A court may have personal jurisdiction over the defendant in a particular lawsuit because the claims *arise out of* or *relate to* the defendant's contacts with the forum state. This is known as specific jurisdiction or case-linked jurisdiction. Personal jurisdiction was proper in *International Shoe*, for example, because the state's claims arose out of the company's employment of salespeople in the State of Washington.

Once again, a court must have both statutory and constitutional authority to exercise specific personal jurisdiction over a defendant. Recall that statutory authority over an out-of-state defendant typically comes from state "long-arm statutes." Recall also that some state long-arm statutes enumerate bases for specific jurisdiction over out-of-state defendants, and when faced with an enumerated-act long-arm statute, your first step is to ascertain whether the defendant fits within the meaning of the statute. If no, then the court lacks jurisdiction; the analysis is over. If yes, then the long-arm statute provides a basis for jurisdiction, and the next question is whether the assertion of jurisdiction under that statute would be constitutional under the minimum contacts test.

Many state long-arm statutes, as you learned above, permit the exercise of personal jurisdiction to the full extent permitted by the Constitution. Moreover, in some states that have what look to be enumerated long-arm statutes, their courts have *interpreted* them to reach to the full extent of the Due Process Clause. In either scenario—whether stated explicitly in the statutory language or based upon the court's interpretation of the long-arm statute—these "sky's the limit" long-arm statutes permit courts to assert personal jurisdiction over any defendant as long as doing so does not violate due process. When analyzing personal jurisdiction in a state with a long-arm that reaches to the full extent of due process, the statutory step in the analysis merges with the constitutional analysis.

This section will focus primarily on the due process analysis for personal jurisdiction. We will explore three important components of the due process analysis: (a) the minimum contacts test; (b) the reasonableness test; and (c) the requirement that the claims arise out of or relate to the defendant's contacts with the state.

(a) Minimum Contacts

In *International Shoe*, the Supreme Court abandoned the rigid *Pennoyer* territorial test for personal jurisdiction, and announced a new test:

> [D]ue process requires only that in order to subject a defendant to a judgment *in personam*, if he be not present within the territory of the forum, he have certain minimum contacts with it such that the maintenance of the suit does not offend "traditional notions of fair play and substantial justice."

Int'l Shoe, 326 U.S. at 316. The Court, however, did not define "minimum contacts." After *International Shoe*, however, the Court attempted to elucidate—case by case— the meaning of this critical term.

First, the Supreme Court made it clear that the minimum contacts test is not merely about quantity. A single contact might be enough if it is substantial and if the claim arises directly from it. That was the lesson of *McGee v. International Life Ins. Co.*, 355 U.S. 220 (1957), in which a Texas insurance company's sale of a single insurance policy to a single policyholder in California sufficed to give a California court jurisdiction over the insurance company for a dispute involving that particular policy. *McGee* was authored by Justice Black, who, writing for a unanimous Court, laid out an expansive view of what constituted a relevant "contact" under *International Shoe*, and thus a broad view of state power. In so doing, Justice Black merged a "reasonableness" analysis with the contacts analysis. Finally, Justice Black did not focus solely on the fairness or reasonableness to defendant; instead he focused on whether refusing to allow personal jurisdiction would be fair to plaintiffs and to the forum state. This approach is consistent with Justice Black's views in *International Shoe*; in *McGee*, Justice Black was not relegated to a concurrence.

In another post–*International Shoe* case, *Hanson v. Denckla*, 357 U.S. 235 (1958), the Supreme Court held that contacts with the forum state must be *purposeful* to count as "minimum contacts." The centrality of purposeful contacts was implicit in *International Shoe* (International Shoe Company purposefully employed persons in Washington), and in *McGee* (International Life Insurance Company purposefully mailed an insurance policy to a policyholder in California). The purposefulness requirement was spelled out explicitly, though, in *Hanson*. The case involved a family dispute over assets in a trust created by Dora Donner. The trust was established in Delaware and the trustee was a Delaware company. Donner subsequently moved to Florida after the formation of the trust. Donner died in Florida, and two of the beneficiaries of Donner's trust brought a lawsuit in Florida in which the Delaware trustee was a necessary defendant. The primary beneficiaries lived in Florida and Donner's will was being administered in Florida. Nonetheless, by a 5-4 vote, the Supreme Court held that the Florida court lacked jurisdiction over the Delaware trustee because personal jurisdiction requires "some act by which the defendant *purposefully avails* itself of the privilege of conducting activities within the forum states, thus invoking the benefits and protections of its laws." *Hanson*, 357 U.S. at 253 (emphasis added). The Court characterized Donner's move to Florida as a "unilateral activity" by Ms. Donner, not a purposeful act by the trustee. *Id.*

Hanson is significant for at least two reasons: First, it officially introduced the (now indispensable) "purposeful availment" requirement in specific jurisdiction cases. Second, by focusing so heavily on the purposefulness of the defendant's contacts with the forum state, the majority downplayed other connections between the dispute and the state, and arguably lost sight of the logic of choosing Florida as the location for adjudicating the dispute. As you read the personal jurisdiction cases that follow, and especially as you see how the "purposeful availment" requirement has been applied, think about the tension between, on the one hand, protecting a defendant from the power of a state with which the defendant has made no purposeful connection, and, on the other hand, finding a sensible and convenient forum for adjudicating a particular dispute. The following four subsections will explore the meaning, contours, and applications of the purposeful availment requirement.

(i) Introduction to Purposeful Availment

"Purposeful availment," as used in *Hanson* and later cases, refers to an act or set of acts that take place in a state or are directed at that state. This subsection explores the Supreme Court's most famous articulation of the purposeful availment requirement: *World-Wide Volkswagen Corp. v. Woodson*, 444 U.S. 286 (1980). As you read *World-Wide Volkswagen*, consider what contacts these defendants have with the forum state. Distinguish the defendants' state contacts that are *related* to the suit from contacts that are unrelated. Also, distinguish the defendants' state contacts that are *purposeful* from those that are fortuitous. Finally, consider whether the Court's focus on purposeful contacts crowds out other considerations that might have come into play to determine whether Oklahoma was an appropriate forum for this dispute.

WORLD-WIDE VOLKSWAGEN CORPORATION v. WOODSON
444 U.S. 286 (1980)

WHITE, J., delivered the opinion of the Court.

The issue before us is whether, consistently with the Due Process Clause of the Fourteenth Amendment, an Oklahoma court may exercise *in personam* jurisdiction over a nonresident automobile retailer and its wholesale distributor in a products-liability action, when the defendants' only connection with Oklahoma is the fact that an automobile sold in New York to New York residents became involved in an accident in Oklahoma.

I

Respondents Harry and Kay Robinson purchased a new Audi automobile from petitioner Seaway Volkswagen, Inc. (Seaway), in Massena, N.Y., in 1976. The following year the Robinson family, who resided in New York, left that State for a new home in Arizona. As they passed through the State of Oklahoma, another car struck their Audi in the rear, causing a fire which severely burned Kay Robinson and her two children.

The Robinsons subsequently brought a products-liability action in the District Court for Creek County, Okla., claiming that their injuries resulted from defective design and placement of the Audi's gas tank and fuel system. They joined as defendants the automobile's manufacturer, Audi NSU Auto Union Aktiengesellschaft (Audi); its importer Volkswagen of America, Inc. (Volkswagen); its regional distributor, petitioner World-Wide Volkswagen Corp. (World-Wide); and its retail dealer, petitioner Seaway. Seaway and World-Wide entered special appearances, claiming that Oklahoma's exercise of jurisdiction over them would offend the limitations on the State's jurisdiction imposed by the Due Process Clause of the Fourteenth Amendment.

The facts presented to the District Court showed that World-Wide is incorporated and has its business office in New York. It distributes vehicles, parts, and accessories, under contract with Volkswagen, to retail dealers in New York, New Jersey, and Connecticut. Seaway, one of these retail dealers, is incorporated and has its place of business in New York. Insofar as the record reveals, Seaway and World-Wide are fully independent corporations whose relations with each other and with Volkswagen and Audi are contractual only. Respondents adduced no evidence that either World-Wide or Seaway does any business in Oklahoma, ships or sells any products to or in that State, has an agent to receive process there, or purchases advertisements in any media calculated to reach Oklahoma. In fact, as respondents' counsel conceded at oral argument, there was no showing that any automobile sold by World-Wide or Seaway has ever entered Oklahoma with the single exception of the vehicle involved in the present case.

Despite the apparent paucity of contacts between petitioners and Oklahoma, the District Court rejected their constitutional claim and reaffirmed that ruling in denying petitioners' motion for reconsideration. Petitioners then sought a writ of prohibition in the Supreme Court of Oklahoma to restrain the District Judge, respondent Charles S. Woodson, from exercising *in personam* jurisdiction over them. They renewed their contention that, because they had no "minimal contacts" with the State of

Oklahoma, the actions of the District Judge were in violation of their rights under the Due Process Clause.

The Supreme Court of Oklahoma denied the writ, 585 P.2d 351 (1978), holding that personal jurisdiction over petitioners was authorized by Oklahoma's "long-arm" statute Okla. Stat., Tit. 12, §1701.03(a)(4).[7] Although the court noted that the proper approach was to test jurisdiction against both statutory and constitutional standards, its analysis did not distinguish these questions, probably because §1701.03(a)(4) has been interpreted as conferring jurisdiction to the limits permitted by the United States Constitution. The court's rationale was contained in the following paragraph, 585 P.2d at 354:

> In the case before us, the product being sold and distributed by the petitioners is by its very design and purpose so mobile that petitioners can foresee its possible use in Oklahoma. This is especially true of the distributor, who has the exclusive right to distribute such automobile in New York, New Jersey and Connecticut. The evidence presented below demonstrated that goods sold and distributed by the petitioners were used in the State of Oklahoma, and under the facts we believe it reasonable to infer, given the retail value of the automobile, that the petitioners derive substantial income from automobiles which from time to time are used in the State of Oklahoma. This being the case, we hold that under the facts presented, the trial court was justified in concluding that the petitioners derive substantial revenue from goods used or consumed in this State.

We granted certiorari to consider an important constitutional question with respect to state-court jurisdiction and to resolve a conflict between the Supreme Court of Oklahoma and the highest courts of at least four other States. We reverse.

II

The Due Process Clause of the Fourteenth Amendment limits the power of a state court to render a valid personal judgment against a nonresident defendant. A judgment rendered in violation of due process is void in the rendering State and is not entitled to full faith and credit elsewhere. *Pennoyer v. Neff*, 95 U.S. 714. Due process requires that the defendant be given adequate notice of the suit, *Mullane v. Central Hanover Trust Co.*, 339 U.S. 306 (1950), and be subject to the personal jurisdiction of the court, *Int'l Shoe*, 326 U.S. 310. In the present case, it is not contended that notice was inadequate; the only question is whether these particular petitioners were subject to the jurisdiction of the Oklahoma courts.

As has long been settled, and as we reaffirm today, a state court may exercise personal jurisdiction over a nonresident defendant only so long as there exist "minimum contacts" between the defendant and the forum State. *Int'l Shoe*, 326 U.S. at 316. The concept of minimum contacts, in turn, can be seen to perform two related, but distinguishable, functions. It protects the defendant against the burdens of litigating

---

[7] This subsection provides:

"A court may exercise personal jurisdiction over a person, who acts directly or by an agent, as to a cause of action or claim for relief arising from the person's ... causing tortious injury in this state by an act or omission outside this state if he regularly does or solicits business or engages in any other persistent course of conduct, or derives substantial revenue from goods used or consumed or services rendered, in this state. . . ."

Rule

in a distant or inconvenient forum. And it acts to ensure that the States through their courts, do not reach out beyond the limits imposed on them by their status as coequal sovereigns in a federal system.

The protection against inconvenient litigation is typically described in terms of "reasonableness" or "fairness." *Id.* We have said that the defendant's contacts with the forum State must be such that maintenance of the suit "does not offend traditional notions of fair play and substantial justice." *Id.* The relationship between the defendant and the forum must be such that it is "reasonable . . . to require the corporation to defend the particular suit which is brought there." *Id.* at 317. Implicit in this emphasis on reasonableness is the understanding that the burden on the defendant, while always a primary concern, will in an appropriate case be considered in light of other relevant factors, including the forum State's interest in adjudicating the dispute; the plaintiff's interest in obtaining convenient and effective relief, at least when that interest is not adequately protected by the plaintiff's power to choose the forum; the interstate judicial system's interest in obtaining the most efficient resolution of controversies; and the shared interest of the several States in furthering fundamental substantive social policies.

The limits imposed on state jurisdiction by the Due Process Clause, in its role as a guarantor against inconvenient litigation, have been substantially relaxed over the years. As we noted in *McGee v. International Life Ins. Co.*, 335 U.S. 220, 222-23 (1957), this trend is largely attributable to a fundamental transformation in the American economy:

Today many commercial transactions touch two or more States and may involve parties separated by the full continent. With this increasing nationalization of commerce has come a great increase in the amount of business conducted by mail across state lines. At the same time modern transportation and communication have made it much less burdensome for a party sued to defend himself in a State where he engages in economic activity.

The historical developments noted in *McGee*, of course, have only accelerated in the generation since that case was decided. Nevertheless, we have never accepted the proposition that state lines are irrelevant for jurisdictional purposes, nor could we, and remain faithful to the principles of interstate federalism embodied in the Constitution. The economic interdependence of the States was foreseen and desired by the Framers. In the Commerce Clause, they provided that the Nation was to be a common market, a "free trade unit" in which the States are debarred from acting as separable economic entities. *H.P. Hood & Sons, Inc. v. Du Mond*, 336 U.S. 525, 538 (1949). But the Framers also intended that the States retain many essential attributes of sovereignty, including, in particular, the sovereign power to try causes in their courts. The sovereignty of each State, in turn, implied a limitation on the sovereignty of all of its sister States—a limitation express or implicit in both the original scheme of the Constitution and the Fourteenth Amendment. . . . [Indeed, w]e emphasized [in *International Shoe*] that the reasonableness of asserting jurisdiction over the defendant must be assessed "in the context of our federal system of government." 326 U.S. at 317. . . .

Thus, the Due Process Clause "does not contemplate that a state may make binding a judgment *in personam* against an individual or corporate defendant with which the state has no contacts, ties, or relations." *Id.* at 319. Even if the defendant would suffer minimal or no inconvenience from being forced to litigate before the tribunals of another State; even if the forum State has a strong interest in applying its law to the controversy; even if the forum State is the most convenient location for litigation, the Due Process Clause, acting as an instrument of interstate federalism, may sometimes act to divest the State of its power to render a valid judgment. *Hanson*, 357 U.S. at 254.

III

Applying these principles to the case at hand, we find in the record before us a total absence of those affiliating circumstances that are a necessary predicate to any exercise of state-court jurisdiction. Petitioners carry on no activity whatsoever in Oklahoma. They close no sales and perform no services there. They avail themselves of none of the privileges and benefits of Oklahoma law. They solicit no business there either through salespersons or through advertising reasonably calculated to reach the State. Nor does the record show that they regularly sell cars at wholesale or retail to Oklahoma customers or residents or that they indirectly, through others, serve or seek to serve the Oklahoma market. In short, respondents seek to base jurisdiction on one, isolated occurrence and whatever inferences can be drawn therefrom: the fortuitous circumstance that a single Audi automobile, sold in New York to New York residents, happened to suffer an accident while passing through Oklahoma.

It is argued, however, that because an automobile is mobile by its very design and purpose it was "foreseeable" that the Robinsons' Audi would cause injury in Oklahoma. Yet "foreseeability" alone has never been a sufficient benchmark for personal jurisdiction under the Due Process Clause.

If foreseeability were the criterion, a local California tire retailer could be forced to defend in Pennsylvania when a blowout occurs there; a Wisconsin seller of a defective automobile jack could be haled before a distant court for damage caused in New Jersey; or a Florida soft-drink concessionaire could be summoned to Alaska to account for injuries happening there. Every seller of chattels would in effect appoint the chattel his agent for service of process. His amenability to suit would travel with the chattel. . . .

This is not to say, of course, that foreseeability is wholly irrelevant. But the foreseeability that is critical to due process analysis is not the mere likelihood that a product will find its way into the forum State. Rather, it is that the defendant's conduct and connection with the forum State are such that he should reasonably anticipate being haled into court there. The Due Process Clause, by ensuring the "orderly administration of the laws," *Int'l Shoe*, 326 U.S. at 319, gives a degree of predictability to the legal system that allows potential defendants to structure their primary conduct with some minimum assurance as to where that conduct will and will not render them liable to suit.

When a corporation "purposefully avails itself of the privilege of conducting activities within the forum State," *Hanson*, 357 U.S. at 253, it has clear notice that it is subject to suit there, and can act to alleviate the risk of burdensome litigation by procuring insurance, passing the expected costs on to customers, or, if the risks are too great, severing its connection with the State. Hence if the sale of a product of a manufacturer or distributor such as Audi or Volkswagen is not simply an isolated occurrence, but arises from the efforts of the manufacturer or distributor to serve directly or indirectly, the market for its product in other States, it is not unreasonable to subject it to suit in one of those States if its allegedly defective merchandise has there been the source of injury to its owner or to others. The forum State does not exceed its powers under the Due Process Clause if it asserts personal jurisdiction over a corporation that delivers its products into the stream of commerce with the expectation that they will be purchased by consumers in the forum State. *Cf. Gray v. American Radiator & Standard Sanitary Corp.*, 176 N.E.2d 761 (Ill. 1961).

But there is no such or similar basis for Oklahoma jurisdiction over World-Wide or Seaway in this case. Seaway's sales are made in Massena, N.Y. World-Wide's market, although substantially larger, is limited to dealers in New York, New Jersey, and Connecticut. There is no evidence of record that any automobiles distributed by World-Wide are sold to retail customers outside this tri-state area. It is foreseeable that the purchasers of automobiles sold by World-Wide and Seaway may take them to Oklahoma. But the mere "unilateral activity of those who claim some relationship with a nonresident defendant cannot satisfy the requirement of contact with the forum State." *Hanson*, 357 U.S. at 253.

[It is contended] . . . that the purchase of automobiles in New York, from which the petitioners earn substantial revenue, would not occur *but for* the fact that the automobiles are capable of use in distant States like Oklahoma. Respondents observe that the very purpose of an automobile is to travel, and that travel of automobiles sold by petitioners is facilitated by an extensive chain of Volkswagen service centers throughout the country, including some in Oklahoma. However, financial benefits accruing to the defendant from a collateral relation to the forum State will not support jurisdiction if they do not stem from a constitutionally cognizable contact with that State. In our view, whatever marginal revenues petitioners may receive by virtue of the fact that their products are capable of use in Oklahoma is far too attenuated a contact to justify that State's exercise of *in personam* jurisdiction over them.

Because we find that petitioners have no "contacts, ties, or relations" with the State of Oklahoma, the judgment of the Supreme Court of Oklahoma is

Reversed.

BRENNAN, J., dissenting.

The Court holds that the Due Process Clause of the Fourteenth Amendment bars [Oklahoma] from asserting jurisdiction over the defendants. . . . The Court so decides because it fails to find the "minimum contacts" that have been required since *Int'l Shoe*, 326 U.S. at 316. Because I believe that the Court reads *International Shoe* and its progeny too narrowly, and because I believe that the standards enunciated by those cases may already be obsolete as constitutional boundaries, I dissent.

I

The Court's opinion focuses tightly on the existence of contacts between the forum and the defendant. In so doing, they accord too little weight to the strength of the forum State's interest in the case and fail to explore whether there would be any actual inconvenience to the defendant. The essential inquiry in locating the constitutional limits on state-court jurisdiction over absent defendants is whether the particular exercise of jurisdiction offends "traditional notions of fair play and substantial justice." *Int'l Shoe*, 326 U.S. at 316. . . . The existence of contacts, so long as there were some, was merely one way of giving content to the determination of fairness and reasonableness.

Surely *International Shoe* contemplated that the significance of the contacts necessary to support jurisdiction would diminish if some other consideration helped establish that jurisdiction would be fair and reasonable. The interests of the State and other parties in proceeding with the case in a particular forum are such considerations. *McGee*, 355 U.S. at 223, for instance, accorded great importance to a State's "manifest interest in providing effective means of redress" for its citizens.

Another consideration is the actual burden a defendant must bear in defending the suit in the forum. . . . The burden, of course, must be of constitutional dimension. Due process limits on jurisdiction do not protect a defendant from all inconvenience of travel, *id.* at 224, and it would not be sensible to make the constitutional rule turn solely on the number of miles the defendant must travel to the courtroom. Instead, the constitutionally significant "burden" to be analyzed relates to the mobility of the defendant's defense. For instance, if having to travel to a foreign forum would hamper the defense because witnesses or evidence or the defendant himself were immobile, or if there were a disproportionately large number of witnesses or amount of evidence that would have to be transported at the defendant's expense, or if being away from home for the duration of the trial would work some special hardship on the defendant, then the Constitution would require special consideration for the defendant's interests. . . . The Constitution does not require that trial be held in the State which has the best contacts with the defendant.

II

. . . I would [also] find that the forum State has an interest in permitting the litigation to go forward, the litigation is connected to the forum, the defendant is linked to the forum, and the burden of defending is not unreasonable. Accordingly, I would hold that it is neither unfair nor unreasonable to require these defendants to defend in the forum State. . . .

The interest of the forum State and its connection to the litigation is strong. The automobile accident underlying the litigation occurred in Oklahoma. The plaintiffs were hospitalized in Oklahoma when they brought suit. Essential witnesses and evidence were in Oklahoma. The State has a legitimate interest in enforcing its laws designed to keep its highway system safe, and the trial can proceed at least as efficiently in Oklahoma as anywhere else.

The petitioners are not unconnected with the forum. Although both sell automobiles within limited sales territories, each sold the automobile which in fact was driven to Oklahoma where it was involved in an accident. It may be true, as the Court suggests, that each sincerely intended to limit its commercial impact to the limited territory, and that each intended to accept the benefits and protection of the laws only of those States within the territory. But obviously these were unrealistic hopes that cannot be treated as an automatic constitutional shield.

An automobile simply is not a stationary item or one designed to be used in one place. An automobile is *intended* to be moved around. Someone in the business of selling large numbers of automobiles can hardly plead ignorance of their mobility or pretend that the automobiles stay put after they are sold. It is not merely that a dealer in automobiles foresees that they will move. The dealer actually intends that the purchasers will use the automobiles to travel to distant States where the dealer does not directly "do business." The sale of an automobile does *purposefully* inject the vehicle into the stream of interstate commerce so that it can travel to distant States. *See Hanson*, 357 U.S. 235, 253 (1958)....

The Court accepts that a State may exercise jurisdiction over a distributor which "serves" that State "indirectly" by "deliver[ing] its products into the stream of commerce with the expectation that they will be purchased by consumers in the forum State." It is difficult to see why the Constitution should distinguish between a case involving goods which reach a distant State through a chain of distribution and a case involving goods which reach the same State because a consumer, using them as the dealer knew the customer would, took them there. In each case the seller purposefully injects the goods into the stream of commerce and those goods predictably are used in the forum State.

Furthermore, an automobile seller derives substantial benefits from States other than its own. A large part of the value of automobiles is the extensive, nationwide network of highways. Significant portions of that network have been constructed by and are maintained by the individual States, including Oklahoma. The States, through their highway programs, contribute in a very direct and important way to the value of petitioners' businesses. Additionally, a network of other related dealerships with their service departments operates throughout the country under the protection of the laws of the various States, including Oklahoma, and enhances the value of petitioners' businesses by facilitating their customers' traveling....

III

It may be that affirmance of the judgments in these cases would approach the outer limits of *International Shoe*'s jurisdictional principle. But that principle, with its almost exclusive focus on the rights of defendants, may be outdated....

As the Court acknowledges . . . both the nationalization of commerce and the ease of transportation and communication have [changed] [t]he model of society on which the *International Shoe* Court based its opinion.... Business people, no matter how local their businesses, cannot assume that goods remain in the business' locality. Customers and goods can be anywhere else in the country usually in a matter of hours and always in a matter of a very few days.

In answering the question whether or not it is fair and reasonable to allow a particular forum to hold a trial binding on a particular defendant, the interests of the forum State and other parties loom large in today's world and surely are entitled to as much weight as are the interests of the defendant.... The conclusion I draw is that constitutional concepts of fairness no longer require the extreme concern for defendants that was once necessary....

The Court's opinion suggests that the defendant ought to be subject to a State's jurisdiction only if he has contacts with the State "such that he should reasonably anticipate being haled into court there." There is nothing unreasonable or unfair, however, about recognizing commercial reality.... [While] I would not abolish limits on jurisdiction or strip state boundaries of all significance . . . I would . . . strip the defendant of an unjustified veto power over certain very appropriate fora—a power the defendant justifiably enjoyed long ago when communication and travel over long distances were slog and unpredictable and when notions of state sovereignty were impractical and exaggerated....

The plaintiffs . . . brought suit in a forum with which they had significant contacts and which had significant contact with the litigation. I am not convinced that the defendant would suffer any heavy and disproportionate burden in defending the suits.... The constitution should not shield the defendants from appearing and defending in the plaintiff's chosen fora.

[The dissent of Justice Marshall, with whom Justice Blackmun joins, is omitted.]

Notes & Questions

1. The Robinsons sued four defendants. Which two defendants objected to personal jurisdiction in Oklahoma? Where was each of these defendants located, and what was the scope of their business?

2. Despite the fact that their businesses were located far from Oklahoma, World-Wide and Seaway had one very important contact with Oklahoma, didn't they? They sold an automobile to the Robinsons that caught fire in Oklahoma in a collision, allegedly due to a defective design, causing serious injuries to the Robinsons. Why, according to the majority, was this insufficient to establish personal jurisdiction? How would the majority distinguish the Robinsons' case from *McGee v. International Life Ins. Co.*, 355 U.S. 220 (1957), discussed above, in which the Court upheld personal jurisdiction where the plaintiff's claim arose out of a defendant's single contact with the forum state? In the majority's view, is the Robinsons' case more like *McGee* or more like *Hanson v. Denckla*, 357 U.S. 235 (1958)? Why?

3. In addition to the fact that they sold the car that injured the Robinsons in Oklahoma, what other contacts did World-Wide and Seaway have with Oklahoma? The majority and dissent offer rather different views on what counts as sufficiently purposeful contacts, don't they?

4. The majority gives little discussion to the connection between the plaintiffs and Oklahoma—plaintiffs who were hospitalized at the time they filed suit. Should plaintiffs' interests be taken into account in the due process analysis? What about Oklahoma's interests?

5. *World-Wide Volkswagen* was a 6-3 decision. The first vigorous dissent is by Justice Brennan. He argues that "the Court reads *International Shoe* and its progeny too narrowly." How so? He also says "the standards enunciated by those cases may already be obsolete as constitutional boundaries." What does he mean? The *International Shoe* test was a great leap toward modernity as compared with the traditional bases for jurisdiction embraced by *Pennoyer*. Has the *International Shoe* test, as well, outlived its usefulness?

6. Make sure you understand—based on the opinions of both the majority and the dissent—the connections between purposeful availment and foreseeability, as well as the differences between them. Why did Justice Brennan think that

foreseeability supported a finding that the defendants purposefully availed themselves of Oklahoma? Why, according to the majority, did this sort of foreseeability fail to meet the minimum contacts test?

7. Justice Marshall, joined by Justice Blackmun, penned a separate dissent criticizing the majority for failing to focus on the economic benefits petitioners received from Oklahoma (as well as from every other contiguous state in the United States). If a distributor or retailer sells products that may be used in every state, and if it benefits economically from this, how should the economic benefit figure into the personal jurisdiction analysis? And if the dissenters are correct that the economic benefit to defendants should count as purposeful contact, should that mean that the Robinsons could have sued World-Wide and Seaway in *any* state, or just that they could have sued in Oklahoma, where the accident occurred?

8. You have now learned about four of the most famous cases in the minimum contacts canon—*International Shoe, McGee, Hanson,* and *World-Wide Volkswagen.* The latter three apply and attempt to define the contours of the test set forth in *International Shoe.* But do these latter three cases interpret and apply the minimum contacts test the same way? Do they emphasize the same values? To help you think about these questions, analyze *World-Wide Volkswagen* as the Court in *McGee* likely would have, and vice versa. Do the same with *Hanson* and *World-Wide Volkswagen.*

(ii) Application of Purposeful Availment

Purposeful Availment by Intentional Acts Directed at the Forum. The Supreme Court's decisions in *Hanson* and *World-Wide Volkswagen* made it clear that, to satisfy the minimum contacts test, what is needed is "purposeful availment." The case must arise out of something the defendant did that was directed at the forum state. The mere foreseeability of a car making its way from New York to Oklahoma does not suffice. Does this mean that a defendant can never be subject to specific jurisdiction based on conduct that occurred outside the state? What if the defendant's out-of-state conduct was both intentional and could foreseeably cause harmful effects in the forum state? Consider the following case.

CALDER v. JONES
465 U.S. 783 (1984)

REHNQUIST, J., delivered the opinion of the Court.

Respondent Shirley Jones brought suit in California Superior Court claiming that she had been libeled in an article written and edited by petitioners in Florida. The article was published in a national magazine with a large circulation in California. Petitioners were served with process by mail in Florida and caused special appearances to be entered on their behalf, moving to quash the service of process for lack of personal jurisdiction. . . .

Respondent lives and works in California. She and her husband brought this suit against the National Enquirer, Inc., its local distributing company, and petitioners for libel, invasion of privacy, and intentional infliction of emotional harm. The Enquirer is a Florida corporation with its principal place of business in Florida. It publishes a national weekly newspaper with a total circulation of over 5 million. About 600,000 of those copies, almost twice the level of the next highest State, are sold in California. Respondent's and her husband's claims were based on an article that appeared in the Enquirer's October 9, 1979, issue. Both the Enquirer and the distributing company answered the complaint and made no objection to the jurisdiction of the California court.

Petitioner South is a reporter employed by the Enquirer. He is a resident of Florida, though he frequently [(6-12 times per year)] travels to California on business. South wrote the first draft of the challenged article, and his byline appeared on it. He did most of his research in Florida, relying on phone calls to sources in California for the information contained in the article. Shortly before publication, South called respondent's home and read to her husband a draft of the article so as to elicit his comments upon it. Aside from his frequent trips and phone calls, South has no other relevant contacts with California.

Petitioner Calder is also a Florida resident. He has been to California only twice—once, on a pleasure trip, prior to the publication of the article and once after to testify in an unrelated trial. Calder is president and editor of the Enquirer. He "oversee[s] just about every function of the Enquirer." He reviewed and approved the initial evaluation of the subject of the article and edited it in its final form. He also declined to print a retraction requested by respondent. Calder has no other relevant contacts with California.

In considering petitioners' motion to quash service of process, the Superior Court surmised that the actions of petitioners in Florida, causing injury to respondent in California, would ordinarily be sufficient to support an assertion of jurisdiction over them [under] California['s long arm statute.][5] But the [Superior Court] felt special solicitude was necessary because of the potential "chilling effect" on reporters and editors which would result from requiring them to appear in remote jurisdictions to answer for the content of articles upon which they worked.

The California Court of Appeal reversed . . . [and] rejected the Superior Court's conclusion that First Amendment considerations must be weighed in the scale against jurisdiction. . . .

The Due Process Clause of the Fourteenth Amendment to the United States Constitution permits personal jurisdiction over a defendant in any State with which the defendant has "certain minimum contacts . . . such that the maintenance of the suit does not offend traditional notions of fair play and substantial justice." *Int'l Shoe*, 326 U.S. at 316. In judging minimum contacts, a court properly focuses on "the relationship among the defendant, the forum, and the litigation." *Shaffer v. Heitner*, 438 U.S. 186, 204 (1977). The plaintiff's lack of

---

[5] California's "long-arm" statute . . . provides that "A court of this state may exercise jurisdiction on any basis not inconsistent with the Constitution of this state or of the United States." [Cal. Code Civ. Proc. §410.10.]

contacts will not defeat otherwise proper jurisdiction, but they may be so manifold as to permit jurisdiction when it would not exist in their absence. Here, the plaintiff is the focus of the activities of the defendants out of which the suit arises. *See McGee*, 355 U.S. at 220.

The allegedly libelous story concerned the California activities of a California resident. It impugned the professionalism of an entertainer whose television career was centered in California. The article was drawn from California sources, and the brunt of the harm, in terms both of respondent's emotional distress and the injury to her professional reputation, was suffered in California. In sum, California is the focal point both of the story and of the harm suffered. Jurisdiction over petitioners is therefore proper in California based on the "effects" of their Florida conduct in California. *World-Wide Volkswagen*, 444 U.S. at 297-98.

Petitioners argue that they are not responsible for the circulation of the article in California. A reporter and an editor, they claim, have no direct economic stake in their employer's sales in a distant State. Nor are ordinary employees able to control their employer's marketing activity. The mere fact that they can "foresee" that the article will be circulated and have an effect in California is not sufficient for an assertion of jurisdiction. *World-Wide Volkswagen*, 444 U.S. at 295. Petitioners liken themselves to a welder employed in Florida who works on a boiler which subsequently explodes in California. Cases which hold that jurisdiction will be proper over the manufacturer, should not be applied to the welder who has no control over and derives no direct benefit from his employer's sales in that distant State.

Petitioners' analogy does not wash. Whatever the status of their hypothetical welder, petitioners are not charged with mere untargeted negligence. Rather, their intentional, and allegedly tortious, actions were expressly aimed at California. Petitioner South wrote and petitioner Calder edited an article that they knew would have a potentially devastating impact upon respondent. And they knew that the brunt of that injury would be felt by respondent in the State in which she lives and works and in which the *National Enquirer* has its largest circulation. Under the circumstances, petitioners must "reasonably anticipate being haled into court there" to answer for the truth of the statements made in their article. *World-Wide Volkswagen*, 444 U.S. at 297. An individual injured in California need not go to Florida to seek redress from persons who, though remaining in Florida, knowingly cause the injury in California. . . .

Petitioners are correct that their contacts with California are not to be judged according to their employer's activities there. On the other hand, their status as employees does not somehow insulate them from jurisdiction. Each defendant's contacts with the forum State must be assessed individually. In this case, petitioners are primary participants in an alleged wrongdoing intentionally directed at a California resident, and jurisdiction over them is proper on that basis.

We hold that jurisdiction over petitioners in California is proper because of their intentional conduct in Florida calculated to cause injury to respondent in California. The judgment of the California Court of Appeal is

Affirmed.

Notes & Questions

1. The same day as *Calder*, the Supreme Court decided *Keeton v. Hustler Magazine, Inc.*, 465 U.S. 770 (1984), another case raising a question of personal jurisdiction over a defendant magazine accused of libel. Plaintiff Kathy Keeton, a resident of New York, sued defendant Hustler Magazine, an Ohio corporation with a principal place of business in California. At the time of Keeton's suit, the statute of limitations in Ohio and other states had already run, so she opted to sue in New Hampshire. Hustler Magazine objected on personal jurisdiction grounds, arguing that its contacts with the state were insufficient. Hustler's only connection to New Hampshire was that between 10,000 and 15,000 copies of its nationally distributed magazine were sold in the state each month. The Supreme Court unanimously held that New Hampshire could exercise personal jurisdiction over Hustler, reasoning that by choosing to circulate the allegedly libelous magazines in New Hampshire, Hustler had "purposefully directed" its actions at New Hampshire and "inevitably affected persons in the state." *Id.* at 774. Notably, the Court pointed out that New Hampshire had a sufficiently strong interest to justify personal jurisdiction over Hustler in this case because New Hampshire had the right to protect its citizens from deceptive material.

2. Why didn't the Supreme Court's holding in *Keeton* suffice to answer the question in *Calder*? (Hint: In *Calder*, which defendants objected to personal jurisdiction?) Note that Shirley Jones sued the National Enquirer along with the individual defendants. Did the Supreme Court case address whether California had personal jurisdiction over the company? If it had addressed that issue, what would the answer have been?

3. On the surface, *Calder* resembles *World-Wide Volkswagen*. In each case, defendants engaged in out-of-state conduct that was alleged to have caused a harmful effect in the forum state. Yet the Court unanimously reached the opposite result in *Calder* from its answer in *World-Wide Volkswagen*. Why? In *Calder*, is the Court relaxing its approach to minimum contacts set forth in *World-Wide Volkswagen*, or are the cases distinguishable? Consider two possible ways to distinguish the cases. First, consider the *types of claims* in these two cases. One case involves an intentional tort; the other does not. Why would that matter to the personal jurisdiction analysis? Second, consider the *directedness* of the contact. One case involves a fortuitous effect in the forum state that could as easily have occurred in any other state; the other involves a non-fortuitous and predictably greater effect in the forum state. After you are comfortable that you see how the Court could distinguish the two cases, ask yourself whether you are convinced that these differences *should* matter to the due process analysis.

4. Consider the following passage in *Calder*: "The plaintiff's lack of contacts will not defeat otherwise proper jurisdiction, but they may be so manifold as to permit jurisdiction when it would not exist in their absence." What does the Court mean by this? Can specific jurisdiction be premised on forum contacts of the *plaintiff* rather than the defendant? Or do the plaintiff's contacts matter only as a way

to help determine the *defendant's* purposeful availment? Is this what the *Calder* Court means by its very next sentence ("Here, the plaintiff is the focus of the activities of the defendants out of which the suit arises.")? To what extent does *Calder* open up the possibility of arguing for personal jurisdiction based on plaintiffs' connections to the forum state?

Perhaps *Walden v. Fiore*, 571 U.S. 277 (2014), can help you answer that question. In *Walden*, two professional gamblers, Fiore and Gipson, were passing through the Atlanta, Georgia airport on their way home to Nevada. While in Atlanta, DEA Agent Walden searched the pair and seized $97,000 in cash from their luggage. Walden, still in Georgia, later drafted an affidavit asserting (falsely, it turned out) probable cause for the seizure of Fiore's and Gipson's money. The pair then filed suit against Walden in the U.S. District Court for the District of Nevada, claiming that Walden intentionally filed a false affidavit. The Supreme Court held that Nevada could not exercise personal jurisdiction over Walden. While both *Calder* and *Walden* involved claims for intentional acts, and both involved claims of harmful effects suffered by plaintiffs in the forum state, what was lacking in *Walden*, the Court said, was purposeful availment by the defendant:

> *Calder* made clear that mere injury to a forum resident is not a sufficient connection to the forum. Regardless of where a plaintiff lives or works, an injury is jurisdictionally relevant only insofar as it shows that the defendant has formed a contact with the forum State. The proper question is not where the plaintiff experienced a particular injury or effect but whether the defendant's conduct connects him to the forum in a meaningful way.

Walden, 571 U.S. at 283. Though Walden's actions in Georgia *affected* plaintiffs while they were in Nevada, the Court held that Walden had not directed his conduct toward Nevada in the ways that the writer and editor in *Calder* had directed their conduct toward California. Do you see the difference? Are you persuaded by it?

Purposeful Availment in Business Relationships. A great deal of litigation involves business relationships, many of which cross state lines (and international boundaries as well). Thus, it is critical to learn what sorts of business contacts constitute purposeful availment. Begin by studying the following case.

BURGER KING CORPORATION v. RUDZEWICZ
471 U.S. 462 (1985)

BRENNAN, J., delivered the opinion of the Court.

The State of Florida's long-arm statute extends jurisdiction to "[a]ny person, whether or not a citizen or resident of this state," who, *inter alia*, "[b]reach[es] a contract in this state by failing to perform acts required by the contract to be performed in this state," so long as the cause of action arises from the alleged contractual breach. Fla. Stat. §48.193(1)(g). The United States District Court for the Southern District of Florida, sitting in diversity, relied on this provision in exercising personal jurisdiction over a Michigan resident who allegedly had breached a franchise agreement with a Florida corporation by failing to make required payments in Florida. The question presented is whether this exercise of long-arm jurisdiction offended "traditional conception[s] of fair play and substantial justice" embodied in the Due Process Clause of the Fourteenth Amendment. *Int'l Shoe*, 326 U.S. at 320.

I

A

Burger King Corporation is a Florida corporation whose principal offices are in Miami.... Burger King licenses its franchisees to use its trademarks and service marks for a period of 20 years and leases standardized restaurant facilities to them for the same term....

The instant litigation grows out of Burger King's termination of one of its franchisees.... The appellee John Rudzewicz, a Michigan citizen and resident... along with Brian MacShara, the son of a business acquaintance... jointly appl[ied] to Burger King for a franchise in the Detroit area [believing the idea offered attractive investment and tax-deferral opportunities].

Rudzewicz and MacShara jointly applied for a franchise to Burger King's Birmingham, Michigan, district office in the autumn of 1978. Their application was forwarded to Burger King's Miami headquarters, which entered into a preliminary agreement with them in February 1979. During the ensuing four months it was agreed that Rudzewicz and MacShara would assume operation of an existing facility in Drayton Plains, Michigan. MacShara attended the prescribed management courses in Miami during this period, and the franchisees purchased $165,000 worth of restaurant equipment from Burger King's Davmor Industries division in Miami. Even before the final agreements were signed, however, the parties began to disagree over site-development fees, building design, computation of monthly rent, and whether the franchisees would be able to assign their liabilities to a corporation they had formed. During these disputes Rudzewicz and MacShara negotiated both with the Birmingham district office and with the Miami headquarters. With some misgivings, Rudzewicz and MacShara finally obtained limited concessions from the Miami headquarters, signed the final agreements, and commenced operations in June 1979. By signing the final agreements, Rudzewicz obligated himself personally to payments exceeding $1 million over the 20-year franchise relationship.

The Drayton Plains facility apparently enjoyed steady business during the summer of 1979, but patronage declined after a recession began later that year. Rudzewicz and MacShara soon fell far behind in their monthly payments to Miami. Headquarters sent notices of default, and an extended period of negotiations began among the franchisees, the Birmingham district office, and the Miami headquarters. [After unsuccessful negotiations], headquarters terminated the franchise and ordered Rudzewicz and MacShara to vacate the premises. They refused and continued to occupy and operate the facility as a Burger King restaurant.

B

Burger King commenced the instant action in the United States District Court for the Southern District of Florida... alleg[ing] that Rudzewicz and MacShara had [*inter alia*] breached their franchise obligations "within [the jurisdiction of] this district court" by failing to make the required payments "at plaintiff's place of business in Miami, Dade County, Florida." ... Rudzewicz and MacShara entered special appearances and argued, *inter alia*, that because they were Michigan residents and because Burger King's claim did not "arise" within the Southern District of Florida, the District Court lacked personal jurisdiction over them. The District Court denied their motions ... [and] [a]fter a 3-day bench trial ... [found] that Rudzewicz and MacShara had breached their franchise agreements with Burger King.... [T]he court entered judgment against them, jointly and severally, for $228,875 in contract damages....

Rudzewicz appealed to the Court of Appeals for the Eleventh Circuit, [which] reversed the judgment....

II

A

The Due Process Clause protects an individual's liberty interest in not being subject to the binding judgments of a forum with which he has established no meaningful "contacts, ties, or relations." *Int'l Shoe*, 326 U.S. at 319. By requiring that individuals have "fair warning that a particular activity may subject [them] to the jurisdiction of a foreign sovereign," *Shaffer v. Heitner*, 433 U.S. 186, 218 (1977) (Stevens, J., concurring in judgment), the Due Process Clause "gives a degree of predictability to the legal system that allows potential defendants to structure their primary conduct with some minimum assurance as to where that conduct will and will not render them liable to suit," *World-Wide Volkswagen*, 444 U.S. at 297.

Where a forum seeks to assert specific jurisdiction over an out-of-state defendant who has not consented to suit there, this "fair warning" requirement is satisfied if the defendant has "purposefully directed"

his activities at residents of the forum, *Keeton v. Hustler Magazine, Inc.*, 465 U.S. 770, 774 (1984), and the litigation results from alleged injuries that "arise out of or relate to" those activities, *Helicopteros Nacionales de Colombia, S.A. v. Hall*, 466 U.S. 408, 414.... [W]ith respect to interstate contractual obligations, we have emphasized that parties who "reach out beyond one state and create continuing relationships and obligations with citizens of another state" are subject to regulation and sanctions in the other State for the consequences of their activities. *Travelers Health Ass'n v. Virginia*, 339 U.S. 643, 647 (1950).

We have noted several reasons why a forum legitimately may exercise personal jurisdiction over a nonresident who "purposefully directs" his activities toward forum residents. A State generally has a "manifest interest" in providing its residents with a convenient forum for redressing injuries inflicted by out-of-state actors. [*McGee v. Int'l Life Ins. Co.*, 355 U.S. 220, 223 (1957).] Moreover, where individuals "purposefully derive benefit" from their interstate activities, *Kulko v. Cal. Superior Court*, 436 U.S. 84, 96 (1978), it may well be unfair to allow them to escape having to account in other States for consequences that arise proximately from such activities; the Due Process Clause may not readily be wielded as a territorial shield to avoid interstate obligations that have been voluntarily assumed. And because "modern transportation and communications have made it much less burdensome for a party sued to defend himself in a State where he engages in economic activity," it usually will not be unfair to subject him to the burdens of litigating in another forum for disputes relating to such activity. *McGee*, 355 U.S. at 223.

Notwithstanding these considerations, the constitutional touchstone remains whether the defendant purposefully established "minimum contacts" in the forum State. *Int'l Shoe*, 326 U.S. at 316. Although it has been argued that foreseeability of causing *injury* in another State should be sufficient to establish such contacts there when policy considerations so require, the Court has consistently held that this kind of foreseeability is not a "sufficient benchmark" for exercising personal jurisdiction. *World-Wide Volkswagen*, 444 U.S. at 295. Instead, "the foreseeability that is critical to due process analysis . . . is that the defendant's conduct and connection with the forum State are such that he should reasonably anticipate being haled into court there." *Id.* at 297. In defining when it is that a potential defendant should "reasonably anticipate" out-of-state litigation, the Court frequently has drawn from the reasoning of *Hanson*, 357 U.S. at 253:

> The unilateral activity of those who claim some relationship with a nonresident defendant cannot satisfy the requirement of contact with the forum State. The application of that rule will vary with the quality and nature of the defendant's activity, but it is essential in each case that there be some act by which the defendant purposefully avails itself of the privilege of conducting activities within the forum State, thus invoking the benefits and protections of its laws.

This "purposeful availment" requirement ensures that a defendant will not be haled into a jurisdiction solely as a result of "random," "fortuitous," or "attenuated" contacts, *World-Wide Volkswagen*, 444 U.S. at 299, or of the "unilateral activity of another party or a third person." *Helicopteros*, 466 U.S. at 417. Jurisdiction is proper, however, where the contacts proximately result from actions by the defendant *himself* that create

a "substantial connection" with the forum State. *McGee*, 355 U.S. at 223. Thus where the defendant "deliberately" has engaged in significant activities within a State, *Keeton*, 465 U.S. at 781, or has created "continuing obligations" between himself and residents of the forum, *Travelers Health Ass'n*, 339 U.S. at 648, he manifestly has availed himself of the privilege of conducting business there, and because his activities are shielded by the benefits and protections of the forum's laws it is presumptively not unreasonable to require him to submit to the burdens of litigation in that forum as well.

Jurisdiction in these circumstances may not be avoided merely because the defendant did not *physically* enter the forum State. Although territorial presence frequently will enhance a potential defendant's affiliation with a State and reinforce the reasonable foreseeability of suit there, it is an inescapable fact of modern commercial life that a substantial amount of business is transacted solely by mail and wire communications across state lines, thus obviating the need for physical presence within a State in which business is conducted. So long as a commercial actor's efforts are "purposefully directed" toward residents of another State, we have consistently rejected the notion that an absence of physical contacts can defeat personal jurisdiction there. *See, e.g., Keeton*, 465 U.S. at 774-75; *Calder*, 465 U.S. at 778-90; *McGee*, 355 U.S. at 222-23.

Once it has been decided that a defendant purposefully established minimum contacts within the forum State, these contacts may be considered in light of other factors to determine whether the assertion of personal jurisdiction would comport with "fair play and substantial justice." *Int'l Shoe*, 326 U.S. at 320. Thus courts in "appropriate case[s]" may evaluate "the burden on the defendant," "the forum

State's interest in adjudicating the dispute," "the plaintiff's interest in obtaining convenient and effective relief," "the interstate judicial system's interest in obtaining the most efficient resolution of controversies," and the "shared interest of the several States in furthering fundamental substantive social policies." *World-Wide Volkswagen*, 444 U.S. at 292. These considerations sometimes serve to establish the reasonableness of jurisdiction upon a lesser showing of minimum contacts than would otherwise be required.

On the other hand, where a defendant who purposefully has directed his activities at forum residents seeks to defeat jurisdiction, he must present a compelling case that the presence of some other considerations would render jurisdiction unreasonable [(though] [m]ost such considerations usually may be accommodated through means short of finding jurisdiction unconstitutional, [such as venue change)]. Nevertheless, minimum requirements inherent in the concept of "fair play and substantial justice" may defeat the reasonableness of jurisdiction even if the defendant has purposefully engaged in forum activities. *Id.*

B
1

Applying these principles to the case at hand, we believe there is substantial record evidence supporting the District Court's conclusion that the assertion of personal jurisdiction over Rudzewicz in Florida for the alleged breach of his franchise agreement did not offend due process. At the outset, we note . . . [that an] individual's contract with an out-of-state party *alone* can[not] automatically establish sufficient minimum contacts in the other party's home forum. The Court long ago rejected the notion that personal jurisdiction might

turn on "mechanical" tests, *Int'l Shoe*, 326 U.S. at 319, or on "conceptualistic theories of the place of contracting or of performance." *Hoopeston Canning Co. v. Cullen*, 318 U.S. 313, 316 (1943). Instead, we have emphasized the need for a "highly realistic" approach that recognizes that a "contract" is "ordinarily but an intermediate step serving to tie up prior business negotiations with future consequences which themselves are the real object of the business transaction." *Id.* at 316-17. It is these factors—prior negotiations and contemplated future consequences, along with the terms of the contract and the parties' actual course of dealing—that must be evaluated in determining whether the defendant purposefully established minimum contacts within the forum.

In this case, no physical ties to Florida can be attributed to Rudzewicz other than MacShara's brief training course in Miami. Rudzewicz did not maintain offices in Florida and, for all that appears from the record, has never even visited there. Yet this franchise dispute grew directly out of "a contract which had a *substantial* connection with that State." *McGee*, 355 U.S. at 223. [R]udzewicz deliberately "reach[ed] out beyond" Michigan and negotiated with a Florida corporation for the purchase of a long-term franchise and the manifold benefits that would derive from affiliation with a nationwide organization. *Travelers Health Ass'n*, 339 U.S. at 647. Upon approval, he entered into a carefully structured 20-year relationship that envisioned continuing and wide-reaching contacts with Burger King in Florida. In light of Rudzewicz' voluntary acceptance of the long-term and exacting regulation of his business from Burger King's Miami headquarters, the "quality and nature" of his relationship to the company in Florida can in no sense be viewed as "random," "fortuitous," or "attenuated." *Hanson*, 357 U.S. at 253. Rudzewicz' refusal to make the contractually required payments in

Miami, and his continued use of Burger King's trademarks and confidential business information after his termination, caused foreseeable injuries to the corporation in Florida. For these reasons it was, at the very least, presumptively reasonable for Rudzewicz to be called to account there for such injuries.

The Court of Appeals concluded, however, that in light of the supervision emanating from Burger King's district office in Birmingham, Rudzewicz reasonably believed that "the Michigan office was for all intents and purposes the embodiment of Burger King" and that he therefore had no "reason to anticipate a Burger King suit outside of Michigan." This reasoning overlooks substantial record evidence indicating that Rudzewicz most certainly knew that he was affiliating himself with an enterprise based primarily in Florida. The contract documents themselves emphasize that Burger King's operations are conducted and supervised from the Miami headquarters, that all relevant notices and payments must be sent there, and that the agreements were made in and enforced from Miami. Moreover, the parties' actual course of dealing repeatedly confirmed that decision-making authority was vested in the Miami headquarters and that the district office served largely as an intermediate link between the headquarters and the franchisees. When problems arose over building design, site-development fees, rent computation, and the defaulted payments, Rudzewicz and MacShara learned that the Michigan office was powerless to resolve their disputes and could only channel their communications to Miami. [Further] . . . it was the Miami headquarters that made the key negotiating decisions out of which the instant litigation arose.

Moreover, we believe the Court of Appeals gave insufficient weight to provisions in the various franchise documents providing that all disputes would be governed by Florida law. . . . Although such a provision standing alone would be insufficient to confer jurisdiction, we believe that, when combined with the 20-year interdependent relationship Rudzewicz established with Burger King's Miami headquarters, it reinforced his deliberate affiliation with the forum State and the reasonable foreseeability of possible litigation there. As Judge Johnson argued in his dissent below, Rudzewicz "purposefully availed himself of the benefits and protections of Florida's laws" by entering into contracts expressly providing that those laws would govern franchise disputes.

2

Nor has Rudzewicz pointed to other factors that can be said persuasively to outweigh the considerations discussed above and to establish the *unconstitutionality* of Florida's assertion of jurisdiction. We cannot conclude that Florida had no "legitimate interest in holding [Rudzewicz] answerable on a claim related to" the contacts he had established in that State. *Keeton*, 465 U.S. at 776. Moreover, although Rudzewicz has argued at some length that Michigan's Franchise Investment Law governs many aspects of this franchise relationship, he has not demonstrated how Michigan's acknowledged interest might possibly render jurisdiction in Florida *unconstitutional*. [Finally,] even to the extent that it is inconvenient for a party who has minimum contacts with a forum to litigate there [a finding we do not make here], such considerations most frequently can be accommodated through a change of venue. Although the Court has suggested that inconvenience may at some point become so substantial as to achieve *constitutional* magnitude, this is not such a case.

The Court of Appeals also concluded, however, that the parties' dealings involved "a characteristic disparity of bargaining power" and "elements of surprise," and that

Rudzewicz "lacked fair notice" of the potential for litigation in Florida because the contractual provisions suggesting to the contrary were merely "boilerplate declarations in a lengthy printed contract." . . . [To the contrary, the District Court remarked that] Rudzewicz and his associates "were and are experienced and sophisticated businessmen," who for five months negotiated the franchise contract with Burger King to secure a "reduction in rent and other concessions from Miami headquarters." . . .

Justice STEVENS, with whom Justice WHITE joins, dissenting.

In my opinion there is a significant element of unfairness in requiring a franchisee to defend a case of this kind in the forum chosen by the franchisor. It is undisputed that appellee maintained no place of business in Florida, that he had no employees in that State, and that he was not licensed to do business there. Appellee did not prepare his French fries, shakes, and hamburgers in Michigan, and then deliver them into the stream of commerce "with the expectation that they [would] be purchased by consumers in" Florida. To the contrary, appellee did business only in Michigan, his business, property, and payroll taxes were payable in that State, and he sold all of his products there.

[Justice Stevens then quoted the opinion of the court of appeals, noting (among other things) that all references to Florida in the relevant documents were boilerplate, and that "[t]here is no evidence that Rudzewicz ever negotiated with anyone in Miami or even sent mail there during negotiations. He maintained no staff in the state of Florida, and as far as the record reveals, he has never even visited the state."]

Accordingly, I respectfully dissent.

Notes & Questions

1. As far as we know, has John Rudzewicz ever been to Florida? He ran a couple of fast-food franchises in Michigan. What is the argument that he has sufficient contacts with Florida to hale him into court there?

2. Burger King Corporation is headquartered in Florida. But Burger King is the *plaintiff*. Remember that in *Walden v. Fiore*, 571 U.S. 277 (2014), discussed above in Note 4 after *Calder v. Jones*, the Supreme Court rejected personal jurisdiction based solely on the plaintiff's connection with the forum state. Is *Burger King* distinguishable from *Walden*? What are the most salient facts to distinguish it?

   Further, recall that although the Court in *Calder* upheld jurisdiction in the plaintiff's home state of California, *Calder* involved an intentional tort. This is unlike *Burger King*, which was a breach-of-contract case. Focusing on the nature of the defendants' conduct and the relationship of that conduct to the forum state, do you see how *Calder* and *Burger King* can come out one way while *Walden* comes out the other way?

3. *Burger King* attempts to clarify the relationship between the "minimum contacts" part of the due process test for personal jurisdiction and the reasonableness prong of the test. How do the two function separately, according to the Court in *Burger King*? How do they work together?

4. How is Rudzewicz's relationship with Florida different from World-Wide Volks-wagen's relationship with Oklahoma?

5. The Court notes that Rudzewicz and MacShara were "experienced and sophisti-cated" businessmen. Does the court define what it means to be a "sophisticated" party for these purposes? And what if they had not been sophisticated business-people? Different result? Even if they were sophisticated, isn't there a significant difference between the parties in this case in terms of power and resources? How, if at all, should that fact bear on the question of jurisdiction?

6. Note that the contract between Rudzewicz and Burger King contained a choice-of-law clause. A choice-of-law clause specifies which state's substantive law will apply to the dispute. The Burger King franchise agreement specified that the con-tract was governed by Florida law. Although some contracts contain forum-selec-tion clauses that specify the court where a lawsuit must be brought, the Burger King franchise agreement did not do this. The choice-of-law clause only deter-mined the applicable law; it did not dictate the forum. Yet the choice-of-law clause played a role in the decision. What was that role, and why should it mat-ter? Be sure you see the difference between *choice of law* and *choice of forum*, and always keep the two questions distinct in your mind. At the same time, it is important to see how the two questions can be linked, in both directions. Choice of forum can affect which substantive law applies (even though the forum state does not necessarily apply its *own* substantive law), as we will explore in Chapter 12. And choice of law can affect the jurisdictional analysis for choice of forum, as we see in *Burger King.*

Purposeful Availment Involving Products Placed in the Stream of Commerce. In today's economy, goods routinely cross state lines and international boundaries. If a plaintiff is injured by a product made by an out-of-state defendant, can the plaintiff sue the defendant in the state where the plaintiff was injured? In some cases, the answer is a clear yes or a clear no. In other cases, as you will see, the answer remains quite murky. Try your hand at the following hypotheticals, using the cases you have already encountered.

> Example 1: An Ohio manufacturer sells one of its products, a water heater, to a consumer in Illinois. The company delivers the product to the consumer's home in Illinois, where the water heater later explodes, causing injury. The consumer brings a lawsuit in Illinois against the manufacturer. The manufacturer moves to dismiss for lack of personal jurisdiction.

> Example 2: An Ohio manufacturer sells one of its products, a water heater, to a consumer from Illinois who is visiting the company's factory store in Ohio. The seller has no reason to know where the consumer lives. The consumer trans-ports the water heater in her pick-up truck back to Illinois, where it later explodes, causing injury. The consumer brings a lawsuit in Illinois against the

manufacturer. The manufacturer moves to dismiss for lack of personal jurisdiction.

Example 3: An Ohio manufacturer sells water heaters wholesale to a company in Pennsylvania that owns a chain of home-improvement stores throughout the United States. The home-improvement chain sells one of these water heaters to a consumer in Illinois. The water heater later explodes, causing injury. The consumer brings a lawsuit in Illinois against the manufacturer. The manufacturer moves to dismiss for lack of personal jurisdiction.

Example 4: A valve manufacturer in Ohio sells valves to a water heater manufacturer in Pennsylvania, which uses the valves as a component part in its water heaters. The manufacturer sells a water heater to a consumer in Illinois. The water heater explodes, causing injury. The consumer brings a lawsuit in Illinois against the valve manufacturer. The valve manufacturer moves to dismiss for lack of personal jurisdiction.

Example 1 offers a straightforward example of specific jurisdiction. The defendant purposefully availed itself of Illinois by selling its product to a consumer there, and the plaintiff's claim arises out of the defendant's purposeful contact with the state. The minimum contacts test is easily satisfied.

Example 2 provides a straightforward application of *World-Wide Volkswagen*. The defendant sold its product in Ohio, not in Illinois. The plaintiff's "unilateral act" of taking the product to Illinois is not a purposeful act of the defendant toward the forum state. Even this straightforward example can get murky quickly, though. What if the hypothetical were altered such that the defendant was *aware* that the water heater was going to Illinois (say the purchaser order so stated)? What if the defendant made an arrangement with its independent delivery company to have it shipped to Ohio?

Examples 3 and 4 are quite difficult. In both examples, the defendant did not sell the product in Illinois. Indeed, the defendants have *no* direct contact with the forum state. But unlike Example 2, it is likely that the defendants could have foreseen that its product or part might have ended up in the forum state. Defendants in Examples 3 and 4 intended to enter a nationwide market and benefit from nationwide sales. Indeed, they knew (and hoped!) that their products would make their way into other states. Is that sufficient to satisfy the purposeful availment requirement?

All of these examples deal with companies putting their products into the *stream of commerce*—a scenario that courts have grappled with for decades in the context of personal jurisdiction. Indeed, *Gray v. American Radiator*, 176 N.E. 2d 761 (Ill. 1961), an early stream-of-commerce case, *is* Example 4. In *Gray*, the Illinois Supreme Court held that the Ohio valve manufacturer was subject to specific jurisdiction in Illinois because the defendant had purposefully placed its valves into the stream of commerce, knowing that they could float down that stream into Illinois. The Supreme Court actually cited *Gray* in dicta in *World-Wide Volkswagen* for the proposition that "[t]he forum state does not exceed its powers under the Due Process Clause if it asserts personal jurisdiction over a corporation that delivers its products into the stream of commerce with the expectation that they will be purchased by consumers in the forum state." 444 U.S. at 297-98.

When faced with the stream-of-commerce question once more in 1987, the Supreme Court did not re-commit to the position in *Gray*. However, neither did the Court clarify the test for purposeful availment in stream-of-commerce cases. In *Asahi Metal Industry Co. v. Superior Court*, 480 U.S. 102 (1987), Asahi, a Japanese tire valve manufacturer, sold valves to Cheng Shin, a Taiwanese tire manufacturer. Cheng Shin tires, with Asahi valves, ended up in Gary Zurcher's motorcycle in California, where Zurcher was injured in a tire-related accident. Zurcher sued a number of defendants, including Cheng Shin. Cheng Shin filed a third-party complaint against Asahi for contribution. Asahi argued that it was not subject to personal jurisdiction in California. This set-up looks strikingly similar to Example 4 and *Gray*.

While Asahi did not sell the valve directly to California, Asahi did place its valves in the stream of commerce, and it could foresee that many of its valves would end up in tires in California. The Court split 4-4 on the question of whether Asahi's placement of valves in the stream of commerce for economic gain, paired with its reasonable expectation that its valves would end up in tires in California, constituted "purposeful availment." Four Justices, in an opinion authored by Justice Brennan, answered yes. Four Justices, in an opinion authored by Justice O'Connor, answered no, asserting that the minimum contacts test requires some additional act directed at the forum state.

However, the entire Court agreed that California could not exercise personal jurisdiction over Asahi, eight of them agreeing that even if the minimum contacts test were met, it would be unreasonable under these circumstances to permit jurisdiction. At that point in the case, everything had settled except the third-party claim by Taiwanese Cheng Shin against Japanese Asahi. How to satisfy minimum contacts in a stream-of-commerce case thus remained a question for another time.

That time arrived in 2011, when the Supreme Court was presented with the stream-of-commerce case of *J. McIntyre Machinery v. Nicastro*, 564 U.S. 873 (2011). By 2011, the Supreme Court had shifted in a conservative direction on a number of issues, as compared with where it had been at the time of *World-Wide Volkswagen* or *Asahi*. As you read *Nicastro*, consider whether the change in Court composition affected either the result or the reasoning. Moreover, ask yourself whether *Nicastro* resolved the minimum contacts question in stream-of-commerce cases left open after *Asahi*.

J. McINTYRE MACHINERY, LTD. v. NICASTRO
564 U.S. 873 (2011)

Justice KENNEDY announced the judgment of the Court and delivered an opinion, in which Chief Justice ROBERTS, Justice SCALIA, and Justice THOMAS join.

Whether a person or entity is subject to the jurisdiction of a state court despite not having been present in the State either at the time of suit or at the time of the alleged injury, and despite not having consented to the exercise of jurisdiction, is a question that arises with great frequency in the routine course of litigation. The rules and standards for determining when a State does or does not have jurisdiction over an absent party have been unclear because of decades-old questions left open in *Asahi Metal Industry Co. v. Superior Court of California*, 480 U.S. 102 (1987).

Here, the Supreme Court of New Jersey, relying in part on *Asahi*, held that New Jersey's courts can exercise jurisdiction over a foreign manufacturer of a product so long as the manufacturer "knows or reasonably should know that its products are distributed through a nationwide distribution system that might lead to those products being sold in any of the fifty states." Applying that test, the court concluded that a British manufacturer of scrap metal machines was subject to jurisdiction in New Jersey, even though at no time had it advertised in, sent goods to, or in any relevant sense targeted the State.

That decision cannot be sustained. Although the New Jersey Supreme Court issued an extensive opinion with careful attention to this Court's cases and to its own precedent, the "stream of commerce" metaphor carried the decision far afield. Due process protects the defendant's right not to be coerced except by lawful judicial power. As a general rule, the exercise of judicial power is not lawful unless the defendant "purposefully avails itself of the privilege of conducting activities within the forum State, thus invoking the benefits and protections of its laws." *Hanson v. Denckla*, 357 U.S. 235 (1958). There may be exceptions, say, for instance, in cases involving an intentional tort. But the general rule is applicable in this products-liability case, and the so-called "stream-of-commerce" doctrine cannot displace it.

I

This case arises from a products-liability suit filed in New Jersey state court. Robert Nicastro seriously injured his hand while using a metal-shearing machine manufactured by J. McIntyre Machinery, Ltd. (J. McIntyre). The accident occurred in New Jersey, but the machine was manufactured in England, where J. McIntyre is incorporated and operates. The question here is whether the New Jersey courts have jurisdiction over J. McIntyre, notwithstanding the fact that the company at no time either marketed goods in the State or shipped them there. Nicastro was a plaintiff in the New Jersey trial court and is the respondent here; J. McIntyre was a defendant and is now the petitioner.

At oral argument in this Court, Nicastro's counsel stressed three primary facts in defense of New Jersey's assertion of jurisdiction over J. McIntyre. First, an independent company agreed to sell J. McIntyre's machines in the United States. J. McIntyre itself did not sell its machines to buyers in this country beyond the U.S. distributor, and there is no allegation that the distributor was under J. McIntyre's control. Second, J. McIntyre officials attended annual conventions for the scrap recycling industry to advertise J. McIntyre's machines alongside the distributor. The conventions took place in various States, but never in New Jersey. Third, no more than four machines (the record suggests only one), including the machine that caused the injuries that are the basis for this suit, ended up in New Jersey.

In addition to these facts emphasized by respondent, the New Jersey Supreme Court noted that J. McIntyre held both United States and European patents on its recycling technology. It also noted that the U.S. distributor "structured [its] advertising and sales efforts in accordance with" J. McIntyre's "direction and guidance whenever possible," and that "at least some of the machines were sold on consignment to" the distributor.

In light of these facts, the New Jersey Supreme Court concluded that New Jersey courts could exercise jurisdiction over petitioner without contravention of the Due Process Clause. Jurisdiction was proper, in that court's view, because the injury occurred in New Jersey; because petitioner knew or reasonably should have known "that its products are distributed through a nationwide distribution system that might lead to those products being sold in any of the fifty states"; and because petitioner failed to "take some reasonable step to prevent the distribution of its products in this State."

Both the New Jersey Supreme Court's holding and its account of what it called "[t]he stream-of-commerce doctrine of jurisdiction," were incorrect, however. This Court's *Asahi* decision may be responsible in part for that court's error regarding the stream of commerce, and this case presents an opportunity to provide greater clarity.

II

The Due Process Clause protects an individual's right to be deprived of life, liberty, or property only by the exercise of lawful power. This is no less true with respect to the power of a sovereign to resolve disputes through judicial process than with respect to the power of a sovereign to prescribe rules of conduct for those within its sphere. As a general rule, neither statute nor judicial decree may bind strangers to the State.

A court may subject a defendant to judgment only when the defendant has sufficient contacts with the sovereign "such that the maintenance of the suit does not offend 'traditional notions of fair play and substantial justice.'" *Int'l Shoe*, 326 U.S. at 316. Freeform notions of fundamental fairness divorced from traditional practice cannot transform a judgment rendered in the absence of authority into law. As a general rule, the sovereign's exercise of power requires some act by which the defendant "purposefully avails itself of the privilege of conducting activities within the forum State, thus invoking the benefits and protections of its laws," *Hanson*, 357 U.S. at 253, though in some cases, as with an intentional tort, the defendant might well fall within the State's authority by reason of his attempt to obstruct its laws. In products-liability cases like this one, it is the defendant's purposeful availment that makes jurisdiction consistent with "traditional notions of fair play and substantial justice."

A person may submit to a State's authority in a number of ways. There is, of course, explicit consent. Presence within a State at the time suit commences through service of process is another example. Citizenship or domicile—or, by analogy, incorporation or principal place of business for corporations—also indicates general submission to a State's powers. Each of these examples reveals circumstances, or a course of conduct, from which it is proper to infer an intention to benefit from and thus an intention to submit to the laws of the forum State. These examples support exercise of the general jurisdiction of the State's courts and allow the State to resolve both matters that originate within the State and those based on activities and events elsewhere. By contrast, those who live or operate primarily outside a State have a due process right not to be subjected to judgment in its courts as a general matter.

There is also a more limited form of submission to a State's authority for disputes that "arise out of or are connected with the activities within the state." *Int'l Shoe Co., supra,* at 319. Where a defendant "purposefully avails itself of the privilege of conducting activities within the forum

State, thus invoking the benefits and protections of its laws," *Hanson*, 375 U.S. at 253, it submits to the judicial power of an otherwise foreign sovereign to the extent that power is exercised in connection with the defendant's activities touching on the State. . . .

The imprecision arising from *Asahi*, for the most part, results from its statement of the relation between jurisdiction and the "stream of commerce." The stream of commerce, like other metaphors, has its deficiencies as well as its utility. It refers to the movement of goods from manufacturers through distributors to consumers, yet beyond that descriptive purpose its meaning is far from exact. This Court has stated that a defendant's placing goods into the stream of commerce "with the expectation that they will be purchased by consumers within the forum State" may indicate purposeful availment. *World-Wide Volkswagen*, 444 U.S. at 298. But that statement does not amend the general rule of personal jurisdiction. It merely observes that a defendant may in an appropriate case be subject to jurisdiction without entering the forum—itself an unexceptional proposition—as where manufacturers or distributors "seek to serve" a given State's market. *Id.* at 295. . . .

The principal inquiry in cases of this sort is whether the defendant's activities manifest an intention to submit to the power of a sovereign. In other words, the defendant must "purposefully avai[l] itself of the privilege of conducting activities within the forum State, thus invoking the benefits and protections of its laws." *Hanson*, 375 U.S. at 253. Sometimes a defendant does so by sending its goods rather than its agents. The defendant's transmission of goods permits the exercise of jurisdiction only where the defendant can be said to have targeted the forum; as a

general rule, it is not enough that the defendant might have predicted that its goods will reach the forum State. . . .

Were general fairness considerations the touchstone of jurisdiction, a lack of purposeful availment might be excused where carefully crafted judicial procedures could otherwise protect the defendant's interests, or where the plaintiff would suffer substantial hardship if forced to litigate in a foreign forum. That such considerations have not been deemed controlling is instructive.

Two principles are implicit in the foregoing. First, personal jurisdiction requires a forum-by-forum, or sovereign-by-sovereign, analysis. The question is whether a defendant has followed a course of conduct directed at the society or economy existing within the jurisdiction of a given sovereign, so that the sovereign has the power to subject the defendant to judgment concerning that conduct. Personal jurisdiction, of course, restricts "judicial power not as a matter of sovereignty, but as a matter of individual liberty," for due process protects the individual's right to be subject only to lawful power. *Ins. Corp. of Ireland v. Compagnie des Bauxites de Guinee*, 456 U.S. 694, 702 (1982). But whether a judicial judgment is lawful depends on whether the sovereign has authority to render it.

The second principle is a corollary of the first. Because the United States is a distinct sovereign, a defendant may in principle be subject to the jurisdiction of the courts of the United States but not of any particular State. . . . For jurisdiction, a litigant may have the requisite relationship with the United States Government but not with the government of any individual State. That would be an exceptional case, however. If the defendant is a domestic domiciliary, the courts of its home State are available and can exercise general jurisdiction. And if another State were to assert jurisdiction in an inappropriate case, it would upset the federal balance, which posits that each State has a sovereignty that is not subject to unlawful intrusion by other States. Furthermore, foreign corporations will often target or concentrate on particular States, subjecting them to specific jurisdiction in those forums. . . .

III

In this case, petitioner directed marketing and sales efforts at the United States. Here the question concerns the authority of a New Jersey state court to exercise jurisdiction, so it is petitioner's purposeful contacts with New Jersey, not with the United States, that alone are relevant. That circumstance is not presented in this case. . . .

Respondent has not established that J. McIntyre engaged in conduct purposefully directed at New Jersey. Recall that respondent's claim of jurisdiction centers on three facts: The distributor agreed to sell J. McIntyre's machines in the United States; J. McIntyre officials attended trade shows in several States but not in New Jersey; and up to four machines ended up in New Jersey. The British manufacturer had no office in New Jersey; it neither paid taxes nor owned property there; and it neither advertised in, nor sent any employees to, the State. Indeed, after discovery the trial court found that the "defendant does not have a single contact with New Jersey short of the machine in question ending up in this state." These facts may reveal an intent to serve the U.S. market, but they do not show that J. McIntyre purposefully availed itself of the New Jersey market. It is notable that the New Jersey Supreme Court appears to agree. . . .

* * *

Due process protects petitioner's right to be subject only to lawful authority. At no time did petitioner engage in any activities in New Jersey that reveal an intent to invoke or benefit from the protection of its laws. New Jersey is without power to adjudge the rights and liabilities of J. McIntyre, and its exercise of jurisdiction would violate due process. The contrary judgment of the New Jersey Supreme Court is

Reversed.

Justice BREYER, with whom Justice ALITO joins, concurring in the judgment.

The Supreme Court of New Jersey adopted a broad understanding of the scope of personal jurisdiction based on its view that "[t]he increasingly fast-paced globalization of the world economy has removed national borders as barriers to trade." I do not doubt that there have been many recent changes in commerce and communication, many of which are not anticipated by our precedents. But this case does not present any of those issues. So I think it unwise to announce a rule of broad applicability without full consideration of the modern-day consequences.

In my view, the outcome of this case is determined by our precedents. Based on the facts found by the New Jersey courts, respondent Nicastro failed to meet his burden to demonstrate that it was constitutionally proper to exercise jurisdiction over petitioner J. McIntyre Machinery, Ltd. (British Manufacturer), a British firm that manufactures scrap-metal machines in Great Britain and sells them through an independent distributor in the United States (American Distributor). On that basis, I agree with the plurality that the contrary judgment of the Supreme Court of New Jersey should be reversed.

I

In asserting jurisdiction over the British Manufacturer, the Supreme Court of New Jersey relied most heavily on three primary facts as providing constitutionally sufficient "contacts" with New Jersey, thereby making it fundamentally fair to hale the British Manufacturer before its courts: (1) The American Distributor on one occasion sold and shipped one machine to a New Jersey customer, namely, Mr. Nicastro's employer, Mr. Curcio; (2) the British Manufacturer permitted, indeed wanted, its independent American Distributor to sell its machines to anyone in America willing to buy them; and (3) representatives of the British Manufacturer attended trade shows in "such cities as Chicago, Las Vegas, New Orleans, Orlando, San Diego, and San Francisco." In my view, these facts do not provide contacts between the British firm and the State of New Jersey constitutionally sufficient to support New Jersey's assertion of jurisdiction in this case.

None of our precedents finds that a single isolated sale, even if accompanied by the kind of sales effort indicated here, is sufficient. . . .

Here, the relevant facts found by the New Jersey Supreme Court show no "regular . . . flow" or "regular course" of sales in New Jersey; and there is no "something more," such as special state-related design, advertising, advice, marketing, or anything else. Mr. Nicastro, who here bears the burden of proving jurisdiction, has shown no specific effort by the British Manufacturer to sell in New Jersey. He has introduced no list of potential New Jersey customers who might, for example, have regularly attended trade shows. And he has not otherwise shown that the British Manufacturer "purposefully avail[ed] itself of the privilege of conducting activities" within New Jersey,

or that it delivered its goods in the stream of commerce "with the expectation that they will be purchased" by New Jersey users. *World-Wide Volkswagen, supra* at 297-98. . . .

II

I would not go further. Because the incident at issue in this case does not implicate modern concerns, and because the factual record leaves many open questions, this is an unsuitable vehicle for making broad pronouncements that refashion basic jurisdictional rules.

A

The plurality seems to state strict rules that limit jurisdiction where a defendant does not "inten[d] to submit to the power of a sovereign" and cannot "be said to have targeted the forum." But what do those standards mean when a company targets the world by selling products from its Web site? And does it matter if, instead of shipping the products directly, a company consigns the products through an intermediary (say, Amazon.com) who then receives and fulfills the orders? And what if the company markets its products through popup advertisements that it knows will be viewed in a forum? Those issues have serious commercial consequences but are totally absent in this case.

B

But though I do not agree with the plurality's seemingly strict no-jurisdiction rule, I am not persuaded by the absolute approach adopted by the New Jersey Supreme Court . . . [that] a producer is subject to jurisdiction for a products-liability action so long as it "knows or reasonably should know that its products are distributed through a nationwide distribution system that *might* lead to those products being sold in any of the fifty states." In the context of this case, I cannot agree.

For one thing, to adopt this view would abandon the heretofore accepted inquiry of whether, focusing upon the relationship between "the defendant, the *forum*, and the litigation," it is fair, in light of the defendant's contacts *with that forum*, to subject the defendant to suit there. *Shaffer v. Heitner*, 433 U.S. 186, 204 (1977) (emphasis added). It would ordinarily rest jurisdiction instead upon no more than the occurrence of a product-based accident in the forum State. But this Court has rejected the notion that a defendant's amenability to suit "travel[s] with the chattel." *World-Wide Volkswagen*, 444 U.S. at 296.

For another, I cannot reconcile so automatic a rule with the constitutional demand for "minimum contacts" and "purposefu[l] avail[ment]," each of which rest upon a particular notion of defendant-focused fairness. *Id.* at 291, 297. A rule like the New Jersey Supreme Court's would permit every State to assert jurisdiction in a products-liability suit against any domestic manufacturer who sells its products (made anywhere in the United States) to a national distributor, no matter how large or small the manufacturer, no matter how distant the forum, and no matter how few the number of items that end up in the particular forum at issue. What might appear fair in the case of a large manufacturer which specifically seeks, or expects, an equal-sized distributor to sell its product in a distant State might seem unfair in the case of a small manufacturer (say, an Appalachian potter) who sells his product (cups and saucers) exclusively to a large distributor, who resells a single item (a coffee mug) to a buyer from a distant

State (Hawaii). I know too little about the range of these or in-between possibilities to abandon in favor of the more absolute rule what has previously been this Court's less absolute approach. . . .

It may be that a larger firm can readily "alleviate the risk of burdensome litigation by procuring insurance, passing the expected costs on to customers, or, if the risks are too great, severing its connection with the State." *World-Wide Volkswagen*, 444 U.S. at 297. But manufacturers come in many shapes and sizes. It may be fundamentally unfair to require a small Egyptian shirt maker, a Brazilian manufacturing cooperative, or a Kenyan coffee farmer, selling its products through international distributors, to respond to products-liability tort suits in virtually every State in the United States, even those in respect to which the foreign firm has no connection at all but the sale of a single (allegedly defective) good. And a rule like the New Jersey Supreme Court suggests would require every product manufacturer, large or small, selling to American distributors to understand not only the tort law of every State, but also the wide variance in the way courts within different States apply that law.

C

At a minimum, I would not work such a change to the law in the way either the plurality or the New Jersey Supreme Court suggests without a better understanding of the relevant contemporary commercial circumstances. . . . This case presents no such occasion . . . [thus] I concur only in the judgment of that opinion and not its reasoning.

Justice GINSBURG, with whom Justice SOTOMAYOR and Justice KAGAN join, dissenting.

A foreign industrialist seeks to develop a market in the United States for machines it manufactures. It hopes to derive substantial revenue from sales it makes to United States purchasers. Where in the United States buyers reside does not matter to this manufacturer. Its goal is simply to sell as much as it can, wherever it can. It excludes no region or State from the market it wishes to reach. But, all things considered, it prefers to avoid products liability litigation in the United States. To that end, it engages a U.S. distributor to ship its machines stateside. Has it succeeded in escaping personal jurisdiction in a State where one of its products is sold and causes injury or even death to a local user?

Under this Court's pathmarking precedent in *International Shoe*, 326 U.S. 310 (1945), and subsequent decisions, one would expect the answer to be unequivocally, "No." But instead, six Justices of this Court, in divergent opinions, tell us that the manufacturer has avoided the jurisdiction of our state courts, except perhaps in States where its products are sold in sizeable quantities. Inconceivable as it may have seemed yesterday, the splintered majority today "turn[s] the clock back to the days before modern long-arm statutes when a manufacturer, to avoid being haled into court where a user is injured, need only Pilate-like wash its hands of a product by having independent distributors market it." Weintraub, *A Map Out of the Personal Jurisdiction Labyrinth*, 28 U.C. D. L. Rev. 531, 555 (1995).

I

On October 11, 2001, a three-ton metal shearing machine severed four fingers on Robert Nicastro's right hand. Alleging that the machine was a dangerous product defectively made, Nicastro sought compensation from the machine's manufacturer, J. McIntyre Machinery Ltd. (McIntyre UK). . . .

The machine that injured Nicastro, a "McIntyre Model 640 Shear," sold in the United States for $24,900 in 1995, and features a "massive cutting capacity." . . . In 2008, New Jersey recycling facilities processed 2,013,730 tons of scrap iron, steel, aluminum, and other metals—more than any other State—outpacing Kentucky, its nearest competitor, by nearly 30 percent.

Nicastro operated the 640 Shear in the course of his employment at Curcio Scrap Metal (CSM) in Saddle Brook, New Jersey. CSM's owner, Frank Curcio, "first heard of [McIntyre UK's] machine while attending an Institute of Scrap Metal Industries [(ISRI)] convention—the world's largest [annual] scrap recycling trade show—in Las Vegas in 1994 or 1995, where [McIntyre UK] was an exhibitor. . . . McIntyre UK exhibited its products at ISRI trade shows [every year from 1990 to 2005]. [T]he company acknowledged [it did so] hoping to reach "anyone interested in the machine from anywhere in the United States." . . .

From at least 1995 until 2001, McIntyre UK retained an Ohio-based company, McIntyre Machinery America, Ltd. (McIntyre America), "as its exclusive distributor for the entire United States." Though similarly named, the two companies were separate and independent entities with "no commonality of ownership or management." In invoices and other written communications, [however,] McIntyre America described itself as McIntyre UK's national distributor, "America's Link" to "Quality Metal Processing Equipment" from England. In a November 23, 1999, letter to McIntyre America, McIntyre UK's president spoke plainly about the manufacturer's objective in authorizing the exclusive distributorship: "All we wish to do is sell our products in the [United] States—and get paid!"...

In sum, McIntyre UK's regular attendance and exhibitions at conventions was surely a purposeful step to reach customers for its products "anywhere in the United States." At least as purposeful was McIntyre UK's engagement of McIntyre America as the conduit for sales of McIntyre UK's machines to buyers "throughout the United States." Given McIntyre UK's endeavors to reach and profit from the United States market as a whole, Nicastro's suit, I would hold, has been brought in a forum entirely appropriate for the adjudication of his claim. He alleges that McIntyre UK's shear machine was defectively designed or manufactured and, as a result, caused injury to him at his workplace. The machine arrived in Nicastro's New Jersey workplace not randomly or fortuitously, but as a result of the U.S. connections and distribution system that McIntyre UK deliberately arranged. On what sensible view of the allocation of adjudicatory authority could the place of Nicastro's injury within the United States be deemed off limits for his products liability claim against a foreign manufacturer who targeted the United States (including all the States that constitute the Nation) as the territory it sought to develop?

II

... [No] issue of the fair and reasonable allocation of adjudicatory authority among States of the United States is present in this case. New Jersey's exercise of personal jurisdiction over a foreign manufacturer... does not tread on the domain, or diminish the sovereignty, of any other state....

[T]he constitutional limits on a state court's adjudicatory authority derive from considerations of due process, not state sovereignty.... [I]n *International Shoe* itself, and decisions thereafter, the Court has made plain that legal fictions, notably "presence" and "implied consent," should be discarded, for they conceal the actual bases on which jurisdiction rests. "[T]he relationship among the defendant, the forum, and the litigation" determines whether due process permits the exercise of personal jurisdiction over a defendant. *Shaffer*, 433 U.S. at 204....

III

This case is illustrative of marketing arrangements for sales in the United States common in today's commercial world. A foreign-country manufacturer engages a U.S. company to promote and distribute the manufacturer's products, not in any particular State, but anywhere and everywhere in the United States the distributor can attract purchasers. The product proves defective and injures a user in the State where the user lives or works. Often, as here, the manufacturer will have liability insurance covering personal injuries caused by its products.

When industrial accidents happen, a long-arm statute in the State where the injury occurs generally permits assertion of jurisdiction, upon giving proper notice, over the foreign manufacturer....

The modern approach to jurisdiction over corporations and other legal entities, ushered in by *International Shoe*, gave prime place to reason and fairness. Is it not fair and reasonable, given the mode of trading of which this case is an example, to require the international seller to defend at the place its products cause injury? Do not litigational convenience and choice-of-law considerations point in that direction? On what measure of reason and fairness can it be considered undue to require McIntyre UK to defend in New Jersey as an incident of its efforts to develop a market for its industrial machines anywhere and everywhere in the United States? Is not the burden on McIntyre UK to defend in New Jersey fair, *i.e.*, a reasonable cost of transacting business internationally, in comparison to the burden on Nicastro to go to Nottingham, England to gain recompense for an injury he sustained using McIntyre's product at his workplace in Saddle Brook, New Jersey?

McIntyre UK dealt with the United States as a single market. Like most foreign manufacturers, it was concerned not with the prospect of suit in State X as opposed to State Y, but rather with its subjection to suit anywhere in the United States. As a McIntyre UK officer wrote in an e-mail to McIntyre America: "American law—who needs it?!" If McIntyre UK is answerable in the United States at all, is it not "perfectly appropriate to permit the exercise of that jurisdiction . . . at the place of injury"?

In sum, McIntyre UK, by engaging McIntyre America to promote and sell its machines in the United States, "purposefully availed itself" of the United States market nationwide, not a market in a single State or a discrete collection of States. McIntyre UK thereby availed itself of the market of all States in which its products were sold by its exclusive distributor. "Th[e] purposeful availment requirement," this Court has explained, simply "ensures that a defendant will not be haled into a jurisdiction solely as a result of 'random,' 'fortuitous,' or 'attenuated' contacts." *Burger King*, 471 U.S. at 475. Adjudicatory authority is appropriately exercised where "actions by the defendant *himself*" give rise to the affiliation with the forum. *Ibid.* How could McIntyre UK not have intended, by its actions targeting a national market, to sell products in . . . the largest scrap metal market [in the United States]?

[As many] [c]ourts . . . have held, it would undermine principles of fundamental fairness to insulate the foreign manufacturer from accountability in court at the place within the United States where the manufacturer's products caused injury.

[In Section IV, Justice Ginsburg asserts that neither *World-Wide Volkswagen* nor *Asahi* compelled the plurality's result, and then points out that the plurality's holding puts United States plaintiffs at a disadvantage compared to similarly situated complainants elsewhere in the world.]

* * *

For the reasons stated, I would hold McIntyre UK answerable in New Jersey for the harm Nicastro suffered at his workplace in that State using McIntyre UK's shearing machine. While I dissent from the Court's judgment, I take heart that the plurality opinion does not speak for the Court, for that opinion would take a giant step away from the "notions of fair play and substantial justice" underlying *International Shoe*, 326 U.S. at 316.

Notes & Questions

1. In *Nicastro* (and other stream-of-commerce cases), the defendant's core argument resembles the argument made by World-Wide and Seaway in *World-Wide Volkswagen*: We sold a product in state A, and through someone *else's* act, the product ended up in state B, where it is alleged to have caused injury; we did not *ourselves* make a purposeful contact with state B, therefore we cannot be said

to have minimum contacts there. In *World-Wide Volkswagen*, the defendants sold a car in New York, and the plaintiffs drove the car to Oklahoma. In *Nicastro*, the defendant in the United Kingdom sold a machine to a distributor in Ohio, and the distributor sold it to the plaintiff's employer in New Jersey. In each case, the *product* contacted the forum state, but the *defendant* arguably did not. If you represented Robert Nicastro, how would you distinguish *World-Wide Volkswagen*? What is the strongest argument that J. McIntyre Machinery Company "purposefully availed" itself of the benefits of New Jersey?

2. What is the holding of *Nicastro*? To be precise, after *Nicastro*, what is the due process test in stream-of-commerce cases? Does it suffice, for purposes of the minimum contacts test, to show that a defendant placed a product into the stream of commerce with knowledge the product could be sold to someone in the forum state? Or is something more required?

Do not be too quick to answer what the holding is. Is there a majority opinion? How many Justices agree with Justice Kennedy's opinion? How many agree with Justice Ginsburg's opinion? One thing is certain: A majority of the Court (six Justices) agree that, under the circumstances of *Nicastro*, in which perhaps only a single machine made its way to New Jersey through an Ohio distributor, it would violate due process to hale the United Kingdom manufacturer into court in New Jersey. What is much less certain is the *reasoning*. Justice Kennedy's view failed to command a majority. But neither did the others.

Looking at the three opinions, how many of the Justices would agree that the minimum contacts test is satisfied if a defendant places its product in the stream of commerce *plus* engages in some additional conduct targeting the forum? Thus, it is easy to describe some circumstances that *would* meet the minimum contacts test. The disagreement among the Justices is about what *would not* meet the test. Specifically, they disagree about whether placing the product in the stream of commerce (and the product foreseeably ending up in the forum state), without more, is enough.

On that question, what does Justice Kennedy say? In this regard, his opinion picks up on the position taken by Justice O'Connor in *Asahi*. What does Justice Ginsburg say? Her opinion picks up on the position taken by Justice Brennan in *Asahi*, albeit with much greater emphasis on the idea that the defendant targeted the United States as a whole.

What about Justice Breyer, whose opinion was joined by Justice Alito? He agreed with the plurality that, on the facts of this case with a "single, isolated sale," personal jurisdiction should be rejected. Justice Breyer, however, does not go further. Why does Justice Breyer see this case as a poor vehicle for answering the big question about stream-of-commerce jurisdiction? What sort of case would he consider suitable for addressing that question? Although only two Justices signed onto this opinion, some courts have treated Justice Breyer's concurrence as the controlling opinion in *Nicastro* because there was no majority opinion and Justice Breyer's offers the narrowest grounds to support the conclusion that jurisdiction in this case was improper. *Cf. Marks v. United States*, 430 U.S. 188,

193 (1977) ("When a fragmented Court decides a case and no single rationale explaining the result enjoys the assent of five Justices, 'the holding of the Court may be viewed as that position taken by those Members who concurred in the judgments on the narrowest grounds.'").

3. The dissent goes out of its way to emphasize that the Due Process Clause, as it relates to personal jurisdiction, is about individual liberty, not state sovereignty or state boundaries. Is the plurality's focus on state sovereignty reminiscent of *Pennoyer*? Regardless of your answer to that question, can the plurality's focus on territoriality and state sovereignty co-exist with the other touchstones of due process the Court developed in *International Shoe* and its progeny, including *McGee, Hanson, World-Wide Volkswagen,* and *Calder*?

4. If interstate highways and global product distribution make *Pennoyer*'s focus on territoriality seem unworkable and outdated, the Internet makes it seem downright obsolete. Justice Breyer's concurrence in *Nicastro* emphasized that issues of personal jurisdiction when a company "targets the world" by selling from its own website, selling via an e-commerce intermediary, or marketing through Internet advertising, "are totally absent in this case." When deciding whether an out-of-state company is subject to specific jurisdiction, how should courts treat contacts through the Internet? Can these issues be answered by applying the existing minimum contacts test with some refinements or do they require a new personal jurisdiction doctrine that recognizes modern realities of non-territoriality?

   For over 20 years, lower courts have been dealing with the question of whether the Internet requires a separate personal jurisdiction analysis, and for the most part they have gotten by with applying standard principles of purposeful availment and reasonableness. The opinion in *Zippo Mfg. Co. v. Zippo Dot Com, Inc.*, 925 F. Supp. 1119 (W.D. Pa. 1997), became the seminal case regarding personal jurisdiction based on the operation of an Internet website. Under *Zippo*, whether the exercise of personal jurisdiction is proper depends upon where on a sliding scale of commercial interactivity a website falls. Some cases are relatively easy: First, if the case *arises out of* a defendant's decision to conduct a transaction of business online with a customer in the forum state, that constitutes purposeful availment. Conversely, if the defendant did nothing more than post information online that was read in the forum state, that usually is not enough of a contact, even if the posted information had an effect in the forum state.

   What about the middle of the sliding scale? Internet-contact cases that exist in the vast middle ground of the *Zippo*-sliding scale are more difficult. Many websites are "commercially interactive"—customers can come onto the website and, if they like, purchase items from the website owner. Is the possibility of commercial activity in a forum state, through a "commercially interactive" website, enough to constitute purposeful availment? The United States Court of Appeals for the Third Circuit answered no. In *Toys "R" Us, Inc. v. Step Two, S.A.*, 318 F.3d 446 (3d Cir. 2002), Toys "R" Us, Inc., brought an action in New Jersey alleging that Step Two used its websites to engage, *inter alia*, in trademark infringement. The Third Circuit first observed the widely accepted view that a website must reflect intentional interaction with the forum state in order for personal jurisdiction to be proper, and that in determining whether there was such intentional interaction, courts may consider both Internet and non-Internet activities. The Third Circuit did not officially decide whether Step Two had purposefully availed itself of the forum state, but in its remand order for jurisdictional discovery, the court expressed skepticism: "Step Two's websites, while commercial and interactive, do not appear to have been designed or intended to reach customers in New Jersey. Step Two's web sites are entirely in Spanish; prices for its merchandise are in pesetas or Euros, and merchandise can be shipped only to addresses within Spain. Most important, none of the portions of Step Two's web sites are designed to accommodate addresses within the United States." *Id.* Do you think *Zippo*'s "sliding scale" for website interactivity did any work in that case? Does it add anything meaningful to the *International Shoe* framework?

STRATEGY SESSION

Disputes over personal jurisdiction—played out mostly on motions to dismiss—raise not only legal questions but also factual questions: What contacts did the defendant have with the forum state? What was the causal connection, if any, between the defendant's contacts with the state and the claims in the lawsuit? If you represent a plaintiff, to respond to a defendant's motion to dismiss for lack of personal jurisdiction, you may need to gather information about the defendant and its conduct. This is when you will seek *jurisdictional discovery*. The discovery rules you learned about in Chapter 3 can be deployed, when needed, to gather information relevant to threshold issues including personal jurisdiction. How might that affect your strategy as a plaintiff's lawyer? In specific jurisdiction cases, the claims arise out of the contacts, so information about minimum contacts may bear on the very conduct at issue in the lawsuit. In light of *Twombly* and *Iqbal*, it might be helpful to get quasi-merits discovery in the early stage of a case, particularly if the case involves co-conspirators or another situation in which information about wrongdoing might be uniquely in the hands of the defendant.

(b) Reasonableness

Thus far, you have learned a great deal about "minimum contacts." In several of the cases you have read, though, the Court has looked not only to whether the defendant had purposeful contacts with the forum state, but also (to greater and lesser degrees) to the broader question of whether asserting jurisdiction in the state would be "reasonable." *See, e.g., Int'l Shoe*, 326 U.S. at 316; *Burger King*, 471 U.S. at 476-78; *Asahi*, 480 U.S. at 108. In some of these cases, the Court framed its reasonableness analysis in terms of the "fair play and substantial justice" language that has been central to the jurisdictional analysis since *International Shoe*. In *International Shoe*, "minimum contacts" and "fair play and substantial justice" arrived in a single sentence and appeared to be a single idea. Since then, however, the reasonableness analysis—or "fair play and substantial justice"—has taken on a life of its own. In *Burger King* and *Asahi*, in particular, the Court clearly separated them into two separate prongs of the due process analysis, stating that, even if a defendant has purposeful contacts with the forum state that are related to the plaintiff's claim, under the circumstances of a particular case it might nonetheless be unreasonable for the court to exercise jurisdiction over the defendant.

The Supreme Court has looked to a variety of factors in determining whether personal jurisdiction would be unreasonable: (1) the burden on the defendant to litigate in the forum state; (2) plaintiff's interest in litigating in the forum state; (3) the forum state's interests in resolving disputes that arose there; and (4) the overall judicial system's interest in the efficient resolution of controversies. *See, e.g.*, *Asahi*, 480 U.S. at 113. Even though the Court does not always analyze all of these factors, as a lawyer today, you must be prepared to address the reasonableness prong as an independent piece of a personal jurisdiction analysis. But do not get carried away. The reasonableness analysis remains closely connected to the question of whether the claim arises out of defendant's contacts with the state, and reasonableness has only rarely determined the outcome of a personal jurisdiction dispute. Indeed, you have seen examples of cases—*Hanson* and *Nicastro* come to mind—in which the Court rejected the assertion of jurisdiction even though a reasonableness analysis would have pointed the other way.

Any reasonableness analysis requires careful attention to *Asahi, Burger King,* and *World-Wide Volkswagen*. Starting with *Asahi*: There was no holding on minimum contacts, but the Court agreed that jurisdiction was unreasonable, for two key reasons. One was the international component: It is a bigger burden for a defendant to litigate across the Pacific Ocean and across language barriers than to litigate across state lines. The other was the peculiar procedural posture of the *Asahi* case. By the time the personal jurisdiction issue was being decided, Zurcher (the injured motorcyclist) had settled with the defendants, so the only remaining claim in the case was Cheng Shin's third-party claim against Asahi—a Taiwanese company's indemnity claim against a Japanese company. Thus, in *Asahi*, the defendant's burden was significant. The "plaintiff's interest" was nil. Zurcher, the original plaintiff, had already settled. And third-party plaintiff Cheng Shin had no legitimate interest in litigating its claim in California; it was a Taiwanese company asserting a claim against a Japanese corporation. The forum state, California, had a significant interest in the original lawsuit because it involved a highway accident within the state, but now that its citizen's claim had settled, California had no real interest in the indemnification claim between Cheng Shin and Asahi.

Now, compare the reasonableness analysis in *Asahi* with those in *Burger King* and *World-Wide Volkswagen*. In *Burger King*, Defendant Rudzewicz's burden, while real, did not include crossing international borders or an ocean. Plaintiff Burger King had an interest in litigating in its home state of Florida. The forum state had an interest in adjudicating a franchise dispute involving a Florida company, especially since the agreement was governed by Florida law. Now look at *World-Wide Volkswagen*. There, the plaintiff's interests were very strong—the family was hospitalized for an extraordinarily long time in Oklahoma, having suffered serious injuries. The forum state's interests were also strong: The accident occurred in Oklahoma, and Oklahoma has an interest in preventing dangerous conditions from affecting its roadways and its citizen motorists. The defendant's burden was not as severe as that in *Asahi*. Ultimately, though, the Court found purposeful availment lacking. Why the difference in outcomes? When analyzing the reasonableness inquiry, draw upon these and other cases to ask yourself whether the reasonableness inquiry, as well as its relationship to purposeful availment, looks more like *Asahi*, more like *Burger King*, or more like *World-Wide Volkswagen*.

THE BIG PICTURE

If you are familiar with the political leanings of Supreme Court Justices, you might have noticed that personal jurisdiction often splits the Justices along liberal-conservative lines. In closely divided personal jurisdiction cases, the more "liberal" Justices tend to allow personal jurisdiction while the more "conservative" Justices tend to reject it. What is so *political* about personal jurisdiction? Part of the answer is that a narrow view of personal jurisdiction gives defendants an edge in civil litigation, while a broader view of personal jurisdiction favors plaintiffs. Much (but certainly not all) litigation pits individual plaintiffs against corporate or government defendants, and pro-plaintiff policies are often described as more liberal, while pro-defendant policies are often described as more pro-business or conservative. Tight restrictions on personal jurisdiction make it hard for plaintiffs to choose their most favorable forum, increase the likelihood that a plaintiff will have to sue the defendant in the defendant's home state, and may make it inconvenient or expensive for plaintiffs to sue.

(c) Relatedness

The Due Process Clause permits a state court to exercise specific jurisdiction over a defendant only when the plaintiff's claims "arise out of or relate to" the defendant's forum activities. *Burger King Corp. v. Rudzewicz*, 471 U.S. 462, 472 (1985). In *International Shoe*, the plaintiff's claim arose out of the defendant's employment of salespersons in the State of Washington. In *Burger King*, the plaintiff's claim arose out of the defendant's business relationship with a Florida company. In *Calder*, the plaintiff's claim arose out of the defendants' writing and editing of an article about a California celebrity. In most cases, courts do not state explicitly that they are conducting a "relatedness" inquiry; the connection between defendant's contacts with the forum and plaintiff's claims are often rather obvious. Nonetheless, every example of specific jurisdiction, by definition, involves jurisdiction over a defendant facing claims that arise out of or relate to the defendant's contacts with the forum state. The next case you will read, *Bristol-Myers Squibb Co. v. Superior Court of California*, 137 S. Ct. 1337 (2017), is the Supreme Court's first significant opinion on the relatedness requirement of specific jurisdiction.

To understand the relatedness requirement of specific jurisdiction, though, you need to understand that the significance of the relatedness requirement is that it is the fundamental distinction between specific jurisdiction and general jurisdiction. Recall from *International Shoe* that there may be some instances in which a defendants' contacts with the forum state are so continuous and systematic as to render that defendant amenable to suit *for any claim* in that state, regardless of the claim's relationship with the defendant's contacts with the forum. The exercise of personal jurisdiction in such a scenario is called general jurisdiction. While it is easy to think of the distinction between general and specific jurisdiction as involving the defendants' *quantity* of contacts with the forum, that misses the fundamental point—namely, that the key distinction between whether you are undertaking a specific or general jurisdiction analysis is the *relatedness* of the contacts to the claim. Keep this in mind as you read *Bristol-Myers Squibb*.

BRISTOL-MYERS SQUIBB CO. v. SUPERIOR COURT OF CALIFORNIA
137 S. Ct. 1773 (2017)

ALITO, J., delivered the opinion of the Court.

More than 600 plaintiffs, most of whom are not California residents, filed this civil action in a California state court against Bristol-Myers Squibb Company (BMS), asserting a variety of state-law claims based on injuries allegedly caused by a BMS drug called Plavix. The California Supreme Court held that the California courts have specific jurisdiction to entertain the nonresidents' claims. We now reverse.

I
A

BMS, a large pharmaceutical company, is incorporated in Delaware and headquartered in New York, and it maintains substantial operations in both New York and New Jersey. Over 50 percent of BMS's work force in the United States is employed in those two States.

BMS also engages in business activities in other jurisdictions, including California. Five of the company's research and laboratory facilities, which employ a total of around 160 employees, are located there. BMS also employs about 250 sales representatives in California and maintains a small state-government advocacy office in Sacramento.

One of the pharmaceuticals that BMS manufactures and sells is Plavix, a prescription drug that thins the blood and inhibits blood clotting. BMS did not develop Plavix in California, did not create a marketing strategy for Plavix in California, and did not manufacture, label, package, or work on the regulatory approval of the product in California. BMS instead engaged in all of these activities in either New York or New Jersey. But BMS does sell Plavix in California. Between 2006 and 2012, it sold almost 187 million Plavix pills in the State and took in more than $900 million from those sales. This amounts to a little over one percent of the company's nationwide sales revenue.

B

A group of plaintiffs—consisting of 86 California residents and 592 residents from 33 other States—filed eight separate complaints in California Superior Court, alleging that Plavix had damaged their health. All the complaints asserted 13 claims under California law, including products liability, negligent misrepresentation, and misleading advertising claims. The nonresident plaintiffs did not allege that they obtained Plavix through California physicians or from any other California source; nor did they claim that they were injured by Plavix or were treated for their injuries in California.

Asserting lack of personal jurisdiction, BMS moved to quash service of summons on the nonresidents' claims, but the California Superior Court denied this motion, finding that the California courts had general jurisdiction over BMS "[b]ecause [it] engages in extensive activities in California." [T]he California Supreme Court instructed the Court of Appeal [to reconsider in light of new Supreme Court precedent regarding general jurisdiction]. The Court of Appeal then changed its decision on the question of general jurisdiction, [holding that] general jurisdiction was clearly lacking, but [going] on to find that the California courts had specific jurisdiction over the nonresidents' claims against BMS.

The California Supreme Court affirmed. The court unanimously agreed with the Court of Appeal [that there was no general jurisdiction], but the court was divided on the question of specific jurisdiction. The majority applied a "sliding scale approach to specific jurisdiction." Under this approach, "the more wide ranging the defendant's forum contacts, the more readily is shown a connection between the forum contacts and the claim." Applying this test, the majority concluded that "BMS's extensive contacts with California" permitted the exercise of specific jurisdiction [over nonresident plaintiffs] "based on a less direct connection between BMS's forum activities and plaintiffs' claims than might otherwise be required." . . . And while acknowledging that "there is no claim that Plavix itself was designed and developed in [BMS's California research facilities]," the court thought it significant that other research was done in the State.

We granted certiorari to decide whether the California courts' exercise of jurisdiction in this case violates the Due Process Clause of the Fourteenth Amendment.

II

It has long been established that the Fourteenth Amendment limits the personal jurisdiction of state courts. *See, e.g., World-Wide Volkswagen Corp. v. Woodson*, 444 U.S. 286, 291 (1980); *International Shoe Co. v. Washington*, 326 U.S. 310, 316-317 (1945); *Pennoyer v. Neff*, 95 U.S. 714, 733 (1878). . . . The primary focus of our personal jurisdiction inquiry is the defendant's relationship to the forum State. *See Walden v. Fiore*, 571 U.S. 277 (2014).

Since our seminal decision in *International Shoe*, our decisions have recognized two types of personal jurisdiction: "general" (sometimes called "all-purpose") jurisdiction and "specific" (sometimes called "case-linked") jurisdiction. *Goodyear Dunlop Tires Op's, S.A. v. Brown*, 564 U.S. 915,

918 (2011). . . . A court with general jurisdiction may hear any claim against that defendant, even if all the incidents underlying the claim occurred in a different State. . . .

Specific jurisdiction is very different. In order for a state court to exercise specific jurisdiction, "the *suit*" must "aris[e] out of or relat[e] to the defendant's contacts with the *forum*." *Burger King*, 471 U.S. 462, 472-73. In other words, there must be "an affiliation between the forum and the underlying controversy, principally, [an] activity or an occurrence that takes place in the forum State and is therefore subject to the State's regulation." *Goodyear*, 564 U.S. at 919. For this reason, "specific jurisdiction is confined to adjudication of issues deriving from, or connected with, the very controversy that establishes jurisdiction." *Ibid.* . . .

III

Our settled principles regarding specific jurisdiction control this case. In order for a court to exercise specific jurisdiction over a claim, there must be an "affiliation between the forum and the underlying controversy, principally, [an] activity or an occurrence that takes place in the forum State." *Goodyear*, 564 U.S. at 919. When there is no such connection, specific jurisdiction is lacking regardless of the extent of a defendant's unconnected activities in the State. *See id.* at 931, n.6 ("[E]ven regularly occurring sales of a product in a State do not justify the exercise of jurisdiction over a claim unrelated to those sales").

For this reason, the California Supreme Court's "sliding scale approach" is difficult to square with our precedents. Under the California approach, the strength of the requisite connection between the forum and the specific claims at issue is relaxed if the defendant has extensive forum contacts that are unrelated to those claims. Our cases provide no support for this approach. . . . For specific jurisdiction . . . [a defendant's] "continuous activity of some sorts within a state . . . is not enough to support the demand that the corporation be amenable to suits unrelated to that activity." *Int'l Shoe*, 326 U.S. at 318.

The present case illustrates the danger of the California approach. The State Supreme Court found that specific jurisdiction was present without identifying any adequate link between the State and the nonresidents' claims. As noted, the nonresidents were not prescribed Plavix in California, did not purchase Plavix in California, did not ingest Plavix in California, and were not injured by Plavix in California. The mere fact that other plaintiffs were prescribed, obtained, and ingested Plavix in California—and allegedly sustained the same injuries as did the nonresidents—does not allow the State to assert specific jurisdiction over the nonresidents' claims. . . . This remains true even when third parties (here, the plaintiffs who reside in California) can bring claims similar to those brought by the nonresidents. Nor is it sufficient—or even relevant—that BMS conducted research in California on matters unrelated to Plavix. What is needed—and what is missing here—is a connection between the forum and the specific claims at issue. . . .

Our decision in *Walden* illustrates this requirement. In that case, Nevada plaintiffs sued an out-of-state defendant for conducting an allegedly unlawful search of the plaintiffs while they were in Georgia preparing to board a plane bound for Nevada. We held that the Nevada courts lacked specific jurisdiction even though the plaintiffs were Nevada residents and "suffered foreseeable harm in Nevada." Because the "*relevant conduct occurred entirely in Georgi[a]* . . .

the mere fact that [this] conduct affected plaintiffs with connections to the forum State d[id] not suffice to authorize jurisdiction." *Walden*, 134 S. Ct. at 1126.

In today's case, the connection between the nonresidents' claims and the forum is even weaker. The relevant plaintiffs are not California residents and do not claim to have suffered harm in that State. In addition, as in *Walden*, all the conduct giving rise to the nonresidents' claims occurred elsewhere. It follows that the California courts cannot claim specific jurisdiction....

In a last ditch contention, respondents contend that BMS's "decision to contract with a California company [McKesson] to distribute [Plavix] nationally" provides a sufficient basis for personal jurisdiction. But as we have explained, "[t]he requirements of *International Shoe* ... must be met as to each defendant over whom a state court exercises jurisdiction." *Walden*, 134 S. Ct. at 1123. In this case, it is not alleged that BMS engaged in relevant acts together with McKesson in California. Nor is it alleged that BMS is derivatively liable for McKesson's conduct in California. And the nonresidents "have adduced no evidence to show how or by whom the Plavix they took was distributed to the pharmacies that dispensed it to them." The bare fact that BMS contracted with a California distributor is not enough to establish personal jurisdiction in the State.

IV

Our straightforward application in this case of settled principles of personal jurisdiction will not result in the parade of horribles that respondents conjure up. Our decision does not prevent the California and out-of-state plaintiffs from joining together in a consolidated action in the States that have general jurisdiction over BMS. BMS concedes that such suits could be brought in either New York or Delaware. Alternatively, the plaintiffs who are residents of a particular State—for example, the 92 plaintiffs from Texas and the 71 from Ohio—could probably sue together in their home States....

* * *

The judgment of the California Supreme Court is reversed, and the case is remanded for further proceedings not inconsistent with this opinion.

Justice SOTOMAYOR, dissenting.

Three years ago, the Court imposed substantial curbs on the exercise of general jurisdiction in its decision in *Daimler AG v. Bauman*, 571 U.S. 117 (2014). Today, the Court takes its first step toward a similar contraction of specific jurisdiction by holding that a corporation that engages in a nationwide course of conduct cannot be held accountable in a state court by a group of injured people unless all of those people were injured in the forum State.

I fear the consequences of the Court's decision today will be substantial. The majority's rule will make it difficult to aggregate the claims of plaintiffs across the country whose claims may be worth little alone. It will make it impossible to bring a nationwide mass action in state court against defendants who are [subject to general jurisdiction] in different States [from one another]. And it will result in piecemeal litigation and the bifurcation of claims. None of this is necessary. A core concern in this Court's personal jurisdiction cases is fairness. And there is nothing unfair about subjecting a massive corporation to suit in a State for a nationwide course of conduct that injures both forum residents and nonresidents alike.

I

Bristol-Myers Squibb is a Fortune 500 pharmaceutical company incorporated in Delaware and headquartered in New York. It employs approximately 25,000 people worldwide and earns annual revenues of over $15 billion.... Bristol-Myers... conducted a single nationwide advertising campaign for Plavix, using television, magazine, and Internet ads to broadcast its message. A consumer in California heard the same advertisement as a consumer in Maine about the benefits of Plavix. Bristol-Myers distribution of Plavix also proceeded through nationwide channels: Consistent with its usual practice, it relied on a small number of wholesalers to distribute Plavix throughout the country.

The 2005 publication of an article in the New England Journal of Medicine questioning the efficacy and safety of Plavix put Bristol-Myers on the defensive, as consumers around the country began to claim that they were injured by the drug. The plaintiffs in these consolidated cases are 86 people who allege they were injured by Plavix in California and several hundred others who say they were injured by the drug in other states. They filed their suits in California Superior Court, raising product-liability claims against Bristol-Myers and McKesson [Bristol-Myers' primary distributor]. Their claims are "materially identical," as Bristol-Myers concedes.... The question is whether Bristol-Myers is subject to suit in California only on the residents' claims, or whether a state court may also hear the non-residents' "identical" claims.

II
A

... Our cases have set out three conditions for the exercise of specific jurisdiction over a nonresident defendant. First, the defendant must have "purposefully avail[ed] itself of the privilege of conducting activities within the forum State" or have purposefully directed its conduct into the forum State. *J. McIntyre Machinery, Ltd. v. Nicastro*, 564 U.S. 873, 877 (2011) (plurality opinion). Second, the plaintiff's claim must "arise out of or relate to" the defendant's forum conduct. *Helicopteros*, 466 U.S. at 414. Finally, the exercise of jurisdiction must be reasonable under the circumstances. *Asahi Metal Industry Co. v. Superior Court of Cal.*, 480 U.S. 102, 113-14 (1987). The factors relevant to such an analysis include "the burden on the defendant, the forum State's interest in adjudicating the dispute, the plaintiff's interest in obtaining convenient and effective relief, the interstate judicial system's interest in obtaining the most efficient resolution of controversies, and the shared interest of the several States in furthering fundamental substantive social policies." *Burger King*, 471 U.S. at 477.

B

Viewed through this framework, the California courts appropriately exercised specific jurisdiction over respondents' claims.

First, there is no dispute that Bristol-Myers "purposefully avail[ed] itself," of California and its substantial pharmaceutical market. Bristol-Myers employs over 400 people in California and maintains half a dozen facilities in the State engaged in research, development, and policymaking. It contracts with a California-based distributor, McKesson, whose sales account for a significant portion of its revenue. And it markets and sells its drugs, including Plavix, in California, resulting in total Plavix sales in that State of nearly $1 billion during the period relevant to this suit.

Second, respondents' claims "relate to" Bristol-Myers' in-state conduct. A claim "relates to" a defendant's forum conduct if it has a "connect[ion] with" that conduct. *Int'l Shoe*, 326 U.S. at 319. So respondents could not, for instance, hale Bristol-Myers into court in California for negligently maintaining the sidewalk outside its New York headquarters—a claim that has no connection to acts Bristol-Myers took in California. Respondents' claims against Bristol-Myers concern conduct materially identical to acts the company took in California: its marketing and distribution of Plavix, which it undertook on a nationwide basis in all 50 States. That respondents were allegedly injured by this nationwide course of conduct in Indiana, Oklahoma, and Texas, and not California, does not mean that their claims do not "relate to" the advertising and distribution efforts that Bristol-Myers undertook in that State. All of the plaintiffs—residents and nonresidents alike—allege that they were injured by the same essential acts. Our cases require no connection more direct than that.

Finally, and importantly, there is no serious doubt that the exercise of jurisdiction over the nonresidents' claims is reasonable. . . .

III

Bristol-Myers does not dispute that it has purposefully availed itself of California's markets, nor—remarkably—did it argue below that it would be "unreasonable" for a California court to hear respondents' claims. Instead, Bristol-Myers contends that respondents' claims do not "arise out of or relate to" its California conduct. The majority agrees, explaining that no "adequate link" exists "between the State and the nonresidents' claims,"—a result that it says follows from "settled principles [of] specific jurisdiction." But our precedents do not require this result, and common sense says that it cannot be correct. . . .

I fear the consequences of the majority's decision today will be substantial. Even absent a rigid requirement that a defendant's in-state conduct must actually cause a plaintiff's claim,[3] the upshot of today's opinion is that plaintiffs cannot join their claims together and sue a defendant in a State in which only some of them have been injured. That rule is likely to have consequences far beyond this case.

First, and most prominently, the Court's opinion in this case will make it profoundly difficult for plaintiffs who are injured in different States by a defendant's nationwide course of conduct to sue that defendant in a single, consolidated action. . . . The effect of the Court's opinion today is to eliminate nationwide mass actions in any State other than those in which a defendant is "essentially at home" [and thus subject to general jurisdiction]. Such a rule hands one more tool to corporate defendants determined to prevent the aggregation of individual claims, and forces injured plaintiffs to bear the burden of bringing suit in what will often be far flung jurisdictions.

Second, the Court's opinion today may make it impossible to bring certain mass actions at all. After this case, it is difficult to imagine where it might be possible to bring a nationwide mass action against two or more defendants headquartered and incorporated in different States. . . . What about a nationwide mass action brought against a

---

[3] Bristol-Myers urges such a rule upon us, but its adoption would have consequences far beyond those that follow from today's factbound opinion. Among other things, it might call into question whether even a plaintiff *injured* in a State by an item identical to those sold by a defendant in that State could avail himself of that State's courts to redress his injuries. That question, and others like it, appears to await another case.

defendant not headquartered or incorporated in the United States? . . .

The majority chides respondents for conjuring a "parade of horribles," but says nothing about how suits like those described here will survive its opinion in this case. The answer is simple: They will not.

* * *

It "does not offend 'traditional notions of fair play and substantial justice,'" *Int'l Shoe*, 326 U.S. at 316, to permit plaintiffs to aggregate claims arising out of a single nationwide course of conduct in a single suit in a single State where some, but not all, were injured. But that is exactly what the Court holds today is barred by the Due Process Clause.

This is not a rule the Constitution has required before. I respectfully dissent.

Notes & Questions

1. In what state is Bristol-Myers Squibb incorporated? Where is it headquartered? Where did it develop and manufacture Plavix? Of the 678 plaintiffs, how many bought and used Plavix in California? For specific jurisdiction, a plaintiff's claims must "arise out of or relate to" the defendant's contacts with the forum state. What is the strongest argument that these 678 plaintiffs' claims meet this requirement? Why did the Supreme Court reject this argument?

2. Until *Bristol-Myers Squibb*, the Supreme Court had never elaborated on what it meant for a claim to "arise out of or relate to" a defendant's forum activities for purposes of specific jurisdiction. For decades, however, lower courts have been split among at least four different tests for "relatedness." The first test, and the most restrictive, requires that defendant's forum activities "*proximately cause*" plaintiffs' injuries. *See, e.g., O'Connor v. Sandy Lane Hotel Co.*, 496 F.3d 312, 318 (3d Cir. 2007). The second test, a slightly less restrictive version of the first, is known as the "*substantial relevance*" test, under which the defendant's forum contacts must be substantially relevant to the merits of plaintiffs' claims. *See, e.g., Mass. Sch. of Law at Andover, Inc. v. Am. Bar Ass'n*, 142 F.3d 26, 35 (1st Cir. 1998). The third test is the "*but-for*" causation test for relatedness. *Id.* Finally, the fourth, and least restrictive, test is the "*substantial relationship*," "*logical relationship*," or "*substantial connection*" test—different names for the same test—the test that rejects a cause-in-fact requirement for relatedness. *See, e.g., Bristol-Myers Squibb Company v. Superior Court of California*, 1 Cal. 5th 783, 800 (Cal. 2016); *TV Azteca v. Ruiz*, 490 S.W.3d 29, 52 (Tex. 2016). Which one (or more) of these relatedness tests best describes the Supreme Court's holding in *Bristol-Myers Squibb*?

   Note that some courts, in applying the "substantial relationship" test, applied the "sliding scale" approach described in BMS to determine whether the "substantial relationship" test was satisfied. Recall that the "sliding scale" test instructs that the intensity of the defendant's contacts is inversely proportional to the relatedness required. Does that sliding scale survive *Bristol-Myers Squibb*?

   In 2020, the Supreme Court granted certiorari in a pair of cases that could further define the relatedness requirement of specific jurisdiction. *See Ford Motor*

Co. v. Bandemer, 2020 WL 254152 (Jan. 17, 2020) (cert. granted), *Ford Motor Co. v. Mont. Eighth Jud. Dist.*, 2020 WL 254155 (Jan. 17, 2020) (cert. granted).

3. Assume, contrary to the facts of *Bristol-Myers Squibb*, that the bulk of the research regarding Plavix *had* occurred in California. Different result vis-à-vis the nonresident plaintiffs? Would your answer change if the plaintiffs' claims had not involved allegations that Plavix was defective, but instead involved allegations that BMS conspired to artificially inflate the price of Plavix?

4. Viewed together, *Nicastro* and *Bristol-Myers Squibb* reveal a rather strong re-commitment to the notion that state power over parties derives from its territorial boundaries—a notion that seemed to have been abandoned in the years following *Pennoyer*. What is the likely effect of this heightened territoriality focus on plaintiffs' choices of forum? On defendants' exposure to liability?

5. *Bristol-Myers Squibb* comes up in the context of a non-class mass tort action. A mass tort action is an aggregate lawsuit, but it lacks the formalities of the class action that you learned about in Chapter 7. However, there is a significant question after *Bristol-Myers Squibb* regarding whether its holding applies to class actions. So far, courts are split on the issue. *Compare, e.g., DeBernardis v. NBTY, Inc.*, 2018 WL 4162228 (N.D. Ill. Jan. 18, 2018) (*Bristol-Myers Squibb* applies with equal force to class actions), *with Mussat v. IQVIA, Inc.*, 953 F.3d 441 (7th Cir. 2020) (the different nature of class actions under Rule 23 makes *Bristol-Myers Squibb* inapplicable). If *Bristol-Myers Squibb* does apply to class actions, what might happen to class actions involving nationwide harm? How might the decision in *Bristol-Myers Squibb* affect the values of efficiency and judicial economy sought to be effectuated by Fed. R. Civ. P. 23? If *Bristol-Myers Squibb* does *not* apply to class actions, what, precisely is the nature and scope of the due process protection for defendants articulated in *Bristol-Myers Squibb*?

6. As you have likely already surmised, *Bristol-Myers Squibb* left open many questions about relatedness. This means you will have to think creatively when faced with relatedness questions in practice. Try this one for starters, using real facts:

At the height of her career, a Mexican recording artist known as Gloria Trevi, sometimes referred to as "Mexico's Madonna," was criminally charged with kidnapping and sexual assault for allegedly luring underaged girls into sexual relationships with her manager and then-boyfriend. *TV Azteca v. Ruiz*, 490 S.W.3d 29, 35 (Tex. 2016). Ms. Trevi eventually served time in prison in Mexico. In 2004, after four years and eight months' incarceration, a Mexican judge dismissed the criminal case, citing a lack of evidence (though Ms. Trevi was never acquitted). TV Azteca, a Mexican national television network, produces and airs a popular entertainment program, *Ventaneando*, in Mexico. In 2009, on the ten-year anniversary of criminal charges against Ms. Trevi, *Ventaneando* produced a series of reports regarding the events related to those criminal charges. *Id.* at 49-50. The reports were made in Mexico, by Mexican journalists, for Mexican viewers, relying upon Mexican sources, and they concerned the activities of Mexican citizens (including Ms. Trevi). However, two television stations owned by TV Azteca in

Northeast Mexico broadcast the *Ventaneando* reports using over-the-air signals that involuntarily crossed into the United States and reached viewers along the south Texas border. Ms. Trevi, her husband, and her son claim that they viewed the broadcasts in Texas, where they were temporarily living on a three-year O-1 visa. *TV Azteca v. Ruiz*, 494 S.W.3d 109, 119 (Tex. Ct. App. 2014). Ms. Trevi filed claims against TV Azteca in Texas, and TV Azteca moved to dismiss for lack of personal jurisdiction. Before reading the next paragraph, craft your best arguments for Ms. Trevi *and* for TV Azteca on the personal jurisdiction issue, relying on the cases you have read so far and using the tests of relatedness you learned about in Note 1. Then read on to see how the Texas Supreme Court came out on the relatedness issue, and more importantly, why.

Ultimately, the Texas Supreme Court found that her claims "arose out of" TV Azteca's contacts with Texas, on the grounds that TV Azteca derived "substantial revenue and other benefits by selling advertising time to Texas businesses," and that TV Azteca made "substantial and successful efforts to distribute their programs and increase their popularity in Texas." 490 S.W.3d at 49, 52. In making these findings, the Texas Supreme Court pointed to the existence of TV Azteca's affiliate, Azteca America, which had programming in the United States as an additional basis for exercising specific jurisdiction over TV Azteca. *Id.* at 50-51. These contacts, the court held, constituted a "substantial connection between [defendant's forum state] contacts and the operative facts of the litigation." *Id.* at 52. TV Azteca's petition for certiorari, filed in 2016, was denied (around the same time that the Supreme Court granted certiorari in *Bristol-Myers Squibb*). Which test for relatedness did the Texas Supreme Court apply? Would the Texas Supreme Court's decision be upheld after *Bristol-Myers Squibb*? Is that question answerable? What questions left open by *Bristol-Myers Squibb* are cast into stark relief by the facts of *TV Azteca*?

7. The Court in *Bristol-Myers Squibb* draws the important distinction between specific jurisdiction, which you have been studying extensively in this chapter, and general jurisdiction, which you first heard about in *International Shoe*. By studying the relatedness requirement of specific jurisdiction, you already know something very important about general jurisdiction—namely, that it does *not* have a relatedness requirement. What, then, is required for a court to have general jurisdiction over a defendant? What does it mean, as the Court put it in *International Shoe*, for a defendant's contacts with a forum state to be so "continuous" and "substantial" as to support general jurisdiction?

(2) General Jurisdiction

So far, you have studied a court's power to exercise jurisdiction over a defendant when the defendant's contacts with the forum state that *relate* to the claims in the suit are of such a nature that the defendant can be said to have "purposefully availed" itself of the forum state. Sometimes, however, a state court may have jurisdiction over the defendant for *any and all claims*, regardless of whether the claims arose out of anything that happened in the state. Suppose, for instance, someone wishes to sue

General Motors Corporation. General Motors is headquartered in Michigan. There is no doubt that the Michigan courts would have power over General Motors—even if the claims did not arise out of General Motor's activity in Michigan. Imagine, now, that someone wishes to sue Mr. X, who is a citizen of Nebraska. There is likewise no doubt that Nebraska courts would have power over Mr. X, even if the dispute arose elsewhere. That is *general jurisdiction*, also referred to as *all-purpose jurisdiction*. The defendant's connection with the forum state is so significant that the courts of that state have power over the defendant without regard to whether the claims arise out of or relate to the defendant's contact with the state.

For an individual, general jurisdiction is based upon *domicile. Milliken v. Meyer*, 311 U.S. 57 (1940). If an individual is domiciled in a state, then the courts of that state have *in personam* jurisdiction over that person for *any* claim, regardless of where it may have arisen. A person, however, can only have one domicile. In determining whether a person is "domiciled" in given state, courts look to physical presence in that state and intent to remain in that state. *See, e.g., Mississippi Band of Choctaw Indians v. Holyfield*, 490 U.S. 30, 48 (1989). We explored the test for domicile with the case of *Aponte-Dávila v. Municipality of Caguas*, 828 F.3d 40 (1st Cir. 2016), in Chapter 9 as a basis for determining citizenship for purposes of diversity jurisdiction.

Terminology Tip

You saw the term *general jurisdiction* in the previous chapter regarding subject matter jurisdiction. "General jurisdiction" in the context of subject matter jurisdiction means something *entirely different* from the same term in personal jurisdiction. In the context of subject matter jurisdiction, we refer to state trial courts as *courts of general jurisdiction*, because they can hear any type of case, as distinct from courts of *limited jurisdiction*, including federal courts. In personal jurisdiction, *general jurisdiction* (or all-purpose jurisdiction) refers to a court's power over a defendant regardless of where the claim arose, as opposed to *specific jurisdiction* (or case-specific jurisdiction).

For a corporation, general jurisdiction requires a similarly strong presence in the state. Although *International Shoe* was a case of specific jurisdiction (recall that the dispute involved unemployment fund contributions based on the defendant's employment of workers within the State of Washington), the Court decision also suggested the idea of general jurisdiction over corporations when the defendant had such "continuous corporate operations within a state . . . so substantial and of such a nature as to justify suit . . . on causes of action arising from dealings entirely distinct from those activities." *Int'l Shoe*, 326 U.S. at 318. After *International Shoe*, the Court has decided numerous cases involving questions of *specific* jurisdiction. By contrast, it has decided very few directly involving questions of general or all-purpose jurisdiction. *See Perkins v. Benguet Mining Co.*, 342 U.S. 437 (1952) (finding that a Philippine mining corporation was subject to the general jurisdiction of Ohio because it had temporarily relocated its offices to Ohio while the Philippines were occupied by the Japanese during WWII); *Helicopteros Nacionales v. Hall*, 466 U.S. 408 (1984) (finding defendant's repeated business contacts with Texas insufficient to confer general jurisdiction).

In 2011, in *Goodyear Dunlop Tires Operations, S.A. v. Brown*, the Court defined what it meant to have "continuous and systematic" contacts with a state for purposes of general jurisdiction, stating that "[a] court may assert general jurisdiction over foreign (sister-state or foreign-country) corporations to hear any and all claims against them when their affiliations with the State are so continuous and systematic *as to render them essentially at home* in the forum State." 564 U.S. 915, 919 (2011) (emphasis added). However, that still leaves open a key question: What degree of affiliations are required to render an entity "at home" in the forum state? Certainly, the state of incorporation makes a corporation "at home" and gives that state general jurisdiction over it. Similarly, a company is "at home" in the state in which it is headquartered (for instance General Motors would be subject to general jurisdiction in Michigan, where it is headquartered). What if a company is not incorporated or headquartered in the state, but does substantial business there? Is that enough for general jurisdiction?

Consider the following case, *Daimler AG v. Bauman*, 571 U.S. 117 (2014), the most recent in the Supreme Court's (thin) general jurisdiction jurisprudence. As you read, see whether and how *Daimler* defines what it means to be "at home" in a state. Further, although *Daimler* represents the current state of the law with regard to all-purpose jurisdiction, pay close attention to the Court's recounting of prior general jurisdiction cases in *Daimler*, as they, along with *Daimler* itself, comprise the entire set of Supreme Court proclamations on general jurisdiction. Indeed, think of the cases in the Supreme Court's general jurisdiction canon as tools for crafting your own general jurisdiction arguments, and for understanding the permissible boundaries of those potential arguments.

DAIMLER AG v. BAUMAN
571 U.S. 117 (2014)

Justice GINSBURG delivered the opinion of the Court.

This case concerns the authority of a court in the United States to entertain a claim brought by foreign plaintiffs against a foreign defendant based on events occurring entirely outside the United States. The litigation commenced in 2004, when twenty-two Argentinian residents filed a complaint in the United States District Court for the Northern District of California against DaimlerChrysler Aktiengesellschaft (Daimler), a German public stock company, that manufactures Mercedes-Benz vehicles in Germany. The complaint alleged that during Argentina's 1976-1983 "Dirty War," Daimler's Argentinian subsidiary, Mercedes-Benz Argentina (MB Argentina) collaborated with state security forces to kidnap, detain, torture, and kill certain MB Argentina workers, among them, plaintiffs or persons closely related to plaintiffs. Damages for the alleged human-rights violations were sought from Daimler under the laws of the United States, California, and Argentina. Jurisdiction over the lawsuit was predicated on the California contacts of Mercedes-Benz USA, LLC (MBUSA), a subsidiary of Daimler incorporated in Delaware with its principal place of business in New Jersey. MBUSA distributes Daimler-manufactured vehicles to independent dealerships throughout the United States, including California.

The question presented is whether the Due Process Clause of the Fourteenth Amendment precludes the District Court from exercising jurisdiction over Daimler in this case, given the absence of any California connection to the atrocities, perpetrators, or victims described in the complaint. Plaintiffs invoked the court's general or all-purpose jurisdiction. California, they urge, is a place where Daimler may be sued on any and all claims against it, wherever in the world the claims may arise. For example, under the proffered jurisdictional theory, if a Daimler-manufactured vehicle overturned in Poland, injuring a Polish driver and passenger, the injured parties could maintain a design defect suit in California. Exercises of personal jurisdiction so exorbitant, we hold, are barred by due process constraints on the assertion of adjudicatory authority.

In *Goodyear Dunlop Tires Operations, S.A. v. Brown*, 564 U.S. 915 (2011), we addressed the distinction between general or all-purpose jurisdiction, and specific or conduct-linked jurisdiction. As to the former, we held that a court may assert jurisdiction over a foreign corporation "to hear any and all claims against [it]" only when the corporation's affiliations with the State in which suit is brought are so constant and pervasive "as to render [it] essentially at home in the forum State." *Id.* Instructed by *Goodyear*, we conclude Daimler is not "at home" in California, and cannot be sued there for injuries plaintiffs attribute to MB Argentina's conduct in Argentina.

I

In 2004, plaintiffs (respondents here) filed suit in the United States District Court for the Northern District of California, alleging that MB Argentina collaborated with Argentinian state security forces to kidnap, detain, torture, and kill plaintiffs and their relatives during the military dictatorship in place there from 1976 through 1983, a period known as Argentina's "Dirty War." Based on those allegations, plaintiffs asserted claims under the Alien Tort Statute, and the Torture Victim Protection Act of 1991, as well as claims for wrongful death and intentional infliction of emotional distress under the laws of California and Argentina. The incidents recounted in the complaint center on MB Argentina's plant in González Catán, Argentina; no part of MB Argentina's alleged collaboration with Argentinian authorities took place in California or anywhere else in the United States.

Plaintiffs' operative complaint names only one corporate defendant: Daimler, the petitioner here. Plaintiffs seek to hold Daimler vicariously liable for MB Argentina's alleged malfeasance. Daimler is a German *Aktiengesellschaft* (public stock company) that manufactures Mercedes-Benz vehicles primarily in Germany and has its headquarters in Stuttgart. At times relevant to this case, MB Argentina was a subsidiary wholly owned by Daimler's predecessor in interest.

Daimler moved to dismiss the action for want of personal jurisdiction. Opposing the motion, plaintiffs submitted declarations and exhibits purporting to demonstrate the presence of Daimler itself in California. Alternatively, plaintiffs maintained that jurisdiction over Daimler could be founded on the California contacts of MBUSA, a distinct corporate entity that, according to plaintiffs, should be treated as Daimler's agent for jurisdictional purposes.

MBUSA, an indirect subsidiary of Daimler, is a Delaware limited liability corporation. MBUSA serves as Daimler's exclusive importer and distributor in the United States, purchasing Mercedes-Benz automobiles from Daimler in Germany, then importing those vehicles, and ultimately distributing them to independent dealerships located throughout the Nation. Although MBUSA's principal place of business is in New Jersey, MBUSA has multiple California-based facilities, including a regional office in Costa Mesa, a Vehicle Preparation Center in Carson, and a Classic Center in Irvine. According to the record developed below, MBUSA is the largest supplier of luxury vehicles to the California market. In particular, over 10% of all sales of new vehicles in the United States take place in California, and MBUSA's California sales account for 2.4% of Daimler's worldwide sales. . . .

The District Court granted Daimler's motion to dismiss. Daimler's own affiliations with California . . . were insufficient to support the exercise of all-purpose jurisdiction over the corporation. Next, the court declined to attribute MBUSA's California contacts to Daimler . . . concluding that plaintiffs failed to demonstrate that MBUSA acted as Daimler's agent. The Ninth Circuit at first affirmed . . . [but upon petition for rehearing, concluded that] the agency test was satisfied and considerations of reasonableness did not bar the exercise of [general] jurisdiction. . . .

II

Federal courts ordinarily follow state law in determining the bounds of their jurisdiction over persons. *See* Fed. Rule Civ. Proc. 4(k)(1)(A) (service of process is effective to establish personal jurisdiction over a defendant "who is subject to the jurisdiction of a court of general jurisdiction in the state where the district court is located"). . . . California's long-arm statute allows the exercise of personal jurisdiction to the full extent permissible under the U.S. Constitution. We therefore inquire whether the Ninth Circuit's holding comports with the limits imposed by federal due process.

III

. . . "The canonical opinion [regarding a state's jurisdiction over persons] remains *International Shoe*, in which we held that a State may authorize its courts to exercise personal jurisdiction over an out-of-state defendant if the defendant has 'certain minimum contacts with [the State] such that the maintenance of the suit does not offend "traditional notions of fair play and substantial justice." ' " *Goodyear*, 564 U.S. at 923 (quoting *Int'l Shoe Co. v. Washington*, 326 U.S. 310, 316 (1945)). Following *International Shoe*, "the relationship among the defendant, the forum, and the litigation, rather than the mutually exclusive sovereignty of the States on which the rules of *Pennoyer* rest, became the central concern of the inquiry into personal jurisdiction." *Shaffer v. Heitner*, 433 U.S. 186, 204 (1977).

International Shoe's conception of "fair play and substantial justice" presaged the development of two categories of personal jurisdiction. The first category is represented by *International Shoe* itself, a case in which the in-state activities of the corporate defendant "ha[d] not only been continuous and systematic, but also g[a]ve rise to the liabilities sued on." 326 U.S. at 317. . . . Adjudicatory authority of this order, in which the suit "aris[es] out of or relate[s] to the defendant's contacts with the forum," *Helicopteros Nacionales de Colombia, S.A. v. Hall*, 466 U.S. 408, 414, n.8 (1984), is today called "specific jurisdiction." *See Goodyear*, 564 U.S. at 919.

International Shoe distinguished between, on the one hand, exercises of specific jurisdiction, as just described, and on the other, situations where a foreign corporation's "continuous corporate operations within a state [are] so substantial and of such a nature as to justify suit against it on causes of action arising from dealings entirely distinct from those activities." 326 U.S. at 318. As we have since explained, "[a] court may assert general jurisdiction over foreign (sister-state or foreign-country) corporations to hear any and all claims against them when their affiliations with the State are so 'continuous and systematic' as to render them essentially at home in the forum State." *Goodyear*, 564 U.S. at 919.

Since *International Shoe*, "specific jurisdiction has become the centerpiece of modern jurisdiction theory, while general jurisdiction [has played] a reduced role." *Goodyear*, 564 U.S. at 925. *International Shoe*'s momentous departure from *Pennoyer*'s rigidly territorial focus, we have noted, unleashed a rapid expansion of tribunals' ability to hear claims against out-of-state defendants when the episode-in-suit occurred in the forum or the defendant purposefully availed itself of the forum. . . .

Our post-*International Shoe* opinions on general jurisdiction, by comparison, are few. "[The Court's] 1952 decision in *Perkins v. Benguet Consol. Mining Co.*, 342 U.S. 437 (1952), remains the textbook case of general jurisdiction appropriately exercised over a foreign corporation that has not consented to suit in the forum." *Goodyear*, 564 U.S. at 927-28. The defendant in *Perkins*, Benguet, was a company incorporated under the laws of the Philippines, where it operated gold and silver mines. Benguet ceased its mining operations during the Japanese occupation of the Philippines in World War II; its president moved to Ohio, where he kept an office, maintained the company's files, and oversaw the company's activities. 342 U.S. at 448. The plaintiff, an Ohio resident, sued Benguet on a claim that neither arose in Ohio nor related to the corporation's activities in that State. We held that the Ohio courts could exercise general jurisdiction

over Benguet without offending due process. That was so, we later noted, because "Ohio was the corporation's principal, if temporary, place of business." *Keeton v. Hustler Magazine, Inc.*, 465 U.S. 770, 780 n.11 (1984).

The next case on point, *Helicopteros*, 466 U.S. 408, arose from a helicopter crash in Peru. Four U.S. citizens perished in that accident; their survivors and representatives brought suit in Texas state court against the helicopter's owner and operator, a Colombian corporation. That company's contacts with Texas were confined to "sending its chief executive officer to Houston for a contract-negotiation session; accepting into its New York bank account checks drawn on a Houston bank; purchasing helicopters, equipment, and training services from [a Texas-based helicopter company] for substantial sums; and sending personnel to [Texas] for training." *Id.* at 416. Notably, those contacts bore no apparent relationship to the accident that gave rise to the suit. We held that the company's Texas connections did not resemble the "continuous and systematic general business contacts . . . found to exist in *Perkins*." *Ibid.* "[M]ere purchases, even if occurring at regular intervals," we clarified, "are not enough to warrant a State's assertion of *in personam* jurisdiction over a nonresident corporation in a cause of action not related to those purchase transactions." *Id.* at 418.

Most recently, in *Goodyear*, we answered the question: "Are foreign subsidiaries of a United States parent corporation amenable to suit in state court on claims unrelated to any activity of the subsidiaries in the forum State?" 564 U.S. at 918. That case arose from a bus accident outside Paris that killed two boys from North Carolina. The boys' parents brought a wrongful-death suit in North Carolina state court alleging that the bus's tire was defectively manufactured. The complaint named as defendants not only The Goodyear Tire and Rubber Company (Goodyear), an Ohio corporation, but also Goodyear's Turkish, French, and Luxembourgian subsidiaries. Those foreign subsidiaries, which manufactured tires for sale in Europe and Asia, lacked any affiliation with North Carolina. A small percentage of tires manufactured by the foreign subsidiaries were distributed in North Carolina, however, and on that ground, the North Carolina Court of Appeals held the subsidiaries amenable to the general jurisdiction of North Carolina courts.

We reversed, observing that the North Carolina court's analysis "elided the essential difference between case-specific and all-purpose (general) jurisdiction." *Id.* at 927. Although the placement of a product into the stream of commerce "may bolster an affiliation germane to *specific* jurisdiction," we explained, such contacts "do not warrant a determination that, based on those ties, the forum has *general* jurisdiction over a defendant." *Id.* As *International Shoe* itself teaches, a corporation's "continuous activity of some sorts within a state is not enough to support the demand that the corporation be amenable to suits unrelated to that activity." 326 U.S. at 318. Because Goodyear's foreign subsidiaries were "in no sense at home in North Carolina," we held, those subsidiaries could not be required to submit to the general jurisdiction of that State's courts. *Goodyear*, 564 U.S. at 929.

As is evident from *Perkins*, *Helicopteros*, and *Goodyear*, general and specific jurisdiction have followed markedly different trajectories post-*International Shoe*. Specific jurisdiction has been cut loose from *Pennoyer*'s sway, but we have declined to stretch general jurisdiction beyond limits

traditionally recognized. As this Court has increasingly trained on the "relationship among the defendant, the forum, and the litigation," *Shaffer*, 433 U.S. at 204, *i.e.*, specific jurisdiction, general jurisdiction has come to occupy a less dominant place in the contemporary scheme.

IV

With this background, we turn directly to the question whether Daimler's affiliations with California are sufficient to subject it to the general (all-purpose) personal jurisdiction of that State's courts. In the proceedings below, the parties agreed on, or failed to contest, certain points we now take as given. Plaintiffs have never attempted to fit this case into the *specific* jurisdiction category. Nor did plaintiffs challenge on appeal the District Court's holding that Daimler's own contacts with California were, by themselves, too sporadic to justify the exercise of general jurisdiction. While plaintiffs ultimately persuaded the Ninth Circuit to impute MBUSA's California contacts to Daimler on an agency theory, at no point have they maintained that MBUSA is an alter ego of Daimler.

Daimler, on the other hand, failed to object below to plaintiffs' assertion that the California courts could exercise all-purpose jurisdiction over MBUSA. We will assume then, for purposes of this decision only, that MBUSA qualifies as at home in California.

A

In sustaining the exercise of general jurisdiction over Daimler, the Ninth Circuit relied on an agency theory, determining that MBUSA acted as Daimler's agent for jurisdictional purposes and then attributing MBUSA's California contacts to Daimler. . . .

This Court has not yet addressed whether a foreign corporation may be subjected to a court's general jurisdiction based on the contacts of its in-state subsidiary . . . [b]ut we need not pass judgment on invocation of an agency theory in the context of general jurisdiction, for in no event can the appeals court's analysis be sustained.

The Ninth Circuit's agency finding rested primarily on its observation that MBUSA's services were "important" to Daimler, as gauged by Daimler's hypothetical readiness to perform those services itself if MBUSA did not exist. Formulated this way, the inquiry into importance stacks the deck, for it will always yield a pro-jurisdiction answer. . . . The Ninth Circuit's agency theory thus appears to subject foreign corporations to general jurisdiction whenever they have an in-state subsidiary or affiliate, an outcome that would sweep beyond even the "sprawling view of general jurisdiction" we rejected in *Goodyear*, 564 U.S. at 929.

B

Even if we were to assume that MBUSA is at home in California, and further to assume MBUSA's contacts are imputable to Daimler, there would still be no basis to subject Daimler to general jurisdiction in California, for Daimler's slim contacts with the State hardly render it at home there. *Goodyear* made clear that only a limited set of affiliations with a forum will render a defendant amenable to all-purpose jurisdiction there. "For an individual, the paradigm forum for the exercise of general jurisdiction is the individual's domicile; for a corporation, it is an equivalent place, one in which the corporation is fairly regarded as at home." 564 U.S. at 924. With respect to a corporation, the place of incorporation and principal place of business are

"paradig[m] bases for general jurisdiction." Brilmayer et al., *A General Look at General Jurisdiction*, Texas L. Rev. 721, 735 (1988). Those affiliations have the virtue of being unique—that is, each ordinarily indicates only one place—as well as easily ascertainable. *Cf. Hertz Corp. v. Friend*, 559 U.S. 77, 94 (2010) ("Simple jurisdictional rules . . . promote greater predictability."). These bases afford plaintiffs recourse to at least one clear and certain forum in which a corporate defendant may be sued on any and all claims.

Goodyear did not hold that a corporation may be subject to general jurisdiction *only* in a forum where it is incorporated or has its principal place of business; it simply typed those places paradigm all-purpose forums. Plaintiffs would have us look beyond the exemplar bases *Goodyear* identified, and approve the exercise of general jurisdiction in every State in which a corporation "engages in a substantial, continuous, and systematic course of business." That formulation, we hold, is unacceptably grasping.

[T]he words "continuous and systematic" were used in *International Shoe* to describe instances in which the exercise of *specific* jurisdiction would be appropriate. *See* 326 U.S. at 317 (jurisdiction can be asserted where a corporation's in-state activities are not only "continuous and systematic, but also give rise to the liabilities sued on"). Turning to all-purpose jurisdiction, in contrast, *International Shoe* speaks of "instances in which the continuous corporate operations within a state [are] so substantial and of such a nature as to justify suit . . . *on causes of action arising from dealings entirely distinct from those activities*." *Id.* at 318 (emphasis added). Accordingly, the inquiry under *Goodyear* is not whether a foreign corporation's in-forum contacts can be said to be in some sense "continuous and systematic," it is whether that corporation's "affiliations with the State are so 'continuous and systematic' as to render [it] essentially at home in the forum State." 564 U.S. at 919.[19]

Here, neither Daimler nor MBUSA is incorporated in California, nor does either entity have its principal place of business there. If Daimler's California activities sufficed to allow adjudication of this Argentina-rooted case in California, the same global reach would presumably be available in every other State in which MBUSA's sales are sizable. Such exorbitant exercises of all-purpose jurisdiction would scarcely permit out-of-state defendants "to structure their primary conduct with some minimum assurance as to where that conduct will and will not render them liable to suit." *Burger King Corp. v. Rudzewicz*, 471 U.S. 462, 472 (1985).

It was therefore error for the Ninth Circuit to conclude that Daimler, even with MBUSA's contacts attributed to it, was at home in California, and hence subject to suit there on claims by foreign plaintiffs having nothing to do with anything that occurred or had its principal impact in California....

Justice SOTOMAYOR, concurring in the judgment.

I agree with the Court's conclusion that the Due Process Clause prohibits the exercise of personal jurisdiction over Daimler in light of the unique circumstances of this case. I concur only in the judgment, however, because I cannot agree with the path the Court takes to arrive at that result....

I begin with the point on which the majority and I agree: The Ninth Circuit's decision should be reversed.

Our personal jurisdiction precedents call for a two-part analysis. The contacts prong asks whether the defendant has sufficient contacts with the forum State to support personal jurisdiction; the reasonableness prong asks whether the exercise of jurisdiction would be unreasonable under the circumstances. *Burger King*, 471 U.S. at 475-478. As the majority points out, all of the cases in which we have applied the reasonableness prong have involved specific as opposed to general jurisdiction. Whether the reasonableness prong should apply in the general jurisdiction context is therefore a question we have never decided,[1] and it is one on which I can appreciate the arguments on both sides. But it would be imprudent to decide that question in this case given that respondents have failed to argue against the application of the reasonableness prong during the entire 8-year history of this litigation. As a result, I would decide this case under the reasonableness prong without foreclosing future consideration of whether that prong should be limited to the specific jurisdiction context.[2]

---

[19] We do not foreclose the possibility that in an exceptional case, *see, e.g., Perkins*, a corporation's operations in a forum other than its formal place of incorporation or principal place of business may be so substantial and of such a nature as to render the corporation at home in that State. But this case presents no occasion to explore that question, because Daimler's activities in California plainly do not approach that level. It is one thing to hold a corporation answerable for operations in the forum State, quite another to expose it to suit on claims having no connection whatever to the forum State.

---

[1] The Courts of Appeals have uniformly held that the reasonableness prong does in fact apply in the general jurisdiction context (citing cases).

[2] While our decisions rejecting the exercise of personal jurisdiction have typically done so under the minimum-contacts prong, we have never required that prong to be decided first. *See Asahi Metal Industry Co.*, 480 U.S. at 121....

We identified the factors that bear on reasonableness in *Asahi Metal Industry Co.* . . . [and ultimately held that] it would be "unreasonable and unfair" for a California court to exercise jurisdiction over a claim between a Taiwanese plaintiff and a Japanese defendant that arose out of a transaction in Taiwan, particularly where the Taiwanese plaintiff had not shown that it would be more convenient to litigate in California than in Taiwan or Japan. 480 U.S. at 113-14.

The same considerations resolve this case. It involves Argentine plaintiffs suing a German defendant for conduct that took place in Argentina. Like the plaintiffs in *Asahi*, respondents have failed to show that it would be more convenient to litigate in California than in Germany, a sovereign with a far greater interest in resolving the dispute. *Asahi* thus makes clear that it would be unreasonable for a court in California to subject Daimler to its jurisdiction.

While the majority's decisional process is problematic enough, I fear that process leads it to an even more troubling result.

Until today, our precedents had established a straightforward test for general jurisdiction: Does the defendant have "continuous corporate operations within a state" that are "so substantial and of such a nature as to justify suit against it on causes of action arising from dealings entirely distinct from those activities?" *Int'l Shoe*, 326 U.S. at 318. In every case where we have applied this test, we have focused solely on the magnitude of the defendant's in-state contacts, not the relative magnitude of those contacts in comparison to the defendant's contacts with other States. . . .

This approach follows from the touchstone principle of due process in this field, the concept of reciprocal fairness. When a corporation chooses to invoke the benefits and protections of a State in which it operates, the State acquires the authority to subject the company to suit in its courts. The majority's focus on the extent of a corporate defendant's out-of-forum contacts is untethered from this rationale. [The proper focus in on the corporation's] interactions with [the forum] State. . . .

Had the majority applied our settled approach, it would have had little trouble concluding that Daimler's California contacts rise to the requisite level, given the majority's assumption that MBUSA's contacts may be attributed to Daimler and given Daimler's concession that those contacts render MBUSA "at home" in California. . . .

Referring to the "continuous and systematic" contacts inquiry that has been taught to generations of first-year law students as "unacceptably grasping," the majority announces the new rule that in order for a foreign defendant to be subject to general jurisdiction, it must not only possess continuous and systematic contacts with a forum State, but those contacts must also surpass some unspecified level when viewed in comparison to the company's "nationwide and worldwide" activities. . . .

[The majority asserts that] its approach is necessary for predictability. . . . But there is nothing unpredictable about a rule that instructs multinational corporations that if they engage in continuous and substantial contacts with more than one State, they will be subject to general jurisdiction in each one. The majority may not favor that rule as a matter of policy, but such disagreement does not render an otherwise routine test unpredictable. . . .

The majority's concern for the consequences of its decision should have led it the other way, because the rule that it adopts will produce deep injustice in at least four respects.

First, the majority's approach unduly curtails the States' sovereign authority to adjudicate disputes against corporate defendants who have engaged in continuous and substantial business operations within their boundaries. The majority does not dispute that a State can exercise general jurisdiction where a corporate defendant has its corporate headquarters, and hence its principal place of business within the State. *Cf. Hertz Corp.*, 559 U.S. at 93. Yet it never explains why the State should lose that power when, as is increasingly common, a corporation "divide[s] [its] command and coordinating functions among officers who work at several different locations." *Id.* at 95-96. . . .

[Further], it should be obvious that the ultimate effect of the majority's approach will be to shift the risk of loss from multinational corporations to the individuals harmed by their actions. . . .

* * *

The Court rules against respondents today on a ground that no court has considered in the history of this case, that this Court did not grant certiorari to decide, and that Daimler raised only in a footnote of its brief. In doing so, the Court adopts a new rule of constitutional law that is unmoored from decades of precedent. Because I would reverse the Ninth Circuit's decision on the narrower ground that the exercise of jurisdiction over Daimler would be unreasonable in any event, I respectfully concur in the judgment only.

Notes & Questions

1. What makes a corporation "at home" for purposes of general jurisdiction? The Court in *Daimler* makes it clear that, at least, a corporation is at home in its state of incorporation and the state where the company is headquartered. Does that mean that the number of home states is capped at two? Consider this example: Amazon announced in 2018 that it is opening a second headquarters, dubbed HQ2, in in Arlington, Virginia, to supplement its original headquarters in Seattle, Washington. Will Amazon be at home both in Washington and in Virginia (as well as Delaware, where it is incorporated)?

2. More broadly, what do you make of footnote 19? After *Daimler*, to what extent may a corporation be subject to general jurisdiction in a state where it does a substantial volume of business and has a substantial physical presence?

    As we mentioned in Chapter 9, Starbucks Corporation is headquartered in Washington, but the greatest number of Starbucks coffee shops is in California. Would Starbucks be considered "at home" in California, under *Daimler*? (And would your answer change if the most Starbucks stores were, surprisingly, in a small state like Rhode Island?) Do the facts of either *Daimler* or *Goodyear* prove helpful in thinking about hypotheticals involving Starbucks, Amazon, or other domestic corporations?

    To make the question more concrete, suppose a customer fell on a slippery floor in a Starbucks store in Wisconsin, and the customer sues the company for negligence, alleging that Starbucks' employees carelessly failed to clean up a spilled Frappuccino. If the plaintiff were to sue in Wisconsin, then of course the court would have specific jurisdiction. If the plaintiff were to sue in Washington, then of course the court would have general jurisdiction. But suppose the Wisconsin plaintiff chooses to sue Starbucks *in California*. Would the California court have personal jurisdiction over Starbucks for the claim of the Wisconsin slip-and-fall plaintiff?

The *Daimler* court tells us how to analyze this question, but does it necessarily tell us the answer? Under *Daimler*, the California court has general jurisdiction over Starbucks only if Starbucks is "at home" in California. Is this the sort of "exceptional case" that fits the description in footnote 19, or would a court simply answer that Starbucks is not at home in California because it is neither incorporated nor headquartered there?

3. Does it even make sense to talk about where Starbucks or Daimler is "at home"? The concept of *home* has meaning for most individuals. Can the same be said of corporations? In your study of law, you will have multiple encounters with the idea of corporate *personhood*. Indeed, throughout this book, you have seen that corporations may sue and be sued just like individuals, and most of the rules on pleadings, discovery, and other procedures apply to corporate litigants and other entities just as they apply to individual litigants. Even if the idea of corporate personhood works reasonably well for many aspects of civil procedure, is it an awkward fit in the realm of personal jurisdiction? You have seen the Supreme Court apply its minimum contacts test to a series of corporations—International Shoe Co., World-Wide Volkswagen Corp., J. McIntyre Machinery, Ltd., and Bristol-Myers Squibb Co.—just as it applied the test to John Rudzewicz, Ian Calder, and other individuals. Does the personhood analogy work equally well for specific jurisdiction and for general jurisdiction? If we go back to the origins of constitutional personal jurisdiction analysis, *Pennoyer v. Neff* introduced concepts of "presence" and "consent" in the context of whether a court had jurisdiction over Marcus Neff. What would it mean for a corporation to be present in a state? By what sort of conduct does a corporation indicate its consent to a state's power? In *Daimler*, for purposes of describing the modern doctrine of general jurisdiction, the Supreme Court leans heavily on the analogy of individual domicile. As you learn to apply the "at home" test for general jurisdiction over corporations, and more broadly as you think about personal jurisdiction over corporations, be cognizant of the difficulties that can arise when concepts are imported from one context to another.

4. The majority in *Daimler* points out that specific jurisdiction has been "cut loose" from *Pennoyer*'s traditional territorial limits, but that general jurisdiction has not (and should not, in the majority's opinion) "stretched beyond" those traditional limits. What might justify such a distinction? In other words, why should general jurisdiction hew to the traditional territorial limitations on jurisdiction set out in *Pennoyer*, while specific jurisdiction need not? Moreover, what do you make of Justice Sotomayor's statement in BMS that the Court is not just contracting the power of states in the context of all-purpose jurisdiction by reverting to

Pennoyer-esque notions of territorial limits on jurisdiction, but also that the Court is contracting specific jurisdiction in a very similar way? Does a return to more *Pennoyer*-like territorial limitations seem woefully out of step with our modern commercial world? Or is there something to commend a return to more traditional restraints on personal jurisdiction, not in spite of, but because of, various features of our modern commercial world?

THE BIG PICTURE

The overall effect of the Supreme Court's recent personal jurisdiction jurisprudence in *Nicastro* (2011), *Goodyear* (2011), *Daimler* (2014), *Walden* (2014), and *Bristol-Myers Squibb* (2017) has been to make it harder for a court to conclude that the exercise of personal jurisdiction is proper in any given case. For plaintiffs, that means that there are fewer courts in which they can originally file a case. For defendants, the retrenchment of personal jurisdiction limits the number of places in which they can be sued, and increases the likelihood that they will be given a "home court advantage."

The Supreme Court's jurisprudence has led some to worry that it has become too difficult for some plaintiffs to sue, thus impeding enforcement of substantive law. Others see the trend as sensible protection against suits in plaintiff-friendly forums that lack sufficient connection to the defendant or the dispute. Whether this trend represents a troubling assault on access to justice, or, on the contrary, a needed antidote to overlitigation, depends mightily on one's point of view about litigation as a mechanism for access to justice and for enforcing the substantive law. In any event, the Court's ever-evolving views on personal jurisdiction reveal how difficult it is to articulate a truly coherent view of what due process protects in the context of personal jurisdiction.

(3) Property-Based Jurisdiction

In *International Shoe*, the Supreme Court did away with *Pennoyer*'s requirement of actual presence in the territory for *in personam* jurisdiction. However, the facts of *International Shoe* provided no occasion to opine on whether *one*, a defendant's property within a state would be sufficient to confer *in rem* jurisdiction; or *two*, the attachment of a defendant's property in the forum state would be sufficient to confer jurisdiction over that defendant, at least to the extent of the value of the property, under a *quasi-in-rem* theory. What remains of these two forms of property-based jurisdiction? Having studied *International Shoe* and specific jurisdiction, you may well be able to predict—right now—the ultimate fate of *in rem* and *quasi-in-rem* jurisdiction. Read the following case to see if your predictions, and your reasoning behind them, were correct.

SHAFFER v. HEITNER
433 U.S. 186 (1977)

MARSHALL, J., delivered the opinion of the Court.

The controversy in this case concerns the constitutionality of a Delaware statute that allows a court of that State to take jurisdiction of a lawsuit by sequestering any property of the defendant that happens to be located in Delaware. Appellants contend that the sequestration statute as applied in this case violates the Due Process Clause of the Fourteenth Amendment both because it permits the state courts to exercise jurisdiction despite the absence of sufficient contacts among the defendants, the litigation, and the State of Delaware....

I

Appellee Heitner, a nonresident of Delaware, is the owner of one share of stock in the Greyhound Corp., a business incorporated under the laws of Delaware with its principal place of business in Phoenix, Ariz. On May 22, 1974, he filed a shareholder's derivative suit in the Court of Chancery for New Castle County, Del., in which he named as defendants . . . 28 present or former officers or directors of [Greyhound]. In essence, Heitner alleged that the individual defendants had violated their duties to Greyhound by causing it and its subsidiary to engage in actions that resulted in the corporations being held liable for substantial damages in a private antitrust suit and a large fine in a criminal contempt action. The activities which led to these penalties took place in Oregon.

Simultaneously with his complaint, Heitner filed a motion for an order of sequestration of the Delaware property of the individual defendants pursuant to Del. Code Ann., Tit. 10, s. 366 (1975). This motion was accompanied by a supporting affidavit of counsel which stated that the individual defendants were nonresidents of Delaware. The affidavit identified the property to be sequestered as "common stock, 3% Second Cumulative Preferenced Stock and stock unit credits of the Defendant Greyhound Corporation, a Delaware corporation...."

The requested sequestration order was signed the day the motion was filed. Pursuant to that order, the sequestrator "seized" approximately 82,000 shares of Greyhound common stock [and options] belonging to [21 defendants].... The stock was considered to be in Delaware, and so subject to seizure, by virtue of Del. Code Ann., Tit. 8, s. 169 (1975), which makes Delaware the situs of ownership of all stock in Delaware corporations.

All 28 defendants were notified of the initiation of the suit by certified mail directed to their last known addresses and by publication in a New Castle County newspaper. The 21 defendants whose property was seized (hereafter referred to as appellants) responded by entering a special appearance for the purpose of moving to quash service of process and to vacate the sequestration order.... In addition, appellants asserted that under the rule of *International Shoe Co. v. Washington*, 326 U.S. 310 (1945), they did not have sufficient contacts with Delaware to sustain the jurisdiction of that State's courts.

The Court of Chancery rejected [appellant's] arguments . . . [and] held that the statutory Delaware situs of the stock provided a sufficient basis for the exercise of *quasi in rem* jurisdiction by a Delaware court. On appeal, the Delaware Supreme Court affirmed. . . .

II

The Delaware courts rejected appellants' jurisdictional challenge by noting that this suit was brought as a *quasi-in-rem* proceeding. Since *quasi-in-rem* jurisdiction is traditionally based on attachment or seizure of property present in the jurisdiction, not on contacts between the defendant and the State, the courts [below] considered appellants' claimed lack of contacts with Delaware to be unimportant. This categorical analysis assumes the continued soundness of the conceptual structure founded on the century-old case of *Pennoyer v. Neff*, 95 U.S. 714 (1878). . . .

As we have noted, under *Pennoyer*, state authority to adjudicate was based on the jurisdiction's power over either persons or property. This fundamental concept is embodied in the very vocabulary which we use to describe judgments. If a court's jurisdiction is based on its authority over the defendant's person, the action and judgment are denominated *in personam* and can impose a personal obligation on the defendant in favor of the plaintiff. If jurisdiction is based on the court's power over property within its territory, the action is called *in rem* or *quasi-in-rem*. . . .

By concluding that "[t]he authority of every tribunal is necessarily restricted by the territorial limits of the State in which it is established," 95 U.S. at 720, *Pennoyer* sharply limited the availability of *in personam* jurisdiction over defendants not resident in the forum State. If a nonresident defendant could not be found in a State, he could not be sued there. On the other hand, since the State in which property was located was considered to have exclusive sovereignty over that property, *in rem* actions could proceed regardless of the owner's location. . . .

The *Pennoyer* rules generally favored nonresident defendants by making them harder to sue. This advantage was reduced, however, by the ability of a resident plaintiff to satisfy a claim against a nonresident defendant by bringing into court any property of the defendant located in the plaintiff's State. . . .

[Over time, the rigidity of *Pennoyer* came under strain] and absorbed much judicial energy. While the essentially quantitative tests which emerged from . . . cases [attempting to bend the rigidity of *Pennoyer*] purported simply to identify circumstances under which presence or consent could be attributed to [a defendant], it became clear that they were in fact attempting to ascertain "what dealings make it just to subject a foreign [defendant] to local suit." *Hutchinson v. Chase & Gilbert*, 45 F.2d 139, 141 (2d Cir. 1930) (L. Hand, J.). In *International Shoe*, we acknowledged that fact.

The question in *International Shoe* was whether the corporation was subject to the judicial and taxing jurisdiction of Washington. Mr. Chief Justice Stone's opinion for the Court began its analysis of that question by noting that the historical basis of *in personam* jurisdiction was a court's power over the defendant's person. That [territorial] power, however, was no longer the central concern:

> But now . . . due process requires only that in order to subject a defendant to a judgment *in personam*, if he be not present within the territory of the forum, he have certain minimum contacts with it such that the maintenance of the suit does not offend traditional notions of fair play and substantial justice. 326 U.S. at 316.

. . . Mechanical or quantitative evaluations of the defendant's activities in the forum could not resolve the question of reasonableness:

> Whether due process is satisfied must depend rather upon the quality and nature of the activity in relation to the fair and orderly administration of the laws which it was the purpose of the due process clause to insure. That clause does not contemplate that a state may make binding a judgment *in personam* against an individual or corporate defendant with which the state has no contacts, ties, or relations. *Id.* at 319.

. . . The immediate effect of this departure from *Pennoyer*'s conceptual apparatus was to increase the ability of the state courts to obtain personal jurisdiction over nonresident defendants.

No equally dramatic change has occurred in the law governing jurisdiction *in rem*. There have, however, been intimations that the collapse of the *in personam* wing of *Pennoyer* has not left that decision unweakened as a foundation for *in rem* jurisdiction. . . .

Although this Court has not addressed [the status of *in rem* jurisdiction] directly, we have held that property cannot be subjected to a court's judgment unless reasonable and appropriate efforts have been made to give the property owners actual notice of the action. *See, e.g., Mullane v. Central Hanover Bank & Trust Co.,* 339 U.S. 306 (1950). This conclusion recognizes, contrary to *Pennoyer,* that an adverse judgment *in rem* directly affects the property owner by divesting him of his rights in the property before the court. . . . [Indeed,] the law of state-court jurisdiction no longer stands securely on the foundation established in *Pennoyer.* We think that the time is ripe to consider whether the standard of fairness and substantial justice set forth in *International Shoe* should be held to govern actions *in rem* as well as *in personam.*

III

The case for applying to jurisdiction *in rem* the same test of "fair play and substantial justice" as governs assertions of jurisdiction *in personam* is simple and straightforward. It is premised on recognition that "(t)he phrase, *judicial jurisdiction over a thing,* is a customary elliptical way of referring to jurisdiction over the interests of persons in a thing." Rest. (2d) of Conflict of Laws §56 (1971). This recognition leads to the conclusion that in order to justify an exercise of jurisdiction *in rem,* the basis for jurisdiction must be sufficient to justify exercising "jurisdiction over the interests of persons in a thing." *Id.* The standard for determining whether an exercise of jurisdiction over the interests of persons is consistent with the Due Process Clause is the minimum-contacts standard elucidated in *International Shoe.*

This argument, of course, does not ignore the fact that the presence of property in a State may bear on the existence of jurisdiction by providing contacts among the forum State, the defendant, and the litigation. For example, when claims to the property itself are the source of the underlying controversy between the plaintiff and the defendant, it would be unusual for the State where the property is located not to have jurisdiction. In such cases, the defendant's claim to property located in the State would normally indicate that he expected to benefit from the State's protection of his interest. The State's strong interests in assuring the marketability of property within its borders and in providing a procedure for peaceful resolution of disputes about the possession of that property would also support jurisdiction, as would the likelihood that important records and witnesses will be found in the State. The presence of property may also favor jurisdiction in cases such as suits for injury suffered on the land of an absentee owner, where the defendant's ownership of the property is conceded but the cause of action is otherwise related to rights and duties growing out of that ownership.

It appears, therefore, that jurisdiction over many types of actions which now are or might be brought *in rem* would not be affected by a holding that any assertion of state-court jurisdiction must satisfy the *International Shoe* standard. For the type of *quasi-in-rem* action typified . . . by the present case, however, accepting the proposed analysis would result in significant change. [This is a case] where the property which now serves as the basis for state-court jurisdiction is completely unrelated to the plaintiff's cause of action. Thus, although the presence of the defendant's property in a State might suggest the existence of other ties among the defendant, the State, and the litigation, the presence of the property alone would not support the State's jurisdiction. . . .

[I]n cases such as this one, the only role played by the property is to provide the basis for bringing the defendant into court. Indeed, the express purpose of the Delaware sequestration procedure is to compel the defendant to enter a personal appearance. In such cases, if a direct assertion of personal jurisdiction over the defendant would violate the Constitution, it would seem that an indirect assertion of that jurisdiction should be equally impermissible.

The primary rationale for treating the presence of property as a sufficient basis for jurisdiction to adjudicate claims over which the State would not have jurisdiction

if *International Shoe* applied is that a wrongdoer "should not be able to avoid payment of his obligations by the expedient of removing his assets to a place where he is not subject to an *in personam* suit."

This justification, however, does not explain why jurisdiction should be recognized without regard to whether the property is present in the State because of an effort to avoid the owner's obligations. Nor does it support jurisdiction to adjudicate the underlying claim. At most, it suggests that a State in which property is located should have jurisdiction to attach that property, by use of proper procedures, as security for a judgment being sought in a forum where the litigation can be maintained consistently with *International Shoe*. Moreover, we know of nothing to justify the assumption that a debtor can avoid paying his obligations by removing his property to a State in which his creditor cannot obtain personal jurisdiction over him. The Full Faith and Credit Clause, after all, makes the valid *in personam* judgment of one State enforceable in all other States.

It might also be suggested that allowing *in rem* jurisdiction avoids the uncertainty inherent in the *International Shoe* standard and assures a plaintiff of a forum. We believe, however, that the fairness standard of *International Shoe* can be easily applied in the vast majority of cases. Moreover, when the existence of jurisdiction in a particular forum under International Shoe is unclear, the cost of simplifying the litigation by avoiding the jurisdictional question may be the sacrifice of "fair play and substantial justice." That cost is too high.

[Nonetheless] . . . we have never held that the presence of property in a State does not automatically confer jurisdiction over the owner's interest in that property. This history must be considered . . . but it is not decisive. "(T)raditional notions of fair play and substantial justice" can be as readily offended by the perpetuation of ancient forms that are no longer justified as by the adoption of new procedures that are inconsistent with the basic values of our constitutional heritage. The fiction that an assertion of jurisdiction over property is anything but an assertion of jurisdiction over the owner of the property supports an ancient form without substantial modern justification. Its continued acceptance would serve only to allow state-court jurisdiction that is fundamentally unfair to the defendant.

We therefore conclude that all assertions of state-court jurisdiction must be evaluated according to the standards set forth in *International Shoe* and its progeny.

IV

The Delaware courts based their assertion of jurisdiction in this case solely on the statutory presence of appellants' property in Delaware. Yet that property is not the subject matter of this litigation, nor is the underlying cause of action related to the property. Appellants' holdings in Greyhound do not, therefore, provide contacts with Delaware sufficient to support the jurisdiction of that State's courts over appellants. If it exists, that jurisdiction must have some other foundation.

Appellee Heitner did not [point to any other contacts between defendants and Delaware]. . . . Nevertheless, he contends that appellants' positions as directors and officers of a corporation chartered in Delaware provide sufficient "contacts, ties, or relations," *Int'l Shoe*, 326 U.S. at 319, with that State to give its courts jurisdiction over appellants in this stockholder's derivative action. This argument is based primarily on what Heitner asserts to be the strong interest of Delaware in supervising the management of a Delaware corporation. . . .

[E]ven if Heitner's assessment of the importance of Delaware's interest is accepted, his argument fails to demonstrate that Delaware is a fair forum for this litigation. . . . Appellee suggests that by accepting positions as officers or directors of a Delaware corporation, appellants performed the acts required by *Hanson v. Denckla*[,] not[ing] that Delaware law provides substantial benefits to corporate officers and directors. But . . . this line of reasoning establishes only that it is appropriate for Delaware law to govern the obligations of appellants to Greyhound and its stockholders. It does not demonstrate that appellants have "purposefully avail[ed themselves] of the privilege of conducting activities within the forum state, *Hanson, supra* at 253, in a way that would justify bring them before a Delaware tribunal. Appellants [who were not even required to acquire interest in Greyhound in order to hold their positions] simply had nothing to do with Delaware.

. . . The judgment of the Delaware Supreme Court must, therefore, be reversed.

BRENNAN, J., concurring in part and dissenting in part.

I join Parts I-III of the Court's opinion. I fully agree that the minimum-contacts analysis developed in *International Shoe Co. v. Washington*, 326 U.S. 310 (1945), represents a far more sensible construct for the exercise of state-court jurisdiction than the patchwork of legal and factual fictions that has been generated from the decision in *Pennoyer v. Neff*, 95 U.S. 714 (1878). It is precisely because the inquiry into minimum contacts is now of such overriding importance, however, that I must respectfully dissent from Part IV of the Court's opinion.

[Section I, in which Justice Brennan asserts that the majority opinion is merely advisory because arguments regarding minimum contacts were not raised, and therefore the factual record vis-à-vis minimum contacts was not developed, is omitted.]

II

Nonetheless, because the Court rules on the minimum-contacts question, I feel impelled to express my view. While evidence derived through discovery might satisfy me that minimum contacts are lacking in a given case, I am convinced that as a general rule a state forum has jurisdiction to adjudicate a shareholder derivative action centering on the conduct and policies of the directors and officers of a corporation chartered by that State. Unlike the Court, I therefore would not foreclose Delaware from asserting jurisdiction over appellants were it persuaded to do so on the basis of minimum contacts.

It is well settled that a derivative lawsuit as presented here does not inure primarily to the benefit of the named plaintiff. Rather, the primary beneficiaries are the corporation and its owners, the shareholders. "The cause of action is not his own but the corporation's." . . . *Koster v. Lumbermens Mut. Cas. Co.*, 330 U.S. 518, 522 (1947).

Viewed in this light, the chartering State has an unusually powerful interest in insuring the availability of a convenient forum for litigating claims involving a possible multiplicity of defendant fiduciaries and for vindicating the State's substantive policies regarding the management of its domestic corporations. I believe that our cases fairly establish that the States' valid substantive interests are important considerations in assessing whether it constitutionally may claim jurisdiction over a given cause of action.

In this instance, Delaware can point to at least three interrelated public policies that are furthered by its assertion of jurisdiction.

First, the State has a substantial interest in providing restitution for its local corporations that allegedly have been victimized by fiduciary misconduct, even if the managerial decisions occurred outside the State. . . . Second, state courts have legitimately read their jurisdiction expansively when a cause of action centers in an area in which the forum State possesses a manifest regulatory interest. *E.g.*, *McGee*, 355 U.S. at 220 (insurance regulation); *Travelers Health Ass'n v. Virginia*, 339 U.S. 643 (1950) (blue sky laws). . . . Finally, a State like Delaware has a recognized interest in affording a convenient forum for supervising and overseeing the affairs of an entity that is purely the creation of that State's law. . . .

I, of course, am not suggesting that Delaware's varied interests would justify its acceptance of jurisdiction over any transaction touching upon the affairs of its domestic corporations. But a derivative action which raises allegations of abuses of the basic management of an institution whose existence is created by the State and whose powers and duties are defined by state law fundamentally implicates the public policies of that forum. . . .

I, therefore, would approach the minimum-contacts analysis differently than does the Court. Crucial to me is the fact that appellants voluntarily associated themselves with the State of Delaware, "invoking the benefits and protections of its laws," *Hanson*, 357 U.S. at 253, by entering into a long-term and fragile relationship with one of its domestic corporations. . . . [W]e are concerned solely with "minimum" contacts, not the "best" contacts. I thus do not believe that it is unfair to insist that appellants make themselves available to suit in a competent forum that Delaware might create for vindication of its important public policies directly pertaining to appellants' fiduciary association with the State.

Notes & Questions

1. In *Shaffer*, the Court held that there was no personal jurisdiction over the defendants. What was the purported statutory authorization for personal jurisdiction in *Shaffer*? Which basis for personal jurisdiction was lacking—statutory or constitutional?

2. What becomes of the constitutional status of *in rem* jurisdiction after *Shaffer*? *Quasi in rem* jurisdiction?

3. After *Shaffer*, what relevance, if any, does in-state property have to an *in personam* jurisdiction analysis? An *in rem* jurisdiction analysis? Relatedly, after *Shaffer*, what role, if any, may a state sequestration statute play in obtaining personal jurisdiction over an out-of-state defendant with in-state property?

4. Did *Shaffer* expand or constrict the range of cases in which a defendant could be subject to personal jurisdiction?

5. *In rem* cases today can often be recognized by their captions. They purport to be actions against the property itself, whether real property (land) or other things. For instance, the case *United States v. 1,500 Cases More or Less, Tomato Paste*, 236 F.2d 208 (7th Cir. 1956), was an *in rem* action to determine ownership of—you guessed it—about 1,500 cases, give or take, of tomato paste. Just as in *Pennoyer*, the authority of the court over the tomato paste—the *res*—derives from the *res* being located within the territorial boundaries of the forum.

   With an example like that, the territorial basis of a court's authority over a *res* sounds simple to satisfy, but it can sometimes be quite complicated. One complication is whether a court can exercise *in rem* jurisdiction when part of, but not the whole of, the *res* is within the forum state's territory. Indeed, think about how the *Pennoyer* Court would have treated this situation: In *Odyssey Marine Exploration, Inc. v. Unidentified, Wrecked, and Abandoned Sailing Vessel*, 727 F. Supp. 2d 1341 (2012), a plaintiff brought suit in Florida district court claiming ownership of a sunken ship submerged in the English Channel. In order to stake its claim to the property, the plaintiff brought a few small artifacts (including a piece of glass and a ship's bell) from the sunken ship with them to court. Plaintiff, however, did *not* manage to move the entire ship into Florida waters. What result? In the end, plaintiff got ownership over its recovered knick-knacks that were in Florida, but the court found that it lacked the power to decide who had property rights over the ship itself, which remained in the English Channel.

   Another complication with *in rem* jurisdiction: What if you can't precisely pinpoint the location of a *res*? For instance, an Internet domain, as a *res*, is not physically located in a single place. To deal with this problem, Congress enacted the federal Anticybersquatting Consumer Protection Act, 15 U.S.C. §1125(d)(2)(A), which permits plaintiffs to file actions *in rem* against the domain names themselves, as the *res*, in the place where the registrar of the domain name is located. *See, e.g., Porsche Cars N. Am. v. Porsche.net & Porsch.com,* 302 F.3d 248 (4th Cir. 2002) (permitting Porsche to sue a British defendant *in rem* in Virginia regarding the defendant's registration of domain names in Virginia). However, under the statute, plaintiffs may use this *in rem* option *only* if the person who registered the domain name is *not* subject to *in personam* jurisdiction in the United States. This feature of the anticybersquatting statute is in keeping with the modern preference for *in personam* proceedings.

(4) Jurisdiction Based on In-State Service

In the days of *Pennoyer,* the Supreme Court took it as a given that if a defendant was personally served with process within a state, the state courts had jurisdiction over the defendant. Even if the defendant was in the state for only a brief visit, or merely passing through, jurisdiction could be established by handing the defendant a summons and complaint while the defendant was within the state borders. Fast-forward to 1959 and the case of *Grace v. MacArthur,* 170 F. Supp. 442 (E.D. Ark. 1959), decided 14 years after *International Shoe,* and you have the spectacle of a defendant, on a non-stop flight from Memphis to Dallas, being served with process on the airplane while flying over Arkansas in order to establish personal jurisdiction in Arkansas (it worked).

After the Supreme Court decided *Shaffer v. Heitner, supra,* in 1977, many lawyers wondered whether jurisdiction via in-state service of process remained valid. Recall that the Court in *Shaffer* stated that "*all* assertions of state-court jurisdiction must be evaluated according to the standards set forth in *International Shoe* and its progeny." *Id.* at 212 (emphasis added). If the *International Shoe* standard means minimum contacts, then how can that test be satisfied if the defendant's only contact with the state is that he happened to step over the state line and someone handed him a summons? With that in mind, consider the next case.

BURNHAM v. SUPERIOR COURT OF CALIFORNIA
495 U.S. 604 (1990)

Justice SCALIA announced the judgment of the Court and delivered an opinion in which Chief Justice REHNQUIST and Justice KENNEDY join, and in which Justice WHITE joins with respect to Parts I, II-A, II-B, and II-C.

The question presented is whether the Due Process Clause of the Fourteenth Amendment denies California courts jurisdiction over a nonresident, who was personally served with process while temporarily in that State, in a suit unrelated to his activities in the State.

I

Petitioner Dennis Burnham married Francie Burnham in 1976 in West Virginia. In 1977 the couple moved to New Jersey, where their two children were born. In July 1987 the Burnhams decided to separate.

They agreed that Mrs. Burnham, who intended to move to California, would take custody of the children. . . . Mrs. Burnham . . . brought suit for divorce in California state court in early January 1988.

In late January, petitioner visited southern California on business, after which he went north to visit his children in the San Francisco Bay area, where his wife resided. He took the older child to San Francisco for the weekend. Upon returning the child to Mrs. Burnham's home on January 24, 1988, petitioner was served with a California court summons and a copy of Mrs. Burnham's divorce petition. He then returned to New Jersey.

Later that year, petitioner made a special appearance in the California Superior Court, moving to quash the service of process on the ground that the court lacked personal jurisdiction over him because his only contacts with California were a few short visits to the State for the purposes of conducting business and visiting his children. The Superior Court denied the motion, and the California Court of Appeal denied mandamus relief, rejecting petitioner's contention that the Due Process Clause prohibited California courts from asserting jurisdiction over him because he lacked "minimum contacts" with the State. The court held it to be "a valid jurisdictional predicate for *in personam* jurisdiction" that the "defendant [was] present in the forum state and personally served with process." We granted certiorari.

II
A

. . . To determine whether the assertion of personal jurisdiction is consistent with due process, we have long relied on the principles traditionally followed by American courts in marking out the territorial limits of each State's authority. That criterion [of territoriality] was first announced in *Pennoyer v. Neff* . . . [and] in what has become the classic expression of the criterion, we said in *International Shoe Co. v. Washington*, 326 U.S. 310 (1945), that a state court's assertion of personal jurisdiction satisfies the Due Process Clause if it does not violate "traditional notions of fair play and substantial justice." Since *International Shoe*, we have only been called upon to decide whether these "traditional notions" permit States to exercise jurisdiction over absent defendants in a manner that deviates from the rules of jurisdiction applied in the 19th century. We have held such deviations permissible, but only with respect to suits arising out of the absent defendant's contacts with the State. The question we must decide today is whether due process requires a similar connection between the litigation and the defendant's contacts with the State in cases where the defendant is physically present in the State at the time process is served upon him.

B

Among the most firmly established principles of personal jurisdiction in American tradition is that the courts of a State have jurisdiction over nonresidents who are physically present in the State. The view developed early that each State had the power to hale before its courts any individual who could be found within its borders, and that once having acquired jurisdiction over such a person by properly serving him with process, the State could retain jurisdiction to enter judgment against him, no matter how fleeting his visit. That view had antecedents in English common-law practice [and traces back as far as ancient Rome]. . . .

Decisions of the courts of many States in the 19th and early 20th centuries held that personal service upon a physically present defendant sufficed to confer jurisdiction without regard to whether the defendant was only briefly in the State or whether the cause of action was related to his activities there.... Most States, moreover, had statutes or common-law rules that exempted from service of process individuals who were brought into the forum by force or fraud, or who were there as a party or witness in unrelated judicial proceedings. These exceptions obviously rested upon the premise that service of process conferred jurisdiction....

This American jurisdictional practice is, moreover, not merely old; it is continuing. It remains the practice of, not only a substantial number of the States, but as far as we are aware all the States and the Federal Government—if one disregards (as one must for this purpose) the few opinions since 1978 that have erroneously said, on grounds similar to those that petitioner presses here, that this Court's due process decisions render the practice unconstitutional. We do not know of a single state or federal statute, or a single judicial decision resting upon state law, that has abandoned in-state service as a basis of jurisdiction. Many recent cases reaffirm it.

C

Despite this formidable body of precedent, petitioner contends, in reliance on our decisions applying the *International Shoe* standard, that in the absence of "continuous and systematic" contacts with the forum, a nonresident defendant can be subjected to judgment only as to matters that arise out of or relate to his contacts with the forum. This argument rests on a thorough misunderstanding of our cases.

The view of most courts in the 19th century was that a court simply could not exercise *in personam* jurisdiction over a nonresident who had not been personally served with process in the forum. *See Pennoyer*, 95 U.S. at 733....

Later years, however, saw the weakening of the *Pennoyer* rule. In the late 19th and early 20th centuries, changes in the technology of transportation and communication, and the tremendous growth of interstate business activity, led to an "inevitable relaxation of the strict limits on state jurisdiction" over nonresident individuals and corporations. *See, e.g., Hanson v. Denckla*, 357 U.S. 235, 260 (1958) (Black, J., dissenting).... Our opinion in *International Shoe* ... [finally] made explicit the underlying basis of the post-*Pennoyer* decisions: Due process does not necessarily *require* the States to adhere to the unbending territorial limits on jurisdiction set forth in *Pennoyer*. The validity of assertion of jurisdiction over a nonconsenting defendant who is not present in the forum depends upon whether "the quality and nature of [his] activity" in relation to the forum, 326 U.S. at 319, renders such jurisdiction consistent with "traditional notions of fair play and substantial justice." *Id.* at 316. Subsequent cases have derived from the *International Shoe* standard the general rule that a State may dispense with in-forum personal service on nonresident defendants in suits arising out of their activities in the State. As *International Shoe* suggests, the defendant's litigation-related "minimum contacts" may take the place of physical presence as the basis for jurisdiction....

Nothing in *International Shoe* or the cases that have followed it, however, offers support for the very different proposition petitioner seeks to establish today: that a defendant's presence in the forum is not only unnecessary to validate novel, nontraditional assertions of jurisdiction, but is itself no longer sufficient to establish jurisdiction. That proposition is unfaithful to both elementary logic and the foundations of our due process jurisprudence. . . .

The short of the matter is that jurisdiction based on physical presence alone constitutes due process because it is one of the continuing traditions of our legal system that define the due process standard of "traditional notions of fair play and substantial justice." That standard was developed by *analogy* to "physical presence," and it would be perverse to say it could now be turned against that touchstone of jurisdiction.

D

Petitioner's strongest argument, though we ultimately reject it, relies upon our decision in *Shaffer*, 433 U.S. at 186. [There], we concluded that the normal rules we had developed under *International Shoe* for jurisdiction over suits against absent defendants should apply—viz., Delaware could not hear the suit because the defendants' sole contact with the State (ownership of property there) was unrelated to the lawsuit. 433 U.S. at 213-15.

[However, it] goes too far to say, as petitioner contends, that *Shaffer* compels the conclusion that a State lacks jurisdiction over an individual unless the litigation arises out of his activities in the State. *Shaffer*, like *International Shoe*, involved jurisdiction over an *absent defendant*, and it stands for nothing more than the proposition that when the "minimum contact" that is a substitute for physical presence consists of property ownership it must, like other minimum contacts, be related to the litigation. Petitioner wrenches out of its context our statement in *Shaffer* that "all assertions of state-court jurisdiction must be evaluated according to the standards set forth in *International Shoe* and its progeny," 433 U.S. at 212. . . . When read together with the two sentences that preceded it, the meaning of this statement becomes clear:

> The fiction that an assertion of jurisdiction over property is anything but an assertion of jurisdiction over the owner of the property supports an ancient form without substantial modification. Its continued acceptance would serve only to allow state-court jurisdiction that is fundamentally unfair to the defendant. *Ibid.*

Shaffer was saying, in other words, not that all bases for the assertion of *in personam* jurisdiction (including, presumably, in-state service) must be treated alike and subjected to the "minimum contacts" analysis of *International Shoe*; but rather that *quasi-in-rem* jurisdiction . . . and *in personam* jurisdiction are really one and the same and must be treated alike—leading to the conclusion that *quasi-in-rem* jurisdiction, *i.e.*, that form of *in personam* jurisdiction based upon a "property ownership" contact and by definition unaccompanied by personal, in-state service, must satisfy the litigation-relatedness requirement of *International Shoe*. The logic of *Shaffer*'s holding—which places all suits against absent nonresidents on the same constitutional footing, regardless of whether a separate Latin label is attached to one particular basis of contact—does not compel the conclusion that physically present defendants must be treated identically to absent ones. As we have demonstrated at length, our tradition has treated the two classes of defendants quite differently, and it is unreasonable to read *Shaffer* as casually obliterating that distinction. . . .

It is fair to say, however, that while our holding today does not contradict *Shaffer*, our basic approach to the due process question is different. We have conducted no independent inquiry into the desirability or fairness of the prevailing in-state service rule, leaving that judgment to the legislatures that are free to amend it; for our purposes, its validation is its pedigree, as the phrase "*traditional notions* of fair play and substantial justice" makes clear. *Shaffer* did conduct such an independent inquiry, asserting that " 'traditional notions of fair play and substantial justice' can be as readily offended by the perpetuation of ancient forms that are no longer justified as by the adoption of new procedures that are inconsistent with the basic values of our constitutional heritage." 433 U.S. at 212. Perhaps that assertion can be sustained when the perpetuation of ancient forms is engaged in by only a very small minority of the States. Where, however, as in the present case, a jurisdictional principle is both firmly approved by tradition and still favored, it is impossible to imagine what standard we could appeal to for the judgment that it is no longer justified. While in no way receding from or casting doubt upon the holding of *Shaffer* or any other case, we reaffirm today our time-honored approach. For new procedures, hitherto unknown, the Due Process Clause requires analysis to determine whether "traditional notions of fair play and substantial justice" have been offended. *Int'l Shoe*, 326 U.S. at 316. But a doctrine of personal jurisdiction that dates back to the adoption of the Fourteenth Amendment and is still generally observed unquestionably meets that standard.

III

A few words in response to Justice Brennan's opinion concurring in the judgment: It insists that we apply "contemporary notions of due process" to determine the constitutionality of California's assertion of jurisdiction. But . . . [the] "contemporary notions of due process" applicable to personal jurisdiction are the enduring "*traditional* notions of fair play and substantial justice" established as the test by *International Shoe*. By its very language, that test is satisfied if a state court adheres to jurisdictional rules that are generally applied and have always been applied in the United States.

But the concurrence's proposed standard of "contemporary notions of due process" requires more: It measures state-court jurisdiction not only against traditional doctrines in this country, including current state-court practice, but also against each Justice's subjective assessment of what is fair and just. [Yet] [a]uthority for that seductive standard is . . . an outright break with the test of "traditional notions of fair play and substantial justice," which would have to be reformulated "*our* notions of fair play and substantial justice."

The subjectivity, and hence inadequacy, of this approach becomes apparent when the concurrence tries to explain *why* the assertion of jurisdiction in the present case meets its standard of continuing-American-tradition-*plus*-innate-fairness. Justice Brennan lists the "benefits" Mr. Burnham derived from the State of California—the fact that, during the few days he was there, "[h]is health and safety [were] guaranteed by the State's police, fire, and emergency medical services; he [was] free to travel on the State's roads and waterways; he likely enjoy[ed] the fruits of the State's economy." Three days' worth of these benefits strike us as powerfully inadequate to establish, as an abstract matter, that it is "fair" for California to decree the ownership of all Mr. Burnham's worldly goods acquired during the 10 years of his marriage, and the custody over his children. . . .

Even less persuasive are the other "fairness" factors alluded to by Justice Brennan. It would create "an asymmetry," we are told, if Burnham were *permitted* (as he is) to appear in California courts as a plaintiff, but were not *compelled* to appear in California courts as defendant; and travel being as easy as it is nowadays, and modern procedural devices being so convenient, it is no great hardship to appear in California courts. The problem with these assertions is that they justify the exercise of jurisdiction over *everyone, whether or not* he ever comes to California. The only "fairness" elements setting Mr. Burnham apart from the rest of the world are the three days' "benefits" referred to above—and even those do not set him apart from many other people who have enjoyed three days in the Golden State but who were fortunate enough not to be served with process while they were there. . . . In other words, even if one agreed with Justice Brennan's conception of an equitable bargain, the "benefits" we have been discussing would explain why it is "fair" to assert general jurisdiction over Burnham-returned-to-New-Jersey-after-service only at the expense of proving that it is also "fair" to assert general jurisdiction over Burnham-returned-to-New-Jersey-*without*-service—which we *know* does not conform with "contemporary notions of due process."

There is, we must acknowledge, one factor mentioned by Justice Brennan that *both* relates distinctively to the assertion of jurisdiction on the basis of personal in-state service *and* is fully persuasive—namely, the fact that a defendant voluntarily present in a particular State has a "reasonable expectatio[n]" that he is subject to suit there. By formulating it as a "reasonable expectation" Justice Brennan makes that seem like a "fairness" factor; but in reality, of course, it is just tradition masquerading

as "fairness." The only reason for charging Mr. Burnham with the reasonable expectation of being subject to suit is that the States of the Union assert adjudicatory jurisdiction over the person, and have always asserted adjudicatory jurisdiction over the person, by serving him with process during his temporary physical presence in their territory. That continuing tradition, which anyone entering California should have known about, renders it "fair" for Mr. Burnham, who voluntarily entered California, to be sued there for divorce—at least "fair" in the limited sense that he has no one but himself to blame. Justice Brennan's long journey is a circular one, leaving him, at the end of the day, in complete reliance upon the very factor he sought to avoid: The existence of a continuing tradition is not enough, fairness also must be considered; fairness exists here because there is a continuing tradition. . . .

The difference between us and Justice Brennan has nothing to do with whether [the legal system will progress]. It has to do with whether changes are to be adopted as progressive by the American people or decreed as progressive by the Justices of this Court. Nothing we say today prevents individual States from limiting or entirely abandoning the in-state-service basis of jurisdiction. And nothing prevents an overwhelming majority of them from doing so, with the consequence that the "traditional notions of fairness" that this Court applies may change. But the States have overwhelmingly declined to adopt such limitation or abandonment, evidently not considering it to be progress. The question is whether, armed with no authority other than individual Justices' perceptions of fairness that conflict with both past and current practice, this Court can compel the States to make such a change on the ground that "due process" requires it. We hold that it cannot.

Because the Due Process Clause does not prohibit the California courts from exercising jurisdiction over petitioner based on the fact of in-state service of process, the judgment is

Affirmed.

[The opinion of Justice White, concurring in part and concurring in the judgment, is omitted.]

Justice BRENNAN, with whom Justice MARSHALL, Justice BLACKMUN, and Justice O'CONNOR join, concurring in the judgment.

I agree with Justice Scalia that the Due Process Clause of the Fourteenth Amendment generally permits a state court to exercise jurisdiction over a defendant if he is served with process while voluntarily present in the forum State.[1] [I do not agree, however, that a jurisdictional rule] automatically comports with due process simply by virtue of its "pedigree." Although I agree that history is an important factor in establishing whether a jurisdictional rule satisfies due process requirements, . . . I would [also] undertake an "independent inquiry into the . . . fairness of the prevailing in-state service rule." I therefore concur only in the judgment.

I

I believe that the approach adopted by Justice Scalia's opinion today—reliance solely on historical pedigree—is foreclosed by our decisions in *International Shoe Co.*

v. Washington, 326 U.S. 310 (1945), and *Shaffer v. Heitner,* 433 U.S. 186 (1977). In *International Shoe,* we held that a state court's assertion of personal jurisdiction does not violate the Due Process Clause if it is consistent with "traditional notions of fair play and substantial justice."[2] In *Shaffer,* we stated that "*all* assertions of state-court jurisdiction must be evaluated according to the standards set forth in *International Shoe* and its progeny." 433 U.S. at 212 (emphasis added). The critical insight of *Shaffer* is that all rules of jurisdiction, even ancient ones, must satisfy contemporary notions of due process. Indeed, that we were willing in *Shaffer* to examine anew the appropriateness of the *quasi-in-rem* rule—until that time dutifully accepted by American courts for at least a century—demonstrates that we did not believe that the "pedigree" of a jurisdictional practice was dispositive in deciding whether it was consistent with due process. . . . Lower courts, commentators, and the American Law Institute all have interpreted *International Shoe* and *Shaffer* to mean that *every* assertion of state-court jurisdiction . . . must comport with contemporary notions of due process. Notwithstanding the nimble gymnastics of Justice Scalia's opinion today, it is not faithful to our decision in *Shaffer.*

II

Tradition, though alone not dispositive, is of course *relevant* to the question whether the rule of transient jurisdiction is

---

[1] I use the term "transient jurisdiction" to refer to jurisdiction premised solely on the fact that a person is served with process while physically present in the forum State.

[2] Our reference in *International Shoe* to "traditional notions of fair play and substantial justice," 326 U.S. at 316, meant simply that those concepts are indeed traditional ones, not that, as Justice Scalia's opinion suggests, their specific *content* was to be determined by tradition alone. We recognized that contemporary societal norms must play a role in our analysis.

consistent with due process. Tradition is salient not in the sense that practices of the past are automatically reasonable today; indeed, under such a standard, the legitimacy of transient jurisdiction would be called into question because the rule's historical "pedigree" is a matter of intense debate.... Rather, I find the historical background relevant because, however murky the jurisprudential origins of transient jurisdiction, the fact that American courts have announced the rule for perhaps a century provides a defendant voluntarily present in a particular State *today* "clear notice that [he] is subject to suit" in the forum. *World-Wide Volkswagen Corp. v. Woodson*, 444 U.S. at 297. Regardless of whether [the lengthy historical] account of the rule's genesis is mythical, our common understanding *now*, fortified by a century of judicial practice, is that jurisdiction is often a function of geography. The transient rule is consistent with reasonable expectations and is entitled to a strong presumption that it comports with due process. "If I visit another State... I knowingly assume some risk that the State will exercise its power over my property or my person while there. My contact with the State, though minimal, gives rise to predictable risks." *Shaffer*, 433 U.S. at 218 (Stevens, J., concurring in judgment).

[Further, by] visiting the forum State, a transient defendant actually "avail[s]" himself, *Burger King*, 471 U.S. at 476, of significant benefits provided by the State. His health and safety are guaranteed by the State's police, fire, and emergency medical services; he is free to travel on the State's roads and waterways; he likely enjoys the fruits of the State's economy as well....

[Moreover, the] potential burdens on a transient defendant are slight. "[M]odern transportation and communications have made it much less burdensome for a party

sued to defend himself" in a State outside his place of residence. *McGee v. International Life Ins. Co.*, 355 U.S. 220, 223 (1957). That the defendant has already journeyed at least once before to the forum—as evidenced by the fact that he was served with process there—is an indication that suit in the forum likely would not be prohibitively inconvenient. Finally, any burdens that do arise can be ameliorated by a variety of procedural devices.[13] For these reasons, as a rule the exercise of personal jurisdiction over a defendant based on his voluntary presence in the forum will satisfy the requirements of due process.

In this case, it is undisputed that petitioner was served with process while voluntarily and knowingly in the State of California. I therefore concur in the judgment.

Justice STEVENS, concurring in the judgment.

... For me, it is sufficient to note that the historical evidence and consensus identified by Justice Scalia, the considerations of fairness identified by Justice Brennan, and the common sense displayed by Justice White, all combine to demonstrate that this is, indeed, a very easy case. Accordingly, I agree that the judgment should be affirmed.

---

[13] For example, in the federal system, a transient defendant can avoid protracted litigation of a spurious suit through a motion to dismiss for failure to state a claim or through a motion for summary judgment. Fed. Rules Civ. Proc. 12(b)(6) and 56. He can use relatively inexpensive methods of discovery, such as oral deposition by telephone (Rule 30(b)(7)), deposition upon written questions (Rule 31), interrogatories (Rule 33), and requests for admission (Rule 36), while enjoying protection from harassment (Rule 26(c)), and possibly obtaining costs and attorney's fees for some of the work involved (Rules 37(a)(4), (b)-(d)). Moreover, a change of venue may be possible. 28 U.S.C. §1404. In state court, many of the same procedural protections are available, as is the doctrine of *forum non conveniens*, under which the suit may be dismissed.

Notes & Questions

1. In *Burnham*, how many Justices agreed that in-state service sufficed to establish personal jurisdiction over Dennis Burnham in California? If they agree with each other, why do Justices Scalia and Brennan seem to be fighting so hard? Make sure you understand the difference between Justice Scalia's and Justice Brennan's approaches to analyzing the constitutionality of jurisdiction via in-state service. Then, pick any current hot-button issue of constitutional law, try applying Justice Scalia's and Justice Brennan's very different modes of constitutional analysis, and see where they lead.

2. Both Justice Scalia and Justice Brennan invoke the phrase "traditional notions of fair play and substantial justice," which has been a centerpiece of the law of personal jurisdiction since *International Shoe*, quoting *Milliken v. Meyer*, enshrined it alongside the minimum contacts test. Are Justice Scalia and Justice Brennan using the same definition of "traditional notions of fair play and substantial justice"? Which word in that phrase does Justice Scalia emphasize? Justice Brennan? Make sure to consider footnote 2 in Justice Brennan's concurrence in your analysis.

3. Imagine that you are asleep on a plane trip from New York to Los Angeles, and you are unceremoniously awakened and served with process over the airspace of Kansas regarding a dispute with your ex-spouse, who lives in Kansas. What result, under Justice Scalia's approach to jurisdiction via in-state service? If you find that result unduly harsh, what result under Justice Brennan's approach? If you are happier with the result under Justice Brennan's approach in that instance, does that mean you necessarily agree with it more generally? Change the facts slightly to test your views: Imagine your plane had to make an emergency landing in Kansas for maintenance. Your next available opportunity to get to Los Angeles is late the following day. So you eat dinner in Kansas, take a taxi to a hotel where you rent a hotel room, and you take a taxi the next morning to have breakfast with an old college buddy at a diner before returning to the airport. During breakfast, you are served with a summons and complaint to appear in Kansas state court. Would you be subject to personal jurisdiction in Kansas under Justice Brennan's view? If so, is there really a meaningful difference between Justice Scalia's and Justice Brennan's approach? More fundamentally, where does this leave your thought process regarding jurisdiction via in-state service generally? Do the procedural

> **Terminology Tip**
>
> Some lawyers even call this form of obtaining jurisdiction over a defendant *tag jurisdiction*, as in "tag, you're it." Others call it *transient* jurisdiction because the defendant was served while in the forum state on a transient basis. Some simply call it, as here, jurisdiction based on in-state service of process.

options available to a transient defendant served with process outlined in footnote 13 of Justice Brennan's opinion soften your view regarding jurisdiction via in-state service (which would exist regardless of whether you were served in-flight or on the ground in Kansas)?

4. In *Burnham*, Justice Scalia mentioned that states have long protected against in-state service obtained by fraud or force. What does that mean? An example illustrates: In *Tickle v. Barton*, 95 S.E.2d 427 (W. Va. 1956), the plaintiff induced a Virginia defendant to cross state lines into West Virginia by having her attorney call Barton at his home in Virginia and wrongfully represent to Barton that he was invited to a championship banquet for his son's football team in West Virginia. Barton believed the invitation was in good faith and entered his son's school on the banquet's purported date. There were no football players present and no banquet at his son's school. There was, however, a process server waiting for Barton. The server promptly handed Barton a summons and complaint. While Barton did know of the underlying action pending against him, he was not aware that he would be served with process by accepting an invitation to the football banquet. West Virginia's highest court voided the service on the grounds that service of process is invalid if effectuated by fraud, artifice, or trickery. Such cases are rare, but they happen. Relatedly, states also provide defendants with temporary immunity from service of process in one proceeding when appearing in a state as a party or witness to a separate judicial proceeding.

(5) Jurisdiction Based on Consent

A court may exercise personal jurisdiction over any defendant that consents to that court's power over it. Recall from the beginning of the chapter that the limit on personal jurisdiction, under the Due Process Clause, is derived from the liberty interest that belongs to the defendant—the interest not to be subject to the judicial power of an unrelated sovereign. If the defendant does not object to the court's power, then there is no infringement of the defendant's liberty interest.

Most of what you have read in this chapter so far involves situations in which a defendant did *not* wish to consent to the court's personal jurisdiction. Recall that in such situations, a defendant has options: One, the defendant can simply decide not to show up and the court will enter a default judgment, as described in Chapter 4. When the plaintiff tries to enforce that judgment against the defendant, as described in Chapter 8, the defendant can attack the judgment, in a separate ("collateral") proceeding, on the grounds that the first court lacked personal jurisdiction and thus the judgment is a nullity. *Pennoyer* involved this very scenario. Collateral attack worked for Neff, but defaulting is a risky approach. If the enforcing court finds that the first court had jurisdiction, then the defendant will have forfeited his chance to dispute the claim on the merits.

A second, less risky, option, is for the defendant to make a special appearance to contest jurisdiction. As you learned earlier in this chapter, the defendant's special appearance in the state cannot be used to obtain personal jurisdiction through a form of "gotcha," whereby the plaintiff would serve the defendant with process in-state during her special appearance. Under modern federal practice, a defendant need not appear specially and await a court decision on personal jurisdiction. Now, she can object to personal jurisdiction—either in the answer or in a pre-answer motion to dismiss for lack of personal jurisdiction—*and* proceed to litigate without thereby consenting to the court's power. *See, e.g.,* Fed. R. Civ. P. 7(a)(2); 8(b); 12(b)(2).

If none of those options are exercised (and recall, objections to personal jurisdiction are waivable), the defendant has consented to the court's power once the lawsuit starts. This consent occurs when the defendant appears to litigate the case without objecting to the court's personal jurisdiction. This has traditionally been called a *general appearance*.

A party may also consent *in advance* to the personal jurisdiction of a court. For instance, a party can provide consent to personal jurisdiction in advance by contract. For instance, a party might agree to a *consent-to-jurisdiction* clause. In *National Equipment Rental, Ltd. v. Szukhent*, 375 U.S. 311 (1964), for example, defendants were Michigan farmers who leased farm equipment from National Equipment Rental, a New York company. The lease, which was a form contract, stated that the lessees must appoint a particular person as their agent for service of process in New York. When the company sued the Szukhents in New York for lease payments, the company served the summons and complaint to the named agent, who forwarded them to the Szukhents. The Supreme Court upheld personal jurisdiction over the Szukhents in New York on the grounds that by signing a lease that contained a provision appointing a New York agent for service of process in New York (the consent-to-jurisdiction clause), the Szukhents had consented to personal jurisdiction in New York should a dispute arise.

Some contracts go a step further than specifying where litigation *could* be brought and specify where litigation *must* be brought. This is achieved by means of a *forum-selection clause*, also known as a *choice-of-forum clause*. The Supreme Court famously enforced a such a clause in *Carnival Cruise Lines v. Shute*, 499 U.S. 585 (1991). The cruise contract, which was printed on passengers' tickets and not presented to the Shutes until after they had purchased the cruise tickets, stated that any dispute arising out of the cruise must be litigated, if at all, in Florida (where Carnival Cruise Lines is headquartered). When the Shutes filed a slip-and-fall lawsuit against Carnival in a court in the plaintiffs' home state of Washington, Carnival argued that the case must be thrown out of the Washington court because of the forum-selection clause. The Supreme Court agreed. *See also Atlantic Marine Constr. v. U.S. District Court*, 571 U.S. 49, 63 (2013) (reaffirming acceptance of *ex ante* litigation clauses in form contracts by unanimously agreeing to enforce a forum-selection clause in the parties' contract).

Note the difference between the contractual clauses in *Carnival Cruise* and *Atlantic Marine* on the one hand, and in *Szukhent* on the other. In *Carnival Cruise* and *Atlantic Marine*, the forum-selection clauses eliminated forum options that would have otherwise been available. The consent-to-jurisdiction clause in *Szukhent*, by contrast, added a forum option that might not otherwise have been available (New York), as National Equipment Rental assuredly could have sued the Szukhents in Michigan.

STRATEGY SESSION

One lesson from *Szukhent* and *Carnival Cruise*, as well as *Burger King*, is that lawyers and clients need to think about personal jurisdiction *before* litigation ensues. Thus, personal jurisdiction matters to lawyers who may never see the inside of a courtroom. If you are negotiating a contract on behalf of your client, you should consider whether it would serve your client's interests to insert contractual provisions that specify what will happen if a dispute ensues. National Equipment Rental's lawyers included a *consent-to-jurisdiction clause* to ensure that the company could sue its rental clients in New York. Carnival Cruise's lawyers included a *forum-selection clause* to ensure that cruise passengers could only sue in Florida. Burger King's lawyers included a *choice-of-law clause* to ensure that Florida law would govern its franchise agreements. That choice-of-law clause did not dictate the forum, but recall that it was relevant to the minimum contacts analysis. Some contracts may well include *all* of these provisions and more. One reason to include such clauses is to provide your clients with predictability. It is easier to structure and conduct business if the company knows which state's laws govern its conduct, and where it may be subject to litigation. Moreover, it is easier to litigate in a familiar setting.

Note also that the Supreme Court's consent-based personal jurisdiction jurisprudence has followed the basic trend of its contacts-based jurisprudence. In particular, its opinions have had the effect of restricting the number of states in which a plaintiff may sue; the corollary of this is that the Court has restricted the number of states in which a defendant can be sued. More than that, though, the Court has given defendants in contractual relationships the lion's share of control over the forums in which suits may be brought. Defendants have (naturally) taken full advantage of this control in a wide swath of contracts governing potential disputes.

States have recently attempted to respond to the overall trend in personal jurisdiction jurisprudence toward restricting the number of states in which a defendant can be sued (and especially the Court's decision in *Daimler*) by using what are known as *registration statutes* to obtain personal jurisdiction over corporations doing in business in their states. Registration statutes, which exist in all 50 states, require foreign corporations to "register" with the state before they may conduct business there. The personal jurisdiction upshot: Some courts have held recently that "registration" constitutes *consent* by the corporation to all-purpose personal jurisdiction in the state in which it registered. *See, e.g., Webb-Benjamin, LLC v. Int'l Rug Group, LLC*, 192 A.2d 1133 (Pa. Super. (2018). Corporations have objected to these decisions on the grounds that registering to do business in a state does not make them "at home" there, as required by *Daimler*. The Supreme Court has not addressed the question, but lower courts have distinguished *Daimler* on the grounds that registration statutes establish personal jurisdiction on the basis of consent, not contacts. Corporations have also objected to the constitutionality of these decisions on the grounds that registration in the state is not voluntary if they wish to do business there.

(6) Personal Jurisdiction in Federal Court

Personal jurisdiction focuses on state boundaries (or, in international litigation, national boundaries) and territorial limits on state power over parties. But what about federal court "boundaries"? You know from Chapter 2 that a defendant may assert an objection to personal jurisdiction in federal court either in the answer or by making a pre-answer motion to dismiss under Rule 12(b)(2). You also know that defendants often pair the 12(b)(2) motion with a Rule 12(b)(5) motion to dismiss for insufficient service of process (part of the due process requirement of notice for personal jurisdiction, explored in Part C of this chapter). Thus, logically, you know that personal jurisdiction limitations *must* constrain federal courts.

Here's the rub, though. If personal jurisdiction is all about limits on state power, do the *same* restrictions apply in federal court? The answer is simple: Usually, yes. From that point, though, things get more complex.

Start with Rule 4(k)(1)(A), which is actually a federal long-arm statute. It provides that service of process establishes personal jurisdiction over a defendant "who is subject to the jurisdiction of a court of general jurisdiction in the state where the district court is located." In other words, if the state court would have personal jurisdiction over the defendant, then so do the federal courts in that state. Even though 4(k)(1)(A) directs you to state long-arms, however, a proper analysis of whether a federal court has personal jurisdiction over a defendant *begins* with a citation to Rule 4(k)(1)(A); without it, you cannot authorize the federal court to look to a state long-arm. As a practical matter, though, federal-court personal jurisdiction analysis under 4(k)(1)(A) will look very similar to that performed in state court. Specifically, if personal jurisdiction is authorized by an enumerated state long-arm, or if the state long-arm's reach is coterminous with the due process analysis for personal jurisdiction, the statutory component of the analysis is met. At that point, the analysis proceeds to the constitutional due process inquiry. U.S. Const. amend. XIV.

Not too bad so far. Now, for some more complexity. Rule 4(k) contains three other provisions that, in appropriate instances, *extend* the reach of personal jurisdiction in federal courts beyond that of the states. First, Rule 4(k)(1)(B) gives a federal court personal jurisdiction over a defendant "who is a party joined under Rule 14 or 19 and is served within a judicial district of the United States and not more than 100 miles from where the summons was issued." Recall from Chapter 2 that the place from which "the summons [is] issued" is the court in which the case was filed. And recall from Chapter 7 that Rule 14 permits a defendant to assert a third-party claim (that is, a claim that brings into the case a person who may be liable to indemnify the defendant or to pay contribution if the defendant is held liable to the plaintiff), and Rule 19 empowers the court to order that certain persons be joined as required parties where it would be unjust to proceed without them. Thus, 4(k)(1)(B), known as the *hundred-mile bulge* provision, allows a federal court to exercise personal jurisdiction over parties joined by a third-party complaint under Rule 14 or as a required party under Rule 19, *even if those parties are served out of state*, so long as they are properly served within one hundred miles of the federal court. The hundred-mile bulge rule is thus a rather limited extension of the territorial power of a federal court, but it is quite useful, especially in metropolitan areas like New York City or Washington, D.C.—metropolitan areas that tend to cross state lines and include multiple federal juridical districts.

Second, Rule 4(k)(1)(C) provides for nationwide (or even worldwide, if authorized by law) service of process "when authorized by federal statute." In other words, if exterritorial service of process is properly executed upon a defendant per express authorization in a federal statute, the statutory requirement for the exercise of jurisdiction in any federal court in the United States is satisfied. Examples of such explicit authorization include the Federal Interpleader Act, which provides for nationwide personal jurisdiction in federal courts for interpleader (a complex form of joinder explained in Chapter 7), as well as the Clayton Antitrust Act, federal securities statutes, and a few others. An example helps illustrate the operation of 4(k)(1)(C). Assume defendant business X (from California) is accused of violating the Clayton Antitrust Act, which provides for nationwide service of process. 15 U.S.C. §22. Plaintiffs bring suit in New York, with which business X has very few contacts. Rule 4(k)(1)(C) provides statutory authorization for the exercise of jurisdiction in New York. Moreover, even though the federal court in New York court must still perform the constitutional minimum contacts analysis, the relevant minimum contacts under 4(k)(1)(C) lie with the United States as a whole, not the forum state. U.S. Const. amend. V. Strategically, think about what a powerful forum-selection tool this is for plaintiffs bringing claims under statutes that provide for nationwide or worldwide service of process (plaintiffs who can then add state law claims if supplemental jurisdiction permits!).

Finally, Rule 4(k)(2) fills a small, but important, gap in personal jurisdiction. Suppose a plaintiff sues a foreign defendant for "claim[s] that arise under federal law." Rule 4(k)(2). The foreign defendant has substantial contacts with the United States, but those contacts are so dispersed that "the defendant is not subject to jurisdiction in any state's court of general jurisdiction." Rule 4(k)(2)(A). Obviously, Rule 4(k)(1)(A) cannot help the plaintiff; that long-arm's reach is coterminous with the reach of the long-arm of the state in which the federal court sits. Rule 4(k)(1)(C) is of little help, for two slightly less obvious reasons. First, presumably a plaintiff is not looking to 4(k)(2) if she is suing under a statute that authorizes nationwide (or worldwide) service of process. Second, very few defendants properly served with nationwide process will simultaneously lack minimum contacts with *any* particular state. Now can you see the gap? A foreign defendant facing federal law claims has sufficient contacts with the United States as a whole to satisfy due process under a nationwide minimum contacts analysis, but nonetheless lacks "minimum contacts" with any particular state, and is subject to a suit arising under federal law, but not under a federal law that authorizes nationwide or worldwide service. Without 4(k)(2), that defendant cannot be subject to the power of *any* United States court, state or federal.

As a matter of federal court power, that gap is troubling: The federal courts are instruments of the United States government. Should their power not extend to a defendant that meets minimum contacts with the *United States*, at least for *claims arising under federal law*? Rule 4(k)(2) says that it should. The rule ensures that whenever a foreign defendant has sufficient contacts with the United States to meet the minimum contacts test *vis-à-vis the United States as a whole* (Rule 4(k)(2)(B), *some* federal court will be able to assert power over that defendant for purposes of federal clams.

To put all of this together, think back to *Nicastro*, and consider three hypotheticals, wherein Nicastro sues not in New Jersey state court, but in the federal district court in New Jersey:

1. Nicastro files claims under federal law against J. McIntyre. Could Rule 4(k)(1)(A) be used by the federal court to exercise personal jurisdiction over J. McIntyre? What about 4(k)(1)(C)?
2. Nicastro files claims that arise under a federal statute authorizing worldwide service of process. Can 4(k)(1)(C) be used by the federal court to obtain personal jurisdiction over J. McIntyre?
3. Nicastro files claims that arise under federal statute, but not any that authorize worldwide service of process. Can Rule 4(k)(2) be used to obtain personal jurisdiction over J. McIntyre by the federal court in New Jersey?

As you go through these hypotheticals, take the analysis step by step. Proceed methodically through the federal long-arm. In hypothetical 1, Rule 4(k)(1)(A) is clearly unavailing; it instructs the court to look to the state-long arm (in *Nicastro*, the New Jersey long-arm), which would lead right back to Court's conclusion that J. McIntyre's contacts with New Jersey were insufficient. Without a federal statute authorizing worldwide service, 4(k)(1)(C) is equally unavailing. In hypothetical 2, you no doubt noted that worldwide service of process is authorized by federal statute as required by 4(k)(1)(C). Does that mean the exercise of personal jurisdiction over J. McIntyre by the New Jersey federal court is proper? What else must you evaluate? Use the facts in the various opinions in *Nicastro* to perform the constitutional analysis. As to hypothetical 3, the federal law requirement is clearly met, but what about the requirement that the defendant not have minimum contacts with *any* state? Is that requirement satisfied? If not, why not? If so, what else must you evaluate?

One final point: Although the due process analysis for personal jurisdiction is similar between state and federal courts, you might have noticed that the citations in this section to the *source* of the due process protection for defendants in federal court sometimes differs from that in state court. Recall that the Constitution contains *two* Due Process Clauses. The Fifth Amendment (part of the Bill of Rights) prohibits the *federal* government from depriving citizens without due process of law. The Fourteenth Amendment (enacted after the Civil War) prohibits the *states* from depriving citizens without due process of law. *Pennoyer, International Shoe*, and most of the other famous personal jurisdiction cases spoke in terms of the Fourteenth Amendment's Due Process Clause because they involved the constitutional limits of *state* court power. Thus, to the extent federal courts permit personal jurisdiction *within* the confines Rule 4(k)(1)(A), which directs the analysis to that which would be conducted in the state in which the federal court sits, the relevant constitutional constraint comes from the Fourteenth Amendment. However, to the extent that federal courts permit personal jurisdiction beyond that which is allowed under Rule 4(k)(1)(A), the constitutional constraint comes from the Fifth Amendment.

C. NOTICE

Territorial power is one part of personal jurisdiction. The other part—equally important and equally grounded in the Due Process Clause—is *notice*. At the constitutional level, the requirement of notice is meant to ensure that parties have an opportunity to be heard before they are subjected to a court's binding determination of their rights or obligations. At the statutory level, the requirement of notice gets implemented through rather detailed rules on service of process. For a court to have personal jurisdiction over a defendant, the plaintiff must serve the summons and complaint on the defendant in the way required by rule or statute, and the means of notice also must comply with due process. Note the parallel with the two-step personal jurisdiction analysis you have studied so far: A court's assertion of power over a party must satisfy statutory requirements as well as the requirements of constitutional due process.

(1) The Due Process Requirement of Notice

If due process means anything, it means that if a proceeding is going to affect a party's interests, the party should have an opportunity to be heard. Further, that opportunity to be heard cannot manifest unless the party has been notified about the proceeding. In the landmark case of *Mullane v. Central Hanover Bank & Trust Co.*, 339 U.S. 306 (1950), the Supreme Court explained the due process requirement of notice. Notice, the Court emphasized, is no mere technicality. "An elementary and fundamental requirement of due process in any proceedings which is to be accorded finality is notice reasonably calculated, under all the circumstances, to apprise interested parties of the pendency of the action and afford them an opportunity to present their objections." *Id.* at 314. What does it mean for notice to be *reasonably calculated* to apprise parties of the proceedings? The Court in *Mullane* explained the idea in common-sense terms: "The means employed must be such as one desirous of actually informing the absentee might reasonably adopt to accomplish it." *Id.* at 315. This explanation is remarkably helpful. Instead of instructing courts to get mired in procedural technicalities, the *Mullane* formulation instructs them to apply a due process standard that emphasizes, as a practical matter, whether the means of notice are likely to reach the intended recipients and to inform them of what they need to know about the proceeding.

Jones v. Flowers, 547 U.S. 220 (2006), provides a prime example of this common-sense approach to notice. In *Jones*, a state commissioner seized Gary Jones' house after property taxes had gone unpaid. The commissioner attempted to notify Jones twice by certified mail, but each time the letter was returned by the post office marked "unclaimed." Jones never saw the letters because he had moved out of the house when he separated from his spouse. When Jones later found out that the state had taken possession of his property and sold it, he brought a lawsuit arguing that the sale violated his right to due process, as he had never received notice of the state's action against his property. The Arkansas courts considered the sale valid and found that the notice requirement had been satisfied by the commissioner's sending of a certified letter to Jones. The Supreme Court, however, agreed with Jones. When the letters were returned unclaimed, the commissioner *knew* that Jones had not received them. *Mullane* made clear that to satisfy the due process notice requirement, the means employed for notification must be such as what one would do if one actually wished to inform the absentee of the proceeding. If you were actually trying to reach someone by certified mail and the letter came back unclaimed, you would try again or try some other method, wouldn't you? The commissioner and the Arkansas courts made the mistake of treating notice as a mere technicality. The Supreme Court took the opportunity to reemphasize that, constitutionally, notice is all about giving the party an opportunity to be heard.

Pay attention, however, to what *Mullane* and *Jones* do *not* say. They do not say that due process always requires *actual* notice for a party to be bound by a judgment. What those cases require is "notice reasonably calculated" to reach the party. There are circumstances in which personal service is impossible and notice by some other means—say, by publication—may well be sufficient to reach the parties, and there are other circumstances in which, for whatever reason, a defendant may not *actually* learn about the proceeding. The inquiry will be highly fact-dependent. As long as the notice complies with applicable rules and is reasonably calculated to reach the defendant, a judgment may bind the defendant without offending due process.

(2) Service of Process

For a court to assert power over a party, not only must the means of notice meet the baseline standard of constitutional due process, it also must comply with applicable statutes or rules. For civil litigation, this means that the plaintiff must *serve* the summons and complaint on the defendant in compliance with the rules on service of process. Recall from Chapter 2 that, along with the complaint, the defendant gets served with a summons. The summons can be prepared by the plaintiff but it is signed by the clerk of court; its function is to summon the defendant to appear to respond to the plaintiff's claims, by order of the court.

Service of process in federal court is governed by Rule 4, and motions objecting either to the content of the summons or the manner of service are contained in Rules 12(b)(4) and (5), respectively. We have already looked at Rule 4(k), which governs the territorial limits of service for purposes of obtaining personal jurisdiction over a party. Other portions of Rule 4 address the *formalities* of how one must serve process on various types of defendants for it to be constitutionally sufficient. Specifically, Rule 4(a) and (b) set forth the requirements for the contents and issuance of the summons. Rule 4(c) specifies what must be served and by whom. Rule 4(e)-(j) sets forth the acceptable methods of serving different types of parties: individuals within the United States (4(e)); individuals in a foreign country (4(f)); minors (4(g)); corporations (4(h)); U.S. governmental entities (4(i)); and foreign, state, or local governments (4(j)). Make sure you take careful note of the differences in acceptable methods of service, depending on the type of party being served, prescribed by the subsections of Rule 4. Also take careful note of Rule 4(d), which governs the process by which parties may waive service—a practice used commonly among those entities that are frequently involved in litigation, and a process you will likely see often in practice. Consider the following case, which grapples with the challenge of reaching an elusive defendant and examines service by e-mail both as a Rule 4 matter and in terms of the strictures of due process.

LIBERTY MEDIA HOLDINGS, LLC v. GAN
2012 WL 122862 (D. Colo. Jan. 17, 2012)

TAFOYA, Magistrate Judge.

This matter is before the court on "Plaintiff's *Ex Parte* Motion for Alternative Service." In its Motion, Plaintiff seeks a court order permitting it to serve Defendant Sheng Gan . . . by email, pursuant to Federal Rule of Civil Procedure 4(f)(3) and 4(h)(2).

[According to the complaint, Sheng Gan, a Chinese national residing in Costa Rica, ran a website called SiteRipKing.com. "Site ripping" refers to copying an entire website and making it available to others. Liberty Media produces and distributes "adult entertainment" products, including Internet pornography. Liberty Media sued Sheng Gan

for copyright and trademark infringement, seeking money damages and an injunction.]

Federal Rule of Civil Procedure 4(f)(3) authorizes service upon an individual in a foreign country "by . . . means not prohibited by international agreement, as the court orders." Rule 4(h)(2) provides that a foreign corporation, partnership or association may be served in "any manner prescribed by Rule 4(f) for serving an individual, except personal delivery under (f)(2)(C)(i)." Plaintiff maintains that since *Rio Properties, Inc. v. Rio International Interlink*, 284 F.3d 1007 (9th Cir. 2002), courts have widely approved of service via email pursuant to subsections (f)(3) and (h)(2) of Rule 4.

In *Rio Properties*, the plaintiff sought to complete service of process via email after it was unable to conventionally serve the defendant, a Costa Rican entity that conducted business solely via the internet. The plaintiff first attempted to serve the defendant at a Florida address it had used to register its website; however that address[] housed the defendant's international courier. Although the courier agreed to forward the summons and complaint on to the defendant, it was not authorized to accept service on the defendant's behalf. Shortly thereafter, the plaintiff was contacted by an attorney who represented to the plaintiff that the defendant had received the summons and complaint, and had contacted him, the attorney, regarding how to respond. The plaintiff inquired if the attorney would accept process on the defendant's behalf; however, the attorney declined.

Consequently, the plaintiff filed a motion for alternate service of process seeking, among other things, to serve the defendant via an email address through which the defendant preferred to receive communications. The district court granted the plaintiff's motion and permitted service of process to be completed via email.

In affirming that email service was appropriate, the Ninth Circuit first looked to Rule 4(f)(3) itself. The court noted that the plain language of Rule 4(f)(3) provided only two limitations on alternate means of service of process on a foreign individual—it "must be (1) directed by the court; and (2) not prohibited by international agreement." 284 F.3d 1007, 1014 (9th Cir. 2002). The court further acknowledged that "even if facially permitted by Rule 4(f)(3), a method of service of process must also comport with constitutional notions of due process." *Id.* at 1016. To meet this requirement, the method of service crafted by a district court must be "reasonably calculated, under all the circumstances, to apprise interested parties of the pendency of the action and afford them an opportunity to present their objections." *Mullane v. Cent. Hanover Bank & Trust Co.*, 339 U.S. 306, 314 (1950).

While acknowledging that it was "tread[ing] upon untrodden ground," the *Rio Properties* court noted that the broad constitutional principle that service be "'reasonably calculated to provide notice and an opportunity to respond'... unshackles the federal courts from anachronistic methods of service and permits them entry into the technological renaissance." *Id.* at 1017. The Ninth Circuit urged that "Courts... cannot be blind to changes and advances in technology." *Id.*

Consequently, on the facts in *Rio*, the court found that not only was service of process via email proper, but was, in fact, "the method of service most likely to reach [the defendant]." *Id.* The court noted that the defendant had "embraced the modern e-business model and profited immensely from it" and "had neither an office nor a door; it had only a computer terminal." *Id.* The defendant had thus "structured its business such that it could be contacted *only* via its email address." *Id.* at 1018. Consequently, the court concluded that "[i]f any method of communication [was] reasonably calculated to provide [the defendant] with notice, surely it [was] email.... [I]t was a means reasonably calculated to apprise [the defendant] of the pendency of the lawsuit, and the Constitution requires nothing more." *Id.*

Notably, however, while the *Rio Properties* court endorsed service of process by email in that case... [the court] noted [the limitation that] often there is no way to confirm that an email message, along with all its attachments, was actually received. Accordingly, the court acknowledged that a district court must exercise discretion in balancing "the limitations of email service against its benefits in any particular case." *Id.*

Plaintiff points out that since *Rio Properties*, a number of courts have approved of service by email pursuant to Rule 4(f)(3). There has been some mild disagreement, however, over whether a court should ordinarily require a plaintiff to attempt to conventionally serve the defendant before authorizing alternate service of process. . . . The court need not detain itself with this question, however, because the court finds that Plaintiff has taken more than reasonable measures to attempt to serve Defendant. While early discovery served upon Name.com turned up that Defendant is the owner and operator of the siteripking.com website at issue in this case, his actual street address and geographical location are still unknown. Both the Costa Rica address more recently associated with the domain name SiteRipKing.com, and the China address originally used to register the domain name are incomplete. Moreover, Plaintiff has made extensive efforts to uncover more precise information about Defendant's physical locale to no avail. Plaintiff has only been able to uncover two email addresses associated with Defendant and the siteripking.com website—support@siteripking.com and kankaqi@gmail.com. Accordingly, regardless of whether making reasonable efforts to serve the defendant without court intervention is a prerequisite to pursuing alternate service under Rule 4(f)(3), the court finds that Plaintiff has fulfilled this potential requirement. . . .

Finally, the court must find that service of process by email in this case complies with constitutional notions of due process. Here, the court finds a hang-up. Plaintiff's proposal for alternative service, at least as presently fashioned, falls short of complying with due process because the limitations of service of process by email

identified by the *Rio Properties* court are acute in this case. More specifically, although Plaintiff analogizes this case to *Rio Properties*—where the court found that the defendant was playing "hide-and-seek" with the federal court by receiving the complaint and summons through its courier and attorney, but refusing to accept service of process—there is no indication that Defendant Gan is independently aware of the pendency of this litigation.

Additionally, unlike in *Rio Properties*, where the defendant designated, and utilized, its email address as its preferred method of contact, here there is no indicia of the extent to which Defendant uses either the support@siteripking.com or the kankaqi@gmail.com email address. Nor is there any indication that Defendant has held these addresses out to the public as a preferred means of contact; rather, Plaintiff admits that it only learned of them when Defendant's privacy services stripped Defendant's anonymity from its records.

More to the point, there is no reasonable assurance that Plaintiff's emailed complaint and summons will be received on the other end. Defendant's conduct in this case, as alleged by Plaintiff, is certainly surreptitious. This is further corroborated by the fact that Defendant provided Name.com with incomplete physical addresses and the fact that the allegedly offending SiteRip King.com site has now been dismantled. In light of these facts, the court has little reason to believe that Defendant has not likewise abandoned both of the email addresses by which Plaintiff proposes to effect service. While the court acknowledges that email may be Plaintiff's last resort, to allow Plaintiff to complete service of process by emailing the complaint and summons to these email addresses without any confirmation of receipt would be akin to allowing Plaintiff to slide a complaint and summon under the front door of what appears to be an abandoned residence. Ultimately, the court finds that due process requires more.

While the court would be warranted to deny Plaintiff's Motion for this reason, in order to conserve party and judicial resources, the court elects another course. In *Williams v. Advertising Sex LLC*, 231 F.R.D. 483, 488 (N.D. W. Va. 2005), the court found that the reliability of email service was likely to be enhanced by the plaintiff's use of the website service "Proof of Service-electronic" ("PoS-e"). That service offered "encrypted on-line delivery of documents and returns a digitally signed proof of delivery once the document has been received by the target e-mail." *Id.* The court finds that if Plaintiff's proposal for service of process via email were similarly enhanced, it would be far more likely to pass constitutional muster.

Accordingly, rather than outright deny Plaintiff's Motion and have Plaintiff file a renewed motion addressing the court's concerns, the court will allow Plaintiff to supplement to its present motion with a proposed method for serving Defendant via email that, as in *Williams*, would further assure that the email message featuring Plaintiff's complaint and summons is actually received.

Notes & Questions

1. *In personam* jurisdiction over Sheng Gan, as a matter of the state's territorial power over Gan, was based on the fact that Gan had registered domain names with name.com, a Colorado business. Nonetheless, the court also required that service of process be accomplished for exercise of jurisdiction to be proper. Why require service of process? That is, what procedural policies—independent of personal jurisdiction in the sense of territorial power—are advanced by the requirement that the summons and complaint be delivered according to specific rules?

2. Why didn't Liberty Media serve Gan by having the summons and complaint personally delivered to him?

3. What did the court in *Rio Properties* conclude about the permissibility of service by e-mail under Rule 4? What did the court in *Liberty Media Holdings* conclude on that issue? Do the holdings in either or both of those cases mean that service via e-mail is permissible generally under Rule 4?

4. Make sure you separate the two courts' analyses of whether service by e-mail was permitted by Rule 4 and their analyses of whether service via e-mail satisfied the *Mullane* due process standard. What was the court's holding on the constitutional issue in *Rio*? In *Liberty Media Holdings*? What explains any differences between the two holdings?

5. Formal service of process, such as personal delivery or other methods approved by Rule 4, can be costly and time-consuming because they may involve hiring a

process server and tracking down the defendant. But the rule suggests a cheaper and easier alternative: *waiver of service.* Rule 4(d) allows a plaintiff to notify the defendant about the action and "request that the defendant waive service of a summons." To make this request, the plaintiff simply sends the defendant a copy of the complaint by first-class mail or other reliable means, along with a form that the defendant can return to waive the requirement of formal service. Why would the defendant agree to this? Look carefully at Rule 4(d) for both a carrot and a stick vis-à-vis waiver of formal service of process.

6. Now that you have reached the end of this chapter, think about how you might put together the various pieces of the personal jurisdiction puzzle. Remember that you have to think about *both* power and notice. For a court to assert *in personam* jurisdiction over a defendant, the defendant must fall within the court's power *and* the defendant must have been adequately notified. Further, each of these components has both a statutory and a constitutional aspect. Thus, keeping in mind both aspects of both components, you might organize the broad framework of your analysis this way:

   (1) Does the court's power reach the defendant:

      (a) as a statutory matter (applying Rule 4(k), state long-arm statutes, etc.), *and*

      (b) as a constitutional matter (applying, among other things, the *International Shoe* minimum contacts test)?

   (2) Was the defendant properly notified:

      (a) as a statutory matter (applying rules and statutes on service of process), *and*

      (b) as a constitutional matter (applying the *Mullane* due process test)?

Each step in this framework, of course, has its own complications. We have spent the bulk of this chapter exploring the most difficult piece—the minimum contacts test and other parts of the due process analysis to determine the circumstances under which a court's power may extend to out-of-state defendants. However, even as you ponder the mysteries of the minimum contacts test for personal jurisdiction, be sure to step back and see how that test is one part of at least a four-part inquiry.

CHAPTER 11

Venue

Federal courts are divided into 94 districts around the country, and state courts are spread among the counties or regions of each state. Where, among these courts, should a lawsuit be heard? The choice of forum is determined, in part, by the jurisdictional constraints covered in Chapters 9 and 10. But jurisdiction doctrines provide, at best, only a partial answer to the question of where particular disputes *ought* to be heard. *Venue* further narrows forum options. More directly than jurisdictional doctrines, which ultimately concern the power of states over persons (personal jurisdiction) and the institutional limits of federal court power (subject matter jurisdiction), venue focuses on determining appropriate and convenient *locations*. In state court, venue statutes ordinarily determine the county or counties where a case may be brought. In federal court, venue statutes determine the district or districts where a case may be brought. If you enjoyed learning subject matter jurisdiction and personal jurisdiction, with their constitutional foundations and multilayered analyses, you may find the topic of venue disappointingly shallow. But sometimes it is comforting to reencounter the old KISS principle (keep it simple, stupid). After the complexities of jurisdiction, we think you will find venue refreshingly straightforward.

First, let's place venue in context as one of several forum-selection doctrines. For a case to be brought in a particular court, that court must have subject matter jurisdiction over the action, must have personal jurisdiction over the parties, and must be a proper venue under applicable federal or state venue rules. Whereas subject matter and personal jurisdiction address the court's power and boast constitutional underpinnings—Article III for federal

> **Terminology Tip**
>
> The word *venue* refers to a set of legal rules that constrain the choice of forum, but also to the forum itself. In this regard, the word functions analogously to *jurisdiction*, which can refer either to the legal principles explored in Chapters 9 and 10 or to the state. As used in the chapter title above, *venue* refers to a set of statutory rules for determining which forums are available, as in the sentence, "She moved to dismiss for improper venue." But the word also refers to the forum itself, as in, "She chose the District of Massachusetts as the venue for her case." The latter use corresponds to the non-legal use of the word, as in a concert venue or sports venue.

subject matter jurisdiction, the Due Process Clause for personal jurisdiction—venue operates on a more mundane level as a purely statutory constraint on forum choices.

One way to think about forum selection is to picture a Venn diagram with overlapping circles representing subject matter jurisdiction, personal jurisdiction, and venue. Where all three circles intersect, the court may hear the case. At least, that is the starting point for the analysis. Later in the chapter, when we address venue transfer and the doctrine of forum non conveniens, you will see that even if a case falls in the intersection, the court nonetheless has discretion to decline to hear a case that would be more appropriately heard elsewhere.

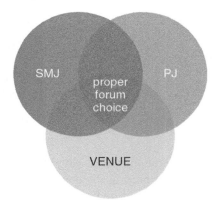

In the practice of law, however, we doubt you will experience these circles as a Venn diagram. More likely, you will find that the circles feel like hoops you have to jump through to establish the legitimacy of a chosen forum. Hoop one: In federal court, the plaintiff's complaint or the defendant's notice of removal must state the basis for the court's subject matter jurisdiction. Hoop two: In either state or federal court, if a defendant objects that the court lacks personal jurisdiction, the plaintiff must show the basis for the court's power. Hoop three: If a party objects to venue, the plaintiff will have to show that the district is a permitted location for the case under the applicable venue statute. A careful lawyer, of course, has anticipated all of these hoops before filing the action.

A. VENUE IN STATE COURT

Venue rules for state courts vary from state to state and are generally regulated by state statutes. These statutes determine where within a state—which county, parish, or district—cases can be brought. In this book, we will keep it brief. Just keep in mind that when you litigate in any state's courts, you need to learn the state's venue rules to determine which venues are proper and what mechanisms are provided for dismissal or transfer.

Often, state venue statutes permit a court to hear a case in the county, parish, or district of the plaintiff's residence, the defendant's residence, where a contract was signed or was to be carried out, or where a substantial part of the events leading to the dispute occurred. Many state venue statutes retain the old common law distinction between local and transitory actions. *Local actions* are those that concern real property, such as lawsuits to determine property ownership, to gain possession of land, or sometimes for trespass. A local action must be brought in the court where the property is located. *Transitory actions* include all other lawsuits and can be brought wherever permitted by the general venue rules as long as the defendant is subject to personal jurisdiction. The notion behind the local-transitory distinction is that a transitory action could have arisen anywhere, whereas a local action, because it involves a specific piece of real property, could have arisen only in one place. If you do not find this a terribly satisfying distinction, you are not alone. Of course it is true that a specific property dispute arises in a specific place. But can't the same be said of automobile accidents, barroom brawls, employment disputes, or a host of other "transitory" actions? Satisfying or not, in most courts, lawsuits involving real property are considered local actions and must be brought in the county, parish, or district where the property is found.

B. VENUE IN FEDERAL COURT

Federal venue statutes determine which of the 94 federal judicial districts are appropriate places to hear a particular case. To figure out which districts are proper venues for a case in federal court, you will usually look at the general federal venue statute, 28 U.S.C. §1391. The three disjunctive subsections of section 1391(b) spell out in general where venue is proper for a lawsuit or, to use the lawyerly terminology, where venue *may be laid*. Section 1391 covers most venue questions in federal district court. Be aware, however, that a few types of cases have their own specific venue statutes, such as 28 U.S.C. §1397 (interpleader venue) and 28 U.S.C. §1400 (patent venue).

To test your reading of the federal venue statute (and for a little review of subject matter jurisdiction and personal jurisdiction), try applying 28 U.S.C. §1391 to the following problem:

X, Y, and Z get into a three-car collision on a highway in Maryland. X is an individual domiciled in Maryland. Y is an individual domiciled in Delaware. Z is an individual domiciled in Pennsylvania (within the Middle District of Pennsylvania). At the time of the accident, Z was driving on company business for her employer, ABC Corporation, which is incorporated in Delaware and headquartered in Pennsylvania. X claims that Y and Z drove negligently and that their negligence caused X harm in excess of $75,000.

(a) X sues Y and Z in the U.S. District Court for the District of Maryland. Start with the first two hoops and then turn to venue: Does the court have subject matter jurisdiction over the action? Does the court have personal jurisdiction over each defendant? Is venue properly laid in this district?

(b) X sues Y and Z in the U.S. District Court for the Middle District of Pennsylvania. Does the court have subject matter jurisdiction over the action? Does the court have personal jurisdiction over each defendant? Is venue properly laid in this district?

(c) X sues Z and ABC Corp. in the U.S. District Court for the Middle District of Pennsylvania. X claims that ABC is vicariously liable for the negligence of its employee in the course of employment. Does the court have subject matter jurisdiction over the action? Does the court have personal jurisdiction over each defendant? Is venue properly laid in this district?

(d) X sues Y, Z, and ABC Corp. in the U.S. District Court for the District of Delaware. Z is personally served with a summons and complaint in X's lawsuit while in Delaware for business. Does the court have subject matter jurisdiction over the action? Does the court have personal jurisdiction over each defendant? Is venue properly laid in this district?

STRATEGY SESSION

Do not think of venue as a question of finding "the" appropriate district for a particular dispute. When you determine forum options in a particular dispute by analyzing subject matter jurisdiction, personal jurisdiction, and venue, often there are multiple places where the lawsuit could be brought. It is up to the plaintiff, as the "master of her complaint," to choose where to file among permissible venues. After the case is filed, the defendant can decide whether to move to transfer to another proper venue. In that situation, the court must decide whether the defendant's arguments in favor of an alternative venue overcome the deference ordinarily given to the plaintiff's choice. However, some controversies must be brought in a particular district, leaving little room for strategic forum choices by either side. Under the federal venue statute, for example, if the defendant resides in the same district where all the substantial events occurred, then the suit must be brought in that district. And in some cases, the choice of forum is dictated by a forum-selection clause or arbitration clause to which the parties have previously agreed.

(1) Defendant's Residence

Section 1 (28 U.S.C. §1391(b)(1)) permits a case to be brought in "a judicial district in which any defendant resides, if all defendants are residents of the State in which the district is located." In a lawsuit against one individual, this section is extremely straightforward: The case may be brought in the district where the defendant resides (residence is defined in section 1391(c)). But in a case involving multiple defendants, section 1 applies only if all defendants reside in the same state. The logic is that if all the defendants reside in Connecticut, then they have no basis to gripe about venue if the plaintiff files the lawsuit in the District of Connecticut. But if one defendant resides in Connecticut, one in Georgia, and one in Oregon, then it makes more sense to base venue on where the relevant events occurred, rather than on the defendants' residences.

The other twist—and this may be the single most important thing for you to remember about the federal venue statute—is the statute's surprising definition of "reside" for a corporation or other entity. Individuals "reside" where they are domiciled, *see* 28 U.S.C. §1391(c)(1), but the definition of corporate residence is not so intuitive. If you were to look only at section 1391(b)(1), you might assume that a corporation resides wherever it is headquartered. Or maybe you would assume that corporate "residence" would be defined just like corporate "citizenship" under the diversity jurisdiction statute, looking at state of incorporation plus principal place of business. But if you assumed this (as countless students have done on civil procedure exams), you would be wrong. Rather, the venue statute provides that an entity "shall be deemed to reside, if a defendant, in any judicial district in which such defendant is subject to the court's personal jurisdiction with respect to the civil action in question." 28 U.S.C. §1391(c)(2). In other words, if a state has personal jurisdiction over a corporation, then the corporation is deemed to "reside" in that state for purposes of the venue provision in section 1391(b)(1).

If a case involves only a single defendant, and it is a corporation or other entity, then as a practical matter, this definition merges the venue inquiry with the personal jurisdiction inquiry. With a single corporate defendant, if the defendant is subject to personal jurisdiction in a district, then federal venue in that district would be proper under section 1391(b)(1).

If a case involves multiple defendants, then to determine venue under section 1391(b)(1), take two steps: First, see where each defendant "resides" by figuring out where each individual is domiciled and where each corporation or other entity is subject to personal jurisdiction. Second, compare to see if there is a state in which all of the defendants are deemed to reside.

Be careful in how you use section 1391(c). It does *not* state where venue is proper. All it does is provide a definition of "reside." Do not make the mistake of saying that "section 1391(c) establishes that venue is proper in this district because the defendant is subject to personal jurisdiction here." Rather, be precise: "Section 1391(c) establishes that the defendant 'resides' in this district because it is subject to personal jurisdiction here; venue is proper in this district under section 1391(b)(1) because all defendants reside here."

(2) Events or Property

Section 2 is the most intuitive part of the venue statute. It permits a case to be brought in "a judicial district in which a substantial part of the events or omissions giving rise to the claim occurred, or a substantial part of property that is the subject of the action is situated." 28 U.S.C. §1391(b)(2).

Many cases invite a straightforward application of section 2. If a dispute involves ownership of a piece of property, venue is proper in the district where the property is located. If a dispute involves an accident, venue is proper in the district where the accident occurred.

Often, however, disputes cross state borders or district borders. If a New Yorker negotiates a contract with a Californian concerning a business in Oklahoma, and a dispute ensues, then section 2 could point to multiple permissible venues, depending on where substantial negotiations and other relevant events occurred. Similarly, if a defective product is sold in New York and causes injury in Oklahoma, section 2 could point to both as appropriate venues.

(3) Fallback Provision

You will never use section 3. Fine, it is theoretically *possible* you might, but in your career as a lawyer, it is unlikely you will ever actually work on a case in which venue is based on section 3. Section 3 (28 U.S.C. §1391(b)(3)) applies only if there is no proper venue under either section 1 or 2. Section 1391(b)(3) provides that "if there is no district in which an action may otherwise be brought as provided in this section," then the action may be brought in "any judicial district in which any defendant is subject to the court's personal jurisdiction with respect to such action."

Think about how unlikely it is that "there is no district in which an action may otherwise be brought" under the other two subsections of the venue statute. That would mean that not only do the defendants not reside in the same state, but *none* of the substantial events took place in *any* judicial district within the United States. Indeed, try to think of a situation that would not fall within either section 1 or section 2. It would be a case where all of the substantial events took place outside the country (yet the plaintiff chose to file in a U.S. court), and the defendants do not reside in the same state (even with the broad definition of "reside" for corporate defendants). If you happen to face that situation, then section 3 allows venue wherever you can get personal jurisdiction. *See, e.g., RMS Titanic, Inc. v. Zaller*, 978 F. Supp. 2d 1275, 1303 (N.D. Ga. 2013) (finding that venue would be proper under section 1391(b)(3) in the Northern District of Georgia, even if a non-Georgia defendant were included in the action, for claims arising in Macau).

C. VENUE TRANSFER

Sometimes, it makes sense for a court to transfer a case from one place to another within a judicial system. Within a state court system, a case might be transferred from one county to another. Within the federal court system, a case might be transferred from one district to another, whether within a state (say, from the Southern District of California to the Northern District of California) or between states (from the Southern District of California to the Eastern District of Pennsylvania). This is known as venue transfer. The first court is called the *transferor court*, and the second court is the *transferee court*. As an attorney, if you think your client would be better off in a different venue where the case could have been brought, consider bringing a motion to transfer venue to your preferred location.

Three different federal venue transfer statutes figure prominently in U.S. litigation. The most basic one—28 U.S.C. §1404—deals with cases that are filed in a court that has jurisdiction and where venue is proper, but under circumstances in which it would be more convenient for the case to be heard somewhere else. The second venue transfer statute—28 U.S.C. §1406—deals with cases that are filed in a venue that is *not* proper and permits a federal court to transfer from the impermissible venue to another federal court that is a permissible venue. Third, the multidistrict litigation statute—28 U.S.C. §1407—deals with situations in which related cases have been filed in multiple federal district courts; it offers a way to bring the cases together so they can be handled more efficiently. We addressed section 1407 in Chapter 7 in connection with joinder and consolidation. Here, we will focus on sections 1404 and 1406.

(1) Transfer from a Proper Forum

The basic federal venue transfer statute, 28 U.S.C. §1404(a), gives federal judges discretion to transfer an action to a more appropriate district: "For the convenience of parties and witnesses, in the interest of justice, a district court may transfer any civil action to any other district or division where it might have been brought or to any district or division to which all parties have consented."

When deciding whether to grant a motion to transfer venue, judges consider a range of factors including where the parties are based, where the witnesses reside, where the evidence can be found, and where the relevant events occurred. If, considering these factors, the dispute's center of gravity is somewhere other than where the lawsuit was filed, then it may be a good candidate for venue transfer. Courts give some deference to plaintiffs' choice of forum, sometimes invoking the old adage that "the plaintiff is the master of the complaint." Keep in mind, however, that venue transfer is highly discretionary. The words of the statute—particularly the key word "may" and the phrase "in the interest of justice"—give the district court plenty of leeway in deciding whether to grant a transfer of venue.

Under section 1404(a), a court may transfer an action to another district "where it might have been brought." This means a district where the court has personal jurisdiction over the defendants and where venue is proper under the applicable federal venue statute. The Supreme Court originally interpreted the "where it might have been brought" language to mean that a defendant could not obtain transfer to a different district by waiving its objection to personal jurisdiction in the transferee court, *see Hoffman v. Blaski*, 363 U.S. 335 (1960), but in 2011 Congress added language to 28 U.S.C. §1404(a) to permit transfer to a district "to which all parties have consented."

To see how venue transfer under section 1404 works—and also to see more clearly how venue and venue transfer fit together with subject matter jurisdiction and personal jurisdiction—consider this hypothetical lawsuit for employment discrimination:

Example 1: An employee is fired from working for a company in Houston, Texas; he believes he was fired because of his race. The fired employee then moves to Delaware. The company is incorporated in Delaware, but its headquarters and most of its employees are in Texas. The employee brings an employment discrimination lawsuit against the company in U.S. District Court for the District of Delaware, asserting claims under federal employment discrimination law.

To see whether the lawsuit in Example 1 was properly filed in the District of Delaware, consider each of the three hoops. First, does the federal court have *subject matter jurisdiction*? Yes, based on federal question jurisdiction. Second, does the court in Delaware have *personal jurisdiction* over the defendant? Yes, Delaware has general jurisdiction over the company because it is incorporated in that state. Third, is *venue* proper in the District of Delaware? Yes, venue is proper under section 1391(b)(1) because the company is deemed to reside in the District of Delaware based on section 1391(c)'s special definition of corporate residence for venue. If the company were to move to dismiss for lack of subject matter jurisdiction, lack of personal jurisdiction, or improper venue, the court would deny those motions.

Terminology Tip

The words *transfer* and *removal* are not interchangeable. Transfer occurs within a single judicial system, rather than between different systems such as federal courts and state courts. A case may be removed from state court to federal court if federal subject matter jurisdiction exists, as you learned in Chapter 9. But don't call that transfer; it's removal. No mechanism exists for moving a case from federal court to state court, except when a case is improperly removed and the federal court then *remands* the case back to state court.

But even though the case was properly filed in the District of Delaware (in the sense of jumping through all three hoops), does it make sense for the case to be heard there? Does adjudicating the case there serve "the interest of justice" and "the convenience of parties and witnesses"? Probably not. The dispute concerns the firing of an employee at a Houston location of a Texas-based company. The plaintiff has since moved to Delaware, but nearly all the other witnesses and evidence will be in Houston. Therefore, the company could reasonably move to transfer venue under section 1404(a) to the Southern District of Texas (the federal district that encompasses Houston), and the court might grant the motion.

(2) Transfer from an Improper Forum

What if a plaintiff files an action in the wrong venue? One option is for the court to dismiss the action for improper venue. Indeed, Federal Rule of Civil Procedure 12(b)(3) lists improper venue as a defense that can be raised on a motion to dismiss.

But rather than dismiss the case, maybe the judge thinks it makes more sense to transfer the case to a proper venue. That is where the other venue transfer statute, 28 U.S.C. §1406(a), comes into play. Section 1406 lets the court decide whether to transfer or dismiss: "The district court of a district in which is filed a case laying venue in the wrong division or district shall dismiss, or if it be in the interest of justice, transfer such case to any district or division in which it could have been brought." Although the language of section 1406 appears to apply only to improper venue, the Supreme Court has interpreted it to allow transfer of a case in which both venue and personal jurisdiction are missing. *See Goldlawr, Inc. v. Heiman*, 369 U.S. 463 (1962).

Let's modify Example 1 to see how transfer works under section 1406:

Example 2: Same employment discrimination lawsuit as in Example 1, except that this time, the employee sues two defendants—the company and the Houston supervisor who was responsible for the firing.

As in Example 1, the federal court has subject matter jurisdiction based on federal question jurisdiction, and the court has personal jurisdiction over the company based on the company's incorporation in Delaware. But in Example 2, the court lacks personal jurisdiction over the boss (unless the boss consents to jurisdiction or is served in state). Moreover, under the venue statute, venue would not be proper under section 1391(b)(1) because both defendants do not reside in Delaware, nor would venue be proper under section 1391(b)(2) because no substantial part of the events took place in Delaware.

Because venue is improper in the District of Delaware, the court could simply dismiss the case. Or, under section 1406(a), the court could decide instead to transfer the case to the Southern District of Texas. The Southern District of Texas constitutes a district where the case "could have been brought" because the court would have personal jurisdiction over both defendants and proper venue under both section 1391(b)(1) and section 1391(b)(2).

To see the federal venue statute and venue transfer statute in operation, consider the following case.

ASTRO-MED, INC. v. NIHON KOHDEN AMERICA, INC.
591 F.3d 1 (1st Cir. 2009)

WOODCOCK, District Judge.*

Astro-Med, Inc. (Astro-Med) and Nihon Kohden America, Inc. (Nihon Kohden) are rivals in the highly competitive life sciences equipment market, and in October 2006, when Nihon Kohden hired away Kevin Plant, a valuable Astro-Med employee, Astro-Med reviewed its legal options. When first hired at Astro-Med in 2002, Plant signed an employee agreement that contained non-competition and non-disclosure provisions. Relying in large part on those provisions, in December 2006, Astro-Med filed suit against

Plant alleging breach of contract and misappropriation of trade secrets. Astro-Med later added a third claim of unfair competition against Plant and joined Nihon Kohden as a defendant, against whom it alleged claims of tortious interference and misappropriation of trade secrets.[1] The lawsuit was especially hard-fought, and Nihon Kohden and Plant were disappointed on April 7, 2008, when a jury returned a verdict against them,

---

[1] Astro-Med originally filed suit in Kent County Superior Court in Rhode Island. Asserting diversity jurisdiction, Plant timely removed the case to the United States District Court for the District of Rhode Island.

---

*Of the District of Maine, sitting by designation.

awarding $375,800 in damages in favor of Astro-Med. Following the verdict, on July 25, 2008, the district court awarded exemplary damages against Nihon Kohden and Plant in the amount of $560,000, added an award of attorney's fees and costs, and imposed a sanction pursuant to Federal Rule of Civil Procedure 37. All told, the judgment against Nihon Kohden and Plant equals $1,159,823.60. On appeal, Nihon Kohden and Plant wage a frontal assault against the judgment, itemizing nine separate claims of legal error. After careful consideration, we reject each of Nihon Kohden's and Plant's contentions and affirm.

I. BACKGROUND

Astro-Med is a Rhode Island corporation with its principal place of business in West Warwick, Rhode Island. Its Grass Technologies product group manufactures, sells, and distributes instruments for sleep and neurological research and clinical applications of sleep science and brain wave recording and analysis. Although the identity of some of its customers is well known, Astro-Med's financial arrangements with its sales people, its marketing strategy, and its pricing and cost structures are all highly confidential, and Astro-Med makes strenuous efforts to protect its trade secrets and other confidential information.

In October 2002, even though Plant had no prior experience in the medical industry or in medical equipment sales, Astro-Med hired him as a Product Specialist, responsible for the demonstration and training of its Grass Technologies product line. Astro-Med provided Plant with extensive training about its business, products, customers, and competitors, and it was Astro-Med's training that later made him marketable to Nihon Kohden. When Astro-Med hired Plant, he signed an Employee Agreement, which contains a non-competition clause [prohibiting Plant from working for a competitor within one year of terminating his employment at the company, and] a trade secrets clause [prohibiting Plant from disclosing certain information about the company to anyone outside the company].

The Employee Agreement also contained a choice-of-law and forum-selection clause, which stated that it shall be governed by the laws of the state of Rhode Island and that Plant consented to jurisdiction in Rhode Island for any dispute arising out of the Agreement.

Subsequently, Plant asked to be transferred to the state of Florida and become a field sales representative; Astro-Med granted his request and paid to relocate him to Florida. On July 12, 2004, Astro-Med promoted Plant to District Sales Manager for sales of Grass Technologies products. As District Sales Manager, Plant had access to and used Astro-Med's trade secrets, including confidential marketing, pricing, and customer information. He became intimately familiar with Astro-Med's [customers, pricing strategy, cost data, suppliers, and research and development].

Nihon Kohden, a California corporation, has its principal place of business in Foothill Ranch, California. As a manufacturer of instrumentation for patient monitoring, sleep assessment, and neurology, Nihon Kohden competes directly with Astro-Med. . . .

Before offering Plant employment, Nihon Kohden became aware of the Astro-Med Employment Agreement with Plant and referred the contract to counsel for review. Nihon Kohden's lawyer advised Nihon Kohden that there was some minimal risk in hiring Plant; notwithstanding that advice, Nihon Kohden hired Plant to sell its products in competition with Astro-Med in the sales territory he had covered for Astro-Med.

II. DISCUSSION

A. THE JURISDICTIONAL ISSUE

From the very outset of this litigation, Nihon Kohden has vigorously maintained that, as a California business, it should not have been haled into court in Rhode Island to defend its hiring of a Florida resident to sell its product in Florida.[2] . . .

1. LEGAL STANDARDS

. . . Early on, Nihon Kohden moved to dismiss the lawsuit under Federal Rule of Civil Procedure 12(b)(2) on the ground that the district court did not have personal jurisdiction. The district court denied the motion. . . . Since we conclude that the district court correctly concluded it had specific jurisdiction, we will address only that issue.

2. SPECIFIC JURISDICTION

This circuit "divides [the] minimum contacts analysis into three inquiries: relatedness, purposeful availment, and reasonableness." *N. Laminate Sales, Inc. v. Davis*, 403 F.3d 14, 25 (1st Cir. 2005). . . .

(a) Relatedness

The first inquiry, relatedness, asks whether "the claim underlying the litigation . . . directly arise[s] out of, or, or relate[s] to, the defendant's forum state activities." *N. Laminate Sales*, 403 F.3d at 25. . . .

Before Nihon Kohden hired Plant, it knew that Astro-Med was located in Rhode Island, that Plant had entered into the Employee Agreement in Rhode Island, that the contract specified it would be governed by Rhode Island law, that the contract contained non-competition and non-disclosure provisions, and that by virtue of the contract, Plant had consented to the exclusive jurisdiction of the courts of Rhode Island over any disputes related to the contract. Further, Nihon Kohden had sought and obtained legal advice that by hiring Plant, it was exposing itself to some legal risk. Thus, Nihon Kohden knew that by employing Plant, it was running the risk that Plant would thereby have breached his Rhode Island contract with a Rhode Island company and any ensuing suit would be initiated in Rhode Island and interpreted under Rhode Island law.

. . . Consistent with *Calder v. Jones*, 465 U.S. 783, 789 (1984), a defendant "need not be physically present in the forum state to cause injury (and thus 'activity' for jurisdictional purposes) in the forum state." *N. Laminate Sales*, 403 F.3d at 25. Nihon Kohden's conduct in Florida and California was a cause of the breach of contract—the actual injury—that occurred in Rhode Island. That in-forum injury was clearly related to Astro-Med's tortious interference claim, satisfying the first prong of the minimum contacts analysis.

(b) Purposeful Availment

[The court determined that Nihon Kohden purposefully directed its conduct toward Rhode Island. Although Nihon Kohden's conduct occurred in Florida and California, its conduct that gave rise to the lawsuit was directed at Rhode Island and Nihon Kohden was aware of the employee agreement's Rhode Island provisions.]

(c) Reasonableness

[The court determined that exercising personal jurisdiction over Nihon Kohden in Rhode Island was reasonable.] . . .

---

[2] Neither Nihon Kohden nor Plant contests the district court's exercise of jurisdiction over Plant.

B. VENUE

Nihon Kohden argues that Rhode Island was not the proper venue for Astro-Med's lawsuit, and the district court should have either dismissed the claim or transferred the case to a different district in accordance with 28 U.S.C. §1404.[5]

1. DETERMINING VENUE

The applicable venue provision of Title 28 states [that a civil action may be brought in (1) a judicial district in which any defendant resides, if all defendants reside in the same state; (2) a judicial district in which a substantial part of the events or omissions giving rise to the claim occurred; or (3) if there is no district in which the action may otherwise be brought, a judicial district in which any defendant is subject to personal jurisdiction. 28 U.S.C. §1391.]

Although Nihon Kohden is a California business, it resides for purposes of venue in Rhode Island.[6] Plant is a resident of Florida. As the defendants reside in different states, subsection (1) does not apply.

Under subsection (2), the question becomes whether the District of Rhode Island is "a judicial district in which a substantial part of the events . . . giving rise to the claim occurred." *Id.* In determining whether Rhode Island is a district in which a substantial part of the events occurred, we look "not to a single 'triggering event' prompting the action, but to the entire sequence of events underlying the claim." *Uffner v. La Reunion Francaise, S.A.*, 244 F.3d 38, 42 (1st Cir. 2001). In addition, we do not focus on the actions of one party. Rather, our approach takes a "holistic view of the acts underlying a claim." *Id.* at 43 n.6. Furthermore, we are not required to determine the best venue, merely a proper venue. Thus, even though Plant was a resident of Florida when he was hired by Nihon Kohden, a California corporation, venue in Rhode Island may still be proper.

Astro-Med and Plant entered into an employment contract in Rhode Island, the district in which Astro-Med was headquartered, that contained the non-compete and non-disclosure clauses at issue here. With full knowledge of the Employee Agreement and its contents, Nihon Kohden hired away Plant, thereby interfering with Astro-Med's contract and misappropriating its trade secrets. Because Astro-Med was headquartered in Rhode Island, this district is one of the places where the tortious interference and misappropriation of trade secrets occurred and where the harms from these torts were felt. In addition, Rhode Island was the forum selected by the Employee Agreement to resolve disputes. Taken together, these facts constitute a substantial part of Astro-Med's claims against Nihon Kohden.

Further, Plant did not contest venue in Rhode Island and that portion of the lawsuit was, for venue purposes, going to proceed in Rhode Island. Thus, the convenience of the parties strongly militated in favor of retention of venue in Rhode Island. Given that a substantial part of Astro-Med's claims involved Rhode Island and proceeding in Rhode Island would not thwart the underlying purpose of the venue statute, we conclude that the district court did not

---

[5] Plant has not challenged the court's venue decision.

[6] With regard to corporations, 28 U.S.C. §1391(c) provides that, "[for] purposes of venue under this chapter, a defendant that is a corporation shall be deemed to reside in any judicial district in which it is subject to personal jurisdiction at the time the action is commenced." Because we have concluded that Nihon Kohden is subject to personal jurisdiction in Rhode Island, we can also conclude that Nihon Kohden, a corporation, "resides" in Rhode Island pursuant to 28 U.S.C. §1391(c).

err in refusing to dismiss the claims pending against Nihon Kohden in Rhode Island for improper venue.

2. TRANSFER OF VENUE

Nihon Kohden also appeals the district court's denial of its motion for change of venue under 28 U.S.C. §1404(a). "Section 1404(a) is intended to place discretion in the district court to adjudicate motions for transfer according to an 'individualized, case-by-case consideration of convenience and fairness.'" *Stewart Org., Inc. v. Ricoh Corp.*, 487 U.S. 22, 29 (1988) (quoting *Van Dusen v. Barrack*, 376 U.S. 612, 622 (1964)). Where the contract between the parties, here speaking of Astro-Med and Plant, contains a forum-selection clause, the clause "will be a significant factor that figures centrally in the District Court's calculus." *Royal Bed & Spring Co. v. Famossul Indústria e Comércio de Móveis Ltda.*, 906 F.2d 45, 51 (1st Cir. 1990). We review a "district court's decision on transfer of venue for an abuse of discretion." *Coady v. Ashcraft & Gerel*, 223 F.3d 1, 11 (1st Cir. 2000). Not only does the burden of proof rest with the party seeking to transfer; there is a "strong presumption in favor of the plaintiff's choice of forum." *Id.* In the circumstances of this case, the district court did not abuse its discretion in denying Nihon Kohden's motion for transfer of venue.

[In Parts C and D, the court rejected the defendants' additional arguments on appeal, including its contentions that the district court erred on judgment a matter of law, new trial, and evidentiary rulings.]

III. CONCLUSION

The district court judgment is affirmed.

Notes & Questions

1. The court's venue analysis in *Astro-Med* is not particularly difficult, but it gives you a chance to observe and internalize a step-by-step application of the federal venue statute. First, understand Nihon Kohden's venue objection at a common-sense level: The defendant was a California company that was sued over its hiring of an employee to work in Florida, and it objected that it should not be required to litigate the dispute in the District of Rhode Island. Next, apply the federal venue statute. Why was section 1 of the venue statute (§1391(b)(1)) inapplicable? Why did the court find venue proper under section 2 (§1391(b)(2))? Note, too, that section 3 (§1391(b)(3)) was inapplicable—do you see why?

2. For more practice applying the venue statute alongside other forum-selection doctrines, try this problem:

   a. A (a Connecticut domiciliary) and B (a New Jersey domiciliary) get into an auto accident in New York City. A sues B in U.S. District Court for the District of Connecticut, seeking $100,000 in damages, and serves B with process while B is in Connecticut on a business trip. First, does the court have subject matter jurisdiction? Second, does the court have personal jurisdiction? Third, is this district a proper venue? What are all the districts where this action properly could be brought?

b. Now, let's change the hypothetical case: There is a three-car collision in New York City among A, B, and C. A is domiciled in Connecticut, B is domiciled in New Jersey, and C is domiciled in New York. If A sues B and C in federal court, what are all the districts where the action properly could be brought?

3. Venue is a waivable objection. Thus, if a defendant does not object to the plaintiff's chosen district, then the court may go ahead and hear the case. Rule 12(h)(1) provides that the defense of improper venue, like the defense of personal jurisdiction, is waived if not asserted at the outset of the litigation. In *Astro-Med*, although the court noted that one of the defendants (Plant) did not object to venue, the other defendant (Nihon Kohden) raised its venue objection at the outset.

4. Where did Astro-Med originally file this lawsuit? (Hint: See footnote 1.) Recall from Chapter 9 that a defendant may remove a case from state court to federal court if federal subject matter jurisdiction exists, and that removal is a common way for cases to end up in federal court. Removal alters the venue analysis. The removal statute states that an action may be removed "to the district court of the United States for the district and division embracing the place where such action is pending." 28 U.S.C. §1441(a). In other words, if a defendant removes an action from the New York state court in Manhattan, the case goes to the Southern District of New York, regardless of whether section 1391 would have permitted that venue originally. The removal statute, not the general federal venue statute, governs venue upon removal. *See Polizzi v. Cowles Magazines, Inc.*, 345 U.S. 663 (1953).

If that is so, then how was Nihon Kohden able to challenge venue under section 1391? Why didn't the First Circuit simply state that venue was proper in the District of Rhode Island since the case was removed from Rhode Island state court? The answer is that Astro-Med's original complaint named only Plant as a defendant; after Plant removed the case to federal court, Astro-Med amended its complaint to name Nihon Kohden as an additional defendant. Nihon Kohden, as a newly added party, could object to venue under 28 U.S.C. §1391. *See, e.g., Lyngholm v. FedEx Ground Package Sys. Inc.*, 827 F. Supp. 2d 912 (S.D. Iowa 2011) (holding that a defendant who is joined after removal may object to venue under section 1391).

5. In addition to objecting to venue under section 1391, Nihon Kohden asked the court to transfer venue under section 1404. Defendants commonly make these motions in the alternative. That is, they move to dismiss under Rule 12(b)(3) for improper venue, or, in the alternative, to transfer venue to [a particular district] under 28 U.S.C. §1404. The idea is that even if the judge finds venue technically proper under section 1391, the judge may agree that another district would be more appropriate.

In *Astro-Med*, the motion to transfer venue was rather weak. Would the motion have been stronger if Nihon Kohden had been sued alone, rather than as a co-defendant with Plant?

6. One interesting twist on venue transfer involves choice of law. In Chapter 12, you will learn that federal courts in diversity cases must apply the same law that would be applied in state court. You also will learn that state courts do not always apply the law of their own state. A New York court might apply Alabama law (or Albania law) where appropriate, and each state has its own "choice-of-law rules" to determine which law to apply in a given situation. To put these two ideas together, a federal court sitting in diversity must apply the same law that would be applied by a state court in the state where it sits, but the law that would be applied might *not* be the law of that state. Now, let's add venue transfer to the picture. If a case is transferred from one federal district to a district in a different state, which state's law should the federal court apply? In *Van Dusen v. Barrack*, 376 U.S. 612 (1964), the Supreme Court held that if a case is transferred under section 1404, the transferee court should apply the same law that the transferor court would have applied. That way, when a court is deciding whether to transfer venue, it can focus on the location of the parties and witnesses, rather than worrying about whether transfer would alter the applicable substantive law.

   But here's the catch. The *Van Dusen* rule applies only to section 1404 venue transfer (transfer from a proper forum), not to section 1406 venue transfer (transfer from an improper forum). Do you see the logic behind this distinction? In the 1404 situation, where the plaintiff chose a court where jurisdiction and venue were proper, a transfer should not deprive the plaintiff of the benefit of the substantive law that would have applied in the proper forum chosen by the plaintiff. That is the *Van Dusen* rule. By contrast, the 1406 situation presents a different picture. If the plaintiff originally filed the case in an improper forum—one where the court lacks personal jurisdiction or where venue is wrong under the venue statute—then the plaintiff should not get the benefit of the substantive law that would be applied in that first court. Rather, after a section 1406 transfer, the transferee court treats the case as if it were filed initially in the transferee district.

7. In *Astro-Med*, the court pointed to a forum-selection clause as part of its reasoning to affirm the district court's denial of the motion to transfer venue. Was Nihon Kohden a party to the contract that contained the forum-selection clause? Why did the court nonetheless consider the clause relevant to its consideration of Nihon Kohden's motion to transfer venue?

   Parties to contracts often insert provisions that specify where disputes will be resolved if they arise. Some contracts provide for disputes to be resolved by private decision makers rather than by the courts; these are known as *arbitration clauses*. Other contracts select forums within the judicial system; these are known as *forum-selection clauses* or *choice-of-forum clauses*. We mentioned forum-selection clauses in Chapter 10 in the context of advance consent to personal jurisdiction. As the *Astro-Med* case shows, these clauses also come up in the context of venue transfer.

In *Astro-Med*, the forum-selection clause supported the plaintiff's choice of forum. Consider the reverse situation: A plaintiff files a lawsuit in a district other than the one named in a forum-selection clause, and a defendant points to the clause in support of its motion to transfer. In *Atlantic Marine Construction Co. v. U.S. District Court*, 571 U.S. 49 (2013), the Supreme Court held that a forum-selection clause may be enforced by a motion to transfer venue under section 1404. In *Atlantic Marine*, when a payment dispute erupted between a Virginia-based construction company and a Texas-based subcontractor, the subcontractor sued in federal court in Texas. The defendant pointed to their contract, which stated that all disputes between them "shall be litigated in the Circuit Court for the City of Norfolk, Virginia, or the United States District Court for the Eastern District of Virginia, Norfolk Division." *Id.* at 52. The Supreme Court held that when a party moves to transfer venue based on such a clause, "a valid forum-selection clause [should be] given controlling weight in all but the most exceptional cases." *Id.* at 58 (quoting *Stewart Organization v. Ricoh Corp.*, 487 U.S. 22, 33 (1988) (Kennedy, J., concurring)). The Court contrasted this situation with a transfer motion in the absence of any forum-selection clause, where a court would look at the convenience of the parties as well as public interest factors. When there is a valid forum-selection clause, the Court said, a judge should not defer to the plaintiff's choice of forum and should not consider the convenience of the parties. A judge may consider arguments about public interest factors, but the Court made it clear that it would be rare for these factors to overcome a valid forum-selection clause.

As to choice of law, the Supreme Court in *Atlantic Marine* held that the *Van Dusen* rule does not apply to transfers based on forum-selection clauses. *See id.* at 582-83. Rather than apply the choice-of-law rules of the plaintiff's original forum, a court should apply whatever substantive law would be applied by the state designated in the forum-selection clause, since the transferee is the forum that was selected by the parties. In other words, for purposes of the *Van Dusen* rule about choice of law after venue transfer, think of forum-selection-clause transfers essentially as transfers from improper forums, rather than transfers from proper forums, even though under *Atlantic Marine* it is technically a section 1404 motion as long as venue was "proper" under section 1391 in the original forum.

8. Having read this case about *federal* venue transfer, you might wonder whether a case can be transferred from a *state* court to a court in a different state. The answer is not yet, and not in the foreseeable future. Venue transfer occurs *within* a single judicial system. Cases can be transferred from one federal district court to another because those courts are part of the federal judicial system, just as cases can be transferred from one location to another within a single state's court system. Even if a case is moved from the District of Alaska to the Southern District of Florida, the transfer occurs within the single system of U.S. federal courts.

But in the state courts, no mechanism exists for transferring a case from one state to another. It could happen, in theory. A statute proposed in the 1990s—the Uniform Transfer of Litigation Act (UTLA)—would enable state courts to transfer cases to other states. But UTLA got little traction in state legislatures, so for now venue transfer occurs only within each system. Turning to the global version of the same question, the same obstacle exists—there is no mechanism to transfer a case from a court in the United States to a court in another country. Regarding both the interstate and international versions of the question, one can imagine a world in which judicial proceedings could be moved efficiently from one forum to another, but that is not the world we live in. While transfer within a single system such as the U.S. federal court system is relatively easy, transfer among separate sovereign entities is another matter entirely.

How, then, would a case filed in Arizona state court get to a more appropriate forum if none of the significant interests and evidence are in Arizona? How would a case filed in the United States get to a more appropriate forum if the interests and evidence are in another country? In such situations, *transfer* is not an option. Rather, the solution is to dismiss the case under the doctrine of forum non conveniens, which we explore in the next section.

D. FORUM NON CONVENIENS

You don't have to know Latin to figure out that *forum non conveniens* means that the forum is not convenient. The doctrine of forum non conveniens gives courts a basis to dismiss actions that should more appropriately be brought in a different court.

Forum non conveniens only comes into play when the more appropriate forum is an entirely different court system. This basically means two situations: a case filed in state court that ought to be brought in a different state or a case filed in the United States (either state or federal court) that ought to be brought in another country.

Further, forum non conveniens applies only if the first court has power over the case. As the Supreme Court said in *Gulf Oil Corp. v. Gilbert*, 330 U.S. 501, 504 (1947), "the doctrine of forum non conveniens can never apply if there is absence of jurisdiction or mistake of venue." If the court lacks jurisdiction, it should dismiss for lack of jurisdiction. If venue is improper, it should dismiss for improper venue (or, in federal court, it can transfer to a proper venue). In other words, recalling the "hoops" from the beginning of the chapter, if the plaintiff has not cleared the hoops of subject matter jurisdiction, personal jurisdiction, and venue, the case never gets to forum non conveniens. This doctrine is reserved for the situation where jurisdiction and venue are proper, but nonetheless there is another forum where the case should more appropriately be brought.

When applying the doctrine of forum non conveniens, federal courts follow the analysis laid out by the Supreme Court in *Piper Aircraft v. Reyno*, 454 U.S. 235

(1981). The *Piper Aircraft* case involved the crash of a small plane in the highlands of Scotland. The families of the Scottish victims brought a wrongful death action against the manufacturers of the airplane and the propeller. They filed the suit in California state court, even though the case had nothing to do with California. The defendants removed the case to federal court. The federal court in the Central District of California transferred the case to the Middle District of Pennsylvania because that was where the airplane manufacturer was located, and the propeller manufacturer was in nearby Ohio. But all of this forum maneuvering was merely a lead-up to the big question: Did the case belong in the United States at all? The defendants moved to dismiss on grounds of forum non conveniens, arguing that even though the federal court in Pennsylvania had subject matter jurisdiction, personal jurisdiction, and venue, the case really belonged in Scotland. The Supreme Court agreed that dismissal was warranted because Scotland was a more appropriate forum.

In reaching that decision, the Supreme Court in *Piper Aircraft* applied a three-part analysis to determine whether dismissal for forum non conveniens was proper: (1) Is there an adequate alternative forum? (2) Do private interest factors counsel in favor of dismissal? (3) Do public interest factors counsel in favor of dismissal?

First, is there an adequate alternative forum? If not, the court should deny the motion. The point of forum non conveniens is that the case should be brought somewhere else rather than where the plaintiff brought it. If you represent a defendant moving to dismiss on grounds of forum non conveniens, you had better be prepared to state where that somewhere else is and to show that the case can be brought there. In *Piper Aircraft*, the Supreme Court held that even if courts in Scotland might apply substantive law that is less favorable to the plaintiff, they offered an adequate alternative forum.

If an adequate forum exists, then the court decides whether to grant dismissal based on two sets of factors, addressing private and public interests. Regarding private interest factors in *Piper Aircraft*, the accident site was in Scotland, as were the relatives of the decedents and the witnesses who had trained the pilot and serviced the plane. Potential third-party defendants were in Scotland as well, including the airplane's owners, the airplane charter company, and the pilot's estate. This outweighed the private interest factors that pointed to Pennsylvania, including evidence concerning the manufacture of the airplane. The public interest factors in *Piper Aircraft* pointed both ways. Scotland had a strong interest in the dispute because it involved a local accident with local victims. But the United States and Pennsylvania had an interest in whether their own manufacturers produced defective products. The court, however, had its own interest in avoiding the complex choice-of-law issues that would have been presented if the case were litigated in the United States. Thus, the Supreme Court concluded that dismissal was appropriate.

In the end, the doctrine of forum non conveniens leaves courts a fair amount of discretion to decide whether another forum is clearly more convenient and appropriate. In the following case, consider each of the three parts of the test and identify the strongest arguments for and against dismissal.

HEFFERAN v. ETHICON ENDO-SURGERY, INC.
828 F.3d 488 (6th Cir. 2016)

Boggs, Circuit Judge.

Brandon and Sabine Hefferan, an American husband and German wife, have lived together in Germany since 2002. They seek damages for complications that arose when a surgical stapler manufactured by American corporation Ethicon Endo-Surgery allegedly malfunctioned during a surgery that Brandon Hefferan underwent in Germany. The district court granted Ethicon's motion to dismiss on the ground of forum non conveniens in favor of litigating in Germany. That decision was not an abuse of the court's discretion. We therefore affirm.

I

Since 2002, Brandon and Sabine Hefferan have lived as a married couple in Germany. In 2012, complications arose during a surgery that Brandon Hefferan underwent there. As a result, he has allegedly endured twenty follow-up surgeries and sustained severe permanent injuries. The Hefferans point the finger at a surgical stapler used during his initial procedure, which they claim malfunctioned. The stapler was manufactured in Mexico by Ethicon Endo-Surgery, which is incorporated and headquartered in Ohio.

In 2014, the Hefferans filed suit in the District of New Jersey against Ethicon and its sole shareholder Johnson & Johnson, which is incorporated and headquartered in New Jersey (collectively "Ethicon"). Ethicon moved to dismiss based on forum non conveniens. Instead of ruling on the motion, the New Jersey court transferred the case to the Southern District of Ohio. The Hefferans filed an amended complaint in the Ohio federal court stating claims for negligence, loss of consortium, and violations of Ohio product-liability law. Ethicon again moved to dismiss on forum non conveniens grounds in favor of proceeding in Germany. The district court granted the motion and the Hefferans appealed.

II

"Under the common law doctrine of forum non conveniens, a district court may decline to exercise its jurisdiction, even though the court has jurisdiction and venue." *Rustal Trading U.S., Inc. v. Makki*, 17 Fed. Appx. 331, 335 (6th Cir. 2001). Forum non conveniens dismissal involves a three-step analysis. After the court determines the degree of deference owed the plaintiff's forum choice, the defendant carries the burden of establishing an adequate alternative forum and showing that the plaintiff's chosen forum is unnecessarily burdensome based on public and private interests.

We review a district court's forum non conveniens determination for abuse of discretion. *Piper Aircraft Co. v. Reyno*, 454 U.S. 235, 257 (1981). . . . In forum non conveniens cases, the district court's decision deserves substantial deference when the court has considered all relevant public- and private-interest factors, and has balanced those factors reasonably.

The Hefferans appeal the grant of Ethicon's forum non conveniens motion on three grounds. They contend that: (1) their choice of forum was not accorded proper deference; (2) Germany is inadequate as an alternative forum; and (3) the court erroneously weighed the public- and private-interest factors. For reasons that follow, we uphold the district court's order.

A

Since each forum non conveniens case "turns on its facts," the Supreme Court has "repeatedly rejected the use of *per se* rules in applying the doctrine." *Am. Dredging Co. v. Miller*, 510 U.S. 443, 455 (1994). Nonetheless, we have found useful a few basic observations about a plaintiff's choice of forum. When a domestic plaintiff initiates a suit in his home forum, that choice is normally entitled great deference because it is presumptively convenient for the plaintiff. In contrast, a foreign plaintiff's forum choice is usually accorded less deference because the assumption of convenience is "much less reasonable." *Piper Aircraft*, 454 U.S. at 256. . . .

The deference normally accorded an American plaintiff's forum choice is based on the premise that holds in some, but not all, cases that the decision to bring suit in one's home forum is a matter of convenience. *Piper Aircraft*, 454 U.S. at 255-56. . . . Underlying the convenience presumption is a concern that defendants will uproot plaintiffs as a form of litigation strategy. The degree of deference owed a plaintiff's forum choice will inevitably vary with circumstances, even among plaintiffs who claim the United States as home. . . .

The district court acted within its discretion when it concluded that the Hefferans' forum choice is entitled to less deference than those of American plaintiffs living in the United States. A person's true home, the centuries-old concept of domicile, requires physical presence and intent to remain: that is, "residence at a particular place accompanied with positive or presumptive proof of an intention to remain there for an unlimited time." *Mitchell v.*

United States, 88 U.S. 21 (1874). Once established, domicile continues until it is superseded. The Hefferans advise that they "may move back to the United States." . . . [However], the Hefferans are still domiciled in Germany and had been for twelve years when they filed suit. What is more, Sabine Hefferan is a German citizen whose only apparent connection to the United States was a brief stint as a foreign exchange student over a dozen years ago. The Hefferans have not shown that their decision to file suit in the United States was motived by a legitimate reason such as convenience or the ability to obtain jurisdiction over the defendants rather than tactical advantage. The presumption of convenience therefore applies with less force to their choice of the United States as a forum.

B

An alternative forum is adequate when the defendant is amenable to process in another jurisdiction that may remedy the alleged harm. *Piper Aircraft*, 454 U.S. at 254-55. In extraordinary cases, an unfavorable difference in law is relevant to the inquiry. If the available remedy in the alternative forum is "clearly inadequate or unsatisfactory"—for example, the jurisdiction "does not permit litigation of the subject matter of the dispute"—dismissal would thwart the interest of justice. *Id.* at 254 & n.22. Law that is simply less favorable to the plaintiff in the alternative forum is not so extraordinary as to render that forum inadequate.

Ethicon has consented to service in Germany and the Hefferans do not contend that a German court would lack subject-matter jurisdiction over their claims. Nonetheless, the Hefferans maintain that Germany is an inadequate forum for two reasons.

1

First, Germany's legal system operates differently than that of the United States, in ways that make it an inadequate alternative forum according to the Hefferans. For example, the German system employs court-appointed experts, has lower average damages awards for pain and suffering than the United States, and lacks jury trials, party-directed pretrial discovery, and punitive damages. That a foreign legal system has its own procedures and idiosyncrasies is to be expected. The relevant question for purposes of forum non conveniens is whether those differences render the possible remedy so clearly inadequate that forcing a plaintiff to bring suit there would be unjust.

Like many civil-law jurisdictions, Germany relies on judges to investigate the facts, appoint experts, and serve as factfinder. To be sure, the investigatory and decision-making power of its judiciary means that tort claims are litigated differently in Germany than the United States. But the Hefferans do not show how that would limit their access to critical evidence, let alone deprive them of an adequate remedy if forced to bring suit there. Nor is a forum inadequate simply because of the likelihood of lesser damages. If that were a sufficient ground to defeat the motion, then a district court might never be within its power to dismiss a tort suit for forum non conveniens in favor of a German court. *See Smith Kline & French Lab. Ltd. v. Bloch*, 1 W.L.R. 730, 733 (C.A. 1983) (Eng.) ("As a moth is drawn to the light, so is a litigant drawn to the United States."). The differences in Germany's legal system do not reveal an alternative forum that provides a remedy "so clearly inadequate or unsatisfactory" that it is "no remedy at all." *Piper Aircraft*, 454 U.S. at 254.

2

Second, German law does not allow Sabine Hefferan to recover for loss of consortium. The district court concluded, based on a dictum from the unpublished opinion of another circuit that inability to pursue a claim for loss of consortium does not render a forum inadequate. We do not reach that question because we agree with the district court's alternative finding: Even if litigated in a United States district court, Sabine Hefferan's claim would be governed by German substantive law.

Like nearly all states, New Jersey recognizes a spouse's right to sue for loss of consortium. According to the Hefferans' expert (with whom Ethicon apparently agrees), German law does not permit a comparable claim when the victim-spouse survives. An actual conflict between New Jersey and German loss-of-consortium law raises the question whether dismissal in favor of proceedings in Germany would result in an unfavorable difference in law. Germany might be an inadequate alternative forum if dismissal deprives Sabine Hefferan of a remedy that would be available if the suit remained in the United States. *See Piper Aircraft*, 454 U.S. at 254-55. But that would be the case only if her right to recover would be determined by the law of a jurisdiction that does compensate for loss of consortium, rather than Germany's.

If the case remained in the United States, the district court would need to determine which jurisdiction's choice-of-law rules would dictate the law to be applied in deciding Sabine Hefferan's right to recover. In cases of voluntary transfer, the transferee forum applies the laws of the transferor court. *Ferens v. John Deere Co.*, 494 U.S. 516, 523 (1990). Thus, transfer of a diversity action between federal district courts pursuant to 28 U.S.C. §1404(a) does not change the applicable choice-of-law rules in American courts—in this case, those of New Jersey.

In personal-injury cases where a conflict of laws arises, New Jersey courts apply the "most significant relationship" test from the Restatement (Second) of Conflicts. . . . To determine the jurisdiction with the most significant relationship, [the court takes into account the place where the injury occurred; the place where the conduct causing the injury occurred; the domicile, residence, nationality, place of incorporation and place of business of the parties; and the place where the relationship, if any, between the parties is centered. Restatement (Second) of Conflict of Laws §145(2).] . . .

For purposes of forum non conveniens, the district properly anticipated that a New Jersey court would probably apply German law to this claim. For Sabine Hefferan's loss-of-consortium claim, most of the contacts are clear cut. The parties do not dispute that the alleged injury occurred in Germany where the Hefferans live. The residence-of-the-parties factor does not clearly point toward or away from Germany. Both appellees are incorporated and headquartered in the United States; Sabine Hefferan is a German citizen living in Germany. To the extent the parties have a relationship, Germany appears to be its locus. Although the stapler's alleged defect originated in the United States or Mexico, it was purchased and used in Germany. As to the "place where the conduct causing the injury occurred," the facts point away from Germany, but not necessarily toward the United States alone. . . . Ethicon's alleged misconduct in manufacturing a defective product occurred in Ohio and Mexico.

Germany has the most significant relationship to the parties and occurrence.

The injury occurred there and it is the place of the parties' relationship. Sabine Hefferan is a German citizen living at home. Although the defendants are United States corporations and the conduct causing the injury occurred at least partially in the United States, those contacts do not outweigh Germany's. Moreover, the interests of comity and judicial administration favor application of German law to a question of liability flowing from an injury that occurred within its borders caused by a product sold and used there. . . .

Litigating in Germany would not result in an unfavorable change in law for Sabine Hefferan on her loss-of-consortium claim because the federal court in Ohio would likely apply German law. This case therefore does not present those "rare circumstances" where a forum's "clearly unsatisfactory" remedy renders it an inadequate alternative. *Piper Aircraft*, 454 U.S. at 254 n.22.

C

The onus of showing that a plaintiff's choice of forum is unnecessarily burdensome falls on the defendant. That inquiry is guided by public- and private-interest factors set forth by the Supreme Court in *Gulf Oil Corp. v. Gilbert*, 330 U.S. 501 (1947). . . . The Hefferans argue that the district court abused its discretion because, on the whole, it erroneously weighed the factors. Although a different court may have given the factors different weight, the district court's balancing was not unreasonable.

1

Private-interest factors include "the relative ease of access to sources of proof; availability of compulsory process for attendance of unwilling, and the cost of obtaining attendance of willing, witnesses; possibility of view of premises, if view would be appropriate to the action; and all other practical problems that make trial of a case easy, expeditious and inexpensive." *Gulf Oil*, 330 U.S. at 508. To examine them, "the district court must scrutinize the substance of the dispute between the parties to evaluate what proof is required, and determine whether the pieces of evidence cited by the parties are critical, or even relevant, to the plaintiff's cause of action and to any potential defenses to the action." *Van Cauwenberghe v. Biard*, 486 U.S. 517, 528 (1988).

Ease of Access to Sources of Proof

The charge to examine the relative ease of access to sources of proof requires courts to dig into the substance of the dispute to assess the relevant evidence. The district court here found that accessing witnesses would be easier in Germany. Most of the Hefferans' proposed witnesses, including "all of the medical witnesses"—five specific physicians and the "doctors and medical providers" of two medical facilities—are in Germany. Ethicon disclosed only two witnesses with discoverable information relating to the stapler's design, application, and manufacture, both apparently located in the United States.

According to the Hefferans, the district court's analysis did not sufficiently focus on the issues likely to be tried. All of the Hefferans' claims center on Ethicon's liability for an allegedly defective stapler. That will require a close examination of the surgery and the harm attributable to the stapler as opposed to other potential causes. Accordingly, the district court properly took into account the location of potential witnesses involved in Brandon Hefferan's surgery and subsequent medical care. The court also properly determined that the surgeons who actually used the device were critical to the Hefferans' claims. . . .

Availability of Compulsory Process

This factor is "properly considered when witnesses are unwilling" to appear. *Duha v. Agium, Inc.*, 448 F.3d 867, 877 (6th Cir. 2006). However, it receives less weight "when it has not been alleged or shown that any witness would be unwilling to testify." *Id.* Ethicon speculates that if trial proceeded in federal district court, they would be "severely restricted" in obtaining the testimony of German witnesses. But they do not allege, much less show, that any witness is unwilling to testify, and that compulsory process is therefore needed.

Similarly, a foreign forum's more burdensome procedures for compelling the production of evidence receives less weight when the defendant has neither alleged nor shown the need to avail itself of that process. To be sure, "[m]utual knowledge of all the relevant facts gathered by both parties is essential to proper litigation." *Hickman v. Taylor*, 329 U.S. 495, 507 (1947). And the district court may have been correct that in foreign proceedings, it is easier to compel the production of evidence located in the United States through 28 U.S.C. §1782 than evidence in Germany through the Hague Evidence Convention. But the Hague Convention is not a "rule of exclusivity" that deprives district courts of other methods of obtaining evidence from abroad. *Société Nationale Industrielle Aérospatiale v. U.S. District Court*, 482 U.S. 522, 539 (1987). Germany's more taxing process for compelling discovery for foreign proceedings receives less weight than if Ethicon had shown that litigating in the United States would in fact produce an evidentiary imbalance.

Other Practical Problems

The list of private-interest factors includes a catch-all for "practical problems that make trial of a case easy, expeditious and inexpensive." *Gulf Oil*, 330 U.S. at 508. This includes a plaintiff's financial ability to practicably bring suit in the alternative forum. However, this factor receives less weight when a plaintiff does not demonstrate its inability to shoulder the cost of litigating in the alternative forum.

The Hefferans point to three costs that allegedly weigh against dismissal. First, their expert asserts that in German court, upfront filing fees can be significant for personal-injury claims. Although the Hefferans submitted evidence suggesting that German filing fees can be significant, they did not establish that these fees would be greater than the out-of-pocket costs they might incur if the case proceeded in the United States. Next, they point to a bond required of claimants who file suit in Germany but who do not have a "habitual place of residence" in the European Union. It is not clear that such a bond would even apply to the Hefferans, both of whom are domiciled in Germany. Besides, Ethicon has agreed to waive the requirement.

Last, the unavailability of contingency-fee arrangements in Germany will, by the Hefferans' estimation, "likely amount to at least tens of thousands of dollars" in additional costs for them. Contingency payment of legal fees certainly opens a litigation system to otherwise priced-out plaintiffs. However, the Hefferans do not support their assertion with evidence of the fees that they would avoid if the case proceeded in the United States.

The district court's conclusion was not in error. Relative ease of access to sources of proof and the availability of compulsory process for proceedings abroad support dismissal.

2

Public-interest factors include "administrative difficulties flowing from court congestion; the 'local interest in having localized controversies decided at home'; the interest in having the trial of a diversity case in a forum that is at home with the law that must govern the action; the avoidance of unnecessary problems in conflict of laws, or in the application of foreign law; and the unfairness of burdening citizens in an unrelated forum with jury duty." *Piper Aircraft*, 454 U.S. at 241 n.6 (quoting *Gulf Oil*, 330 U.S. at 509). To evaluate them, district courts "must consider the locus of the alleged culpable conduct, often a disputed issue, and the connection of that conduct to the plaintiff's chosen forum." *Van Cauwenberghe*, 486 U.S. at 528. These factors will typically "thrust the court into the merits of the underlying dispute." *Id.*

Local Interest in Deciding a Local Controversy

The primary local-interest considerations are the parties' connections to the local forum and the location of the injury. For example, when a case pits an American manufacturer against foreign nationals injured at home by a product sold there, the "incremental deterrence" of trial in the United States usually cannot overcome the foreign forum's interest in the dispute. *Piper Aircraft*, 454 U.S. at 260. Adding an American plaintiff to the mix does not necessarily tip the scales. . . .

Here, the stapler's design and manufacture by an American company does not outweigh Germany's interest in the controversy, to say nothing of the Hefferans'

German domicile. The country where a product is sold, used, and regulated has a strong interest, often an insurmountably strong interest, in litigation involving that product.

Conflict of Laws

As with the loss-of-consortium claim, Part II.B.2, *supra*, the Hefferans' right to recover on their other claims would likely be decided by German law. The United States does have an additional contact to Brandon Hefferan. He is an American citizen. Yet like his wife, Brandon Hefferan lives and works in Germany. In light of his longtime German domicile, Brandon Hefferan's American citizenship does not increase United States contacts enough to give it a greater interest in his claims. The district court correctly concluded that the interest of proceeding in a forum whose law will decide the parties' rights and liabilities supports dismissal. . . .

III

Where a district court has considered all relevant public- and private-interest factors, and has reasonably balanced those factors, its decision deserves substantial deference. The court here correctly concluded that Ethicon met its burden of showing that if the case remained in the Southern District of Ohio, the vexation it would endure and trouble to the court would be out of proportion to the Hefferans' minimal convenience.

The district court did not specify whether its dismissal was with or without prejudice. However, when the appropriate disposition is well established, we read ambiguity according to that convention. It is well established that the appropriate disposition of a granted forum non conveniens motion is dismissal without prejudice to filing in the alternative forum. We therefore read the district court's order as such and AFFIRM without prejudice to the case being refiled in Germany.

Notes & Questions

1. Think about how many locations are involved in this dispute. What is Brandon Hefferan's domicile? His national citizenship? How about Sabine Hefferan? Where is Ethicon incorporated and headquartered? Where is Johnson & Johnson incorporated and headquartered? Where was the stapler manufactured? Where did the surgery take place? Are some of these questions more significant than others for purposes of determining an appropriate forum? In thinking about the relative significance of these questions, do not lose sight of the actual dispute between the parties and the issues likely to be litigated in the action.

2. We have seen cases where parties, predictably, have sought a "home court" advantage. In *Astro-Med v. Nihon Kohden*, for example, Astro-Med filed its lawsuit at home in Rhode Island and the California defendant objected to venue. And recall from Chapter 10 that in *Burger King v. Rudzewicz*, Burger King filed the case in its home state of Florida and the Michigan defendant objected to personal jurisdiction. But, as you see in *Hefferan*, parties do not always prefer their home court. In *Hefferan*, who chose the U.S. forum? Who argued that the case belongs in Germany instead of the United States?

3. The *Hefferan* court applied the three-part test of *Piper Aircraft v. Reyno*. First, is there an adequate alternative forum? In some cases, parties dispute the fundamental adequacy of the legal system in the alternative forum, particularly if the other country's legal processes are underdeveloped or if the system is mired in corruption. Germany's court system was not susceptible to this type of argument in *Hefferan*. What arguments did the Hefferans muster to suggest that Germany would not provide an adequate forum? Why did the court reject these arguments? The adequacy of an alternative forum could be questioned if the court lacks personal jurisdiction over the defendants or if the case would be barred under the statute of limitations. As a practical matter, however, these rarely present a problem because defendants are generally willing to waive personal jurisdiction and timeliness defenses in the alternative forum if doing so will persuade the court to grant the dismissal on grounds of forum non conveniens. Note that in *Hefferan*, Ethicon consented to service in Germany and agreed to waive the German requirement that certain plaintiffs post a bond.

4. Next, the *Hefferan* court examined the private interest factors and public interest factors. Which way did the private interest factors cut? Which way did the public interest factors cut? Courts often mention deference to plaintiff's choice of forum as a significant factor, either as a private interest factor or as a separate consideration. Why didn't the *Hefferan* court defer to plaintiffs' chosen forum? In *Piper Aircraft*, the Supreme Court named a number of private and public factors to consider:

> The factors pertaining to the private interests of the litigants included the "relative ease of access to sources of proof; availability of compulsory process for attendance of unwilling, and the cost of obtaining attendance of willing, witnesses; possibility of view of premises, if view would be appropriate to the action; and all other practical problems that make trial of a case easy, expeditious and inexpensive." The public factors bearing on the question included the administrative difficulties flowing from court congestion; the "local interest in having localized controversies decided at home"; the interest in having the trial of a diversity case in a forum that is at home with the law that must govern the action; the avoidance of unnecessary problems in conflict of laws, or in the application of foreign law; and the unfairness of burdening citizens in an unrelated forum with jury duty.

Piper Aircraft v. Reyno, 454 U.S. 235, 241 n.6 (1981) (quoting *Gulf Oil v. Gilbert*, 330 U.S. 501, 508-09 (1947)). The *Hefferan* court quoted much of this language in its analysis. Which of these factors mattered most in *Hefferan*?

5. The Hefferans are a global couple living in an increasingly global world. Think about the problem in broader perspective. As the world shrinks and particularly as global commerce grows, how should legal doctrine keep up? Human interactions and economic reality transcend state and national borders, but court systems continue to exist largely on a state-by-state, nation-by-nation basis. In such a world, given that plaintiffs often seek adjudication in U.S. courts for claims that arise elsewhere, consider several configurations: Under what

circumstances is it appropriate to allow a U.S. plaintiff to sue a foreign defendant in a U.S. court? How about a foreign plaintiff suing a U.S. defendant? Finally, how about a foreign plaintiff suing a foreign defendant? Does the answer depend mostly on where the dispute arose, rather than on who the parties are? Under what circumstances, if any, is it appropriate for a U.S. court to adjudicate an action between a foreign plaintiff and a foreign defendant on a dispute that arose outside of the country?

THE BIG PICTURE

Why did the plaintiffs in *Hefferan* prefer a United States forum? And why did the defendants prefer to litigate in Germany? Similarly, why did the plaintiffs in *Piper Aircraft* prefer a United States forum, and why did the defendants prefer to litigate in Scotland? The *Hefferan* court quotes Lord Denning's famous dictum, "As a moth is drawn to the light, so is a litigant drawn to the United States." Although it is easy to exaggerate the differences, and there has been some convergence in recent years, most lawyers would agree that U.S. courts provide a number of perceived advantages to plaintiffs, as compared with the courts of most other countries. Depending on the case, the advantages may include jury trial, broad discovery, contingent fees, class actions, and relatively large awards of compensatory and sometimes punitive damages. Also, U.S. law includes certain legal doctrines favorable to plaintiffs, such as strict liability, although U.S. courts do not necessarily apply their own substantive law to foreign disputes. Because of these features of U.S. courts, foreign plaintiffs often choose to sue in the United States rather than in their home countries, and defendants often fight to get out. Forum non conveniens, along with personal jurisdiction, is an important doctrinal battleground on which these forum wars are fought.

CHAPTER 12

Choice of Law

A. INTRODUCTION TO CHOICE OF LAW

Up until this point, you have learned that a case could be brought in a number of different forums depending upon a combination of court authority and party preference. Getting a dispute to a particular and appropriate court, however, does not necessarily answer the critical question of what substantive law will apply.

While you might wonder how any judge can ever apply the law of some other government, courts apply the laws of other sovereigns all the time. In appropriate cases, New Mexico courts apply Arizona law. Federal courts apply state law. State courts apply federal law. U.S. courts apply French law. And so on. Having learned subject matter jurisdiction, you know that federal question jurisdiction is largely *concurrent* jurisdiction; those cases can be brought either in federal court or state court. State courts therefore often decide cases governed by federal substantive law. Having learned about diversity jurisdiction and supplemental jurisdiction, you know that federal courts often adjudicate state law claims, and therefore must apply state law. And having learned about personal jurisdiction, you know that there can be multiple states where a dispute could be adjudicated, so courts often handle claims that require application of another state's substantive law. When a court faces a choice between which of two or more different jurisdictions' laws to apply, that court is said to be faced with a "choice-of-law" problem.

The study of conflict of laws, which grapples with these choice-of-law questions, is the subject of an upper-level course at most law schools. For purposes of learning civil procedure, however, you should be aware of a few basic principles. These principles concern both the choice among different states' laws ("horizontal" choice-of-law questions), which we will cover briefly, and the choice between federal and state law ("vertical" choice-of-law questions), which we will address in some detail.

A horizontal conflict of law is a conflict involving the rules of two or more states. These issues arise both at the *interstate* level and at the *international* level. Thus, a court may face a choice-of-law decision between New York and California law or a choice-of-law decision between New York and Canadian law. To resolve a horizontal conflict of law, the court must look to what are known as "choice-of-law rules" to determine which of the various states' substantive laws to apply. In the United States, these choice-of-law rules are primarily matters of state law, and the court faced with a choice-of-law problem applies the choice-of-law rules of the state in which it sits. Do not let the phrase "choice-of-law rules" deceive you into thinking these rules are codified like rules of civil procedure or rules of evidence. For the most part, choice-of-law rules are part of each state's common law, embodied in judicial decisions.

States have adopted different choice-of-law approaches. Broadly, these choice-of-law rules can be broken down into two categories. There are traditional approaches, most prominently the "vested rights" approach embodied in the First Restatement of the Law of Conflict of Laws (Restatement (First) (1935)), and various and more flexible modern approaches.

According to the traditional "vested rights" approach, a legal right vests in the place where a particular event happens. Thus, if a contract was executed in Georgia, under the "vested rights" approach, the laws of Georgia govern that contract. Similarly, if a New York resident commits the tort of battery in Connecticut, the laws of Connecticut govern the dispute that arose from that battery. The "vested rights" approach is often referred to by shorthand Latin names such as *lex loci contractus* (the place of the contract, for contract suits); *lex loci delicti* (the place of the wrong, for tort suits); *lex loci incorporationis* (the place of incorporation, for issues of corporate law), *lex loci rei sitae* or *lex situs* (the place where property is located, for property disputes), and so on for other sorts of substantive issues.

Some cases are simple enough for the vested rights approach to yield straightforward answers. In a negligence lawsuit about an automobile accident, the relevant tort law almost certainly is the law of the state where the accident occurred. In a dispute about ownership of real property, the relevant property law almost certainly is the law of the state where the property is situated. And in a dispute over corporate governance, the relevant corporate law almost certainly is the law of the state where the entity is incorporated.

But plenty of cases involve multiple states and raise harder questions under the traditional approach. To illustrate, assume that Tom's Toasters manufactures toaster ovens in Maryland. Peter Parker bought one of these toasters in Delaware, and he was injured when it caught fire in his home in Virginia. Parker sues Tom's Toasters for products liability in Virginia state court, alleging that the toaster oven was defectively manufactured. The choice-of-law rules of the state of Virginia follow the traditional approach for torts—*lex loci delicti*. Therefore the court must apply the law of the place of the *delict*, or the wrong. But what is the place of the wrong? Is it Virginia, where the toaster caught fire and injured Parker? Or is it Maryland, where the allegedly defective toaster was manufactured? Or is it Delaware, where Parker bought the toaster? Answering this question may depend on how one conceives of the tort— whether the wrong is making a defective product, selling a defective product, or causing an injury. Declaring a simple rule of *lex loci delicti* alone does not resolve the question.

Indeed, the traditional "vested rights" approach revealed itself to be problematic. Simple rules sometimes fail to capture the complex interests at stake. The First Restatement, for example, directed courts to apply the law of the state in which the last act required to complete the cause of action occurred, but the "last act" test could lead to arbitrary results. With the toaster oven example, should Peter Parker's claim be governed by Virginia law and every other consumer's claim be governed by the law of wherever they suffered injury, even though the product was manufactured in Maryland? Would Maryland not have a strong interest in having its laws govern the manufacture of products within its borders? Under the *lex loci delicti* approach, if the last act is what matters, Tom's Toasters is potentially subject to the varying tort laws of all 50 states.

Though a few states still follow the traditional "vested rights" approach, most states have abandoned that approach in favor of various modern approaches. As a brief overview, three of the principal modern approaches bear mention here. First, some states use a *governmental interest analysis* approach, now embraced by the Draft Restatement (Third) of Conflict of Laws. Under this approach, the court must first determine the governmental policy expressed by the law of the forum. The second step is then to apply forum law if doing so would promote that governmental purpose. However, if applying forum law in a given case would *not* promote the governmental interest, the court should instead apply the law of the other relevant jurisdiction if doing so would further the relevant governmental policy behind *that state's* law. This approach is not widely used.

Instead, the most popular approach to choice-of-law problems is that of the Restatement (Second) of Conflict of Laws, which provides a flexible set of choice-of-law rules that give judges a fair bit of discretion in selecting which substantive law to apply. For example, for torts, the Second Restatement requires application of the law of the state with the "most significant relationship" with the occurrence and with the parties. Restatement (Second) of Conflict of Laws §145. For contracts, the Second Restatement expresses a preference for the law that would validate the contract at issue, as well as any choice-of-law provision contained in that contract. Restatement (Second) of Conflict of Laws §§187-188. The Second Restatement provides similar principles for other areas of law.

In addition, some states apply a third approach, known as the *better law* approach, under which judges are supposed to choose the "better" law, explaining their choice with criteria such as avoidance of unfair surprise, economic benefits, uniformity, advancement of the forum state's interests, and other rational criteria. Finally, some states apply a combination of these approaches.

Regardless of which choice-of-law rules a particular state follows, all courts are bound by outer constitutional limits in determining which substantive law will apply. The key constitutional limitations on the choice-of-law process are the Due Process Clause and the Full Faith and Credit Clause. The Due Process Clause and Equal Protection Clause of the Fourteenth Amendment provide: "[N]or shall any State deprive any person of life, liberty, or property, without due process of law; nor deny to any person within its jurisdiction the equal protection of the laws...." U.S. Const. amend. XIV, §1. The essence of the due process limitation on choice of law is that a state must have some connection to the dispute in order to apply its own law to the case. *See, e.g., Phillips Petroleum Co. v. Shutts*, 472 U.S. 797 (1985). The Full Faith and Credit Clause provides: "Full Faith and Credit shall be given in each State to the public Acts, records and judicial Proceedings of every other State. . . ." U.S. Const. art. IV, §1. Generally, the due process and full faith and credit analysis in the choice-of law context has merged. In one case, the Supreme Court suggested that the two clauses might do independent work in the choice-of-law context. *Order of Commercial Travelers v. Wolfe*, 331 U.S. 586 (1947) (holding that the Full Faith and Credit Clause required a state to apply a foreign state's law instead of its own law, even when there were minimum contacts with the forum that satisfied due process, on the grounds that the foreign state had compelling interests in the dispute—namely, significantly stronger contacts with the action as well as a significantly stronger interest in having its law apply). Since then, however, the Court has largely rejected the notion that a state with enough contacts to satisfy due process could be prevented by the Full Faith and Credit Clause from applying its own law to a dispute. The application of forum law meets constitutional muster so long as its choice of law "is neither arbitrary nor fundamentally unfair." *Allstate Ins. Co. v. Hague*, 449 U.S. 302 (1981).

STRATEGY SESSION

As you have already learned, there are tactical considerations in deciding where to file a complaint. Choice-of-law rules are yet another one. Consider one (oversimplified) example. Suppose you represent a plaintiff with a product-liability claim against a manufacturer. The product was manufactured in state A and your client was injured at home in state B. The tort law of state B applies strict liability to such claims, which is good for your client. The tort law of state A does not apply strict liability, so you would have to prove negligence, which is worse for your client. Obviously, you want state B's tort law to apply. Does that mean you should file the lawsuit in state B? Not necessarily. Remember that a state court does not automatically apply the substantive laws of its own state, but rather follows its state's choice-of-law rules. When you research the choice-of-law cases in each state, you find that in product-liability cases, courts of state A generally apply the law of the state where the injury occurred, while courts of state B apply the law of the state where the product was manufactured. Thus, in order to get state B's tort law applied, you are better off filing the action in state A. This choice-of-law consideration would go into the hopper along with other questions—where can you get personal jurisdiction over the manufacturer, how important is it to your client to sue in the client's home state, etc.—as you decide where to file the action. The bottom line is the choice of law matters, and to obtain your preferred substantive law, you do not simply file in the state whose law you prefer, but rather in the state whose choice-of-law rules are most likely to point to the law you prefer.

In contrast with horizontal choice of law, which involves conflicts between the substantive laws of one or more states in state or federal court, vertical choice of law involves the choice between federal and state law. More specifically, it involves whether a federal court should apply federal law or state law. Keep in mind that diversity jurisdiction permits federal courts to hear many claims that do not arise under federal law. Vertical choice-of-law problems are usually dealt with through what is known as the *Erie* doctrine, named for the famous case of *Erie Railroad v. Tompkins*, 304 U.S. 64 (1938). The remainder of this chapter is devoted to this topic.

B. THE *ERIE* DOCTRINE

(1) Introduction to the *Erie* Doctrine

Suppose you are litigating a common law case and the precedents in the courts of the state go against your client. Can you avoid those unfavorable precedents by litigating in federal court instead of state court (assuming the federal court has subject matter jurisdiction over the case)? That is the initial question behind the *Erie* doctrine. *See Erie Railroad v. Tompkins*, 304 U.S. 64 (1938). The basic answer to that question is no—you cannot avoid state law by litigating in federal court. Unless some specific federal statute or rule applies, the federal court must apply state substantive law. Federal courts apply federal law in matters governed by federal statutes, such as securities, antitrust, and civil rights cases. They apply state law not only in cases under state statutes, but also in common law cases such as contract, tort, or property disputes.

Beyond these very basic precepts, however, is a much more complicated picture. Even though federal courts are bound to apply state substantive law, the federal courts apply their own procedural rules. Attorneys in federal court therefore must know how to tell the difference between substance and procedure, which is far trickier than you might expect. This chapter teaches you how to deal with these vertical choice-of-law problems. In so doing, it forces you to grapple at a more sophisticated level with the question we opened with in Chapter 1: What is civil procedure?

Most of what a competent attorney needs to know about the *Erie* doctrine can be expressed in a single sentence: On state law claims, federal courts apply state substantive law and federal procedural law. As a practical matter, that covers roughly 90 percent of what lawyers need to know about the *Erie* doctrine. Most of this chapter addresses the remaining 10 percent—the situations in which it is not obvious whether a federal court will apply state or federal law in federal court.

In most cases, the *Erie* question is not terribly difficult. Suppose you are litigating a negligence case involving a car accident in Nashville, Tennessee, and the case is brought in the federal court for the Middle District of Tennessee based on diversity jurisdiction. According to the *Erie* doctrine, the federal court must apply the substantive tort law of Tennessee. Thus, if there are substantive law questions such as the standard of care, the defense of comparative fault, or caps on damages, the federal court will look to the statutes and common law decisions of Tennessee. As a federal tribunal, however, the federal court will use federal procedural law. For things like pleading requirements, discovery, summary judgment, jury selection, trial processes, and the time limit for filing an appeal, the court will look to the Federal Rules of Civil Procedure and other federal procedural law.

Some situations and some cases involve a more complex and subtle analysis, however. These are the cases that have proven difficult for the Supreme Court over the years, and which can be difficult to understand as attorneys. To be able to handle these harder cases, you need to understand the *Erie* doctrine as it has developed through a series of Supreme Court decisions.

(2) The Development of the *Erie* Doctrine

Before the *Erie* decision in 1938, there was almost a century of jurisprudence that established the complete opposite principle regarding the application of state law (or not) in federal court. In 1842, the Supreme Court decided *Swift v. Tyson*, 41 U.S. 1, which involved a commercial law dispute in federal court in New York. The federal court had subject matter jurisdiction based on diversity of citizenship. The parties disputed an issue of contract law—specifically, whether the discharge of a debt can be consideration for a contract. The precedents in New York's state courts said no. The question was whether the federal judge was required to follow the New York precedents, as opposed to following federal court precedents or making up his own mind about the legal issue. In other words, must the federal court apply state common law?

The Rules of Decision Act (RDA), 28 U.S.C. §1652, a federal statute that has been around since 1789, seemed to answer the question:

> The laws of the several states, except where the Constitution or treaties of the United States or Acts of Congress otherwise require or provide, shall be regarded as rules of decision in civil actions in the courts of the United States, in cases where they apply.

If the "laws of the several states" must be used as the "rules of decision" in federal courts, then does it not follow that the federal court in *Swift* must follow the New York precedents about contract law?

According to the Supreme Court in *Swift*, the answer was no. The Court held that "laws of the several states" in the RDA meant statutes and regulations of the states, but *not* general common law (like contract, tort, and property law). Instead, the federal courts should "ascertain upon general reasoning and legal analogies . . . what is the just rule furnished by the principles of commercial law to govern the case." *Swift*, 41 U.S. at 19. In other words, the federal courts should engage in their own common law reasoning and generate their own body of common law precedents. In 1938, everything changed.

ERIE RAILROAD CO. v. TOMPKINS
304 U.S. 64 (1938)

Justice BRANDEIS delivered the opinion of the Court.

The question for decision is whether the oft-challenged doctrine of *Swift v. Tyson* shall now be disapproved.

Tompkins, a citizen of Pennsylvania, was injured on a dark night by a passing freight train of the Erie Railroad Company ("The Erie") while walking along its right of way at Hughestown in that state. He claimed that the accident occurred through negligence in the operation, or maintenance, of the train; that he was rightfully on the premises as licensee because on a commonly used beaten footpath which ran for a short distance alongside the tracks; and that he was struck by something which looked like a door projecting from one of the moving cars. To enforce that claim he brought an action in the federal court for Southern New York, which had jurisdiction because the company is a corporation of that state. It denied liability; and the case was tried by a jury.

The Erie insisted that its duty to Tompkins was no greater than that owed to a trespasser. It contended that its duty to Tompkins, and hence its liability, should be determined in accordance with the Pennsylvania law; that under the law of Pennsylvania, as declared by its highest court, persons who use pathways along the railroad right of way—that is, a longitudinal pathway as distinguished from a crossing—are to be deemed trespassers; and that the railroad is not liable for injuries to undiscovered trespassers resulting from its negligence, unless it be wanton or willful. Tompkins denied that any such rule had been established by the decisions of the Pennsylvania courts; and contended that, since there was no statute of the state on the subject, the railroad's duty and liability is to be determined in federal courts as a matter of general law.

The trial judge refused to rule that the applicable law precluded recovery. The jury brought in a verdict of $30,000; and the judgment entered thereon was affirmed by the Circuit Court of Appeals, which held that it was unnecessary to consider whether the law of Pennsylvania was as contended, because the question was one not of local, but of general, law, and that

> upon questions of general law the federal courts are free, in absence of a local statute, to exercise their independent judgment as to what the law is; and it is well settled that the question of the responsibility of a railroad for injuries caused by its servants is one of general law.... Where the public has made open and notorious use of a railroad right of way for a long period of time and without objection, the company owes to persons on such permissive pathway a duty of care in the operation of its trains.... It is likewise generally recognized law that a jury may find that negligence exists toward a pedestrian using a permissive path on the railroad right of way if he is hit by some object projecting from the side of the train. 90 F.2d 603, 604.

The Erie had contended that application of the Pennsylvania rule was required, among other things, by Section 34 of the Federal Judiciary Act of September 24, 1789, which provides: "The laws of the several States, except where the Constitution, treaties, or statutes of the United States otherwise require or provide, shall be regarded as rules of decision in trials at common law, in the courts of the United States, in cases where they apply." 28 U.S.C. §725.

Because of the importance of the question whether the federal court was free to disregard the alleged rule of the Pennsylvania common law, we granted certiorari.

Swift v. Tyson, 16 Pet. 1, 18 (1842), held that federal courts exercising jurisdiction on the ground of diversity of citizenship need not, in matters of general jurisprudence, apply the unwritten law of the state as declared by its highest court; that they are free to exercise an independent judgment as to what the common law of the state is—or should be; and [as Justice Story states in *Swift*]:

> the true interpretation of the 34th section limited its application to state laws, strictly local, that is to say, to the positive statutes of the state, and the construction thereof adopted by the local tribunals, and to rights and titles to things having a permanent locality. . . . It never has been supposed by us, that the section did apply, or was intended to apply, to questions of a more general nature, not at all dependent upon local statutes or local usages of a fixed and permanent operation, as, for example, to the construction of ordinary contracts or other written instruments, and especially to questions of general commercial law, where the state tribunals are called upon to . . . ascertain, upon general reasoning and legal analogies, what is the true exposition of the contract or instrument, or what is the just rule furnished by the principles of commercial law to govern the case.

The Court in applying the rule of section 34 to equity cases said: "The statute, however, is merely declarative of the rule which would exist in the absence of the statute." *Mason v. United States*, 260 U.S. 545, 559 (1923). The federal courts assumed, in the broad field of "general law," the power to declare rules of decision which Congress was without power to enact as statutes. Doubt was repeatedly expressed as to the correctness of the construction given section 34, and as to the soundness of the rule which it introduced. But it was the more recent research of a competent scholar, who examined the original document, which established that the construction given to it by the Court was erroneous; and that the purpose of the section was merely to make certain that, in all matters except those in which some federal law is controlling, the federal courts exercising jurisdiction in diversity of citizenship cases would apply as their rules of decision the law of the state, unwritten as well as written. Charles Warren, *New Light on the History of the Federal Judiciary Act of 1789* (1923), 37 Harv. L. Rev. 49, 51-52, 81-88, 108.

Criticism of the doctrine became widespread after the decision of *Black & White Taxicab & Transfer Co. v. Brown & Yellow Taxicab & Transfer Co.*, 276 U.S. 518 (1928). There, Brown & Yellow, a Kentucky corporation owned by Kentuckians, and the Louisville & Nashville Railroad, also a Kentucky corporation, wished that the former should have the exclusive privilege of soliciting passenger and baggage transportation at the Bowling Green, Kentucky, Railroad station; and that the Black & White, a competing Kentucky corporation, should be prevented from interfering with that privilege. Knowing that such a contract would be void under the common law of Kentucky, it was arranged that the Brown

& Yellow reincorporate under the law of Tennessee, and that the contract with the railroad should be executed there. The suit was then brought by the Tennessee corporation in the federal court for Western Kentucky to enjoin competition by the Black & White; an injunction issued by the District Court was sustained by the Court of Appeals; and this Court, citing many decisions in which the doctrine of *Swift v. Tyson* had been applied, affirmed the decree.

Experience in applying the doctrine of *Swift v. Tyson* had revealed its defects, political and social; the benefits expected to flow from the rule did not accrue. Persistence of state courts in their own opinions on questions of common law prevented uniformity; and the impossibility of discovering a satisfactory line of demarcation between the province of general law and that of local law developed a new well of uncertainties.

On the other hand, the mischievous results of the doctrine had become apparent. Diversity of citizenship jurisdiction was conferred in order to prevent apprehended discrimination in state courts against those not citizens of the state. *Swift v. Tyson* introduced grave discrimination by noncitizens against citizens. It made rights enjoyed under the unwritten "general law" vary according to whether enforcement was sought in the state or in the federal court; and the privilege of selecting the court in which the right should be determined was conferred upon the noncitizen. Thus, the doctrine rendered impossible equal protection of the law. . . .

The injustice and confusion incident to the doctrine of *Swift v. Tyson* have been repeatedly urged as reasons for abolishing or limiting diversity of citizenship jurisdiction. Other legislative relief has been proposed [to abrogate the doctrine of *Swift v.*

Tyson]. If only a question of statutory construction were involved, we should not be prepared to abandon a doctrine so widely applied through nearly a century. But the unconstitutionality of the course pursued has now been made clear, and compels us to do so.

Except in matters governed by the Federal Constitution or by acts of Congress, the law to be applied in any case is the law of the state. And whether the law of the state shall be declared by its Legislature in a statute or by its highest court in a decision is not a matter of federal concern. There is no federal general common law. Congress has no power to declare substantive rules of common law applicable in a state whether they be local in their nature or "general," be they commercial law or a part of the law of torts. And no clause in the Constitution purports to confer such a power upon the federal courts. . . .

The fallacy underlying the rule declared in *Swift v. Tyson* is made clear by Mr. Justice Holmes [in *Black & White Taxicab*, 276 U.S. at 532-36]. The doctrine rests upon the assumption that there is "a transcendental body of law outside of any particular State but obligatory within it unless and until changed by statute," that federal courts have the power to use their judgment as to what the rules of common law are; and that in the federal courts "the parties are entitled to an independent judgment on matters of general law":

But law in the sense in which courts speak of it today does not exist without some definite authority behind it. The common law so far as it is enforced in a State, whether called common law or not, is not the common law generally but the law of that State existing by the authority of that State.... The authority and only authority is the State, and if that be so, the voice adopted by the State as its own [whether it be of its Legislature or of its Supreme Court] should utter the last word.

Thus the doctrine of *Swift v. Tyson* is, as Mr. Justice Holmes said, "an unconstitutional assumption of powers by the Courts of the United States which no lapse of time or respectable array of opinion should make us hesitate to correct." [*Id.*] In disapproving that doctrine we do not hold unconstitutional section 34 of the Federal Judiciary Act of 1789 or any other act of Congress. We merely declare that in applying the doctrine this Court and the lower courts have invaded rights which in our opinion are reserved by the Constitution to the several states.

... The Circuit Court of Appeals ruled that the question of liability is one of general law; and on that ground declined to decide the issue of [Pennsylvania] state law. As we hold this was error, the judgment is reversed and the case remanded to it for further proceedings in conformity with our opinion.

Reversed.

Justice REED (concurring in part).

I concur in the conclusion reached in this case, in the disapproval of the doctrine of *Swift v. Tyson*, and in the reasoning of the majority opinion, except in so far as it relies upon the unconstitutionality of the "course pursued" by the federal courts.

The "doctrine of *Swift v. Tyson*," as I understand it, is that the words "the laws," as used in section 34, line 1, of the Federal Judiciary Act of September 24, 1789, 28 U.S.C.A. §725, do not include[] in their meaning "the decisions of the local tribunals." Mr. Justice Story, in deciding that point, said, "Undoubtedly, the decisions of the local tribunals upon such subjects are entitled to, and will receive, the most deliberate attention and respect of this court; but they cannot furnish positive rules, or conclusive authority, by which our own judgments are to be bound up and governed." *Swift v. Tyson*, 41 U.S. 1 (1842)....

The "unconstitutional" course referred to in the majority opinion is apparently the ruling in *Swift v. Tyson* that the supposed omission of Congress to legislate as to the effect of decisions leaves federal courts free to interpret general law for themselves. I am not at all sure whether, in the absence of federal statutory direction, federal courts would be compelled to follow state decisions. There was sufficient doubt about the matter in 1789 to induce the first Congress to legislate. No former opinions of this Court have passed upon it. Mr. Justice Holmes evidently saw nothing "unconstitutional" which required the overruling of *Swift v. Tyson*, for he said in the very opinion quoted by the majority, "I should leave *Swift* undisturbed, as I indicated in *Kuhn v. Fairmont Coal Co.*, but I would not allow it to spread the assumed dominion into new fields." *Black & White Taxicab Co. v. Brown & Yellow Taxicab Co.*, 276 U.S. 518, 535 (1928). If the opinion commits this Court to the position that the Congress is without power to declare what rules of substantive law shall govern the federal courts, that conclusion also seems questionable. The line between procedural and substantive law is hazy, but no one doubts federal power over procedure....

Notes & Questions

1. Start by making sure you understand the issue of tort law on which Tompkins' case depended, and thus the importance of choice of law to the outcome. Harry Tompkins sued the railroad for negligence. When the accident occurred, Tompkins was walking alongside the railroad tracks, on the railroad's "right of way." According to the railroad, under Pennsylvania law as declared by Pennsylvania's highest court, what duty is owed by a railroad to a trespasser on its right of way? In other words, according to the defendant, what would Tompkins have to prove to win his tort claim against the railroad? The federal district court and court of appeals, however, applied federal common law, permitting Tompkins to assert a claim for simple negligence—a standard of "ordinary care." On the facts of Tompkins' injury, a jury found the railroad liable for negligence. How likely was it, on the facts of this case, that Harry Tompkins could prove "wanton or willful" misconduct, as opposed to simple negligence?

2. Thus, the outcome of the case likely depended on a choice-of-law question. Now, turn to the choice-of-law arguments. Which party wanted the court to apply Pennsylvania law? Which party wanted the court to apply federal common law? How did the Rules of Decision Act, 28 U.S.C. §1652, support the railroad's position? How did *Swift v. Tyson* support Tompkins' position?

3. The legal theory underlying *Swift v. Tyson* was the notion, widely held at the time, that judges do not make the law; rather, they discover it. The law is the law, and the judge's job in a common law case is to use reasoning and analogies to figure out what the law is. Given that understanding of the common law, it made sense to say that federal judges were free to reject state court precedents, since federal court judges could use their minds to discover the law just as well as state judges. *Swift* was the law for nearly a century, during which time a large body of federal common law developed. Note the reliance in *Erie* on proclamations in various *dissents* by Justice Oliver Wendell Holmes, who had long been a critic of *Swift v. Tyson* and the theory of jurisprudence underlying it. He expressed his disapproval most prominently in *Black & White Taxicab v. Brown & Yellow Taxicab*. Holmes' dissents—and particularly his views on legal theory—took a foothold in law schools, among legal academics, and among critics of the Supreme Court in the first part of the twentieth century. *Erie* was decided in an era of legal realism, where it was no longer tenable to assert that law is a "brooding omnipresence in the sky" waiting to be discovered. *Erie* represented, in many ways, the culmination of this theoretical shift. Why would this change in legal theory dictate the result in *Erie*? Does it *have* to dictate the result in *Erie*? In other words, could the *result* in *Swift* stand, even in an era of legal realism, perhaps with different reasoning?

4. What sort of functional problems did the opinion in *Swift* create? What forum-shopping strategies did it enable? In what way did it produce "discrimination" between in-state and out-of-state citizens?

5. What are the key *principles* underlying the decision in *Erie*, according to Justice Brandeis? What is the *legal basis* for the decision in *Erie*? Do all of the Justices agree on the legal basis for *Erie*? Why does it matter? To the extent *Erie* is a constitutional decision, what part of the Constitution compels the *Erie* decision?

6. After *Erie*, is it the rule that the federal court always must apply the substantive law of the state in which the federal court sits? No. The *Erie* case provides a perfect example. Harry Tompkins brought the case in the Southern District of New York, but the court applied Pennsylvania state law. What *Erie* requires is that the federal court follow the *choice-of-law* rules of the state in which it sits. Often, the choice-of-law rules of the state in which the federal court sits will dictate that the substantive law of *that* state be applied, leading the federal court to apply the substantive law of the state in which it sits. However, choice-of-law rules might dictate that *another state's* substantive law apply. The Supreme Court spelled this out in *Klaxon v. Stentor*, 313 U.S. 487 (1941), which held that the federal court must apply whichever substantive law would be applied by the state court where the federal court sits. Returning to the example of *Erie* itself, stated as precisely as possible in *Klaxon* terms: Tompkins brought his case in the federal court for the Southern District of New York. The federal court in New York was required to apply whatever state tort law a New York state court would have applied. A New York state court would have applied Pennsylvania's tort law, since, according to New York choice-of-law rules, the law that applies is the law of the state where the accident happened (*lex loci delicti*). Therefore, the Southern District of New York federal court in *Erie* was required to apply Pennsylvania tort law.

7. The same year the decision in *Erie* came down, the Federal Rules of Civil Procedure went into effect. *Erie* did *not* involve a dispute over procedure; instead, it involved a question of whether to apply state judge-made common law or federal judge-made common law in the substantive area of torts. However, when the Court held in *Erie* that federal courts must apply state law in diversity cases, did this mean that federal courts should not apply the new Federal Rules of Civil Procedure?

Three years later, in *Sibbach v. Wilson*, 312 U.S. 1 (1941), the Supreme Court addressed the validity of the new federal rules. Sibbach sued Wilson in federal court in Illinois for injuries sustained in Indiana. Wilson moved under Federal Rule of Civil Procedure 35 to require Sibbach to submit to a physical examination, and the court granted the motion. Sibbach argued that such an order was not permitted under Illinois state law and refused to comply with the order. The district court then held Sibbach in contempt under Federal Rule of Civil Procedure 37. The court of appeals upheld the orders, and the Supreme Court granted certiorari on the question of whether the Supreme Court had the authority to promulgate Federal Rules 35 and 37. The Supreme Court, under the Rules Enabling Act, 28 U.S.C. §2071, is permitted by Congress to promulgate "general rules of practice and procedure," so long as "[s]uch rules do not abridge, enlarge or modify any substantive right."... The Supreme Court in *Sibbach* held that both Rules 35 and 37 regulated procedure, not substance, and therefore did not run afoul of the Rules Enabling Act. The Court made no mention of *Erie* in *Sibbach*. What do you make of that omission?

8. *Erie* stands for the proposition that federal courts must apply state substantive law. In *Erie*, this rule was easy enough to apply: The railroad's duty of care was governed by Pennsylvania state tort law. How would the new rule play out in situations where the issue was *less* clearly substantive than a railroad's duty of care? Consider the following case.

GUARANTY TRUST CO. OF NEW YORK v. YORK
326 U.S. 99 (1945)

Justice FRANKFURTER delivered the opinion of the Court.

[This suit was instituted as a class action in federal court on behalf of bondholders against a trustee for breach of fiduciary duty. The district court granted summary judgment in favor of petitioner, Guaranty Trust. On appeal, the Circuit Court of Appeals affirmed, finding that the federal court had not been required to apply the state statute of limitations that would have otherwise foreclosed petitioner's suit in state court even though the exclusive basis of federal jurisdiction is diversity of citizenship.]

Our only concern is with the holding that the federal courts in a suit like this are not bound by local law. . . .

Our starting point must be the policy of federal jurisdiction which *Erie R[ailroad] Co. v. Tompkins*, 304 U.S. 64 (1938), embodies. In overruling *Swift v. Tyson, Erie R. Co. v. Tompkins* did not merely overrule a venerable case. It overruled a particular way of looking at law which dominated the judicial process long after its inadequacies had been laid bare. Law was conceived as a "brooding omnipresence" of Reason, of which decisions were merely evidence and not themselves the controlling formulations. Accordingly,

federal courts deemed themselves free to ascertain what Reason, and therefore Law, required wholly independent of authoritatively declared State law, even in cases where a legal right as the basis for relief was created by State authority and could not be created by federal authority and the case got into a federal court merely because it was "between Citizens of different States" under Art. III, §2 of the Constitution of the United States. . . .

The [*Swift*] doctrine was congenial to the jurisprudential climate of the time. Once established, judicial momentum kept it going. Since it was conceived that there was "a transcendental body of law outside of any particular State but obligatory within it unless and until changed by statute," [*Black & White Taxi Cab & Transfer Co. v. Brown & Yellow Taxicab & Transfer Co.*], 276 U.S. 518, 532, 533, State court decisions were not "the law" but merely someone's opinion—to be sure an opinion to be respected—concerning the content of this all-pervading law. Not unnaturally, the federal courts assumed power to find for themselves the content of such a body of law. The notion was stimulated by the attractive vision of a uniform body of federal law. To such sentiments for uniformity of decision and freedom from diversity in State law the federal courts gave currency, particularly in cases where equitable remedies were sought, because equitable doctrines are so often cast in terms of universal applicability when close analysis of the source of legal enforceability is not demanded. . . .

And so this case reduces itself to the narrow question whether, when no recovery could be had in a State court because the action is barred by the statute of limitations, a federal court in equity can take cognizance of the suit because there is diversity of citizenship between the parties. Is the outlawry, according to State law, of a claim created by the States a matter of "substantive rights" to be respected by a federal court of equity when that court's jurisdiction is dependent on the fact that there is a State-created right, or is such statute of "a mere remedial character," *Henrietta Mills v. Rutherford Co.*, 281 U.S. 121, 128 (1930), which a federal court may disregard?

Matters of "substance" and matters of "procedure" are much talked about in the books as though they defined a great divide cutting across the whole domain of law. But, of course, "substance" and "procedure" are the same key-words to very different problems. Neither "substance" nor "procedure" represents the same invariants. Each implies different variables depending upon the particular problem for which it is used. . . .

Here we are dealing with a right to recover derived not from the United States but from one of the States. When, because the plaintiff happens to be a nonresident, such a right is enforceable in a federal as well as in a State court, the forms and mode of enforcing the right may at times, naturally enough, vary because the two judicial systems are not identic. But since a federal court adjudicating a state-created right solely because of the diversity of citizenship of the parties is for that purpose, in effect, only another court of the State, it cannot afford recovery if the right to recover is made unavailable by the State nor can it substantially affect the enforcement of the right as given by the State.

And so the question is not whether a statute of limitations is deemed a matter of "procedure" in some sense. The question is whether such a statute concerns merely the manner and the means by which a right to recover, as recognized by the State, is enforced, or whether such statutory limitation is a matter of substance in the aspect that alone is relevant to our problem, namely, does it significantly affect the result of a litigation for a federal court to disregard a law of a State that would be controlling in an action upon the same claim by the same parties in a State court?

It is therefore immaterial whether statutes of limitation are characterized either as "substantive" or "procedural" in State court opinions in any use of those terms unrelated to the specific issue before us. *Erie R. Co. v. Tompkins* was not an endeavor to formulate scientific legal terminology. It expressed a policy that touches vitally the proper distribution of judicial power between State and federal courts. In essence, the intent of that decision was to insure that, in all cases where a federal court is exercising jurisdiction solely because of the diversity of citizenship of the parties, the outcome of the litigation in the federal court should be substantially the same, so far as legal rules determine the outcome of a litigation, as it would be if tried in a State court. The nub of the policy that underlies *Erie R. Co. v. Tompkins* is that for the same transaction the accident of a suit by a non-resident litigant in a federal court instead of in a State court a block away, should not lead to a substantially different result. And so, putting to one side abstractions regarding "substance" and "procedure," we have held that in diversity cases the federal courts must follow the law of the State as to burden of proof, *Cities Service Oil Co. v. Dunlap*, 308 U.S. 208 (1939), as to conflict of laws, *Klaxon v. Stentor Co.*, 313 U.S. 487 (1941), [and] as to contributory negligence, *Palmer v. Hoffman*, 318 U.S. 109 (1943). *Erie R. Co. v. Tompkins* has been applied with an eye alert to essentials in avoiding disregard of State law in diversity cases in the federal courts. A policy so important to our federalism must be kept free from entanglements with analytical or terminological niceties.

Plainly enough, a statute that would completely bar recovery in a suit if brought in a State court bears on a State created right vitally and not merely formally or negligibly. As to consequences that so intimately affect recovery or non-recovery a federal court in a diversity case should follow State law. The fact that under New York law a statute of limitations might be lengthened or shortened, that a security may be foreclosed though the debt be barred, that a barred debt may be used as a set-off, are all matters of local law properly to be respected by federal courts sitting in New York when their incidence comes into play there. Such particular rules of local law, however, do not in the slightest change the crucial consideration that if a plea of the statute of limitations would bar recovery in a State court, a federal court ought not to afford recovery....

To make an exception to *Erie R. Co. v. Tompkins* on the equity side of a federal court is to reject the considerations of policy which, after long travail, led to that decision. Judge Augustus N. Hand thus summarized below the fatal objection to such inroad upon *Erie R. Co. v. Tompkins*:

"In my opinion it would be a mischievous practice to disregard state statutes of limitation whenever federal courts think that the result of adopting them may be inequitable. Such procedure would promote the choice of United States rather than of state courts in order to gain the advantage of different laws." ... *York v. Guaranty Trust Co. of New York*, 143 F.2d 503, 529 (1944).

Diversity jurisdiction is founded on assurance to non-resident litigants of courts free from susceptibility to potential local bias. The Framers of the Constitution, according to Marshall, entertained "apprehensions" lest distant suitors be subjected to local bias in State courts, or, at least, viewed with "indulgence the possible fears and apprehensions" of such suitors. *Bank of the United States v. Devaux*, 9 U.S. 61 (1809). And so Congress afforded out-of-State litigants another tribunal, not another body of law. The operation of a double system of conflicting laws in the same State is plainly hostile to the reign of law. Certainly, the fortuitous circumstance of residence out of a State of one of the parties to a litigation ought not to give rise to a discrimination against others equally concerned but locally resident. The source of substantive rights enforced by a federal court under diversity jurisdiction, it cannot be said too often, is the law of the States. Whenever that law is authoritatively declared by a State, whether its voice be the legislature or its highest court, such law ought to govern in litigation founded on that law, whether the forum of application is a State or a federal court and whether the remedies be sought at law or may be had in equity....

The judgment is reversed and the case is remanded for proceedings not inconsistent with this opinion.

Reversed.

Notes & Questions

1. After *Erie*, it was clear that the federal court must apply New York substantive law to York's claim against Guaranty Trust for breach of fiduciary duty. But what about *procedural* law? Remember that the brand-new Federal Rules of Civil Procedure went into effect in 1938, the very year the Supreme Court decided *Erie*. Surely, *Erie* did not require federal courts to ignore federal procedural law in diversity cases, or did it? And if federal courts were expected to apply state substantive law and federal procedural law, is it always easy to tell the difference? Is a statute of limitations "substantive" or "procedural"? In what ways does a statute of limitations advance procedural policies? In what way does it advance substantive policies?

2. The Court in *Guaranty Trust* held that statutes of limitations were "substantive" because there would be a different "outcome" under the federal doctrine of laches than under the state statute. Under *Guaranty Trust*, what exactly counts as an "outcome-determinative" difference between federal and state law? Think of it this way: If the Court applied the doctrine of laches and allowed the case to go forward, would that have guaranteed a plaintiff victory? Yet, if this difference between federal and state law counts as outcome-determinative under the *Guaranty Trust* test, what does it tell you about the breadth of this test?

3. The outcome-determinativeness test, as set forth in *Guaranty Trust*, turned out to be far too blunt an instrument for carving up the nuanced differences between substance and procedure, much less for providing a mechanism for balancing federal and state power. This became clear four years later when the Supreme Court decided a trilogy of *Erie* cases: First, in *Ragan v. Merchants Transfer*, 337 U.S. 530 (1949), the Court grappled with the issue of whether a federal court must apply state law to the question of when an action has been "commenced" for purposes of complying with the statute of limitations. Second, in *Woods v. Interstate Realty Co.*, 337 U.S. 535 (1949), the Court faced the issue of whether a federal court must apply a state law providing that in order to sue in the Mississippi courts, a corporation must be registered to do business in Mississippi. Third, in *Cohen v. Beneficial Indus. Loan Corp.*, 337 U.S. 541 (1949), the Court faced the question whether a federal court must apply a state law requiring an unsuccessful plaintiff in a shareholder derivative suit to pay all attorneys' fees and costs, and thus to post a security bond at the start of the suit. You could convincingly argue that each of these state laws raise matters of procedure that federal courts could and should decide for themselves. However, applying the *Guaranty Trust* outcome-determinativeness test, the Supreme Court held in all three cases that the relevant state rule could determine the outcome and thus must be applied by the federal court. After this trilogy, it seemed like the *Guaranty Trust* rule meant that just about *everything* was outcome-determinative.

4. Over a decade after *Guaranty Trust*, the Supreme Court took a step back from what was developing into an all-encompassing outcome-determinativeness rule for *Erie* cases. In *Byrd v. Blue Ridge Rural Electric Cooperative*, 356 U.S. 525 (1958), the issue was whether the plaintiff's employment status should be decided by the judge or jury. Byrd, a construction worker, sued Blue Ridge for an injury he sustained on the job. Employees, unlike independent contractors, cannot bring tort suits against their employers for workplace injuries because, under state statutes, workers' compensation is their exclusive remedy. Byrd argued that he was an independent contractor, but Blue Ridge contended that Byrd should be treated as an employee because he was doing the same work as employees, making Blue Ridge immune from this suit under South Carolina workers' compensation statute. This tees up the *Erie* issue: Blue Ridge wanted the judge to decide Byrd's employment status and cited a South Carolina state court case supporting its view that the issue should be decided by the judge. Under *Erie* and the Rules of Decision Act, Blue Ridge argued, the federal court must do what a South Carolina court would do. Byrd, on the other hand, wanted a jury to decide his employment status, perhaps expecting that a jury would more likely allow him to go forward with his personal-injury suit. He argued that in federal court, the jury should decide the question.

Is the choice between judge and jury in *Byrd* outcome-determinative in the *Guaranty Trust* sense? Are there arguments both ways? Even if the choice is considered outcome-determinative, is that the end of the inquiry? The Court in *Byrd*, backing off from a sweeping view of outcome-determinativeness, said no:

> [C]ases following *Erie* have evinced a . . . policy to the effect that the federal courts should conform as near as may be—in the absence of other considerations—to state rules even of form and mode where the state rules may bear substantially on the question whether the litigation would come out one way in the federal court and another way in the state court if the federal court failed to apply a particular local rule. *E.g.*, *Guaranty Trust Co. of New York v. York*, 326 U.S. 99 (1945). Concededly the nature of the tribunal which tries issues may be important in the enforcement of the parcel of rights making up a cause of action or defense, and bear significantly upon achievement of uniform enforcement of the right. It may well be that in the instant personal-injury case the outcome would be substantially affected by whether the issue of [Blue Ridge's] immunity is decided by a judge or a jury. Therefore, were "outcome" the only consideration, a strong case might appear for saying that the federal court should follow state practice.
>
> But there are affirmative countervailing considerations at work here. The federal system is an independent system for administering justice to litigants who properly invoke its jurisdiction. An essential characteristic of that system is the manner in which, in civil common-law actions, it distributes between judge and jury and, under the influence—if not the command—of the Seventh Amendment, assigns the questions of disputed questions of fact to the jury. The policy of uniform enforcement of state-created rights and obligations cannot in every case exact compliance with a state rule—not bound up with rights and obligations—which disrupts

the federal system of allocating functions between judge and jury. Thus the inquiry here is whether the federal policy favoring jury decisions of disputed fact questions should yield to the state rule in the interest of furthering the objective that the litigation should not come out one way in the federal court and another way in the state court.

We think that in the circumstances of this case the federal court should not follow the state rule.

Byrd v. Blue Ridge Rural Elec. Co-op, Inc., 356 U.S. at 536-38. The Supreme Court held that even if the choice between judge and jury could be outcome-determinative, there is more to the *Erie* doctrine—and the distinction between substance and procedure for purposes of determining the scope of federal court power— than outcome-determinativeness. Specifically, the Court in *Byrd* identified a "countervailing interest" in the allocation of power between a judge and jury in federal court:

> Perhaps even more clearly in light of the influence of the Seventh Amendment, the function assigned to the jury "is an essential factor in the process for which the Federal Constitution provides." *Herron v. So. Pacific Co.*, 283 U.S. 91, 95 (1931). Concededly the Herron case was decided before *Erie R. Co. v. Tompkins*, but even when *Swift v. Tyson* was governing law and allowed federal courts sitting in diversity cases to disregard state decisional law, it was never thought that state statutes or constitutions were similarly to be disregarded. Yet *Herron* held that state statutes and constitutional provisions could not disrupt or alter the essential character or function of a federal court.

Byrd, 356 U.S. at 539.

The Supreme Court further noted that the South Carolina court's practice of allowing the judge to decide immunity was not "bound up with [state-created] rights and obligations." *Id.* at 535. That language suggests the existence of a threshold question, in an *Erie* analysis, about the nature of the state law at issue. Keep that question—whether an issue is bound up with state-created rights and obligations—in mind as you read the cases in the remainder of this chapter.

5. In 1965, in *Hanna v. Plumer*, 380 U.S. 460, the Supreme Court refined the *Erie* test and articulated the version of that test that operates in cases today. Read *Hanna* carefully, as it is the single most important case for understanding how to apply *Erie*—even more important than *Erie* itself. As you read *Hanna* and its progeny, ask yourself what becomes of the various cases you have learned about already—particularly *Erie*, *Guaranty Trust*, *Ragan*, *Sibbach*, and *Byrd*.

HANNA v. PLUMER
380 U.S. 460 (1965)

Chief Justice WARREN delivered the opinion of the Court.

The question to be decided is whether, in a civil action where the jurisdiction of the United States district court is based upon diversity of citizenship between the parties, service of process shall be made in the manner prescribed by state law or that set forth in Rule 4(d)(1)* of the Federal Rules of Civil Procedure.

On February 6, 1963, petitioner, a citizen of Ohio, filed her complaint in the District Court for the District of Massachusetts, claiming damages in excess of $10,000 for personal injuries resulting from an automobile accident in South Carolina, allegedly caused by the negligence of one Louise Plumer Osgood, a Massachusetts citizen deceased at the time of the filing of the complaint. Respondent, Mrs. Osgood's executor and also a Massachusetts citizen, was named as defendant. On February 8, service was made by leaving copies of the summons and the complaint with respondent's wife at his residence, concededly in compliance with Rule 4(d)(1), [which permits service] "by leaving copies [of the summons and complaint at the party's] dwelling house or usual place of abode with some person of suitable age and discretion then residing therein."

Respondent filed his answer on February 26, alleging, *inter alia*, that the action could not be maintained because it had been brought "contrary to and in violation of the provisions of Massachusetts General Laws Chapter 197, Section 9." That section provides [that service on an executor or administrator must be effectuated by] ... "delivery in hand upon such executor or administrator...." Mass. Gen. Laws. Ann., c.197, §9 (1958). On October 17, 1963, the District Court granted respondent's motion for summary judgment, citing *Ragan v. Merchants Transfer Co.*, 337 U.S. 530 (1949), and *Guaranty Trust Co. of New York v. York*, 326 U.S. 99 (1945), in support of its conclusion that the adequacy of the service was to be measured by §9, with which, the court held, petitioner had not complied. On appeal, petitioner admitted noncompliance with §9, but argued that Rule 4(d)(1) defines the method by which service of process is to be effected in diversity actions. The Court of Appeals for the First Circuit, finding that "(r)elatively recent amendments (to §9) evince a clear legislative purpose to require personal notification within the year,"[1] concluded that the conflict of state and federal rules was over "a substantive rather than a procedural matter," and unanimously affirmed. 331 F.2d 157. Because of the threat to the goal of uniformity of federal procedure posed by the decision below, we granted certiorari.

We conclude that the adoption of Rule 4(d)(1), designed to control service of process in diversity actions, neither exceeded the congressional mandate embodied in the Rules Enabling Act nor transgressed

---

Editors' Note: Rule 4 has been amended and renumbered; this provision is now found in Rule 4(e)(2)(B).

[1] The purpose of this part of the statute is to insure that executors will receive actual notice of claims. Actual notice is of course also the goal of Rule 4(d)(1); however, the Federal Rule reflects a determination that this goal can be achieved by a method less cumbersome than that prescribed in §9. In this case the goal seems to have been achieved; although the affidavit filed by respondent in the District Court asserts that he had not been served in hand nor had he accepted service, it does not allege lack of actual notice.

constitutional bounds, and that the Rule is therefore the standard against which the District Court should have measured the adequacy of the service. Accordingly, we reverse the decision of the Court of Appeals.

The Rules Enabling Act, 28 U.S.C. §2072 (1958 ed.), provides, in pertinent part:

> The Supreme Court shall have the power to prescribe, by general rules, the forms of process, writs, pleadings, and motions, and the practice and procedure of the district courts of the United States in civil actions. Such rules shall not abridge, enlarge or modify any substantive right. . . .

Under the cases construing the scope of the Enabling Act, Rule 4(d)(1) clearly passes muster. Prescribing the manner in which a defendant is to be notified that a suit has been instituted against him, it relates to the "practice and procedure of the district courts." *Cf. Insurance Co. v. Bangs*, 103 U.S. 435 (1880).

"The test must be whether a rule really regulates procedure,—the judicial process for enforcing rights and duties recognized by substantive law and for justly administering remedy and redress for disregard or infraction of them." *Sibbach v. Wilson & Co.*, 312 U.S. 1 (1941). . . .

[W]ere there no conflicting state procedure, Rule 4(d)(1) would clearly control. However, respondent, focusing on the contrary Massachusetts rule, calls to the Court's attention another line of cases, a line which—like the Federal Rules—had its birth in 1938. *Erie R. Co. v. Tompkins*, overruling *Swift v. Tyson*, 41 U.S. 1 (1842), held that federal courts sitting in diversity cases, when deciding questions of "substantive" law, are bound by state court decisions as well as state statutes. The broad command of *Erie* was therefore identical to that of the Enabling Act: federal courts are to apply state substantive law and federal procedural law. However, as subsequent cases sharpened the distinction between substance and procedure, the line of cases following *Erie* diverged markedly from the line construing the Enabling Act. *Guaranty Trust* made it clear that *Erie*-type problems were not to be solved by reference to any traditional or common-sense substance-procedure distinction:

> And so the question is not whether a statute of limitations is deemed a matter of "procedure" in some sense. The question is . . . does it significantly affect the result of a litigation for a federal court to disregard a law of a State that would be controlling in an action upon the same claim by the same parties in a State court? 326 U.S. 109.

Respondent, by placing primary reliance on *York* and *Ragan*, suggests that the *Erie* doctrine acts as a check on the Federal Rules of Civil Procedure, that despite the clear command of Rule 4(d)(1), *Erie* and its progeny demand the application of the Massachusetts rule. Reduced to essentials, the argument is: (1) *Erie*, as refined in *York*, demands that federal courts apply state law whenever application of federal law in its stead will alter the outcome of the case. (2) In this case, a determination that the Massachusetts service requirements obtain will result in immediate victory for respondent. If, on the other hand, it should be held that Rule 4(d)(1) is applicable, the litigation will continue, with possible victory for petitioner. (3) Therefore, *Erie* demands application of the Massachusetts rule. The syllogism possesses an appealing simplicity, but is for several reasons invalid.

In the first place, it is doubtful that, even if there were no Federal Rule making it clear that in-hand service is not required in diversity actions, the *Erie* rule would have obligated the District Court to follow the Massachusetts procedure. "Outcome-determination" analysis was never intended to serve as a talisman. *Byrd v. Blue Ridge Rural Elec. Cooperative*, 356 U.S. 525 (1958). Indeed, the message of *York* itself is that choices between state and federal law are to be made not by application of any automatic, "litmus paper" criterion, but rather by reference to the policies underlying the *Erie* rule. *York*, 326 U.S. at 108-11.

The *Erie* rule is rooted in part in a realization that it would be unfair for the character of result of a litigation materially to differ because the suit had been brought in a federal court. . . .

The [*Erie*] decision was also in part a reaction to the practice of "forum-shopping" which had grown up in response to the rule of *Swift v. Tyson*, 304 U.S. at 73-74. That the *York* test was an attempt to effectuate these policies is demonstrated by the fact that the opinion framed the inquiry in terms of "substantial" variations between state and federal litigation. 326 U.S. at 109. Not only are nonsubstantial, or trivial, variations not likely to raise the sort of equal protection problems which troubled the Court in *Erie*; they are also unlikely to influence the choice of a forum. The "outcome-determination" test therefore cannot be read without reference to the twin aims of the *Erie* rule: discouragement of forum-shopping and avoidance of inequitable administration of the laws.[9]

The difference between the conclusion that the Massachusetts rule is applicable, and the conclusion that it is not, is of course at this point "outcome-determinative" in the sense that if we hold the state rule to apply, respondent prevails, whereas if we hold that Rule 4(d)(1) governs, the litigation will continue. But in this sense every procedural variation is "outcome-determinative." For example, having brought suit in a federal court, a plaintiff cannot then insist on the right to file subsequent pleadings in accord with the time limits applicable in state courts, even though enforcement of the federal timetable will, if he continues to insist that he must meet only the state time limit, result in determination of the controversy against him. So it is here. Though choice of the federal or state rule will at this point have a marked effect upon the outcome of the litigation, the difference between the two rules would be of scant, if any, relevance to the choice of a forum. Petitioner, in choosing her forum, was not presented with a situation where application of the state rule would wholly bar recovery; rather, adherence to the state rule would have resulted only in altering the way in which process was served. Moreover, it is difficult to argue that permitting service of defendant's wife to take the place of in-hand service of defendant himself alters the mode of enforcement of state-created rights in a fashion sufficiently "substantial" to raise the sort of equal protection problems to which the *Erie* opinion alluded.

There is, however, a more fundamental flaw in respondent's syllogism: the incorrect assumption that the rule of *Erie R. Co. v.*

---

[9] The Court of Appeals seemed to frame the inquiry in terms of how "important" §9 is to the State. . . . [However,] *Erie* and its progeny make clear that when a federal court sitting in a diversity case is faced with a question of whether or not to apply state law, the importance of a state rule is indeed relevant, but only in the context of asking whether application of the rule would make so important a difference to the character

or result of the litigation that failure to enforce it would unfairly discriminate against citizens of the forum State, or whether application of the rule would have so important an effect upon the fortunes of one or both of the litigants that failure to enforce it would be likely to cause a plaintiff to choose the federal court.

Tompkins constitutes the appropriate test of the validity and therefore the applicability of a Federal Rule of Civil Procedure. The *Erie* rule has never been invoked to void a Federal Rule. It is true that there have been cases where this Court has held applicable a state rule in the face of an argument that the situation was governed by one of the Federal Rules. But the holding of each such case was not that *Erie* commanded displacement of a Federal Rule by an inconsistent state rule, but rather that the scope of the Federal Rule was not as broad as the losing party urged, and therefore, there being no Federal Rule which covered the point in dispute, *Erie* commanded the enforcement of state law. . . . (Here, of course, the clash is unavoidable; Rule 4(d)(1) says—implicitly, but with unmistakable clarity—that in-hand service is not required in federal courts.) At the same time, in cases adjudicating the validity of Federal Rules, we have not applied the *York* rule or other refinements of *Erie*, but have to this day continued to decide questions concerning the scope of the Enabling Act and the constitutionality of specific Federal Rules in light of the distinction set forth in *Sibbach*.

Nor has the development of two separate lines of cases been inadvertent. The line between "substance" and "procedure" shifts as the legal context changes. "Each implies different variables depending upon the particular problem for which it is used." *York, supra*, 326 U.S. at 108. It is true that both the Enabling Act and the *Erie* rule say, roughly, that federal courts are to apply state "substantive" law and federal "procedural" law, but from that it need not follow that the tests are identical. For they were designed to control very different sorts of decisions. When a situation is covered by one of the Federal Rules, the question facing the court is a far cry from the typical, relatively unguided *Erie* choice: the court

has been instructed to apply the Federal Rule, and can refuse to do so only if the Advisory Committee, this Court, and Congress erred in their prima facie judgment that the Rule in question transgresses neither the terms of the Enabling Act nor constitutional restrictions.

. . . [T]he opinion in *Erie*, which involved no Federal Rule and dealt with a question which was "substantive" in every traditional sense (whether the railroad owed a duty of care to Tompkins as a trespasser or a licensee), surely neither said nor implied that measures like Rule 4(d)(1) are unconstitutional. For the constitutional provision for a federal court system (augmented by the Necessary and Proper Clause) carries with it congressional power to make rules governing the practice and pleading in those courts, which in turn includes a power to regulate matters which, though falling within the uncertain area between substance and procedure, are rationally capable of classification as either. Neither *York* nor the cases following it ever suggested that the rule there laid down for coping with situations where no Federal Rule applies is coextensive with the limitation on Congress to which *Erie* had adverted. Although this Court has never before been confronted with a case where the applicable Federal Rule is in direct collision with the law of the relevant State, courts of appeals faced with such clashes have rightly discerned the implications of our decisions.

"One of the shaping purposes of the Federal Rules is to bring about uniformity in the federal courts by getting away from local rules. This is especially true in matters which relate to the administration of legal proceedings, an area in which federal courts have traditionally exerted strong inherent power, completely aside from the powers Congress expressly conferred in the Rules. The purpose of the *Erie* doctrine, even as extended in *York* and *Ragan*, was never to bottle up federal courts with 'outcome-determinative' . . . stoppers—when there are 'affirmative countervailing (federal) considerations' and when there is a Congressional mandate (the Rules) supported by constitutional authority." *Lumbermen's Mutual Casualty Co. v. Wright*, 322 F.2d 759, 764 (5th Cir. 1963).

Erie and its offspring cast no doubt on the long-recognized power of Congress to prescribe housekeeping rules for federal courts even though some of those rules will inevitably differ from comparable state rules. "When, because the plaintiff happens to be a non-resident, such a right is enforceable in a federal as well as in a State court, the forms and mode of enforcing the right may at times, naturally enough, vary because the two judicial systems are not identic." *York, supra*, 326 U.S. at 108. Thus, though a court, in measuring a Federal Rule against the standards contained in the Enabling Act and the Constitution, need not wholly blind itself to the degree to which the Rule makes the character and result of the federal litigation stray from the course it would follow in state courts, it cannot be forgotten that the *Erie* rule, and the guidelines suggested in *York*, were created to serve another purpose altogether. To hold that a Federal Rule of Civil Procedure must cease to function whenever it alters the mode of enforcing state-created rights would be to disembowel either the Constitution's grant of power over federal procedure or Congress' attempt to exercise that power in the Enabling Act. Rule 4(d)(1) is valid and controls the instant case.

Reversed.

Justice HARLAN, concurring.

It is unquestionably true that up to now *Erie* and the cases following it have not succeeded in articulating a workable doctrine governing choice of law in diversity actions. I respect the Court's effort to clarify the situation in today's opinion. However, in doing so I think it has misconceived the constitutional premises of *Erie* and has failed to deal adequately with those past decisions upon which the courts below relied.

Erie was something more than an opinion which worried about "forum-shopping and avoidance of inequitable administration of the laws," although to be sure these were important elements of the decision. I have always regarded that decision as one of the modern cornerstones of our federalism, expressing policies that profoundly touch the allocation of judicial power between the state and federal systems. *Erie* recognized that there should not be two conflicting systems of law controlling the primary activity of citizens, for such alternative governing authority must necessarily give rise to a debilitating uncertainty in the planning of everyday affairs. And it recognized that the scheme of our Constitution envisions an allocation of law-making functions between state and federal legislative processes which is undercut if the federal judiciary can make substantive law affecting state affairs beyond the bounds of congressional legislative powers in this regard. Thus, in diversity cases *Erie* commands that it be the state law governing primary private activity which prevails.

. . . The Court is quite right in stating that the "outcome-determinative" test of *York*, 326 U.S. 99, if taken literally, proves too much, for any rule, no matter how clearly "procedural," can affect the outcome of litigation if it is not obeyed. In turning from the "outcome" test of *York* back to the unadorned forum-shopping rationale of *Erie*, however, the Court falls prey to like oversimplification, for a simple forum-shopping rule also proves too much; litigants often choose a federal forum merely to obtain what they consider the advantages of the Federal Rules of Civil Procedure or to try their cases before a supposedly more favorable judge. To my mind the proper line of approach in determining whether to apply a state or a federal rule, whether "substantive" or "procedural," is to stay close to basic principles by inquiring if the choice of rule would substantially affect those primary decisions respecting human conduct which our constitutional system leaves to state regulation. If so, *Erie* and the Constitution require that the state rule prevail, even in the face of a conflicting federal rule.

The Court weakens, if indeed it does not submerge, this basic principle by finding, in effect, a grant of substantive legislative power in the constitutional provision for a federal court system, and through it, setting up the Federal Rules as a body of law inviolate.

> (T)he constitutional provision for a federal court system . . . carries with it congressional power . . . to regulate matters which, though falling within the uncertain area between substance and procedure, *are rationally capable of classification as either.* (Emphasis supplied).

So long as a reasonable man could characterize any duly adopted federal rule as "procedural," the Court, unless I misapprehend what is said, would have it apply no matter how seriously it frustrated a State's substantive regulation of the primary conduct and affairs of its citizens. Since the members of the Advisory Committee, the Judicial Conference, and this Court who formulated the Federal Rules are presumably reasonable men, it follows that the integrity of the Federal Rules is absolute. Whereas the unadulterated outcome and forum-shopping tests may err too far toward honoring state rules, I submit that the Court's "arguably procedural, ergo constitutional" test moves too fast and far in the other direction.

The courts below relied upon this Court's decisions in *Ragan v. Merchants*

Transfer & Warehouse Co., 337 U.S. 530 (1949), and *Cohen v. Beneficial Indus. Loan Corp.*, 337 U.S. 541 (1949). Those cases deserve more attention than this Court has given them, particularly *Ragan*. . . .

In *Ragan*, a Kansas statute of limitations provided that an action was deemed commenced when service was made on the defendant. Despite Federal Rule 3, which provides that an action commences with the filing of the complaint, the Court [applied the state rule]. . . . I think that the decision was wrong. . . . The choice of the Federal Rule would have had no effect on the primary stages of private activity from which torts arise, and only the most minimal effect on behavior following the commission of the tort. In such circumstances, the interest of the federal system in proceeding under its own rules should have prevailed. . . . [T]he Court attributes such overriding force to the Federal Rules that it is hard to think of a case where a conflicting state rule would be allowed to operate, even though the state rule reflected policy considerations, which, under *Erie*, would lie within the realm of state legislative authority.

It remains to apply what has been said to the present case. . . . If the Federal District Court in Massachusetts applies Rule 4(d)(1) of the Federal Rules of Civil Procedure instead of the Massachusetts service rule, what effect would that have on the speed and assurance with which estates are distributed? As I see it, the effect would not be substantial. It would mean simply that an executor would have to check at his own house or the federal courthouse as well as the registry of probate before he could distribute the estate with impunity. As this does not seem enough to give rise to any real impingement on the vitality of the state policy which the Massachusetts rule is intended to serve, I concur in the judgment of the Court.

Notes & Questions

1. *Swift* and *Erie* concerned the application of the Rules of Decision Act. In *Hanna*, Chief Justice Warren says the case should be decided based on a different statute—the Rules Enabling Act. Why? According to *Hanna*, if a particular issue is addressed by a valid Federal Rule of Civil Procedure, does a court need to conduct an *Erie* analysis to decide whether to apply state law that contradicts the federal rule?

2. What test does the majority in *Hanna* set forth for determining whether a Federal Rule of Civil Procedure is valid under the Rules Enabling Act? Does Justice Harlan endorse that test? Does he disagree that there are two separate analyses—one under the Rules Enabling Act and one under the Rules of Decision Act? In thinking about this question, consider Justice Harlan's discussion of how he would have analyzed the issue in *Ragan*.

3. Under *Hanna*, the choice-of-law consequence of a conflict between a valid federal procedural rule and a state law is that the court must apply the valid federal rule. This same logic applies to federal statutes. If Congress has enacted a valid statute—a statute that is not unconstitutional—then federal courts must enforce that statute, regardless of conflicting state law. The Supremacy Clause of the Constitution makes duly enacted federal law "the supreme law of the land." U.S. Const. art. VI. *Hanna* recognizes that federal courts are bound to uphold legitimately enacted federal rules and statutes.

4. Thus, one important move in *Hanna* is the idea that federal rules and statutes are treated differently, for *Erie* purposes, from federal practices that are not embodied in rules and statutes. But that is not the only important move. Even if the federal approach to service of process had been a matter of case law rather than embodied in a Federal Rule of Civil Procedure, would the majority have reached a different result on whether a federal court must apply the Massachusetts service rule? How about Justice Harlan?

5. Was the conflict between state and federal law in *Hanna* outcome-determinative in the *Guaranty Trust* sense? More importantly, does it matter to the majority whether it is or not? How does Chief Justice Warren reframe that test? How do *Guaranty Trust* and *Byrd* fit into the reframed analysis?

6. One of the key things to come out of *Hanna* is the Court's articulation of the "twin aims of *Erie*." What are those twin aims? While these "twin aims" come at the vertical choice-of-law problem from different angles, both ultimately make the same point: If the difference between state and federal law matters enough that litigants would choose one court over the other to get a different application of the law, then the federal court must apply state law. Maybe they are identical twins.

7. Throughout this book, we have highlighted forum-selection strategy. You might even say that this book has *encouraged* you to engage thoughtfully in forum

shopping on behalf of your clients. Yet *Hanna* emphasizes the goal of *discouraging* forum shopping. What does the Court mean, and what is special about the *Erie-Hanna* context? The concern in *Hanna* about forum shopping is not that lawyers should refrain from choosing the best forum for their clients, but rather that the legal system should set things up so that the choice between federal and state court does not yield substantively different legal norms. That is actually a pretty limited concern, and thus a limited constraint. For vertical forum shopping, *Erie* removes differences in substantive law but has no effect on many other strategic reasons why one might choose federal or state court, such as judges, jury pools, or discovery rules. And *Erie* does nothing to reduce horizontal forum shopping—discussed earlier in this chapter, the choice between one state and another.

8. *Hanna* transformed the *Erie* analysis; indeed, many now call it *Erie-Hanna* analysis. While *Hanna* seems to make application of the *Erie* principle more straightforward, there is a difficult complication built into the *Erie-Hanna* analysis. Specifically, federal courts are to apply any valid federal rule or statute that is directly on point. Here is the rub: When is a federal rule "directly on point" or in "direct conflict" with the state law? And does that analysis leave room for discretionary interpretation in some cases (answer: yes). Indeed, might a federal court that prefers state law construe a federal rule narrowly so that it is not "directly on point"? *See, e.g., Walker v. Armco Steel*, 446 U.S. 740 (1980) (finding that Federal Rule of Civil Procedure 3, which states that an action is commenced by filing a complaint for statutes of limitation purposes, did not "directly collide" with Oklahoma law providing that an action was commenced when process was served, and thus *Erie* commanded the enforcement of state law) (reaffirming *Ragan v. Merchants Transfer*, 337 U.S. 530 (1949), but characterizing *Ragan* as not involving a "direct conflict" between a state and federal rule).

   Conversely, might a federal court eager to apply federal law stretch to find that the federal rule is in "direct conflict" with state law? For example, in *Burlington Northern Railroad Co. v. Woods*, 480 U.S. 1 (1987), the Court was faced with a question of which rule—federal or state—to apply regarding damages awards for frivolous appeals. Under Alabama law, such damages were mandatory. Under Rule 38 of the Federal Rules of Appellate Procedure, however, such sanctions for frivolous appeals are left to the court's discretion. The Court held that Rule 38 came into "direct collision" with the Alabama law, was valid under the Constitution and the Rules Enabling Act, and thus applied in *Woods*. How could you argue that Alabama law does not directly conflict with Rule 38, and thus that the Alabama rule should apply? *See also Stewart Organization v. Ricoh Corp.*, 487 U.S. 22 (1988) (in a case involving a motion for venue transfer based on a forum-selection clause, the Court held that the federal venue statute, 28 U.S.C. §1404, came into direct conflict with state law that disfavored enforcement of forum-selection clauses).

9. Another problem that comes up in determining whether there is a direct conflict between the federal rule and state law is that the court must ascertain what the

content of a particular state's law actually is. In some instances, determining state law is a simple piece of legal research that involves little more than reading a relevant state statute. And the court will have the benefit of both sides' briefs on any disputed legal issues. However, sometimes the law is not so clear or the parties dispute the interpretation. In those situations, state law is whatever the state high court says it is, or, more precisely, what the state high court would decide if faced with the issue. When applying state law, federal courts must apply the law exactly as they believe the relevant state's high court would. The court therefore looks to see if the state supreme court has decided the issue, and if so, it follows that ruling unless there is a very good reason to believe that the state supreme court would no longer decide it the same way. If there is no state supreme court decision on point, then the federal court looks at intermediate appellate decisions from that state, or other sources that the state high court would consider, such as decisions from other states or secondary sources.

(3) Application of the Modern *Erie* Doctrine

GASPERINI v. CENTER FOR HUMANITIES, INC.
518 U.S. 415 (1996)

GINSBURG, J., delivered the opinion of the Court, in which O'CONNOR, KENNEDY, SOUTER, and BREYER, JJ., joined.

Under the law of New York, appellate courts are empowered to review the size of jury verdicts and to order new trials when the jury's award "deviates materially from what would be reasonable compensation." N.Y. Civ. Prac. Law and Rules (CPLR) §5501(c). Under the Seventh Amendment, which governs proceedings in federal court, but not in state court, "the right of trial by jury shall be preserved, and no fact tried by a jury, shall be otherwise re-examined in any Court of the United States, than according to the rules of the common law." U.S. Const. Amdt. 7. The compatibility of these provisions, in an action based on New York law but tried in federal court by reason of the parties' diverse citizenship, is the issue we confront in this case. We hold that New York's law controlling compensation awards for excessiveness or inadequacy can be given effect, without detriment to the Seventh Amendment, if the review standard set out in CPLR §5501(c) is applied by the federal trial court judge, with appellate control of the trial court's ruling limited to review for "abuse of discretion."

I

Petitioner William Gasperini, a journalist for CBS News and the Christian Science Monitor, began reporting on events in Central America in 1984. He earned his living primarily in radio and print media and only occasionally sold his photographic work. During the course of his seven-year stint in Central America, Gasperini took over 5,000 slide transparencies, depicting active war zones, political leaders, and scenes from daily life. In 1990, Gasperini agreed to supply his original color transparencies to The Center for Humanities, Inc. (Center) for use in an educational videotape, *Conflict in Central America.* Gasperini selected 300 of his slides for the Center; its videotape included 110 of them. The Center agreed to return the original transparencies, but upon the completion of the project, it could not find them.

Gasperini commenced suit in the United States District Court for the Southern District of New York, invoking the court's diversity jurisdiction pursuant to 28 U.S.C. §1332. He alleged several state-law claims for relief, including breach of contract, conversion, and negligence. The Center conceded liability for the lost transparencies and the issue of damages was tried before a jury.

At trial, Gasperini's expert witness testified that the "industry standard" within the photographic publishing community valued a lost transparency at $1,500. . . . Gasperini estimated that his earnings from photography totaled just over $10,000 for the period from 1984 through 1993. He also testified that he intended to produce a book containing his best photographs from Central America.

After a three-day trial, the jury awarded Gasperini $450,000 in compensatory damages. This sum, the jury foreperson announced, "is [$]1500 each, for 300 slides." Moving for a new trial under Federal Rule of Civil Procedure 59, the Center attacked the verdict on various grounds, including excessiveness. Without comment, the District Court denied the motion.

The Court of Appeals for the Second Circuit vacated the judgment entered on the jury's verdict. Mindful that New York law governed the controversy, the Court of Appeals endeavored to apply CPLR §5501(c), which instructs that, when a jury returns an itemized verdict, as the jury did in this case, the New York Appellate Division "shall determine that an award is excessive or inadequate if it deviates materially from what would be reasonable compensation." . . . The Second Circuit concluded that testimony on industry standard alone was insufficient to justify [the] verdict; prime among other factors warranting consideration were the uniqueness of the slides' subject matter and the photographer's earning level. . . .

[T]he Second Circuit held that the $450,000 verdict "materially deviates from what is reasonable compensation." 66 F.3d at 431. . . . Absent evidence showing significant earnings from photographic endeavors or concrete plans to publish a book, the court further determined, any damage award above $100 each for the remaining slides would be excessive. . . . [T]he Second Circuit set aside the $450,000 verdict and ordered a new trial, unless Gasperini agreed to an award of $100,000.

This case presents an important question regarding the standard a federal court uses to measure the alleged excessiveness of a jury's verdict in an action for damages based on state law. We therefore granted certiorari.

II

Before 1986, state and federal courts in New York generally invoked the same judge-made formulation in responding to excessiveness attacks on jury verdicts: courts would not disturb an award unless the amount was so exorbitant that it "shocked the conscience of the court." *See Consorti v. Armstrong World Industries, Inc.,* 64 F.3d 781, 1012-13.

In both state and federal courts, trial judges made the excessiveness assessment in the first instance, and appellate judges ordinarily deferred to the trial court's judgment.

In 1986, as part of a series of tort reform measures, New York codified a standard for judicial review of the size of jury awards. Placed in CPLR §5501(c), the prescription reads:

> In reviewing a money judgment . . . in which it is contended that the award is excessive or inadequate and that a new trial should have been granted unless a stipulation is entered to a different award, the appellate division shall determine that an award is excessive or inadequate if it deviates materially from what would be reasonable compensation. . . .

The [New York legislative record revealed that] lawmakers found the "shocks the conscience" test an insufficient check on damage awards; the legislature therefore installed a standard "invit[ing] more careful appellate scrutiny." Ch. 266, 1986 N.Y. Laws 470. . . . New York state-court opinions confirm that §5501(c)'s "deviates materially" standard calls for closer surveillance than "shock the conscience" oversight. Although phrased as a direction to New York's intermediate appellate courts, §5501(c)'s "deviates materially" standard, as construed by New York's courts, instructs state trial judges as well. . . . Application of §5501(c) at the trial level is key to this case. . . .

III

In cases like Gasperini's, in which New York law governs the claims for relief, does New York law also supply the test for federal-court review of the size of the verdict? The Center answers yes. The "deviates materially" standard, it argues, is a substantive standard that must be applied by federal appellate courts in diversity cases. The Second Circuit agreed. Gasperini, emphasizing that §5501(c) trains on the New York Appellate Division, characterizes

the provision as procedural, an allocation of decisionmaking authority regarding damages, not a hard cap on the amount recoverable. Correctly comprehended, Gasperini urges, §5501(c)'s direction to the Appellate Division cannot be given effect by federal appellate courts without violating the Seventh Amendment's Re-examination Clause.

As the parties' arguments suggest, CPLR §5501(c), appraised under *Erie R. Co. v. Tompkins*, 304 U.S. 64 (1938), and decisions in *Erie*'s path, is both "substantive" and "procedural": "substantive" in that §5501(c)'s "deviates materially" standard controls how much a plaintiff can be awarded; "procedural" in that §5501(c) assigns decisionmaking authority to New York's Appellate Division. Parallel application of §5501(c) at the federal appellate level would be out of sync with the federal system's division of trial and appellate court functions, an allocation weighted by the Seventh Amendment. The dispositive question, therefore, is whether federal courts can give effect to the substantive thrust of §5501(c) without untoward alteration of the federal scheme for the trial and decision of civil cases.

A

Federal diversity jurisdiction provides an alternative forum for the adjudication of state-created rights, but it does not carry with it generation of rules of substantive law. As *Erie* read the Rules of Decision Act: "Except in matters governed by the Federal Constitution or by Acts of Congress, the law to be applied in any case is the law of the State." 304 U.S. at 78. Under the *Erie* doctrine, federal courts sitting in diversity apply state substantive law and federal procedural law. Classification of a law as "substantive" or "procedural" for *Erie* purposes is sometimes a challenging endeavor. . . .

[Here], we address the question whether New York's "deviates materially" standard, codified in CPLR §5501(c), is outcome affective in this sense: Would "application of the [standard] . . . have so important an effect upon the fortunes of one or both of the litigants that failure to [apply] it would [unfairly discriminate against citizens of the forum State, or] be likely to cause a plaintiff to choose the federal court"? *Hanna, supra* at 468 n.9.

We start from a point the parties do not debate. Gasperini acknowledges that a statutory cap on damages would supply substantive law for *Erie* purposes. Although CPLR §5501(c) is less readily classified, it was designed to provide an analogous control.

New York's Legislature codified in §5501(c) a new standard, one that requires closer court review than the common-law "shock the conscience" test. [Further,] to foster predictability, the legislature required the reviewing court, when overturning a verdict under §5501(c), to state its reasons, including the factors it considered relevant. We think it a fair conclusion that CPLR §5501(c) differs from a statutory cap "in that the maximum amount recoverable is not set forth by statute, but rather is determined by case law." In sum, §5501(c) contains a procedural instruction, but the State's objective is manifestly substantive.

It thus appears that if federal courts ignore the change in the New York standard and persist in applying the "shock the conscience" test to damage awards on claims governed by New York law, "'substantial' variations between state and federal [money judgments]" may be expected. *See Hanna*, 380 U.S. at 467-468. We therefore agree with the Second Circuit that New York's check on excessive damages implicates what we have called *Erie*'s "twin aims." Just as the *Erie* principle precludes a federal court from giving a state-created claim "longer life . . . than [the claim] would have had in the state court," *Ragan*, 337 U.S. at 533-34, so *Erie* precludes a recovery in federal court significantly larger than the recovery that would have been tolerated in state court.

B

CPLR §5501(c), as earlier noted, is phrased as a direction to the New York Appellate Division. Acting essentially as a surrogate for a New York appellate forum, the Court of Appeals reviewed Gasperini's award to determine if it "deviate[d] materially" from damage awards the Appellate Division permitted in similar circumstances. The Court of Appeals performed this task without benefit of an opinion from the District Court, which had denied "without comment" the Center's Rule 59 motion. Concentrating on the authority §5501(c) gives to the Appellate Division, Gasperini urges that the provision shifts fact-finding responsibility from the jury and the trial judge to the appellate court. Assigning such responsibility to an appellate court, he maintains, is incompatible with the Seventh Amendment's Reexamination Clause, and therefore, Gasperini concludes, §5501(c) cannot be given effect in federal court. Although we reach a different conclusion than Gasperini, we agree that the Second Circuit did not attend to "[a]n essential characteristic of [the federal court] system," *Byrd v. Blue Ridge Rural Elec. Cooperative, Inc.*, 356 U.S. 525, 537 (1958), when it used §5501(c) as "the standard for [federal] appellate review."

That "essential characteristic" was described in *Byrd* . . . [in which the] Court held that, despite the state practice, the plaintiff was entitled to a jury trial in federal court. In so ruling, the Court said that the *Guaranty Trust* "outcome-determination" test was an insufficient guide in cases presenting countervailing federal interests. *See Byrd*, 356 U.S. at 537. . . .

The Seventh Amendment, which governs proceedings in federal court, but not in state court, bears not only on the allocation of trial functions between judge and jury, the issue in *Byrd*; it also controls the allocation of authority to review verdicts, the issue of concern here. The [Re-examination clause of the] Amendment reads: "[N]o fact tried by a jury, shall be re-examined in any Court of the United States, than according to the rules of the common law." U.S. Const., Amdt. 7.

. . . In keeping with the historic understanding, the Reexamination Clause does not inhibit the authority of trial judges to grant new trials "for any of the reasons for which new trials have heretofore been granted in actions at law in the courts of the United States." Fed. Rule Civ. Proc. 59(a). That authority is large. "The trial judge in the federal system," we have reaffirmed, "has . . . discretion to grant a new trial if the verdict appears to [the judge] to be against the weight of the evidence." *Byrd*, 356 U.S. at 540. This discretion includes overturning verdicts for excessiveness and ordering a new trial without qualification, or conditioned on the verdict winner's refusal to agree to a reduction (remittitur).

In contrast, appellate review of a federal trial court's denial of a motion to set aside a jury's verdict as excessive is a . . . less secure development [as a matter of the Seventh Amendment Re-Examination Clause]. . . .

C

In *Byrd*, the Court faced a one-or-the-other choice: trial by judge as in state court, or trial by jury according to the federal practice. In the case before us, a choice of

that order is not required, for the principal state and federal interests can be accommodated. The Second Circuit correctly recognized that when New York substantive law governs a claim for relief, New York law and decisions guide the allowable damages. But that court did not take into account the characteristic of the federal court system that caused us to reaffirm: "The proper role of the trial and appellate courts in the federal system in reviewing the size of jury verdicts is . . . a matter of federal law." *Donovan v. Penn Shipping Co.*, 429 U.S. 648, 649 (1977).

New York's dominant interest can be respected, without disrupting the federal system, once it is recognized that the federal district court is capable of performing the checking function, *i.e.*, that court can apply the State's "deviates materially" standard in line with New York case law evolving under CPLR §5501(c).[22] We recall, in this regard, that the "deviates materially" standard serves as the guide to be applied in trial as well as appellate courts in New York.

Within the federal system, practical reasons combine with Seventh Amendment constraints to lodge in the district court, not the court of appeals, primary responsibility for application of §5501(c)'s "deviates materially" check. Trial judges have the "unique opportunity to consider the evidence in the living courtroom context,"

---

[22] Justice Scalia finds in Federal Rule of Civil Procedure 59 a "federal standard" for new trial motions in "direct collision" with, and "leaving no room for the operation of," a state law like CPLR §5501(c). The relevant prescription, Rule 59(a), has remained unchanged since the adoption of the Federal Rules by this Court in 1937. . . . [The ground] for a Rule 59 motion is that the damages are excessive. Whether damages are excessive for the claim-in-suit must be governed by *some law*. And there is no candidate for that governance other than the law that gives rise to the claim for relief—here, the law of New York.

Taylor v. Washington Terminal Co., 409 F.2d 145, 148 (D.C. Cir. 1969), while appellate judges see only the "cold paper record." 66 F.3d at 431.

District court applications of the "deviates materially" standard would be subject to appellate review under the standard the Circuits now employ when inadequacy or excessiveness is asserted on appeal: abuse of discretion. . . .

IV

It does not appear that the District Court checked the jury's verdict against the relevant New York decisions demanding more than "industry standard" testimony to support an award of the size the jury returned in this case. As the Court of Appeals recognized, the uniqueness of the photographs and the plaintiff's earnings as photographer—past and reasonably projected—are factors relevant to appraisal of the award. Accordingly, we vacate the judgment of the Court of Appeals and instruct that court to remand the case to the District Court so that the trial judge, revisiting his ruling on the new trial motion, may test the jury's verdict against CPLR §5501(c)'s "deviates materially" standard.

[The dissenting opinion of Justice Stevens, wherein he agreed with most of the Court's reasoning but disagreed that the Seventh Amendment limits the power of a federal appellate court sitting in diversity to decide whether damages exceeds a state's limit, is omitted.]

Justice SCALIA, with whom Chief Justice REHNQUIST and Justice THOMAS join, dissenting.

Today the Court overrules a longstanding and well-reasoned line of precedent that has for years prohibited federal appellate courts from reviewing refusals by district courts to set aside civil jury awards as contrary to the weight of the evidence. . . .

The Court also holds today that a state practice that relates to the division of duties between state judges and juries must be followed by federal courts in diversity cases. On this issue, too, our prior cases are directly to the contrary.

As I would reverse the judgment of the Court of Appeals, I respectfully dissent.

I

Granting appellate courts authority to decide whether an award is "excessive or inadequate" in the manner of CPLR §5501(c) may reflect a sound understanding of the capacities of modern juries and trial judges. That is to say, the people of the State of New York may well be correct that such a rule contributes to a more just legal system. But the practice of *federal* appellate reexamination of facts found by a jury is precisely what the People of the several States considered *not* to be good legal policy in 1791. Indeed, so fearful were they of such a practice that they constitutionally prohibited it by means of the Seventh Amendment. . . .

[I]t is not possible to review [a denial of a new trial motion] without engaging in a "reexamin[ation]" of the "facts tried by the jury" in a manner "otherwise" than allowed at common law. Determining whether a particular award is excessive requires that one first determine the nature and extent of the harm—which undeniably requires reviewing the facts of the case. That the court's review also entails application of a legal standard (whether "shocks the conscience," "deviates materially," or some other) makes no difference, for what is necessarily *also* required is *reexamination of facts* found by the jury. . . .

II

The Court's holding that federal courts of appeals may review district-court denials of motions for new trials for error of fact is not the only novel aspect of today's decision. The Court also directs that the case be remanded to the District Court, so that it may "test the jury's verdict against CPLR §5501(c)'s 'deviates materially' standard." This disposition contradicts the principle that "[t]he proper role of the trial and appellate courts in the federal system in reviewing the size of jury verdicts is . . . a matter of federal law." *Donovan v. Penn Shipping Co.*, 429 U.S. 648, 649 (1977). . . . [In sum], the . . . Court's *Erie* analysis is [fundamentally] flawed.

But in my view, one does not even reach the *Erie* question in this case. The standard to be applied by a district court in ruling on a motion for a new trial is set forth in Rule 59 of the Federal Rules of Civil Procedure, which provides that "[a] new trial may be granted . . . for any of the reasons for which new trials have heretofore been granted in actions at law *in the courts of the United States*." (Emphasis added.) That is undeniably a federal standard.[12] Federal District Courts in the Second Circuit have interpreted that standard to permit the granting of new trials where "it is quite clear that the jury has reached a seriously erroneous result" and letting the verdict stand would result in a "miscarriage of justice." *Bevevino v. Saydjari*, 574 F.2d 676, 684 (2d Cir. 1978). Assuming (as we have no reason to question) that this is a correct interpretation of what Rule 59 requires, it is undeniable that the Federal Rule is "sufficiently broad to cause a direct collision with the state law or, implicitly, to control the issue before the court, thereby leaving no room for the operation of that law." *Burlington Northern R. Co. v. Woods*, 480 U.S. 1, 4-5 (1987). It is simply not possible to give controlling effect both to the federal standard and the state standard in reviewing the jury's award. That being so, the court has no choice but to apply the Federal Rule, which is an exercise of what we have called Congress's "power to regulate matters which, though falling within the uncertain area between substance and procedure, are rationally capable of classification as either," *Hanna*, 380 U.S. at 472. . . .

When there is added to the revision of the Seventh Amendment the Court's precedent-setting disregard of Congress's instructions in Rule 59, one must conclude that this is a bad day for the Constitution's distinctive Article III courts in general, and for the role of the jury in those courts in particular. I respectfully dissent.

---

[12] I agree with the Court's entire progression of reasoning in its footnote 22, leading to the conclusion that *state* law must determine whether damages are excessive. But the question whether damages are excessive is quite separate from the question of when a jury award may be set aside for excessiveness. It is the latter that is governed by Rule 59. . . .

Notes & Questions

1. Again, the Court faced a question of whether to apply federal or state law in a diversity case. William Gasperini's claims against the center were state law claims, so under *Erie*, of course, the court must apply New York state law regarding breach of contract, conversion, and negligence. But what law should govern

how an appellate court reviews whether damages are excessive? Is it substantive or procedural? As Justice Ginsburg says in the understatement of the century, "[c]lassification of a law as 'substantive' or 'procedural' for *Erie* purposes is sometimes a challenging endeavor."

2. The question of how an appellate court reviews damages can be broken down into two separate issues, and each of them had been treated differently by New York courts and federal courts. Thus, there are *two* vertical conflicts of law in *Gasperini*. Precisely what are they? In applying the *Erie-Hanna* analysis, does the Court treat them the same way?

3. What role does the majority in *Gasperini* suggest that *Byrd* might play in the Rules of Decision Act analysis? Is its role limited to the context of the Seventh Amendment? Can you think of any other federal interests that a court might find compelling enough to consider in the Rules of Decision Act analysis?

4. *Gasperini* involves the application of both the Rules Enabling Act analysis and the Rules of Decision Act analysis. Justice Scalia contends that the Rules Enabling Act analysis should have disposed of the question in *Gasperini*. How? Why does the majority reject this position?

SHADY GROVE ORTHOPEDIC ASSOCIATES, P.A. v. ALLSTATE INSURANCE CO.
559 U.S. 393 (2010)

Justice SCALIA announced the judgment of the Court and delivered the opinion of the Court with respect to Parts I and II-A, an opinion with respect to Parts II-B and II-D, in which Chief Justice ROBERTS, Justice THOMAS, and Justice SOTOMAYOR join, and an opinion with respect to Part II-C, in which Chief Justice ROBERTS and Justice THOMAS join.

New York law prohibits class actions in suits seeking penalties or statutory minimum damages. We consider whether this precludes a federal district court sitting in diversity from entertaining a class action under Federal Rule of Civil Procedure 23.

I

The petitioner's complaint alleged the following: Shady Grove Orthopedic Associates,

P.A., provided medical care to Sonia E. Galvez for injuries she suffered in an automobile accident. As partial payment for that care, Galvez assigned to Shady Grove her rights to insurance benefits under a policy issued in New York by Allstate Insurance Co. Shady Grove tendered a claim for the assigned benefits to Allstate, which under New York law had 30 days to pay the claim or deny it. Allstate apparently paid, but not on time, and it refused to pay the statutory interest that accrued on the overdue benefits (at two percent per month).

Shady Grove filed this diversity suit in the Eastern District of New York to recover the unpaid statutory interest. Alleging that Allstate routinely refuses to pay interest on overdue benefits, Shady Grove sought relief on behalf of itself and a class of all others to whom Allstate owes interest. The District

Court dismissed the suit for lack of jurisdiction. It reasoned that N.Y. Civ. Prac. Law Ann. §901(b), which precludes a suit to recover a "penalty" from proceeding as a class action, applies in diversity suits in federal court, despite Federal Rule of Civil Procedure 23. Concluding that statutory interest is a "penalty" under New York law, it held that §901(b) prohibited the proposed class action. And, since Shady Grove conceded that its individual claim (worth roughly $500) fell far short of the amount-in-controversy requirement for individual suits under 28 U.S.C. §1332(a), the suit did not belong in federal court.

The Second Circuit affirmed. The court did not dispute that a federal rule adopted in compliance with the Rules Enabling Act would control if it conflicted with §901(b). But there was no conflict because (as we will describe in more detail below) the Second Circuit concluded that Rule 23 and §901(b) address different issues. Finding no federal rule on point, the Court of Appeals held that §901(b) is "substantive" within the meaning of *Erie R. Co. v. Tompkins*, 304 U.S. 64 (1938), and thus must be applied by federal courts sitting in diversity.

We granted certiorari, 556 U.S. 1220 (2009).

II

The framework for our decision is familiar. We must first determine whether Rule 23 answers the question in dispute. If it does, it governs—New York's law notwithstanding—unless it exceeds statutory authorization or Congress's rulemaking power. *See Hanna v. Plumer*, 380 U.S. 460, 463-464 (1965). We do not wade into *Erie*'s murky waters unless the federal rule is inapplicable or invalid. *See* 380 U.S. at 469-471.

A

The question in dispute is whether Shady Grove's suit may proceed as a class action. Rule 23 provides an answer. It states that "[a] class action may be maintained" if two conditions are met: The suit must satisfy the criteria set forth in subdivision (a) (*i.e.*, numerosity, commonality, typicality, and adequacy of representation), and it also must fit into one of the three categories described in subdivision (b). Fed. Rule Civ. Proc. 23(b). By its terms this creates a categorical rule entitling a plaintiff whose suit meets the specified criteria to pursue his claim as a class action. Thus, Rule 23 provides a one-size-fits-all formula for deciding the class-action question. Because §901(b) attempts to answer the same question—*i.e.*, it states that Shady Grove's suit "may *not* be maintained as a class action" (emphasis added) because of the relief it seeks—it cannot apply in diversity suits unless Rule 23 is ultra vires.

The Second Circuit believed that §901(b) and Rule 23 do not conflict because they address different issues. Rule 23, it said, concerns only the criteria for determining whether a given class can and should be certified; section 901(b), on the other hand, addresses an antecedent question: whether the particular type of claim is eligible for class treatment in the first place—a question on which Rule 23 is silent. Allstate embraces this analysis.

We disagree. To begin with, the line between eligibility and certifiability is entirely artificial. Both are preconditions for maintaining a class action. Allstate suggests that eligibility must depend on the "particular cause of action" asserted, instead of some other attribute of the suit. But that is not so. Congress could, for example, provide that only claims involving more than a certain number of plaintiffs are "eligible" for class treatment in federal court. In other words, relabeling Rule 23(a)'s prerequisites "eligibility criteria" would obviate Allstate's objection—a sure sign that its eligibility-certifiability distinction is made-to-order.

There is no reason, in any event, to read Rule 23 as addressing only whether claims made eligible for class treatment by some *other* law should be certified as class actions. Allstate asserts that Rule 23 neither explicitly nor implicitly empowers a federal court "to certify a class in each and every case" where the Rule's criteria are met. But that is *exactly* what Rule 23 does: It says that if the prescribed preconditions are satisfied "[a] class action *may be maintained*" (emphasis added)—not "*a class action may be permitted*." Courts do not maintain actions; litigants do. The discretion suggested by Rule 23's "may" is discretion residing in the plaintiff: He may bring his claim in a class action if he wishes. And like the rest of the Federal Rules of Civil Procedure, Rule 23 *automatically* applies "in all civil actions and proceedings in the United States district courts," Fed. Rule Civ. Proc. 1. . . .

The dissent argues that §901(b) has nothing to do with whether Shady Grove may maintain its suit as a class action, but affects only the *remedy* it may obtain if it wins. Whereas "Rule 23 governs procedural aspects of class litigation" by "prescrib[ing] the considerations relevant to class certification and postcertification proceedings," §901(b) addresses only "the size of a monetary award a class plaintiff may pursue." Accordingly, the dissent says, Rule 23 and New York's law may coexist in peace.

We need not decide whether a state law that limits the remedies available in an existing class action would conflict with Rule 23; that is not what §901(b) does. By its terms, the provision precludes a plaintiff

from "maintain[ing]" a class action seeking statutory penalties. Unlike a law that sets a ceiling on damages (or puts other remedies out of reach) in properly filed class actions, §901(b) says nothing about what remedies a court may award; it prevents the class actions it covers from coming into existence at all. Consequently, a court bound by §901(b) could not certify a class action seeking both statutory penalties and other remedies even if it announces in advance that it will refuse to award the penalties in the event the plaintiffs prevail; to do so would violate the statute's clear prohibition on "maintain[ing]" such suits as class actions. . . .

But while the dissent does indeed artificially narrow the scope of §901(b) by finding that it pursues only substantive policies, that is not the central difficulty of the dissent's position. The central difficulty is that even artificial narrowing cannot render §901(b) compatible with Rule 23. *Whatever* the policies they pursue, they flatly contradict each other. Allstate asserts (and the dissent implies) that we can (and must) *interpret* Rule 23 in a manner that avoids overstepping its authorizing statute. If the Rule were susceptible of two meanings—one that would violate §2072(b) and another that would not—we would agree. But it is not. Rule 23 unambiguously authorizes *any* plaintiff, in *any* federal civil proceeding, to maintain a class action if the Rule's prerequisites are met. We cannot contort its text, even to avert a collision with state law that might render it invalid. What the dissent's approach achieves is not the avoiding of a "conflict between Rule 23 and §901(b)," but rather the invalidation of Rule 23 (pursuant to §2072(b) of the Rules Enabling Act) to the extent that it conflicts with the substantive policies of §901. There is no other way to reach the dissent's destination. We must therefore confront head-on whether Rule 23 falls within the statutory authorization.

B

Erie involved the constitutional power of federal courts to supplant state law with judge-made rules. In that context, it made no difference whether the rule was technically one of substance or procedure; the touchstone was whether it "significantly affect[s] the result of a litigation." *Guaranty Trust Co. v. York*, 326 U.S. 99 (1945). That is not the test for either the constitutionality or the statutory validity of a Federal Rule of Procedure. Congress has undoubted power to supplant state law, and undoubted power to prescribe rules for the courts it has created, so long as those rules regulate matters "rationally capable of classification" as procedure. *Hanna*, 380 U.S. at 472. In the Rules Enabling Act, Congress authorized this Court to promulgate rules of procedure subject to its review, but with the limitation that those rules "shall not abridge, enlarge or modify any substantive right," §2072(b).

We have long held that this limitation means that the Rule must "really regulat[e] procedure,—the judicial process for enforcing rights and duties recognized by substantive law and for justly administering remedy and redress for disregard or infraction of them," *Sibbach*, 312 U.S. at 14. The test is not whether the rule affects a litigant's substantive rights; most procedural rules do. What matters is what the rule itself regulates: If it governs only "the manner and the means" by which the litigants' rights are "enforced," it is valid; if it alters "the rules of decision by which [the] court will adjudicate [those] rights," it is not. *Mississippi Publishing Corp. v. Murphree*, 326 U.S. 438, 446 (1946).

Applying that test, we have rejected every statutory challenge to a Federal Rule that has come before us. We have found to be in compliance with §2072(b) rules prescribing methods for serving process, *see Hanna, supra* at 463-465 (Fed. Rule Civ. Proc. 4(d)(1)), and requiring litigants whose mental or physical condition is in dispute to submit to examinations, *see Sibbach, supra* at 14-16 (Fed. Rule Civ. Proc. 35). Likewise, we have upheld rules authorizing imposition of sanctions upon those who file frivolous appeals, *see Burlington, supra* at 8 (Fed. Rule App. Proc. 38), or who sign court papers without a reasonable inquiry into the facts asserted, *see Business Guides, Inc. v. Chromatic Communications Enterprises, Inc.*, 498 U.S. 533, 551-554 (1991) (Fed. Rule Civ. Proc. 11). Each of these rules had some practical effect on the parties' rights, but each undeniably regulated only the process for enforcing those rights; none altered the rights themselves, the available remedies, or the rules of decision by which the court adjudicated either.

Applying that criterion, we think it obvious that rules allowing multiple claims (and claims by or against multiple parties) to be litigated together are also valid. *See, e.g.*, Fed. Rules Civ. Proc. 18 (joinder of claims), 20 (joinder of parties), 42(a) (consolidation of actions). Such rules neither change plaintiffs' separate entitlements to relief nor abridge defendants' rights; they alter only how the claims are processed. For the same reason, Rule 23—at least insofar as it allows willing plaintiffs to join their separate claims against the same defendants in a class action—falls within §2072(b)'s authorization. A class action, no less than traditional joinder (of which it is a species), merely enables a federal court to adjudicate claims of multiple parties at once, instead of in separate suits. And like traditional joinder, it leaves the parties' legal rights and duties intact and the rules of decision unchanged.

Allstate contends that the authorization of class actions is not substantively neutral: Allowing Shady Grove to sue on behalf of a class "transform[s] [the] dispute over a five *hundred* dollar penalty into a dispute over a five *million* dollar penalty." Allstate's aggregate liability, however, does not depend on whether the suit proceeds as a class action. Each of the 1,000-plus members of the putative class could (as Allstate acknowledges) bring a freestanding suit asserting his individual claim. It is undoubtedly true that some plaintiffs who would not bring individual suits for the relatively small sums involved will choose to join a class action. That has no bearing, however, on Allstate's or the plaintiffs' legal rights. The likelihood that some (even many) plaintiffs will be induced to sue by the availability of a class action is just the sort of "incidental effec[t]" we have long held does not violate §2072(b). *Mississippi Publishing, supra* at 445.

Allstate argues that Rule 23 violates §2072(b) because the state law it displaces, §901(b), creates a right that the Federal Rule abridges—namely, a "substantive right . . . not to be subjected to aggregated class-action liability" in a single suit. To begin with, we doubt that that is so. Nothing in the text of §901(b) (which is to be found in New York's procedural code) confines it to claims under New York law; and of course New York has no power to alter substantive rights and duties created by other sovereigns. As we have said, the *consequence* of excluding certain class actions may be to cap the damages a defendant can face in a single suit, but the law itself alters only procedure. In that respect, §901(b) is no different from a state law forbidding simple joinder. As a fallback argument, Allstate argues that even if §901(b) is a procedural provision, it was enacted "for *substantive reasons.*" Its end was not to improve "the conduct of the litigation process itself" but to alter "the outcome of that process."

The fundamental difficulty with both these arguments is that the substantive nature of New York's law, or its substantive purpose, *makes no difference.* A Federal Rule of Procedure is not valid in some jurisdictions and invalid in others—or valid in some cases and invalid in others—depending upon whether its effect is to frustrate a state substantive law (or a state procedural law enacted for substantive purposes). . . .

In sum, it is not the substantive or procedural nature or purpose of the affected state law that matters, but the substantive or procedural nature of the Federal Rule. We have held since *Sibbach*, and reaffirmed repeatedly, that the validity of a Federal Rule depends entirely upon whether it regulates procedure. *See Sibbach, supra* at 14; *Hanna, supra* at 464; *Burlington*, 480 U.S. at 8. If it does, it is authorized by §2072 and is valid in all jurisdictions, with respect to all claims, regardless of its incidental effect upon state-created rights.

C

. . . The concurrence would decide this case on the basis, not that Rule 23 is procedural, but that the state law it displaces is procedural, in the sense that it does not "function as a part of the State's definition of substantive rights and remedies." A state procedural rule is not preempted, according to the concurrence, so long as it is "so bound up with," or "sufficiently intertwined with," a substantive state-law right or remedy "that it defines the scope of that substantive right or remedy."

This analysis squarely conflicts with *Sibbach*, which established the rule we apply. The concurrence contends that *Sibbach* did not rule out its approach, but that is not so. Recognizing the impracticability of a test that turns on the idiosyncrasies of state law, *Sibbach* adopted and applied a rule with a single criterion: whether the Federal Rule "really regulates procedure." 312 U.S. at 14. . . .

D

We must acknowledge the reality that keeping the federal-court door open to class actions that cannot proceed in state court will produce forum shopping. That is unacceptable when it comes as the consequence of judge-made rules created to fill supposed "gaps" in positive federal law. *See Hanna*, 380 U.S. at 471-472. For where neither the Constitution, a treaty, nor a statute provides the rule of decision or authorizes a federal court to supply one, "state law must govern because there can be no other law." *Ibid.* But divergence from state law, with the attendant consequence of forum shopping, is the inevitable (indeed, one might say the intended) result of a uniform system of federal procedure. Congress itself has created the possibility that the same case may follow a different course if filed in federal instead of state court. The short of the matter is that a Federal Rule governing procedure is valid whether or not it alters the outcome of the case in a way that induces forum shopping. To hold otherwise would be to "disembowel either the Constitution's grant of power over federal procedure" or Congress's exercise of it. *Hanna, supra* at 473-74.

* * *

The judgment of the Court of Appeals is reversed, and the case is remanded for further proceedings.

Justice STEVENS, concurring in part and concurring in the judgment.

The New York law at issue, N.Y. Civ. Prac. Law Ann. (CPLR) §901(b), is a procedural rule that is not part of New York's substantive law. Accordingly, I agree with Justice Scalia that Federal Rule of Civil Procedure 23 must apply in this case and join Parts I and II-A of the Court's opinion. But I also agree with Justice Ginsburg that there are some state procedural rules that federal courts must apply in diversity cases because they function as a part of the State's definition of substantive rights and remedies.

I

It is a long-recognized principle that federal courts sitting in diversity "apply state substantive law and federal procedural law." *Hanna v. Plumer*, 380 U.S. 460, 465 (1965). . . . [W]hen a situation is covered by a federal rule, the . . . Rules Enabling Act (Enabling Act) controls. *See* 28 U.S.C. §2072.

That does not mean, however, that the federal rule always governs. Congress has provided for a system of uniform federal rules under which federal courts sitting in diversity operate as "an independent system for administering justice to litigants who properly invoke its jurisdiction," *Byrd v. Blue Ridge Rural Elec. Cooperative, Inc.*, 356 U.S. 525, 537 (1958), and not as state-court clones that assume all aspects of state tribunals but are managed by Article III judges. *See Hanna*, 380 U.S. at 473-474. But while Congress may have the *constitutional* power to prescribe procedural rules that interfere with state substantive law in any number of respects, that is not what Congress has done (emphasis added). Instead, it has provided in the Enabling Act that although "[t]he Supreme Court" may "prescribe general rules of practice and procedure," §2072(a), those rules "shall not abridge, enlarge or modify any substantive right," §2072(b). The Enabling Act's limitation does not mean that federal rules cannot displace state policy judgments; it means only that federal rule cannot displace a State's definition of its own rights or remedies. *See Sibbach*, 312 U.S. at 13-14.

Congress has thus struck a balance: "[H]ousekeeping rules for federal courts" will generally apply in diversity cases, notwithstanding that some federal rules "will inevitably differ" from state rules. *Hanna*, 380 U.S. at 473. But . . . federal rules must be interpreted with some degree of "sensitivity to important state interests and regulatory policies," *Gasperini*, 518 U.S. at 427 n.7, and applied to diversity cases against the background of Congress' command that such rules not alter substantive rights and with consideration of "the degree to which the Rule makes the character and result of the federal litigation stray from the course it would follow in state courts," *Hanna*, 380 U.S. at 473. This can be a tricky balance to implement.

It is important to observe that the balance Congress has struck turns, in part, on the nature of the state law that is being displaced by a federal rule. And in my view, the application of that balance does not necessarily turn on whether the state law at issue takes the *form* of what is traditionally described as substantive or procedural. Rather, it turns on whether the state law actually is part of a State's framework of substantive rights or remedies. *See* §2072(b); *cf. Hanna*, 380 U.S. at 471 ("The line between 'substance' and 'procedure' shifts as the legal context changes"); *York*, 326 U.S. at 108 (noting that the words "substance" and "procedure" "[e]ach impl[y] different variables depending upon the particular problem for which [they] are used").

. . . A "state procedural rule, though undeniably 'procedural' in the ordinary sense of the term," may exist "to influence substantive outcomes," *S.A. Healy Co. v. Milwaukee Metro. Sewerage Dist.*, 60 F.3d 305, 310 (7th Cir. 1995) (Posner, J.), and may in some instances become so bound up with the state-created right or remedy that it defines the scope of that substantive right or remedy. Such laws, for example, may be seemingly procedural rules that make it significantly more difficult to bring or to prove a claim, thus serving to limit the scope of that claim. *See, e.g., Cohen*, 337 U.S. at 555 (state "procedure" that required plaintiffs to post bond before suing); *Guaranty Trust Co.*, 326 U.S. 99 (state statute of limitations). Such "procedural rules" may also define the amount of recovery. *See, e.g., Gasperini*, 518 U.S. at 427 (state procedure for examining jury verdicts as means of capping the available remedy).

In our federalist system, Congress has not mandated that federal courts dictate to state legislatures the form that their substantive law must take. And were federal courts to ignore those portions of substantive state law that operate as procedural devices, it could in many instances limit the ways that sovereign States may define their rights and remedies. When a State chooses to use a traditionally procedural vehicle as a means of defining the scope of substantive rights or remedies, federal courts must recognize and respect that choice.

II

When both a federal rule and a state law appear to govern a question before a federal court sitting in diversity, our precedents have set out a two-step framework for federal courts to negotiate this thorny area. At both steps of the inquiry, there is a critical question about what the state law and the federal rule mean.

The court must first determine whether the scope of the federal rule is "sufficiently broad" to "control the issue" before the court, "thereby leaving no room for the operation" of seemingly conflicting state law. *See Burlington Northern*, 480 U.S. at 4-5. If the federal rule does not apply or can operate alongside the state rule, then there is no "Ac[t] of Congress" governing that particular question, 28 U.S.C. §1652, and the court must engage in the traditional Rules of Decision Act inquiry under *Erie* and its progeny.

If, on the other hand, the federal rule is "sufficiently broad to control the issue before the Court," such that there is a "direct collision," *Walker*, 446 U.S. at 749-50, the court must decide whether application of the federal rule "represents a valid exercise" of the "rulemaking authority . . . bestowed on this Court by the Rules Enabling Act." *Burlington Northern*, 480 U.S. at 5. . . . Unlike Justice Scalia, I believe that an application of a federal rule that effectively abridges, enlarges, or modifies a state-created right or remedy violates this command. . . .

Thus, the second step of the inquiry may well bleed back into the first. When a federal rule appears to abridge, enlarge, or modify a substantive right, federal courts must consider whether the rule can reasonably be interpreted to avoid that impermissible result. And when such a "saving" construction is not possible and the rule would violate the Enabling Act, federal courts cannot apply the rule. A federal rule, therefore, cannot govern a particular case in which the rule would displace a state law that is procedural in the ordinary use of the term but is so intertwined with a state right or remedy that it functions to define the scope of the state-created right. And absent a governing federal rule, a federal court must engage in the traditional Rules of Decision Act inquiry, under the *Erie* line of cases. This application of the Enabling Act shows "sensitivity to important state interests" and "regulatory policies," but it does so as Congress authorized, by ensuring that federal rules that ordinarily "prescribe general rules of practice and procedure," §2072(a), do "not abridge, enlarge or modify any substantive right," §2072(b).

Justice Scalia believes that the sole Enabling Act question is whether the federal rule "really regulates procedure," which means, apparently, whether it regulates "the manner and means by which litigants' rights are enforced." I respectfully disagree. This interpretation of the Enabling Act is consonant with the Act's first limitation to "general rules of practice and procedure," §2072(a). But it ignores the second limitation that such rules also "not abridge, enlarge or modify *any* substantive right," §2072(b) (emphasis added), and in so doing ignores the balance that Congress struck between uniform rules of federal procedure and respect for a State's construction of its own rights and remedies. It also ignores the separation-of-powers presumption and federalism presumption that counsel against judicially created rules displacing state substantive law. . . .

Although Justice Scalia may generally prefer easily administrable, bright-line rules, his preference does not give us license to adopt a second-best interpretation of the Rules Enabling Act. Courts cannot ignore text and context in the service of simplicity. . . .

III

. . . I [therefore] readily acknowledge that if a federal rule displaces a state rule that is " 'procedural' in the ordinary sense of the term," *S.A. Healy Co.*, 60 F.3d at

310, but sufficiently interwoven with the scope of a substantive right or remedy, there would be an Enabling Act problem, and the federal rule would have to give way. In my view, [the bar for finding an Enabling Act problem is a high one;] this is not such a case. . . .

Justice GINSBURG, with whom Justice KEN-NEDY, Justice BREYER, and Justice ALITO join, dissenting.

The Court today approves Shady Grove's attempt to transform a $500 case into a $5,000,000 award, although the State creating the right to recover has proscribed this alchemy. If Shady Grove had filed suit in New York state court, the 2% interest payment authorized by New York Ins. Law Ann. §5106(a) (West 2009) as a penalty for overdue benefits would, by Shady Grove's own measure, amount to no more than $500. By instead filing in federal court based on the parties' diverse citizenship and requesting class certification, Shady Grove hopes to recover, for the class, statutory damages of more than $5,000,000. The New York Legislature has barred this remedy, instructing that, unless specifically permitted, "an action to recover a penalty, or minimum measure of recovery created or imposed by statute may not be maintained as a class action." N.Y. Civ. Prac. Law Ann. (CPLR) §901(b) (West 2006). The Court nevertheless holds that Federal Rule of Civil Procedure 23, which prescribes procedures for the conduct of class actions in federal courts, preempts the application of §901(b) in diversity suits.

The Court reads Rule 23 relentlessly to override New York's restriction on the availability of statutory damages. Our decisions, however, caution us to ask, before undermining state legislation: Is this conflict really necessary? Had the Court

engaged in that inquiry, it would not have read Rule 23 to collide with New York's legitimate interest in keeping certain monetary awards reasonably bounded. I would continue to interpret Federal Rules with awareness of, and sensitivity to, important state regulatory policies. Because today's judgment radically departs from that course, I dissent.

I

A

. . . If a Federal Rule controls an issue and directly conflicts with a state law, the Rule, so long as it is consonant with the Rules Enabling Act, applies in diversity suits. *See Hanna*, 380 U.S. at 469-74. If however, no Federal Rule or statute governs the issue, the Rules of Decision Act, as interpreted in *Erie*, controls. That Act directs federal courts, in diversity cases, to apply state law when failure to do so would invite forum shopping and yield markedly disparate litigation outcomes. *See Gasperini*, 518 U.S. at 428; *Hanna*, 380 U.S. at 468. Recognizing that the Rules of Decision Act and the Rules Enabling Act simultaneously frame and inform the *Erie* analysis, we have endeavored in diversity suits to remain safely within the bounds of both Congressional directives.

B

In our prior decisions in point, many of them not mentioned in the Court's opinion, we have avoided immoderate interpretations of the Federal Rules that would trench on state prerogatives without serving any countervailing federal interest. "Application of the *Hanna* analysis," we have said, "is premised on a 'direct collision' between the Federal Rule and the state law." *Walker v. Armco Steel Corp.*, 446 U.S. 740, 749-50

(1980) (quoting *Hanna*, 380 U.S. at 472). To displace state law, a Federal Rule, "when fairly construed," must be "sufficiently broad" so as "to control the issue before the court, thereby leaving *no room* for the operation of that law." *Burlington Northern*, 480 U.S. at 4-5. . . .

Following *Hanna*, we [have] continued to "interpre[t] the federal rules to avoid conflict with important state regulatory policies." Hart & Wechsler 593. . . . [Indeed,] both before and after *Hanna*, federal courts have been cautioned by this Court to "interpre[t] the Federal Rules . . . with sensitivity to important state interests," *Gasperini*, 518 U.S. at 427 n.7, and a will "to avoid conflict with important state regulatory policies," *id.* at 438 n.22. The Court veers away from that approach—and conspicuously, its most recent reiteration in *Gasperini*—in favor of a mechanical reading of Federal Rules, insensitive to state interests and productive of discord.

C

Our decisions instruct over and over again that, in the adjudication of diversity cases, state interests—whether advanced in a statute or a procedural rule—warrant our respectful consideration. Yet today, the Court gives no quarter to New York's limitation on statutory damages and requires the lower courts to thwart the regulatory policy at stake: To prevent excessive damages, New York's law controls the penalty to which a defendant may be exposed in a single suit. . . .

Section 901(a) allows courts leeway in deciding whether to certify a class, but §901(b) rejects the use of the class mechanism to pursue the particular remedy of statutory damages. The limitation was not designed with the fair conduct or efficiency of litigation in mind. Indeed, suits seeking statutory damages are arguably *best* suited to the class device because individual proof of actual damages is unnecessary. New York's decision instead to block class-action proceedings for statutory damages therefore makes scant sense, except as a means to a manifestly substantive end: Limiting a defendant's liability in a single lawsuit in order to prevent the exorbitant inflation of penalties—remedies the New York Legislature created with individual suits in mind.

D

Shady Grove contends—and the Court today agrees—that Rule 23 unavoidably preempts New York's prohibition on the recovery of statutory damages in class actions. The Federal Rule, the Court emphasizes, states that Shady Grove's suit "may be" maintained as a class action, which conflicts with §901(b)'s instruction that it "may not" so proceed. Accordingly, the Court insists, §901(b) "cannot apply in diversity suits unless Rule 23 is ultra vires." Concluding that Rule 23 does not violate the Rules Enabling Act, the Court holds that the federal provision controls Shady Grove's ability to seek, on behalf of a class, a statutory penalty of over $5,000,000.

The Court, I am convinced, finds conflict where none is necessary. Mindful of the history behind §901(b)'s enactment, the thrust of our precedent, and the substantive-rights limitation in the Rules Enabling Act, I conclude, as did the Second Circuit and every District Court to have considered the question in any detail, that Rule 23 does not collide with §901(b). As the Second Circuit well understood, Rule 23 prescribes the considerations relevant to class certification and postcertification proceedings—but it does not command that a particular remedy be available when a party sues in a representative capacity.

Section 901(b), in contrast, trains on that latter issue. Sensibly read, Rule 23 governs procedural aspects of class litigation, but allows state law to control the size of a monetary award a class plaintiff may pursue.

In other words, Rule 23 describes a method of enforcing a claim for relief, while §901(b) defines the dimensions of the claim itself. In this regard, it is immaterial that §901(b) bars statutory penalties in wholesale, rather than retail, fashion. The New York Legislature could have embedded the limitation in every provision creating a cause of action for which a penalty is authorized; §901(b) operates as shorthand to the same effect. It is as much a part of the delineation of the claim for relief as it would be were it included claim by claim in the New York Code.

The Court single-mindedly focuses on whether a suit "may" or "may not" be maintained as a class action. Putting the question that way, the Court does not home in on the reason *why*. Rule 23 authorizes class treatment for suits satisfying its prerequisites because the class mechanism generally affords a fair and efficient way to aggregate claims for adjudication. Section 901(b) responds to an entirely different concern; it does not allow class members to recover statutory damages because the New York Legislature considered the result of adjudicating such claims en masse to be exorbitant. The fair and efficient *conduct* of class litigation is the legitimate concern of Rule 23; the *remedy* for an infraction of state law, however, is the legitimate concern of the State's lawmakers and not of the federal rulemakers. . . .

The absence of an inevitable collision between Rule 23 and §901(b) becomes evident once it is comprehended that a federal court sitting in diversity can accord due respect to both state and federal prescriptions. Plaintiffs seeking to vindicate claims

for which the State has provided a statutory penalty may pursue relief through a class action if they forgo statutory damages and instead seek actual damages or injunctive or declaratory relief; any putative class member who objects can opt out and pursue actual damages, if available, and the statutory penalty in an individual action. In this manner, the Second Circuit explained, "Rule 23's procedural requirements for class actions can be applied along with the substantive requirement of CPLR 901(b)." 549 F.3d at 144. In sum, while phrased as responsive to the question whether certain class actions may begin, §901(b) is unmistakably aimed at controlling how those actions must end. On that remedial issue, Rule 23 is silent.

Any doubt whether Rule 23 leaves §901(b) in control of the remedial issue at the core of this case should be dispelled by our *Erie* jurisprudence, including *Hanna*, which counsels us to read Federal Rules moderately and cautions against stretching a rule to cover every situation it could conceivably reach. . . . Is there any reason to read Rule 23 as authorizing a claim for relief when the State that created the remedy disallows its pursuit on behalf of a class? None at all is the answer our federal system should give. . . .

By finding a conflict without considering whether Rule 23 rationally should be read to avoid any collision, the Court unwisely and unnecessarily retreats from the federalism principles undergirding *Erie*. Had the Court reflected on the respect for state regulatory interests endorsed in our decisions, it would have found no cause to interpret Rule 23 so woodenly—and every reason not to do so.

II

Because I perceive no unavoidable conflict between Rule 23 and §901(b), I would decide this case by inquiring "whether application of the [state] rule would have so important an effect upon the fortunes of one or both of the litigants that failure to [apply] it would be likely to cause a plaintiff to choose the federal court." *Hanna*, 380 U.S. at 468 n.9. . . .

Seeking to pretermit that inquiry, Shady Grove urges that the class-action bar in §901(b) must be regarded as "procedural" because it is contained the CPLR, which "govern[s] the *procedure* in civil judicial proceedings *in all courts of the state.*" Placement in the CPLR is hardly dispositive. The provision held "substantive" for *Erie* purposes in *Gasperini* is also contained in the CPLR (§5501(c)), as are limitations periods, §201 *et seq.*, prescriptions plainly "substantive" for *Erie* purposes however they may be characterized for other purposes, *see York*, 326 U.S. at 109. . . .

It is beyond debate that "a statutory cap on damages would supply substantive law for *Erie* purposes." *Gasperini*, 518 U.S. at 428. . . . *Gasperini*'s observations apply with full force in this case. By barring the recovery of statutory damages in a class action, §901(b) controls a defendant's maximum liability in a suit seeking such a remedy. The remedial provision could have been written as an explicit cap: "In any class action seeking statutory damages, relief is limited to the amount the named plaintiff would have recovered in an individual suit." That New York's Legislature used other words to express the very same meaning should be inconsequential. . . .

III

The Court's erosion of *Erie*'s federalism grounding impels me to point out the large irony in today's judgment. Shady Grove is able to pursue its claim in federal court only by virtue of the recent enactment of the Class Action Fairness Act of 2005 (CAFA), 28 U.S.C. §1332(d). In CAFA, Congress opened federal-court doors to state-law-based class actions so long as there is minimal diversity, at least 100 class members, and at least $5,000,000 in controversy. *Ibid.* By providing a federal forum, Congress sought to check what it considered to be the overreadiness of some state courts to certify class actions. *See, e.g.*, S. Rep. No. 109-14, p. 4 (2005) (CAFA prevents lawyers from "gam[ing]" the procedural rules [to] keep nationwide or multi-state class actions in state courts whose judges have reputations for readily certifying classes."); *id.* at 22 (disapproving "the 'I never met a class action I didn't like' approach to class certification" that "is prevalent in state courts in some localities"). In other words, Congress envisioned fewer—not more—class actions overall. Congress surely never anticipated that CAFA would make federal courts a mecca for suits of the kind Shady Grove has launched: class actions seeking state-created penalties for claims arising under state law—claims that would be barred from class treatment in the State's own courts.

* * *

I would continue to approach *Erie* questions in a manner mindful of the purposes underlying the Rules of Decision Act and the Rules Enabling Act, faithful to precedent, and respectful of important state interests. I would therefore hold that the New York Legislature's limitation on the recovery of statutory damages applies in this case, and would affirm the Second Circuit's judgment.

Notes & Questions

1. Again, we see Justice Ginsburg and Justice Scalia bringing different modes of analysis to an *Erie* problem, just as we saw in *Gasperini*. Before turning to their disagreements, however, note what they agree on. Look at the step-by-step analysis each of them offers, and notice the extent to which they apply the same analytical structure for their *Erie* analyses, separating the Rules Enabling Act and Rules of Decision Act questions. Thus, the basic framework of *Erie* analysis is well established, even as the Justices diverge in how they apply it in hard cases. What is the state of the law regarding *Erie* analysis after *Shady Grove*, given that there is no majority opinion?

2. The plurality and the dissent in *Shady Grove* first disagree about whether there is a "direct conflict" between Federal Rule of Procedure 23 and New York's CPLR §901(b). What is the analytical consequence of finding a "direct conflict"?

3. Justice Stevens concurs with a great deal of the plurality opinion. What, precisely, is his point of disagreement with the plurality? Specifically, what would a Rules Enabling Act analysis look like under Justice Stevens' approach?

4. All three opinions grapple with the characterization of "substance" and "procedure." Note, however, that the Justices do not fully agree on precisely *what* must be evaluated as "substantive" or "procedural." For Justice Scalia and the plurality, the only relevant inquiry under the Rules Enabling Act is whether the *federal* rule is "procedural." Why does Justice Scalia conclude that Rule 23 is "procedural"? For Justice Stevens in concurrence, and for Justice Ginsburg and the dissenters (and thus for a majority of the nine Justices), the Rules Enabling Act inquiry should go further and look at whether the *state* rule is "substantive" or "procedural."

   First, consider the difference between the Scalia group's view (that it does not matter whether New York's section 901(b) is substantive) and the Stevens-Ginsburg group's view (that it does matter whether section 901(b) is substantive). What is the argument for each position?

   Next, consider the difference between Justice Stevens' view (that section 901(b) is *not* substantive) and Justice Ginsburg's view (that section 901(b) *is* substantive). What is the argument for each position?

5. Why do Justice Stevens and the dissenting Justices disagree on the "procedural" or "substantive" nature of section 901(b)? What would Justice Stevens need to see in order to find that section 901(b) is "substantive"? Finally, if section 901(b) fit Justice Stevens' criteria for being substantive, would the plurality's decision come out any differently?

6. Both the plurality and the dissent discuss the separation-of-powers considerations at work in *Shady Grove*. The plurality, however, engages in a formalistic analysis that defers largely to the federal enactments of Congress, while the dissent sets out a more functional analysis that attempts to be more accommodating of state interests and federalism values. Think all the way back to the *Erie* opinion itself. Does *Shady Grove* reveal that the *Erie* doctrine is still looking for its constitutional footing?

CHAPTER 13

Settlement, Mediation, and Arbitration

After 12 chapters devoted to understanding the litigation-adjudication process, we conclude our exploration of civil procedure by stepping outside of both litigation and adjudication. We will step outside in several ways.

First, we will step outside of *adjudication* to focus on settlement as a means of dispute resolution. By adjudication, we mean a court decision that determines the parties' rights and liabilities. This definition of adjudication includes not only judgments based on verdicts at trial, but also judgments reached by granting a motion to dismiss or summary judgment, as well as any other resolution of a dispute through the entry of a court judgment based on the court's determinations of facts, law, or both. *Settlement*, by contrast, is when the parties take the determination of their dispute into their own hands. Whereas adjudication involves judicial determination of facts, determination of law, and application of law to facts, settlement simply involves the parties' agreeing on a mutually acceptable resolution. The possibility of settlement, of course, has been a subtext throughout the book. Whenever you represent a client in litigation, you will experience each step in the litigation-adjudication process as infused with the possibility of a negotiated resolution. But at this point in the book, rather than treating settlement as something important to be aware of in the background, we will consider settlement as a topic of its own.

Next, we will turn to several forms of what many people call "alternative dispute resolution" or "ADR." We resist calling it this because we do not believe that litigation is rightly understood as the *normal* way to resolve disputes. Humans (and entities, too) have disputes every day, ranging from petty matters to weighty ones. The vast majority of disputes get resolved without litigation, and for that matter without *any* formally conceived process. Even among disputes that undergo a relatively formal process for resolution, litigation is only one of several ways to go. As a lawyer, you want to be aware of all of your client's options. In any event, many lawyers and others use the label ADR to refer to mediation, arbitration, and related practices. Regardless of the label, lawyers must be familiar with at least four mechanisms for resolving disputes: litigation, negotiation, mediation, and arbitration. Do not think of each merely as a stand-alone option; these mechanisms often function together in an interwoven process for resolving any particular dispute. In this chapter, after examining settlement, we will turn to *mediation*, in which a neutral person facilitates settlement, and finally we will turn to *arbitration*, in which a private decision maker renders a binding decision to resolve a dispute.

Our brief exploration of forms of dispute resolution will give you a hint of the panoply of options available to clients. We intend for this chapter not only to help you think about negotiation, mediation, and arbitration, but also to help you think about what is unique and important about civil litigation and adjudication in the public courts. In addition, by looking at things from different angles, we hope the chapter will enhance your appreciation of procedural design, procedural choices, and procedural strategy.

A. SETTLEMENT

(1) Settlement as Contract

A settlement is a contract, and for the most part settlements of litigated disputes are governed by ordinary principles of contract law. Often, one party agrees to pay a certain amount of money and the other party agrees to release its claim and drop the lawsuit. The details may vary: Sometimes there are multiple parties. Sometimes the remedy is something other than money. Sometimes there are counterclaims so releases may go both ways. Sometimes the payouts are structured as a series of installments over time. But, at bottom, the settlement is a contract, a binding agreement by the parties to resolve their dispute on terms reached by negotiation.

Start by reading the following settlement agreement, a pretty standard example of the genre.

GENERAL RELEASE AND SETTLEMENT AGREEMENT

This General Release and Settlement Agreement (this "**Agreement**") is entered into as of this 20th day of January, 2012 (the "**Effective Date**"), by and between Kid Brands, Inc., ("**KID**"), and The Realty Associates Fund VIII, L.P. ("**Fund VIII**") (KID and Fund VIII are at times hereafter collectively referred to as the "**Parties**," and each individually, a "**Party**").

RECITALS

WHEREAS, on or about July 18, 2011, Fund VIII filed a civil action against KID in the Superior Court of New Jersey, Law Division: Middlesex County, Docket No. L 5153-11 for breach of contract (the "**Action**"); and

WHEREAS, KID denies all liability to Fund VIII for the claims asserted in the Action; and

WHEREAS, the Parties wish to settle their dispute, as well as all other claims, disputes and matters that could have been litigated or asserted in the Action, without any admission of liability, as of the Effective Date, in the interest of conserving resources, time, fees and costs in connection with the Action and otherwise; and

NOW, THEREFORE, in consideration of the mutual releases, promises, covenants, representations, and warranties contained in this Agreement, and other good and valuable consideration, the receipt and sufficiency of which are hereby acknowledged, the Parties hereby agree as follows.

AGREEMENT

1. Settlement Payment. KID shall pay Fund VIII the total sum of $1,400,000 within thirty (30) days of execution of this Agreement by delivering a cashier's or certified check payable to Fund VIII, and to such address as shall be requested by Fund VIII (the "**Settlement Payment**"). The Settlement Payment is in full and final satisfaction and settlement of all claims asserted by Fund VIII against KID in the Action, and as consideration for the release set forth in Paragraph 3 below.

2. Dismissal of the Action. Within ten (10) days of receipt of the Settlement Payment, Fund VIII shall dismiss the Action with prejudice against KID.

3. Release by Plaintiff. Fund VIII, on behalf of itself and its officers, managers, directors, stockholders, members, employees, general or limited partners, joint venturers, insurers, agents, representatives and attorneys and all persons acting by, through, under or in concert with them (the "**Releasing Parties**"), hereby irrevocably and unconditionally releases and forever discharges KID and its officers, managers, directors, stockholders, members, employees insurers, agents, representatives and attorneys and all persons acting by, through, under or in concert with them (the "**Releasees**"), or any of them, from any and all actions, causes of action, suits, claims, rights, damages, losses, costs, expenses (including attorneys' fees and costs actually incurred), contracts, agreements or controversies of any nature whatsoever, known or unknown, liquidated or unliquidated, suspected or unsuspected, fixed or contingent in law or in equity (hereinafter "**Claim**" or "**Claims**") that the Releasing Parties now have, own or hold, or at any time heretofore ever had, owned or held, or could have had, owned or held against the Releasees, including, without limiting the generality of the foregoing: any Claims that arise out of or are related to the matters asserted in the Action or which could have been asserted in the Action.

4. Representations, Warranties, and Covenants. Each Party hereby represents and warrants to and covenants to the other Party that such Party [has read and understood the Agreement, has had the opportunity to consult with legal counsel, has the legal authority to enter this Agreement, and agrees to be bound by the Agreement]. In addition, Fund VIII represents and warrants that there is no other person or entity that owns or holds any rights in connection with or related to the Claims released in this Agreement or which were or could have been asserted in the Action.

5. No Admission: The Parties agree that this Agreement and its contents, and any and all statements, negotiations, documents and discussions associated with it, shall not be deemed or construed to be an admission or evidence of any violation of any statute or law or of any liability or wrongdoing or of the truth of any of the claims or allegations asserted in this Action or any other action or proceeding. . . .

7. Miscellaneous.

[The Agreement includes provisions addressing severability, modification, transfer, and survival of representations.]

(e) Attorney's Fees in the Event of Dispute. If any legal action, dispute, or other proceeding arises or is commenced to interpret, enforce or recover damages for the breach of any term of this Agreement, the prevailing Party shall be entitled to recover from the non-prevailing Party all of its fees and costs in connection therewith, including, without limitation, its attorneys' fees and costs and costs of suit.

(f) Participation in Drafting. Each Party has participated in, cooperated in, or contributed to the drafting and preparation of this Agreement. In any construction of this Agreement, the same shall not be construed for, or against, any Party, but shall be construed fairly according to its plain meaning.

[The Agreement includes several more miscellaneous provisions, stating that the parties will execute further documents, that the Agreement may be executed in counterparts and electronically, that this constitutes the entire agreement of the parties, and that the Agreement is governed by New Jersey law.]

IN WITNESS WHEREOF, the Parties have each approved and executed this Agreement as of the Effective Date.

KID BRANDS, INC.

By: /s/ Raphael Benaroya
    Name: Raphael Benaroya
    Its: Acting CEO

THE REALTY ASSOCIATES FUND VIII, L.P.

By: /s/ James P. Knowles
    Name: James P. Knowles
    Its: Regional Director

Notes & Questions

1. If you have already had a course on contracts, apply your knowledge of contract law to the settlement agreement between Fund VIII and KID and the negotiations that led to the agreement. Among other things, you might think about offer and acceptance, consideration, statute of frauds, and defenses such as fraud, duress, and unconscionability. *See generally Mallory v. Eyrich*, 922 F.2d 1273, 1279-80 (6th Cir. 1991) (noting, with regard to Rule 68 offers of judgment—a special form of settlement that will be discussed later in the chapter—that traditional contract principles apply to the formation of the agreement and to defenses for avoiding an otherwise binding agreement); *Vulgamott v. Perry*, 154 S.W.3d 382 (Mo. Ct. App. 2004) (enforcing settlement agreement based on contract principles regarding offer and acceptance, consideration, and statute of frauds).

2. As to consideration (the thing of value received by each party in the exchange), what exactly was the consideration for the contract between Fund VIII and KID? Obviously, the contract provided something of value to Fund VIII: a payment of $1.4 million. But what did KID get in exchange? The way to understand settlements, fundamentally, is to see the value of what KID got in the deal. Would the consideration have been valid for the formation of a contract even if Fund VIII's claim probably would have lost on the merits had the case gone to trial? *See Vulgamott*, 154 S.W.3d at 390 ("Compromise of even a doubtful claim is sufficient consideration for a settlement agreement.").

3. What if one of the parties, after signing this agreement, regretted the decision? Suppose KID decided $1.4 is too much money and it would prefer to fight the claims in court. Or suppose Fund VIII decided $1.4 million was too little in light of the strength of its claim. Could the regretful party have wiggled out of the agreement by arguing the settlement was unfair? Not likely. Even if a settlement seems unfair in hindsight, that rarely makes the agreement "unconscionable" as a matter of contract law.

     In *Pursley v. Pursley*, 144 S.W.3d 820 (Ky. 2004), an ex-spouse attempted to get out of a divorce settlement in which he had agreed to pay much more in child support than would ordinarily be required. The Supreme Court of Kentucky rejected his argument:

> "[A] bad bargain and unconscionability [are] . . . not synonymous." Although we recognize that William Pursley provided Sharen Pursley generous child support, [we defer to the trial court's ruling that the agreement was not unconscionable.] "Parties to a divorce action often have perfectly valid motives for agreeing to what appear to be bad bargains." Here, ostensibly, William Pursley wanted to provide generous support for his children and to ensure their future education. And, perhaps, he had cathartic reasons for agreeing to such generous child support. "If so, what appears on the surface to be a bad bargain may not be so bad after all. In such a case, it is not manifestly unfair or inequitable to let a party lie in the bed he or she has freely made." Although for

> William Pursley the Agreement appears to be a bad bargain on its face, . . . [w]e hold that the trial court's findings were not clearly erroneous, and therefore, the Pursleys' Agreement is enforceable.

Id. at 827-28 (footnotes omitted).

4. Paragraph 1 of the agreement states the remedy that KID agreed to provide—a single payment of $1.4 million. Such monetary payments are the typical remedy offered in litigation settlements, but they are not the only option.

     Some settlements provide—instead of or on top of a monetary remedy—that a party will undertake or refrain from engaging in certain conduct. The option of "injunctive" types of remedies in settlements mirrors to some extent the possibility of injunctive relief in court, but settlements can be more creative in this direction. Whereas judges are constrained by law concerning available remedies when adjudicating claims, parties who settle have more room to negotiate whatever (legal) terms they find mutually acceptable. Later in the chapter, in our discussion of judicial approval of settlements, we will note that consent decrees or consent judgments may involve ongoing judicial supervision to enforce injunctive remedies in settlements.

     One variation on monetary payments is a *structured settlement*. Rather than make a single payment as required of KID in Paragraph 1, a structured settlement requires a series of payments over time. Although lump sum settlements are more common, lawyers may recommend structured settlements for some clients because they can provide tax advantages and reduce the risk of the client mismanaging the money.

5. Paragraph 2 of the settlement agreement requires that Fund VIII dismiss the action. In federal court, such a dismissal would be a Rule 41(a) voluntary dismissal, which we discussed in Chapter 4. Note what the agreement says about whether the dismissal is *with prejudice* or *without prejudice*. For obvious reasons, only one of these options is acceptable to most defendants when settling disputes.

6. In Paragraph 3 of the settlement agreement, Fund VIII releases KID from liability. This provision, along with the required payment in Paragraph 1, is the heart of the settlement agreement. Note the breadth of the release. Who are the parties who are giving up their claims? Who are the parties against whom claims are given up? What is the scope of the claims that are given up? Consider the positions of the parties when negotiating this aspect of the settlement. In general, defendants prefer the broadest possible release and plaintiffs prefer a narrower release, but plaintiffs may agree to the sort of language in Paragraph 3 to induce defendants to settle. What is essential for both sides, though, is clarity about the scope of the release so that the parties know what the settlement covers.

7. Plea bargains are the criminal analogue to civil settlements. A plea bargain is an agreement between a criminal defendant and a prosecutor in which the

defendant agrees to plead guilty to criminal charges in exchange for concessions from the prosecutor such as dropping other charges or recommending a lighter sentence. Plea bargains and civil settlements have much in common: Both involve a compromise in which the parties avoid trial by reaching agreement about the outcome. Just as most civil cases are resolved by settlements, most criminal cases end with plea bargains. However, one important difference is that a plea deal must be presented to a judge, who ultimately holds the power to impose the sentence. Moreover, a plea bargain requires a plea of guilty or no contest. Look at Paragraph 5 of the settlement agreement between Fund VIII and KID, as well as the second "Whereas" recital, in which KID denies liability. Such language about denial of liability—the very opposite of pleading guilty—is common in civil settlements. So, while it is reasonable to think of plea bargains as a kind of settlement of criminal liability and some of the same principles apply, keep in mind the differences between the civil and criminal contexts.

8. Fund VIII and KID reached their settlement about six months after Fund VIII filed the lawsuit. The timing of settlement varies. Parties often reach settlement on the eve of trial—sometimes literally. As trial nears, the risk of liability for a defendant and the risk of total loss for a plaintiff become palpable, making many parties amenable to deal making. For similar reasons, settlements may occur during trial, for example during jury deliberations. But a settlement can happen at *any* point during or before litigation. Many cases settle in discovery, as information emerges and as costs mount. As we suggested in a Strategy Session in Chapter 4, the threat or denial of summary judgment can spur settlement. Also in Chapter 4, we saw that Schwarzer and Hirsch advise judges to encourage early settlement, rather than allow litigation costs to accumulate. At the opposite end of the timeline, settlements may occur pending appeal.

   Do not forget that a settlement may occur *before* any litigation has commenced. Even before Fund VIII filed its complaint against KID in New Jersey Superior Court, it could have contacted KID about its claim and negotiations could have begun. A letter from Fund VIII's lawyer, describing the basis for the claim and stating that Fund VIII was considering filing a lawsuit, could have gotten the ball rolling. If this had been such a pre-complaint settlement, what language, if any, would change in the settlement agreement?

9. Why did Fund VIII and KID choose to settle, rather than allow the court to adjudicate the claim? In other words, for the parties, what are the benefits of settlement? For a party asserting a claim, the obvious benefit is the remedy provided, such as the $1.4 million for Fund VIII. For a party against whom a claim is asserted, the obvious benefit is the release from liability. Presumably, Fund VIII decided that getting $1.4 million was worth giving up its chance at an even larger judgment by taking the claim to trial. And presumably KID decided that the benefit of the predictability of this payment was more appealing than the possibility of prevailing at trial with the risk of facing even greater liability. Risk aversion is a prime driver of settlements.

For most parties, however, the benefits of settlement go beyond risk aversion concerning liability. For one thing, settlement reduces litigation expenses. The earlier the settlement, the bigger the savings. Trial, in particular, demands a lot of lawyer time, and lawyer time is expensive. If the client is paying the lawyer on an hourly-fee basis (like many civil litigation defendants), early settlement can mean substantial savings for the client. If the client is paying the lawyer on a contingent-fee basis (like many civil litigation plaintiffs), early settlement can mean substantial savings for the lawyer in addition to cost savings for the client.

For another thing, settlements may help parties maintain privacy. Although the agreement between Fund VIII and KID became public because KID attached it to a filing with the Securities and Exchange Commission, many settlement agreements include confidentiality clauses. Settlements also may help parties maintain relationships, as a negotiated resolution avoids some of the adversarialism of litigation. While the value of relationship maintenance may matter little to two strangers litigating an auto accident claim, it may matter greatly to business partners, family members, or others who expect an ongoing relationship after the conclusion of a particular dispute.

10. Despite these benefits of settlement, what are some reasons why a party might not settle? One reason is simply a failure to reach agreement on mutually acceptable terms. The negotiating parties may have failed to converge on a settlement zone, which could result from different beliefs about the facts, different analyses of the law, different predictions about the success of the claims and defenses, or a failure of negotiation. Optimism bias can infect lawyers' advice just as it infects other human decision making, and studies have shown that lawyers tend to be overconfident about their clients' positions and likely outcomes.

   But there are other, more basic, reasons why parties may resist settlement. A plaintiff who feels wronged may insist upon holding a defendant accountable in court. A defendant who feels that a plaintiff's claim is meritless may insist that it should have zero liability. A repeat-player defendant may resist settlement to avoid encouraging similar plaintiffs to pursue claims. Finally, consider the role of public interest organizations and others pursing impact litigation. If the plaintiffs' goal is reform of a particular institution (such as a prison's policies or a corporation's hiring practices), settlement may provide a satisfactory resolution. But if the plaintiffs' goal is reform of the law, as is often the goal of organizations such as the American Civil Liberties Union and the NAACP Legal Defense and Education Fund, then they may be unsatisfied with anything other than adjudication.

11. As between lawyers and clients, who gets to decide what constitutes an acceptable settlement? Lawyers often take the lead in negotiating settlements. But ultimately the decision of whether to settle, and on what terms, belongs to the client. Indeed, professional ethics rules specifically list settlement as a subject within client control. *See* ABA Model Rule of Professional Conduct 1.2(a) ("A

lawyer shall abide by a client's decision whether to settle a matter."). Thus, if KID's lawyer had reached out to Fund VIII's lawyer to offer a settlement, Fund VIII's lawyer could not have simply accepted the deal, but rather would have conveyed the offer to the client, offered advice, and followed the client's decision whether to accept the settlement or to continue litigating. Clients may authorize their lawyer in advance to agree to a settlement on their behalf, and may specify in advance terms that would be acceptable or unacceptable. If a lawyer negotiates a settlement on behalf of multiple clients, special rules apply. *See* ABA Model Rule of Professional Conduct 1.8(g) (requiring disclosure and informed consent for aggregate settlements).

12. What if a party does not comply with the terms of a settlement agreement? Suppose KID failed to make the promised payment. Or suppose Fund VIII failed to dismiss the action as promised. There are several ways parties may enforce a settlement agreement. The most basic response is that a party may sue for breach of contract. Suing for breach of contract, however, means filing a separate action, which can involve additional expense and delay. If a party prefers the simpler path of asking the original court to enforce the contract, this may be accomplished in a couple of ways. If the original lawsuit is still proceeding—for example, if the settlement agreement resolved one part of a larger action that has not yet concluded—then the court still has power over the matter. In that circumstance, a party may file a motion to enforce the settlement agreement in the pending action. *See, e.g., Vulgamott v. Perry*, 154 S.W.3d 382, 387 (Mo. Ct. App. 2004) ("Settlement agreements are a species of contract. A motion to compel settlement adds to a pending action a collateral action for specific performance of the settlement agreement.").

    Alternatively, the parties may ask the judge in the original proceeding to enter a consent decree or consent judgment that embodies the parties' settlement agreement. If the court agrees to do this—which generally requires persuading the judge of the fairness of the settlement and the need for such a decree—then the agreement may be enforced not merely as a private contract, but as a court order over which the court retains jurisdiction.

13. An interesting twist on the problem of settlement enforcement involves federal subject matter jurisdiction. Recall from Chapter 9 that federal courts have limited jurisdiction. Suppose parties are litigating an action in federal court and the parties lack citizenship diversity but the court has federal question jurisdiction under 28 U.S.C. §1331 because the claim arises under federal law. The parties reach a settlement, sign the agreement, and dismiss the action with prejudice. Then one party fails to comply with the agreement. The other party wishes to return to the federal court to enforce the settlement agreement. Does the federal court have power to enforce the agreement? The court lacks diversity jurisdiction. Does the court have federal question jurisdiction over the state law breach-of-contract claim to enforce the settlement agreement? Or suppose the court had diversity jurisdiction over the original action, but the settlement amount is not greater than $75,000. Again, would a federal court have subject

matter jurisdiction to decide a claim that one party breached the settlement agreement? In *Kokkonen v. Guardian Life Ins. Co.*, 511 U.S. 375 (1994), the Supreme Court held that federal courts lack inherent power to adjudicate claims for breach of private settlement agreements. The Court explained, "The short of the matter is this: The suit involves a claim for breach of a contract, part of the consideration for which was dismissal of an earlier federal suit. No federal statute makes that connection (if it constitutionally could) the basis for federal court jurisdiction over the contract dispute." *Id.* at 381. But the Court suggested in dicta that parties could return to federal court to enforce a settlement if the judge explicitly retained jurisdiction or incorporated the terms into a court order:

> The situation would be quite different if the parties' obligation to comply with the terms of the settlement agreement had been made part of the order of dismissal—either by separate provision (such as a provision "retaining jurisdiction" over the settlement agreement) or by incorporating the terms of the settlement agreement in the order. In that event, a breach of the agreement would be a violation of the order, and ancillary jurisdiction to enforce the agreement would therefore exist. That, however, was not the case here. The judge's mere awareness and approval of the terms of the settlement agreement do not suffice to make them part of his order.

Id. The Court concluded, "[W]e think the court is authorized to embody the settlement contract in its dismissal order (or, what has the same effect, retain jurisdiction over the settlement contract) if the parties agree. Absent such action, however, enforcement of the settlement agreement is for state courts, unless there is some independent basis for federal jurisdiction." *Id.* at 381-82.

14. Disputes involving particular substantive statutes that provide attorneys' fees and costs to "prevailing parties"—such as civil rights statutes, *see, e.g.*, 42 U.S.C. §1988—create hard questions in the context of settlement. If an action brought under such a statute results in a settlement offer, must the plaintiff nonetheless press on and "prevail" at trial in order to collect fees and costs? The Supreme Court has held that a favorable settlement—even one that brings about a change in the defendant's behavior—is insufficient to confer "prevailing party" status for purposes of fee shifting. *Buckhannon Board & Care Home, Inc. v. West Va. Dep't of Health & Human Resources*, 532 U.S. 598 (2001). To be a "prevailing party," the plaintiff must obtain either a judgment on the merits *or* a court-ordered consent decree embodying the settlement. *Id.* Even a private settlement followed by a court order of dismissal is insufficient, absent certain features, to confer "prevailing party" status. *Compare, e.g., Bill M. v. Nebraska Dep't of Health & Human Servs.*, 570 F.3d 1001 (8th Cir. 2009), *with Roberson v. Giuliani*, 346 F.3d 75 (2d Cir. 2003) (holding that an order of dismissal that does not incorporate the terms of the settlement but nonetheless retained the court's jurisdiction over its enforcement *was* sufficient to confer prevailing party status); *Perez v. Westchester Dep't of Corrections*, 597 F.3d 143 (2d Cir. 2009) (holding that significant judicial involvement in the creation of the settlement and resulting dismissal order suffices to confer prevailing party status, even in

the absence of retention of jurisdiction, incorporation of settlement terms, consent decree, and any admission of liability).

15. In Note 9 above, we mentioned that settlement agreements often include confidentiality clauses. Consider why each party may agree to confidentiality. Trials are public events. Documents filed with the court and transcripts of court proceedings are public unless a judge orders the records sealed. When parties fail to settle and a claim reaches adjudication, information about the claim and its resolution are public information. Suppose a defendant agrees to pay a plaintiff $1 million for an injury the plaintiff claims was caused by the defendant's product. The defendant prefers not to publicize the claim that its product caused injury and that it was willing to pay a million dollars. As for the plaintiff, she may prefer not to publicize her injury, and may prefer not to announce that she suddenly has a lot of money. Even if the plaintiff does not care whether everyone knows about her injury and wealth, the plaintiff does care about getting compensated for her injury, and she knows that confidentiality has value to the defendant. So, for example, if the defendant were willing to pay $500,000 without confidentiality or $1 million with confidentiality, or if the defendant were willing to settle only on condition of confidentiality, most plaintiffs would accept the confidentiality provision.

16. Settlement confidentiality often is attractive to the parties, but how about as a matter of public policy? Consider the following newspaper account:

> Harvey Weinstein used them. So did R. Kelly, Bill O'Reilly and many less famous men.
> When these men were accused of sexual abuse or harassment, they would use a legal tool that was practically magical in its power to make their problems disappear: a nondisclosure agreement. That, along with a substantial payment, would be enough to ensure that no one outside a handful of people would ever know what they had been accused of.
> Such agreements have been a requirement for years in virtually every out-of-court settlement for sexual misconduct. But after the #MeToo movement took off in late 2017, there were calls around the country to restrict or ban such agreements, and thunderous outrage over their secrecy.

Elizabeth A. Harris, *Despite #MeToo Glare, Efforts to Ban Secret Settlements Stop Short*, N.Y. Times, June 14, 2019, at A1. The article goes on to describe efforts in 26 states, with varying levels of success, to impose statutory restrictions on confidentiality regarding sexual harassment and sexual assault.

Earlier statutory efforts—often called "Sunshine in Litigation" laws—were not limited to sexual misconduct cases. For example, Florida's Sunshine in Litigation Act, Fla. Stat. §69.081, enacted in 1990, prohibits secret settlements involving government entities, prohibits courts from entering any order or judgment that would conceal a public hazard, and prohibits agreements that would conceal public hazards: "Any portion of an agreement or contract which has the purpose or effect of concealing a public hazard . . . is void, contrary to public policy, and may not be enforced." Fla. Stat. §69.081(4). The Florida act and other early sunshine laws were driven, in part, by concerns about secrecy regarding product-liability litigation.

What is the strongest argument in favor of banning confidentiality provisions in settlements in at least some categories of cases? What is the strongest argument against banning such confidentiality provisions? Suppose you were persuaded that confidentiality facilitates settlements, but you were also persuaded that confidentiality reduces the public's ability to protect itself from dangerous persons, products, or conditions. How would you weigh these benefits and costs? And whose responsibility is it to do the weighing? If you were a legislator considering a bill to ban secret settlements, you would consider the overall costs and benefits. What about clients and lawyers in particular disputes? If you represented a client who was offered a settlement on terms of confidentiality, what would be the circumstances, if any, where you might advise your client to refuse to settle on such terms because of concerns about harm to others? And how would you approach that conversation with the client? *Cf.* ABA Model Rules of Professional Conduct 1.2(a) ("[A] lawyer shall abide by a client's decisions concerning the objectives of representation and . . . shall consult with the client as to the means by which they are to be pursued."), 2.1 ("In rendering advice, a lawyer may refer not only to law but to other considerations such as moral, economic, social and political factors, that may be relevant to the client's situation.").

(2) Judicial Encouragement of Settlement

(a) Judges as Settlement Promoters

Chapter 4 included an excerpt from Schwarzer & Hirsch, *The Elements of Case Management* (Federal Judicial Center, 3d ed. 2017). Recall their emphasis on the judge's role in encouraging and facilitating settlement:

> It is useful for a judge to inquire about settlement whenever meeting with the lawyers. Lawyers are often interested in settling (particularly in view of the rising cost of litigation), but may consider raising the subject an admission of weakness. A judge's questions offer a graceful opening.

Id. at 8. Their advice to judges in most cases is to find ways to nudge the parties toward settling. This may involve urging the parties to negotiate, ordering phased discovery, focusing the parties' attention on the realistic strengths and weaknesses of their cases, sending the parties to court-connected mediation, or other techniques. They note that some cases may not be suitable for settlement, stating that "[j]udges should facilitate, not coerce, settlement." *Id.* at 7. We will explore mediation and other settlement-facilitation processes in Part B of this chapter; here in Part A, we focus specifically on the role of the courts with regard to settlement.

Schwarzer and Hirsch particularly encourage judges to use Rule 16 as a settlement tool. Recall from Chapter 4 that Rule 16 creates a structure for judges to conduct pretrial conferences with parties and their attorneys. Rule 16 explicitly mentions settlement as one of the objectives of pretrial conferences and as one of the topics for discussion. *See* Rule 16(a)(5), 16(c)(1), and 16(c)(2)(I). Schwarzer and Hirsch build on this: "The Rule 16 conference also should explore the possibility of settlement, and in most cases it should include a specific discussion of an appropriate time for and process of alternative dispute resolution. . . . The Rule 16 conference should provide lawyers with a 'reality check,' and discussion about settlement should focus their attention on what would be an acceptable outcome for the client." *Id.* at 8.

Schwarzer and Hirsch distinguish two types of judges: those who personally get involved in settlement negotiations in their own cases, and those who prefer to bring in another district judge or magistrate judge as a "settlement judge" so as not to jeopardize the primary judge's impartiality. In terms of procedural justice and the risk of coercion, isn't there an enormous difference between settlement facilitation/encouragement by a presiding judge, as compared to the same activity by another judge or magistrate judge? As one observer explained, in the situation where a judge offers both settlement assistance and adjudication, "the parties and their lawyers reasonably may fear that the judge's involvement in the settlement session will color her rulings at trial." Nancy A. Welsh, *Magistrate Judges, Settlement, and Procedural Justice*, 16 Nev. L.J. 983, 1032 (2016).

(b) Court-Connected Dispute Resolution

Each federal district court has its own local rules concerning dispute-resolution processes to facilitate settlement. While courts have experimented with various dispute-resolution processes at least since the 1970s, it sped up in the 1990s. The Civil Justice Reform Act of 1990 required courts to develop plans to reduce costs and delays. The Alternative Dispute Resolution Act of 1998 took it a step further, requiring each district court to promote ADR: "Each United States district court shall devise and implement its own alternative dispute resolution program, by local rule adopted under section 2071(a), to encourage and promote the use of alternative dispute resolution in its district." 28 U.S.C. §651(b).

For example, the Northern District of California adopted a set of Alternative Dispute Resolution Local Rules, including a "Multi-Option Program" to which most civil cases are assigned. *See* Northern District of California ADR Local Rule 3-2. The district court's Multi-Option Program offers three options: early neutral evaluation, mediation, or a settlement conference with a magistrate judge. At the initial case management conference, the judge discusses these options with the lawyers and selects one of the processes for the case. The district court maintains a "panel of neutrals," including lawyers and others who have the skills and experience to serve as mediators. *See* ADR L.R. 2-5.

The District of Hawaii adopted a local rule to implement court-sponsored mediation. *See* District of Hawaii Local Rule 88.1 (LR 88.1). Pursuant to LR 88.1, a magistrate judge is appointed to maintain a list of approved mediators. LR 88.1(e) states that "[t]he mediator's job is to facilitate the voluntary resolution of cases," in other words, to help the parties reach a settlement. Parties may stipulate to submit their dispute to mediation, or a judge may order it: "[A]t any time before the entry of final judgment, the court may, on its own motion or at the request of any party after affording the parties an opportunity to express their views, order the parties to participate in mediation and/or any other non-binding ADR process." LR 88.1(d)(2). If the parties cannot agree on the selection of a mediator, the court selects the mediator. Attendance and participation are mandatory. *See* LR 88.1(g) ("Lead counsel and clients, representatives, or third persons with full settlement authority shall attend, in person, all mediation conferences scheduled by the mediator, unless excused by the mediator."); LR 88.1(f) ("Parties shall meaningfully participate in any mediation submitted under this rule.").

Thus, like many similar rules around the country, the District of Hawaii's local rule on court-connected dispute resolution empowers the judge to order that parties engage in a settlement-facilitative process, and states that the parties must attend and "shall meaningfully participate." How far does this power extend? What if a party shows up but refuses to engage in settlement negotiations? Consider the following case from the District of Hawaii.

HTK HAWAII, INC. v. SUN
2016 WL 6917284 (D. Haw. May 12, 2016)

PUGLISI, Magistrate Judge.

Before the Court is Plaintiff's Motion for Sanctions for Failure to Meaningfully Participate in Mediation, filed April 11, 2016 ("Motion"). Defendants filed their Opposition on April 25, 2016. Plaintiff filed its Reply on May 9, 2016. . . . After carefully reviewing the parties' submissions and the relevant legal authority, the Court DENIES Plaintiff's Motion.

BACKGROUND

Plaintiff brought this action against Defendants related to negotiations for a potential expansion of Plaintiff's Hawaii shave ice supply business in California. Plaintiff's Second Amended Complaint asserts claims for declaratory judgment, unjust enrichment, conversion, fraud, breach of

contract, breach of the covenant of good faith and fair dealing, and rescission.

The parties participated in two settlement conferences with the Court on September 11, 2015, and November 16, 2015, which did not result in a settlement between the parties. On January 6, 2016, the trial court held a hearing on Defendants' Motion to Dismiss and Motion to Transfer Venue to California. During the hearing, the court stated, in part, as follows:

> Now, I want to say to all counsel, I am—and I have not said this or done this very often in my 10 years on the bench now. This isn't a big case. It shouldn't be a big case. By "big" I mean dollar figures and resources.
>
> * * *
>
> And when I look at the back and forth between counsel, I see bad

feelings and a lot of hurt between the parties that sort of boils over in part by counsel. The case is being litigated, I think, beyond how it should be litigated. And I have only I think twice ordered a case into mediation, which I have the power to do. And I am inclined to do that in this case. In part because I think things are careening out of control largely.

* * *

I'm just concerned with the actions of counsel and that counsel are channeling the feelings of clients— the clients too much in this case, is what I see. I'm not saying it's unprofessional, but it's bordering on that.

So my intent is to order you folks into mediation. I'll put out an order so you'll have my order, on this—on these motions I mean. I mean that will come out and you will have the benefit of that. But then ordering you into mediation.

Neither party objected to being ordered into mediation. Thereafter, the parties submitted letters to the court indicating that they could not agree on a mediator. The Court issued an Order Regarding Mediation appointing Justice James E. Duffy (ret.) as mediator.... The mediation was held on February 22, 2016, and did not result in settlement of this action.

In the present Motion, Plaintiff argues that Defendants failed to meaningfully participate in mediation and asks the Court to award sanctions against Defendants for their failure to participate in good faith. In support of its contention that Defendants failed to "meaningfully participate," Plaintiff asserts [that Defendants arrived late to the mediation and "left early" from the mediation because they booked return flights to California that afternoon; that Defendants increased their settlement demand at the mediation; and that Defendants represented during mediation that they were not concerned about litigation costs. Plaintiff asks the Court to impose sanctions, including monetary sanctions to cover the costs of the mediation including Plaintiff's attorneys' fees.]

DISCUSSION

Local Rule 88.1(f) provides that "[p]arties shall meaningfully participate in any mediation submitted under this rule." LR88.1(f). Local Rule 11.1 provides that the "[f]ailure of counsel or of a party to comply with any provision of these rules is a ground for imposition of sanctions, including a fine, dismissal, or other appropriate sanction." LR11.1.

Additionally, Federal Rule of Civil Procedure 16(f) authorizes a court to "issue any just orders . . . if a party or its attorney . . . fails to obey a scheduling or other pretrial order." Fed. R. Civ. P. 16(f)(1)(C). Rule 16(f) further provides that "[i]nstead of or in addition to any other sanction, the court must order the party . . . to pay the reasonable expenses—including attorney's fees and costs—incurred because of any noncompliance with this rule, unless the noncompliance was substantially justified or other circumstances make an award of expenses unjust." Fed. R. Civ. P. 16(f)(2).

1. THE COURT REJECTS PLAINTIFF'S ARGUMENT THAT DEFENDANTS FAILED TO MEANINGFULLY PARTICIPATE IN MEDIATION BASED ON DEFENDANTS' ATTENDANCE

In its Motion, Plaintiff argues that Defendants' failure to participate in good faith in the mediation is evident from the fact that Defendants were fifteen minutes late to the mediation, that Defendants "left early" because they booked a return flight to California that afternoon, and that Defendants' local counsel did not participate in the mediation. The Court disagrees that these facts demonstrate Defendants' lack of good faith. [The mediation concluded because it appeared unlikely the parties were going to reach a settlement, not because the Defendants had to leave to make their flight.] . . .

2. THE COURT REJECTS PLAINTIFF'S ARGUMENT THAT DEFENDANTS FAILED TO MEANINGFULLY PARTICIPATE IN MEDIATION BASED ON DEFENDANTS' SETTLEMENT POSITION

In its Motion, Plaintiff argues that Defendants' failure to participate in good faith in the mediation is evident from the fact that Defendants increased their settlement demand at the mediation and that Defendants represented during mediation that they were not concerned about litigation costs because Defendants' new mainland counsel has taken this case on a contingency basis. Again, the Court disagrees that these facts demonstrate Defendants' lack of good faith.

Although the court may encourage and facilitate settlement, the Court cannot punish a party based on their settlement position. As recognized by the Fifth Circuit Court of Appeals, "parties may have valid and principled reasons for not wishing to settle particular cases," which "may not be based necessarily on the merits of a particular case, or the party's possible exposure in it." *Dawson v. United States*, 68 F.3d 886, 897 (5th Cir. 1995) (reversing district court's award of sanctions against the defendant for its failure to make a "good faith" monetary settlement offer).

. . . Although Plaintiff may believe that Defendants' settlement demands were unreasonable, a high settlement demand is not an indication of bad faith. Defendants communicated their demands during the mediation and provided an explanation to support their demands in their mediation brief. There is no indication that Defendants' counsel's conduct during the mediation in communicating these demands was unprofessional or designed to harass. The fact that Defendants increased their demands during mediation is not evidence of . . . failure to meaningfully participate in the mediation. Neither is Defendants' decision to hire new counsel under a contingency agreement evidence of bad faith. Plaintiff argues that Defendants used the substitution of their new counsel "for strategic purposes." However, it is common for parties to consider the cost of litigation in determining their settlement positions. The fact that Defendants may have sought new counsel and negotiated a contingency fee structure to decrease their litigation costs is not sanctionable conduct. . . .

CONCLUSION

In accordance with the foregoing, the Court DENIES Plaintiff's Motion for Sanctions for Failure to Meaningfully Participate in Mediation and DENIES Defendants' request for sanctions pursuant to 28 U.S.C. §1927.

Notes & Questions

1. In *HTK*, what did the judge hope would be accomplished by conducting settlement conferences with the parties on September 11 and November 16, 2015? What are some of the reasons why this effort might not have succeeded at producing a settlement? Then, what did the judge hope to accomplish on January 6, by deciding to send the parties to mediation? In thinking about it, consider the difference between what parties might be willing to say in the presence of a judge, as opposed to what they might be willing to say in a confidential mediation session. Consider also that mediators bring a particular set of skills and experience to the process, which we will consider in Part B below.

2. In *Gray v. Eggert*, 635 N.W.2d 667 (Wis. Ct. App. 2001), a driver who collided with a bus sued the bus company. The judge ordered the parties to participate in mediation, which they did, but it did not result in a settlement. On the date set for trial, the judge learned that the defendant bus company had not offered any money to settle the case. The company said that it had offered nothing because its bus was standing still when the plaintiff ran into it and therefore the company had "absolutely no liability." The judge instructed the parties to attempt to negotiate, pointing to the court's scheduling order that said "counsel are expected to confer and make a good faith effort to settle the case." The bus company then offered $100. The judge was not happy, and punished the defendant by entering judgment for the plaintiff: "For failure to comply in good faith with the scheduling order to sit and confer and try to settle the case in good faith, the court strikes the answer and responsive pleadings of the defendant, [and] enters judgment in favor of the plaintiff in the amount of five thousand dollars."

   The bus company appealed, and the Court of Appeals reversed the trial judge's ruling. Under a Wisconsin statute, the appellate court explained, "a trial court has authority to order parties in civil litigation to attempt mediation or other settlement processes to resolve a case. . . . Nowhere, however, does [the statute] provide a court the authority to require resolution." *Id.* at 671. "Thus, when Gray and Milwaukee Transport arrived in court for their trial, nothing yet established any violation of the scheduling order. Simply stated, the parties had complied with the order for mediation, but mediation had not produced a settlement. At that point, the court, understandably, instructed the parties to make one last effort to reach resolution. But the court had no authority to require resolution or to sanction either party for failing to agree." *Id.* at 672.

3. "I see bad feelings and a lot of hurt between the parties." This was part of the judge's rationale for sending the parties to mediation in *HTK*. Presumably, the judge hoped that a skilled mediator could help the parties get past bad feelings that were clouding their judgment and help them to negotiate a resolution that would make economic sense for both of them. As the judge described it, this was a relatively low-stakes dispute but the litigation was "careening out of control." Suppose it is true that one or both parties refused to settle on economically

rational terms because of bad feelings or other emotional factors. As a judge, would you see it as part of your responsibility to help the parties get past emotional or psychological barriers that can impede settlement? Most judges would probably take this view. Or would you allow the parties to litigate as they see fit within the rules of procedure, and keep moving the case toward adjudication on the merits? These are hard questions. On the one hand, it can be painful to watch parties make irrational decisions, expending both private and public resources to litigate claims that could have been settled more cheaply than the cost of litigation. On the other hand, one of the benefits of a public system of civil dispute resolution is that it allows parties to channel aggressions and to resolve disputes in non-violent ways. If a party has a nonfrivolous claim or defense, who gets to decide whether the party's reasons for continuing to litigate are rational—the party or the judge?

4. In *HTK*, Judge Puglisi seems to have treated it as axiomatic that he should encourage settlement; the only question really was whether he should sanction the defendants for their lack of enthusiasm. His efforts to encourage settlement were in keeping with the spirit of the district's local rule on dispute resolution and the Alternative Dispute Resolution Act. The maxim seems to be: Settlement is good, therefore judges should do all they can to help the parties reach a negotiated resolution of their dispute. Supposing that this is the maxim that motivates judges to conduct settlement conferences, to order parties into mediation, and to take other actions to drive settlements, do you agree with the maxim? We will look at different perspectives on this question in Part A(4) below.

(c) Formal Offers of Judgment

Alongside the judicial settlement-encouragement methods described above, there is a settlement-encouragement provision built into the Federal Rules of Civil Procedure. Rule 68 is the most explicitly pro-settlement provision in the rules. Under Rule 68, a defending party may make a formal "offer to allow judgment on specified terms." In other words, the defendant may say to the plaintiff that the defendant agrees to have judgment entered against it for a certain amount of money. If the plaintiff agrees to the offer, then the court enters judgment on those terms.

The incentive comes in Rule 68(d): "If the judgment that the offeree finally obtains is not more favorable than the unaccepted offer, the offeree must pay the costs incurred after the offer was made." For example, suppose a defendant makes a Rule 68 formal offer of judgment for $100,000. If the plaintiff accepts the offer, then the court enters judgment against the defendant for $100,000. If the plaintiff declines the offer and ends up winning a judgment for $150,000, the plaintiff simply gets the $150,000 judgment. But if the plaintiff declines the offer and ends up winning a judgment for $50,000, the plaintiff must pay the defendant's costs of litigating after the offer was declined. Note that, in general, the "costs" covered by Rule 68 do not include attorneys' fees. Even so, the cost-shifting provision of Rule 68 creates an incentive for defendants to make formal settlement offers and for plaintiffs to accept such offers if reasonable.

In *Marek v. Chesny*, 473 U.S. 1, 5 (1985), the Supreme Court explained, "The plain purpose of Rule 68 is to encourage settlement and avoid litigation. The Rule prompts both parties to a suit to evaluate the risks and costs of litigation, and to balance them against the likelihood of success upon trial on the merits." The Court in *Marek* decided that the "costs" covered by Rule 68 include attorneys' fees awarded under fee-shifting provisions in federal civil rights statutes.

(3) Judicial Approval of Settlement

Although in general settlements are simply contracts between the parties and do not need anyone else's approval, certain types of settlements require approval by the judge. These include settlements involving minors, class action settlements, and consent judgments.

Keeping in mind that a settlement is a contract, consider the problem that not every person has the capacity to enter into binding contracts. Minors do not have that capacity. In most states, the age of majority for purposes of contracts is 18 years of age. Similarly, persons with mental impairment due to age or mental illness may lack the capacity to enter contracts. Therefore, to settle a claim in which one of the parties is a minor, mentally incompetent, or otherwise lacks the capacity to enter a contract, the parties must obtain the court's approval.

For the same fundamental reason, class action settlements require judicial approval. Recall from Chapter 7 that class representatives and class counsel litigate a class action on behalf of the entire defined class, and the outcome is binding on all of the class members even though the "absent class members" did not participate in the litigation. In this regard, for purposes of consent to a settlement, the absent class members resemble minors or other persons who lack capacity to consent. This is because the absent class members did not personally agree to the settlement that purports to bind them. Thus, a class settlement binds the class members only if approved by the judge. Under Rule 23(e), "[t]he claims, issues, or defenses of a certified class—or a class proposed to be certified for purposes of settlement—may be settled, voluntarily dismissed, or compromised only with the court's approval." The rule goes on to specify the procedures for notifying the class of the proposed settlement and for giving class members the opportunity to object to the proposal. The judge may approve the proposed class settlement only if the judge finds it "fair, reasonable, and adequate." Fed. R. Civ. P. 23(e)(2). The rule spells out factors for the judge to consider, including "whether the class representatives and class counsel have adequately represented the class," whether the relief provided is adequate in light of "the costs, risks, and delay of trial and appeal," and whether "the proposal treats class members equitably relative to each other." Fed. R. Civ. P. 23(e)(2)(A)-(D).

As we discussed in Chapter 7, some class settlements are negotiated even before the class has been certified. These cases—known as *settlement class actions*—are presented to the court for simultaneous ruling on both class certification and settlement approval. For defendants, settlement class actions can offer an appealing way to resolve potential mass liability. When a defendant pays to settle a mass dispute, the defendant often prefers to wrap it up neatly rather than to leave large numbers of potential plaintiffs who can still sue the defendant. The Supreme Court has expressed concerns about potential unfairness in settlement class actions, but has held that they are permitted as long as they satisfy the usual requirements for class certification other than trial manageability. *See Amchem Products, Inc. v. Windsor*, 521 U.S. 591 (1997).

In addition to settlements that require court approval because of lack of genuine consent due to minority, incapacity, or status as absent class members, there is another type of settlement that requires a judge's approval. This is when the parties want the court to have the power of ongoing supervision and enforcement. When parties negotiate a settlement agreement that includes an injunctive component and when they want the court to have the power to enforce it, they ask the court to enter a decree or judgment that embodies the terms of their agreement. Because the parties have agreed to the terms, these are known as *consent decrees* or *consent judgments*.

(4) Settlement Versus Adjudication

(a) Adjudication as Failure to Reach Settlement

As you have learned civil procedure, perhaps you have viewed litigation and procedural policy mostly in terms of whether civil procedure rules are well designed to achieve fair and efficient adjudications based on accurate fact-finding and fidelity to substantive law. This view probably captures, reasonably well, the thinking of the drafters of the original Federal Rules of Civil Procedure, as well as the thinking of many lawyers and judges when looking at each component part of civil procedure. Consider the litigation process step by step as a process designed for adjudication: Pleadings notify parties of the claims and defenses and narrow which issues are in dispute, thus defining what the court needs to resolve. Joinder brings parties and claims together to enhance the efficiency, fairness, and finality of determinations. Motions to dismiss determine the legal validity of the claims. Discovery reveals information the parties need in order to prove their claims and defenses, so that adjudication will be fact-based. Summary judgment provides an opportunity to adjudicate claims that have only one reasonable outcome as a matter of law. Finally, for disputes that require factual determinations, trial is the moment when each side presents its evidence and makes its arguments so that a judge or jury can determine who prevails under the facts and law. This, in a nutshell, is the story of civil procedure from the perspective of adjudication.

But there is another way to view the litigation process, another way to think about the highest function of the law of civil procedure. Consider the possibility that the process is aimed at giving the parties what they need to reach settlement fairly and efficiently. Professors Samuel Gross and Kent Syverud put the argument this way:

> A trial is a failure. Although we celebrate it as the centerpiece of our system of justice, we know that trial is not only an uncommon method of resolving disputes, but a disfavored one. With some notable exceptions, lawyers, judges, and commentators agree that pretrial settlement is almost always cheaper, faster, and better than trial. Much of our civil procedure is justified by the desire to promote settlement and avoid trial. More important, the nature of our civil process drives parties to settle so as to avoid the costs, delays, and uncertainties of trial, and, in many cases, to agree upon terms that are beyond the power or competence of courts to dictate. These are powerful forces, and they produce settlement in a very high proportion of litigated disputes. Once in a while, however, the process fails and a case goes to trial.

Samuel R. Gross & Kent D. Syverud, *Getting to No: A Study of Settlement Negotiations and the Selection of Cases for Trial*, 90 MICH. L. REV. 319, 320 (1991).

Look again at this line from Gross and Syverud: "Much of our civil procedure is justified by the desire to promote settlement and avoid trial." *Id.* With this perspective in mind, consider again the litigation process, step by step. This time, instead of thinking of it as a process moving toward adjudication, look at it as a process moving toward settlement. Pleadings inform the parties of the other side's claims and defenses, so that both parties know what needs to be negotiated and can begin to evaluate the strength of the other side's position. Joinder brings in the parties who should be at the negotiating table, and announces the various claims that should be part of the discussion, some of which might cancel each other out or result in a different net settlement value. Motions to dismiss help to limit the discussion to the claims that have some chance of success and provide information about the judge's positions on the legal issues, which are relevant to settlement value. Discovery allows the parties to work from a common base of information and to obtain a realistic picture of the strengths and weaknesses of each other's claims and defenses, which in turn allows the parties to assess the value of the claims for purposes of determining an appropriate settlement range. Summary judgment, if the litigation reaches this point, creates another opportunity to narrow the discussion to claims that have a chance of success; when a claim survives a summary judgment motion, it means that the judge thinks a reasonable jury could go either way, which invites the parties to consider a compromise. Finally, trial is the threat that motivates both parties to settle. The defendant knows that a trial could result in a favorable verdict for the plaintiff for a larger, perhaps much larger, amount than might have been paid in settlement. And the plaintiff knows that a trial could result in a judgment for the defendant, in which case the plaintiff gets zero. In the "game of chicken" of litigation, trial is the explosive finish that both sides fear, and settlement is the way to avoid disaster. If a good settlement is one that accurately reflects each party's likelihood of success in light of the law and the facts, it is hard to imagine a more perfect motivator than the threat of a fully informed adjudication. This is the story of civil procedure from the perspective of settlement. From this perspective, the process is designed to provide the parties with information and incentives so that settlement negotiations will be productive.

If you could design the rules of civil procedure to maximize the likelihood of fair settlements, what would the rules look like? Consider this critique of the current federal rules:

> The world of settlement is here to stay, and it is time to face it head-on. The Federal Rules of Civil Procedure, designed for a bygone world of trials, are increasingly unable to fulfill their animating goal that cases be resolved on their merits, as defined by the governing substantive law. Procedural reform is needed to grapple with the unique difficulties generated by settlement as the dominant form of case resolution in achieving this objective.

J. Maria Glover, *The Federal Rules of Civil Settlement*, 87 N.Y.U. L. Rev. 1713, 1778 (2012). Professor Glover argues that "procedural mechanisms should be harnessed to provide meaningful merits-based information to guide parties' settlement decisions." *Id.* at 1718. For example, she suggests discovery rules could be reformed to target information most likely to aid settlement negotiations, rather than the current system of plenary discovery that increases costs in a way that distorts settlements. And pretrial procedures such as motions to dismiss and motions for summary judgment could be reformed to provide better judicial guidance on the merits of claims and defenses. *Id.* at 1752-68.

(b) Settlement as Failure to Reach Adjudication

Now consider the opposite point of view. Rather than view settlement as the best outcome of the litigation process because it is mutually satisfactory to the parties, consider the possibility that settlement is a betrayal of the purpose of the court system. This point of view was famously expressed by Professor Owen Fiss in a 1984 law review article called *Against Settlement*. By the time he wrote this article, judges had turned toward embracing their role as settlement facilitators and the legal profession had turned toward new types of dispute-resolution processes. Fiss argued that this was a wrong turn:

> The dispute-resolution story makes settlement appear as a perfect substitute for judgment . . . by trivializing the remedial dimensions of a lawsuit, and also by reducing the social function of the lawsuit to one of resolving private disputes: In that story, settlement appears to achieve exactly the same purpose as judgment—peace between the parties—but at considerably less expense to society. The two quarreling neighbors turn to a court in order to resolve their dispute, and society makes courts available because it wants to aid in the achievement of their private ends or to secure the peace.
>
> In my view, however, the purpose of adjudication should be understood in broader terms. Adjudication uses public resources, and employs not strangers chosen by the parties but public officials chosen by a process in which the public participates. These officials, like members of the legislative and executive branches, possess a power that has been defined and conferred by public law, not by private agreement. Their job is not to maximize the ends of private parties, nor simply to secure the peace, but to explicate

and give force to the values embodied in authoritative texts such as the Constitution and statutes: to interpret those values and to bring reality into accord with them. This duty is not discharged when the parties settle.

Owen M. Fiss, *Against Settlement*, 93 YALE L.J. 1073, 1085 (1984). According to Fiss, "[p]arties might settle while leaving justice undone." *Id.* On this view, adjudication—reasoned decision making by judges and juries as public officials or publicly constituted bodies with public duties—represents the best outcome of civil litigation; it represents Fiss' conception of justice. Lawyers, judges, and scholars have continued to debate Fiss' point of view. *See, e.g., Symposium, Against Settlement: Twenty-Five Years Later*, 78 FORDHAM L. REV. 1117 (2009).

What you think of the settlement-versus-adjudication debate may depend upon how you conceive of litigation. To whom does the lawsuit "belong"—the disputants or the public? Is litigation a process for *resolving disputes*? Is it a process for *enforcing the law*? Both? Why is litigation a *public* process (both in the sense of being non-secret and in the sense of being supported by the taxpayer dollars that pay for the court system)?

As you think back on what you have learned about civil procedure, and as you move forward into a legal career, try to remain open to both points of view regarding settlement and adjudication, and try to see beyond that binary choice. Surely justice and peace are not mutually exclusive, and sometimes justice can be achieved by negotiated resolutions. And surely some disputes, especially disputes with reasonable arguments both ways on the facts or law, or disputes with complex remedial questions, are *more* likely to reach sensible outcomes in a compromise settlement than in an all-or-nothing adjudication. And just as surely, there are situations where justice is unfulfilled by compromise and where justice demands that a court determine, declare, and enforce the outcome. Professor Carrie Menkel-Meadow suggests that "the question is not 'for or against' settlement (since settlement has become the 'norm' for our system), but *when, how, and under what circumstances* should cases be settled?" Carrie Menkel-Meadow, *Whose Dispute Is It Anyway?: A Philosophical and Democratic Defense of Settlement (In Some Cases)*, 83 GEO. L.J. 2663, 2664-65 (1995). Both adjudication and settlement can offer satisfying or unsatisfying processes, and both can reach sound or unsound outcomes. In thinking about these issues, do not be too quick to assume that there is only one legitimate way to conceive of justice.

THE BIG PICTURE

Whatever you conclude on the settlement-versus-adjudication debate, note that either way, justice depends on a system of civil procedure that can move disputes efficiently and fairly toward binding judgments on the merits. If the ultimate outcome is *adjudication*, procedural rules must provide a process that defines the issues in dispute, facilitates the search for truth, and answers questions of law and fact. If the ultimate outcome is *settlement*, again procedural rules must provide a process that defines the issues and facilitates the search for truth. And if settlements are to reflect the merits of claims and defenses, they must be negotiated with an expectation that, in the absence of agreement, a court would reach an outcome informed by facts and law. The *expectation of judgment* motivates settlement, so a procedural system that favors one side will almost inevitably produce skewed settlements. And *litigation expenses* motivate settlement, so a procedural system that is unduly expensive will produce settlements that reflect fear of the cost rather than the merits. Outcomes driven by cost avoidance are particularly problematic where parties have resource imbalances or face asymmetrical litigation expenses. Thus, regardless of whether one considers adjudication or settlement the best way for disputes to end, justice requires procedural rules that provide an effective and efficient path. This is not to say that the procedural rules described in this book accomplish this perfectly or anything close. We would be fools to believe that the law of civil procedure delivers perfect truth, justice, or efficiency. But we would be even more foolish to think that it doesn't matter.

B. MEDIATION AND OTHER SETTLEMENT-FACILITATIVE PROCESSES

Already, we have seen mediation as one of several tools used by courts to help parties reach settlement. Here, we will explore mediation in greater detail. The idea behind mediation is that there may be a potential resolution that would be mutually beneficial for the parties, but the parties need a neutral third-party facilitator to help them get there. A skilled mediator can get the parties where they want to go, even if the parties had been unable to get there on their own. Sometimes mediation occurs as a court-affiliated process, as in *HTK Hawaii v. Sun*, which we saw earlier in this chapter. Sometimes, mediation happens independently as a process voluntarily entered by the parties. The following brief description explains a few of the benefits, common techniques, and typical ground rules of mediation. As you read it, think about the types of situations where you would find mediation to be a superior alternative or a useful adjunct to litigation.

Morton Denlow,* *MEDIATION 101: A PRIMER*
JAMS ADR Blog (Aug. 3, 2017)

The growth in the use of mediation to settle a wide variety of disputes means more and more parties—and their lawyers—are considering this alternative to litigation. As mediation grows in popularity, it might be beneficial to review the characteristics of this type of alternative dispute resolution and how the process works.

Editors' Note: Morton Denlow served as a U.S. Magistrate Judge in the Northern District of Illinois from 1996 to 2012, and then became a mediator for JAMS, an organization that provides mediation and arbitration services.

Not Litigation

Mediation is a consensual process that bears no resemblance to litigation. The mediator has no independent power to resolve the dispute, which can only be concluded through the mutual agreement of the parties. The mediator conducts a series of joint sessions and separate caucuses with the litigants to facilitate agreement. The parties rarely submit evidence or witnesses, because evidence has no legal significance in the outcome of mediation. The mediator can explore a wide variety of issues and concerns in helping the parties address the underlying problems that gave rise to their dispute. Mediators meet separately with the parties as an ordinary part of the mediation process. In the event an agreement is reached, a term sheet is ordinarily prepared.

In the event no agreement is reached, the mediator may follow up at a later date, but cannot resolve the dispute without agreement by the parties. Mediation is most effective when the parties have sufficient information to exchange settlement proposals and when party representatives with full authority are present at the mediation.

Timing and Speed of Mediation

Mediation can be instituted at any time, even prior to the filing of a lawsuit.

Information transmitted to the mediator during the private caucuses is kept confidential by the mediator, unless permission to disclose is otherwise given. Therefore, a party can safely disclose to the mediator information that it would not ordinarily disclose to the other side at an early stage in the negotiation process. Candor enhances clarity of understanding, facilitating settlement.

Absent mediation, neither side might be expected to reveal its true concerns at an early stage in the litigation. A mediator is able to obtain this information without compromising the negotiating position of either side, because the mediator will keep the information confidential.

Consensus and Confidentiality

Mediation is consensual, and the ultimate solution is in the hands of the parties. The mediator can create a casual atmosphere in which creative problem-solving takes place. Clients are encouraged to speak and be a part of the process.

Mediation is also confidential. There are two components of confidentiality. First, the communications between the parties and the mediator in their separate caucuses are kept confidential, unless a party permits the mediator to make disclosure to the other side.

Moreover, the entire process remains confidential. A party can avoid hanging out "dirty laundry" for competitors and others to observe—no public pleadings, depositions, or transcripts. Mediation is generally conducted in the privacy of an office and the parties determine who will be in attendance. Confidentiality can be extremely important in preserving trade secrets and the value of a business while issues are resolved.

Problem-Solving Approach

Mediation focuses on problem-solving, rather than truth-seeking. The mediator's primary focus is to help create solutions, not to assign blame. Mediation does not seek to resolve issues of "right" and "wrong," but rather focuses on resolving the dispute in a constructive fashion. . . .

Notes & Questions

1. Whenever mediation succeeds—that is, whenever it results in a resolution of the dispute—it means that there was a settlement that was satisfactory to both sides. It means there was a set of terms that the parties could agree on. If so, why didn't the parties reach settlement on their own, without going to the trouble and expense of hiring a mediator? Think of reasons why parties might not be able to reach an agreement on their own, even if a set of settlement terms exists that both parties would find acceptable. For each of the reasons you think of, in what ways might a mediator help the parties break their impasse?

2. The objective of mediation is to help the parties reach a negotiated resolution, not to impose a resolution on them. Mediation can involve *evaluative* elements, helping parties to be more realistic about the strengths, weaknesses, and values of their cases, as well as *facilitative* or *elicitive* elements, helping the parties to understand their own interests and to reach agreement based on their objectives and points of view. As Judge Denlow explains, "the mediator has no independent power to resolve the dispute." In this regard, it differs from litigation and arbitration. Litigation, of course, may produce an enforceable judgment. And arbitration, as we will see below in Part C, results in an enforceable decision by the arbitrator. Thus, in litigation and arbitration, the end of the dispute may arrive by a third-party decision maker's determination of who wins, who loses, and by how much. By contrast, the only way mediation ends a dispute is if the parties reach agreement. Mediation is assisted negotiation.

3. In addition to mediation, lawyers and others have invented a wide range of mechanisms to facilitate settlement negotiations. Just like mediation, each of these mechanisms is intended to help parties reach agreement on a settlement of their dispute. These mechanisms facilitate settlement by helping parties and their lawyers to see the strength of the other side's case, to work from a common pool of information, and to predict the outcome more accurately if the dispute were to go to trial. Some of these processes are offered or imposed as court-connected processes under local rules, while others are conducted independently.

   a. *Non-binding arbitration.* In Part C below, we will discuss arbitration as a process of reaching a binding decision, but many courts have created processes for *non-binding* arbitration. In non-binding arbitration, parties present their cases and obtain an arbitrator's decision on the merits, but the decision is merely advisory. Often this occurs early in the litigation process, and often as a court-connected process. Even though the parties are not bound by the decision, the idea is that the process and result may facilitate settlement by helping parties to anticipate how a judge or jury might see their case. If the parties are satisfied with the arbitrator's decision, they can choose to accept it and voluntarily resolve their dispute on those terms.

Many courts have established mandatory programs of non-binding arbitration, at least for certain categories of disputes. The state trial court in Cook County, Illinois, for example, describes its program as follows:

> The Mandatory Arbitration Program was approved by the Illinois Supreme Court in January 1990 as a joint effort of the judiciary, attorneys and public to help resolve disputes in a more efficient way. The Cook County Mandatory Arbitration Program resolves approximately fifty percent of cases before they reach a jury trial.
>
> The court uses mandatory arbitration for certain types of small civil cases in which the plaintiff is seeking only money. The objective of the program is to enable the parties to quickly resolve their dispute, without resorting to a formal trial with a judge or jury, through the use of high-quality, economical hearings.
>
> A mandatory arbitration hearing is a legal proceeding held before a panel of three Illinois-licensed attorneys (called "arbitrators") who have taken a court certified arbitrator training program. The hearing is conducted like a trial where the parties may be represented by an attorney, or they may represent themselves. The arbitrators act in place of a judge and render a decision (called "award") at the conclusion of the hearing.
>
> If one of the parties disagrees with the award, that party may file a rejection within 30 days of the arbitration hearing. Unless a party is indigent, there is a $200 fee paid to the Clerk of the Circuit Court at the time of filing a rejection. The case is then assigned to a trial room and the dispute will be heard in court before a judge and jury.

Introduction, Cook County Mandatory Arbitration, http://www.cookcountycourt. org/ABOUTTHECOURT/OfficeoftheChiefJudge/CourtRelatedServices/Mandatory Arbitration.aspx. What do you think about using mandatory non-binding arbitration as a means to improve the efficiency of dispute resolution in the courts? Are you troubled by the fee for rejecting the arbitrator's decision?

As you think about non-binding arbitration such as the program described here, keep in mind the crucial difference between this and the sort of arbitration we will cover below in Part C, in which arbitrators have the power to render binding decisions.

b. *Early neutral evaluation.* Similar to non-binding arbitration, early neutral evaluation (ENE) offers parties a candid, neutral assessment of their cases early in the litigation process. But in contrast to arbitration, which often looks like an adjudicative proceeding, ENE resembles mediation in that it looks more like a meeting or discussion. The ENE evaluator is generally an experienced lawyer with expertise in the subject area.

c. *Summary jury trial.* Like non-binding arbitration and ENE, this process allows the parties to test run their cases, helping them to predict the outcome at trial if they fail to reach agreement. But summary jury trial is much more elaborate than either non-binding arbitration or ENE. In a summary jury trial, the court actually assembles a jury from people in the court's jury pool. The "trial" occurs in a real courtroom with a real judge. The lawyers present an abbreviated version of their case, and the jury renders a non-binding "verdict." In essence, the jury functions as a focus group, helping the parties to see how a real jury might view the case if there were to be a full-fledged trial.

d. *Mini-trial.* There is a process that dispute-resolution specialists call a "mini-trial," but really it is not a trial at all. Like a summary jury trial, a mini-trial gives each side the opportunity to present a short version of the case. But rather than assemble a mock jury using the power of the court, a mini-trial is driven directly by counsel, who bring together the principals for each side. In a dispute between corporations, for example, the lawyers might present their case to two business executives, one from each side, who have settlement authority. After the presentations, the principals attempt to settle the dispute.

e. *Online dispute resolution.* A relatively new entrant to the dispute-resolution scene, online dispute resolution (ODR) uses technology to resolve disputes. ODR involves aspects of negotiation, mediation, and arbitration; what makes it distinctive is that the process takes place via the Internet, often without the participation of lawyers, and sometimes without any human mediator or decision maker. ODR was developed for disputes over online transactions, particularly high-volume, low-value transactions on e-commerce sites such as eBay. Although it originated as an online tool for resolving online disputes, ODR has grown beyond its origins and some courts in the United States and elsewhere have incorporated ODR as a tool for resolution of a variety of disputes. Some observers see in this development the potential for deep changes in how courts function and how parties resolve disputes:

> While the adoption of ODR processes may seem like an extension of existing court operations, merely improving courts' convenience and accessibility, it is our contention that the adoption of full-fledged ODR systems could transform courts as we know them. Courts will shift from institutions that rely on physical presence and geography; employ human decision-making; and resolve individual cases as a channel for enforcing and developing the law, to ones that increasingly rely on digital communication, employ algorithms, and prevent disputes from arising as a means of enforcing existing norms and establishing the need for new law.

Orna Rabinovitch-Einy & Ethan Katsh, *The New New Courts*, 67 Am. U. L. Rev. 165, 188 (2017).

C. ARBITRATION

(1) Arbitration as Private Dispute Resolution

The majority of this course has focused on litigation and dispute resolution within the confines of our public judicial system—the federal and state courts in the United States. Indeed, litigation in the courts, funded by taxpayers, is the default for legal dispute resolution in the United States. Our public courts are not the only forums resolving legal disputes, however. Since the early part of the twentieth century, scholars, judge, attorneys, and litigants have criticized the civil litigation system as cumbersome, expensive, and time-consuming. These criticisms led many to search for alternatives to that system. In the prior section, you learned about mediation. In this section, you will be introduced to binding arbitration, the most formal alternative to litigation in the United States.

Arbitration is a private process whereby parties agree, via contract, that a third-party neutral arbitrator (or group of arbitrators) will make a decision about the dispute after reviewing evidence and hearing arguments. Agreements to arbitrate are found in contracts that govern the relevant relationship between the contracting parties out of which any legal dispute may arise. These agreements are embodied in what are known as *pre-dispute arbitration clauses*. They are so named because they make clear that any dispute that *may arise in the future* between the contracting parties relating to their contractual relationship will be resolved in arbitration.

Generally speaking, there are many potential advantages to private arbitration. For one, arbitration is often quicker and less formal than a trial. Arbitration is often less costly and more efficient than court proceedings. Further, particularly for some types of disputes, the private nature of arbitration is quite appealing to one or more of the parties. Arbitration also provides parties with the ability to indicate that any disputes will be resolved before an arbitrator who has expertise in the field relevant to those potential disputes. Above, we discussed non-binding arbitration as a process for encouraging voluntary resolutions. In this section, however, we focus on binding arbitration. In binding arbitration, the decision of the arbitrator is final, can be enforced by a court, and can only be vacated or annulled on narrow grounds. *See* Federal Arbitration Act (FAA), 9 U.S.C. §10.

In the early twentieth century, contractual agreements to arbitrate were not received warmly by the courts. In order to encourage the enforcement of arbitration contracts, Congress in 1925 passed the FAA, 9 U.S.C. §§1-16. The key provisions of the FAA are sections 2 and 10. Section 2 of the FAA states that parties' agreement to arbitration will be enforced in federal court and "shall be valid, irrevocable and enforceable, save upon such grounds as exist at law or in equity for the revocation of any contract." 9 U.S.C. §2 (1994). An arbitral award can only be vacated by a district court on very limited grounds: if it was the product of fraud, corruption, or partiality, 9 U.S.C. §§10(a)(1)-(2); if the arbitrators were guilty of specified forms of misconduct, §10(a)(3); or if the arbitrator "exceeded [its] powers," §10(a)(4).

Arbitration is a matter of contract, and that—combined with the Supreme Court's increasingly strong embrace of freedom-of-contract principles—gives parties (or at least the contract drafters) a great deal of control in designing the procedures for any resulting arbitration. Before a dispute even arises, parties to the contract can design the arbitration process almost any way they wish by so specifying in their arbitration agreement. Many arbitration agreements simply specify that a particular organization's rules apply, such as those of the American Arbitration Association (AAA) or JAMS (formerly known as Judicial Arbitration and Mediation Services, Inc.).

But contracting parties are also free to specify their own rules. An arbitration agreement can spell out what is required in a statement of a claim, what sort of joinder is permitted, how much discovery is available, and so on. In other words, in arbitration contracts, contracting parties can *design their own procedures*. The only catches are *one*, the parties must agree to the procedures (which can be tricky when dealing with, say, two powerful corporations attempting to set up procedures for a future dispute), and *two*, the procedural provisions must be reflected in an arbitration agreement that the court will enforce under FAA section 2. Section 2 of the FAA provides that arbitration agreements "shall be valid, irrevocable, and enforceable, save upon such grounds as exist in law or equity for the revocation of any contract."

(2) Arbitration as Litigation Avoidance

The power to design one's own dispute-resolution procedures, discussed in the last section, does not play out evenly for all parties. In this regard, there is a big difference between, on the one hand, arbitration agreements among sophisticated businesses, and on the other hand, arbitration agreements between parties of unequal power, such as businesses and consumers or employers and employees. Some parties are repeat players; others are more likely to be one-time claimants. Some parties are likely to be the drafters of arbitration agreements; others are more likely to be handed a contract containing an arbitration agreement on a take-it-or-leave-it basis. The opportunity to design one's own procedures—by specifying rules about claims, discovery, joinder, remedies, decision makers, and other matters in an arbitration agreement—holds powerful allure for parties who defend regularly against claims. Frequent defendants are not big fans of litigation. Given the willingness of courts to enforce arbitration clauses under the FAA, it is no surprise that banks, businesses, and others availed themselves of the opportunity to design their own dispute-resolution procedures for disputes with customers and employees. Why would such repeat-player defendants want to design their own dispute-resolution processes? First, starting with the least cynical explanation, perhaps they simply want to resolve disputes efficiently and privately. Second, a bit more cynically, perhaps they prefer a process that systematically favors their interests and reduces the likelihood or extent of liability. Third, and most cynically, perhaps they prefer to avoid the claims altogether; perhaps they expect that, if customers or employees lack access to the public litigation process and its procedural rules, some potential claimants will choose not to (or be unable to) pursue their claims at all.

To what extent do courts enforce arbitration agreements that constrain procedural rights? Consider both "catches" we mentioned above—party agreement and arbitration-agreement enforceability under the FAA. Start with the question of whether an arbitration clause reflects an *agreement* of the parties. Congress passed the FAA in 1925, against a backdrop in which arbitration clauses were contained in contracts between parties of roughly equal bargaining power (businesses, merchants, unions and management, etc.). Thus, party agreement was not just required by the FAA; it was a feature of the arbitration-contract negotiation process. Indeed, before the FAA was enacted, some members of Congress expressed concern that the FAA might be used to enforce non-negotiated arbitration agreements, but they were assured by the bill's supporters that the Act was not intended to facilitate arbitration agreements "offered on a take-it-or-leave-it basis to captive customers or consumers." *See Hearing on S. 4213 and S. 4214 Before the Subcomm. of the S. Comm. on the Judiciary*, 67th Cong. 9-11 (1923). Supreme Court jurisprudence was in accord with that legislative view. *See Wilko v. Swan*, 346 U.S. 427, 435-36 (1953) (refusing to enforce an arbitration agreement governing federal securities law claims, and emphasizing that the FAA "was drafted with an eye to the disadvantages under which buyers labor").

Several decades later, the Supreme Court changed course. *See Rodriguez de Quijas v. Shearson/American Express, Inc.*, 490 U.S. 477, 481 (1989) (reversing *Wilko* in a 5-4 decision and enforcing an arbitration agreement drafted by securities brokerage houses in a dispute with investors); *Gilmer v. Interstate/Johnson Lane Corp.*, 500 U.S. 20 (1991) (enforcing an arbitration clause in a discrimination dispute between an employer and employee). The Supreme Court has made it clear that *actual agreement* to an arbitration clause is not required for the clause to be enforceable. Thus, parties no longer tend to succeed on arguments that an arbitration agreement drafted by one party (usually a potential defendant) and offered in a contract of adhesion to another party (usually a potential plaintiff such as a consumer or employee) fails for lack of agreement. Unsurprisingly, then, in the decade and a half or so after *Wilko*'s reversal, corporations rushed to insert arbitration agreements into contracts previously thought off limits, including consumer, employment, financial product, and franchise contracts. Very likely, you are a party to some of these arbitration provisions; think about consumer contracts you have signed and for which you have clicked your "agreement" to online terms and conditions.

What about the second "catch"—that an arbitration agreement may be struck down under FAA section 2 when the procedures in that agreement are so unfairly one-sided as to be unconscionable under state contract-law doctrine? Recall that FAA section 2 provides that arbitration agreements are enforceable "save upon such grounds as exist in law or equity for the revocation of any contract." To what extent does that "catch" ensnare arbitration agreements contained in contracts of adhesion? As businesses added arbitration clauses to consumer contracts and others after

Wilko's reversal, some of them included numerous one-sided provisions in their arbitration agreements that, for instance, imposed exorbitant arbitration fees on potential plaintiffs, demanded that plaintiffs travel to far-flung forums, shortened statutes of limitations, and barred many forms of relief. Some of the provisions in these so-called first-generation arbitration agreements were struck down under FAA section 2 as unconscionable. *See* Richard A. Nagareda, *The Litigation-Arbitration Dichotomy Meets the Class Action*, 86 Notre Dame L. Rev. 1019 (2011) (describing how arbitration clauses went through multiple "generations" in order to respond to lower-court restrictions on the contours of arbitration agreements).

Businesses responded in two basic ways to the unconscionability decisions issued by lower courts (and even action by some state legislatures). One: Businesses went on defense. In an attempt to survive FAA section 2 challenges to mandatory arbitration agreements, many businesses revised their arbitration agreements by removing the most clearly unconscionable provisions.

Two: Businesses went on offense, in at least three ways. First, they clung to the one provision they seemed to want most: the provision that prohibited class actions or other aggregated proceedings. Second, they fought for the enforcement of class-prohibition provisions by vigorously challenging state rules and holdings that restrained the enforcement of arbitration agreements "according to their terms" on the grounds that the FAA superseded—"preempted"—those state rules. They did not win all of these preemption arguments, but they won some, and more than that, certain businesses kept their eye on the long game: a preemption fight before the Supreme Court. Third, businesses not only mounted challenges to lower court opinions striking down their arbitration agreements, but they also included in their arbitration agreements "consumer-friendly" clauses to make the class-action prohibition more palatable. One might call it a "Mary Poppins" strategy: A spoonful of sugar helps the medicine go down.

The following case represents the culmination of these efforts. It involves a preemption challenge by AT&T to the decisions of the California Court of Appeal, the California Supreme Court, and the United States Court of Appeals for the Ninth Circuit that AT&T's arbitration agreement—which contained a class-action waiver—was unconscionable as a matter of state contract law and therefore unenforceable under FAA section 2. AT&T argued that the California rule regarding unconscionability was preempted by the FAA, and that its arbitration agreement, class-action waiver and all, must be enforced according to its terms. AT&T also wasted no opportunity in pointing out the "consumer-friendly" provisions it included in its arbitration agreement. As you read, think about three key questions: One, why was AT&T (and other businesses) so intent upon preserving the class-action prohibition in its arbitration agreement when it was willing to part with control over other procedures? Two, why were these businesses indeed so intent on preserving the class-action prohibition that they were willing to include numerous claimant-friendly provisions in their arbitration agreements? Three, in what ways (or not) does California's unconscionability rule regarding class prohibitions conflict with the FAA?

AT&T MOBILITY LLC v. CONCEPCION
563 U.S. 333 (2011)

SCALIA, J., delivered the opinion of the Court.

Section 2 of the Federal Arbitration Act (FAA) makes agreements to arbitrate "valid, irrevocable, and enforceable, save upon such grounds as exist at law or in equity for the revocation of any such contract." 9 U.S.C. §2. We consider whether the FAA prohibits States from conditioning the enforceability of certain arbitration agreements on the availability of classwide arbitration procedures.

I

In February 2022, Vincent and Liza Concepcion entered into an agreement for the sale and servicing of cellular telephones with AT&T Mobility LLC (AT&T). The contract provided for arbitration of all disputes between the parties, but required that claims be brought in the parties' "individual capacity, and not as a plaintiff or class member in any purported class or representative proceeding." The agreement authorized AT&T to make unilateral amendments, which it did to the arbitration provision on several occasions. . . .

The revised agreement provides that customers may initiate dispute proceedings by completing a one-page Notice of Dispute form available on AT&T's Web site. In the event the parties proceed to arbitration, the agreement specifies that AT&T must pay all costs for nonfrivolous claims; that arbitration must take place in the county in which the customer is billed; that, for claims of $10,000 or less, the customer may choose whether the arbitration proceeds in person, by telephone, or based only on submissions; that either party may bring a claim in small claims court in lieu of arbitration; and that the arbitrator may award any form of individual relief, including injunctions and presumably punitive damages. The agreement, moreover, denies AT&T any ability to seek reimbursement of its attorney's fees, and, in the event that a customer receives an arbitration award greater than AT&T's last written settlement offer, requires AT&T to pay a $7,500 minimum recovery and twice the amount of the claimant's attorney's fees.

The Concepcions purchased AT&T service, which was advertised as including the provision of free phones; they were not charged for the phones, but they were charged $30.22 in sales tax based on the phones' retail value. In March 2006, the Concepcions filed a complaint against AT&T in the United States District Court for the Southern District of California. The complaint was later consolidated with a putative class action, alleging, among other things, that AT&T had engaged in false advertising and fraud by charging sales tax on phones it advertised as free.

In March 2008, AT&T moved to compel arbitration under the terms of its contract with the Concepcions. The Concepcions opposed the motion, contending that the arbitration agreement was unconscionable and unlawfully exculpatory under California law because it disallowed classwide procedures. The District Court denied AT&T's motion. . . . [R]elying on the California Supreme Court's decision in *Discover Bank v. Superior Court*, 113 P.3d 1100 (2005), the court found that the arbitration provision was unconscionable because AT&T had not shown that bilateral arbitration adequately substituted for the deterrent effects of the class action.

The Ninth Circuit affirmed, also finding the provision unconscionable under California law as announced in *Discover Bank*. *Laster v. AT&T Mobility LLC*, 584 F.3d 849, 855 (2009). It also held that the *Discover Bank* rule was not preempted by the FAA because that rule was simply "a refinement of the unconscionability analysis applicable to contracts generally in California." 584 F.3d at 857. . . .

II

The FAA was enacted in 1925 in response to widespread judicial hostility to arbitration agreements. Section 2, the "primary substantive provision of the Act," *Moses H. Cone Memorial Hospital v. Mercury Constr. Corp.*, 460 U.S. 1, 24 (1983), provides, in relevant part, as follows:

> A written provision in any maritime transaction or a contract evidencing a transaction involving commerce to settle by arbitration a controversy thereafter arising out of such contract or transaction . . . shall be valid, irrevocable, and enforceable, save upon such grounds as exist at law or in equity for the revocation of any contract. 9 U.S.C. §2.

We have described this provision as reflecting both a "liberal federal policy favoring arbitration," *Moses H. Cone, supra*, at 24, and the "fundamental principle that arbitration is a matter of contract," *Rent-A-Center, West, Inc. v. Jackson*, 561 U.S. 63, 67 (2010). In line with these principles, courts must place arbitration agreements on an equal footing with other contracts, and enforce them according to their terms.

The final phrase of §2, however, permits arbitration agreements to be declared unenforceable "upon such grounds as exist at law or in equity for the revocation of any contract." This saving clause permits agreements to arbitrate to be invalidated by "generally applicable contract defenses, such as fraud, duress, or unconscionability," but not by defenses that apply only to arbitration or that derive their meaning from the fact that an agreement to arbitrate is at issue. *Doctor's Associates, Inc. v. Casarotto*, 517 U.S. 681, 687 (1996). The question in this case is whether §2 preempts California's rule classifying most collective-arbitration waivers in consumer contracts as unconscionable. We refer to this as the *Discover Bank* rule.

Under California law, courts may refuse to enforce any contract found "to have been unconscionable at the time it was made," or may "limit the application of any unconscionable clause." Cal. Civ. Code Ann. §1670.5(a) (West 1985). A finding of unconscionability requires "a procedural and a substantive element, the former focusing on oppression and surprise due to unequal bargaining power, the latter on the overly harsh or one-sided results." *Discover Bank*, 113 P.3d at 1108.

In *Discover Bank*, the California Supreme Court applied this framework to class-action waivers in arbitration agreements and held as follows: "When the waiver is found in a consumer contract of adhesion in a setting in which disputes between the contracting parties predictably involved small amounts of damages, and when it is alleged that the party with the superior bargaining power has carried out a scheme to deliberately cheat large numbers of consumers out of individually small sums of money, then . . . the waiver becomes in practice the exemption of the party from responsibility from [its] own fraud, or willful injury to the person or property of another. Under these circumstances, such waivers are unconscionable under California law and should not be enforced." *Id.* at 1110.

III

A

The Concepcions argue that the *Discover Bank* rule, given its origins in California's unconscionability doctrine and California's policy against exculpation, is a ground that "exist[s] at law or in equity for the revocation of any contract" under FAA §2. Moreover, they argue that even if we construe the *Discover Bank* rule as a prohibition on collective-action waivers rather than simply an application of unconscionability, the rule would still be applicable to all dispute-resolution contracts, since California prohibits waivers of class litigation as well.

When state law prohibits outright the arbitration of a particular type of claim, the analysis is straightforward: The conflicting rule is displaced by the FAA. But the inquiry becomes more complex when a doctrine normally thought to be generally applicable, such as duress, or as relevant here, unconscionability, is alleged to have been applied in a fashion that disfavors arbitration. . . .

An obvious illustration of this point would be a case finding unconscionable or unenforceable as against public policy consumer arbitration agreements that fail to provide for judicially monitored discovery. The rationalizations for such a holding are neither difficult to imagine nor different in kind from those articulated in *Discover Bank*. A court might reason that no consumer would knowingly waive his right to full discovery, as this would enable companies to hide their wrongdoing. Or the court might simply say that such agreements are exculpatory—restricting discovery would be of greater benefit to the company than the consumer, since the former is more likely to be sued than to sue. And, that reasoning would continue, because such a rule applies the general principle of unconscionability or public-policy disapproval of exculpatory agreements, it is applicable to "any" contract and thus preserved by §2 of the FAA. In practice, of course, the rule would have a disproportionate impact on arbitration agreements; but it would presumably apply to contracts purporting to restrict discovery in litigation as well. Other examples are easy to imagine. . . .

The Concepcions suggest that all this is just a parade of horribles, and no genuine worry. "Rules aimed at destroying arbitration" or "demanding procedures incompatible with arbitration," they concede, "would be preempted by the FAA because they cannot sensibly be reconciled with Section 2." The "grounds" available under §2's saving clause, they admit, "should not be construed to include a State's mere preference for procedures that are incompatible with arbitration and would wholly eviscerate arbitration agreements."

We largely agree. Although §2's saving clause preserves generally applicable contract defenses, nothing in it suggests an intent to preserve state-law rules that stand as an obstacle to the accomplishment of the FAA's objectives. As we have said, a federal statute's saving clause "cannot in reason be construed as [allowing] a common law right, the continued existence of which would be absolutely inconsistent with the provisions of the act. In other words, the act cannot be held to destroy itself." *Am. Telephone & Telegraph Co. v. Central Office Telephone, Inc.*, 524 U.S. 214, 227-28 (1998).

We differ with the Concepcions only in the application of this analysis to the matter before us. . . . Requiring the availability of classwide arbitration interferes with fundamental attributes of arbitration and thus creates a scheme inconsistent with the FAA.

B

The "principal purpose" of the FAA is to "ensur[e] that private arbitration agreements are enforced according to their terms." *Stolt-Nielsen S.A. v. AnimalFeeds Int'l Corp.*, 559 U.S. 662, 681-82 (2010). This purpose is readily apparent from the FAA's text. Section 2 makes arbitration agreements "valid, irrevocable, and enforceable" as written (subject, of course to the saving clause), §3 requires courts to stay litigation of arbitral claims pending arbitration of those claims "in accordance with the terms of the agreement. . . ."

The point of affording parties discretion in designing arbitration processes is to allow for efficient, streamlined procedures tailored to the type of dispute. It can be specified, for example, that the decisionmaker be a specialist in the relevant field, or that proceedings be kept confidential to keep trade secrets. And the informality of arbitral proceedings is itself desirable, reducing the cost and increasing the speed of dispute resolution. . . .

Contrary to the dissent's view, our cases place it beyond dispute that the FAA was designed to promote arbitration. . . . [Yet] California's *Discover Bank* rule interferes with arbitration. Although the rule does not require classwide arbitration, it allows any party to a consumer contract to demand it ex post. The rule is limited to adhesion contracts, *Discover Bank*, 113 P.3d at 1110, but the times in which consumer contracts were anything other than adhesive are long past. The rule also requires that damages be predictably small, and that the consumer allege a scheme to cheat consumers. The former requirement, however, is toothless and malleable . . . and the latter has no limiting effect, as all that is required is an allegation. Consumers remain free to bring and resolve their disputes on a bilateral basis under *Discover Bank*, and some may well do so; but there is little incentive for lawyers to arbitrate on behalf of individuals when they may do so for a class and reap far higher fees in the process. And faced with inevitable class arbitration, companies would have less incentive to continue resolving potentially duplicative claims on an individual basis.

Although we have had little occasion to examine classwide arbitration, our decision in *Stolt-Nielsen* is instructive. In that case we held that an arbitration panel exceeded its power under §10(a)(4) of the FAA by imposing class procedures based on policy judgments rather than the arbitration agreement itself or some background principle of contract law that would affect its interpretation. 559 U.S. at 684-87. We then held that the agreement at issue, which was silent on the question of class procedures, could not be interpreted to allow them because the "changes brought by the shift from bilateral arbitration to class-action arbitration" are "fundamental." *Id.* at 686. This is obvious as a structural matter: Classwide arbitration includes absent parties, necessitating additional and different procedures and involving higher stakes. Confidentiality becomes more difficult. And while it is theoretically possible to select an arbitrator with some expertise relevant to the class-certification question, arbitrators are not generally knowledgeable in the often-dominant procedural aspects of certification, such as the protection of absent parties. The conclusion follows that class arbitration, to the extent it is manufactured by *Discover Bank* rather than consensual, is inconsistent with the FAA.

First, the switch from bilateral to class arbitration sacrifices the principal advantage of arbitration—its informality—and makes the process slower, more costly, and more likely to generate procedural morass than final judgment. . . . According to the American Arbitration Association (AAA), the average consumer arbitration between January and August 2007 resulted in a disposition on the merits in six months, four months if the arbitration was conducted by documents only. As of September 2009, the AAA had opened 283 class arbitrations. Of those, 121 remained active, and 162 had been settled, withdrawn, or dismissed. Not a single one, however, had resulted in a final award on the merits. For those cases that were no longer active, the median time from filing to settlement, withdrawal, or dismissal—not judgment on the merits—was 583 days, and the mean was 630 days.

Second, class arbitration requires procedural formality. The AAA's rules governing class arbitrations mimic the Federal Rules of Civil Procedure for class litigation. And while parties can alter those procedures by contract, an alternative is not obvious. If procedures are too informal, absent class members would not be bound by the arbitration. . . .

We find it unlikely that in passing the FAA Congress meant to leave the disposition of these procedural requirements to an arbitrator. Indeed, class arbitration was not even envisioned by Congress when it passed the FAA in 1925; as the California Supreme Court admitted in *Discover Bank*, class arbitration is a "relatively recent development." 113 P.3d at 1110. And it is at least odd to think that an arbitrator would be entrusted with ensuring that third parties' due process rights are satisfied.

Third, class arbitration greatly increases risks to defendants. Informal procedures do of course have a cost: The absence of multilayered review makes it more likely that errors will go uncorrected. Defendants are willing to accept the costs of these errors in arbitration, since their impact is limited to the size of individual disputes, and presumably outweighed by savings from avoiding the courts. But when damages allegedly owed to tens of thousands of potential claimants are aggregated and decided at once, the risk of error will often become unacceptable. Faced with even a small chance of devastating loss, defendants will be pressured into settling questionable claims. Other courts have noted the risk of "in terrorem" settlements that class actions entail, and class arbitration would be no different. . . .

The dissent claims that class proceedings are necessary to prosecute small-dollar claims that might otherwise slip through the legal system. But States cannot require a procedure that is inconsistent with the FAA, even if it is desirable for unrelated reasons. Moreover, the claim here was most unlikely to go unresolved [given AT&T's "consumer-friendly" arbitration clause]. . . .

Because it "stands as an obstacle to the accomplishment and execution of the full purposes and objectives of Congress," *Hines v. Davidowitz*, 312 U.S. 52, 67 (1941), California's *Discover Bank* rule is preempted by the FAA. The judgment of the Ninth Circuit is reversed, and the case is remanded for further proceedings consistent with this opinion.

[The concurrence of Justice Thomas is omitted.]

Justice BREYER, with whom Justice GINSBURG, Justice SOTOMAYOR, and Justice KAGAN join, dissenting.

The Federal Arbitration Act says that an arbitration agreement "shall be valid irrevocable, and enforceable, *save upon such grounds as exist at law or in equity for the revocation of any contract.*" 9 U.S.C. §2 (emphasis added). California law sets forth certain circumstances in which "class action waivers" in *any* contract are unenforceable. In my view, this rule of state law is consistent with the federal Act's language and primary objective. It does not "stan[d] as an obstacle" to the Act's "accomplishment and execution." *Hines*, 312 U.S. at 67. And the Court is wrong to hold that the federal Act pre-empts the rule of state law.

I

The California law in question consists of an authoritative state-court interpretation of two provisions of the California Civil Code. The first provision makes unlawful all contracts "which have for their object, directly or indirectly, to exempt anyone from responsibility for his own . . . violation of the law." Cal. Civ. Code Ann. §1668 (West 1985). The second provision authorizes courts to "limit the application of any unconscionable clause" in a contract so "as to avoid any unconscionable result." §1670.5(a).

The specific rule of state law in question consists of the California Supreme Court's application of these principles to hold that "some" (but not "all") "class action waivers" in consumer contracts are exculpatory and unconscionable under California "law." *Discover Bank*, 113 P.3d at 1110. . . .

The *Discover Bank* rule does not create a "blanket policy in California against class action waivers in the consumer context." *Provencher v. Dell, Inc.*, 409 F. Supp. 2d 1201 (C.D. Cal. 2006). Instead, it represents the "application of a more general [unconscionability] principle." *Gentry v. Superior Court*, 165 P.3d 556, 564 (2007). Courts applying California law have enforced class-action waivers where they satisfy general unconscionability standards. And even when they fail, the parties remain free to

devise other dispute mechanisms, including informal mechanisms, that in context, will not prove unconscionable.

II

A

The *Discover Bank* rule is consistent with the federal Act's language. It "applies equally to class action litigation waivers in contracts without arbitration agreements as it does to class arbitration waivers in contracts with such agreements." 113 P.3d at 1112. Linguistically speaking, it falls directly within the scope of the Act's exception permitting courts to refuse to enforce arbitration agreements on the grounds that exist "for the revocation of *any* contract." 9 U.S.C. §2 (emphasis added). The majority agrees.

B

The *Discover Bank* rule is also consistent with the basic purpose behind the Act. We have described that purpose as one of "ensur[ing] judicial enforcement" of arbitration agreements. *Dean Witter Reynolds Inc. v. Byrd*, 470 U.S. 213, 219 (1985). . . . The Act sought to eliminate [judicial hostility toward arbitration] by placing agreements "*upon the same footing as other contracts.*" H.R. Rep. No. 96, at 2 (emphasis added). . . .

Thus, insofar as we seek to implement Congress' intent, we should think more than twice before invalidating a state law that does just what §2 requires, namely, puts agreements to arbitrate and agreements to litigate "upon the same footing."

III

The majority's contrary view (that *Discover Bank* stands as an "obstacle" to the accomplishment of the federal law's objective), rests primarily upon its claims that the *Discover Bank* rule increases the complexity of arbitration procedures, thereby discouraging parties from entering into arbitration agreements, and to that extent discriminating in practice against arbitration. These claims are not well founded.

For one thing, a state rule of law that would sometimes set aside as unconscionable a contract term that forbids class arbitration is not (as the majority claims) like a rule that would require ... "judicially monitored discovery...." Unlike the majority's examples, class arbitration is consistent with the use of arbitration. It is a form of arbitration that is well known in California and followed elsewhere. American Arbitration Association (AAA), Supplementary Rules for Class Arbitrations (2003); JAMS, The Resolution Experts, Class Action Procedures (2009). And unlike the majority's examples, the *Discover Bank* rule imposes equivalent limitations on litigation; hence it cannot fairly be characterized as a targeted attack on arbitration.

Where does the majority get its contrary idea—that individual, rather than class, arbitration is a "fundamental attribut[e]" of arbitration? The majority does not explain. And it is unlikely to be able to trace its present view to the history of the arbitration statute itself.

When Congress enacted the Act, arbitration procedures had not yet been fully developed. Insofar as Congress considered detailed forms of arbitration at all, it may well have thought that arbitration would be used primarily where merchants sought to resolve disputes of fact, not law, under the customs of their industries, where the parties possessed roughly equivalent bargaining power. *See* Joint Hearings on S. 1005 and H.R. 646 before the Subcommittees of the Committees on the Judiciary, 68th Cong., 1st Sess., 15 (1924); Hearing on S. 4213 and S. 4214 before a Subcommittee of the Senate Committee on the Judiciary, 67th Cong., 4th Sess., 9-10 (1923).... This last mentioned feature of the history—roughly equivalent bargaining power—suggests, if anything, that California's statute is consistent with, and indeed may help to further, the objectives that Congress had in mind.

Regardless, if neither the history nor present practice suggests that class arbitration is fundamentally incompatible with arbitration itself, then on what basis can the majority hold California's law pre-empted?

For another thing, the majority's argument that the *Discover Bank* rule will discourage arbitration rests critically upon the wrong comparison. The majority compares the complexity of class arbitration with that of bilateral arbitration. And it finds the former more complex. But, if incentives are at issue, the *relevant* comparison is not "arbitration with arbitration" but a comparison between class arbitration and judicial class actions. After all, in respect to the relevant set of contracts, the *Discover Bank* rule similarly and equally sets aside clauses that forbid class procedures—whether arbitration procedures or ordinary judicial procedures are at issue.

Why would a typical defendant (say, a business) prefer a judicial class action to class arbitration? AAA statistics "suggest that class arbitration proceedings take more time than the average commercial arbitration, but may take *less time* than the average class action in court." AAA *Amicus Brief* 24 (emphasis added). Data from California courts confirm that class arbitrations can take considerably less time than in-court proceedings in which class certification is sought. And single class proceeding is surely more efficient than thousands of separate proceedings for identical claims. Thus, if speedy resolution of disputes were all that mattered, then the *Discover Bank* rule would reinforce, not obstruct, that objective of the Act. . . .

[T]he majority highlights the disadvantages of class arbitrations, as it sees them. But class proceedings have countervailing advantages. In general agreements that forbid the consolidation of claims can lead small-dollar claimants to abandon their claims rather than to litigate. I suspect that is true even here, for as the Court of Appeals recognized, AT&T can avoid the $7,500 payout (the payout that supposedly makes the Concepcions' arbitration worthwhile) simply by paying the claim's face value, such that the "maximum gain to a customer for the hassle of arbitrating a $30.22 dispute is still just $30.22." *Laster v. AT&T Mobility LLC*, 584 F.3d 849, 855, 859 (9th Cir. 2009).

What rational lawyer would have signed on to represent the Concepcions in litigation for the possibility of fees stemming from a $30.22 claim? In California's perfectly rational view, nonclass arbitration over such sums will also sometimes have the effect of depriving claimants of their claims (say, for example, where claiming the $30.22 were to involve filling out many forms that require technical legal knowledge or waiting at great length while a call is placed on hold). *Discover Bank* sets forth circumstances in which the California courts believe that the terms of consumer contracts can be manipulated to insulate an agreement's author from liability for its own frauds by "deliberately cheat[ing] large numbers of consumers out of individually small sums of money." 113 P.3d at 1110. Why is this kind of decision—weighing the pros and cons of all class proceedings—not California's to make? . . .

IV

By using the words "save upon such grounds as exist at law or in equity for the revocation of any contract," Congress retained for the States an important role incident to agreements to arbitrate. 9 U.S.C. §2. Through those words Congress reiterated a basic federal idea that has long informed the nature of this Nation's laws. We have often expressed this idea in opinions that set forth presumptions. But federalism is as much a question of deeds as words. It often takes the form of a concrete decision by this Court that respects the legitimacy of a State's action in an individual case. Here, recognition of that federalist ideal, embodied in specific language in this particular statute, should lead us to uphold California's law, not to strike it down. We do not honor federalist principles in their breach.

With respect, I dissent.

Notes & Questions

1. The core holding in *Concepcion* is that the Federal Arbitration Act (FAA) preempted California contract law, including the state's *Discover Bank* rule. The preemption doctrine derives from the Supremacy Clause of the United States Constitution, and it provides that federal law supersedes conflicting state laws. In what way did the *Discover Bank* rule conflict with the FAA? Did it conflict with the statutory text (express preemption)? The Court says that the *Discover Bank* rule posed an "obstacle to the accomplishment of Congress's objectives."

Which of Congress's objectives did the *Discover Bank* rule conflict with? Where were those objectives stated or implied in the FAA?

2. The majority states that "[t]he point of affording parties discretion in designing arbitration processes is to allow for efficient, streamlined procedures tailored to the type of dispute." Think about the purposes of class actions and the purposes of arbitration. Do some of the purposes overlap? If so, why are class arbitration proceedings incompatible with arbitration, according to the majority? Would it depend on the facts? What about a case like *Concepcion*, where an individual claim was worth $30.22 and where "the class is so numerous that joinder of all members is impracticable"? Fed. R. Civ. P. 23(a)(1). What about a case where individual claims are worth thousands, but joinder of all claimants is nonetheless impracticable?

3. The majority worries about the "in terrorem" settlement pressure that class arbitration would place upon defendants. Would that pressure be any different in class litigation? *See, e.g., In re Rhone-Poulenc Rorer Pharmaceuticals, Inc.*, 51 F.3d 1293 (7th Cir. 1995) (Posner, J.) (describing the "in terrorem" settlement effect of the class action on defendants). If so, how? If not (or not meaningfully), is that a concern properly addressed indirectly through FAA preemption jurisprudence? How might that concern be addressed directly in Rule 23 (either as it exists or might be amended)?

   Assuming class proceedings in arbitration do produce "in terrorem" settlement pressure (a point of debate among courts and scholars), should that pressure be balanced against the risks to plaintiffs created by the removal of the class device from arbitration? Should *either* of these considerations be part of the Court's interpretation of the FAA? Does your answer depend on which theory of statutory interpretation you endorse?

4. Arbitration has sometimes been heralded as providing streamlined proceedings. This raises two questions. First, are arbitration proceedings necessarily more streamlined than litigation? Arbitration proceedings vary from one context to another, and some types of arbitration strongly resemble litigation in terms of procedures, complexity, delay, and expense. Second, does enforcement of arbitration agreements according to their terms necessarily facilitate proceedings at all? To put the point differently, is the choice between streamlined proceedings and complex class arbitration (as the majority contends), or is it between class arbitration and no proceedings whatsoever? Do the specific provisions in AT&T's arbitration clause affect your answer?

5. *Concepcion* involved state law claims. How would the Court treat a mandatory arbitration agreement with a class waiver in the context of a federal law claims, where the preemption doctrine is not at issue? In *American Express Co. v. Italian Colors Restaurant*, 570 U.S. 228 (2013), the Court's most sweeping FAA decision to date, the majority held that an arbitration agreement containing a class-action waiver was enforceable under the FAA even though enforcing the arbitration clause with the waiver would mean that plaintiffs could not, as an

economical matter, bring *federal* antitrust claims. In *Italian Colors*, the Court no longer touted the virtues of cost-effective, efficient arbitration proceedings. Instead, the Court divorced the freedom-of-contract justification for arbitration from the streamlined-arbitration-proceedings justification. The arbitration clause at issue in *Italian Colors* would not promote arbitration at all, and as Justice Kagan put it in her dissent, the majority simply found it "[t]oo darn bad" that plaintiffs would never be able to seek vindication of their federal statutory rights, in any forum. *Id.*

6. Many state leaders were displeased with the Court's decisions in *Concepcion* and *Italian Colors*. In the wake of those decisions, some state legislatures, lawyers, and political leaders looked for ways to create clever workarounds. One such workaround was to enact or increase the use of what are known as Private Attorneys General Acts (PAGAs). A PAGA is a piece of legislation that authorizes a private citizen to act as an attorney general of the state and sue a company to recover civil penalties for certain types of claims. In other words, rather than sue in her private capacity, the individual takes on the mantle of the state attorney general and acts in a quasi-law enforcement role. As a reward for the individual's law-enforcement service to the state, that individual is entitled to a portion of the penalty recovered. PAGAs are intended to incentivize individuals to bring suits that would otherwise not be financially feasible, both because providing such incentives helps ensure that laws are adequately enforced in a world of scarce state resources, and because states with PAGAs have recognized that other law-enforcement-incentivizing devices like the class action are frequently not available due to the proliferation of mandatory arbitration agreements with class-action waivers. Even though the individual may be subject to a mandatory arbitration agreement, the state is not, enabling the individual—acting as a private attorney general—to bring her suit in a representative capacity without running afoul of the arbitration agreement. *See Iskanian v. CLS Transportation Los Angeles, LLC*, 59 Cal. 4th 348, 378-92 (2014) (state is not a signatory, and therefore not bound, by arbitration contract between employer and employee). In California in particular, the number of PAGA claims have skyrocketed in the years following *Concepcion*, ballooning from a couple hundred cases annually to over 5,700 in 2018, suggesting that PAGA is not only becoming more important as a means of law enforcement for the state, but also as a means for individuals to vindicate their rights when the contours of their arbitration agreements would otherwise prevent them from doing so.

7. In 2015, the Consumer Financial Protection Bureau (CFPB) (an administrative agency created by Congress) concluded a years-long study on the use of arbitration agreements for consumer financial products and services. Congress had ordered the CFPB to undertake this study so that it and the public could better understand the advantages and disadvantages of moving consumer financial disputes out of the judicial system and into private arbitration. Some of the CFPB's key findings include, one, that tens of millions of consumers are subject to mandatory arbitration agreements (including, for instance, 92 percent of

prepaid card consumers, 99.9 percent of wireless mobile customers, and 85.7 percent of borrowers of private student loans). Two, almost all of the mandatory pre-dispute arbitration clauses contained class-action waivers (93.9 percent of credit card arbitration clauses; 88.5 percent of checking account arbitration clauses; 97.9 percent of prepaid card arbitration clauses; 88.7 percent of the storefront payday loan arbitration clauses; 100 percent of private student loan arbitration clauses; and 85.7 percent of the mobile wireless arbitration clauses). Three, the CFPB found that few consumers had any idea whether their contracts included arbitration agreements; indeed, fewer than 7 percent of credit card consumers knew that they could not sue their credit card company in court. Relatedly, more than half of consumers thought that they could participate in a class action if they had a dispute with the consumer financial product provider. Perhaps most fundamentally, virtually no consumers knew what arbitration was.

8. Informed by its findings about financial consumer arbitration, the CFPB crafted a rule that (1) "prohibit[ed] . . . providers of certain consumer financial products and services from using an agreement with a consumer that provides for arbitration of any future dispute between the parties to bar the consumer from filing or participating in a class action concerning the covered consumer financial product or service"; and (2) "require[d] covered providers that are involved in an arbitration pursuant to a pre-dispute arbitration agreement to submit specified arbitral records to the Bureau and also to submit specified court records." 82 Fed. Reg. 33210 (July 19, 2017). In July of 2017, the House voted 231-190 in favor of a resolution to eliminate the CFPB regulation. H.J. Res. 111 (July 2017). In October of the same year, the Senate voted 51-50 in favor of the resolution. Vice-President Pence provided the tie-breaking vote.

9. By rejecting the CFPB's arbitration rule, Congress left in place the status quo, embodied in various opinions of the Supreme Court interpreting the FAA. To briefly summarize, in *Stolt-Nielsen S.A. v. Animal Feeds Int'l Corp.*, 559 U.S. 662 (2010), referenced in *Concepcion*, the Supreme Court construed the meaning and fundamental attributes of "arbitration" in the FAA as inconsistent with class proceedings. Building on that judicial interpretation of the meaning and nature of "arbitration" in the FAA, the Supreme Court in *Concepcion* held that a state rule disfavoring class-action waivers constituted an obstacle to the achievement of the FAA's objective of promoting "arbitration," as defined in *Stolt-Nielsen*. Then, in *Italian Colors*, the Supreme Court held that a class-action waiver was enforceable under the FAA even though plaintiffs' federal statutory claims could not be effectuated on an individual basis and even though there would be no "arbitration," whatever its attributes. In three cases, the Court cemented an interpretation of arbitration under the FAA as a contract for private (and typically individualized) dispute resolution in an arbitral forum, whose procedures are almost entirely subject to the terms of the contract. It is important to note two key points about the institutional dynamics of the future of the FAA: First, a later Supreme Court could revisit and even change the

existing interpretations of the FAA. Second, and perhaps more importantly, a future Congress could change the current state of affairs with the stroke of a pen. Past efforts by Congress to do so have been unsuccessful, but continued efforts to amend the FAA are underway, even now. *See* Arbitration Fairness for Consumers Act, S. 630, 116th Cong. (2019-20).

STRATEGY SESSION

In litigation, there is the short game, the long game, and the very long game. The short game is about winning a particular motion or issue. One long game is about winning the lawsuit or improving settlement position. Beyond the particular lawsuit, however, litigants and lawyers can play what you might call the *very long game*. One of these very long games is about crafting the law over the course of multiple cases and multiple years. In *Concepcion*, the law moved in a direction that was decidedly unfavorable for class-action plaintiffs and favorable for businesses that want to avoid class actions. Class waivers and mandatory arbitration agreements were (and remain) a hot-button issue at the time the attorneys in *Concepcion* filed the class complaint. The plaintiffs' attorneys in *Concepcion* arguably failed to consider the very long game (or misjudged it). How so? For one, the facts in *Concepcion* are not particularly appealing for the plaintiffs; they paid $30.22 in taxes on an otherwise free phone. Moreover, the arbitration agreement in *Concepcion was* particularly appealing, and purposely so. AT&T's provision was designed to be as consumer-friendly as possible without sacrificing the thing AT&T cared about: the class waiver. AT&T (and others) were playing a very long game: a game for rules. At the end of the day, plaintiffs' attorneys lost their case *and* provided the platform for one of the broadest pro-arbitration holdings in the history of the Court. One might look at this and say the plaintiffs ought not have filed the case, because it ended up harming other would-be plaintiffs subject to arbitration agreements. If the plaintiffs' goal was to get rid of class-action prohibitions, then filing the *Concepcion* case was counterproductive. As one scholar memorably put it, "Hogs get slaughtered at the Supreme Court." Suzanna Sherry, *Hogs Get Slaughtered at the Supreme Court*, 2011 Sup. Ct. Rev. 1. On the other hand, was it Vincent and Liza Concepcion's duty to worry about the future of class actions? And, supposing they just wanted their money back, would it have been ethically permissible for their *lawyers* to play the litigation differently for fear of what might happen if the case reached the Supreme Court? Does your answer depend on whether the Concepcions sought out the lawyers or vice versa? AT&T, as a repeat player in litigation, played the *Concepcion* case in a way that maximized its long-term interests. The Concepcions, as probable one-time litigants, may have had a different view, and their lawyer may have cared about the future of class actions but may have focused primarily on this particular case. The bottom line is that lawyers think differently about how to litigate when they are playing the very long game.

10. Like settlement, arbitration has been criticized by some as depriving the dispute-resolution system of various public goods—development of the law, disclosure of wrongdoing, and democratic and procedural legitimacy, to name a few. *See, e.g.,* Judith Resnik, *Diffusing Disputes: The Public in the Private of Arbitration, the Private in Courts, and the Erasure of Rights,* 124 Yale L.J. 2084 (2015). At least when disputes can realistically be arbitrated, do those concerns outweigh the benefits of arbitration to the parties? Might the cost-benefit analysis differ depending on the type of case, with some cases better suited to private arbitration than others?

D. CONCLUDING THOUGHTS

At the start of this book, we told you—a bit grandiloquently, perhaps—that this was a book about justice, about truth, and about peace. And we told you it was a book about hard choices and trade-offs.

Having made it to the end of the book, and presumably having reached the conclusion of your civil procedure course, we hope you have seen how *procedural choices matter.* We hope you have seen, in case after case, the impact of procedure on the ability of parties to pursue claims and defenses. We hope you have seen the impact of procedure on the ability of courts to adjudicate fairly and the ability of the legal system to handle disputes efficiently. And we hope you have seen the power of the litigation process to foster a climate—or not—in which negotiated settlements may reflect the merits of claims and defenses and the legitimate interests of parties.

When we say that *procedural choices matter,* we are referring to least two different kinds of choices. First, we mean choices of *procedural design* embedded in the rules and doctrines that govern the litigation process. The Federal Rules of Civil Procedure, which have occupied the bulk of this book's attention, reflect a particular set of choices of procedural design. If parties have not otherwise agreed to a process for determining the outcome of their dispute, they turn to the courts and they rely on the process established by the courts. In this sense, one can think of the Federal Rules of Civil Procedure, as well as state rules and other law governing procedure, as a kind of default setting. When parties have not established any other mechanism for resolving their dispute—which is most of the time—the state and federal courts provide processes by which the parties can litigate their disputes, by which courts can adjudicate those disputes, and in the shadow of which they can negotiate a possible resolution by settlement.

Baked into the Federal Rules of Civil Procedure and their state counterparts, as well as other sources of procedural law, are thousands of choices of procedural design. Some of these are fundamental structural choices about the function of the litigation-adjudication process and the course of litigation, while others are detailed choices about how each aspect of the litigation process works. How easy should it be for plaintiffs to start a lawsuit? How should factual information be gathered?

Under what circumstances should courts resolve disputes prior to trial? How should evidence be presented and how should decision-making power be allocated? What rights of review should be available for disappointed litigants? How should the system handle disputes with multiple claims or multiple parties? How should judgments be enforced, and what is the scope of their binding effect? How should power be allocated among different courts, and how much choice should parties have when selecting a forum? As you have seen, these matters of procedural design continue to develop every year. Changes come from those involved in amending the Federal Rules of Civil Procedure and from judges who decide how to interpret and apply the rules, as well as judges deciding matters of constitutional law and procedural common law. Choices of procedural design continue to be made, as well, by Congress and by state legislatures, state rule makers, and state judges. The cases in this book have provided plenty of opportunity for you to consider the merits and pitfalls of a wide range of procedural design choices. We encourage you to think back through the topics we have covered—pleadings, discovery, pretrial, trial, appeals, joinder, preclusion, subject matter jurisdiction, personal jurisdiction, venue, choice of law, and dispute resolution—and consider the hard choices embodied in every detail.

Second, when we say that procedural choices matter, we also mean the *strategic choices* made by lawyers and litigants in the course of litigation. It is one thing for the rules of procedure to open up opportunities for discovery or joinder or pretrial adjudication, it is another thing for lawyers to decide how to avail themselves of these opportunities. Just as the cases in this book have given you perspectives on choices of procedural design, so have they given you moments to consider choices of procedural strategy. Again, we encourage you to think back through the chapters and the cases and to think about how procedural rules create ways for you to serve clients' interests and to pursue justice, truth, and peace on their behalf.

In this concluding chapter, we have stepped outside the litigation-adjudication process. Or, at least, we have looked at aspects of it that go beyond the traditional conception of litigation and adjudication. But this does not mean that we have stepped away from choices of procedural design and strategy. Think back to our last topic of arbitration. When thinking about procedural design, consider the significance of arbitration agreements and their presumptive enforceability under the FAA even when they contain provisions (such as the joinder and class action prohibition in *Concepcion*) that differ from the rules of litigation. The enforceability of arbitration agreements means that parties have wide latitude to design their own dispute-resolution process. If both parties agree (or, in light of *Concepcion*, if the parties' "agreement" is embodied in a contractual clause that courts will enforce), then the contract governs the process by which the parties may resolve their dispute. In the absence of such an agreement, the Federal Rules of Civil Procedure, their state counterparts, and other procedural law governs the process by which the parties may resolve their dispute. Either way, the litigants and lawyers have opportunities to deploy procedural rules in service of clients. In sum, whether practicing within the confines of the Federal Rules of Civil Procedure, the rules of the various state courts, or the rules of private dispute-resolution mechanisms invoked by agreement of the parties, a careful lawyer must understand the importance of procedural design and the importance of strategic choices in deploying procedural opportunities.

Perhaps this sounds daunting. Perhaps it sounds exciting. As you embark upon your career as an attorney, it assuredly will be both. At any particular time, in any particular context, the contours of a civil dispute-resolution system may or may not strike the right balance among goals such as justice, truth, and peace. But the only hope for the effectiveness of a civil dispute-resolution system is that it be deployed by lawyers who understand the process. Welcome, again, to civil procedure.

TABLE OF CASES

TABLE OF STATUTES AND RULES

Federal District Court Local Rules

American Bar Association Model Rules of Professional Conduct